A COURSE IN MIRACLES

COMBINED VOLUME

A COURSE IN MIRACLES

COMBINED VOLUME
Third Edition

PREFACE
TEXT
WORKBOOK FOR STUDENTS
MANUAL FOR TEACHERS
CLARIFICATION OF TERMS
SUPPLEMENTS

FOUNDATION FOR INNER PEACE

Published by the Foundation for Inner Peace
P.O. Box 598
Mill Valley, CA 94942
www.acim.org

A Course in Miracles was first published in three volumes in June, 1976
by the Foundation for Inner Peace

Manufactured in the United States of America

12 13 14 15 16 - 22 21 20 19 18 17 16

ISBN 978-1-883360-25-2 Hard cover
ISBN 978-1-883360-24-5 Softcover
ISBN 978-1-883360-26-9 Paperback

Library of Congress Catalog Card Number 79-20363

PREFACE

This Preface was written in 1977, in response to many requests for a brief introduction to *A Course in Miracles*. The first two parts—*How It Came; What It Is*—Helen Schucman wrote herself; the final part—*What It Says*—was written by the process of inner dictation described in the Preface.

How It Came

A Course in Miracles began with the sudden decision of two people to join in a common goal. Their names were Helen Schucman and William Thetford, Professors of Medical Psychology at Columbia University's College of Physicians and Surgeons in New York City. It does not matter who they were, except that the story shows that with God all things are possible. They were anything but spiritual. Their relationship with each other was difficult and often strained, and they were concerned with personal and professional acceptance and status. In general, they had considerable investment in the values of the world. Their lives were hardly in accord with anything that the Course advocates. Helen, the one who received the material, describes herself:

> *Psychologist, educator, conservative in theory and atheistic in belief, I was working in a prestigious and highly academic setting. And then something happened that triggered a chain of events I could never have predicted. The head of my department unexpectedly announced that he was tired of the angry and aggressive feelings our attitudes reflected, and concluded that "there must be another way." As if on cue, I agreed to help him find it. Apparently this Course is the other way.*

Although their intention was serious, they had great difficulty in starting out on their joint venture. But they had given the Holy Spirit the "little willingness" that, as the Course itself was to emphasize again and again, is sufficient to enable Him to use any situation for His purposes and provide it with His power.

To continue Helen's first-person account:

> *Three startling months preceded the actual writing, during which time Bill suggested that I write down the highly symbolic dreams*

*and descriptions of the strange images that were coming to me.
Although I had grown more accustomed to the unexpected by that
time, I was still very surprised when I wrote, "This is a course in
miracles." That was my introduction to the Voice. It made no
sound, but seemed to be giving me a kind of rapid, inner dictation
which I took down in a shorthand notebook. The writing was never
automatic. It could be interrupted at any time and later picked up
again. It made me very uncomfortable, but it never seriously occurred to me to stop. It seemed to be a special assignment I had
somehow, somewhere agreed to complete. It represented a truly collaborative venture between Bill and myself, and much of its signifi-
cance, I am sure, lies in that. I would take down what the Voice
"said" and read it to him the next day, and he typed it from my
dictation. I expect he had his special assignment, too. Without his
encouragement and support I would never have been able to fulfill
mine. The whole process took about seven years. The Text came
first, then the Workbook for Students, and finally the Manual for
Teachers. Only a few minor changes have been made. Chapter titles
and subheadings have been inserted in the Text, and some of the
more personal references that occurred at the beginning have been
omitted. Otherwise the material is substantially unchanged.*

The names of the collaborators in the recording of the Course
do not appear on the cover because the Course can and should
stand on its own. It is not intended to become the basis for another cult. Its only purpose is to provide a way in which some
people will be able to find their own Internal Teacher.

What It Is

As its title implies, the Course is arranged throughout as a
teaching device. It consists of three books: a 669-page Text, a 488-
page Workbook for Students, and a 92-page Manual for Teachers.
The order in which students choose to use the books, and the
ways in which they study them, depend on their particular needs
and preferences.

The curriculum the Course proposes is carefully conceived
and is explained, step by step, at both the theoretical and practical levels. It emphasizes application rather than theory, and experience rather than theology. It specifically states that "a universal

theology is impossible, but a universal experience is not only possible but necessary" (Manual, p. 77). Although Christian in statement, the Course deals with universal spiritual themes. It emphasizes that it is but one version of the universal curriculum. There are many others, this one differing from them only in form. They all lead to God in the end.

The Text is largely theoretical, and sets forth the concepts on which the Course's thought system is based. Its ideas contain the foundation for the Workbook's lessons. Without the practical application the Workbook provides, the Text would remain largely a series of abstractions which would hardly suffice to bring about the thought reversal at which the Course aims.

The Workbook includes 365 lessons, one for each day of the year. It is not necessary, however, to do the lessons at that tempo, and one might want to remain with a particularly appealing lesson for more than one day. The instructions urge only that not more than one lesson a day should be attempted. The practical nature of the Workbook is underscored by the introduction to its lessons, which emphasizes experience through application rather than a prior commitment to a spiritual goal:

> Some of the ideas the workbook presents you will find hard to believe, and others may seem to be quite startling. This does not matter. You are merely asked to apply the ideas as you are directed to do. You are not asked to judge them at all. You are asked only to use them. It is their use that will give them meaning to you, and will show you that they are true.

> Remember only this; you need not believe the ideas, you need not accept them, and you need not even welcome them. Some of them you may actively resist. None of this will matter, or decrease their efficacy. But do not allow yourself to make exceptions in applying the ideas the workbook contains, and whatever your reactions to the ideas may be, use them. Nothing more than that is required (Workbook, p. 2).

Finally, the Manual for Teachers, which is written in question and answer form, provides answers to some of the more likely questions a student might ask. It also includes a clarification of a number of the terms the Course uses, explaining them within the theoretical framework of the Text.

The Course makes no claim to finality, nor are the Workbook lessons intended to bring the student's learning to completion. At the end, the reader is left in the hands of his or her own Internal

Teacher, Who will direct all subsequent learning as He sees fit. While the Course is comprehensive in scope, truth cannot be limited to any finite form, as is clearly recognized in the statement at the end of the Workbook:

> This Course is a beginning, not an end...No more specific lessons are assigned, for there is no more need of them. Henceforth, hear but the Voice for God...He will direct your efforts, telling you exactly what to do, how to direct your mind, and when to come to Him in silence, asking for His sure direction and His certain Word (Workbook, p. 487).

What It Says

Nothing real can be threatened.
Nothing unreal exists.
Herein lies the peace of God.

This is how *A Course in Miracles* begins. It makes a fundamental distinction between the real and the unreal; between knowledge and perception. Knowledge is truth, under one law, the law of love or God. Truth is unalterable, eternal and unambiguous. It can be unrecognized, but it cannot be changed. It applies to everything that God created, and only what He created is real. It is beyond learning because it is beyond time and process. It has no opposite; no beginning and no end. It merely is.

The world of perception, on the other hand, is the world of time, of change, of beginnings and endings. It is based on interpretation, not on facts. It is the world of birth and death, founded on the belief in scarcity, loss, separation and death. It is learned rather than given, selective in its perceptual emphases, unstable in its functioning, and inaccurate in its interpretations.

From knowledge and perception respectively, two distinct thought systems arise which are opposite in every respect. In the realm of knowledge no thoughts exist apart from God, because God and His Creation share one Will. The world of perception, however, is made by the belief in opposites and separate wills, in perpetual conflict with each other and with God. What perception sees and hears appears to be real because it permits into awareness only what conforms to the wishes of the perceiver. This leads to a world of illusions, a world which needs constant defense precisely *because* it is not real.

When you have been caught in the world of perception you are caught in a dream. You cannot escape without help, because everything your senses show merely witnesses to the reality of the dream. God has provided the Answer, the only Way out, the true Helper. It is the function of His Voice, His Holy Spirit, to mediate between the two worlds. He can do this because, while on the one hand He knows the truth, on the other He also recognizes our illusions, but without believing in them. It is the Holy Spirit's goal to help us escape from the dream world by teaching us how to reverse our thinking and unlearn our mistakes. Forgiveness is the Holy Spirit's great learning aid in bringing this thought reversal about. However, the Course has its own definition of what forgiveness really is just as it defines the world in its own way.

The world we see merely reflects our own internal frame of reference—the dominant ideas, wishes and emotions in our minds. "Projection makes perception" (Text, p. 445). We look inside first, decide the kind of world we want to see and then project that world outside, making it the truth *as we see it*. We make it true by our interpretations of what it is we are seeing. If we are using perception to justify our own mistakes—our anger, our impulses to attack, our lack of love in whatever form it may take— we will see a world of evil, destruction, malice, envy and despair. All this we must learn to forgive, not because we are being "good" and "charitable," but because what we are seeing is not true. We have distorted the world by our twisted defenses, and are therefore seeing what is not there. As we learn to recognize our perceptual errors, we also learn to look past them or "forgive." At the same time we are forgiving ourselves, looking past our distorted self-concepts to the Self That God created in us and as us.

Sin is defined as "lack of love" (Text, p. 11). Since love is all there is, sin in the sight of the Holy Spirit is a mistake to be corrected, rather than an evil to be punished. Our sense of inadequacy, weakness and incompletion comes from the strong investment in the "scarcity principle" that governs the whole world of illusions. From that point of view, we seek in others what we feel is wanting in ourselves. We "love" another in order to get something ourselves. That, in fact, is what passes for love in the dream world. There can be no greater mistake than that, for love is incapable of asking for anything.

Only minds can really join, and whom God has joined no man can put asunder (Text, p. 356). It is, however, only at the level of Christ Mind that true union is possible, and has, in fact, never been lost. The "little I" seeks to enhance itself by external approval, external possessions and external "love." The Self That God created needs nothing. It is forever complete, safe, loved and loving. It seeks to share rather than to get; to extend rather than project. It has no needs and wants to join with others out of their mutual awareness of abundance.

The special relationships of the world are destructive, selfish and childishly egocentric. Yet, if given to the Holy Spirit, these relationships can become the holiest things on earth—the miracles that point the way to the return to Heaven. The world uses its special relationships as a final weapon of exclusion and a demonstration of separateness. The Holy Spirit transforms them into perfect lessons in forgiveness and in awakening from the dream. Each one is an opportunity to let perceptions be healed and errors corrected. Each one is another chance to forgive oneself by forgiving the other. And each one becomes still another invitation to the Holy Spirit and to the remembrance of God.

Perception is a function of the body, and therefore represents a limit on awareness. Perception sees through the body's eyes and hears through the body's ears. It evokes the limited responses which the body makes. The body appears to be largely self-motivated and independent, yet it actually responds only to the intentions of the mind. If the mind wants to use it for attack in any form, it becomes prey to sickness, age and decay. If the mind accepts the Holy Spirit's purpose for it instead, it becomes a useful way of communicating with others, invulnerable as long as it is needed, and to be gently laid by when its use is over. Of itself it is neutral, as is everything in the world of perception. Whether it is used for the goals of the ego or the Holy Spirit depends entirely on what the mind wants.

The opposite of seeing through the body's eyes is the vision of Christ, which reflects strength rather than weakness, unity rather than separation, and love rather than fear. The opposite of hearing through the body's ears is communication through the Voice for God, the Holy Spirit, which abides in each of us. His Voice seems distant and difficult to hear because the ego, which speaks for the little, separated self, seems to be much louder. This is actually reversed. The Holy Spirit speaks with unmistakable clarity and overwhelming appeal. No one who does not choose to identify with the body could possibly be deaf to His messages of release and hope, nor could he fail to accept joyously the vision of Christ in glad exchange for his miserable picture of himself.

Christ's vision is the Holy Spirit's gift, God's alternative to the illusion of separation and to the belief in the reality of sin, guilt and death. It is the one correction for all errors of perception; the reconciliation of the seeming opposites on which this world is based. Its kindly light shows all things from another point of view, reflecting the thought system that arises from knowledge and making return to God not only possible but inevitable. What was regarded as injustices done to one by someone else now becomes a call for help and for union. Sin, sickness and attack are seen as misperceptions calling for remedy through gentleness and love. Defenses are laid down because where there is no attack there is no need for them. Our brothers' needs become our own, because they are taking the journey with us as we go to God. Without us they would lose their way. Without them we could never find our own.

Forgiveness is unknown in Heaven, where the need for it would be inconceivable. However, in this world, forgiveness is a necessary correction for all the mistakes that we have made. To offer forgiveness is the only way for us to have it, for it reflects the law of Heaven that giving and receiving are the same. Heaven is the natural state of all the Sons of God as He created them. Such is their reality forever. It has not changed because it has been forgotten.

Forgiveness is the means by which we will remember. Through forgiveness the thinking of the world is reversed. The forgiven world becomes the gate of Heaven, because by its mercy we can at last forgive ourselves. Holding no one prisoner to guilt, we become free. Acknowledging Christ in all our brothers, we recognize His Presence in ourselves. Forgetting all our misperceptions, and with nothing from the past to hold us back, we can remember God. Beyond this, learning cannot go. When we are ready, God Himself will take the final step in our return to Him.

A COURSE IN MIRACLES

TEXT

FOUNDATION FOR INNER PEACE

CONTENTS

Chapter 29   THE AWAKENING

Chapter 30   THE NEW BEGINNING

Chapter 31   THE FINAL VISION

INTRODUCTION

1. This is a course in miracles. ²It is a required course. ³Only the time you take it is voluntary. ⁴Free will does not mean that you can establish the curriculum. ⁵It means only that you can elect what you want to take at a given time. ⁶The course does not aim at teaching the meaning of love, for that is beyond what can be taught. ⁷It does aim, however, at removing the blocks to the awareness of love's presence, which is your natural inheritance. ⁸The opposite of love is fear, but what is all-encompassing can have no opposite.

2. This course can therefore be summed up very simply in this way:

> ²**Nothing real can be threatened.**
> ³**Nothing unreal exists.**

⁴Herein lies the peace of God.

Chapter 1

THE MEANING OF MIRACLES

I. Principles of Miracles

1. There is no order of difficulty in miracles. ²One is not "harder" or "bigger" than another. ³They are all the same. ⁴All expressions of love are maximal.

2. Miracles as such do not matter. ²The only thing that matters is their Source, which is far beyond evaluation.

3. Miracles occur naturally as expressions of love. ²The real miracle is the love that inspires them. ³In this sense everything that comes from love is a miracle.

4. All miracles mean life, and God is the Giver of life. ²His Voice will direct you very specifically. ³You will be told all you need to know.

5. Miracles are habits, and should be involuntary. ²They should not be under conscious control. ³Consciously selected miracles can be misguided.

6. Miracles are natural. ²When they do not occur something has gone wrong.

7. Miracles are everyone's right, but purification is necessary first.

8. Miracles are healing because they supply a lack; they are performed by those who temporarily have more for those who temporarily have less.

9. Miracles are a kind of exchange. ²Like all expressions of love, which are always miraculous in the true sense, the exchange reverses the physical laws. ³They bring more love both to the giver *and* the receiver.

10. The use of miracles as spectacles to induce belief is a misunderstanding of their purpose.

11. Prayer is the medium of miracles. ²It is a means of communication of the created with the Creator. ³Through prayer love is received, and through miracles love is expressed.

12. Miracles are thoughts. ²Thoughts can represent the lower or bodily level of experience, or the higher or spiritual level of experience. ³One makes the physical, and the other creates the spiritual.

3

13. Miracles are both beginnings and endings, and so they alter the temporal order. ²They are always affirmations of rebirth, which seem to go back but really go forward. ³They undo the past in the present, and thus release the future.

14. Miracles bear witness to truth. ²They are convincing because they arise from conviction. ³Without conviction they deteriorate into magic, which is mindless and therefore destructive; or rather, the uncreative use of mind.

15. Each day should be devoted to miracles. ²The purpose of time is to enable you to learn how to use time constructively. ³It is thus a teaching device and a means to an end. ⁴Time will cease when it is no longer useful in facilitating learning.

16. Miracles are teaching devices for demonstrating it is as blessed to give as to receive. ²They simultaneously increase the strength of the giver and supply strength to the receiver.

17. Miracles transcend the body. ²They are sudden shifts into invisibility, away from the bodily level. ³That is why they heal.

18. A miracle is a service. ²It is the maximal service you can render to another. ³It is a way of loving your neighbor as yourself. ⁴You recognize your own and your neighbor's worth simultaneously.

19. Miracles make minds one in God. ²They depend on cooperation because the Sonship is the sum of all that God created. ³Miracles therefore reflect the laws of eternity, not of time.

20. Miracles reawaken the awareness that the spirit, not the body, is the altar of truth. ²This is the recognition that leads to the healing power of the miracle.

21. Miracles are natural signs of forgiveness. ²Through miracles you accept God's forgiveness by extending it to others.

22. Miracles are associated with fear only because of the belief that darkness can hide. ²You believe that what your physical eyes cannot see does not exist. ³This leads to a denial of spiritual sight.

23. Miracles rearrange perception and place all levels in true perspective. ²This is healing because sickness comes from confusing the levels.

24. Miracles enable you to heal the sick and raise the dead because you made sickness and death yourself, and can therefore abolish both. ²*You* are a miracle, capable of creating in the likeness of your Creator. ³Everything else is your own nightmare, and does not exist. ⁴Only the creations of light are real.

25. Miracles are part of an interlocking chain of forgiveness which, when completed, is the Atonement. ²Atonement works all the

time and in all the dimensions of time.

26. Miracles represent freedom from fear. ²"Atoning" means "undoing." ³The undoing of fear is an essential part of the Atonement value of miracles.

27. A miracle is a universal blessing from God through me to all my brothers. ²It is the privilege of the forgiven to forgive.

28. Miracles are a way of earning release from fear. ²Revelation induces a state in which fear has already been abolished. ³Miracles are thus a means and revelation is an end.

29. Miracles praise God through you. ²They praise Him by honoring His creations, affirming their perfection. ³They heal because they deny body-identification and affirm spirit-identification.

30. By recognizing spirit, miracles adjust the levels of perception and show them in proper alignment. ²This places spirit at the center, where it can communicate directly.

31. Miracles should inspire gratitude, not awe. ²You should thank God for what you really are. ³The children of God are holy and the miracle honors their holiness, which can be hidden but never lost.

32. I inspire all miracles, which are really intercessions. ²They intercede for your holiness and make your perceptions holy. ³By placing you beyond the physical laws they raise you into the sphere of celestial order. ⁴In this order you *are* perfect.

33. Miracles honor you because you are lovable. ²They dispel illusions about yourself and perceive the light in you. ³They thus atone for your errors by freeing you from your nightmares. ⁴By releasing your mind from the imprisonment of your illusions, they restore your sanity.

34. Miracles restore the mind to its fullness. ²By atoning for lack they establish perfect protection. ³The spirit's strength leaves no room for intrusions.

35. Miracles are expressions of love, but they may not always have observable effects.

36. Miracles are examples of right thinking, aligning your perceptions with truth as God created it.

37. A miracle is a correction introduced into false thinking by me. ²It acts as a catalyst, breaking up erroneous perception and reorganizing it properly. ³This places you under the Atonement principle, where perception is healed. ⁴Until this has occurred, knowledge of the Divine Order is impossible.

38. The Holy Spirit is the mechanism of miracles. ²He recognizes

both God's creations and your illusions. ³He separates the true from the false by His ability to perceive totally rather than selectively.

39. The miracle dissolves error because the Holy Spirit identifies error as false or unreal. ²This is the same as saying that by perceiving light, darkness automatically disappears.

40. The miracle acknowledges everyone as your brother and mine. ²It is a way of perceiving the universal mark of God.

41. Wholeness is the perceptual content of miracles. ²They thus correct, or atone for, the faulty perception of lack.

42. A major contribution of miracles is their strength in releasing you from your false sense of isolation, deprivation and lack.

43. Miracles arise from a miraculous state of mind, or a state of miracle-readiness.

44. The miracle is an expression of an inner awareness of Christ and the acceptance of His Atonement.

45. A miracle is never lost. ²It may touch many people you have not even met, and produce undreamed of changes in situations of which you are not even aware.

46. The Holy Spirit is the highest communication medium. ²Miracles do not involve this type of communication, because they are *temporary* communication devices. ³When you return to your original form of communication with God by direct revelation, the need for miracles is over.

47. The miracle is a learning device that lessens the need for time. ²It establishes an out-of-pattern time interval not under the usual laws of time. ³In this sense it is timeless.

48. The miracle is the only device at your immediate disposal for controlling time. ²Only revelation transcends it, having nothing to do with time at all.

49. The miracle makes no distinction among degrees of misperception. ²It is a device for perception correction, effective quite apart from either the degree or the direction of the error. ³This is its true indiscriminateness.

50. The miracle compares what you have made with creation, accepting what is in accord with it as true, and rejecting what is out of accord as false.

II. Revelation, Time and Miracles

1. Revelation induces complete but temporary suspension of doubt and fear. [2]It reflects the original form of communication between God and His creations, involving the extremely personal sense of creation sometimes sought in physical relationships. [3]Physical closeness cannot achieve it. [4]Miracles, however, are genuinely interpersonal, and result in true closeness to others. [5]Revelation unites you directly with God. [6]Miracles unite you directly with your brother. [7]Neither emanates from consciousness, but both are experienced there. [8]Consciousness is the state that induces action, though it does not inspire it. [9]You are free to believe what you choose, and what you do attests to what you believe.

2. Revelation is intensely personal and cannot be meaningfully translated. [2]That is why any attempt to describe it in words is impossible. [3]Revelation induces only experience. [4]Miracles, on the other hand, induce action. [5]They are more useful now because of their interpersonal nature. [6]In this phase of learning, working miracles is important because freedom from fear cannot be thrust upon you. [7]Revelation is literally unspeakable because it is an experience of unspeakable love.

3. Awe should be reserved for revelation, to which it is perfectly and correctly applicable. [2]It is not appropriate for miracles because a state of awe is worshipful, implying that one of a lesser order stands before his Creator. [3]You are a perfect creation, and should experience awe only in the Presence of the Creator of perfection. [4]The miracle is therefore a sign of love among equals. [5]Equals should not be in awe of one another because awe implies inequality. [6]It is therefore an inappropriate reaction to me. [7]An elder brother is entitled to respect for his greater experience, and obedience for his greater wisdom. [8]He is also entitled to love because he is a brother, and to devotion if he is devoted. [9]It is only my devotion that entitles me to yours. [10]There is nothing about me that you cannot attain. [11]I have nothing that does not come from God. [12]The difference between us now is that I have nothing else. [13]This leaves me in a state which is only potential in you.

4. "No man cometh unto the Father but by me" does not mean that I am in any way separate or different from you except in time, and time does not really exist. [2]The statement is more meaningful in terms of a vertical rather than a horizontal axis.

³You stand below me and I stand below God. ⁴In the process of "rising up," I am higher because without me the distance between God and man would be too great for you to encompass. ⁵I bridge the distance as an elder brother to you on the one hand, and as a Son of God on the other. ⁶My devotion to my brothers has placed me in charge of the Sonship, which I render complete because I share it. ⁷This may appear to contradict the statement "I and my Father are one," but there are two parts to the statement in recognition that the Father is greater.

5.   Revelations are indirectly inspired by me because I am close to the Holy Spirit, and alert to the revelation-readiness of my brothers. ²I can thus bring down to them more than they can draw down to themselves. ³The Holy Spirit mediates higher to lower communication, keeping the direct channel from God to you open for revelation. ⁴Revelation is not reciprocal. ⁵It proceeds from God to you, but not from you to God.

6.   The miracle minimizes the need for time. ²In the longitudinal or horizontal plane the recognition of the equality of the members of the Sonship appears to involve almost endless time. ³However, the miracle entails a sudden shift from horizontal to vertical perception. ⁴This introduces an interval from which the giver and receiver both emerge farther along in time than they would otherwise have been. ⁵The miracle thus has the unique property of abolishing time to the extent that it renders the interval of time it spans unnecessary. ⁶There is no relationship between the time a miracle takes and the time it covers. ⁷The miracle substitutes for learning that might have taken thousands of years. ⁸It does so by the underlying recognition of perfect equality of giver and receiver on which the miracle rests. ⁹The miracle shortens time by collapsing it, thus eliminating certain intervals within it. ¹⁰It does this, however, within the larger temporal sequence.

III. Atonement and Miracles

1.   I am in charge of the process of Atonement, which I undertook to begin. ²When you offer a miracle to any of my brothers, you do it to *yourself* and me. ³The reason you come before me is that I do not need miracles for my own Atonement, but I stand at the end in case you fail temporarily. ⁴My part in the Atonement is the

cancelling out of all errors that you could not otherwise correct. ⁵When you have been restored to the recognition of your original state, you naturally become part of the Atonement yourself. ⁶As you share my unwillingness to accept error in yourself and others, you must join the great crusade to correct it; listen to my voice, learn to undo error and act to correct it. ⁷The power to work miracles belongs to you. ⁸I will provide the opportunities to do them, but you must be ready and willing. ⁹Doing them will bring conviction in the ability, because conviction comes through accomplishment. ¹⁰The ability is the potential, the achievement is its expression, and the Atonement, which is the natural profession of the children of God, is the purpose.

2. "Heaven and earth shall pass away" means that they will not continue to exist as separate states. ²My word, which is the resurrection and the life, shall not pass away because life is eternal. ³You are the work of God, and His work is wholly lovable and wholly loving. ⁴This is how a man must think of himself in his heart, because this is what he is.

3. The forgiven are the means of the Atonement. ²Being filled with spirit, they forgive in return. ³Those who are released must join in releasing their brothers, for this is the plan of the Atonement. ⁴Miracles are the way in which minds that serve the Holy Spirit unite with me for the salvation or release of all of God's creations.

4. I am the only one who can perform miracles indiscriminately, because I am the Atonement. ²You have a role in the Atonement which I will dictate to you. ³Ask me which miracles you should perform. ⁴This spares you needless effort, because you will be acting under direct communication. ⁵The impersonal nature of the miracle is an essential ingredient, because it enables me to direct its application, and under my guidance miracles lead to the highly personal experience of revelation. ⁶A guide does not control but he does direct, leaving it up to you to follow. ⁷"Lead us not into temptation" means "Recognize your errors and choose to abandon them by following my guidance."

5. Error cannot really threaten truth, which can always withstand it. ²Only the error is actually vulnerable. ³You are free to establish your kingdom where you see fit, but the right choice is inevitable if you remember this:

> ⁴*Spirit is in a state of grace forever.*
> ⁵*Your reality is only spirit.*
> ⁶*Therefore you are in a state of grace forever.*

⁷Atonement undoes all errors in this respect, and thus uproots the source of fear. ⁸Whenever you experience God's reassurances as threat, it is always because you are defending misplaced or misdirected loyalty. ⁹When you project this to others you imprison them, but only to the extent to which you reinforce errors they have already made. ¹⁰This makes them vulnerable to the distortions of others, since their own perception of themselves is distorted. ¹¹The miracle worker can only bless them, and this undoes their distortions and frees them from prison.

6. You respond to what you perceive, and as you perceive so shall you behave. ²The Golden Rule asks you to do unto others as you would have them do unto you. ³This means that the perception of both must be accurate. ⁴The Golden Rule is the rule for appropriate behavior. ⁵You cannot behave appropriately unless you perceive correctly. ⁶Since you and your neighbor are equal members of one family, as you perceive both so you will do to both. ⁷You should look out from the perception of your own holiness to the holiness of others.

7. Miracles arise from a mind that is ready for them. ²By being united this mind goes out to everyone, even without the awareness of the miracle worker himself. ³The impersonal nature of miracles is because the Atonement itself is one, uniting all creations with their Creator. ⁴As an expression of what you truly are, the miracle places the mind in a state of grace. ⁵The mind then naturally welcomes the Host within and the stranger without. ⁶When you bring in the stranger, he becomes your brother.

8. That the miracle may have effects on your brothers that you may not recognize is not your concern. ²The miracle will always bless *you*. ³Miracles you are not asked to perform have not lost their value. ⁴They are still expressions of your own state of grace, but the action aspect of the miracle should be controlled by me because of my complete awareness of the whole plan. ⁵The impersonal nature of miracle-mindedness ensures your grace, but only I am in a position to know where they can be bestowed.

9. Miracles are selective only in the sense that they are directed towards those who can use them for themselves. ²Since this makes it inevitable that they will extend them to others, a strong chain of

10

Atonement is welded. ³However, this selectivity takes no account of the magnitude of the miracle itself, because the concept of size exists on a plane that is itself unreal. ⁴Since the miracle aims at restoring the awareness of reality, it would not be useful if it were bound by laws that govern the error it aims to correct.

IV. The Escape from Darkness

1. The escape from darkness involves two stages: First, the recognition that darkness cannot hide. ²This step usually entails fear. ³Second, the recognition that there is nothing you want to hide even if you could. ⁴This step brings escape from fear. ⁵When you have become willing to hide nothing, you will not only be willing to enter into communion but will also understand peace and joy.

2. Holiness can never be really hidden in darkness, but you can deceive yourself about it. ²This deception makes you fearful because you realize in your heart it *is* a deception, and you exert enormous efforts to establish its reality. ³The miracle sets reality where it belongs. ⁴Reality belongs only to spirit, and the miracle acknowledges only truth. ⁵It thus dispels illusions about yourself, and puts you in communion with yourself and God. ⁶The miracle joins in the Atonement by placing the mind in the service of the Holy Spirit. ⁷This establishes the proper function of the mind and corrects its errors, which are merely lacks of love. ⁸Your mind can be possessed by illusions, but spirit is eternally free. ⁹If a mind perceives without love, it perceives an empty shell and is unaware of the spirit within. ¹⁰But the Atonement restores spirit to its proper place. ¹¹The mind that serves spirit *is* invulnerable.

3. Darkness is lack of light as sin is lack of love. ²It has no unique properties of its own. ³It is an example of the "scarcity" belief, from which only error can proceed. ⁴Truth is always abundant. ⁵Those who perceive and acknowledge that they have everything have no needs of any kind. ⁶The purpose of the Atonement is to restore everything to you; or rather, to restore it to your awareness. ⁷You were given everything when you were created, just as everyone was.

4. The emptiness engendered by fear must be replaced by forgiveness. ²That is what the Bible means by "There is no death," and why I could demonstrate that death does not exist. ³I came to

fulfill the law by reinterpreting it. ⁴The law itself, if properly understood, offers only protection. ⁵It is those who have not yet changed their minds who brought the "hell-fire" concept into it. ⁶I assure you that I will witness for anyone who lets me, and to whatever extent he permits it. ⁷Your witnessing demonstrates your belief, and thus strengthens it. ⁸Those who witness for me are expressing, through their miracles, that they have abandoned the belief in deprivation in favor of the abundance they have learned belongs to them.

V. Wholeness and Spirit

1. The miracle is much like the body in that both are learning aids for facilitating a state in which they become unnecessary. ²When spirit's original state of direct communication is reached, neither the body nor the miracle serves any purpose. ³While you believe you are in a body, however, you can choose between loveless and miraculous channels of expression. ⁴You can make an empty shell, but you cannot express nothing at all. ⁵You can wait, delay, paralyze yourself, or reduce your creativity almost to nothing. ⁶But you cannot abolish it. ⁷You can destroy your medium of communication, but not your potential. ⁸You did not create yourself.

2. The basic decision of the miracle-minded is not to wait on time any longer than is necessary. ²Time can waste as well as be wasted. ³The miracle worker, therefore, accepts the time-control factor gladly. ⁴He recognizes that every collapse of time brings everyone closer to the ultimate release from time, in which the Son and the Father are One. ⁵Equality does not imply equality *now.* ⁶When everyone recognizes that he has everything, individual contributions to the Sonship will no longer be necessary.

3. When the Atonement has been completed, all talents will be shared by all the Sons of God. ²God is not partial. ³All His children have His total Love, and all His gifts are freely given to everyone alike. ⁴"Except ye become as little children" means that unless you fully recognize your complete dependence on God, you cannot know the real power of the Son in his true relationship with the Father. ⁵The specialness of God's Sons does not stem from exclusion but from inclusion. ⁶All my brothers are special. ⁷If they believe they are deprived of anything, their perception becomes distorted. ⁸When this occurs the whole family of

God, or the Sonship, is impaired in its relationships.

4. Ultimately, every member of the family of God must return. [2]The miracle calls him to return because it blesses and honors him, even though he may be absent in spirit. [3]"God is not mocked" is not a warning but a reassurance. [4]God *would* be mocked if any of His creations lacked holiness. [5]The creation is whole, and the mark of wholeness is holiness. [6]Miracles are affirmations of Sonship, which is a state of completion and abundance.

5. Whatever is true is eternal, and cannot change or be changed. [2]Spirit is therefore unalterable because it is already perfect, but the mind can elect what it chooses to serve. [3]The only limit put on its choice is that it cannot serve two masters. [4]If it elects to do so, the mind can become the medium by which spirit creates along the line of its own creation. [5]If it does not freely elect to do so, it retains its creative potential but places itself under tyrannous rather than Authoritative control. [6]As a result it imprisons, because such are the dictates of tyrants. [7]To change your mind means to place it at the disposal of *true* Authority.

6. The miracle is a sign that the mind has chosen to be led by me in Christ's service. [2]The abundance of Christ is the natural result of choosing to follow Him. [3]All shallow roots must be uprooted, because they are not deep enough to sustain you. [4]The illusion that shallow roots can be deepened, and thus made to hold, is one of the distortions on which the reverse of the Golden Rule rests. [5]As these false underpinnings are given up, the equilibrium is temporarily experienced as unstable. [6]However, nothing is less stable than an upside-down orientation. [7]Nor can anything that holds it upside down be conducive to increased stability.

VI. The Illusion of Needs

1. You who want peace can find it only by complete forgiveness. [2]No learning is acquired by anyone unless he wants to learn it and believes in some way that he needs it. [3]While lack does not exist in the creation of God, it is very apparent in what you have made. [4]It is, in fact, the essential difference between them. [5]Lack implies that you would be better off in a state somehow different from the one you are in. [6]Until the "separation," which is the meaning of the "fall," nothing was lacking. [7]There were no needs at all. [8]Needs arise only when you deprive yourself. [9]You act

according to the particular order of needs you establish. [10]This, in turn, depends on your perception of what you are.

2.   A sense of separation from God is the only lack you really need correct. [2]This sense of separation would never have arisen if you had not distorted your perception of truth, and had thus perceived yourself as lacking. [3]The idea of order of needs arose because, having made this fundamental error, you had already fragmented yourself into levels with different needs. [4]As you integrate you become one, and your needs become one accordingly. [5]Unified needs lead to unified action, because this produces a lack of conflict.

3.   The idea of orders of need, which follows from the original error that one can be separated from God, requires correction at its own level before the error of perceiving levels at all can be corrected. [2]You cannot behave effectively while you function on different levels. [3]However, while you do, correction must be introduced vertically from the bottom up. [4]This is because you think you live in space, where concepts such as "up" and "down" are meaningful. [5]Ultimately, space is as meaningless as time. [6]Both are merely beliefs.

4.   The real purpose of this world is to use it to correct your unbelief. [2]You can never control the effects of fear yourself, because you made fear, and you believe in what you made. [3]In attitude, then, though not in content, you resemble your Creator, Who has perfect faith in His creations *because* He created them. [4]Belief produces the acceptance of existence. [5]That is why you can believe what no one else thinks is true. [6]It is true for you because it was made by you.

5.   All aspects of fear are untrue because they do not exist at the creative level, and therefore do not exist at all. [2]To whatever extent you are willing to submit your beliefs to this test, to that extent are your perceptions corrected. [3]In sorting out the false from the true, the miracle proceeds along these lines:

> [4]*Perfect love casts out fear.*
> [5]*If fear exists,*
> *Then there is not perfect love.*

> [6]*But:*

> [7]*Only perfect love exists.*
> [8]*If there is fear,*
> *It produces a state that does not exist.*

⁹Believe this and you will be free. ¹⁰Only God can establish this solution, and this faith *is* His gift.

VII. Distortions of Miracle Impulses

1. Your distorted perceptions produce a dense cover over miracle impulses, making it hard for them to reach your own awareness. ²The confusion of miracle impulses with physical impulses is a major perceptual distortion. ³Physical impulses are misdirected miracle impulses. ⁴All real pleasure comes from doing God's Will. ⁵This is because *not* doing it is a denial of Self. ⁶Denial of Self results in illusions, while correction of the error brings release from it. ⁷Do not deceive yourself into believing that you can relate in peace to God or to your brothers with anything external.

2. Child of God, you were created to create the good, the beautiful and the holy. ²Do not forget this. ³The Love of God, for a little while, must still be expressed through one body to another, because vision is still so dim. ⁴You can use your body best to help you enlarge your perception so you can achieve real vision, of which the physical eye is incapable. ⁵Learning to do this is the body's only true usefulness.

3. Fantasy is a distorted form of vision. ²Fantasies of any kind are distortions, because they always involve twisting perception into unreality. ³Actions that stem from distortions are literally the reactions of those who know not what they do. ⁴Fantasy is an attempt to control reality according to false needs. ⁵Twist reality in any way and you are perceiving destructively. ⁶Fantasies are a means of making false associations and attempting to obtain pleasure from them. ⁷But although you can perceive false associations, you can never make them real except to yourself. ⁸You believe in what you make. ⁹If you offer miracles, you will be equally strong in your belief in them. ¹⁰The strength of your conviction will then sustain the belief of the miracle receiver. ¹¹Fantasies become totally unnecessary as the wholly satisfying nature of reality becomes apparent to both giver and receiver. ¹²Reality is "lost" through usurpation, which produces tyranny. ¹³As long as a single "slave" remains to walk the earth, your release is not complete. ¹⁴Complete restoration of the Sonship is the only goal of the miracle-minded.

4. This is a course in mind training. ²All learning involves attention and study at some level. ³Some of the later parts of the course rest too heavily on these earlier sections not to require their careful study. ⁴You will also need them for preparation. ⁵Without this, you may become much too fearful of what is to come to make constructive use of it. ⁶However, as you study these earlier sections, you will begin to see some of the implications that will be amplified later on.

5. A solid foundation is necessary because of the confusion between fear and awe to which I have already referred, and which is often made. ²I have said that awe is inappropriate in connection with the Sons of God, because you should not experience awe in the presence of your equals. ³However, it was also emphasized that awe is proper in the Presence of your Creator. ⁴I have been careful to clarify my role in the Atonement without either over- or understating it. ⁵I am also trying to do the same with yours. ⁶I have stressed that awe is not an appropriate reaction to me because of our inherent equality. ⁷Some of the later steps in this course, however, involve a more direct approach to God Himself. ⁸It would be unwise to start on these steps without careful preparation, or awe will be confused with fear, and the experience will be more traumatic than beatific. ⁹Healing is of God in the end. ¹⁰The means are being carefully explained to you. ¹¹Revelation may occasionally reveal the end to you, but to reach it the means are needed.

Chapter 2

THE SEPARATION AND THE ATONEMENT

I. The Origins of Separation

1. To extend is a fundamental aspect of God which He gave to His Son. [2]In the creation, God extended Himself to His creations and imbued them with the same loving Will to create. [3]You have not only been fully created, but have also been created perfect. [4]There is no emptiness in you. [5]Because of your likeness to your Creator you are creative. [6]No child of God can lose this ability because it is inherent in what he is, but he can use it inappropriately by projecting. [7]The inappropriate use of extension, or projection, occurs when you believe that some emptiness or lack exists in you, and that you can fill it with your own ideas instead of truth. [8]This process involves the following steps:

[9]First, you believe that what God created can be changed by your own mind.

[10]Second, you believe that what is perfect can be rendered imperfect or lacking.

[11]Third, you believe that you can distort the creations of God, including yourself.

[12]Fourth, you believe that you can create yourself, and that the direction of your own creation is up to you.

2. These related distortions represent a picture of what actually occurred in the separation, or the "detour into fear." [2]None of this existed before the separation, nor does it actually exist now. [3]Everything God created is like Him. [4]Extension, as undertaken by God, is similar to the inner radiance that the children of the Father inherit from Him. [5]Its real source is internal. [6]This is as true of the Son as of the Father. [7]In this sense the creation includes both the creation of the Son by God, and the Son's creations when his mind is healed. [8]This requires God's endowment of the Son with free will, because all loving creation is freely given in one continuous line, in which all aspects are of the same order.

3. The Garden of Eden, or the pre-separation condition, was a state of mind in which nothing was needed. [2]When Adam listened to the "lies of the serpent," all he heard was untruth. [3]You

17

do not have to continue to believe what is not true unless you choose to do so. [4]All that can literally disappear in the twinkling of an eye because it is merely a misperception. [5]What is seen in dreams seems to be very real. [6]Yet the Bible says that a deep sleep fell upon Adam, and nowhere is there reference to his waking up. [7]The world has not yet experienced any comprehensive reawakening or rebirth. [8]Such a rebirth is impossible as long as you continue to project or miscreate. [9]It still remains within you, however, to extend as God extended His Spirit to you. [10]In reality this is your only choice, because your free will was given you for your joy in creating the perfect.

4.   All fear is ultimately reducible to the basic misperception that you have the ability to usurp the power of God. [2]Of course, you neither can nor have been able to do this. [3]Here is the real basis for your escape from fear. [4]The escape is brought about by your acceptance of the Atonement, which enables you to realize that your errors never really occurred. [5]Only after the deep sleep fell upon Adam could he experience nightmares. [6]If a light is suddenly turned on while someone is dreaming a fearful dream, he may initially interpret the light itself as part of his dream and be afraid of it. [7]However, when he awakens, the light is correctly perceived as the release from the dream, which is then no longer accorded reality. [8]This release does not depend on illusions. [9]The knowledge that illuminates not only sets you free, but also shows you clearly that you *are* free.

5.   Whatever lies you may believe are of no concern to the miracle, which can heal any of them with equal ease. [2]It makes no distinctions among misperceptions. [3]Its sole concern is to distinguish between truth on the one hand, and error on the other. [4]Some miracles may seem to be of greater magnitude than others. [5]But remember the first principle in this course; there is no order of difficulty in miracles. [6]In reality you are perfectly unaffected by all expressions of lack of love. [7]These can be from yourself and others, from yourself to others, or from others to you. [8]Peace is an attribute *in* you. [9]You cannot find it outside. [10]Illness is some form of external searching. [11]Health is inner peace. [12]It enables you to remain unshaken by lack of love from without and capable, through your acceptance of miracles, of correcting the conditions proceeding from lack of love in others.

II. The Atonement as Defense

1. You can do anything I ask. [2]I have asked you to perform miracles, and have made it clear that miracles are natural, corrective, healing and universal. [3]There is nothing they cannot do, but they cannot be performed in the spirit of doubt or fear. [4]When you are afraid of anything, you are acknowledging its power to hurt you. [5]Remember that where your heart is, there is your treasure also. [6]You believe in what you value. [7]If you are afraid, you are valuing wrongly. [8]Your understanding will then inevitably value wrongly, and by endowing all thoughts with equal power will inevitably destroy peace. [9]That is why the Bible speaks of "the peace of God which passeth understanding." [10]This peace is totally incapable of being shaken by errors of any kind. [11]It denies the ability of anything not of God to affect you. [12]This is the proper use of denial. [13]It is not used to hide anything, but to correct error. [14]It brings all error into the light, and since error and darkness are the same, it corrects error automatically.

2. True denial is a powerful protective device. [2]You can and should deny any belief that error can hurt you. [3]This kind of denial is not a concealment but a correction. [4]Your right mind depends on it. [5]Denial of error is a strong defense of truth, but denial of truth results in miscreation, the projections of the ego. [6]In the service of the right mind the denial of error frees the mind, and re-establishes the freedom of the will. [7]When the will is really free it cannot miscreate, because it recognizes only truth.

3. You can defend truth as well as error. [2]The means are easier to understand after the value of the goal is firmly established. [3]It is a question of what it is *for*. [4]Everyone defends his treasure, and will do so automatically. [5]The real questions are, what do you treasure, and how much do you treasure it? [6]Once you have learned to consider these questions and to bring them into all your actions, you will have little difficulty in clarifying the means. [7]The means are available whenever you ask. [8]You can, however, save time if you do not protract this step unduly. [9]The correct focus will shorten it immeasurably.

4. The Atonement is the only defense that cannot be used destructively because it is not a device you made. [2]The Atonement *principle* was in effect long before the Atonement began. [3]The principle was love and the Atonement was an *act* of love. [4]Acts were not necessary before the separation, because belief in

19

space and time did not exist. ⁵It was only after the separation that the Atonement and the conditions necessary for its fulfillment were planned. ⁶Then a defense so splendid was needed that it could not be misused, although it could be refused. ⁷Refusal could not, however, turn it into a weapon of attack, which is the inherent characteristic of other defenses. ⁸The Atonement thus becomes the only defense that is not a two-edged sword. ⁹It can only heal.

5. The Atonement was built into the space-time belief to set a limit on the need for the belief itself, and ultimately to make learning complete. ²The Atonement is the final lesson. ³Learning itself, like the classrooms in which it occurs, is temporary. ⁴The ability to learn has no value when change is no longer necessary. ⁵The eternally creative have nothing to learn. ⁶You can learn to improve your perceptions, and can become a better and better learner. ⁷This will bring you into closer and closer accord with the Sonship; but the Sonship itself is a perfect creation and perfection is not a matter of degree. ⁸Only while there is a belief in differences is learning meaningful.

6. Evolution is a process in which you seem to proceed from one degree to the next. ²You correct your previous missteps by stepping forward. ³This process is actually incomprehensible in temporal terms, because you return as you go forward. ⁴The Atonement is the device by which you can free yourself from the past as you go ahead. ⁵It undoes your past errors, thus making it unnecessary for you to keep retracing your steps without advancing to your return. ⁶In this sense the Atonement saves time, but like the miracle it serves, does not abolish it. ⁷As long as there is need for Atonement, there is need for time. ⁸But the Atonement as a completed plan has a unique relationship to time. ⁹Until the Atonement is complete, its various phases will proceed in time, but the whole Atonement stands at time's end. ¹⁰At that point the bridge of return has been built.

7. The Atonement is a total commitment. ²You may still think this is associated with loss, a mistake all the separated Sons of God make in one way or another. ³It is hard to believe a defense that cannot attack is the best defense. ⁴This is what is meant by "the meek shall inherit the earth." ⁵They will literally take it over because of their strength. ⁶A two-way defense is inherently weak precisely because it has two edges, and can be turned against you very unexpectedly. ⁷This possibility cannot be controlled

except by miracles. ⁸The miracle turns the defense of Atonement to your real protection, and as you become more and more secure you assume your natural talent of protecting others, knowing yourself as both a brother and a Son.

III. The Altar of God

1. The Atonement can only be accepted within you by releasing the inner light. ²Since the separation, defenses have been used almost entirely to defend *against* the Atonement, and thus maintain the separation. ³This is generally seen as a need to protect the body. ⁴The many body fantasies in which minds engage arise from the distorted belief that the body can be used as a means for attaining "atonement." ⁵Perceiving the body as a temple is only the first step in correcting this distortion, because it alters only part of it. ⁶It *does* recognize that Atonement in physical terms is impossible. ⁷The next step, however, is to realize that a temple is not a structure at all. ⁸Its true holiness lies at the inner altar around which the structure is built. ⁹The emphasis on beautiful structures is a sign of the fear of Atonement, and an unwillingness to reach the altar itself. ¹⁰The real beauty of the temple cannot be seen with the physical eye. ¹¹Spiritual sight, on the other hand, cannot see the structure at all because it is perfect vision. ¹²It can, however, see the altar with perfect clarity.

2. For perfect effectiveness the Atonement belongs at the center of the inner altar, where it undoes the separation and restores the wholeness of the mind. ²Before the separation the mind was invulnerable to fear, because fear did not exist. ³Both the separation and the fear are miscreations that must be undone for the restoration of the temple, and for the opening of the altar to receive the Atonement. ⁴This heals the separation by placing within you the one effective defense against all separation thoughts and making you perfectly invulnerable.

3. The acceptance of the Atonement by everyone is only a matter of time. ²This may appear to contradict free will because of the inevitability of the final decision, but this is not so. ³You can temporize and you are capable of enormous procrastination, but you cannot depart entirely from your Creator, Who set the limits on your ability to miscreate. ⁴An imprisoned will engenders a situation which, in the extreme, becomes altogether intolerable.

⁵Tolerance for pain may be high, but it is not without limit. ⁶Eventually everyone begins to recognize, however dimly, that there *must* be a better way. ⁷As this recognition becomes more firmly established, it becomes a turning point. ⁸This ultimately reawakens spiritual vision, simultaneously weakening the investment in physical sight. ⁹The alternating investment in the two levels of perception is usually experienced as conflict, which can become very acute. ¹⁰But the outcome is as certain as God.

4. Spiritual vision literally cannot see error, and merely looks for Atonement. ²All solutions the physical eye seeks dissolve. ³Spiritual vision looks within and recognizes immediately that the altar has been defiled and needs to be repaired and protected. ⁴Perfectly aware of the right defense it passes over all others, looking past error to truth. ⁵Because of the strength of its vision, it brings the mind into its service. ⁶This re-establishes the power of the mind and makes it increasingly unable to tolerate delay, realizing that it only adds unnecessary pain. ⁷As a result, the mind becomes increasingly sensitive to what it would once have regarded as very minor intrusions of discomfort.

5. The children of God are entitled to the perfect comfort that comes from perfect trust. ²Until they achieve this, they waste themselves and their true creative powers on useless attempts to make themselves more comfortable by inappropriate means. ³But the real means are already provided, and do not involve any effort at all on their part. ⁴The Atonement is the only gift that is worthy of being offered at the altar of God, because of the value of the altar itself. ⁵It was created perfect and is entirely worthy of receiving perfection. ⁶God and His creations are completely dependent on Each Other. ⁷He depends on them *because* He created them perfect. ⁸He gave them His peace so they could not be shaken and could not be deceived. ⁹Whenever you are afraid you *are* deceived, and your mind cannot serve the Holy Spirit. ¹⁰This starves you by denying you your daily bread. ¹¹God is lonely without His Sons, and they are lonely without Him. ¹²They must learn to look upon the world as a means of healing the separation. ¹³The Atonement is the guarantee that they will ultimately succeed.

IV. Healing as Release from Fear

1. Our emphasis is now on healing. ²The miracle is the means, the Atonement is the principle, and healing is the result. ³To speak of "a miracle of healing" is to combine two orders of reality inappropriately. ⁴Healing is not a miracle. ⁵The Atonement, or the final miracle, is a remedy and any type of healing is a result. ⁶The kind of error to which Atonement is applied is irrelevant. ⁷All healing is essentially the release from fear. ⁸To undertake this you cannot be fearful yourself. ⁹You do not understand healing because of your own fear.

2. A major step in the Atonement plan is to undo error at all levels. ²Sickness or "not-right-mindedness" is the result of level confusion, because it always entails the belief that what is amiss on one level can adversely affect another. ³We have referred to miracles as the means of correcting level confusion, for all mistakes must be corrected at the level on which they occur. ⁴Only the mind is capable of error. ⁵The body can act wrongly only when it is responding to misthought. ⁶The body cannot create, and the belief that it can, a fundamental error, produces all physical symptoms. ⁷Physical illness represents a belief in magic. ⁸The whole distortion that made magic rests on the belief that there is a creative ability in matter which the mind cannot control. ⁹This error can take two forms; it can be believed that the mind can miscreate in the body, or that the body can miscreate in the mind. ¹⁰When it is understood that the mind, the only level of creation, cannot create beyond itself, neither type of confusion need occur.

3. Only the mind can create because spirit has already been created, and the body is a learning device for the mind. ²Learning devices are not lessons in themselves. ³Their purpose is merely to facilitate learning. ⁴The worst a faulty use of a learning device can do is to fail to facilitate learning. ⁵It has no power in itself to introduce actual learning errors. ⁶The body, if properly understood, shares the invulnerability of the Atonement to two-edged application. ⁷This is not because the body is a miracle, but because it is not inherently open to misinterpretation. ⁸The body is merely part of your experience in the physical world. ⁹Its abilities can be and frequently are overevaluated. ¹⁰However, it is almost impossible to deny its existence in this world. ¹¹Those who do so are engaging in a particularly unworthy form of denial. ¹²The term "unworthy" here implies only that it is not necessary

to protect the mind by denying the unmindful. [13]If one denies this unfortunate aspect of the mind's power, one is also denying the power itself.

4. All material means that you accept as remedies for bodily ills are restatements of magic principles. [2]This is the first step in believing that the body makes its own illness. [3]It is a second misstep to attempt to heal it through non-creative agents. [4]It does not follow, however, that the use of such agents for corrective purposes is evil. [5]Sometimes the illness has a sufficiently strong hold over the mind to render a person temporarily inaccessible to the Atonement. [6]In this case it may be wise to utilize a compromise approach to mind and body, in which something from the outside is temporarily given healing belief. [7]This is because the last thing that can help the non-right-minded, or the sick, is an increase in fear. [8]They are already in a fear-weakened state. [9]If they are prematurely exposed to a miracle, they may be precipitated into panic. [10]This is likely to occur when upside-down perception has induced the belief that miracles are frightening.

5. The value of the Atonement does not lie in the manner in which it is expressed. [2]In fact, if it is used truly, it will inevitably be expressed in whatever way is most helpful to the receiver. [3]This means that a miracle, to attain its full efficacy, must be expressed in a language that the recipient can understand without fear. [4]This does not necessarily mean that this is the highest level of communication of which he is capable. [5]It does mean, however, that it is the highest level of communication of which he is capable *now*. [6]The whole aim of the miracle is to raise the level of communication, not to lower it by increasing fear.

V. The Function of the Miracle Worker

1. Before miracle workers are ready to undertake their function in this world, it is essential that they fully understand the fear of release. [2]Otherwise they may unwittingly foster the belief that release is imprisonment, a belief that is already very prevalent. [3]This misperception arises in turn from the belief that harm can be limited to the body. [4]That is because of the underlying fear that the mind can hurt itself. [5]None of these errors is meaningful, because the miscreations of the mind do not really exist. [6]This

recognition is a far better protective device than any form of level confusion, because it introduces correction at the level of the error. [7]It is essential to remember that only the mind can create, and that correction belongs at the thought level. [8]To amplify an earlier statement, spirit is already perfect and therefore does not require correction. [9]The body does not exist except as a learning device for the mind. [10]This learning device is not subject to errors of its own, because it cannot create. [11]It is obvious, then, that inducing the mind to give up its miscreations is the only application of creative ability that is truly meaningful.

2. Magic is the mindless or the miscreative use of mind. [2]Physical medications are forms of "spells," but if you are afraid to use the mind to heal, you should not attempt to do so. [3]The very fact that you are afraid makes your mind vulnerable to miscreation. [4]You are therefore likely to misunderstand any healing that might occur, and because egocentricity and fear usually occur together, you may be unable to accept the real Source of the healing. [5]Under these conditions, it is safer for you to rely temporarily on physical healing devices, because you cannot misperceive them as your own creations. [6]As long as your sense of vulnerability persists, you should not attempt to perform miracles.

3. I have already said that miracles are expressions of miracle-mindedness, and miracle-mindedness means right-mindedness. [2]The right-minded neither exalt nor depreciate the mind of the miracle worker or the miracle receiver. [3]However, as a correction, the miracle need not await the right-mindedness of the receiver. [4]In fact, its purpose is to restore him *to* his right mind. [5]It is essential, however, that the miracle worker be in his right mind, however briefly, or he will be unable to re-establish right-mindedness in someone else.

4. The healer who relies on his own readiness is endangering his understanding. [2]You are perfectly safe as long as you are completely unconcerned about your readiness, but maintain a consistent trust in mine. [3]If your miracle working inclinations are not functioning properly, it is always because fear has intruded on your right-mindedness and has turned it upside down. [4]All forms of not-right-mindedness are the result of refusal to accept the Atonement for yourself. [5]If you do accept it, you are in a position to recognize that those who need healing are simply those who have not realized that right-mindedness *is* healing.

5. *The sole responsibility of the miracle worker is to accept the Atone-*

ment for himself. ²This means you recognize that mind is the only creative level, and that its errors are healed by the Atonement. ³Once you accept this, your mind can only heal. ⁴By denying your mind any destructive potential and reinstating its purely constructive powers, you place yourself in a position to undo the level confusion of others. ⁵The message you then give to them is the truth that their minds are similarly constructive, and their miscreations cannot hurt them. ⁶By affirming this you release the mind from overevaluating its own learning device, and restore the mind to its true position as the learner.

6. It should be emphasized again that the body does not learn any more than it creates. ²As a learning device it merely follows the learner, but if it is falsely endowed with self-initiative, it becomes a serious obstruction to the very learning it should facilitate. ³Only the mind is capable of illumination. ⁴Spirit is already illuminated and the body in itself is too dense. ⁵The mind, however, can bring its illumination to the body by recognizing that it is not the learner, and is therefore unamenable to learning. ⁶The body is, however, easily brought into alignment with a mind that has learned to look beyond it toward the light.

7. Corrective learning always begins with the awakening of spirit, and the turning away from the belief in physical sight. ²This often entails fear, because you are afraid of what your spiritual sight will show you. ³I said before that the Holy Spirit cannot see error, and is capable only of looking beyond it to the defense of Atonement. ⁴There is no doubt that this may produce discomfort, yet the discomfort is not the final outcome of the perception. ⁵When the Holy Spirit is permitted to look upon the defilement of the altar, He also looks immediately toward the Atonement. ⁶Nothing He perceives can induce fear. ⁷Everything that results from spiritual awareness is merely channelized toward correction. ⁸Discomfort is aroused only to bring the need for correction into awareness.

8. The fear of healing arises in the end from an unwillingness to accept unequivocally that healing is necessary. ²What the physical eye sees is not corrective, nor can error be corrected by any device that can be seen physically. ³As long as you believe in what your physical sight tells you, your attempts at correction will be misdirected. ⁴The real vision is obscured, because you cannot endure to see your own defiled altar. ⁵But since the altar has been defiled, your state becomes doubly dangerous unless it

is perceived.

9. Healing is an ability that developed after the separation, before which it was unnecessary. [2]Like all aspects of the belief in space and time, it is temporary. [3]However, as long as time persists, healing is needed as a means of protection. [4]This is because healing rests on charity, and charity is a way of perceiving the perfection of another even if you cannot perceive it in yourself. [5]Most of the loftier concepts of which you are capable now are time-dependent. [6]Charity is really a weaker reflection of a much more powerful love-encompassment that is far beyond any form of charity you can conceive of as yet. [7]Charity is essential to right-mindedness in the limited sense in which it can now be attained.

10. Charity is a way of looking at another as if he had already gone far beyond his actual accomplishments in time. [2]Since his own thinking is faulty he cannot see the Atonement for himself, or he would have no need of charity. [3]The charity that is accorded him is both an acknowledgment that he needs help, and a recognition that he will accept it. [4]Both of these perceptions clearly imply their dependence on time, making it apparent that charity still lies within the limitations of this world. [5]I said before that only revelation transcends time. [6]The miracle, as an expression of charity, can only shorten it. [7]It must be understood, however, that whenever you offer a miracle to another, you are shortening the suffering of both of you. [8]This corrects retroactively as well as progressively.

A. Special Principles of Miracle Workers

11. (1) The miracle abolishes the need for lower-order concerns. [2]Since it is an out-of-pattern time interval, the ordinary considerations of time and space do not apply. [3]When you perform a miracle, I will arrange both time and space to adjust to it.

12. (2) A clear distinction between what is created and what is made is essential. [2]All forms of healing rest on this fundamental correction in level perception.

13. (3) Never confuse right- and wrong-mindedness. [2]Responding to any form of error with anything except a desire to heal is an expression of this confusion.

14. (4) The miracle is always a denial of this error and an affirmation of the truth. [2]Only right-mindedness can correct in a way that has any real effect. [3]Pragmatically, what has no real effect

has no real existence. ⁴Its effect, then, is emptiness. ⁵Being without substantial content, it lends itself to projection.

15. (5) The level-adjustment power of the miracle induces the right perception for healing. ²Until this has occurred healing cannot be understood. ³Forgiveness is an empty gesture unless it entails correction. ⁴Without this it is essentially judgmental, rather than healing.

16. (6) Miracle-minded forgiveness is *only* correction. ²It has no element of judgment at all. ³The statement "Father forgive them for they know not what they do" in no way evaluates *what* they do. ⁴It is an appeal to God to heal their minds. ⁵There is no reference to the outcome of the error. ⁶That does not matter.

17. (7) The injunction "Be of one mind" is the statement for revelation-readiness. ²My request "Do this in remembrance of me" is the appeal for cooperation from miracle workers. ³The two statements are not in the same order of reality. ⁴Only the latter involves an awareness of time, since to remember is to recall the past in the present. ⁵Time is under my direction, but timelessness belongs to God. ⁶In time we exist for and with each other. ⁷In timelessness we coexist with God.

18. (8) You can do much on behalf of your own healing and that of others if, in a situation calling for help, you think of it this way:

> ²*I am here only to be truly helpful.*
> ³*I am here to represent Him Who sent me.*
> ⁴*I do not have to worry about what to say or what*
>   *to do, because He Who sent me will direct me.*
> ⁵*I am content to be wherever He wishes, knowing*
>   *He goes there with me.*
> ⁶*I will be healed as I let Him teach me to heal.*

VI. Fear and Conflict

1. Being afraid seems to be involuntary; something beyond your own control. ²Yet I have said already that only constructive acts should be involuntary. ³My control can take over everything that does not matter, while my guidance can direct everything that does, if you so choose. ⁴Fear cannot be controlled by me, but it can be self-controlled. ⁵Fear prevents me from giving you my control. ⁶The presence of fear shows that you have raised body

thoughts to the level of the mind. [7]This removes them from my control, and makes you feel personally responsible for them. [8]This is an obvious confusion of levels.

2.   I do not foster level confusion, but you must choose to correct it. [2]You would not excuse insane behavior on your part by saying you could not help it. [3]Why should you condone insane thinking? [4]There is a confusion here that you would do well to look at clearly. [5]You may believe that you are responsible for what you do, but not for what you think. [6]The truth is that you are responsible for what you think, because it is only at this level that you can exercise choice. [7]What you do comes from what you think. [8]You cannot separate yourself from the truth by "giving" autonomy to behavior. [9]This is controlled by me automatically as soon as you place what you think under my guidance. [10]Whenever you are afraid, it is a sure sign that you have allowed your mind to miscreate and have not allowed me to guide it.

3.   It is pointless to believe that controlling the outcome of misthought can result in healing. [2]When you are fearful, you have chosen wrongly. [3]That is why you feel responsible for it. [4]You must change your mind, not your behavior, and this *is* a matter of willingness. [5]You do not need guidance except at the mind level. [6]Correction belongs only at the level where change is possible. [7]Change does not mean anything at the symptom level, where it cannot work.

4.   The correction of fear *is* your responsibility. [2]When you ask for release from fear, you are implying that it is not. [3]You should ask, instead, for help in the conditions that have brought the fear about. [4]These conditions always entail a willingness to be separate. [5]At that level you *can* help it. [6]You are much too tolerant of mind wandering, and are passively condoning your mind's miscreations. [7]The particular result does not matter, but the fundamental error does. [8]The correction is always the same. [9]Before you choose to do anything, ask me if your choice is in accord with mine. [10]If you are sure that it is, there will be no fear.

5.   Fear is always a sign of strain, arising whenever what you want conflicts with what you do. [2]This situation arises in two ways: First, you can choose to do conflicting things, either simultaneously or successively. [3]This produces conflicted behavior, which is intolerable to you because the part of the mind that wants to do something else is outraged. [4]Second, you can behave as you think you should, but without entirely wanting to do so.

⁵This produces consistent behavior, but entails great strain. ⁶In both cases, the mind and the behavior are out of accord, resulting in a situation in which you are doing what you do not wholly want to do. ⁷This arouses a sense of coercion that usually produces rage, and projection is likely to follow. ⁸Whenever there is fear, it is because you have not made up your mind. ⁹Your mind is therefore split, and your behavior inevitably becomes erratic. ¹⁰Correcting at the behavioral level can shift the error from the first to the second type, but will not obliterate the fear.

6. It is possible to reach a state in which you bring your mind under my guidance without conscious effort, but this implies a willingness that you have not developed as yet. ²The Holy Spirit cannot ask more than you are willing to do. ³The strength to do comes from your undivided decision. ⁴There is no strain in doing God's Will as soon as you recognize that it is also your own. ⁵The lesson here is quite simple, but particularly apt to be overlooked. ⁶I will therefore repeat it, urging you to listen. ⁷Only your mind can produce fear. ⁸It does so whenever it is conflicted in what it wants, producing inevitable strain because wanting and doing are discordant. ⁹This can be corrected only by accepting a unified goal.

7. The first corrective step in undoing the error is to know first that the conflict is an expression of fear. ²Say to yourself that you must somehow have chosen not to love, or the fear could not have arisen. ³Then the whole process of correction becomes nothing more than a series of pragmatic steps in the larger process of accepting the Atonement as the remedy. ⁴These steps may be summarized in this way:

⁵Know first that this is fear.
⁶Fear arises from lack of love.
⁷The only remedy for lack of love is perfect love.
⁸Perfect love is the Atonement.

8. I have emphasized that the miracle, or the expression of Atonement, is always a sign of respect *from* the worthy *to* the worthy. ²The recognition of this worth is re-established by the Atonement. ³It is obvious, then, that when you are afraid, you have placed yourself in a position where you need Atonement. ⁴You have done something loveless, having chosen without love. ⁵This is precisely the situation for which the Atonement was offered. ⁶The need for the remedy inspired its establishment. ⁷As long as you recognize only the need for the remedy, you will

remain fearful. [8]However, as soon as you accept the remedy, you have abolished the fear. [9]This is how true healing occurs.

9. Everyone experiences fear. [2]Yet it would take very little right thinking to realize why fear occurs. [3]Few appreciate the real power of the mind, and no one remains fully aware of it all the time. [4]However, if you hope to spare yourself from fear there are some things you must realize, and realize fully. [5]The mind is very powerful, and never loses its creative force. [6]It never sleeps. [7]Every instant it is creating. [8]It is hard to recognize that thought and belief combine into a power surge that can literally move mountains. [9]It appears at first glance that to believe such power about yourself is arrogant, but that is not the real reason you do not believe it. [10]You prefer to believe that your thoughts cannot exert real influence because you are actually afraid of them. [11]This may allay awareness of the guilt, but at the cost of perceiving the mind as impotent. [12]If you believe that what you think is ineffectual you may cease to be afraid of it, but you are hardly likely to respect it. [13]There *are* no idle thoughts. [14]All thinking produces form at some level.

VII. Cause and Effect

1. You may still complain about fear, but you nevertheless persist in making yourself fearful. [2]I have already indicated that you cannot ask me to release you from fear. [3]I know it does not exist, but you do not. [4]If I intervened between your thoughts and their results, I would be tampering with a basic law of cause and effect; the most fundamental law there is. [5]I would hardly help you if I depreciated the power of your own thinking. [6]This would be in direct opposition to the purpose of this course. [7]It is much more helpful to remind you that you do not guard your thoughts carefully enough. [8]You may feel that at this point it would take a miracle to enable you to do this, which is perfectly true. [9]You are not used to miracle-minded thinking, but you can be trained to think that way. [10]All miracle workers need that kind of training.

2. I cannot let you leave your mind unguarded, or you will not be able to help me. [2]Miracle working entails a full realization of the power of thought in order to avoid miscreation. [3]Otherwise a miracle will be necessary to set the mind itself straight, a circular process that would not foster the time collapse for which the

miracle was intended. [4]The miracle worker must have genuine respect for true cause and effect as a necessary condition for the miracle to occur.

3. Both miracles and fear come from thoughts. [2]If you are not free to choose one, you would also not be free to choose the other. [3]By choosing the miracle you *have* rejected fear, if only temporarily. [4]You have been fearful of everyone and everything. [5]You are afraid of God, of me and of yourself. [6]You have misperceived or miscreated Us, and believe in what you have made. [7]You would not have done this if you were not afraid of your own thoughts. [8]The fearful *must* miscreate, because they misperceive creation. [9]When you miscreate you are in pain. [10]The cause and effect principle now becomes a real expediter, though only temporarily. [11]Actually, "Cause" is a term properly belonging to God, and His "Effect" is His Son. [12]This entails a set of Cause and Effect relationships totally different from those you introduce into miscreation. [13]The fundamental conflict in this world, then, is between creation and miscreation. [14]All fear is implicit in the second, and all love in the first. [15]The conflict is therefore one between love and fear.

4. It has already been said that you believe you cannot control fear because you yourself made it, and your belief in it seems to render it out of your control. [2]Yet any attempt to resolve the error through attempting the mastery of fear is useless. [3]In fact, it asserts the power of fear by the very assumption that it need be mastered. [4]The true resolution rests entirely on mastery through love. [5]In the interim, however, the sense of conflict is inevitable, since you have placed yourself in a position where you believe in the power of what does not exist.

5. Nothing and everything cannot coexist. [2]To believe in one is to deny the other. [3]Fear is really nothing and love is everything. [4]Whenever light enters darkness, the darkness is abolished. [5]What you believe is true for you. [6]In this sense the separation *has* occurred, and to deny it is merely to use denial inappropriately. [7]However, to concentrate on error is only a further error. [8]The initial corrective procedure is to recognize temporarily that there is a problem, but only as an indication that immediate correction is needed. [9]This establishes a state of mind in which the Atonement can be accepted without delay. [10]It should be emphasized, however, that ultimately no compromise is possible between everything and nothing. [11]Time is essentially a device by

which all compromise in this respect can be given up. ¹²It only seems to be abolished by degrees, because time itself involves intervals that do not exist. ¹³Miscreation made this necessary as a corrective device. ¹⁴The statement "For God so loved the world that he gave his only begotten Son, that whosoever believeth in him should not perish but have everlasting life" needs only one slight correction to be meaningful in this context; "He gave it *to* His only begotten Son."

6. It should especially be noted that God has only *one* Son. ²If all His creations are His Sons, every one must be an integral part of the whole Sonship. ³The Sonship in its Oneness transcends the sum of its parts. ⁴However, this is obscured as long as any of its parts is missing. ⁵That is why the conflict cannot ultimately be resolved until all the parts of the Sonship have returned. ⁶Only then can the meaning of wholeness in the true sense be understood. ⁷Any part of the Sonship can believe in error or incompleteness if he so chooses. ⁸However, if he does so, he is believing in the existence of nothingness. ⁹The correction of this error is the Atonement.

7. I have already briefly spoken about readiness, but some additional points might be helpful here. ²Readiness is only the prerequisite for accomplishment. ³The two should not be confused. ⁴As soon as a state of readiness occurs, there is usually some degree of desire to accomplish, but it is by no means necessarily undivided. ⁵The state does not imply more than a potential for a change of mind. ⁶Confidence cannot develop fully until mastery has been accomplished. ⁷We have already attempted to correct the fundamental error that fear can be mastered, and have emphasized that the only real mastery is through love. ⁸Readiness is only the beginning of confidence. ⁹You may think this implies that an enormous amount of time is necessary between readiness and mastery, but let me remind you that time and space are under my control.

VIII. The Meaning of the Last Judgment

1. One of the ways in which you can correct the magic-miracle confusion is to remember that you did not create yourself. ²You are apt to forget this when you become egocentric, and this puts you in a position where a belief in magic is virtually inevitable.

³Your will to create was given you by your Creator, Who was expressing the same Will in His creation. ⁴Since creative ability rests in the mind, everything you create is necessarily a matter of will. ⁵It also follows that whatever you alone make is real in your own sight, though not in the Mind of God. ⁶This basic distinction leads directly into the real meaning of the Last Judgment.

2. The Last Judgment is one of the most threatening ideas in your thinking. ²This is because you do not understand it. ³Judgment is not an attribute of God. ⁴It was brought into being only after the separation, when it became one of the many learning devices to be built into the overall plan. ⁵Just as the separation occurred over millions of years, the Last Judgment will extend over a similarly long period, and perhaps an even longer one. ⁶Its length can, however, be greatly shortened by miracles, the device for shortening but not abolishing time. ⁷If a sufficient number become truly miracle-minded, this shortening process can be virtually immeasurable. ⁸It is essential, however, that you free yourself from fear quickly, because you must emerge from the conflict if you are to bring peace to other minds.

3. The Last Judgment is generally thought of as a procedure undertaken by God. ²Actually it will be undertaken by my brothers with my help. ³It is a final healing rather than a meting out of punishment, however much you may think that punishment is deserved. ⁴Punishment is a concept totally opposed to right-mindedness, and the aim of the Last Judgment is to restore right-mindedness to you. ⁵The Last Judgment might be called a process of right evaluation. ⁶It simply means that everyone will finally come to understand what is worthy and what is not. ⁷After this, the ability to choose can be directed rationally. ⁸Until this distinction is made, however, the vacillations between free and imprisoned will cannot but continue.

4. The first step toward freedom involves a sorting out of the false from the true. ²This is a process of separation in the constructive sense, and reflects the true meaning of the Apocalypse. ³Everyone will ultimately look upon his own creations and choose to preserve only what is good, just as God Himself looked upon what He had created and knew that it was good. ⁴At this point, the mind can begin to look with love on its own creations because of their worthiness. ⁵At the same time the mind will inevitably disown its miscreations which, without belief, will no longer exist.

5. The term "Last Judgment" is frightening not only because it has been projected onto God, but also because of the association of "last" with death. [2]This is an outstanding example of upside-down perception. [3]If the meaning of the Last Judgment is objectively examined, it is quite apparent that it is really the doorway to life. [4]No one who lives in fear is really alive. [5]Your own last judgment cannot be directed toward yourself, because you are not your own creation. [6]You can, however, apply it meaningfully and at any time to everything you have made, and retain in your memory only what is creative and good. [7]This is what your right-mindedness cannot but dictate. [8]The purpose of time is solely to "give you time" to achieve this judgment. [9]It is your own perfect judgment of your own perfect creations. [10]When everything you retain is lovable, there is no reason for fear to remain with you. [11]This is your part in the Atonement.

Chapter 3

THE INNOCENT PERCEPTION

I. Atonement without Sacrifice

1. A further point must be perfectly clear before any residual fear still associated with miracles can disappear. [2]The crucifixion did not establish the Atonement; the resurrection did. [3]Many sincere Christians have misunderstood this. [4]No one who is free of the belief in scarcity could possibly make this mistake. [5]If the crucifixion is seen from an upside-down point of view, it does appear as if God permitted and even encouraged one of His Sons to suffer because he was good. [6]This particularly unfortunate interpretation, which arose out of projection, has led many people to be bitterly afraid of God. [7]Such anti-religious concepts enter into many religions. [8]Yet the real Christian should pause and ask, "How could this be?" [9]Is it likely that God Himself would be capable of the kind of thinking which His Own words have clearly stated is unworthy of His Son?

2. The best defense, as always, is not to attack another's position, but rather to protect the truth. [2]It is unwise to accept any concept if you have to invert a whole frame of reference in order to justify it. [3]This procedure is painful in its minor applications and genuinely tragic on a wider scale. [4]Persecution frequently results in an attempt to "justify" the terrible misperception that God Himself persecuted His Own Son on behalf of salvation. [5]The very words are meaningless. [6]It has been particularly difficult to overcome this because, although the error itself is no harder to correct than any other, many have been unwilling to give it up in view of its prominent value as a defense. [7]In milder forms a parent says, "This hurts me more than it hurts you," and feels exonerated in beating a child. [8]Can you believe our Father really thinks this way? [9]It is so essential that all such thinking be dispelled that we must be sure that nothing of this kind remains in your mind. [10]I was not "punished" because *you* were bad. [11]The wholly benign lesson the Atonement teaches is lost if it is tainted with this kind of distortion in any form.

3. The statement "Vengeance is mine, saith the Lord" is a misperception by which one assigns his own "evil" past to God.

²The "evil" past has nothing to do with God. ³He did not create it and He does not maintain it. ⁴God does not believe in retribution. ⁵His Mind does not create that way. ⁶He does not hold your "evil" deeds against you. ⁷Is it likely that He would hold them against me? ⁸Be very sure that you recognize how utterly impossible this assumption is, and how entirely it arises from projection. ⁹This kind of error is responsible for a host of related errors, including the belief that God rejected Adam and forced him out of the Garden of Eden. ¹⁰It is also why you may believe from time to time that I am misdirecting you. ¹¹I have made every effort to use words that are almost impossible to distort, but it is always possible to twist symbols around if you wish.

4. Sacrifice is a notion totally unknown to God. ²It arises solely from fear, and frightened people can be vicious. ³Sacrificing in any way is a violation of my injunction that you should be merciful even as your Father in Heaven is merciful. ⁴It has been hard for many Christians to realize that this applies to themselves. ⁵Good teachers never terrorize their students. ⁶To terrorize is to attack, and this results in rejection of what the teacher offers. ⁷The result is learning failure.

5. I have been correctly referred to as "the lamb of God who taketh away the sins of the world," but those who represent the lamb as blood-stained do not understand the meaning of the symbol. ²Correctly understood, it is a very simple symbol that speaks of my innocence. ³The lion and the lamb lying together symbolize that strength and innocence are not in conflict, but naturally live in peace. ⁴"Blessed are the pure in heart for they shall see God" is another way of saying the same thing. ⁵A pure mind knows the truth and this is its strength. ⁶It does not confuse destruction with innocence because it associates innocence with strength, not with weakness.

6. Innocence is incapable of sacrificing anything, because the innocent mind has everything and strives only to protect its wholeness. ²It cannot project. ³It can only honor other minds, because honor is the natural greeting of the truly loved to others who are like them. ⁴The lamb "taketh away the sins of the world" in the sense that the state of innocence, or grace, is one in which the meaning of the Atonement is perfectly apparent. ⁵The Atonement is entirely unambiguous. ⁶It is perfectly clear because it exists in light. ⁷Only the attempts to shroud it in darkness have made it inaccessible to those who do not choose to see.

7.   The Atonement itself radiates nothing but truth. ²It therefore epitomizes harmlessness and sheds only blessing. ³It could not do this if it arose from anything but perfect innocence. ⁴Innocence is wisdom because it is unaware of evil, and evil does not exist. ⁵It is, however, perfectly aware of everything that is true. ⁶The resurrection demonstrated that nothing can destroy truth. ⁷Good can withstand any form of evil, as light abolishes forms of darkness. ⁸The Atonement is therefore the perfect lesson. ⁹It is the final demonstration that all the other lessons I taught are true. ¹⁰If you can accept this one generalization now, there will be no need to learn from many smaller lessons. ¹¹You are released from all errors if you believe this.

8.   The innocence of God is the true state of the mind of His Son. ²In this state your mind knows God, for God is not symbolic; He is Fact. ³Knowing His Son as he is, you realize that the Atonement, not sacrifice, is the only appropriate gift for God's altar, where nothing except perfection belongs. ⁴The understanding of the innocent is truth. ⁵That is why their altars are truly radiant.

II. Miracles as True Perception

1.   I have stated that the basic concepts referred to in this course are not matters of degree. ²Certain fundamental concepts cannot be understood in terms of opposites. ³It is impossible to conceive of light and darkness or everything and nothing as joint possibilities. ⁴They are all true or all false. ⁵It is essential that you realize your thinking will be erratic until a firm commitment to one or the other is made. ⁶A firm commitment to darkness or nothingness, however, is impossible. ⁷No one has ever lived who has not experienced *some* light and *some* thing. ⁸No one, therefore, is able to deny truth totally, even if he thinks he can.

2.   Innocence is not a partial attribute. ²It is not real *until* it is total. ³The partly innocent are apt to be quite foolish at times. ⁴It is not until their innocence becomes a viewpoint with universal application that it becomes wisdom. ⁵Innocent or true perception means that you never misperceive and always see truly. ⁶More simply, it means that you never see what does not exist, and always see what does.

3.   When you lack confidence in what someone will do, you are attesting to your belief that he is not in his right mind. ²This is

hardly a miracle-based frame of reference. ³It also has the disastrous effect of denying the power of the miracle. ⁴The miracle perceives everything as it is. ⁵If nothing but the truth exists, right-minded seeing cannot see anything but perfection. ⁶I have said that only what God creates or what you create with the same Will has any real existence. ⁷This, then, is all the innocent can see. ⁸They do not suffer from distorted perception.

4. You are afraid of God's Will because you have used your own mind, which He created in the likeness of His Own, to miscreate. ²The mind can miscreate only when it believes it is not free. ³An "imprisoned" mind is not free because it is possessed, or held back, by itself. ⁴It is therefore limited, and the will is not free to assert itself. ⁵To be one is to be of one mind or will. ⁶When the Will of the Sonship and the Father are one, their perfect accord is Heaven.

5. Nothing can prevail against a Son of God who commends his spirit into the Hands of his Father. ²By doing this the mind awakens from its sleep and remembers its Creator. ³All sense of separation disappears. ⁴The Son of God is part of the Holy Trinity, but the Trinity Itself is One. ⁵There is no confusion within Its Levels, because They are of one Mind and one Will. ⁶This single purpose creates perfect integration and establishes the peace of God. ⁷Yet this vision can be perceived only by the truly innocent. ⁸Because their hearts are pure, the innocent defend true perception instead of defending themselves against it. ⁹Understanding the lesson of the Atonement they are without the wish to attack, and therefore they see truly. ¹⁰This is what the Bible means when it says, "When he shall appear (or be perceived) we shall be like him, for we shall see him as he is."

6. The way to correct distortions is to withdraw your faith in them and invest it only in what is true. ²You cannot make untruth true. ³If you are willing to accept what is true in everything you perceive, you let it be true for you. ⁴Truth overcomes all error, and those who live in error and emptiness can never find lasting solace. ⁵If you perceive truly you are cancelling out misperceptions in yourself and in others simultaneously. ⁶Because you see them as they are, you offer them your acceptance of their truth so they can accept it for themselves. ⁷This is the healing that the miracle induces.

III. Perception versus Knowledge

1. We have been emphasizing perception, and have said very little about knowledge as yet. ²This is because perception must be straightened out before you can know anything. ³To know is to be certain. ⁴Uncertainty means that you do not know. ⁵Knowledge is power because it is certain, and certainty is strength. ⁶Perception is temporary. ⁷As an attribute of the belief in space and time, it is subject to either fear or love. ⁸Misperceptions produce fear and true perceptions foster love, but neither brings certainty because all perception varies. ⁹That is why it is not knowledge. ¹⁰True perception is the basis for knowledge, but knowing is the affirmation of truth and beyond all perceptions.

2. All your difficulties stem from the fact that you do not recognize yourself, your brother or God. ²To recognize means to "know again," implying that you knew before. ³You can see in many ways because perception involves interpretation, and this means that it is not whole or consistent. ⁴The miracle, being a way of perceiving, is not knowledge. ⁵It is the right answer to a question, but you do not question when you know. ⁶Questioning illusions is the first step in undoing them. ⁷The miracle, or the right answer, corrects them. ⁸Since perceptions change, their dependence on time is obvious. ⁹How you perceive at any given time determines what you do, and actions must occur in time. ¹⁰Knowledge is timeless, because certainty is not questionable. ¹¹You know when you have ceased to ask questions.

3. The questioning mind perceives itself in time, and therefore looks for future answers. ²The closed mind believes the future and the present will be the same. ³This establishes a seemingly stable state that is usually an attempt to counteract an underlying fear that the future will be worse than the present. ⁴This fear inhibits the tendency to question at all.

4. True vision is the natural perception of spiritual sight, but it is still a correction rather than a fact. ²Spiritual sight is symbolic, and therefore not a device for knowing. ³It is, however, a means of right perception, which brings it into the proper domain of the miracle. ⁴A "vision of God" would be a miracle rather than a revelation. ⁵The fact that perception is involved at all removes the experience from the realm of knowledge. ⁶That is why visions, however holy, do not last.

5. The Bible tells you to know yourself, or to be certain. ²Certainty

is always of God. ³When you love someone you have perceived him as he is, and this makes it possible for you to know him. ⁴Until you first perceive him as he is you cannot know him. ⁵While you ask questions about him you are clearly implying that you do not know God. ⁶Certainty does not require action. ⁷When you say you are acting on the basis of knowledge, you are really confusing knowledge with perception. ⁸Knowledge provides the strength for creative thinking, but not for right doing. ⁹Perception, miracles and doing are closely related. ¹⁰Knowledge is the result of revelation and induces only thought. ¹¹Even in its most spiritualized form perception involves the body. ¹²Knowledge comes from the altar within and is timeless because it is certain. ¹³To perceive the truth is not the same as to know it.

6.   Right perception is necessary before God can communicate directly to His altars, which He established in His Sons. ²There He can communicate His certainty, and His knowledge will bring peace without question. ³God is not a stranger to His Sons, and His Sons are not strangers to each other. ⁴Knowledge preceded both perception and time, and will ultimately replace them. ⁵That is the real meaning of "Alpha and Omega, the beginning and the end," and "Before Abraham was I am." ⁶Perception can and must be stabilized, but knowledge *is* stable. ⁷"Fear God and keep His commandments" becomes "Know God and accept His certainty."

7.   If you attack error in another, you will hurt yourself. ²You cannot know your brother when you attack him. ³Attack is always made upon a stranger. ⁴You are making him a stranger by misperceiving him, and so you cannot know him. ⁵It is because you have made him a stranger that you are afraid of him. ⁶Perceive him correctly so that you can know him. ⁷There are no strangers in God's creation. ⁸To create as He created you can create only what you know, and therefore accept as yours. ⁹God knows His children with perfect certainty. ¹⁰He created them by knowing them. ¹¹He recognizes them perfectly. ¹²When they do not recognize each other, they do not recognize Him.

IV. Error and the Ego

1.   The abilities you now possess are only shadows of your real strength. ²All of your present functions are divided and open to question and doubt. ³This is because you are not certain how you

will use them, and are therefore incapable of knowledge. ⁴You are also incapable of knowledge because you can still perceive love-lessly. ⁵Perception did not exist until the separation introduced degrees, aspects and intervals. ⁶Spirit has no levels, and all con-flict arises from the concept of levels. ⁷Only the Levels of the Trinity are capable of unity. ⁸The levels created by the separation cannot but conflict. ⁹This is because they are meaningless to each other.

2. Consciousness, the level of perception, was the first split intro-duced into the mind after the separation, making the mind a per-ceiver rather than a creator. ²Consciousness is correctly identified as the domain of the ego. ³The ego is a wrong-minded attempt to perceive yourself as you wish to be, rather than as you are. ⁴Yet you can know yourself only as you are, because that is all you can be sure of. ⁵Everything else *is* open to question.

3. The ego is the questioning aspect of the post-separation self, which was made rather than created. ²It is capable of asking questions but not of perceiving meaningful answers, because these would involve knowledge and cannot be perceived. ³The mind is therefore confused, because only One-mindedness can be without confusion. ⁴A separated or divided mind *must* be con-fused. ⁵It is necessarily uncertain about what it is. ⁶It has to be in conflict because it is out of accord with itself. ⁷This makes its aspects strangers to each other, and this is the essence of the fear-prone condition, in which attack is always possible. ⁸You have every reason to feel afraid as you perceive yourself. ⁹This is why you cannot escape from fear until you realize that you did not and could not create yourself. ¹⁰You can never make your misper-ceptions true, and your creation is beyond your own error. ¹¹That is why you must eventually choose to heal the separation.

4. Right-mindedness is not to be confused with the knowing mind, because it is applicable only to right perception. ²You can be right-minded or wrong-minded, and even this is subject to degrees, clearly demonstrating that knowledge is not involved. ³The term "right-mindedness" is properly used as the correction for "wrong-mindedness," and applies to the state of mind that induces accurate perception. ⁴It is miracle-minded because it heals misperception, and this is indeed a miracle in view of how you perceive yourself.

5. Perception always involves some misuse of mind, because it brings the mind into areas of uncertainty. ²The mind is very

active. ³When it chooses to be separated it chooses to perceive. ⁴Until then it wills only to know. ⁵Afterwards it can only choose ambiguously, and the only way out of ambiguity is clear perception. ⁶The mind returns to its proper function only when it wills to know. ⁷This places it in the service of spirit, where perception is changed. ⁸The mind chooses to divide itself when it chooses to make its own levels. ⁹But it could not entirely separate itself from spirit, because it is from spirit that it derives its whole power to make or create. ¹⁰Even in miscreation the mind is affirming its Source, or it would merely cease to be. ¹¹This is impossible, because the mind belongs to spirit which God created and which is therefore eternal.

6. The ability to perceive made the body possible, because you must perceive *something* and *with* something. ²That is why perception involves an exchange or translation, which knowledge does not need. ³The interpretative function of perception, a distorted form of creation, then permits you to interpret the body as yourself in an attempt to escape from the conflict you have induced. ⁴Spirit, which knows, could not be reconciled with this loss of power, because it is incapable of darkness. ⁵This makes spirit almost inaccessible to the mind and entirely inaccessible to the body. ⁶Thereafter, spirit is perceived as a threat, because light abolishes darkness merely by showing you it is not there. ⁷Truth will always overcome error in this way. ⁸This cannot be an active process of correction because, as I have already emphasized, knowledge does not do anything. ⁹It can be perceived as an attacker, but it cannot attack. ¹⁰What you perceive as its attack is your own vague recognition that knowledge can always be remembered, never having been destroyed.

7. God and His creations remain in surety, and therefore know that no miscreation exists. ²Truth cannot deal with errors that you want. ³I was a man who remembered spirit and its knowledge. ⁴As a man I did not attempt to counteract error with knowledge, but to correct error from the bottom up. ⁵I demonstrated both the powerlessness of the body and the power of the mind. ⁶By uniting my will with that of my Creator, I naturally remembered spirit and its real purpose. ⁷I cannot unite your will with God's for you, but I can erase all misperceptions from your mind if you will bring it under my guidance. ⁸Only your misperceptions stand in your way. ⁹Without them your choice is certain. ¹⁰Sane perception induces sane choosing. ¹¹I cannot choose for you, but I

can help you make your own right choice. [12]"Many are called but few are chosen" should be, "All are called but few choose to listen." [13]Therefore, they do not choose right. [14]The "chosen ones" are merely those who choose right sooner. [15]Right minds can do this now, and they will find rest unto their souls. [16]God knows you only in peace, and this *is* your reality.

V. Beyond Perception

1. I have said that the abilities you possess are only shadows of your real strength, and that perception, which is inherently judgmental, was introduced only after the separation. [2]No one has been sure of anything since. [3]I have also made it clear that the resurrection was the means for the return to knowledge, which was accomplished by the union of my will with the Father's. [4]We can now establish a distinction that will clarify some of our subsequent statements.

2. Since the separation, the words "create" and "make" have become confused. [2]When you make something, you do so out of a specific sense of lack or need. [3]Anything made for a specific purpose has no true generalizability. [4]When you make something to fill a perceived lack, you are tacitly implying that you believe in separation. [5]The ego has invented many ingenious thought systems for this purpose. [6]None of them is creative. [7]Inventiveness is wasted effort even in its most ingenious form. [8]The highly specific nature of invention is not worthy of the abstract creativity of God's creations.

3. Knowing, as we have already observed, does not lead to doing. [2]The confusion between your real creation and what you have made of yourself is so profound that it has become literally impossible for you to know anything. [3]Knowledge is always stable, and it is quite evident that you are not. [4]Nevertheless, you are perfectly stable as God created you. [5]In this sense, when your behavior is unstable, you are disagreeing with God's idea of your creation. [6]You can do this if you choose, but you would hardly want to do it if you were in your right mind.

4. The fundamental question you continually ask yourself cannot properly be directed to yourself at all. [2]You keep asking what it is you are. [3]This implies that the answer is not only one you know, but is also one that is up to you to supply. [4]Yet you cannot per-

ceive yourself correctly. [5]You have no image to be perceived. [6]The word "image" is always perception-related, and not a part of knowledge. [7]Images are symbolic and stand for something else. [8]The idea of "changing your image" recognizes the power of perception, but also implies that there is nothing stable to know.

5. Knowing is not open to interpretation. [2]You may try to "interpret" meaning, but this is always open to error because it refers to the *perception* of meaning. [3]Such incongruities are the result of attempts to regard yourself as separated and unseparated at the same time. [4]It is impossible to make so fundamental a confusion without increasing your overall confusion still further. [5]Your mind may have become very ingenious, but as always happens when method and content are separated, it is utilized in a futile attempt to escape from an inescapable impasse. [6]Ingenuity is totally divorced from knowledge, because knowledge does not require ingenuity. [7]Ingenious thinking is *not* the truth that shall set you free, but you are free of the need to engage in it when you are willing to let it go.

6. Prayer is a way of asking for something. [2]It is the medium of miracles. [3]But the only meaningful prayer is for forgiveness, because those who have been forgiven have everything. [4]Once forgiveness has been accepted, prayer in the usual sense becomes utterly meaningless. [5]The prayer for forgiveness is nothing more than a request that you may be able to recognize what you already have. [6]In electing perception instead of knowledge, you placed yourself in a position where you could resemble your Father only by perceiving miraculously. [7]You have lost the knowledge that you yourself are a miracle of God. [8]Creation is your Source and your only real function.

7. The statement "God created man in his own image and likeness" needs reinterpretation. [2]"Image" can be understood as "thought," and "likeness" as "of a like quality." [3]God did create spirit in His Own Thought and of a quality like to His Own. [4]There *is* nothing else. [5]Perception, on the other hand, is impossible without a belief in "more" and "less." [6]At every level it involves selectivity. [7]Perception is a continual process of accepting and rejecting, organizing and reorganizing, shifting and changing. [8]Evaluation is an essential part of perception, because judgments are necessary in order to select.

8. What happens to perceptions if there are no judgments and nothing but perfect equality? [2]Perception becomes impossible.

³Truth can only be known. ⁴All of it is equally true, and knowing any part of it is to know all of it. ⁵Only perception involves partial awareness. ⁶Knowledge transcends the laws governing perception, because partial knowledge is impossible. ⁷It is all one and has no separate parts. ⁸You who are really one with it need but know yourself and your knowledge is complete. ⁹To know God's miracle is to know Him.

9. Forgiveness is the healing of the perception of separation. ²Correct perception of your brother is necessary, because minds have chosen to see themselves as separate. ³Spirit knows God completely. ⁴That is its miraculous power. ⁵The fact that each one has this power completely is a condition entirely alien to the world's thinking. ⁶The world believes that if anyone has everything, there is nothing left. ⁷But God's miracles are as total as His Thoughts because they *are* His Thoughts.

10. As long as perception lasts prayer has a place. ²Since perception rests on lack, those who perceive have not totally accepted the Atonement and given themselves over to truth. ³Perception is based on a separated state, so that anyone who perceives at all needs healing. ⁴Communion, not prayer, is the natural state of those who know. ⁵God and His miracle are inseparable. ⁶How beautiful indeed are the Thoughts of God who live in His light! ⁷Your worth is beyond perception because it is beyond doubt. ⁸Do not perceive yourself in different lights. ⁹Know yourself in the One Light where the miracle that is you is perfectly clear.

VI. Judgment and the Authority Problem

1. We have already discussed the Last Judgment, but in insufficient detail. ²After the Last Judgment there will be no more. ³Judgment is symbolic because beyond perception there is no judgment. ⁴When the Bible says "Judge not that ye be not judged," it means that if you judge the reality of others you will be unable to avoid judging your own.

2. The choice to judge rather than to know is the cause of the loss of peace. ²Judgment is the process on which perception but not knowledge rests. ³I have discussed this before in terms of the selectivity of perception, pointing out that evaluation is its obvious prerequisite. ⁴Judgment always involves rejection. ⁵It never emphasizes only the positive aspects of what is judged, whether

in you or in others. [6]What has been perceived and rejected, or judged and found wanting, remains in your mind because it has been perceived. [7]One of the illusions from which you suffer is the belief that what you judged against has no effect. [8]This cannot be true unless you also believe that what you judged against does not exist. [9]You evidently do not believe this, or you would not have judged against it. [10]In the end it does not matter whether your judgment is right or wrong. [11]Either way you are placing your belief in the unreal. [12]This cannot be avoided in any type of judgment, because it implies the belief that reality is yours to select *from*.

3. You have no idea of the tremendous release and deep peace that comes from meeting yourself and your brothers totally without judgment. [2]When you recognize what you are and what your brothers are, you will realize that judging them in any way is without meaning. [3]In fact, their meaning is lost to you precisely *because* you are judging them. [4]All uncertainty comes from the belief that you are under the coercion of judgment. [5]You do not need judgment to organize your life, and you certainly do not need it to organize yourself. [6]In the presence of knowledge all judgment is automatically suspended, and this is the process that enables recognition to replace perception.

4. You are very fearful of everything you have perceived but have refused to accept. [2]You believe that, because you have refused to accept it, you have lost control over it. [3]This is why you see it in nightmares, or in pleasant disguises in what seem to be your happier dreams. [4]Nothing that you have refused to accept can be brought into awareness. [5]It is not dangerous in itself, but you have made it seem dangerous to you.

5. When you feel tired, it is because you have judged yourself as capable of being tired. [2]When you laugh at someone, it is because you have judged him as unworthy. [3]When you laugh at yourself you must laugh at others, if only because you cannot tolerate the idea of being more unworthy than they are. [4]All this makes you feel tired because it is essentially disheartening. [5]You are not really capable of being tired, but you are very capable of wearying yourself. [6]The strain of constant judgment is virtually intolerable. [7]It is curious that an ability so debilitating would be so deeply cherished. [8]Yet if you wish to be the author of reality, you will insist on holding on to judgment. [9]You will also regard judgment with fear, believing that it will someday be used against

you. ¹⁰This belief can exist only to the extent that you believe in the efficacy of judgment as a weapon of defense for your own authority.

6. God offers only mercy. ²Your words should reflect only mercy, because that is what you have received and that is what you should give. ³Justice is a temporary expedient, or an attempt to teach you the meaning of mercy. ⁴It is judgmental only because you are capable of injustice.

7. I have spoken of different symptoms, and at that level there is almost endless variation. ²There is, however, only one cause for all of them: the authority problem. ³This *is* "the root of all evil." ⁴Every symptom the ego makes involves a contradiction in terms, because the mind is split between the ego and the Holy Spirit, so that whatever the ego makes is incomplete and contradictory. ⁵This untenable position is the result of the authority problem which, because it accepts the one inconceivable thought as its premise, can produce only ideas that are inconceivable.

8. The issue of authority is really a question of authorship. ²When you have an authority problem, it is always because you believe you are the author of yourself and project your delusion onto others. ³You then perceive the situation as one in which others are literally fighting you for your authorship. ⁴This is the fundamental error of all those who believe they have usurped the power of God. ⁵This belief is very frightening to them, but hardly troubles God. ⁶He is, however, eager to undo it, not to punish His children, but only because He knows that it makes them unhappy. ⁷God's creations are given their true Authorship, but you prefer to be anonymous when you choose to separate yourself from your Author. ⁸Being uncertain of your true Authorship, you believe that your creation was anonymous. ⁹This leaves you in a position where it sounds meaningful to believe that you created yourself. ¹⁰The dispute over authorship has left such uncertainty in your mind that it may even doubt whether you really exist at all.

9. Only those who give over all desire to reject can know that their own rejection is impossible. ²You have not usurped the power of God, but you *have* lost it. ³Fortunately, to lose something does not mean that it has gone. ⁴It merely means that you do not remember where it is. ⁵Its existence does not depend on your ability to identify it, or even to place it. ⁶It is possible to look on reality without judgment and merely know that it is there.

10. Peace is a natural heritage of spirit. ²Everyone is free to refuse to accept his inheritance, but he is not free to establish what his inheritance is. ³The problem everyone must decide is the fundamental question of authorship. ⁴All fear comes ultimately, and sometimes by way of very devious routes, from the denial of Authorship. ⁵The offense is never to God, but only to those who deny Him. ⁶To deny His Authorship is to deny yourself the reason for your peace, so that you see yourself only in segments. ⁷This strange perception *is* the authority problem.

11. There is no one who does not feel that he is imprisoned in some way. ²If this is the result of his own free will he must regard his will as not free, or the circular reasoning in this position would be quite apparent. ³Free will must lead to freedom. ⁴Judgment always imprisons because it separates segments of reality by the unstable scales of desire. ⁵Wishes are not facts. ⁶To wish is to imply that willing is not sufficient. ⁷Yet no one in his right mind believes that what is wished is as real as what is willed. ⁸Instead of "Seek ye first the Kingdom of Heaven" say, "*Will* ye first the Kingdom of Heaven," and you have said, "I know what I am and I accept my own inheritance."

VII. Creating versus the Self-Image

1. Every system of thought must have a starting point. ²It begins with either a making or a creating, a difference we have already discussed. ³Their resemblance lies in their power as foundations. ⁴Their difference lies in what rests upon them. ⁵Both are cornerstones for systems of belief by which one lives. ⁶It is a mistake to believe that a thought system based on lies is weak. ⁷Nothing made by a child of God is without power. ⁸It is essential to realize this, because otherwise you will be unable to escape from the prison you have made.

2. You cannot resolve the authority problem by depreciating the power of your mind. ²To do so is to deceive yourself, and this will hurt you because you really understand the strength of the mind. ³You also realize that you cannot weaken it, any more than you can weaken God. ⁴The "devil" is a frightening concept because he seems to be extremely powerful and extremely active. ⁵He is perceived as a force in combat with God, battling Him for possession of His creations. ⁶The devil deceives by lies, and

builds kingdoms in which everything is in direct opposition to God. [7]Yet he attracts men rather than repels them, and they are willing to "sell" him their souls in return for gifts of no real worth. [8]This makes absolutely no sense.

3. We have discussed the fall or separation before, but its meaning must be clearly understood. [2]The separation is a system of thought real enough in time, though not in eternity. [3]All beliefs are real to the believer. [4]The fruit of only one tree was "forbidden" in the symbolic garden. [5]But God could not have forbidden it, or it could not have *been* eaten. [6]If God knows His children, and I assure you that He does, would He have put them in a position where their own destruction was possible? [7]The "forbidden tree" was named the "tree of knowledge." [8]Yet God created knowledge and gave it freely to His creations. [9]The symbolism here has been given many interpretations, but you may be sure that any interpretation that sees either God or His creations as capable of destroying Their Own purpose is in error.

4. Eating of the fruit of the tree of knowledge is a symbolic expression for usurping the ability for self-creating. [2]This is the only sense in which God and His creations are not co-creators. [3]The belief that they are is implicit in the "self-concept," or the tendency of the self to make an image of itself. [4]Images are perceived, not known. [5]Knowledge cannot deceive, but perception can. [6]You can perceive yourself as self-creating, but you cannot do more than believe it. [7]You cannot make it true. [8]And, as I said before, when you finally perceive correctly you can only be glad that you cannot. [9]Until then, however, the belief that you can is the foundation stone in your thought system, and all your defenses are used to attack ideas that might bring it to light. [10]You still believe you are an image of your own making. [11]Your mind is split with the Holy Spirit on this point, and there is no resolution while you believe the one thing that is literally inconceivable. [12]That is why you cannot create and are filled with fear about what you make.

5. The mind can make the belief in separation very real and very fearful, and this belief *is* the "devil." [2]It is powerful, active, destructive and clearly in opposition to God, because it literally denies His Fatherhood. [3]Look at your life and see what the devil has made. [4]But realize that this making will surely dissolve in the light of truth, because its foundation is a lie. [5]Your creation by God is the only Foundation that cannot be shaken, because the

light is in it. ⁶Your starting point is truth, and you must return to your Beginning. ⁷Much has been seen since then, but nothing has really happened. ⁸Your Self is still in peace, even though your mind is in conflict. ⁹You have not yet gone back far enough, and that is why you become so fearful. ¹⁰As you approach the Beginning, you feel the fear of the destruction of your thought system upon you as if it were the fear of death. ¹¹There is no death, but there *is* a belief in death.

6. The branch that bears no fruit will be cut off and will wither away. ²Be glad! ³The light will shine from the true Foundation of life, and your own thought system will stand corrected. ⁴It cannot stand otherwise. ⁵You who fear salvation are choosing death. ⁶Life and death, light and darkness, knowledge and perception, are irreconcilable. ⁷To believe that they can be reconciled is to believe that God and His Son can *not*. ⁸Only the oneness of knowledge is free of conflict. ⁹Your Kingdom is not of this world because it was given you from beyond this world. ¹⁰Only in this world is the idea of an authority problem meaningful. ¹¹The world is not left by death but by truth, and truth can be known by all those for whom the Kingdom was created, and for whom it waits.

Chapter 4

THE ILLUSIONS OF THE EGO

Introduction

1.   The Bible says that you should go with a brother twice as far as he asks. ²It certainly does not suggest that you set him back on his journey. ³Devotion to a brother cannot set you back either. ⁴It can lead only to mutual progress. ⁵The result of genuine devotion is inspiration, a word which properly understood is the opposite of fatigue. ⁶To be fatigued is to be dis-spirited, but to be inspired is to be in the spirit. ⁷To be egocentric is to be dis-spirited, but to be Self-centered in the right sense is to be inspired or in spirit. ⁸The truly inspired are enlightened and cannot abide in darkness.

2.   You can speak from the spirit or from the ego, as you choose. ²If you speak from spirit you have chosen to "Be still and know that I am God." ³These words are inspired because they reflect knowledge. ⁴If you speak from the ego you are disclaiming knowledge instead of affirming it, and are thus dis-spiriting yourself. ⁵Do not embark on useless journeys, because they are indeed in vain. ⁶The ego may desire them, but spirit cannot embark on them because it is forever unwilling to depart from its Foundation.

3.   The journey to the cross should be the last "useless journey." ²Do not dwell upon it, but dismiss it as accomplished. ³If you can accept it as your own last useless journey, you are also free to join my resurrection. ⁴Until you do so your life is indeed wasted. ⁵It merely re-enacts the separation, the loss of power, the futile attempts of the ego at reparation, and finally the crucifixion of the body, or death. ⁶Such repetitions are endless until they are voluntarily given up. ⁷Do not make the pathetic error of "clinging to the old rugged cross." ⁸The only message of the crucifixion is that you can overcome the cross. ⁹Until then you are free to crucify yourself as often as you choose. ¹⁰This is not the gospel I intended to offer you. ¹¹We have another journey to undertake, and if you will read these lessons carefully they will help prepare you to undertake it.

I. Right Teaching and Right Learning

1. A good teacher clarifies his own ideas and strengthens them by teaching them. ²Teacher and pupil are alike in the learning process. ³They are in the same order of learning, and unless they share their lessons conviction will be lacking. ⁴A good teacher must believe in the ideas he teaches, but he must meet another condition; he must believe in the students to whom he offers the ideas.

2. Many stand guard over their ideas because they want to protect their thought systems as they are, and learning means change. ²Change is always fearful to the separated, because they cannot conceive of it as a move towards healing the separation. ³They always perceive it as a move toward further separation, because the separation was their first experience of change. ⁴You believe that if you allow no change to enter into your ego you will find peace. ⁵This profound confusion is possible only if you maintain that the same thought system can stand on two foundations. ⁶Nothing can reach spirit from the ego, and nothing can reach the ego from spirit. ⁷Spirit can neither strengthen the ego nor reduce the conflict within it. ⁸The ego *is* a contradiction. ⁹Your self and God's Self *are* in opposition. ¹⁰They are opposed in source, in direction and in outcome. ¹¹They are fundamentally irreconcilable, because spirit cannot perceive and the ego cannot know. ¹²They are therefore not in communication and can never be in communication. ¹³Nevertheless, the ego can learn, even though its maker can be misguided. ¹⁴He cannot, however, make the totally lifeless out of the life-given.

3. Spirit need not be taught, but the ego must be. ²Learning is ultimately perceived as frightening because it leads to the relinquishment, not the destruction, of the ego to the light of spirit. ³This is the change the ego must fear, because it does not share my charity. ⁴My lesson was like yours, and because I learned it I can teach it. ⁵I will never attack your ego, but I am trying to teach you how its thought system arose. ⁶When I remind you of your true creation, your ego cannot but respond with fear.

4. Teaching and learning are your greatest strengths now, because they enable you to change your mind and help others to change theirs. ²Refusing to change your mind will not prove that the separation has not occurred. ³The dreamer who doubts the reality of his dream while he is still dreaming is not really healing

his split mind. [4]You dream of a separated ego and believe in a world that rests upon it. [5]This is very real to you. [6]You cannot undo it by not changing your mind about it. [7]If you are willing to renounce the role of guardian of your thought system and open it to me, I will correct it very gently and lead you back to God.

5. Every good teacher hopes to give his students so much of his own learning that they will one day no longer need him. [2]This is the one true goal of the teacher. [3]It is impossible to convince the ego of this, because it goes against all of its own laws. [4]But remember that laws are set up to protect the continuity of the system in which the lawmaker believes. [5]It is natural for the ego to try to protect itself once you have made it, but it is not natural for you to want to obey its laws unless *you* believe them. [6]The ego cannot make this choice because of the nature of its origin. [7]You can, because of the nature of yours.

6. Egos can clash in any situation, but spirit cannot clash at all. [2]If you perceive a teacher as merely "a larger ego" you will be afraid, because to enlarge an ego would be to increase anxiety about separation. [3]I will teach with you and live with you if you will think with me, but my goal will always be to absolve you finally from the need for a teacher. [4]This is the opposite of the ego-oriented teacher's goal. [5]He is concerned with the effect of his ego on other egos, and therefore interprets their interaction as a means of ego preservation. [6]I would not be able to devote myself to teaching if I believed this, and you will not be a devoted teacher as long as you believe it. [7]I am constantly being perceived as a teacher either to be exalted or rejected, but I do not accept either perception for myself.

7. Your worth is not established by teaching or learning. [2]Your worth is established by God. [3]As long as you dispute this everything you do will be fearful, particularly any situation that lends itself to the belief in superiority and inferiority. [4]Teachers must be patient and repeat their lessons until they are learned. [5]I am willing to do this, because I have no right to set your learning limits for you. [6]Again,—nothing you do or think or wish or make is necessary to establish your worth. [7]This point is not debatable except in delusions. [8]Your ego is never at stake because God did not create it. [9]Your spirit is never at stake because He did. [10]Any confusion on this point is delusional, and no form of devotion is possible as long as this delusion lasts.

8. The ego tries to exploit all situations into forms of praise for

itself in order to overcome its doubts. [2]It will remain doubtful as long as you believe in its existence. [3]You who made it cannot trust it, because in your right mind you realize it is not real. [4]The only sane solution is not to try to change reality, which is indeed a fearful attempt, but to accept it as it is. [5]You are part of reality, which stands unchanged beyond the reach of your ego but within easy reach of spirit. [6]When you are afraid, be still and know that God is real, and you are His beloved Son in whom He is well pleased. [7]Do not let your ego dispute this, because the ego cannot know what is as far beyond its reach as you are.

9. God is not the author of fear. [2]You are. [3]You have chosen to create unlike Him, and have therefore made fear for yourself. [4]You are not at peace because you are not fulfilling your function. [5]God gave you a very lofty function that you are not meeting. [6]Your ego has chosen to be afraid instead of meeting it. [7]When you awaken you will not be able to understand this, because it is literally incredible. [8]*Do not believe the incredible now.* [9]Any attempt to increase its believableness is merely to postpone the inevitable. [10]The word "inevitable" is fearful to the ego, but joyous to the spirit. [11]God is inevitable, and you cannot avoid Him any more than He can avoid you.

10. The ego is afraid of the spirit's joy, because once you have experienced it you will withdraw all protection from the ego, and become totally without investment in fear. [2]Your investment is great now because fear is a witness to the separation, and your ego rejoices when you witness to it. [3]Leave it behind! [4]Do not listen to it and do not preserve it. [5]Listen only to God, Who is as incapable of deception as is the spirit He created. [6]Release yourself and release others. [7]Do not present a false and unworthy picture of yourself to others, and do not accept such a picture of them yourself.

11. The ego has built a shabby and unsheltering home for you, because it cannot build otherwise. [2]Do not try to make this impoverished house stand. [3]Its weakness is your strength. [4]Only God could make a home that is worthy of His creations, who have chosen to leave it empty by their own dispossession. [5]Yet His home will stand forever, and is ready for you when you choose to enter it. [6]Of this you can be wholly certain. [7]God is as incapable of creating the perishable as the ego is of making the eternal.

12. Of your ego you can do nothing to save yourself or others, but

of your spirit you can do everything for the salvation of both. [2]Humility is a lesson for the ego, not for the spirit. [3]Spirit is beyond humility, because it recognizes its radiance and gladly sheds its light everywhere. [4]The meek shall inherit the earth because their egos are humble, and this gives them truer perception. [5]The Kingdom of Heaven is the spirit's right, whose beauty and dignity are far beyond doubt, beyond perception, and stand forever as the mark of the Love of God for His creations, who are wholly worthy of Him and only of Him. [6]Nothing else is sufficiently worthy to be a gift for a creation of God Himself.

13.   I will substitute for your ego if you wish, but never for your spirit. [2]A father can safely leave a child with an elder brother who has shown himself responsible, but this involves no confusion about the child's origin. [3]The brother can protect the child's body and his ego, but he does not confuse himself with the father because he does this. [4]I can be entrusted with your body and your ego only because this enables you not to be concerned with them, and lets me teach you their unimportance. [5]I could not understand their importance to you if I had not once been tempted to believe in them myself. [6]Let us undertake to learn this lesson together so we can be free of them together. [7]I need devoted teachers who share my aim of healing the mind. [8]Spirit is far beyond the need of your protection or mine. [9]Remember this:

[10]*In this world you need not have tribulation because I have overcome the world.* [11]*That is why you should be of good cheer.*

II. The Ego and False Autonomy

1.   It is reasonable to ask how the mind could ever have made the ego. [2]In fact, it is the best question you could ask. [3]There is, however, no point in giving an answer in terms of the past because the past does not matter, and history would not exist if the same errors were not being repeated in the present. [4]Abstract thought applies to knowledge because knowledge is completely impersonal, and examples are irrelevant to its understanding. [5]Perception, however, is always specific, and therefore quite concrete.

2.   Everyone makes an ego or a self for himself, which is subject to enormous variation because of its instability. [2]He also makes an ego for everyone else he perceives, which is equally variable.

³Their interaction is a process that alters both, because they were not made by or with the Unalterable. ⁴It is important to realize that this alteration can and does occur as readily when the interaction takes place in the mind as when it involves physical proximity. ⁵Thinking about another ego is as effective in changing relative perception as is physical interaction. ⁶There could be no better example that the ego is only an idea and not a fact.

3. Your own state of mind is a good example of how the ego was made. ²When you threw knowledge away it is as if you never had it. ³This is so apparent that one need only recognize it to see that it does happen. ⁴If this occurs in the present, why is it surprising that it occurred in the past? ⁵Surprise is a reasonable response to the unfamiliar, though hardly to something that occurs with such persistence. ⁶But do not forget that the mind need not work that way, even though it does work that way now.

4. Think of the love of animals for their offspring, and the need they feel to protect them. ²That is because they regard them as part of themselves. ³No one dismisses something he considers part of himself. ⁴You react to your ego much as God does to His creations,—with love, protection and charity. ⁵Your reactions to the self you made are not surprising. ⁶In fact, they resemble in many ways how you will one day react to your real creations, which are as timeless as you are. ⁷The question is not how you respond to the ego, but what you believe you are. ⁸Belief is an ego function, and as long as your origin is open to belief you are regarding it from an ego viewpoint. ⁹When teaching is no longer necessary you will merely know God. ¹⁰Belief that there is another way of perceiving is the loftiest idea of which ego thinking is capable. ¹¹That is because it contains a hint of recognition that the ego is not the Self.

5. Undermining the ego's thought system must be perceived as painful, even though this is anything but true. ²Babies scream in rage if you take away a knife or scissors, although they may well harm themselves if you do not. ³In this sense you are still a baby. ⁴You have no sense of real self-preservation, and are likely to decide that you need precisely what would hurt you most. ⁵Yet whether or not you recognize it now, you have agreed to cooperate in the effort to become both harmless and helpful, attributes that must go together. ⁶Your attitudes even toward this are necessarily conflicted, because all attitudes are ego-based. ⁷This will not last. ⁸Be patient a while and remember that the outcome is as

certain as God.

6. Only those who have a real and lasting sense of abundance can be truly charitable. ²This is obvious when you consider what is involved. ³To the ego, to give anything implies that you will have to do without it. ⁴When you associate giving with sacrifice, you give only because you believe that you are somehow getting something better, and can therefore do without the thing you give. ⁵"Giving to get" is an inescapable law of the ego, which always evaluates itself in relation to other egos. ⁶It is therefore continually preoccupied with the belief in scarcity that gave rise to it. ⁷Its whole perception of other egos as real is only an attempt to convince itself that *it* is real. ⁸"Self-esteem" in ego terms means nothing more than that the ego has deluded itself into accepting its reality, and is therefore temporarily less predatory. ⁹This "self-esteem" is always vulnerable to stress, a term which refers to any perceived threat to the ego's existence.

7. The ego literally lives by comparisons. ²Equality is beyond its grasp, and charity becomes impossible. ³The ego never gives out of abundance, because it was made as a substitute for it. ⁴That is why the concept of "getting" arose in the ego's thought system. ⁵Appetites are "getting" mechanisms, representing the ego's need to confirm itself. ⁶This is as true of body appetites as it is of the so-called "higher ego needs." ⁷Body appetites are not physical in origin. ⁸The ego regards the body as its home, and tries to satisfy itself through the body. ⁹But the idea that this is possible is a decision of the mind, which has become completely confused about what is really possible.

8. The ego believes it is completely on its own, which is merely another way of describing how it thinks it originated. ²This is such a fearful state that it can only turn to other egos and try to unite with them in a feeble attempt at identification, or attack them in an equally feeble show of strength. ³It is not free, however, to open the premise to question, because the premise is its foundation. ⁴The ego is the mind's belief that it is completely on its own. ⁵The ego's ceaseless attempts to gain the spirit's acknowledgment and thus establish its own existence are useless. ⁶Spirit in its knowledge is unaware of the ego. ⁷It does not attack it; it merely cannot conceive of it at all. ⁸While the ego is equally unaware of spirit, it does perceive itself as being rejected by something greater than itself. ⁹This is why self-esteem in ego terms must be delusional. ¹⁰The creations of God do not create myths,

although creative effort can be turned to mythology. [11]It can do so, however, only under one condition; what it makes is then no longer creative. [12]Myths are entirely perceptual, and so ambiguous in form and characteristically good-and-evil in nature that the most benevolent of them is not without fearful connotations.

9. Myths and magic are closely associated, since myths are usually related to ego origins, and magic to the powers the ego ascribes to itself. [2]Mythological systems generally include some account of "the creation," and associate this with its particular form of magic. [3]The so-called "battle for survival" is only the ego's struggle to preserve itself, and its interpretation of its own beginning. [4]This beginning is usually associated with physical birth, because it is hard to maintain that the ego existed before that point in time. [5]The more "religiously" ego-oriented may believe that the soul existed before, and will continue to exist after a temporary lapse into ego life. [6]Some even believe that the soul will be punished for this lapse. [7]However, salvation does not apply to spirit, which is not in danger and does not need to be salvaged.

10. Salvation is nothing more than "right-mindedness," which is not the One-mindedness of the Holy Spirit, but which must be achieved before One-mindedness is restored. [2]Right-mindedness leads to the next step automatically, because right perception is uniformly without attack, and therefore wrong-mindedness is obliterated. [3]The ego cannot survive without judgment, and is laid aside accordingly. [4]The mind then has only one direction in which it can move. [5]Its direction is always automatic, because it cannot but be dictated by the thought system to which it adheres.

11. It cannot be emphasized too often that correcting perception is merely a temporary expedient. [2]It is necessary only because misperception is a block to knowledge, while accurate perception is a steppingstone towards it. [3]The whole value of right perception lies in the inevitable realization that *all* perception is unnecessary. [4]This removes the block entirely. [5]You may ask how this is possible as long as you appear to be living in this world. [6]That is a reasonable question. [7]You must be careful, however, that you really understand it. [8]Who is the "you" who are living in this world? [9]Spirit is immortal, and immortality is a constant state. [10]It is as true now as it ever was or ever will be, because it implies no change at all. [11]It is not a continuum, nor is it understood by

being compared to an opposite. [12]Knowledge never involves comparisons. [13]That is its main difference from everything else the mind can grasp.

III. Love without Conflict

1. It is hard to understand what "The Kingdom of Heaven is within you" really means. [2]This is because it is not understandable to the ego, which interprets it as if something outside is inside, and this does not mean anything. [3]The word "within" is unnecessary. [4]The Kingdom of Heaven *is* you. [5]What else *but* you did the Creator create, and what else *but* you is His Kingdom? [6]This is the whole message of the Atonement; a message which in its totality transcends the sum of its parts. [7]You, too, have a Kingdom that your spirit created. [8]It has not ceased to create because of the ego's illusions. [9]Your creations are no more fatherless than you are. [10]Your ego and your spirit will never be co-creators, but your spirit and your Creator will always be. [11]Be confident that your creations are as safe as you are.

[12]*The Kingdom is perfectly united and perfectly protected, and the ego will not prevail against it.* [13]*Amen.*

2. This is written in the form of a prayer because it is useful in moments of temptation. [2]It is a declaration of independence. [3]You will find it very helpful if you understand it fully. [4]The reason you need my help is because you have denied your own Guide and therefore need guidance. [5]My role is to separate the true from the false, so truth can break through the barriers the ego has set up and can shine into your mind. [6]Against our united strength the ego cannot prevail.

3. It is surely apparent by now why the ego regards spirit as its "enemy." [2]The ego arose from the separation, and its continued existence depends on your continuing belief in the separation. [3]The ego must offer you some sort of reward for maintaining this belief. [4]All it can offer is a sense of temporary existence, which begins with its own beginning and ends with its own ending. [5]It tells you this life is your existence because it is its own. [6]Against this sense of temporary existence spirit offers you the knowledge of permanence and unshakable being. [7]No one who has experi-

enced the revelation of this can ever fully believe in the ego again. [8]How can its meager offering to you prevail against the glorious gift of God?

4. You who identify with your ego cannot believe God loves you. [2]You do not love what you made, and what you made does not love you. [3]Being made out of the denial of the Father, the ego has no allegiance to its maker. [4]You cannot conceive of the real relationship that exists between God and His creations because of your hatred for the self you made. [5]You project onto the ego the decision to separate, and this conflicts with the love you feel for the ego because you made it. [6]No love in this world is without this ambivalence, and since no ego has experienced love without ambivalence the concept is beyond its understanding. [7]Love will enter immediately into any mind that truly wants it, but it must want it truly. [8]This means that it wants it without ambivalence, and this kind of wanting is wholly without the ego's "drive to get."

5. There is a kind of experience so different from anything the ego can offer that you will never want to cover or hide it again. [2]It is necessary to repeat that your belief in darkness and hiding is why the light cannot enter. [3]The Bible gives many references to the immeasurable gifts which are for you, but for which you must ask. [4]This is not a condition as the ego sets conditions. [5]It is the glorious condition of what you are.

6. No force except your own will is strong enough or worthy enough to guide you. [2]In this you are as free as God, and must remain so forever. [3]Let us ask the Father in my name to keep you mindful of His Love for you and yours for Him. [4]He has never failed to answer this request, because it asks only for what He has already willed. [5]Those who call truly are always answered. [6]Thou shalt have no other gods before Him because there *are* none.

7. It has never really entered your mind to give up every idea you ever had that opposes knowledge. [2]You retain thousands of little scraps of fear that prevent the Holy One from entering. [3]Light cannot penetrate through the walls you make to block it, and it is forever unwilling to destroy what you have made. [4]No one can see through a wall, but I can step around it. [5]Watch your mind for the scraps of fear, or you will be unable to ask me to do so. [6]I can help you only as our Father created us. [7]I will love you and honor you and maintain complete respect for what you have made, but I will not uphold it unless it is true. [8]I will never

forsake you any more than God will, but I must wait as long as you choose to forsake yourself. ⁹Because I wait in love and not in impatience, you will surely ask me truly. ¹⁰I will come in response to a single unequivocal call.

8. Watch carefully and see what it is you are really asking for. ²Be very honest with yourself in this, for we must hide nothing from each other. ³If you will really try to do this, you have taken the first step toward preparing your mind for the Holy One to enter. ⁴We will prepare for this together, for once He has come, you will be ready to help me make other minds ready for Him. ⁵How long will you deny Him His Kingdom?

9. In your own mind, though denied by the ego, is the declaration of your release. ²*God has given you everything.* ³This one fact means the ego does not exist, and this makes it profoundly afraid. ⁴In the ego's language, "to have" and "to be" are different, but they are identical to the Holy Spirit. ⁵The Holy Spirit knows that you both *have* everything and *are* everything. ⁶Any distinction in this respect is meaningful only when the idea of "getting," which implies a lack, has already been accepted. ⁷That is why we make no distinction between *having* the Kingdom of God. and *being* the Kingdom of God.

10. The calm being of God's Kingdom, which in your sane mind is perfectly conscious, is ruthlessly banished from the part of the mind the ego rules. ²The ego is desperate because it opposes literally invincible odds, whether you are asleep or awake. ³Consider how much vigilance you have been willing to exert to protect your ego, and how little to protect your right mind. ⁴Who but the insane would undertake to believe what is not true, and then protect this belief at the cost of truth?

IV. This Need Not Be

1. If you cannot hear the Voice for God, it is because you do not choose to listen. ²That you *do* listen to the voice of your ego is demonstrated by your attitudes, your feelings and your behavior. ³Yet this is what you want. ⁴This is what you are fighting to keep, and what you are vigilant to save. ⁵Your mind is filled with schemes to save the face of your ego, and you do not seek the face of Christ. ⁶The glass in which the ego seeks to see its face is dark indeed. ⁷How can it maintain the trick of its existence except with

mirrors? [8]But where you look to find yourself is up to you.

2. I have said that you cannot change your mind by changing your behavior, but I have also said, and many times, that you *can* change your mind. [2]When your mood tells you that you have chosen wrongly, and this is so whenever you are not joyous, then *know this need not be.* [3]In every case you have thought wrongly about some brother God created, and are perceiving images your ego makes in a darkened glass. [4]Think honestly what you have thought that God would not have thought, and what you have not thought that God would have you think. [5]Search sincerely for what you have done and left undone accordingly, and then change your mind to think with God's. [6]This may seem hard to do, but it is much easier than trying to think against it. [7]Your mind is one with God's. [8]Denying this and thinking otherwise has held your ego together, but has literally split your mind. [9]As a loving brother I am deeply concerned with your mind, and urge you to follow my example as you look at yourself and at your brother, and see in both the glorious creations of a glorious Father.

3. When you are sad, *know this need not be.* [2]Depression comes from a sense of being deprived of something you want and do not have. [3]Remember that you are deprived of nothing except by your own decisions, and then decide otherwise.

4. When you are anxious, realize that anxiety comes from the capriciousness of the ego, and *know this need not be.* [2]You can be as vigilant against the ego's dictates as for them.

5. When you feel guilty, remember that the ego has indeed violated the laws of God, but *you* have not. [2]Leave the "sins" of the ego to me. [3]That is what Atonement is for. [4]But until you change your mind about those whom your ego has hurt, the Atonement cannot release you. [5]While you feel guilty your ego is in command, because only the ego can experience guilt. [6]*This need not be.*

6. Watch your mind for the temptations of the ego, and do not be deceived by it. [2]It offers you nothing. [3]When you have given up this voluntary dis-spiriting, you will see how your mind can focus and rise above fatigue and heal. [4]Yet you are not sufficiently vigilant against the demands of the ego to disengage yourself. [5]*This need not be.*

7. The habit of engaging with God and His creations is easily made if you actively refuse to let your mind slip away. [2]The problem is not one of concentration; it is the belief that no one, includ-

ing yourself, is worth consistent effort. ³Side with me consistently against this deception, and do not permit this shabby belief to pull you back. ⁴The disheartened are useless to themselves and to me, but only the ego can *be* disheartened.

8.   Have you really considered how many opportunities you have had to gladden yourself, and how many of them you have refused? ²There is no limit to the power of a Son of God, but he can limit the expression of his power as much as he chooses. ³Your mind and mine can unite in shining your ego away, releasing the strength of God into everything you think and do. ⁴Do not settle for anything less than this, and refuse to accept anything but this as your goal. ⁵Watch your mind carefully for any beliefs that hinder its accomplishment, and step away from them. ⁶Judge how well you have done this by your own feelings, for this is the one right use of judgment. ⁷Judgment, like any other defense, can be used to attack or protect; to hurt or to heal. ⁸The ego *should* be brought to judgment and found wanting there. ⁹Without your own allegiance, protection and love, the ego cannot exist. ¹⁰Let it be judged truly and you must withdraw allegiance, protection and love from it.

9.   You are a mirror of truth, in which God Himself shines in perfect light. ²To the ego's dark glass you need but say, "I will not look there because I know these images are not true." ³Then let the Holy One shine on you in peace, knowing that this and only this must be. ⁴His Mind shone on you in your creation and brought your mind into being. ⁵His Mind still shines on you and must shine through you. ⁶Your ego cannot prevent Him from shining on you, but it can prevent you from letting Him shine through you.

10.   The First Coming of Christ is merely another name for the creation, for Christ is the Son of God. ²The Second Coming of Christ means nothing more than the end of the ego's rule and the healing of the mind. ³I was created like you in the First, and I have called you to join with me in the Second. ⁴I am in charge of the Second Coming, and my judgment, which is used only for protection, cannot be wrong because it never attacks. ⁵Yours may be so distorted that you believe I was mistaken in choosing you. ⁶I assure you this is a mistake of your ego. ⁷Do not mistake it for humility. ⁸Your ego is trying to convince you that it is real and I am not, because if I am real, I am no more real than you are. ⁹That knowledge, and I assure you that it *is* knowledge, means that

Christ has come into your mind and healed it.

11. I do not attack your ego. ²I do work with your higher mind, the home of the Holy Spirit, whether you are asleep or awake, just as your ego does with your lower mind, which is its home. ³I am your vigilance in this, because you are too confused to recognize your own hope. ⁴I am not mistaken. ⁵Your mind will elect to join with mine, and together we are invincible. ⁶You and your brother will yet come together in my name, and your sanity will be restored. ⁷I raised the dead by knowing that life is an eternal attribute of everything that the living God created. ⁸Why do you believe it is harder for me to inspire the dis-spirited or to stabilize the unstable? ⁹I do not believe that there is an order of difficulty in miracles; you do. ¹⁰I have called and you will answer. ¹¹I understand that miracles are natural, because they are expressions of love. ¹²My calling you is as natural as your answer, and as inevitable.

V. The Ego-Body Illusion

1. All things work together for good. ²There are no exceptions except in the ego's judgment. ³The ego exerts maximal vigilance about what it permits into awareness, and this is not the way a balanced mind holds together. ⁴The ego is thrown further off balance because it keeps its primary motivation from your awareness, and raises control rather than sanity to predominance. ⁵The ego has every reason to do this, according to the thought system which gave rise to it and which it serves. ⁶Sane judgment would inevitably judge against the ego, and must be obliterated by the ego in the interest of its self-preservation.

2. A major source of the ego's off-balanced state is its lack of discrimination between the body and the Thoughts of God. ²Thoughts of God are unacceptable to the ego, because they clearly point to the nonexistence of the ego itself. ³The ego therefore either distorts them or refuses to accept them. ⁴It cannot, however, make them cease to be. ⁵It therefore tries to conceal not only "unacceptable" body impulses, but also the Thoughts of God, because both are threatening to it. ⁶Being concerned primarily with its own preservation in the face of threat, the ego perceives them as the same. ⁷By perceiving them as the same, the ego attempts to save itself from being swept away, as it would surely be in the

presence of knowledge.

3.   Any thought system that confuses God and the body must be insane. ²Yet this confusion is essential to the ego, which judges only in terms of threat or non-threat to itself. ³In one sense the ego's fear of God is at least logical, since the idea of Him does dispel the ego. ⁴But fear of the body, with which the ego identifies so closely, makes no sense at all.

4.   The body is the ego's home by its own election. ²It is the only identification with which the ego feels safe, since the body's vulnerability is its own best argument that you cannot be of God. ³This is the belief that the ego sponsors eagerly. ⁴Yet the ego hates the body, because it cannot accept it as good enough to be its home. ⁵Here is where the mind becomes actually dazed. ⁶Being told by the ego that it is really part of the body and that the body is its protector, the mind is also told that the body cannot protect it. ⁷Therefore, the mind asks, "Where can I go for protection?" to which the ego replies, "Turn to me." ⁸The mind, and not without cause, reminds the ego that it has itself insisted that it is identified with the body, so there is no point in turning to *it* for protection. ⁹The ego has no real answer to this because there is none, but it does have a typical solution. ¹⁰It obliterates the question from the mind's awareness. ¹¹Once out of awareness the question can and does produce uneasiness, but it cannot be answered because it cannot be asked.

5.   This is the question that *must* be asked: "Where can I go for protection?" ²"Seek and ye shall find" does not mean that you should seek blindly and desperately for something you would not recognize. ³Meaningful seeking is consciously undertaken, consciously organized and consciously directed. ⁴The goal must be formulated clearly and kept in mind. ⁵Learning and wanting to learn are inseparable. ⁶You learn best when you believe what you are trying to learn is of value to you. ⁷However, not everything you may want to learn has lasting value. ⁸Indeed, many of the things you want to learn may be chosen *because* their value will not last.

6.   The ego thinks it is an advantage not to commit itself to anything that is eternal, because the eternal must come from God. ²Eternalness is the one function the ego has tried to develop, but has systematically failed to achieve. ³The ego compromises with the issue of the eternal, just as it does with all issues touching on the real question in any way. ⁴By becoming involved with tangen-

tial issues, it hopes to hide the real question and keep it out of mind. ⁵The ego's characteristic busyness with nonessentials is for precisely that purpose. ⁶Preoccupations with problems set up to be incapable of solution are favorite ego devices for impeding learning progress. ⁷In all these diversionary tactics, however, the one question that is never asked by those who pursue them is, "What for?" ⁸This is the question that *you* must learn to ask in connection with everything. ⁹What is the purpose? ¹⁰Whatever it is, it will direct your efforts automatically. ¹¹When you make a decision of purpose, then, you have made a decision about your future effort; a decision that will remain in effect unless you change your mind.

VI. The Rewards of God

1. The ego does not recognize the real source of "threat," and if you associate yourself with the ego, you do not understand the situation as it is. ²Only your allegiance to it gives the ego any power over you. ³I have spoken of the ego as if it were a separate thing, acting on its own. ⁴This was necessary to persuade you that you cannot dismiss it lightly, and must realize how much of your thinking is ego-directed. ⁵We cannot safely let it go at that, however, or you will regard yourself as necessarily conflicted as long as you are here, or as long as you believe that you are here. ⁶The ego is nothing more than a part of your belief about your-self. ⁷Your other life has continued without interruption, and has been and always will be totally unaffected by your attempts to dissociate it.

2. In learning to escape from illusions, your debt to your brother is something you must never forget. ²It is the same debt that you owe to me. ³Whenever you act egotistically towards another, you are throwing away the graciousness of your indebtedness and the holy perception it would produce. ⁴The term "holy" can be used here because, as you learn how much you are indebted to the whole Sonship, which includes me, you come as close to knowledge as perception can. ⁵The gap is then so small that knowledge can easily flow across it and obliterate it forever.

3. You have very little trust in me as yet, but it will increase as you turn more and more often to me instead of to your ego for guidance. ²The results will convince you increasingly that this

choice is the only sane one you can make. [3]No one who learns from experience that one choice brings peace and joy while another brings chaos and disaster needs additional convincing. [4]Learning through rewards is more effective than learning through pain, because pain is an ego illusion, and can never induce more than a temporary effect. [5]The rewards of God, however, are immediately recognized as eternal. [6]Since this recognition is made by you and not the ego, the recognition itself establishes that you and your ego cannot be identical. [7]You may believe that you have already accepted this difference, but you are by no means convinced as yet. [8]The fact that you believe you must escape from the ego shows this; but you cannot escape from the ego by humbling it or controlling it or punishing it.

4. The ego and the spirit do not know each other. [2]The separated mind cannot maintain the separation except by dissociating. [3]Having done this, it denies all truly natural impulses, not because the ego is a separate thing, but because you want to believe that *you* are. [4]The ego is a device for maintaining this belief, but it is still only your decision to use the device that enables it to endure.

5. How can you teach someone the value of something he has deliberately thrown away? [2]He must have thrown it away because he did not value it. [3]You can only show him how miserable he is without it, and slowly bring it nearer so he can learn how his misery lessens as he approaches it. [4]This teaches him to associate his misery with its absence, and the opposite of misery with its presence. [5]It gradually becomes desirable as he changes his mind about its worth. [6]I am teaching you to associate misery with the ego and joy with the spirit. [7]You have taught yourself the opposite. [8]You are still free to choose, but can you really want the rewards of the ego in the presence of the rewards of God?

6. My trust in you is greater than yours in me at the moment, but it will not always be that way. [2]Your mission is very simple. [3]You are asked to live so as to demonstrate that you are not an ego, and I do not choose God's channels wrongly. [4]The Holy One shares my trust, and accepts my Atonement decisions because my will is never out of accord with His. [5]I have said before that I am in charge of the Atonement. [6]This is only because I completed my part in it as a man, and can now complete it through others. [7]My chosen channels cannot fail, because I will lend them my strength as long as theirs is wanting.

7. I will go with you to the Holy One, and through my perception He can bridge the little gap. ²Your gratitude to your brother is the only gift I want. ³I will bring it to God for you, knowing that to know your brother *is* to know God. ⁴If you are grateful to your brother, you are grateful to God for what He created. ⁵Through your gratitude you come to know your brother, and one moment of real recognition makes everyone your brother because each of them is of your Father. ⁶Love does not conquer all things, but it does set all things right. ⁷Because you are the Kingdom of God I can lead you back to your own creations. ⁸You do not recognize them now, but what has been dissociated is still there.

8. As you come closer to a brother you approach me, and as you withdraw from him I become distant to you. ²Salvation is a collaborative venture. ³It cannot be undertaken successfully by those who disengage themselves from the Sonship, because they are disengaging themselves from me. ⁴God will come to you only as you will give Him to your brothers. ⁵Learn first of them and you will be ready to hear God. ⁶That is because the function of love is one.

VII. Creation and Communication

1. It is clear that while the content of any particular ego illusion does not matter, its correction is more helpful in a specific context. ²Ego illusions are quite specific, although the mind is naturally abstract. ³Part of the mind becomes concrete, however, when it splits. ⁴The concrete part believes in the ego, because the ego depends on the concrete. ⁵The ego is the part of the mind that believes your existence is defined by separation.

2. Everything the ego perceives is a separate whole, without the relationships that imply being. ²The ego is thus against communication, except insofar as it is utilized to establish separateness rather than to abolish it. ³The communication system of the ego is based on its own thought system, as is everything else it dictates. ⁴Its communication is controlled by its need to protect itself, and it will disrupt communication when it experiences threat. ⁵This disruption is a reaction to a specific person or persons. ⁶The specificity of the ego's thinking, then, results in spurious generalization which is really not abstract at all. ⁷It merely responds in certain specific ways to everything it perceives as related.

3. In contrast, spirit reacts in the same way to everything it knows is true, and does not respond at all to anything else. [2]Nor does it make any attempt to establish what is true. [3]It knows that what is true is everything that God created. [4]It is in complete and direct communication with every aspect of creation, because it is in complete and direct communication with its Creator. [5]This communication is the Will of God. [6]Creation and communication are synonymous. [7]God created every mind by communicating His Mind to it, thus establishing it forever as a channel for the reception of His Mind and Will. [8]Since only beings of a like order can truly communicate, His creations naturally communicate with Him and like Him. [9]This communication is perfectly abstract, since its quality is universal in application and not subject to any judgment, any exception or any alteration. [10]God created you by this and for this. [11]The mind can distort its function, but it cannot endow itself with functions it was not given. [12]That is why the mind cannot totally lose the ability to communicate, even though it may refuse to utilize it on behalf of being.

4. Existence as well as being rests on communication. [2]Existence, however, is specific in how, what and with whom communication is judged to be worth undertaking. [3]Being is completely without these distinctions. [4]It is a state in which the mind is in communication with everything that is real. [5]To whatever extent you permit this state to be curtailed you are limiting your sense of your own reality, which becomes total only by recognizing all reality in the glorious context of its real relationship to you. [6]This is your reality. [7]Do not desecrate it or recoil from it. [8]It is your real home, your real temple and your real Self.

5. God, Who encompasses all being, created beings who have everything individually, but who want to share it to increase their joy. [2]Nothing real can be increased except by sharing. [3]That is why God created you. [4]Divine Abstraction takes joy in sharing. [5]That is what creation means. [6]"How," "what" and "to whom" are irrelevant, because real creation gives everything, since it can create only like itself. [7]Remember that in the Kingdom there is no difference between *having* and *being*, as there is in existence. [8]In the state of being the mind gives everything always.

6. The Bible repeatedly states that you should praise God. [2]This hardly means that you should tell Him how wonderful He is. [3]He has no ego with which to accept such praise, and no perception with which to judge it. [4]But unless you take your part in the

creation, His joy is not complete because yours is incomplete. [5]And this He does know. [6]He knows it in His Own Being and its experience of His Son's experience. [7]The constant going out of His Love is blocked when His channels are closed, and He is lonely when the minds He created do not communicate fully with Him.

7. God has kept your Kingdom for you, but He cannot share His joy with you until you know it with your whole mind. [2]Revelation is not enough, because it is only communication *from* God. [3]God does not need revelation returned to Him, which would clearly be impossible, but He does want it brought to others. [4]This cannot be done with the actual revelation; its content cannot be expressed, because it is intensely personal to the mind that receives it. [5]It can, however, be returned by that mind to other minds, through the attitudes the knowledge from the revelation brings.

8. God is praised whenever any mind learns to be wholly helpful. [2]This is impossible without being wholly harmless, because the two beliefs must coexist. [3]The truly helpful are invulnerable, because they are not protecting their egos and so nothing can hurt them. [4]Their helpfulness is their praise of God, and He will return their praise of Him because they are like Him, and they can rejoice together. [5]God goes out to them and through them, and there is great joy throughout the Kingdom. [6]Every mind that is changed adds to this joy with its individual willingness to share in it. [7]The truly helpful are God's miracle workers, whom I direct until we are all united in the joy of the Kingdom. [8]I will direct you to wherever you can be truly helpful, and to whoever can follow my guidance through you.

Chapter 5

HEALING AND WHOLENESS

Introduction

1. To heal is to make happy. ²I have told you to think how many opportunities you have had to gladden yourself, and how many you have refused. ³This is the same as telling you that you have refused to heal yourself. ⁴The light that belongs to you is the light of joy. ⁵Radiance is not associated with sorrow. ⁶Joy calls forth an integrated willingness to share it, and promotes the mind's natural impulse to respond as one. ⁷Those who attempt to heal without being wholly joyous themselves call forth different kinds of responses at the same time, and thus deprive others of the joy of responding wholeheartedly.

2. To be wholehearted you must be happy. ²If fear and love cannot coexist, and if it is impossible to be wholly fearful and remain alive, the only possible whole state is that of love. ³There is no difference between love and joy. ⁴Therefore, the only possible whole state is the wholly joyous. ⁵To heal or to make joyous is therefore the same as to integrate and to make one. ⁶That is why it makes no difference to what part or by what part of the Sonship the healing is offered. ⁷Every part benefits, and benefits equally.

3. You are being blessed by every beneficent thought of any of your brothers anywhere. ²You should want to bless them in return, out of gratitude. ³You need not know them individually, or they you. ⁴The light is so strong that it radiates throughout the Sonship and returns thanks to the Father for radiating His joy upon it. ⁵Only God's holy children are worthy channels of His beautiful joy, because only they are beautiful enough to hold it by sharing it. ⁶It is impossible for a child of God to love his neighbor except as himself. ⁷That is why the healer's prayer is:

⁸*Let me know this brother as I know myself.*

I. The Invitation to the Holy Spirit

1.   Healing is a thought by which two minds perceive their one-ness and become glad. ²This gladness calls to every part of the Sonship to rejoice with them, and lets God go out into them and through them. ³Only the healed mind can experience revelation with lasting effect, because revelation is an experience of pure joy. ⁴If you do not choose to be wholly joyous, your mind cannot have what it does not choose to be. ⁵Remember that spirit knows no difference between *having* and *being*. ⁶The higher mind thinks according to the laws spirit obeys, and therefore honors only the laws of God. ⁷To spirit getting is meaningless and giving is all. ⁸Having everything, spirit holds everything by giving it, and thus creates as the Father created. ⁹While this kind of thinking is to-tally alien to having things, even to the lower mind it is quite comprehensible in connection with ideas. ¹⁰If you share a physi-cal possession, you do divide its ownership. ¹¹If you share an idea, however, you do not lessen it. ¹²All of it is still yours al-though all of it has been given away. ¹³Further, if the one to whom you give it accepts it as his, he reinforces it in your mind and thus increases it. ¹⁴If you can accept the concept that the world is one of ideas, the whole belief in the false association the ego makes between giving and losing is gone.

2.   Let us start our process of reawakening with just a few simple concepts:

> ²*Thoughts increase by being given away.*
> ³*The more who believe in them the stronger they become.*
> ⁴*Everything is an idea.*
> ⁵*How, then, can giving and losing be associated?*

3.   This is the invitation to the Holy Spirit. ²I have said already that I can reach up and bring the Holy Spirit down to you, but I can bring Him to you only at your own invitation. ³The Holy Spirit is in your right mind, as He was in mine. ⁴The Bible says, "May the mind be in you that was also in Christ Jesus," and uses this as a blessing. ⁵It is the blessing of miracle-mindedness. ⁶It asks that you may think as I thought, joining with me in Christ thinking.

4.   The Holy Spirit is the only part of the Holy Trinity that has a symbolic function. ²He is referred to as the Healer, the Comforter and the Guide. ³He is also described as something "separate,"

apart from the Father and from the Son. [4]I myself said, "If I go I will send you another Comforter and he will abide with you." [5]His symbolic function makes the Holy Spirit difficult to understand, because symbolism is open to different interpretations. [6]As a man and also one of God's creations, my right thinking, which came from the Holy Spirit or the Universal Inspiration, taught me first and foremost that this Inspiration is for all. [7]I could not have It myself without knowing this. [8]The word "know" is proper in this context, because the Holy Spirit is so close to knowledge that He calls it forth; or better, allows it to come. [9]I have spoken before of the higher or "true" perception, which is so near to truth that God Himself can flow across the little gap. [10]Knowledge is always ready to flow everywhere, but it cannot oppose. [11]Therefore you can obstruct it, although you can never lose it.

5. The Holy Spirit is the Christ Mind which is aware of the knowledge that lies beyond perception. [2]He came into being with the separation as a protection, inspiring the Atonement principle at the same time. [3]Before that there was no need for healing, for no one was comfortless. [4]The Voice of the Holy Spirit is the Call to Atonement, or the restoration of the integrity of the mind. [5]When the Atonement is complete and the whole Sonship is healed there will be no Call to return. [6]But what God creates is eternal. [7]The Holy Spirit will remain with the Sons of God, to bless their creations and keep them in the light of joy.

6. God honored even the miscreations of His children because they had made them. [2]But He also blessed His children with a way of thinking that could raise their perceptions so high they could reach almost back to Him. [3]The Holy Spirit is the Mind of the Atonement. [4]He represents a state of mind close enough to One-mindedness that transfer to it is at last possible. [5]Perception is not knowledge, but it can be transferred to knowledge, or cross over into it. [6]It might even be more helpful here to use the literal meaning of transferred or "carried over," since the last step is taken by God.

7. The Holy Spirit, the shared Inspiration of all the Sonship, induces a kind of perception in which many elements are like those in the Kingdom of Heaven itself:

[2]First, its universality is perfectly clear, and no one who attains it could believe for one instant that sharing it involves anything but gain.

[3]Second, it is incapable of attack and is therefore truly open.

⁴This means that although it does not engender knowledge, it does not obstruct it in any way.

⁵Finally, it points the way beyond the healing that it brings, and leads the mind beyond its own integration toward the paths of creation. ⁶It is at this point that sufficient quantitative change occurs to produce a real qualitative shift.

II. The Voice for God

1. Healing is not creating; it is reparation. ²The Holy Spirit promotes healing by looking beyond it to what the children of God were before healing was needed, and will be when they have been healed. ³This alteration of the time sequence should be quite familiar, because it is very similar to the shift in the perception of time that the miracle introduces. ⁴The Holy Spirit is the motivation for miracle-mindedness; the decision to heal the separation by letting it go. ⁵Your will is still in you because God placed it in your mind, and although you can keep it asleep you cannot obliterate it. ⁶God Himself keeps your will alive by transmitting it from His Mind to yours as long as there is time. ⁷The miracle itself is a reflection of this union of Will between Father and Son.

2. The Holy Spirit is the spirit of joy. ²He is the Call to return with which God blessed the minds of His separated Sons. ³This is the vocation of the mind. ⁴The mind had no calling until the separation, because before that it had only being, and would not have understood the Call to right thinking. ⁵The Holy Spirit is God's Answer to the separation; the means by which the Atonement heals until the whole mind returns to creating.

3. The principle of Atonement and the separation began at the same time. ²When the ego was made, God placed in the mind the Call to joy. ³This Call is so strong that the ego always dissolves at Its sound. ⁴That is why you must choose to hear one of two voices within you. ⁵One you made yourself, and that one is not of God. ⁶But the other is given you by God, Who asks you only to listen to it. ⁷The Holy Spirit is in you in a very literal sense. ⁸His is the Voice that calls you back to where you were before and will be again. ⁹It is possible even in this world to hear only that Voice and no other. ¹⁰It takes effort and great willingness to learn. ¹¹It is the final lesson that I learned, and God's Sons are as equal as

learners as they are as Sons.

4.   You *are* the Kingdom of Heaven, but you have let the belief in darkness enter your mind and so you need a new light. [2]The Holy Spirit is the radiance that you must let banish the idea of darkness. [3]His is the glory before which dissociation falls away, and the Kingdom of Heaven breaks through into its own. [4]Before the separation you did not need guidance. [5]You knew as you will know again, but as you do not know now.

5.   God does not guide, because He can share only perfect knowledge. [2]Guidance is evaluative, because it implies there is a right way and also a wrong way, one to be chosen and the other to be avoided. [3]By choosing one you give up the other. [4]The choice for the Holy Spirit is the choice for God. [5]God is not in you in a literal sense; you are part of Him. [6]When you chose to leave Him He gave you a Voice to speak for Him because He could no longer share His knowledge with you without hindrance. [7]Direct communication was broken because you had made another voice.

6.   The Holy Spirit calls you both to remember and to forget. [2]You have chosen to be in a state of opposition in which opposites are possible. [3]As a result, there are choices you must make. [4]In the holy state the will is free, so that its creative power is unlimited and choice is meaningless. [5]Freedom to choose is the same power as freedom to create, but its application is different. [6]Choosing depends on a split mind. [7]The Holy Spirit is one way of choosing. [8]God did not leave His children comfortless, even though they chose to leave Him. [9]The voice they put in their minds was not the Voice for His Will, for which the Holy Spirit speaks.

7.   The Voice of the Holy Spirit does not command, because It is incapable of arrogance. [2]It does not demand, because It does not seek control. [3]It does not overcome, because It does not attack. [4]It merely reminds. [5]It is compelling only because of what It reminds you *of*. [6]It brings to your mind the other way, remaining quiet even in the midst of the turmoil you may make. [7]The Voice for God is always quiet, because It speaks of peace. [8]Peace is stronger than war because it heals. [9]War is division, not increase. [10]No one gains from strife. [11]What profiteth it a man if he gain the whole world and lose his own soul? [12]If you listen to the wrong voice you *have* lost sight of your soul. [13]You cannot lose it, but you can not know it. [14]It is therefore "lost" to you until you choose right.

8.   The Holy Spirit is your Guide in choosing. [2]He is in the part of

your mind that always speaks for the right choice, because He speaks for God. ³He is your remaining communication with God, which you can interrupt but cannot destroy. ⁴The Holy Spirit is the way in which God's Will is done on earth as it is in Heaven. ⁵Both Heaven and earth are in you, because the call of both is in your mind. ⁶The Voice for God comes from your own altars to Him. ⁷These altars are not things; they are devotions. ⁸Yet you have other devotions now. ⁹Your divided devotion has given you the two voices, and you must choose at which altar you want to serve. ¹⁰The call you answer now is an evaluation because it is a decision. ¹¹The decision is very simple. ¹²It is made on the basis of which call is worth more to you.

9. My mind will always be like yours, because we were created as equals. ²It was only my decision that gave me all power in Heaven and earth. ³My only gift to you is to help you make the same decision. ⁴This decision is the choice to share it, because the decision itself *is* the decision to share. ⁵It is made by giving, and is therefore the one choice that resembles true creation. ⁶I am your model for decision. ⁷By deciding for God I showed you that this decision can be made, and that you can make it.

10. I have assured you that the Mind that decided for me is also in you, and that you can let it change you just as it changed me. ²This Mind is unequivocal, because it hears only one Voice and answers in only one way. ³You are the light of the world with me. ⁴Rest does not come from sleeping but from waking. ⁵The Holy Spirit is the Call to awaken and be glad. ⁶The world is very tired, because it is the idea of weariness. ⁷Our task is the joyous one of waking it to the Call for God. ⁸Everyone will answer the Call of the Holy Spirit, or the Sonship cannot be as one. ⁹What better vocation could there be for any part of the Kingdom than to restore it to the perfect integration that can make it whole? ¹⁰Hear only this through the Holy Spirit within you, and teach your brothers to listen as I am teaching you.

11. When you are tempted by the wrong voice, call on me to remind you how to heal by sharing my decision and making it stronger. ²As we share this goal, we increase its power to attract the whole Sonship, and to bring it back into the oneness in which it was created. ³Remember that "yoke" means "join together," and "burden" means "message." ⁴Let us restate "My yoke is easy and my burden light" in this way; "Let us join together, for my message is light."

12. I have enjoined you to behave as I behaved, but we must respond to the same Mind to do this. ²This Mind is the Holy Spirit, Whose Will is for God always. ³He teaches you how to keep me as the model for your thought, and to behave like me as a result. ⁴The power of our joint motivation is beyond belief, but not beyond accomplishment. ⁵What we can accomplish together has no limits, because the Call for God is the Call to the unlimited. ⁶Child of God, my message is for you, to hear and give away as you answer the Holy Spirit within you.

III. The Guide to Salvation

1. The way to recognize your brother is by recognizing the Holy Spirit in him. ²I have already said that the Holy Spirit is the Bridge for the transfer of perception to knowledge, so we can use the terms as if they were related, because in His Mind they are. ³This relationship must be in His Mind because, unless it were, the separation between the two ways of thinking would not be open to healing. ⁴He is part of the Holy Trinity, because His Mind is partly yours and also partly God's. ⁵This needs clarification, not in statement but in experience.

2. The Holy Spirit is the idea of healing. ²Being thought, the idea gains as it is shared. ³Being the Call *for* God, it is also the idea *of* God. ⁴Since you are part of God it is also the idea of yourself, as well as of all His creations. ⁵The idea of the Holy Spirit shares the property of other ideas because it follows the laws of the universe of which it is a part. ⁶It is strengthened by being given away. ⁷It increases in you as you give it to your brother. ⁸Your brother does not have to be aware of the Holy Spirit in himself or in you for this miracle to occur. ⁹He may have dissociated the Call for God, just as you have. ¹⁰This dissociation is healed in both of you as you become aware of the Call for God in him, and thus acknowledge Its being.

3. There are two diametrically opposed ways of seeing your brother. ²They must both be in your mind, because you are the perceiver. ³They must also be in his, because you are perceiving him. ⁴See him through the Holy Spirit in his mind, and you will recognize Him in yours. ⁵What you acknowledge in your brother you are acknowledging in yourself, and what you share you strengthen.

4.   The Voice of the Holy Spirit is weak in you. ²That is why you must share It. ³It must be increased in strength before you can hear It. ⁴It is impossible to hear It in yourself while It is so weak in your mind. ⁵It is not weak in Itself, but It is limited by your unwillingness to hear It. ⁶If you make the mistake of looking for the Holy Spirit in yourself alone your thoughts will frighten you because, by adopting the ego's viewpoint, you are undertaking an ego-alien journey with the ego as guide. ⁷This is bound to produce fear.

5.   Delay is of the ego, because time is its concept. ²Both time and delay are meaningless in eternity. ³I have said before that the Holy Spirit is God's Answer to the ego. ⁴Everything of which the Holy Spirit reminds you is in direct opposition to the ego's notions, because true and false perceptions are themselves opposed. ⁵The Holy Spirit has the task of undoing what the ego has made. ⁶He undoes it at the same level on which the ego operates, or the mind would be unable to understand the change.

6.   I have repeatedly emphasized that one level of the mind is not understandable to another. ²So it is with the ego and the Holy Spirit; with time and eternity. ³Eternity is an idea of God, so the Holy Spirit understands it perfectly. ⁴Time is a belief of the ego, so the lower mind, which is the ego's domain, accepts it without question. ⁵The only aspect of time that is eternal is *now*.

7.   The Holy Spirit is the Mediator between the interpretations of the ego and the knowledge of the spirit. ²His ability to deal with symbols enables Him to work with the ego's beliefs in its own language. ³His ability to look beyond symbols into eternity enables Him to understand the laws of God, for which He speaks. ⁴He can therefore perform the function of reinterpreting what the ego makes, not by destruction but by understanding. ⁵Understanding is light, and light leads to knowledge. ⁶The Holy Spirit is in light because He is in you who are light, but you yourself do not know this. ⁷It is therefore the task of the Holy Spirit to reinterpret you on behalf of God.

8.   You cannot understand yourself alone. ²This is because you have no meaning apart from your rightful place in the Sonship, and the rightful place of the Sonship is God. ³This is your life, your eternity and your Self. ⁴It is of this that the Holy Spirit reminds you. ⁵It is this that the Holy Spirit sees. ⁶This vision frightens the ego because it is so calm. ⁷Peace is the ego's greatest enemy because, according to its interpretation of reality, war is the

guarantee of its survival. [8]The ego becomes strong in strife. [9]If you believe there is strife you will react viciously, because the idea of danger has entered your mind. [10]The idea itself is an appeal to the ego. [11]The Holy Spirit is as vigilant as the ego to the call of danger, opposing it with His strength just as the ego welcomes it. [12]The Holy Spirit counters this welcome by welcoming peace. [13]Eternity and peace are as closely related as are time and war.

9.   Perception derives meaning from relationships. [2]Those you accept are the foundations of your beliefs. [3]The separation is merely another term for a split mind. [4]The ego is the symbol of separation, just as the Holy Spirit is the symbol of peace. [5]What you perceive in others you are strengthening in yourself. [6]You may let your mind misperceive, but the Holy Spirit lets your mind reinterpret its own misperceptions.

10.   The Holy Spirit is the perfect Teacher. [2]He uses only what your mind already understands to teach you that you do not understand it. [3]The Holy Spirit can deal with a reluctant learner without going counter to his mind, because part of it is still for God. [4]Despite the ego's attempts to conceal this part, it is still much stronger than the ego, although the ego does not recognize it. [5]The Holy Spirit recognizes it perfectly because it is His Own dwelling place; the place in the mind where He is at home. [6]You are at home there, too, because it is a place of peace, and peace is of God. [7]You who are part of God are not at home except in His peace. [8]If peace is eternal, you are at home only in eternity.

11.   The ego made the world as it perceives it, but the Holy Spirit, the reinterpreter of what the ego made, sees the world as a teaching device for bringing you home. [2]The Holy Spirit must perceive time, and reinterpret it into the timeless. [3]He must work through opposites, because He must work with and for a mind that is in opposition. [4]Correct and learn, and be open to learning. [5]You have not made truth, but truth can still set you free. [6]Look as the Holy Spirit looks, and understand as He understands. [7]His understanding looks back to God in remembrance of me. [8]He is in communion with God always, and He is part of you. [9]He is your Guide to salvation, because He holds the remembrance of things past and to come, and brings them to the present. [10]He holds this gladness gently in your mind, asking only that you increase it in His Name by sharing it to increase His joy in you.

IV. Teaching and Healing

1.   What fear has hidden still is part of you. ²Joining the Atonement is the way out of fear. ³The Holy Spirit will help you reinterpret everything that you perceive as fearful, and teach you that only what is loving is true. ⁴Truth is beyond your ability to destroy, but entirely within your ability to accept. ⁵It belongs to you because, as an extension of God, you created it with Him. ⁶It is yours because it is part of you, just as you are part of God because He created you. ⁷Nothing that is good can be lost because it comes from the Holy Spirit, the Voice for creation. ⁸Nothing that is not good was ever created, and therefore cannot be protected. ⁹The Atonement is the guarantee of the safety of the Kingdom, and the union of the Sonship is its protection. ¹⁰The ego cannot prevail against the Kingdom because the Sonship is united. ¹¹In the presence of those who hear the Holy Spirit's Call to be as one, the ego fades away and is undone.

2.   What the ego makes it keeps to itself, and so it is without strength. ²Its existence is unshared. ³It does not die; it was merely never born. ⁴Physical birth is not a beginning; it is a continuing. ⁵Everything that continues has already been born. ⁶It will increase as you are willing to return the unhealed part of your mind to the higher part, returning it undivided to creation. ⁷I have come to give you the foundation, so your own thoughts can make you really free. ⁸You have carried the burden of unshared ideas that are too weak to increase, but having made them you did not realize how to undo them. ⁹You cannot cancel out your past errors alone. ¹⁰They will not disappear from your mind without the Atonement, a remedy not of your making. ¹¹The Atonement must be understood as a pure act of sharing. ¹²That is what I meant when I said it is possible even in this world to listen to one Voice. ¹³If you are part of God and the Sonship is one, you cannot be limited to the self the ego sees.

3.   Every loving thought held in any part of the Sonship belongs to every part. ²It is shared *because* it is loving. ³Sharing is God's way of creating, and also yours. ⁴The ego can keep you in exile from the Kingdom, but in the Kingdom itself it has no power. ⁵Ideas of the spirit do not leave the mind that thinks them, nor can they conflict with each other. ⁶However, ideas of the ego can conflict because they occur at different levels and also include opposite thoughts at the same level. ⁷*It is impossible to share*

opposing thoughts. ⁸You can share only the thoughts that are of God and that He keeps for you. ⁹And of such is the Kingdom of Heaven. ¹⁰The rest remains with you until the Holy Spirit has reinterpreted them in the light of the Kingdom, making them, too, worthy of being shared. ¹¹When they have been sufficiently purified He lets you give them away. ¹²The decision to share them *is* their purification.

4. I heard one Voice because I understood that I could not atone for myself alone. ²Listening to one Voice implies the decision to share It in order to hear It yourself. ³The Mind that was in me is still irresistibly drawn to every mind created by God, because God's Wholeness is the Wholeness of His Son. ⁴You cannot be hurt, and do not want to show your brother anything except your wholeness. ⁵Show him that he cannot hurt you and hold nothing against him, or you hold it against yourself. ⁶This is the meaning of "turning the other cheek."

5. Teaching is done in many ways, above all by example. ²Teaching should be healing, because it is the sharing of ideas and the recognition that to share ideas is to strengthen them. ³I cannot forget my need to teach what I have learned, which arose in me *because* I learned it. ⁴I call upon you to teach what you have learned, because by so doing you can depend on it. ⁵Make it dependable in my name because my name is the Name of God's Son. ⁶What I learned I give you freely, and the Mind that was in me rejoices as you choose to hear it.

6. The Holy Spirit atones in all of us by undoing, and thus lifts the burden you have placed in your mind. ²By following Him you are led back to God where you belong, and how can you find the way except by taking your brother with you? ³My part in the Atonement is not complete until you join it and give it away. ⁴As you teach so shall you learn. ⁵I will never leave you or forsake you, because to forsake you would be to forsake myself and God Who created me. ⁶You forsake yourself and God if you forsake any of your brothers. ⁷You must learn to see them as they are, and understand they belong to God as you do. ⁸How could you treat your brother better than by rendering unto God the things that are God's?

7. The Atonement gives you the power of a healed mind, but the power to create is of God. ²Therefore, those who have been forgiven must devote themselves first to healing because, having received the idea of healing, they must give it to hold it. ³The full

power of creation cannot be expressed as long as any of God's ideas is withheld from the Kingdom. ⁴The joint will of the Sonship is the only creator that can create like the Father, because only the complete can think completely, and the thinking of God lacks nothing. ⁵Everything you think that is not through the Holy Spirit *is* lacking.

8. How can you who are so holy suffer? ²All your past except its beauty is gone, and nothing is left but a blessing. ³I have saved all your kindnesses and every loving thought you ever had. ⁴I have purified them of the errors that hid their light, and kept them for you in their own perfect radiance. ⁵They are beyond destruction and beyond guilt. ⁶They came from the Holy Spirit within you, and we know what God creates is eternal. ⁷You can indeed depart in peace because I have loved you as I loved myself. ⁸You go with my blessing and for my blessing. ⁹Hold it and share it, that it may always be ours. ¹⁰I place the peace of God in your heart and in your hands, to hold and share. ¹¹The heart is pure to hold it, and the hands are strong to give it. ¹²We cannot lose. ¹³My judgment is as strong as the wisdom of God, in Whose Heart and Hands we have our being. ¹⁴His quiet children are His blessed Sons. ¹⁵The Thoughts of God are with you.

V. The Ego's Use of Guilt

1. Perhaps some of our concepts will become clearer and more personally meaningful if the ego's use of guilt is clarified. ²The ego has a purpose, just as the Holy Spirit has. ³The ego's purpose is fear, because only the fearful can be egotistic. ⁴The ego's logic is as impeccable as that of the Holy Spirit, because your mind has the means at its disposal to side with Heaven or earth, as it elects. ⁵But again, remember that both are in you.

2. In Heaven there is no guilt, because the Kingdom is attained through the Atonement, which releases you to create. ²The word "create" is appropriate here because, once what you have made is undone by the Holy Spirit, the blessed residue is restored and therefore continues in creation. ³What is truly blessed is incapable of giving rise to guilt, and must give rise to joy. ⁴This makes it invulnerable to the ego because its peace is unassailable. ⁵It is invulnerable to disruption because it is whole. ⁶Guilt is *always* disruptive. ⁷Anything that engenders fear is divisive because it

obeys the law of division. [8]If the ego is the symbol of the separation, it is also the symbol of guilt. [9]Guilt is more than merely not of God. [10]It is the symbol of attack on God. [11]This is a totally meaningless concept except to the ego, but do not underestimate the power of the ego's belief in it. [12]This is the belief from which all guilt really stems.

3.   The ego is the part of the mind that believes in division. [2]How could part of God detach itself without believing it is attacking Him? [3]We spoke before of the authority problem as based on the concept of usurping God's power. [4]The ego believes that this is what you did because it believes that it *is* you. [5]If you identify with the ego, you must perceive yourself as guilty. [6]Whenever you respond to your ego you will experience guilt, and you will fear punishment. [7]The ego is quite literally a fearful thought. [8]However ridiculous the idea of attacking God may be to the sane mind, never forget that the ego is not sane. [9]It represents a delusional system, and speaks for it. [10]Listening to the ego's voice means that you believe it is possible to attack God, and that a part of Him has been torn away by you. [11]Fear of retaliation from without follows, because the severity of the guilt is so acute that it must be projected.

4.   Whatever you accept into your mind has reality for you. [2]It is your acceptance of it that makes it real. [3]If you enthrone the ego in your mind, your allowing it to enter makes it your reality. [4]This is because the mind is capable of creating reality or making illusions. [5]I said before that you must learn to think with God. [6]To think with Him is to think like Him. [7]This engenders joy, not guilt, because it is natural. [8]Guilt is a sure sign that your thinking is unnatural. [9]Unnatural thinking will always be attended with guilt, because it is the belief in sin. [10]The ego does not perceive sin as a lack of love, but as a positive act of assault. [11]This is necessary to the ego's survival because, as soon as you regard sin as a lack, you will automatically attempt to remedy the situation. [12]And you will succeed. [13]The ego regards this as doom, but you must learn to regard it as freedom.

5.   The guiltless mind cannot suffer. [2]Being sane, the mind heals the body because *it* has been healed. [3]The sane mind cannot conceive of illness because it cannot conceive of attacking anyone or anything. [4]I said before that illness is a form of magic. [5]It might be better to say that it is a form of magical solution. [6]The ego believes that by punishing itself it will mitigate the punishment

of God. ⁷Yet even in this it is arrogant. ⁸It attributes to God a punishing intent, and then takes this intent as its own prerogative. ⁹It tries to usurp all the functions of God as it perceives them, because it recognizes that only total allegiance can be trusted.

6. The ego cannot oppose the laws of God any more than you can, but it can interpret them according to what it wants, just as you can. ²That is why the question, "What do you want?" must be answered. ³You are answering it every minute and every second, and each moment of decision is a judgment that is anything but ineffectual. ⁴Its effects will follow automatically until the decision is changed. ⁵Remember, though, that the alternatives themselves are unalterable. ⁶The Holy Spirit, like the ego, is a decision. ⁷Together they constitute all the alternatives the mind can accept and obey. ⁸The Holy Spirit and the ego are the only choices open to you. ⁹God created one, and so you cannot eradicate it. ¹⁰You made the other, and so you can. ¹¹Only what God creates is irreversible and unchangeable. ¹²What you made can always be changed because, when you do not think like God, you are not really thinking at all. ¹³Delusional ideas are not real thoughts, although you can believe in them. ¹⁴But you are wrong. ¹⁵The function of thought comes from God and is in God. ¹⁶As part of His Thought, you *cannot* think apart from Him.

7. Irrational thought is disordered thought. ²God Himself orders your thought because your thought was created by Him. ³Guilt feelings are always a sign that you do not know this. ⁴They also show that you believe you can think apart from God, and want to. ⁵Every disordered thought is attended by guilt at its inception, and maintained by guilt in its continuance. ⁶Guilt is inescapable by those who believe they order their own thoughts, and must therefore obey their dictates. ⁷This makes them feel responsible for their errors without recognizing that, by accepting this responsibility, they are reacting irresponsibly. ⁸If the sole responsibility of the miracle worker is to accept the Atonement for himself, and I assure you that it is, then the responsibility for *what* is atoned for cannot be yours. ⁹The dilemma cannot be resolved except by accepting the solution of undoing. ¹⁰You *would* be responsible for the effects of all your wrong thinking if it could not be undone. ¹¹The purpose of the Atonement is to save the past in purified form only. ¹²If you accept the remedy for disordered thought, a remedy whose efficacy is beyond doubt, how

can its symptoms remain?

8. The continuing decision to remain separated is the only possible reason for continuing guilt feelings. ²We have said this before, but did not emphasize the destructive results of the decision. ³Any decision of the mind will affect both behavior and experience. ⁴What you want you expect. ⁵This is not delusional. ⁶Your mind *does* make your future, and it will turn it back to full creation at any minute if it accepts the Atonement first. ⁷It will also return to full creation the instant it has done so. ⁸Having given up its disordered thought, the proper ordering of thought becomes quite apparent.

VI. Time and Eternity

1. God in His knowledge is not waiting, but His Kingdom is bereft while *you* wait. ²All the Sons of God are waiting for your return, just as you are waiting for theirs. ³Delay does not matter in eternity, but it is tragic in time. ⁴You have elected to be in time rather than eternity, and therefore believe you *are* in time. ⁵Yet your election is both free and alterable. ⁶You do not belong in time. ⁷Your place is only in eternity, where God Himself placed you forever.

2. Guilt feelings are the preservers of time. ²They induce fears of retaliation or abandonment, and thus ensure that the future will be like the past. ³This is the ego's continuity. ⁴It gives the ego a false sense of security by believing that you cannot escape from it. ⁵But you can and must. ⁶God offers you the continuity of eternity in exchange. ⁷When you choose to make this exchange, you will simultaneously exchange guilt for joy, viciousness for love, and pain for peace. ⁸My role is only to unchain your will and set it free. ⁹Your ego cannot accept this freedom, and will oppose it at every possible moment and in every possible way. ¹⁰And as its maker, you recognize what it can do because you gave it the power to do it.

3. Remember the Kingdom always, and remember that you who are part of the Kingdom cannot be lost. ²The Mind that was in me *is* in you, for God creates with perfect fairness. ³Let the Holy Spirit remind you always of His fairness, and let me teach you how to share it with your brothers. ⁴How else can the chance to claim it for yourself be given you? ⁵The two voices speak for

different interpretations of the same thing simultaneously; or almost simultaneously, for the ego always speaks first. [6]Alternate interpretations were unnecessary until the first one was made.

4. The ego speaks in judgment, and the Holy Spirit reverses its decision, much as a higher court has the power to reverse a lower court's decisions in this world. [2]The ego's decisions are always wrong, because they are based on the error they were made to uphold. [3]Nothing the ego perceives is interpreted correctly. [4]Not only does the ego cite Scripture for its purpose, but it even interprets Scripture as a witness for itself. [5]The Bible is a fearful thing in the ego's judgment. [6]Perceiving it as frightening, it interprets it fearfully. [7]Being afraid, you do not appeal to the Higher Court because you believe its judgment would also be against you.

5. There are many examples of how the ego's interpretations are misleading, but a few will suffice to show how the Holy Spirit can reinterpret them in His Own light.

6. "As ye sow, so shall ye reap" He interprets to mean what you consider worth cultivating you will cultivate in yourself. [2]Your judgment of what is worthy makes it worthy for you.

7. "Vengeance is mine, saith the Lord" is easily reinterpreted if you remember that ideas increase only by being shared. [2]The statement emphasizes that vengeance cannot be shared. [3]Give it therefore to the Holy Spirit, Who will undo it in you because it does not belong in your mind, which is part of God.

8. "I will visit the sins of the fathers unto the third and fourth generation," as interpreted by the ego, is particularly vicious. [2]It becomes merely an attempt to guarantee the ego's own survival. [3]To the Holy Spirit, the statement means that in later generations He can still reinterpret what former generations had misunderstood, and thus release the thoughts from the ability to produce fear.

9. "The wicked shall perish" becomes a statement of Atonement, if the word "perish" is understood as "be undone." [2]Every loveless thought must be undone, a word the ego cannot even understand. [3]To the ego, to be undone means to be destroyed. [4]The ego will not be destroyed because it is part of your thought, but because it is uncreative and therefore unsharing, it will be reinterpreted to release you from fear. [5]The part of your mind that you have given to the ego will merely return to the Kingdom, where your whole mind belongs. [6]You can delay the completion of the Kingdom, but you cannot introduce the

concept of fear into it.

10. You need not fear the Higher Court will condemn you. ²It will merely dismiss the case against you. ³There can be no case against a child of God, and every witness to guilt in God's creations is bearing false witness to God Himself. ⁴Appeal everything you believe gladly to God's Own Higher Court, because it speaks for Him and therefore speaks truly. ⁵It will dismiss the case against you, however carefully you have built it up. ⁶The case may be fool-proof, but it is not God-proof. ⁷The Holy Spirit will not hear it, because He can only witness truly. ⁸His verdict will always be "thine is the Kingdom," because He was given to you to remind you of what you are.

11. When I said "I am come as a light into the world," I meant that I came to share the light with you. ²Remember my reference to the ego's dark glass, and remember also that I said, "Do not look there." ³It is still true that where you look to find yourself is up to you. ⁴Your patience with your brother is your patience with yourself. ⁵Is not a child of God worth patience? ⁶I have shown you infinite patience because my will is that of our Father, from Whom I learned of infinite patience. ⁷His Voice was in me as It is in you, speaking for patience towards the Sonship in the Name of its Creator.

12. Now you must learn that only infinite patience produces immediate effects. ²This is the way in which time is exchanged for eternity. ³Infinite patience calls upon infinite love, and by producing results *now* it renders time unnecessary. ⁴We have repeatedly said that time is a learning device to be abolished when it is no longer useful. ⁵The Holy Spirit, Who speaks for God in time, also knows that time is meaningless. ⁶He reminds you of this in every passing moment of time, because it is His special function to return you to eternity and remain to bless your creations there. ⁷He is the only blessing you can truly give, because He is truly blessed. ⁸Because He has been given you freely by God, you must give Him as you received Him.

VII. The Decision for God

1. Do you really believe you can make a voice that can drown out God's? ²Do you really believe you can devise a thought system that can separate you from Him? ³Do you really believe you can

plan for your safety and joy better than He can? ⁴You need be neither careful nor careless; you need merely cast your cares upon Him because He careth for you. ⁵You are His care because He loves you. ⁶His Voice reminds you always that all hope is yours because of His care. ⁷You cannot choose to escape His care because that is not His Will, but you can choose to accept His care and use the infinite power of His care for all those He created by it.

2. There have been many healers who did not heal themselves. ²They have not moved mountains by their faith because their faith was not whole. ³Some of them have healed the sick at times, but they have not raised the dead. ⁴Unless the healer heals himself, he cannot believe that there is no order of difficulty in miracles. ⁵He has not learned that every mind God created is equally worthy of being healed *because* God created it whole. ⁶You are merely asked to return to God the mind as He created it. ⁷He asks you only for what He gave, knowing that this giving will heal you. ⁸Sanity is wholeness, and the sanity of your brothers is yours.

3. Why should you listen to the endless insane calls you think are made upon you, when you can know the Voice for God is in you? ²God commended His Spirit to you, and asks that you commend yours to Him. ³He wills to keep it in perfect peace, because you are of one mind and spirit with Him. ⁴Excluding yourself from the Atonement is the ego's last-ditch defense of its own existence. ⁵It reflects both the ego's need to separate, and your willingness to side with its separateness. ⁶This willingness means that you do not want to be healed.

4. But the time is now. ²You have not been asked to work out the plan of salvation yourself because, as I told you before, the remedy could not be of your making. ³God Himself gave you the perfect Correction for everything you made that is not in accord with His holy Will. ⁴I am making His plan perfectly explicit to you, and will also tell you of your part in it, and how urgent it is to fulfill it. ⁵God weeps at the "sacrifice" of His children who believe they are lost to Him.

5. Whenever you are not wholly joyous, it is because you have reacted with a lack of love to one of God's creations. ²Perceiving this as "sin" you become defensive because you expect attack. ³The decision to react in this way is yours, and can therefore be undone. ⁴It cannot be undone by repentance in the usual sense,

because this implies guilt. ⁵If you allow yourself to feel guilty, you will reinforce the error rather than allow it to be undone for you.

6. Decision cannot be difficult. ²This is obvious, if you realize that you must already have decided not to be wholly joyous if that is how you feel. ³Therefore, the first step in the undoing is to recognize that you actively decided wrongly, but can as actively decide otherwise. ⁴Be very firm with yourself in this, and keep yourself fully aware that the undoing process, which does not come from you, is nevertheless within you because God placed it there. ⁵Your part is merely to return your thinking to the point at which the error was made, and give it over to the Atonement in peace. ⁶Say this to yourself as sincerely as you can, remembering that the Holy Spirit will respond fully to your slightest invitation:

> ⁷*I must have decided wrongly, because I am not at peace.*
> ⁸*I made the decision myself, but I can also decide otherwise.*
> ⁹*I want to decide otherwise, because I want to be at peace.*
> ¹⁰*I do not feel guilty, because the Holy Spirit will undo all the consequences of my wrong decision if I will let Him.*
> ¹¹*I choose to let Him, by allowing Him to decide for God for me.*

Chapter 6

THE LESSONS OF LOVE

Introduction

1. The relationship of anger to attack is obvious, but the relationship of anger to fear is not always so apparent. ²Anger always involves projection of separation, which must ultimately be accepted as one's own responsibility, rather than being blamed on others. ³Anger cannot occur unless you believe that you have been attacked, that your attack is justified in return, and that you are in no way responsible for it. ⁴Given these three wholly irrational premises, the equally irrational conclusion that a brother is worthy of attack rather than of love must follow. ⁵What can be expected from insane premises except an insane conclusion? ⁶The way to undo an insane conclusion is to consider the sanity of the premises on which it rests. ⁷You cannot *be* attacked, attack *has* no justification, and you *are* responsible for what you believe.

2. You have been asked to take me as your model for learning, since an extreme example is a particularly helpful learning device. ²Everyone teaches, and teaches all the time. ³This is a responsibility you inevitably assume the moment you accept any premise at all, and no one can organize his life without some thought system. ⁴Once you have developed a thought system of any kind, you live by it and teach it. ⁵Your capacity for allegiance to a thought system may be misplaced, but it is still a form of faith and can be redirected.

I. The Message of the Crucifixion

1. For learning purposes, let us consider the crucifixion again. ²I did not dwell on it before because of the fearful connotations you may associate with it. ³The only emphasis laid upon it so far has been that it was not a form of punishment. ⁴Nothing, however, can be explained in negative terms only. ⁵There is a positive interpretation of the crucifixion that is wholly devoid of fear, and therefore wholly benign in what it teaches, if it is properly understood.

2.   The crucifixion is nothing more than an extreme example. ²Its value, like the value of any teaching device, lies solely in the kind of learning it facilitates. ³It can be, and has been, misunderstood. ⁴This is only because the fearful are apt to perceive fearfully. ⁵I have already told you that you can always call on me to share my decision, and thus make it stronger. ⁶I have also told you that the crucifixion was the last useless journey the Sonship need take, and that it represents release from fear to anyone who understands it. ⁷While I emphasized only the resurrection before, the purpose of the crucifixion and how it actually led to the resurrection was not clarified then. ⁸Nevertheless, it has a definite contribution to make to your own life, and if you will consider it without fear, it will help you understand your own role as a teacher.

3.   You have probably reacted for years as if you were being crucified. ²This is a marked tendency of the separated, who always refuse to consider what they have done to themselves. ³Projection means anger, anger fosters assault, and assault promotes fear. ⁴The real meaning of the crucifixion lies in the *apparent* intensity of the assault of some of the Sons of God upon another. ⁵This, of course, is impossible, and must be fully understood *as* impossible. ⁶Otherwise, I cannot serve as a model for learning.

4.   Assault can ultimately be made only on the body. ²There is little doubt that one body can assault another, and can even destroy it. ³Yet if destruction itself is impossible, anything that is destructible cannot be real. ⁴Its destruction, therefore, does not justify anger. ⁵To the extent to which you believe that it does, you are accepting false premises and teaching them to others. ⁶The message the crucifixion was intended to teach was that it is not necessary to perceive any form of assault in persecution, because you cannot *be* persecuted. ⁷If you respond with anger, you must be equating yourself with the destructible, and are therefore regarding yourself insanely.

5.   I have made it perfectly clear that I am like you and you are like me, but our fundamental equality can be demonstrated only through joint decision. ²You are free to perceive yourself as persecuted if you choose. ³When you do choose to react that way, however, you might remember that I was persecuted as the world judges, and did not share this evaluation for myself. ⁴And because I did not share it, I did not strengthen it. ⁵I therefore offered

a different interpretation of attack, and one which I want to share with you. [6]If you will believe it, you will help me teach it.

6. As I have said before, "As you teach so shall you learn." [2]If you react as if you are persecuted, you are teaching persecution. [3]This is not a lesson a Son of God should want to teach if he is to realize his own salvation. [4]Rather, teach your own perfect immunity, which is the truth in you, and realize that it cannot *be* assailed. [5]Do not try to protect it yourself, or you are believing that it is assailable. [6]You are not asked to be crucified, which was part of my own teaching contribution. [7]You are merely asked to follow my example in the face of much less extreme temptations to misperceive, and not to accept them as false justifications for anger. [8]There can be no justification for the unjustifiable. [9]Do not believe there is, and do not teach that there is. [10]Remember always that what you believe you will teach. [11]Believe with me, and we will become equal as teachers.

7. Your resurrection is your reawakening. [2]I am the model for rebirth, but rebirth itself is merely the dawning on your mind of what is already in it. [3]God placed it there Himself, and so it is true forever. [4]I believed in it, and therefore accepted it as true for me. [5]Help me to teach it to our brothers in the name of the Kingdom of God, but first believe that it is true for you, or you will teach amiss. [6]My brothers slept during the so-called "agony in the garden," but I could not be angry with them because I knew I could not *be* abandoned.

8. I am sorry when my brothers do not share my decision to hear only one Voice, because it weakens them as teachers and as learners. [2]Yet I know they cannot really betray themselves or me, and that it is still on them that I must build my church. [3]There is no choice in this, because only you can be the foundation of God's church. [4]A church is where an altar is, and the presence of the altar is what makes the church holy. [5]A church that does not inspire love has a hidden altar that is not serving the purpose for which God intended it. [6]I must found His church on you, because those who accept me as a model are literally my disciples. [7]Disciples are followers, and if the model they follow has chosen to save them pain in all respects, they are unwise not to follow him.

9. I elected, for your sake and mine, to demonstrate that the most outrageous assault, as judged by the ego, does not matter. [2]As the world judges these things, but not as God knows them, I was betrayed, abandoned, beaten, torn, and finally killed. [3]It was

clear that this was only because of the projection of others onto me, since I had not harmed anyone and had healed many.

10.   We are still equal as learners, although we do not need to have equal experiences. ²The Holy Spirit is glad when you can learn from mine, and be reawakened by them. ³That is their only purpose, and that is the only way in which I can be perceived as the way, the truth and the life. ⁴When you hear only one Voice you are never called on to sacrifice. ⁵On the contrary, by being able to hear the Holy Spirit in others you can learn from their experiences, and can gain from them without experiencing them directly yourself. ⁶That is because the Holy Spirit is one, and anyone who listens is inevitably led to demonstrate His way for all.

11.   You are not persecuted, nor was I. ²You are not asked to repeat my experiences because the Holy Spirit, Whom we share, makes this unnecessary. ³To use my experiences constructively, however, you must still follow my example in how to perceive them. ⁴My brothers and yours are constantly engaged in justifying the unjustifiable. ⁵My one lesson, which I must teach as I learned it, is that no perception that is out of accord with the judgment of the Holy Spirit can be justified. ⁶I undertook to show this was true in an extreme case, merely because it would serve as a good teaching aid to those whose temptation to give in to anger and assault would not be so extreme. ⁷I will with God that none of His Sons should suffer.

12.   The crucifixion cannot be shared because it is the symbol of projection, but the resurrection is the symbol of sharing because the reawakening of every Son of God is necessary to enable the Sonship to know its Wholeness. ²Only this is knowledge.

13.   The message of the crucifixion is perfectly clear:

²Teach only love, for that is what you are.

14.   If you interpret the crucifixion in any other way, you are using it as a weapon for assault rather than as the call for peace for which it was intended. ²The Apostles often misunderstood it, and for the same reason that anyone misunderstands it. ³Their own imperfect love made them vulnerable to projection, and out of their own fear they spoke of the "wrath of God" as His retaliatory weapon. ⁴Nor could they speak of the crucifixion entirely without anger, because their sense of guilt had made them angry.

15. These are some of the examples of upside-down thinking in the New Testament, although its gospel is really only the message of love. ²If the Apostles had not felt guilty, they never could have quoted me as saying, "I come not to bring peace but a sword." ³This is clearly the opposite of everything I taught. ⁴Nor could they have described my reactions to Judas as they did, if they had really understood me. ⁵I could not have said, "Betrayest thou the Son of man with a kiss?" unless I believed in betrayal. ⁶The whole message of the crucifixion was simply that I did not. ⁷The "punishment" I was said to have called forth upon Judas was a similar mistake. ⁸Judas was my brother and a Son of God, as much a part of the Sonship as myself. ⁹Was it likely that I would condemn him when I was ready to demonstrate that condemnation is impossible?

16. As you read the teachings of the Apostles, remember that I told them myself that there was much they would understand later, because they were not wholly ready to follow me at the time. ²I do not want you to allow any fear to enter into the thought system toward which I am guiding you. ³I do not call for martyrs but for teachers. ⁴No one is punished for sins, and the Sons of God are not sinners. ⁵Any concept of punishment involves the projection of blame, and reinforces the idea that blame is justified. ⁶The result is a lesson in blame, for all behavior teaches the beliefs that motivate it. ⁷The crucifixion was the result of clearly opposed thought systems; the perfect symbol of the "conflict" between the ego and the Son of God. ⁸This conflict seems just as real now, and its lessons must be learned now as well as then.

17. I do not need gratitude, but you need to develop your weakened ability to be grateful, or you cannot appreciate God. ²He does not need your appreciation, but *you* do. ³You cannot love what you do not appreciate, for fear makes appreciation impossible. ⁴When you are afraid of what you are you do not appreciate it, and will therefore reject it. ⁵As a result, you will teach rejection.

18. The power of the Sons of God is present all the time, because they were created as creators. ²Their influence on each other is without limit, and must be used for their joint salvation. ³Each one must learn to teach that all forms of rejection are meaningless. ⁴The separation is the notion of rejection. ⁵As long as you teach this you will believe it. ⁶This is not as God thinks, and you must think as He thinks if you are to know Him again.

19.   Remember that the Holy Spirit is the Communication Link between God the Father and His separated Sons. ²If you will listen to His Voice you will know that you cannot either hurt or be hurt, and that many need your blessing to help them hear this for themselves. ³When you perceive only this need in them, and do not respond to any other, you will have learned of me and will be as eager to share your learning as I am.

II. The Alternative to Projection

1.   Any split in mind must involve a rejection of part of it, and this *is* the belief in separation. ²The Wholeness of God, which is His peace, cannot be appreciated except by a whole mind that recognizes the Wholeness of God's creation. ³By this recognition it knows its Creator. ⁴Exclusion and separation are synonymous, as are separation and dissociation. ⁵We have said before that the separation was and is dissociation, and that once it occurs projection becomes its main defense, or the device that keeps it going. ⁶The reason, however, may not be so obvious as you think.

2.   What you project you disown, and therefore do not believe is yours. ²You are excluding yourself by the very judgment that you are different from the one on whom you project. ³Since you have also judged against what you project, you continue to attack it because you continue to keep it separated. ⁴By doing this unconsciously, you try to keep the fact that you attacked yourself out of awareness, and thus imagine that you have made yourself safe.

3.   Yet projection will always hurt you. ²It reinforces your belief in your own split mind, and its only purpose is to keep the separation going. ³It is solely a device of the ego to make you feel different from your brothers and separated from them. ⁴The ego justifies this on the grounds that it makes you seem "better" than they are, thus obscuring your equality with them still further. ⁵Projection and attack are inevitably related, because projection is always a means of justifying attack. ⁶Anger without projection is impossible. ⁷The ego uses projection only to destroy your perception of both yourself and your brothers. ⁸The process begins by excluding something that exists in you but which you do not want, and leads directly to excluding you from your brothers.

4.   We have learned, however, that there *is* an alternative to projection. ²Every ability of the ego has a better use, because its abili-

ties are directed by the mind, which has a better Voice. ³The Holy Spirit extends and the ego projects. ⁴As their goals are opposed, so is the result.

5. The Holy Spirit begins by perceiving you as perfect. ²Knowing this perfection is shared He recognizes it in others, thus strengthening it in both. ³Instead of anger this arouses love for both, because it establishes inclusion. ⁴Perceiving equality, the Holy Spirit perceives equal needs. ⁵This invites Atonement automatically, because Atonement is the one need in this world that is universal. ⁶To perceive yourself this way is the only way in which you can find happiness in the world. ⁷That is because it is the acknowledgment that you are not in this world, for the world *is* unhappy.

6. How else can you find joy in a joyless place except by realizing that you are not there? ²You cannot be anywhere God did not put you, and God created you as part of Him. ³That is both where you are and what you are. ⁴It is completely unalterable. ⁵It is total inclusion. ⁶You cannot change it now or ever. ⁷It is forever true. ⁸It is not a belief, but a Fact. ⁹Anything that God created is as true as He is. ¹⁰Its truth lies only in its perfect inclusion in Him Who alone is perfect. ¹¹To deny this is to deny yourself and Him, since it is impossible to accept one without the other.

7. The perfect equality of the Holy Spirit's perception is the reflection of the perfect equality of God's knowing. ²The ego's perception has no counterpart in God, but the Holy Spirit remains the Bridge between perception and knowledge. ³By enabling you to use perception in a way that reflects knowledge, you will ultimately remember it. ⁴The ego would prefer to believe that this memory is impossible, yet it is *your* perception the Holy Spirit guides. ⁵Your perception will end where it began. ⁶Everything meets in God, because everything was created by Him and in Him.

8. God created His Sons by extending His Thought, and retaining the extensions of His Thought in His Mind. ²All His Thoughts are thus perfectly united within themselves and with each other. ³The Holy Spirit enables you to perceive this wholeness *now.* ⁴God created you to create. ⁵You cannot extend His Kingdom until you know of its wholeness.

9. Thoughts begin in the mind of the thinker, from which they reach outward. ²This is as true of God's Thinking as it is of yours. ³Because your mind is split, you can perceive as well as think.

[4]Yet perception cannot escape the basic laws of mind. [5]You perceive from your mind and project your perceptions outward. [6]Although perception of any kind is unreal, you made it and the Holy Spirit can therefore use it well. [7]He can inspire perception and lead it toward God. [8]This convergence seems to be far in the future only because your mind is not in perfect alignment with the idea, and therefore does not want it now.

10.   The Holy Spirit uses time, but does not believe in it. [2]Coming from God He uses everything for good, but He does not believe in what is not true. [3]Since the Holy Spirit is in your mind, your mind can also believe only what is true. [4]The Holy Spirit can speak only for this, because He speaks for God. [5]He tells you to return your whole mind to God, because it has never left Him. [6]If it has never left Him, you need only perceive it as it is to be returned. [7]The full awareness of the Atonement, then, is the recognition that *the separation never occurred*. [8]The ego cannot prevail against this because it is an explicit statement that the ego never occurred.

11.   The ego can accept the idea that return is necessary because it can so easily make the idea seem difficult. [2]Yet the Holy Spirit tells you that even return is unnecessary, because what never happened cannot be difficult. [3]However, you can *make* the idea of return both necessary and difficult. [4]Yet it is surely clear that the perfect need nothing, and you cannot experience perfection as a difficult accomplishment, because that is what you are. [5]This is the way in which you must perceive God's creations, bringing all of your perceptions into the one line the Holy Spirit sees. [6]This line is the direct line of communication with God, and lets your mind converge with His. [7]There is no conflict anywhere in this perception, because it means that all perception is guided by the Holy Spirit, Whose Mind is fixed on God. [8]Only the Holy Spirit can resolve conflict, because only the Holy Spirit is conflict-free. [9]He perceives only what is true in your mind, and extends outward only to what is true in other minds.

12.   The difference between the ego's projection and the Holy Spirit's extension is very simple. [2]The ego projects to exclude, and therefore to deceive. [3]The Holy Spirit extends by recognizing Himself in every mind, and thus perceives them as one. [4]Nothing conflicts in this perception, because what the Holy Spirit perceives is all the same. [5]Wherever He looks He sees Himself, and because He is united He offers the whole Kingdom always. [6]This

is the one message God gave to Him and for which He must speak, because that is what He is. [7]The peace of God lies in that message, and so the peace of God lies in you. [8]The great peace of the Kingdom shines in your mind forever, but it must shine outward to make you aware of it.

13. The Holy Spirit was given you with perfect impartiality, and only by recognizing Him impartially can you recognize Him at all. [2]The ego is legion, but the Holy Spirit is one. [3]No darkness abides anywhere in the Kingdom, but your part is only to allow no darkness to abide in your own mind. [4]This alignment with light is unlimited, because it is in alignment with the light of the world. [5]Each of us is the light of the world, and by joining our minds in this light we proclaim the Kingdom of God together and as one.

III. The Relinquishment of Attack

1. As we have already emphasized, every idea begins in the mind of the thinker. [2]Therefore, what extends from the mind is still in it, and from *what* it extends it knows itself. [3]The word "knows" is correct here, because the Holy Spirit still holds knowledge safe in your mind through His impartial perception. [4]By attacking nothing, He presents no barrier to the communication of God. [5]Therefore, being is never threatened. [6]Your Godlike mind can never be defiled. [7]The ego never was and never will be part of it, but through the ego you can hear and teach and learn what is not true. [8]You have taught yourself to believe that you are not what you are. [9]You cannot teach what you have not learned, and what you teach you strengthen in yourself because you are sharing it. [10]Every lesson you teach you are learning.

2. That is why you must teach only one lesson. [2]If you are to be conflict-free yourself, you must learn only from the Holy Spirit and teach only by Him. [3]You are only love, but when you deny this, you make what you are something you must learn to remember. [4]I said before that the message of the crucifixion was, "Teach only love, for that is what you are." [5]This is the one lesson that is perfectly unified, because it is the only lesson that is one. [6]Only by teaching it can you learn it. [7]"As you teach so will you learn." [8]If that is true, and it is true indeed, do not forget that what you teach is teaching you. [9]And what you project

or extend you believe.

3.   The only safety lies in extending the Holy Spirit, because as you see His gentleness in others your own mind perceives itself as totally harmless. [2]Once it can accept this fully, it sees no need to protect itself. [3]The protection of God then dawns upon it, assuring it that it is perfectly safe forever. [4]The perfectly safe are wholly benign. [5]They bless because they know that they are blessed. [6]Without anxiety the mind is wholly kind, and because it extends beneficence it is beneficent. [7]Safety is the complete relinquishment of attack. [8]No compromise is possible in this. [9]Teach attack in any form and you have learned it, and it will hurt you. [10]Yet this learning is not immortal, and you can unlearn it by not teaching it.

4.   Since you cannot *not* teach, your salvation lies in teaching the exact opposite of everything the ego believes. [2]This is how you will learn the truth that will set you free, and will keep you free as others learn it of you. [3]The only way to have peace is to teach peace. [4]By teaching peace you must learn it yourself, because you cannot teach what you still dissociate. [5]Only thus can you win back the knowledge that you threw away. [6]An idea that you share you must have. [7]It awakens in your mind through the conviction of teaching it. [8]Everything you teach you are learning. [9]Teach only love, and learn that love is yours and you are love.

IV. The Only Answer

1.   Remember that the Holy Spirit is the Answer, not the question. [2]The ego always speaks first. [3]It is capricious and does not mean its maker well. [4]It believes, and correctly, that its maker may withdraw his support from it at any moment. [5]If it meant you well it would be glad, as the Holy Spirit will be glad when He has brought you home and you no longer need His guidance. [6]The ego does not regard itself as part of you. [7]Herein lies its primary error, the foundation of its whole thought system.

2.   When God created you He made you part of Him. [2]That is why attack within the Kingdom is impossible. [3]You made the ego without love, and so it does not love you. [4]You could not remain within the Kingdom without love, and since the Kingdom *is* love, you believe that you are without it. [5]This enables the ego to regard itself as separate and outside its maker, thus speaking for

the part of your mind that believes *you* are separate and outside the Mind of God. [6]The ego, then, raised the first question that was ever asked, but one it can never answer. [7]That question, "What are you?" was the beginning of doubt. [8]The ego has never answered any questions since, although it has raised a great many. [9]The most inventive activities of the ego have never done more than obscure the question, because you have the answer and *the ego is afraid of you.*

3. You cannot understand the conflict until you fully understand the basic fact that the ego cannot know anything. [2]The Holy Spirit does not speak first, *but He always answers*. [3]Everyone has called upon Him for help at one time or another and in one way or another, and has been answered. [4]Since the Holy Spirit answers truly He answers for all time, which means that everyone has the answer *now*.

4. The ego cannot hear the Holy Spirit, but it does believe that part of the mind that made it is against it. [2]It interprets this as a justification for attacking its maker. [3]It believes that the best defense is attack, and wants *you* to believe it. [4]Unless you do believe it you will not side with it, and the ego feels badly in need of allies, though not of brothers. [5]Perceiving something alien to itself in your mind, the ego turns to the body as its ally, because the body is *not* part of you. [6]This makes the body the ego's friend. [7]It is an alliance frankly based on separation. [8]If you side with this alliance you will be afraid, because you are siding with an alliance of fear.

5. The ego uses the body to conspire against your mind, and because the ego realizes that its "enemy" can end them both merely by recognizing they are not part of you, they join in the attack together. [2]This is perhaps the strangest perception of all, if you consider what it really involves. [3]The ego, which is not real, attempts to persuade the mind, which *is* real, that the mind is the ego's learning device; and further, that the body is more real than the mind is. [4]No one in his right mind could possibly believe this, and no one in his right mind does believe it.

6. Hear, then, the one answer of the Holy Spirit to all the questions the ego raises: You are a child of God, a priceless part of His Kingdom, which He created as part of Him. [2]Nothing else exists and only this is real. [3]You have chosen a sleep in which you have had bad dreams, but the sleep is not real and God calls you to awake. [4]There will be nothing left of your dream when you hear

Him, because you will awaken. ⁵Your dreams contain many of the ego's symbols and they have confused you. ⁶Yet that was only because you were asleep and did not know. ⁷When you wake you will see the truth around you and in you, and you will no longer believe in dreams because they will have no reality for you. ⁸Yet the Kingdom and all that you have created there will have great reality for you, because they are beautiful and true.

7. In the Kingdom, where you are and what you are is perfectly certain. ²There is no doubt, because the first question was never asked. ³Having finally been wholly answered, *it has never been.* ⁴*Being* alone lives in the Kingdom, where everything lives in God without question. ⁵The time spent on questioning in the dream has given way to creation and to its eternity. ⁶You are as certain as God because you are as true as He is, but what was once certain in your mind has become only the ability for certainty.

8. The introduction of abilities into being was the beginning of uncertainty, because abilities are potentials, not accomplishments. ²Your abilities are useless in the presence of God's accomplishments, and also of yours. ³Accomplishments are results that have been achieved. ⁴When they are perfect, abilities are meaningless. ⁵It is curious that the perfect must now be perfected. ⁶In fact, it is impossible. ⁷Remember, however, that when you put yourself in an impossible situation you believe that the impossible *is* possible.

9. Abilities must be developed before you can use them. ²This is not true of anything that God created, but it is the kindest solution possible for what you made. ³In an impossible situation, you can develop your abilities to the point where they can get you out of it. ⁴You have a Guide to how to develop them, but you have no commander except yourself. ⁵This leaves you in charge of the Kingdom, with both a Guide to find it and a means to keep it. ⁶You have a model to follow who will strengthen your command, and never detract from it in any way. ⁷You therefore retain the central place in your imagined enslavement, which in itself demonstrates that you are not enslaved.

10. You are in an impossible situation only because you think it is possible to be in one. ²You *would* be in an impossible situation if God showed you your perfection, and proved to you that you were wrong. ³This would demonstrate that the perfect are inadequate to bring themselves to the awareness of their perfection, and thus side with the belief that those who have everything

need help and are therefore helpless. ⁴This is the kind of "reasoning" in which the ego engages. ⁵God, Who knows that His creations are perfect, does not affront them. ⁶This would be as impossible as the ego's notion that it has affronted Him.

11. That is why the Holy Spirit never commands. ²To command is to assume inequality, which the Holy Spirit demonstrates does not exist. ³Fidelity to premises is a law of mind, and everything God created is faithful to His laws. ⁴Fidelity to other laws is also possible, however, not because the laws are true, but because you made them. ⁵What would be gained if God proved to you that you have thought insanely? ⁶Can God lose His Own certainty? ⁷I have frequently said that what you teach you are. ⁸Would you have God teach you that you have sinned? ⁹If He confronted the self you made with the truth He created for you, what could you be but afraid? ¹⁰You would doubt your right mind, which is the only place where you can find the sanity He gave you.

12. God does not teach. ²To teach is to imply a lack, which God knows is not there. ³God is not conflicted. ⁴Teaching aims at change, but God created only the changeless. ⁵The separation was not a loss of perfection, but a failure in communication. ⁶A harsh and strident form of communication arose as the ego's voice. ⁷It could not shatter the peace of God, but it could shatter *yours*. ⁸God did not blot it out, because to eradicate it would be to attack it. ⁹Being questioned, He did not question. ¹⁰He merely gave the Answer. ¹¹His Answer is your Teacher.

V. The Lessons of the Holy Spirit

1. Like any good teacher, the Holy Spirit knows more than you do now, but He teaches only to make you equal with Him. ²You had already taught yourself wrongly, having believed what was not true. ³You did not believe in your own perfection. ⁴Would God teach you that you had made a split mind, when He knows your mind only as whole? ⁵What God does know is that His communication channels are not open to Him, so that He cannot impart His joy and know that His children are wholly joyous. ⁶Giving His joy is an ongoing process, not in time but in eternity. ⁷God's extending outward, though not His completeness, is blocked when the Sonship does not communicate with Him as one. ⁸So He thought, "My children sleep and must be awakened."

2. How can you wake children in a more kindly way than by a gentle Voice that will not frighten them, but will merely remind them that the night is over and the light has come? [2]You do not inform them that the nightmares that frightened them so badly are not real, because children believe in magic. [3]You merely reassure them that they are safe *now*. [4]Then you train them to recognize the difference between sleeping and waking, so they will understand they need not be afraid of dreams. [5]And so when bad dreams come, they will themselves call on the light to dispel them.

3. A wise teacher teaches through approach, not avoidance. [2]He does not emphasize what you must avoid to escape from harm, but what you need to learn to have joy. [3]Consider the fear and confusion a child would experience if he were told, "Do not do this because it will hurt you and make you unsafe; but if you do that instead, you will escape from harm and be safe, and then you will not be afraid." [4]It is surely better to use only three words: "Do only that!" [5]This simple statement is perfectly clear, easily understood and very easily remembered.

4. The Holy Spirit never itemizes errors because He does not frighten children, and those who lack wisdom *are* children. [2]Yet He always answers their call, and His dependability makes them more certain. [3]Children *do* confuse fantasy and reality, and they are frightened because they do not recognize the difference. [4]The Holy Spirit makes no distinction among dreams. [5]He merely shines them away. [6]His light is always the Call to awaken, whatever you have been dreaming. [7]Nothing lasting lies in dreams, and the Holy Spirit, shining with the light from God Himself, speaks only for what lasts forever.

A. To Have, Give All to All

1. When your body and your ego and your dreams are gone, you will know that you will last forever. [2]Perhaps you think this is accomplished through death, but nothing is accomplished through death, because death is nothing. [3]Everything is accomplished through life, and life is of the mind and in the mind. [4]The body neither lives nor dies, because it cannot contain you who are life. [5]If we share the same mind, you can overcome death because I did. [6]Death is an attempt to resolve conflict by not deciding at all. [7]Like any other impossible solution the ego

attempts, *it will not work.*

2. God did not make the body, because it is destructible, and therefore not of the Kingdom. ²The body is the symbol of what you think you are. ³It is clearly a separation device, and therefore does not exist. ⁴The Holy Spirit, as always, takes what you have made and translates it into a learning device. ⁵Again as always, He reinterprets what the ego uses as an argument for separation into a demonstration against it. ⁶If the mind can heal the body, but the body cannot heal the mind, then the mind must be stronger than the body. ⁷Every miracle demonstrates this.

3. I have said that the Holy Spirit is the motivation for miracles. ²He always tells you that only the mind is real, because only the mind can be shared. ³The body is separate, and therefore cannot be part of you. ⁴To be of one mind is meaningful, but to be one body is meaningless. ⁵By the laws of mind, then, the body is meaningless.

4. To the Holy Spirit, there is no order of difficulty in miracles. ²This is familiar enough to you by now, but it has not yet become believable. ³Therefore, you do not understand it and cannot use it. ⁴We have too much to accomplish on behalf of the Kingdom to let this crucial concept slip away. ⁵It is a real foundation stone of the thought system I teach and want you to teach. ⁶You cannot perform miracles without believing it, because it is a belief in perfect equality. ⁷Only one equal gift can be offered to the equal Sons of God, and that is full appreciation. ⁸Nothing more and nothing less. ⁹Without a range, order of difficulty is meaningless, and there must be no range in what you offer to your brother.

5. The Holy Spirit, Who leads to God, translates communication into being, just as He ultimately translates perception into knowledge. ²You do not lose what you communicate. ³The ego uses the body for attack, for pleasure and for pride. ⁴The insanity of this perception makes it a fearful one indeed. ⁵The Holy Spirit sees the body only as a means of communication, and because communicating is sharing it becomes communion. ⁶Perhaps you think that fear as well as love can be communicated; and therefore can be shared. ⁷Yet this is not so real as it may appear. ⁸Those who communicate fear are promoting attack, and attack always breaks communication, making it impossible. ⁹Egos do join together in temporary allegiance, but always for what each one can get *separately.* ¹⁰The Holy Spirit communicates only what each one can give to all. ¹¹He never takes anything back, because He

wants you to keep it. [12]Therefore, His teaching begins with the lesson:

[13]*To have, give all to all.*

6.   This is a very preliminary step, and the only one you must take for yourself. [2]It is not even necessary that you complete the step yourself, but it is necessary that you turn in that direction. [3]Having chosen to go that way, you place yourself in charge of the journey, where you and only you must remain. [4]This step may appear to exacerbate conflict rather than resolve it, because it is the beginning step in reversing your perception and turning it right-side up. [5]This conflicts with the upside-down perception you have not yet abandoned, or the change in direction would not have been necessary. [6]Some remain at this step for a long time, experiencing very acute conflict. [7]At this point they may try to accept the conflict, rather than take the next step towards its resolution. [8]Having taken the first step, however, they will be helped. [9]Once they have chosen what they cannot complete alone, they are no longer alone.

B. To Have Peace, Teach Peace to Learn It

1.   All who believe in separation have a basic fear of retaliation and abandonment. [2]They believe in attack and rejection, so that is what they perceive and teach and learn. [3]These insane ideas are clearly the result of dissociation and projection. [4]What you teach you are, but it is quite apparent that you can teach wrongly, and can therefore teach yourself wrong. [5]Many thought I was attacking them, even though it was apparent I was not. [6]An insane learner learns strange lessons. [7]What you must recognize is that when you do not share a thought system, you are weakening it. [8]Those who believe in it therefore perceive this as an attack on them. [9]This is because everyone identifies himself with his thought system, and every thought system centers on what you believe you are. [10]If the center of the thought system is true, only truth extends from it. [11]But if a lie is at its center, only deception proceeds from it.

2.   All good teachers realize that only fundamental change will last, but they do not begin at that level. [2]Strengthening motivation for change is their first and foremost goal. [3]It is also their last

and final one. ⁴Increasing motivation for change in the learner is all that a teacher need do to guarantee change. ⁵Change in motivation is a change of mind, and this will inevitably produce fundamental change because the mind *is* fundamental.

3.   The first step in the reversal or undoing process is the undoing of the getting concept. ²Accordingly, the Holy Spirit's first lesson was "To have, give all to all." ³I said that this is apt to increase conflict temporarily, and we can clarify this still further now. ⁴At this point, the equality of *having* and *being* is not yet perceived. ⁵Until it is, *having* appears to be the opposite of *giving*. ⁶Therefore, the first lesson seems to contain a contradiction, since it is being learned by a conflicted mind. ⁷This means conflicting motivation, and so the lesson cannot be learned consistently as yet. ⁸Further, the mind of the learner projects its own conflict, and thus does not perceive consistency in the minds of others, making him suspicious of their motivation. ⁹This is the real reason why, in many respects, the first lesson is the hardest to learn. ¹⁰Still strongly aware of the ego in yourself, and responding primarily to the ego in others, you are being taught to react to both as if what you do believe is not true.

4.   Upside down as always, the ego perceives the first lesson as insane. ²In fact, this is its only alternative since the other possibility, which would be much less acceptable to it, would obviously be that *it* is insane. ³The ego's judgment, here as always, is predetermined by what it is. ⁴The fundamental change will still occur with the change of mind in the thinker. ⁵Meanwhile, the increasing clarity of the Holy Spirit's Voice makes it impossible for the learner not to listen. ⁶For a time, then, he is receiving conflicting messages and accepting both.

5.   The way out of conflict between two opposing thought systems is clearly to choose one and relinquish the other. ²If you identify with your thought system, and you cannot escape this, and if you accept two thought systems which are in complete disagreement, peace of mind is impossible. ³If you teach both, which you will surely do as long as you accept both, you are teaching conflict and learning it. ⁴Yet you do want peace, or you would not have called upon the Voice for peace to help you. ⁵Its lesson is not insane; the conflict is.

6.   There can be no conflict between sanity and insanity. ²Only one is true, and therefore only one is real. ³The ego tries to persuade you that it is up to you to decide which voice is true, but

107

the Holy Spirit teaches you that truth was created by God, and your decision cannot change it. ⁴As you begin to realize the quiet power of the Holy Spirit's Voice, and Its perfect consistency, it must dawn on your mind that you are trying to undo a decision that was irrevocably made for you. ⁵That is why I suggested before that you remind yourself to allow the Holy Spirit to decide for God for you.

7. You are not asked to make insane decisions, although you can think you are. ²It must, however, be insane to believe that it is up to you to decide what God's creations are. ³The Holy Spirit perceives the conflict exactly as it is. ⁴Therefore, His second lesson is:

> ⁵*To have peace, teach peace to learn it.*

8. This is still a preliminary step, since *having* and *being* are still not equated. ²It is, however, more advanced than the first step, which is really only the beginning of the thought reversal. ³The second step is a positive affirmation of what you want. ⁴This, then, is a step in the direction out of conflict, since it means that alternatives have been considered, and one has been chosen as more desirable. ⁵Nevertheless, the term "more desirable" still implies that the desirable has degrees. ⁶Therefore, although this step is essential for the ultimate decision, it is clearly not the final one. ⁷Lack of order of difficulty in miracles has not yet been accepted, because nothing is difficult that is *wholly* desired. ⁸To desire wholly is to create, and creating cannot be difficult if God Himself created you as a creator.

9. The second step, then, is still perceptual, although it is a giant step toward the unified perception that reflects God's knowing. ²As you take this step and hold this direction, you will be pushing toward the center of your thought system, where the fundamental change will occur. ³At the second step progress is intermittent, but the second step is easier than the first because it follows. ⁴Realizing that it *must* follow is a demonstration of a growing awareness that the Holy Spirit will lead you on.

C. Be Vigilant Only for God and His Kingdom

1. We said before that the Holy Spirit is evaluative, and must be. ²He sorts out the true from the false in your mind, and teaches you to judge every thought you allow to enter it in the light of

what God put there. ³Whatever is in accord with this light He retains, to strengthen the Kingdom in you. ⁴What is partly in accord with it He accepts and purifies. ⁵But what is out of accord entirely He rejects by judging against. ⁶This is how He keeps the Kingdom perfectly consistent and perfectly unified. ⁷Remember, however, that what the Holy Spirit rejects the ego accepts. ⁸This is because they are in fundamental disagreement about everything, being in fundamental disagreement about what you are. ⁹The ego's beliefs on this crucial issue vary, and that is why it promotes different moods. ¹⁰The Holy Spirit never varies on this point, and so the one mood He engenders is joy. ¹¹He protects it by rejecting everything that does not foster joy, and so He alone can keep you wholly joyous.

2. The Holy Spirit does not teach you to judge others, because He does not want you to teach error and learn it yourself. ²He would hardly be consistent if He allowed you to strengthen what you must learn to avoid. ³In the mind of the thinker, then, He *is* judgmental, but only in order to unify the mind so it can perceive without judgment. ⁴This enables the mind to teach without judgment, and therefore to learn to *be* without judgment. ⁵The undoing is necessary only in your mind, so that you will not project, instead of extend. ⁶God Himself has established what you can extend with perfect safety. ⁷Therefore, the Holy Spirit's third lesson is:

⁸*Be vigilant only for God and His Kingdom.*

3. This is a major step toward fundamental change. ²Yet it still has an aspect of thought reversal, since it implies that there is something you must be vigilant *against*. ³It has advanced far from the first lesson, which is merely the beginning of the thought reversal, and also from the second, which is essentially the identification of what is more desirable. ⁴This step, which follows from the second as the second follows from the first, emphasizes the dichotomy between the desirable and the undesirable. ⁵It therefore makes the ultimate choice inevitable.

4. While the first step seems to increase conflict and the second may still entail conflict to some extent, this step calls for consistent vigilance against it. ²I have already told you that you can be as vigilant against the ego as for it. ³This lesson teaches not only that you can be, but that you *must* be. ⁴It does not concern itself

with order of difficulty, but with clear-cut priority for vigilance. [5]This lesson is unequivocal in that it teaches there must be no exceptions, although it does not deny that the temptation to make exceptions will occur. [6]Here, then, your consistency is called on despite chaos. [7]Yet chaos and consistency cannot coexist for long, since they are mutually exclusive. [8]As long as you must be vigilant against anything, however, you are not recognizing this mutual exclusiveness, and still believe that you can choose either one. [9]By teaching *what* to choose, the Holy Spirit will ultimately teach you that you need not choose at all. [10]This will finally liberate your mind from choice, and direct it towards creation within the Kingdom.

5.   Choosing through the Holy Spirit will lead you to the Kingdom. [2]You create by your true being, but what you are you must learn to remember. [3]The way to remember it is inherent in the third step, which brings together the lessons implied in the others, and goes beyond them towards real integration. [4]If you allow yourself to have in your mind only what God put there, you are acknowledging your mind as God created it. [5]Therefore, you are accepting it as it is. [6]Since it is whole, you are teaching peace *because* you believe in it. [7]The final step will still be taken for you by God, but by the third step the Holy Spirit has prepared you for God. [8]He is getting you ready for the translation of *having* into *being* by the very nature of the steps you must take with Him.

6.   You learn first that *having* rests on giving, and not on getting. [2]Next you learn that you learn what you teach, and that you want to learn peace. [3]This is the condition for identifying with the Kingdom, since it is the condition *of* the Kingdom. [4]You have believed that you are without the Kingdom, and have therefore excluded yourself from it in your belief. [5]It is therefore essential to teach you that you must be included, and that the belief that you are not is the only thing that you must exclude.

7.   The third step is thus one of protection for your mind, allowing you to identify only with the center, where God placed the altar to Himself. [2]Altars are beliefs, but God and His creations are beyond belief because they are beyond question. [3]The Voice for God speaks only for belief beyond question, which is the preparation for *being* without question. [4]As long as belief in God and His Kingdom is assailed by any doubts in your mind, His perfect accomplishment is not apparent to you. [5]This is why you must be

vigilant on God's behalf. 6The ego speaks against His creation, and therefore engenders doubt. 7You cannot go beyond belief until you believe fully.

8. To teach the whole Sonship without exception demonstrates that you perceive its wholeness, and have learned that it is one. 2Now you must be vigilant to hold its oneness in your mind because, if you let doubt enter, you will lose awareness of its wholeness and will be unable to teach it. 3The wholeness of the Kingdom does not depend on your perception, but your awareness of its wholeness does. 4It is only your awareness that needs protection, since being cannot be assailed. 5Yet a real sense of being cannot be yours while you are doubtful of what you are. 6This is why vigilance is essential. 7Doubts about being must not enter your mind, or you cannot know what you are with certainty. 8Certainty is of God for you. 9Vigilance is not necessary for truth, but it is necessary against illusions.

9. Truth is without illusions and therefore within the Kingdom. 2Everything outside the Kingdom is illusion. 3When you threw truth away you saw yourself as if you were without it. 4By making another kingdom that you valued, you did not keep *only* the Kingdom of God in your mind, and thus placed part of your mind outside it. 5What you made has imprisoned your will, and given you a sick mind that must be healed. 6Your vigilance against this sickness is the way to heal it. 7Once your mind is healed it radiates health, and thereby teaches healing. 8This establishes you as a teacher who teaches like me. 9Vigilance was required of me as much as of you, and those who choose to teach the same thing must be in agreement about what they believe.

10. The third step, then, is a statement of what you want to believe, and entails a willingness to relinquish everything else. 2The Holy Spirit will enable you to take this step, if you follow Him. 3Your vigilance is the sign that you *want* Him to guide you. 4Vigilance does require effort, but only until you learn that effort itself is unnecessary. 5You have exerted great effort to preserve what you made because it was not true. 6Therefore, you must now turn your effort against it. 7Only this can cancel out the need for effort, and call upon the being which you both *have* and *are*. 8This recognition is wholly without effort since it is already true and needs no protection. 9It is in the perfect safety of God. 10Therefore, inclusion is total and creation is without limit.

Chapter 7

THE GIFTS OF THE KINGDOM

I. The Last Step

1. The creative power of God and His creations is limitless, but they are not in reciprocal relationship. ²You communicate fully with God, as He does with you. ³This is an ongoing process in which you share, and because you share it, you are inspired to create like God. ⁴Yet in creation you are not in a reciprocal relation to God, since He created you but you did not create Him. ⁵I have already told you that only in this respect your creative power differs from His. ⁶Even in this world there is a parallel. ⁷Parents give birth to children, but children do not give birth to parents. ⁸They do, however, give birth to their children, and thus give birth as their parents do.

2. If you created God and He created you, the Kingdom could not increase through its own creative thought. ²Creation would therefore be limited, and you would not be co-creator with God. ³As God's creative Thought proceeds from Him to you, so must your creative thought proceed from you to your creations. ⁴Only in this way can all creative power extend outward. ⁵God's accomplishments are not yours, but yours are like His. ⁶He created the Sonship and you increase it. ⁷You have the power to add to the Kingdom, though not to add to the Creator of the Kingdom. ⁸You claim this power when you become vigilant only for God and His Kingdom. ⁹By accepting this power as yours you have learned to remember what you are.

3. Your creations belong in you, as you belong in God. ²You are part of God, as your sons are part of His Sons. ³To create is to love. ⁴Love extends outward simply because it cannot be contained. ⁵Being limitless it does not stop. ⁶It creates forever, but not in time. ⁷God's creations have always been, because He has always been. ⁸Your creations have always been, because you can create only as God creates. ⁹Eternity is yours, because He created you eternal.

4. The ego, on the other hand, always demands reciprocal rights, because it is competitive rather than loving. ²It is always willing to strike a bargain, but it cannot understand that to be like

another means that no bargains are possible. ³To gain you must give, not bargain. ⁴To bargain is to limit giving, and this is not God's Will. ⁵To will with God is to create like Him. ⁶God does not limit His gifts in any way. ⁷You *are* His gifts, and so your gifts must be like His. ⁸Your gifts to the Kingdom must be like His gifts to you.

5.   I gave only love to the Kingdom because I believed that was what I was. ²What you believe you are determines your gifts, and if God created you by extending Himself as you, you can only extend yourself as He did. ³Only joy increases forever, since joy and eternity are inseparable. ⁴God extends outward beyond limits and beyond time, and you who are co-creator with Him extend His Kingdom forever and beyond limit. ⁵Eternity is the indelible stamp of creation. ⁶The eternal are in peace and joy forever.

6.   To think like God is to share His certainty of what you are, and to create like Him is to share the perfect Love He shares with you. ²To this the Holy Spirit leads you, that your joy may be complete because the Kingdom of God is whole. ³I have said that the last step in the reawakening of knowledge is taken by God. ⁴This is true, but it is hard to explain in words because words are symbols, and nothing that is true need be explained. ⁵However, the Holy Spirit has the task of translating the useless into the useful, the meaningless into the meaningful, and the temporary into the timeless. ⁶He can therefore tell you something about this last step.

7.   God does not take steps, because His accomplishments are not gradual. ²He does not teach, because His creations are changeless. ³He does nothing last, because He created first and for always. ⁴It must be understood that the word "first" as applied to Him is not a time concept. ⁵He is first in the sense that He is the First in the Holy Trinity Itself. ⁶He is the Prime Creator, because He created His co-creators. ⁷Because He did, time applies neither to Him nor to what He created. ⁸The "last step" that God will take was therefore true in the beginning, is true now, and will be true forever. ⁹What is timeless is always there, because its being is eternally changeless. ¹⁰It does not change by increase, because it was forever created to increase. ¹¹If you perceive it as not increasing you do not know what it is. ¹²You also do not know Who created it. ¹³God does not reveal this to you because it was never hidden. ¹⁴His light was never obscured, because it is His Will to

share it. [15]How can what is fully shared be withheld and then revealed?

II. The Law of the Kingdom

1. To heal is the only kind of thinking in this world that resembles the Thought of God, and because of the elements they share, can transfer easily to it. [2]When a brother perceives himself as sick, he is perceiving himself as not whole, and therefore in need. [3]If you, too, see him this way, you are seeing him as if he were absent from the Kingdom or separated from it, thus making the Kingdom itself obscure to both of you. [4]Sickness and separation are not of God, but the Kingdom is. [5]If you obscure the Kingdom, you are perceiving what is not of God.

2. To heal, then, is to correct perception in your brother and yourself by sharing the Holy Spirit with him. [2]This places you both within the Kingdom, and restores its wholeness in your mind. [3]This reflects creation, because it unifies by increasing and integrates by extending. [4]What you project or extend is real for you. [5]This is an immutable law of the mind in this world as well as in the Kingdom. [6]However, the content is different in this world, because the thoughts it governs are very different from the Thoughts in the Kingdom. [7]Laws must be adapted to circumstances if they are to maintain order. [8]The outstanding characteristic of the laws of mind as they operate in this world is that by obeying them, and I assure you that you must obey them, you can arrive at diametrically opposed results. [9]This is because the laws have been adapted to the circumstances of this world, in which diametrically opposed outcomes seem possible because you can respond to two conflicting voices.

3. Outside the Kingdom, the law that prevails inside is adapted to "What you project you believe." [2]This is its teaching form, because outside the Kingdom learning is essential. [3]This form implies that you will learn what you are from what you have projected onto others, and therefore believe they are. [4]In the Kingdom there is no teaching or learning, because there is no belief. [5]There is only certainty. [6]God and His Sons, in the surety of being, know that what you extend you are. [7]That form of the law is not adapted at all, being the law of creation. [8]God Himself created the law by creating *by* it. [9]And His Sons, who create like

Him, follow it gladly, knowing that the increase of the Kingdom depends on it, just as their own creation did.

4. Laws must be communicated if they are to be helpful. [2]In effect, they must be translated for those who speak different languages. [3]Nevertheless, a good translator, although he must alter the form of what he translates, never changes the meaning. [4]In fact, his whole purpose is to change the form so that the original meaning is retained. [5]The Holy Spirit is the Translator of the laws of God to those who do not understand them. [6]You could not do this yourself because a conflicted mind cannot be faithful to one meaning, and will therefore change the meaning to preserve the form.

5. The Holy Spirit's purpose in translating is exactly the opposite. [2]He translates only to preserve the original meaning in all respects and in all languages. [3]Therefore, He opposes the idea that differences in form are meaningful, emphasizing always that *these differences do not matter*. [4]The meaning of His message is always the same; only the meaning matters. [5]God's law of creation does not involve the use of truth to convince His Sons of truth. [6]The extension of truth, which *is* the law of the Kingdom, rests only on the knowledge of what truth is. [7]This is your inheritance and requires no learning at all, but when you disinherited yourself you became a learner of necessity.

6. No one questions the connection of learning and memory. [2]Learning is impossible without memory since it must be consistent to be remembered. [3]That is why the Holy Spirit's teaching is a lesson in remembering. [4]I said before that He teaches remembering and forgetting, but the forgetting is only to make the remembering consistent. [5]You forget in order to remember better. [6]You will not understand His translations while you listen to two ways of interpreting them. [7]Therefore you must forget or relinquish one to understand the other. [8]This is the only way you can learn consistency, so that you can finally *be* consistent.

7. What can the perfect consistency of the Kingdom mean to those who are confused? [2]It is apparent that confusion interferes with meaning, and therefore prevents the learner from appreciating it. [3]There is no confusion in the Kingdom, because there is only one meaning. [4]This meaning comes from God and *is* God. [5]Because it is also you, you share it and extend it as your Creator did. [6]This needs no translation because it is perfectly understood, but it does need extension because it *means* extension. [7]Communication is

perfectly direct and perfectly united. ⁸It is totally free, because nothing discordant ever enters. ⁹That is why it is the Kingdom of God. ¹⁰It belongs to Him and is therefore like Him. ¹¹That is its reality, and nothing can assail it.

III. The Reality of the Kingdom

1. The Holy Spirit teaches one lesson, and applies it to all individuals in all situations. ²Being conflict-free, He maximizes all efforts and all results. ³By teaching the power of the Kingdom of God Himself, He teaches you that all power is yours. ⁴Its application does not matter. ⁵It is always maximal. ⁶Your vigilance does not establish it as yours, but it does enable you to use it always and in all ways. ⁷When I said "I am with you always," I meant it literally. ⁸I am not absent to anyone in any situation. ⁹Because I am always with you, *you* are the way, the truth and the life. ¹⁰You did not make this power, any more than I did. ¹¹It was created to be shared, and therefore cannot be meaningfully perceived as belonging to anyone at the expense of another. ¹²Such a perception makes it meaningless by eliminating or overlooking its real and only meaning.

2. God's meaning waits in the Kingdom, because that is where He placed it. ²It does not wait in time. ³It merely rests in the Kingdom because it belongs there, as you do. ⁴How can you who are God's meaning perceive yourself as absent from it? ⁵You can see yourself as separated from your meaning only by experiencing yourself as unreal. ⁶This is why the ego is insane; it teaches that you are not what you are. ⁷That is so contradictory it is clearly impossible. ⁸It is therefore a lesson you cannot really learn, and therefore cannot really teach. ⁹Yet you are always teaching. ¹⁰You must, therefore, be teaching something else, even though the ego does not know what it is. ¹¹The ego, then, is always being undone, and does suspect your motives. ¹²Your mind cannot be unified in allegiance to the ego, because the mind does not belong to it. ¹³Yet what is "treacherous" to the ego is faithful to peace. ¹⁴The ego's "enemy" is therefore your friend.

3. I said before that the ego's friend is not part of you, because the ego perceives itself at war and therefore in need of allies. ²You who are not at war must look for brothers and recognize all whom you see as brothers, because only equals are at peace. ³Because

God's equal Sons have everything, they cannot compete. ⁴Yet if they perceive any of their brothers as anything other than their perfect equals, the idea of competition has entered their minds. ⁵Do not underestimate your need to be vigilant *against* this idea, because all your conflicts come from it. ⁶It *is* the belief that conflicting interests are possible, and therefore you have accepted the impossible as true. ⁷Is that different from saying you perceive yourself as unreal?

4. To be in the Kingdom is merely to focus your full attention on it. ²As long as you believe you can attend to what is not true, you are accepting conflict as your choice. ³Is it really a choice? ⁴It seems to be, but seeming and reality are hardly the same. ⁵You who *are* the Kingdom are not concerned with seeming. ⁶Reality is yours because you are reality. ⁷This is how *having* and *being* are ultimately reconciled, not in the Kingdom, but in your mind. ⁸The altar there is the only reality. ⁹The altar is perfectly clear in thought, because it is a reflection of perfect Thought. ¹⁰Your right mind sees only brothers, because it sees only in its own light.

5. God has lit your mind Himself, and keeps your mind lit by His light because His light is what your mind is. ²This is totally beyond question, and when you question it you are answered. ³The Answer merely undoes the question by establishing the fact that to question reality is to question meaninglessly. ⁴That is why the Holy Spirit never questions. ⁵His sole function is to undo the questionable and thus lead to certainty. ⁶The certain are perfectly calm, because they are not in doubt. ⁷They do not raise questions, because nothing questionable enters their minds. ⁸This holds them in perfect serenity, because this is what they share, knowing what they are.

IV. Healing as the Recognition of Truth

1. Truth can only *be* recognized and *need* only be recognized. ²Inspiration is of the Holy Spirit, and certainty is of God according to His laws. ³Both, therefore, come from the same Source, since inspiration comes from the Voice for God and certainty comes from the laws of God. ⁴Healing does not come directly from God, Who knows His creations as perfectly whole. ⁵Yet healing is still of God, because it proceeds from His Voice and from His laws. ⁶It is their result, in a state of mind that does not know Him. ⁷The

state is unknown to Him and therefore does not exist, but those who sleep are unaware. [8]Because they are unaware, they do not know.

2.   The Holy Spirit must work *through* you to teach you He is *in* you. [2]This is an intermediary step toward the knowledge that you are in God because you are part of Him. [3]The miracles the Holy Spirit inspires can have no order of difficulty, because every part of creation is of one order. [4]This is God's Will and yours. [5]The laws of God establish this, and the Holy Spirit reminds you of it. [6]When you heal, you are remembering the laws of God and forgetting the laws of the ego. [7]I said before that forgetting is merely a way of remembering better. [8]It is therefore not the opposite of remembering when it is properly perceived. [9]Perceived improperly, it induces a perception of conflict with something else, as all incorrect perception does. [10]Properly perceived, it can be used as a way out of conflict, as all proper perception can.

3.   The ego does not want to teach everyone all it has learned, because that would defeat its purpose. [2]Therefore it does not really learn at all. [3]The Holy Spirit teaches you to use what the ego has made, to teach the opposite of what the ego has "learned." [4]The kind of learning is as irrelevant as is the particular ability that was applied to the learning. [5]All you need do is make the effort to learn, for the Holy Spirit has a unified goal for the effort. [6]If different abilities are applied long enough to one goal, the abilities themselves become unified. [7]This is because they are channelized in one direction, or in one way. [8]Ultimately, then, they all contribute to one result, and by so doing, their similarity rather than their differences is emphasized.

4.   All abilities should therefore be given over to the Holy Spirit, Who understands how to use them properly. [2]He uses them only for healing, because He knows you only as whole. [3]By healing you learn of wholeness, and by learning of wholeness you learn to remember God. [4]You have forgotten Him, but the Holy Spirit understands that your forgetting must be translated into a way of remembering.

5.   The ego's goal is as unified as the Holy Spirit's, and it is because of this that their goals can never be reconciled in any way or to any extent. [2]The ego always seeks to divide and separate. [3]The Holy Spirit always seeks to unify and heal. [4]As you heal you are healed, because the Holy Spirit sees no order of difficulty in healing. [5]Healing is the way to undo the belief in differences,

118

being the only way of perceiving the Sonship as one. ⁶This perception is therefore in accord with the laws of God, even in a state of mind that is out of accord with His. ⁷The strength of right perception is so great that it brings the mind into accord with His, because it serves His Voice, which is in all of you.

6. To think you can oppose the Will of God is a real delusion. ²The ego believes that it can, and that it can offer you its own "will" as a gift. ³*You do not want it.* ⁴It is not a gift. ⁵It is nothing at all. ⁶God has given you a gift that you both *have* and *are*. ⁷When you do not use it, you forget that you have it. ⁸By not remembering it, you do not know what you are. ⁹Healing, then, is a way of approaching knowledge by thinking in accordance with the laws of God, and recognizing their universality. ¹⁰Without this recognition, you have made the laws meaningless to you. ¹¹Yet the laws are not meaningless, since all meaning is contained by them and in them.

7. Seek ye first the Kingdom of Heaven, because that is where the laws of God operate truly, and they can operate only truly because they are the laws of truth. ²But seek this only, because you can find nothing else. ³There *is* nothing else. ⁴God is All in all in a very literal sense. ⁵All being is in Him Who is all Being. ⁶You are therefore in Him since your being is His. ⁷Healing is a way of forgetting the sense of danger the ego has induced in you, by not recognizing its existence in your brother. ⁸This strengthens the Holy Spirit in both of you, because it is a refusal to acknowledge fear. ⁹Love needs only this invitation. ¹⁰It comes freely to all the Sonship, being what the Sonship is. ¹¹By your awakening to it, you are merely forgetting what you are not. ¹²This enables you to remember what you are.

V. Healing and the Changelessness of Mind

1. The body is nothing more than a framework for developing abilities, which is quite apart from what they are used for. ²*That* is a decision. ³The effects of the ego's decision in this matter are so apparent that they need no elaboration, but the Holy Spirit's decision to use the body only for communication has such a direct connection with healing that it does need clarification. ⁴The unhealed healer obviously does not understand his own vocation.

2.   Only minds communicate. [2]Since the ego cannot obliterate the impulse to communicate because it is also the impulse to create, it can only teach you that the body can both communicate and create, and therefore does not need the mind. [3]The ego thus tries to teach you that the body can act like the mind, and is therefore self-sufficient. [4]Yet we have learned that behavior is not the level for either teaching or learning, since you can act in accordance with what you do not believe. [5]To do this, however, will weaken you as a teacher and a learner because, as has been repeatedly emphasized, you teach what you *do* believe. [6]An inconsistent lesson will be poorly taught and poorly learned. [7]If you teach both sickness *and* healing, you are both a poor teacher and a poor learner.

3.   Healing is the one ability everyone can develop and must develop if he is to be healed. [2]Healing is the Holy Spirit's form of communication in this world, and the only one He accepts. [3]He recognizes no other, because He does not accept the ego's confusion of mind and body. [4]Minds can communicate, but they cannot hurt. [5]The body in the service of the ego can hurt other bodies, but this cannot occur unless the body has already been confused with the mind. [6]This situation, too, can be used either for healing or for magic, but you must remember that magic always involves the belief that healing is harmful. [7]This belief is its totally insane premise, and so it proceeds accordingly.

4.   Healing only strengthens. [2]Magic always tries to weaken. [3]Healing perceives nothing in the healer that everyone else does not share with him. [4]Magic always sees something "special" in the healer, which he believes he can offer as a gift to someone who does not have it. [5]He may believe that the gift comes from God to him, but it is quite evident that he does not understand God if he thinks he has something that others lack.

5.   The Holy Spirit does not work by chance, and healing that is of Him *always* works. [2]Unless the healer always heals by Him the results will vary. [3]Yet healing itself is consistent, since only consistency is conflict-free, and only the conflict-free are whole. [4]By accepting exceptions and acknowledging that he can sometimes heal and sometimes not, the healer is obviously accepting inconsistency. [5]He is therefore in conflict, and is teaching conflict. [6]Can anything of God not be for all and for always? [7]Love is incapable of any exceptions. [8]Only if there is fear does the idea of exceptions seem to be meaningful. [9]Exceptions are fearful because they

are made by fear. [10]The "fearful healer" is a contradiction in terms, and is therefore a concept that only a conflicted mind could possibly perceive as meaningful.

6. Fear does not gladden. [2]Healing does. [3]Fear always makes exceptions. [4]Healing never does. [5]Fear produces dissociation, because it induces separation. [6]Healing always produces harmony, because it proceeds from integration. [7]It is predictable because it can be counted on. [8]Everything that is of God can be counted on, because everything of God is wholly real. [9]Healing can be counted on because it is inspired by His Voice, and is in accord with His laws. [10]Yet if healing is consistent it cannot be inconsistently understood. [11]Understanding means consistency because God means consistency. [12]Since that is His meaning, it is also yours. [13]Your meaning cannot be out of accord with His, because your whole meaning and your only meaning comes from His and is like His. [14]God cannot be out of accord with Himself, and you cannot be out of accord with Him. [15]You cannot separate your Self from your Creator, Who created you by sharing His Being with you.

7. The unhealed healer wants gratitude from his brothers, but he is not grateful to them. [2]That is because he thinks he is giving something to them, and is not receiving something equally desirable in return. [3]His teaching is limited because he is learning so little. [4]His healing lesson is limited by his own ingratitude, which is a lesson in sickness. [5]True learning is constant, and so vital in its power for change that a Son of God can recognize his power in one instant and change the world in the next. [6]That is because, by changing his mind, he has changed the most powerful device that was ever given him for change. [7]This in no way contradicts the changelessness of mind as God created it, but you think that you have changed it as long as you learn through the ego. [8]This places you in a position of needing to learn a lesson that seems contradictory;—you must learn to change your mind about your mind. [9]Only by this can you learn that it *is* changeless.

8. When you heal, that is exactly what you *are* learning. [2]You are recognizing the changeless mind in your brother by realizing that he could not have changed his mind. [3]That is how you perceive the Holy Spirit in him. [4]It is only the Holy Spirit in him that never changes His Mind. [5]He himself may think he can, or he would not perceive himself as sick. [6]He therefore does not know what his Self is. [7]If you see only the changeless in him you have not

really changed him. ⁸By changing your mind about his *for* him, you help him undo the change his ego thinks it has made in him.

9. As you can hear two voices, so you can see in two ways. ²One way shows you an image, or an idol that you may worship out of fear, but will never love. ³The other shows you only truth, which you will love because you will understand it. ⁴Understanding is appreciation, because what you understand you can identify with, and by making it part of you, you have accepted it with love. ⁵That is how God Himself created you; in understanding, in appreciation and in love. ⁶The ego is totally unable to understand this, because it does not understand what it makes, does not appreciate it and does not love it. ⁷It incorporates to take away. ⁸It literally believes that every time it deprives someone of something, it has increased. ⁹I have spoken often of the increase of the Kingdom by your creations, which can only be created as you were. ¹⁰The whole glory and perfect joy that *is* the Kingdom lies in you to give. ¹¹Do you not want to give it?

10. You cannot forget the Father because I am with you, and I cannot forget Him. ²To forget me is to forget yourself and Him Who created you. ³Our brothers are forgetful. ⁴That is why they need your remembrance of me and of Him Who created me. ⁵Through this remembrance, you can change their minds about themselves, as I can change yours. ⁶Your mind is so powerful a light that you can look into theirs and enlighten them, as I can enlighten yours. ⁷I do not want to share my body in communion because this is to share nothing. ⁸Would I try to share an illusion with the most holy children of a most holy Father? ⁹Yet I do want to share my mind with you because we are of one Mind, and that Mind is ours. ¹⁰See only this Mind everywhere, because only this is everywhere and in everything. ¹¹It is everything because it encompasses all things within itself. ¹²Blessed are you who perceive only this, because you perceive only what is true.

11. Come therefore unto me, and learn of the truth in you. ²The mind we share is shared by all our brothers, and as we see them truly they will be healed. ³Let your mind shine with mine upon their minds, and by our gratitude to them make them aware of the light in them. ⁴This light will shine back upon you and on the whole Sonship, because this is your proper gift to God. ⁵He will accept it and give it to the Sonship, because it is acceptable to Him and therefore to His Sons. ⁶This is true communion with the Holy Spirit, Who sees the altar of God in every-

one, and by bringing it to your appreciation, He calls upon you to love God and His creation. [7]You can appreciate the Sonship only as one. [8]This is part of the law of creation, and therefore governs all thought.

VI. From Vigilance to Peace

1. Although you can love the Sonship only as one, you can perceive it as fragmented. [2]It is impossible, however, to see something in part of it that you will not attribute to all of it. [3]That is why attack is never discrete, and why it must be relinquished entirely. [4]If it is not relinquished entirely it is not relinquished at all. [5]Fear and love make or create, depending on whether the ego or the Holy Spirit begets or inspires them, but they *will* return to the mind of the thinker and they will affect his total perception. [6]That includes his concept of God, of His creations and of his own. [7]He will not appreciate any of Them if he regards Them fearfully. [8]He will appreciate all of Them if he regards Them with love.

2. The mind that accepts attack cannot love. [2]That is because it believes it can destroy love, and therefore does not understand what love is. [3]If it does not understand what love is, it cannot perceive itself as loving. [4]This loses the awareness of being, induces feelings of unreality and results in utter confusion. [5]Your thinking has done this because of its power, but your thinking can also save you from this because its power is not of your making. [6]Your ability to direct your thinking as you choose is part of its power. [7]If you do not believe you can do this you have denied the power of your thought, and thus rendered it powerless in your belief.

3. The ingeniousness of the ego to preserve itself is enormous, but it stems from the very power of the mind the ego denies. [2]This means that the ego attacks what is preserving it, which must result in extreme anxiety. [3]That is why the ego never recognizes what it is doing. [4]It is perfectly logical but clearly insane. [5]The ego draws upon the one source that is totally inimical to its existence *for* its existence. [6]Fearful of perceiving the power of this source, it is forced to depreciate it. [7]This threatens its own existence, a state which it finds intolerable. [8]Remaining logical but still insane, the ego resolves this completely insane dilemma in a completely insane way. [9]It does not perceive *its* existence as

threatened by projecting the threat onto *you*, and perceiving your being as nonexistent. [10]This ensures its continuance if you side with it, by guaranteeing that you will not know your own safety.

4. The ego cannot afford to know anything. [2]Knowledge is total, and the ego does not believe in totality. [3]This unbelief is its origin, and while the ego does not love you it *is* faithful to its own antecedents, begetting as it was begotten. [4]Mind always reproduces as it was produced. [5]Produced by fear, the ego reproduces fear. [6]This is its allegiance, and this allegiance makes it treacherous to love because you *are* love. [7]Love is your power, which the ego must deny. [8]It must also deny everything this power gives you *because* it gives you everything. [9]No one who has everything wants the ego. [10]Its own maker, then, does not want it. [11]Rejection is therefore the only decision the ego could possibly encounter, if the mind that made it knew itself. [12]And if it recognized any part of the Sonship, it *would* know itself.

5. The ego therefore opposes all appreciation, all recognition, all sane perception and all knowledge. [2]It perceives their threat as total, because it senses that all commitments the mind makes are total. [3]Forced, therefore, to detach itself from you, it is willing to attach itself to anything else. [4]But there *is* nothing else. [5]The mind can, however, make up illusions, and if it does so it will believe in them, because that is how it made them.

6. The Holy Spirit undoes illusions without attacking them, because He cannot perceive them at all. [2]They therefore do not exist for Him. [3]He resolves the apparent conflict they engender by perceiving conflict as meaningless. [4]I have said before that the Holy Spirit perceives the conflict exactly as it is, and it *is* meaningless. [5]The Holy Spirit does not want you to understand conflict; He wants you to realize that, because conflict is meaningless, it is not understandable. [6]As I have already said, understanding brings appreciation and appreciation brings love. [7]Nothing else can be understood, because nothing else is real and therefore nothing else has meaning.

7. If you will keep in mind what the Holy Spirit offers you, you cannot be vigilant for anything *but* God and His Kingdom. [2]The only reason you may find this hard to accept is because you may still think there is something else. [3]Belief does not require vigilance unless it is conflicted. [4]If it is, there are conflicting components within it that have led to a state of war, and vigilance has therefore become essential. [5]Vigilance has no place in peace. [6]It is

necessary against beliefs that are not true, and would never have been called upon by the Holy Spirit if you had not believed the untrue. [7]When you believe something, you have made it true for you. [8]When you believe what God does not know, your thought seems to contradict His, and this makes it appear as if you are attacking Him.

8. I have repeatedly emphasized that the ego does believe it can attack God, and tries to persuade you that you have done this. [2]If the mind cannot attack, the ego proceeds perfectly logically to the belief that you must be a body. [3]By not seeing you as you are, it can see itself as it wants to be. [4]Aware of its weakness the ego wants your allegiance, but not as you really are. [5]The ego therefore wants to engage your mind in its own delusional system, because otherwise the light of your understanding would dispel it. [6]It wants no part of truth, because the ego itself is not true. [7]If truth is total, the untrue cannot exist. [8]Commitment to either must be total; they cannot coexist in your mind without splitting it. [9]If they cannot coexist in peace, and if you want peace, you must give up the idea of conflict entirely and for all time. [10]This requires vigilance only as long as you do not recognize what is true. [11]While you believe that two totally contradictory thought systems share truth, your need for vigilance is apparent.

9. Your mind is dividing its allegiance between two kingdoms, and you are totally committed to neither. [2]Your identification with the Kingdom is totally beyond question except by you, when you are thinking insanely. [3]What you are is not established by your perception, and is not influenced by it at all. [4]Perceived problems in identification at any level are not problems of fact. [5]They are problems of understanding, since their presence implies a belief that what you are is up to you to decide. [6]The ego believes this totally, being fully committed to it. [7]It is not true. [8]The ego therefore is totally committed to untruth, perceiving in total contradiction to the Holy Spirit and to the knowledge of God.

10. You can be perceived with meaning only by the Holy Spirit because your being *is* the knowledge of God. [2]Any belief you accept apart from this will obscure God's Voice in you, and will therefore obscure God to you. [3]Unless you perceive His creation truly you cannot know the Creator, since God and His creation are not separate. [4]The Oneness of the Creator and the creation is your wholeness, your sanity and your limitless power. [5]This limitless power is God's gift to you, because it is what you are. [6]If

you dissociate your mind from it you are perceiving the most powerful force in the universe as if it were weak, because you do not believe you are part of it.

11.   Perceived without your part in it, God's creation is seen as weak, and those who see themselves as weakened do attack. [2]The attack must be blind, however, because there is nothing to attack. [3]Therefore they make up images, perceive them as unworthy and attack them for their unworthiness. [4]That is all the world of the ego is. [5]Nothing. [6]It has no meaning. [7]It does not exist. [8]Do not try to understand it because, if you do, you are believing that it can be understood and is therefore capable of being appreciated and loved. [9]That would justify its existence, which cannot be justified. [10]You cannot make the meaningless meaningful. [11]This can only be an insane attempt.

12.   Allowing insanity to enter your mind means that you have not judged sanity as wholly desirable. [2]If you want something else you will make something else, but because it is something else, it will attack your thought system and divide your allegiance. [3]You cannot create in this divided state, and you must be vigilant against this divided state because only peace can be extended. [4]Your divided mind is blocking the extension of the Kingdom, and its extension is your joy. [5]If you do not extend the Kingdom, you are not thinking with your Creator and creating as He created.

13.   In this depressing state the Holy Spirit reminds you gently that you are sad because you are not fulfilling your function as cocreator with God, and are therefore depriving yourself of joy. [2]This is not God's choice but yours. [3]If your mind could be out of accord with God's, you would be willing without meaning. [4]Yet because God's Will is unchangeable, no conflict of will is possible. [5]This is the Holy Spirit's perfectly consistent teaching. [6]Creation, not separation, is your will *because* it is God's, and nothing that opposes this means anything at all. [7]Being a perfect accomplishment, the Sonship can only accomplish perfectly, extending the joy in which it was created, and identifying itself with both its Creator and its creations, knowing They are One.

VII. The Totality of the Kingdom

1. Whenever you deny a blessing to a brother *you* will feel deprived, because denial is as total as love. ²It is as impossible to deny part of the Sonship as it is to love it in part. ³Nor is it possible to love it totally at times. ⁴You cannot be totally committed sometimes. ⁵Denial has no power in itself, but you can give it the power of your mind, whose power is without limit. ⁶If you use it to deny reality, reality is gone for you. ⁷*Reality cannot be partly appreciated.* ⁸That is why denying any part of it means you have lost the awareness of all of it. ⁹Yet denial is a defense, and so it is as capable of being used positively as well as negatively. ¹⁰Used negatively it will be destructive, because it will be used for attack. ¹¹But in the service of the Holy Spirit, it can help you recognize part of reality, and thus appreciate all of it. ¹²Mind is too powerful to be subject to exclusion. ¹³You will never be able to exclude yourself from your thoughts.

2. When a brother acts insanely, he is offering you an opportunity to bless him. ²His need is yours. ³You need the blessing you can offer him. ⁴There is no way for you to have it except by giving it. ⁵This is the law of God, and it has no exceptions. ⁶What you deny you lack, not because it is lacking, but because you have denied it in another and are therefore not aware of it in yourself. ⁷Every response you make is determined by what you think you are, and what you want to be *is* what you think you are. ⁸What you want to be, then, must determine every response you make.

3. You do not need God's blessing because that you have forever, but you do need yours. ²The ego's picture of you is deprived, unloving and vulnerable. ³You cannot love this. ⁴Yet you can very easily escape from this image by leaving it behind. ⁵You are not there and that is not you. ⁶Do not see this picture in anyone, or you have accepted it *as* you. ⁷All illusions about the Sonship are dispelled together as they were made together. ⁸Teach no one that he is what you would not want to be. ⁹Your brother is the mirror in which you see the image of yourself as long as perception lasts. ¹⁰And perception will last until the Sonship knows itself as whole. ¹¹You made perception and it must last as long as you want it.

4. Illusions are investments. ²They will last as long as you value them. ³Values are relative, but they are powerful because they are mental judgments. ⁴The only way to dispel illusions is to

withdraw all investment from them, and they will have no life for you because you will have put them out of your mind. ⁵While you include them in it, you are giving life to them. ⁶Except there is nothing there to receive your gift.

5. The gift of life is yours to give, because it was given you. ²You are unaware of your gift because you do not give it. ³You cannot make nothing live, since nothing cannot be enlivened. ⁴Therefore, you are not extending the gift you both *have* and *are*, and so you do not know your being. ⁵All confusion comes from not extending life, because that is not the Will of your Creator. ⁶You can do nothing apart from Him, and you *do* do nothing apart from Him. ⁷Keep His way to remember yourself, and teach His way lest you forget yourself. ⁸Give only honor to the Sons of the living God, and count yourself among them gladly.

6. Only honor is a fitting gift for those whom God Himself created worthy of honor, and whom He honors. ²Give them the appreciation God accords them always, because they are His beloved Sons in whom He is well pleased. ³You cannot be apart from them because you are not apart from Him. ⁴Rest in His Love and protect your rest by loving. ⁵But love everything He created, of which you are a part, or you cannot learn of His peace and accept His gift for yourself and as yourself. ⁶You cannot know your own perfection until you have honored all those who were created like you.

7. One child of God is the only teacher sufficiently worthy to teach another. ²One Teacher is in all minds and He teaches the same lesson to all. ³He always teaches you the inestimable worth of every Son of God, teaching it with infinite patience born of the infinite Love for which He speaks. ⁴Every attack is a call for His patience, since His patience can translate attack into blessing. ⁵Those who attack do not know they are blessed. ⁶They attack because they believe they are deprived. ⁷Give, therefore, of your abundance, and teach your brothers theirs. ⁸Do not share their illusions of scarcity, or you will perceive yourself as lacking.

8. Attack could never promote attack unless you perceived it as a means of depriving you of something you want. ²Yet you cannot lose anything unless you do not value it, and therefore do not want it. ³This makes you feel deprived of it, and by projecting your own rejection you then believe that others are taking it from you. ⁴You must be fearful if you believe that your brother is attacking you to tear the Kingdom of Heaven from you. ⁵This is the

ultimate basis for all the ego's projection.

9. Being the part of your mind that does not believe it is responsible for itself, and being without allegiance to God, the ego is incapable of trust. ²Projecting its insane belief that you have been treacherous to your Creator, it believes that your brothers, who are as incapable of this as you are, are out to take God from you. ³Whenever a brother attacks another, that *is* what he believes. ⁴Projection always sees your wishes in others. ⁵If you choose to separate yourself from God, that is what you will think others are doing to you.

10. You *are* the Will of God. ²Do not accept anything else as your will, or you are denying what you are. ³Deny this and you will attack, believing you have been attacked. ⁴But see the Love of God in you, and you will see it everywhere because it *is* everywhere. ⁵See His abundance in everyone, and you will know that you are in Him with them. ⁶They are part of you, as you are part of God. ⁷You are as lonely without understanding this as God Himself is lonely when His Sons do not know Him. ⁸The peace of God is understanding this. ⁹There is only one way out of the world's thinking, just as there was only one way into it. ¹⁰Understand totally by understanding totality.

11. Perceive any part of the ego's thought system as wholly insane, wholly delusional and wholly undesirable, and you have correctly evaluated all of it. ²This correction enables you to perceive any part of creation as wholly real, wholly perfect and wholly desirable. ³Wanting this only you will *have* this only, and giving this only you will *be* only this. ⁴The gifts you offer to the ego are always experienced as sacrifices, but the gifts you offer to the Kingdom are gifts to you. ⁵They will always be treasured by God because they belong to His beloved Sons, who belong to Him. ⁶All power and glory are yours because the Kingdom is His.

VIII. The Unbelievable Belief

1. We have said that without projection there can be no anger, but it is also true that without extension there can be no love. ²These reflect a fundamental law of the mind, and therefore one that always operates. ³It is the law by which you create and were created. ⁴It is the law that unifies the Kingdom, and keeps it in the Mind of God. ⁵To the ego, the law is perceived as a means of

getting rid of something it does not want. [6]To the Holy Spirit, it is the fundamental law of sharing, by which you give what you value in order to keep it in your mind. [7]To the Holy Spirit it is the law of extension. [8]To the ego it is the law of deprivation. [9]It therefore produces abundance or scarcity, depending on how you choose to apply it. [10]This choice is up to you, but it is not up to you to decide whether or not you will utilize the law. [11]Every mind must project or extend, because that is how it lives, and every mind is life.

2.   The ego's use of projection must be fully understood before the inevitable association between projection and anger can be finally undone. [2]The ego always tries to preserve conflict. [3]It is very ingenious in devising ways that seem to diminish conflict, because it does not want you to find conflict so intolerable that you will insist on giving it up. [4]The ego therefore tries to persuade you that *it* can free you of conflict, lest you give the ego up and free yourself. [5]Using its own warped version of the laws of God, the ego utilizes the power of the mind only to defeat the mind's real purpose. [6]It projects conflict from your mind to other minds, in an attempt to persuade you that you have gotten rid of the problem.

3.   There are two major errors involved in this attempt. [2]First, strictly speaking, conflict cannot be projected because it cannot be shared. [3]Any attempt to keep part of it and get rid of another part does not really mean anything. [4]Remember that a conflicted teacher is a poor teacher and a poor learner. [5]His lessons are confused, and their transfer value is limited by his confusion. [6]The second error is the idea that you can get rid of something you do not want by giving it away. [7]Giving it is how you *keep* it. [8]The belief that by seeing it outside you have excluded it from within is a complete distortion of the power of extension. [9]That is why those who project are vigilant for their own safety. [10]They are afraid that their projections will return and hurt them. [11]Believing they have blotted their projections from their own minds, they also believe their projections are trying to creep back in. [12]Since the projections have not left their minds, they are forced to engage in constant activity in order not to recognize this.

4.   You cannot perpetuate an illusion about another without perpetuating it about yourself. [2]There is no way out of this, because it is impossible to fragment the mind. [3]To fragment is to break into pieces, and mind cannot attack or be attacked. [4]The belief

that it can, an error the ego always makes, underlies its whole use of projection. [5]It does not understand what mind is, and therefore does not understand what *you* are. [6]Yet its existence is dependent on your mind, because the ego is your belief. [7]The ego is a confusion in identification. [8]Never having had a consistent model, it never developed consistently. [9]It is the product of the misapplication of the laws of God by distorted minds that are misusing their power.

5. *Do not be afraid of the ego.* [2]It depends on your mind, and as you made it by believing in it, so you can dispel it by withdrawing belief from it. [3]Do not project the responsibility for your belief in it onto anyone else, or you will preserve the belief. [4]When you are willing to accept sole responsibility for the ego's existence you will have laid aside all anger and all attack, because they come from an attempt to project responsibility for your own errors. [5]But having accepted the errors as yours, do not keep them. [6]Give them over quickly to the Holy Spirit to be undone completely, so that all their effects will vanish from your mind and from the Sonship as a whole.

6. The Holy Spirit will teach you to perceive beyond your belief, because truth is beyond belief and His perception is true. [2]The ego can be completely forgotten at any time, because it is a totally incredible belief, and no one can keep a belief he has judged to be unbelievable. [3]The more you learn about the ego, the more you realize that it cannot be believed. [4]The incredible cannot be understood because it is unbelievable. [5]The meaninglessness of perception based on the unbelievable is apparent, but it may not be recognized as being beyond belief, because it is made *by* belief.

7. The whole purpose of this course is to teach you that the ego is unbelievable and will forever be unbelievable. [2]You who made the ego by believing the unbelievable cannot make this judgment alone. [3]By accepting the Atonement for yourself, you are deciding against the belief that you can be alone, thus dispelling the idea of separation and affirming your true identification with the whole Kingdom as literally part of you. [4]This identification is as beyond doubt as it is beyond belief. [5]Your wholeness has no limits because being is infinity.

131

IX. The Extension of the Kingdom

1. Only you can limit your creative power, but God wills to release it. ²He no more wills you to deprive yourself of your creations than He wills to deprive Himself of His. ³Do not withhold your gifts to the Sonship, or you withhold yourself from God! ⁴Selfishness is of the ego, but Self-fullness is of spirit because that is how God created it. ⁵The Holy Spirit is in the part of the mind that lies between the ego and the spirit, mediating between them always in favor of the spirit: ⁶To the ego this is partiality, and it responds as if it were being sided against. ⁷To spirit this is truth, because it knows its fullness and cannot conceive of any part from which it is excluded.

2. Spirit knows that the awareness of all its brothers is included in its own, as it is included in God. ²The power of the whole Sonship and of its Creator is therefore spirit's own fullness, rendering its creations equally whole and equal in perfection. ³The ego cannot prevail against a totality that includes God, and any totality *must* include God. ⁴Everything He created is given all His power, because it is part of Him and shares His Being with Him. ⁵Creating is the opposite of loss, as blessing is the opposite of sacrifice. ⁶Being *must* be extended. ⁷That is how it retains the knowledge of itself. ⁸Spirit yearns to share its being as its Creator did. ⁹Created by sharing, its will is to create. ¹⁰It does not wish to contain God, but wills to extend His Being.

3. The extension of God's Being is spirit's only function. ²Its fullness cannot be contained, any more than can the fullness of its Creator. ³Fullness is extension. ⁴The ego's whole thought system blocks extension, and thus blocks your only function. ⁵It therefore blocks your joy, so that you perceive yourself as unfulfilled. ⁶Unless you create you *are* unfulfilled, but God does not know unfulfillment and therefore you must create. ⁷You may not know your own creations, but this can no more interfere with their reality than your unawareness of your spirit can interfere with its being.

4. The Kingdom is forever extending because it is in the Mind of God. ²You do not know your joy because you do not know your own Self-fullness. ³Exclude any part of the Kingdom from yourself and you are not whole. ⁴A split mind cannot perceive its fullness, and needs the miracle of its wholeness to dawn upon it and heal it. ⁵This reawakens the wholeness in it, and restores it to the

Kingdom because of its acceptance of wholeness. ⁶The full appreciation of the mind's Self-fullness makes selfishness impossible and extension inevitable. ⁷That is why there is perfect peace in the Kingdom. ⁸Spirit is fulfilling its function, and only complete fulfillment is peace.

5. Your creations are protected for you because the Holy Spirit, Who is in your mind, knows of them and can bring them into your awareness whenever you will let Him. ²They are there as part of your own being, because your fulfillment includes them. ³The creations of every Son of God are yours, since every creation belongs to everyone, being created for the Sonship as a whole.

6. You have not failed to increase the inheritance of the Sons of God, and thus have not failed to secure it for yourself. ²Since it was the Will of God to give it to you, He gave it forever. ³Since it was His Will that you have it forever, He gave you the means for keeping it. ⁴*And you have done so.* ⁵Disobeying God's Will is meaningful only to the insane. ⁶In truth it is impossible. ⁷Your Self-fullness is as boundless as God's. ⁸Like His, It extends forever and in perfect peace. ⁹Its radiance is so intense that It creates in perfect joy, and only the whole can be born of Its Wholeness.

7. Be confident that you have never lost your Identity and the extensions which maintain It in wholeness and peace. ²Miracles are an expression of this confidence. ³They are reflections of both your proper identification with your brothers, and of your awareness that your identification is maintained by extension. ⁴The miracle is a lesson in total perception. ⁵By including any part of totality in the lesson, you have included the whole.

X. The Confusion of Pain and Joy

1. The Kingdom is the result of premises, just as this world is. ²You may have carried the ego's reasoning to its logical conclusion, which is total confusion about everything. ³If you really saw this result you could not want it. ⁴The only reason you could possibly want any part of it is because you do not see the whole of it. ⁵You are willing to look at the ego's premises, but not at their logical outcome. ⁶Is it not possible that you have done the same thing with the premises of God? ⁷Your creations are the logical outcome of His premises. ⁸His thinking has established them for you. ⁹They are exactly where they belong. ¹⁰They belong

in your mind as part of your identification with His, but your state of mind and your recognition of what is in it depend on what you believe about your mind. [11]Whatever these beliefs may be, they are the premises that will determine what you accept into your mind.

2. It is surely clear that you can both accept into your mind what is not there, and deny what is. [2]Yet the function God Himself gave your mind through His you may deny, but you cannot prevent. [3]It is the logical outcome of what you are. [4]The ability to see a logical outcome depends on the willingness to see it, but its truth has nothing to do with your willingness. [5]Truth is God's Will. [6]Share His Will and you share what He knows. [7]Deny His Will as yours, and you are denying His Kingdom *and* yours.

3. The Holy Spirit will direct you only so as to avoid pain. [2]Surely no one would object to this goal if he recognized it. [3]The problem is not whether what the Holy Spirit says is true, but whether you want to listen to what He says. [4]You no more recognize what is painful than you know what is joyful, and are, in fact, very apt to confuse the two. [5]The Holy Spirit's main function is to teach you to tell them apart. [6]What is joyful to you is painful to the ego, and as long as you are in doubt about what you are, you will be confused about joy and pain. [7]This confusion is the cause of the whole idea of sacrifice. [8]Obey the Holy Spirit, and you will be giving up the ego. [9]But you will be sacrificing nothing. [10]On the contrary, you will be gaining everything. [11]If you believed this, there would be no conflict.

4. That is why you need to demonstrate the obvious to yourself. [2]It is not obvious to you. [3]You believe that doing the opposite of God's Will can be better for you. [4]You also believe that it is possible to *do* the opposite of God's Will. [5]Therefore, you believe that an impossible choice is open to you, and one which is both fearful and desirable. [6]Yet God wills. [7]He does not wish. [8]Your will is as powerful as His because it *is* His. [9]The ego's wishes do not mean anything, because the ego wishes for the impossible. [10]You can wish for the impossible, but you can will only with God. [11]This is the ego's weakness and your strength.

5. The Holy Spirit always sides with you and with your strength. [2]As long as you avoid His guidance in any way, you want to be weak. [3]Yet weakness is frightening. [4]What else, then, can this decision mean except that you want to be fearful? [5]The Holy Spirit never asks for sacrifice, but the ego always does. [6]When you are

confused about this distinction in motivation, it can only be due to projection. ⁷Projection is a confusion in motivation, and given this confusion, trust becomes impossible. ⁸No one gladly obeys a guide he does not trust, but this does not mean that the guide is untrustworthy. ⁹In this case, it always means that the follower is. ¹⁰However, this, too, is merely a matter of his own belief. ¹¹Believing that he can betray, he believes that everything can betray him. ¹²Yet this is only because he has elected to follow false guidance. ¹³Unable to follow this guidance without fear, he associates fear with guidance, and refuses to follow any guidance at all. ¹⁴If the result of this decision is confusion, this is hardly surprising.

6. The Holy Spirit is perfectly trustworthy, as you are. ²God Himself trusts you, and therefore your trustworthiness is beyond question. ³It will always remain beyond question, however much you may question it. ⁴I said before that you are the Will of God. ⁵His Will is not an idle wish, and your identification with His Will is not optional, since it is what you are. ⁶Sharing His Will with me is not really open to choice, though it may seem to be. ⁷The whole separation lies in this error. ⁸The only way out of the error is to decide that you do not have to decide anything. ⁹Everything has been given you by God's decision. ¹⁰That is His Will, and you cannot undo it.

7. Even the relinquishment of your false decision-making prerogative, which the ego guards so jealously, is not accomplished by your wish. ²It was accomplished for you by the Will of God, Who has not left you comfortless. ³His Voice will teach you how to distinguish between pain and joy, and will lead you out of the confusion you have made. ⁴There is no confusion in the mind of a Son of God, whose will must be the Will of the Father, because the Father's Will *is* His Son.

8. Miracles are in accord with the Will of God, Whose Will you do not know because you are confused about what *you* will. ²This means that you are confused about what you are. ³If you are God's Will and do not accept His Will, you are denying joy. ⁴The miracle is therefore a lesson in what joy is. ⁵Being a lesson in sharing it is a lesson in love, which *is* joy. ⁶Every miracle is thus a lesson in truth, and by offering truth you are learning the difference between pain and joy.

XI. The State of Grace

1. The Holy Spirit will always guide you truly, because your joy is His. ²This is His Will for everyone because He speaks for the Kingdom of God, which *is* joy. ³Following Him is therefore the easiest thing in the world, and the only thing that is easy, because it is not of the world. ⁴It is therefore natural. ⁵The world goes against your nature, being out of accord with God's laws. ⁶The world perceives orders of difficulty in everything. ⁷This is because the ego perceives nothing as wholly desirable. ⁸By demonstrating to yourself there is no order of difficulty in miracles, you will convince yourself that, in your natural state, there is no difficulty at all *because* it is a state of grace.

2. Grace is the natural state of every Son of God. ²When he is not in a state of grace, he is out of his natural environment and does not function well. ³Everything he does becomes a strain, because he was not created for the environment that he has made. ⁴He therefore cannot adapt to it, nor can he adapt it to him. ⁵There is no point in trying. ⁶A Son of God is happy only when he knows he is with God. ⁷That is the only environment in which he will not experience strain, because that is where he belongs. ⁸It is also the only environment that is worthy of him, because his own worth is beyond anything he can make.

3. Consider the kingdom you have made and judge its worth fairly. ²Is it worthy to be a home for a child of God? ³Does it protect his peace and shine love upon him? ⁴Does it keep his heart untouched by fear, and allow him to give always, without any sense of loss? ⁵Does it teach him that this giving is his joy, and that God Himself thanks him for his giving? ⁶That is the only environment in which you can be happy. ⁷You cannot make it, any more than you can make yourself. ⁸It has been created for you, as you were created for it. ⁹God watches over His children and denies them nothing. ¹⁰Yet when they deny Him they do not know this, because they deny themselves everything. ¹¹You who could give the Love of God to everything you see and touch and remember, are literally denying Heaven to yourself.

4. I call upon you to remember that I have chosen you to teach the Kingdom *to* the Kingdom. ²There are no exceptions to this lesson, because the lack of exceptions *is* the lesson. ³Every Son who returns to the Kingdom with this lesson in his heart has healed the Sonship and given thanks to God. ⁴Everyone who

learns this lesson has become the perfect teacher, because he has learned it of the Holy Spirit.

5.   When a mind has only light, it knows only light. [2]Its own radiance shines all around it, and extends out into the darkness of other minds, transforming them into majesty. [3]The Majesty of God is there, for you to recognize and appreciate and know. [4]Recognizing the Majesty of God as your brother is to accept your own inheritance. [5]God gives only equally. [6]If you recognize His gift in anyone, you have acknowledged what He has given you. [7]Nothing is so easy to recognize as truth. [8]This is the recognition that is immediate, clear and natural. [9]You have trained yourself not to recognize it, and this has been very difficult for you.

6.   Out of your natural environment you may well ask, "What is truth?" since truth is the environment by which and for which you were created. [2]You do not know yourself, because you do not know your Creator. [3]You do not know your creations because you do not know your brothers, who created them with you. [4]I have already said that only the whole Sonship is worthy to be co-creator with God, because only the whole Sonship can create like Him. [5]Whenever you heal a brother by recognizing his worth, you are acknowledging his power to create and yours. [6]He cannot have lost what you recognize, and you must have the glory you see in him. [7]He is a co-creator with God with you. [8]Deny his creative power, and you are denying yours and that of God Who created you.

7.   You cannot deny part of truth. [2]You do not know your creations because you do not know their creator. [3]You do not know yourself because you do not know yours. [4]Your creations cannot establish your reality, any more than you can establish God's. [5]But you can *know* both. [6]Being is known by sharing. [7]Because God shared His Being with you, you can know Him. [8]But you must also know all He created, to know what they have shared. [9]Without your Father you will not know your fatherhood. [10]The Kingdom of God includes all His Sons and their children, who are as like the Sons as they are like the Father. [11]Know, then, the Sons of God, and you will know all creation.

Chapter 8

THE JOURNEY BACK

I. The Direction of the Curriculum

1. Knowledge is not the motivation for learning this course. ²Peace is. ³This is the prerequisite for knowledge only because those who are in conflict are not peaceful, and peace is the condition of knowledge because it is the condition of the Kingdom. ⁴Knowledge can be restored only when you meet its conditions. ⁵This is not a bargain made by God, Who makes no bargains. ⁶It is merely the result of your misuse of His laws on behalf of an imaginary will that is not His. ⁷Knowledge *is* His Will. ⁸If you are opposing His Will, how can you have knowledge? ⁹I have told you what knowledge offers you, but perhaps you do not yet regard this as wholly desirable. ¹⁰If you did you would not be so ready to throw it away when the ego asks for your allegiance.

2. The distractions of the ego may seem to interfere with your learning, but the ego has no power to distract you unless you give it the power to do so. ²The ego's voice is an hallucination. ³You cannot expect it to say "I am not real." ⁴Yet you are not asked to dispel your hallucinations alone. ⁵You are merely asked to evaluate them in terms of their results to you. ⁶If you do not want them on the basis of loss of peace, they will be removed from your mind for you.

3. Every response to the ego is a call to war, and war does deprive you of peace. ²Yet in this war there is no opponent. ³This is the reinterpretation of reality that you must make to secure peace, and the only one you need ever make. ⁴Those whom you perceive as opponents are part of your peace, which you are giving up by attacking them. ⁵How can you have what you give up? ⁶You share to have, but you do not give it up yourself. ⁷When you give up peace, you are excluding yourself from it. ⁸This is a condition so alien to the Kingdom that you cannot understand the state that prevails within it.

4. Your past learning must have taught you the wrong things, simply because it has not made you happy. ²On this basis alone its value should be questioned. ³If learning aims at change, and that is always its purpose, are you satisfied with the changes

your learning has brought you? [4]Dissatisfaction with learning outcomes is a sign of learning failure, since it means that you did not get what you wanted.

5. The curriculum of the Atonement is the opposite of the curriculum you have established for yourself, but so is its outcome. [2]If the outcome of yours has made you unhappy, and if you want a different one, a change in the curriculum is obviously necessary. [3]The first change to be introduced is a change in direction. [4]A meaningful curriculum cannot be inconsistent. [5]If it is planned by two teachers, each believing in diametrically opposed ideas, it cannot be integrated. [6]If it is carried out by these two teachers simultaneously, each one merely interferes with the other. [7]This leads to fluctuation, but not to change. [8]The volatile have no direction. [9]They cannot choose one because they cannot relinquish the other, even if it does not exist. [10]Their conflicted curriculum teaches them that *all* directions exist, and gives them no rationale for choice.

6. The total senselessness of such a curriculum must be fully recognized before a real change in direction becomes possible. [2]You cannot learn simultaneously from two teachers who are in total disagreement about everything. [3]Their joint curriculum presents an impossible learning task. [4]They are teaching you entirely different things in entirely different ways, which might be possible except that both are teaching you about yourself. [5]Your reality is unaffected by both, but if you listen to both, your mind will be split about what your reality is.

II. The Difference between Imprisonment and Freedom

1. There *is* a rationale for choice. [2]Only one Teacher knows what your reality is. [3]If learning to remove the obstacles to that knowledge is the purpose of the curriculum, you must learn it of Him. [4]The ego does not know what it is trying to teach. [5]It is trying to teach you what you are without knowing what you are. [6]It is expert only in confusion. [7]It does not understand anything else. [8]As a teacher, then, the ego is totally confused and totally confusing. [9]Even if you could disregard the Holy Spirit entirely, which is impossible, you could still learn nothing from the ego, because the ego knows nothing.

2. Is there any possible reason for choosing a teacher such as this?

²Does the total disregard of anything it teaches make anything but sense? ³Is this the teacher to whom a Son of God should turn to find himself? ⁴The ego has never given you a sensible answer to anything. ⁵Simply on the grounds of your own experience with its teaching, should not this alone disqualify it as your future teacher? ⁶Yet the ego has done more harm to your learning than this alone. ⁷Learning is joyful if it leads you along your natural path, and facilitates the development of what you have. ⁸When you are taught against your nature, however, you will lose by your learning because your learning will imprison you. ⁹Your will is *in* your nature, and therefore cannot go against it.

3. The ego cannot teach you anything as long as your will is free, because you will not listen to it. ²It is not your will to be imprisoned because your will is free. ³That is why the ego is the denial of free will. ⁴It is never God Who coerces you, because He shares His Will with you. ⁵His Voice teaches only in accordance with His Will, but that is not the Holy Spirit's lesson because that is what you *are*. ⁶The lesson is that your will and God's cannot be out of accord because they are one. ⁷This is the undoing of everything the ego tries to teach. ⁸It is not, then, only the direction of the curriculum that must be unconflicted, but also the content.

4. The ego tries to teach that you want to oppose God's Will. ²This unnatural lesson cannot be learned, and the attempt to learn it is a violation of your own freedom, making you afraid of your will *because* it is free. ³The Holy Spirit opposes any imprisoning of the will of a Son of God, knowing that the Will of the Son is the Father's. ⁴The Holy Spirit leads you steadily along the path of freedom, teaching you how to disregard or look beyond everything that would hold you back.

5. We have said that the Holy Spirit teaches you the difference between pain and joy. ²That is the same as saying He teaches you the difference between imprisonment and freedom. ³You cannot make this distinction without Him because you have taught yourself that imprisonment is freedom. ⁴Believing them to be the same, how can you tell them apart? ⁵Can you ask the part of your mind that taught you to believe they are the same, to teach you how they are different?

6. The Holy Spirit's teaching takes only *one* direction and has only *one* goal. ²His direction is freedom and His goal is God. ³Yet He cannot conceive of God without you, because it is not God's Will to *be* without you. ⁴When you have learned that your will is

God's, you could no more will to be without Him than He could will to be without you. ⁵This is freedom and this is joy. ⁶Deny yourself this and you are denying God His Kingdom, because He created you for this.

7. When I said, "All power and glory are yours because the Kingdom is His," this is what I meant: The Will of God is without limit, and all power and glory lie within it. ²It is boundless in strength and in love and in peace. ³It has no boundaries because its extension is unlimited, and it encompasses all things because it created all things. ⁴By creating all things, it made them part of itself. ⁵You are the Will of God because that is how you were created. ⁶Because your Creator creates only like Himself, you are like Him. ⁷You are part of Him Who is all power and glory, and are therefore as unlimited as He is.

8. To what else except all power and glory can the Holy Spirit appeal to restore God's Kingdom? ²His appeal, then, is merely to what the Kingdom is, and for its own acknowledgment of what it is. ³When you acknowledge this you bring the acknowledgment automatically to everyone, because you *have* acknowledged everyone. ⁴By your recognition you awaken theirs, and through theirs yours is extended. ⁵Awakening runs easily and gladly through the Kingdom, in answer to the Call for God. ⁶This is the natural response of every Son of God to the Voice for his Creator, because It is the Voice for his creations and for his own extension.

III. The Holy Encounter

1. Glory to God in the highest, and to you because He has so willed it. ²Ask and it shall be given you, because it has already *been* given. ³Ask for light and learn that you *are* light. ⁴If you want understanding and enlightenment you will learn it, because your decision to learn it is the decision to listen to the Teacher Who knows of light, and can therefore teach it to you. ⁵There is no limit on your learning because there is no limit on your mind. ⁶There is no limit on His teaching because He was created to teach. ⁷Understanding His function perfectly He fulfills it perfectly, because that is His joy and yours.

2. To fulfill the Will of God perfectly is the only joy and peace that can be fully known, because it is the only function that can be fully experienced. ²When this is accomplished, then, there is no

141

other experience. ³Yet the wish for other experience will block its accomplishment, because God's Will cannot be forced upon you, being an experience of total willingness. ⁴The Holy Spirit understands how to teach this, but you do not. ⁵That is why you need Him, and why God gave Him to you. ⁶Only His teaching will release your will to God's, uniting it with His power and glory and establishing them as yours. ⁷You share them as God shares them, because this is the natural outcome of their being.

3.   The Will of the Father and of the Son are One, by Their extension. ²Their extension is the result of Their Oneness, holding Their unity together by extending Their joint Will. ³This is perfect creation by the perfectly created, in union with the perfect Creator. ⁴The Father must give fatherhood to His Son, because His Own Fatherhood must be extended outward. ⁵You who belong in God have the holy function of extending His Fatherhood by placing no limits upon it. ⁶Let the Holy Spirit teach you how to do this, for you can know what it means only of God Himself.

4.   When you meet anyone, remember it is a holy encounter. ²As you see him you will see yourself. ³As you treat him you will treat yourself. ⁴As you think of him you will think of yourself. ⁵Never forget this, for in him you will find yourself or lose yourself. ⁶Whenever two Sons of God meet, they are given another chance at salvation. ⁷Do not leave anyone without giving salvation to him and receiving it yourself. ⁸For I am always there with you, in remembrance of *you*.

5.   The goal of the curriculum, regardless of the teacher you choose, is "Know thyself." ²There is nothing else to seek. ³Everyone is looking for himself and for the power and glory he thinks he has lost. ⁴Whenever you are with anyone, you have another opportunity to find them. ⁵Your power and glory are in him because they are yours. ⁶The ego tries to find them in yourself alone, because it does not know where to look. ⁷The Holy Spirit teaches you that if you look only at yourself you cannot find yourself, because that is not what you are. ⁸Whenever you are with a brother, you are learning what you are because you are teaching what you are. ⁹He will respond either with pain or with joy, depending on which teacher you are following. ¹⁰He will be imprisoned or released according to your decision, and so will you. ¹¹Never forget your responsibility to him, because it is your responsibility to yourself. ¹²Give him his place in the Kingdom and you will have yours.

6. The Kingdom cannot be found alone, and you who are the Kingdom cannot find yourself alone. [2]To achieve the goal of the curriculum, then, you cannot listen to the ego, whose purpose is to defeat its own goal. [3]The ego does not know this, because it does not know anything. [4]But you can know it, and you will know it if you are willing to look at what the ego would make of you. [5]This is your responsibility, because once you have really looked at it you *will* accept the Atonement for yourself. [6]What other choice could you make? [7]Having made this choice you will understand why you once believed that, when you met someone else, you thought he *was* someone else. [8]And every holy encounter in which you enter fully will teach you this is not so.

7. You can encounter only part of yourself because you are part of God, Who is everything. [2]His power and glory are everywhere, and you cannot be excluded from them. [3]The ego teaches that your strength is in you alone. [4]The Holy Spirit teaches that all strength is in God and *therefore* in you. [5]God wills no one suffer. [6]He does not will anyone to suffer for a wrong decision, including you. [7]That is why He has given you the means for undoing it. [8]Through His power and glory all your wrong decisions are undone completely, releasing you and your brother from every imprisoning thought any part of the Sonship holds. [9]Wrong decisions have no power, because they are not true. [10]The imprisonment they seem to produce is no more true than they are.

8. Power and glory belong to God alone. [2]So do you. [3]God gives whatever belongs to Him because He gives of Himself, and everything belongs to Him. [4]Giving of yourself is the function He gave you. [5]Fulfilling it perfectly will let you remember what you *have* of Him, and by this you will remember also what you *are* in Him. [6]You cannot be powerless to do this, because this is your power. [7]Glory is God's gift to you, because that is what He is. [8]See this glory everywhere to remember what you are.

IV. The Gift of Freedom

1. If God's Will for you is complete peace and joy, unless you experience only this you must be refusing to acknowledge His Will. [2]His Will does not vacillate, being changeless forever. [3]When you are not at peace it can only be because you do not believe you are in Him. [4]Yet He is All in all. [5]His peace is complete, and you must

be included in it. ⁶His laws govern you because they govern everything. ⁷You cannot exempt yourself from His laws, although you can disobey them. ⁸Yet if you do, and only if you do, you will feel lonely and helpless, because you are denying yourself everything.

2.   I am come as a light into a world that does deny itself everything. ²It does this simply by dissociating itself from everything. ³It is therefore an illusion of isolation, maintained by fear of the same loneliness that *is* its illusion. ⁴I said that I am with you always, even unto the end of the world. ⁵That is why I am the light of the world. ⁶If I am with you in the loneliness of the world, the loneliness is gone. ⁷You cannot maintain the illusion of loneliness if you are not alone. ⁸My purpose, then, is still to overcome the world. ⁹I do not attack it, but my light must dispel it because of what it is. ¹⁰Light does not attack darkness, but it does shine it away. ¹¹If my light goes with you everywhere, you shine it away with me. ¹²The light becomes ours, and you cannot abide in darkness any more than darkness can abide wherever you go. ¹³The remembrance of me is the remembrance of yourself, and of Him Who sent me to you.

3.   You were in darkness until God's Will was done completely by any part of the Sonship. ²When this was done, it was perfectly accomplished by all. ³How else could it be perfectly accomplished? ⁴My mission was simply to unite the will of the Sonship with the Will of the Father by being aware of the Father's Will myself. ⁵This is the awareness I came to give you, and your problem in accepting it is the problem of this world. ⁶Dispelling it is salvation, and in this sense I *am* the salvation of the world. ⁷The world must therefore despise and reject me, because the world *is* the belief that love is impossible. ⁸If you will accept the fact that I am with you, you are denying the world and accepting God. ⁹My will is His, and your decision to hear me is the decision to hear His Voice and abide in His Will. ¹⁰As God sent me to you so will I send you to others. ¹¹And I will go to them with you, so we can teach them peace and union.

4.   Do you not think the world needs peace as much as you do? ²Do you not want to give it to the world as much as you want to receive it? ³For unless you do, you will not receive it. ⁴If you want to have it of me, you must give it. ⁵Healing does not come from anyone else. ⁶You must accept guidance from within. ⁷The guidance must be what you want, or it will be meaningless to you.

8That is why healing is a collaborative venture. 9I can tell you what to do, but you must collaborate by believing that I know what you should do. 10Only then will your mind choose to follow me. 11Without this choice you could not be healed because you would have decided against healing, and this rejection of my decision for you makes healing impossible.

5. Healing reflects our joint will. 2This is obvious when you consider what healing is for. 3Healing is the way in which the separation is overcome. 4Separation is overcome by union. 5It cannot be overcome by separating. 6The decision to unite must be unequivocal, or the mind itself is divided and not whole. 7Your mind is the means by which you determine your own condition, because mind is the mechanism of decision. 8It is the power by which you separate or join, and experience pain or joy accordingly. 9My decision cannot overcome yours, because yours is as powerful as mine. 10If it were not so the Sons of God would be unequal. 11All things are possible through our joint decision, but mine alone cannot help you. 12Your will is as free as mine, and God Himself would not go against it. 13I cannot will what God does not will. 14I can offer my strength to make yours invincible, but I cannot oppose your decision without competing with it and thereby violating God's Will for you.

6. Nothing God created can oppose your decision, as nothing God created can oppose His Will. 2God gave your will its power, which I can only acknowledge in honor of His. 3If you want to be like me I will help you, knowing that we are alike. 4If you want to be different, I will wait until you change your mind. 5I can teach you, but only you can choose to listen to my teaching. 6How else can it be, if God's Kingdom is freedom? 7Freedom cannot be learned by tyranny of any kind, and the perfect equality of all God's Sons cannot be recognized through the dominion of one mind over another. 8God's Sons are equal in will, all being the Will of their Father. 9This is the only lesson I came to teach.

7. If your will were not mine it would not be our Father's. 2This would mean you have imprisoned yours, and have not let it be free. 3Of yourself you can do nothing, because of yourself you *are* nothing. 4I am nothing without the Father and you are nothing without me, because by denying the Father you deny yourself. 5I will always remember you, and in my remembrance of you lies your remembrance of yourself. 6In our remembrance of each other lies our remembrance of God. 7And in this remembrance

lies your freedom because your freedom is in Him. ⁸Join, then, with me in praise of Him and you whom He created. ⁹This is our gift of gratitude to Him, which He will share with all His creations, to whom He gives equally whatever is acceptable to Him. ¹⁰Because it is acceptable to Him it is the gift of freedom, which is His Will for all His Sons. ¹¹By offering freedom you will be free.

8.   Freedom is the only gift you can offer to God's Sons, being an acknowledgment of what they are and what He is. ²Freedom is creation, because it is love. ³Whom you seek to imprison you do not love. ⁴Therefore, when you seek to imprison anyone, including yourself, you do not love him and you cannot identify with him. ⁵When you imprison yourself you are losing sight of your true identification with me and with the Father. ⁶Your identification is with the Father *and* with the Son. ⁷It cannot be with One and not the Other. ⁸If you are part of One you must be part of the Other, because They are One. ⁹The Holy Trinity is holy *because* It is One. ¹⁰If you exclude yourself from this union, you are perceiving the Holy Trinity as separated. ¹¹You must be included in It, because It is everything. ¹²Unless you take your place in It and fulfill your function as part of It, the Holy Trinity is as bereft as you are. ¹³No part of It can be imprisoned if Its truth is to be known.

V. The Undivided Will of the Sonship

1.   Can you be separated from your identification and be at peace? ²Dissociation is not a solution; it is a delusion. ³The delusional believe that truth will assail them, and they do not recognize it because they prefer the delusion. ⁴Judging truth as something they do not want, they perceive their illusions which block knowledge. ⁵Help them by offering them your unified mind on their behalf, as I am offering you mine on behalf of yours. ⁶Alone we can do nothing, but together our minds fuse into something whose power is far beyond the power of its separate parts. ⁷By not being separate, the Mind of God is established in ours and as ours. ⁸This Mind is invincible because it is undivided.

2.   The undivided will of the Sonship is the perfect creator, being wholly in the likeness of God, Whose Will it is. ²You cannot be exempt from it if you are to understand what it is and what you

are. ³By the belief that your will is separate from mine, you are exempting yourself from the Will of God which *is* yourself. ⁴Yet to heal is still to make whole. ⁵Therefore, to heal is to unite with those who are like you, because perceiving this likeness is to recognize the Father. ⁶If your perfection is in Him and only in Him, how can you know it without recognizing Him? ⁷The recognition of God is the recognition of yourself. ⁸There is no separation of God and His creation. ⁹You will realize this when you understand that there is no separation between your will and mine. ¹⁰Let the Love of God shine upon you by your acceptance of me. ¹¹My reality is yours and His. ¹²By joining your mind with mine you are signifying your awareness that the Will of God is One.

3. God's Oneness and ours are not separate, because His Oneness encompasses ours. ²To join with me is to restore His power to you because we are sharing it. ³I offer you only the recognition of His power in you, but in that lies all truth. ⁴As we unite, we unite with Him. ⁵Glory be to the union of God and His holy Sons! ⁶All glory lies in Them *because* They are united. ⁷The miracles we do bear witness to the Will of the Father for His Son, and to our joy in uniting with His Will for us.

4. When you unite with me you are uniting without the ego, because I have renounced the ego in myself and therefore cannot unite with yours. ²Our union is therefore the way to renounce the ego in you. ³The truth in both of us is beyond the ego. ⁴Our success in transcending the ego is guaranteed by God, and I share this confidence for both of us and all of us. ⁵I bring God's peace back to all His children because I received it of Him for us all. ⁶Nothing can prevail against our united wills because nothing can prevail against God's.

5. Would you know the Will of God for you? ²Ask it of me who know it for you and you will find it. ³I will deny you nothing, as God denies me nothing. ⁴Ours is simply the journey back to God Who is our home. ⁵Whenever fear intrudes anywhere along the road to peace, it is because the ego has attempted to join the journey with us and cannot do so. ⁶Sensing defeat and angered by it, the ego regards itself as rejected and becomes retaliative. ⁷You are invulnerable to its retaliation because I am with you. ⁸On this journey you have chosen me as your companion *instead* of the ego. ⁹Do not attempt to hold on to both, or you will try to go in different directions and will lose the way.

6. The ego's way is not mine, but it is also not yours. ²The Holy Spirit has one direction for all minds, and the one He taught me is yours. ³Let us not lose sight of His direction through illusions, for only illusions of another direction can obscure the one for which God's Voice speaks in all of us. ⁴Never accord the ego the power to interfere with the journey. ⁵It has none, because the journey is the way to what is true. ⁶Leave all illusions behind, and reach beyond all attempts of the ego to hold you back. ⁷I go before you because I am beyond the ego. ⁸Reach, therefore, for my hand because you want to transcend the ego. ⁹My strength will never be wanting, and if you choose to share it you will do so. ¹⁰I give it willingly and gladly, because I need you as much as you need me.

VI. The Treasure of God

1. We are the joint will of the Sonship, whose Wholeness is for all. ²We begin the journey back by setting out together, and gather in our brothers as we continue together. ³Every gain in our strength is offered for all, so they too can lay aside their weakness and add their strength to us. ⁴God's welcome waits for us all, and He will welcome us as I am welcoming you. ⁵Forget not the Kingdom of God for anything the world has to offer.
2. The world can add nothing to the power and the glory of God and His holy Sons, but it can blind the Sons to the Father if they behold it. ²You cannot behold the world and know God. ³Only one is true. ⁴I am come to tell you that the choice of which is true is not yours to make. ⁵If it were, you would have destroyed yourself. ⁶Yet God did not will the destruction of His creations, having created them for eternity. ⁷His Will has saved you, not from yourself but from your illusion of yourself. ⁸He has saved you *for* yourself.
3. Let us glorify Him Whom the world denies, for over His Kingdom the world has no power. ²No one created by God can find joy in anything except the eternal; not because he is deprived of anything else, but because nothing else is worthy of him. ³What God and His Sons create is eternal, and in this and this only is Their joy.
4. Listen to the story of the prodigal son, and learn what God's treasure is and yours: This son of a loving father left his home

and thought he had squandered everything for nothing of any value, although he had not understood its worthlessness at the time. [2]He was ashamed to return to his father, because he thought he had hurt him. [3]Yet when he came home the father welcomed him with joy, because the son himself *was* his father's treasure. [4]He wanted nothing else.

5. God wants only His Son because His Son is His only treasure. [2]You want your creations as He wants His. [3]Your creations are your gift to the Holy Trinity, created in gratitude for your creation. [4]They do not leave you any more than you left your Creator, but they extend your creation as God extended Himself to you. [5]Can the creations of God Himself take joy in what is not real? [6]And what is real except the creations of God and those that are created like His? [7]Your creations love you as you love your Father for the gift of creation. [8]There is no other gift that is eternal, and therefore there is no other gift that is true. [9]How, then, can you accept anything else or give anything else, and expect joy in return? [10]And what else but joy would you want? [11]You made neither yourself nor your function. [12]You made only the decision to be unworthy of both. [13]Yet you cannot make yourself unworthy because you are the treasure of God, and what He values is valuable. [14]There can be no question of its worth, because its value lies in God's sharing Himself with it and establishing its value forever.

6. Your function is to add to God's treasure by creating yours. [2]His Will *to* you is His Will *for* you. [3]He would not withhold creation from you because His joy is in it. [4]You cannot find joy except as God does. [5]His joy lay in creating you, and He extends His Fatherhood to you so that you can extend yourself as He did. [6]You do not understand this because you do not understand Him. [7]No one who does not accept his function can understand what it is, and no one can accept his function unless he knows what *he* is. [8]Creation is the Will of God. [9]His Will created you to create. [10]Your will was not created separate from His, and so you must will as He wills.

7. An "unwilling will" does not mean anything, being a contradiction in terms that actually means nothing. [2]When you think you are unwilling to will with God, you are not thinking. [3]God's Will *is* Thought. [4]It cannot be contradicted *by* thought. [5]God does not contradict Himself, and His Sons, who are like Him, cannot contradict themselves or Him. [6]Yet their thought is so powerful

that they can even imprison the mind of God's Son, if they so choose. [7]This choice does make the Son's function unknown to him, but never to his Creator. [8]And because it is not unknown to his Creator, it is forever knowable to him.

8. There is no question but one you should ever ask of yourself;— "Do I want to know my Father's Will for me?" [2]He will not hide it. [3]He has revealed it to me because I asked it of Him, and learned of what He had already given. [4]Our function is to work together, because apart from each other we cannot function at all. [5]The whole power of God's Son lies in all of us, but not in any of us alone. [6]God would not have us be alone because *He* does not will to be alone. [7]That is why He created His Son, and gave him the power to create with Him. [8]Our creations are as holy as we are, and we are the Sons of God Himself, as holy as He is. [9]Through our creations we extend our love, and thus increase the joy of the Holy Trinity. [10]You do not understand this, because you who are God's Own treasure do not regard yourself as valuable. [11]Given this belief, you cannot understand anything.

9. I share with God the knowledge of the value He puts upon you. [2]My devotion to you is of Him, being born of my knowledge of myself and Him. [3]We cannot be separated. [4]Whom God has joined cannot be separated, and God has joined all His Sons with Himself. [5]Can you be separated from your life and your being? [6]The journey to God is merely the reawakening of the knowledge of where you are always, and what you are forever. [7]It is a journey without distance to a goal that has never changed. [8]Truth can only be experienced. [9]It cannot be described and it cannot be explained. [10]I can make you aware of the conditions of truth, but the experience is of God. [11]Together we can meet its conditions, but truth will dawn upon you of itself.

10. What God has willed for you *is* yours. [2]He has given His Will to His treasure, whose treasure it is. [3]Your heart lies where your treasure is, as His does. [4]You who are beloved of God are wholly blessed. [5]Learn this of me, and free the holy will of all those who are as blessed as you are.

VII. The Body as a Means of Communication

VII. The Body as a Means of Communication

1. Attack is always physical. ²When attack in any form enters your mind you are equating yourself with a body, since this is the ego's interpretation of the body. ³You do not have to attack physically to accept this interpretation. ⁴You are accepting it simply by the belief that attack can get you something you want. ⁵If you did not believe this, the idea of attack would have no appeal for you. ⁶When you equate yourself with a body you will always experience depression. ⁷When a child of God thinks of himself in this way he is belittling himself, and seeing his brothers as similarly belittled. ⁸Since he can find himself only in them, he has cut himself off from salvation.

2. Remember that the Holy Spirit interprets the body only as a means of communication. ²Being the Communication Link between God and His separated Sons, the Holy Spirit interprets everything you have made in the light of what He is. ³The ego separates through the body. ⁴The Holy Spirit reaches through it to others. ⁵You do not perceive your brothers as the Holy Spirit does, because you do not regard bodies solely as a means of joining minds and uniting them with yours and mine. ⁶This interpretation of the body will change your mind entirely about its value. ⁷Of itself it has none.

3. If you use the body for attack, it is harmful to you. ²If you use it only to reach the minds of those who believe they are bodies, and teach them *through* the body that this is not so, you will understand the power of the mind that is in you. ³If you use the body for this and only for this, you cannot use it for attack. ⁴In the service of uniting it becomes a beautiful lesson in communion, which has value until communion *is*. ⁵This is God's way of making unlimited what you have limited. ⁶The Holy Spirit does not see the body as you do, because He knows the only reality of anything is the service it renders God on behalf of the function He gives it.

4. Communication ends separation. ²Attack promotes it. ³The body is beautiful or ugly, peaceful or savage, helpful or harmful, according to the use to which it is put. ⁴And in the body of another you will see the use to which you have put yours. ⁵If the body becomes a means you give to the Holy Spirit to use on behalf of union of the Sonship, you will not see anything physical except as what it is. ⁶Use it for truth and you will see it truly.

151

⁷Misuse it and you will misunderstand it, because you have already done so *by* misusing it. ⁸Interpret anything apart from the Holy Spirit and you will mistrust it. ⁹This will lead you to hatred and attack and loss of peace.

5. Yet all loss comes only from your own misunderstanding. ²Loss of any kind is impossible. ³But when you look upon a brother as a physical entity, his power and glory are "lost" to you and so are yours. ⁴You have attacked him, but you must have attacked yourself first. ⁵Do not see him this way for your own salvation, which must bring him his. ⁶Do not allow him to belittle himself in your mind, but give him freedom from his belief in littleness, and thus escape from yours. ⁷As part of you, he is holy. ⁸As part of me, you are. ⁹To communicate with part of God Himself is to reach beyond the Kingdom to its Creator, through His Voice which He has established as part of you.

6. Rejoice, then, that of yourself you can do nothing. ²You are not *of* yourself. ³He of Whom you are has willed your power and glory for you, with which you can perfectly accomplish His holy Will for you when you accept it for yourself. ⁴He has not withdrawn His gifts from you, but you believe you have withdrawn them from Him. ⁵Let no Son of God remain hidden for His Name's sake, because His Name is yours.

7. The Bible says, "The Word (or thought) was made flesh." ²Strictly speaking this is impossible, since it seems to involve the translation of one order of reality into another. ³Different orders of reality merely appear to exist, just as different orders of miracles do. ⁴Thought cannot be made into flesh except by belief, since thought is not physical. ⁵Yet thought is communication, for which the body can be used. ⁶This is the only natural use to which it can be put. ⁷To use the body unnaturally is to lose sight of the Holy Spirit's purpose, and thus to confuse the goal of His curriculum.

8. There is nothing so frustrating to a learner as a curriculum he cannot learn. ²His sense of adequacy suffers, and he must become depressed. ³Being faced with an impossible learning situation is the most depressing thing in the world. ⁴In fact, it is ultimately why the world itself is depressing. ⁵The Holy Spirit's curriculum is never depressing, because it is a curriculum of joy. ⁶Whenever the reaction to learning is depression, it is because the true goal of the curriculum has been lost sight of.

9. In this world, not even the body is perceived as whole. ²Its

purpose is seen as fragmented into many functions with little or no relationship to each other, so that it appears to be ruled by chaos. ³Guided by the ego, it *is*. ⁴Guided by the Holy Spirit, it is not. ⁵It becomes a means by which the part of the mind you tried to separate *from* spirit can reach beyond its distortions and return *to* spirit. ⁶The ego's temple thus becomes the temple of the Holy Spirit, where devotion to Him replaces devotion to the ego. ⁷In this sense the body does become a temple to God; His Voice abides in it by directing the use to which it is put.

10. Healing is the result of using the body solely for communication. ²Since this is natural it heals by making whole, which is also natural. ³All mind is whole, and the belief that part of it is physical, or not mind, is a fragmented or sick interpretation. ⁴Mind cannot be made physical, but it can be made manifest *through* the physical if it uses the body to go beyond itself. ⁵By reaching out, the mind extends itself. ⁶It does not stop at the body, for if it does it is blocked in its purpose. ⁷A mind that has been blocked has allowed itself to be vulnerable to attack, because it has turned against itself.

11. The removal of blocks, then, is the only way to guarantee help and healing. ²Help and healing are the normal expressions of a mind that is working through the body, but not *in* it. ³If the mind believes the body is its goal it will distort its perception of the body, and by blocking its own extension beyond it, will induce illness by fostering separation. ⁴Perceiving the body as a separate entity cannot but foster illness, because it is not true. ⁵A medium of communication loses its usefulness if it is used for anything else. ⁶To use a medium of communication as a medium of attack is an obvious confusion in purpose.

12. To communicate is to join and to attack is to separate. ²How can you do both simultaneously with the same thing and not suffer? ³Perception of the body can be unified only by one purpose. ⁴This releases the mind from the temptation to see the body in many lights, and gives it over entirely to the One Light in which it can be really understood. ⁵To confuse a learning device with a curriculum goal is a fundamental confusion that blocks the understanding of both. ⁶Learning must lead beyond the body to the re-establishment of the power of the mind in it. ⁷This can be accomplished only if the mind extends to other minds, and does not arrest itself in its extension. ⁸This arrest is the cause of all illness, because only extension is the mind's function.

13.   The opposite of joy is depression. [2]When your learning promotes depression instead of joy, you cannot be listening to God's joyous Teacher and learning His lessons. [3]To see a body as anything except a means of communication is to limit your mind and to hurt yourself. [4]Health is therefore nothing more than united purpose. [5]If the body is brought under the purpose of the mind, it becomes whole because the mind's purpose is one. [6]Attack can only be an assumed purpose of the body, because apart from the mind the body has no purpose at all.

14.   You are not limited by the body, and thought cannot be made flesh. [2]Yet mind can be manifested through the body if it goes beyond it and does not interpret it as limitation. [3]Whenever you see another as limited to or by the body, you are imposing this limit on yourself. [4]Are you willing to accept this, when your whole purpose for learning should be to escape from limitations? [5]To conceive of the body as a means of attack and to believe that joy could possibly result, is a clear-cut indication of a poor learner. [6]He has accepted a learning goal in obvious contradiction to the unified purpose of the curriculum, and one that is interfering with his ability to accept its purpose as his own.

15.   Joy is unified purpose, and unified purpose is only God's. [2]When yours is unified it is His. [3]Believe you can interfere with His purpose, and you need salvation. [4]You have condemned yourself, but condemnation is not of God. [5]Therefore it is not true. [6]No more are any of its seeming results. [7]When you see a brother as a body, you are condemning him because you have condemned yourself. [8]Yet if all condemnation is unreal, and it must be unreal since it is a form of attack, then it can *have* no results.

16.   Do not allow yourself to suffer from imagined results of what is not true. [2]Free your mind from the belief that this is possible. [3]In its complete impossibility lies your only hope for release. [4]But what other hope would you want? [5]Freedom from illusions lies only in not believing them. [6]There is no attack, but there *is* unlimited communication and therefore unlimited power and wholeness. [7]The power of wholeness is extension. [8]Do not arrest your thought in this world, and you will open your mind to creation in God.

VIII. The Body as Means or End

1. Attitudes toward the body are attitudes toward attack. [2]The ego's definitions of anything are childish, and are always based on what it believes the thing is *for*. [3]This is because it is incapable of true generalizations, and equates what it sees with the function it ascribes to it. [4]It does not equate it with what it *is*. [5]To the ego the body is to attack *with*. [6]Equating you with the body, it teaches that *you* are to attack with. [7]The body, then, is not the source of its own health. [8]The body's condition lies solely in your interpretation of its function. [9]Functions are part of being since they arise from it, but the relationship is not reciprocal. [10]The whole does define the part, but the part does not define the whole. [11]Yet to know in part is to know entirely because of the fundamental difference between knowledge and perception. [12]In perception the whole is built up of parts that can separate and reassemble in different constellations. [13]But knowledge never changes, so its constellation is permanent. [14]The idea of part-whole relationships has meaning only at the level of perception, where change is possible. [15]Otherwise, there is no difference between the part and whole.

2. The body exists in a world that seems to contain two voices fighting for its possession. [2]In this perceived constellation the body is seen as capable of shifting its allegiance from one to the other, making the concepts of both health and sickness meaningful. [3]The ego makes a fundamental confusion between means and end as it always does. [4]Regarding the body as an end, the ego has no real use for it because it is *not* an end. [5]You must have noticed an outstanding characteristic of every end that the ego has accepted as its own. [6]When you have achieved it, *it has not satisfied you*. [7]This is why the ego is forced to shift ceaselessly from one goal to another, so that you will continue to hope it can yet offer you something.

3. It has been particularly difficult to overcome the ego's belief in the body as an end, because it is synonymous with the belief in attack as an end. [2]The ego has a profound investment in sickness. [3]If you are sick, how can you object to the ego's firm belief that you are not invulnerable? [4]This is an appealing argument from the ego's point of view, because it obscures the obvious attack that underlies the sickness. [5]If you recognized this and also decided against attack, you could not give this false witness

to the ego's stand.

4. It is hard to perceive sickness as a false witness, because you do not realize that it is entirely out of keeping with what you want. ²This witness, then, appears to be innocent and trustworthy because you have not seriously cross-examined him. ³If you had, you would not consider sickness such a strong witness on behalf of the ego's views. ⁴A more honest statement would be that those who want the ego are predisposed to defend it. ⁵Therefore, their choice of witnesses should be suspect from the beginning. ⁶The ego does not call upon witnesses who would disagree with its case, nor does the Holy Spirit. ⁷I have said that judgment is the function of the Holy Spirit, and one He is perfectly equipped to fulfill. ⁸The ego as a judge gives anything but an impartial judgment. ⁹When the ego calls on a witness, it has already made the witness an ally.

5. It is still true that the body has no function of itself, because it is not an end. ²The ego, however, establishes it as an end because, as such, its true function is obscured. ³This is the purpose of everything the ego does. ⁴Its sole aim is to lose sight of the function of everything. ⁵A sick body does not make any sense. ⁶It could not make sense because sickness is not what the body is for. ⁷Sickness is meaningful only if the two basic premises on which the ego's interpretation of the body rests are true; that the body is for attack, and that you are a body. ⁸Without these premises sickness is inconceivable.

6. Sickness is a way of demonstrating that you can be hurt. ²It is a witness to your frailty, your vulnerability, and your extreme need to depend on external guidance. ³The ego uses this as its best argument for your need for *its* guidance. ⁴It dictates endless prescriptions for avoiding catastrophic outcomes. ⁵The Holy Spirit, perfectly aware of the same situation, does not bother to analyze it at all. ⁶If data are meaningless there is no point in analyzing them. ⁷The function of truth is to collect information that is true. ⁸*Any* way you handle error results in nothing. ⁹The more complicated the results become the harder it may be to recognize their nothingness, but it is not necessary to examine all possible outcomes to which premises give rise in order to judge them truly.

7. A learning device is not a teacher. ²It cannot tell you how you feel. ³You do not know how you feel because you have accepted the ego's confusion, and you therefore believe that a learning

device *can* tell you how you feel. ⁴Sickness is merely another example of your insistence on asking guidance of a teacher who does not know the answer. ⁵The ego is incapable of knowing how you feel. ⁶When I said that the ego does not know anything, I said the one thing about the ego that is wholly true. ⁷But there is a corollary; if only knowledge has being and the ego has no knowledge, then the ego has no being.

8. You might well ask how the voice of something that does not exist can be so insistent. ²Have you thought about the distorting power of something you want, even if it is not real? ³There are many instances of how what you want distorts perception. ⁴No one can doubt the ego's skill in building up false cases. ⁵Nor can anyone doubt your willingness to listen until you choose not to accept anything except truth. ⁶When you lay the ego aside, it will be gone. ⁷The Holy Spirit's Voice is as loud as your willingness to listen. ⁸It cannot be louder without violating your freedom of choice, which the Holy Spirit seeks to restore, never to undermine.

9. The Holy Spirit teaches you to use your body only to reach your brothers, so He can teach His message through you. ²This will heal them and therefore heal you. ³Everything used in accordance with its function as the Holy Spirit sees it cannot be sick. ⁴Everything used otherwise is. ⁵Do not allow the body to be a mirror of a split mind. ⁶Do not let it be an image of your own perception of littleness. ⁷Do not let it reflect your decision to attack. ⁸Health is seen as the natural state of everything when interpretation is left to the Holy Spirit, Who perceives no attack on anything. ⁹Health is the result of relinquishing all attempts to use the body lovelessly. ¹⁰Health is the beginning of the proper perspective on life under the guidance of the one Teacher Who knows what life is, being the Voice for Life Itself.

IX. Healing as Corrected Perception

1. I said before that the Holy Spirit is the Answer. ²He is the Answer to everything, because He knows what the answer to everything is. ³The ego does not know what a real question is, although it asks an endless number. ⁴Yet you can learn this as you learn to question the value of the ego, and thus establish your ability to evaluate its questions. ⁵When the ego tempts you to

sickness do not ask the Holy Spirit to heal the body, for this would merely be to accept the ego's belief that the body is the proper aim of healing. ⁶Ask, rather, that the Holy Spirit teach you the right *perception* of the body, for perception alone can be distorted. ⁷Only perception can be sick, because only perception can be wrong.

2. Wrong perception is the wish that things be as they are not. ²The reality of everything is totally harmless, because total harmlessness is the condition of its reality. ³It is also the condition of your awareness of its reality. ⁴You do not have to seek reality. ⁵It will seek you and find you when you meet its conditions. ⁶Its conditions are part of what it is. ⁷And this part only is up to you. ⁸The rest is of itself. ⁹You need do so little because your little part is so powerful that it will bring the whole to you. ¹⁰Accept, then, your little part, and let the whole be yours.

3. Wholeness heals because it is of the mind. ²All forms of sickness, even unto death, are physical expressions of the fear of awakening. ³They are attempts to reinforce sleeping out of fear of waking. ⁴This is a pathetic way of trying not to see by rendering the faculties for seeing ineffectual. ⁵"Rest in peace" is a blessing for the living, not the dead, because rest comes from waking, not from sleeping. ⁶Sleep is withdrawing; waking is joining. ⁷Dreams are illusions of joining, because they reflect the ego's distorted notions about what joining is. ⁸Yet the Holy Spirit, too, has use for sleep, and can use dreams on behalf of waking if you will let Him.

4. How you wake is the sign of how you have used sleep. ²To whom did you give it? ³Under which teacher did you place it? ⁴Whenever you wake dispiritedly, it was not given to the Holy Spirit. ⁵Only when you awaken joyously have you utilized sleep according to His purpose. ⁶You can indeed be "drugged" by sleep, if you have misused it on behalf of sickness. ⁷Sleep is no more a form of death than death is a form of unconsciousness. ⁸Complete unconsciousness is impossible. ⁹You can rest in peace only because you are awake.

5. Healing is release from the fear of waking and the substitution of the decision to wake. ²The decision to wake is the reflection of the will to love, since all healing involves replacing fear with love. ³The Holy Spirit cannot distinguish among degrees of error, for if He taught that one form of sickness is more serious than another, He would be teaching that one error can be more real

than another. ⁴His function is to distinguish only between the false and the true, replacing the false with the true.

6. The ego, which always wants to weaken the mind, tries to separate it from the body in an attempt to destroy it. ²Yet the ego actually believes that it is protecting it. ³This is because the ego believes that mind is dangerous, and that to make mindless is to heal. ⁴But to make mindless is impossible, since it would mean to make nothing out of what God created. ⁵The ego despises weakness, even though it makes every effort to induce it. ⁶The ego wants only what it hates. ⁷To the ego this is perfectly sensible. ⁸Believing in the power of attack, the ego wants attack.

7. The Bible enjoins you to be perfect, to heal all errors, to take no thought of the body as separate and to accomplish all things in my name. ²This is not my name alone, for ours is a shared identification. ³The Name of God's Son is one, and you are enjoined to do the works of love because we share this Oneness. ⁴Our minds are whole because they are one. ⁵If you are sick you are withdrawing from me. ⁶Yet you cannot withdraw from me alone. ⁷You can only withdraw from yourself *and* me.

8. You have surely begun to realize that this is a very practical course, and one that means exactly what it says. ²I would not ask you to do things you cannot do, and it is impossible that I could do things you cannot do. ³Given this, and given this quite literally, nothing can prevent you from doing exactly what I ask, and everything argues *for* your doing it. ⁴I give you no limits because God lays none upon you. ⁵When you limit yourself we are not of one mind, and that is sickness. ⁶Yet sickness is not of the body, but of the mind. ⁷All forms of sickness are signs that the mind is split, and does not accept a unified purpose.

9. The unification of purpose, then, is the Holy Spirit's only way of healing. ²This is because it is the only level at which healing means anything. ³The re-establishing of meaning in a chaotic thought system *is* the way to heal it. ⁴Your task is only to meet the conditions for meaning, since meaning itself is of God. ⁵Yet your return to meaning is essential to His, because your meaning is part of His. ⁶Your healing, then, is part of His health, since it is part of His Wholeness. ⁷He cannot lose this, but you *can* not know it. ⁸Yet it is still His Will for you, and His Will must stand forever and in all things.

Chapter 9

THE ACCEPTANCE OF THE ATONEMENT

I. The Acceptance of Reality

1. Fear of the Will of God is one of the strangest beliefs the human mind has ever made. ²It could not possibly have occurred unless the mind were already profoundly split, making it possible for it to be afraid of what it really is. ³Reality cannot "threaten" anything except illusions, since reality can only uphold truth. ⁴The very fact that the Will of God, which is what you are, is perceived as fearful, demonstrates that you *are* afraid of what you are. ⁵It is not, then, the Will of God of which you are afraid, but yours.

2. Your will is not the ego's, and that is why the ego is against you. ²What seems to be the fear of God is really the fear of your own reality. ³It is impossible to learn anything consistently in a state of panic. ⁴If the purpose of this course is to help you remember what you are, and if you believe that what you are is fearful, then it must follow that you will not learn this course. ⁵Yet the reason for the course is that you do not know what you are.

3. If you do not know what your reality is, why would you be so sure that it is fearful? ²The association of truth and fear, which would be highly artificial at most, is particularly inappropriate in the minds of those who do not know what truth is. ³All this could mean is that you are arbitrarily associating something beyond your awareness with something you do not want. ⁴It is evident, then, that you are judging something of which you are totally unaware. ⁵You have set up this strange situation so that it is impossible to escape from it without a Guide Who *does* know what your reality is. ⁶The purpose of this Guide is merely to remind you of what you want. ⁷He is not attempting to force an alien will upon you. ⁸He is merely making every possible effort, within the limits you impose on Him, to re-establish your own will in your awareness.

4. You have imprisoned your will beyond your own awareness, where it remains, but cannot help you. ²When I said that the Holy Spirit's function is to sort out the true from the false in your mind, I meant that He has the power to look into what you have

hidden and recognize the Will of God there. ³His recognition of this Will can make it real to you because He is in your mind, and therefore He is your reality. ⁴If, then, His perception of your mind brings its reality to you, He *is* helping you to remember what you are. ⁵The only source of fear in this process is what you think you will lose. ⁶Yet it is only what the Holy Spirit sees that you can possibly have.

5.   I have emphasized many times that the Holy Spirit will never call upon you to sacrifice anything. ²But if you ask the sacrifice of reality of yourself, the Holy Spirit must remind you that this is not God's Will because it is not yours. ³There is no difference between your will and God's. ⁴If you did not have a split mind, you would recognize that willing is salvation because it is communication.

6.   It is impossible to communicate in alien tongues. ²You and your Creator can communicate through creation, because that, and only that is Your joint Will. ³A divided mind cannot communicate, because it speaks for different things to the same mind. ⁴This loses the ability to communicate simply because confused communication does not mean anything. ⁵A message cannot be communicated unless it makes sense. ⁶How sensible can your messages be, when you ask for what you do not want? ⁷Yet as long as you are afraid of your will, that is precisely what you are asking for.

7.   You may insist that the Holy Spirit does not answer you, but it might be wiser to consider the kind of questioner you are. ²You do not ask only for what you want. ³This is because you are afraid you might receive it, and you would. ⁴That is why you persist in asking the teacher who could not possibly give you what you want. ⁵Of him you can never learn what it is, and this gives you the illusion of safety. ⁶Yet you cannot be safe *from* truth, but only *in* truth. ⁷Reality is the only safety. ⁸Your will is your salvation because it is the same as God's. ⁹The separation is nothing more than the belief that it is different.

8.   No right mind can believe that its will is stronger than God's. ²If, then, a mind believes that its will is different from His, it can only decide either that there is no God or that God's Will is fearful. ³The former accounts for the atheist and the latter for the martyr, who believes that God demands sacrifices. ⁴Either of these insane decisions will induce panic, because the atheist believes he is alone, and the martyr believes that God is crucifying him. ⁵Yet no

one really wants either abandonment or retaliation, even though many may seek both. ⁶Can you ask the Holy Spirit for "gifts" such as these, and actually expect to receive them? ⁷He cannot give you something you do not want. ⁸When you ask the Universal Giver for what you do not want, you are asking for what cannot be given because it was never created. ⁹It was never created, because it was never your will for *you*.

9.   Ultimately everyone must remember the Will of God, because ultimately everyone must recognize himself. ²This recognition is the recognition that his will and God's are one. ³In the presence of truth, there are no unbelievers and no sacrifices. ⁴In the security of reality, fear is totally meaningless. ⁵To deny what is can only *seem* to be fearful. ⁶Fear cannot be real without a cause, and God is the only Cause. ⁷God is Love and you do want Him. ⁸This *is* your will. ⁹Ask for this and you will be answered, because you will be asking only for what belongs to you.

10.   When you ask the Holy Spirit for what would hurt you He cannot answer because nothing can hurt you, and so you are asking for nothing. ²Any wish that stems from the ego is a wish for nothing, and to ask for it is not a request. ³It is merely a denial in the form of a request. ⁴The Holy Spirit is not concerned with form, being aware only of meaning. ⁵The ego cannot ask the Holy Spirit for anything, because there is complete communication failure between them. ⁶Yet *you* can ask for everything of the Holy Spirit, because your requests to Him are real, being of your right mind. ⁷Would the Holy Spirit deny the Will of God? ⁸And could He fail to recognize it in His Son?

11.   You do not recognize the enormous waste of energy you expend in denying truth. ²What would you say of someone who persists in attempting the impossible, believing that to achieve it is to succeed? ³The belief that you must have the impossible in order to be happy is totally at variance with the principle of creation. ⁴God could not will that happiness depended on what you could never have. ⁵The fact that God is Love does not require belief, but it does require acceptance. ⁶It is indeed possible for you to deny facts, although it is impossible for you to change them. ⁷If you hold your hands over your eyes, you will not see because you are interfering with the laws of seeing. ⁸If you deny love, you will not know it because your cooperation is the law of its being. ⁹You cannot change laws you did not make, and the laws of happiness were created for you, not by you.

12. Any attempt to deny what *is* must be fearful, and if the attempt is strong it will induce panic. ²Willing against reality, though impossible, can be made into a very persistent goal even though you do not want it. ³But consider the result of this strange decision. ⁴You are devoting your mind to what you do not want. ⁵How real can this devotion be? ⁶If you do not want it, it was never created. ⁷If it were never created, it is nothing. ⁸Can you really devote yourself to nothing?

13. God in His devotion to you created you devoted to everything, and gave you what you are devoted *to*. ²Otherwise you would not have been created perfect. ³Reality is everything, and you have everything because you are real. ⁴You cannot make the unreal because the absence of reality is fearful, and fear cannot be created. ⁵As long as you believe that fear is possible, you will not create. ⁶Opposing orders of reality make reality meaningless, and reality *is* meaning.

14. Remember, then, that God's Will is already possible, and nothing else will ever be. ²This is the simple acceptance of reality, because only that is real. ³You cannot distort reality and know what it is. ⁴And if you do distort reality you will experience anxiety, depression and ultimately panic, because you are trying to make yourself unreal. ⁵When you feel these things, do not try to look beyond yourself for truth, for truth can only be within you. ⁶Say, therefore:

> ⁷*Christ is in me, and where He is God must be,*
> *for Christ is part of Him.*

II. The Answer to Prayer

1. Everyone who ever tried to use prayer to ask for something has experienced what appears to be failure. ²This is not only true in connection with specific things that might be harmful, but also in connection with requests that are strictly in line with this course. ³The latter in particular might be incorrectly interpreted as "proof" that the course does not mean what it says. ⁴You must remember, however, that the course states, and repeatedly, that its purpose is the escape from fear.

2. Let us suppose, then, that what you ask of the Holy Spirit is what you really want, but you are still afraid of it. ²Should this be

the case, your attainment of it would no longer *be* what you want. ³This is why certain specific forms of healing are not achieved, even when the state of healing is. ⁴An individual may ask for physical healing because he is fearful of bodily harm. ⁵At the same time, if he were healed physically, the threat to his thought system might be considerably more fearful to him than its physical expression. ⁶In this case he is not really asking for release from fear, but for the removal of a symptom that he himself selected. ⁷This request is, therefore, not for healing at all.

3.   The Bible emphasizes that all prayer is answered, and this is indeed true. ²The very fact that the Holy Spirit has been asked for anything will ensure a response. ³Yet it is equally certain that no response given by Him will ever be one that would increase fear. ⁴It is possible that His answer will not be heard. ⁵It is impossible, however, that it will be lost. ⁶There are many answers you have already received but have not yet heard. ⁷I assure you that they are waiting for you.

4.   If you would know your prayers are answered, never doubt a Son of God. ²Do not question him and do not confound him, for your faith in him is your faith in yourself. ³If you would know God and His Answer, believe in me whose faith in you cannot be shaken. ⁴Can you ask of the Holy Spirit truly, and doubt your brother? ⁵Believe his words are true because of the truth that is in him. ⁶You will unite with the truth in him, and his words will *be* true. ⁷As you hear him you will hear me. ⁸Listening to truth is the only way you can hear it now, and finally know it.

5.   The message your brother gives you is up to you. ²What does he say to you? ³What would you have him say? ⁴Your decision about him determines the message you receive. ⁵Remember that the Holy Spirit is in him, and His Voice speaks to you through him. ⁶What can so holy a brother tell you except truth? ⁷But are you listening to it? ⁸Your brother may not know who he is, but there is a light in his mind that does know. ⁹This light can shine into yours, giving truth to his words and making you able to hear them. ¹⁰His words are the Holy Spirit's answer to you. ¹¹Is your faith in him strong enough to let you hear?

6.   You can no more pray for yourself alone than you can find joy for yourself alone. ²Prayer is the restatement of inclusion, directed by the Holy Spirit under the laws of God. ³Salvation is of your brother. ⁴The Holy Spirit extends from your mind to his, and answers *you*. ⁵You cannot hear the Voice for God in yourself

alone, because you are not alone. [6]And His answer is only for what you are. [7]You will not know the trust I have in you unless you extend it. [8]You will not trust the guidance of the Holy Spirit, or believe that it is for you unless you hear it in others. [9]It must be for your brother *because* it is for you. [10]Would God have created a Voice for you alone? [11]Could you hear His answer except as He answers all of God's Sons? [12]Hear of your brother what you would have me hear of you, for you would not want me to be deceived.

7. I love you for the truth in you, as God does. [2]Your deceptions may deceive you, but they cannot deceive me. [3]Knowing what you are, I cannot doubt you. [4]I hear only the Holy Spirit in you, Who speaks to me through you. [5]If you would hear me, hear my brothers in whom God's Voice speaks. [6]The answer to all prayers lies in them. [7]You will be answered as you hear the answer in everyone. [8]Do not listen to anything else or you will not hear truly.

8. Believe in your brothers because I believe in you, and you will learn that my belief in you is justified. [2]Believe in me *by* believing in them, for the sake of what God gave them. [3]They will answer you if you learn to ask only truth of them. [4]Do not ask for blessings without blessing them, for only in this way can you learn how blessed you are. [5]By following this way you are seeking the truth in you. [6]This is not going beyond yourself but toward yourself. [7]Hear only God's Answer in His Sons, and you are answered.

9. To disbelieve is to side against, or to attack. [2]To believe is to accept, and to side with. [3]To believe is not to be credulous, but to accept and appreciate. [4]What you do not believe you do not appreciate, and you cannot be grateful for what you do not value. [5]There is a price you will pay for judgment, because judgment is the setting of a price. [6]And as you set it you will pay it.

10. If paying is equated with getting, you will set the price low but demand a high return. [2]You will have forgotten, however, that to price is to value, so that your return is in proportion to your judgment of worth. [3]If paying is associated with giving it cannot be perceived as loss, and the reciprocal relationship of giving and receiving will be recognized. [4]The price will then be set high, because of the value of the return. [5]The price for getting is to lose sight of value, making it inevitable that you will not value what you receive. [6]Valuing it little, you will not appreciate it and you will not want it.

11. Never forget, then, that you set the value on what you receive,

and price it by what you give. [2]To believe that it is possible to get much for little is to believe that you can bargain with God. [3]God's laws are always fair and perfectly consistent. [4]By giving you receive. [5]But to receive is to accept, not to get. [6]It is impossible not to have, but it is possible not to know you have. [7]The recognition of having is the willingness for giving, and only by this willingness can you recognize what you have. [8]What you give is therefore the value you put on what you have, being the exact measure of the value you put upon it. [9]And this, in turn, is the measure of how much you want it.

12.   You can ask of the Holy Spirit, then, only by giving to Him, and you can give to Him only where you recognize Him. [2]If you recognize Him in everyone, consider how much you will be asking of Him, and how much you will receive. [3]He will deny you nothing because you have denied Him nothing, and so you can share everything. [4]This is the way, and the only way to have His answer, because His answer is all you can ask for and want. [5]Say, then, to everyone:

> [6]*Because I will to know myself, I see you as God's Son and my brother.*

III. The Correction of Error

1.   The alertness of the ego to the errors of other egos is not the kind of vigilance the Holy Spirit would have you maintain. [2]Egos are critical in terms of the kind of "sense" they stand for. [3]They understand this kind of sense, because it is sensible to them. [4]To the Holy Spirit it makes no sense at all.

2.   To the ego it is kind and right and good to point out errors and "correct" them. [2]This makes perfect sense to the ego, which is unaware of what errors are and what correction is. [3]Errors are of the ego, and correction of errors lies in the relinquishment of the ego. [4]When you correct a brother, you are telling him that he is wrong. [5]He may be making no sense at the time, and it is certain that, if he is speaking from the ego, he will not be making sense. [6]But your task is still to tell him he is right. [7]You do not tell him this verbally, if he is speaking foolishly. [8]He needs correction at another level, because his error is at another level. [9]He is still right, because he is a Son of God. [10]His ego is always wrong, no

matter what it says or does.

3. If you point out the errors of your brother's ego you must be seeing through yours, because the Holy Spirit does not perceive his errors. ²This *must* be true, since there is no communication between the ego and the Holy Spirit. ³The ego makes no sense, and the Holy Spirit does not attempt to understand anything that arises from it. ⁴Since He does not understand it, He does not judge it, knowing that nothing the ego makes means anything.

4. When you react at all to errors, you are not listening to the Holy Spirit. ²He has merely disregarded them, and if you attend to them you are not hearing Him. ³If you do not hear Him, you are listening to your ego and making as little sense as the brother whose errors you perceive. ⁴This cannot be correction. ⁵Yet it is more than merely a lack of correction for him. ⁶It is the giving up of correction in yourself.

5. When a brother behaves insanely, you can heal him only by perceiving the sanity in him. ²If you perceive his errors and accept them, you are accepting yours. ³If you want to give yours over to the Holy Spirit, you must do this with his. ⁴Unless this becomes the one way in which you handle all errors, you cannot understand how all errors are undone. ⁵How is this different from telling you that what you teach you learn? ⁶Your brother is as right as you are, and if you think he is wrong you are condemning yourself.

6. *You* cannot correct yourself. ²Is it possible, then, for you to correct another? ³Yet you can see him truly, because it is possible for you to see yourself truly. ⁴It is not up to you to change your brother, but merely to accept him as he is. ⁵His errors do not come from the truth that is in him, and only this truth is yours. ⁶His errors cannot change this, and can have no effect at all on the truth in you. ⁷To perceive errors in anyone, and to react to them as if they were real, is to make them real to you. ⁸You will not escape paying the price for this, not because you are being punished for it, but because you are following the wrong guide and will therefore lose your way.

7. Your brother's errors are not of him, any more than yours are of you. ²Accept his errors as real, and you have attacked yourself. ³If you would find your way and keep it, see only truth beside you for you walk together. ⁴The Holy Spirit in you forgives all things in you and in your brother. ⁵His errors are forgiven with yours. ⁶Atonement is no more separate than love. ⁷Atonement

cannot be separate because it comes from love. [8]Any attempt you make to correct a brother means that you believe correction by you is possible, and this can only be the arrogance of the ego. [9]Correction is of God, Who does not know of arrogance.

8. The Holy Spirit forgives everything because God created everything. [2]Do not undertake His function, or you will forget yours. [3]Accept only the function of healing in time, because that is what time is for. [4]God gave you the function to create in eternity. [5]You do not need to learn that, but you do need to learn to want it. [6]For that all learning was made. [7]This is the Holy Spirit's use of an ability that you do not need, but that you made. [8]Give it to Him! [9]You do not understand how to use it. [10]He will teach you how to see yourself without condemnation, by learning how to look on everything without it. [11]Condemnation will then not be real to you, and all your errors will be forgiven.

IV. The Holy Spirit's Plan of Forgiveness

1. Atonement is for all, because it is the way to undo the belief that anything is for you alone. [2]To forgive is to overlook. [3]Look, then, beyond error and do not let your perception rest upon it, for you will believe what your perception holds. [4]Accept as true only what your brother is, if you would know yourself. [5]Perceive what he is not and you cannot know what you are, because you see him falsely. [6]Remember always that your Identity is shared, and that Its sharing is Its reality.

2. You have a part to play in the Atonement, but the plan of the Atonement is beyond you. [2]You do not understand how to overlook errors, or you would not make them. [3]It would merely be further error to believe either that you do not make them, or that you can correct them without a Guide to correction. [4]And if you do not follow this Guide, your errors will not be corrected. [5]The plan is not yours because of your limited ideas about what you are. [6]This sense of limitation is where all errors arise. [7]The way to undo them, therefore, is not *of* you but *for* you.

3. The Atonement is a lesson in sharing, which is given you because *you have forgotten how to do it*. [2]The Holy Spirit merely reminds you of the natural use of your abilities. [3]By reinterpreting the ability to attack into the ability to share, He translates what you have made into what God created. [4]If you would accomplish

this through Him you cannot look on your abilities through the eyes of the ego, or you will judge them as *it* does. [5]All their harmfulness lies in the ego's judgment. [6]All their helpfulness lies in the judgment of the Holy Spirit.

4. The ego, too, has a plan of forgiveness because you are asking for one, though not of the right teacher. [2]The ego's plan, of course, makes no sense and will not work. [3]By following its plan you will merely place yourself in an impossible situation, to which the ego always leads you. [4]The ego's plan is to have you see error clearly first, and then overlook it. [5]Yet how can you overlook what you have made real? [6]By seeing it clearly, you have made it real and *cannot* overlook it. [7]This is where the ego is forced to appeal to "mysteries," insisting that you must accept the meaningless to save yourself. [8]Many have tried to do this in my name, forgetting that my words make perfect sense because they come from God. [9]They are as sensible now as they ever were, because they speak of ideas that are eternal.

5. Forgiveness that is learned of me does not use fear to undo fear. [2]Nor does it make real the unreal and then destroy it. [3]Forgiveness through the Holy Spirit lies simply in looking beyond error from the beginning, and thus keeping it unreal for you. [4]Do not let any belief in its realness enter your mind, or you will also believe that you must undo what you have made in order to be forgiven. [5]What has no effect does not exist, and to the Holy Spirit the effects of error are nonexistent. [6]By steadily and consistently cancelling out all its effects, everywhere and in all respects, He teaches that the ego does not exist and proves it.

6. Follow the Holy Spirit's teaching in forgiveness, then, because forgiveness is His function and He knows how to fulfill it perfectly. [2]That is what I meant when I said that miracles are natural, and when they do not occur something has gone wrong. [3]Miracles are merely the sign of your willingness to follow the Holy Spirit's plan of salvation, recognizing that you do not understand what it is. [4]His work is not your function, and unless you accept this you cannot learn what your function is.

7. The confusion of functions is so typical of the ego that you should be quite familiar with it by now. [2]The ego believes that all functions belong to it, even though it has no idea what they are. [3]This is more than mere confusion. [4]It is a particularly dangerous combination of grandiosity and confusion that makes the ego likely to attack anyone and anything for no reason at all. [5]This is

exactly what the ego does. ⁶It is unpredictable in its responses, because it has no idea of what it perceives.

8. If you have no idea what is happening, how appropriately can you expect to react? ²You might ask yourself, regardless of how you may account for the reaction, whether its unpredictability places the ego in a sound position as your guide. ³Let me repeat that the ego's qualifications as a guide are singularly unfortunate, and that it is a remarkably poor choice as a teacher of salvation. ⁴Anyone who elects a totally insane guide must be totally insane himself. ⁵Nor is it true that you do not realize the guide is insane. ⁶You realize it because I realize it, and you have judged it by the same standard I have.

9. The ego literally lives on borrowed time, and its days are numbered. ²Do not fear the Last Judgment, but welcome it and do not wait, for the ego's time is "borrowed" from your eternity. ³This is the Second Coming that was made for you as the First was created. ⁴The Second Coming is merely the return of sense. ⁵Can this possibly be fearful?

10. What can be fearful but fantasy, and who turns to fantasy unless he despairs of finding satisfaction in reality? ²Yet it is certain that you will never find satisfaction in fantasy, so that your only hope is to change your mind about reality. ³Only if the decision that reality is fearful is wrong can God be right. ⁴And I assure you that God *is* right. ⁵Be glad, then, that you have been wrong, but this was only because you did not know who you were. ⁶Had you known, you could no more have been wrong than God can.

11. The impossible can happen only in fantasy. ²When you search for reality in fantasies you will not find it. ³The symbols of fantasy are of the ego, and of these you will find many. ⁴But do not look for meaning in them. ⁵They have no more meaning than the fantasies into which they are woven. ⁶Fairy tales can be pleasant or fearful, but no one calls them true. ⁷Children may believe them, and so, for a while, the tales are true for them. ⁸Yet when reality dawns, the fantasies are gone. ⁹Reality has not gone in the meanwhile. ¹⁰The Second Coming is the awareness of reality, not its return.

12. Behold, my child, reality is here. ²It belongs to you and me and God, and is perfectly satisfying to all of Us. ³Only this awareness heals, because it is the awareness of truth.

V. The Unhealed Healer

1. The ego's plan for forgiveness is far more widely used than God's. [2]This is because it is undertaken by unhealed healers, and is therefore of the ego. [3]Let us consider the unhealed healer more carefully now. [4]By definition, he is trying to give what he has not received. [5]If an unhealed healer is a theologian, for example, he may begin with the premise, "I am a miserable sinner, and so are you." [6]If he is a psychotherapist, he is more likely to start with the equally incredible belief that attack is real for both himself and the patient, but that it does not matter for either of them.

2. I have repeatedly said that beliefs of the ego cannot be shared, and this is why they are unreal. [2]How, then, can "uncovering" them make them real? [3]Every healer who searches fantasies for truth must be unhealed, because he does not know where to look for truth, and therefore does not have the answer to the problem of healing.

3. There is an advantage to bringing nightmares into awareness, but only to teach that they are not real, and that anything they contain is meaningless. [2]The unhealed healer cannot do this because he does not believe it. [3]All unhealed healers follow the ego's plan for forgiveness in one form or another. [4]If they are theologians they are likely to condemn themselves, teach condemnation and advocate a fearful solution. [5]Projecting condemnation onto God, they make Him appear retaliative, and fear His retribution. [6]What they have done is merely to identify with the ego, and by perceiving what *it* does, condemn themselves because of this confusion. [7]It is understandable that there have been revolts against this concept, but to revolt against it is still to believe in it.

4. Some newer forms of the ego's plan are as unhelpful as the older ones, because form does not matter and the content has not changed. [2]In one of the newer forms, for example, a psychotherapist may interpret the ego's symbols in a nightmare, and then use them to prove that the nightmare is real. [3]Having made it real, he then attempts to dispel its effects by depreciating the importance of the dreamer. [4]This would be a healing approach if the dreamer were also identified as unreal. [5]Yet if the dreamer is equated with the mind, the mind's corrective power through the Holy Spirit is denied. [6]This is a contradiction even in the ego's terms, and one which it usually notes even in its confusion.

5. If the way to counteract fear is to reduce the importance of the mind, how can this build ego strength? [2]Such evident inconsistencies account for why no one has really explained what happens in psychotherapy. [3]Nothing really does. [4]Nothing real has happened to the unhealed healer, and he must learn from his own teaching. [5]His ego will always seek to get something from the situation. [6]The unhealed healer therefore does not know how to give, and consequently cannot share. [7]He cannot correct because he is not working correctively. [8]He believes that it is up to him to teach the patient what is real, although he does not know it himself.

6. What, then, should happen? [2]When God said, "Let there be light," there *was* light. [3]Can you find light by analyzing darkness, as the psychotherapist does, or like the theologian, by acknowledging darkness in yourself and looking for a distant light to remove it, while emphasizing the distance? [4]Healing is not mysterious. [5]Nothing will change unless it is understood, since light *is* understanding. [6]A "miserable sinner" cannot be healed without magic, nor can an "unimportant mind" esteem itself without magic.

7. Both forms of the ego's approach, then, must arrive at an impasse; the characteristic "impossible situation" to which the ego always leads. [2]It may help someone to point out where he is heading, but the point is lost unless he is also helped to change his direction. [3]The unhealed healer cannot do this for him, since he cannot do it for himself. [4]The only meaningful contribution the healer can make is to present an example of one whose direction has been changed *for* him, and who no longer believes in nightmares of any kind. [5]The light in his mind will therefore answer the questioner, who must decide with God that there is light *because* he sees it. [6]And by his acknowledgment the healer knows it is there. [7]That is how perception ultimately is translated into knowledge. [8]The miracle worker begins by perceiving light, and translates his perception into sureness by continually extending it and accepting its acknowledgment. [9]Its effects assure him it is there.

8. A therapist does not heal; *he lets healing be.* [2]He can point to darkness but he cannot bring light of himself, for light is not of him. [3]Yet, being *for* him, it must also be for his patient. [4]The Holy Spirit is the only Therapist. [5]He makes healing clear in any situation in which He is the Guide. [6]You can only let Him fulfill His

function. ⁷He needs no help for this. ⁸He will tell you exactly what to do to help anyone He sends to you for help, and will speak to him through you if you do not interfere. ⁹Remember that you choose the guide for helping, and the wrong choice will not help. ¹⁰But remember also that the right one will. ¹¹Trust Him, for help is His function, and He is of God. ¹²As you awaken other minds to the Holy Spirit through Him, and not yourself, you will understand that you are not obeying the laws of this world. ¹³But the laws you are obeying work. ¹⁴"The good is what works" is a sound though insufficient statement. ¹⁵Only the good *can* work. ¹⁶Nothing else works at all.

9.   This course offers a very direct and a very simple learning situation, and provides the Guide Who tells you what to do. ²If you do it, you will see that it works. ³Its results are more convincing than its words. ⁴They will convince you that the words are true. ⁵By following the right Guide, you will learn the simplest of all lessons:

> ⁶*By their fruits ye shall know them, and they shall know themselves.*

VI. The Acceptance of Your Brother

1.   How can you become increasingly aware of the Holy Spirit in you except by His effects? ²You cannot see Him with your eyes nor hear Him with your ears. ³How, then, can you perceive Him at all? ⁴If you inspire joy and others react to you with joy, even though you are not experiencing joy yourself there must be something in you that is capable of producing it. ⁵If it is in you and can produce joy, and if you see that it does produce joy in others, you must be dissociating it in yourself.

2.   It seems to you that the Holy Spirit does not produce joy consistently in you only because you do not consistently arouse joy in others. ²Their reactions to you are your evaluations of His consistency. ³When you are inconsistent you will not always give rise to joy, and so you will not always recognize His consistency. ⁴What you offer to your brother you offer to Him, because He cannot go beyond your offering in His giving. ⁵This is not because He limits His giving, but simply because you have limited your receiving. ⁶The decision to receive is the decision to accept.

3. If your brothers are part of you, will you accept them? ²Only they can teach you what you are, for your learning is the result of what you taught them. ³What you call upon in them you call upon in yourself. ⁴And as you call upon it in them it becomes real to you. ⁵God has but one Son, knowing them all as one. ⁶Only God Himself is more than they but they are not less than He is. ⁷Would you know what this means? ⁸If what you do to my brother you do to me, and if you do everything for yourself because we are part of you, everything we do belongs to you as well. ⁹Everyone God created is part of you and shares His glory with you. ¹⁰His glory belongs to Him, but it is equally yours. ¹¹You cannot, then, be less glorious than He is.

4. God is more than you only because He created you, but not even this would He keep from you. ²Therefore you can create as He did, and your dissociation will not alter this. ³Neither God's light nor yours is dimmed because you do not see. ⁴Because the Sonship must create as one, you remember creation whenever you recognize part of creation. ⁵Each part you remember adds to your wholeness because each part *is* whole. ⁶Wholeness is indivisible, but you cannot learn of your wholeness until you see it everywhere. ⁷You can know yourself only as God knows His Son, for knowledge is shared with God. ⁸When you awake in Him you will know your magnitude by accepting His limitlessness as yours. ⁹But meanwhile you will judge it as you judge your brother's, and will accept it as you accept his.

5. You are not yet awake, but you can learn how to awaken. ²Very simply, the Holy Spirit teaches you to awaken others. ³As you see them waken you will learn what waking means, and because you have chosen to wake them, their gratitude and their appreciation of what you have given them will teach you its value. ⁴They will become the witnesses to your reality, as you were created witness to God's. ⁵Yet when the Sonship comes together and accepts its Oneness it will be known by its creations, who witness to its reality as the Son does to the Father.

6. Miracles have no place in eternity, because they are reparative. ²Yet while you still need healing, your miracles are the only witnesses to your reality that you can recognize. ³You cannot perform a miracle for yourself, because miracles are a way of giving acceptance and receiving it. ⁴In time the giving comes first, though they are simultaneous in eternity, where they cannot be separated. ⁵When you have learned they are the same, the need

for time is over.

7. Eternity is one time, its only dimension being "always." ²This cannot mean anything to you until you remember God's open Arms, and finally know His open Mind. ³Like Him, *you* are "always"; in His Mind and with a mind like His. ⁴In your open mind are your creations, in perfect communication born of perfect understanding. ⁵Could you but accept one of them you would not want anything the world has to offer. ⁶Everything else would be totally meaningless. ⁷God's meaning is incomplete without you, and you are incomplete without your creations. ⁸Accept your brother in this world and accept nothing else, for in him you will find your creations because he created them with you. ⁹You will never know that you are co-creator with God until you learn that your brother is co-creator with you.

VII. The Two Evaluations

1. God's Will is your salvation. ²Would He not have given you the means to find it? ³If He wills you to have it, He must have made it possible and easy to obtain it. ⁴Your brothers are everywhere. ⁵You do not have to seek far for salvation. ⁶Every minute and every second gives you a chance to save yourself. ⁷Do not lose these chances, not because they will not return, but because delay of joy is needless. ⁸God wills you perfect happiness now. ⁹Is it possible that this is not also your will? ¹⁰And is it possible that this is not also the will of your brothers?

2. Consider, then, that in this joint will you are all united, and in this only. ²There may be disagreement on anything else, but not on this. ³This, then, is where peace abides. ⁴And you abide in peace when you so decide. ⁵Yet you cannot abide in peace unless you accept the Atonement, because the Atonement *is* the way to peace. ⁶The reason is very simple, and so obvious that it is often overlooked. ⁷The ego is afraid of the obvious, since obviousness is the essential characteristic of reality. ⁸Yet *you* cannot overlook it unless you are not looking.

3. It is perfectly obvious that if the Holy Spirit looks with love on all He perceives, He looks with love on you. ²His evaluation of you is based on His knowledge of what you are, and so He evaluates you truly. ³And this evaluation must be in your mind, because He is. ⁴The ego is also in your mind, because you have

accepted it there. [5]Its evaluation of you, however, is the exact opposite of the Holy Spirit's, because the ego does not love you. [6]It is unaware of what you are, and wholly mistrustful of everything it perceives because its perceptions are so shifting. [7]The ego is therefore capable of suspiciousness at best and viciousness at worst. [8]That is its range. [9]It cannot exceed it because of its uncertainty. [10]And it can never go beyond it because it can never *be* certain.

4. You, then, have two conflicting evaluations of yourself in your mind, and they cannot both be true. [2]You do not yet realize how completely different these evaluations are, because you do not understand how lofty the Holy Spirit's perception of you really is. [3]He is not deceived by anything you do, because He never forgets what you are. [4]The ego is deceived by everything you do, especially when you respond to the Holy Spirit, because at such times its confusion increases. [5]The ego is, therefore, particularly likely to attack you when you react lovingly, because it has evaluated you as unloving and you are going against its judgment. [6]The ego will attack your motives as soon as they become clearly out of accord with its perception of you. [7]This is when it will shift abruptly from suspiciousness to viciousness, since its uncertainty is increased. [8]Yet it is surely pointless to attack in return. [9]What can this mean except that you are agreeing with the ego's evaluation of what you are?

5. If you choose to see yourself as unloving you will not be happy. [2]You are condemning yourself and must therefore regard yourself as inadequate. [3]Would you look to the ego to help you escape from a sense of inadequacy it has produced, and must maintain for its existence? [4]Can you escape from its evaluation of you by using its methods for keeping this picture intact?

6. You cannot evaluate an insane belief system from within it. [2]Its range precludes this. [3]You can only go beyond it, look back from a point where sanity exists and *see the contrast*. [4]Only by this contrast can insanity be judged as insane. [5]With the grandeur of God in you, you have chosen to be little and to lament your littleness. [6]Within the system that dictated this choice the lament is inevitable. [7]Your littleness is taken for granted there and you do not ask, "Who granted it?" [8]The question is meaningless within the ego's thought system, because it would open the whole thought system to question.

7. I have said that the ego does not know what a real question is.

²Lack of knowledge of any kind is always associated with unwillingness to know, and this produces a total lack of knowledge simply because knowledge is total. ³Not to question your littleness therefore is to deny all knowledge, and keep the ego's whole thought system intact. ⁴You cannot retain part of a thought system, because it can be questioned only at its foundation. ⁵And this must be questioned from beyond it, because within it its foundation does stand. ⁶The Holy Spirit judges against the reality of the ego's thought system merely because He knows its foundation is not true. ⁷Therefore, nothing that arises from it means anything. ⁸He judges every belief you hold in terms of where it comes from. ⁹If it comes from God, He knows it to be true. ¹⁰If it does not, He knows that it is meaningless.

8. Whenever you question your value, say:

²God Himself is incomplete without me.

³Remember this when the ego speaks, and you will not hear it. ⁴The truth about you is so lofty that nothing unworthy of God is worthy of you. ⁵Choose, then, what you want in these terms, and accept nothing that you would not offer to God as wholly fitting for Him. ⁶You do not want anything else. ⁷Return your part to Him, and He will give you all of Himself in exchange for the return of what belongs to Him and renders Him complete.

VIII. Grandeur versus Grandiosity

1. Grandeur is of God, and only of Him. ²Therefore it is in you. ³Whenever you become aware of it, however dimly, you abandon the ego automatically, because in the presence of the grandeur of God the meaninglessness of the ego becomes perfectly apparent. ⁴When this occurs, even though it does not understand it, the ego believes that its "enemy" has struck, and attempts to offer gifts to induce you to return to its "protection." ⁵Self-inflation is the only offering it can make. ⁶The grandiosity of the ego is its alternative to the grandeur of God. ⁷Which will you choose?
2. Grandiosity is always a cover for despair. ²It is without hope because it is not real. ³It is an attempt to counteract your littleness, based on the belief that the littleness is real. ⁴Without this belief grandiosity is meaningless, and you could not possibly

want it. [5]The essence of grandiosity is competitiveness, because it always involves attack. [6]It is a delusional attempt to outdo, but not to undo. [7]We said before that the ego vacillates between suspiciousness and viciousness. [8]It remains suspicious as long as you despair of yourself. [9]It shifts to viciousness when you decide not to tolerate self-abasement and seek relief. [10]Then it offers you the illusion of attack as a "solution."

3. The ego does not understand the difference between grandeur and grandiosity, because it sees no difference between miracle impulses and ego-alien beliefs of its own. [2]I told you that the ego is aware of threat to its existence, but makes no distinctions between these two very different kinds of threat. [3]Its profound sense of vulnerability renders it incapable of judgment except in terms of attack. [4]When the ego experiences threat, its only decision is whether to attack now or to withdraw to attack later. [5]If you accept its offer of grandiosity it will attack immediately. [6]If you do not, it will wait.

4. The ego is immobilized in the presence of God's grandeur, because His grandeur establishes your freedom. [2]Even the faintest hint of your reality literally drives the ego from your mind, because you will give up all investment in it. [3]Grandeur is totally without illusions, and because it is real it is compellingly convincing. [4]Yet the conviction of reality will not remain with you unless you do not allow the ego to attack it. [5]The ego will make every effort to recover and mobilize its energies against your release. [6]It will tell you that you are insane, and argue that grandeur cannot be a real part of you because of the littleness in which it believes. [7]Yet your grandeur is not delusional because you did not make it. [8]You made grandiosity and are afraid of it because it is a form of attack, but your grandeur is of God, Who created it out of His Love.

5. From your grandeur you can only bless, because your grandeur is your abundance. [2]By blessing you hold it in your mind, protecting it from illusions and keeping yourself in the Mind of God. [3]Remember always that you cannot be anywhere except in the Mind of God. [4]When you forget this, you *will* despair and you *will* attack.

6. The ego depends solely on your willingness to tolerate it. [2]If you are willing to look upon your grandeur you cannot despair, and therefore you cannot want the ego. [3]Your grandeur is God's answer to the ego, because it is true. [4]Littleness and grandeur

cannot coexist, nor is it possible for them to alternate. [5]Littleness and grandiosity can and must alternate, since both are untrue and are therefore on the same level. [6]Being the level of shift, it is experienced as shifting and extremes are its essential characteristic.

7. Truth and littleness are denials of each other because grandeur is truth. [2]Truth does not vacillate; it is always true. [3]When grandeur slips away from you, you have replaced it with something you have made. [4]Perhaps it is the belief in littleness; perhaps it is the belief in grandiosity. [5]Yet it must be insane because it is not true. [6]Your grandeur will never deceive you, but your illusions always will. [7]Illusions are deceptions. [8]You cannot triumph, but you *are* exalted. [9]And in your exalted state you seek others like you and rejoice with them.

8. It is easy to distinguish grandeur from grandiosity, because love is returned and pride is not. [2]Pride will not produce miracles, and will therefore deprive you of the true witnesses to your reality. [3]Truth is not obscure nor hidden, but its obviousness to you lies in the joy you bring to its witnesses, who show it to you. [4]They attest to your grandeur, but they cannot attest to pride because pride is not shared. [5]God wants you to behold what He created because it is His joy.

9. Can your grandeur be arrogant when God Himself witnesses to it? [2]And what can be real that has no witnesses? [3]What good can come of it? [4]And if no good can come of it the Holy Spirit cannot use it. [5]What He cannot transform to the Will of God does not exist at all. [6]Grandiosity is delusional, because it is used to replace your grandeur. [7]Yet what God has created cannot be replaced. [8]God is incomplete without you because His grandeur is total, and you cannot be missing from it.

10. You are altogether irreplaceable in the Mind of God. [2]No one else can fill your part in it, and while you leave your part of it empty your eternal place merely waits for your return. [3]God, through His Voice, reminds you of it, and God Himself keeps your extensions safe within it. [4]Yet you do not know them until you return to them. [5]You cannot replace the Kingdom, and you cannot replace yourself. [6]God, Who knows your value, would not have it so, and so it is not so. [7]Your value is in God's Mind, and therefore not in yours alone. [8]To accept yourself as God created you cannot be arrogance, because it is the denial of arrogance. [9]To accept your littleness *is* arrogant, because it means that you believe your evaluation of yourself is truer than God's.

11.   Yet if truth is indivisible, your evaluation of yourself must *be* God's. [2]You did not establish your value and it needs no defense. [3]Nothing can attack it nor prevail over it. [4]It does not vary. [5]It merely *is*. [6]Ask the Holy Spirit what it is and He will tell you, but do not be afraid of His answer, because it comes from God. [7]It is an exalted answer because of its Source, but the Source is true and so is Its answer. [8]Listen and do not question what you hear, for God does not deceive. [9]He would have you replace the ego's belief in littleness with His Own exalted Answer to what you are, so that you can cease to question it and know it for what it is.

Chapter 10

THE IDOLS OF SICKNESS

Introduction

1. Nothing beyond yourself can make you fearful or loving, because nothing *is* beyond you. ²Time and eternity are both in your mind, and will conflict until you perceive time solely as a means to regain eternity. ³You cannot do this as long as you believe that anything happening to you is caused by factors outside yourself. ⁴You must learn that time is solely at your disposal, and that nothing in the world can take this responsibility from you. ⁵You can violate God's laws in your imagination, but you cannot escape from them. ⁶They were established for your protection and are as inviolate as your safety.

2. God created nothing beside you and nothing beside you exists, for you are part of Him. ²What except Him can exist? ³Nothing beyond Him can happen, because nothing except Him is real. ⁴Your creations add to Him as you do, but nothing is added that is different because everything has always been. ⁵What can upset you except the ephemeral, and how can the ephemeral be real if you are God's only creation and He created you eternal? ⁶Your holy mind establishes everything that happens to you. ⁷Every response you make to everything you perceive is up to you, because your mind determines your perception of it.

3. God does not change His Mind about you, for He is not uncertain of Himself. ²And what He knows can be known, because He does not know it only for Himself. ³He created you for Himself, but He gave you the power to create for yourself so you would be like Him. ⁴That is why your mind is holy. ⁵Can anything exceed the Love of God? ⁶Can anything, then, exceed your will? ⁷Nothing can reach you from beyond it because, being in God, you encompass everything. ⁸Believe this, and you will realize how much is up to you. ⁹When anything threatens your peace of mind, ask yourself, "Has God changed His Mind about me?" ¹⁰Then accept His decision, for it is indeed changeless, and refuse to change your mind about yourself. ¹¹God will never decide against you, or He would be deciding against Himself.

I. At Home in God

1.   You do not know your creations simply because you would decide against them as long as your mind is split, and to attack what you have created is impossible. ²But remember that *it is as impossible for God*. ³The law of creation is that you love your creations as yourself, because they are part of you. ⁴Everything that was created is therefore perfectly safe, because the laws of God protect it by His Love. ⁵Any part of your mind that does not know this has banished itself from knowledge, because it has not met its conditions. ⁶Who could have done this but you? ⁷Recognize this gladly, for in this recognition lies the realization that your banishment is not of God, and therefore does not exist.

2.   You are at home in God, dreaming of exile but perfectly capable of awakening to reality. ²Is it your decision to do so? ³You recognize from your own experience that what you see in dreams you think is real while you are asleep. ⁴Yet the instant you waken you realize that everything that seemed to happen in the dream did not happen at all. ⁵You do not think this strange, even though all the laws of what you awaken to were violated while you slept. ⁶Is it not possible that you merely shifted from one dream to another, without really waking?

3.   Would you bother to reconcile what happened in conflicting dreams, or would you dismiss both together if you discovered that reality is in accord with neither? ²You do not remember being awake. ³When you hear the Holy Spirit you may feel better because loving then seems possible to you, but you do not remember yet that it once was so. ⁴And it is in this remembering that you will know it can be so again. ⁵What is possible has not yet been accomplished. ⁶Yet what has once been is so now, if it is eternal. ⁷When you remember, you will know that what you remember is eternal, and therefore is now.

4.   You will remember everything the instant you desire it wholly, for if to desire wholly is to create, you will have willed away the separation, returning your mind simultaneously to your Creator and your creations. ²Knowing Them you will have no wish to sleep, but only the desire to waken and be glad. ³Dreams will be impossible because you will want only truth, and being at last your will, it will be yours.

II. The Decision to Forget

1. Unless you first know something you cannot dissociate it. [2]Knowledge must precede dissociation, so that dissociation is nothing more than a decision to forget. [3]What has been forgotten then appears to be fearful, but only because the dissociation is an attack on truth. [4]You are fearful *because* you have forgotten. [5]And you have replaced your knowledge by an awareness of dreams because you are afraid of your dissociation, not of what you have dissociated. [6]When what you have dissociated is accepted, it ceases to be fearful.

2. Yet to give up the dissociation of reality brings more than merely lack of fear. [2]In this decision lie joy and peace and the glory of creation. [3]Offer the Holy Spirit only your willingness to remember, for He retains the knowledge of God and of yourself for you, waiting for your acceptance. [4]Give up gladly everything that would stand in the way of your remembering, for God is in your memory. [5]His Voice will tell you that you are part of Him when you are willing to remember Him and know your own reality again. [6]Let nothing in this world delay your remembering of Him, for in this remembering is the knowledge of yourself.

3. To remember is merely to restore to your mind *what is already there*. [2]You do not make what you remember; you merely accept again what is already there, but was rejected. [3]The ability to accept truth in this world is the perceptual counterpart of creating in the Kingdom. [4]God will do His part if you will do yours, and His return in exchange for yours is the exchange of knowledge for perception. [5]Nothing is beyond His Will for you. [6]But signify your will to remember Him, and behold! [7]He will give you everything but for the asking.

4. When you attack, you are denying yourself. [2]You are specifically teaching yourself that you are not what you are. [3]Your denial of reality precludes the acceptance of God's gift, because you have accepted something else in its place. [4]If you understand that this is always an attack on truth, and truth is God, you will realize why it is always fearful. [5]If you further recognize that you are part of God, you will understand why it is that you always attack yourself first.

5. All attack is Self attack. [2]It cannot be anything else. [3]Arising from your own decision not to be what you are, it is an attack on your identification. [4]Attack is thus the way in which your identi-

fication is lost, because when you attack, you must have forgotten what you are. ⁵And if your reality is God's, when you attack you are not remembering Him. ⁶This is not because He is gone, but because you are actively choosing not to remember Him.

6. If you realized the complete havoc this makes of your peace of mind you could not make such an insane decision. ²You make it only because you still believe it can get you something you want. ³It follows, then, that you want something other than peace of mind, but you have not considered what it must be. ⁴Yet the logical outcome of your decision is perfectly clear, if you will only look at it. ⁵By deciding against your reality, you have made yourself vigilant *against* God and His Kingdom. ⁶And it is this vigilance that makes you afraid to remember Him.

III. The God of Sickness

1. You have not attacked God and you do love Him. ²Can you change your reality? ³No one can will to destroy himself. ⁴When you think you are attacking yourself, it is a sure sign that you hate what you *think* you are. ⁵And this, and only this, can be attacked by you. ⁶What you think you are can be very hateful, and what this strange image makes you do can be very destructive. ⁷Yet the destruction is no more real than the image, although those who make idols do worship them. ⁸The idols are nothing, but their worshippers are the Sons of God in sickness. ⁹God would have them released from their sickness and returned to His Mind. ¹⁰He will not limit your power to help them, because He has given it to you. ¹¹Do not be afraid of it, because it is your salvation.

2. What Comforter can there be for the sick children of God except His power through you? ²Remember that it does not matter where in the Sonship He is accepted. ³He is always accepted for all, and when your mind receives Him the remembrance of Him awakens throughout the Sonship. ⁴Heal your brothers simply by accepting God for them. ⁵Your minds are not separate, and God has only one channel for healing because He has but one Son. ⁶God's remaining Communication Link with all His children joins them together, and them to Him. ⁷To be aware of this is to heal them because it is the awareness that no one is separate, and so no one is sick.

3.   To believe that a Son of God can be sick is to believe that part of God can suffer. ²Love cannot suffer, because it cannot attack. ³The remembrance of love therefore brings invulnerability with it. ⁴Do not side with sickness in the presence of a Son of God even if he believes in it, for your acceptance of God in him acknowledges the Love of God he has forgotten. ⁵Your recognition of him as part of God reminds him of the truth about himself, which he is denying. ⁶Would you strengthen his denial of God and thus lose sight of yourself? ⁷Or would you remind him of his wholeness and remember your Creator with him?

4.   To believe a Son of God is sick is to worship the same idol he does. ²God created love, not idolatry. ³All forms of idolatry are caricatures of creation, taught by sick minds too divided to know that creation shares power and never usurps it. ⁴Sickness is idolatry, because it is the belief that power can be taken from you. ⁵Yet this is impossible, because you are part of God, Who is all power. ⁶A sick god must be an idol, made in the image of what its maker thinks he is. ⁷And that is exactly what the ego does perceive in a Son of God; a sick god, self-created, self-sufficient, very vicious and very vulnerable. ⁸Is this the idol you would worship? ⁹Is this the image you would be vigilant to save? ¹⁰Are you really afraid of losing this?

5.   Look calmly at the logical conclusion of the ego's thought system and judge whether its offering is really what you want, for this *is* what it offers you. ²To obtain this you are willing to attack the Divinity of your brothers, and thus lose sight of yours. ³And you are willing to keep it hidden, to protect an idol you think will save you from the dangers for which it stands, but which do not exist.

6.   There are no idolaters in the Kingdom, but there is great appreciation for everything that God created, because of the calm knowledge that each one is part of Him. ²God's Son knows no idols, but he does know his Father. ³Health in this world is the counterpart of value in Heaven. ⁴It is not my merit that I contribute to you but my love, for you do not value yourself. ⁵When you do not value yourself you become sick, but my value of you can heal you, because the value of God's Son is one. ⁶When I said, "My peace I give unto you," I meant it. ⁷Peace comes from God through me to you. ⁸It is for you although you may not ask for it.

7.   When a brother is sick it is because he is not asking for peace, and therefore does not know he has it. ²The acceptance of peace is

185

the denial of illusion, and sickness *is* an illusion. [3]Yet every Son of God has the power to deny illusions anywhere in the Kingdom, merely by denying them completely in himself. [4]I can heal you because I know you. [5]I know your value for you, and it is this value that makes you whole. [6]A whole mind is not idolatrous, and does not know of conflicting laws. [7]I will heal you merely because I have only one message, and it is true. [8]Your faith in it will make you whole when you have faith in me.

8.   I do not bring God's message with deception, and you will learn this as you learn that you always receive as much as you accept. [2]You could accept peace now for everyone, and offer them perfect freedom from all illusions because you heard His Voice. [3]But have no other gods before Him or you will not hear. [4]God is not jealous of the gods you make, but you are. [5]You would save them and serve them, because you believe that they made you. [6]You think they are your father, because you are projecting onto them the fearful fact that you made them to replace God. [7]Yet when they seem to speak to you, remember that nothing can replace God, and whatever replacements you have attempted are nothing.

9.   Very simply, then, you may believe you are afraid of nothingness, but you are really afraid of nothing. [2]And in that awareness you are healed. [3]You will hear the god you listen to. [4]You made the god of sickness, and by making him you made yourself able to hear him. [5]Yet you did not create him, because he is not the Will of the Father. [6]He is therefore not eternal and will be unmade for you the instant you signify your willingness to accept only the eternal.

10.   If God has but one Son, there is but one God. [2]You share reality with Him, because reality is not divided. [3]To accept other gods before Him is to place other images before yourself. [4]You do not realize how much you listen to your gods, and how vigilant you are on their behalf. [5]Yet they exist only because you honor them. [6]Place honor where it is due, and peace will be yours. [7]It is your inheritance from your real Father. [8]You cannot make your Father, and the father you made did not make you. [9]Honor is not due to illusions, for to honor them is to honor nothing. [10]Yet fear is not due them either, for nothing cannot be fearful. [11]You have chosen to fear love because of its perfect harmlessness, and because of this fear you have been willing to give up your own perfect helpfulness and your own perfect Help.

11. Only at the altar of God will you find peace. ²And this altar is in you because God put it there. ³His Voice still calls you to return, and He will be heard when you place no other gods before Him. ⁴You can give up the god of sickness for your brothers; in fact, you would have to do so if you give him up for yourself. ⁵For if you see the god of sickness anywhere, you have accepted him. ⁶And if you accept him you will bow down and worship him, because he was made as God's replacement. ⁷He is the belief that you can choose which god is real. ⁸Although it is clear this has nothing to do with reality, it is equally clear that it has everything to do with reality as you perceive it.

IV. The End of Sickness

1. All magic is an attempt at reconciling the irreconcilable. ²All religion is the recognition that the irreconcilable cannot be reconciled. ³Sickness and perfection are irreconcilable. ⁴If God created you perfect, you *are* perfect. ⁵If you believe you can be sick, you have placed other gods before Him. ⁶God is not at war with the god of sickness you made, but you are. ⁷He is the symbol of deciding against God, and you are afraid of him because he cannot be reconciled with God's Will. ⁸If you attack him, you will make him real to you. ⁹But if you refuse to worship him in whatever form he may appear to you, and wherever you think you see him, he will disappear into the nothingness out of which he was made.

2. Reality can dawn only on an unclouded mind. ²It is always there to be accepted, but its acceptance depends on your willingness to have it. ³To know reality must involve the willingness to judge unreality for what it is. ⁴To overlook nothingness is merely to judge it correctly, and because of your ability to evaluate it truly, to let it go. ⁵Knowledge cannot dawn on a mind full of illusions, because truth and illusions are irreconcilable. ⁶Truth is whole, and cannot be known by part of a mind.

3. The Sonship cannot be perceived as partly sick, because to perceive it that way is not to perceive it at all. ²If the Sonship is one, it is one in all respects. ³Oneness cannot be divided. ⁴If you perceive other gods your mind is split, and you will not be able to limit the split, because it is the sign that you have removed part of your mind from God's Will. ⁵This means it is out of control. ⁶To

be out of control is to be out of reason, and then the mind does become unreasonable. [7]By defining the mind wrongly, you perceive it as functioning wrongly.

4. God's laws will keep your mind at peace because peace is His Will, and His laws are established to uphold it. [2]His are the laws of freedom, but yours are the laws of bondage. [3]Since freedom and bondage are irreconcilable, their laws cannot be understood together. [4]The laws of God work only for your good, and there are no other laws beside His. [5]Everything else is merely lawless and therefore chaotic. [6]Yet God Himself has protected everything He created by His laws. [7]Everything that is not under them does not exist. [8]"Laws of chaos" is a meaningless term. [9]Creation is perfectly lawful, and the chaotic is without meaning because it is without God. [10]You have "given" your peace to the gods you made, but they are not there to take it from you, and you cannot give it to them.

5. You are not free to give up freedom, but only to deny it. [2]You cannot do what God did not intend, because what He did not intend does not happen. [3]Your gods do not bring chaos; you are endowing them with chaos, and accepting it of them. [4]All this has never been. [5]Nothing but the laws of God has ever been, and nothing but His Will will ever be. [6]You were created through His laws and by His Will, and the manner of your creation established you a creator. [7]What you have made is so unworthy of you that you could hardly want it, if you were willing to see it as it is. [8]You will see nothing at all. [9]And your vision will automatically look beyond it, to what is in you and all around you. [10]Reality cannot break through the obstructions you interpose, but it will envelop you completely when you let them go.

6. When you have experienced the protection of God, the making of idols becomes inconceivable. [2]There are no strange images in the Mind of God, and what is not in His Mind cannot be in yours, because you are of one mind and that mind belongs to Him. [3]It is yours *because* it belongs to Him, for to Him ownership is sharing. [4]And if it is so for Him, it is so for you. [5]His definitions *are* His laws, for by them He established the universe as what it is. [6]No false gods you attempt to interpose between yourself and your reality affect truth at all. [7]Peace is yours because God created you. [8]And He created nothing else.

7. The miracle is the act of a Son of God who has laid aside all false gods, and calls on his brothers to do likewise. [2]It is an act of

faith, because it is the recognition that his brother can do it. ³It is a call to the Holy Spirit in his mind, a call that is strengthened by joining. ⁴Because the miracle worker has heard God's Voice, he strengthens It in a sick brother by weakening his belief in sickness, which he does not share. ⁵The power of one mind can shine into another, because all the lamps of God were lit by the same spark. ⁶It is everywhere and it is eternal.

8. In many only the spark remains, for the Great Rays are obscured. ²Yet God has kept the spark alive so that the Rays can never be completely forgotten. ³If you but see the little spark you will learn of the greater light, for the Rays are there unseen. ⁴Perceiving the spark will heal, but knowing the light will create. ⁵Yet in the returning the little light must be acknowledged first, for the separation was a descent from magnitude to littleness. ⁶But the spark is still as pure as the Great Light, because it is the remaining call of creation. ⁷Put all your faith in it, and God Himself will answer you.

V. The Denial of God

1. The rituals of the god of sickness are strange and very demanding. ²Joy is never permitted, for depression is the sign of allegiance to him. ³Depression means that you have forsworn God. ⁴Many are afraid of blasphemy, but they do not understand what it means. ⁵They do not realize that to deny God is to deny their own Identity, and in this sense the wages of sin *is* death. ⁶The sense is very literal; denial of life perceives its opposite, as all forms of denial replace what is with what is not. ⁷No one can really do this, but that you can think you can and believe you have is beyond dispute.

2. Do not forget, however, that to deny God will inevitably result in projection, and you will believe that others and not yourself have done this to you. ²You must receive the message you give because it is the message you want. ³You may believe that you judge your brothers by the messages they give you, but you have judged them by the message you give to them. ⁴Do not attribute your denial of joy to them, or you cannot see the spark in them that would bring joy to you. ⁵It is the denial of the spark that brings depression, for whenever you see your brothers without it, you are denying God.

3. Allegiance to the denial of God is the ego's religion. ²The god of sickness obviously demands the denial of health, because health is in direct opposition to its own survival. ³But consider what this means to you. ⁴Unless you are sick you cannot keep the gods you made, for only in sickness could you possibly want them. ⁵Blasphemy, then, is *self*-destructive, not God-destructive. ⁶It means that you are willing not to know yourself in order to be sick. ⁷This is the offering your god demands because, having made him out of your insanity, he is an insane idea. ⁸He has many forms, but although he may seem to be many different things he is but one idea;—the denial of God.

4. Sickness and death seemed to enter the mind of God's Son against His Will. ²The "attack on God" made His Son think he was Fatherless, and out of his depression he made the god of depression. ³This was his alternative to joy, because he would not accept the fact that, although he was a creator, he had been created. ⁴Yet the Son *is* helpless without the Father, Who alone is his Help.

5. I said before that of yourself you can do nothing, but you are not *of* yourself. ²If you were, what you have made would be true, and you could never escape. ³It is because you did not make yourself that you need be troubled over nothing. ⁴Your gods are nothing, because your Father did not create them. ⁵You cannot make creators who are unlike your Creator, any more than He could have created a Son who was unlike Him. ⁶If creation is sharing, it cannot create what is unlike itself. ⁷It can share only what it is. ⁸Depression is isolation, and so it could not have been created.

6. Son of God, you have not sinned, but you have been much mistaken. ²Yet this can be corrected and God will help you, knowing that you could not sin against Him. ³You denied Him because you loved Him, knowing that if you recognized your love for Him, you could not deny Him. ⁴Your denial of Him therefore means that you love Him, and that you know He loves you. ⁵Remember that what you deny you must have once known. ⁶And if you accept denial, you can accept its undoing.

7. Your Father has not denied you. ²He does not retaliate, but He does call to you to return. ³When you think He has not answered your call, you have not answered His. ⁴He calls to you from every part of the Sonship, because of His Love for His Son. ⁵If you hear His message He has answered you, and you will learn of Him if

you hear aright. ⁶The Love of God is in everything He created, for His Son is everywhere. ⁷Look with peace upon your brothers, and God will come rushing into your heart in gratitude for your gift to Him.

8. Do not look to the god of sickness for healing but only to the God of love, for healing is the acknowledgment of Him. ²When you acknowledge Him you will know that He has never ceased to acknowledge you, and that in His acknowledgment of you lies your being. ³You are not sick and you cannot die. ⁴But you can confuse yourself with things that do. ⁵Remember, though, that to do this is blasphemy, for it means that you are looking without love on God and His creation, from which He cannot be separated.

9. Only the eternal can be loved, for love does not die. ²What is of God is His forever, and you are of God. ³Would He allow Himself to suffer? ⁴And would He offer His Son anything that is not acceptable to Him? ⁵If you will accept yourself as God created you, you will be incapable of suffering. ⁶Yet to do this you must acknowledge Him as your Creator. ⁷This is not because you will be punished otherwise. ⁸It is merely because your acknowledgment of your Father is the acknowledgment of yourself as you are. ⁹Your Father created you wholly without sin, wholly without pain and wholly without suffering of any kind. ¹⁰If you deny Him you bring sin, pain and suffering into your own mind because of the power He gave it. ¹¹Your mind is capable of creating worlds, but it can also deny what it creates because it is free.

10. You do not realize how much you have denied yourself, and how much God, in His Love, would not have it so. ²Yet He would not interfere with you, because He would not know His Son if he were not free. ³To interfere with you would be to attack Himself, and God is not insane. ⁴When you deny Him *you* are insane. ⁵Would you have Him share your insanity? ⁶God will never cease to love His Son, and His Son will never cease to love Him. ⁷That was the condition of His Son's creation, fixed forever in the Mind of God. ⁸To know that is sanity. ⁹To deny it is insanity. ¹⁰God gave Himself to you in your creation, and His gifts are eternal. ¹¹Would you deny yourself to Him?

11. Out of your gifts to Him the Kingdom will be restored to His Son. ²His Son removed himself from His gift by refusing to accept what had been created for him, and what he had created in the Name of his Father. ³Heaven waits for his return, for it was cre-

ated as the dwelling place of God's Son. [4]You are not at home anywhere else, or in any other condition. [5]Do not deny yourself the joy that was created for you for the misery you have made for yourself. [6]God has given you the means for undoing what you have made. [7]Listen, and you will learn how to remember what you are.

12.   If God knows His children as wholly sinless, it is blasphemous to perceive them as guilty. [2]If God knows His children as wholly without pain, it is blasphemous to perceive suffering anywhere. [3]If God knows His children to be wholly joyous, it is blasphemous to feel depressed. [4]All of these illusions, and the many other forms that blasphemy may take, are refusals to accept creation as it is. [5]If God created His Son perfect, that is how you must learn to see him to learn of his reality. [6]And as part of the Sonship, that is how you must see yourself to learn of yours.

13.   Do not perceive anything God did not create or you are denying Him. [2]His is the only Fatherhood, and it is yours only because He has given it to you. [3]Your gifts to yourself are meaningless, but your gifts to your creations are like His, because they are given in His Name. [4]That is why your creations are as real as His. [5]Yet the real Fatherhood must be acknowledged if the real Son is to be known. [6]You believe that the sick things you have made are your real creations, because you believe that the sick images you perceive are the Sons of God. [7]Only if you accept the Fatherhood of God will you have anything, because His Fatherhood gave you everything. [8]That is why to deny Him is to deny yourself.

14.   Arrogance is the denial of love, because love shares and arrogance withholds. [2]As long as both appear to you to be desirable the concept of choice, which is not of God, will remain with you. [3]While this is not true in eternity it *is* true in time, so that while time lasts in your mind there will be choices. [4]Time itself is your choice. [5]If you would remember eternity, you must look only on the eternal. [6]If you allow yourself to become preoccupied with the temporal, you are living in time. [7]As always, your choice is determined by what you value. [8]Time and eternity cannot both be real, because they contradict each other. [9]If you will accept only what is timeless as real, you will begin to understand eternity and make it yours.

Chapter 11

GOD OR THE EGO

Introduction

1. Either God or the ego is insane. ²If you will examine the evidence on both sides fairly, you will realize this must be true. ³Neither God nor the ego proposes a partial thought system. ⁴Each is internally consistent, but they are diametrically opposed in all respects so that partial allegiance is impossible. ⁵Remember, too, that their results are as different as their foundations, and their fundamentally irreconcilable natures cannot be reconciled by vacillations between them. ⁶Nothing alive is Fatherless, for life is creation. ⁷Therefore, your decision is always an answer to the question, "Who is my father?" ⁸And you will be faithful to the father you choose.

2. Yet what would you say to someone who believed this question really involves conflict? ²If you made the ego, how can the ego have made you? ³The authority problem is still the only source of conflict, because the ego was made out of the wish of God's Son to father Him. ⁴The ego, then, is nothing more than a delusional system in which you made your own father. ⁵Make no mistake about this. ⁶It sounds insane when it is stated with perfect honesty, but the ego never looks on what it does with perfect honesty. ⁷Yet that is its insane premise, which is carefully hidden in the dark cornerstone of its thought system. ⁸And either the ego, which you made, *is* your father, or its whole thought system will not stand.

3. You make by projection, but God creates by extension. ²The cornerstone of God's creation is you, for His thought system is light. ³Remember the Rays that are there unseen. ⁴The more you approach the center of His thought system, the clearer the light becomes. ⁵The closer you come to the foundation of the ego's thought system, the darker and more obscure becomes the way. ⁶Yet even the little spark in your mind is enough to lighten it. ⁷Bring this light fearlessly with you, and bravely hold it up to the foundation of the ego's thought system. ⁸Be willing to judge it with perfect honesty. ⁹Open the dark cornerstone of terror on which it rests, and bring it out into the light. ¹⁰There you will see

that it rested on meaninglessness, and that everything of which you have been afraid was based on nothing.

4.   My brother, you are part of God and part of me. ²When you have at last looked at the ego's foundation without shrinking you will also have looked upon ours. ³I come to you from our Father to offer you everything again. ⁴Do not refuse it in order to keep a dark cornerstone hidden, for its protection will not save you. ⁵I give you the lamp and I will go with you. ⁶You will not take this journey alone. ⁷I will lead you to your true Father, Who hath need of you, as I have. ⁸Will you not answer the call of love with joy?

I. The Gifts of Fatherhood

1.   You have learned your need of healing. ²Would you bring anything else to the Sonship, recognizing your need of healing for yourself? ³For in this lies the beginning of the return to knowledge; the foundation on which God will help build again the thought system you share with Him. ⁴Not one stone you place upon it but will be blessed by Him, for you will be restoring the holy dwelling place of His Son, where He wills His Son to be and where he is. ⁵In whatever part of the mind of God's Son you restore this reality, you restore it to yourself. ⁶You dwell in the Mind of God with your brother, for God Himself did not will to be alone.

2.   To be alone is to be separated from infinity, but how can this be if infinity has no end? ²No one can be beyond the limitless, because what has no limits must be everywhere. ³There are no beginnings and no endings in God, Whose universe is Himself. ⁴Can you exclude yourself from the universe, or from God Who *is* the universe? ⁵I and my Father are one with you, for you are part of Us. ⁶Do you really believe that part of God can be missing or lost to Him?

3.   If you were not part of God, His Will would not be unified. ²Is this conceivable? ³Can part of His Mind contain nothing? ⁴If your place in His Mind cannot be filled by anyone except you, and your filling it was your creation, without you there would be an empty place in God's Mind. ⁵Extension cannot be blocked, and it has no voids. ⁶It continues forever, however much it is denied. ⁷Your denial of its reality may arrest it in time, but not in eternity. ⁸That is why your creations have not ceased to be extended, and

why so much is waiting for your return.

4. Waiting is possible only in time, but time has no meaning. [2]You who made delay can leave time behind simply by recognizing that neither beginnings nor endings were created by the Eternal, Who placed no limits on His creation or upon those who create like Him. [3]You do not know this simply because you have tried to limit what He created, and so you believe that all creation is limited. [4]How, then, could you know your creations, having denied infinity?

5. The laws of the universe do not permit contradiction. [2]What holds for God holds for you. [3]If you believe you are absent from God, you will believe that He is absent from you. [4]Infinity is meaningless without you, and you are meaningless without God. [5]There is no end to God and His Son, for we *are* the universe. [6]God is not incomplete, and He is not childless. [7]Because He did not will to be alone, He created a Son like Himself. [8]Do not deny Him His Son, for your unwillingness to accept His Fatherhood has denied you yours. [9]See His creations as His Son, for yours were created in honor of Him. [10]The universe of love does not stop because you do not see it, nor have your closed eyes lost the ability to see. [11]Look upon the glory of His creation, and you will learn what God has kept for you.

6. God has given you a place in His Mind that is yours forever. [2]Yet you can keep it only by giving it, as it was given you. [3]Could you be alone there, when it was given you because God did not will to be alone? [4]God's Mind cannot be lessened. [5]It can only be increased, for everything He creates has the function of creating. [6]Love does not limit, and what it creates is not limited. [7]To give without limit is God's Will for you, because only this can bring you the joy that is His and that He wills to share with you. [8]Your love is as boundless as His because it *is* His.

7. Could any part of God be without His Love, and could any part of His Love be contained? [2]God is your heritage, because His one gift is Himself. [3]How can you give except like Him if you would know His gift to you? [4]Give, then, without limit and without end, to learn how much He has given you. [5]Your ability to accept Him depends on your willingness to give as He gives. [6]Your fatherhood and your Father are one. [7]God wills to create, and your will is His. [8]It follows, then, that you will to create, since your will follows from His. [9]And being an extension of His Will, yours must be the same.

8.   Yet what you will you do not know. ²This is not strange when you realize that to deny is to "not know." ³God's Will is that you are His Son. ⁴By denying this you deny your own will, and therefore do not know what it is. ⁵You must ask what God's Will is in everything, because it is yours. ⁶You do not know what it is, but the Holy Spirit remembers it for you. ⁷Ask Him, therefore, what God's Will is for you, and He will tell you yours. ⁸It cannot be too often repeated that you do not know it. ⁹Whenever what the Holy Spirit tells you appears to be coercive, it is only because you have not recognized your will.

9.   The projection of the ego makes it appear as if God's Will is outside yourself, and therefore not yours. ²In this interpretation it seems possible for God's Will and yours to conflict. ³God, then, may seem to demand of you what you do not want to give, and thus deprive you of what you want. ⁴Would God, Who wants only your will, be capable of this? ⁵Your will is His life, which He has given to you. ⁶Even in time you cannot live apart from Him. ⁷Sleep is not death. ⁸What He created can sleep, but cannot die. ⁹Immortality is His Will for His Son, and His Son's will for himself. ¹⁰God's Son cannot will death for himself because his Father is life, and His Son is like Him. ¹¹Creation is your will *because* it is His.

10.   You cannot be happy unless you do what you will truly, and you cannot change this because it is immutable. ²It is immutable by God's Will and yours, for otherwise His Will would not be extended. ³You are afraid to know God's Will, because you believe it is not yours. ⁴This belief is your whole sickness and your whole fear. ⁵Every symptom of sickness and fear arises here, because this is the belief that makes you *want* not to know. ⁶Believing this you hide in darkness, denying that the light is in you.

11.   You are asked to trust the Holy Spirit only because He speaks for you. ²He is the Voice for God, but never forget that God did not will to be alone. ³He shares His Will with you; He does not thrust it upon you. ⁴Always remember that what He gives He keeps, so that nothing He gives can contradict Him. ⁵You who share His life must share it to know it, for sharing *is* knowing. ⁶Blessed are you who learn that to hear the Will of your Father is to know your own. ⁷For it is your will to be like Him, Whose Will it is that it be so. ⁸God's Will is that His Son be one, and united with Him in His Oneness. ⁹That is why healing is the beginning of the recognition that your will is His.

II. The Invitation to Healing

1. If sickness is separation, the decision to heal and to be healed is the first step toward recognizing what you truly want. [2]Every attack is a step away from this, and every healing thought brings it closer. [3]The Son of God *has* both Father and Son, because he *is* both Father and Son. [4]To unite *having* and *being* is to unite your will with His, for He wills you Himself. [5]And you will yourself to Him because, in your perfect understanding of Him, you know there is but one Will. [6]Yet when you attack any part of God and His Kingdom your understanding is not perfect, and what you really want is therefore lost to you.

2. Healing thus becomes a lesson in understanding, and the more you practice it the better teacher and learner you become. [2]If you have denied truth, what better witnesses to its reality could you have than those who have been healed by it? [3]But be sure to count yourself among them, for in your willingness to join them is your healing accomplished. [4]Every miracle that you accomplish speaks to you of the Fatherhood of God. [5]Every healing thought that you accept, either from your brother or in your own mind, teaches you that you are God's Son. [6]In every hurtful thought you hold, wherever you perceive it, lies the denial of God's Fatherhood and of your Sonship.

3. And denial is as total as love. [2]You cannot deny part of yourself, because the rest will seem to be separate and therefore without meaning. [3]And being without meaning to you, you will not understand it. [4]To deny meaning is to fail to understand. [5]You can heal only yourself, for only God's Son needs healing. [6]You need it because you do not understand yourself, and therefore know not what you do. [7]Having forgotten your will, you do not know what you really want.

4. Healing is a sign that you want to make whole. [2]And this willingness opens your ears to the Voice of the Holy Spirit, Whose message is wholeness. [3]He will enable you to go far beyond the healing you would undertake, for beside your small willingness to make whole He will lay His Own complete Will and make yours whole. [4]What can the Son of God not accomplish with the Fatherhood of God in him? [5]And yet the invitation must come from you, for you have surely learned that whom you invite as your guest will abide with you.

5. The Holy Spirit cannot speak to an unwelcoming host, because

He will not be heard. ²The Eternal Guest remains, but His Voice grows faint in alien company. ³He needs your protection, only because your care is a sign that you want Him. ⁴Think like Him ever so slightly, and the little spark becomes a blazing light that fills your mind so that He becomes your only Guest. ⁵Whenever you ask the ego to enter, you lessen His welcome. ⁶He will remain, but you have allied yourself against Him. ⁷Whatever journey you choose to take, He will go with you, waiting. ⁸You can safely trust His patience, for He cannot leave a part of God. ⁹Yet you need far more than patience.

6. You will never rest until you know your function and fulfill it, for only in this can your will and your Father's be wholly joined. ²To have Him is to be like Him, and He has given Himself to you. ³You who have God must be as God, for His function became yours with His gift. ⁴Invite this knowledge back into your mind, and let nothing that obscures it enter. ⁵The Guest Whom God sent you will teach you how to do this, if you but recognize the little spark and are willing to let it grow. ⁶Your willingness need not be perfect, because His is. ⁷If you will merely offer Him a little place, He will lighten it so much that you will gladly let it be increased. ⁸And by this increase, you will begin to remember creation.

7. Would you be hostage to the ego or host to God? ²You will accept only whom you invite. ³You are free to determine who shall be your guest, and how long he shall remain with you. ⁴Yet this is not real freedom, for it still depends on how you see it. ⁵The Holy Spirit is there, although He cannot help you without your invitation. ⁶And the ego is nothing, whether you invite it in or not. ⁷Real freedom depends on welcoming reality, and of your guests only the Holy Spirit is real. ⁸Know, then, Who abides with you merely by recognizing what is there already, and do not be satisfied with imaginary comforters, for the Comforter of God is in you.

III. From Darkness to Light

1. When you are weary, remember you have hurt yourself. ²Your Comforter will rest you, but you cannot. ³You do not know how, for if you did you could never have grown weary. ⁴Unless you hurt yourself you could never suffer in any way, for that is not God's Will for His Son. ⁵Pain is not of Him, for He knows no

attack and His peace surrounds you silently. [6]God is very quiet, for there is no conflict in Him. [7]Conflict is the root of all evil, for being blind it does not see whom it attacks. [8]Yet it always attacks the Son of God, and the Son of God is you.

2.   God's Son is indeed in need of comfort, for he knows not what he does, believing his will is not his own. [2]The Kingdom is his, and yet he wanders homeless. [3]At home in God he is lonely, and amid all his brothers he is friendless. [4]Would God let this be real, when He did not will to be alone Himself? [5]And if your will is His it cannot be true of you, because it is not true of Him.

3.   O my child, if you knew what God wills for you, your joy would be complete! [2]And what He wills has happened, for it was always true. [3]When the light comes and you have said, "God's Will is mine," you will see such beauty that you will know it is not of you. [4]Out of your joy you will create beauty in His Name, for your joy could no more be contained than His. [5]The bleak little world will vanish into nothingness, and your heart will be so filled with joy that it will leap into Heaven, and into the Presence of God. [6]I cannot tell you what this will be like, for your heart is not ready. [7]Yet I can tell you, and remind you often, that what God wills for Himself He wills for you, and what He wills for you is yours.

4.   The way is not hard, but it *is* very different. [2]Yours is the way of pain, of which God knows nothing. [3]That way is hard indeed, and very lonely. [4]Fear and grief are your guests, and they go with you and abide with you on the way. [5]But the dark journey is not the way of God's Son. [6]Walk in light and do not see the dark companions, for they are not fit companions for the Son of God, who was created *of* light and *in* light. [7]The Great Light always surrounds you and shines out from you. [8]How can you see the dark companions in a light such as this? [9]If you see them, it is only because you are denying the light. [10]But deny them instead, for the light is here and the way is clear.

5.   God hides nothing from His Son, even though His Son would hide himself. [2]Yet the Son of God cannot hide his glory, for God wills him to be glorious, and gave him the light that shines in him. [3]You will never lose your way, for God leads you. [4]When you wander, you but undertake a journey that is not real. [5]The dark companions, the dark way, are all illusions. [6]Turn toward the light, for the little spark in you is part of a light so great that it can sweep you out of all darkness forever. [7]For your Father *is*

your Creator, and you *are* like Him.

6. The children of light cannot abide in darkness, for darkness is not in them. ²Do not be deceived by the dark comforters, and never let them enter the mind of God's Son, for they have no place in His temple. ³When you are tempted to deny Him remember that there *are* no other gods to place before Him, and accept His Will for you in peace. ⁴For you cannot accept it otherwise.

7. Only God's Comforter can comfort you. ²In the quiet of His temple, He waits to give you the peace that is yours. ³Give His peace, that you may enter the temple and find it waiting for you. ⁴But be holy in the Presence of God, or you will not know that you are there. ⁵For what is unlike God cannot enter His Mind, because it was not His Thought and therefore does not belong to Him. ⁶And your mind must be as pure as His, if you would know what belongs to you. ⁷Guard carefully His temple, for He Himself dwells there and abides in peace. ⁸You cannot enter God's Presence with the dark companions beside you, but you also cannot enter alone. ⁹All your brothers must enter with you, for until you have accepted them *you* cannot enter. ¹⁰For you cannot understand wholeness unless you are whole, and no part of the Son can be excluded if he would know the Wholeness of his Father.

8. In your mind you can accept the whole Sonship and bless it with the light your Father gave it. ²Then you will be worthy to dwell in the temple with Him, because it is your will not to be alone. ³God blessed His Son forever. ⁴If you will bless him in time, you will be in eternity. ⁵Time cannot separate you from God if you use it on behalf of the eternal.

IV. The Inheritance of God's Son

1. Never forget that the Sonship is your salvation, for the Sonship is your Self. ²As God's creation It is yours, and belonging to you It is His. ³Your Self does not need salvation, but your mind needs to learn what salvation is. ⁴You are not saved *from* anything, but you are saved *for* glory. ⁵Glory is your inheritance, given you by your Creator that you might extend it. ⁶Yet if you hate part of your Self all your understanding is lost, because you are looking on what God created as yourself without love. ⁷And since what He created is part of Him, you are denying Him His place in His Own altar.

2. Could you try to make God homeless and know that you are at home? ²Can the Son deny the Father without believing that the Father has denied him? ³God's laws hold only for your protection, and they never hold in vain. ⁴What you experience when you deny your Father is still for your protection, for the power of your will cannot be lessened without the intervention of God against it, and any limitation on your power is not the Will of God. ⁵Therefore, look only to the power that God gave to save you, remembering that it is yours *because* it is His, and join with your brothers in His peace.

3. Your peace lies in its limitlessness. ²Limit the peace you share, and your Self must be unknown to you. ³Every altar to God is part of you, because the light He created is one with Him. ⁴Would you cut off a brother from the light that is yours? ⁵You would not do so if you realized that you can darken only your own mind. ⁶As you bring him back, so will you return. ⁷That is the law of God, for the protection of the Wholeness of His Son.

4. *Only you can deprive yourself of anything.* ²Do not oppose this realization, for it is truly the beginning of the dawn of light. ³Remember also that the denial of this simple fact takes many forms, and these you must learn to recognize and to oppose steadfastly, without exception. ⁴This is a crucial step in the reawakening. ⁵The beginning phases of this reversal are often quite painful, for as blame is withdrawn from without, there is a strong tendency to harbor it within. ⁶It is difficult at first to realize that this is exactly the same thing, for there is no distinction between within and without.

5. If your brothers are part of you and you blame them for your deprivation, you are blaming yourself. ²And you cannot blame yourself without blaming them. ³That is why blame must be undone, not seen elsewhere. ⁴Lay it to yourself and you cannot know yourself, for only the ego blames at all. ⁵Self-blame is therefore ego identification, and as much an ego defense as blaming others. ⁶*You cannot enter God's Presence if you attack His Son.* ⁷When His Son lifts his voice in praise of his Creator, he will hear the Voice for his Father. ⁸Yet the Creator cannot be praised without His Son, for Their glory is shared and They are glorified together.

6. Christ is at God's altar, waiting to welcome His Son. ²But come wholly without condemnation, for otherwise you will believe that the door is barred and you cannot enter. ³The door is not barred, and it is impossible that you cannot enter the place where

God would have you be. ⁴But love yourself with the Love of Christ, for so does your Father love you. ⁵You can refuse to enter, but you cannot bar the door that Christ holds open. ⁶Come unto me who hold it open for you, for while I live it cannot be shut, and I live forever. ⁷God is my life and yours, and nothing is denied by God to His Son.

7. At God's altar Christ waits for the restoration of Himself in you. ²God knows His Son as wholly blameless as Himself, and He is approached through the appreciation of His Son. ³Christ waits for your acceptance of Him as yourself, and of His Wholeness as yours. ⁴For Christ is the Son of God, Who lives in His Creator and shines with His glory. ⁵Christ is the extension of the Love and the loveliness of God, as perfect as His Creator and at peace with Him.

8. Blessed is the Son of God whose radiance is of his Father, and whose glory he wills to share as his Father shares it with him. ²There is no condemnation in the Son, for there is no condemnation in the Father. ³Sharing the perfect Love of the Father the Son must share what belongs to Him, for otherwise he will not know the Father or the Son. ⁴Peace be unto you who rest in God, and in whom the whole Sonship rests.

V. The "Dynamics" of the Ego

1. No one can escape from illusions unless he looks at them, for not looking is the way they are protected. ²There is no need to shrink from illusions, for they cannot be dangerous. ³We are ready to look more closely at the ego's thought system because together we have the lamp that will dispel it, and since you realize you do not want it, you must be ready. ⁴Let us be very calm in doing this, for we are merely looking honestly for truth. ⁵The "dynamics" of the ego will be our lesson for a while, for we must look first at this to see beyond it, since you have made it real. ⁶We will undo this error quietly together, and then look beyond it to truth.

2. What is healing but the removal of all that stands in the way of knowledge? ²And how else can one dispel illusions except by looking at them directly, without protecting them? ³Be not afraid, therefore, for what you will be looking at is the source of fear, and you are beginning to learn that fear is not real. ⁴You are also

learning that its effects can be dispelled merely by denying their reality. [5]The next step is obviously to recognize that what has no effects does not exist. [6]Laws do not operate in a vacuum, and what leads to nothing has not happened. [7]If reality is recognized by its extension, what leads to nothing could not be real. [8]Do not be afraid, then, to look upon fear, for it cannot be seen. [9]Clarity undoes confusion by definition, and to look upon darkness through light must dispel it.

3. Let us begin this lesson in "ego dynamics" by understanding that the term itself does not mean anything. [2]It contains the very contradiction in terms that makes it meaningless. [3]"Dynamics" implies the power to do something, and the whole separation fallacy lies in the belief that the ego *has* the power to do anything. [4]The ego is fearful to you because you believe this. [5]Yet the truth is very simple:

> [6]*All power is of God.*
> [7]*What is not of Him has no power to do anything.*

4. When we look at the ego, then, we are not considering dynamics but delusions. [2]You can surely regard a delusional system without fear, for it cannot have any effects if its source is not real. [3]Fear becomes more obviously inappropriate if you recognize the ego's goal, which is so clearly senseless that any effort on its behalf is necessarily expended on nothing. [4]The ego's goal is quite explicitly ego autonomy. [5]From the beginning, then, its purpose is to be separate, sufficient unto itself and independent of any power except its own. [6]This is why it is the symbol of separation.

5. Every idea has a purpose, and its purpose is always the natural outcome of what it is. [2]Everything that stems from the ego is the natural outcome of its central belief, and the way to undo its results is merely to recognize that their source is not natural, being out of accord with your true nature. [3]I said before that to will contrary to God is wishful thinking and not real willing. [4]His Will is One *because* the extension of His Will cannot be unlike itself. [5]The real conflict you experience, then, is between the ego's idle wishes and the Will of God, which you share. [6]Can this be a real conflict?

6. Yours is the independence of creation, not of autonomy. [2]Your whole creative function lies in your complete dependence on

203

God, Whose function He shares with you. [3]By His willingness to share it, He became as dependent on you as you are on Him. [4]Do not ascribe the ego's arrogance to Him Who wills not to be independent of you. [5]He has included you in His Autonomy. [6]Can you believe that autonomy is meaningful apart from Him? [7]The belief in ego autonomy is costing you the knowledge of your dependence on God, in which your freedom lies. [8]The ego sees all dependency as threatening, and has twisted even your longing for God into a means of establishing itself. [9]But do not be deceived by its interpretation of your conflict.

7. The ego always attacks on behalf of separation. [2]Believing it has the power to do this it does nothing else, because its goal of autonomy *is* nothing else. [3]The ego is totally confused about reality, but it does not lose sight of its goal. [4]It is much more vigilant than you are, because it is perfectly certain of its purpose. [5]You are confused because you do not recognize yours.

8. You must recognize that the last thing the ego wishes you to realize is that you are afraid of it. [2]For if the ego could give rise to fear, it would diminish your independence and weaken your power. [3]Yet its one claim to your allegiance is that it can give power to you. [4]Without this belief you would not listen to it at all. [5]How, then, can its existence continue if you realize that, by accepting it, you are belittling yourself and depriving yourself of power?

9. The ego can and does allow you to regard yourself as supercilious, unbelieving, "lighthearted," distant, emotionally shallow, callous, uninvolved and even desperate, but not really afraid. [2]Minimizing fear, but not its undoing, is the ego's constant effort, and is indeed a skill at which it is very ingenious. [3]How can it preach separation without upholding it through fear, and would you listen to it if you recognized this is what it is doing?

10. Your recognition that whatever seems to separate you from God is only fear, regardless of the form it takes and quite apart from how the ego wants you to experience it, is therefore the basic ego threat. [2]Its dream of autonomy is shaken to its foundation by this awareness. [3]For though you may countenance a false idea of independence, you will not accept the cost of fear if you recognize it. [4]Yet this is the cost, and the ego cannot minimize it. [5]If you overlook love you are overlooking yourself, and you must fear unreality *because* you have denied yourself. [6]By believing that you have successfully attacked truth, you are believing that

attack has power. [7]Very simply, then, you have become afraid of yourself. [8]And no one wants to find what he believes would destroy him.

11. If the ego's goal of autonomy could be accomplished God's purpose could be defeated, and this is impossible. [2]Only by learning what fear is can you finally learn to distinguish the possible from the impossible and the false from the true. [3]According to the ego's teaching, *its* goal can be accomplished and God's purpose can *not*. [4]According to the Holy Spirit's teaching, *only* God's purpose can be accomplished, and it is accomplished already.

12. God is as dependent on you as you are on Him, because His Autonomy encompasses yours, and is therefore incomplete without it. [2]You can only establish your autonomy by identifying with Him, and fulfilling your function as it exists in truth. [3]The ego believes that to accomplish its goal is happiness. [4]But it is given you to know that God's function is yours, and happiness cannot be found apart from Your joint Will. [5]Recognize only that the ego's goal, which you have pursued so diligently, has merely brought you fear, and it becomes difficult to maintain that fear is happiness. [6]Upheld by fear, this is what the ego would have you believe. [7]Yet God's Son is not insane, and cannot believe it. [8]Let him but recognize it and he will not accept it. [9]For only the insane would choose fear in place of love, and only the insane could believe that love can be gained by attack. [10]But the sane realize that only attack could produce fear, from which the Love of God completely protects them.

13. The ego analyzes; the Holy Spirit accepts. [2]The appreciation of wholeness comes only through acceptance, for to analyze means to break down or to separate out. [3]The attempt to understand totality by breaking it down is clearly the characteristically contradictory approach of the ego to everything. [4]The ego believes that power, understanding and truth lie in separation, and to establish this belief it must attack. [5]Unaware that the belief cannot be established, and obsessed with the conviction that separation is salvation, the ego attacks everything it perceives by breaking it into small, disconnected parts, without meaningful relationships and therefore without meaning. [6]The ego will always substitute chaos for meaning, for if separation is salvation, harmony is threat.

14. The ego's interpretations of the laws of perception are, and

would have to be, the exact opposite of the Holy Spirit's. [2]The ego focuses on error and overlooks truth. [3]It makes real every mistake it perceives, and with characteristically circular reasoning concludes that because of the mistake consistent truth must be meaningless. [4]The next step, then, is obvious. [5]If consistent truth is meaningless, inconsistency must be true. [6]Holding error clearly in mind, and protecting what it has made real, the ego proceeds to the next step in its thought system: Error is real and truth is error.

15. The ego makes no attempt to understand this, and it is clearly not understandable, but the ego does make every attempt to demonstrate it, and this it does constantly. [2]Analyzing to attack meaning, the ego succeeds in overlooking it and is left with a series of fragmented perceptions which it unifies on behalf of itself. [3]This, then, becomes the universe it perceives. [4]And it is this universe which, in turn, becomes its demonstration of its own reality.

16. Do not underestimate the appeal of the ego's demonstrations to those who would listen. [2]Selective perception chooses its witnesses carefully, and its witnesses are consistent. [3]The case for insanity is strong to the insane. [4]For reasoning ends at its beginning, and no thought system transcends its source. [5]Yet reasoning without meaning cannot demonstrate anything, and those who are convinced by it must be deluded. [6]Can the ego teach truly when it overlooks truth? [7]Can it perceive what it has denied? [8]Its witnesses do attest to its denial, but hardly to what it has denied. [9]The ego looks straight at the Father and does not see Him, for it has denied His Son.

17. Would *you* remember the Father? [2]Accept His Son and you will remember Him. [3]Nothing can demonstrate that His Son is unworthy, for nothing can prove that a lie is true. [4]What you see of His Son through the eyes of the ego is a demonstration that His Son does not exist, yet where the Son is the Father must be. [5]Accept what God does not deny, and it will demonstrate its truth. [6]The witnesses for God stand in His light and behold what He created. [7]Their silence is the sign that they have beheld God's Son, and in the Presence of Christ they need demonstrate nothing, for Christ speaks to them of Himself and of His Father. [8]They are silent because Christ speaks to them, and it is His words they speak.

18. Every brother you meet becomes a witness for Christ or for the

ego, depending on what you perceive in him. ²Everyone convinces you of what you want to perceive, and of the reality of the kingdom you have chosen for your vigilance. ³Everything you perceive is a witness to the thought system you want to be true. ⁴Every brother has the power to release you, if you choose to be free. ⁵You cannot accept false witness of him unless you have evoked false witnesses against him. ⁶If he speaks not of Christ to you, you spoke not of Christ to him. ⁷You hear but your own voice, and if Christ speaks through you, you will hear Him.

VI. Waking to Redemption

1. It is impossible not to believe what you see, but it is equally impossible to see what you do not believe. ²Perceptions are built up on the basis of experience, and experience leads to beliefs. ³It is not until beliefs are fixed that perceptions stabilize. ⁴In effect, then, what you believe you *do* see. ⁵That is what I meant when I said, "Blessed are ye who have not seen and still believe," for those who believe in the resurrection will see it. ⁶The resurrection is the complete triumph of Christ over the ego, not by attack but by transcendence. ⁷For Christ does rise above the ego and all its works, and ascends to the Father and His Kingdom.

2. Would you join in the resurrection or the crucifixion? ²Would you condemn your brothers or free them? ³Would you transcend your prison and ascend to the Father? ⁴These questions are all the same, and are answered together. ⁵There has been much confusion about what perception means, because the word is used both for awareness and for the interpretation of awareness. ⁶Yet you cannot be aware without interpretation, for what you perceive *is* your interpretation.

3. This course is perfectly clear. ²If you do not see it clearly, it is because you are interpreting against it, and therefore do not believe it. ³And since belief determines perception, you do not perceive what it means and therefore do not accept it. ⁴Yet different experiences lead to different beliefs, and with them different perceptions. ⁵For perceptions are learned *with* beliefs, and experience does teach. ⁶I am leading you to a new kind of experience that you will become less and less willing to deny. ⁷Learning of Christ is easy, for to perceive with Him involves no strain at all. ⁸His perceptions are your natural awareness, and it

is only the distortions you introduce that tire you. ⁹Let the Christ in you interpret for you, and do not try to limit what you see by narrow little beliefs that are unworthy of God's Son. ¹⁰For until Christ comes into His Own, the Son of God will see himself as Fatherless.

4. I am *your* resurrection and *your* life. ²You live in me because you live in God. ³And everyone lives in you, as you live in everyone. ⁴Can you, then, perceive unworthiness in a brother and not perceive it in yourself? ⁵And can you perceive it in yourself and not perceive it in God? ⁶Believe in the resurrection because it has been accomplished, and it has been accomplished in you. ⁷This is as true now as it will ever be, for the resurrection is the Will of God, which knows no time and no exceptions. ⁸But make no exceptions yourself, or you will not perceive what has been accomplished for you. ⁹For we ascend unto the Father together, as it was in the beginning, is now and ever shall be, for such is the nature of God's Son as his Father created him.

5. Do not underestimate the power of the devotion of God's Son, nor the power the god he worships has over him. ²For he places himself at the altar of his god, whether it be the god he made or the God Who created him. ³That is why his slavery is as complete as his freedom, for he will obey only the god he accepts. ⁴The god of crucifixion demands that he crucify, and his worshippers obey. ⁵In his name they crucify themselves, believing that the power of the Son of God is born of sacrifice and pain. ⁶The God of resurrection demands nothing, for He does not will to take away. ⁷He does not require obedience, for obedience implies submission. ⁸He would only have you learn your will and follow it, not in the spirit of sacrifice and submission, but in the gladness of freedom.

6. Resurrection must compel your allegiance gladly, because it is the symbol of joy. ²Its whole compelling power lies in the fact that it represents what you want to be. ³The freedom to leave behind everything that hurts you and humbles you and frightens you cannot be thrust upon you, but it can be offered you through the grace of God. ⁴And you can accept it by His grace, for God is gracious to His Son, accepting him without question as His Own. ⁵Who, then, is *your* own? ⁶The Father has given you all that is His, and He Himself is yours with them. ⁷Guard them in their resurrection, for otherwise you will not awake in God, safely surrounded by what is yours forever.

7. You will not find peace until you have removed the nails from

the hands of God's Son, and taken the last thorn from his forehead. [2]The Love of God surrounds His Son whom the god of crucifixion condemns. [3]Teach not that I died in vain. [4]Teach rather that I did not die by demonstrating that I live in you. [5]For the undoing of the crucifixion of God's Son is the work of the redemption, in which everyone has a part of equal value. [6]God does not judge His guiltless Son. [7]Having given Himself to him, how could it be otherwise?

8. You have nailed yourself to a cross, and placed a crown of thorns upon your own head. [2]Yet you cannot crucify God's Son, for the Will of God cannot die. [3]His Son has been redeemed from his own crucifixion, and you cannot assign to death whom God has given eternal life. [4]The dream of crucifixion still lies heavy on your eyes, but what you see in dreams is not reality. [5]While you perceive the Son of God as crucified, you are asleep. [6]And as long as you believe that you can crucify him, you are only having nightmares. [7]You who are beginning to wake are still aware of dreams, and have not yet forgotten them. [8]The forgetting of dreams and the awareness of Christ come with the awakening of others to share your redemption.

9. You will awaken to your own call, for the Call to awake is within you. [2]If I live in you, you are awake. [3]Yet you must see the works I do through you, or you will not perceive that I have done them unto you. [4]Do not set limits on what you believe I can do through you, or you will not accept what I can do *for* you. [5]Yet it is done already, and unless you give all that you have received you will not know that your redeemer liveth, and that you have awakened with him. [6]Redemption is recognized only by sharing it.

10. God's Son *is* saved. [2]Bring only this awareness to the Sonship, and you will have a part in the redemption as valuable as mine. [3]For your part must be like mine if you learn it of me. [4]If you believe that yours is limited, you are limiting mine. [5]There is no order of difficulty in miracles because all of God's Sons are of equal value, and their equality is their oneness. [6]The whole power of God is in every part of Him, and nothing contradictory to His Will is either great or small. [7]What does not exist has no size and no measure. [8]To God all things are possible. [9]And to Christ it is given to be like the Father.

VII. The Condition of Reality

1. The world as you perceive it cannot have been created by the Father, for the world is not as you see it. [2]God created only the eternal, and everything you see is perishable. [3]Therefore, there must be another world that you do not see. [4]The Bible speaks of a new Heaven and a new earth, yet this cannot be literally true, for the eternal are not re-created. [5]To perceive anew is merely to perceive again, implying that before, or in the interval between, you were not perceiving at all. [6]What, then, is the world that awaits your perception when you see it?

2. Every loving thought that the Son of God ever had is eternal. [2]The loving thoughts his mind perceives in this world are the world's only reality. [3]They are still perceptions, because he still believes that he is separate. [4]Yet they are eternal because they are loving. [5]And being loving they are like the Father, and therefore cannot die. [6]The real world can actually be perceived. [7]All that is necessary is a willingness to perceive nothing else. [8]For if you perceive both good and evil, you are accepting both the false and the true and making no distinction between them.

3. The ego may see some good, but never only good. [2]That is why its perceptions are so variable. [3]It does not reject goodness entirely, for that you could not accept. [4]But it always adds something that is not real to the real, thus confusing illusion and reality. [5]For perceptions cannot be partly true. [6]If you believe in truth and illusion, you cannot tell which is true. [7]To establish your personal autonomy you tried to create unlike your Father, believing that what you made is capable of being unlike Him. [8]Yet everything true *is* like Him. [9]Perceiving only the real world will lead you to the real Heaven, because it will make you capable of understanding it.

4. The perception of goodness is not knowledge, but the denial of the opposite of goodness enables you to recognize a condition in which opposites do not exist. [2]And this *is* the condition of knowledge. [3]Without this awareness you have not met its conditions, and until you do you will not know it is yours already. [4]You have made many ideas that you have placed between yourself and your Creator, and these beliefs are the world as you perceive it. [5]Truth is not absent here, but it is obscure. [6]You do not know the difference between what you have made and what God created, and so you do not know the difference between what you have

made and what *you* have created. ⁷To believe that you can perceive the real world is to believe that you can know yourself. ⁸You can know God because it is His Will to be known. ⁹The real world is all that the Holy Spirit has saved for you out of what you have made, and to perceive only this is salvation, because it is the recognition that reality is only what is true.

VIII. The Problem and the Answer

1. This is a very simple course. ²Perhaps you do not feel you need a course which, in the end, teaches that only reality is true. ³But do you believe it? ⁴When you perceive the real world, you will recognize that you did not believe it. ⁵Yet the swiftness with which your new and only real perception will be translated into knowledge will leave you but an instant to realize that this alone is true. ⁶And then everything you made will be forgotten; the good and the bad, the false and the true. ⁷For as Heaven and earth become one, even the real world will vanish from your sight. ⁸The end of the world is not its destruction, but its translation into Heaven. ⁹The reinterpretation of the world is the transfer of all perception to knowledge.

2. The Bible tells you to become as little children. ²Little children recognize that they do not understand what they perceive, and so they ask what it means. ³Do not make the mistake of believing that you understand what you perceive, for its meaning is lost to you. ⁴Yet the Holy Spirit has saved its meaning for you, and if you will let Him interpret it, He will restore to you what you have thrown away. ⁵Yet while you think you know its meaning, you will see no need to ask it of Him.

3. You do not know the meaning of anything you perceive. ²Not one thought you hold is wholly true. ³The recognition of this is your firm beginning. ⁴You are not misguided; you have accepted no guide at all. ⁵Instruction in perception is your great need, for you understand nothing. ⁶Recognize this but do not accept it, for understanding is your inheritance. ⁷Perceptions are learned, and you are not without a Teacher. ⁸Yet your willingness to learn of Him depends on your willingness to question everything you learned of yourself, for you who learned amiss should not be your own teacher.

4. No one can withhold truth except from himself. ²Yet God will

not refuse you the Answer He gave. ³Ask, then, for what is yours, but which you did not make, and do not defend yourself against truth. ⁴You made the problem God has answered. ⁵Ask yourself, therefore, but one simple question:

⁶*Do I want the problem or do I want the answer?*

⁷Decide for the answer and you will have it, for you will see it as it is, and it is yours already.

5. You may complain that this course is not sufficiently specific for you to understand and use. ²Yet perhaps you have not done what it specifically advocates. ³This is not a course in the play of ideas, but in their practical application. ⁴Nothing could be more specific than to be told that if you ask you will receive. ⁵The Holy Spirit will answer every specific problem as long as you believe that problems are specific. ⁶His answer is both many and one, as long as you believe that the one is many. ⁷You may be afraid of His specificity, for fear of what you think it will demand of you. ⁸Yet only by asking will you learn that nothing of God demands anything of you. ⁹God gives; He does not take. ¹⁰When you refuse to ask, it is because you believe that asking is taking rather than sharing.

6. The Holy Spirit will give you only what is yours, and will take nothing in return. ²For what is yours is everything, and you share it with God. ³That is its reality. ⁴Would the Holy Spirit, Who wills only to restore, be capable of misinterpreting the question you must ask to learn His answer? ⁵You *have* heard the answer, but you have misunderstood the question. ⁶You believe that to ask for guidance of the Holy Spirit is to ask for deprivation.

7. Little child of God, you do not understand your Father. ²You believe in a world that takes, because you believe that you can get by taking. ³And by that perception you have lost sight of the real world. ⁴You are afraid of the world as you see it, but the real world is still yours for the asking. ⁵Do not deny it to yourself, for it can only free you. ⁶Nothing of God will enslave His Son whom He created free and whose freedom is protected by His Being. ⁷Blessed are you who are willing to ask the truth of God without fear, for only thus can you learn that His answer is the release from fear.

8. Beautiful child of God, you are asking only for what I promised you. ²Do you believe I would deceive you? ³The Kingdom of

Heaven *is* within you. ⁴Believe that the truth is in me, for I know that it is in you. ⁵God's Sons have nothing they do not share. ⁶Ask for truth of any Son of God, and you have asked it of me. ⁷Not one of us but has the answer in him, to give to anyone who asks it of him.

9. Ask anything of God's Son and his Father will answer you, for Christ is not deceived in His Father and His Father is not deceived in Him. ²Do not, then, be deceived in your brother, and see only his loving thoughts as his reality, for by denying that his mind is split you will heal yours. ³Accept him as his Father accepts him and heal him unto Christ, for Christ is his healing and yours. ⁴Christ is the Son of God Who is in no way separate from His Father, Whose every thought is as loving as the Thought of His Father by which He was created. ⁵Be not deceived in God's Son, for thereby you must be deceived in yourself. ⁶And being deceived in yourself you are deceived in your Father, in Whom no deceit is possible.

10. In the real world there is no sickness, for there is no separation and no division. ²Only loving thoughts are recognized, and because no one is without your help, the Help of God goes with you everywhere. ³As you become willing to accept this Help by asking for It, you will give It because you want It. ⁴Nothing will be beyond your healing power, because nothing will be denied your simple request. ⁵What problems will not disappear in the Presence of God's Answer? ⁶Ask, then, to learn of the reality of your brother, because this is what you will perceive in him, and you will see your beauty reflected in his.

11. Do not accept your brother's variable perception of himself for his split mind is yours, and you will not accept your healing without his. ²For you share the real world as you share Heaven, and his healing is yours. ³To love yourself is to heal yourself, and you cannot perceive part of you as sick and achieve your goal. ⁴Brother, we heal together as we live together and love together. ⁵Be not deceived in God's Son, for he is one with himself and one with his Father. ⁶Love him who is beloved of his Father, and you will learn of the Father's Love for you.

12. If you perceive offense in a brother pluck the offense from your mind, for you are offended by Christ and are deceived in Him. ²Heal in Christ and be not offended by Him, for there is no offense in Him. ³If what you perceive offends you, you are offended in yourself and are condemning God's Son whom God

condemneth not. [4]Let the Holy Spirit remove all offenses of God's Son against himself and perceive no one but through His guidance, for He would save you from all condemnation. [5]Accept His healing power and use it for all He sends you, for He wills to heal the Son of God, in whom He is not deceived.

13.   Children perceive frightening ghosts and monsters and dragons, and they are terrified. [2]Yet if they ask someone they trust for the meaning of what they perceive, and are willing to let their own interpretations go in favor of reality, their fear goes with them. [3]When a child is helped to translate his "ghost" into a curtain, his "monster" into a shadow, and his "dragon" into a dream he is no longer afraid, and laughs happily at his own fear.

14.   You, my child, are afraid of your brothers and of your Father and of yourself. [2]But you are merely deceived in them. [3]Ask what they are of the Teacher of reality, and hearing His answer, you too will laugh at your fears and replace them with peace. [4]For fear lies not in reality, but in the minds of children who do not understand reality. [5]It is only their lack of understanding that frightens them, and when they learn to perceive truly they are not afraid. [6]And because of this they will ask for truth again when they are frightened. [7]It is not the reality of your brothers or your Father or yourself that frightens you. [8]You do not know what they are, and so you perceive them as ghosts and monsters and dragons. [9]Ask what their reality is from the One Who knows it, and He will tell you what they are. [10]For you do not understand them, and because you are deceived by what you see you need reality to dispel your fears.

15.   Would you not exchange your fears for truth, if the exchange is yours for the asking? [2]For if God is not deceived in you, you can be deceived only in yourself. [3]Yet you can learn the truth about yourself from the Holy Spirit, Who will teach you that, as part of God, deceit in you is impossible. [4]When you perceive yourself without deceit, you will accept the real world in place of the false one you have made. [5]And then your Father will lean down to you and take the last step for you, by raising you unto Himself.

Chapter 12

THE HOLY SPIRIT'S CURRICULUM

I. The Judgment of the Holy Spirit

1. You have been told not to make error real, and the way to do this is very simple. ²If you want to believe in error, you would have to make it real because it is not true. ³But truth is real in its own right, and to believe in truth *you do not have to do anything*. ⁴Understand that you do not respond to anything directly, but to your interpretation of it. ⁵Your interpretation thus becomes the justification for the response. ⁶That is why analyzing the motives of others is hazardous to you. ⁷If you decide that someone is really trying to attack you or desert you or enslave you, you will respond as if he had actually done so, having made his error real to you. ⁸To interpret error is to give it power, and having done this you will overlook truth.

2. The analysis of ego motivation is very complicated, very obscuring, and never without your own ego involvement. ²The whole process represents a clear-cut attempt to demonstrate your own ability to understand what you perceive. ³This is shown by the fact that you react to your interpretations as if they were correct. ⁴You may then control your reactions behaviorally, but not emotionally. ⁵This would obviously be a split or an attack on the integrity of your mind, pitting one level within it against another.

3. There is but one interpretation of motivation that makes any sense. ²And because it is the Holy Spirit's judgment it requires no effort at all on your part. ³Every loving thought is true. ⁴Everything else is an appeal for healing and help, regardless of the form it takes. ⁵Can anyone be justified in responding with anger to a brother's plea for help? ⁶No response can be appropriate except the willingness to give it to him, for this and only this is what he is asking for. ⁷Offer him anything else, and you are assuming the right to attack his reality by interpreting it as you see fit. ⁸Perhaps the danger of this to your own mind is not yet fully apparent. ⁹If you believe that an appeal for help is something else you will react to something else. ¹⁰Your response will therefore be inappropriate to reality as it is, but not to your perception of it.

4. There is nothing to prevent you from recognizing all calls for

help as exactly what they are except your own imagined need to attack. [2]It is only this that makes you willing to engage in endless "battles" with reality, in which you deny the reality of the need for healing by making it unreal. [3]You would not do this except for your unwillingness to accept reality as it is, and which you therefore withhold from yourself.

5.	It is surely good advice to tell you not to judge what you do not understand. [2]No one with a personal investment is a reliable witness, for truth to him has become what he wants it to be. [3]If you are unwilling to perceive an appeal for help as what it is, it is because you are unwilling to give help and to receive it. [4]To fail to recognize a call for help is to refuse help. [5]Would you maintain that you do not need it? [6]Yet this is what you are maintaining when you refuse to recognize a brother's appeal, for only by answering his appeal *can* you be helped. [7]Deny him your help and you will not recognize God's Answer to you. [8]The Holy Spirit does not need your help in interpreting motivation, but you do need His.

6.	Only appreciation is an appropriate response to your brother. [2]Gratitude is due him for both his loving thoughts and his appeals for help, for both are capable of bringing love into your awareness if you perceive them truly. [3]And all your sense of strain comes from your attempts not to do just this. [4]How simple, then, is God's plan for salvation. [5]There is but one response to reality, for reality evokes no conflict at all. [6]There is but one Teacher of reality, Who understands what it is. [7]He does not change His Mind about reality because reality does not change. [8]Although your interpretations of reality are meaningless in your divided state, His remain consistently true. [9]He gives them to you because they are *for* you. [10]Do not attempt to "help" a brother in your way, for you cannot help yourself. [11]But hear his call for the Help of God, and you will recognize your own need for the Father.

7.	Your interpretations of your brother's needs are your interpretation of yours. [2]By giving help you are asking for it, and if you perceive but one need in yourself you will be healed. [3]For you will recognize God's Answer as you want It to be, and if you want It in truth, It will be truly yours. [4]Every appeal you answer in the Name of Christ brings the remembrance of your Father closer to your awareness. [5]For the sake of your need, then, hear every call for help as what it is, so God can answer *you*.

8.   By applying the Holy Spirit's interpretation of the reactions of others more and more consistently, you will gain an increasing awareness that His criteria are equally applicable to you. ²For to recognize fear is not enough to escape from it, although the recognition is necessary to demonstrate the need for escape. ³The Holy Spirit must still translate the fear into truth. ⁴If you were left with the fear, once you had recognized it, you would have taken a step away from reality, not towards it. ⁵Yet we have repeatedly emphasized the need to recognize fear and face it without disguise as a crucial step in the undoing of the ego. ⁶Consider how well the Holy Spirit's interpretation of the motives of others will serve you then. ⁷Having taught you to accept only loving thoughts in others and to regard everything else as an appeal for help, He has taught you that fear itself is an appeal for help. ⁸This is what recognizing fear really means. ⁹If you do not protect it, He will reinterpret it. ¹⁰That is the ultimate value in learning to perceive attack as a call for love. ¹¹We have already learned that fear and attack are inevitably associated. ¹²If only attack produces fear, and if you see attack as the call for help that it is, the unreality of fear must dawn on you. ¹³For fear *is* a call for love, in unconscious recognition of what has been denied.

9.   Fear is a symptom of your own deep sense of loss. ²If when you perceive it in others you learn to supply the loss, the basic cause of fear is removed. ³Thereby you teach yourself that fear does not exist in you. ⁴The means for removing it is in yourself, and you have demonstrated this by giving it. ⁵Fear and love are the only emotions of which you are capable. ⁶One is false, for it was made out of denial; and denial depends on the belief in what is denied for its own existence. ⁷By interpreting fear correctly as a positive affirmation of the underlying belief it masks, you are undermining its perceived usefulness by rendering it useless. ⁸Defenses that do not work at all are automatically discarded. ⁹If you raise what fear conceals to clear-cut unequivocal predominance, fear becomes meaningless. ¹⁰You have denied its power to conceal love, which was its only purpose. ¹¹The veil that you have drawn across the face of love has disappeared.

10.   If you would look upon love, which *is* the world's reality, how could you do better than to recognize, in every defense against it, the underlying appeal *for* it? ²And how could you better learn of its reality than by answering the appeal for it by giving it? ³The Holy Spirit's interpretation of fear does dispel it, for the aware-

ness of truth cannot be denied. ⁴Thus does the Holy Spirit replace fear with love and translate error into truth. ⁵And thus will you learn of Him how to replace your dream of separation with the fact of unity. ⁶For the separation is only the denial of union, and correctly interpreted, attests to your eternal knowledge that union is true.

II. The Way to Remember God

1. Miracles are merely the translation of denial into truth. ²If to love oneself is to heal oneself, those who are sick do not love themselves. ³Therefore, they are asking for the love that would heal them, but which they are denying to themselves. ⁴If they knew the truth about themselves they could not be sick. ⁵The task of the miracle worker thus becomes *to deny the denial of truth*. ⁶The sick must heal themselves, for the truth is in them. ⁷Yet having obscured it, the light in another mind must shine into theirs because that light *is* theirs.

2. The light in them shines as brightly regardless of the density of the fog that obscures it. ²If you give no power to the fog to obscure the light, it has none. ³For it has power only if the Son of God gives power to it. ⁴He must himself withdraw that power, remembering that all power is of God. ⁵You can remember this for all the Sonship. ⁶Do not allow your brother not to remember, for his forgetfulness is yours. ⁷But your remembering is his, for God cannot be remembered alone. ⁸*This is what you have forgotten*. ⁹To perceive the healing of your brother as the healing of yourself is thus the way to remember God. ¹⁰For you forgot your brothers with Him, and God's Answer to your forgetting is but the way to remember.

3. Perceive in sickness but another call for love, and offer your brother what he believes he cannot offer himself. ²Whatever the sickness, there is but one remedy. ³You will be made whole as you make whole, for to perceive in sickness the appeal for health is to recognize in hatred the call for love. ⁴And to give a brother what he really wants is to offer it unto yourself, for your Father wills you to know your brother as yourself. ⁵Answer his call for love, and yours is answered. ⁶Healing is the Love of Christ for His Father and for Himself.

4. Remember what was said about the frightening perceptions of

little children, which terrify them because they do not understand them. ²If they ask for enlightenment and accept it, their fears vanish. ³But if they hide their nightmares they will keep them. ⁴It is easy to help an uncertain child, for he recognizes that he does not understand what his perceptions mean. ⁵Yet you believe that you do understand yours. ⁶Little child, you are hiding your head under the cover of the heavy blankets you have laid upon yourself. ⁷You are hiding your nightmares in the darkness of your own false certainty, and refusing to open your eyes and look at them.

5.   Let us not save nightmares, for they are not fitting offerings for Christ, and so they are not fit gifts for you. ²Take off the covers and look at what you are afraid of. ³Only the anticipation will frighten you, for the reality of nothingness cannot be frightening. ⁴Let us not delay this, for your dream of hatred will not leave you without help, and Help is here. ⁵Learn to be quiet in the midst of turmoil, for quietness is the end of strife and this is the journey to peace. ⁶Look straight at every image that rises to delay you, for the goal is inevitable because it is eternal. ⁷The goal of love is but your right, and it belongs to you despite your dreams.

6.   You still want what God wills, and no nightmare can defeat a child of God in his purpose. ²For your purpose was given you by God, and you must accomplish it because it is His Will. ³Awake and remember your purpose, for it is your will to do so. ⁴What has been accomplished for you must be yours. ⁵Do not let your hatred stand in the way of love, for nothing can withstand the Love of Christ for His Father, or His Father's Love for Him.

7.   A little while and you will see me, for I am not hidden because *you* are hiding. ²I will awaken you as surely as I awakened myself, for I awoke for you. ³In my resurrection is your release. ⁴Our mission is to escape from crucifixion, not from redemption. ⁵Trust in my help, for I did not walk alone, and I will walk with you as our Father walked with me. ⁶Do you not know that I walked with Him in peace? ⁷And does not that mean that peace goes with *us* on the journey?

8.   There is no fear in perfect love. ²We will but be making perfect to you what is already perfect in you. ³You do not fear the unknown but the known. ⁴You will not fail in your mission because I did not fail in mine. ⁵Give me but a little trust in the name of the complete trust I have in you, and we will easily accomplish the goal of perfection together. ⁶For perfection *is*, and cannot be

denied. [7]To deny the denial of perfection is not so difficult as to deny truth, and what we can accomplish together will be believed when you see it as accomplished.

9. You who have tried to banish love have not succeeded, but you who choose to banish fear must succeed. [2]The Lord is with you, but you know it not. [3]Yet your Redeemer liveth, and abideth in you in the peace out of which He was created. [4]Would you not exchange this awareness for the awareness of fear? [5]When we have overcome fear—not by hiding it, not by minimizing it, and not by denying its full import in any way—this is what you will really see. [6]You cannot lay aside the obstacles to real vision without looking upon them, for to lay aside means to judge against. [7]If you will look, the Holy Spirit will judge, and He will judge truly. [8]Yet He cannot shine away what you keep hidden, for you have not offered it to Him and He cannot take it from you.

10. We are therefore embarking on an organized, well-structured and carefully planned program aimed at learning how to offer to the Holy Spirit everything you do not want. [2]He knows what to do with it. [3]You do not understand how to use what He knows. [4]Whatever is given Him that is not of God is gone. [5]Yet you must look at it yourself in perfect willingness, for otherwise His knowledge remains useless to you. [6]Surely He will not fail to help you, since help is His only purpose. [7]Do you not have greater reason for fearing the world as you perceive it, than for looking at the cause of fear and letting it go forever?

III. The Investment in Reality

1. I once asked you to sell all you have and give to the poor and follow me. [2]This is what I meant: If you have no investment in anything in this world, you can teach the poor where their treasure is. [3]The poor are merely those who have invested wrongly, and they are poor indeed! [4]Because they are in need it is given you to help them, since you are among them. [5]Consider how perfectly your lesson would be learned if you were unwilling to share their poverty. [6]For poverty is lack, and there is but one lack since there is but one need.

2. Suppose a brother insists on having you do something you think you do not want to do. [2]His very insistence should tell you that he believes salvation lies in it. [3]If you insist on refusing and

experience a quick response of opposition, you are believing that your salvation lies in *not* doing it. ⁴You, then, are making the same mistake he is, and are making his error real to both of you. ⁵Insistence means investment, and what you invest in is always related to your notion of salvation. ⁶The question is always twofold; first, *what* is to be saved? ⁷And second, *how* can it be saved?

3. Whenever you become angry with a brother, for whatever reason, you are believing that the ego is to be saved, and to be saved by attack. ²If he attacks, you are agreeing with this belief; and if you attack, you are reinforcing it. ³*Remember that those who attack are poor.* ⁴Their poverty asks for gifts, not for further impoverishment. ⁵You who could help them are surely acting destructively if you accept their poverty as yours. ⁶If you had not invested as they had, it would never occur to you to overlook their need.

4. *Recognize what does not matter*, and if your brothers ask you for something "outrageous," do it *because* it does not matter. ²Refuse, and your opposition establishes that it does matter to you. ³It is only you, therefore, who have made the request outrageous, and every request of a brother is for you. ⁴Why would you insist in denying him? ⁵For to do so is to deny yourself and impoverish both. ⁶He is asking for salvation, as you are. ⁷Poverty is of the ego, and never of God. ⁸No "outrageous" requests can be made of one who recognizes what is valuable and wants to accept nothing else.

5. Salvation is for the mind, and it is attained through peace. ²This is the only thing that can be saved and the only way to save it. ³Any response other than love arises from a confusion about the "what" and the "how" of salvation, and this is the only answer. ⁴Never lose sight of this, and never allow yourself to believe, even for an instant, that there is another answer. ⁵For you will surely place yourself among the poor, who do not understand that they dwell in abundance and that salvation is come.

6. To identify with the ego is to attack yourself and make yourself poor. ²That is why everyone who identifies with the ego feels deprived. ³What he experiences then is depression or anger, because what he did was to exchange Self-love for self-hate, making him afraid of himself. ⁴He does not realize this. ⁵Even if he is fully aware of anxiety he does not perceive its source as his own ego identification, and he always tries to handle it by making some sort of insane "arrangement" with the world. ⁶He always

perceives this world as outside himself, for this is crucial to his adjustment. [7]He does not realize that he makes this world, for there is no world outside of him.

7.   If only the loving thoughts of God's Son are the world's reality, the real world must be in his mind. [2]His insane thoughts, too, must be in his mind, but an internal conflict of this magnitude he cannot tolerate. [3]A split mind is endangered, and the recognition that it encompasses completely opposed thoughts within itself is intolerable. [4]Therefore the mind projects the split, not the reality. [5]Everything you perceive as the outside world is merely your attempt to maintain your ego identification, for everyone believes that identification is salvation. [6]Yet consider what has happened, for thoughts do have consequences to the thinker. [7]You have become at odds with the world as you perceive it, because you think it is antagonistic to you. [8]This is a necessary consequence of what you have done. [9]You have projected outward what is antagonistic to what is inward, and therefore you would have to perceive it this way. [10]That is why you must realize that your hatred is in your mind and not outside it before you can get rid of it; and why you must get rid of it before you can perceive the world as it really is.

8.   I said before that God so loved the world that He gave it to His only begotten Son. [2]God does love the real world, and those who perceive its reality cannot see the world of death. [3]For death is not of the real world, in which everything reflects the eternal. [4]God gave you the real world in exchange for the one you made out of your split mind, and which is the symbol of death. [5]For if you could really separate yourself from the Mind of God you would die.

9.   The world you perceive is a world of separation. [2]Perhaps you are willing to accept even death to deny your Father. [3]Yet He would not have it so, and so it is not so. [4]You still cannot will against Him, and that is why you have no control over the world you made. [5]It is not a world of will because it is governed by the desire to be unlike God, and this desire is not will. [6]The world you made is therefore totally chaotic, governed by arbitrary and senseless "laws," and without meaning of any kind. [7]For it is made out of what you do not want, projected from your mind because you are afraid of it. [8]Yet this world is only in the mind of its maker, along with his real salvation. [9]Do not believe it is outside of yourself, for only by recognizing where it is will you gain

control over it. [10]For you do have control over your mind, since the mind is the mechanism of decision.

10. If you will recognize that all the attack you perceive is in your own mind and nowhere else, you will at last have placed its source, and where it begins it must end. [2]For in this same place also lies salvation. [3]The altar of God where Christ abideth is there. [4]You have defiled the altar, but not the world. [5]Yet Christ has placed the Atonement on the altar for you. [6]Bring your perceptions of the world to this altar, for it is the altar to truth. [7]There you will see your vision changed, and there you will learn to see truly. [8]From this place, where God and His Son dwell in peace and where you are welcome, you will look out in peace and behold the world truly. [9]Yet to find the place, you must relinquish your investment in the world as you project it, allowing the Holy Spirit to extend the real world to you from the altar of God.

IV. Seeking and Finding

1. The ego is certain that love is dangerous, and this is always its central teaching. [2]It never puts it this way; on the contrary, everyone who believes that the ego is salvation seems to be intensely engaged in the search for love. [3]Yet the ego, though encouraging the search for love very actively, makes one proviso; do not find it. [4]Its dictates, then, can be summed up simply as: "Seek and do *not* find." [5]This is the one promise the ego holds out to you, and the one promise it will keep. [6]For the ego pursues its goal with fanatic insistence, and its judgment, though severely impaired, is completely consistent.

2. The search the ego undertakes is therefore bound to be defeated. [2]And since it also teaches that it is your identification, its guidance leads you to a journey which must end in perceived self-defeat. [3]For the ego cannot love, and in its frantic search for love it is seeking what it is afraid to find. [4]The search is inevitable because the ego is part of your mind, and because of its source the ego is not wholly split off, or it could not be believed at all. [5]For it is your mind that believes in it and gives existence to it. [6]Yet it is also your mind that has the power to deny the ego's existence, and you will surely do so when you realize exactly what the journey is on which the ego sets you.

3. It is surely obvious that no one wants to find what would

utterly defeat him. ²Being unable to love, the ego would be totally inadequate in love's presence, for it could not respond at all. ³Then, you would have to abandon the ego's guidance, for it would be quite apparent that it had not taught you the response you need. ⁴The ego will therefore distort love, and teach you that love really calls forth the responses the ego *can* teach. ⁵Follow its teaching, then, and you will search for love, but will not recognize it.

4. Do you realize that the ego must set you on a journey which cannot but lead to a sense of futility and depression? ²To seek and not to find is hardly joyous. ³Is this the promise you would keep? ⁴The Holy Spirit offers you another promise, and one that will lead to joy. ⁵For His promise is always, "Seek and you *will* find," and under His guidance you cannot be defeated. ⁶His is the journey to accomplishment, and the goal He sets before you He will give you. ⁷For He will never deceive God's Son whom He loves with the Love of the Father.

5. You *will* undertake a journey because you are not at home in this world. ²And you *will* search for your home whether you realize where it is or not. ³If you believe it is outside you the search will be futile, for you will be seeking it where it is not. ⁴You do not remember how to look within for you do not believe your home is there. ⁵Yet the Holy Spirit remembers it for you, and He will guide you to your home because that is His mission. ⁶As He fulfills His mission He will teach you yours, for your mission is the same as His. ⁷By guiding your brothers home you are but following Him.

6. Behold the Guide your Father gave you, that you might learn you have eternal life. ²For death is not your Father's Will nor yours, and whatever is true is the Will of the Father. ³You pay no price for life for that was given you, but you do pay a price for death, and a very heavy one. ⁴If death is your treasure, you will sell everything else to purchase it. ⁵And you will believe that you have purchased it, because you have sold everything else. ⁶Yet you cannot sell the Kingdom of Heaven. ⁷Your inheritance can neither be bought nor sold. ⁸There can be no disinherited parts of the Sonship, for God is whole and all His extensions are like Him.

7. The Atonement is not the price of your wholeness, but it *is* the price of your awareness of your wholeness. ²For what you chose to "sell" had to be kept for you, since you could not "buy" it back. ³Yet you must invest in it, not with money but with spirit.

4For spirit is will, and will is the "price" of the Kingdom. 5Your inheritance awaits only the recognition that you have been redeemed. 6The Holy Spirit guides you into life eternal, but you must relinquish your investment in death, or you will not see life though it is all around you.

V. The Sane Curriculum

1. Only love is strong because it is undivided. 2The strong do not attack because they see no need to do so. 3Before the idea of attack can enter your mind, you must have perceived yourself as weak. 4Because you attacked yourself and believed that the attack was effective, you behold yourself as weakened. 5No longer perceiving yourself and your brothers as equal, and regarding yourself as weaker, you attempt to "equalize" the situation you made. 6You use attack to do so because you believe that attack was successful in weakening you.

2. That is why the recognition of your own invulnerability is so important to the restoration of your sanity. 2For if you accept your invulnerability, you are recognizing that attack has no effect. 3Although you have attacked yourself, you will be demonstrating that nothing really happened. 4Therefore, by attacking you have not done anything. 5Once you realize this you will no longer see any sense in attack, for it manifestly does not work and cannot protect you. 6Yet the recognition of your invulnerability has more than negative value. 7If your attacks on yourself have failed to weaken you, you are still strong. 8You therefore have no need to "equalize" the situation to establish your strength.

3. You will never realize the utter uselessness of attack except by recognizing that your attack on yourself has no effects. 2For others do react to attack if they perceive it, and if you are trying to attack them you will be unable to avoid interpreting this as reinforcement. 3The only place you can cancel out all reinforcement is in yourself. 4For you are always the first point of your attack, and if this has never been, it has no consequences.

4. The Holy Spirit's Love is your strength, for yours is divided and therefore not real. 2You cannot trust your own love when you attack it. 3You cannot learn of perfect love with a split mind, because a split mind has made itself a poor learner. 4You tried to

make the separation eternal, because you wanted to retain the characteristics of creation, but with your own content. ⁵Yet creation is not of you, and poor learners do need special teaching.

5.   You have learning handicaps in a very literal sense. ²There are areas in your learning skills that are so impaired that you can progress only under constant, clear-cut direction, provided by a Teacher Who can transcend your limited resources. ³He becomes your Resource because of yourself you cannot learn. ⁴The learning situation in which you placed yourself is impossible, and in this situation you clearly require a special Teacher and a special curriculum. ⁵Poor learners are not good choices as teachers, either for themselves or for anyone else. ⁶You would hardly turn to them to establish the curriculum by which they can escape from their limitations. ⁷If they understood what is beyond them, they would not be handicapped.

6.   You do not know the meaning of love, and that is your handicap. ²Do not attempt to teach yourself what you do not understand, and do not try to set up curriculum goals where yours have clearly failed. ³Your learning goal has been *not* to learn, and this cannot lead to successful learning. ⁴You cannot transfer what you have not learned, and the impairment of the ability to generalize is a crucial learning failure. ⁵Would you ask those who have failed to learn what learning aids are for? ⁶They do not know. ⁷If they could interpret the aids correctly, they would have learned from them.

7.   I have said that the ego's rule is, "Seek and do not find." ²Translated into curricular terms this means, "Try to learn but do not succeed." ³The result of this curriculum goal is obvious. ⁴Every legitimate teaching aid, every real instruction, and every sensible guide to learning will be misinterpreted, since they are all for facilitating the learning this strange curriculum is against ⁵If you are trying to learn how not to learn, and the aim of your teaching is to defeat itself, what can you expect but confusion? ⁶Such a curriculum does not make sense. ⁷This attempt at "learning" has so weakened your mind that you cannot love, for the curriculum you have chosen is against love, and amounts to a course in how to attack yourself. ⁸A supplementary goal in this curriculum is learning how *not* to overcome the split that makes its primary aim believable. ⁹And you will not overcome the split in this curriculum, for all your learning will be on its behalf. ¹⁰Yet your mind speaks against your learning as your learning speaks

against your mind, and so you fight against all learning and succeed, for that is what you want. [11]But perhaps you do not realize, even yet, that there is something you want to learn, and that you can learn it because it *is* your choice to do so.

8. You who have tried to learn what you do not want should take heart, for although the curriculum you set yourself is depressing indeed, it is merely ridiculous if you look at it. [2]Is it possible that the way to achieve a goal is not to attain it? [3]Resign now as your own teacher. [4]This resignation will not lead to depression. [5]It is merely the result of an honest appraisal of what you have taught yourself, and of the learning outcomes that have resulted. [6]Under the proper learning conditions, which you can neither provide nor understand, you will become an excellent learner and an excellent teacher. [7]But it is not so yet, and will not be so until the whole learning situation as you have set it up is reversed.

9. Your learning potential, properly understood, is limitless because it will lead you to God. [2]You can teach the way to Him and learn it, if you follow the Teacher Who knows the way to Him and understands His curriculum for learning it. [3]The curriculum is totally unambiguous, because the goal is not divided and the means and the end are in complete accord. [4]You need offer only undivided attention. [5]Everything else will be given you. [6]For you really want to learn aright, and nothing can oppose the decision of God's Son. [7]His learning is as unlimited as he is.

VI. The Vision of Christ

1. The ego is trying to teach you how to gain the whole world and lose your own soul. [2]The Holy Spirit teaches that you cannot lose your soul and there is no gain in the world, for of itself it profits nothing. [3]To invest without profit is surely to impoverish yourself, and the overhead is high. [4]Not only is there no profit in the investment, but the cost to you is enormous. [5]For this investment costs you the world's reality by denying yours, and gives you nothing in return. [6]You cannot sell your soul, but you can sell your awareness of it. [7]You cannot perceive your soul, but you will not know it while you perceive something else as more valuable.

2. The Holy Spirit is your strength because He knows nothing but the spirit as you. [2]He is perfectly aware that you do not know yourself, and perfectly aware of how to teach you to remember

what you are. ³Because He loves you, He will gladly teach you what He loves, for He wills to share it. ⁴Remembering you always, He cannot let you forget your worth. ⁵For the Father never ceases to remind Him of His Son, and He never ceases to remind His Son of the Father. ⁶God is in your memory because of Him. ⁷You chose to forget your Father but you do not really want to do so, and therefore you can decide otherwise. ⁸As it was my decision, so is it yours.

3. You do not want the world. ²The only thing of value in it is whatever part of it you look upon with love. ³This gives it the only reality it will ever have. ⁴Its value is not in itself, but yours is in you. ⁵As self-value comes from self-extension, so does the perception of self-value come from the extension of loving thoughts outward. ⁶Make the world real unto yourself, for the real world is the gift of the Holy Spirit, and so it belongs to you.

4. Correction is for all who cannot see. ²To open the eyes of the blind is the Holy Spirit's mission, for He knows that they have not lost their vision, but merely sleep. ³He would awaken them from the sleep of forgetting to the remembering of God. ⁴Christ's eyes are open, and He will look upon whatever you see with love if you accept His vision as yours. ⁵The Holy Spirit keeps the vision of Christ for every Son of God who sleeps. ⁶In His sight the Son of God is perfect, and He longs to share His vision with you. ⁷He will show you the real world because God gave you Heaven. ⁸Through Him your Father calls His Son to remember. ⁹The awakening of His Son begins with his investment in the real world, and by this he will learn to re-invest in himself. ¹⁰For reality is one with the Father and the Son, and the Holy Spirit blesses the real world in Their Name.

5. When you have seen this real world, as you will surely do, you will remember Us. ²Yet you must learn the cost of sleeping, and refuse to pay it. ³Only then will you decide to awaken. ⁴And then the real world will spring to your sight, for Christ has never slept. ⁵He is waiting to be seen, for He has never lost sight of you. ⁶He looks quietly on the real world, which He would share with you because He knows of the Father's Love for Him. ⁷And knowing this, He would give you what is yours. ⁸In perfect peace He waits for you at His Father's altar, holding out the Father's Love to you in the quiet light of the Holy Spirit's blessing. ⁹For the Holy Spirit will lead everyone home to his Father, where Christ waits as his Self.

6. Every child of God is one in Christ, for his being is in Christ as Christ's is in God. [2]Christ's Love for you is His Love for His Father, which He knows because He knows His Father's Love for Him. [3]When the Holy Spirit has at last led you to Christ at the altar to His Father, perception fuses into knowledge because perception has become so holy that its transfer to holiness is merely its natural extension. [4]Love transfers to love without any interference, for the two are one. [5]As you perceive more and more common elements in all situations, the transfer of training under the Holy Spirit's guidance increases and becomes generalized. [6]Gradually you learn to apply it to everyone and everything, for its applicability is universal. [7]When this has been accomplished, perception and knowledge have become so similar that they share the unification of the laws of God.

7. What is one cannot be perceived as separate, and the denial of the separation is the reinstatement of knowledge. [2]At the altar of God, the holy perception of God's Son becomes so enlightened that light streams into it, and the spirit of God's Son shines in the Mind of the Father and becomes one with it. [3]Very gently does God shine upon Himself, loving the extension of Himself that is His Son. [4]The world has no purpose as it blends into the purpose of God. [5]For the real world has slipped quietly into Heaven, where everything eternal in it has always been. [6]There the Redeemer and the redeemed join in perfect love of God and of each other. [7]Heaven is your home, and being in God it must also be in you.

VII. Looking Within

1. Miracles demonstrate that learning has occurred under the right guidance, for learning is invisible and what has been learned can be recognized only by its results. [2]Its generalization is demonstrated as you use it in more and more situations. [3]You will recognize that you have learned there is no order of difficulty in miracles when you apply them to all situations. [4]There is no situation to which miracles do not apply, and by applying them to all situations you will gain the real world. [5]For in this holy perception you will be made whole, and the Atonement will radiate from your acceptance of it for yourself to everyone the Holy Spirit sends you for your blessing. [6]In every child of God His

blessing lies, and in your blessing of the children of God is His blessing to you.

2. Everyone in the world must play his part in its redemption, in order to recognize that the world has been redeemed. ²You cannot see the invisible. ³Yet if you see its effects you know it must be there. ⁴By perceiving what it does, you recognize its being. ⁵And by what it does, you learn what it is. ⁶You cannot see your strengths, but you gain confidence in their existence as they enable you to act. ⁷And the results of your actions you *can* see.

3. The Holy Spirit is invisible, but you can see the results of His Presence, and through them you will learn that He is there. ²What He enables you to do is clearly not of this world, for miracles violate every law of reality as this world judges it. ³Every law of time and space, of magnitude and mass is transcended, for what the Holy Spirit enables you to do is clearly beyond all of them. ⁴Perceiving His results, you will understand where He must be, and finally know what He is.

4. You cannot see the Holy Spirit, but you can see His manifestations. ²And unless you do, you will not realize He is there. ³Miracles are His witnesses, and speak for His Presence. ⁴What you cannot see becomes real to you only through the witnesses that speak for it. ⁵For you can be aware of what you cannot see, and it can become compellingly real to you as its presence becomes manifest through you. ⁶Do the Holy Spirit's work, for you share in His function. ⁷As your function in Heaven is creation, so your function on earth is healing. ⁸God shares His function with you in Heaven, and the Holy Spirit shares His with you on earth. ⁹As long as you believe you have other functions, so long will you need correction. ¹⁰For this belief is the destruction of peace, a goal in direct opposition to the Holy Spirit's purpose.

5. You see what you expect, and you expect what you invite. ²Your perception is the result of your invitation, coming to you as you sent for it. ³Whose manifestations would you see? ⁴Of whose presence would you be convinced? ⁵For you will believe in what you manifest, and as you look out so will you see in. ⁶Two ways of looking at the world are in your mind, and your perception will reflect the guidance you have chosen.

6. I am the manifestation of the Holy Spirit, and when you see me it will be because you have invited Him. ²For He will send you His witnesses if you will but look upon them. ³Remember always that you see what you seek, for what you seek you will find. ⁴The

ego finds what it seeks, and only that. ⁵It does not find love, for that is not what it is seeking. ⁶Yet seeking and finding are the same, and if you seek for two goals you will find them, but you will recognize neither. ⁷You will think they are the same because you want both of them. ⁸The mind always strives for integration, and if it is split and wants to keep the split, it will still believe it has one goal by making it seem to be one.

7. I said before that what you project or extend is up to you, but you must do one or the other, for that is a law of mind, and you must look in before you look out. ²As you look in, you choose the guide for seeing. ³And then you look out and behold his witnesses. ⁴This is why you find what you seek. ⁵What you want in yourself you will make manifest, and you will accept it from the world because you put it there by wanting it. ⁶When you think you are projecting what you do not want, it is still because you *do* want it. ⁷This leads directly to dissociation, for it represents the acceptance of two goals, each perceived in a different place; separated from each other because you made them different. ⁸The mind then sees a divided world outside itself, but not within. ⁹This gives it an illusion of integrity, and enables it to believe that it is pursuing one goal. ¹⁰Yet as long as you perceive the world as split, you are not healed. ¹¹For to be healed is to pursue one goal, because you have accepted only one and want but one.

8. When you want only love you will see nothing else. ²The contradictory nature of the witnesses you perceive is merely the reflection of your conflicting invitations. ³You have looked upon your mind and accepted opposition there, having sought it there. ⁴But do not then believe that the witnesses for opposition are true, for they attest only to your decision about reality, returning to you the messages you gave them. ⁵Love, too, is recognized by its messengers. ⁶If you make love manifest, its messengers will come to you because you invited them.

9. The power of decision is your one remaining freedom as a prisoner of this world. ²You can decide to see it right. ³What you made of it is not its reality, for its reality is only what you give it. ⁴You cannot really give anything but love to anyone or anything, nor can you really receive anything but love from them. ⁵If you think you have received anything else, it is because you have looked within and thought you saw the power to give something else within yourself. ⁶It was only this decision that determined

what you found, for it was the decision for what you sought.

10. You are afraid of me because you looked within and are afraid of what you saw. ²Yet you could not have seen reality, for the reality of your mind is the loveliest of God's creations. ³Coming only from God, its power and grandeur could only bring you peace *if you really looked upon it.* ⁴If you are afraid, it is because you saw something that is not there. ⁵Yet in that same place you could have looked upon me and all your brothers, in the perfect safety of the Mind which created us. ⁶For we are there in the peace of the Father, Who wills to extend His peace through you.

11. When you have accepted your mission to extend peace you will find peace, for by making it manifest you will see it. ²Its holy witnesses will surround you because you called upon them, and they will come to you. ³I have heard your call and I have answered it, but you will not look upon me nor hear the answer that you sought. ⁴That is because you do not yet want *only* that. ⁵Yet as I become more real to you, you will learn that you do want only that. ⁶And you will see me as you look within, and we will look upon the real world together. ⁷Through the eyes of Christ, only the real world exists and only the real world can be seen. ⁸As you decide so will you see. ⁹And all that you see but witnesses to your decision.

12. When you look within and see me, it will be because you have decided to manifest truth. ²And as you manifest it you will see it both without and within. ³You will see it without *because* you saw it first within. ⁴Everything you behold without is a judgment of what you beheld within. ⁵If it is your judgment it will be wrong, for judgment is not your function. ⁶If it is the judgment of the Holy Spirit it will be right, for judgment *is* His function. ⁷You share His function only by judging as He does, reserving no judgment at all for yourself. ⁸You will judge against yourself, but He will judge *for* you.

13. Remember, then, that whenever you look without and react unfavorably to what you see, you have judged yourself unworthy and have condemned yourself to death. ²The death penalty is the ego's ultimate goal, for it fully believes that you are a criminal, as deserving of death as God knows you are deserving of life. ³The death penalty never leaves the ego's mind, for that is what it always reserves for you in the end. ⁴Wanting to kill you as the final expression of its feeling for you, it lets you live but to await death. ⁵It will torment you while you live, but its hatred is not

satisfied until you die. [6]For your destruction is the one end toward which it works, and the only end with which it will be satisfied.

14. The ego is not a traitor to God, to Whom treachery is impossible. [2]But it is a traitor to you who believe that you have been treacherous to your Father. [3]That is why the undoing of guilt is an essential part of the Holy Spirit's teaching. [4]For as long as you feel guilty you are listening to the voice of the ego, which tells you that you have been treacherous to God and therefore deserve death. [5]You will think that death comes from God and not from the ego because, by confusing yourself with the ego, you believe that you want death. [6]And from what you want God does not save you.

15. When you are tempted to yield to the desire for death, *remember that I did not die*. [2]You will realize that this is true when you look within and *see* me. [3]Would I have overcome death for myself alone? [4]And would eternal life have been given me of the Father unless He had also given it to you? [5]When you learn to make me manifest, you will never see death. [6]For you will have looked upon the deathless in yourself, and you will see only the eternal as you look out upon a world that cannot die.

VIII. The Attraction of Love for Love

1. Do you really believe that you can kill the Son of God? [2]The Father has hidden His Son safely within Himself, and kept him far away from your destructive thoughts, but you know neither the Father nor the Son because of them. [3]You attack the real world every day and every hour and every minute, and yet you are surprised that you cannot see it. [4]If you seek love in order to attack it, you will never find it. [5]For if love is sharing, how can you find it except through itself? [6]Offer it and it will come to you, because it is drawn to itself. [7]But offer attack and love will remain hidden, for it can live only in peace.

2. God's Son is as safe as his Father, for the Son knows his Father's protection and cannot fear. [2]His Father's Love holds him in perfect peace, and needing nothing, he asks for nothing. [3]Yet he is far from you whose Self he is, for you chose to attack him and he disappeared from your sight into his Father. [4]He did not change, but you did. [5]For a split mind and all its works were not created by

the Father, and could not live in the knowledge of Him.

3.   When you made visible what is not true, what *is* true became invisible to you. [2]Yet it cannot be invisible in itself, for the Holy Spirit sees it with perfect clarity. [3]It is invisible to you because you are looking at something else. [4]Yet it is no more up to you to decide what is visible and what is invisible, than it is up to you to decide what reality is. [5]What can be seen is what the Holy Spirit sees. [6]The definition of reality is God's, not yours. [7]He created it, and He knows what it is. [8]You who knew have forgotten, and unless He had given you a way to remember you would have condemned yourself to oblivion.

4.   Because of your Father's Love you can never forget Him, for no one can forget what God Himself placed in his memory. [2]You can deny it, but you cannot lose it. [3]A Voice will answer every question you ask, and a vision will correct the perception of everything you see. [4]For what you have made invisible is the only truth, and what you have not heard is the only Answer. [5]God would reunite you with yourself, and did not abandon you in your distress. [6]You are waiting only for Him, and do not know it. [7]Yet His memory shines in your mind and cannot be obliterated. [8]It is no more past than future, being forever always.

5.   You have but to ask for this memory, and you will remember. [2]Yet the memory of God cannot shine in a mind that has obliterated it and wants to keep it so. [3]For the memory of God can dawn only in a mind that chooses to remember, and that has relinquished the insane desire to control reality. [4]You who cannot even control yourself should hardly aspire to control the universe. [5]But look upon what you have made of it, and rejoice that it is not so.

6.   Son of God, be not content with nothing! [2]What is not real cannot be seen and has no value. [3]God could not offer His Son what has no value, nor could His Son receive it. [4]You were redeemed the instant you thought you had deserted Him. [5]Everything you made has never been, and is invisible because the Holy Spirit does not see it. [6]Yet what He does see is yours to behold, and through His vision your perception is healed. [7]You have made invisible the only truth that this world holds. [8]Valuing nothing, you have sought nothing. [9]By making nothing real to you, you have seen it. [10]*But it is not there.* [11]And Christ is invisible to you because of what you have made visible to yourself.

7.   Yet it does not matter how much distance you have tried to

interpose between your awareness and truth. [2]God's Son can be seen because his vision is shared. [3]The Holy Spirit looks upon him, and sees nothing else in you. [4]What is invisible to you is perfect in His sight, and encompasses all of it. [5]He has remembered you because He forgot not the Father. [6]You looked upon the unreal and found despair. [7]Yet by seeking the unreal, what else could you find? [8]The unreal world *is* a thing of despair, for it can never be. [9]And you who share God's Being with Him could never be content without reality. [10]What God did not give you has no power over you, and the attraction of love for love remains irresistible. [11]For it is the function of love to unite all things unto itself, and to hold all things together by extending its wholeness.

8. The real world was given you by God in loving exchange for the world you made and the world you see. [2]Only take it from the hand of Christ and look upon it. [3]Its reality will make everything else invisible, for beholding it is total perception. [4]And as you look upon it you will remember that it was always so. [5]Nothingness will become invisible, for you will at last have seen truly. [6]Redeemed perception is easily translated into knowledge, for only perception is capable of error and perception has never been. [7]Being corrected it gives place to knowledge, which is forever the only reality. [8]The Atonement is but the way back to what was never lost. [9]Your Father could not cease to love His Son.

Chapter 13

THE GUILTLESS WORLD

Introduction

1. If you did not feel guilty you could not attack, for condemnation is the root of attack. ²It is the judgment of one mind by another as unworthy of love and deserving of punishment. ³But herein lies the split. ⁴For the mind that judges perceives itself as separate from the mind being judged, believing that by punishing another, it will escape punishment. ⁵All this is but the delusional attempt of the mind to deny itself, and escape the penalty of denial. ⁶It is not an attempt to relinquish denial, but to hold on to it. ⁷For it is guilt that has obscured the Father to you, and it is guilt that has driven you insane.

2. The acceptance of guilt into the mind of God's Son was the beginning of the separation, as the acceptance of the Atonement is its end. ²The world you see is the delusional system of those made mad by guilt. ³Look carefully at this world, and you will realize that this is so. ⁴For this world is the symbol of punishment, and all the laws that seem to govern it are the laws of death. ⁵Children are born into it through pain and in pain. ⁶Their growth is attended by suffering, and they learn of sorrow and separation and death. ⁷Their minds seem to be trapped in their brain, and its powers to decline if their bodies are hurt. ⁸They seem to love, yet they desert and are deserted. ⁹They appear to lose what they love, perhaps the most insane belief of all. ¹⁰And their bodies wither and gasp and are laid in the ground, and are no more. ¹¹Not one of them but has thought that God is cruel.

3. If this were the real world, God *would* be cruel. ²For no Father could subject His children to this as the price of salvation and *be* loving. ³*Love does not kill to save.* ⁴If it did, attack would be salvation, and this is the ego's interpretation, not God's. ⁵Only the world of guilt could demand this, for only the guilty could conceive of it. ⁶Adam's "sin" could have touched no one, had he not believed it was the Father Who drove him out of Paradise. ⁷For in that belief the knowledge of the Father was lost, since only those who do not understand Him could believe it.

4. This world *is* a picture of the crucifixion of God's Son. ²And

until you realize that God's Son cannot be crucified, this is the world you will see. ³Yet you will not realize this until you accept the eternal fact that God's Son is not guilty. ⁴He deserves only love because he has given only love. ⁵He cannot be condemned because he has never condemned. ⁶The Atonement is the final lesson he need learn, for it teaches him that, never having sinned, he has no need of salvation.

I. Guiltlessness and Invulnerability

1. Earlier, I said that the Holy Spirit shares the goal of all good teachers, whose ultimate aim is to make themselves unnecessary by teaching their pupils all they know. ²The Holy Spirit wants only this, for sharing the Father's Love for His Son, He seeks to remove all guilt from his mind that he may remember his Father in peace. ³Peace and guilt are antithetical, and the Father can be remembered only in peace. ⁴Love and guilt cannot coexist, and to accept one is to deny the other. ⁵Guilt hides Christ from your sight, for it is the denial of the blamelessness of God's Son.

2. In the strange world that you have made the Son of God *has* sinned. ²How could you see him, then? ³By making him invisible, the world of retribution rose in the black cloud of guilt that you accepted, and you hold it dear. ⁴For the blamelessness of Christ is the proof that the ego never was, and can never be. ⁵Without guilt the ego has no life, and God's Son *is* without guilt.

3. As you look upon yourself and judge what you do honestly, you may be tempted to wonder how you can be guiltless. ²Yet consider this: You are not guiltless in time, but in eternity. ³You have "sinned" in the past, but there is no past. ⁴Always has no direction. ⁵Time seems to go in one direction, but when you reach its end it will roll up like a long carpet spread along the past behind you, and will disappear. ⁶As long as you believe the Son of God is guilty you will walk along this carpet, believing that it leads to death. ⁷And the journey will seem long and cruel and senseless, for so it is.

4. The journey the Son of God has set himself is useless indeed, but the journey on which his Father sets him is one of release and joy. ²The Father is not cruel, and His Son cannot hurt himself. ³The retaliation that he fears and that he sees will never touch him, for although he believes in it the Holy Spirit knows it is not

true. ⁴The Holy Spirit stands at the end of time, where you must be because He is with you. ⁵He has already undone everything unworthy of the Son of God, for such was His mission, given Him by God. ⁶And what God gives has always been.

5.   You will see me as you learn the Son of God is guiltless. ²He has always sought his guiltlessness, and he has found it. ³For everyone is seeking to escape from the prison he has made, and the way to find release is not denied him. ⁴Being in him, he has found it. ⁵*When* he finds it is only a matter of time, and time is but an illusion. ⁶For the Son of God is guiltless now, and the brightness of his purity shines untouched forever in God's Mind. ⁷God's Son will always be as he was created. ⁸Deny your world and judge him not, for his eternal guiltlessness is in the Mind of his Father, and protects him forever.

6.   When you have accepted the Atonement for yourself, you will realize there is no guilt in God's Son. ²And only as you look upon him as guiltless can you understand his oneness. ³For the idea of guilt brings a belief in condemnation of one by another, projecting separation in place of unity. ⁴You can condemn only yourself, and by so doing you cannot know that you are God's Son. ⁵You have denied the condition of his being, which is his perfect blamelessness. ⁶Out of love he was created, and in love he abides. ⁷Goodness and mercy have always followed him, for he has always extended the Love of his Father.

7.   As you perceive the holy companions who travel with you, you will realize that there is no journey, but only an awakening. ²The Son of God, who sleepeth not, has kept faith with his Father for you. ³There is no road to travel on, and no time to travel through. ⁴For God waits not for His Son in time, being forever unwilling to be without him. ⁵And so it has always been. ⁶Let the holiness of God's Son shine away the cloud of guilt that darkens your mind, and by accepting his purity as yours, learn of him that it *is* yours.

8.   You are invulnerable because you are guiltless. ²You can hold on to the past only through guilt. ³For guilt establishes that you will be punished for what you have done, and thus depends on one-dimensional time, proceeding from past to future. ⁴No one who believes this can understand what "always" means, and therefore guilt must deprive you of the appreciation of eternity. ⁵You are immortal because you are eternal, and "always" must be now. ⁶Guilt, then, is a way of holding past and future in your

mind to ensure the ego's continuity. ⁷For if what has been will be punished, the ego's continuity is guaranteed. ⁸Yet the guarantee of your continuity is God's, not the ego's. ⁹And immortality is the opposite of time, for time passes away, while immortality is constant.

9. Accepting the Atonement teaches you what immortality is, for by accepting your guiltlessness you learn that the past has never been, and so the future is needless and will not be. ²The future, in time, is always associated with expiation, and only guilt could induce a sense of a need for expiation. ³Accepting the guiltlessness of the Son of God as yours is therefore God's way of reminding you of His Son, and what he is in truth. ⁴For God has never condemned His Son, and being guiltless he is eternal.

10. You cannot dispel guilt by making it real, and then atoning for it. ²This is the ego's plan, which it offers instead of dispelling it. ³The ego believes in atonement through attack, being fully committed to the insane notion that attack is salvation. ⁴And you who cherish guilt must also believe it, for how else but by identifying with the ego could you hold dear what you do not want?

11. The ego teaches you to attack yourself because you are guilty, and this must increase the guilt, for guilt is the result of attack. ²In the ego's teaching, then, there is no escape from guilt. ³For attack makes guilt real, and if it is real there *is* no way to overcome it. ⁴The Holy Spirit dispels it simply through the calm recognition that it has never been. ⁵As He looks upon the guiltless Son of God, He knows that this is true. ⁶And being true for you, you cannot attack yourself, for without guilt attack is impossible. ⁷You, then, are saved because God's Son is guiltless. ⁸And being wholly pure, you are invulnerable.

II. The Guiltless Son of God

1. The ultimate purpose of projection is always to get rid of guilt. ²Yet, characteristically, the ego attempts to get rid of guilt from its viewpoint only, for much as the ego wants to retain guilt *you* find it intolerable, since guilt stands in the way of your remembering God, Whose pull is so strong that you cannot resist it. ³On this issue, then, the deepest split of all occurs, for if you are to retain guilt, as the ego insists, *you cannot be you*. ⁴Only by persuading you that it is you could the ego possibly induce you to project

guilt, and thereby keep it in your mind.

2. Yet consider how strange a solution the ego's arrangement is. ²You project guilt to get rid of it, but you are actually merely concealing it. ³You do experience the guilt, but you have no idea why. ⁴On the contrary, you associate it with a weird assortment of "ego ideals," which the ego claims you have failed. ⁵Yet you have no idea that you are failing the Son of God by seeing him as guilty. ⁶Believing you are no longer you, you do not realize that you are failing yourself.

3. The darkest of your hidden cornerstones holds your belief in guilt from your awareness. ²For in that dark and secret place is the realization that you have betrayed God's Son by condemning him to death. ³You do not even suspect this murderous but insane idea lies hidden there, for the ego's destructive urge is so intense that nothing short of the crucifixion of God's Son can ultimately satisfy it. ⁴It does not know who the Son of God is because it is blind. ⁵Yet let it perceive guiltlessness anywhere, and it will try to destroy it because it is afraid.

4. Much of the ego's strange behavior is directly attributable to its definition of guilt. ²To the ego, *the guiltless are guilty.* ³Those who do not attack are its "enemies" because, by not valuing its interpretation of salvation, they are in an excellent position to let it go. ⁴They have approached the darkest and deepest cornerstone in the ego's foundation, and while the ego can withstand your raising all else to question, it guards this one secret with its life, for its existence depends on keeping this secret. ⁵So it is this secret that we must look upon, for the ego cannot protect you against truth, and in its presence the ego is dispelled.

5. In the calm light of truth, let us recognize that you believe you have crucified God's Son. ²You have not admitted to this "terrible" secret because you would still wish to crucify him if you could find him. ³Yet the wish has hidden him from you because it is very fearful, and so you are afraid to find him. ⁴You have handled this wish to kill yourself by not knowing who you are, and identifying with something else. ⁵You have projected guilt blindly and indiscriminately, but you have not uncovered its source. ⁶For the ego does want to kill you, and if you identify with it you must believe its goal is yours.

6. I have said that the crucifixion is the symbol of the ego. ²When it was confronted with the real guiltlessness of God's Son it did attempt to kill him, and the reason it gave was that guiltlessness

is blasphemous to God. ³To the ego, the *ego* is God, and guiltless-ness must be interpreted as the final guilt that fully justifies mur-der. ⁴You do not yet understand that any fear you may experience in connection with this course stems ultimately from this inter-pretation, but if you will consider your reactions to it you will become increasingly convinced that this is so.

7. This course has explicitly stated that its goal for you is happi-ness and peace. ²Yet you are afraid of it. ³You have been told again and again that it will set you free, yet you sometimes react as if it is trying to imprison you. ⁴You often dismiss it more readily than you dismiss the ego's thought system. ⁵To some extent, then, you must believe that by not learning the course you are protecting yourself. ⁶And you do not realize that it is only your guiltlessness that *can* protect you.

8. The Atonement has always been interpreted as the release from guilt, and this is correct if it is understood. ²Yet even when I inter-pret it for you, you may reject it and do not accept it for yourself. ³You have perhaps recognized the futility of the ego and its offer-ings, but though you do not want them, you may not yet look upon the alternative with gladness. ⁴In the extreme, you are afraid of redemption and you believe it will kill you. ⁵Make no mistake about the depth of this fear. ⁶For you believe that, in the presence of truth, you might turn on yourself and destroy yourself.

9. Little child, this is not so. ²Your "guilty secret" is nothing, and if you will but bring it to the light, the light will dispel it. ³And then no dark cloud will remain between you and the remem-brance of your Father, for you will remember His guiltless Son, who did not die because he is immortal. ⁴And you will see that you were redeemed with him, and have never been separated from him. ⁵In this understanding lies your remembering, for it is the recognition of love without fear. ⁶There will be great joy in Heaven on your homecoming, and the joy will be yours. ⁷For the redeemed son of man is the guiltless Son of God, and to recog-nize him *is* your redemption.

III. The Fear of Redemption

1. You may wonder why it is so crucial that you look upon your hatred and realize its full extent. ²You may also think that it would be easy enough for the Holy Spirit to show it to you, and to dispel it without the need for you to raise it to awareness yourself. ³Yet there is one more obstacle you have interposed between yourself and the Atonement. ⁴We have said that no one will countenance fear if he recognizes it. ⁵Yet in your disordered state of mind you are not afraid of fear. ⁶You do not like it, but it is not your desire to attack that really frightens you. ⁷You are not seriously disturbed by your hostility. ⁸You keep it hidden because you are more afraid of what it covers. ⁹You could look even upon the ego's darkest cornerstone without fear if you did not believe that, without the ego, you would find within yourself something you fear even more. ¹⁰You are not really afraid of crucifixion. ¹¹Your real terror is of redemption.

2. Under the ego's dark foundation is the memory of God, and it is of this that you are really afraid. ²For this memory would instantly restore you to your proper place, and it is this place that you have sought to leave. ³Your fear of attack is nothing compared to your fear of love. ⁴You would be willing to look even upon your savage wish to kill God's Son, if you did not believe that it saves you from love. ⁵For this wish caused the separation, and you have protected it because you do not want the separation healed. ⁶You realize that, by removing the dark cloud that obscures it, your love for your Father would impel you to answer His Call and leap into Heaven. ⁷You believe that attack is salvation because it would prevent you from this. ⁸For still deeper than the ego's foundation, and much stronger than it will ever be, is your intense and burning love of God, and His for you. ⁹This is what you really want to hide.

3. In honesty, is it not harder for you to say "I love" than "I hate"? ²You associate love with weakness and hatred with strength, and your own real power seems to you as your real weakness. ³For you could not control your joyous response to the call of love if you heard it, and the whole world you thought you made would vanish. ⁴The Holy Spirit, then, seems to be attacking your fortress, for you would shut out God, and He does not will to be excluded.

4. You have built your whole insane belief system because you think you would be helpless in God's Presence, and you would save yourself from His Love because you think it would crush you into nothingness. ²You are afraid it would sweep you away from yourself and make you little, because you believe that magnitude lies in defiance, and that attack is grandeur. ³You think you have made a world God would destroy; and by loving Him, which you do, you would throw this world away, which you *would*. ⁴Therefore, you have used the world to cover your love, and the deeper you go into the blackness of the ego's foundation, the closer you come to the Love that is hidden there. ⁵*And it is this that frightens you.*

5. You can accept insanity because you made it, but you cannot accept love because you did not. ²You would rather be a slave of the crucifixion than a Son of God in redemption. ³Your individual death seems more valuable than your living oneness, for what is given you is not so dear as what you made. ⁴You are more afraid of God than of the ego, and love cannot enter where it is not welcome. ⁵But hatred can, for it enters of its own volition and cares not for yours.

6. You must look upon your illusions and not keep them hidden, because they do not rest on their own foundation. ²In concealment they appear to do so, and thus they seem to be self-sustained. ³This is the fundamental illusion on which the others rest. ⁴For beneath them, and concealed as long as they are hidden, is the loving mind that thought it made them in anger. ⁵And the pain in this mind is so apparent, when it is uncovered, that its need of healing cannot be denied. ⁶Not all the tricks and games you offer it can heal it, for here is the real crucifixion of God's Son.

7. And yet he is not crucified. ²Here is both his pain and his healing, for the Holy Spirit's vision is merciful and His remedy is quick. ³Do not hide suffering from His sight, but bring it gladly to Him. ⁴Lay before His eternal sanity all your hurt, and let Him heal you. ⁵Do not leave any spot of pain hidden from His light, and search your mind carefully for any thoughts you may fear to uncover. ⁶For He will heal every little thought you have kept to hurt you and cleanse it of its littleness, restoring it to the magnitude of God.

8. Beneath all the grandiosity you hold so dear is your real call for help. ²For you call for love to your Father as your Father calls you to Himself. ³In that place which you have hidden, you will

only to unite with the Father, in loving remembrance of Him. [4]You will find this place of truth as you see it in your brothers, for though they may deceive themselves, like you they long for the grandeur that is in them. [5]And perceiving it you will welcome it, and it will be yours. [6]For grandeur is the right of God's Son, and no illusions can satisfy him or save him from what he is. [7]Only his love is real, and he will be content only with his reality.

9. Save him from his illusions that you may accept the magnitude of your Father in peace and joy. [2]But exempt no one from your love, or you will be hiding a dark place in your mind where the Holy Spirit is not welcome. [3]And thus you will exempt yourself from His healing power, for by not offering total love you will not be healed completely. [4]Healing must be as complete as fear, for love cannot enter where there is one spot of fear to mar its welcome.

10. You who prefer separation to sanity cannot obtain it in your right mind. [2]You were at peace until you asked for special favor. [3]And God did not give it for the request was alien to Him, and you could not ask this of a Father Who truly loved His Son. [4]Therefore you made of Him an unloving father, demanding of Him what only such a father could give. [5]And the peace of God's Son was shattered, for he no longer understood his Father. [6]He feared what he had made, but still more did he fear his real Father, having attacked his own glorious equality with Him.

11. In peace he needed nothing and asked for nothing. [2]In war he demanded everything and found nothing. [3]For how could the gentleness of love respond to his demands, except by departing in peace and returning to the Father? [4]If the Son did not wish to remain in peace, he could not remain at all. [5]For a darkened mind cannot live in the light, and it must seek a place of darkness where it can believe it is where it is not. [6]God did not allow this to happen. [7]Yet you demanded that it happen, and therefore believed that it was so.

12. To "single out" is to "make alone," and thus make lonely. [2]God did not do this to you. [3]Could He set you apart, knowing that your peace lies in His Oneness? [4]He denied you only your request for pain, for suffering is not of His creation. [5]Having given you creation, He could not take it from you. [6]He could but answer your insane request with a sane answer that would abide with you in your insanity. [7]And this He did. [8]No one who hears His answer but will give up insanity. [9]For His answer is the refer-

ence point beyond illusions, from which you can look back on them and see them as insane. ¹⁰But seek this place and you will find it, for Love is in you and will lead you there.

IV. The Function of Time

1. And now the reason why you are afraid of this course should be apparent. ²For this is a course on love, because it is about you. ³You have been told that your function in this world is healing, and your function in Heaven is creating. ⁴The ego teaches that your function on earth is destruction, and you have no function at all in Heaven. ⁵It would thus destroy you here and bury you here, leaving you no inheritance except the dust out of which it thinks you were made. ⁶As long as it is reasonably satisfied with you, as its reasoning goes, it offers you oblivion. ⁷When it becomes overtly savage, it offers you hell.

2. Yet neither oblivion nor hell is as unacceptable to you as Heaven. ²Your definition of Heaven *is* hell and oblivion, and the real Heaven is the greatest threat you think you could experience. ³For hell and oblivion are ideas that you made up, and you are bent on demonstrating their reality to establish yours. ⁴If their reality is questioned, you believe that yours is. ⁵For you believe that attack is your reality, and that your destruction is the final proof that you were right.

3. Under the circumstances, would it not be more desirable to have been wrong, even apart from the fact that you were wrong? ²While it could perhaps be argued that death suggests there *was* life, no one would claim that it proves there *is* life. ³Even the past life that death might indicate, could only have been futile if it must come to this, and needs this to prove that it was at all. ⁴You question Heaven, but you do not question this. ⁵Yet you could heal and be healed if you did question it. ⁶And even though you know not Heaven, might it not be more desirable than death? ⁷You have been as selective in your questioning as in your perception. ⁸An open mind is more honest than this.

4. The ego has a strange notion of time, and it is with this notion that your questioning might well begin. ²The ego invests heavily in the past, and in the end believes that the past is the only aspect of time that is meaningful. ³Remember that its emphasis on guilt enables it to ensure its continuity by making the future like the

past, and thus avoiding the present. [4]By the notion of paying for the past in the future, the past becomes the determiner of the future, making them continuous without an intervening present. [5]For the ego regards the present only as a brief transition to the future, in which it brings the past to the future by interpreting the present in past terms.

5. "Now" has no meaning to the ego. [2]The present merely reminds it of past hurts, and it reacts to the present as if it *were* the past. [3]The ego cannot tolerate release from the past, and although the past is over, the ego tries to preserve its image by responding as if it were present. [4]It dictates your reactions to those you meet in the present from a past reference point, obscuring their present reality. [5]In effect, if you follow the ego's dictates you will react to your brother as though he were someone else, and this will surely prevent you from recognizing him as he is. [6]And you will receive messages from him out of your own past because, by making it real in the present, you are forbidding yourself to let it go. [7]You thus deny yourself the message of release that every brother offers you *now*.

6. The shadowy figures from the past are precisely what you must escape. [2]They are not real, and have no hold over you unless you bring them with you. [3]They carry the spots of pain in your mind, directing you to attack in the present in retaliation for a past that is no more. [4]And this decision is one of future pain. [5]Unless you learn that past pain is an illusion, you are choosing a future of illusions and losing the many opportunities you could find for release in the present. [6]The ego would preserve your nightmares, and prevent you from awakening and understanding they are past. [7]Would you recognize a holy encounter if you are merely perceiving it as a meeting with your own past? [8]For you would be meeting no one, and the sharing of salvation, which makes the encounter holy, would be excluded from your sight. [9]The Holy Spirit teaches that you always meet yourself, and the encounter is holy because you are. [10]The ego teaches that you always encounter your past, and because your dreams were not holy, the future cannot be, and the present is without meaning.

7. It is evident that the Holy Spirit's perception of time is the exact opposite of the ego's. [2]The reason is equally clear, for they perceive the goal of time as diametrically opposed. [3]The Holy Spirit interprets time's purpose as rendering the need for time

unnecessary. ⁴He regards the function of time as temporary, serving only His teaching function, which is temporary by definition. ⁵His emphasis is therefore on the only aspect of time that can extend to the infinite, for *now* is the closest approximation of eternity that this world offers. ⁶It is in the reality of "now," without past or future, that the beginning of the appreciation of eternity lies. ⁷For only "now" is here, and only "now" presents the opportunities for the holy encounters in which salvation can be found.

8. The ego, on the other hand, regards the function of time as one of extending itself in place of eternity, for like the Holy Spirit, the ego interprets the goal of time as its own. ²The continuity of past and future, under its direction, is the only purpose the ego perceives in time, and it closes over the present so that no gap in its own continuity can occur. ³Its continuity, then, would keep you in time, while the Holy Spirit would release you from it. ⁴It is His interpretation of the means of salvation that you must learn to accept, if you would share His goal of salvation for you.

9. You, too, will interpret the function of time as you interpret yours. ²If you accept your function in the world of time as one of healing, you will emphasize only the aspect of time in which healing can occur. ³Healing cannot be accomplished in the past. ⁴It must be accomplished in the present to release the future. ⁵This interpretation ties the future to the present, and extends the present rather than the past. ⁶But if you interpret your function as destruction, you will lose sight of the present and hold on to the past to ensure a destructive future. ⁷And time will be as you interpret it, for of itself it is nothing.

V. The Two Emotions

1. I have said you have but two emotions, love and fear. ²One is changeless but continually exchanged, being offered by the eternal to the eternal. ³In this exchange it is extended, for it increases as it is given. ⁴The other has many forms, for the content of individual illusions differs greatly. ⁵Yet they have one thing in common; they are all insane. ⁶They are made of sights that are not seen, and sounds that are not heard. ⁷They make up a private world that cannot be shared. ⁸For they are meaningful only to their maker, and so they have no meaning at all. ⁹In this world their maker moves alone, for only he perceives them.

2. Each one peoples his world with figures from his individual past, and it is because of this that private worlds do differ. ²Yet the figures that he sees were never real, for they are made up only of his reactions to his brothers, and do not include their reactions to him. ³Therefore, he does not see he made them, and that they are not whole. ⁴For these figures have no witnesses, being perceived in one separate mind only.

3. It is through these strange and shadowy figures that the insane relate to their insane world. ²For they see only those who remind them of these images, and it is to them that they relate. ³Thus do they communicate with those who are not there, and it is they who answer them. ⁴And no one hears their answer save him who called upon them, and he alone believes they answered him. ⁵Projection makes perception, and you cannot see beyond it. ⁶Again and again have you attacked your brother, because you saw in him a shadow figure in your private world. ⁷And thus it is you must attack yourself first, for what you attack is not in others. ⁸Its only reality is in your own mind, and by attacking others you are literally attacking what is not there.

4. The delusional can be very destructive, for they do not recognize they have condemned themselves. ²They do not wish to die, yet they will not let condemnation go. ³And so they separate into their private worlds, where everything is disordered, and where what is within appears to be without. ⁴Yet what is within they do not see, for the reality of their brothers they cannot recognize.

5. You have but two emotions, yet in your private world you react to each of them as though it were the other. ²For love cannot abide in a world apart, where when it comes it is not recognized. ³If you see your own hatred as your brother, you are not seeing him. ⁴Everyone draws nigh unto what he loves, and recoils from what he fears. ⁵And you react with fear to love, and draw away from it. ⁶Yet fear attracts you, and believing it is love, you call it to yourself. ⁷Your private world is filled with figures of fear you have invited into it, and all the love your brothers offer you, you do not see.

6. As you look with open eyes upon your world, it must occur to you that you have withdrawn into insanity. ²You see what is not there, and you hear what makes no sound. ³Your manifestations of emotions are the opposite of what the emotions are. ⁴You communicate with no one, and you are as isolated from reality as if you were alone in all the universe. ⁵In your madness you over-

look reality completely, and you see only your own split mind everywhere you look. ⁶God calls you and you do not hear, for you are preoccupied with your own voice. ⁷And the vision of Christ is not in your sight, for you look upon yourself alone.

7. Little child, would you offer this to your Father? ²For if you offer it to yourself, you *are* offering it to Him. ³And He will not return it, for it is unworthy of you because it is unworthy of Him. ⁴Yet He would release you from it and set you free. ⁵His sane Answer tells you what you have offered yourself is not true, but His offering to you has never changed. ⁶You who know not what you do can learn what insanity is, and look beyond it. ⁷It is given you to learn how to deny insanity, and come forth from your private world in peace. ⁸You will see all that you denied in your brothers because you denied it in yourself. ⁹For you will love them, and by drawing nigh unto them you will draw them to yourself, perceiving them as witnesses to the reality you share with God. ¹⁰I am with them as I am with you, and we will draw them from their private worlds, for as we are united so would we unite with them. ¹¹The Father welcomes all of us in gladness, and gladness is what we should offer Him. ¹²For every Son of God is given you to whom God gave Himself. ¹³And it is God Whom you must offer them, to recognize His gift to you.

8. Vision depends on light. ²You cannot see in darkness. ³Yet in darkness, in the private world of sleep, you see in dreams although your eyes are closed. ⁴And it is here that what you see you made. ⁵But let the darkness go and all you made you will no longer see, for sight of it depends upon denying vision. ⁶Yet from denying vision it does not follow you cannot see. ⁷But this is what denial does, for by it you accept insanity, believing you can make a private world and rule your own perception. ⁸Yet for this, light must be excluded. ⁹Dreams disappear when light has come and you can see.

9. Do not seek vision through your eyes, for you made your way of seeing that you might see in darkness, and in this you are deceived. ²Beyond this darkness, and yet still within you, is the vision of Christ, Who looks on all in light. ³Your "vision" comes from fear, as His from love. ⁴And He sees for you, as your witness to the real world. ⁵He is the Holy Spirit's manifestation, looking always on the real world, and calling forth its witnesses and drawing them to you. ⁶He loves what He sees within you, and He would extend it. ⁷And He will not return unto the Father until He

has extended your perception even unto Him. [8]And there perception is no more, for He has returned you to the Father with Him.

10. You have but two emotions, and one you made and one was given you. [2]Each is a way of seeing, and different worlds arise from their different sights. [3]See through the vision that is given you, for through Christ's vision He beholds Himself. [4]And seeing what He is, He knows His Father. [5]Beyond your darkest dreams He sees God's guiltless Son within you, shining in perfect radiance that is undimmed by your dreams. [6]And this *you* will see as you look with Him, for His vision is His gift of love to you, given Him of the Father for you.

11. The Holy Spirit is the light in which Christ stands revealed. [2]And all who would behold Him can see Him, for they have asked for light. [3]Nor will they see Him alone, for He is no more alone than they are. [4]Because they saw the Son, they have risen in Him to the Father. [5]And all this will they understand, because they looked within and saw beyond the darkness the Christ in them, and recognized Him. [6]In the sanity of His vision they looked upon themselves with love, seeing themselves as the Holy Spirit sees them. [7]And with this vision of the truth in them came all the beauty of the world to shine upon them.

VI. Finding the Present

1. To perceive truly is to be aware of all reality through the awareness of your own. [2]But for this no illusions can rise to meet your sight, for reality leaves no room for any error. [3]This means that you perceive a brother only as you see him *now*. [4]His past has no reality in the present, so you cannot see it. [5]Your past reactions to him are also not there, and if it is to them that you react, you see but an image of him that you made and cherish instead of him. [6]In your questioning of illusions, ask yourself if it is really sane to perceive what was as now. [7]If you remember the past as you look upon your brother, you will be unable to perceive the reality that is now.

2. You consider it "natural" to use your past experience as the reference point from which to judge the present. [2]Yet this is *unnatural* because it is delusional. [3]When you have learned to look on everyone with no reference at all to the past, either his or yours as you perceived it, you will be able to learn from what you

see *now*. [4]For the past can cast no shadow to darken the present, *unless you are afraid of light*. [5]And only if you are would you choose to bring darkness with you, and by holding it in your mind, see it as a dark cloud that shrouds your brothers and conceals their reality from your sight.

3. *This darkness is in you*. [2]The Christ as revealed to you now has no past, for He is changeless, and in His changelessness lies your release. [3]For if He is as He was created, there is no guilt in Him. [4]No cloud of guilt has risen to obscure Him, and He stands revealed in everyone you meet because you see Him through Himself. [5]To be born again is to let the past go, and look without condemnation upon the present. [6]The cloud that obscures God's Son to you *is* the past, and if you would have it past and gone, you must not see it now. [7]If you see it now in your illusions, it has not gone from you, although it is not there.

4. Time can release as well as imprison, depending on whose interpretation of it you use. [2]Past, present and future are not continuous, unless you force continuity on them. [3]You can perceive them as continuous, and make them so for you. [4]But do not be deceived, and then believe that this is how it is. [5]For to believe reality is what you would have it be according to your use for it *is* delusional. [6]You would destroy time's continuity by breaking it into past, present and future for your own purposes. [7]You would anticipate the future on the basis of your past experience, and plan for it accordingly. [8]Yet by doing so you are aligning past and future, and not allowing the miracle, which could intervene between them, to free you to be born again.

5. The miracle enables you to see your brother without his past, and so perceive him as born again. [2]His errors are all past, and by perceiving him without them you are releasing him. [3]And since his past is yours, you share in this release. [4]Let no dark cloud out of your past obscure him from you, for truth lies only in the present, and you will find it if you seek it there. [5]You have looked for it where it is not, and therefore have not found it. [6]Learn, then, to seek it where it is, and it will dawn on eyes that see. [7]Your past was made in anger, and if you use it to attack the present, you will not see the freedom that the present holds.

6. Judgment and condemnation are behind you, and unless you bring them with you, you will see that you are free of them. [2]Look lovingly upon the present, for it holds the only things that are forever true. [3]All healing lies within it because its continuity is

real. ⁴It extends to all aspects of the Sonship at the same time, and thus enables them to reach each other. ⁵The present is before time was, and will be when time is no more. ⁶In it are all things that are eternal, and they are one. ⁷Their continuity is timeless and their communication is unbroken, for they are not separated by the past. ⁸Only the past can separate, and it is nowhere.

7. The present offers you your brothers in the light that would unite you with them, and free you from the past. ²Would you, then, hold the past against them? ³For if you do, you are choosing to remain in the darkness that is not there, and refusing to accept the light that is offered you. ⁴For the light of perfect vision is freely given as it is freely received, and can be accepted only without limit. ⁵In this one, still dimension of time that does not change, and where there is no sight of what you were, you look at Christ and call His witnesses to shine on you *because you called them forth.* ⁶And they will not deny the truth in you, because you looked for it in them and found it there.

8. Now is the time of salvation, for now is the release from time. ²Reach out to all your brothers, and touch them with the touch of Christ. ³In timeless union with them is your continuity, unbroken because it is wholly shared. ⁴God's guiltless Son is only light. ⁵There is no darkness in him anywhere, for he is whole. ⁶Call all your brothers to witness to his wholeness, as I am calling you to join with me. ⁷Each voice has a part in the song of redemption, the hymn of gladness and thanksgiving for the light to the Creator of light. ⁸The holy light that shines forth from God's Son is the witness that his light is of his Father.

9. Shine on your brothers in remembrance of your Creator, for you will remember Him as you call forth the witnesses to His creation. ²Those whom you heal bear witness to your healing, for in their wholeness you will see your own. ³And as your hymns of praise and gladness rise to your Creator, He will return your thanks in His clear Answer to your call. ⁴For it can never be that His Son called upon Him and remained unanswered. ⁵His Call to you is but your call to Him. ⁶And in Him you are answered by His peace.

10. Child of Light, you know not that the light is in you. ²Yet you will find it through its witnesses, for having given light to them they will return it. ³Each one you see in light brings your light closer to your awareness. ⁴Love always leads to love. ⁵The sick, who ask for love, are grateful for it, and in their joy they shine

with holy thanks. ⁶And this they offer you who gave them joy. ⁷They are your guides to joy, for having received it of you they would keep it. ⁸You have established them as guides to peace, for you have made it manifest in them. ⁹And seeing it, its beauty calls you home.

11. There is a light that this world cannot give. ²Yet you can give it, as it was given you. ³And as you give it, it shines forth to call you from the world and follow it. ⁴For this light will attract you as nothing in this world can do. ⁵And you will lay aside the world and find another. ⁶This other world is bright with love which you have given it. ⁷And here will everything remind you of your Father and His holy Son. ⁸Light is unlimited, and spreads across this world in quiet joy. ⁹All those you brought with you will shine on you, and you will shine on them in gratitude because they brought you here. ¹⁰Your light will join with theirs in power so compelling, that it will draw the others out of darkness as you look on them.

12. Awaking unto Christ is following the laws of love of your free will, and out of quiet recognition of the truth in them. ²The attraction of light must draw you willingly, and willingness is signified by giving. ³Those who accept love of you become your willing witnesses to the love you gave them, and it is they who hold it out to you. ⁴In sleep you are alone, and your awareness is narrowed to yourself. ⁵And that is why the nightmares come. ⁶You dream of isolation because your eyes are closed. ⁷You do not see your brothers, and in the darkness you cannot look upon the light you gave to them.

13. And yet the laws of love are not suspended because you sleep. ²And you have followed them through all your nightmares, and have been faithful in your giving, for you were not alone. ³Even in sleep has Christ protected you, ensuring the real world for you when you awake. ⁴In your name He has given for you, and given you the gifts He gave. ⁵God's Son is still as loving as his Father. ⁶Continuous with his Father, he has no past apart from Him. ⁷So he has never ceased to be his Father's witness and his own. ⁸Although he slept, Christ's vision did not leave him. ⁹And so it is that he can call unto himself the witnesses that teach him that he never slept.

VII. Attainment of the Real World

1. Sit quietly and look upon the world you see, and tell yourself: "The real world is not like this. ²It has no buildings and there are no streets where people walk alone and separate. ³There are no stores where people buy an endless list of things they do not need. ⁴It is not lit with artificial light, and night comes not upon it. ⁵There is no day that brightens and grows dim. ⁶There is no loss. ⁷Nothing is there but shines, and shines forever."

2. The world you see must be denied, for sight of it is costing you a different kind of vision. ²*You cannot see both worlds*, for each of them involves a different kind of seeing, and depends on what you cherish. ³The sight of one is possible because you have denied the other. ⁴Both are not true, yet either one will seem as real to you as the amount to which you hold it dear. ⁵And yet their power is not the same, because their real attraction to you is unequal.

3. You do not really want the world you see, for it has disappointed you since time began. ²The homes you built have never sheltered you. ³The roads you made have led you nowhere, and no city that you built has withstood the crumbling assault of time. ⁴Nothing you made but has the mark of death upon it. ⁵Hold it not dear, for it is old and tired and ready to return to dust even as you made it. ⁶This aching world has not the power to touch the living world at all. ⁷You could not give it that, and so although you turn in sadness from it, you cannot find in it the road that leads away from it into another world.

4. Yet the real world has the power to touch you even here, because you love it. ²And what you call with love will come to you. ³Love always answers, being unable to deny a call for help, or not to hear the cries of pain that rise to it from every part of this strange world you made but do not want. ⁴All that you need to give this world away in glad exchange for what you did not make is willingness to learn the one you made is false.

5. You have been wrong about the world because you have misjudged yourself. ²From such a twisted reference point, what could you see? ³All seeing starts with the perceiver, who judges what is true and what is false. ⁴And what he judges false he does not see. ⁵You who would judge reality cannot see it, for whenever judgment enters reality has slipped away. ⁶The out of mind *is* out of sight, because what is denied is there but is not recognized.

7Christ is still there, although you know Him not. 8His Being does not depend upon your recognition. 9He lives within you in the quiet present, and waits for you to leave the past behind and enter into the world He holds out to you in love.

6. No one in this distracted world but has seen some glimpses of the other world about him. 2Yet while he still lays value on his own, he will deny the vision of the other, maintaining that he loves what he loves not, and following not the road that love points out. 3Love leads so gladly! 4As you follow Him, you will rejoice that you have found His company, and learned of Him the joyful journey home. 5You wait but for yourself. 6To give this sad world over and exchange your errors for the peace of God is but *your* will. 7And Christ will always offer you the Will of God, in recognition that you share it with Him.

7. It is God's Will that nothing touch His Son except Himself, and nothing else comes nigh unto him. 2He is as safe from pain as God Himself, Who watches over him in everything. 3The world about him shines with love because God placed him in Himself where pain is not, and love surrounds him without end or flaw. 4Disturbance of his peace can never be. 5In perfect sanity he looks on love, for it is all about him and within him. 6He must deny the world of pain the instant he perceives the arms of love around him. 7And from this point of safety he looks quietly about him and recognizes that the world is one with him.

8. The peace of God passeth your understanding only in the past. 2Yet here it *is*, and you can understand it *now*. 3God loves His Son forever, and His Son returns his Father's Love forever. 4The real world is the way that leads you to remembrance of the one thing that is wholly true and wholly yours. 5For all else you have lent yourself in time, and it will fade. 6But this one thing is always yours, being the gift of God unto His Son. 7Your one reality was given you, and by it God created you as one with Him.

9. You will first dream of peace, and then awaken to it. 2Your first exchange of what you made for what you want is the exchange of nightmares for the happy dreams of love. 3In these lie your true perceptions, for the Holy Spirit corrects the world of dreams, where all perception is. 4Knowledge needs no correction. 5Yet the dreams of love lead unto knowledge. 6In them you see nothing fearful, and because of this they are the welcome that you offer knowledge. 7Love waits on welcome, not on time, and the real world is but your welcome of what always was. 8Therefore the

call of joy is in it, and your glad response is your awakening to what you have not lost.

10. Praise, then, the Father for the perfect sanity of His most holy Son. ²Your Father knoweth that you have need of nothing. ³In Heaven this is so, for what could you need in eternity? ⁴In your world you do need things. ⁵It is a world of scarcity in which you find yourself *because* you are lacking. ⁶Yet can you find yourself in such a world? ⁷Without the Holy Spirit the answer would be no. ⁸Yet because of Him the answer is a joyous *yes!* ⁹As Mediator between the two worlds, He knows what you have need of and what will not hurt you. ¹⁰Ownership is a dangerous concept if it is left to you. ¹¹The ego wants to have things for salvation, for possession is its law. ¹²Possession for its own sake is the ego's fundamental creed, a basic cornerstone in the churches it builds to itself. ¹³And at its altar it demands you lay all of the things it bids you get, leaving you no joy in them.

11. Everything the ego tells you that you need will hurt you. ²For although the ego urges you again and again to get, it leaves you nothing, for what you get it will demand of you. ³And even from the very hands that grasped it, it will be wrenched and hurled into the dust. ⁴For where the ego sees salvation it sees separation, and so you lose whatever you have gotten in its name. ⁵Therefore ask not of yourself what you need, for you do not know, and your advice to yourself will hurt you. ⁶For what you think you need will merely serve to tighten up your world against the light, and render you unwilling to question the value that this world can really hold for you.

12. Only the Holy Spirit knows what you need. ²For He will give you all things that do not block the way to light. ³And what else could you need? ⁴In time, He gives you all the things that you need have, and will renew them as long as you have need of them. ⁵He will take nothing from you as long as you have any need of it. ⁶And yet He knows that everything you need is temporary, and will but last until you step aside from all your needs and realize that all of them have been fulfilled. ⁷Therefore He has no investment in the things that He supplies, except to make certain that you will not use them on behalf of lingering in time. ⁸He knows that you are not at home there, and He wills no delay to wait upon your joyous homecoming.

13. Leave, then, your needs to Him. ²He will supply them with no emphasis at all upon them. ³What comes to you of Him comes

safely, for He will ensure it never can become a dark spot, hidden in your mind and kept to hurt you. [4]Under His guidance you will travel light and journey lightly, for His sight is ever on the journey's end, which is His goal. [5]God's Son is not a traveller through outer worlds. [6]However holy his perception may become, no world outside himself holds his inheritance. [7]Within himself he has no needs, for light needs nothing but to shine in peace, and from itself to let the rays extend in quiet to infinity.

14. Whenever you are tempted to undertake a useless journey that would lead away from light, remember what you really want, and say:

> [2]*The Holy Spirit leads me unto Christ, and where else*
> *would I go? [3]What need have I but to awake in Him?*

15. Then follow Him in joy, with faith that He will lead you safely through all dangers to your peace of mind this world may set before you. [2]Kneel not before the altars to sacrifice, and seek not what you will surely lose. [3]Content yourself with what you will as surely keep, and be not restless, for you undertake a quiet journey to the peace of God, where He would have you be in quietness.

16. In me you have already overcome every temptation that would hold you back. [2]We walk together on the way to quietness that is the gift of God. [3]Hold me dear, for what except your brothers can you need? [4]We will restore to you the peace of mind that we must find together. [5]The Holy Spirit will teach you to awaken unto us and to yourself. [6]This is the only real need to be fulfilled in time. [7]Salvation from the world lies only here. [8]My peace I give you. [9]Take it of me in glad exchange for all the world has offered but to take away. [10]And we will spread it like a veil of light across the world's sad face, in which we hide our brothers from the world, and it from them.

17. We cannot sing redemption's hymn alone. [2]My task is not completed until I have lifted every voice with mine. [3]And yet it is not mine, for as it is my gift to you, so was it the Father's gift to me, given me through His Spirit. [4]The sound of it will banish sorrow from the mind of God's most holy Son, where it cannot abide. [5]Healing in time is needed, for joy cannot establish its eternal reign where sorrow dwells. [6]You dwell not here, but in eternity. [7]You travel but in dreams, while safe at home. [8]Give

257

thanks to every part of you that you have taught how to remember you. ⁹Thus does the Son of God give thanks unto his Father for his purity.

VIII. From Perception to Knowledge

1. All healing is release from the past. ²That is why the Holy Spirit is the only Healer. ³He teaches that the past does not exist, a fact which belongs to the sphere of knowledge, and which therefore no one in the world can know. ⁴It would indeed be impossible to be in the world with this knowledge. ⁵For the mind that knows this unequivocally knows also it dwells in eternity, and utilizes no perception at all. ⁶It therefore does not consider where it is, because the concept "where" does not mean anything to it. ⁷It knows that it is everywhere, just as it has everything, and forever.

2. The very real difference between perception and knowledge becomes quite apparent if you consider this: There is nothing partial about knowledge. ²Every aspect is whole, and therefore no aspect is separate. ³You are an aspect of knowledge, being in the Mind of God, Who knows you. ⁴All knowledge must be yours, for in you is all knowledge. ⁵Perception, at its loftiest, is never complete. ⁶Even the perception of the Holy Spirit, as perfect as perception can be, is without meaning in Heaven. ⁷Perception can reach everywhere under His guidance, for the vision of Christ beholds everything in light. ⁸Yet no perception, however holy, will last forever.

3. Perfect perception, then, has many elements in common with knowledge, making transfer to it possible. ²Yet the last step must be taken by God, because the last step in your redemption, which seems to be in the future, was accomplished by God in your creation. ³The separation has not interrupted it. ⁴Creation cannot be interrupted. ⁵The separation is merely a faulty formulation of reality, with no effect at all. ⁶The miracle, without a function in Heaven, is needful here. ⁷Aspects of reality can still be seen, and they will replace aspects of unreality. ⁸Aspects of reality can be seen in everything and everywhere. ⁹Yet only God can gather them together, by crowning them as one with the final gift of eternity.

4. Apart from the Father and the Son, the Holy Spirit has no function. ²He is not separate from Either, being in the Mind of Both,
and knowing that Mind is One. ³He is a Thought of God, and
God has given Him to you because He has no Thoughts He does
not share. ⁴His message speaks of timelessness in time, and that
is why Christ's vision looks on everything with love. ⁵Yet even
Christ's vision is not His reality. ⁶The golden aspects of reality
that spring to light under His loving gaze are partial glimpses of
the Heaven that lies beyond them.

5. This is the miracle of creation; *that it is one forever*. ²Every miracle you offer to the Son of God is but the true perception of one
aspect of the whole. ³Though every aspect *is* the whole, you cannot know this until you see that every aspect is the same, perceived in the same light and therefore one. ⁴Everyone seen
without the past thus brings you nearer to the end of time by
bringing healed and healing sight into the darkness, and enabling the world to see. ⁵For light must come into the darkened
world to make Christ's vision possible even here. ⁶Help Him to
give His gift of light to all who think they wander in the darkness, and let Him gather them into His quiet sight that makes
them one.

6. They are all the same; all beautiful and equal in their holiness.
²And He will offer them unto His Father as they were offered
unto Him. ³There is one miracle, as there is one reality. ⁴And
every miracle you do contains them all, as every aspect of reality
you see blends quietly into the one reality of God. ⁵The only miracle that ever was is God's most holy Son, created in the one
reality that is his Father. ⁶Christ's vision is His gift to you. ⁷His
Being is His Father's gift to Him.

7. Be you content with healing, for Christ's gift you can bestow,
and your Father's gift you cannot lose. ²Offer Christ's gift to
everyone and everywhere, for miracles, offered the Son of God
through the Holy Spirit, attune you to reality. ³The Holy Spirit
knows your part in the redemption, and who are seeking you
and where to find them. ⁴Knowledge is far beyond your individual concern. ⁵You who are part of it and all of it need only
realize that it is of the Father, not of you. ⁶Your role in the redemption leads you to it by re-establishing its oneness in your
mind.

8. When you have seen your brothers as yourself you will be released to knowledge, having learned to free yourself through

Him Who knows of freedom. ²Unite with me under the holy banner of His teaching, and as we grow in strength the power of God's Son will move in us, and we will leave no one untouched and no one left alone. ³And suddenly time will be over, and we will all unite in the eternity of God the Father. ⁴The holy light you saw outside yourself, in every miracle you offered to your brothers, will be returned to you. ⁵And knowing that the light is in you, your creations will be there with you, as you are in your Father.

9. As miracles in this world join you to your brothers, so do your creations establish your fatherhood in Heaven. ²You are the witness to the Fatherhood of God, and He has given you the power to create the witnesses to yours, which is as His. ³Deny a brother here, and you deny the witnesses to your fatherhood in Heaven. ⁴The miracle that God created is perfect, as are the miracles that you established in His Name. ⁵They need no healing, nor do you, when you accept them.

10. Yet in this world your perfection is unwitnessed. ²God knows it, but you do not, and so you do not share His witness to it. ³Nor do you witness unto Him, for reality is witnessed to as one. ⁴God waits your witness to His Son and to Himself. ⁵The miracles you do on earth are lifted up to Heaven and to Him. ⁶They witness to what you do not know, and as they reach the gates of Heaven, God will open them. ⁷For never would He leave His Own beloved Son outside them, and beyond Himself.

IX. The Cloud of Guilt

1. Guilt remains the only thing that hides the Father, for guilt is the attack upon His Son. ²The guilty always condemn, and having done so they will still condemn, linking the future to the past as is the ego's law. ³Fidelity to this law lets no light in, for it demands fidelity to darkness and forbids awakening. ⁴The ego's laws are strict, and breaches are severely punished. ⁵Therefore give no obedience to its laws, for they are laws of punishment. ⁶And those who follow them believe that they are guilty, and so they must condemn. ⁷Between the future and the past the laws of God must intervene, if you would free yourself. ⁸Atonement stands between them, like a lamp shining so brightly that the chain of darkness in which you bound yourself will disappear.

2. Release from guilt is the ego's whole undoing. ²*Make no one fearful*, for his guilt is yours, and by obeying the ego's harsh commandments you bring its condemnation on yourself, and you will not escape the punishment it offers those who obey it. ³The ego rewards fidelity to it with pain, for faith in it *is* pain. ⁴And faith can be rewarded only in terms of the belief in which the faith was placed. ⁵Faith makes the power of belief, and where it is invested determines its reward. ⁶For faith is always given what is treasured, and what is treasured is returned to you.

3. The world can give you only what you gave it, for being nothing but your own projection, it has no meaning apart from what you found in it and placed your faith in. ²Be faithful unto darkness and you will not see, because your faith will be rewarded as you gave it. ³You *will* accept your treasure, and if you place your faith in the past, the future will be like it. ⁴Whatever you hold dear you think is yours. ⁵The power of your valuing will make it so.

4. Atonement brings a re-evaluation of everything you cherish, for it is the means by which the Holy Spirit can separate the false and the true, which you have accepted into your mind without distinction. ²Therefore you cannot value one without the other, and guilt has become as true for you as innocence. ³You do not believe the Son of God is guiltless because you see the past, and see him not. ⁴When you condemn a brother you are saying, "I who was guilty choose to remain so." ⁵You have denied his freedom, and by so doing you have denied the witness unto yours. ⁶You could as easily have freed him from the past, and lifted from his mind the cloud of guilt that binds him to it. ⁷And in his freedom would have been your own.

5. Lay not his guilt upon him, for his guilt lies in his secret thought that he has done this unto you. ²Would you, then, teach him he is right in his delusion? ³The idea that the guiltless Son of God can attack himself and make himself guilty is insane. ⁴In any form, in anyone, *believe this not*. ⁵For sin and condemnation are the same, and the belief in one is faith in the other, calling for punishment instead of love. ⁶Nothing can justify insanity, and to call for punishment upon yourself must be insane.

6. See no one, then, as guilty, and you will affirm the truth of guiltlessness unto yourself. ²In every condemnation that you offer the Son of God lies the conviction of your own guilt. ³If you would have the Holy Spirit make you free of it, accept His offer

of Atonement for all your brothers. [4]For so you learn that it is true for you. [5]Remember always that it is impossible to condemn the Son of God in part. [6]Those whom you see as guilty become the witnesses to guilt in you, and you will see it there, for it *is* there until it is undone. [7]Guilt is always in your mind, which has condemned itself. [8]Project it not, for while you do, it cannot be undone. [9]With everyone whom you release from guilt great is the joy in Heaven, where the witnesses to your fatherhood rejoice.

7. Guilt makes you blind, for while you see one spot of guilt within you, you will not see the light. [2]And by projecting it the world seems dark, and shrouded in your guilt. [3]You throw a dark veil over it, and cannot see it because you cannot look within. [4]You are afraid of what you would see there, but it is not there. [5]*The thing you fear is gone.* [6]If you would look within you would see only the Atonement, shining in quiet and in peace upon the altar to your Father.

8. Do not be afraid to look within. [2]The ego tells you all is black with guilt within you, and bids you not to look. [3]Instead, it bids you look upon your brothers, and see the guilt in them. [4]Yet this you cannot do without remaining blind. [5]For those who see their brothers in the dark, and guilty in the dark in which they shroud them, are too afraid to look upon the light within. [6]Within you is not what you believe is there, and what you put your faith in. [7]Within you is the holy sign of perfect faith your Father has in you. [8]He does not value you as you do. [9]He knows Himself, and knows the truth in you. [10]He knows there is no difference, for He knows not of differences. [11]Can you see guilt where God knows there is perfect innocence? [12]You can deny His knowledge, but you cannot change it. [13]Look, then, upon the light He placed within you, and learn that what you feared was there has been replaced with love.

X. Release from Guilt

1. You are accustomed to the notion that the mind can see the source of pain where it is not. [2]The doubtful service of such displacement is to hide the real source of guilt, and keep from your awareness the full perception that it is insane. [3]Displacement always is maintained by the illusion that the source of guilt, from which attention is diverted, must be true; and must be fearful, or

you would not have displaced the guilt onto what you believed to be less fearful. ⁴You are therefore willing to look upon all kinds of "sources," provided they are not the deeper source to which they bear no real relationship at all.

2. Insane ideas have no real relationships, for that is why they are insane. ²No real relationship can rest on guilt, or even hold one spot of it to mar its purity. ³For all relationships that guilt has touched are used but to avoid the person *and* the guilt. ⁴What strange relationships you have made for this strange purpose! ⁵And you forgot that real relationships are holy, and cannot be used by you at all. ⁶They are used only by the Holy Spirit, and it is that which makes them pure. ⁷If you displace your guilt upon them, the Holy Spirit cannot use them. ⁸For, by pre-empting for your own ends what you should have given Him, He cannot use it for your release. ⁹No one who would unite in any way with anyone for his individual salvation will find it in that strange relationship. ¹⁰It is not shared, and so it is not real.

3. In any union with a brother in which you seek to lay your guilt upon him, or share it with him or perceive his own, *you* will feel guilty. ²Nor will you find satisfaction and peace with him, because your union with him is not real. ³You will see guilt in that relationship because you put it there. ⁴It is inevitable that those who suffer guilt will attempt to displace it, because they do believe in it. ⁵Yet though they suffer, they will not look within and let it go. ⁶They cannot know they love, and cannot understand what loving is. ⁷Their main concern is to perceive the source of guilt outside themselves, beyond their own control.

4. When you maintain that you are guilty but the source of your guilt lies in the past, you are not looking inward. ²The past is not *in* you. ³Your weird associations to it have no meaning in the present. ⁴Yet you let them stand between you and your brothers, with whom you find no real relationships at all. ⁵Can you expect to use your brothers as a means to "solve" the past, and still to see them as they really are? ⁶Salvation is not found by those who use their brothers to resolve problems that are not there. ⁷You wanted not salvation in the past. ⁸Would you impose your idle wishes on the present, and hope to find salvation now?

5. Determine, then, to be not as you were. ²Use no relationship to hold you to the past, but with each one each day be born again. ³A minute, even less, will be enough to free you from the past, and give your mind in peace over to the Atonement. ⁴When everyone

is welcome to you as you would have yourself be welcome to your Father, you will see no guilt in you. ⁵For you will have accepted the Atonement, which shone within you all the while you dreamed of guilt, and would not look within and see it.

6. As long as you believe that guilt is justified in any way, in anyone, whatever he may do, you will not look within, where you would always find Atonement. ²The end of guilt will never come as long as you believe there is a reason for it. ³For you must learn that guilt is always totally insane, and has no reason. ⁴The Holy Spirit seeks not to dispel reality. ⁵If guilt were real, Atonement would not be. ⁶The purpose of Atonement is to dispel illusions, not to establish them as real and then forgive them.

7. The Holy Spirit does not keep illusions in your mind to frighten you, and show them to you fearfully to demonstrate what He has saved you from. ²What He has saved you from is gone. ³Give no reality to guilt, and see no reason for it. ⁴The Holy Spirit does what God would have Him do, and has always done so. ⁵He has seen separation, but knows of union. ⁶He teaches healing, but He also knows of creation. ⁷He would have you see and teach as He does, and through Him. ⁸Yet what He knows you do not know, though it is yours.

8. *Now* it is given you to heal and teach, to make what will be *now*. ²As yet it is not now. ³The Son of God believes that he is lost in guilt, alone in a dark world where pain is pressing everywhere upon him from without. ⁴When he has looked within and seen the radiance there, he will remember how much his Father loves him. ⁵And it will seem incredible that he ever thought his Father loved him not, and looked upon him as condemned. ⁶The moment that you realize guilt is insane, wholly unjustified and wholly without reason, you will not fear to look upon the Atonement and accept it wholly.

9. You who have been unmerciful to yourself do not remember your Father's Love. ²And looking without mercy upon your brothers, you do not remember how much you love Him. ³Yet it is forever true. ⁴In shining peace within you is the perfect purity in which you were created. ⁵Fear not to look upon the lovely truth in you. ⁶Look through the cloud of guilt that dims your vision, and look past darkness to the holy place where you will see the light. ⁷The altar to your Father is as pure as He Who raised it to Himself. ⁸Nothing can keep from you what Christ would have you see. ⁹His Will is like His Father's, and He offers

mercy to every child of God, as He would have you do.

10.   Release from guilt as you would be released. ²There is no other way to look within and see the light of love, shining as steadily and as surely as God Himself has always loved His Son. ³*And as His Son loves Him.* ⁴There is no fear in love, for love is guiltless. ⁵You who have always loved your Father can have no fear, for any reason, to look within and see your holiness. ⁶You cannot be as you believed you were. ⁷Your guilt is without reason because it is not in the Mind of God, where you are. ⁸And this *is* reason, which the Holy Spirit would restore to you. ⁹He would remove only illusions. ¹⁰All else He would have you see. ¹¹And in Christ's vision He would show you the perfect purity that is forever within God's Son.

11.   You cannot enter into real relationships with any of God's Sons unless you love them all and equally. ²Love is not special. ³If you single out part of the Sonship for your love, you are imposing guilt on all your relationships and making them unreal. ⁴You can love only as God loves. ⁵Seek not to love unlike Him, for there is no love apart from His. ⁶Until you recognize that this is true, you will have no idea what love is like. ⁷No one who condemns a brother can see himself as guiltless and in the peace of God. ⁸If he is guiltless and in peace and sees it not, he is delusional, and has not looked upon himself. ⁹To him I say:

   ¹⁰*Behold the Son of God, and look upon his purity and be still.* ¹¹*In quiet look upon his holiness, and offer thanks unto his Father that no guilt has ever touched him.*

12.   No illusion that you have ever held against him has touched his innocence in any way. ²His shining purity, wholly untouched by guilt and wholly loving, is bright within you. ³Let us look upon him together and love him. ⁴For in love of him is your guiltlessness. ⁵But look upon yourself, and gladness and appreciation for what you see will banish guilt forever. ⁶I thank You, Father, for the purity of Your most holy Son, whom You have created guiltless forever.

13.   Like you, my faith and my belief are centered on what I treasure. ²The difference is that I love *only* what God loves with me, and because of this I treasure you beyond the value that you set on yourself, even unto the worth that God has placed upon you. ³I love all that He created, and all my faith and my belief I offer

unto it. [4]My faith in you is as strong as all the love I give my Father. [5]My trust in you is without limit, and without the fear that you will hear me not. [6]I thank the Father for your loveliness, and for the many gifts that you will let me offer to the Kingdom in honor of its wholeness that is of God.

14. Praise be to you who make the Father one with His Own Son. [2]Alone we are all lowly, but together we shine with brightness so intense that none of us alone can even think of it. [3]Before the glorious radiance of the Kingdom guilt melts away, and transformed into kindness will never more be what it was. [4]Every reaction you experience will be so purified that it is fitting as a hymn of praise unto your Father. [5]See only praise of Him in what He has created, for He will never cease His praise of you. [6]United in this praise we stand before the gates of Heaven where we will surely enter in our sinlessness. [7]God loves you. [8]Could I, then, lack faith in you and love Him perfectly?

XI. The Peace of Heaven

1. Forgetfulness and sleep and even death become the ego's best advice for dealing with the perceived and harsh intrusion of guilt on peace. [2]Yet no one sees himself in conflict and ravaged by a cruel war unless he believes that both opponents in the war are real. [3]Believing this he must escape, for such a war would surely end his peace of mind, and so destroy him. [4]Yet if he could but realize the war is between real and unreal powers, he could look upon himself and see his freedom. [5]No one finds himself ravaged and torn in endless battles if he himself perceives them as wholly without meaning.

2. God would not have His Son embattled, and so His Son's imagined "enemy" is totally unreal. [2]You are but trying to escape a bitter war from which you *have* escaped. [3]The war is gone. [4]For you have heard the hymn of freedom rising unto Heaven. [5]Gladness and joy belong to God for your release, because you made it not. [6]Yet as you made not freedom, so you made not a war that could endanger freedom. [7]Nothing destructive ever was or will be. [8]The war, the guilt, the past are gone as one into the unreality from which they came.

3. When we are all united in Heaven, you will value nothing that you value here. [2]For nothing that you value here do you value

wholly, and so you do not value it at all. ³Value is where God placed it, and the value of what God esteems cannot be judged, for it has been established. ⁴It is wholly of value. ⁵It can merely be appreciated or not. ⁶To value it partially is not to know its value. ⁷In Heaven is everything God values, and nothing else. ⁸Heaven is perfectly unambiguous. ⁹Everything is clear and bright, and calls forth one response. ¹⁰There is no darkness and there is no contrast. ¹¹There is no variation. ¹²There is no interruption. ¹³There is a sense of peace so deep that no dream in this world has ever brought even a dim imagining of what it is.

4. Nothing in this world can give this peace, for nothing in this world is wholly shared. ²Perfect perception can merely show you what is capable of being wholly shared. ³It can also show you the results of sharing, while you still remember the results of not sharing. ⁴The Holy Spirit points quietly to the contrast, knowing that you will finally let Him judge the difference for you, allowing Him to demonstrate which must be true. ⁵He has perfect faith in your final judgment, because He knows that He will make it for you. ⁶To doubt this would be to doubt that His mission will be fulfilled. ⁷How is this possible, when His mission is of God?

5. You whose mind is darkened by doubt and guilt, remember this: God gave the Holy Spirit to you, and gave Him the mission to remove all doubt and every trace of guilt that His dear Son has laid upon himself. ²It is impossible that this mission fail. ³Nothing can prevent what God would have accomplished from accomplishment. ⁴Whatever your reactions to the Holy Spirit's Voice may be, whatever voice you choose to listen to, whatever strange thoughts may occur to you, God's Will *is* done. ⁵You will find the peace in which He has established you, because He does not change His Mind. ⁶He is invariable as the peace in which you dwell, and of which the Holy Spirit reminds you.

6. You will not remember change and shift in Heaven. ²You have need of contrast only here. ³Contrast and differences are necessary teaching aids, for by them you learn what to avoid and what to seek. ⁴When you have learned this, you will find the answer that makes the need for any differences disappear. ⁵Truth comes of its own will unto its own. ⁶When you have learned that you belong to truth, it will flow lightly over you without a difference of any kind. ⁷For you will need no contrast to help you realize that this is what you want, and only this. ⁸Fear not the Holy Spirit will fail in what your Father has given Him to do. ⁹The Will of

God can fail in nothing.

7. Have faith in only this one thing, and it will be sufficient: God wills you be in Heaven, and nothing can keep you from it, or it from you. ²Your wildest misperceptions, your weird imaginings, your blackest nightmares all mean nothing. ³They will not prevail against the peace God wills for you. ⁴The Holy Spirit will restore your sanity because insanity is not the Will of God. ⁵If that suffices Him, it is enough for you. ⁶You will not keep what God would have removed, because it breaks communication with you with whom He would communicate. ⁷His Voice *will* be heard.

8. The Communication Link that God Himself placed within you, joining your mind with His, cannot be broken. ²You may believe you want It broken, and this belief does interfere with the deep peace in which the sweet and constant communication God would share with you is known. ³Yet His channels of reaching out cannot be wholly closed and separated from Him. ⁴Peace will be yours because His peace still flows to you from Him Whose Will is peace. ⁵You have it now. ⁶The Holy Spirit will teach you how to use it, and by extending it, to learn that it is in you. ⁷God willed you Heaven, and will always will you nothing else. ⁸The Holy Spirit knows only of His Will. ⁹There is no chance that Heaven will not be yours, for God is sure, and what He wills is as sure as He is.

9. You will learn salvation because you will learn how to save. ²It will not be possible to exempt yourself from what the Holy Spirit wants to teach you. ³Salvation is as sure as God. ⁴His certainty suffices. ⁵Learn that even the darkest nightmare that disturbs the mind of God's sleeping Son holds no power over him. ⁶He will learn the lesson of awaking. ⁷God watches over him and light surrounds him.

10. Can God's Son lose himself in dreams, when God has placed within him the glad Call to waken and be glad? ²He cannot separate himself from what is in him. ³His sleep will not withstand the Call to wake. ⁴The mission of redemption will be fulfilled as surely as the creation will remain unchanged throughout eternity. ⁵You do not have to know that Heaven is yours to make it so. ⁶It *is* so. ⁷Yet to know it, the Will of God must be accepted as your will.

11. The Holy Spirit will undo for you everything you have learned that teaches that what is not true must be reconciled with truth. ²This is the reconciliation the ego would substitute for your

reconciliation to sanity and to peace. ³The Holy Spirit has a very different kind of reconciliation in His Mind for you, and one He will effect as surely as the ego will not effect what it attempts. ⁴Failure is of the ego, not of God. ⁵From Him you cannot wander, and there is no possibility that the plan the Holy Spirit offers *to* everyone, for the salvation *of* everyone, will not be perfectly accomplished. ⁶You will be released, and you will not remember anything you made that was not created for you and by you in return. ⁷For how can you remember what was never true, or not remember what has always been? ⁸It is this reconciliation with truth, and only truth, in which the peace of Heaven lies.

Chapter 14

TEACHING FOR TRUTH

Introduction

1. Yes, you are blessed indeed. ²Yet in this world you do not know it. ³But you have the means for learning it and seeing it quite clearly. ⁴The Holy Spirit uses logic as easily and as well as does the ego, except that His conclusions are not insane. ⁵They take a direction exactly opposite, pointing as clearly to Heaven as the ego points to darkness and to death. ⁶We have followed much of the ego's logic, and have seen its logical conclusions. ⁷And having seen them, we have realized that they cannot be seen except in illusions, for there alone their seeming clearness seems to be clearly seen. ⁸Let us now turn away from them, and follow the simple logic by which the Holy Spirit teaches the simple conclusions that speak for truth, and only truth.

I. The Conditions of Learning

1. If you are blessed and do not know it, you need to learn it must be so. ²The knowledge is not taught, but its conditions must be acquired for it is they that have been thrown away. ³You can learn to bless, and cannot give what you have not. ⁴If, then, you offer blessing, it must have come first to yourself. ⁵And you must also have accepted it as yours, for how else could you give it away? ⁶That is why miracles offer *you* the testimony that you are blessed. ⁷If what you offer is complete forgiveness you must have let guilt go, accepting the Atonement for yourself and learning you are guiltless. ⁸How could you learn what has been done for you, unknown to you, unless you do what you would have to do if it *had* been done for you?

2. Indirect proof of truth is needed in a world made of denial and without direction. ²You will perceive the need for this if you realize that to deny is the decision not to know. ³The logic of the world must therefore lead to nothing, for its goal is nothing. ⁴If you decide to have and give and be nothing except a dream, you must direct your thoughts unto oblivion. ⁵And if you have and

270

give and are everything, and all this has been denied, your thought system is closed off and wholly separated from the truth. ⁶This *is* an insane world, and do not underestimate the extent of its insanity. ⁷There is no area of your perception that it has not touched, and your dream *is* sacred to you. ⁸That is why God placed the Holy Spirit in you, where you placed the dream.

3. Seeing is always outward. ²Were your thoughts wholly of you, the thought system you made would be forever dark. ³The thoughts the mind of God's Son projects or extends have all the power that he gives to them. ⁴The thoughts he shares with God are beyond his belief, but those he made *are* his beliefs. ⁵And it is these, and not the truth, that he has chosen to defend and love. ⁶They will not be taken from him. ⁷But they can be given up *by* him, for the Source of their undoing is in him. ⁸There is nothing in the world to teach him that the logic of the world is totally insane and leads to nothing. ⁹Yet in him who made this insane logic there is One Who knows it leads to nothing, for He knows everything.

4. Any direction that would lead you where the Holy Spirit leads you not, goes nowhere. ²Anything you deny that He knows to be true you have denied yourself, and He must therefore teach you not to deny it. ³Undoing *is* indirect, as doing is. ⁴You were created only to create, neither to see nor do. ⁵These are but indirect expressions of the will to live, which has been blocked by the capricious and unholy whim of death and murder that your Father does not share with you. ⁶You have set yourself the task of sharing what cannot be shared. ⁷And while you think it possible to learn to do this, you will not believe all that *is* possible to learn to do.

5. The Holy Spirit, therefore, must begin His teaching by showing you what you can never learn. ²His message is not indirect, but He must introduce the simple truth into a thought system which has become so twisted and so complex you cannot see that it means nothing. ³He merely looks at its foundation and dismisses it. ⁴But you who cannot undo what you have made, nor escape the heavy burden of its dullness that lies upon your mind, cannot see through it. ⁵It deceives you, because you chose to deceive yourself. ⁶Those who choose to be deceived will merely attack direct approaches, because they seem to encroach upon deception and strike at it.

II. The Happy Learner

1. The Holy Spirit needs a happy learner, in whom His mission can be happily accomplished. [2]You who are steadfastly devoted to misery must first recognize that you are miserable and not happy. [3]The Holy Spirit cannot teach without this contrast, for you believe that misery *is* happiness. [4]This has so confused you that you have undertaken to learn to do what you can never do, believing that unless you learn it you will not be happy. [5]You do not realize that the foundation on which this most peculiar learning goal depends means absolutely nothing. [6]Yet it may still make sense to you. [7]Have faith in nothing and you will find the "treasure" that you seek. [8]Yet you will add another burden to your already burdened mind. [9]You will believe that nothing is of value, and will value it. [10]A little piece of glass, a speck of dust, a body or a war are one to you. [11]For if you value one thing made of nothing, you have believed that nothing can be precious, and that you *can* learn how to make the untrue true.

2. The Holy Spirit, seeing where you are but knowing you are elsewhere, begins His lesson in simplicity with the fundamental teaching that *truth is true*. [2]This is the hardest lesson you will ever learn, and in the end the only one. [3]Simplicity is very difficult for twisted minds. [4]Consider all the distortions you have made of nothing; all the strange forms and feelings and actions and reactions that you have woven out of it. [5]Nothing is so alien to you as the simple truth, and nothing are you less inclined to listen to. [6]The contrast between what is true and what is not is perfectly apparent, yet you do not see it. [7]The simple and the obvious are not apparent to those who would make palaces and royal robes of nothing, believing they are kings with golden crowns because of them.

3. All this the Holy Spirit sees, and teaches, simply, that all this is not true. [2]To those unhappy learners who would teach themselves nothing, and delude themselves into believing that it is not nothing, the Holy Spirit says, with steadfast quietness:

> [3]*The truth is true.* [4]*Nothing else matters, nothing else is real, and everything beside it is not there.* [5]*Let Me make the one distinction for you that you cannot make, but need to learn.* [6]*Your faith in nothing is deceiving you.* [7]*Offer your faith to Me, and I will place it gently in the holy*

place where it belongs. ⁸You will find no deception there,
but only the simple truth. ⁹And you will love it because
you will understand it.

4. Like you, the Holy Spirit did not make truth. ²Like God, He
knows it to be true. ³He brings the light of truth into the darkness,
and lets it shine on you. ⁴And as it shines your brothers see it, and
realizing that this light is not what you have made, they see in you
more than you see. ⁵They will be happy learners of the lesson this
light brings to them, because it teaches them release from nothing
and from all the works of nothing. ⁶The heavy chains that seem to
bind them to despair they do not see as nothing, until you bring
the light to them. ⁷And then they see the chains have disappeared,
and so they *must* have been nothing. ⁸And you will see it with
them. ⁹Because you taught them gladness and release, they will
become your teachers in release and gladness.

5. When you teach anyone that truth is true, you learn it with
him. ²And so you learn that what seemed hardest was the easiest.
³Learn to be a happy learner. ⁴You will never learn how to make
nothing everything. ⁵Yet see that this has been your goal, and
recognize how foolish it has been. ⁶Be glad it is undone, for when
you look at it in simple honesty, it *is* undone. ⁷I said before, "Be
not content with nothing," for you have believed that nothing
could content you. ⁸*It is not so.*

6. If you would be a happy learner, you must give everything
you have learned to the Holy Spirit, to be unlearned for you.
²And then begin to learn the joyous lessons that come quickly on
the firm foundation that truth is true. ³For what is builded there *is*
true, and built on truth. ⁴The universe of learning will open up
before you in all its gracious simplicity. ⁵With truth before you,
you will not look back.

7. The happy learner meets the conditions of learning here, as he
meets the conditions of knowledge in the Kingdom. ²All this lies
in the Holy Spirit's plan to free you from the past, and open up
the way to freedom for you. ³For truth *is* true. ⁴What else could
ever be, or ever was? ⁵This simple lesson holds the key to the
dark door that you believe is locked forever. ⁶You made this door
of nothing, and behind it *is* nothing. ⁷The key is only the light that
shines away the shapes and forms and fears of nothing. ⁸Accept
this key to freedom from the hands of Christ Who gives it to you,
that you may join Him in the holy task of bringing light. ⁹For, like

your brothers, you do not realize the light has come and freed you from the sleep of darkness.

8.   Behold your brothers in their freedom, and learn of them how to be free of darkness. ²The light in you will waken them, and they will not leave you asleep. ³The vision of Christ is given the very instant that it is perceived. ⁴Where everything is clear, it is all holy. ⁵The quietness of its simplicity is so compelling that you will realize it is impossible to deny the simple truth. ⁶For there is nothing else. ⁷God is everywhere, and His Son is in Him with everything. ⁸Can he sing the dirge of sorrow when this is true?

III. The Decision for Guiltlessness

1.   The happy learner cannot feel guilty about learning. ²This is so essential to learning that it should never be forgotten. ³The guiltless learner learns easily because his thoughts are free. ⁴Yet this entails the recognition that guilt is interference, not salvation, and serves no useful function at all.

2.   Perhaps you are accustomed to using guiltlessness merely to offset the pain of guilt, and do not look upon it as having value in itself. ²You believe that guilt and guiltlessness are both of value, each representing an escape from what the other does not offer you. ³You do not want either alone, for without both you do not see yourself as whole and therefore happy. ⁴Yet you are whole only in your guiltlessness, and only in your guiltlessness can you be happy. ⁵There is no conflict here. ⁶To wish for guilt in any way, in any form, will lose appreciation of the value of your guiltlessness, and push it from your sight.

3.   There is no compromise that you can make with guilt, and escape the pain that only guiltlessness allays. ²Learning is living here, as creating is being in Heaven. ³Whenever the pain of guilt seems to attract you, remember that if you yield to it, you are deciding against your happiness, and will not learn how to be happy. ⁴Say therefore, to yourself, gently, but with the conviction born of the Love of God and of His Son:

> ⁵*What I experience I will make manifest.*
> ⁶*If I am guiltless, I have nothing to fear.*
> ⁷*I choose to testify to my acceptance of the*
>   *Atonement, not to its rejection.*

⁸*I would accept my guiltlessness by making it
manifest and sharing it.*
⁹*Let me bring peace to God's Son from his Father.*

4. Each day, each hour and minute, even each second, you are deciding between the crucifixion and the resurrection; between the ego and the Holy Spirit. ²The ego is the choice for guilt; the Holy Spirit the choice for guiltlessness. ³The power of decision is all that is yours. ⁴What you can decide between is fixed, because there are no alternatives except truth and illusion. ⁵And there is no overlap between them, because they are opposites which cannot be reconciled and cannot both be true. ⁶You are guilty or guiltless, bound or free, unhappy or happy.

5. The miracle teaches you that you have chosen guiltlessness, freedom and joy. ²It is not a cause, but an effect. ³It is the natural result of choosing right, attesting to your happiness that comes from choosing to be free of guilt. ⁴Everyone you offer healing to returns it. ⁵Everyone you attack keeps it and cherishes it by holding it against you. ⁶Whether he does this or does it not will make no difference; you will think he does. ⁷It is impossible to offer what you do not want without this penalty. ⁸The cost of giving *is* receiving. ⁹Either it is a penalty from which you suffer, or the happy purchase of a treasure to hold dear.

6. No penalty is ever asked of God's Son except by himself and of himself. ²Every chance given him to heal is another opportunity to replace darkness with light and fear with love. ³If he refuses it he binds himself to darkness, because he did not choose to free his brother and enter light with him. ⁴By giving power to nothing, he throws away the joyous opportunity to learn that nothing has no power. ⁵And by not dispelling darkness, he became afraid of darkness and of light. ⁶The joy of learning that darkness has no power over the Son of God is the happy lesson the Holy Spirit teaches, and would have you teach with Him. ⁷It is His joy to teach it, as it will be yours.

7. The way to teach this simple lesson is merely this: Guiltlessness is invulnerability. ²Therefore, make your invulnerability manifest to everyone. ³Teach him that, whatever he may try to do to you, your perfect freedom from the belief that you can be harmed shows him that he is guiltless. ⁴He can do nothing that can hurt you, and by refusing to allow him to think he can, you teach him that the Atonement, which you have accepted for

275

yourself, is also his. ⁵There is nothing to forgive. ⁶No one can hurt the Son of God. ⁷His guilt is wholly without cause, and being without cause, cannot exist.

8.   God is the only Cause, and guilt is not of Him. ²Teach no one he has hurt you, for if you do, you teach yourself that what is not of God has power over you. ³*The causeless cannot be.* ⁴Do not attest to it, and do not foster belief in it in any mind. ⁵Remember always that mind is one, and cause is one. ⁶You will learn communication with this oneness only when you learn to deny the causeless, and accept the Cause of God as yours. ⁷The power that God has given to His Son *is* his, and nothing else can His Son see or choose to look upon without imposing on himself the penalty of guilt, in place of all the happy teaching the Holy Spirit would gladly offer him.

9.   Whenever you choose to make decisions for yourself you are thinking destructively, and the decision will be wrong. ²It will hurt you because of the concept of decision that led to it. ³It is not true that you can make decisions by yourself or for yourself alone. ⁴No thought of God's Son can be separate or isolated in its effects. ⁵Every decision is made for the whole Sonship, directed in and out, and influencing a constellation larger than anything you ever dreamed of.

10.   Those who accept the Atonement *are* invulnerable. ²But those who believe they are guilty will respond to guilt, because they think it is salvation, and will not refuse to see it and side with it. ³They believe that increasing guilt is self-protection. ⁴And they will fail to understand the simple fact that what they do not want must hurt them. ⁵All this arises because they do not believe that what they want is good. ⁶Yet will was given them because it is holy, and will bring to them all that they need, coming as naturally as peace that knows no limits. ⁷There is nothing their will fails to provide that offers them anything of value. ⁸Yet because they do not understand their will, the Holy Spirit quietly understands it for them, and gives them what they want without effort, strain, or the impossible burden of deciding what they want and need alone.

11.   It will never happen that you must make decisions for yourself. ²You are not bereft of help, and Help that knows the answer. ³Would you be content with little, which is all that you alone can offer yourself, when He Who gives you everything will simply offer it to you? ⁴He will never ask what you have done to make

you worthy of the gift of God. ⁵Ask it not therefore of yourself. ⁶Instead, accept His answer, for He knows that you are worthy of everything God wills for you. ⁷Do not try to escape the gift of God He so freely and so gladly offers you. ⁸He offers you but what God gave Him for you. ⁹You need not decide whether or not you are deserving of it. ¹⁰God knows you are.

12. Would you deny the truth of God's decision, and place your pitiful appraisal of yourself in place of His calm and unswerving value of His Son? ²Nothing can shake God's conviction of the perfect purity of everything that He created, for it *is* wholly pure. ³Do not decide against it, for being of Him it must be true. ⁴Peace abides in every mind that quietly accepts the plan God set for its Atonement, relinquishing its own. ⁵You know not of salvation, for you do not understand it. ⁶Make no decisions about what it is or where it lies, but ask the Holy Spirit everything, and leave all decisions to His gentle counsel.

13. The One Who knows the plan of God that God would have you follow can teach you what it is. ²Only His wisdom is capable of guiding you to follow it. ³Every decision you undertake alone but signifies that you would define what salvation *is*, and what you would be saved *from*. ⁴The Holy Spirit knows that all salvation is escape from guilt. ⁵You have no other "enemy," and against this strange distortion of the purity of the Son of God the Holy Spirit is your only Friend. ⁶He is the strong protector of the innocence that sets you free. ⁷And it is His decision to undo everything that would obscure your innocence from your unclouded mind.

14. Let Him, therefore, be the only Guide that you would follow to salvation. ²He knows the way, and leads you gladly on it. ³With Him you will not fail to learn that what God wills for you *is* your will. ⁴Without His guidance you will think you know alone, and will decide against your peace as surely as you decided that salvation lay in you alone. ⁵Salvation is of Him to Whom God gave it for you. ⁶He has not forgotten it. ⁷Forget Him not and He will make every decision for you, for your salvation and the peace of God in you.

15. Seek not to appraise the worth of God's Son whom He created holy, for to do so is to evaluate his Father and judge against Him. ²And you *will* feel guilty for this imagined crime, which no one in this world or Heaven could possibly commit. ³The Holy Spirit teaches only that the "sin" of self-replacement on the throne of

God is not a source of guilt. [4]What cannot happen can have no effects to fear. [5]Be quiet in your faith in Him Who loves you, and would lead you out of insanity. [6]Madness may be your choice, but not your reality. [7]Never forget the Love of God, Who has remembered you. [8]For it is quite impossible that He could ever let His Son drop from the loving Mind wherein he was created, and where his abode was fixed in perfect peace forever.

16. Say to the Holy Spirit only, "Decide for me," and it is done. [2]For His decisions are reflections of what God knows about you, and in this light, error of any kind becomes impossible. [3]Why would you struggle so frantically to anticipate all you cannot know, when all knowledge lies behind every decision the Holy Spirit makes for you? [4]Learn of His wisdom and His Love, and teach His answer to everyone who struggles in the dark. [5]For you decide for them and for yourself.

17. How gracious it is to decide all things through Him Whose equal Love is given equally to all alike! [2]He leaves you no one outside you. [3]And so He gives you what is yours, because your Father would have you share it with Him. [4]In everything be led by Him, and do not reconsider. [5]Trust Him to answer quickly, surely, and with Love for everyone who will be touched in any way by the decision. [6]And everyone will be. [7]Would you take unto yourself the sole responsibility for deciding what can bring only good to everyone? [8]Would you know this?

18. You taught yourself the most unnatural habit of not communicating with your Creator. [2]Yet you remain in close communication with Him, and with everything that is within Him, as it is within yourself. [3]Unlearn isolation through His loving guidance, and learn of all the happy communication that you have thrown away but could not lose.

19. Whenever you are in doubt what you should do, think of His Presence in you, and tell yourself this, and only this:

> [2]*He leadeth me and knows the way, which I know not.*
> [3]*Yet He will never keep from me what He would have me learn.*
> [4]*And so I trust Him to communicate to me all that He knows for me.*

[5]Then let Him teach you quietly how to perceive your guiltlessness, which is already there.

IV. Your Function in the Atonement

1. When you accept a brother's guiltlessness you will see the Atonement in him. ²For by proclaiming it in him you make it yours, and you will see what you sought. ³You will not see the symbol of your brother's guiltlessness shining within him while you still believe it is not there. ⁴His guiltlessness is *your* Atonement. ⁵Grant it to him, and you will see the truth of what you have acknowledged. ⁶Yet truth is offered first to be received, even as God gave it first to His Son. ⁷The first in time means nothing, but the First in eternity is God the Father, Who is both First and One. ⁸Beyond the First there is no other, for there is no order, no second or third, and nothing but the First.

2. You who belong to the First Cause, created by Him like unto Himself and part of Him, are more than merely guiltless. ²The state of guiltlessness is only the condition in which what is not there has been removed from the disordered mind that thought it was. ³This state, and only this, must you attain, with God beside you. ⁴For until you do, you will still think that you are separate from Him. ⁵You can perhaps feel His Presence next to you, but cannot know that you are one with Him. ⁶This cannot be taught. ⁷Learning applies only to the condition in which it happens of itself.

3. When you have let all that obscured the truth in your most holy mind be undone for you, and therefore stand in grace before your Father, He will give Himself to you as He has always done. ²Giving Himself is all He knows, and so it is all knowledge. ³For what He knows not cannot be, and therefore cannot be given. ⁴Ask not to be forgiven, for this has already been accomplished. ⁵Ask, rather, to learn how to forgive, and to restore what always was to your unforgiving mind. ⁶Atonement becomes real and visible to those who use it. ⁷On earth this is your only function, and you must learn that it is all you want to learn. ⁸You will feel guilty till you learn this. ⁹For in the end, whatever form it takes, your guilt arises from your failure to fulfill your function in God's Mind with all of yours. ¹⁰Can you escape this guilt by failing to fulfill your function here?

4. You need not understand creation to do what must be done before that knowledge would be meaningful to you. ²God breaks no barriers; neither did He make them. ³When you release them they are gone. ⁴God will not fail, nor ever has in anything.

[5]Decide that God is right and you are wrong about yourself. [6]He created you out of Himself, but still within Him. [7]He knows what you are. [8]Remember that there is no second to Him. [9]There cannot, therefore, be anyone without His Holiness, nor anyone unworthy of His perfect Love. [10]Fail not in your function of loving in a loveless place made out of darkness and deceit, for thus are darkness and deceit undone. [11]Fail not yourself, but instead offer to God and you His blameless Son. [12]For this small gift of appreciation for His Love, God will Himself exchange your gift for His.

5.   Before you make any decisions for yourself, remember that you have decided against your function in Heaven, and then consider carefully whether you want to make decisions here. [2]Your function here is only to decide against deciding what you want, in recognition that you do not know. [3]How, then, can you decide what you should do? [4]Leave all decisions to the One Who speaks for God, and for your function as He knows it. [5]So will He teach you to remove the awful burden you have laid upon yourself by loving not the Son of God, and trying to teach him guilt instead of love. [6]Give up this frantic and insane attempt that cheats you of the joy of living with your God and Father, and of waking gladly to His Love and Holiness that join together as the truth in you, making you one with Him.

6.   When you have learned how to decide with God, all decisions become as easy and as right as breathing. [2]There is no effort, and you will be led as gently as if you were being carried down a quiet path in summer. [3]Only your own volition seems to make deciding hard. [4]The Holy Spirit will not delay in answering your every question what to do. [5]He knows. [6]And He will tell you, and then do it for you. [7]You who are tired will find this is more restful than sleep. [8]For you can bring your guilt into sleeping, but not into this.

7.   Unless you are guiltless you cannot know God, Whose Will is that you know Him. [2]Therefore, you *must* be guiltless. [3]Yet if you do not accept the necessary conditions for knowing Him, you have denied Him and do not recognize Him, though He is all around you. [4]He cannot be known without His Son, whose guiltlessness is the condition for knowing Him. [5]Accepting His Son as guilty is denial of the Father so complete, that knowledge is swept away from recognition in the very mind where God Himself has placed it. [6]If you would but listen, and learn how

impossible this is! [7]Do not endow Him with attributes you understand. [8]You made Him not, and anything you understand is not of Him.

8. Your task is not to make reality. [2]It is here without your making, but not without you. [3]You who have tried to throw yourself away and valued God so little, hear me speak for Him and for yourself. [4]You cannot understand how much your Father loves you, for there is no parallel in your experience of the world to help you understand it. [5]There is nothing on earth with which it can compare, and nothing you have ever felt apart from Him resembles it ever so faintly. [6]You cannot even give a blessing in perfect gentleness. [7]Would you know of One Who gives forever, and Who knows of nothing except giving?

9. The children of Heaven live in the light of the blessing of their Father, because they know that they are sinless. [2]The Atonement was established as the means of restoring guiltlessness to minds that have denied it, and thus denied Heaven to themselves. [3]Atonement teaches you the true condition of the Son of God. [4]It does not teach you what you are, or what your Father is. [5]The Holy Spirit, Who remembers this for you, merely teaches you how to remove the blocks that stand between you and what you know. [6]His memory is yours. [7]If you remember what you have made, you are remembering nothing. [8]Remembrance of reality is in Him, and therefore in you.

10. The guiltless and the guilty are totally incapable of understanding one another. [2]Each perceives the other as like himself, making both unable to communicate, because each sees the other unlike the way he sees himself. [3]God can communicate only to the Holy Spirit in your mind, because only He shares the knowledge of what you are with God. [4]And only the Holy Spirit can answer God for you, for only He knows what God is. [5]Everything else that you have placed within your mind cannot exist, for what is not in communication with the Mind of God has never been. [6]Communication with God is life. [7]Nothing without it is at all.

V. The Circle of Atonement

1.   The only part of your mind that has reality is the part that links you still with God. [2]Would you have all of it transformed into a radiant message of God's Love, to share with all the lonely ones who have denied Him? [3]*God makes this possible.* [4]Would you deny His yearning to be known? [5]You yearn for Him, as He for you. [6]This is forever changeless. [7]Accept, then, the immutable. [8]Leave the world of death behind, and return quietly to Heaven. [9]There is nothing of value here, and everything of value there. [10]Listen to the Holy Spirit, and to God through Him. [11]He speaks of you to *you.* [12]There is no guilt in you, for God is blessed in His Son as the Son is blessed in Him.

2.   Everyone has a special part to play in the Atonement, but the message given to each one is always the same; *God's Son is guiltless.* [2]Each one teaches the message differently, and learns it differently. [3]Yet until he teaches it and learns it, he will suffer the pain of dim awareness that his true function remains unfulfilled in him. [4]The burden of guilt is heavy, but God would not have you bound by it. [5]His plan for your awaking is as perfect as yours is fallible. [6]You know not what you do, but He Who knows is with you. [7]His gentleness is yours, and all the love you share with God He holds in trust for you. [8]He would teach you nothing except how to be happy.

3.   Blessed Son of a wholly blessing Father, joy was created for you. [2]Who can condemn whom God has blessed? [3]There is nothing in the Mind of God that does not share His shining innocence. [4]Creation is the natural extension of perfect purity. [5]Your only calling here is to devote yourself, with active willingness, to the denial of guilt in all its forms. [6]To accuse is *not to understand.* [7]The happy learners of the Atonement become the teachers of the innocence that is the right of all that God created. [8]Deny them not what is their due, for you will not withhold it from them alone.

4.   The inheritance of the Kingdom is the right of God's Son, given him in his creation. [2]Do not try to steal it from him, or you will ask for guilt and will experience it. [3]Protect his purity from every thought that would steal it away and keep it from his sight. [4]Bring innocence to light, in answer to the call of the Atonement. [5]Never allow purity to remain hidden, but shine away the heavy veils of guilt within which the Son of God has

hidden himself from his own sight.

5. We are all joined in the Atonement here, and nothing else can unite us in this world. ²So will the world of separation slip away, and full communication be restored between the Father and the Son. ³The miracle acknowledges the guiltlessness that must have been denied to produce the need of healing. ⁴Do not withhold this glad acknowledgment, for hope of happiness and release from suffering of every kind lie in it. ⁵Who is there but wishes to be free of pain? ⁶He may not yet have learned how to exchange guilt for innocence, nor realize that only in this exchange can freedom from pain be his. ⁷Yet those who have failed to learn need teaching, not attack. ⁸To attack those who have need of teaching is to fail to learn from them.

6. Teachers of innocence, each in his own way, have joined together, taking their part in the unified curriculum of the Atonement. ²There is no unity of learning goals apart from this. ³There is no conflict in this curriculum, which has one aim however it is taught. ⁴Each effort made on its behalf is offered for the single purpose of release from guilt, to the eternal glory of God and His creation. ⁵And every teaching that points to this points straight to Heaven, and the peace of God. ⁶There is no pain, no trial, no fear that teaching this can fail to overcome. ⁷The power of God Himself supports this teaching, and guarantees its limitless results.

7. Join your own efforts to the power that cannot fail and must result in peace. ²No one can be untouched by teaching such as this. ³You will not see yourself beyond the power of God if you teach only this. ⁴You will not be exempt from the effects of this most holy lesson, which seeks but to restore what is the right of God's creation. ⁵From everyone whom you accord release from guilt you will inevitably learn your innocence. ⁶The circle of Atonement has no end. ⁷And you will find ever-increasing confidence in your safe inclusion in the circle with everyone you bring within its safety and its perfect peace.

8. Peace, then, be unto everyone who becomes a teacher of peace. ²For peace is the acknowledgment of perfect purity, from which no one is excluded. ³Within its holy circle is everyone whom God created as His Son. ⁴Joy is its unifying attribute, with no one left outside to suffer guilt alone. ⁵The power of God draws everyone to its safe embrace of love and union. ⁶Stand quietly within this circle, and attract all tortured minds to join with you in the safety of its peace and holiness. ⁷Abide with me

within it, as a teacher of Atonement, not of guilt.

9.   Blessed are you who teach with me. [2]Our power comes not of us, but of our Father. [3]In guiltlessness we know Him, as He knows us guiltless. [4]I stand within the circle, calling you to peace. [5]Teach peace with me, and stand with me on holy ground. [6]Remember for everyone your Father's power that He has given him. [7]Believe not that you cannot teach His perfect peace. [8]Stand not outside, but join with me within. [9]Fail not the only purpose to which my teaching calls you. [10]Restore to God His Son as He created him, by teaching him his innocence.

10.   The crucifixion had no part in the Atonement. [2]Only the resurrection became my part in it. [3]That is the symbol of the release from guilt by guiltlessness. [4]Whom you perceive as guilty you would crucify. [5]Yet you restore guiltlessness to whomever you see as guiltless. [6]Crucifixion is always the ego's aim. [7]It sees everyone as guilty, and by its condemnation it would kill. [8]The Holy Spirit sees only guiltlessness, and in His gentleness He would release from fear and re-establish the reign of love. [9]The power of love is in His gentleness, which is of God and therefore cannot crucify nor suffer crucifixion. [10]The temple you restore becomes your altar, for it was rebuilt through you. [11]And everything you give to God is yours. [12]Thus He creates, and thus must you restore.

11.   Each one you see you place within the holy circle of Atonement or leave outside, judging him fit for crucifixion or for redemption. [2]If you bring him into the circle of purity, you will rest there with him. [3]If you leave him without, you join him there. [4]Judge not except in quietness which is not of you. [5]Refuse to accept anyone as without the blessing of Atonement, and bring him into it by blessing him. [6]Holiness must be shared, for therein lies everything that makes it holy. [7]Come gladly to the holy circle, and look out in peace on all who think they are outside. [8]Cast no one out, for here is what he seeks along with you. [9]Come, let us join him in the holy place of peace which is for all of us, united as one within the Cause of peace.

VI. The Light of Communication

1. The journey that we undertake together is the exchange of dark for light, of ignorance for understanding. ²Nothing you understand is fearful. ³It is only in darkness and in ignorance that you perceive the frightening, and shrink away from it to further darkness. ⁴And yet it is only the hidden that can terrify, not for what it is, but for its hiddenness. ⁵The obscure is frightening because you do not understand its meaning. ⁶If you did, it would be clear and you would be no longer in the dark. ⁷Nothing has hidden value, for what is hidden cannot be shared, and so its value is unknown. ⁸The hidden is kept apart, but value always lies in joint appreciation. ⁹What is concealed cannot be loved, and so it must be feared.

2. The quiet light in which the Holy Spirit dwells within you is merely perfect openness, in which nothing is hidden and therefore nothing is fearful. ²Attack will always yield to love if it is brought to love, not hidden from it. ³There is no darkness that the light of love will not dispel, unless it is concealed from love's beneficence. ⁴What is kept apart from love cannot share its healing power, because it has been separated off and kept in darkness. ⁵The sentinels of darkness watch over it carefully, and you who made these guardians of illusion out of nothing are now afraid of them.

3. Would you continue to give imagined power to these strange ideas of safety? ²They are neither safe nor unsafe. ³They do not protect; neither do they attack. ⁴They do nothing at all, being nothing at all. ⁵As guardians of darkness and of ignorance look to them only for fear, for what they keep obscure *is* fearful. ⁶But let them go, and what was fearful will be so no longer. ⁷Without protection of obscurity only the light of love remains, for only this has meaning and can live in light. ⁸Everything else must disappear.

4. Death yields to life simply because destruction is not true. ²The light of guiltlessness shines guilt away because, when they are brought together, the truth of one must make the falsity of its opposite perfectly clear. ³Keep not guilt and guiltlessness apart, for your belief that you can have them both is meaningless. ⁴All you have done by keeping them apart is lose their meaning by confusing them with each other. ⁵And so you do not realize that only one means anything. ⁶The other is wholly without sense of any kind.

5. You have regarded the separation as a means for breaking your

communication with your Father. ²The Holy Spirit reinterprets it as a means of re-establishing what was not broken, but *has* been made obscure. ³All things you made have use to Him, for His most holy purpose. ⁴He knows you are not separate from God, but He perceives much in your mind that lets you think you are. ⁵All this and nothing else would He separate from you. ⁶The power of decision, which you made in place of the power of creation, He would teach you how to use on your behalf. ⁷You who made it to crucify yourself must learn of Him how to apply it to the holy cause of restoration.

6. You who speak in dark and devious symbols do not understand the language you have made. ²It has no meaning, for its purpose is not communication, but rather the disruption of communication. ³If the purpose of language is communication, how can this tongue mean anything? ⁴Yet even this strange and twisted effort to communicate through not communicating holds enough of love to make it meaningful if its Interpreter is not its maker. ⁵You who made it are but expressing conflict, from which the Holy Spirit would release you. ⁶Leave what you would communicate to Him. ⁷He will interpret it to you with perfect clarity, for He knows with Whom you are in perfect communication.

7. You know not what you say, and so you know not what is said to you. ²Yet your Interpreter perceives the meaning in your alien language. ³He will not attempt to communicate the meaningless. ⁴But He will separate out all that has meaning, dropping off the rest and offering your true communication to those who would communicate as truly with you. ⁵You speak two languages at once, and this must lead to unintelligibility. ⁶Yet if one means nothing and the other everything, only that one is possible for purposes of communication. ⁷The other but interferes with it.

8. The Holy Spirit's function is entirely communication. ²He therefore must remove whatever interferes with communication in order to restore it. ³Therefore, keep no source of interference from His sight, for He will not attack your sentinels. ⁴But bring them to Him and let His gentleness teach you that, in the light, they are not fearful, and cannot serve to guard the dark doors behind which nothing at all is carefully concealed. ⁵We must open all doors and let the light come streaming through. ⁶There are no hidden chambers in God's temple. ⁷Its gates are open wide to greet His Son. ⁸No one can fail to come where God has called him, if he close not the door himself upon his Father's welcome.

VII. Sharing Perception with the Holy Spirit

1. What do you want? ²Light or darkness, knowledge or ignorance are yours, but not both. ³Opposites must be brought together, not kept apart. ⁴For their separation is only in your mind, and they are reconciled by union, as you are. ⁵In union, everything that is not real must disappear, for truth *is* union. ⁶As darkness disappears in light, so ignorance fades away when knowledge dawns. ⁷Perception is the medium by which ignorance is brought to knowledge. ⁸Yet the perception must be without deceit, for otherwise it becomes the messenger of ignorance rather than a helper in the search for truth.

2. The search for truth is but the honest searching out of everything that interferes with truth. ²Truth *is*. ³It can neither be lost nor sought nor found. ⁴It is there, wherever you are, being within you. ⁵Yet it can be recognized or unrecognized, real or false to you. ⁶If you hide it, it becomes unreal to you *because* you hid it and surrounded it with fear. ⁷Under each cornerstone of fear on which you have erected your insane system of belief, the truth lies hidden. ⁸Yet you cannot know this, for by hiding truth in fear, you see no reason to believe that the more you look at fear the less you see it, and the clearer what it conceals becomes.

3. It is not possible to convince the unknowing that they know. ²From their point of view it is not true. ³Yet it is true because God knows it. ⁴These are clearly opposite viewpoints on what the "unknowing" are. ⁵To God, unknowing is impossible. ⁶It is therefore not a point of view at all, but merely a belief in something that does not exist. ⁷It is only this belief that the unknowing have, and by it they are wrong about themselves. ⁸They have defined themselves as they were not created. ⁹Their creation was not a point of view, but rather a certainty. ¹⁰Uncertainty brought to certainty does not retain any conviction of reality.

4. Our emphasis has been on bringing what is undesirable to the desirable; what you do not want to what you do. ²You will realize that salvation must come to you this way, if you consider what dissociation is. ³Dissociation is a distorted process of thinking whereby two systems of belief which cannot coexist are both maintained. ⁴If they are brought together, their joint acceptance becomes impossible. ⁵But if one is kept in darkness from the other, their separation seems to keep them both alive and equal in their reality. ⁶Their joining thus becomes the source of fear, for

if they meet, acceptance must be withdrawn from one of them. [7]You cannot have them both, for each denies the other. [8]Apart, this fact is lost from sight, for each in a separate place can be endowed with firm belief. [9]Bring them together, and the fact of their complete incompatibility is instantly apparent. [10]One will go, because the other is seen in the same place.

5.   Light cannot enter darkness when a mind believes in darkness, and will not let it go. [2]Truth does not struggle against ignorance, and love does not attack fear. [3]What needs no protection does not defend itself. [4]Defense is of your making. [5]God knows it not. [6]The Holy Spirit uses defenses on behalf of truth only because you made them against it. [7]His perception of them, according to His purpose, merely changes them into a call for what you have attacked with them. [8]Defenses, like everything you made, must be gently turned to your own good, translated by the Holy Spirit from means of self-destruction to means of preservation and release. [9]His task is mighty, but the power of God is with Him. [10]Therefore, to Him it is so easy that it was accomplished the instant it was given Him for you. [11]Do not delay in your return to peace by wondering how He can fulfill what God has given Him to do. [12]Leave that to Him Who knows. [13]You are not asked to do mighty tasks yourself. [14]You are merely asked to do the little He suggests you do, trusting Him only to the small extent of believing that, if He asks it, you can do it. [15]You will see how easily all that He asks can be accomplished.

6.   The Holy Spirit asks of you but this; bring to Him every secret you have locked away from Him. [2]Open every door to Him, and bid Him enter the darkness and lighten it away. [3]At your request He enters gladly. [4]He brings the light to darkness if you make the darkness open to Him. [5]But what you hide He cannot look upon. [6]He sees for you, and unless you look with Him He cannot see. [7]The vision of Christ is not for Him alone, but for Him with you. [8]Bring, therefore, all your dark and secret thoughts to Him, and look upon them with Him. [9]He holds the light, and you the darkness. [10]They cannot coexist when both of You together look on them. [11]His judgment must prevail, and He will give it to you as you join your perception to His.

7.   Joining with Him in seeing is the way in which you learn to share with Him the interpretation of perception that leads to knowledge. [2]You cannot see alone. [3]Sharing perception with Him Whom God has given you teaches you how to recognize what

you see. ⁴It is the recognition that nothing you see means any-thing alone. ⁵Seeing with Him will show you that all meaning, including yours, comes not from double vision, but from the gen-tle fusing of everything into *one* meaning, *one* emotion and *one* purpose. ⁶God has one purpose which He shares with you. ⁷The single vision which the Holy Spirit offers you will bring this one-ness to your mind with clarity and brightness so intense you could not wish, for all the world, not to accept what God would have you have. ⁸Behold your will, accepting it as His, with all His Love as yours. ⁹All honor to you through Him, and through Him unto God.

VIII. The Holy Meeting Place

1. In the darkness you have obscured the glory God gave you, and the power He bestowed upon His guiltless Son. ²All this lies hidden in every darkened place, shrouded in guilt and in the dark denial of innocence. ³Behind the dark doors you have closed lies nothing, because nothing can obscure the gift of God. ⁴It is the closing of the doors that interferes with recognition of the power of God that shines in you. ⁵Banish not power from your mind, but let all that would hide your glory be brought to the judgment of the Holy Spirit, and there undone. ⁶Whom He would save for glory *is* saved for it. ⁷He has promised the Father that through Him you would be released from littleness to glory. ⁸To what He promised God He is wholly faithful, for He shares with God the promise that was given Him to share with you.

2. He shares it still, for you. ²Everything that promises otherwise, great or small, however much or little valued, He will replace with the one promise given unto Him to lay upon the altar to your Father and His Son. ³No altar stands to God without His Son. ⁴And nothing brought there that is not equally worthy of Both, but will be replaced by gifts wholly acceptable to Father and to Son. ⁵Can you offer guilt to God? ⁶You cannot, then, offer it to His Son. ⁷For They are not apart, and Gifts to One are offered to the Other. ⁸You know not God because you know not this. ⁹And yet you do know God and also this. ¹⁰All this is safe within you, where the Holy Spirit shines. ¹¹He shines not in division, but in the meeting place where God, united with His Son, speaks to His Son through Him. ¹²Communication between what cannot be

divided cannot cease. [13]The holy meeting place of the unseparated Father and His Son lies in the Holy Spirit and in you. [14]All interference in the communication that God Himself wills with His Son is quite impossible here. [15]Unbroken and uninterrupted love flows constantly between the Father and the Son, as Both would have it be. [16]And so it is.

3. Let your mind wander not through darkened corridors, away from light's center. [2]You and your brother may choose to lead yourselves astray, but you can be brought together only by the Guide appointed for you. [3]He will surely lead you to where God and His Son await your recognition. [4]They are joined in giving you the gift of oneness, before which all separation vanishes. [5]Unite with what you are. [6]You cannot join with anything except reality. [7]God's glory and His Son's belong to you in truth. [8]They have no opposite, and nothing else can you bestow upon yourself.

4. There is no substitute for truth. [2]And truth will make this plain to you as you are brought into the place where you must meet with truth. [3]And there you must be led, through gentle understanding which can lead you nowhere else. [4]Where God is, there are you. [5]Such is the truth. [6]Nothing can change the knowledge, given you by God, into unknowingness. [7]Everything God created knows its Creator. [8]For this is how creation is accomplished by the Creator and by His creations. [9]In the holy meeting place are joined the Father and His creations, and the creations of His Son with Them together. [10]There is one link that joins Them all together, holding Them in the oneness out of which creation happens.

5. The link with which the Father joins Himself to those He gives the power to create can never be dissolved. [2]Heaven itself is union with all of creation, and with its one Creator. [3]And Heaven remains the Will of God for you. [4]Lay no gifts other than this upon your altars, for nothing can coexist with it. [5]Here your little offerings are brought together with the gift of God, and only what is worthy of the Father will be accepted by the Son, for whom it is intended. [6]To whom God gives Himself, He *is* given. [7]Your little gifts will vanish on the altar, where He has placed His Own.

IX. The Reflection of Holiness

1. The Atonement does not make holy. ²You were created holy. ³It merely brings unholiness to holiness; or what you made to what you are. ⁴Bringing illusion to truth, or the ego to God, is the Holy Spirit's only function. ⁵Keep not your making from your Father, for hiding it has cost you knowledge of Him and of yourself. ⁶The knowledge is safe, but where is your safety apart from it? ⁷The making of time to take the place of timelessness lay in the decision to be not as you are. ⁸Thus truth was made past, and the present was dedicated to illusion. ⁹And the past, too, was changed and interposed between what always was and now. ¹⁰The past that you remember never was, and represents only the denial of what always was.

2. Bringing the ego to God is but to bring error to truth, where it stands corrected because it is the opposite of what it meets. ²It is undone because the contradiction can no longer stand. ³How long can contradiction stand when its impossible nature is clearly revealed? ⁴What disappears in light is not attacked. ⁵It merely vanishes because it is not true. ⁶Different realities are meaningless, for reality must be one. ⁷It cannot change with time or mood or chance. ⁸Its changelessness is what makes it real. ⁹This cannot be undone. ¹⁰Undoing is for unreality. ¹¹And this reality will do for you.

3. Merely by being what it is, does truth release you from everything that it is not. ²The Atonement is so gentle you need but whisper to it, and all its power will rush to your assistance and support. ³You are not frail with God beside you. ⁴Yet without Him you are nothing. ⁵The Atonement offers you God. ⁶The gift that you refused is held by Him in you. ⁷The Holy Spirit holds it there for you. ⁸God has not left His altar, though His worshippers placed other gods upon it. ⁹The temple still is holy, for the Presence that dwells within it *is* Holiness.

4. In the temple, Holiness waits quietly for the return of them that love it. ²The Presence knows they will return to purity and to grace. ³The graciousness of God will take them gently in, and cover all their sense of pain and loss with the immortal assurance of their Father's Love. ⁴There, fear of death will be replaced with joy of life. ⁵For God is life, and they abide in life. ⁶Life is as holy as the Holiness by which it was created. ⁷The Presence of Holiness lives in everything that lives, for Holiness created life,

and leaves not what It created holy as Itself.

5.   In this world you can become a spotless mirror, in which the Holiness of your Creator shines forth from you to all around you. ²You can reflect Heaven here. ³Yet no reflections of the images of other gods must dim the mirror that would hold God's reflection in it. ⁴Earth can reflect Heaven or hell; God or the ego. ⁵You need but leave the mirror clean and clear of all the images of hidden darkness you have drawn upon it. ⁶God will shine upon it of Himself. ⁷Only the clear reflection of Himself can be perceived upon it.

6.   Reflections are seen in light. ²In darkness they are obscure, and their meaning seems to lie only in shifting interpretations, rather than in themselves. ³The reflection of God needs no interpretation. ⁴It is clear. ⁵Clean but the mirror, and the message that shines forth from what the mirror holds out for everyone to see, no one can fail to understand. ⁶It is the message that the Holy Spirit is holding to the mirror that is in him. ⁷He recognizes it because he has been taught his need for it, but knows not where to look to find it. ⁸Let him, then, see it in you and share it with you.

7.   Could you but realize for a single instant the power of healing that the reflection of God, shining in you, can bring to all the world, you could not wait to make the mirror of your mind clean to receive the image of the holiness that heals the world. ²The image of holiness that shines in your mind is not obscure, and will not change. ³Its meaning to those who look upon it is not obscure, for everyone perceives it as the same. ⁴All bring their different problems to its healing light, and all their problems find but healing there.

8.   The response of holiness to any form of error is always the same. ²There is no contradiction in what holiness calls forth. ³Its one response is healing, without regard for what is brought to it. ⁴Those who have learned to offer only healing, because of the reflection of holiness in them, are ready at last for Heaven. ⁵There, holiness is not a reflection, but rather the actual condition of what was but reflected to them here. ⁶God is no image, and His creations, as part of Him, hold Him in them in truth. ⁷They do not merely reflect truth, for they *are* truth.

X. The Equality of Miracles

1. When no perception stands between God and His creations, or between His children and their own, the knowledge of creation must continue forever. [2]The reflections you accept into the mirror of your mind in time but bring eternity nearer or farther. [3]But eternity itself is beyond all time. [4]Reach out of time and touch it, with the help of its reflection in you. [5]And you will turn from time to holiness, as surely as the reflection of holiness calls everyone to lay all guilt aside. [6]Reflect the peace of Heaven here, and bring this world to Heaven. [7]For the reflection of truth draws everyone to truth, and as they enter into it they leave all reflections behind.

2. In Heaven reality is shared and not reflected. [2]By sharing its reflection here, its truth becomes the only perception the Son of God accepts. [3]And thus, remembrance of his Father dawns on him, and he can no longer be satisfied with anything but his own reality. [4]You on earth have no conception of limitlessness, for the world you seem to live in is a world of limits. [5]In this world, it is not true that anything without order of difficulty can occur. [6]The miracle, therefore, has a unique function, and is motivated by a unique Teacher Who brings the laws of another world to this one. [7]The miracle is the one thing you can do that transcends order, being based not on differences but on equality.

3. Miracles are not in competition, and the number of them that you can do is limitless. [2]They can be simultaneous and legion. [3]This is not difficult to understand, once you conceive of them as possible at all. [4]What is more difficult to grasp is the lack of order of difficulty that stamps the miracle as something that must come from elsewhere, not from here. [5]From the world's viewpoint, this is impossible.

4. Perhaps you have been aware of lack of competition among your thoughts, which even though they may conflict, can occur together and in great numbers. [2]You may indeed be so used to this that it causes you little surprise. [3]Yet you are also used to classifying some of your thoughts as more important, larger or better, wiser, or more productive and valuable than others. [4]This is true of the thoughts that cross the mind of those who think they live apart. [5]For some are reflections of Heaven, while others are motivated by the ego, which but seems to think.

5. The result is a weaving, changing pattern that never rests and

293

is never still. ²It shifts unceasingly across the mirror of your mind, and the reflections of Heaven last but a moment and grow dim, as darkness blots them out. ³Where there was light, darkness removes it in an instant, and alternating patterns of light and darkness sweep constantly across your mind. ⁴The little sanity that still remains is held together by a sense of order that you establish. ⁵Yet the very fact that you can do this, and bring any order into chaos shows you that you are not an ego, and that more than an ego must be in you. ⁶For the ego *is* chaos, and if it were all of you, no order at all would be possible. ⁷Yet though the order you impose upon your mind limits the ego, it also limits you. ⁸To order is to judge, and to arrange by judgment. ⁹Therefore it is not your function, but the Holy Spirit's.

6. It will seem difficult for you to learn that you have no basis at all for ordering your thoughts. ²This lesson the Holy Spirit teaches by giving you the shining examples of miracles to show you that your way of ordering is wrong, but that a better way is offered you. ³The miracle offers exactly the same response to every call for help. ⁴It does not judge the call. ⁵It merely recognizes what it is, and answers accordingly. ⁶It does not consider which call is louder or greater or more important. ⁷You may wonder how you who are still bound to judgment can be asked to do that which requires no judgment of your own. ⁸The answer is very simple. ⁹The power of God, and not of you, engenders miracles. ¹⁰The miracle itself is but the witness that you have the power of God in you. ¹¹That is the reason why the miracle gives equal blessing to all who share in it, and that is also why everyone shares in it. ¹²The power of God is limitless. ¹³And being always maximal, it offers everything to every call from anyone. ¹⁴There is no order of difficulty here. ¹⁵A call for help is given help.

7. The only judgment involved is the Holy Spirit's one division into two categories; one of love, and the other the call for love. ²You cannot safely make this division, for you are much too confused either to recognize love, or to believe that everything else is nothing but a call for love. ³You are too bound to form, and not to content. ⁴What you consider content is not content at all. ⁵It is merely form, and nothing else. ⁶For you do not respond to what a brother really offers you, but only to the particular perception of his offering by which the ego judges it.

8. The ego is incapable of understanding content, and is totally

unconcerned with it. ²To the ego, if the form is acceptable the content must be. ³Otherwise it will attack the form. ⁴If you believe you understand something of the "dynamics" of the ego, let me assure you that you understand nothing of it. ⁵For of yourself you could not understand it. ⁶The study of the ego is not the study of the mind. ⁷In fact, the ego enjoys studying itself, and thoroughly approves the undertakings of students who would "analyze" it, thus approving its importance. ⁸Yet they but study form with meaningless content. ⁹For their teacher is senseless, though careful to conceal this fact behind impressive sounding words, but which lack any consistent sense when they are put together.

9. This is characteristic of the ego's judgments. ²Separately, they seem to hold, but put them together and the system of thought that arises from joining them is incoherent and utterly chaotic. ³For form is not enough for meaning, and the underlying lack of content makes a cohesive system impossible. ⁴Separation therefore remains the ego's chosen condition. ⁵For no one alone can judge the ego truly. ⁶Yet when two or more join together in searching for truth, the ego can no longer defend its lack of content. ⁷The fact of union tells them it is not true.

10. It is impossible to remember God in secret and alone. ²For remembering Him means you are not alone, and are willing to remember it. ³Take no thought for yourself, for no thought you hold *is* for yourself. ⁴If you would remember your Father, let the Holy Spirit order your thoughts and give only the answer with which He answers you. ⁵Everyone seeks for love as you do, but knows it not unless he joins with you in seeking it. ⁶If you undertake the search together, you bring with you a light so powerful that what you see is given meaning. ⁷The lonely journey fails because it has excluded what it would find.

11. As God communicates to the Holy Spirit in you, so does the Holy Spirit translate His communications through you, so you can understand them. ²God has no secret communications, for everything of Him is perfectly open and freely accessible to all, being for all. ³Nothing lives in secret, and what you would hide from the Holy Spirit is nothing. ⁴Every interpretation you would lay upon a brother is senseless. ⁵Let the Holy Spirit show him to you, and teach you both his love and his call for love. ⁶Neither his mind nor yours holds more than these two orders of thought.

12. The miracle is the recognition that this is true. ²Where there is love, your brother must give it to you because of what it is. ³But

where there is a call for love, you must give it because of what you are. ⁴Earlier I said this course will teach you how to remember what you are, restoring to you your Identity. ⁵We have already learned that this Identity is shared. ⁶The miracle becomes the means of sharing It. ⁷By supplying your Identity wherever It is not recognized, you will recognize It. ⁸And God Himself, Who wills to be with His Son forever, will bless each recognition of His Son with all the Love He holds for him. ⁹Nor will the power of all His Love be absent from any miracle you offer to His Son. ¹⁰How, then, can there be any order of difficulty among them?

XI. The Test of Truth

1. Yet the essential thing is learning that *you do not know*. ²Knowledge is power, and all power is of God. ³You who have tried to keep power for yourself have "lost" it. ⁴You still have the power, but you have interposed so much between it and your awareness of it that you cannot use it. ⁵Everything you have taught yourself has made your power more and more obscure to you. ⁶You know not what it is, nor where. ⁷You have made a semblance of power and a show of strength so pitiful that it must fail you. ⁸For power is not a seeming strength, and truth is beyond semblance of any kind. ⁹Yet all that stands between you and the power of God in you is but your learning of the false, and of your attempts to undo the true.

2. Be willing, then, for all of it to be undone, and be glad that you are not bound to it forever. ²For you have taught yourself how to imprison the Son of God, a lesson so unthinkable that only the insane, in deepest sleep, could even dream of it. ³Can God learn how not to be God? ⁴And can His Son, given all power by Him, learn to be powerless? ⁵What have you taught yourself that you can possibly prefer to keep, in place of what you *have* and what you *are*?

3. Atonement teaches you how to escape forever from everything that you have taught yourself in the past, by showing you only what you are *now*. ²Learning has been accomplished before its effects are manifest. ³Learning is therefore in the past, but its influence determines the present by giving it whatever meaning it holds for you. ⁴*Your* learning gives the present no meaning at all. ⁵Nothing you have ever learned can help you understand the

present, or teach you how to undo the past. ⁶Your past is what you have taught yourself. ⁷*Let it all go.* ⁸Do not attempt to understand any event or anything or anyone in its "light," for the darkness in which you try to see can only obscure. ⁹Put no confidence at all in darkness to illuminate your understanding, for if you do you contradict the light, and thereby think you see the darkness. ¹⁰Yet darkness cannot be seen, for it is nothing more than a condition in which seeing becomes impossible.

4. You who have not yet brought all of the darkness you have taught yourself into the light in you, can hardly judge the truth and value of this course. ²Yet God did not abandon you. ³And so you have another lesson sent from Him, already learned for every child of light by Him to Whom God gave it. ⁴This lesson shines with God's glory, for in it lies His power, which He shares so gladly with His Son. ⁵Learn of His happiness, which is yours. ⁶But to accomplish this, all your dark lessons must be brought willingly to truth, and joyously laid down by hands open to receive, not closed to take. ⁷Every dark lesson that you bring to Him Who teaches light He will accept from you, because you do not want it. ⁸And He will gladly exchange each one for the bright lesson He has learned for you. ⁹Never believe that any lesson you have learned apart from Him means anything.

5. You have one test, as sure as God, by which to recognize if what you learned is true. ²If you are wholly free of fear of any kind, and if all those who meet or even think of you share in your perfect peace, then you can be sure that you have learned God's lesson, and not your own. ³Unless all this is true, there are dark lessons in your mind that hurt and hinder you, and everyone around you. ⁴The absence of perfect peace means but one thing: You think you do not will for God's Son what his Father wills for him. ⁵Every dark lesson teaches this, in one form or another. ⁶And each bright lesson with which the Holy Spirit will replace the dark ones you do not accept, teaches you that you will with the Father and His Son.

6. Do not be concerned about how you can learn a lesson so completely different from everything that you have taught yourself. ²How would you know? ³Your part is very simple. ⁴You need only recognize that everything you learned you do not want. ⁵Ask to be taught, and do not use your experiences to confirm what you have learned. ⁶When your peace is threatened or disturbed in any way, say to yourself:

> *7I do not know what anything, including this, means. 8And so I do not know how to respond to it. 9And I will not use my own past learning as the light to guide me now.*

10By this refusal to attempt to teach yourself what you do not know, the Guide Whom God has given you will speak to you. 11He will take His rightful place in your awareness the instant you abandon it, and offer it to Him.

7. You cannot be your guide to miracles, for it is you who made them necessary. 2And because you did, the means on which you can depend for miracles has been provided for you. 3God's Son can make no needs his Father will not meet, if he but turn to Him ever so little. 4Yet He cannot compel His Son to turn to Him and remain Himself. 5It is impossible that God lose His Identity, for if He did, you would lose yours. 6And being yours He cannot change Himself, for your Identity is changeless. 7The miracle acknowledges His changelessness by seeing His Son as he always was, and not as he would make himself. 8The miracle brings the effects that only guiltlessness can bring, and thus establishes the fact that guiltlessness must be.

8. How can you, so firmly bound to guilt and committed so to remain, establish for yourself your guiltlessness? 2That is impossible. 3But be sure that you are willing to acknowledge that it *is* impossible. 4It is only because you think that you can run some little part, or deal with certain aspects of your life alone, that the guidance of the Holy Spirit is limited. 5Thus would you make Him undependable, and use this fancied undependability as an excuse for keeping certain dark lessons from Him. 6And by so limiting the guidance that you would accept, you are unable to depend on miracles to answer all your problems for you.

9. Do you think that what the Holy Spirit would have you give He would withhold from you? 2You have no problems that He cannot solve by offering you a miracle. 3Miracles are for you. 4And every fear or pain or trial you have has been undone. 5He has brought all of them to light, having accepted them instead of you, and recognized they never were. 6There are no dark lessons He has not already lightened for you. 7The lessons you would teach yourself He has corrected already. 8They do not exist in His Mind at all. 9For the past binds Him not, and therefore binds not you. 10He does not see time as you do. 11And each miracle He offers you corrects your use of time, and makes it His.

10. He Who has freed you from the past would teach you are free of it. ²He would but have you accept His accomplishments as yours, because He did them for you. ³And because He did, they *are* yours. ⁴He has made you free of what you made. ⁵You can deny Him, but you cannot call on Him in vain. ⁶He always gives His gifts in place of yours. ⁷He would establish His bright teaching so firmly in your mind, that no dark lesson of guilt can abide in what He has established as holy by His Presence. ⁸Thank God that He is there and works through you. ⁹And all His works are yours. ¹⁰He offers you a miracle with every one you let Him do through you.

11. God's Son will always be indivisible. ²As we are held as one in God, so do we learn as one in Him. ³God's Teacher is as like to His Creator as is His Son, and through His Teacher does God proclaim His Oneness and His Son's. ⁴Listen in silence, and do not raise your voice against Him. ⁵For He teaches the miracle of oneness, and before His lesson division disappears. ⁶Teach like Him here, and you will remember that you have always created like your Father. ⁷The miracle of creation has never ceased, having the holy stamp of immortality upon it. ⁸This is the Will of God for all creation, and all creation joins in willing this.

12. Those who remember always that they know nothing, and who have become willing to learn everything, will learn it. ²But whenever they trust themselves, they will not learn. ³They have destroyed their motivation for learning by thinking they already know. ⁴Think not you understand anything until you pass the test of perfect peace, for peace and understanding go together and never can be found alone. ⁵Each brings the other with it, for it is the law of God they be not separate. ⁶They are cause and effect, each to the other, so where one is absent the other cannot be.

13. Only those who recognize they cannot know unless the effects of understanding are with them, can really learn at all. ²For this it must be peace they want, and nothing else. ³Whenever you think you know, peace will depart from you, because you have abandoned the Teacher of peace. ⁴Whenever you fully realize that you know not, peace will return, for you will have invited Him to do so by abandoning the ego on behalf of Him. ⁵Call not upon the ego for anything; it is only this that you need do. ⁶The Holy Spirit will, of Himself, fill every mind that so makes room for Him.

14. If you want peace you must abandon the teacher of attack. ²The Teacher of peace will never abandon you. ³You can desert

Him but He will never reciprocate, for His faith in you is His understanding. [4]It is as firm as is His faith in His Creator, and He knows that faith in His Creator must encompass faith in His creation. [5]In this consistency lies His Holiness which He cannot abandon, for it is not His Will to do so. [6]With your perfection ever in His sight, He gives the gift of peace to everyone who perceives the need for peace, and who would have it. [7]Make way for peace, and it will come. [8]For understanding is in you, and from it peace must come.

15.   The power of God, from which they both arise, is yours as surely as it is His. [2]You think you know Him not, only because, alone, it is impossible to know Him. [3]Yet see the mighty works that He will do through you, and you must be convinced you did them through Him. [4]It is impossible to deny the Source of effects so powerful they could not be of you. [5]Leave room for Him, and you will find yourself so filled with power that nothing will prevail against your peace. [6]And this will be the test by which you recognize that you have understood.

Chapter 15

THE HOLY INSTANT

I. The Two Uses of Time

1. Can you imagine what it means to have no cares, no worries, no anxieties, but merely to be perfectly calm and quiet all the time? ²Yet that is what time is for; to learn just that and nothing more. ³God's Teacher cannot be satisfied with His teaching until it constitutes all your learning. ⁴He has not fulfilled His teaching function until you have become such a consistent learner that you learn only of Him. ⁵When this has happened, you will no longer need a teacher or time in which to learn.

2. One source of perceived discouragement from which you may suffer is your belief that this takes time, and that the results of the Holy Spirit's teaching are far in the future. ²This is not so. ³For the Holy Spirit uses time in His Own way, and is not bound by it. ⁴Time is His friend in teaching. ⁵It does not waste Him, as it does you. ⁶And all the waste that time seems to bring with it is due but to your identification with the ego, which uses time to support its belief in destruction. ⁷The ego, like the Holy Spirit, uses time to convince you of the inevitability of the goal and end of teaching. ⁸To the ego the goal is death, which *is* its end. ⁹But to the Holy Spirit the goal is life, which *has* no end.

3. The ego is an ally of time, but not a friend. ²For it is as mistrustful of death as it is of life, and what it wants for you it cannot tolerate. ³The ego wants *you* dead, but not itself. ⁴The outcome of its strange religion must therefore be the conviction that it can pursue you beyond the grave. ⁵And out of its unwillingness for you to find peace even in death, it offers you immortality in hell. ⁶It speaks to you of Heaven, but assures you that Heaven is not for you. ⁷How can the guilty hope for Heaven?

4. The belief in hell is inescapable to those who identify with the ego. ²Their nightmares and their fears are all associated with it. ³The ego teaches that hell is in the future, for this is what all its teaching is directed to. ⁴Hell is its goal. ⁵For although the ego aims at death and dissolution as an end, it does not believe it. ⁶The goal of death, which it craves for you, leaves it unsatisfied. ⁷No one who follows the ego's teaching is without the fear of

301

death. ⁸Yet if death were thought of merely as an end to pain, would it be feared? ⁹We have seen this strange paradox in the ego's thought system before, but never so clearly as here. ¹⁰For the ego must seem to keep fear from you to hold your allegiance. ¹¹Yet it must engender fear in order to maintain itself. ¹²Again the ego tries, and all too frequently succeeds, in doing both, by using dissociation for holding its contradictory aims together so that they seem to be reconciled. ¹³The ego teaches thus: Death is the end as far as hope of Heaven goes. ¹⁴Yet because you and the ego cannot be separated, and because it cannot conceive of its own death, it will pursue you still, because guilt is eternal. ¹⁵Such is the ego's version of immortality. ¹⁶And it is this the ego's version of time supports.

5. The ego teaches that Heaven is here and now because the future is hell. ²Even when it attacks so savagely that it tries to take the life of someone who thinks its is the only voice, it speaks of hell even to him. ³For it tells him hell is here as well, and bids him leap from hell into oblivion. ⁴The only time the ego allows anyone to look upon with equanimity is the past. ⁵And even there, its only value is that it is no more.

6. How bleak and despairing is the ego's use of time! ²And how terrifying! ³For underneath its fanatical insistence that the past and future be the same is hidden a far more insidious threat to peace. ⁴The ego does not advertise its final threat, for it would have its worshippers still believe that it can offer them escape. ⁵But the belief in guilt must lead to the belief in hell, and always does. ⁶The only way in which the ego allows the fear of hell to be experienced is to bring hell here, but always as a foretaste of the future. ⁷For no one who considers himself as deserving of hell can believe that punishment will end in peace.

7. The Holy Spirit teaches thus: There is no hell. ²Hell is only what the ego has made of the present. ³The belief in hell is what prevents you from understanding the present, because you are afraid of it. ⁴The Holy Spirit leads as steadily to Heaven as the ego drives to hell. ⁵For the Holy Spirit, Who knows only the present, uses it to undo the fear by which the ego would make the present useless. ⁶There is no escape from fear in the ego's use of time. ⁷For time, according to its teaching, is nothing but a teaching device for compounding guilt until it becomes all-encompassing, demanding vengeance forever.

8. The Holy Spirit would undo all of this *now*. ²Fear is not of the

present, but only of the past and future, which do not exist. [3]There is no fear in the present when each instant stands clear and separated from the past, without its shadow reaching out into the future. [4]Each instant is a clean, untarnished birth, in which the Son of God emerges from the past into the present. [5]And the present extends forever. [6]It is so beautiful and so clean and free of guilt that nothing but happiness is there. [7]No darkness is remembered, and immortality and joy are now.

9. This lesson takes no time. [2]For what is time without a past and future? [3]It has taken time to misguide you so completely, but it takes no time at all to be what you are. [4]Begin to practice the Holy Spirit's use of time as a teaching aid to happiness and peace. [5]Take this very instant, now, and think of it as all there is of time. [6]Nothing can reach you here out of the past, and it is here that you are completely absolved, completely free and wholly without condemnation. [7]From this holy instant wherein holiness was born again you will go forth in time without fear, and with no sense of change with time.

10. Time is inconceivable without change, yet holiness does not change. [2]Learn from this instant more than merely that hell does not exist. [3]In this redeeming instant lies Heaven. [4]And Heaven will not change, for the birth into the holy present is salvation from change. [5]Change is an illusion, taught by those who cannot see themselves as guiltless. [6]There is no change in Heaven because there is no change in God. [7]In the holy instant, in which you see yourself as bright with freedom, you will remember God. [8]For remembering Him *is* to remember freedom.

11. If you are tempted to be dispirited by thinking how long it would take to change your mind so completely, ask yourself, "How long is an instant?" [2]Could you not give so short a time to the Holy Spirit for your salvation? [3]He asks no more, for He has no need of more. [4]It takes far longer to teach you to be willing to give Him this than for Him to use this tiny instant to offer you the whole of Heaven. [5]In exchange for this instant He stands ready to give you the remembrance of eternity.

12. You will never give this holy instant to the Holy Spirit on behalf of your release while you are unwilling to give it to your brothers on behalf of theirs. [2]For the instant of holiness is shared, and cannot be yours alone. [3]Remember, then, when you are tempted to attack a brother, that his instant of release is yours. [4]Miracles are the instants of release you offer, and will receive.

[5]They attest to your willingness to *be* released, and to offer time to the Holy Spirit for His use of it.

13. How long is an instant? [2]It is as short for your brother as it is for you. [3]Practice giving this blessed instant of freedom to all who are enslaved by time, and thus make time their friend for them. [4]The Holy Spirit gives their blessed instant to you through your giving it. [5]As you give it, He offers it to you. [6]Be not unwilling to give what you would receive of Him, for you join with Him in giving. [7]In the crystal cleanness of the release you give is your instantaneous escape from guilt. [8]You must be holy if you offer holiness.

14. How long is an instant? [2]As long as it takes to re-establish perfect sanity, perfect peace and perfect love for everyone, for God and for yourself. [3]As long as it takes to remember immortality, and your immortal creations who share it with you. [4]As long as it takes to exchange hell for Heaven. [5]Long enough to transcend all of the ego's making, and ascend unto your Father.

15. Time is your friend, if you leave it to the Holy Spirit to use. [2]He needs but very little to restore God's whole power to you. [3]He Who transcends time for you understands what time is for. [4]Holiness lies not in time, but in eternity. [5]There never was an instant in which God's Son could lose his purity. [6]His changeless state is beyond time, for his purity remains forever beyond attack and without variability. [7]Time stands still in his holiness, and changes not. [8]And so it is no longer time at all. [9]For caught in the single instant of the eternal sanctity of God's creation, it is transformed into forever. [10]Give the eternal instant, that eternity may be remembered for you, in that shining instant of perfect release. [11]Offer the miracle of the holy instant through the Holy Spirit, and leave His giving it to you to Him.

II. The End of Doubt

1. The Atonement is *in* time, but not *for* time. [2]Being in you, it is eternal. [3]What holds remembrance of God cannot be bound by time. [4]No more are you. [5]For unless God is bound, you cannot be. [6]An instant offered to the Holy Spirit is offered to God on your behalf, and in that instant you will awaken gently in Him. [7]In the blessed instant you will let go all your past learning, and the Holy Spirit will quickly offer you the whole lesson of peace.

⁸What can take time, when all the obstacles to learning it have been removed? ⁹Truth is so far beyond time that all of it happens at once. ¹⁰For as it was created one, so its oneness depends not on time at all.

2. Do not be concerned with time, and fear not the instant of holiness that will remove all fear. ²For the instant of peace is eternal *because* it is without fear. ³It will come, being the lesson God gives you, through the Teacher He has appointed to translate time into eternity. ⁴Blessed is God's Teacher, Whose joy it is to teach God's holy Son his holiness. ⁵His joy is not contained in time. ⁶His teaching is for you because His joy is yours. ⁷Through Him you stand before God's altar, where He gently translates hell into Heaven. ⁸For it is only in Heaven that God would have you be.

3. How long can it take to be where God would have you? ²For you are where you have forever been and will forever be. ³All that you have, you have forever. ⁴The blessed instant reaches out to encompass time, as God extends Himself to encompass you. ⁵You who have spent days, hours and even years in chaining your brothers to your ego in an attempt to support it and uphold its weakness, do not perceive the Source of strength. ⁶In this holy instant you will unchain all your brothers, and refuse to support either their weakness or your own.

4. You do not realize how much you have misused your brothers by seeing them as sources of ego support. ²As a result, they witness to the ego in your perception, and seem to provide reasons for not letting it go. ³Yet they are far stronger and much more compelling witnesses for the Holy Spirit. ⁴And they support His strength. ⁵It is, therefore, your choice whether they support the ego or the Holy Spirit in you. ⁶And you will recognize which you have chosen by *their* reactions. ⁷A Son of God who has been released through the Holy Spirit in a brother is always recognized. ⁸He cannot be denied. ⁹If you remain uncertain, it is only because you have not given complete release. ¹⁰And because of this, you have not given a single instant completely to the Holy Spirit. ¹¹For when you have, you will be sure you have. ¹²You will be sure because the witness to Him will speak so clearly of Him that you will hear and understand. ¹³You will doubt until you hear one witness whom you have wholly released through the Holy Spirit. ¹⁴And then you will doubt no more.

5. The holy instant has not yet happened to you. ²Yet it will, and

you will recognize it with perfect certainty. ³No gift of God is recognized in any other way. ⁴You can practice the mechanics of the holy instant, and will learn much from doing so. ⁵Yet its shining and glittering brilliance, which will literally blind you to this world by its own vision, you cannot supply. ⁶And here it is, all in this instant, complete, accomplished and given wholly.

6.   Start now to practice your little part in separating out the holy instant. ²You will receive very specific instructions as you go along. ³To learn to separate out this single second, and to experience it as timeless, is to begin to experience yourself as not separate. ⁴Fear not that you will not be given help in this. ⁵God's Teacher and His lesson will support your strength. ⁶It is only your weakness that will depart from you in this practice, for it is the practice of the power of God in you. ⁷Use it but for one instant, and you will never deny it again. ⁸Who can deny the Presence of what the universe bows to, in appreciation and gladness? ⁹Before the recognition of the universe that witnesses to It, your doubts must disappear.

III. Littleness versus Magnitude

1.   Be not content with littleness. ²But be sure you understand what littleness is, and why you could never be content with it. ³Littleness is the offering you give yourself. ⁴You offer this in place of magnitude, and you accept it. ⁵Everything in this world is little because it is a world made out of littleness, in the strange belief that littleness can content you. ⁶When you strive for anything in this world in the belief that it will bring you peace, you are belittling yourself and blinding yourself to glory. ⁷Littleness and glory are the choices open to your striving and your vigilance. ⁸You will always choose one at the expense of the other.

2.   Yet what you do not realize, each time you choose, is that your choice is your evaluation of yourself. ²Choose littleness and you will not have peace, for you will have judged yourself unworthy of it. ³And whatever you offer as a substitute is much too poor a gift to satisfy you. ⁴It is essential that you accept the fact, and accept it gladly, that there is no form of littleness that can ever content you. ⁵You are free to try as many as you wish, but all you will be doing is to delay your homecoming. ⁶For you will be content only in magnitude, which is your home.

3.   There is a deep responsibility you owe yourself, and one you must learn to remember all the time. ²The lesson may seem hard at first, but you will learn to love it when you realize that it is true and is but a tribute to your power. ³You who have sought and found littleness, remember this: Every decision you make stems from what you think you are, and represents the value that you put upon yourself. ⁴Believe the little can content you, and by limiting yourself you will not be satisfied. ⁵For your function is not little, and it is only by finding your function and fulfilling it that you can escape from littleness.

4.   There is no doubt about what your function is, for the Holy Spirit knows what it is. ²There is no doubt about its magnitude, for it reaches you through Him *from* Magnitude. ³You do not have to strive for it, because you have it. ⁴All your striving must be directed against littleness, for it does require vigilance to protect your magnitude in this world. ⁵To hold your magnitude in perfect awareness in a world of littleness is a task the little cannot undertake. ⁶Yet it is asked of you, in tribute to your magnitude and not your littleness. ⁷Nor is it asked of you alone. ⁸The power of God will support every effort you make on behalf of His dear Son. ⁹Search for the little, and you deny yourself His power. ¹⁰God is not willing that His Son be content with less than everything. ¹¹For He is not content without His Son, and His Son cannot be content with less than his Father has given him.

5.   I asked you earlier, "Would you be hostage to the ego or host to God?" ²Let this question be asked you by the Holy Spirit every time you make a decision. ³For every decision you make does answer this, and invites sorrow or joy accordingly. ⁴When God gave Himself to you in your creation, He established you as host to Him forever. ⁵He has not left you, and you have not left Him. ⁶All your attempts to deny His magnitude, and make His Son hostage to the ego, cannot make little whom God has joined with Him. ⁷Every decision you make is for Heaven or for hell, and brings you the awareness of what you decided for.

6.   The Holy Spirit can hold your magnitude, clean of all littleness, clearly and in perfect safety in your mind, untouched by every little gift the world of littleness would offer you. ²But for this, you cannot side against Him in what He wills for you. ³Decide for God through Him. ⁴For littleness, and the belief that you can be content with littleness, are decisions you make about yourself. ⁵The power and the glory that lie in you from God are

for all who, like you, perceive themselves as little, and believe that littleness can be blown up into a sense of magnitude that can content them. ⁶Neither give littleness, nor accept it. ⁷All honor is due the host of God. ⁸Your littleness deceives you, but your magnitude is of Him Who dwells in you, and in Whom you dwell. ⁹Touch no one, then, with littleness in the Name of Christ, eternal Host unto His Father.

7. In this season (Christmas) which celebrates the birth of holiness into this world, join with me who decided for holiness for you. ²It is our task together to restore the awareness of magnitude to the host whom God appointed for Himself. ³It is beyond all your littleness to give the gift of God, but not beyond you. ⁴For God would give Himself *through* you. ⁵He reaches from you to everyone and beyond everyone to His Son's creations, but without leaving you. ⁶Far beyond your little world but still in you, He extends forever. ⁷Yet He brings all His extensions to you, as host to Him.

8. Is it a sacrifice to leave littleness behind, and wander not in vain? ²It is not sacrifice to wake to glory. ³But it is sacrifice to accept anything less than glory. ⁴Learn that you must be worthy of the Prince of Peace, born in you in honor of Him Whose host you are. ⁵You know not what love means because you have sought to purchase it with little gifts, thus valuing it too little to understand its magnitude. ⁶Love is not little and love dwells in you, for you are host to Him. ⁷Before the greatness that lives in you, your poor appreciation of yourself and all the little offerings you give slip into nothingness.

9. Holy child of God, when will you learn that only holiness can content you and give you peace? ²Remember that you learn not for yourself alone, no more than I did. ³It is because I learned for you that you can learn of me. ⁴I would but teach you what is yours, so that together we can replace the shabby littleness that binds the host of God to guilt and weakness with the glad awareness of the glory that is in him. ⁵My birth in you is your awakening to grandeur. ⁶Welcome me not into a manger, but into the altar to holiness, where holiness abides in perfect peace. ⁷My Kingdom is not of this world because it is in you. ⁸And you are of your Father. ⁹Let us join in honoring you, who must remain forever beyond littleness.

10. Decide with me, who has decided to abide with you. ²I will as my Father wills, knowing His Will is constant and at peace for-

ever with itself. [3]You will be content with nothing but His Will. [4]Accept no less, remembering that everything I learned is yours. [5]What my Father loves I love as He does, and I can no more accept it as what it is not, than He can. [6]And no more can you. [7]When you have learned to accept what you are, you will make no more gifts to offer to yourself, for you will know you are complete, in need of nothing, and unable to accept anything for yourself. [8]But you will gladly give, having received. [9]The host of God need not seek to find anything.

11. If you are wholly willing to leave salvation to the plan of God and unwilling to attempt to grasp for peace yourself, salvation will be given you. [2]Yet think not you can substitute your plan for His. [3]Rather, join with me in His, that we may release all those who would be bound, proclaiming together that the Son of God is host to Him. [4]Thus will we let no one forget what you would remember. [5]And thus will you remember it.

12. Call forth in everyone only the remembrance of God, and of the Heaven that is in him. [2]For where you would have your brother be, there will you think you are. [3]Hear not his appeal to hell and littleness, but only his call for Heaven and greatness. [4]Forget not that his call is yours, and answer him with me. [5]God's power is forever on the side of His host, for it protects only the peace in which He dwells. [6]Lay not littleness before His holy altar, which rises above the stars and reaches even to Heaven, because of what is given it.

IV. Practicing the Holy Instant

1. This course is not beyond immediate learning, unless you believe that what God wills takes time. [2]And this means only that you would rather delay the recognition that His Will is so. [3]The holy instant is this instant and every instant. [4]The one you want it to be it is. [5]The one you would not have it be is lost to you. [6]You must decide when it is. [7]Delay it not. [8]For beyond the past and future, where you will not find it, it stands in shimmering readiness for your acceptance. [9]Yet you cannot bring it into glad awareness while you do not want it, for it holds the whole release from littleness.

2. Your practice must therefore rest upon your willingness to let all littleness go. [2]The instant in which magnitude dawns upon

you is but as far away as your desire for it. [3]As long as you desire it not and cherish littleness instead, by so much is it far from you. [4]By so much as you want it will you bring it nearer. [5]Think not that you can find salvation in your own way and have it. [6]Give over every plan you have made for your salvation in exchange for God's. [7]His will content you, and nothing else can bring you peace. [8]For peace is of God, and no one beside Him.

3. Be humble before Him, and yet great *in* Him. [2]And value no plan of the ego before the plan of God. [3]For you leave empty your place in His plan, which you must fill if you would join with me, by your decision to join in any plan but His. [4]I call you to fulfill your holy part in the plan that He has given to the world for its release from littleness. [5]God would have His host abide in perfect freedom. [6]Every allegiance to a plan of salvation apart from Him diminishes the value of His Will for you in your own mind. [7]And yet it is your mind that is the host to Him.

4. Would you learn how perfect and immaculate is the holy altar on which your Father has placed Himself? [2]This you will recognize in the holy instant, in which you willingly and gladly give over every plan but His. [3]For there lies peace, perfectly clear because you have been willing to meet its conditions. [4]You can claim the holy instant any time and anywhere you want it. [5]In your practice, try to give over every plan you have accepted for finding magnitude in littleness. [6]*It is not there.* [7]Use the holy instant only to recognize that you alone cannot know where it is, and can only deceive yourself.

5. I stand within the holy instant, as clear as you would have me. [2]And the extent to which you learn to accept me is the measure of the time in which the holy instant will be yours. [3]I call to you to make the holy instant yours at once, for the release from littleness in the mind of the host of God depends on willingness, and not on time.

6. The reason this course is simple is that truth is simple. [2]Complexity is of the ego, and is nothing more than the ego's attempt to obscure the obvious. [3]You could live forever in the holy instant, beginning now and reaching to eternity, but for a very simple reason. [4]Do not obscure the simplicity of this reason, for if you do, it will be only because you prefer not to recognize it and not to let it go. [5]The simple reason, simply stated, is this: The holy instant is a time in which you receive and give perfect communication. [6]This means, however, that it is a time in which your mind

is open, both to receive and give. ⁷It is the recognition that all minds are in communication. ⁸It therefore seeks to change nothing, but merely to accept everything.

7. How can you do this when you would prefer to have private thoughts and keep them? ²The only way you could do that would be to deny the perfect communication that makes the holy instant what it is. ³You believe you can harbor thoughts you would not share, and that salvation lies in keeping thoughts to yourself alone. ⁴For in private thoughts, known only to yourself, you think you find a way to keep what you would have alone, and share what *you* would share. ⁵And then you wonder why it is that you are not in full communication with those around you, and with God Who surrounds all of you together.

8. Every thought you would keep hidden shuts communication off, because you would have it so. ²It is impossible to recognize perfect communication while breaking communication holds value to you. ³Ask yourself honestly, "Would I want to have perfect communication, and am I wholly willing to let everything that interferes with it go forever?" ⁴If the answer is no, then the Holy Spirit's readiness to give it to you is not enough to make it yours, for you are not ready to share it with Him. ⁵And it cannot come into a mind that has decided to oppose it. ⁶For the holy instant is given and received with equal willingness, being the acceptance of the single Will that governs all thought.

9. The necessary condition for the holy instant does not require that you have no thoughts that are not pure. ²But it does require that you have none that you would keep. ³Innocence is not of your making. ⁴It is given you the instant you would have it. ⁵Atonement would not be if there were no need for it. ⁶You will not be able to accept perfect communication as long as you would hide it from yourself. ⁷For what you would hide *is* hidden from you. ⁸In your practice, then, try only to be vigilant against deception, and seek not to protect the thoughts you would keep to yourself. ⁹Let the Holy Spirit's purity shine them away, and bring all your awareness to the readiness for purity He offers you. ¹⁰Thus will He make you ready to acknowledge that you are host to God, and hostage to no one and to nothing.

V. The Holy Instant and Special Relationships

1.   The holy instant is the Holy Spirit's most useful learning device for teaching you love's meaning. ²For its purpose is to suspend judgment entirely. ³Judgment always rests on the past, for past experience is the basis on which you judge. ⁴Judgment becomes impossible without the past, for without it you do not understand anything. ⁵You would make no attempt to judge, because it would be quite apparent to you that you do not understand what anything means. ⁶You are afraid of this because you believe that without the ego, all would be chaos. ⁷Yet I assure you that without the ego, all would be love.

2.   The past is the ego's chief learning device, for it is in the past that you learned to define your own needs and acquired methods for meeting them on your own terms. ²We have said that to limit love to part of the Sonship is to bring guilt into your relationships, and thus make them unreal. ³If you seek to separate out certain aspects of the totality and look to them to meet your imagined needs, you are attempting to use separation to save you. ⁴How, then, could guilt not enter? ⁵For separation is the source of guilt, and to appeal to it for salvation is to believe you are alone. ⁶To be alone *is* to be guilty. ⁷For to experience yourself as alone is to deny the Oneness of the Father and His Son, and thus to attack reality.

3.   You cannot love parts of reality and understand what love means. ²If you would love unlike to God, Who knows no special love, how can you understand it? ³To believe that *special* relationships, with *special* love, can offer you salvation is the belief that separation is salvation. ⁴For it is the complete equality of the Atonement in which salvation lies. ⁵How can you decide that special aspects of the Sonship can give you more than others? ⁶The past has taught you this. ⁷Yet the holy instant teaches you it is not so.

4.   Because of guilt, all special relationships have elements of fear in them. ²This is why they shift and change so frequently. ³They are not based on changeless love alone. ⁴And love, where fear has entered, cannot be depended on because it is not perfect. ⁵In His function as Interpreter of what you made, the Holy Spirit uses special relationships, which you have chosen to support the ego, as learning experiences that point to truth. ⁶Under His teaching, every relationship becomes a lesson in love.

5.   The Holy Spirit knows no one is special. [2]Yet He also perceives that you have made special relationships, which He would purify and not let you destroy. [3]However unholy the reason you made them may be, He can translate them into holiness by removing as much fear as you will let Him. [4]You can place any relationship under His care and be sure that it will not result in pain, if you offer Him your willingness to have it serve no need but His. [5]All the guilt in it arises from your use of it. [6]All the love from His. [7]Do not, then, be afraid to let go your imagined needs, which would destroy the relationship. [8]Your only need is His.

6.   Any relationship you would substitute for another has not been offered to the Holy Spirit for His use. [2]There *is* no substitute for love. [3]If you would attempt to substitute one aspect of love for another, you have placed less value on one and more on the other. [4]You have not only separated them, but you have also judged against both. [5]Yet you had judged against yourself first, or you would never have imagined that you needed your brothers as they were not. [6]Unless you had seen yourself as without love, you could not have judged them so like you in lack.

7.   The ego's use of relationships is so fragmented that it frequently goes even farther; one part of one aspect suits its purposes, while it prefers different parts of another aspect. [2]Thus does it assemble reality to its own capricious liking, offering for your seeking a picture whose likeness does not exist. [3]For there is nothing in Heaven or earth that it resembles, and so, however much you seek for its reality, you cannot find it because it is not real.

8.   Everyone on earth has formed special relationships, and although this is not so in Heaven, the Holy Spirit knows how to bring a touch of Heaven to them here. [2]In the holy instant no one is special, for your personal needs intrude on no one to make your brothers seem different. [3]Without the values from the past, you would see them all the same and like yourself. [4]Nor would you see any separation between yourself and them. [5]In the holy instant, you see in each relationship what it will be when you perceive only the present.

9.   God knows you *now.* [2]He remembers nothing, having always known you exactly as He knows you now. [3]The holy instant reflects His knowing by bringing all perception out of the past, thus removing the frame of reference you have built by which to judge your brothers. [4]Once this is gone, the Holy Spirit substi-

tutes His frame of reference for it. [5]His frame of reference is simply God. [6]The Holy Spirit's timelessness lies only here. [7]For in the holy instant, free of the past, you see that love is in you, and you have no need to look without and snatch love guiltily from where you thought it was.

10. All your relationships are blessed in the holy instant, because the blessing is not limited. [2]In the holy instant the Sonship gains as one, and united in your blessing it becomes one to you. [3]The meaning of love is the meaning God gave to it. [4]Give to it any meaning apart from His, and it is impossible to understand it. [5]God loves every brother as He loves you; neither less nor more. [6]He needs them all equally, and so do you. [7]In time, you have been told to offer miracles as I direct, and let the Holy Spirit bring to you those who are seeking you. [8]Yet in the holy instant you unite directly with God, and all your brothers join in Christ. [9]Those who are joined in Christ are in no way separate. [10]For Christ is the Self the Sonship shares, as God shares His Self with Christ.

11. Think you that you can judge the Self of God? [2]God has created It beyond judgment, out of His need to extend His Love. [3]With love in you, you have no need except to extend it. [4]In the holy instant there is no conflict of needs, for there is only one. [5]For the holy instant reaches to eternity, and to the Mind of God. [6]And it is only there love has meaning, and only there can it be understood.

VI. The Holy Instant and the Laws of God

1. It is impossible to use one relationship at the expense of another and not to suffer guilt. [2]And it is equally impossible to condemn part of a relationship and find peace within it. [3]Under the Holy Spirit's teaching all relationships are seen as total commitments, yet they do not conflict with one another in any way. [4]Perfect faith in each one, for its ability to satisfy you completely, arises only from perfect faith in yourself. [5]And this you cannot have while guilt remains. [6]And there will be guilt as long as you accept the possibility, and cherish it, that you can make a brother into what he is not, because you would have him so.

2. You have so little faith in yourself because you are unwilling to accept the fact that perfect love is in you. [2]And so you seek with-

out for what you cannot find without. ³I offer you my perfect faith in you, in place of all your doubts. ⁴But forget not that my faith must be as perfect in all your brothers as it is in you, or it would be a limited gift to you. ⁵In the holy instant we share our faith in God's Son because we recognize, together, that he is wholly worthy of it, and in our appreciation of his worth we cannot doubt his holiness. ⁶And so we love him.

3. All separation vanishes as holiness is shared. ²For holiness is power, and by sharing it, it gains in strength. ³If you seek for satisfaction in gratifying your needs as you perceive them, you must believe that strength comes from another, and what you gain he loses. ⁴Someone must always lose if you perceive yourself as weak. ⁵Yet there is another interpretation of relationships that transcends the concept of loss of power completely.

4. You do not find it difficult to believe that when another calls on God for love, your call remains as strong. ²Nor do you think that when God answers him, your hope of answer is diminished. ³On the contrary, you are more inclined to regard his success as witness to the possibility of yours. ⁴That is because you recognize, however dimly, that God is an idea, and so your faith in Him is strengthened by sharing. ⁵What you find difficult to accept is the fact that, like your Father, *you* are an idea. ⁶And like Him, you can give yourself completely, wholly without loss and only with gain. ⁷Herein lies peace, for here there *is* no conflict.

5. In the world of scarcity, love has no meaning and peace is impossible. ²For gain and loss are both accepted, and so no one is aware that perfect love is in him. ³In the holy instant you recognize the idea of love in you, and unite this idea with the Mind that thought it, and could not relinquish it. ⁴By holding it within itself, there *is* no loss. ⁵The holy instant thus becomes a lesson in how to hold all of your brothers in your mind, experiencing not loss but completion. ⁶From this it follows you can only give. ⁷And this *is* love, for this alone is natural under the laws of God. ⁸In the holy instant the laws of God prevail, and only they have meaning. ⁹The laws of this world cease to hold any meaning at all. ¹⁰When the Son of God accepts the laws of God as what he gladly wills, it is impossible that he be bound, or limited in any way. ¹¹In that instant he is as free as God would have him be. ¹²For the instant he refuses to be bound, he is not bound.

6. In the holy instant nothing happens that has not always been. ²Only the veil that has been drawn across reality is lifted. ³Noth-

ing has changed. ⁴Yet the awareness of changelessness comes swiftly as the veil of time is pushed aside. ⁵No one who has not yet experienced the lifting of the veil, and felt himself drawn irresistibly into the light behind it, can have faith in love without fear. ⁶Yet the Holy Spirit gives you this faith, because He offered it to me and I accepted it. ⁷Fear not the holy instant will be denied you, for I denied it not. ⁸And through me the Holy Spirit gives it unto you, as you will give it. ⁹Let no need you perceive obscure your need of this. ¹⁰For in the holy instant you will recognize the only need the Sons of God share equally, and by this recognition you will join with me in offering what is needed.

7.   It is through *us* that peace will come. ²Join me in the idea of peace, for in ideas minds can communicate. ³If you would give yourself as your Father gives His Self, you will learn to understand Selfhood. ⁴And therein is love's meaning understood. ⁵But remember that understanding is of the mind, and only of the mind. ⁶Knowledge is therefore of the mind, and its conditions are in the mind with it. ⁷If you were not an idea, and nothing but an idea, you could not be in full communication with all that ever was. ⁸Yet as long as you prefer to be something else, or would attempt to be nothing else and something else together, you will not remember the language of communication, which you know perfectly.

8.   In the holy instant God is remembered, and the language of communication with all your brothers is remembered with Him. ²For communication is remembered together, as is truth. ³There is no exclusion in the holy instant because the past is gone, and with it goes the whole basis for exclusion. ⁴Without its source exclusion vanishes. ⁵And this permits your Source, and that of all your brothers, to replace it in your awareness. ⁶God and the power of God will take Their rightful place in you, and you will experience the full communication of ideas with ideas. ⁷Through your ability to do this you will learn what you must be, for you will begin to understand what your Creator is, and what His creation is along with Him.

VII. The Needless Sacrifice

1. Beyond the poor attraction of the special love relationship, and always obscured by it, is the powerful attraction of the Father for His Son. ²There is no other love that can satisfy you, because there *is* no other love. ³This is the only love that is fully given and fully returned. ⁴Being complete, it asks nothing. ⁵Being wholly pure, everyone joined in it has everything. ⁶This is not the basis for any relationship in which the ego enters. ⁷For every relationship on which the ego embarks *is* special.

2. The ego establishes relationships only to get something. ²And it would keep the giver bound to itself through guilt. ³It is impossible for the ego to enter into any relationship without anger, for the ego believes that anger makes friends. ⁴This is not its statement, but it *is* its purpose. ⁵For the ego really believes that it can get and keep *by making guilty*. ⁶This is its one attraction; an attraction so weak that it would have no hold at all, except that no one recognizes it. ⁷For the ego always seems to attract through love, and has no attraction at all to anyone who perceives that it attracts through guilt.

3. The sick attraction of guilt must be recognized for what it is. ²For having been made real to you, it is essential to look at it clearly, and by withdrawing your investment in it, to learn to let it go. ³No one would choose to let go what he believes has value. ⁴Yet the attraction of guilt has value to you only because you have not looked at what it is, and have judged it completely in the dark. ⁵As we bring it to light, your only question will be why it was you ever wanted it. ⁶You have nothing to lose by looking open-eyed, for ugliness such as this belongs not in your holy mind. ⁷This host of God can have no real investment here.

4. We said before that the ego attempts to maintain and increase guilt, but in such a way that you do not recognize what it would do to you. ²For it is the ego's fundamental doctrine that what you do to others you have escaped. ³The ego wishes no one well. ⁴Yet its survival depends on your belief that you are exempt from its evil intentions. ⁵It counsels, therefore, that if you are host to it, it will enable you to direct its anger outward, thus protecting you. ⁶And thus it embarks on an endless, unrewarding chain of special relationships, forged out of anger and dedicated to but one insane belief; that the more anger you invest outside yourself, the safer you become.

5.   It is this chain that binds the Son of God to guilt, and it is this chain the Holy Spirit would remove from his holy mind. ²For the chain of savagery belongs not around the chosen host of God, who cannot make himself host to the ego. ³In the name of his release, and in the Name of Him Who would release him, let us look more closely at the relationships the ego contrives, and let the Holy Spirit judge them truly. ⁴For it is certain that if you will look at them, you will offer them gladly to Him. ⁵What He can make of them you do not know, but you will become willing to find out, if you are willing first to perceive what you have made of them.

6.   In one way or another, every relationship the ego makes is based on the idea that by sacrificing itself, it becomes bigger. ²The "sacrifice," which it regards as purification, is actually the root of its bitter resentment. ³For it would prefer to attack directly, and avoid delaying what it really wants. ⁴Yet the ego acknowledges "reality" as it sees it, and recognizes that no one could interpret direct attack as love. ⁵Yet to make guilty *is* direct attack, although it does not seem to be. ⁶For the guilty expect attack, and having asked for it they are attracted to it.

7.   In such insane relationships, the attraction of what you do not want seems to be much stronger than the attraction of what you do want. ²For each one thinks that he has sacrificed something to the other, and hates him for it. ³Yet this is what he thinks he wants. ⁴He is not in love with the other at all. ⁵He merely believes he is in love with sacrifice. ⁶And for this sacrifice, which he demands of himself, he demands that the other accept the guilt and sacrifice himself as well. ⁷Forgiveness becomes impossible, for the ego believes that to forgive another is to lose him. ⁸It is only by attack without forgiveness that the ego can ensure the guilt that holds all its relationships together.

8.   Yet they only *seem* to be together. ²For relationships, to the ego, mean only that bodies are together. ³It is always this that the ego demands, and it does not object where the mind goes or what it thinks, for this seems unimportant. ⁴As long as the body is there to receive its sacrifice, it is content. ⁵To the ego the mind is private, and only the body can be shared. ⁶Ideas are basically of no concern, except as they bring the body of another closer or farther. ⁷And it is in these terms that it evaluates ideas as good or bad. ⁸What makes another guilty and holds him through guilt is "good." ⁹What releases him from guilt is "bad," because he

would no longer believe that bodies communicate, and so he would be "gone."

9. Suffering and sacrifice are the gifts with which the ego would "bless" all unions. [2]And those who are united at its altar accept suffering and sacrifice as the price of union. [3]In their angry alliances, born of the fear of loneliness and yet dedicated to the continuance of loneliness, each seeks relief from guilt by increasing it in the other. [4]For each believes that this decreases guilt in him. [5]The other seems always to be attacking and wounding him, perhaps in little ways, perhaps "unconsciously," yet never without demand of sacrifice. [6]The fury of those joined at the ego's altar far exceeds your awareness of it. [7]For what the ego really wants you do not realize.

10. Whenever you are angry, you can be sure that you have formed a special relationship which the ego has "blessed," for anger *is* its blessing. [2]Anger takes many forms, but it cannot long deceive those who will learn that love brings no guilt at all, and what brings guilt cannot be love and *must* be anger. [3]All anger is nothing more than an attempt to make someone feel guilty, and this attempt is the only basis the ego accepts for special relationships. [4]Guilt is the only need the ego has, and as long as you identify with it, guilt will remain attractive to you. [5]Yet remember this; to be with a body is not communication. [6]And if you think it is, you will feel guilty about communication and will be afraid to hear the Holy Spirit, recognizing in His Voice your own need to communicate.

11. The Holy Spirit cannot teach through fear. [2]And how can He communicate with you, while you believe that to communicate is to make yourself alone? [3]It is clearly insane to believe that by communicating you will be abandoned. [4]And yet many do believe it. [5]For they think their minds must be kept private or they will lose them, but if their bodies are together their minds remain their own. [6]The union of bodies thus becomes the way in which they would keep minds apart. [7]For bodies cannot forgive. [8]They can only do as the mind directs.

12. The illusion of the autonomy of the body and its ability to overcome loneliness is but the working of the ego's plan to establish its own autonomy. [2]As long as you believe that to be with a body is companionship, you will be compelled to attempt to keep your brother in his body, held there by guilt. [3]And you will see safety in guilt and danger in communication. [4]For the ego will

always teach that loneliness is solved by guilt, and that communication is the cause of loneliness. [5]And despite the evident insanity of this lesson, many have learned it.

13. Forgiveness lies in communication as surely as damnation lies in guilt. [2]It is the Holy Spirit's teaching function to instruct those who believe communication to be damnation that communication is salvation. [3]And He will do so, for the power of God in Him and you is joined in a real relationship so holy and so strong, that it can overcome even this without fear.

14. It is through the holy instant that what seems impossible is accomplished, making it evident that it is not impossible. [2]In the holy instant guilt holds no attraction, since communication has been restored. [3]And guilt, whose only purpose is to disrupt communication, has no function here. [4]Here there is no concealment, and no private thoughts. [5]The willingness to communicate attracts communication to it, and overcomes loneliness completely. [6]There is complete forgiveness here, for there is no desire to exclude anyone from your completion, in sudden recognition of the value of his part in it. [7]In the protection of your wholeness, all are invited and made welcome. [8]And you understand that your completion is God's, Whose only need is to have you be complete. [9]For your completion makes you His in your awareness. [10]And here it is that you experience yourself as you were created, and as you are.

VIII. The Only Real Relationship

1. The holy instant does not replace the need for learning, for the Holy Spirit must not leave you as your Teacher until the holy instant has extended far beyond time. [2]For a teaching assignment such as His, He must use everything in this world for your release. [3]He must side with every sign or token of your willingness to learn of Him what the truth must be. [4]He is swift to utilize whatever you offer Him on behalf of this. [5]His concern and care for you are limitless. [6]In the face of your fear of forgiveness, which He perceives as clearly as He knows forgiveness is release, He will teach you to remember that forgiveness is not loss, but your salvation. [7]And that in complete forgiveness, in which you recognize that there is nothing to forgive, you are absolved completely.

2. Hear Him gladly, and learn of Him that you have need of no special relationships at all. ²You but seek in them what you have thrown away. ³And through them you will never learn the value of what you have cast aside, but still desire with all your heart. ⁴Let us join together in making the holy instant all that there is, by desiring that it *be* all that there is. ⁵God's Son has such great need of your willingness to strive for this that you cannot conceive of need so great. ⁶Behold the only need that God and His Son share, and will to meet together. ⁷You are not alone in this. ⁸The will of your creations calls to you, to share your will with them. ⁹Turn, then, in peace from guilt to God and them.

3. Relate only with what will never leave you, and what you can never leave. ²The loneliness of God's Son is the loneliness of his Father. ³Refuse not the awareness of your completion, and seek not to restore it to yourself. ⁴Fear not to give redemption over to your Redeemer's Love. ⁵He will not fail you, for He comes from One Who cannot fail. ⁶Accept your sense of failure as nothing more than a mistake in who you are. ⁷For the holy host of God is beyond failure, and nothing that he wills can be denied. ⁸You are forever in a relationship so holy that it calls to everyone to escape from loneliness, and join you in your love. ⁹And where you are must everyone seek, and find you there.

4. Think but an instant on this: God gave the Sonship to you, to ensure your perfect creation. ²This was His gift, for as He withheld Himself not from you, He withheld not His creation. ³Nothing that ever was created but is yours. ⁴Your relationships are with the universe. ⁵And this universe, being of God, is far beyond the petty sum of all the separate bodies you perceive. ⁶For all its parts are joined in God through Christ, where they become like to their Father. ⁷Christ knows of no separation from His Father, Who is His one relationship, in which He gives as His Father gives to Him.

5. The Holy Spirit is God's attempt to free you of what He does not understand. ²And because of the Source of the attempt, it will succeed. ³The Holy Spirit asks you to respond as God does, for He would teach you what you do not understand. ⁴God would respond to every need, whatever form it takes. ⁵And so He keeps this channel open to receive His communication to you, and yours to Him. ⁶God does not understand your problem in communication, for He does not share it with you. ⁷It is only you who believe that it is understandable. ⁸The Holy Spirit knows that it is

not understandable, and yet He understands it because you made it.

6. In the Holy Spirit alone lies the awareness of what God cannot know, and what you do not understand. ²It is His holy function to accept them both, and by removing every element of disagreement, to join them into one. ³He will do this because it is His function. ⁴Leave, then, what seems to you to be impossible, to Him Who knows it must be possible because it is the Will of God. ⁵And let Him Whose teaching is only of God teach you the only meaning of relationships. ⁶For God created the only relationship that has meaning, and that is His relationship with you.

IX. The Holy Instant and the Attraction of God

1. As the ego would limit your perception of your brothers to the body, so would the Holy Spirit release your vision and let you see the Great Rays shining from them, so unlimited that they reach to God. ²It is this shift to vision that is accomplished in the holy instant. ³Yet it is needful for you to learn just what this shift entails, so you will become willing to make it permanent. ⁴Given this willingness it will not leave you, for it *is* permanent. ⁵Once you have accepted it as the only perception you want, it is translated into knowledge by the part that God Himself plays in the Atonement, for it is the only step in it He understands. ⁶Therefore, in this there will be no delay when you are ready for it. ⁷God is ready now, but you are not.

2. Our task is but to continue, as fast as possible, the necessary process of looking straight at all the interference and seeing it exactly as it is. ²For it is impossible to recognize as wholly without gratification what you think you want. ³The body is the symbol of the ego, as the ego is the symbol of the separation. ⁴And both are nothing more than attempts to limit communication, and thereby to make it impossible. ⁵For communication must be unlimited in order to have meaning, and deprived of meaning, it will not satisfy you completely. ⁶Yet it remains the only means by which you can establish real relationships, which have no limits, having been established by God.

3. In the holy instant, where the Great Rays replace the body in awareness, the recognition of relationships without limits is given you. ²But in order to see this, it is necessary to give up

every use the ego has for the body, and to accept the fact that the ego has no purpose you would share with it. ³For the ego would limit everyone to a body for its own purposes, and while you think it has a purpose, you will choose to utilize the means by which it tries to turn its purpose into accomplishment. ⁴This will never be accomplished. ⁵Yet you have surely recognized that the ego, whose goals are altogether unattainable, will strive for them with all its might, and will do so with the strength that you have given it.

4. It is impossible to divide your strength between Heaven and hell, God and the ego, and release your power to creation, which is the only purpose for which it was given you. ²Love would always give increase. ³Limits are demanded by the ego, and represent its demands to make little and ineffectual. ⁴Limit your sight of a brother to his body, which you will do as long as you would not release him from it, and you have denied his gift to you. ⁵His body cannot give it. ⁶And seek it not through yours. ⁷Yet your minds are already continuous, and their union need only be accepted and the loneliness in Heaven is gone.

5. If you would but let the Holy Spirit tell you of the Love of God for you, and the need your creations have to be with you forever, you would experience the attraction of the eternal. ²No one can hear Him speak of this and long remain willing to linger here. ³For it is your will to be in Heaven, where you are complete and quiet, in such sure and loving relationships that any limit is impossible. ⁴Would you not exchange your little relationships for this? ⁵For the body *is* little and limited, and only those whom you would see without the limits the ego would impose on them can offer you the gift of freedom.

6. You have no conception of the limits you have placed on your perception, and no idea of all the loveliness that you could see. ²But this you must remember; the attraction of guilt opposes the attraction of God. ³His attraction for you remains unlimited, but because your power, being His, is as great as His, you can turn away from love. ⁴What you invest in guilt you withdraw from God. ⁵And your sight grows weak and dim and limited, for you have attempted to separate the Father from the Son, and limit Their communication. ⁶Seek not Atonement in further separation. ⁷And limit not your vision of God's Son to what interferes with his release, and what the Holy Spirit must undo to set him free. ⁸For his belief in limits *has* imprisoned him.

7.   When the body ceases to attract you, and when you place no value on it as a means of getting anything, then there will be no interference in communication and your thoughts will be as free as God's. ²As you let the Holy Spirit teach you how to use the body only for purposes of communication, and renounce its use for separation and attack which the ego sees in it, you will learn you have no need of a body at all. ³In the holy instant there are no bodies, and you experience only the attraction of God. ⁴Accepting it as undivided you join Him wholly, in an instant, for you would place no limits on your union with Him. ⁵The reality of this relationship becomes the only truth that you could ever want. ⁶All truth *is* here.

X. The Time of Rebirth

1.   It is in your power, in time, to delay the perfect union of the Father and the Son. ²For in this world, the attraction of guilt does stand between them. ³Neither time nor season means anything in eternity. ⁴But here it is the Holy Spirit's function to use them both, though not as the ego uses them. ⁵This is the season when you would celebrate my birth into the world. ⁶Yet you know not how to do it. ⁷Let the Holy Spirit teach you, and let me celebrate *your* birth through Him. ⁸The only gift I can accept of you is the gift I gave to you. ⁹Release me as I choose your own release. ¹⁰The time of Christ we celebrate together, for it has no meaning if we are apart.

2.   The holy instant is truly the time of Christ. ²For in this liberating instant no guilt is laid upon the Son of God, and his unlimited power is thus restored to him. ³What other gift can you offer me, when only this I choose to offer you? ⁴And to see me is to see me in everyone, and offer everyone the gift you offer me. ⁵I am as incapable of receiving sacrifice as God is, and every sacrifice you ask of yourself you ask of me. ⁶Learn now that sacrifice of any kind is nothing but a limitation imposed on giving. ⁷And by this limitation you have limited acceptance of the gift I offer you.

3.   We who are one cannot give separately. ²When you are willing to accept our relationship as real, guilt will hold no attraction for you. ³For in our union you will accept all of our brothers. ⁴The gift of union is the only gift that I was born to give. ⁵Give it to me,

that you may have it. ⁶The time of Christ is the time appointed for the gift of freedom, offered to everyone. ⁷And by your acceptance of it, you offer it to everyone.

4. It is in your power to make this season holy, for it is in your power to make the time of Christ be now. ²It is possible to do this all at once because there is but one shift in perception that is necessary, for you made but one mistake. ³It seems like many, but it is all the same. ⁴For though the ego takes many forms, it is always the same idea. ⁵What is not love is always fear, and nothing else.

5. It is not necessary to follow fear through all the circuitous routes by which it burrows underground and hides in darkness, to emerge in forms quite different from what it is. ²Yet it *is* necessary to examine each one as long as you would retain the principle that governs all of them. ³When you are willing to regard them, not as separate, but as different manifestations of the same idea, and one you do not want, they go together. ⁴The idea is simply this: You believe it is possible to be host to the ego or hostage to God. ⁵This is the choice you think you have, and the decision you believe that you must make. ⁶You see no other alternatives, for you cannot accept the fact that sacrifice gets nothing. ⁷Sacrifice is so essential to your thought system that salvation apart from sacrifice means nothing to you. ⁸Your confusion of sacrifice and love is so profound that you cannot conceive of love without sacrifice. ⁹And it is this that you must look upon; sacrifice is attack, not love. ¹⁰If you would accept but this one idea, your fear of love would vanish. ¹¹Guilt cannot last when the idea of sacrifice has been removed. ¹²For if there is sacrifice, someone must pay and someone must get. ¹³And the only question that remains is how much is the price, and for getting what.

6. As host to the ego, you believe that you can give all your guilt away whenever you want, and thereby purchase peace. ²And the payment does not seem to be yours. ³While it is obvious that the ego does demand payment it never seems to be demanding it of you. ⁴You are unwilling to recognize that the ego, which you invited, is treacherous only to those who think they are its host. ⁵The ego will never let you perceive this, since this recognition would make it homeless. ⁶For when the recognition dawns clearly, you will not be deceived by any form the ego takes to protect itself from your sight. ⁷Each form will be recognized as but a cover for the one idea that hides behind them all; that love

demands sacrifice, and is therefore inseparable from attack and fear. [8]And that guilt is the price of love, which must be paid by fear.

7. How fearful, then, has God become to you, and how great a sacrifice do you believe His Love demands! [2]For total love would demand total sacrifice. [3]And so the ego seems to demand less of you than God, and of the two is judged as the lesser of two evils, one to be feared a little, perhaps, but the other to be destroyed. [4]For you see love as destructive, and your only question is who is to be destroyed, you or another? [5]You seek to answer this question in your special relationships, in which you seem to be both destroyer and destroyed in part, but able to be neither completely. [6]And this you think saves you from God, Whose total Love would completely destroy you.

8. You think that everyone outside yourself demands your sacrifice, but you do not see that only you demand sacrifice, and only of yourself. [2]Yet the demand of sacrifice is so savage and so fearful that you cannot accept it where it is. [3]The real price of not accepting this has been so great that you have given God away rather than look at it. [4]For if God would demand total sacrifice of you, it seems safer to project Him outward and away from you, and not be host to Him. [5]To Him you ascribed the ego's treachery, inviting it to take His place to protect you from Him. [6]And you do not recognize that it is what you invited in that would destroy you, and does demand total sacrifice of you. [7]No partial sacrifice will appease this savage guest, for it is an invader who but seems to offer kindness, but always to make the sacrifice complete.

9. You will not succeed in being partial hostage to the ego, for it keeps no bargains and would leave you nothing. [2]Nor can you be partial host to it. [3]You must choose between total freedom and total bondage, for there are no alternatives but these. [4]You have tried many compromises in the attempt to avoid recognizing the one decision you must make. [5]And yet it is the recognition of the decision, *just as it is*, that makes the decision so easy. [6]Salvation is simple, being of God, and therefore very easy to understand. [7]Do not try to project it from you and see it outside yourself. [8]In you are both the question and the answer; the demand for sacrifice and the peace of God.

XI. Christmas as the End of Sacrifice

1. Fear not to recognize the whole idea of sacrifice as solely of your making. [2]And seek not safety by attempting to protect yourself from where it is not. [3]Your brothers and your Father have become very fearful to you. [4]And you would bargain with them for a few special relationships, in which you think you see some scraps of safety. [5]Do not try longer to keep apart your thoughts and the Thought that has been given you. [6]When they are brought together and perceived where they are, the choice between them is nothing more than a gentle awakening, and as simple as opening your eyes to daylight when you have no more need of sleep.

2. The sign of Christmas is a star, a light in darkness. [2]See it not outside yourself, but shining in the Heaven within, and accept it as the sign the time of Christ has come. [3]He comes demanding nothing. [4]No sacrifice of any kind, of anyone, is asked by Him. [5]In His Presence the whole idea of sacrifice loses all meaning. [6]For He is Host to God. [7]And you need but invite Him in Who is there already, by recognizing that His Host is One, and no thought alien to His Oneness can abide with Him there. [8]Love must be total to give Him welcome, for the Presence of Holiness creates the holiness that surrounds it. [9]No fear can touch the Host Who cradles God in the time of Christ, for the Host is as holy as the perfect Innocence which He protects, and Whose power protects Him.

3. This Christmas give the Holy Spirit everything that would hurt you. [2]Let yourself be healed completely that you may join with Him in healing, and let us celebrate our release together by releasing everyone with us. [3]Leave nothing behind, for release is total, and when you have accepted it with me you will give it with me. [4]All pain and sacrifice and littleness will disappear in our relationship, which is as innocent as our relationship with our Father, and as powerful. [5]Pain will be brought to us and disappear in our presence, and without pain there can be no sacrifice. [6]And without sacrifice there love *must* be.

4. You who believe that sacrifice is love must learn that sacrifice is separation from love. [2]For sacrifice brings guilt as surely as love brings peace. [3]Guilt is the condition of sacrifice, as peace is the condition for the awareness of your relationship with God. [4]Through guilt you exclude your Father and your brothers from

yourself. [5]Through peace you invite them back, realizing that they are where your invitation bids them be. [6]What you exclude from yourself seems fearful, for you endow it with fear and try to cast it out, though it is part of you. [7]Who can perceive part of himself as loathsome, and live within himself in peace? [8]And who can try to resolve the "conflict" of Heaven and hell in him by casting Heaven out and giving it the attributes of hell, without experiencing himself as incomplete and lonely?

5. As long as you perceive the body as your reality, so long will you perceive yourself as lonely and deprived. [2]And so long will you also perceive yourself as a victim of sacrifice, justified in sacrificing others. [3]For who could thrust Heaven and its Creator aside without a sense of sacrifice and loss? [4]And who could suffer sacrifice and loss without attempting to restore himself? [5]Yet how could you accomplish this yourself, when the basis of your attempts is the belief in the reality of the deprivation? [6]Deprivation breeds attack, being the belief that attack is justified. [7]And as long as you would retain the deprivation, attack becomes salvation and sacrifice becomes love.

6. So is it that, in all your seeking for love, you seek for sacrifice and find it. [2]Yet you find not love. [3]It is impossible to deny what love is and still recognize it. [4]The meaning of love lies in what you have cast outside yourself, and it has no meaning apart from you. [5]It is what you prefer to keep that has no meaning, while all that you would keep away holds all the meaning of the universe, and holds the universe together in its meaning. [6]Unless the universe were joined in you it would be apart from God, and to be without Him *is* to be without meaning.

7. In the holy instant the condition of love is met, for minds are joined without the body's interference, and where there is communication there is peace. [2]The Prince of Peace was born to reestablish the condition of love by teaching that communication remains unbroken even if the body is destroyed, provided that you see not the body as the necessary means of communication. [3]And if you understand this lesson, you will realize that to sacrifice the body is to sacrifice nothing, and communication, which must be of the mind, cannot be sacrificed. [4]Where, then, *is* sacrifice? [5]The lesson I was born to teach, and still would teach to all my brothers, is that sacrifice is nowhere and love is everywhere. [6]For communication embraces everything, and in the peace it reestablishes, love comes of itself.

8. Let no despair darken the joy of Christmas, for the time of Christ is meaningless apart from joy. ²Let us join in celebrating peace by demanding no sacrifice of anyone, for so you offer me the love I offer you. ³What can be more joyous than to perceive we are deprived of nothing? ⁴Such is the message of the time of Christ, which I give you that you may give it and return it to the Father, Who gave it to me. ⁵For in the time of Christ communication is restored, and He joins us in the celebration of His Son's creation.

9. God offers thanks to the holy host who would receive Him, and lets Him enter and abide where He would be. ²And by your welcome does He welcome you into Himself, for what is contained in you who welcome Him is returned to Him. ³And we but celebrate His Wholeness as we welcome Him into ourselves. ⁴Those who receive the Father are one with Him, being host to Him Who created them. ⁵And by allowing Him to enter, the remembrance of the Father enters with Him, and with Him they remember the only relationship they ever had, and ever want to have.

10. This is the time in which a new year will soon be born from the time of Christ. ²I have perfect faith in you to do all that you would accomplish. ³Nothing will be lacking, and you will make complete and not destroy. ⁴Say, then, to your brother:

> ⁵*I give you to the Holy Spirit as part of myself.*
> ⁶*I know that you will be released, unless I want to use you*
>   *to imprison myself.*
> ⁷*In the name of my freedom I choose your release, because*
>   *I recognize that we will be released together.*

⁸So will the year begin in joy and freedom. ⁹There is much to do, and we have been long delayed. ¹⁰Accept the holy instant as this year is born, and take your place, so long left unfulfilled, in the Great Awakening. ¹¹Make this year different by making it all the same. ¹²And let all your relationships be made holy for you. ¹³This is our will. ¹⁴Amen.

Chapter 16

THE FORGIVENESS OF ILLUSIONS

I. True Empathy

1. To empathize does not mean to join in suffering, for that is what you must *refuse* to understand. [2]That is the ego's interpretation of empathy, and is always used to form a special relationship in which the suffering is shared. [3]The capacity to empathize is very useful to the Holy Spirit, provided you let Him use it in His way. [4]His way is very different. [5]He does not understand suffering, and would have you teach it is not understandable. [6]When He relates through you, He does not relate through your ego to another ego. [7]He does not join in pain, understanding that healing pain is not accomplished by delusional attempts to enter into it, and lighten it by sharing the delusion.

2. The clearest proof that empathy as the ego uses it is destructive lies in the fact that it is applied only to certain types of problems and in certain people. [2]These it selects out, and joins with. [3]And it never joins except to strengthen itself. [4]Having identified with what it thinks it understands, the ego sees itself and would increase itself by sharing what is like itself. [5]Make no mistake about this maneuver; the ego always empathizes to weaken, and to weaken is always to attack. [6]You do not know what empathizing means. [7]Yet of this you may be sure; if you will merely sit quietly by and let the Holy Spirit relate through you, you will empathize with strength, and will gain in strength and not in weakness.

3. Your part is only to remember this; you do not want anything you value to come of a relationship. [2]You choose neither to hurt it nor to heal it in your own way. [3]You do not know what healing is. [4]All you have learned of empathy is from the past. [5]And there is nothing from the past that you would share, for there is nothing from the past that you would keep. [6]Do not use empathy to make the past real, and so perpetuate it. [7]Step gently aside, and let healing be done for you. [8]Keep but one thought in mind and do not lose sight of it, however tempted you may be to judge any situation, and to determine your response *by* judging it. [9]Focus your mind only on this:

330

> ¹⁰*I am not alone, and I would not intrude the past*
> *upon my Guest.*
> ¹¹*I have invited Him, and He is here.*
> ¹²*I need do nothing except not to interfere.*

4. True empathy is of Him Who knows what it is. ²You will learn His interpretation of it if you let Him use your capacity for strength, and not for weakness. ³He will not desert you, but be sure that you desert not Him. ⁴Humility is strength in this sense only; that to recognize and accept the fact that you do not know is to recognize and accept the fact that He *does* know. ⁵You are not sure that He will do His part, because you have never yet done yours completely. ⁶You cannot know how to respond to what you do not understand. ⁷Be tempted not in this, and yield not to the ego's triumphant use of empathy for its glory.

5. The triumph of weakness is not what you would offer to a brother. ²And yet you recognize no triumph but this. ³This is not knowledge, and the form of empathy which would bring this about is so distorted that it would imprison what it would release. ⁴The unredeemed cannot redeem, yet they have a Redeemer. ⁵Attempt to teach Him not. ⁶You are the learner; He the Teacher. ⁷Do not confuse your role with His, for this will never bring peace to anyone. ⁸Offer your empathy to Him for it is *His* perception and *His* strength that you would share. ⁹And let Him offer you His strength and His perception, to be shared through you.

6. The meaning of love is lost in any relationship that looks to weakness, and hopes to find love there. ²The power of love, which *is* its meaning, lies in the strength of God that hovers over it and blesses it silently by enveloping it in healing wings. ³Let this be, and do not try to substitute your "miracle" for this. ⁴I have said that if a brother asks a foolish thing of you to do it. ⁵But be certain that this does not mean to do a foolish thing that would hurt either him or you, for what would hurt one will hurt the other. ⁶Foolish requests are foolish merely because they conflict, since they always contain some element of specialness. ⁷Only the Holy Spirit recognizes foolish needs as well as real ones. ⁸And He will teach you how to meet both without losing either.

7. *You* will attempt to do this only in secrecy. ²And you will think that by meeting the needs of one you do not jeopardize another,

because you keep them separate and secret from each other. ³That is not the way, for it leads not to life and truth. ⁴No needs will long be left unmet if you leave them all to Him Whose function is to meet them. ⁵That is His function, and not yours. ⁶He will not meet them secretly, for He would share everything you give through Him. ⁷That is why He gives it. ⁸What you give through Him is for the whole Sonship, not for part of it. ⁹Leave Him His function, for He will fulfill it if you but ask Him to enter your relationships, and bless them for you.

II. The Power of Holiness

1. You may still think that holiness is impossible to understand, because you cannot see how it can be extended to include everyone. ²And you have been told that it must include everyone to *be* holy. ³Concern yourself not with the extension of holiness, for the nature of miracles you do not understand. ⁴Nor do you do them. ⁵It is their extension, far beyond the limits you perceive, that demonstrates you do not do them. ⁶Why should you worry how the miracle extends to all the Sonship when you do not understand the miracle itself? ⁷One attribute is no more difficult to understand than is the whole. ⁸If miracles *are* at all, their attributes would have to be miraculous, being part of them.

2. There is a tendency to fragment, and then to be concerned about the truth of just a little part of the whole. ²And this is but a way of avoiding, or looking away from the whole, to what you think you might be better able to understand. ³For this is but another way in which you would still try to keep understanding to yourself. ⁴A better and far more helpful way to think of miracles is this: You do not understand them, either in part or in whole. ⁵Yet they have been done through you. ⁶Therefore your understanding cannot be necessary. ⁷Yet it is still impossible to accomplish what you do not understand. ⁸And so there must be Something in you that *does* understand.

3. To you the miracle cannot seem natural, because what you have done to hurt your mind has made it so unnatural that it does not remember what is natural to it. ²And when you are told what is natural, you cannot understand it. ³The recognition of the part as whole, and of the whole in every part is perfectly natural, for it is the way God thinks, and what is natural to Him is natural

to you. ⁴Wholly natural perception would show you instantly that order of difficulty in miracles is quite impossible, for it involves a contradiction of what miracles mean. ⁵And if you could understand their meaning, their attributes could hardly cause you perplexity.

4. You have done miracles, but it is quite apparent that you have not done them alone. ²You have succeeded whenever you have reached another mind and joined with it. ³When two minds join as one and share one idea equally, the first link in the awareness of the Sonship as one has been made. ⁴When you have made this joining as the Holy Spirit bids you, and have offered it to Him to use as He sees fit, His natural perception of your gift enables Him to understand it, and you to use His understanding on your behalf. ⁵It is impossible to convince you of the reality of what has clearly been accomplished through your willingness while you believe that you must understand it or else it is not real.

5. How can faith in reality be yours while you are bent on making it unreal? ²And are you really safer in maintaining the reality of illusions than you would be in joyously accepting truth for what it is, and giving thanks for it? ³Honor the truth that has been given you, and be glad you do not understand it. ⁴Miracles are natural to the One Who speaks for God. ⁵For His task is to translate the miracle into the knowledge which it represents, and which is hidden to you. ⁶Let His understanding of the miracle be enough for you, and do not turn away from all the witnesses that He has given you to His reality.

6. No evidence will convince you of the truth of what you do not want. ²Yet your relationship with Him is real. ³Regard this not with fear, but with rejoicing. ⁴The One you called upon *is* with you. ⁵Bid Him welcome, and honor the witnesses who bring you the glad tidings He has come. ⁶It is true, just as you fear, that to acknowledge Him is to deny all that you think you know. ⁷But what you think you know was never true. ⁸What gain is there to you in clinging to it, and denying the evidence for truth? ⁹For you have come too near to truth to renounce it now, and you *will* yield to its compelling attraction. ¹⁰You can delay this now, but only a little while. ¹¹The Host of God has called to you, and you have heard. ¹²Never again will you be wholly willing not to listen.

7. This is a year of joy, in which your listening will increase and peace will grow with its increase. ²The power of holiness and the weakness of attack are both being brought into your awareness.

³And this has been accomplished in a mind firmly convinced that holiness is weakness and attack is power. ⁴Should not this be a sufficient miracle to teach you that your Teacher is not of you? ⁵But remember also that whenever you listened to His interpretation the results have brought you joy. ⁶Would you prefer the results of your interpretation, considering honestly what they have been? ⁷God wills you better. ⁸Could you not look with greater charity on whom God loves with perfect Love?

8. Do not interpret against God's Love, for you have many witnesses that speak of it so clearly that only the blind and deaf could fail to see and hear them. ²This year determine not to deny what has been given you by God. ³Awake and share it, for that is the only reason He has called to you. ⁴His Voice has spoken clearly, and yet you have so little faith in what you heard, because you have preferred to place still greater faith in the disaster you have made. ⁵Today, let us resolve together to accept the joyful tidings that disaster is not real and that reality is not disaster. ⁶Reality is safe and sure, and wholly kind to everyone and everything. ⁷There is no greater love than to accept this and be glad. ⁸For love asks only that you be happy, and will give you everything that makes for happiness.

9. You have never given any problem to the Holy Spirit He has not solved for you, nor will you ever do so. ²You have never tried to solve anything yourself and been successful. ³Is it not time you brought these facts together and made sense of them? ⁴This is the year for the application of the ideas that have been given you. ⁵For the ideas are mighty forces, to be used and not held idly by. ⁶They have already proved their power sufficiently for you to place your faith in them, and not in their denial. ⁷This year invest in truth, and let it work in peace. ⁸Have faith in Him Who has faith in you. ⁹Think what you have really seen and heard, and recognize it. ¹⁰Can you be alone with witnesses like these?

III. The Reward of Teaching

1. We have already learned that everyone teaches, and teaches all the time. ²You may have taught well, and yet you may not have learned how to accept the comfort of your teaching. ³If you will consider what you have taught, and how alien it is to what you thought you knew, you will be compelled to realize that your

Teacher came from beyond your thought system. ⁴Therefore He could look upon it fairly, and perceive it was untrue. ⁵He must have done so from the basis of a very different thought system, and one with nothing in common with yours. ⁶For certainly what He has taught, and what you have taught through Him, have nothing in common with what you taught before He came. ⁷And the results have been to bring peace where there was pain, and suffering has disappeared to be replaced by joy.

2. You may have taught freedom, but you have not learned how to be free. ²I said earlier, "By their fruits ye shall know them, and they shall know themselves." ³For it is certain that you judge yourself according to your teaching. ⁴The ego's teaching produces immediate results, because its decisions are immediately accepted as your choice. ⁵And this acceptance means that you are willing to judge yourself accordingly. ⁶Cause and effect are very clear in the ego's thought system, because all your learning has been directed toward establishing the relationship between them. ⁷And would you not have faith in what you have so diligently taught yourself to believe? ⁸Yet remember how much care you have exerted in choosing its witnesses, and in avoiding those which spoke for the cause of truth and its effects.

3. Does not the fact that you have not learned what you have taught show you that you do not perceive the Sonship as one? ²And does it not also show you that you do not regard *yourself* as one? ³For it is impossible to teach successfully wholly without conviction, and it is equally impossible that conviction be outside of you. ⁴You could never have taught freedom unless you did believe in it. ⁵And it must be that what you taught came from yourself. ⁶Yet this Self you clearly do not know, and do not recognize It even though It functions. ⁷What functions must be there. ⁸And it is only if you deny what It has done that you could possibly deny Its Presence.

4. This is a course in how to know yourself. ²You have taught what you are, but have not let what you are teach you. ³You have been very careful to avoid the obvious, and not to see the real cause and effect relationship that is perfectly apparent. ⁴Yet within you is everything you taught. ⁵What can it be that has not learned it? ⁶It must be this part that is really outside yourself, not by your own projection, but in truth. ⁷And it is this part that you have taken in that is not you. ⁸What you accept into your mind does not really change it. ⁹Illusions are but beliefs in what is not

there. [10]And the seeming conflict between truth and illusion can only be resolved by separating yourself from the illusion and not from truth.

5. Your teaching has already done this, for the Holy Spirit is part of you. [2]Created by God, He left neither God nor His creation. [3]He is both God and you, as you are God and Him together. [4]For God's Answer to the separation added more to you than you tried to take away. [5]He protected both your creations and you together, keeping one with you what you would exclude. [6]And they will take the place of what you took in to replace them. [7]They are quite real, as part of the Self you do not know. [8]They communicate to you through the Holy Spirit, and their power and gratitude to you for their creation they offer gladly to your teaching of yourself, who is their home. [9]You who are host to God are also host to them. [10]For nothing real has ever left the mind of its creator. [11]And what is not real was never there.

6. You are not two selves in conflict. [2]What is beyond God? [3]If you who hold Him and whom He holds are the universe, all else must be outside, where nothing is. [4]You have taught this, and from far off in the universe, yet not beyond yourself, the witnesses to your teaching have gathered to help you learn. [5]Their gratitude has joined with yours and God's to strengthen your faith in what you taught. [6]For what you taught is true. [7]Alone, you stand outside your teaching and apart from it. [8]But with them you must learn that you but taught yourself, and learned from the conviction you shared with them.

7. This year you will begin to learn, and make learning commensurate with teaching. [2]You have chosen this by your own willingness to teach. [3]Though you seemed to suffer for it, the joy of teaching will yet be yours. [4]For the joy of teaching is in the learner, who offers it to the teacher in gratitude, and shares it with him. [5]As you learn, your gratitude to your Self, Who teaches you what He is, will grow and help you honor Him. [6]And you will learn His power and strength and purity, and love Him as His Father does. [7]His Kingdom has no limits and no end, and there is nothing in Him that is not perfect and eternal. [8]All this is *you*, and nothing outside of this *is* you.

8. To your most holy Self all praise is due for what you are, and for what He is Who created you as you are. [2]Sooner or later must everyone bridge the gap he imagines exists between his selves. [3]Each one builds this bridge, which carries him across the gap as

soon as he is willing to expend some little effort on behalf of bridging it. ⁴His little efforts are powerfully supplemented by the strength of Heaven, and by the united will of all who make Heaven what it is, being joined within it. ⁵And so the one who would cross over is literally transported there.

9. Your bridge is builded stronger than you think, and your foot is planted firmly on it. ²Have no fear that the attraction of those who stand on the other side and wait for you will not draw you safely across. ³For you will come where you would be, and where your Self awaits you.

IV. The Illusion and the Reality of Love

1. Be not afraid to look upon the special hate relationship, for freedom lies in looking at it. ²It would be impossible not to know the meaning of love, except for this. ³For the special love relationship, in which the meaning of love is hidden, is undertaken solely to offset the hate, but not to let it go. ⁴Your salvation will rise clearly before your open eyes as you look on this. ⁵You cannot limit hate. ⁶The special love relationship will not offset it, but will merely drive it underground and out of sight. ⁷It is essential to bring it into sight, and to make no attempt to hide it. ⁸For it is the attempt to balance hate with love that makes love meaningless to you. ⁹The extent of the split that lies in this you do not realize. ¹⁰And until you do the split will remain unrecognized, and therefore unhealed.

2. The symbols of hate against the symbols of love play out a conflict that does not exist. ²For symbols stand for something else, and the symbol of love is without meaning if love is everything. ³You will go through this last undoing quite unharmed, and will at last emerge as yourself. ⁴This is the last step in the readiness for God. ⁵Be not unwilling now; you are too near, and you will cross the bridge in perfect safety, translated quietly from war to peace. ⁶For the illusion of love will never satisfy, but its reality, which awaits you on the other side, will give you everything.

3. The special love relationship is an attempt to limit the destructive effects of hate by finding a haven in the storm of guilt. ²It makes no attempt to rise above the storm, into the sunlight. ³On the contrary, it emphasizes the guilt outside the haven by attempting to build barricades against it, and keep within them.

337

[4]The special love relationship is not perceived as a value in itself, but as a place of safety from which hatred is split off and kept apart. [5]The special love partner is acceptable only as long as he serves this purpose. [6]Hatred can enter, and indeed is welcome in some aspects of the relationship, but it is still held together by the illusion of love. [7]If the illusion goes, the relationship is broken or becomes unsatisfying on the grounds of disillusionment.

4. Love is not an illusion. [2]It is a fact. [3]Where disillusionment is possible, there was not love but hate. [4]For hate *is* an illusion, and what can change was never love. [5]It is sure that those who select certain ones as partners in any aspect of living, and use them for any purpose which they would not share with others, are trying to live with guilt rather than die of it. [6]This is the choice they see. [7]And love, to them, is only an escape from death. [8]They seek it desperately, but not in the peace in which it would gladly come quietly to them. [9]And when they find the fear of death is still upon them, the love relationship loses the illusion that it is what it is not. [10]When the barricades against it are broken, fear rushes in and hatred triumphs.

5. There are no triumphs of love. [2]Only hate is at all concerned with the "triumph of love." [3]The illusion of love can triumph over the illusion of hate, but always at the price of making both illusions. [4]As long as the illusion of hatred lasts, so long will love be an illusion to you. [5]And then the only choice remaining possible is which illusion you prefer. [6]There *is* no conflict in the choice between truth and illusion. [7]Seen in these terms, no one would hesitate. [8]But conflict enters the instant the choice seems to be one between illusions, but this choice does not matter. [9]Where one choice is as dangerous as the other, the decision must be one of despair.

6. Your task is not to seek for love, but merely to seek and find all of the barriers within yourself that you have built against it. [2]It is not necessary to seek for what is true, but it *is* necessary to seek for what is false. [3]Every illusion is one of fear, whatever form it takes. [4]And the attempt to escape from one illusion into another must fail. [5]If you seek love outside yourself you can be certain that you perceive hatred within, and are afraid of it. [6]Yet peace will never come from the illusion of love, but only from its reality.

7. Recognize this, for it is true, and truth must be recognized if it is to be distinguished from illusion: The special love relationship is an attempt to bring love into separation. [2]And, as such, it is

nothing more than an attempt to bring love into fear, and make it real in fear. ³In fundamental violation of love's one condition, the special love relationship would accomplish the impossible. ⁴How but in illusion could this be done? ⁵It is essential that we look very closely at exactly what it is you think you can do to solve the dilemma which seems very real to you, but which does not exist. ⁶You have come close to truth, and only this stands between you and the bridge that leads you into it.

8. Heaven waits silently, and your creations are holding out their hands to help you cross and welcome them. ²For it is they you seek. ³You seek but for your own completion, and it is they who render you complete. ⁴The special love relationship is but a shabby substitute for what makes you whole in truth, not in illusion. ⁵Your relationship with them is without guilt, and this enables you to look on all your brothers with gratitude, because your creations were created in union with them. ⁶Acceptance of your creations is the acceptance of the Oneness of creation, without which you could never be complete. ⁷No specialness can offer you what God has given, and what you are joined with Him in giving.

9. Across the bridge is your completion, for you will be wholly in God, willing for nothing special, but only to be wholly like to Him, completing Him by your completion. ²Fear not to cross to the abode of peace and perfect holiness. ³Only there is the completion of God and of His Son established forever. ⁴Seek not for this in the bleak world of illusion, where nothing is certain and where everything fails to satisfy. ⁵In the Name of God, be wholly willing to abandon all illusions. ⁶In any relationship in which you are wholly willing to accept completion, and only this, there is God completed, and His Son with Him.

10. The bridge that leads to union in yourself *must* lead to knowledge, for it was built with God beside you, and will lead you straight to Him where your completion rests, wholly compatible with His. ²Every illusion you accept into your mind by judging it to be attainable removes your own sense of completion, and thus denies the Wholeness of your Father. ³Every fantasy, be it of love or hate, deprives you of knowledge for fantasies are the veil behind which truth is hidden. ⁴To lift the veil that seems so dark and heavy, it is only needful to value truth beyond all fantasy, and to be entirely unwilling to settle for illusion in place of truth.

11. Would you not go through fear to love? ²For such the journey

seems to be. [3]Love calls, but hate would have you stay. [4]Hear not the call of hate, and see no fantasies. [5]For your completion lies in truth, and nowhere else. [6]See in the call of hate, and in every fantasy that rises to delay you, but the call for help that rises ceaselessly from you to your Creator. [7]Would He not answer you whose completion is His? [8]He loves you, wholly without illusion, as you must love. [9]For love *is* wholly without illusion, and therefore wholly without fear. [10]Whom God remembers must be whole. [11]And God has never forgotten what makes Him whole. [12]In your completion lie the memory of His Wholeness and His gratitude to you for His completion. [13]In His link with you lie both His inability to forget and your ability to remember. [14]In Him are joined your willingness to love and all the Love of God, Who forgot you not.

12. Your Father can no more forget the truth in you than you can fail to remember it. [2]The Holy Spirit is the Bridge to Him, made from your willingness to unite with Him and created by His joy in union with you. [3]The journey that seemed endless is almost complete, for what *is* endless is very near. [4]You have almost recognized it. [5]Turn with me firmly away from all illusions now, and let nothing stand in the way of truth. [6]We will take the last useless journey away from truth together, and then together we go straight to God, in joyous answer to His Call for His completion.

13. If special relationships of any kind would hinder God's completion, can they have any value to you? [2]What would interfere with God must interfere with you. [3]Only in time does interference in God's completion seem to be possible. [4]The bridge that He would carry you across lifts you from time into eternity. [5]Waken from time, and answer fearlessly the Call of Him Who gave eternity to you in your creation. [6]On this side of the bridge to timelessness you understand nothing. [7]But as you step lightly across it, upheld *by* timelessness, you are directed straight to the Heart of God. [8]At its center, and only there, you are safe forever, because you are complete forever. [9]There is no veil the Love of God in us together cannot lift. [10]The way to truth is open. [11]Follow it with me.

V. The Choice for Completion

1. In looking at the special relationship, it is necessary first to realize that it involves a great amount of pain. ²Anxiety, despair, guilt and attack all enter into it, broken into by periods in which they seem to be gone. ³All these must be understood for what they are. ⁴Whatever form they take, they are always an attack on the self to make the other guilty. ⁵I have spoken of this before, but there are some aspects of what is really being attempted that have not been touched upon.

2. Very simply, the attempt to make guilty is always directed against God. ²For the ego would have you see Him, and Him alone, as guilty, leaving the Sonship open to attack and unprotected from it. ³The special love relationship is the ego's chief weapon for keeping you from Heaven. ⁴It does not appear to be a weapon, but if you consider how you value it and why, you will realize what it must be.

3. The special love relationship is the ego's most boasted gift, and one which has the most appeal to those unwilling to relinquish guilt. ²The "dynamics" of the ego are clearest here, for counting on the attraction of this offering, the fantasies that center around it are often quite overt. ³Here they are usually judged to be acceptable and even natural. ⁴No one considers it bizarre to love and hate together, and even those who believe that hate is sin merely feel guilty, but do not correct it. ⁵This is the "natural" condition of the separation, and those who learn that it is not natural at all seem to be the unnatural ones. ⁶For this world *is* the opposite of Heaven, being made to be its opposite, and everything here takes a direction exactly opposite of what is true. ⁷In Heaven, where the meaning of love is known, love is the same as union. ⁸Here, where the illusion of love is accepted in love's place, love is perceived as separation and exclusion.

4. It is in the special relationship, born of the hidden wish for special love from God, that the ego's hatred triumphs. ²For the special relationship is the renunciation of the Love of God, and the attempt to secure for the self the specialness that He denied. ³It is essential to the preservation of the ego that you believe this specialness is not hell, but Heaven. ⁴For the ego would never have you see that separation could only be loss, being the one condition in which Heaven could not be.

5. To everyone Heaven is completion. ²There can be no disagree-

ment on this, because both the ego and the Holy Spirit accept it. [3]They are, however, in complete disagreement on what completion is, and how it is accomplished. [4]The Holy Spirit knows that completion lies first in union, and then in the extension of union. [5]To the ego completion lies in triumph, and in the extension of the "victory" even to the final triumph over God. [6]In this it sees the ultimate freedom of the self, for nothing would remain to interfere with the ego. [7]This is its idea of Heaven. [8]And therefore union, which is a condition in which the ego cannot interfere, must be hell.

6. The special relationship is a strange and unnatural ego device for joining hell and Heaven, and making them indistinguishable. [2]And the attempt to find the imagined "best" of both worlds has merely led to fantasies of both, and to the inability to perceive either as it is. [3]The special relationship is the triumph of this confusion. [4]It is a kind of union from which union is excluded, and the basis for the attempt at union rests on exclusion. [5]What better example could there be of the ego's maxim, "Seek but do not find"?

7. Most curious of all is the concept of the self which the ego fosters in the special relationship. [2]This "self" seeks the relationship to make itself complete. [3]Yet when it finds the special relationship in which it thinks it can accomplish this it gives itself away, and tries to "trade" itself for the self of another. [4]This is not union, for there is no increase and no extension. [5]Each partner tries to sacrifice the self he does not want for one he thinks he would prefer. [6]And he feels guilty for the "sin" of taking, and of giving nothing of value in return. [7]How much value can he place upon a self that he would give away to get a "better" one?

8. The "better" self the ego seeks is always one that is more special. [2]And whoever seems to possess a special self is "loved" for what can be taken from him. [3]Where both partners see this special self in each other, the ego sees "a union made in Heaven." [4]For neither one will recognize that he has asked for hell, and so he will not interfere with the ego's illusion of Heaven, which it offered him to interfere with Heaven. [5]Yet if all illusions are of fear, and they can be of nothing else, the illusion of Heaven is nothing more than an "attractive" form of fear, in which the guilt is buried deep and rises in the form of "love."

9. The appeal of hell lies only in the terrible attraction of guilt, which the ego holds out to those who place their faith in littleness.

²The conviction of littleness lies in every special relationship, for only the deprived could value specialness. ³The demand for specialness, and the perception of the giving of specialness as an act of love, would make love hateful. ⁴The real purpose of the special relationship, in strict accordance with the ego's goals, is to destroy reality and substitute illusion. ⁵For the ego is itself an illusion, and only illusions can be the witnesses to its "reality."

10. If you perceived the special relationship as a triumph over God, would you want it? ²Let us not think of its fearful nature, nor of the guilt it must entail, nor of the sadness and the loneliness. ³For these are only attributes of the whole religion of separation, and of the total context in which it is thought to occur. ⁴The central theme in its litany to sacrifice is that God must die so you can live. ⁵And it is this theme that is acted out in the special relationship. ⁶Through the death of your self you think you can attack another self, and snatch it from the other to replace the self that you despise. ⁷And you despise it because you do not think it offers the specialness that you demand. ⁸And hating it you have made it little and unworthy, because you are afraid of it.

11. How can you grant unlimited power to what you think you have attacked? ²So fearful has the truth become to you that unless it is weak and little, and unworthy of value, you would not dare to look upon it. ³You think it safer to endow the little self you made with power you wrested from truth, triumphing over it and leaving it helpless. ⁴See how exactly is this ritual enacted in the special relationship. ⁵An altar is erected in between two separate people, on which each seeks to kill his self, and on his body raise another self to take its power from his death. ⁶Over and over and over this ritual is enacted. ⁷And it is never completed, nor ever will be completed. ⁸The ritual of completion cannot complete, for life arises not from death, nor Heaven from hell.

12. Whenever any form of special relationship tempts you to seek for love in ritual, remember love is content, and not form of any kind. ²The special relationship is a ritual of form, aimed at raising the form to take the place of God at the expense of content. ³There is no meaning in the form, and there will never be. ⁴The special relationship must be recognized for what it is; a senseless ritual in which strength is extracted from the death of God, and invested in His killer as the sign that form has triumphed over content, and love has lost its meaning. ⁵Would you want this to be possible, even apart from its evident impossibility? ⁶If it were

possible, you would have made yourself helpless. [7]God is not angry. [8]He merely could not let this happen. [9]You cannot change His Mind. [10]No rituals that you have set up in which the dance of death delights you can bring death to the eternal. [11]Nor can your chosen substitute for the Wholeness of God have any influence at all upon it.

13. See in the special relationship nothing more than a meaningless attempt to raise other gods before Him, and by worshipping them to obscure their tininess and His greatness. [2]In the name of your completion you do not want this. [3]For every idol that you raise to place before Him stands before *you*, in place of what you are.

14. Salvation lies in the simple fact that illusions are not fearful because they are not true. [2]They but seem to be fearful to the extent to which you fail to recognize them for what they are; and you will fail to do this to the extent to which you *want* them to be true. [3]And to the same extent you are denying truth, and so are failing to make the simple choice between truth and illusion; God and fantasy. [4]Remember this, and you will have no difficulty in perceiving the decision as just what it is, and nothing more.

15. The core of the separation illusion lies simply in the fantasy of destruction of love's meaning. [2]And unless love's meaning is restored to you, you cannot know yourself who share its meaning. [3]Separation is only the decision *not* to know yourself. [4]This whole thought system is a carefully contrived learning experience, designed to lead away from truth and into fantasy. [5]Yet for every learning that would hurt you, God offers you correction and complete escape from all its consequences.

16. The decision whether or not to listen to this course and follow it is but the choice between truth and illusion. [2]For here is truth, separated from illusion and not confused with it at all. [3]How simple does this choice become when it is perceived as only what it is. [4]For only fantasies make confusion in choosing possible, and they are totally unreal.

17. This year is thus the time to make the easiest decision that ever confronted you, and also the only one. [2]You will cross the bridge into reality simply because you will recognize that God is on the other side, and nothing at all is here. [3]It is impossible not to make the natural decision as this is realized.

VI. The Bridge to the Real World

1. The search for the special relationship is the sign that you equate yourself with the ego and not with God. ²For the special relationship has value only to the ego. ³To the ego, unless a relationship has special value it has no meaning, for it perceives all love as special. ⁴Yet this cannot be natural, for it is unlike the relationship of God and His Son, and all relationships that are unlike this one *must* be unnatural. ⁵For God created love as He would have it be, and gave it as it is. ⁶Love has no meaning except as its Creator defined it by His Will. ⁷It is impossible to define it otherwise and understand it.

2. Love is freedom. ²To look for it by placing yourself in bondage is to separate yourself from it. ³For the Love of God, no longer seek for union in separation, nor for freedom in bondage! ⁴As you release, so will you be released. ⁵Forget this not, or Love will be unable to find you and comfort you.

3. There is a way in which the Holy Spirit asks your help, if you would have His. ²The holy instant is His most helpful aid in protecting you from the attraction of guilt, the real lure in the special relationship. ³You do not recognize that this is its real appeal, for the ego has taught you that freedom lies in it. ⁴Yet the closer you look at the special relationship, the more apparent it becomes that it must foster guilt and therefore must imprison.

4. The special relationship is totally meaningless without a body. ²If you value it, you must also value the body. ³And what you value you will keep. ⁴The special relationship is a device for limiting your self to a body, and for limiting your perception of others to theirs. ⁵The Great Rays would establish the total lack of value of the special relationship, if they were seen. ⁶For in seeing them the body would disappear, because its value would be lost. ⁷And so your whole investment in seeing it would be withdrawn from it.

5. You see the world you value. ²On this side of the bridge you see the world of separate bodies, seeking to join each other in separate unions and to become one by losing. ³When two individuals seek to become one, they are trying to decrease their magnitude. ⁴Each would deny his power, for the separate union excludes the universe. ⁵Far more is left outside than would be taken in, for God is left without and *nothing* taken in. ⁶If one such union were made in perfect faith, the universe would enter into it. ⁷Yet the special relationship the ego seeks does not include

345

even one whole individual. [8]The ego wants but part of him, and sees only this part and nothing else.

6. Across the bridge it is so different! [2]For a time the body is still seen, but not exclusively, as it is seen here. [3]The little spark that holds the Great Rays within it is also visible, and this spark cannot be limited long to littleness. [4]Once you have crossed the bridge, the value of the body is so diminished in your sight that you will see no need at all to magnify it. [5]For you will realize that the only value the body has is to enable you to bring your brothers to the bridge with you, and to be released together there.

7. The bridge itself is nothing more than a transition in the perspective of reality. [2]On this side, everything you see is grossly distorted and completely out of perspective. [3]What is little and insignificant is magnified, and what is strong and powerful cut down to littleness. [4]In the transition there is a period of confusion, in which a sense of actual disorientation may occur. [5]But fear it not, for it means only that you have been willing to let go your hold on the distorted frame of reference that seemed to hold your world together. [6]This frame of reference is built around the special relationship. [7]Without this illusion there could be no meaning you would still seek here.

8. Fear not that you will be abruptly lifted up and hurled into reality. [2]Time is kind, and if you use it on behalf of reality, it will keep gentle pace with you in your transition. [3]The urgency is only in dislodging your mind from its fixed position here. [4]This will not leave you homeless and without a frame of reference. [5]The period of disorientation, which precedes the actual transition, is far shorter than the time it took to fix your mind so firmly on illusions. [6]Delay will hurt you now more than before, only because you realize it *is* delay, and that escape from pain is really possible. [7]Find hope and comfort, rather than despair, in this: You could not long find even the illusion of love in any special relationship here. [8]For you are no longer wholly insane, and you would soon recognize the guilt of self-betrayal for what it is.

9. Nothing you seek to strengthen in the special relationship is really part of you. [2]And you cannot keep part of the thought system that taught you it was real, and understand the Thought that *knows* what you are. [3]You have allowed the Thought of your reality to enter your mind, and because you invited it, it will abide with you. [4]Your love for it will not allow you to betray yourself, and you could not enter into a relationship where it could not go

with you, for you would not want to be apart from it.

10. Be glad you have escaped the mockery of salvation the ego offered you, and look not back with longing on the travesty it made of your relationships. ²Now no one need suffer, for you have come too far to yield to the illusion of the beauty and holiness of guilt. ³Only the wholly insane could look on death and suffering, sickness and despair, and see it thus. ⁴What guilt has wrought is ugly, fearful and very dangerous. ⁵See no illusion of truth and beauty there. ⁶And be you thankful that there *is* a place where truth and beauty wait for you. ⁷Go on to meet them gladly, and learn how much awaits you for the simple willingness to give up nothing *because* it is nothing.

11. The new perspective you will gain from crossing over will be the understanding of where Heaven *is*. ²From this side, it seems to be outside and across the bridge. ³Yet as you cross to join it, it will join with you and become one with you. ⁴And you will think, in glad astonishment, that for all this you gave up *nothing*! ⁵The joy of Heaven, which has no limit, is increased with each light that returns to take its rightful place within it. ⁶Wait no longer, for the Love of God and *you*. ⁷And may the holy instant speed you on the way, as it will surely do if you but let it come to you.

12. The Holy Spirit asks only this little help of you: Whenever your thoughts wander to a special relationship which still attracts you, enter with Him into a holy instant, and there let Him release you. ²He needs only your willingness to share His perspective to give it to you completely. ³And your willingness need not be complete because His is perfect. ⁴It is His task to atone for your unwillingness by His perfect faith, and it is His faith you share with Him there. ⁵Out of your recognition of your unwillingness for your release, His perfect willingness is given you. ⁶Call upon Him, for Heaven is at His Call. ⁷And let Him call on Heaven for you.

VII. The End of Illusions

1. It is impossible to let the past go without relinquishing the special relationship. ²For the special relationship is an attempt to re-enact the past and change it. ³Imagined slights, remembered pain, past disappointments, perceived injustices and deprivations all enter into the special relationship, which becomes a way

in which you seek to restore your wounded self-esteem. ⁴What basis would you have for choosing a special partner without the past? ⁵Every such choice is made because of something "evil" in the past to which you cling, and for which must someone else atone.

2.   The special relationship takes vengeance on the past. ²By seeking to remove suffering in the past, it overlooks the present in its preoccupation with the past and its total commitment to it. ³No special relationship is experienced in the present. ⁴Shades of the past envelop it, and make it what it is. ⁵It has no meaning in the present, and if it means nothing now, it cannot have any real meaning at all. ⁶How can you change the past except in fantasy? ⁷And who can give you what you think the past deprived you of? ⁸The past is nothing. ⁹Do not seek to lay the blame for deprivation on it, for the past is gone. ¹⁰You cannot really *not* let go what has already gone. ¹¹It must be, therefore, that you are maintaining the illusion that it has not gone because you think it serves some purpose that you want fulfilled. ¹²And it must also be that this purpose could not be fulfilled in the present, but only in the past.

3.   Do not underestimate the intensity of the ego's drive for vengeance on the past. ²It is completely savage and completely insane. ³For the ego remembers everything you have done that has offended it, and seeks retribution of you. ⁴The fantasies it brings to its chosen relationships in which to act out its hate are fantasies of your destruction. ⁵For the ego holds the past against you, and in your escape from the past it sees itself deprived of the vengeance it believes you so justly merit. ⁶Yet without your alliance in your own destruction, the ego could not hold you to the past. ⁷In the special relationship you are allowing your destruction to be. ⁸That this is insane is obvious. ⁹But what is less obvious is that the present is useless to you while you pursue the ego's goal as its ally.

4.   The past is gone; seek not to preserve it in the special relationship that binds you to it, and would teach you salvation is past and so you must return to the past to find salvation. ²There is no fantasy that does not contain the dream of retribution for the past. ³Would you act out the dream, or let it go?

5.   In the special relationship it does not seem to be an acting out of vengeance that you seek. ²And even when the hatred and the savagery break briefly through, the illusion of love is not profoundly shaken. ³Yet the one thing the ego never allows to reach

awareness is that the special relationship is the acting out of vengeance on yourself. ⁴Yet what else could it be? ⁵In seeking the special relationship, you look not for glory in yourself. ⁶You have denied that it is there, and the relationship becomes your substitute for it. ⁷And vengeance becomes your substitute for Atonement, and the escape from vengeance becomes your loss.

6. Against the ego's insane notion of salvation the Holy Spirit gently lays the holy instant. ²We said before that the Holy Spirit must teach through comparisons, and uses opposites to point to truth. ³The holy instant is the opposite of the ego's fixed belief in salvation through vengeance for the past. ⁴In the holy instant it is understood that the past is gone, and with its passing the drive for vengeance has been uprooted and has disappeared. ⁵The stillness and the peace of *now* enfold you in perfect gentleness. ⁶Everything is gone except the truth.

7. For a time you may attempt to bring illusions into the holy instant, to hinder your full awareness of the complete difference, in all respects, between your experience of truth and illusion. ²Yet you will not attempt this long. ³In the holy instant the power of the Holy Spirit will prevail, because you joined Him. ⁴The illusions you bring with you will weaken the experience of Him for a while, and will prevent you from keeping the experience in your mind. ⁵Yet the holy instant is eternal, and your illusions of time will not prevent the timeless from being what it is, nor you from experiencing it as it is.

8. What God has given you is truly given, and will be truly received. ²For God's gifts have no reality apart from your receiving them. ³Your receiving completes His giving. ⁴You will receive *because* it is His Will to give. ⁵He gave the holy instant to be given you, and it is impossible that you receive it not *because* He gave it. ⁶When He willed that His Son be free, His Son *was* free. ⁷In the holy instant is His reminder that His Son will always be exactly as he was created. ⁸And everything the Holy Spirit teaches is to remind you that you have received what God has given you.

9. There is nothing you can hold against reality. ²All that must be forgiven are the illusions you have held against your brothers. ³Their reality has no past, and only illusions can be forgiven. ⁴God holds nothing against anyone, for He is incapable of illusions of any kind. ⁵Release your brothers from the slavery of their illusions by forgiving them for the illusions you perceive in them. ⁶Thus will you learn that you have been forgiven, for it is you

who offered them illusions. [7]In the holy instant this is done for you in time, to bring you the true condition of Heaven.

10. Remember that you always choose between truth and illusion; between the real Atonement that would heal and the ego's "atonement" that would destroy. [2]The power of God and all His Love, without limit, will support you as you seek only your place in the plan of Atonement arising from His Love. [3]Be an ally of God and not the ego in seeking how Atonement can come to you. [4]His help suffices, for His Messenger understands how to restore the Kingdom to you, and to place all your investment in salvation in your relationship with Him.

11. Seek and *find* His message in the holy instant, where all illusions are forgiven. [2]From there the miracle extends to bless everyone and to resolve all problems, be they perceived as great or small, possible or impossible. [3]There is nothing that will not give place to Him and to His Majesty. [4]To join in close relationship with Him is to accept relationships as real, and through their reality to give over all illusions for the reality of your relationship with God. [5]Praise be to your relationship with Him and to no other. [6]The truth lies there and nowhere else. [7]You choose this or nothing.

12. *Forgive us our illusions, Father, and help us to accept our true relationship with You, in which there are no illusions, and where none can ever enter. [2]Our holiness is Yours. [3]What can there be in us that needs forgiveness when Yours is perfect? [4]The sleep of forgetfulness is only the unwillingness to remember Your forgiveness and Your Love. [5]Let us not wander into temptation, for the temptation of the Son of God is not Your Will. [6]And let us receive only what You have given, and accept but this into the minds which You created and which You love. [7]Amen.*

Chapter 17

FORGIVENESS AND THE HOLY RELATIONSHIP

I. Bringing Fantasy to Truth

1. The betrayal of the Son of God lies only in illusions, and all his "sins" are but his own imagining. [2]His reality is forever sinless. [3]He need not be forgiven but awakened. [4]In his dreams he has betrayed himself, his brothers and his God. [5]Yet what is done in dreams has not been really done. [6]It is impossible to convince the dreamer that this is so, for dreams are what they are *because* of their illusion of reality. [7]Only in waking is the full release from them, for only then does it become perfectly apparent that they had no effect upon reality at all, and did not change it. [8]Fantasies change reality. [9]That is their purpose. [10]They cannot do so in reality, but they *can* do so in the mind that would have reality be different.

2. It is, then, only your wish to change reality that is fearful, because by your wish you think you have accomplished what you wish. [2]This strange position, in a sense, acknowledges your power. [3]Yet by distorting it and devoting it to "evil," it also makes it unreal. [4]You cannot be faithful to two masters who ask conflicting things of you. [5]What you use in fantasy you deny to truth. [6]Yet what you give to truth to use for you is safe from fantasy.

3. When you maintain that there must be an order of difficulty in miracles, all you mean is that there are some things you would withhold from truth. [2]You believe truth cannot deal with them only because you would keep them from truth. [3]Very simply, your lack of faith in the power that heals all pain arises from your wish to retain some aspects of reality for fantasy. [4]If you but realized what this must do to your appreciation of the whole! [5]What you reserve for yourself, you take away from Him Who would release you. [6]Unless you give it back, it is inevitable that your perspective on reality be warped and uncorrected.

4. As long as you would have it so, so long will the illusion of an order of difficulty in miracles remain with you. [2]For you have established this order in reality by giving some of it to one teacher, and some to another. [3]And so you learn to deal with part of the truth in one way, and in another way the other part. [4]To

351

fragment truth is to destroy it by rendering it meaningless. ⁵Orders of reality is a perspective without understanding; a frame of reference for reality to which it cannot really be compared at all.

5.   Think you that you can bring truth to fantasy, and learn what truth means from the perspective of illusions? ²Truth *has* no meaning in illusion. ³The frame of reference for its meaning must be itself. ⁴When you try to bring truth to illusions, you are trying to make illusions real, and keep them by justifying your belief in them. ⁵But to give illusions to truth is to enable truth to teach that the illusions are unreal, and thus enable you to escape from them. ⁶Reserve not one idea aside from truth, or you establish orders of reality that must imprison you. ⁷There is no order in reality, because everything there is true.

6.   Be willing, then, to give all you have held outside the truth to Him Who knows the truth, and in Whom all is brought to truth. ²Salvation from separation would be complete, or will not be at all. ³Be not concerned with anything except your willingness to have this be accomplished. ⁴He will accomplish it; not you. ⁵But forget not this: When you become disturbed and lose your peace of mind because another is attempting to solve his problems through fantasy, you are refusing to forgive yourself for just this same attempt. ⁶And you are holding both of you away from truth and from salvation. ⁷As you forgive him, you restore to truth what was denied by both of you. ⁸And you will see forgiveness where you have given it.

II. The Forgiven World

1.   Can you imagine how beautiful those you forgive will look to you? ²In no fantasy have you ever seen anything so lovely. ³Nothing you see here, sleeping or waking, comes near to such loveliness. ⁴And nothing will you value like unto this, nor hold so dear. ⁵Nothing that you remember that made your heart sing with joy has ever brought you even a little part of the happiness this sight will bring you. ⁶For you will see the Son of God. ⁷You will behold the beauty the Holy Spirit loves to look upon, and which He thanks the Father for. ⁸He was created to see this for you, until you learned to see it for yourself. ⁹And all His teaching leads to seeing it and giving thanks with Him.

2.   This loveliness is not a fantasy. ²It is the real world, bright and

clean and new, with everything sparkling under the open sun. [3]Nothing is hidden here, for everything has been forgiven and there are no fantasies to hide the truth. [4]The bridge between that world and this is so little and so easy to cross, that you could not believe it is the meeting place of worlds so different. [5]Yet this little bridge is the strongest thing that touches on this world at all. [6]This little step, so small it has escaped your notice, is a stride through time into eternity, beyond all ugliness into beauty that will enchant you, and will never cease to cause you wonderment at its perfection.

3. This step, the smallest ever taken, is still the greatest accomplishment of all in God's plan of Atonement. [2]All else is learned, but this is given, complete and wholly perfect. [3]No one but Him Who planned salvation could complete it thus. [4]The real world, in its loveliness, you learn to reach. [5]Fantasies are all undone, and no one and nothing remain still bound by them, and by your own forgiveness you are free to see. [6]Yet what you see is only what you made, with the blessing of your forgiveness on it. [7]And with this final blessing of God's Son upon himself, the real perception, born of the new perspective he has learned, has served its purpose.

4. The stars will disappear in light, and the sun that opened up the world to beauty will vanish. [2]Perception will be meaningless when it has been perfected, for everything that has been used for learning will have no function. [3]Nothing will ever change; no shifts nor shadings, no differences, no variations that made perception possible will still occur. [4]The perception of the real world will be so short that you will barely have time to thank God for it. [5]For God will take the last step swiftly, when you have reached the real world and have been made ready for Him.

5. The real world is attained simply by the complete forgiveness of the old, the world you see without forgiveness. [2]The great Transformer of perception will undertake with you the careful searching of the mind that made this world, and uncover to you the seeming reasons for your making it. [3]In the light of the real reason that He brings, as you follow Him, He will show you that there is no reason here at all. [4]Each spot His reason touches grows alive with beauty, and what seemed ugly in the darkness of your lack of reason is suddenly released to loveliness. [5]Not even what the Son of God made in insanity could be without a hidden spark of beauty that gentleness could release.

6. All this beauty will rise to bless your sight as you look upon the world with forgiving eyes. ²For forgiveness literally transforms vision, and lets you see the real world reaching quietly and gently across chaos, removing all illusions that had twisted your perception and fixed it on the past. ³The smallest leaf becomes a thing of wonder, and a blade of grass a sign of God's perfection.

7. From the forgiven world the Son of God is lifted easily into his home. ²And there he knows that he has always rested there in peace. ³Even salvation will become a dream, and vanish from his mind. ⁴For salvation is the end of dreams, and with the closing of the dream will have no meaning. ⁵Who, awake in Heaven, could dream that there could ever be need of salvation?

8. How much do you want salvation? ²It will give you the real world, trembling with readiness to be given you. ³The eagerness of the Holy Spirit to give you this is so intense He would not wait, although He waits in patience. ⁴Meet His patience with your impatience at delay in meeting Him. ⁵Go out in gladness to meet with your Redeemer, and walk with Him in trust out of this world, and into the real world of beauty and forgiveness.

III. Shadows of the Past

1. To forgive is merely to remember only the loving thoughts you gave in the past, and those that were given you. ²All the rest must be forgotten. ³Forgiveness is a selective remembering, based not on your selection. ⁴For the shadow figures you would make immortal are "enemies" of reality. ⁵Be willing to forgive the Son of God for what he did not do. ⁶The shadow figures are the witnesses you bring with you to demonstrate he did what he did not. ⁷Because you bring them, you will hear them. ⁸And you who keep them by your own selection do not understand how they came into your mind, and what their purpose is. ⁹They represent the evil that you think was done to you. ¹⁰You bring them with you only that you may return evil for evil, hoping that their witness will enable you to think guiltily of another and not harm yourself. ¹¹They speak so clearly for the separation that no one not obsessed with keeping separation could hear them. ¹²They offer you the "reasons" why you should enter into unholy alliances to support the ego's goals, and make your relationships the witness to its power.

354

2. It is these shadow figures that would make the ego holy in your sight, and teach you what you do to keep it safe is really love. ²The shadow figures always speak for vengeance, and all relationships into which they enter are totally insane. ³Without exception, these relationships have as their purpose the exclusion of the truth about the other, and of yourself. ⁴This is why you see in both what is not there, and make of both the slaves of vengeance. ⁵And why whatever reminds you of your past grievances attracts you, and seems to go by the name of love, no matter how distorted the associations by which you arrive at the connection may be. ⁶And finally, why all such relationships become attempts at union through the body, for only bodies can be seen as means for vengeance. ⁷That bodies are central to all unholy relationships is evident. ⁸Your own experience has taught you this. ⁹But what you may not realize are all the reasons that go to make the relationship unholy. ¹⁰For unholiness seeks to reinforce itself, as holiness does, by gathering to itself what it perceives as like itself.

3. In the unholy relationship, it is not the body of the other with which union is attempted, but the bodies of those who are not there. ²For even the body of the other, already a severely limited perception of him, is not the central focus as it is, or in entirety. ³What can be used for fantasies of vengeance, and what can be most readily associated with those on whom vengeance is really sought, is centered on and separated off as being the only parts of value. ⁴Every step taken in the making, the maintaining and the breaking off of the unholy relationship is a move toward further fragmentation and unreality. ⁵The shadow figures enter more and more, and the one in whom they seem to be decreases in importance.

4. Time is indeed unkind to the unholy relationship. ²For time *is* cruel in the ego's hands, as it is kind when used for gentleness. ³The attraction of the unholy relationship begins to fade and to be questioned almost at once. ⁴Once it is formed, doubt must enter in, because its purpose is impossible. ⁵The "ideal" of the unholy relationship thus becomes one in which the reality of the other does not enter at all to "spoil" the dream. ⁶And the less the other really brings to the relationship, the "better" it becomes. ⁷Thus, the attempt at union becomes a way of excluding even the one with whom the union was sought. ⁸For it was formed to get him out of it, and join with fantasies in uninterrupted "bliss."

5. How can the Holy Spirit bring His interpretation of the body

as a means of communication into relationships whose only purpose is separation from reality? ²What forgiveness *is* enables Him to do so. ³If all but loving thoughts have been forgotten, what remains is eternal. ⁴And the transformed past is made like the present. ⁵No longer does the past conflict with *now*. ⁶This continuity extends the present by increasing its reality and its value in your perception of it. ⁷In these loving thoughts is the spark of beauty hidden in the ugliness of the unholy relationship where hatred is remembered; yet there to come alive as the relationship is given to Him Who gives it life and beauty. ⁸That is why Atonement centers on the past, which is the source of separation, and where it must be undone. ⁹For separation must be corrected where it was made.

6. The ego seeks to "resolve" its problems, not at their source, but where they were not made. ²And thus it seeks to guarantee there will be no solution. ³The Holy Spirit wants only to make His resolutions complete and perfect, and so He seeks and finds the source of problems where it is, and there undoes it. ⁴And with each step in His undoing is the separation more and more undone, and union brought closer. ⁵He is not at all confused by any "reasons" for separation. ⁶All He perceives in separation is that it must be undone. ⁷Let Him uncover the hidden spark of beauty in your relationships, and show it to you. ⁸Its loveliness will so attract you that you will be unwilling ever to lose the sight of it again. ⁹And you will let this spark transform the relationship so you can see it more and more. ¹⁰For you will want it more and more, and become increasingly unwilling to let it be hidden from you. ¹¹And you will learn to seek for and establish the conditions in which this beauty can be seen.

7. All this you will do gladly, if you but let Him hold the spark before you, to light your way and make it clear to you. ²God's Son is one. ³Whom God has joined as one, the ego cannot put asunder. ⁴The spark of holiness must be safe, however hidden it may be, in every relationship. ⁵For the Creator of the one relationship has left no part of it without Himself. ⁶This is the only part of the relationship the Holy Spirit sees, because He knows that only this is true. ⁷You have made the relationship unreal, and therefore unholy, by seeing it where it is not and as it is not. ⁸Give the past to Him Who can change your mind about it for you. ⁹But first, be sure you fully realize what you have made the past to represent, and why.

8.   The past becomes the justification for entering into a continuing, unholy alliance with the ego against the present. ²For the present *is* forgiveness. ³Therefore, the relationships the unholy alliance dictates are not perceived nor felt as *now*. ⁴Yet the frame of reference to which the present is referred for meaning is an *illusion* of the past, in which those elements that fit the purpose of the unholy alliance are retained, and all the rest let go. ⁵And what is thus let go is all the truth the past could ever offer to the present as witnesses for its reality. ⁶What is kept but witnesses to the reality of dreams.

9.   It is still up to you to choose to join with truth or with illusion. ²But remember that to choose one is to let the other go. ³Which one you choose you will endow with beauty and reality, because the choice depends on which you value more. ⁴The spark of beauty or the veil of ugliness, the real world or the world of guilt and fear, truth or illusion, freedom or slavery—it is all the same. ⁵For you can never choose except between God and the ego. ⁶Thought systems are but true or false, and all their attributes come simply from what they are. ⁷Only the Thoughts of God are true. ⁸And all that follows from them comes from what they are, and is as true as is the holy Source from which they came.

10.   My holy brother, I would enter into all your relationships, and step between you and your fantasies. ²Let my relationship to you be real to you, and let me bring reality to your perception of your brothers. ³They were not created to enable you to hurt yourself through them. ⁴They were created to create with you. ⁵This is the truth that I would interpose between you and your goal of madness. ⁶Be not separate from me, and let not the holy purpose of Atonement be lost to you in dreams of vengeance. ⁷Relationships in which such dreams are cherished have excluded me. ⁸Let me enter in the Name of God and bring you peace, that you may offer peace to me.

IV. The Two Pictures

1.   God established His relationship with you to make you happy, and nothing you do that does not share His purpose can be real. ²The purpose God ascribed to anything is its only function. ³Because of His reason for creating His relationship with you, the function of relationships became forever "to make happy." ⁴*And*

nothing else. ⁵To fulfill this function you relate to your creations as God to His. ⁶For nothing God created is apart from happiness, and nothing God created but would extend happiness as its Creator did. ⁷Whatever does not fulfill this function cannot be real.

2.   In this world it is impossible to create. ²Yet it *is* possible to make happy. ³I have said repeatedly that the Holy Spirit would not deprive you of your special relationships, but would transform them. ⁴And all that is meant by that is that He will restore to them the function given them by God. ⁵The function you have given them is clearly not to make happy. ⁶But the holy relationship shares God's purpose, rather than aiming to make a substitute for it. ⁷Every special relationship you have made is a substitute for God's Will, and glorifies yours instead of His because of the illusion that they are different.

3.   You have made very real relationships even in this world. ²Yet you do not recognize them because you have raised their substitutes to such predominance that, when truth calls to you, as it does constantly, you answer with a substitute. ³Every special relationship you have made has, as its fundamental purpose, the aim of occupying your mind so completely that you will not hear the call of truth.

4.   In a sense, the special relationship was the ego's answer to the creation of the Holy Spirit, Who was God's Answer to the separation. ²For although the ego did not understand what had been created, it was aware of threat. ³The whole defense system the ego evolved to protect the separation from the Holy Spirit was in response to the gift with which God blessed it, and by His blessing enabled it to be healed. ⁴This blessing holds within itself the truth about everything. ⁵And the truth is that the Holy Spirit is in close relationship with you, because in Him is your relationship with God restored to you. ⁶The relationship with Him has never been broken, because the Holy Spirit has not been separate from anyone since the separation. ⁷And through Him have all your holy relationships been carefully preserved, to serve God's purpose for you.

5.   The ego is always alert to threat, and the part of your mind into which the ego was accepted is very anxious to preserve its reason, as it sees it. ²It does not realize that it is totally insane. ³And you must realize just what this means if you would be restored to sanity. ⁴The insane protect their thought systems, but

they do so insanely. [5]And all their defenses are as insane as what they are supposed to protect. [6]The separation has nothing in it, no part, no "reason," and no attribute that is not insane. [7]And its "protection" is part of it, as insane as the whole. [8]The special relationship, which is its chief defense, must therefore be insane.

6. You have but little difficulty now in realizing that the thought system the special relationship protects is but a system of delusions. [2]You recognize, at least in general terms, that the ego is insane. [3]Yet the special relationship still seems to you somehow to be "different." [4]Yet we have looked at it far closer than we have at many other aspects of the ego's thought system that you have been more willing to let go. [5]While this one remains, you will not let the others go. [6]For this one is not different. [7]Retain this one, and you have retained the whole.

7. It is essential to realize that all defenses *do* what they would defend. [2]The underlying basis for their effectiveness is that they offer what they defend. [3]What they defend is placed in them for safe-keeping, and as they operate they bring it to you. [4]Every defense operates by giving gifts, and the gift is always a miniature of the thought system the defense protects, set in a golden frame. [5]The frame is very elaborate, all set with jewels, and deeply carved and polished. [6]Its purpose is to be of value *in itself*, and to divert your attention from what it encloses. [7]But the frame without the picture you cannot have. [8]Defenses operate to make you think you can.

8. The special relationship has the most imposing and deceptive frame of all the defenses the ego uses. [2]Its thought system is offered here, surrounded by a frame so heavy and so elaborate that the picture is almost obliterated by its imposing structure. [3]Into the frame are woven all sorts of fanciful and fragmented illusions of love, set with dreams of sacrifice and self-aggrandizement, and interlaced with gilded threads of self-destruction. [4]The glitter of blood shines like rubies, and the tears are faceted like diamonds and gleam in the dim light in which the offering is made.

9. Look at the *picture*. [2]Do not let the frame distract you. [3]This gift is given you for your damnation, and if you take it you will believe that you *are* damned. [4]You cannot have the frame without the picture. [5]What you value is the frame, for there you see no conflict. [6]Yet the frame is only the wrapping for the gift of conflict. [7]The frame is not the gift. [8]Be not deceived by the most

superficial aspects of this thought system, for these aspects enclose the whole, complete in every aspect. ⁹Death lies in this glittering gift. ¹⁰Let not your gaze dwell on the hypnotic gleaming of the frame. ¹¹Look at the picture, and realize that death is offered you.

10. That is why the holy instant is so important in the defense of truth. ²The truth itself needs no defense, but you do need defense against your acceptance of the gift of death. ³When you who are truth accept an idea so dangerous to truth, you threaten truth with destruction. ⁴And your defense must now be undertaken, to keep truth whole. ⁵The power of Heaven, the Love of God, the tears of Christ, and the joy of His eternal Spirit are marshalled to defend you from your own attack. ⁶For you attack Them, being part of Them, and They must save you, for They love Themselves.

11. The holy instant is a miniature of Heaven, sent you *from* Heaven. ²It is a picture, too, set in a frame. ³Yet if you accept this gift you will not see the frame at all, because the gift can only be accepted through your willingness to focus all your attention on the picture. ⁴The holy instant is a miniature of eternity. ⁵It is a picture of timelessness, set in a frame of time. ⁶If you focus on the picture, you will realize that it was only the frame that made you think it *was* a picture. ⁷Without the frame, the picture is seen as what it represents. ⁸For as the whole thought system of the ego lies in its gifts, so the whole of Heaven lies in this instant, borrowed from eternity and set in time for you.

12. Two gifts are offered you. ²Each is complete, and cannot be partially accepted. ³Each is a picture of all that you can have, seen very differently. ⁴You cannot compare their value by comparing a picture to a frame. ⁵It must be the pictures only that you compare, or the comparison is wholly without meaning. ⁶Remember that it is the picture that is the gift. ⁷And only on this basis are you really free to choose. ⁸Look at the pictures. ⁹Both of them. ¹⁰One is a tiny picture, hard to see at all beneath the heavy shadows of its enormous and disproportionate enclosure. ¹¹The other is lightly framed and hung in light, lovely to look upon for what it is.

13. You who have tried so hard, and are still trying, to fit the better picture into the wrong frame and so combine what cannot be combined, accept this and be glad: These pictures are each framed perfectly for what they represent. ²One is framed to be out of focus and not seen. ³The other is framed for perfect clarity. ⁴The picture of darkness and of death grows less convincing as

you search it out amid its wrappings. ⁵As each senseless stone that seems to shine from the frame in darkness is exposed to light, it becomes dull and lifeless, and ceases to distract you from the picture. ⁶And finally you look upon the picture itself, seeing at last that, unprotected by the frame, it has no meaning.

14. The other picture is lightly framed, for time cannot contain eternity. ²There is no distraction here. ³The picture of Heaven and eternity grows more convincing as you look at it. ⁴And now, by real comparison, a transformation of both pictures can at last occur. ⁵And each is given its rightful place when both are seen in relation to each other. ⁶The dark picture, brought to light, is not perceived as fearful, but the fact that it is just a picture is brought home at last. ⁷And what you see there you will recognize as what it is; a picture of what you thought was real, and nothing more. ⁸For beyond this picture you will see nothing.

15. The picture of light, in clear-cut and unmistakable contrast, is transformed into what lies beyond the picture. ²As you look on this, you realize that it is not a picture, but a reality. ³This is no figured representation of a thought system, but the Thought itself. ⁴What it represents is there. ⁵The frame fades gently and God rises to your remembrance, offering you the whole of creation in exchange for your little picture, wholly without value and entirely deprived of meaning.

16. As God ascends into His rightful place and you to yours, you will experience again the meaning of relationship and know it to be true. ²Let us ascend in peace together to the Father, by giving Him ascendance in our minds. ³We will gain everything by giving Him the power and the glory, and keeping no illusions of where they are. ⁴They are in us, through His ascendance. ⁵What He has given is His. ⁶It shines in every part of Him, as in the whole. ⁷The whole reality of your relationship with Him lies in our relationship to one another. ⁸The holy instant shines alike on all relationships, for in it they *are* one. ⁹For here is only healing, already complete and perfect. ¹⁰For here is God, and where He is only the perfect and complete can be.

V. The Healed Relationship

1. The holy relationship is the expression of the holy instant in living in this world. ²Like everything about salvation, the holy instant is a practical device, witnessed to by its results. ³The holy instant never fails. ⁴The experience of it is always felt. ⁵Yet without expression it is not remembered. ⁶The holy relationship is a constant reminder of the experience in which the relationship became what it is. ⁷And as the unholy relationship is a continuing hymn of hate in praise of its maker, so is the holy relationship a happy song of praise to the Redeemer of relationships.

2. The holy relationship, a major step toward the perception of the real world, is learned. ²It is the old, unholy relationship, transformed and seen anew. ³The holy relationship is a phenomenal teaching accomplishment. ⁴In all its aspects, as it begins, develops and becomes accomplished, it represents the reversal of the unholy relationship. ⁵Be comforted in this; the only difficult phase is the beginning. ⁶For here, the goal of the relationship is abruptly shifted to the exact opposite of what it was. ⁷This is the first result of offering the relationship to the Holy Spirit, to use for His purposes.

3. This invitation is accepted immediately, and the Holy Spirit wastes no time in introducing the practical results of asking Him to enter. ²At once His goal replaces yours. ³This is accomplished very rapidly, but it makes the relationship seem disturbed, disjunctive and even quite distressing. ⁴The reason is quite clear. ⁵For the relationship as it *is* is out of line with its own goal, and clearly unsuited to the purpose that has been accepted for it. ⁶In its unholy condition, *your* goal was all that seemed to give it meaning. ⁷Now it seems to make no sense. ⁸Many relationships have been broken off at this point, and the pursuit of the old goal re-established in another relationship. ⁹For once the unholy relationship has accepted the goal of holiness, it can never again be what it was.

4. The temptation of the ego becomes extremely intense with this shift in goals. ²For the relationship has not as yet been changed sufficiently to make its former goal completely without attraction, and its structure is "threatened" by the recognition of its inappropriateness for meeting its new purpose. ³The conflict between the goal and the structure of the relationship is so apparent that they cannot coexist. ⁴Yet now the goal will not be changed.

⁵Set firmly in the unholy relationship, there is no course except to change the relationship to fit the goal. ⁶Until this happy solution is seen and accepted as the only way out of the conflict, the relationship may seem to be severely strained.

5. It would not be kinder to shift the goal more slowly, for the contrast would be obscured, and the ego given time to reinterpret each slow step according to its liking. ²Only a radical shift in purpose could induce a complete change of mind about what the whole relationship is for. ³As this change develops and is finally accomplished, it grows increasingly beneficent and joyous. ⁴But at the beginning, the situation is experienced as very precarious. ⁵A relationship, undertaken by two individuals for their unholy purposes, suddenly has holiness for its goal. ⁶As these two contemplate their relationship from the point of view of this new purpose, they are inevitably appalled. ⁷Their perception of the relationship may even become quite disorganized. ⁸And yet, the former organization of their perception no longer serves the purpose they have agreed to meet.

6. This is the time for *faith*. ²You let this goal be set for you. ³That was an act of faith. ⁴Do not abandon faith, now that the rewards of faith are being introduced. ⁵If you believed the Holy Spirit was there to accept the relationship, why would you now not still believe that He is there to purify what He has taken under His guidance? ⁶Have faith in your brother in what but seems to be a trying time. ⁷The goal *is* set. ⁸And your relationship has sanity as its purpose. ⁹For now you find yourself in an insane relationship, recognized as such in the light of its goal.

7. Now the ego counsels thus; substitute for this another relationship to which your former goal was quite appropriate. ²You can escape from your distress only by getting rid of your brother. ³You need not part entirely if you choose not to do so. ⁴But you must exclude major areas of fantasy from your brother, to save your sanity. ⁵*Hear not this now!* ⁶Have faith in Him Who answered you. ⁷He heard. ⁸Has He not been very explicit in His answer? ⁹You are not now wholly insane. ¹⁰Can you deny that He has given you a most explicit statement? ¹¹Now He asks for faith a little longer, even in bewilderment. ¹²For this will go, and you will see the justification for your faith emerge, to bring you shining conviction. ¹³Abandon Him not now, nor your brother. ¹⁴This relationship has been reborn as holy.

8. Accept with gladness what you do not understand, and let it

be explained to you as you perceive its purpose work in it to make it holy. ²You will find many opportunities to blame your brother for the "failure" of your relationship, for it will seem at times to have no purpose. ³A sense of aimlessness will come to haunt you, and to remind you of all the ways you once sought for satisfaction and thought you found it. ⁴Forget not now the misery you really found, and do not breathe life into your failing ego. ⁵For your relationship has not been disrupted. ⁶It has been saved.

9.   You are very new in the ways of salvation, and think you have lost your way. ²*Your* way *is* lost, but think not this is loss. ³In your newness, remember that you and your brother have started again, *together*. ⁴And take his hand, to walk together along a road far more familiar than you now believe. ⁵Is it not certain that you will remember a goal unchanged throughout eternity? ⁶For you have chosen but the goal of God, from which your true intent was never absent.

10.   Throughout the Sonship is the song of freedom heard, in joyous echo of your choice. ²You have joined with many in the holy instant, and they have joined with you. ³Think not your choice will leave you comfortless, for God Himself has blessed your holy relationship. ⁴Join in His blessing, and withhold not yours upon it. ⁵For all it needs now is your blessing, that you may see that in it rests salvation. ⁶Condemn salvation not, for it has come to you. ⁷And welcome it together, for it has come to join you and your brother together in a relationship in which all the Sonship is together blessed.

11.   You undertook, together, to invite the Holy Spirit into your relationship. ²He could not have entered otherwise. ³Although you may have made many mistakes since then, you have also made enormous efforts to help Him do His work. ⁴And He has not been lacking in appreciation for all you have done for Him. ⁵Nor does He see the mistakes at all. ⁶Have you been similarly grateful to your brother? ⁷Have you consistently appreciated the good efforts, and overlooked mistakes? ⁸Or has your appreciation flickered and grown dim in what seemed to be the light of the mistakes? ⁹Perhaps you are now entering upon a campaign to blame him for the discomfort of the situation in which you find yourself. ¹⁰And by this lack of thanks and gratitude you make yourself unable to express the holy instant, and thus lose sight of it.

12.   The experience of an instant, however compelling it may be, is

easily forgotten if you allow time to close over it. ²It must be kept shining and gracious in your awareness of time, but not concealed within it. ³The instant remains. ⁴But where are you? ⁵To give thanks to your brother is to appreciate the holy instant, and thus enable its results to be accepted and shared. ⁶To attack your brother is not to lose the instant, but to make it powerless in its effects.

13. You *have* received the holy instant, but you may have established a condition in which you cannot use it. ²As a result, you do not realize that it is with you still. ³And by cutting yourself off from its expression, you have denied yourself its benefit. ⁴You reinforce this every time you attack your brother, for the attack must blind you to yourself. ⁵And it is impossible to deny yourself, and to recognize what has been given and received by you.

14. You and your brother stand together in the holy presence of truth itself. ²Here is the goal, together with you. ³Think you not the goal itself will gladly arrange the means for its accomplishment? ⁴It is just this same discrepancy between the purpose that has been accepted and the means as they stand now which seems to make you suffer, but which makes Heaven glad. ⁵If Heaven were outside you, you could not share in its gladness. ⁶Yet because it is within, the gladness, too, is yours. ⁷You *are* joined in purpose, but remain still separate and divided on the means. ⁸Yet the goal is fixed, firm and unalterable, and the means will surely fall in place because the goal is sure. ⁹And you will share the gladness of the Sonship that it is so.

15. As you begin to recognize and accept the gifts you have so freely given to your brother, you will also accept the effects of the holy instant and use them to correct all your mistakes and free you from their results. ²And learning this, you will have also learned how to release all the Sonship, and offer it in gladness and thanksgiving to Him Who gave you your release, and Who would extend it through you.

VI. Setting the Goal

1. The practical application of the Holy Spirit's purpose is extremely simple, but it is unequivocal. ²In fact, in order to be simple it *must* be unequivocal. ³The simple is merely what is easily understood, and for this it is apparent that it must be clear. ⁴The

setting of the Holy Spirit's goal is general. ⁵Now He will work with you to make it specific, for application *is* specific. ⁶There are certain very specific guidelines He provides for any situation, but remember that you do not yet realize their universal application. ⁷Therefore, it is essential at this point to use them in each situation separately, until you can more safely look beyond each situation, in an understanding far broader than you now possess.

2. In any situation in which you are uncertain, the first thing to consider, very simply, is "What do I want to come of this? ²What is it *for?*" ³The clarification of the goal belongs at the beginning, for it is this which will determine the outcome. ⁴In the ego's procedure this is reversed. ⁵The situation becomes the determiner of the outcome, which can be anything. ⁶The reason for this disorganized approach is evident. ⁷The ego does not know what it wants to come of the situation. ⁸It is aware of what it does not want, but only that. ⁹It has no positive goal at all.

3. Without a clear-cut, positive goal, set at the outset, the situation just seems to happen, and makes no sense until it has already happened. ²Then you look back at it, and try to piece together what it must have meant. ³And you will be wrong. ⁴Not only is your judgment in the past, but you have no idea what should happen. ⁵No goal was set with which to bring the means in line. ⁶And now the only judgment left to make is whether or not the ego likes it; is it acceptable, or does it call for vengeance? ⁷The absence of a criterion for outcome, set in advance, makes understanding doubtful and evaluation impossible.

4. The value of deciding in advance what you want to happen is simply that you will perceive the situation as a means to *make* it happen. ²You will therefore make every effort to overlook what interferes with the accomplishment of your objective, and concentrate on everything that helps you meet it. ³It is quite noticeable that this approach has brought you closer to the Holy Spirit's sorting out of truth and falsity. ⁴The true becomes what can be used to meet the goal. ⁵The false becomes the useless from this point of view. ⁶The situation now has meaning, but only because the goal has made it meaningful.

5. The goal of truth has further practical advantages. ²If the situation is used for truth and sanity, its outcome must be peace. ³And this is quite apart from what the outcome *is*. ⁴If peace is the condition of truth and sanity, and cannot be without them, where

peace is they must be. ⁵Truth comes of itself. ⁶If you experience peace, it is because the truth has come to you and you will see the outcome truly, for deception cannot prevail against you. ⁷You will recognize the outcome *because* you are at peace. ⁸Here again you see the opposite of the ego's way of looking, for the ego believes the situation brings the experience. ⁹The Holy Spirit knows that the situation is as the goal determines it, and is experienced according to the goal.

6. The goal of truth requires faith. ²Faith is implicit in the acceptance of the Holy Spirit's purpose, and this faith is all-inclusive. ³Where the goal of truth is set, there faith must be. ⁴The Holy Spirit sees the situation as a whole. ⁵The goal establishes the fact that everyone involved in it will play his part in its accomplishment. ⁶This is inevitable. ⁷No one will fail in anything. ⁸This seems to ask for faith beyond you, and beyond what you can give. ⁹Yet this is so only from the viewpoint of the ego, for the ego believes in "solving" conflict through fragmentation, and does not perceive the situation as a whole. ¹⁰Therefore, it seeks to split off segments of the situation and deal with them separately, for it has faith in separation and not in wholeness.

7. Confronted with any aspect of the situation that seems to be difficult, the ego will attempt to take this aspect elsewhere, and resolve it there. ²And it will seem to be successful, except that this attempt conflicts with unity, and must obscure the goal of truth. ³And peace will not be experienced except in fantasy. ⁴Truth has not come because faith has been denied, being withheld from where it rightfully belonged. ⁵Thus do you lose the understanding of the situation the goal of truth would bring. ⁶For fantasy solutions bring but the illusion of experience, and the illusion of peace is not the condition in which truth can enter.

VII. The Call for Faith

1. The substitutes for aspects of the situation are the witnesses to your lack of faith. ²They demonstrate that you did not believe the situation and the problem were in the same place. ³The problem *was* the lack of faith, and it is this you demonstrate when you remove it from its source and place it elsewhere. ⁴As a result, you do not see the problem. ⁵Had you not lacked faith that it could be solved, the problem would be gone. ⁶And the situation would

have been meaningful to you, because the interference in the way of understanding would have been removed. [7]To remove the problem elsewhere is to keep it, for you remove yourself from it and make it unsolvable.

2. There is no problem in any situation that faith will not solve. [2]There is no shift in any aspect of the problem but will make solution impossible. [3]For if you shift part of the problem elsewhere the meaning of the problem must be lost, and the solution to the problem is inherent in its meaning. [4]Is it not possible that all your problems have been solved, but you have removed yourself from the solution? [5]Yet faith must be where something has been done, and where you see it done.

3. A situation is a relationship, being the joining of thoughts. [2]If problems are perceived, it is because the thoughts are judged to be in conflict. [3]But if the goal is truth, this is impossible. [4]Some idea of bodies must have entered, for minds cannot attack. [5]The thought of bodies is the sign of faithlessness, for bodies cannot solve anything. [6]It is their intrusion on the relationship, an error in your thoughts about the situation, which then becomes the justification for your lack of faith. [7]You will make this error, but be not at all concerned with that. [8]The error does not matter. [9]Faithlessness brought to faith will never interfere with truth. [10]But faithlessness used *against* truth will always destroy faith. [11]If you lack faith, ask that it be restored where it was lost, and seek not to have it made up to you elsewhere, as if you had been unjustly deprived of it.

4. Only what *you* have not given can be lacking in any situation. [2]But remember this; the goal of holiness was set for your relationship, and not by you. [3]You did not set it because holiness cannot be seen except through faith, and your relationship was not holy because your faith in your brother was so limited and little. [4]Your faith must grow to meet the goal that has been set. [5]The goal's reality will call this forth, for you will see that peace and faith will not come separately. [6]What situation can you be in without faith, and remain faithful to your brother?

5. Every situation in which you find yourself is but a means to meet the purpose set for your relationship. [2]See it as something else and you are faithless. [3]Use not your faithlessness. [4]Let it enter and look upon it calmly, but do not use it. [5]Faithlessness is the servant of illusion, and wholly faithful to its master. [6]Use it, and it will carry you straight to illusions. [7]Be tempted not by what it

offers you. [8]It interferes, not with the goal, but with the value of the goal to you. [9]Accept not the illusion of peace it offers, but look upon its offering and recognize it *is* illusion.

6. The goal of illusion is as closely tied to faithlessness as faith to truth. [2]If you lack faith in anyone to fulfill, and perfectly, his part in any situation dedicated in advance to truth, your dedication is divided. [3]And so you have been faithless to your brother, and used your faithlessness against him. [4]No relationship is holy unless its holiness goes with it everywhere. [5]As holiness and faith go hand in hand, so must its faith go everywhere with it. [6]The goal's reality will call forth and accomplish every miracle needed for its fulfillment. [7]Nothing too small or too enormous, too weak or too compelling, but will be gently turned to its use and purpose. [8]The universe will serve it gladly, as it serves the universe. [9]But do not interfere.

7. The power set in you in whom the Holy Spirit's goal has been established is so far beyond your little conception of the infinite that you have no idea how great the strength that goes with you. [2]And you can use *this* in perfect safety. [3]Yet for all its might, so great it reaches past the stars and to the universe that lies beyond them, your little faithlessness can make it useless, if you would use the faithlessness instead.

8. Yet think on this, and learn the cause of faithlessness: You think you hold against your brother what he has done to you. [2]But what you really blame him for is what *you* did to *him*. [3]It is not his past but yours you hold against him. [4]And you lack faith in him because of what you were. [5]Yet you are as innocent of what you were as he is. [6]What never was is causeless, and is not there to interfere with truth. [7]There is no cause for faithlessness, but there *is* Cause for faith. [8]That Cause has entered any situation that shares Its purpose. [9]The light of truth shines from the center of the situation, and touches everyone to whom the situation's purpose calls. [10]It calls to everyone. [11]There is no situation that does not involve your whole relationship, in every aspect and complete in every part. [12]You can leave nothing of yourself outside it and keep the situation holy. [13]For it shares the purpose of your whole relationship, and derives its meaning from it.

9. Enter each situation with the faith you give your brother, or you are faithless to your own relationship. [2]Your faith will call the others to share your purpose, as the same purpose called forth the faith in you. [3]And you will see the means you once

employed to lead you to illusions transformed to means for truth. ⁴Truth calls for faith, and faith makes room for truth. ⁵When the Holy Spirit changed the purpose of your relationship by exchanging yours for His, the goal He placed there was extended to every situation in which you enter, or will ever enter. ⁶And every situation was thus made free of the past, which would have made it purposeless.

10. You call for faith because of Him Who walks with you in every situation. ²You are no longer wholly insane, and no longer alone. ³For loneliness in God must be a dream. ⁴You whose relationship shares the Holy Spirit's goal are set apart from loneliness because the truth has come. ⁵Its call for faith is strong. ⁶Use not your faithlessness against it, for it calls you to salvation and to peace.

VIII. The Conditions of Peace

1. The holy instant is nothing more than a special case, or an extreme example, of what every situation is meant to be. ²The meaning that the Holy Spirit's purpose has given it is also given to every situation. ³It calls forth just the same suspension of faithlessness, withheld and left unused, that faith might answer to the call of truth. ⁴The holy instant is the shining example, the clear and unequivocal demonstration of the meaning of every relationship and every situation, seen as a whole. ⁵Faith has accepted every aspect of the situation, and faithlessness has not forced any exclusion on it. ⁶It is a situation of perfect peace, simply because you have let it be what it is.

2. This simple courtesy is all the Holy Spirit asks of you. ²Let truth be what it is. ³Do not intrude upon it, do not attack it, do not interrupt its coming. ⁴Let it encompass every situation and bring you peace. ⁵Not even faith is asked of you, for truth asks nothing. ⁶Let it enter, and it will call forth and secure for you the faith you need for peace. ⁷But rise you not against it, for against your opposition it cannot come.

3. Would you not want to make a holy instant of every situation? ²For such is the gift of faith, freely given wherever faithlessness is laid aside, unused. ³And then the power of the Holy Spirit's purpose is free to use instead. ⁴This power instantly transforms all situations into one sure and continuous means for establishing His purpose, and demonstrating its reality. ⁵What has been demonstrated has called for faith, and has been given it. ⁶Now it becomes a

fact, from which faith can no longer be withheld. [7]The strain of refusing faith to truth is enormous, and far greater than you realize. [8]But to answer truth with faith entails no strain at all.

4. To you who have acknowledged the Call of your Redeemer, the strain of not responding to His Call seems to be greater than before. [2]This is not so. [3]Before, the strain was there, but you attributed it to something else, believing that the "something else" produced it. [4]This was never true. [5]For what the "something else" produced was sorrow and depression, sickness and pain, darkness and dim imaginings of terror, cold fantasies of fear and fiery dreams of hell. [6]And it was nothing but the intolerable strain of refusing to give faith to truth, and see its evident reality.

5. Such was the crucifixion of the Son of God. [2]His faithlessness did this to him. [3]Think carefully before you let yourself use faithlessness against him. [4]For he is risen, and you have accepted the Cause of his awakening as yours. [5]You have assumed your part in his redemption, and you are now fully responsible to him. [6]Fail him not now, for it has been given you to realize what your lack of faith in him must mean to you. [7]His salvation is your only purpose. [8]See only this in every situation, and it will be a means for bringing only this.

6. When you accepted truth as the goal for your relationship, you became a giver of peace as surely as your Father gave peace to you. [2]For the goal of peace cannot be accepted apart from its conditions, and you had faith in it for no one accepts what he does not believe is real. [3]Your purpose has not changed, and will not change, for you accepted what can never change. [4]And nothing that it needs to be forever changeless can you now withhold from it. [5]Your release is certain. [6]Give as you have received. [7]And demonstrate that you have risen far beyond any situation that could hold you back, and keep you separate from Him Whose Call you answered.

Chapter 18

THE PASSING OF THE DREAM

I. The Substitute Reality

1. To substitute is to accept instead. ²If you would but consider exactly what this entails, you would perceive at once how much at variance this is with the goal the Holy Spirit has given you, and would accomplish for you. ³To substitute is to choose between, renouncing one aspect of the Sonship in favor of the other. ⁴For this special purpose, one is judged more valuable and the other is replaced by him. ⁵The relationship in which the substitution occurred is thus fragmented, and its purpose split accordingly. ⁶To fragment is to exclude, and substitution is the strongest defense the ego has for separation.

2. The Holy Spirit never uses substitutes. ²Where the ego perceives one person as a replacement for another, the Holy Spirit sees them joined and indivisible. ³He does not judge between them, knowing they are one. ⁴Being united, they are one because they are the same. ⁵Substitution is clearly a process in which they are perceived as different. ⁶One would unite; the other separate. ⁷Nothing can come between what God has joined and what the Holy Spirit sees as one. ⁸But everything *seems* to come between the fragmented relationships the ego sponsors to destroy.

3. The one emotion in which substitution is impossible is love. ²Fear involves substitution by definition, for it is love's replacement. ³Fear is both a fragmented and fragmenting emotion. ⁴It seems to take many forms, and each one seems to require a different form of acting out for satisfaction. ⁵While this appears to introduce quite variable behavior, a far more serious effect lies in the fragmented perception from which the behavior stems. ⁶No one is seen complete. ⁷The body is emphasized, with special emphasis on certain parts, and used as the standard for comparison of acceptance or rejection for acting out a special form of fear.

4. You who believe that God is fear made but one substitution. ²It has taken many forms, because it was the substitution of illusion for truth; of fragmentation for wholeness. ³It has become so splintered and subdivided and divided again, over and over, that it is now almost impossible to perceive it once was one, and still is

what it was. ⁴That one error, which brought truth to illusion, infinity to time, and life to death, was all you ever made. ⁵Your whole world rests upon it. ⁶Everything you see reflects it, and every special relationship that you have ever made is part of it.

5.   You may be surprised to hear how very different is reality from what you see. ²You do not realize the magnitude of that one error. ³It was so vast and so completely incredible that from it a world of total unreality *had* to emerge. ⁴What else could come of it? ⁵Its fragmented aspects are fearful enough, as you begin to look at them. ⁶But nothing you have seen begins to show you the enormity of the original error, which seemed to cast you out of Heaven, to shatter knowledge into meaningless bits of disunited perceptions, and to force you to make further substitutions.

6.   That was the first projection of error outward. ²The world arose to hide it, and became the screen on which it was projected and drawn between you and the truth. ³For truth extends inward, where the idea of loss is meaningless and only increase is conceivable. ⁴Do you really think it strange that a world in which everything is backwards and upside down arose from this projection of error? ⁵It was inevitable. ⁶For truth brought to this could only remain within in quiet, and take no part in all the mad projection by which this world was made. ⁷Call it not sin but madness, for such it was and so it still remains. ⁸Invest it not with guilt, for guilt implies it was accomplished in reality. ⁹And above all, *be not afraid of it.*

7.   When you seem to see some twisted form of the original error rising to frighten you, say only, "God is not fear, but Love," and it will disappear. ²The truth will save you. ³It has not left you, to go out into the mad world and so depart from you. ⁴Inward is sanity; insanity is outside you. ⁵You but believe it is the other way; that truth is outside, and error and guilt within. ⁶Your little, senseless substitutions, touched with insanity and swirling lightly off on a mad course like feathers dancing insanely in the wind, have no substance. ⁷They fuse and merge and separate, in shifting and totally meaningless patterns that need not be judged at all. ⁸To judge them individually is pointless. ⁹Their tiny differences in form are no real differences at all. ¹⁰None of them matters. ¹¹*That* they have in common and nothing else. ¹²Yet what else is necessary to make them all the same?

8.   Let them all go, dancing in the wind, dipping and turning till they disappear from sight, far, far outside of you. ²And turn you

to the stately calm within, where in holy stillness dwells the living God you never left, and Who never left you. ³The Holy Spirit takes you gently by the hand, and retraces with you your mad journey outside yourself, leading you gently back to the truth and safety within. ⁴He brings all your insane projections and the wild substitutions that you have placed outside you to the truth. ⁵Thus He reverses the course of insanity and restores you to reason.

9. In your relationship with your brother, where He has taken charge of everything at your request, He has set the course inward to the truth you share. ²In the mad world outside you nothing can be shared but only substituted, and sharing and substituting have nothing in common in reality. ³Within yourself you love your brother with a perfect love. ⁴Here is holy ground, in which no substitution can enter, and where only the truth in your brother can abide. ⁵Here you are joined in God, as much together as you are with Him. ⁶The original error has not entered here, nor ever will. ⁷Here is the radiant truth, to which the Holy Spirit has committed your relationship. ⁸Let Him bring it here, where *you* would have it be. ⁹Give Him but a little faith in your brother, to help Him show you that no substitute you made for Heaven can keep you from it.

10. In you there is no separation, and no substitute can keep you from your brother. ²Your reality was God's creation, and has no substitute. ³You are so firmly joined in truth that only God is there. ⁴And He would never accept something else instead of you. ⁵He loves you both, equally and as one. ⁶And as He loves you, so you are. ⁷You are not joined together in illusions, but in the Thought so holy and so perfect that illusions cannot remain to darken the holy place in which you stand together. ⁸God is with you, my brother. ⁹Let us join in Him in peace and gratitude, and accept His gift as our most holy and perfect reality, which we share in Him.

11. Heaven is restored to all the Sonship through your relationship, for in it lies the Sonship, whole and beautiful, safe in your love. ²Heaven has entered quietly, for all illusions have been gently brought unto the truth in you, and love has shined upon you, blessing your relationship with truth. ³God and His whole creation have entered it together. ⁴How lovely and how holy is your relationship, with the truth shining upon it! ⁵Heaven beholds it, and rejoices that you have let it come to you. ⁶And God Himself is

glad that your relationship is as it was created. ⁷The universe within you stands with you, together with your brother. ⁸And Heaven looks with love on what is joined in it, along with its Creator.

12.   Whom God has called should hear no substitutes. ²Their call is but an echo of the original error that shattered Heaven. ³And what became of peace in those who heard? ⁴Return with me to Heaven, walking together with your brother out of this world and through another, to the loveliness and joy the other holds within it. ⁵Would you still further weaken and break apart what is already broken and hopeless? ⁶Is it here that you would look for happiness? ⁷Or would you not prefer to heal what has been broken, and join in making whole what has been ravaged by separation and disease?

13.   You have been called, together with your brother, to the most holy function this world contains. ²It is the only one that has no limits, and reaches out to every broken fragment of the Sonship with healing and uniting comfort. ³This is offered you, in your holy relationship. ⁴Accept it here, and you will give as you have accepted. ⁵The peace of God is given you with the glowing purpose in which you join with your brother. ⁶The holy light that brought you and him together must extend, as you accepted it.

II. The Basis of the Dream

1.   Does not a world that seems quite real arise in dreams? ²Yet think what this world is. ³It is clearly not the world you saw before you slept. ⁴Rather it is a distortion of the world, planned solely around what you would have preferred. ⁵Here, you are "free" to make over whatever seemed to attack you, and change it into a tribute to your ego, which was outraged by the "attack." ⁶This would not be your wish unless you saw yourself as one with the ego, which always looks upon itself, and therefore on you, as under attack and highly vulnerable to it.

2.   Dreams are chaotic because they are governed by your conflicting wishes, and therefore they have no concern with what is true. ²They are the best example you could have of how perception can be utilized to substitute illusions for truth. ³You do not take them seriously on awaking because the fact that reality is so outrageously violated in them becomes apparent. ⁴Yet they are a

way of looking at the world, and changing it to suit the ego better. ⁵They provide striking examples, both of the ego's inability to tolerate reality, and of your willingness to change reality on its behalf.

3. You do not find the differences between what you see in sleep and on awaking disturbing. ²You recognize that what you see on waking is blotted out in dreams. ³Yet on awakening, you do not expect it to be gone. ⁴In dreams *you* arrange everything. ⁵People become what you would have them be, and what they do you order. ⁶No limits on substitution are laid upon you. ⁷For a time it seems as if the world were given you, to make it what you wish. ⁸You do not realize you are attacking it, trying to triumph over it and make it serve you.

4. Dreams are perceptual temper tantrums, in which you literally scream, "I want it thus!" ²And thus it seems to be. ³And yet the dream cannot escape its origin. ⁴Anger and fear pervade it, and in an instant the illusion of satisfaction is invaded by the illusion of terror. ⁵For the dream of your ability to control reality by substituting a world that you prefer *is* terrifying. ⁶Your attempts to blot out reality are very fearful, but this you are not willing to accept. ⁷And so you substitute the fantasy that reality is fearful, not what you would do to it. ⁸And thus is guilt made real.

5. Dreams show you that you have the power to make a world as you would have it be, and that because you want it you see it. ²And while you see it you do not doubt that it is real. ³Yet here is a world, clearly within your mind, that seems to be outside. ⁴You do not respond to it as though you made it, nor do you realize that the emotions the dream produces must come from you. ⁵It is the figures in the dream and what they do that seem to make the dream. ⁶You do not realize that you are making them act out for you, for if you did the guilt would not be theirs, and the illusion of satisfaction would be gone. ⁷In dreams these features are not obscure. ⁸You seem to waken, and the dream is gone. ⁹Yet what you fail to recognize is that what caused the dream has not gone with it. ¹⁰Your wish to make another world that is not real remains with you. ¹¹And what you seem to waken to is but another form of this same world you see in dreams. ¹²All your time is spent in dreaming. ¹³Your sleeping and your waking dreams have different forms, and that is all. ¹⁴Their content is the same. ¹⁵They are your protest against reality, and your fixed and insane idea that you can change it. ¹⁶In your waking dreams, the special rela-

tionship has a special place. ¹⁷It is the means by which you try to make your sleeping dreams come true. ¹⁸From this, you do not waken. ¹⁹The special relationship is your determination to keep your hold on unreality, and to prevent yourself from waking. ²⁰And while you see more value in sleeping than in waking, you will not let go of it.

6. The Holy Spirit, ever practical in His wisdom, accepts your dreams and uses them as means for waking. ²You would have used them to remain asleep. ³I said before that the first change, before dreams disappear, is that your dreams of fear are changed to happy dreams. ⁴That is what the Holy Spirit does in the special relationship. ⁵He does not destroy it, nor snatch it away from you. ⁶But He does use it differently, as a help to make His purpose real to you. ⁷The special relationship will remain, not as a source of pain and guilt, but as a source of joy and freedom. ⁸It will not be for you alone, for therein lay its misery. ⁹As its unholiness kept it a thing apart, its holiness will become an offering to everyone.

7. Your special relationship will be a means for undoing guilt in everyone blessed through your holy relationship. ²It will be a happy dream, and one which you will share with all who come within your sight. ³Through it, the blessing the Holy Spirit has laid upon it will be extended. ⁴Think not that He has forgotten anyone in the purpose He has given you. ⁵And think not that He has forgotten you to whom He gave the gift. ⁶He uses everyone who calls on Him as means for the salvation of everyone. ⁷And He will waken everyone through you who offered your relationship to Him. ⁸If you but recognized His gratitude! ⁹Or mine through His! ¹⁰For we are joined as in one purpose, being of one mind with Him.

8. Let not the dream take hold to close your eyes. ²It is not strange that dreams can make a world that is unreal. ³It is the *wish* to make it that is incredible. ⁴Your relationship with your brother has now become one in which the wish has been removed, because its purpose has been changed from one of dreams to one of truth. ⁵You are not sure of this because you think it may be this that is the dream. ⁶You are so used to choosing among dreams you do not see that you have made, at last, the choice between the truth and *all* illusions.

9. Yet Heaven is sure. ²This is no dream. ³Its coming means that you have chosen truth, and it has come because you have been

willing to let your special relationship meet its conditions. ⁴In your relationship the Holy Spirit has gently laid the real world; the world of happy dreams, from which awaking is so easy and so natural. ⁵For as your sleeping and your waking dreams represent the same wishes in your mind, so do the real world and the truth of Heaven join in the Will of God. ⁶The dream of waking is easily transferred to its reality. ⁷For this dream reflects your will joined with the Will of God. ⁸And what this Will would have accomplished has never *not* been done.

III. Light in the Dream

1. You who have spent your life in bringing truth to illusion, reality to fantasy, have walked the way of dreams. ²For you have gone from waking to sleeping, and on and on to a yet deeper sleep. ³Each dream has led to other dreams, and every fantasy that seemed to bring a light into the darkness but made the darkness deeper. ⁴Your goal was darkness, in which no ray of light could enter. ⁵And you sought a blackness so complete that you could hide from truth forever, in complete insanity. ⁶What you forgot was simply that God cannot destroy Himself. ⁷The light is *in* you. ⁸Darkness can cover it, but cannot put it out.

2. As the light comes nearer you will rush to darkness, shrinking from the truth, sometimes retreating to the lesser forms of fear, and sometimes to stark terror. ²But you will advance, because your goal is the advance from fear to truth. ³The goal you accepted is the goal of knowledge, for which you signified your willingness. ⁴Fear seems to live in darkness, and when you are afraid you have stepped back. ⁵Let us then join quickly in an instant of light, and it will be enough to remind you that your goal is light.

3. Truth has rushed to meet you since you called upon it. ²If you knew Who walks beside you on the way that you have chosen, fear would be impossible. ³You do not know because the journey into darkness has been long and cruel, and you have gone deep into it. ⁴A little flicker of your eyelids, closed so long, has not yet been sufficient to give you confidence in yourself, so long despised. ⁵You go toward love still hating it, and terribly afraid of its judgment upon you. ⁶And you do not realize that you are not afraid of love, but only of what you have made of it. ⁷You are

advancing to love's meaning, and away from all illusions in which you have surrounded it. ⁸When you retreat to the illusion your fear increases, for there is little doubt that what you think it means *is* fearful. ⁹Yet what is that to us who travel surely and very swiftly away from fear?

4. You who hold your brother's hand also hold mine, for when you joined each other you were not alone. ²Do you believe that I would leave you in the darkness that you agreed to leave with me? ³In your relationship is this world's light. ⁴And fear must disappear before you now. ⁵Be tempted not to snatch away the gift of faith you offered to your brother. ⁶You will succeed only in frightening yourself. ⁷The gift is given forever, for God Himself received it. ⁸You cannot take it back. ⁹You have accepted God. ¹⁰The holiness of your relationship is established in Heaven. ¹¹You do not understand what you accepted, but remember that your understanding is not necessary. ¹²All that was necessary was merely the *wish* to understand. ¹³That wish was the desire to be holy. ¹⁴The Will of God is granted you. ¹⁵For you desire the only thing you ever had, or ever were.

5. Each instant that we spend together will teach you that this goal is possible, and will strengthen your desire to reach it. ²And in your desire lies its accomplishment. ³Your desire is now in complete accord with all the power of the Holy Spirit's Will. ⁴No little, faltering footsteps that you may take can separate your desire from His Will and from His strength. ⁵I hold your hand as surely as you agreed to take your brother's. ⁶You will not separate, for I stand with you and walk with you in your advance to truth. ⁷And where we go we carry God with us.

6. In your relationship you have joined with me in bringing Heaven to the Son of God, who hid in darkness. ²You have been willing to bring the darkness to light, and this willingness has given strength to everyone who would remain in darkness. ³Those who would see *will* see. ⁴And they will join with me in carrying their light into the darkness, when the darkness in them is offered to the light, and is removed forever. ⁵My need for you, joined with me in the holy light of your relationship, is your need for salvation. ⁶Would I not give you what you gave to me? ⁷For when you joined your brother, you answered me.

7. You who are now the bringer of salvation have the function of bringing light to darkness. ²The darkness in you has been brought to light. ³Carry it back to darkness, from the holy instant

379

to which you brought it. ⁴We are made whole in our desire to make whole. ⁵Let not time worry you, for all the fear that you and your brother experience is really past. ⁶Time has been readjusted to help us do, together, what your separate pasts would hinder. ⁷You have gone past fear, for no two minds can join in the desire for love without love's joining them.

8. Not one light in Heaven but goes with you. ²Not one Ray that shines forever in the Mind of God but shines on you. ³Heaven is joined with you in your advance to Heaven. ⁴When such great lights have joined with you to give the little spark of your desire the power of God Himself, can you remain in darkness? ⁵You and your brother are coming home together, after a long and meaningless journey that you undertook apart, and that led nowhere. ⁶You have found your brother, and you will light each other's way. ⁷And from this light will the Great Rays extend back into darkness and forward unto God, to shine away the past and so make room for His eternal Presence, in which everything is radiant in the light.

IV. The Little Willingness

1. The holy instant is the result of your determination to be holy. ²It is the *answer*. ³The desire and the willingness to let it come precede its coming. ⁴You prepare your mind for it only to the extent of recognizing that you want it above all else. ⁵It is not necessary that you do more; indeed, it is necessary that you realize that you cannot do more. ⁶Do not attempt to give the Holy Spirit what He does not ask, or you will add the ego to Him and confuse the two. ⁷He asks but little. ⁸It is He Who adds the greatness and the might. ⁹He joins with you to make the holy instant far greater than you can understand. ¹⁰It is your realization that you need do so little that enables Him to give so much.

2. Trust not your good intentions. ²They are not enough. ³But trust implicitly your willingness, whatever else may enter. ⁴Concentrate only on this, and be not disturbed that shadows surround it. ⁵That is why you came. ⁶If you could come without them you would not need the holy instant. ⁷Come to it not in arrogance, assuming that you must achieve the state its coming brings with it. ⁸The miracle of the holy instant lies in your willingness to let it be what it is. ⁹And in your willingness for this lies

also your acceptance of yourself as you were meant to be.

3. Humility will never ask that you remain content with little-ness. ²But it does require that you be not content with less than greatness that comes not of you. ³Your difficulty with the holy instant arises from your fixed conviction that you are not worthy of it. ⁴And what is this but the determination to be as you would make yourself? ⁵God did not create His dwelling place unworthy of Him. ⁶And if you believe He cannot enter where He wills to be, you must be interfering with His Will. ⁷You do not need the strength of willingness to come from you, but only from His Will.

4. The holy instant does not come from your little willingness alone. ²It is always the result of your small willingness combined with the unlimited power of God's Will. ³You have been wrong in thinking that it is needful to prepare yourself for Him. ⁴It is im-possible to make arrogant preparations for holiness, and not be-lieve that it is up to you to establish the conditions for peace. ⁵God has established them. ⁶They do not wait upon your willing-ness for what they are. ⁷Your willingness is needed only to make it possible to teach you what they are. ⁸If you maintain you are unworthy of learning this, you are interfering with the lesson by believing that you must make the learner different. ⁹You did not make the learner, nor can you make him different. ¹⁰Would you first make a miracle yourself, and then expect one to be made *for* you?

5. You merely ask the question. ²The answer is given. ³Seek not to answer, but merely to receive the answer as it is given. ⁴In prepar-ing for the holy instant, do not attempt to make yourself holy to be ready to receive it. ⁵That is but to confuse your role with God's. ⁶Atonement cannot come to those who think that they must first atone, but only to those who offer it nothing more than simple willingness to make way for it. ⁷Purification is of God alone, and therefore for you. ⁸Rather than seek to prepare your-self for Him, try to think thus:

> ⁹*I who am host to God am worthy of Him.*
> ¹⁰*He Who established His dwelling place in me created it as He would have it be.*
> ¹¹*It is not needful that I make it ready for Him, but only that I do not interfere with His plan to restore to me my own awareness of my readiness, which is eternal.*
> ¹²*I need add nothing to His plan.*

> [13]But to receive it, I must be willing not to substitute my
> own in place of it.

6.   And that is all. [2]Add more, and you will merely take away the
little that is asked. [3]Remember you made guilt, and that your
plan for the escape from guilt has been to bring Atonement to it,
and make salvation fearful. [4]And it is only fear that you will add,
if you prepare yourself for love. [5]The preparation for the holy
instant belongs to Him Who gives it. [6]Release yourself to Him
Whose function is release. [7]Do not assume His function for Him.
[8]Give Him but what He asks, that you may learn how little is
your part, and how great is His.

7.   It is this that makes the holy instant so easy and so natural.
[2]You make it difficult, because you insist there must be more that
you need do. [3]You find it difficult to accept the idea that you need
give so little, to receive so much. [4]And it is very hard for you to
realize it is not personally insulting that your contribution and
the Holy Spirit's are so extremely disproportionate. [5]You are still
convinced that your understanding is a powerful contribution to
the truth, and makes it what it is. [6]Yet we have emphasized that
you need understand nothing. [7]Salvation is easy just *because* it
asks nothing you cannot give right now.

8.   Forget not that it has been your decision to make everything
that is natural and easy for you impossible. [2]If you believe the
holy instant is difficult for you, it is because you have become the
arbiter of what is possible, and remain unwilling to give place to
One Who knows. [3]The whole belief in orders of difficulty in miracles is centered on this. [4]Everything God wills is not only possible, but has already happened. [5]And that is why the past has
gone. [6]It never happened in reality. [7]Only in your mind, which
thought it did, is its undoing needful.

V. The Happy Dream

1.   Prepare you *now* for the undoing of what never was. [2]If you
already understood the difference between truth and illusion, the
Atonement would have no meaning. [3]The holy instant, the holy
relationship, the Holy Spirit's teaching, and all the means by
which salvation is accomplished, would have no purpose. [4]For
they are all but aspects of the plan to change your dreams of fear

to happy dreams, from which you waken easily to knowledge. ⁵Put yourself not in charge of this, for you cannot distinguish between advance and retreat. ⁶Some of your greatest advances you have judged as failures, and some of your deepest retreats you have evaluated as success.

2. Never approach the holy instant after you have tried to remove all fear and hatred from your mind. ²That is *its* function. ³Never attempt to overlook your guilt before you ask the Holy Spirit's help. ⁴That is *His* function. ⁵Your part is only to offer Him a little willingness to let Him remove all fear and hatred, and to be forgiven. ⁶On your little faith, joined with His understanding, He will build your part in the Atonement and make sure that you fulfill it easily. ⁷And with Him, you will build a ladder planted in the solid rock of faith, and rising even to Heaven. ⁸Nor will you use it to ascend to Heaven alone.

3. Through your holy relationship, reborn and blessed in every holy instant you do not arrange, thousands will rise to Heaven with you. ²Can you plan for this? ³Or could you prepare yourself for such a function? ⁴Yet it is possible, because God wills it. ⁵Nor will He change His Mind about it. ⁶The means and purpose both belong to Him. ⁷You have accepted one; the other will be provided. ⁸A purpose such as this, without the means, is inconceivable. ⁹He will provide the means to anyone who shares His purpose.

4. Happy dreams come true, not because they are dreams, but only because they are happy. ²And so they must be loving. ³Their message is, "Thy Will be done," and not, "I want it otherwise." ⁴The alignment of means and purpose is an undertaking impossible for you to understand. ⁵You do not even realize you have accepted the Holy Spirit's purpose as your own, and you would merely bring unholy means to its accomplishment. ⁶The little faith it needed to change the purpose is all that is required to receive the means and use them.

5. It is no dream to love your brother as yourself. ²Nor is your holy relationship a dream. ³All that remains of dreams within it is that it is still a special relationship. ⁴Yet it is very useful to the Holy Spirit, Who *has* a special function here. ⁵It will become the happy dream through which He can spread joy to thousands on thousands who believe that love is fear, not happiness. ⁶Let Him fulfill the function that He gave to your relationship by accepting it for you, and nothing will be wanting that would make of it

what He would have it be.

6.   When you feel the holiness of your relationship is threatened by anything, stop instantly and offer the Holy Spirit your willingness, in spite of fear, to let Him exchange this instant for the holy one that you would rather have. ²He will never fail in this. ³But forget not that your relationship is one, and so it must be that whatever threatens the peace of one is an equal threat to the other. ⁴The power of joining its blessing lies in the fact that it is now impossible for you or your brother to experience fear alone, or to attempt to deal with it alone. ⁵Never believe that this is necessary, or even possible. ⁶Yet just as this is impossible, so is it equally impossible that the holy instant come to either of you without the other. ⁷And it will come to both at the request of either.

7.   Whoever is saner at the time the threat is perceived should remember how deep is his indebtedness to the other and how much gratitude is due him, and be glad that he can pay his debt by bringing happiness to both. ²Let him remember this, and say:

> ³I desire this holy instant for myself, that I may share it
> with my brother, whom I love.
> ⁴It is not possible that I can have it without him, or he
> without me.
> ⁵Yet it is wholly possible for us to share it now.
> ⁶And so I choose this instant as the one to offer to the Holy
> Spirit, that His blessing may descend on us, and keep us
> both in peace.

VI. Beyond the Body

1.   There is nothing outside you. ²That is what you must ultimately learn, for it is the realization that the Kingdom of Heaven is restored to you. ³For God created only this, and He did not depart from it nor leave it separate from Himself. ⁴The Kingdom of Heaven is the dwelling place of the Son of God, who left not his Father and dwells not apart from Him. ⁵Heaven is not a place nor a condition. ⁶It is merely an awareness of perfect Oneness, and the knowledge that there is nothing else; nothing outside this Oneness, and nothing else within.

2.   What could God give but knowledge of Himself? ²What else is

there to give? ³The belief that you could give and get something else, something outside yourself, has cost you the awareness of Heaven and of your Identity. ⁴And you have done a stranger thing than you yet realize. ⁵You have displaced your guilt to your body from your mind. ⁶Yet a body cannot be guilty, for it can do nothing of itself. ⁷You who think you hate your body deceive yourself. ⁸You hate your mind, for guilt has entered into it, and it would remain separate from your brother's, which it cannot do.

3. Minds are joined; bodies are not. ²Only by assigning to the mind the properties of the body does separation seem to be possible. ³And it is mind that seems to be fragmented and private and alone. ⁴Its guilt, which keeps it separate, is projected to the body, which suffers and dies because it is attacked to hold the separation in the mind, and let it not know its Identity. ⁵Mind cannot attack, but it can make fantasies and direct the body to act them out. ⁶Yet it is never what the body does that seems to satisfy. ⁷Unless the mind believes the body is actually acting out its fantasies, it will attack the body by increasing the projection of its guilt upon it.

4. In this, the mind is clearly delusional. ²It cannot attack, but it maintains it can, and uses what it does to hurt the body to prove it can. ³The mind cannot attack, but it can deceive itself. ⁴And this is all it does when it believes it has attacked the body. ⁵It can project its guilt, but it will not lose it through projection. ⁶And though it clearly can misperceive the function of the body, it cannot change its function from what the Holy Spirit establishes it to be. ⁷The body was not made by love. ⁸Yet love does not condemn it and can use it lovingly, respecting what the Son of God has made and using it to save him from illusions.

5. Would you not have the instruments of separation reinterpreted as means for salvation, and used for purposes of love? ²Would you not welcome and support the shift from fantasies of vengeance to release from them? ³Your perception of the body can clearly be sick, but project not this upon the body. ⁴For your wish to make destructive what cannot destroy can have no real effect at all. ⁵What God created is only what He would have it be, being His Will. ⁶You cannot make His Will destructive. ⁷You can make fantasies in which your will conflicts with His, but that is all.

6. It is insane to use the body as the scapegoat for guilt, directing its attack and blaming it for what you wished it to do. ²It is

impossible to act out fantasies. ³For it is still the fantasies you want, and they have nothing to do with what the body does. ⁴It does not dream of them, and they but make it a liability where it could be an asset. ⁵For fantasies have made your body your "enemy"; weak, vulnerable and treacherous, worthy of the hate that you invest in it. ⁶How has this served you? ⁷You have identified with this thing you hate, the instrument of vengeance and the perceived source of your guilt. ⁸You have done this to a thing that has no meaning, proclaiming it to be the dwelling place of God's Son, and turning it against him.

7.   This is the host of God that *you* have made. ²And neither God nor His most holy Son can enter an abode that harbors hate, and where you have sown the seeds of vengeance, violence and death. ³This thing you made to serve your guilt stands between you and other minds. ⁴The minds *are* joined, but you do not identify with them. ⁵You see yourself locked in a separate prison, removed and unreachable, incapable of reaching out as being reached. ⁶You hate this prison you have made, and would destroy it. ⁷But you would not escape from it, leaving it unharmed, without your guilt upon it.

8.   Yet only thus *can* you escape. ²The home of vengeance is not yours; the place you set aside to house your hate is not a prison, but an illusion of yourself. ³The body is a limit imposed on the universal communication that is an eternal property of mind. ⁴But the communication is internal. ⁵Mind reaches to itself. ⁶It is *not* made up of different parts, which reach each other. ⁷It does not go out. ⁸Within itself it has no limits, and there is nothing outside it. ⁹It encompasses everything. ¹⁰It encompasses you entirely; you within it and it within you. ¹¹There is nothing else, anywhere or ever.

9.   The body is outside you, and but seems to surround you, shutting you off from others and keeping you apart from them, and them from you. ²It is not there. ³There is no barrier between God and His Son, nor can His Son be separated from Himself except in illusions. ⁴This is not his reality, though he believes it is. ⁵Yet this could only be if God were wrong. ⁶God would have had to create differently, and to have separated Himself from His Son to make this possible. ⁷He would have had to create different things, and to establish different orders of reality, only some of which were love. ⁸Yet love must be forever like itself, changeless forever, and forever without alternative. ⁹And so it is. ¹⁰You can-

not put a barrier around yourself, because God placed none between Himself and you.

10.   You can stretch out your hand and reach to Heaven. ²You whose hand is joined with your brother's have begun to reach beyond the body, but not outside yourself, to reach your shared Identity together. ³Could this be outside you? ⁴Where God is not? ⁵Is *He* a body, and did He create you as He is not, and where He cannot be? ⁶You are surrounded only by Him. ⁷What limits can there be on you whom He encompasses?

11.   Everyone has experienced what he would call a sense of being transported beyond himself. ²This feeling of liberation far exceeds the dream of freedom sometimes hoped for in special relationships. ³It is a sense of actual escape from limitations. ⁴If you will consider what this "transportation" really entails, you will realize that it is a sudden unawareness of the body, and a joining of yourself and something else in which your mind enlarges to encompass it. ⁵It becomes part of you, as you unite with it. ⁶And both become whole, as neither is perceived as separate. ⁷What really happens is that you have given up the illusion of a limited awareness, and lost your fear of union. ⁸The love that instantly replaces it extends to what has freed you, and unites with it. ⁹And while this lasts you are not uncertain of your Identity, and would not limit It. ¹⁰You have escaped from fear to peace, asking no questions of reality, but merely accepting it. ¹¹You have accepted this instead of the body, and have let yourself be one with something beyond it, simply by not letting your mind be limited by it.

12.   This can occur regardless of the physical distance that seems to be between you and what you join; of your respective positions in space; and of your differences in size and seeming quality. ²Time is not relevant; it can occur with something past, present or anticipated. ³The "something" can be anything and anywhere; a sound, a sight, a thought, a memory, and even a general idea without specific reference. ⁴Yet in every case, you join it without reservation because you love it, and would be with it. ⁵And so you rush to meet it, letting your limits melt away, suspending all the "laws" your body obeys and gently setting them aside.

13.   There is no violence at all in this escape. ²The body is not attacked, but simply properly perceived. ³It does not limit you, merely because you would not have it so. ⁴You are not really "lifted out" of it; it cannot contain you. ⁵You go where you would

387

be, gaining, not losing, a sense of Self. ⁶In these instants of release from physical restrictions, you experience much of what happens in the holy instant; the lifting of the barriers of time and space, the sudden experience of peace and joy, and, above all, the lack of awareness of the body, and of the questioning whether or not all this is possible.

14. It is possible because you want it. ²The sudden expansion of awareness that takes place with your desire for it is the irresistible appeal the holy instant holds. ³It calls to you to be yourself, within its safe embrace. ⁴There are the laws of limit lifted for you, to welcome you to openness of mind and freedom. ⁵Come to this place of refuge, where you can be yourself in peace. ⁶Not through destruction, not through a breaking out, but merely by a quiet melting in. ⁷For peace will join you there, simply because you have been willing to let go the limits you have placed upon love, and joined it where it is and where it led you, in answer to its gentle call to be at peace.

VII. I Need Do Nothing

1. You still have too much faith in the body as a source of strength. ²What plans do you make that do not involve its comfort or protection or enjoyment in some way? ³This makes the body an end and not a means in your interpretation, and this always means you still find sin attractive. ⁴No one accepts Atonement for himself who still accepts sin as his goal. ⁵You have thus not met your *one* responsibility. ⁶Atonement is not welcomed by those who prefer pain and destruction.

2. There is one thing that you have never done; you have not utterly forgotten the body. ²It has perhaps faded at times from your sight, but it has not yet completely disappeared. ³You are not asked to let this happen for more than an instant, yet it is in this instant that the miracle of Atonement happens. ⁴Afterwards you will see the body again, but never quite the same. ⁵And every instant that you spend without awareness of it gives you a different view of it when you return.

3. At no single instant does the body exist at all. ²It is always remembered or anticipated, but never experienced just *now*. ³Only its past and future make it seem real. ⁴Time controls it entirely, for sin is never wholly in the present. ⁵In any single instant

the attraction of guilt would be experienced as pain and nothing else, and would be avoided. ⁶It has no attraction *now.* ⁷Its whole attraction is imaginary, and therefore must be thought of in the past or in the future.

4. It is impossible to accept the holy instant without reservation unless, just for an instant, you are willing to see no past or future. ²You cannot prepare for it without placing it in the future. ³Release is given you the instant you desire it. ⁴Many have spent a lifetime in preparation, and have indeed achieved their instants of success. ⁵This course does not attempt to teach more than they learned in time, but it does aim at saving time. ⁶You may be attempting to follow a very long road to the goal you have accepted. ⁷It is extremely difficult to reach Atonement by fighting against sin. ⁸Enormous effort is expended in the attempt to make holy what is hated and despised. ⁹Nor is a lifetime of contemplation and long periods of meditation aimed at detachment from the body necessary. ¹⁰All such attempts will ultimately succeed because of their purpose. ¹¹Yet the means are tedious and very time consuming, for all of them look to the future for release from a state of present unworthiness and inadequacy.

5. Your way will be different, not in purpose but in means. ²A holy relationship is a means of saving time. ³One instant spent together with your brother restores the universe to both of you. ⁴You *are* prepared. ⁵Now you need but to remember you need do nothing. ⁶It would be far more profitable now merely to concentrate on this than to consider what you should do. ⁷When peace comes at last to those who wrestle with temptation and fight against the giving in to sin; when the light comes at last into the mind given to contemplation; or when the goal is finally achieved by anyone, it always comes with just one happy realization; *"I need do nothing."*

6. Here is the ultimate release which everyone will one day find in his own way, at his own time. ²You do not need this time. ³Time has been saved for you because you and your brother are together. ⁴This is the special means this course is using to save you time. ⁵You are not making use of the course if you insist on using means which have served others well, neglecting what was made for *you.* ⁶Save time for me by only this one preparation, and practice doing nothing else. ⁷"I need do nothing" is a statement of allegiance, a truly undivided loyalty. ⁸Believe it for just one instant, and you will accomplish more than is given to a century

389

of contemplation, or of struggle against temptation.

7. To do anything involves the body. ²And if you recognize you need do nothing, you have withdrawn the body's value from your mind. ³Here is the quick and open door through which you slip past centuries of effort, and escape from time. ⁴This is the way in which sin loses all attraction *right now*. ⁵For here is time denied, and past and future gone. ⁶Who needs do nothing has no need for time. ⁷To do nothing is to rest, and make a place within you where the activity of the body ceases to demand attention. ⁸Into this place the Holy Spirit comes, and there abides. ⁹He will remain when you forget, and the body's activities return to occupy your conscious mind.

8. Yet there will always be this place of rest to which you can return. ²And you will be more aware of this quiet center of the storm than all its raging activity. ³This quiet center, in which you do nothing, will remain with you, giving you rest in the midst of every busy doing on which you are sent. ⁴For from this center will you be directed how to use the body sinlessly. ⁵It is this center, from which the body is absent, that will keep it so in your awareness of it.

VIII. The Little Garden

1. It is only the awareness of the body that makes love seem limited. ²For the body *is* a limit on love. ³The belief in limited love was its origin, and it was made to limit the unlimited. ⁴Think not that this is merely allegorical, for it was made to limit *you*. ⁵Can you who see yourself within a body know yourself as an idea? ⁶Everything you recognize you identify with externals, something outside itself. ⁷You cannot even think of God without a body, or in some form you think you recognize.

2. The body cannot know. ²And while you limit your awareness to its tiny senses, you will not see the grandeur that surrounds you. ³God cannot come into a body, nor can you join Him there. ⁴Limits on love will always seem to shut Him out, and keep you apart from Him. ⁵The body is a tiny fence around a little part of a glorious and complete idea. ⁶It draws a circle, infinitely small, around a very little segment of Heaven, splintered from the whole, proclaiming that within it is your kingdom, where God can enter not.

3. Within this kingdom the ego rules, and cruelly. ²And to defend this little speck of dust it bids you fight against the universe. ³This fragment of your mind is such a tiny part of it that, could you but appreciate the whole, you would see instantly that it is like the smallest sunbeam to the sun, or like the faintest ripple on the surface of the ocean. ⁴In its amazing arrogance, this tiny sunbeam has decided it is the sun; this almost imperceptible ripple hails itself as the ocean. ⁵Think how alone and frightened is this little thought, this infinitesimal illusion, holding itself apart against the universe. ⁶The sun becomes the sunbeam's "enemy" that would devour it, and the ocean terrifies the little ripple and wants to swallow it.

4. Yet neither sun nor ocean is even aware of all this strange and meaningless activity. ²They merely continue, unaware that they are feared and hated by a tiny segment of themselves. ³Even that segment is not lost to them, for it could not survive apart from them. ⁴And what it thinks it is in no way changes its total dependence on them for its being. ⁵Its whole existence still remains in them. ⁶Without the sun the sunbeam would be gone; the ripple without the ocean is inconceivable.

5. Such is the strange position in which those in a world inhabited by bodies seem to be. ²Each body seems to house a separate mind, a disconnected thought, living alone and in no way joined to the Thought by which it was created. ³Each tiny fragment seems to be self-contained, needing another for some things, but by no means totally dependent on its one Creator for everything; needing the whole to give it any meaning, for by itself it does mean nothing. ⁴Nor has it any life apart and by itself.

6. Like to the sun and ocean your Self continues, unmindful that this tiny part regards itself as you. ²It is not missing; it could not exist if it were separate, nor would the whole be whole without it. ³It is not a separate kingdom, ruled by an idea of separation from the rest. ⁴Nor does a fence surround it, preventing it from joining with the rest, and keeping it apart from its Creator. ⁵This little aspect is no different from the whole, being continuous with it and at one with it. ⁶It leads no separate life, because its life *is* the oneness in which its being was created.

7. Do not accept this little, fenced-off aspect as yourself. ²The sun and ocean are as nothing beside what you are. ³The sunbeam sparkles only in the sunlight, and the ripple dances as it rests upon the ocean. ⁴Yet in neither sun nor ocean is the power that

rests in you. ⁵Would you remain within your tiny kingdom, a sorry king, a bitter ruler of all that he surveys, who looks on nothing yet who would still die to defend it? ⁶This little self is not your kingdom. ⁷Arched high above it and surrounding it with love is the glorious whole, which offers all its happiness and deep content to every part. ⁸The little aspect that you think you set apart is no exception.

8. Love knows no bodies, and reaches to everything created like itself. ²Its total lack of limit *is* its meaning. ³It is completely impartial in its giving, encompassing only to preserve and keep complete what it would give. ⁴In your tiny kingdom you have so little! ⁵Should it not, then, be there that you would call on love to enter? ⁶Look at the desert—dry and unproductive, scorched and joyless—that makes up your little kingdom. ⁷And realize the life and joy that love would bring to it from where it comes, and where it would return with you.

9. The Thought of God surrounds your little kingdom, waiting at the barrier you built to come inside and shine upon the barren ground. ²See how life springs up everywhere! ³The desert becomes a garden, green and deep and quiet, offering rest to those who lost their way and wander in the dust. ⁴Give them a place of refuge, prepared by love for them where once a desert was. ⁵And everyone you welcome will bring love with him from Heaven for you. ⁶They enter one by one into this holy place, but they will not depart as they had come, alone. ⁷The love they brought with them will stay with them, as it will stay with you. ⁸And under its beneficence your little garden will expand, and reach out to everyone who thirsts for living water, but has grown too weary to go on alone.

10. Go out and find them, for they bring your Self with them. ²And lead them gently to your quiet garden, and receive their blessing there. ³So will it grow and stretch across the desert, leaving no lonely little kingdoms locked away from love, and leaving you inside. ⁴And you will recognize yourself, and see your little garden gently transformed into the Kingdom of Heaven, with all the Love of its Creator shining upon it.

11. The holy instant is your invitation to love to enter into your bleak and joyless kingdom, and to transform it into a garden of peace and welcome. ²Love's answer is inevitable. ³It will come because you came without the body, and interposed no barriers to interfere with its glad coming. ⁴In the holy instant, you ask of

love only what it offers everyone, neither less nor more. ⁵Asking for everything, you will receive it. ⁶And your shining Self will lift the tiny aspect that you tried to hide from Heaven straight to Heaven. ⁷No part of love calls on the whole in vain. ⁸No Son of God remains outside His Fatherhood.

12. Be sure of this; love has entered your special relationship, and entered fully at your weak request. ²You do not recognize that love has come, because you have not yet let go of all the barriers you hold against your brother. ³And you and he will not be able to give love welcome separately. ⁴You could no more know God alone than He knows you without your brother. ⁵But together you could no more be unaware of love than love could know you not, or fail to recognize itself in you.

13. You have reached the end of an ancient journey, not realizing yet that it is over. ²You are still worn and tired, and the desert's dust still seems to cloud your eyes and keep you sightless. ³Yet He Whom you welcomed has come to you, and would welcome you. ⁴He has waited long to give you this. ⁵Receive it now of Him, for He would have you know Him. ⁶Only a little wall of dust still stands between you and your brother. ⁷Blow on it lightly and with happy laughter, and it will fall away. ⁸And walk into the garden love has prepared for both of you.

IX. The Two Worlds

1. You have been told to bring the darkness to the light, and guilt to holiness. ²And you have also been told that error must be corrected at its source. ³Therefore, it is the tiny part of yourself, the little thought that seems split off and separate, the Holy Spirit needs. ⁴The rest is fully in God's keeping, and needs no guide. ⁵Yet this wild and delusional thought needs help because, in its delusions, it thinks it is the Son of God, whole and omnipotent, sole ruler of the kingdom it set apart to tyrannize by madness into obedience and slavery. ⁶This is the little part you think you stole from Heaven. ⁷Give it back to Heaven. ⁸Heaven has not lost it, but *you* have lost sight of Heaven. ⁹Let the Holy Spirit remove it from the withered kingdom in which you set it off, surrounded by darkness, guarded by attack and reinforced by hate. ¹⁰Within its barricades is still a tiny segment of the Son of God, complete and holy, serene and unaware of what you think surrounds it.

2. Be you not separate, for the One Who does surround it has brought union to you, returning your little offering of darkness to the eternal light. ²How is this done? ³It is extremely simple, being based on what this little kingdom really is. ⁴The barren sands, the darkness and the lifelessness, are seen only through the body's eyes. ⁵Its bleak sight is distorted, and the messages it transmits to you who made it to limit your awareness are little and limited, and so fragmented they are meaningless.

3. From the world of bodies, made by insanity, insane messages seem to be returned to the mind that made it. ²And these messages bear witness to this world, pronouncing it as true. ³For you sent forth these messengers to bring this back to you. ⁴Everything these messages relay to you is quite external. ⁵There are no messages that speak of what lies underneath, for it is not the body that could speak of this. ⁶Its eyes perceive it not; its senses remain quite unaware of it; its tongue cannot relay its messages. ⁷Yet God can bring you there, if you are willing to follow the Holy Spirit through seeming terror, trusting Him not to abandon you and leave you there. ⁸For it is not His purpose to frighten you, but only yours. ⁹You are severely tempted to abandon Him at the outside ring of fear, but He would lead you safely through and far beyond.

4. The circle of fear lies just below the level the body sees, and seems to be the whole foundation on which the world is based. ²Here are all the illusions, all the twisted thoughts, all the insane attacks, the fury, the vengeance and betrayal that were made to keep the guilt in place, so that the world could rise from it and keep it hidden. ³Its shadow rises to the surface, enough to hold its most external manifestations in darkness, and to bring despair and loneliness to it and keep it joyless. ⁴Yet its intensity is veiled by its heavy coverings, and kept apart from what was made to keep it hidden. ⁵The body cannot see this, for the body arose from this for its protection, which depends on keeping it not seen. ⁶The body's eyes will never look on it. ⁷Yet they will see what it dictates.

5. The body will remain guilt's messenger, and will act as it directs as long as you believe that guilt is real. ²For the reality of guilt is the illusion that seems to make it heavy and opaque, impenetrable, and a real foundation for the ego's thought system. ³Its thinness and transparency are not apparent until you see the light behind it. ⁴And then you see it as a fragile veil before the light.

394

6. This heavy-seeming barrier, this artificial floor that looks like rock, is like a bank of low dark clouds that seem to be a solid wall before the sun. ²Its impenetrable appearance is wholly an illusion. ³It gives way softly to the mountain tops that rise above it, and has no power at all to hold back anyone willing to climb above it and see the sun. ⁴It is not strong enough to stop a button's fall, nor hold a feather. ⁵Nothing can rest upon it, for it is but an illusion of a foundation. ⁶Try but to touch it and it disappears; attempt to grasp it and your hands hold nothing.

7. Yet in this cloud bank it is easy to see a whole world rising. ²A solid mountain range, a lake, a city, all rise in your imagination, and from the clouds the messengers of your perception return to you, assuring you that it is there. ³Figures stand out and move about, actions seem real, and forms appear and shift from loveliness to the grotesque. ⁴And back and forth they go, as long as you would play the game of children's make-believe. ⁵Yet however long you play it, and regardless of how much imagination you bring to it, you do not confuse it with the world below, nor seek to make it real.

8. So should it be with the dark clouds of guilt, no more impenetrable and no more substantial. ²You will not bruise yourself against them in traveling through. ³Let your Guide teach you their unsubstantial nature as He leads you past them, for beneath them is a world of light whereon they cast no shadows. ⁴Their shadows lie upon the world beyond them, still further from the light. ⁵Yet from them to the light their shadows cannot fall.

9. This world of light, this circle of brightness is the real world, where guilt meets with forgiveness. ²Here the world outside is seen anew, without the shadow of guilt upon it. ³Here are you forgiven, for here you have forgiven everyone. ⁴Here is the new perception, where everything is bright and shining with innocence, washed in the waters of forgiveness, and cleansed of every evil thought you laid upon it. ⁵Here there is no attack upon the Son of God, and you are welcome. ⁶Here is your innocence, waiting to clothe you and protect you, and make you ready for the final step in the journey inward. ⁷Here are the dark and heavy garments of guilt laid by, and gently replaced by purity and love.

10. Yet even forgiveness is not the end. ²Forgiveness does make

. lovely, but it does not create. ³It is the source of healing, but it is the messenger of love and not its Source. ⁴Here you are led, that God Himself can take the final step unhindered, for here does nothing interfere with love, letting it be itself. ⁵A step beyond this holy place of forgiveness, a step still further inward but the one *you* cannot take, transports you to something completely different. ⁶Here is the Source of light; nothing perceived, forgiven nor transformed. ⁷But merely known.

11.   This course will lead to knowledge, but knowledge itself is still beyond the scope of our curriculum. ²Nor is there any need for us to try to speak of what must forever lie beyond words. ³We need remember only that whoever attains the real world, beyond which learning cannot go, will go beyond it, but in a different way. ⁴Where learning ends there God begins, for learning ends before Him Who is complete where He begins, and where there *is* no end. ⁵It is not for us to dwell on what cannot be attained. ⁶There is too much to learn. ⁷The readiness for knowledge still must be attained.

12.   Love is not learned. ²Its meaning lies within itself. ³And learning ends when you have recognized all it is *not*. ⁴That is the interference; that is what needs to be undone. ⁵Love is not learned, because there never was a time in which you knew it not. ⁶Learning is useless in the Presence of your Creator, Whose acknowledgment of you and yours of Him so far transcend all learning that everything you learned is meaningless, replaced forever by the knowledge of love and its one meaning.

13.   Your relationship with your brother has been uprooted from the world of shadows, and its unholy purpose has been safely brought through the barriers of guilt, washed with forgiveness, and set shining and firmly rooted in the world of light. ²From there it calls to you to follow the course it took, lifted high above the darkness and gently placed before the gates of Heaven. ³The holy instant in which you and your brother were united is but the messenger of love, sent from beyond forgiveness to remind you of all that lies beyond it. ⁴Yet it is through forgiveness that it will be remembered.

14.   And when the memory of God has come to you in the holy place of forgiveness you will remember nothing else, and memory will be as useless as learning, for your only purpose will be creating. ²Yet this you cannot know until every perception has been cleansed and purified, and finally removed forever. ³Forgiveness

removes only the untrue, lifting the shadows from the world and carrying it, safe and sure within its gentleness, to the bright world of new and clean perception. [4]There is your purpose *now*. [5]And it is there that peace awaits you.

Chapter 19

THE ATTAINMENT OF PEACE

I. Healing and Faith

1. We said before that when a situation has been dedicated wholly to truth, peace is inevitable. [2]Its attainment is the criterion by which the wholeness of the dedication can be safely assumed. [3]Yet we also said that peace without faith will never be attained, for what is dedicated to truth as its only goal is brought to truth *by* faith. [4]This faith encompasses everyone involved, for only thus the situation is perceived as meaningful and as a whole. [5]And everyone must be involved in it, or else your faith is limited and your dedication incomplete.

2. Every situation, properly perceived, becomes an opportunity to heal the Son of God. [2]And he is healed *because* you offered faith to him, giving him to the Holy Spirit and releasing him from every demand your ego would make of him. [3]Thus do you see him free, and in this vision does the Holy Spirit share. [4]And since He shares it He has given it, and so He heals through you. [5]It is this joining Him in a united purpose that makes this purpose real, because you make it whole. [6]And this *is* healing. [7]The body is healed because you came without it, and joined the Mind in which all healing rests.

3. The body cannot heal, because it cannot make itself sick. [2]It *needs* no healing. [3]Its health or sickness depends entirely on how the mind perceives it, and the purpose that the mind would use it for. [4]It is obvious that a segment of the mind can see itself as separated from the Universal Purpose. [5]When this occurs the body becomes its weapon, used against this Purpose, to demonstrate the "fact" that separation has occurred. [6]The body thus becomes the instrument of illusion, acting accordingly; seeing what is not there, hearing what truth has never said and behaving insanely, being imprisoned *by* insanity.

4. Do not overlook our earlier statement that faithlessness leads straight to illusions. [2]For faithlessness is the perception of a brother as a body, and the body cannot be used for purposes of union. [3]If, then, you see your brother as a body, you have established a condition in which uniting with him becomes impossible. [4]Your

faithlessness to him has separated you from him, and kept you both apart from being healed. [5]Your faithlessness has thus opposed the Holy Spirit's purpose, and brought illusions, centered on the body, to stand between you. [6]And the body will seem to be sick, for you have made of it an "enemy" of healing and the opposite of truth.

5. It cannot be difficult to realize that faith must be the opposite of faithlessness. [2]Yet the difference in how they operate is less apparent, though it follows directly from the fundamental difference in what they are. [3]Faithlessness would always limit and attack; faith would remove all limitations and make whole. [4]Faithlessness would destroy and separate; faith would unite and heal. [5]Faithlessness would interpose illusions between the Son of God and his Creator; faith would remove all obstacles that seem to rise between them. [6]Faithlessness is wholly dedicated to illusions; faith wholly to truth. [7]Partial dedication is impossible. [8]Truth is the absence of illusion; illusion the absence of truth. [9]Both cannot be together, nor perceived in the same place. [10]To dedicate yourself to both is to set up a goal forever impossible to attain, for part of it is sought through the body, thought of as a means for seeking out reality through attack. [11]The other part would heal, and therefore calls upon the mind and not the body.

6. The inevitable compromise is the belief that the body must be healed, and not the mind. [2]For this divided goal has given both an equal reality, which could be possible only if the mind is limited to the body and divided into little parts of seeming wholeness, but without connection. [3]This will not harm the body, but it *will* keep the delusional thought system in the mind. [4]Here, then, is healing needed. [5]And it is here that healing *is*. [6]For God gave healing not apart from sickness, nor established remedy where sickness cannot be. [7]They are together, and when they are seen together, all attempts to keep both truth and illusion in the mind, where both must be, are recognized as dedication to illusion; and given up when brought to truth, and seen as totally unreconcilable with truth, in any respect or in any way.

7. Truth and illusion have no connection. [2]This will remain forever true, however much you seek to connect them. [3]But illusions are always connected, as is truth. [4]Each is united, a complete thought system, but totally disconnected to each other. [5]And to perceive this is to recognize where separation is, and where it

must be healed. [6]The result of an idea is never separate from its source. [7]The idea of separation produced the body and remains connected to it, making it sick because of the mind's identification with it. [8]You think you are protecting the body by hiding this connection, for this concealment seems to keep your identification safe from the "attack" of truth.

8. If you but understood how much this strange concealment has hurt your mind, and how confused your own identification has become because of it! [2]You do not see how great the devastation wrought by your faithlessness, for faithlessness is an attack that seems to be justified by its results. [3]For by withholding faith you see what is unworthy of it, and cannot look beyond the barrier to what is joined with you.

9. To have faith is to heal. [2]It is the sign that you have accepted the Atonement for yourself, and would therefore share it. [3]By faith, you offer the gift of freedom from the past, which you received. [4]You do not use anything your brother has done before to condemn him now. [5]You freely choose to overlook his errors, looking past all barriers between yourself and him, and seeing them as one. [6]And in that one you see your faith is fully justified. [7]There is no justification for faithlessness, but faith is always justified.

10. Faith is the opposite of fear, as much a part of love as fear is of attack. [2]Faith is the acknowledgment of union. [3]It is the gracious acknowledgment of everyone as a Son of your most loving Father, loved by Him like you, and therefore loved by you as yourself. [4]It is His Love that joins you and your brother, and for His Love you would keep no one separate from yours. [5]Each one appears just as he is perceived in the holy instant, united in your purpose to be released from guilt. [6]You see the Christ in him, and he is healed because you look on what makes faith forever justified in everyone.

11. Faith is the gift of God, through Him Whom God has given you. [2]Faithlessness looks upon the Son of God, and judges him unworthy of forgiveness. [3]But through the eyes of faith, the Son of God is seen already forgiven, free of all the guilt he laid upon himself. [4]Faith sees him only *now* because it looks not to the past to judge him, but would see in him only what it would see in you. [5]It sees not through the body's eyes, nor looks to bodies for its justification. [6]It is the messenger of the new perception, sent forth to gather witnesses unto its coming, and to return their

messages to you.

12. Faith is as easily exchanged for knowledge as is the real world. [2]For faith arises from the Holy Spirit's perception, and is the sign you share it with Him. [3]Faith is a gift you offer to the Son of God through Him, and wholly acceptable to his Father as to Him. [4]And therefore offered you. [5]Your holy relationship, with its new purpose, offers you faith to give unto your brother. [6]Your faithlessness has driven you and him apart, and so you do not recognize salvation in him. [7]Yet faith unites you in the holiness you see, not through the body's eyes, but in the sight of Him Who joined you, and in Whom you are united.

13. Grace is not given to a body, but to a mind. [2]And the mind that receives it looks instantly beyond the body, and sees the holy place where it was healed. [3]There is the altar where the grace was given, in which it stands. [4]Do you, then, offer grace and blessing to your brother, for you stand at the same altar where grace was laid for both of you. [5]And be you healed by grace together, that you may heal through faith.

14. In the holy instant, you and your brother stand before the altar God has raised unto Himself and both of you. [2]Lay faithlessness aside, and come to it together. [3]There will you see the miracle of your relationship as it was made again through faith. [4]And there it is that you will realize that there is nothing faith cannot forgive. [5]No error interferes with its calm sight, which brings the miracle of healing with equal ease to all of them. [6]For what the messengers of love are sent to do they do, returning the glad tidings that it was done to you and your brother who stand together before the altar from which they were sent forth.

15. As faithlessness will keep your little kingdoms barren and separate, so will faith help the Holy Spirit prepare the ground for the most holy garden that He would make of it. [2]For faith brings peace, and so it calls on truth to enter and make lovely what has already been prepared for loveliness. [3]Truth follows faith and peace, completing the process of making lovely that they begin. [4]For faith is still a learning goal, no longer needed when the lesson has been learned. [5]Yet truth will stay forever.

16. Let, then, your dedication be to the eternal, and learn how not to interfere with it and make it slave to time. [2]For what you think you do to the eternal you do to *you.* [3]Whom God created as His Son is slave to nothing, being lord of all, along with his Creator. [4]You can enslave a body, but an idea is free, incapable of being

kept in prison or limited in any way except by the mind that thought it. ⁵For it remains joined to its source, which is its jailer or its liberator, according to which it chooses as its purpose for itself.

II. Sin versus Error

1. It is essential that error be not confused with sin, and it is this distinction that makes salvation possible. ²For error can be corrected, and the wrong made right. ³But sin, were it possible, would be irreversible. ⁴The belief in sin is necessarily based on the firm conviction that minds, not bodies, can attack. ⁵And thus the mind is guilty, and will forever so remain unless a mind not part of it can give it absolution. ⁶Sin calls for punishment as error for correction, and the belief that punishment *is* correction is clearly insane.

2. Sin is not an error, for sin entails an arrogance which the idea of error lacks. ²To sin would be to violate reality, and to succeed. ³Sin is the proclamation that attack is real and guilt is justified. ⁴It assumes the Son of God is guilty, and has thus succeeded in losing his innocence and making himself what God created not. ⁵Thus is creation seen as not eternal, and the Will of God open to opposition and defeat. ⁶Sin is the grand illusion underlying all the ego's grandiosity. ⁷For by it God Himself is changed, and rendered incomplete.

3. The Son of God can be mistaken; he can deceive himself; he can even turn the power of his mind against himself. ²But he *cannot* sin. ³There is nothing he can do that would really change his reality in any way, nor make him really guilty. ⁴That is what sin would do, for such is its purpose. ⁵Yet for all the wild insanity inherent in the whole idea of sin, it is impossible. ⁶For the wages of sin *is* death, and how can the immortal die?

4. A major tenet in the ego's insane religion is that sin is not error but truth, and it is innocence that would deceive. ²Purity is seen as arrogance, and the acceptance of the self as sinful is perceived as holiness. ³And it is this doctrine that replaces the reality of the Son of God as his Father created him, and willed that he be forever. ⁴Is this humility? ⁵Or is it, rather, an attempt to wrest creation away from truth, and keep it separate?

5. Any attempt to reinterpret sin as error is always indefensible

402

to the ego. ²The idea of sin is wholly sacrosanct to its thought system, and quite unapproachable except with reverence and awe. ³It is the most "holy" concept in the ego's system; lovely and powerful, wholly true, and necessarily protected with every defense at its disposal. ⁴For here lies its "best" defense, which all the others serve. ⁵Here is its armor, its protection, and the fundamental purpose of the special relationship in its interpretation.

6.   It can indeed be said the ego made its world on sin. ²Only in such a world could everything be upside down. ³This is the strange illusion that makes the clouds of guilt seem heavy and impenetrable. ⁴The solidness that this world's foundation seems to have is found in this. ⁵For sin has changed creation from an idea of God to an ideal the ego wants; a world it rules, made up of bodies, mindless and capable of complete corruption and decay. ⁶If this is a mistake, it can be undone easily by truth. ⁷Any mistake can be corrected, if truth be left to judge it. ⁸But if the mistake is given the status of truth, to what can it be brought? ⁹The "holiness" of sin is kept in place by just this strange device. ¹⁰As truth it is inviolate, and everything is brought to *it* for judgment. ¹¹As a mistake, *it* must be brought to truth. ¹²It is impossible to have faith in sin, for sin is faithlessness. ¹³Yet it is possible to have faith that a mistake can be corrected.

7.   There is no stone in all the ego's embattled citadel that is more heavily defended than the idea that sin is real; the natural expression of what the Son of God has made himself to be, and what he is. ²To the ego, this is no mistake. ³For this is its reality; this is the "truth" from which escape will always be impossible. ⁴This is his past, his present and his future. ⁵For he has somehow managed to corrupt his Father, and change His Mind completely. ⁶Mourn, then, the death of God, Whom sin has killed! ⁷And this would be the ego's wish, which in its madness it believes it has accomplished.

8.   Would you not rather that all this be nothing more than a mistake, entirely correctable, and so easily escaped from that its whole correction is like walking through a mist into the sun? ²For that is all it is. ³Perhaps you would be tempted to agree with the ego that it is far better to be sinful than mistaken. ⁴Yet think you carefully before you allow yourself to make this choice. ⁵Approach it not lightly, for it is the choice of hell or Heaven.

III. The Unreality of Sin

1.   The attraction of guilt is found in sin, not error. ²Sin will be repeated because of this attraction. ³Fear can become so acute that the sin is denied the acting out. ⁴But while the guilt remains attractive the mind will suffer, and not let go of the idea of sin. ⁵For guilt still calls to it, and the mind hears it and yearns for it, making itself a willing captive to its sick appeal. ⁶Sin is an idea of evil that cannot be corrected, and yet will be forever desirable. ⁷As an essential part of what the ego thinks you are, you will always want it. ⁸And only an avenger, with a mind unlike your own, could stamp it out through fear.

2.   The ego does not think it possible that love, not fear, is really called upon by sin, *and always answers*. ²For the ego brings sin to fear, demanding punishment. ³Yet punishment is but another form of guilt's protection, for what is deserving punishment must have been really done. ⁴Punishment is always the great preserver of sin, treating it with respect and honoring its enormity. ⁵What must be punished, must be true. ⁶And what is true must be eternal, and will be repeated endlessly. ⁷For what you think is real you want, and will not let it go.

3.   An error, on the other hand, is not attractive. ²What you see clearly as a mistake you want corrected. ³Sometimes a sin can be repeated over and over, with obviously distressing results, but without the loss of its appeal. ⁴And suddenly, you change its status from a sin to a mistake. ⁵Now you will not repeat it; you will merely stop and let it go, unless the guilt remains. ⁶For then you will but change the form of sin, granting that it was an error, but keeping it uncorrectable. ⁷This is not really a change in your perception, for it is sin that calls for punishment, not error.

4.   The Holy Spirit cannot punish sin. ²Mistakes He recognizes, and would correct them all as God entrusted Him to do. ³But sin He knows not, nor can He recognize mistakes that cannot be corrected. ⁴For a mistake that cannot be corrected is meaningless to Him. ⁵Mistakes are *for* correction, and they call for nothing else. ⁶What calls for punishment must call for nothing. ⁷Every mistake *must* be a call for love. ⁸What, then, is sin? ⁹What could it be but a mistake you would keep hidden; a call for help that you would keep unheard and thus unanswered?

5.   In time, the Holy Spirit clearly sees the Son of God can make mistakes. ²On this you share His vision. ³Yet you do not share His

recognition of the difference between time and eternity. ⁴And when correction is completed, time *is* eternity. ⁵The Holy Spirit can teach you how to look on time differently and see beyond it, but not while you believe in sin. ⁶In error, yes, for this can be corrected by the mind. ⁷But sin is the belief that your perception is unchangeable, and that the mind must accept as true what it is told through it. ⁸If it does not obey, the mind is judged insane. ⁹The only power that could change perception is thus kept impotent, held to the body by the fear of changed perception which its Teacher, Who is one with it, would bring.

6. When you are tempted to believe that sin is real, remember this: If sin is real, both God and you are not. ²If creation is extension, the Creator must have extended Himself, and it is impossible that what is part of Him is totally unlike the rest. ³If sin is real, God must be at war with Himself. ⁴He must be split, and torn between good and evil; partly sane and partially insane. ⁵For He must have created what wills to destroy Him, and has the power to do so. ⁶Is it not easier to believe that you have been mistaken than to believe in this?

7. While you believe that your reality or your brother's is bounded by a body, you will believe in sin. ²While you believe that bodies can unite, you will find guilt attractive and believe that sin is precious. ³For the belief that bodies limit mind leads to a perception of the world in which the proof of separation seems to be everywhere. ⁴And God and His creation seem to be split apart and overthrown. ⁵For sin would prove what God created holy could not prevail against it, nor remain itself before the power of sin. ⁶Sin is perceived as mightier than God, before which God Himself must bow, and offer His creation to its conqueror. ⁷Is this humility or madness?

8. If sin is real, it must forever be beyond the hope of healing. ²For there would be a power beyond God's, capable of making another will that could attack His Will and overcome it; and give His Son a will apart from His, and stronger. ³And each part of God's fragmented creation would have a different will, opposed to His, and in eternal opposition to Him and to each other. ⁴Your holy relationship has, as its purpose now, the goal of proving this is impossible. ⁵Heaven has smiled upon it, and the belief in sin has been uprooted in its smile of love. ⁶You see it still, because you do not realize that its foundation has gone. ⁷Its source has been removed, and so it can be cherished but a little while before

it vanishes. [8]Only the habit of looking for it still remains.

9.   And yet you look with Heaven's smile upon your lips, and Heaven's blessing on your sight. [2]You will not see sin long. [3]For in the new perception the mind corrects it when it seems to be seen, and it becomes invisible. [4]Errors are quickly recognized and quickly given to correction, to be healed, not hidden. [5]You will be healed of sin and all its ravages the instant that you give it no power over your brother. [6]And you will help him overcome mistakes by joyously releasing him from the belief in sin.

10.   In the holy instant, you will see the smile of Heaven shining on both you and your brother. [2]And you will shine upon him, in glad acknowledgment of the grace that has been given you. [3]For sin will not prevail against a union Heaven has smiled upon. [4]Your perception was healed in the holy instant Heaven gave you. [5]Forget what you have seen, and raise your eyes in faith to what you now can see. [6]The barriers to Heaven will disappear before your holy sight, for you who were sightless have been given vision, and you can see. [7]Look not for what has been removed, but for the glory that has been restored for you to see.

11.   Look upon your Redeemer, and behold what He would show you in your brother, and let not sin arise again to blind your eyes. [2]For sin would keep you separate from him, but your Redeemer would have you look upon your brother as yourself. [3]Your relationship is now a temple of healing; a place where all the weary ones can come and rest. [4]Here is the rest that waits for all, after the journey. [5]And it is brought nearer to all by your relationship.

IV. The Obstacles to Peace

1.   As peace extends from deep inside yourself to embrace all the Sonship and give it rest, it will encounter many obstacles. [2]Some of them you will try to impose. [3]Others will seem to arise from elsewhere; from your brothers, and from various aspects of the world outside. [4]Yet peace will gently cover them, extending past completely unencumbered. [5]The extension of the Holy Spirit's purpose from your relationship to others, to bring them gently in, is the way in which He will bring means and goal in line. [6]The peace He lay, deep within you and your brother, will quietly extend to every aspect of your life, surrounding you and your

brother with glowing happiness and the calm awareness of complete protection. ⁷And you will carry its message of love and safety and freedom to everyone who draws nigh unto your temple, where healing waits for him. ⁸You will not wait to give him this, for you will call to him and he will answer you, recognizing in your call the Call for God. ⁹And you will draw him in and give him rest, as it was given you.

2. All this will you do. ²Yet the peace that already lies deeply within must first expand, and flow across the obstacles you placed before it. ³This will you do, for nothing undertaken with the Holy Spirit remains unfinished. ⁴You can indeed be sure of nothing you see outside you, but of this you *can* be sure: The Holy Spirit asks that you offer Him a resting place where you will rest in Him. ⁵He answered you, and entered your relationship. ⁶Would you not now return His graciousness, and enter into a relationship with Him? ⁷For it is He Who offered your relationship the gift of holiness, without which it would have been forever impossible to appreciate your brother.

3. The gratitude you owe to Him He asks but that you receive for Him. ²And when you look with gentle graciousness upon your brother, you are beholding Him. ³For you are looking where He *is*, and not apart from Him. ⁴You cannot see the Holy Spirit, but you can see your brothers truly. ⁵And the light in them will show you all that you need to see. ⁶When the peace in you has been extended to encompass everyone, the Holy Spirit's function here will be accomplished. ⁷What need is there for seeing, then? ⁸When God has taken the last step Himself, the Holy Spirit will gather all the thanks and gratitude that you have offered Him, and lay them gently before His Creator in the Name of His most holy Son. ⁹And the Father will accept them in His Name. ¹⁰What need is there of seeing, in the presence of His gratitude?

A. The First Obstacle: The Desire to Get Rid of It

1. The first obstacle that peace must flow across is your desire to get rid of it. ²For it cannot extend unless you keep it. ³You are the center from which it radiates outward, to call the others in. ⁴You are its home; its tranquil dwelling place from which it gently reaches out, but never leaving you. ⁵If you would make it homeless, how can it abide within the Son of God? ⁶If it would spread across the whole creation, it must begin with you, and from you

reach to everyone who calls, and bring him rest by joining you.

2.   Why would you want peace homeless? ²What do you think that it must dispossess to dwell with you? ³What seems to be the cost you are so unwilling to pay? ⁴The little barrier of sand still stands between you and your brother. ⁵Would you reinforce it now? ⁶You are not asked to let it go for yourself alone. ⁷Christ asks it of you for Himself. ⁸He would bring peace to everyone, and how can He do this except through you? ⁹Would you let a little bank of sand, a wall of dust, a tiny seeming barrier, stand between your brothers and salvation? ¹⁰And yet, this little remnant of attack you cherish still against your brother *is* the first obstacle the peace in you encounters in its going forth. ¹¹This little wall of hatred would still oppose the Will of God, and keep it limited.

3.   The Holy Spirit's purpose rests in peace within you. ²Yet you are still unwilling to let it join you wholly. ³You still oppose the Will of God, just by a little. ⁴And that little is a limit you would place upon the whole. ⁵God's Will is One, not many. ⁶It has no opposition, for there is none beside it. ⁷What you would still contain behind your little barrier and keep separate from your brother seems mightier than the universe, for it would hold back the universe and its Creator. ⁸This little wall would hide the purpose of Heaven, and keep it *from* Heaven.

4.   Would you thrust salvation away from the giver of salvation? ²For such have you become. ³Peace could no more depart from you than from God. ⁴Fear not this little obstacle. ⁵It cannot contain the Will of God. ⁶Peace will flow across it, and join you without hindrance. ⁷Salvation cannot be withheld from you. ⁸It is your purpose. ⁹You cannot choose apart from this. ¹⁰You have no purpose apart from your brother, nor apart from the one you asked the Holy Spirit to share with you. ¹¹The little wall will fall away so quietly beneath the wings of peace. ¹²For peace will send its messengers from you to all the world, and barriers will fall away before their coming as easily as those that you interpose will be surmounted.

5.   To overcome the world is no more difficult than to surmount your little wall. ²For in the miracle of your holy relationship, without this barrier, is every miracle contained. ³There is no order of difficulty in miracles, for they are all the same. ⁴Each is a gentle winning over from the appeal of guilt to the appeal of love. ⁵How can this fail to be accomplished, wherever it is undertaken?

⁶Guilt can raise no real barriers against it. ⁷And all that seems to stand between you and your brother must fall away because of the appeal you answered. ⁸From you who answered, He Who answered you would call. ⁹His home is in your holy relationship. ¹⁰Do not attempt to stand between Him and His holy purpose, for it is yours. ¹¹But let Him quietly extend the miracle of your relationship to everyone contained in it as it was given.

6.   There is a hush in Heaven, a happy expectancy, a little pause of gladness in acknowledgment of the journey's end. ²For Heaven knows you well, as you know Heaven. ³No illusions stand between you and your brother now. ⁴Look not upon the little wall of shadows. ⁵The sun has risen over it. ⁶How can a shadow keep you from the sun? ⁷No more can you be kept by shadows from the light in which illusions end. ⁸Every miracle is but the end of an illusion. ⁹Such was the journey; such its ending. ¹⁰And in the goal of truth which you accepted must all illusions end.

7.   The little insane wish to get rid of Him Whom you invited in and push Him out *must* produce conflict. ²As you look upon the world, this little wish, uprooted and floating aimlessly, can land and settle briefly upon anything, for it has no purpose now. ³Before the Holy Spirit entered to abide with you it seemed to have a mighty purpose; the fixed and unchangeable dedication to sin and its results. ⁴Now it is aimless, wandering pointlessly, causing no more than tiny interruptions in love's appeal.

8.   This feather of a wish, this tiny illusion, this microscopic remnant of the belief in sin, is all that remains of what once seemed to be the world. ²It is no longer an unrelenting barrier to peace. ³Its pointless wandering makes its results appear to be more erratic and unpredictable than before. ⁴Yet what could be more unstable than a tightly organized delusional system? ⁵Its seeming stability is its pervasive weakness, which extends to everything. ⁶The variability the little remnant induces merely indicates its limited results.

9.   How mighty can a little feather be before the great wings of truth? ²Can it oppose an eagle's flight, or hinder the advance of summer? ³Can it interfere with the effects of summer's sun upon a garden covered by the snow? ⁴See but how easily this little wisp is lifted up and carried away, never to return, and part with it in gladness, not regret. ⁵For it is nothing in itself, and stood for nothing when you had greater faith in its protection. ⁶Would you not rather greet the summer sun than fix your gaze upon a disappearing snowflake, and shiver in remembrance of the winter's cold?

i. The Attraction of Guilt

10. The attraction of guilt produces fear of love, for love would never look on guilt at all. [2]It is the nature of love to look upon only the truth, for there it sees itself, with which it would unite in holy union and completion. [3]As love must look past fear, so must fear see love not. [4]For love contains the end of guilt, as surely as fear depends on it. [5]Love is attracted only to love. [6]Overlooking guilt completely, it sees no fear. [7]Being wholly without attack, it could not be afraid. [8]Fear is attracted to what love sees not, and each believes that what the other looks upon does not exist. [9]Fear looks on guilt with just the same devotion that love looks on itself. [10]And each has messengers which it sends forth, and which return to it with messages written in the language in which their going forth was asked.

11. Love's messengers are gently sent, and return with messages of love and gentleness. [2]The messengers of fear are harshly ordered to seek out guilt, and cherish every scrap of evil and of sin that they can find, losing none of them on pain of death, and laying them respectfully before their lord and master. [3]Perception cannot obey two masters, each asking for messages of different things in different languages. [4]What fear would feed upon, love overlooks. [5]What fear demands, love cannot even see. [6]The fierce attraction that guilt holds for fear is wholly absent from love's gentle perception. [7]What love would look upon is meaningless to fear, and quite invisible.

12. Relationships in this world are the result of how the world is seen. [2]And this depends on which emotion was called on to send its messengers to look upon it, and return with word of what they saw. [3]Fear's messengers are trained through terror, and they tremble when their master calls on them to serve him. [4]For fear is merciless even to its friends. [5]Its messengers steal guiltily away in hungry search of guilt, for they are kept cold and starving and made very vicious by their master, who allows them to feast only upon what they return to him. [6]No little shred of guilt escapes their hungry eyes. [7]And in their savage search for sin they pounce on any living thing they see, and carry it screaming to their master, to be devoured.

13. Send not these savage messengers into the world, to feast upon it and to prey upon reality. [2]For they will bring you word of bones and skin and flesh. [3]They have been taught to seek for the

corruptible, and to return with gorges filled with things decayed and rotted. ⁴To them such things are beautiful, because they seem to allay their savage pangs of hunger. ⁵For they are frantic with the pain of fear, and would avert the punishment of him who sends them forth by offering him what they hold dear.

14. The Holy Spirit has given you love's messengers to send instead of those you trained through fear. ²They are as eager to return to you what they hold dear as are the others. ³If you send them forth, they will see only the blameless and the beautiful, the gentle and the kind. ⁴They will be as careful to let no little act of charity, no tiny expression of forgiveness, no little breath of love escape their notice. ⁵And they will return with all the happy things they found, to share them lovingly with you. ⁶Be not afraid of them. ⁷They offer you salvation. ⁸Theirs are the messages of safety, for they see the world as kind.

15. If you send forth only the messengers the Holy Spirit gives you, wanting no messages but theirs, you will see fear no more. ²The world will be transformed before your sight, cleansed of all guilt and softly brushed with beauty. ³The world contains no fear that you laid not upon it. ⁴And none you cannot ask love's messengers to remove from it, and see it still. ⁵The Holy Spirit has given you His messengers to send to your brother and return to you with what love sees. ⁶They have been given to replace the hungry dogs of fear you sent instead. ⁷And they go forth to signify the end of fear.

16. Love, too, would set a feast before you, on a table covered with a spotless cloth, set in a quiet garden where no sound but singing and a softly joyous whispering is ever heard. ²This is a feast that honors your holy relationship, and at which everyone is welcomed as an honored guest. ³And in a holy instant grace is said by everyone together, as they join in gentleness before the table of communion. ⁴And I will join you there, as long ago I promised and promise still. ⁵For in your new relationship am I made welcome. ⁶And where I am made welcome, there I am.

17. I am made welcome in the state of grace, which means you have at last forgiven me. ²For I became the symbol of your sin, and so I had to die instead of you. ³To the ego sin means death, and so atonement is achieved through murder. ⁴Salvation is looked upon as a way by which the Son of God was killed instead of you. ⁵Yet would I offer you my body, you whom I love, *knowing* its littleness? ⁶Or would I teach that bodies cannot keep us apart?

411

⁷Mine was of no greater value than yours; no better means for communication of salvation, but not its Source. ⁸No one can die for anyone, and death does not atone for sin. ⁹But you can live to show it is not real. ¹⁰The body does appear to be the symbol of sin while you believe that it can get you what you want. ¹¹While you believe that it can give you pleasure, you will also believe that it can bring you pain. ¹²To think you could be satisfied and happy with so little is to hurt yourself, and to limit the happiness that you would have calls upon pain to fill your meager store and make your life complete. ¹³This is completion as the ego sees it. ¹⁴For guilt creeps in where happiness has been removed, and substitutes for it. ¹⁵Communion is another kind of completion, which goes beyond guilt, because it goes beyond the body.

B. The Second Obstacle: The Belief the Body is Valuable for What It Offers

1. We said that peace must first surmount the obstacle of your desire to get rid of it. ²Where the attraction of guilt holds sway, peace is not wanted. ³The second obstacle that peace must flow across, and closely related to the first, is the belief that the body is valuable for what it offers. ⁴For here is the attraction of guilt made manifest in the body, and seen in it.

2. This is the value that you think peace would rob you of. ²This is what you believe that it would dispossess, and leave you homeless. ³And it is this for which you would deny a home to peace. ⁴This "sacrifice" you feel to be too great to make, too much to ask of you. ⁵Is it a sacrifice, or a release? ⁶What has the body really given you that justifies your strange belief that in it lies salvation? ⁷Do you not see that this is the belief in death? ⁸Here is the focus of the perception of Atonement as murder. ⁹Here is the source of the idea that love is fear.

3. The Holy Spirit's messengers are sent far beyond the body, calling the mind to join in holy communion and be at peace. ²Such is the message that I gave them for you. ³It is only the messengers of fear that see the body, for they look for what can suffer. ⁴Is it a sacrifice to be removed from what can suffer? ⁵The Holy Spirit does not demand you sacrifice the hope of the body's pleasure; it *has* no hope of pleasure. ⁶But neither can it bring you fear of pain. ⁷Pain is the only "sacrifice" the Holy Spirit asks, and this He *would* remove.

412

4. Peace is extended from you only to the eternal, and it reaches out from the eternal in you. ²It flows across all else. ³The second obstacle is no more solid than the first. ⁴For you want neither to get rid of peace nor limit it. ⁵What are these obstacles that you would interpose between peace and its going forth but barriers you place between your will and its accomplishment? ⁶You want communion, not the feast of fear. ⁷You want salvation, not the pain of guilt. ⁸And you want your Father, not a little mound of clay, to be your home. ⁹In your holy relationship is your Father's Son. ¹⁰He has not lost communion with Him, nor with himself. ¹¹When you agreed to join your brother, you acknowledged this is so. ¹²This has no cost, but it has release from cost.

5. You have paid very dearly for your illusions, and nothing you have paid for brought you peace. ²Are you not glad that Heaven cannot be sacrificed, and sacrifice cannot be asked of you? ³There is no obstacle that you can place before our union, for in your holy relationship I am there already. ⁴We will surmount all obstacles together, for we stand within the gates and not outside. ⁵How easily the gates are opened from within, to let peace through to bless the tired world! ⁶Can it be difficult for us to walk past barriers together, when you have joined the limitless? ⁷The end of guilt is in your hands to give. ⁸Would you stop now to look for guilt in your brother?

6. Let me be to you the symbol of the end of guilt, and look upon your brother as you would look on me. ²Forgive me all the sins you think the Son of God committed. ³And in the light of your forgiveness he will remember who he is, and forget what never was. ⁴I ask for your forgiveness, for if you are guilty, so must I be. ⁵But if I surmounted guilt and overcame the world, you were with me. ⁶Would you see in me the symbol of guilt or of the end of guilt, remembering that what I signify to you you see within yourself?

7. From your holy relationship truth proclaims the truth, and love looks on itself. ²Salvation flows from deep within the home you offered to my Father and to me. ³And we are there together, in the quiet communion in which the Father and the Son are joined. ⁴O come ye faithful to the holy union of the Father and the Son in you! ⁵And keep you not apart from what is offered you in gratitude for giving peace its home in Heaven. ⁶Send forth to all the world the joyous message of the end of guilt, and all the world will answer. ⁷Think of your happiness as everyone offers

you witness of the end of sin, and shows you that its power is gone forever. ⁸Where can guilt be, when the belief in sin is gone? ⁹And where is death, when its great advocate is heard no more?

8.   Forgive me your illusions, and release me from punishment for what I have not done. ²So will you learn the freedom that I taught by teaching freedom to your brother, and so releasing me. ³I am within your holy relationship, yet you would imprison me behind the obstacles you raise to freedom, and bar my way to you. ⁴Yet it is not possible to keep away One Who is there already. ⁵And in Him it *is* possible that our communion, where we are joined already, will be the focus of the new perception that will bring light to all the world, contained in you.

i. The Attraction of Pain

9.   Your little part is but to give the Holy Spirit the whole idea of sacrifice. ²And to accept the peace He gives instead, without the limits that would hold its extension back, and so would limit your awareness of it. ³For what He gives must be extended if you would have its limitless power, and use it for the Son of God's release. ⁴It is not this you would be rid of, and having it you cannot limit it. ⁵If peace is homeless, so are you and so am I. ⁶And He Who is our home is homeless with us. ⁷Is this your wish? ⁸Would you forever be a wanderer in search of peace? ⁹Would you invest your hope of peace and happiness in what must fail?

10.   Faith in the eternal is always justified, for the eternal is forever kind, infinite in its patience and wholly loving. ²It will accept you wholly, and give you peace. ³Yet it can unite only with what already is at peace in you, immortal as itself. ⁴The body can bring you neither peace nor turmoil; neither joy nor pain. ⁵It is a means, and not an end. ⁶It has no purpose of itself, but only what is given to it. ⁷The body will seem to be whatever is the means for reaching the goal that you assign to it. ⁸Only the mind can set a purpose, and only the mind can see the means for its accomplishment, and justify its use. ⁹Peace and guilt are both conditions of the mind, to be attained. ¹⁰And these conditions are the home of the emotion that calls them forth, and therefore is compatible with them.

11.   But think you which it is that is compatible with you. ²Here is your choice, and it *is* free. ³But all that lies in it will come with it, and what you think you are can never be apart from it. ⁴The body

is the great seeming betrayer of faith. ⁵In it lies disillusionment and the seeds of faithlessness, but only if you ask of it what it cannot give. ⁶Can your mistake be reasonable grounds for depression and disillusionment, and for retaliative attack on what you think has failed you? ⁷Use not your error as the justification for your faithlessness. ⁸You have not sinned, but you have been mistaken in what is faithful. ⁹And the correction of your mistake will give you grounds for faith.

12. It is impossible to seek for pleasure through the body and not find pain. ²It is essential that this relationship be understood, for it is one the ego sees as proof of sin. ³It is not really punitive at all. ⁴It is but the inevitable result of equating yourself with the body, which is the invitation to pain. ⁵For it invites fear to enter and become your purpose. ⁶The attraction of guilt *must* enter with it, and whatever fear directs the body to do is therefore painful. ⁷It will share the pain of all illusions, and the illusion of pleasure will be the same as pain.

13. Is not this inevitable? ²Under fear's orders the body will pursue guilt, serving its master whose attraction to guilt maintains the whole illusion of its existence. ³This, then, is the attraction of pain. ⁴Ruled by this perception the body becomes the servant of pain, seeking it dutifully and obeying the idea that pain is pleasure. ⁵It is this idea that underlies all of the ego's heavy investment in the body. ⁶And it is this insane relationship that it keeps hidden, and yet feeds upon. ⁷To you it teaches that the body's pleasure is happiness. ⁸Yet to itself it whispers, "It is death."

14. Why should the body be anything to you? ²Certainly what it is made of is not precious. ³And just as certainly it has no feeling. ⁴It transmits to you the feelings that you want. ⁵Like any communication medium the body receives and sends the messages that it is given. ⁶It has no feeling for them. ⁷All of the feeling with which they are invested is given by the sender and the receiver. ⁸The ego and the Holy Spirit both recognize this, and both also recognize that here the sender and receiver are the same. ⁹The Holy Spirit tells you this with joy. ¹⁰The ego hides it, for it would keep you unaware of it. ¹¹Who would send messages of hatred and attack if he but understood he sends them to himself? ¹²Who would accuse, make guilty and condemn himself?

15. The ego's messages are always sent away from you, in the belief that for your message of attack and guilt will someone

other than yourself suffer. ²And even if you suffer, yet someone else will suffer more. ³The great deceiver recognizes that this is not so, but as the "enemy" of peace, it urges you to send out all your messages of hate and free yourself. ⁴And to convince you this is possible, it bids the body search for pain in attack upon another, calling it pleasure and offering it to you as freedom *from* attack.

16. Hear not its madness, and believe not the impossible is true. ²Forget not that the ego has dedicated the body to the goal of sin, and places in it all its faith that this can be accomplished. ³Its sad disciples chant the body's praise continually, in solemn celebration of the ego's rule. ⁴Not one but must believe that yielding to the attraction of guilt is the escape from pain. ⁵Not one but must regard the body as himself, without which he would die, and yet within which is his death equally inevitable.

17. It is not given to the ego's disciples to realize that they have dedicated themselves to death. ²Freedom is offered them but they have not accepted it, and what is offered must also be received, to be truly given. ³For the Holy Spirit, too, is a communication medium, receiving from the Father and offering His messages unto the Son. ⁴Like the ego, the Holy Spirit is both the sender and the receiver. ⁵For what is sent through Him returns to Him, seeking itself along the way, and finding what it seeks. ⁶So does the ego find the death *it* seeks, returning it to you.

C. The Third Obstacle: The Attraction of Death

1. To you and your brother, in whose special relationship the Holy Spirit entered, it is given to release and be released from the dedication to death. ²For it was offered you, and you accepted. ³Yet you must learn still more about this strange devotion, for it contains the third obstacle that peace must flow across. ⁴No one can die unless he chooses death. ⁵What seems to be the fear of death is really its attraction. ⁶Guilt, too, is feared and fearful. ⁷Yet it could have no hold at all except on those who are attracted to it and seek it out. ⁸And so it is with death. ⁹Made by the ego, its dark shadow falls across all living things, because the ego is the "enemy" of life.

2. And yet a shadow cannot kill. ²What is a shadow to the living? ³They but walk past and it is gone. ⁴But what of those whose dedication is not to live; the black-draped "sinners," the ego's

mournful chorus, plodding so heavily away from life, dragging their chains and marching in the slow procession that honors their grim master, lord of death? [5]Touch any one of them with the gentle hands of forgiveness, and watch the chains fall away, along with yours. [6]See him throw aside the black robe he was wearing to his funeral, and hear him laugh at death. [7]The sentence sin would lay upon him he can escape through your forgiveness. [8]This is no arrogance. [9]It is the Will of God. [10]What is impossible to you who chose His Will as yours? [11]What is death to you? [12]Your dedication is not to death, nor to its master. [13]When you accepted the Holy Spirit's purpose in place of the ego's you renounced death, exchanging it for life. [14]We know that an idea leaves not its source. [15]And death is the result of the thought we call the ego, as surely as life is the result of the Thought of God.

i. The Incorruptible Body

3. From the ego came sin and guilt and death, in opposition to life and innocence, and to the Will of God Himself. [2]Where can such opposition lie but in the sick minds of the insane, dedicated to madness and set against the peace of Heaven? [3]One thing is sure; God, Who created neither sin nor death, wills not that you be bound by them. [4]He knows of neither sin nor its results. [5]The shrouded figures in the funeral procession march not in honor of their Creator, Whose Will it is they live. [6]They are not following His Will; they are opposing it.

4. And what is the black-draped body they would bury? [2]A body which they dedicated to death, a symbol of corruption, a sacrifice to sin, offered to sin to feed upon and keep itself alive; a thing condemned, damned by its maker and lamented by every mourner who looks upon it as himself. [3]You who believe you have condemned the Son of God to this *are* arrogant. [4]But you who would release him are but honoring the Will of his Creator. [5]The arrogance of sin, the pride of guilt, the sepulchre of separation, all are part of your unrecognized dedication to death. [6]The glitter of guilt you laid upon the body would kill it. [7]For what the ego loves, it kills for its obedience. [8]But what obeys it not, it cannot kill.

5. You have another dedication that would keep the body incorruptible and perfect as long as it is useful for your holy purpose.

417

²The body no more dies than it can feel. ³It does nothing. ⁴Of itself it is neither corruptible nor incorruptible. ⁵It *is* nothing. ⁶It is the result of a tiny, mad idea of corruption that can be corrected. ⁷For God has answered this insane idea with His Own; an Answer which left Him not, and therefore brings the Creator to the awareness of every mind which heard His Answer and accepted It.

6. You who are dedicated to the incorruptible have been given through your acceptance, the power to release from corruption. ²What better way to teach the first and fundamental principle in a course on miracles than by showing you the one that seems to be the hardest can be accomplished first? ³The body can but serve your purpose. ⁴As you look on it, so will it seem to be. ⁵Death, were it true, would be the final and complete disruption of communication, which is the ego's goal.

7. Those who fear death see not how often and how loudly they call to it, and bid it come to save them from communication. ²For death is seen as safety, the great dark savior from the light of truth, the answer to the Answer, the silencer of the Voice that speaks for God. ³Yet the retreat to death is not the end of conflict. ⁴Only God's Answer is its end. ⁵The obstacle of your seeming love for death that peace must flow across seems to be very great. ⁶For in it lie hidden all the ego's secrets, all its strange devices for deception, all its sick ideas and weird imaginings. ⁷Here is the final end of union, the triumph of the ego's making over creation, the victory of lifelessness on Life Itself.

8. Under the dusty edge of its distorted world the ego would lay the Son of God, slain by its orders, proof in his decay that God Himself is powerless before the ego's might, unable to protect the life that He created against the ego's savage wish to kill. ²My brother, child of our Father, this is a *dream* of death. ³There is no funeral, no dark altars, no grim commandments nor twisted rituals of condemnation to which the body leads you. ⁴Ask not release of *it*. ⁵But free it from the merciless and unrelenting orders you laid upon it, and forgive it what you ordered it to do. ⁶In its exaltation you commanded it to die, for only death could conquer life. ⁷And what but insanity could look upon the defeat of God, and think it real?

9. The fear of death will go as its appeal is yielded to love's real attraction. ²The end of sin, which nestles quietly in the safety of your relationship, protected by your union with your brother,

and ready to grow into a mighty force for God is very near. ³The infancy of salvation is carefully guarded by love, preserved from every thought that would attack it, and quietly made ready to fulfill the mighty task for which it was given you. ⁴Your newborn purpose is nursed by angels, cherished by the Holy Spirit and protected by God Himself. ⁵It needs not your protection; it is *yours.* ⁶For it is deathless, and within it lies the end of death.

10. What danger can assail the wholly innocent? ²What can attack the guiltless? ³What fear can enter and disturb the peace of sinlessness? ⁴What has been given you, even in its infancy, is in full communication with God and you. ⁵In its tiny hands it holds, in perfect safety, every miracle you will perform, held out to you. ⁶The miracle of life is ageless, born in time but nourished in eternity. ⁷Behold this infant, to whom you gave a resting place by your forgiveness of your brother, and see in it the Will of God. ⁸Here is the babe of Bethlehem reborn. ⁹And everyone who gives him shelter will follow him, not to the cross, but to the resurrection and the life.

11. When anything seems to you to be a source of fear, when any situation strikes you with terror and makes your body tremble and the cold sweat of fear comes over it, remember it is always for *one* reason; the ego has perceived it as a symbol of fear, a sign of sin and death. ²Remember, then, that neither sign nor symbol should be confused with source, for they must stand for something other than themselves. ³Their meaning cannot lie in them, but must be sought in what they represent. ⁴And they may thus mean everything or nothing, according to the truth or falsity of the idea which they reflect. ⁵Confronted with such seeming uncertainty of meaning, judge it not. ⁶Remember the holy Presence of the One given to you to be the Source of judgment. ⁷Give it to Him to judge for you, and say:

> ⁸*Take this from me and look upon it, judging it for me.*
> ⁹*Let me not see it as a sign of sin and death, nor use it for destruction.*
> ¹⁰*Teach me how **not** to make of it an obstacle to peace, but let You use it for me, to facilitate its coming.*

419

D. The Fourth Obstacle: The Fear of God

1.   What would you see without the fear of death? [2]What would you feel and think if death held no attraction for you? [3]Very simply, you would remember your Father. [4]The Creator of life, the Source of everything that lives, the Father of the universe and of the universe of universes, and of everything that lies even beyond them would you remember. [5]And as this memory rises in your mind, peace must still surmount a final obstacle, after which is salvation completed, and the Son of God entirely restored to sanity. [6]For here your world *does* end.

2.   The fourth obstacle to be surmounted hangs like a heavy veil before the face of Christ. [2]Yet as His face rises beyond it, shining with joy because He is in His Father's Love, peace will lightly brush the veil aside and run to meet Him, and to join with Him at last. [3]For this dark veil, which seems to make the face of Christ Himself like to a leper's, and the bright Rays of His Father's Love that light His face with glory appear as streams of blood, fades in the blazing light beyond it when the fear of death is gone.

3.   This is the darkest veil, upheld by the belief in death and protected by its attraction. [2]The dedication to death and to its sovereignty is but the solemn vow, the promise made in secret to the ego never to lift this veil, not to approach it, nor even to suspect that it is there. [3]This is the secret bargain made with the ego to keep what lies beyond the veil forever blotted out and unremembered. [4]Here is your promise never to allow union to call you out of separation; the great amnesia in which the memory of God seems quite forgotten; the cleavage of your Self from you;—*the fear of God,* the final step in your dissociation.

4.   See how the belief in death would seem to "save" you. [2]For if this were gone, what could you fear but life? [3]It is the attraction of death that makes life seem to be ugly, cruel and tyrannical. [4]You are no more afraid of death than of the ego. [5]These are your chosen friends. [6]For in your secret alliance with them you have agreed never to let the fear of God be lifted, so you could look upon the face of Christ and join Him in His Father.

5.   Every obstacle that peace must flow across is surmounted in just the same way; the fear that raised it yields to the love beyond, and so the fear is gone. [2]And so it is with this. [3]The desire to get rid of peace and drive the Holy Spirit from you fades in the presence of the quiet recognition that you love Him.

⁴The exaltation of the body is given up in favor of the spirit, which you love as you could never love the body. ⁵And the appeal of death is lost forever as love's attraction stirs and calls to you. ⁶From beyond each of the obstacles to love, Love Itself has called. ⁷And each has been surmounted by the power of the attraction of what lies beyond. ⁸Your wanting fear seemed to be holding them in place. ⁹Yet when you heard the Voice of Love beyond them, you answered and they disappeared.

6. And now you stand in terror before what you swore never to look upon. ²Your eyes look down, remembering your promise to your "friends." ³The "loveliness" of sin, the delicate appeal of guilt, the "holy" waxen image of death, and the fear of vengeance of the ego you swore in blood not to desert, all rise and bid you not to raise your eyes. ⁴For you realize that if you look on this and let the veil be lifted, *they* will be gone forever. ⁵All of your "friends," your "protectors" and your "home" will vanish. ⁶Nothing that you remember now will you remember.

7. It seems to you the world will utterly abandon you if you but raise your eyes. ²Yet all that will occur is you will leave the world forever. ³This is the re-establishment of *your* will. ⁴Look upon it, open-eyed, and you will nevermore believe that you are at the mercy of things beyond you, forces you cannot control, and thoughts that come to you against your will. ⁵It *is* your will to look on this. ⁶No mad desire, no trivial impulse to forget again, no stab of fear nor the cold sweat of seeming death can stand against your will. ⁷For what attracts you from beyond the veil is also deep within you, unseparated from it and completely one.

i. The Lifting of the Veil

8. Forget not that you came this far together, you and your brother. ²And it was surely not the ego that led you here. ³No obstacle to peace can be surmounted through its help. ⁴It does not open up its secrets, and bid you look on them and go beyond them. ⁵It would not have you see its weakness, and learn it has no power to keep you from the truth. ⁶The Guide Who brought you here remains with you, and when you raise your eyes you will be ready to look on terror with no fear at all. ⁷But first, lift up your eyes and look on your brother in innocence born of complete forgiveness of his illusions, and through the eyes of faith that sees them not.

9. No one can look upon the fear of God unterrified, unless he has accepted the Atonement and learned illusions are not real. [2]No one can stand before this obstacle alone, for he could not have reached this far unless his brother walked beside him. [3]And no one would dare to look on it without complete forgiveness of his brother in his heart. [4]Stand you here a while and tremble not. [5]You will be ready. [6]Let us join together in a holy instant, here in this place where the purpose, given in a holy instant, has led you. [7]And let us join in faith that He Who brought us here together will offer you the innocence you need, and that you will accept it for my love and His.

10. Nor is it possible to look on this too soon. [2]This is the place to which everyone must come when he is ready. [3]Once he has found his brother he *is* ready. [4]Yet merely to reach the place is not enough. [5]A journey without a purpose is still meaningless, and even when it is over it seems to make no sense. [6]How can you know that it is over unless you realize its purpose is accomplished? [7]Here, with the journey's end before you, you *see* its purpose. [8]And it is here you choose whether to look upon it or wander on, only to return and make the choice again.

11. To look upon the fear of God does need some preparation. [2]Only the sane can look on stark insanity and raving madness with pity and compassion, but not with fear. [3]For only if they share in it does it seem fearful, and you do share in it until you look upon your brother with perfect faith and love and tenderness. [4]Before complete forgiveness you still stand unforgiving. [5]You are afraid of God *because* you fear your brother. [6]Those you do not forgive you fear. [7]And no one reaches love with fear beside him.

12. This brother who stands beside you still seems to be a stranger. [2]You do not know him, and your interpretation of him is very fearful. [3]And you attack him still, to keep what seems to be yourself unharmed. [4]Yet in his hands is your salvation. [5]You see his madness, which you hate because you share it. [6]And all the pity and forgiveness that would heal it gives way to fear. [7]Brother, you need forgiveness of your brother, for you will share in madness or in Heaven together. [8]And you and he will raise your eyes in faith together, or not at all.

13. Beside you is one who offers you the chalice of Atonement, for the Holy Spirit is in him. [2]Would you hold his sins against him, or accept his gift to you? [3]Is this giver of salvation your friend or

enemy? ⁴Choose which he is, remembering that you will receive of him according to your choice. ⁵He has in him the power to forgive your sin, as you for him. ⁶Neither can give it to himself alone. ⁷And yet your savior stands beside each one. ⁸Let him be what he is, and seek not to make of love an enemy.

14. Behold your Friend, the Christ Who stands beside you. ²How holy and how beautiful He is! ³You thought He sinned because you cast the veil of sin upon Him to hide His loveliness. ⁴Yet still He holds forgiveness out to you, to share His Holiness. ⁵This "enemy," this "stranger" still offers you salvation as His Friend. ⁶The "enemies" of Christ, the worshippers of sin, know not Whom they attack.

15. This is your brother, crucified by sin and waiting for release from pain. ²Would you not offer him forgiveness, when only he can offer it to you? ³For his redemption he will give you yours, as surely as God created every living thing and loves it. ⁴And he will give it truly, for it will be both offered and received. ⁵There is no grace of Heaven that you cannot offer to your brother, and receive from your most holy Friend. ⁶Let him withhold it not, for by receiving it you offer it to him. ⁷And he will receive of you what you received of him. ⁸Redemption has been given you to give your brother, and thus receive it. ⁹Whom you forgive is free, and what you give you share. ¹⁰Forgive the sins your brother thinks he has committed, and all the guilt you think you see in him.

16. Here is the holy place of resurrection, to which we come again; to which we will return until redemption is accomplished and received. ²Think who your brother is, before you would condemn him. ³And offer thanks to God that he is holy, and has been given the gift of holiness for you. ⁴Join him in gladness, and remove all trace of guilt from his disturbed and tortured mind. ⁵Help him to lift the heavy burden of sin you laid upon him and he accepted as his own, and toss it lightly and with happy laughter away from him. ⁶Press it not like thorns against his brow, nor nail him to it, unredeemed and hopeless.

17. Give faith to your brother, for faith and hope and mercy are yours to give. ²Into the hands that give, the gift is given. ³Look on your brother, and see in him the gift of God you would receive. ⁴It is almost Easter, the time of resurrection. ⁵Let us give redemption to each other and share in it, that we may rise as one in resurrection, not separate in death. ⁶Behold the gift of freedom that I gave the Holy Spirit for you. ⁷And be you and your brother

423

free together, as you offer to the Holy Spirit this same gift. [8]And giving it, receive it of Him in return for what you gave. [9]He leadeth you and me together, that we might meet here in this holy place, and make the same decision.

18. Free your brother here, as I freed you. [2]Give him the selfsame gift, nor look upon him with condemnation of any kind. [3]See him as guiltless as I look on you, and overlook the sins he thinks he sees within himself. [4]Offer your brother freedom and complete release from sin, here in the garden of seeming agony and death. [5]So will we prepare together the way unto the resurrection of God's Son, and let him rise again to glad remembrance of his Father, Who knows no sin, no death, but only life eternal.

19. Together we will disappear into the Presence beyond the veil, not to be lost but found; not to be seen but known. [2]And knowing, nothing in the plan God has established for salvation will be left undone. [3]This is the journey's purpose, without which is the journey meaningless. [4]Here is the peace of God, given to you eternally by Him. [5]Here is the rest and quiet that you seek, the reason for the journey from its beginning. [6]Heaven is the gift you owe your brother, the debt of gratitude you offer to the Son of God in thanks for what he is, and what his Father created him to be.

20. Think carefully how you would look upon the giver of this gift, for as you look on him so will the gift itself appear to be. [2]As he is seen as either the giver of guilt or of salvation, so will his offering be seen and so received. [3]The crucified give pain because they are in pain. [4]But the redeemed give joy because they have been healed of pain. [5]Everyone gives as he receives, but he must choose what it will *be* that he receives. [6]And he will recognize his choice by what he gives, and what is given him. [7]Nor is it given anything in hell or Heaven to interfere with his decision.

21. You came this far because the journey was your choice. [2]And no one undertakes to do what he believes is meaningless. [3]What you had faith in still is faithful, and watches over you in faith so gentle yet so strong that it would lift you far beyond the veil, and place the Son of God safely within the sure protection of his Father. [4]Here is the only purpose that gives this world, and the long journey through this world, whatever meaning lies in them. [5]Beyond this, they are meaningless. [6]You and your brother stand together, still without conviction they have a purpose. [7]Yet it is given you to see this purpose in your holy Friend, and recognize it as your own.

Chapter 20

THE VISION OF HOLINESS

I. Holy Week

1. This is Palm Sunday, the celebration of victory and the acceptance of the truth. ²Let us not spend this holy week brooding on the crucifixion of God's Son, but happily in the celebration of his release. ³For Easter is the sign of peace, not pain. ⁴A slain Christ has no meaning. ⁵But a risen Christ becomes the symbol of the Son of God's forgiveness on himself; the sign he looks upon himself as healed and whole.

2. This week begins with palms and ends with lilies, the white and holy sign the Son of God is innocent. ²Let no dark sign of crucifixion intervene between the journey and its purpose; between the acceptance of the truth and its expression. ³This week we celebrate life, not death. ⁴And we honor the perfect purity of the Son of God, and not his sins. ⁵Offer your brother the gift of lilies, not the crown of thorns; the gift of love and not the "gift" of fear. ⁶You stand beside your brother, thorns in one hand and lilies in the other, uncertain which to give. ⁷Join now with me and throw away the thorns, offering the lilies to replace them. ⁸This Easter I would have the gift of your forgiveness offered by you to me, and returned by me to you. ⁹We cannot be united in crucifixion and in death. ¹⁰Nor can the resurrection be complete till your forgiveness rests on Christ, along with mine.

3. A week is short, and yet this holy week is the symbol of the whole journey the Son of God has undertaken. ²He started with the sign of victory, the promise of the resurrection, already given him. ³Let him not wander into the temptation of crucifixion, and delay him there. ⁴Help him to go in peace beyond it, with the light of his own innocence lighting his way to his redemption and release. ⁵Hold him not back with thorns and nails when his redemption is so near. ⁶But let the whiteness of your shining gift of lilies speed him on his way to resurrection.

4. Easter is not the celebration of the *cost* of sin, but of its *end*. ²If you see glimpses of the face of Christ behind the veil, looking between the snow-white petals of the lilies you have received and given as your gift, you will behold your brother's face and

recognize it. ³I was a stranger and you took me in, not knowing who I was. ⁴Yet for your gift of lilies you will know. ⁵In your forgiveness of this stranger, alien to you and yet your ancient Friend, lies his release and your redemption with him. ⁶The time of Easter is a time of joy, and not of mourning. ⁷Look on your risen Friend, and celebrate his holiness along with me. ⁸For Easter is the time of your salvation, along with mine.

II. The Gift of Lilies

1. Look upon all the trinkets made to hang upon the body, or to cover it or for its use. ²See all the useless things made for its eyes to see. ³Think on the many offerings made for its pleasure, and remember all these were made to make seem lovely what you hate. ⁴Would you employ this hated thing to draw your brother to you, and to attract his body's eyes? ⁵Learn you but offer him a crown of thorns, not recognizing it for what it is, and trying to justify your own interpretation of its value by his acceptance. ⁶Yet still the gift proclaims his worthlessness to you, as his acceptance and delight acknowledges the lack of value he places on himself.

2. Gifts are not made through bodies, if they be truly given and received. ²For bodies can neither offer nor accept; hold out nor take. ³Only the mind can value, and only the mind decides on what it would receive and give. ⁴And every gift it offers depends on what it wants. ⁵It will adorn its chosen home most carefully, making it ready to receive the gifts it wants by offering them to those who come unto its chosen home, or those it would attract to it. ⁶And there they will exchange their gifts, offering and receiving what their minds judge to be worthy of them.

3. Each gift is an evaluation of the receiver and the *giver*. ²No one but sees his chosen home as an altar to himself. ³No one but seeks to draw to it the worshippers of what he placed upon it, making it worthy of their devotion. ⁴And each has set a light upon his altar, that they may see what he has placed upon it and take it for their own. ⁵Here is the value that you lay upon your brother and on yourself. ⁶Here is your gift to both; your judgment on the Son of God for what he is. ⁷Forget not that it is your savior to whom the gift is offered. ⁸Offer him thorns and *you* are crucified. ⁹Offer him lilies and it is yourself you free.

4. I have great need for lilies, for the Son of God has not forgiven

me. ²And can I offer him forgiveness when he offers thorns to me? ³For he who offers thorns to anyone is against me still, and who is whole without him? ⁴Be you his friend for me, that I may be forgiven and you may look upon the Son of God as whole. ⁵But look you first upon the altar in your chosen home, and see what you have laid upon it to offer me. ⁶If it be thorns whose points gleam sharply in a blood-red light, the body is your chosen home and it is separation that you offer me. ⁷And yet the thorns are gone. ⁸Look you still closer at them now, and you will see your altar is no longer what it was.

5. You look still with the body's eyes, and they can see but thorns. ²Yet you have asked for and received another sight. ³Those who accept the Holy Spirit's purpose as their own share also His vision. ⁴And what enables Him to see His purpose shine forth from every altar now is yours as well as His. ⁵He sees no strangers; only dearly loved and loving friends. ⁶He sees no thorns but only lilies, gleaming in the gentle glow of peace that shines on everything He looks upon and loves.

6. This Easter, look with different eyes upon your brother. ²You *have* forgiven me. ³And yet I cannot use your gift of lilies while you see them not. ⁴Nor can you use what I have given unless you share it. ⁵The Holy Spirit's vision is no idle gift, no plaything to be tossed about a while and laid aside. ⁶Listen and hear this carefully, nor think it but a dream, a careless thought to play with, or a toy you would pick up from time to time and then put by. ⁷For if you do, so will it be to you.

7. You have the vision now to look past all illusions. ²It has been given you to see no thorns, no strangers and no obstacles to peace. ³The fear of God is nothing to you now. ⁴Who is afraid to look upon illusions, knowing his savior stands beside him? ⁵With him, your vision has become the greatest power for the undoing of illusion that God Himself could give. ⁶For what God gave the Holy Spirit, you have received. ⁷The Son of God looks unto you for his release. ⁸For you have asked for and been given the strength to look upon this final obstacle, and see no thorns nor nails to crucify the Son of God, and crown him king of death.

8. Your chosen home is on the other side, beyond the veil. ²It has been carefully prepared for you, and it is ready to receive you now. ³You will not see it with the body's eyes. ⁴Yet all you need you have. ⁵Your home has called to you since time began, nor have you ever failed entirely to hear. ⁶You heard, but knew not

how to look, nor where. ⁷And now you know. ⁸In you the knowledge lies, ready to be unveiled and freed from all the terror that kept it hidden. ⁹There *is* no fear in love. ¹⁰The song of Easter is the glad refrain the Son of God was never crucified. ¹¹Let us lift up our eyes together, not in fear but faith. ¹²And there will be no fear in us, for in our vision will be no illusions; only a pathway to the open door of Heaven, the home we share in quietness and where we live in gentleness and peace, as one together.

9.   Would you not have your holy brother lead you there? ²His innocence will light your way, offering you its guiding light and sure protection, and shining from the holy altar within him where you laid the lilies of forgiveness. ³Let him be to you the savior from illusions, and look on him with the new vision that looks upon the lilies and brings you joy. ⁴We go beyond the veil of fear, lighting each other's way. ⁵The holiness that leads us is within us, as is our home. ⁶So will we find what we were meant to find by Him Who leads us.

10.   This is the way to Heaven and to the peace of Easter, in which we join in glad awareness that the Son of God is risen from the past, and has awakened to the present. ²Now is he free, unlimited in his communion with all that is within him. ³Now are the lilies of his innocence untouched by guilt, and perfectly protected from the cold chill of fear and withering blight of sin alike. ⁴Your gift has saved him from the thorns and nails, and his strong arm is free to guide you safely through them and beyond. ⁵Walk with him now rejoicing, for the savior from illusions has come to greet you, and lead you home with him.

11.   Here is your savior and your friend, released from crucifixion through your vision, and free to lead you now where he would be. ²He will not leave you, nor forsake the savior in his pain. ³And gladly will you and your brother walk the way of innocence together, singing as you behold the open door of Heaven and recognize the home that called to you. ⁴Give joyously to your brother the freedom and the strength to lead you there. ⁵And come before his holy altar where the strength and freedom wait, to offer and receive the bright awareness that leads you home. ⁶The lamp is lit in you for your brother. ⁷And by the hands that gave it to him shall you be led past fear to love.

III. Sin as an Adjustment

1. The belief in sin is an adjustment. ²And an adjustment is a change; a shift in perception, or a belief that what was so before has been made different. ³Every adjustment is therefore a distortion, and calls upon defenses to uphold it against reality. ⁴Knowledge requires no adjustments and, in fact, is lost if any shift or change is undertaken. ⁵For this reduces it at once to mere perception; a way of looking in which certainty is lost and doubt has entered. ⁶To this impaired condition *are* adjustments necessary, because it is not true. ⁷Who need adjust to truth, which calls on only what he is, to understand?

2. Adjustments of any kind are of the ego. ²For it is the ego's fixed belief that all relationships depend upon adjustments, to make of them what it would have them be. ³Direct relationships, in which there are no interferences, are always seen as dangerous. ⁴The ego is the self-appointed mediator of all relationships, making whatever adjustments it deems necessary and interposing them between those who would meet, to keep them separate and prevent their union. ⁵It is this studied interference that makes it difficult for you to recognize your holy relationship for what it is.

3. The holy do not interfere with truth. ²They are not afraid of it, for it is within the truth they recognize their holiness, and rejoice at what they see. ³They look on it directly, without attempting to adjust themselves to it, or it to them. ⁴And so they see that it was in them, not deciding first where they would have it be. ⁵Their looking merely asks a question, and it is what they see that answers them. ⁶You make the world and then adjust to it, and it to you. ⁷Nor is there any difference between yourself and it in your perception, which made them both.

4. A simple question yet remains, and needs an answer. ²Do you like what you have made?—a world of murder and attack, through which you thread your timid way through constant dangers, alone and frightened, hoping at most that death will wait a little longer before it overtakes you and you disappear. ³*You made this up.* ⁴It is a picture of what you think you are; of how you see yourself. ⁵A murderer *is* frightened, and those who kill fear death. ⁶All these are but the fearful thoughts of those who would adjust themselves to a world made fearful by their adjustments. ⁷And they look out in sorrow from what is sad within, and see the sadness there.

5. Have you not wondered what the world is really like; how it would look through happy eyes? ²The world you see is but a judgment on yourself. ³It is not there at all. ⁴Yet judgment lays a sentence on it, justifies it and makes it real. ⁵Such is the world you see; a judgment on yourself, and made by you. ⁶This sickly picture of yourself is carefully preserved by the ego, whose image it is and which it loves, and placed outside you in the world. ⁷And to this world must you adjust as long as you believe this picture is outside, and has you at its mercy. ⁸This world *is* merciless, and were it outside you, you should indeed be fearful. ⁹Yet it was you who made it merciless, and now if mercilessness seems to look back at you, it can be corrected.

6. Who in a holy relationship can long remain unholy? ²The world the holy see is one with them, just as the world the ego looks upon is like itself. ³The world the holy see is beautiful because they see their innocence in it. ⁴They did not tell it what it was; they did not make adjustments to fit their orders. ⁵They gently questioned it and whispered, "What are you?" ⁶And He Who watches over all perception answered. ⁷Take not the judgment of the world as answer to the question, "What am I?" ⁸The world believes in sin, but the belief that made it as you see it is not outside you.

7. Seek not to make the Son of God adjust to his insanity. ²There is a stranger in him, who wandered carelessly into the home of truth and who will wander off. ³He came without a purpose, but he will not remain before the shining light the Holy Spirit offered, and you accepted. ⁴For there the stranger is made homeless and *you* are welcome. ⁵Ask not this transient stranger, "What am I?" ⁶He is the only thing in all the universe that does not know. ⁷Yet it is he you ask, and it is to his answer that you would adjust. ⁸This one wild thought, fierce in its arrogance, and yet so tiny and so meaningless it slips unnoticed through the universe of truth, becomes your guide. ⁹To it you turn to ask the meaning of the universe. ¹⁰And of the one blind thing in all the seeing universe of truth you ask, "How shall I look upon the Son of God?"

8. Does one ask judgment of what is totally bereft of judgment? ²And if you have, would you believe the answer, and adjust to it as if it were the truth? ³The world you look on is the answer that it gave you, and you have given it power to adjust the world to make its answer true. ⁴You asked this puff of madness for the meaning of your unholy relationship, and adjusted it according

to its insane answer. ⁵How happy did it make you? ⁶Did you meet your brother with joy to bless the Son of God, and give him thanks for all the happiness that he held out to you? ⁷Did you recognize your brother as the eternal gift of God to you? ⁸Did you see the holiness that shone in both you and your brother, to bless the other? ⁹That is the purpose of your holy relationship. ¹⁰Ask not the means of its attainment of the one thing that still would have it be unholy. ¹¹Give it no power to adjust the means and end.

9.   Prisoners bound with heavy chains for years, starved and emaciated, weak and exhausted, and with eyes so long cast down in darkness they remember not the light, do not leap up in joy the instant they are made free. ²It takes a while for them to understand what freedom is. ³You groped but feebly in the dust and found your brother's hand, uncertain whether to let it go or to take hold on life so long forgotten. ⁴Strengthen your hold and raise your eyes unto your strong companion, in whom the meaning of your freedom lies. ⁵He seemed to be crucified beside you. ⁶And yet his holiness remained untouched and perfect, and with him beside you, you shall this day enter with him to Paradise, and know the peace of God.

10.   Such is my will for you and your brother, and for each of you for one another and for himself. ²Here there is only holiness and joining without limit. ³For what is Heaven but union, direct and perfect, and without the veil of fear upon it? ⁴Here are we one, looking with perfect gentleness upon each other and on ourselves. ⁵Here all thoughts of any separation between us become impossible. ⁶You who were a prisoner in separation are now made free in Paradise. ⁷And here would I unite with you, my friend, my brother and my Self.

11.   Your gift unto your brother has given me the certainty our union will be soon. ²Share, then, this faith with me, and know that it is justified. ³There is no fear in perfect love *because* it knows no sin, and it must look on others as on itself. ⁴Looking with charity within, what can it fear without? ⁵The innocent see safety, and the pure in heart see God within His Son, and look unto the Son to lead them to the Father. ⁶And where else would they go but where they will to be? ⁷You and your brother now will lead the other to the Father as surely as God created His Son holy, and kept him so. ⁸In your brother is the light of God's eternal promise of your immortality. ⁹See him as sinless, and there can *be* no fear in you.

IV. Entering the Ark

1. Nothing can hurt you unless you give it the power to do so. [2]Yet *you* give power as the laws of this world interpret giving; as you give you lose. [3]It is not up to you to give power at all. [4]Power is of God, given by Him and reawakened by the Holy Spirit, Who knows that as you give you gain. [5]He gives no power to sin, and therefore it has none; nor to its results as this world sees them, — sickness and death and misery and pain. [6]These things have not occurred because the Holy Spirit sees them not, and gives no power to their seeming source. [7]Thus would He keep you free of them. [8]Being without illusion of what you are, the Holy Spirit merely gives everything to God, Who has already given and received all that is true. [9]The untrue He has neither received nor given.

2. Sin has no place in Heaven, where its results are alien and can no more enter than can their source. [2]And therein lies your need to see your brother sinless. [3]In him *is* Heaven. [4]See sin in him instead, and Heaven is lost to you. [5]But see him as he is, and what is yours shines from him to you. [6]Your savior gives you only love, but what you would receive of him is up to you. [7]It lies in him to overlook all your mistakes, and therein lies his own salvation. [8]And so it is with yours. [9]Salvation is a lesson in giving, as the Holy Spirit interprets it. [10]It is the reawakening of the laws of God in minds that have established other laws, and given them power to enforce what God created not.

3. Your insane laws were made to guarantee that you would make mistakes, and give them power over you by accepting their results as your just due. [2]What could this be but madness? [3]And is it this that you would see within your savior from insanity? [4]He is as free from this as you are, and in the freedom that you see in him you see your own. [5]For this you share. [6]What God has given follows His laws, and His alone. [7]Nor is it possible for those who follow them to suffer the results of any other source.

4. Those who choose freedom will experience only its results. [2]Their power is of God, and they will give it only to what God has given, to share with them. [3]Nothing but this can touch them, for they see only this, sharing their power according to the Will of God. [4]And thus their freedom is established and maintained. [5]It is upheld through all temptation to imprison and to be imprisoned. [6]It is of them who learned of freedom that you should ask what

freedom is. [7]Ask not the sparrow how the eagle soars, for those with little wings have not accepted for themselves the power to share with you.

5.   The sinless give as they received. [2]See, then, the power of sinlessness within your brother, and share with him the power of the release from sin you offered him. [3]To each who walks this earth in seeming solitude is a savior given, whose special function here is to release him, and so to free himself. [4]In the world of separation each is appointed separately, though they are all the same. [5]Yet those who know that they are all the same need not salvation. [6]And each one finds his savior when he is ready to look upon the face of Christ, and see Him sinless.

6.   The plan is not of you, nor need you be concerned with anything except the part that has been given you to learn. [2]For He Who knows the rest will see to it without your help. [3]But think not that He does not need your part to help Him with the rest. [4]For in your part lies all of it, without which is no part complete, nor is the whole completed without your part. [5]The ark of peace is entered two by two, yet the beginning of another world goes with them. [6]Each holy relationship must enter here, to learn its special function in the Holy Spirit's plan, now that it shares His purpose. [7]And as this purpose is fulfilled, a new world rises in which sin can enter not, and where the Son of God can enter without fear and where he rests a while, to forget imprisonment and to remember freedom. [8]How can he enter, to rest and to remember, without you? [9]Except you be there, he is not complete. [10]And it is his completion that he remembers there.

7.   This is the purpose given you. [2]Think not that your forgiveness of your brother serves but you two alone. [3]For the whole new world rests in the hands of every two who enter here to rest. [4]And as they rest, the face of Christ shines on them and they remember the laws of God, forgetting all the rest and yearning only to have His laws perfectly fulfilled in them and all their brothers. [5]Think you when this has been achieved that you will rest without them? [6]You could no more leave one of them outside than I could leave you, and forget part of myself.

8.   You may wonder how you can be at peace when, while you are in time, there is so much that must be done before the way to peace is open. [2]Perhaps this seems impossible to you. [3]But ask yourself if it is possible that God would have a plan for your salvation that does not work. [4]Once you accept His plan as the

one function that you would fulfill, there will be nothing else the Holy Spirit will not arrange for you without your effort. [5]He will go before you making straight your path, and leaving in your way no stones to trip on, and no obstacles to bar your way. [6]Nothing you need will be denied you. [7]Not one seeming difficulty but will melt away before you reach it. [8]You need take thought for nothing, careless of everything except the only purpose that you would fulfill. [9]As that was given you, so will its fulfillment be. [10]God's guarantee will hold against all obstacles, for it rests on certainty and not contingency. [11]It rests on *you*. [12]And what can be more certain than a Son of God?

V. Heralds of Eternity

1. In this world, God's Son comes closest to himself in a holy relationship. [2]There he begins to find the certainty his Father has in him. [3]And there he finds his function of restoring his Father's laws to what was held outside them, and finding what was lost. [4]Only in time can anything be lost, and never lost forever. [5]So do the parts of God's Son gradually join in time, and with each joining is the end of time brought nearer. [6]Each miracle of joining is a mighty herald of eternity. [7]No one who has a single purpose, unified and sure, can be afraid. [8]No one who shares his purpose with him can *not* be one with him.

2. Each herald of eternity sings of the end of sin and fear. [2]Each speaks in time of what is far beyond it. [3]Two voices raised together call to the hearts of everyone, to let them beat as one. [4]And in that single heartbeat is the unity of love proclaimed and given welcome. [5]Peace to your holy relationship, which has the power to hold the unity of the Son of God together. [6]You give to your brother for everyone, and in your gift is everyone made glad. [7]Forget not Who has given you the gifts you give, and through your not forgetting this, will you remember Who gave the gifts to Him to give to you.

3. It is impossible to overestimate your brother's value. [2]Only the ego does this, but all it means is that it wants the other for itself, and therefore values him too little. [3]What is inestimable clearly cannot be evaluated. [4]Do you recognize the fear that rises from the meaningless attempt to judge what lies so far beyond your judgment you cannot even see it? [5]Judge not what is invisible to

you or you will never see it, but wait in patience for its coming. ⁶It will be given you to see your brother's worth when all you want for him is peace. ⁷And what you want for him you will receive.

4. How can you estimate the worth of him who offers peace to you? ²What would you want except his offering? ³His worth has been established by his Father, and you will recognize it as you receive his Father's gift through him. ⁴What is in him will shine so brightly in your grateful vision that you will merely love him and be glad. ⁵You will not think to judge him, for who would see the face of Christ and yet insist that judgment still has meaning? ⁶For this insistence is of those who do not see. ⁷Vision or judgment is your choice, but never both of these.

5. Your brother's body is as little use to you as it is to him. ²When it is used only as the Holy Spirit teaches, it has no function. ³For minds need not the body to communicate. ⁴The sight that sees the body has no use which serves the purpose of a holy relationship. ⁵And while you look upon your brother thus, the means and end have not been brought in line. ⁶Why should it take so many holy instants to let this be accomplished, when one would do? ⁷There *is* but one. ⁸The little breath of eternity that runs through time like golden light is all the same; nothing before it, nothing afterwards.

6. You look upon each holy instant as a different point in time. ²It never changes. ³All that it ever held or will ever hold is here right now. ⁴The past takes nothing from it, and the future will add no more. ⁵Here, then, is everything. ⁶Here is the loveliness of your relationship, with means and end in perfect harmony already. ⁷Here is the perfect faith that you will one day offer to your brother already offered you; and here the limitless forgiveness you will give him already given, the face of Christ you yet will look upon already seen.

7. Can you evaluate the giver of a gift like this? ²Would you exchange this gift for any other? ³This gift returns the laws of God to your remembrance. ⁴And merely by remembering them, the laws that held you prisoner to pain and death must be forgotten. ⁵This is no gift your brother's body offers you. ⁶The veil that hides the gift hides him as well. ⁷He *is* the gift, and yet he knows it not. ⁸No more do you. ⁹And yet, have faith that He Who sees the gift in you and your brother will offer and receive it for you both. ¹⁰And through His vision will you see it, and through His understanding recognize it and love it as your own.

8. Be comforted, and feel the Holy Spirit watching over you in love and perfect confidence in what He sees. ²He knows the Son of God, and shares his Father's certainty the universe rests in his gentle hands in safety and in peace. ³Let us consider now what he must learn, to share his Father's confidence in him. ⁴What is he, that the Creator of the universe should offer it to him and know it rests in safety? ⁵He looks upon himself not as his Father knows him. ⁶And yet it is impossible the confidence of God should be misplaced.

VI. The Temple of the Holy Spirit

1. The meaning of the Son of God lies solely in his relationship with his Creator. ²If it were elsewhere it would rest on contingency, but there *is* nothing else. ³And this is wholly loving and forever. ⁴Yet has the Son of God invented an unholy relationship between him and his Father. ⁵His real relationship is one of perfect union and unbroken continuity. ⁶The one he made is partial, self-centered, broken into fragments and full of fear. ⁷The one created by his Father is wholly Self-encompassing and Self-extending. ⁸The one he made is wholly self-destructive and self-limiting.

2. Nothing can show the contrast better than the experience of both a holy and an unholy relationship. ²The first is based on love, and rests on it serene and undisturbed. ³The body does not intrude upon it. ⁴Any relationship in which the body enters is based not on love, but on idolatry. ⁵Love wishes to be known, completely understood and shared. ⁶It has no secrets; nothing that it would keep apart and hide. ⁷It walks in sunlight, open-eyed and calm, in smiling welcome and in sincerity so simple and so obvious it cannot be misunderstood.

3. But idols do not share. ²Idols accept, but never make return. ³They can be loved, but cannot love. ⁴They do not understand what they are offered, and any relationship in which they enter has lost its meaning. ⁵The love of them has made love meaningless. ⁶They live in secrecy, hating the sunlight and happy in the body's darkness, where they can hide and keep their secrets hidden along with them. ⁷And they have no relationships, for no one else is welcome there. ⁸They smile on no one, and those who smile on them they do not see.

4. Love has no darkened temples where mysteries are kept ob-

scure and hidden from the sun. ²It does not seek for power, but for relationships. ³The body is the ego's chosen weapon for seeking power *through* relationships. ⁴And its relationships must be unholy, for what they are it does not even see. ⁵It wants them solely for the offerings on which its idols thrive. ⁶The rest it merely throws away, for all that it could offer is seen as valueless. ⁷Homeless, the ego seeks as many bodies as it can collect to place its idols in, and so establish them as temples to itself.

5. The Holy Spirit's temple is not a body, but a relationship. ²The body is an isolated speck of darkness; a hidden secret room, a tiny spot of senseless mystery, a meaningless enclosure carefully protected, yet hiding nothing. ³Here the unholy relationship escapes reality, and seeks for crumbs to keep itself alive. ⁴Here it would drag its brothers, holding them here in its idolatry. ⁵Here it is "safe," for here love cannot enter. ⁶The Holy Spirit does not build His temples where love can never be. ⁷Would He Who sees the face of Christ choose as His home the only place in all the universe where it can not be seen?

6. You cannot make the body the Holy Spirit's temple, and it will never be the seat of love. ²It is the home of the idolater, and of love's condemnation. ³For here is love made fearful and hope abandoned. ⁴Even the idols that are worshipped here are shrouded in mystery, and kept apart from those who worship them. ⁵This is the temple dedicated to no relationships and no return. ⁶Here is the "mystery" of separation perceived in awe and held in reverence. ⁷What God would have *not* be is here kept "safe" from Him. ⁸But what you do not realize is what you fear within your brother, and would not see in him, is what makes God seem fearful to you, and kept unknown.

7. Idolaters will always be afraid of love, for nothing so severely threatens them as love's approach. ²Let love draw near them and overlook the body, as it will surely do, and they retreat in fear, feeling the seeming firm foundation of their temple begin to shake and loosen. ³Brother, you tremble with them. ⁴Yet what you fear is but the herald of escape. ⁵This place of darkness is not your home. ⁶Your temple is not threatened. ⁷You are an idolater no longer. ⁸The Holy Spirit's purpose lies safe in your relationship, and not your body. ⁹You have escaped the body. ¹⁰Where you are the body cannot enter, for the Holy Spirit has set His temple there.

8. There is no order in relationships. ²They either are or not. ³An

unholy relationship is no relationship. ⁴It is a state of isolation, which seems to be what it is not. ⁵No more than that. ⁶The instant that the mad idea of making your relationship with God unholy seemed to be possible, all your relationships were made meaningless. ⁷In that unholy instant time was born, and bodies made to house the mad idea and give it the illusion of reality. ⁸And so it seemed to have a home that held together for a little while in time, and vanished. ⁹For what could house this mad idea against reality but for an instant?

9.   Idols must disappear, and leave no trace behind their going. ²The unholy instant of their seeming power is frail as is a snowflake, but without its loveliness. ³Is this the substitute you want for the eternal blessing of the holy instant and its unlimited beneficence? ⁴Is the malevolence of the unholy relationship, so seeming powerful and so bitterly misunderstood and so invested in a false attraction your preference to the holy instant, which offers you peace and understanding? ⁵Then lay aside the body and quietly transcend it, rising to welcome what you really want. ⁶And from His holy temple, look you not back on what you have awakened from. ⁷For no illusions can attract the mind that has transcended them, and left them far behind.

10.   The holy relationship reflects the true relationship the Son of God has with his Father in reality. ²The Holy Spirit rests within it in the certainty it will endure forever. ³Its firm foundation is eternally upheld by truth, and love shines on it with the gentle smile and tender blessing it offers to its own. ⁴Here the unholy instant is exchanged in gladness for the holy one of safe return. ⁵Here is the way to true relationships held gently open, through which you and your brother walk together, leaving the body thankfully behind and resting in the Everlasting Arms. ⁶Love's Arms are open to receive you, and give you peace forever.

11.   The body is the ego's idol; the belief in sin made flesh and then projected outward. ²This produces what seems to be a wall of flesh around the mind, keeping it prisoner in a tiny spot of space and time, beholden unto death, and given but an instant in which to sigh and grieve and die in honor of its master. ³And this unholy instant seems to be life; an instant of despair, a tiny island of dry sand, bereft of water and set uncertainly upon oblivion. ⁴Here does the Son of God stop briefly by, to offer his devotion to death's idols and then pass on. ⁵And here he is more dead than living. ⁶Yet it is also here he makes his choice again between

idolatry and love. [7]Here it is given him to choose to spend this instant paying tribute to the body, or let himself be given freedom from it. [8]Here he can accept the holy instant, offered him to replace the unholy one he chose before. [9]And here can he learn relationships are his salvation, and not his doom.

12. You who are learning this may still be fearful, but you are not immobilized. [2]The holy instant is of greater value now to you than its unholy seeming counterpart, and you have learned you really want but one. [3]This is no time for sadness. [4]Perhaps confusion, but hardly discouragement. [5]You have a *real* relationship, and it has meaning. [6]It is as like your real relationship with God as equal things are like unto each other. [7]Idolatry is past and meaningless. [8]Perhaps you fear your brother a little yet; perhaps a shadow of the fear of God remains with you. [9]Yet what is that to those who have been given one true relationship beyond the body? [10]Can they be long held back from looking on the face of Christ? [11]And can they long withhold the memory of their relationship with their Father from themselves, and keep remembrance of His Love apart from their awareness?

VII. The Consistency of Means and End

1. We have said much about discrepancies of means and end, and how these must be brought in line before your holy relationship can bring you only joy. [2]But we have also said the means to meet the Holy Spirit's goal will come from the same Source as does His purpose. [3]Being so simple and direct, this course has nothing in it that is not consistent. [4]The seeming inconsistencies, or parts you find more difficult than others, are merely indications of areas where means and end are still discrepant. [5]And this produces great discomfort. [6]This need not be. [7]This course requires almost nothing of you. [8]It is impossible to imagine one that asks so little, or could offer more.

2. The period of discomfort that follows the sudden change in a relationship from sin to holiness may now be almost over. [2]To the extent you still experience it, you are refusing to leave the means to Him Who changed the purpose. [3]You recognize you want the goal. [4]Are you not also willing to accept the means? [5]If you are not, let us admit that *you* are inconsistent. [6]A purpose is attained by means, and if you want a purpose you must be willing to

want the means as well. ⁷How can one be sincere and say, "I want this above all else, and yet I do not want to learn the means to get it?"

3. To obtain the goal the Holy Spirit indeed asks little. ²He asks no more to give the means as well. ³The means are second to the goal. ⁴And when you hesitate, it is because the purpose frightens you, and not the means. ⁵Remember this, for otherwise you will make the error of believing the means are difficult. ⁶Yet how can they be difficult if they are merely given you? ⁷They guarantee the goal, and they are perfectly in line with it. ⁸Before we look at them a little closer, remember that if you think they are impossible, your wanting of the purpose has been shaken. ⁹For if a goal is possible to reach, the means to do so must be possible as well.

4. It *is* impossible to see your brother as sinless and yet to look upon him as a body. ²Is this not perfectly consistent with the goal of holiness? ³For holiness is merely the result of letting the effects of sin be lifted, so what was always true is recognized. ⁴To see a sinless body is impossible, for holiness is positive and the body is merely neutral. ⁵It is not sinful, but neither is it sinless. ⁶As nothing, which it is, the body cannot meaningfully be invested with attributes of Christ or of the ego. ⁷Either must be an error, for both would place the attributes where they cannot be. ⁸And both must be undone for purposes of truth.

5. The body *is* the means by which the ego tries to make the unholy relationship seem real. ²The unholy instant *is* the time of bodies. ³But the *purpose* here is sin. ⁴It cannot be attained but in illusion, and so the illusion of a brother as a body is quite in keeping with the purpose of unholiness. ⁵Because of this consistency, the means remain unquestioned while the end is cherished. ⁶Seeing adapts to wish, for sight is always secondary to desire. ⁷And if you see the body, you have chosen judgment and not vision. ⁸For vision, like relationships, has no order. ⁹You either see or not.

6. Who sees a brother's body has laid a judgment on him, and sees him not. ²He does not really see him as sinful; he does not see him at all. ³In the darkness of sin he is invisible. ⁴He can but be imagined in the darkness, and it is here that the illusions you hold about him are not held up to his reality. ⁵Here are illusions and reality kept separated. ⁶Here are illusions never brought to truth, and always hidden from it. ⁷And here, in darkness, is your brother's reality imagined as a body, in unholy relationships with

other bodies, serving the cause of sin an instant before he dies.

7. There is indeed a difference between this vain imagining and vision. ²The difference lies not in them, but in their purpose. ³Both are but means, each one appropriate to the end for which it is employed. ⁴Neither can serve the purpose of the other, for each one is a *choice* of purpose, employed on its behalf. ⁵Either is meaningless without the end for which it was intended, nor is it valued as a separate thing apart from the intention. ⁶The means seem real because the goal is valued. ⁷And judgment has no value unless the goal is sin.

8. The body cannot be looked upon except through judgment. ²To see the body is the sign that you lack vision, and have denied the means the Holy Spirit offers you to serve His purpose. ³How can a holy relationship achieve its purpose through the means of sin? ⁴Judgment you taught yourself; vision is learned from Him Who would undo your teaching. ⁵His vision cannot see the body because it cannot look on sin. ⁶And thus it leads you to reality. ⁷Your holy brother, sight of whom is your release, is no illusion. ⁸Attempt to see him not in darkness, for your imaginings about him will seem real there. ⁹You closed your eyes to shut him out. ¹⁰Such was your purpose, and while this purpose seems to have a meaning, the means for its attainment will be evaluated as worth the seeing, and so you will not see.

9. Your question should not be, "How can I see my brother without the body?" ²Ask only, "Do I really wish to see him sinless?" ³And as you ask, forget not that his sinlessness is *your* escape from fear. ⁴Salvation is the Holy Spirit's goal. ⁵The means is vision. ⁶For what the seeing look upon *is* sinless. ⁷No one who loves can judge, and what he sees is free of condemnation. ⁸And what he sees he did not make, for it was given him to see, as was the vision that made his seeing possible.

VIII. The Vision of Sinlessness

1. Vision will come to you at first in glimpses, but they will be enough to show you what is given you who see your brother sinless. ²Truth is restored to you through your desire, as it was lost to you through your desire for something else. ³Open the holy place that you closed off by valuing the "something else," and what was never lost will quietly return. ⁴It has been saved for

you. ⁵Vision would not be necessary had judgment not been made. ⁶Desire now its whole undoing, and it is done for you.

2. Do you not want to know your own Identity? ²Would you not happily exchange your doubts for certainty? ³Would you not willingly be free of misery, and learn again of joy? ⁴Your holy relationship offers all this to you. ⁵As it was given you, so will be its effects. ⁶And as its holy purpose was not made by you, the means by which its happy end is yours is also not of you. ⁷Rejoice in what is yours but for the asking, and think not that you need make either means or end. ⁸All this is given you who would but see your brother sinless. ⁹All this is given, waiting on your desire but to receive it. ¹⁰Vision is freely given to those who ask to see.

3. Your brother's sinlessness is given you in shining light, to look on with the Holy Spirit's vision and to rejoice in along with Him. ²For peace will come to all who ask for it with real desire and sincerity of purpose, shared with the Holy Spirit and at one with Him on what salvation is. ³Be willing, then, to see your brother sinless, that Christ may rise before your vision and give you joy. ⁴And place no value on your brother's body, which holds him to illusions of what he is. ⁵It is his desire to see his sinlessness, as it is yours. ⁶And bless the Son of God in your relationship, nor see in him what you have made of him.

4. The Holy Spirit guarantees that what God willed and gave you shall be yours. ²This is your purpose now, and the vision that makes it yours is ready to be given. ³You have the vision that enables you to see the body not. ⁴And as you look upon your brother, you will see an altar to your Father, holy as Heaven, glowing with radiant purity and sparkling with the shining lilies you laid upon it. ⁵What can you value more than this? ⁶Why do you think the body is a better home, a safer shelter for God's Son? ⁷Why would you rather look on it than on the truth? ⁸How can the engine of destruction be preferred, and chosen to replace the holy home the Holy Spirit offers, where He will dwell with you?

5. The body is the sign of weakness, vulnerability and loss of power. ²Can such a savior help you? ³Would you turn in your distress and need for help unto the helpless? ⁴Is the pitifully little the perfect choice to call upon for strength? ⁵Judgment will seem to make your savior weak. ⁶Yet it is *you* who need his strength. ⁷There is no problem, no event or situation, no perplexity that vision will not solve. ⁸All is redeemed when looked upon with vision. ⁹For this is not *your* sight, and brings with it the laws

beloved of Him Whose sight it is.

6. Everything looked upon with vision falls gently into place, according to the laws brought to it by His calm and certain sight. ²The end for everything He looks upon is always sure. ³For it will meet His purpose, seen in unadjusted form and suited perfectly to meet it. ⁴Destructiveness becomes benign, and sin is turned to blessing under His gentle gaze. ⁵What can the body's eyes perceive, with power to correct? ⁶Its eyes adjust to sin, unable to overlook it in any form and seeing it everywhere, in everything. ⁷Look through its eyes, and everything will stand condemned before you. ⁸All that could save you, you will never see. ⁹Your holy relationship, the source of your salvation, will be deprived of meaning, and its most holy purpose bereft of means for its accomplishment.

7. Judgment is but a toy, a whim, the senseless means to play the idle game of death in your imagination. ²But vision sets all things right, bringing them gently within the kindly sway of Heaven's laws. ³What if you recognized this world is an hallucination? ⁴What if you really understood you made it up? ⁵What if you realized that those who seem to walk about in it, to sin and die, attack and murder and destroy themselves, are wholly unreal? ⁶Could you have faith in what you see, if you accepted this? ⁷And would you see it?

8. Hallucinations disappear when they are recognized for what they are. ²This is the healing and the remedy. ³Believe them not and they are gone. ⁴And all you need to do is recognize that *you* did this. ⁵Once you accept this simple fact and take unto yourself the power you gave them, you are released from them. ⁶One thing is sure; hallucinations serve a purpose, and when that purpose is no longer held they disappear. ⁷Therefore, the question never is whether you want them, but always, do you want the purpose that they serve? ⁸This world seems to hold out many purposes, each different and with different values. ⁹Yet they are all the same. ¹⁰Again there is no order; only a seeming hierarchy of values.

9. Only two purposes are possible. ²And one is sin, the other holiness. ³Nothing is in between, and which you choose determines what you see. ⁴For what you see is merely how you elect to meet your goal. ⁵Hallucinations serve to meet the goal of madness. ⁶They are the means by which the outside world, projected from within, adjusts to sin and seems to witness to its reality. ⁷It still is

443

true that nothing is without. [8]Yet upon nothing are all projections made. [9]For it is the projection that gives the "nothing" all the meaning that it holds.

10. What has no meaning cannot be perceived. [2]And meaning always looks within to find itself, and *then* looks out. [3]All meaning that you give the world outside must thus reflect the sight you saw within; or better, if you saw at all or merely judged against. [4]Vision is the means by which the Holy Spirit translates your nightmares into happy dreams; your wild hallucinations that show you all the fearful outcomes of imagined sin into the calm and reassuring sights with which He would replace them. [5]These gentle sights and sounds are looked on happily, and heard with joy. [6]They are His substitutes for all the terrifying sights and screaming sounds the ego's purpose brought to your horrified awareness. [7]They step away from sin, reminding you that it is not reality which frightens you, and that the errors which you made can be corrected.

11. When you have looked on what seemed terrifying, and seen it change to sights of loveliness and peace; when you have looked on scenes of violence and death, and watched them change to quiet views of gardens under open skies, with clear, life-giving water running happily beside them in dancing brooks that never waste away; who need persuade you to accept the gift of vision? [2]And after vision, who is there who could refuse what must come after? [3]Think but an instant just on this; you can behold the holiness God gave His Son. [4]And never need you think that there is something else for you to see.

Chapter 21

REASON AND PERCEPTION

Introduction

1. Projection makes perception. [2]The world you see is what you gave it, nothing more than that. [3]But though it is no more than that, it is not less. [4]Therefore, to you it is important. [5]It is the witness to your state of mind, the outside picture of an inward condition. [6]As a man thinketh, so does he perceive. [7]Therefore, seek not to change the world, but choose to change your mind about the world. [8]Perception is a result and not a cause. [9]And that is why order of difficulty in miracles is meaningless. [10]Everything looked upon with vision is healed and holy. [11]Nothing perceived without it means anything. [12]And where there is no meaning, there is chaos.

2. Damnation is your judgment on yourself, and this you will project upon the world. [2]See it as damned, and all you see is what you did to hurt the Son of God. [3]If you behold disaster and catastrophe, you tried to crucify him. [4]If you see holiness and hope, you joined the Will of God to set him free. [5]There is no choice that lies between these two decisions. [6]And you will see the witness to the choice you made, and learn from this to recognize which one you chose. [7]The world you see but shows you how much joy you have allowed yourself to see in you, and to accept as yours. [8]And, if this *is* its meaning, then the power to give it joy must lie within you.

I. The Forgotten Song

1. Never forget the world the sightless "see" must be imagined, for what it really looks like is unknown to them. [2]They must infer what could be seen from evidence forever indirect; and reconstruct their inferences as they stumble and fall because of what they did not recognize, or walk unharmed through open doorways that they thought were closed. [3]And so it is with you. [4]You do not see. [5]Your cues for inference are wrong, and so you stumble and fall down upon the stones you did not recognize, but fail

445

to be aware you can go through the doors you thought were closed, but which stand open before unseeing eyes, waiting to welcome you.

2. How foolish is it to attempt to judge what could be seen instead. ²It is not necessary to imagine what the world must look like. ³It must be seen before you recognize it for what it is. ⁴You can be shown which doors are open, and you can see where safety lies; and which way leads to darkness, which to light. ⁵Judgment will always give you false directions, but vision shows you where to go. ⁶Why should you guess?

3. There is no need to learn through pain. ²And gentle lessons are acquired joyously, and are remembered gladly. ³What gives you happiness you want to learn and not forget. ⁴It is not this you would deny. ⁵Your question is whether the means by which this course is learned will bring to you the joy it promises. ⁶If you believed it would, the learning of it would be no problem. ⁷You are not a happy learner yet because you still remain uncertain that vision gives you more than judgment does, and you have learned that both you cannot have.

4. The blind become accustomed to their world by their adjustments to it. ²They think they know their way about in it. ³They learned it, not through joyous lessons, but through the stern necessity of limits they believed they could not overcome. ⁴And still believing this, they hold those lessons dear, and cling to them because they cannot see. ⁵They do not understand the lessons *keep* them blind. ⁶This they do not believe. ⁷And so they keep the world they learned to "see" in their imagination, believing that their choice is that or nothing. ⁸They hate the world they learned through pain. ⁹And everything they think is in it serves to remind them that they are incomplete and bitterly deprived.

5. Thus they define their life and where they live, adjusting to it as they think they must, afraid to lose the little that they have. ²And so it is with all who see the body as all they have and all their brothers have. ³They try to reach each other, and they fail, and fail again. ⁴And they adjust to loneliness, believing that to keep the body is to save the little that they have. ⁵Listen, and try to think if you remember what we will speak of now.

6. Listen,—perhaps you catch a hint of an ancient state not quite forgotten; dim, perhaps, and yet not altogether unfamiliar, like a song whose name is long forgotten, and the circumstances in which you heard completely unremembered. ²Not the whole

song has stayed with you, but just a little wisp of melody, attached not to a person or a place or anything particular. ³But you remember, from just this little part, how lovely was the song, how wonderful the setting where you heard it, and how you loved those who were there and listened with you.

7.   The notes are nothing. ²Yet you have kept them with you, not for themselves, but as a soft reminder of what would make you weep if you remembered how dear it was to you. ³You could remember, yet you are afraid, believing you would lose the world you learned since then. ⁴And yet you know that nothing in the world you learned is half so dear as this. ⁵Listen, and see if you remember an ancient song you knew so long ago and held more dear than any melody you taught yourself to cherish since.

8.   Beyond the body, beyond the sun and stars, past everything you see and yet somehow familiar, is an arc of golden light that stretches as you look into a great and shining circle. ²And all the circle fills with light before your eyes. ³The edges of the circle disappear, and what is in it is no longer contained at all. ⁴The light expands and covers everything, extending to infinity forever shining and with no break or limit anywhere. ⁵Within it everything is joined in perfect continuity. ⁶Nor is it possible to imagine that anything could be outside, for there is nowhere that this light is not.

9.   This is the vision of the Son of God, whom you know well. ²Here is the sight of him who knows his Father. ³Here is the memory of what you are; a part of this, with all of it within, and joined to all as surely as all is joined in you. ⁴Accept the vision that can show you this, and not the body. ⁵You know the ancient song, and know it well. ⁶Nothing will ever be as dear to you as is this ancient hymn of love the Son of God sings to his Father still.

10. And now the blind can see, for that same song they sing in honor of their Creator gives praise to them as well. ²The blindness that they made will not withstand the memory of this song. ³And they will look upon the vision of the Son of God, remembering who he is they sing of. ⁴What is a miracle but this remembering? ⁵And who is there in whom this memory lies not? ⁶The light in one awakens it in all. ⁷And when you see it in your brother, you *are* remembering for everyone.

II. The Responsibility for Sight

1. We have repeated how little is asked of you to learn this course. ²It is the same small willingness you need to have your whole relationship transformed to joy; the little gift you offer to the Holy Spirit for which He gives you everything; the very little on which salvation rests; the tiny change of mind by which the crucifixion is changed to resurrection. ³And being true, it is so simple that it cannot fail to be completely understood. ⁴Rejected yes, but not ambiguous. ⁵And if you choose against it now it will not be because it is obscure, but rather that this little cost seemed, in your judgment, to be too much to pay for peace.

2. This is the only thing that you need do for vision, happiness, release from pain and the complete escape from sin, all to be given you. ²Say only this, but mean it with no reservations, for here the power of salvation lies:

> ³*I am responsible for what I see.*
> ⁴*I choose the feelings I experience, and I decide*
>   *upon the goal I would achieve.*
> ⁵*And everything that seems to happen to me*
>   *I ask for, and receive as I have asked.*

⁶Deceive yourself no longer that you are helpless in the face of what is done to you. ⁷Acknowledge but that you have been mistaken, and all effects of your mistakes will disappear.

3. It is impossible the Son of God be merely driven by events outside of him. ²It is impossible that happenings that come to him were not his choice. ³His power of decision is the determiner of every situation in which he seems to find himself by chance or accident. ⁴No accident nor chance is possible within the universe as God created it, outside of which is nothing. ⁵Suffer, and you decided sin was your goal. ⁶Be happy, and you gave the power of decision to Him Who must decide for God for you. ⁷This is the little gift you offer to the Holy Spirit, and even this He gives to you to give yourself. ⁸For by this gift is given you the power to release your savior, that he may give salvation unto you.

4. Begrudge not then this little offering. ²Withhold it, and you keep the world as now you see it. ³Give it away, and everything you see goes with it. ⁴Never was so much given for so little. ⁵In the holy instant is this exchange effected and maintained. ⁶Here

is the world you do not want brought to the one you do. [7]And here the one you do is given you because you want it. [8]Yet for this, the power of your wanting must first be recognized. [9]You must accept its strength, and not its weakness. [10]You must perceive that what is strong enough to make a world can let it go, and can accept correction if it is willing to see that it was wrong.

5. The world you see is but the idle witness that you were right. [2]This witness is insane. [3]You trained it in its testimony, and as it gave it back to you, you listened and convinced yourself that what it saw was true. [4]You did this to yourself. [5]See only this, and you will also see how circular the reasoning on which your "seeing" rests. [6]This was not given you. [7]This was your gift to you and to your brother. [8]Be willing, then, to have it taken from him and be replaced with truth. [9]And as you look upon the change in him, it will be given you to see it in yourself.

6. Perhaps you do not see the need for you to give this little offering. [2]Look closer, then, at what it is. [3]And, very simply, see in it the whole exchange of separation for salvation. [4]All that the ego is, is an idea that it is possible that things could happen to the Son of God without his will; and thus without the Will of his Creator, Whose Will cannot be separate from his own. [5]This is the Son of God's replacement for his will, a mad revolt against what must forever be. [6]This is the statement that he has the power to make God powerless and so to take it for himself, and leave himself without what God has willed for him. [7]This is the mad idea you have enshrined upon your altars, and which you worship. [8]And anything that threatens this seems to attack your faith, for here is it invested. [9]Think not that you are faithless, for your belief and trust in this is strong indeed.

7. The Holy Spirit can give you faith in holiness and vision to see it easily enough. [2]But you have not left open and unoccupied the altar where the gifts belong. [3]Where they should be, you have set up your idols to something else. [4]This other "will," which seems to tell you what must happen, you give reality. [5]And what would show you otherwise must therefore seem unreal. [6]All that is asked of you is to make room for truth. [7]You are not asked to make or do what lies beyond your understanding. [8]All you are asked to do is *let it in;* only to stop your interference with what will happen of itself; simply to recognize again the presence of what you thought you gave away.

8. Be willing, for an instant, to leave your altars free of what you

placed upon them, and what is really there you cannot fail to see. [2]The holy instant is not an instant of creation, but of recognition. [3]For recognition comes of vision and suspended judgment. [4]Then only it is possible to look within and see what must be there, plainly in sight, and wholly independent of inference and judgment. [5]Undoing is not your task, but it *is* up to you to welcome it or not. [6]Faith and desire go hand in hand, for everyone believes in what he wants.

9. We have already said that wishful thinking is how the ego deals with what it wants, to make it so. [2]There is no better demonstration of the power of wanting, and therefore of faith, to make its goals seem real and possible. [3]Faith in the unreal leads to adjustments of reality to make it fit the goal of madness. [4]The goal of sin induces the perception of a fearful world to justify its purpose. [5]What you desire, you will see. [6]And if its reality is false, you will uphold it by not realizing all the adjustments you have introduced to make it so.

10. When vision is denied, confusion of cause and effect becomes inevitable. [2]The purpose now becomes to keep obscure the cause of the effect, and make effect appear to be a cause. [3]This seeming independence of effect enables it to be regarded as standing by itself, and capable of serving as a cause of the events and feelings its maker thinks it causes. [4]Earlier, we spoke of your desire to create your own creator, and be father and not son to him. [5]This is the same desire. [6]The Son is the Effect, whose Cause he would deny. [7]And so he seems to *be* the cause, producing real effects. [8]Nothing can have effects without a cause, and to confuse the two is merely to fail to understand them both.

11. It is as needful that you recognize you made the world you see, as that you recognize that you did not create yourself. [2]*They are the same mistake.* [3]Nothing created not by your Creator has any influence over you. [4]And if you think what you have made can tell you what you see and feel, and place your faith in its ability to do so, you are denying your Creator and believing that you made yourself. [5]For if you think the world you made has power to make you what it wills, you are confusing Son and Father; effect and Source.

12. The Son's creations are like his Father's. [2]Yet in creating them the Son does not delude himself that he is independent of his Source. [3]His union with It is the source of his creating. [4]Apart from this he has no power to create, and what he makes is mean-

ingless. ⁵It changes nothing in creation, depends entirely upon the madness of its maker, and cannot serve to justify the madness. ⁶Your brother thinks he made the world with you. ⁷Thus he denies creation. ⁸With you, he thinks the world he made, made him. ⁹Thus he denies he made it.

13. Yet the truth is you and your brother were both created by a loving Father, Who created you together and as one. ²See what "proves" otherwise, and you deny your whole reality. ³But grant that everything that seems to stand between you and your brother, keeping you from each other and separate from your Father, you made in secret, and the instant of release has come to you. ⁴All its effects are gone, because its source has been uncovered. ⁵It is its seeming independence of its source that keeps you prisoner. ⁶This is the same mistake as thinking you are independent of the Source by which you were created, and have never left.

III. Faith, Belief and Vision

1. All special relationships have sin as their goal. ²For they are bargains with reality, toward which the seeming union is adjusted. ³Forget not this; to bargain is to set a limit, and any brother with whom you have a limited relationship, you hate. ⁴You may attempt to keep the bargain in the name of "fairness," sometimes demanding payment of yourself, perhaps more often of the other. ⁵Thus in the "fairness" you attempt to ease the guilt that comes from the accepted purpose of the relationship. ⁶And that is why the Holy Spirit must change its purpose to make it useful to Him and harmless to you.

2. If you accept this change, you have accepted the idea of making room for truth. ²The *source* of sin is gone. ³You may imagine that you still experience its effects, but it is not your purpose and you no longer want it. ⁴No one allows a purpose to be replaced while he desires it, for nothing is so cherished and protected as is a goal the mind accepts. ⁵This it will follow, grimly or happily, but always with faith and with the persistence that faith inevitably brings. ⁶The power of faith is never recognized if it is placed in sin. ⁷But it is always recognized if it is placed in love.

3. Why is it strange to you that faith can move mountains? ²This

is indeed a little feat for such a power. ³For faith can keep the Son of God in chains as long as he believes he is in chains. ⁴And when he is released from them it will be simply because he no longer believes in them, withdrawing faith that they can hold him, and placing it in his freedom instead. ⁵It is impossible to place equal faith in opposite directions. ⁶What faith you give to sin you take away from holiness. ⁷And what you offer holiness has been removed from sin.

4. Faith and belief and vision are the means by which the goal of holiness is reached. ²Through them the Holy Spirit leads you to the real world, and away from all illusions where your faith was laid. ³This is His direction; the only one He ever sees. ⁴And when you wander, He reminds you there is but one. ⁵His faith and His belief and vision are all for you. ⁶And when you have accepted them completely instead of yours, you will have need of them no longer. ⁷For faith and vision and belief are meaningful only before the state of certainty is reached. ⁸In Heaven they are unknown. ⁹Yet Heaven is reached through them.

5. It is impossible that the Son of God lack faith, but he can choose where he would have it be. ²Faithlessness is not a lack of faith, but faith in nothing. ³Faith given to illusions does not lack power, for by it does the Son of God believe that he is powerless. ⁴Thus is he faithless to himself, but strong in faith in his illusions about himself. ⁵For faith, perception and belief you made, as means for losing certainty and finding sin. ⁶This mad direction was your choice, and by your faith in what you chose, you made what you desired.

6. The Holy Spirit has a use for all the means for sin by which you sought to find it. ²But as He uses them they lead away from sin, because His purpose lies in the opposite direction. ³He sees the means you use, but not the purpose for which you made them. ⁴He would not take them from you, for He sees their value as a means for what He wills for you. ⁵You made perception that you might choose among your brothers, and seek for sin with them. ⁶The Holy Spirit sees perception as a means to teach you that the vision of a holy relationship is all you *want* to see. ⁷Then will you give your faith to holiness, desiring and believing in it because of your desire.

7. Faith and belief become attached to vision, as all the means that once served sin are redirected now toward holiness. ²For what you think is sin is limitation, and whom you try to limit to

the body you hate because you fear. ³In your refusal to forgive him, you would condemn him to the body because the means for sin are dear to you. ⁴And so the body has your faith and your belief. ⁵But holiness would set your brother free, removing hatred by removing fear, not as a symptom, but at its source.

8. Those who would free their brothers from the body can have no fear. ²They have renounced the means for sin by choosing to let all limitations be removed. ³As they desire to look upon their brothers in holiness, the power of their belief and faith sees far beyond the body, supporting vision, not obstructing it. ⁴But first they chose to recognize how much their faith had limited their understanding of the world, desiring to place its power else-where should another point of view be given them. ⁵The miracles that follow this decision are also born of faith. ⁶For all who choose to look away from sin are given vision, and are led to holiness.

9. Those who believe in sin must think the Holy Spirit asks for sacrifice, for this is how they think *their* purpose is accomplished. ²Brother, the Holy Spirit knows that sacrifice brings nothing. ³He makes no bargains. ⁴And if you seek to limit Him, you will hate Him because you are afraid. ⁵The gift that He has given you is more than anything that stands this side of Heaven. ⁶The instant for its recognition is at hand. ⁷Join your awareness to what has been already joined. ⁸The faith you give your brother can accom-plish this. ⁹For He Who loves the world is seeing it for you, with-out one spot of sin upon it, and in the innocence that makes the sight of it as beautiful as Heaven.

10. Your faith in sacrifice has given it great power in your sight; except you do not realize you cannot see because of it. ²For sacri-fice must be exacted of a body, and by another body. ³The mind could neither ask it nor receive it of itself. ⁴And no more could the body. ⁵The intention is in the mind, which tries to use the body to carry out the means for sin in which the mind believes. ⁶Thus is the joining of mind and body an inescapable belief of those who value sin. ⁷And so is sacrifice invariably a means for limitation, and thus for hate.

11. Think you the Holy Spirit is concerned with this? ²He gives not what it is His purpose to lead you *from*. ³You think He would deprive you for your good. ⁴But "good" and "deprivation" are opposites, and cannot meaningfully join in any way. ⁵It is like saying that the moon and sun are one because they come with

night and day, and so they must be joined. ⁶Yet sight of one is but the sign the other has disappeared from sight. ⁷Nor is it possible that what gives light be one with what depends on darkness to be seen. ⁸Neither demands the sacrifice of the other. ⁹Yet on the absence of the other does each depend.

12.   The body was made to be a sacrifice to sin, and in the darkness so it still is seen. ²Yet in the light of vision it is looked upon quite differently. ³You can have faith in it to serve the Holy Spirit's goal, and give it power to serve as means to help the blind to see. ⁴But in their seeing they look past it, as do you. ⁵The faith and the belief you gave it belongs beyond. ⁶You gave perception and belief and faith from mind to body. ⁷Let them now be given back to what produced them, and can use them still to save itself from what it made.

IV. The Fear to Look Within

1.   The Holy Spirit will never teach you that you are sinful. ²Errors He will correct, but this makes no one fearful. ³You are indeed afraid to look within and see the sin you think is there. ⁴This you would not be fearful to admit. ⁵Fear in association with sin the ego deems quite appropriate, and smiles approvingly. ⁶It has no fear to let you feel ashamed. ⁷It doubts not your belief and faith in sin. ⁸Its temples do not shake because of this. ⁹Your faith that sin is there but witnesses to your desire that it *be* there to see. ¹⁰This merely seems to be the source of fear.

2.   Remember that the ego is not alone. ²Its rule is tempered, and its unknown "enemy," Whom it cannot even see, it fears. ³Loudly the ego tells you not to look inward, for if you do your eyes will light on sin, and God will strike you blind. ⁴This you believe, and so you do not look. ⁵Yet this is not the ego's hidden fear, nor yours who serve it. ⁶Loudly indeed the ego claims it is; too loudly and too often. ⁷For underneath this constant shout and frantic proclamation, the ego is not certain it is so. ⁸Beneath your fear to look within because of sin is yet another fear, and one which makes the ego tremble.

3.   What if you looked within and saw no sin? ²This "fearful" question is one the ego never asks. ³And you who ask it now are threatening the ego's whole defensive system too seriously for it to bother to pretend it is your friend. ⁴Those who have joined

their brothers have detached themselves from their belief that their identity lies in the ego. ⁵A holy relationship is one in which you join with what is part of you in truth. ⁶And your belief in sin has been already shaken, nor are you now entirely unwilling to look within and see it not.

4.   Your liberation still is only partial; still limited and incomplete, yet born within you. ²Not wholly mad, you have been willing to look on much of your insanity and recognize its madness. ³Your faith is moving inward, past insanity and on to reason. ⁴And what your reason tells you now the ego would not hear. ⁵The Holy Spirit's purpose was accepted by the part of your mind the ego knows not of. ⁶No more did you. ⁷And yet this part, with which you now identify, is not afraid to look upon itself. ⁸It knows no sin. ⁹How, otherwise, could it have been willing to see the Holy Spirit's purpose as its own?

5.   This part has seen your brother, and recognized him perfectly since time began. ²And it desired nothing but to join with him and to be free again, as once it was. ³It has been waiting for the birth of freedom; the acceptance of release to come to you. ⁴And now you recognize that it was not the ego that joined the Holy Spirit's purpose, and so there must be something else. ⁵Think not that this is madness. ⁶For this your reason tells you, and it follows perfectly from what you have already learned.

6.   There is no inconsistency in what the Holy Spirit teaches. ²This is the reasoning of the sane. ³You have perceived the ego's madness, and not been made afraid because you did not choose to share in it. ⁴At times it still deceives you. ⁵Yet in your saner moments, its ranting strikes no terror in your heart. ⁶For you have realized that all the gifts it would withdraw from you, in rage at your "presumptuous" wish to look within, you do not want. ⁷A few remaining trinkets still seem to shine and catch your eye. ⁸Yet you would not "sell" Heaven to have them.

7.   And now the ego *is* afraid. ²Yet what it hears in terror, the other part hears as the sweetest music; the song it longed to hear since first the ego came into your mind. ³The ego's weakness is its strength. ⁴The song of freedom, which sings the praises of another world, brings to it hope of peace. ⁵For it remembers Heaven, and now it sees that Heaven has come to earth at last, from which the ego's rule has kept it out so long. ⁶Heaven has come because it found a home in your relationship on earth. ⁷And earth can hold no longer what has been given Heaven as its own.

8. Look gently on your brother, and remember the ego's weakness is revealed in both your sight. ²What it would keep apart has met and joined, and looks upon the ego unafraid. ³Little child, innocent of sin, follow in gladness the way to certainty. ⁴Be not held back by fear's insane insistence that sureness lies in doubt. ⁵This has no meaning. ⁶What matters it to you how loudly it is proclaimed? ⁷The senseless is not made meaningful by repetition and by clamor. ⁸The quiet way is open. ⁹Follow it happily, and question not what must be so.

V. The Function of Reason

1. Perception selects, and makes the world you see. ²It literally picks it out as the mind directs. ³The laws of size and shape and brightness would hold, perhaps, if other things were equal. ⁴They are not equal. ⁵For what you look for you are far more likely to discover than what you would prefer to overlook. ⁶The still, small Voice for God is not drowned out by all the ego's raucous screams and senseless ravings to those who want to hear It. ⁷Perception is a choice and not a fact. ⁸But on this choice depends far more than you may realize as yet. ⁹For on the voice you choose to hear, and on the sights you choose to see, depends entirely your whole belief in what you are. ¹⁰Perception is a witness but to this, and never to reality. ¹¹Yet it can show you the conditions in which awareness of reality is possible, or those where it could never be.

2. Reality needs no cooperation from you to be itself. ²But your awareness of it needs your help, because it is your choice. ³Listen to what the ego says, and see what it directs you see, and it is sure that you will see yourself as tiny, vulnerable and afraid. ⁴You will experience depression, a sense of worthlessness, and feelings of impermanence and unreality. ⁵You will believe that you are helpless prey to forces far beyond your own control, and far more powerful than you. ⁶And you will think the world you made directs your destiny. ⁷For this will be your faith. ⁸But never believe because it is your faith it makes reality.

3. There is another vision and another Voice in which your freedom lies, awaiting but your choice. ²And if you place your faith in Them, you will perceive another self in you. ³This other self sees miracles as natural. ⁴They are as simple and as natural to it as breathing to the body. ⁵They are the obvious response to calls

for help, the only one it makes. ⁶Miracles seem unnatural to the ego because it does not understand how separate minds can influence each other. ⁷Nor *could* they do so. ⁸But minds cannot be separate. ⁹This other self is perfectly aware of this. ¹⁰And thus it recognizes that miracles do not affect another's mind, only its own. ¹¹They always change *your* mind. ¹²There *is* no other.

4. You do not realize the whole extent to which the idea of separation has interfered with reason. ²Reason lies in the other self you have cut off from your awareness. ³And nothing you have allowed to stay in your awareness is capable of reason. ⁴How can the segment of the mind devoid of reason understand what reason is, or grasp the information it would give? ⁵All sorts of questions may arise in it, but if the basic question stems from reason, it will not ask it. ⁶Like all that stems from reason, the basic question is obvious, simple and remains unasked. ⁷But think not reason could not answer it.

5. God's plan for your salvation could not have been established without your will and your consent. ²It must have been accepted by the Son of God, for what God wills for him he must receive. ³For God wills not apart from him, nor does the Will of God wait upon time to be accomplished. ⁴Therefore, what joined the Will of God must be in you now, being eternal. ⁵You must have set aside a place in which the Holy Spirit can abide, and where He is. ⁶He must have been there since the need for Him arose, and was fulfilled in the same instant. ⁷Such would your reason tell you, if you listened. ⁸Yet such is clearly not the ego's reasoning. ⁹Your reason's alien nature to the ego is proof you will not find the answer there. ¹⁰Yet if it must be so, it must exist. ¹¹And if it exists for you, and has your freedom as the purpose given it, you must be free to find it.

6. God's plan is simple; never circular and never self-defeating. ²He has no Thoughts except the Self-extending, and in this your will must be included. ³Thus, there must be a part of you that knows His Will and shares it. ⁴It is not meaningful to ask if what must be is so. ⁵But it is meaningful to ask why you are unaware of what is so, for this must have an answer if the plan of God for your salvation is complete. ⁶And it must be complete, because its Source knows not of incompletion.

7. Where would the answer be but in the Source? ²And where are you but there, where this same answer is? ³Your Identity, as much a true Effect of this same Source as is the answer, must therefore

be together and the same. ⁴O yes, you know this, and more than this alone. ⁵Yet any part of knowledge threatens dissociation as much as all of it. ⁶And all of it will come with any part. ⁷Here is the part you can accept. ⁸What reason points to you can see, because the witnesses on its behalf are clear. ⁹Only the totally insane can disregard them, and you have gone past this. ¹⁰Reason is a means that serves the Holy Spirit's purpose in its own right. ¹¹It is not reinterpreted and redirected from the goal of sin, as are the others. ¹²For reason is beyond the ego's range of means.

8. Faith and perception and belief can be misplaced, and serve the great deceiver's needs as well as truth. ²But reason has no place at all in madness, nor can it be adjusted to fit its end. ³Faith and belief are strong in madness, guiding perception toward what the mind has valued. ⁴But reason enters not at all in this. ⁵For the perception would fall away at once, if reason were applied. ⁶There is no reason in insanity, for it depends entirely on reason's absence. ⁷The ego never uses it, because it does not realize that it exists. ⁸The partially insane have access to it, and only they have need of it. ⁹Knowledge does not depend on it, and madness keeps it out.

9. The part of mind where reason lies was dedicated, by your will in union with your Father's, to the undoing of insanity. ²Here was the Holy Spirit's purpose accepted and accomplished, both at once. ³Reason is alien to insanity, and those who use it have gained a means which cannot be applied to sin. ⁴Knowledge is far beyond attainment of any kind. ⁵But reason can serve to open doors you closed against it.

10. You have come very close to this. ²Faith and belief have shifted, and you have asked the question the ego will never ask. ³Does not your reason tell you now the question must have come from something that you do not know, but must belong to you? ⁴Faith and belief, upheld by reason, cannot fail to lead to changed perception. ⁵And in this change is room made way for vision. ⁶Vision extends beyond itself, as does the purpose that it serves, and all the means for its accomplishment.

VI. Reason versus Madness

1. Reason cannot see sin but can see errors, and leads to their correction. ²It does not value *them,* but their correction. ³Reason will also tell you that when you think you sin, you call for help. ⁴Yet if you will not accept the help you call for, you will not believe that it is yours to give. ⁵And so you will not give it, thus maintaining the belief. ⁶For uncorrected error of any kind deceives you about the power that is in you to make correction. ⁷If it can correct, and you allow it not to do so, you deny it to yourself and to your brother. ⁸And if he shares this same belief you both will think that you are damned. ⁹This you could spare him and yourself. ¹⁰For reason would not make way for correction in you alone.

2. Correction cannot be accepted or refused by you without your brother. ²Sin would maintain it can. ³Yet reason tells you that you cannot see your brother or yourself as sinful and still perceive the other innocent. ⁴Who looks upon himself as guilty and sees a sinless world? ⁵And who can see a sinful world and look upon himself apart from it? ⁶Sin would maintain you and your brother must be separate. ⁷But reason tells you that this must be wrong. ⁸If you and your brother are joined, how could it be that you have private thoughts? ⁹And how could thoughts that enter into what but seems like yours alone have no effect at all on what *is* yours? ¹⁰If minds are joined, this is impossible.

3. No one can think but for himself, as God thinks not without His Son. ²Only were Both in bodies could this be. ³Nor could one mind think only for itself unless the body *were* the mind. ⁴For only bodies can be separate, and therefore unreal. ⁵The home of madness cannot be the home of reason. ⁶Yet it is easy to leave the home of madness if you see reason. ⁷You do not leave insanity by going somewhere else. ⁸You leave it simply by accepting reason where madness was. ⁹Madness and reason see the same things, but it is certain that they look upon them differently.

4. Madness is an attack on reason that drives it out of mind, and takes its place. ²Reason does not attack, but takes the place of madness quietly, replacing madness if it be the choice of the insane to listen to it. ³But the insane know not their will, for they believe they see the body, and let their madness tell them it is real. ⁴Reason would be incapable of this. ⁵And if you would defend the body against your reason, you will not understand the

body or yourself.

5.   The body does not separate you from your brother, and if you think it does you are insane. ²But madness has a purpose, and believes it also has the means to make its purpose real. ³To see the body as a barrier between what reason tells you must be joined must be insane. ⁴Nor could you see it, if you heard the voice of reason. ⁵What can there be that stands between what is continuous? ⁶And if there is nothing in between, how can what enters part be kept away from other parts? ⁷Reason would tell you this. ⁸But think what you must recognize, if it be so.

6.   If you choose sin instead of healing, you would condemn the Son of God to what can never be corrected. ²You tell him, by your choice, that he is damned; separate from you and from his Father forever, without a hope of safe return. ³You teach him this, and you will learn of him exactly what you taught. ⁴For you can teach him only that he is as you would have him, and what you choose he be is but your choice for you. ⁵Yet think not this is fearful. ⁶That you are joined to him is but a fact, not an interpretation. ⁷How can a fact be fearful unless it disagrees with what you hold more dear than truth? ⁸Reason will tell you that this fact is your release.

7.   Neither your brother nor yourself can be attacked alone. ²But neither can accept a miracle instead without the other being blessed by it, and healed of pain. ³Reason, like love, would reassure you, and seeks not to frighten you. ⁴The power to heal the Son of God is given you because he must be one with you. ⁵You *are* responsible for how he sees himself. ⁶And reason tells you it is given you to change his whole mind, which is one with you, in just an instant. ⁷And any instant serves to bring complete correction of his errors and make him whole. ⁸The instant that you choose to let yourself be healed, in that same instant is his whole salvation seen as complete with yours. ⁹Reason is given you to understand that this is so. ¹⁰For reason, kind as is the purpose for which it is the means, leads steadily away from madness toward the goal of truth. ¹¹And here you will lay down the burden of denying truth. ¹²*This* is the burden that is terrible, and not the truth.

8.   That you and your brother are joined is your salvation; the gift of Heaven, not the gift of fear. ²Does Heaven seem to be a burden to you? ³In madness, yes. ⁴And yet what madness sees must be dispelled by reason. ⁵Reason assures you Heaven is what you

want, and all you want. [6]Listen to Him Who speaks with reason, and brings your reason into line with His. [7]Be willing to let reason be the means by which He would direct you how to leave insanity behind. [8]Hide not behind insanity in order to escape from reason. [9]What madness would conceal, the Holy Spirit still holds out for everyone to look upon with gladness.

9. You *are* your brother's savior. [2]He is yours. [3]Reason speaks happily indeed of this. [4]This gracious plan was given love by Love. [5]And what Love plans is like Itself in this: Being united, It would have you learn what you must be. [6]And being one with It, it must be given you to give what It has given, and gives still. [7]Spend but an instant in the glad acceptance of what is given you to give your brother, and learn with him what has been given both of you. [8]To give is no more blessed than to receive. [9]But neither is it less.

10. The Son of God is always blessed as one. [2]And as his gratitude goes out to you who blessed him, reason will tell you that it cannot be you stand apart from blessing. [3]The gratitude he offers you reminds you of the thanks your Father gives you for completing Him. [4]And here alone does reason tell you that you can understand what you must be. [5]Your Father is as close to you as is your brother. [6]Yet what is there that could be nearer you than is your Self?

11. The power you have over the Son of God is not a threat to his reality. [2]It but attests to it. [3]Where could his freedom lie but in himself, if he be free already? [4]And who could bind him but himself, if he deny his freedom? [5]God is not mocked; no more His Son can be imprisoned save by his own desire. [6]And it is by his own desire that he is freed. [7]Such is his strength, and not his weakness. [8]He is at his own mercy. [9]And where he chooses to be merciful, there is he free. [10]But where he chooses to condemn instead, there is he held a prisoner, waiting in chains his pardon on himself to set him free.

VII. The Last Unanswered Question

1. Do you not see that all your misery comes from the strange belief that you are powerless? [2]Being helpless is the cost of sin. [3]Helplessness is sin's condition; the one requirement that it demands to be believed. [4]Only the helpless could believe in it.

[5]Enormity has no appeal save to the little. [6]And only those who first believe that they are little could see attraction there. [7]Treachery to the Son of God is the defense of those who do not identify with him. [8]And you are for him or against him; either you love him or attack him, protect his unity or see him shattered and slain by your attack.

2.   No one believes the Son of God is powerless. [2]And those who see themselves as helpless must believe that they are not the Son of God. [3]What can they be except his enemy? [4]And what can they do but envy him his power, and by their envy make themselves afraid of it? [5]These are the dark ones, silent and afraid, alone and not communicating, fearful the power of the Son of God will strike them dead, and raising up their helplessness against him. [6]They join the army of the powerless, to wage their war of vengeance, bitterness and spite on him, to make him one with them. [7]Because they do not know that they *are* one with him, they know not whom they hate. [8]They are indeed a sorry army, each one as likely to attack his brother or turn upon himself as to remember that they thought they had a common cause.

3.   Frantic and loud and strong the dark ones seem to be. [2]Yet they know not their "enemy," except they hate him. [3]In hatred they have come together, but have not joined each other. [4]For had they done so hatred would be impossible. [5]The army of the powerless must be disbanded in the presence of strength. [6]Those who are strong are never treacherous, because they have no need to dream of power and to act out their dream. [7]How would an army act in dreams? [8]Any way at all. [9]It could be seen attacking anyone with anything. [10]Dreams have no reason in them. [11]A flower turns into a poisoned spear, a child becomes a giant and a mouse roars like a lion. [12]And love is turned to hate as easily. [13]This is no army, but a madhouse. [14]What seems to be a planned attack is bedlam.

4.   The army of the powerless is weak indeed. [2]It has no weapons and it has no enemy. [3]Yes, it can overrun the world and *seek* an enemy. [4]But it can never find what is not there. [5]Yes, it can *dream* it found an enemy, but this will shift even as it attacks, so that it runs at once to find another, and never comes to rest in victory. [6]And as it runs it turns against itself, thinking it caught a glimpse of the great enemy who always eludes its murderous attack by turning into something else. [7]How treacherous does this enemy appear, who changes so it is impossible even to recognize him.

5.   Yet hate must have a target. [2]There can be no faith in sin

without an enemy. ³Who that believes in sin would dare believe he has no enemy? ⁴Could he admit that no one made him powerless? ⁵Reason would surely bid him seek no longer what is not there to find. ⁶Yet first he must be willing to perceive a world where it is not. ⁷It is not necessary that he understand how he can see it. ⁸Nor should he try. ⁹For if he focuses on what he cannot understand, he will but emphasize his helplessness, and let sin tell him that his enemy must be himself. ¹⁰But let him only ask himself these questions, which he must decide, to have it done for him:

> ¹¹Do I desire a world I rule instead of one that rules me?
> ¹²Do I desire a world where I am powerful instead of helpless?
> ¹³Do I desire a world in which I have no enemies and cannot sin?
> ¹⁴And do I want to see what I denied *because* it is the truth?

6. You may already have answered the first three questions, but not yet the last. ²For this one still seems fearful, and unlike the others. ³Yet reason would assure you they are all the same. ⁴We said this year would emphasize the sameness of things that are the same. ⁵This final question, which is indeed the last you need decide, still seems to hold a threat the rest have lost for you. ⁶And this imagined difference attests to your belief that truth may be the enemy you yet may find. ⁷Here, then, would seem to be the last remaining hope of finding sin, and not accepting power.

7. Forget not that the choice of sin or truth, helplessness or power, is the choice of whether to attack or heal. ²For healing comes of power, and attack of helplessness. ³Whom you attack you *cannot* want to heal. ⁴And whom you would have healed must be the one you chose to be protected from attack. ⁵And what is this decision but the choice whether to see him through the body's eyes, or let him be revealed to you through vision? ⁶How this decision leads to its effects is not your problem. ⁷But what you want to see must be your choice. ⁸This is a course in cause and not effect.

8. Consider carefully your answer to the last question you have left unanswered still. ²And let your reason tell you that it must be answered, and is answered in the other three. ³And then it will be clear to you that, as you look on the effects of sin in any form, all you need do is simply ask yourself:

⁴Is this what I would see? ⁵Do I want this?

9.   This is your one decision; this the condition for what occurs. ²It is irrelevant to how it happens, but not to why. ³You *have* control of this. ⁴And if you choose to see a world without an enemy, in which you are not helpless, the means to see it will be given you.

10.   Why is the final question so important? ²Reason will tell you why. ³It is the same as are the other three, except in time. ⁴The others are decisions that can be made, and then unmade and made again. ⁵But truth is constant, and implies a state where vacillations are impossible. ⁶You can desire a world you rule that rules you not, and change your mind. ⁷You can desire to exchange your helplessness for power, and lose this same desire as a little glint of sin attracts you. ⁸And you can want to see a sinless world, and let an "enemy" tempt you to use the body's eyes and change what you desire.

11.   In content all the questions are the same. ²For each one asks if you are willing to exchange the world of sin for what the Holy Spirit sees, since it is this the world of sin denies. ³And therefore those who look on sin are seeing the denial of the real world. ⁴Yet the last question adds the wish for constancy in your desire to see the real world, so the desire becomes the only one you have. ⁵By answering the final question "yes," you add sincerity to the decisions you have already made to all the rest. ⁶For only then have you renounced the option to change your mind again. ⁷When it is this you do not want, the rest are wholly answered.

12.   Why do you think you are unsure the others have been answered? ²Could it be necessary they be asked so often, if they had? ³Until the last decision has been made, the answer is both "yes" and "no." ⁴For you have answered "yes" without perceiving that "yes" must mean "not no." ⁵No one decides against his happiness, but he may do so if he does not see he does it. ⁶And if he sees his happiness as ever changing, now this, now that, and now an elusive shadow attached to nothing, he does decide against it.

13.   Elusive happiness, or happiness in changing form that shifts with time and place, is an illusion that has no meaning. ²Happiness must be constant, because it is attained by giving up the wish for the *in*constant. ³Joy cannot be perceived except through constant vision. ⁴And constant vision can be given only those who wish for constancy. ⁵The power of the Son of God's desire

remains the proof that he is wrong who sees himself as helpless.
[6]Desire what you want, and you will look on it and think it real.
[7]No thought but has the power to release or kill. [8]And none can
leave the thinker's mind, or leave him unaffected.

VIII. The Inner Shift

1. Are thoughts, then, dangerous? [2]To bodies, yes! [3]The thoughts
that seem to kill are those that teach the thinker that he *can* be
killed. [4]And so he "dies" because of what he learned. [5]He goes
from life to death, the final proof he valued the inconstant more
than constancy. [6]Surely he thought he wanted happiness. [7]Yet he
did not desire it *because* it was the truth, and therefore must be
constant.

2. The constancy of joy is a condition quite alien to your understanding. [2]Yet if you could even imagine what it must be, you
would desire it although you understand it not. [3]The constancy
of happiness has no exceptions; no change of any kind. [4]It is unshakable as is the Love of God for His creation. [5]Sure in its vision
as its Creator is in what He knows, happiness looks on everything and sees it is the same. [6]It sees not the ephemeral, for it
desires everything be like itself, and sees it so. [7]Nothing has
power to confound its constancy, because its own desire cannot
be shaken. [8]It comes as surely unto those who see the final question is necessary to the rest, as peace must come to those who
choose to heal and not to judge.

3. Reason will tell you that you cannot ask for happiness incon-
stantly. [2]For if what you desire you receive, and happiness is constant, then you need ask for it but once to have it always. [3]And if
you do not have it always, being what it is, you did not ask for it.
[4]For no one fails to ask for his desire of something he believes
holds out some promise of the power of giving it. [5]He may be
wrong in what he asks, where, and of what. [6]Yet he will ask because desire is a request, an asking for, and made by one whom
God Himself will never fail to answer. [7]God has already given all
that he really wants. [8]Yet what he is uncertain of, God cannot
give. [9]For he does not desire it while he remains uncertain, and
God's giving must be incomplete unless it is received.

4. You who complete God's Will and are His happiness, whose
will is powerful as His, a power that is not lost in your illusions,

think carefully why you have not yet decided how you would answer the final question. ²Your answer to the others has made it possible to help you be already partly sane. ³And yet it is the final one that really asks if you are willing to be wholly sane.

5.   What is the holy instant but God's appeal to you to recognize what He has given you? ²Here is the great appeal to reason; the awareness of what is always there to see, the happiness that could be always yours. ³Here is the constant peace you could experience forever. ⁴Here is what denial has denied revealed to you. ⁵For here the final question is already answered, and what you ask for given. ⁶Here is the future *now*, for time is powerless because of your desire for what will never change. ⁷For you have asked that nothing stand between the holiness of your relationship and your *awareness* of its holiness.

Chapter 22

SALVATION AND THE HOLY RELATIONSHIP

Introduction

1. Take pity on yourself, so long enslaved. ²Rejoice whom God hath joined have come together and need no longer look on sin apart. ³No two can look on sin together, for they could never see it in the same place and time. ⁴Sin is a strictly individual perception, seen in the other yet believed by each to be within himself. ⁵And each one seems to make a different error, and one the other cannot understand. ⁶Brother, it is the same, made by the same, and forgiven for its maker in the same way. ⁷The holiness of your relationship forgives you and your brother, undoing the effects of what you both believed and saw. ⁸And with their going is the need for sin gone with them.

2. Who has need for sin? ²Only the lonely and alone, who see their brothers different from themselves. ³It is this difference, seen but not real, that makes the need for sin, not real but seen, seem justified. ⁴And all this would be real if sin were so. ⁵For an unholy relationship is based on differences, where each one thinks the other has what he has not. ⁶They come together, each to complete himself and rob the other. ⁷They stay until they think that there is nothing left to steal, and then move on. ⁸And so they wander through a world of strangers, unlike themselves, living with their bodies perhaps under a common roof that shelters neither; in the same room and yet a world apart.

3. A holy relationship starts from a different premise. ²Each one has looked within and seen no lack. ³Accepting his completion, he would extend it by joining with another, whole as himself. ⁴He sees no difference between these selves, for differences are only of the body. ⁵Therefore, he looks on nothing he would take. ⁶He denies not his own reality *because* it is the truth. ⁷Just under Heaven does he stand, but close enough not to return to earth. ⁸For this relationship has Heaven's Holiness. ⁹How far from home can a relationship so like to Heaven be?

4. Think what a holy relationship can teach! ²Here is belief in differences undone. ³Here is the faith in differences shifted to sameness. ⁴And here is sight of differences transformed to vision.

467

⁵Reason now can lead you and your brother to the logical conclusion of your union. ⁶It must extend, as you extended when you and he joined. ⁷It must reach out beyond itself, as you reached out beyond the body, to let you and your brother be joined. ⁸And now the sameness that you saw extends and finally removes all sense of differences, so that the sameness that lies beneath them all becomes apparent. ⁹Here is the golden circle where you recognize the Son of God. ¹⁰For what is born into a holy relationship can never end.

I. The Message of the Holy Relationship

1. Let reason take another step. ²If you attack whom God would heal and hate the one He loves, then you and your Creator have a different will. ³Yet if you *are* His Will, what you must then believe is that you are not yourself. ⁴You can indeed believe this, and you do. ⁵And you have faith in this and see much evidence on its behalf. ⁶And where, you wonder, does your strange uneasiness, your sense of being disconnected, and your haunting fear of lack of meaning in yourself arise? ⁷It is as though you wandered in without a plan of any kind except to wander off, for only that seems certain.

2. Yet we have heard a very similar description earlier, but it was not of you. ²But still this strange idea which it does accurately describe, you *think* is you. ³Reason would tell you that the world you see through eyes that are not yours must make no sense to you. ⁴To whom would seeing such as this send back its messages? ⁵Surely not you, whose sight is wholly independent of the eyes that look upon the world. ⁶If this is not your vision, what can it show to you? ⁷The brain cannot interpret what your vision sees. ⁸This *you* would understand. ⁹The brain interprets to the body, of which it is a part. ¹⁰But what it says you cannot understand. ¹¹Yet you have listened to it. ¹²And long and hard you tried to understand its messages.

3. You have not realized it is impossible to understand what fails entirely to reach you. ²You have received no messages at all you understand. ³For you have listened to what can never communicate at all. ⁴Think, then, what happens. ⁵Denying what you are, and firm in faith that you are something else, this "something else" that you have made to be yourself becomes your sight. ⁶Yet

it must be the "something else" that sees, and as *not* you, explains its sight *to* you. [7]Your vision would, of course, render this quite unnecessary. [8]Yet if your eyes are closed and you have called upon this thing to lead you, asking it to explain to you the world it sees, you have no reason not to listen, nor to suspect that what it tells you is not true. [9]Reason would tell you it cannot be true *because* you do not understand it. [10]God has no secrets. [11]He does not lead you through a world of misery, waiting to tell you, at the journey's end, why He did this to you.

4. What could be secret from God's Will? [2]Yet you believe that you have secrets. [3]What could your secrets be except another "will" that is your own, apart from His? [4]Reason would tell you that this is no secret that need be hidden as a sin. [5]But a mistake indeed! [6]Let not your fear of sin protect it from correction, for the attraction of guilt is only fear. [7]Here is the one emotion that you made, whatever it may seem to be. [8]This is the emotion of secrecy, of private thoughts and of the body. [9]This is the one emotion that opposes love, and always leads to sight of differences and loss of sameness. [10]Here is the one emotion that keeps you blind, dependent on the self you think you made to lead you through the world it made for you.

5. Your sight was given you, along with everything that you can understand. [2]You will perceive no difficulty in understanding what this vision tells you, for everyone sees only what he thinks he is. [3]And what your sight would show you, you will understand *because* it is the truth. [4]Only your vision can convey to you what you can see. [5]It reaches you directly, without a need to be interpreted to you. [6]What needs interpretation must be alien. [7]Nor will it ever be made understandable by an interpreter you cannot understand.

6. Of all the messages you have received and failed to understand, this course alone is open to your understanding and can be understood. [2]This is *your* language. [3]You do not understand it yet only because your whole communication is like a baby's. [4]The sounds a baby makes and what he hears are highly unreliable, meaning different things to him at different times. [5]Neither the sounds he hears nor sights he sees are stable yet. [6]But what he hears and does not understand will be his native tongue, through which he will communicate with those around him, and they with him. [7]And the strange, shifting ones he sees about him will become to him his comforters, and he will recognize his home

and see them there with him.

7. So in each holy relationship is the ability to communicate instead of separate reborn. ²Yet a holy relationship, so recently reborn itself from an unholy relationship, and yet more ancient than the old illusion it has replaced, is like a baby now in its rebirth. ³Still in this infant is your vision returned to you, and he will speak the language you can understand. ⁴He is not nurtured by the "something else" you thought was you. ⁵He was not given there, nor was received by anything except yourself. ⁶For no two brothers can unite except through Christ, Whose vision sees them one.

8. Think what is given you, my holy brother. ²This child will teach you what you do not understand, and make it plain. ³For his will be no alien tongue. ⁴He will need no interpreter to you, for it was you who taught him what he knows *because* you knew it. ⁵He could not come to anyone but you, never to "something else." ⁶Where Christ has entered no one is alone, for never could He find a home in separate ones. ⁷Yet must He be reborn into His ancient home, so seeming new and yet as old as He, a tiny newcomer, dependent on the holiness of your relationship to let Him live.

9. Be certain God did not entrust His Son to the unworthy. ²Nothing but what is part of Him is worthy of being joined. ³Nor is it possible that anything not part of Him *can* join. ⁴Communication must have been restored to those who join, for this they could not do through bodies. ⁵What, then, has joined them? ⁶Reason will tell you that they must have seen each other through a vision not of the body, and communicated in a language the body does not speak. ⁷Nor could it be a fearful sight or sound that drew them gently into one. ⁸Rather, in each other saw a perfect shelter where his Self could be reborn in safety and in peace. ⁹Such did his reason tell him; such he believed *because* it was the truth.

10. Here is the first direct perception that you can make. ²You make it through awareness older than perception, and yet reborn in just an instant. ³For what is time to what was always so? ⁴Think what that instant brought; the recognition that the "something else" you thought was you is an illusion. ⁵And truth came instantly, to show you where your Self must be. ⁶It is denial of illusions that calls on truth, for to deny illusions is to recognize that fear is meaningless. ⁷Into the holy home where fear is power-

less love enters thankfully, grateful that it is one with you who joined to let it enter.

11.   Christ comes to what is like Himself; the same, not different. ²For He is always drawn unto Himself. ³What is as like Him as a holy relationship? ⁴And what draws you and your brother together draws Him to you. ⁵Here are His sweetness and His gentle innocence protected from attack. ⁶And here can He return in confidence, for faith in another is always faith in Him. ⁷You are indeed correct in looking on your brother as His chosen home, for here you will with Him and with His Father. ⁸This is your Father's Will for you, and yours with His. ⁹And who is drawn to Christ is drawn to God as surely as Both are drawn to every holy relationship, the home prepared for Them as earth is turned to Heaven.

II. Your Brother's Sinlessness

1.   The opposite of illusions is not disillusionment but truth. ²Only to the ego, to which truth is meaningless, do they appear to be the only alternatives, and different from each other. ³In truth they are the same. ⁴Both bring the same amount of misery, though each one seems to be the way to lose the misery the other brings. ⁵Every illusion carries pain and suffering in the dark folds of the heavy garments in which it hides its nothingness. ⁶Yet by these dark and heavy garments are those who seek illusions covered, and hidden from the joy of truth.

2.   Truth is the opposite of illusions because it offers joy. ²What else but joy could be the opposite of misery? ³To leave one kind of misery and seek another is hardly an escape. ⁴To change illusions is to make no change. ⁵The search for joy in misery is senseless, for how could joy be found in misery? ⁶All that is possible in the dark world of misery is to select some aspects out of it, see them as different, and define the difference as joy. ⁷Yet to perceive a difference where none exists will surely fail to make a difference.

3.   Illusions carry only guilt and suffering, sickness and death, to their believers. ²The form in which they are accepted is irrelevant. ³No form of misery in reason's eyes can be confused with joy. ⁴Joy is eternal. ⁵You can be sure indeed that any seeming happiness that does not last is really fear. ⁶Joy does not turn to sorrow, for the eternal cannot change. ⁷But sorrow can be turned to

joy, for time gives way to the eternal. [8]Only the timeless must remain unchanged, but everything in time can change with time. [9]Yet if the change be real and not imagined, illusions must give way to truth, and not to other dreams that are but equally unreal. [10]This is no difference.

4. Reason will tell you that the only way to escape from misery is to recognize it *and go the other way*. [2]Truth is the same and misery the same, but they are different from each other in every way, in every instance and without exception. [3]To believe that one exception can exist is to confuse what is the same with what is different. [4]One illusion cherished and defended against the truth makes all truth meaningless, and all illusions real. [5]Such is the power of belief. [6]It cannot compromise. [7]And faith in innocence is faith in sin, if the belief excludes one living thing and holds it out, apart from its forgiveness.

5. Both reason and the ego will tell you this, but what they make of it is not the same. [2]The ego will assure you now that it is impossible for you to see no guilt in anyone. [3]And if this seeing is the only means by which escape from guilt can be attained, then the belief in sin must be eternal. [4]Yet reason looks on this another way, for reason sees the source of an idea as what will make it either true or false. [5]This must be so, if the idea is like its source. [6]Therefore, says reason, if escape from guilt was given to the Holy Spirit as His purpose, and by One to Whom nothing He wills can be impossible, the means for its attainment are more than possible. [7]They must be there, and you must have them.

6. This is a crucial period in this course, for here the separation of you and the ego must be made complete. [2]For if you have the means to let the Holy Spirit's purpose be accomplished, they can be used. [3]And through their use will you gain faith in them. [4]Yet to the ego this must be impossible, and no one undertakes to do what holds no hope of ever being done. [5]*You* know what your Creator wills is possible, but what you made believes it is not so. [6]Now must you choose between yourself and an illusion of yourself. [7]Not both, but one. [8]There is no point in trying to avoid this one decision. [9]It must be made. [10]Faith and belief can fall to either side, but reason tells you misery lies only on one side and joy upon the other.

7. Forsake not now your brother. [2]For you who are the same will not decide alone nor differently. [3]Either you give each other life or death; either you are each other's savior or his judge, offering

him sanctuary or condemnation. ⁴This course will be believed entirely or not at all. ⁵For it is wholly true or wholly false, and cannot be but partially believed. ⁶And you will either escape from misery entirely or not at all. ⁷Reason will tell you that there is no middle ground where you can pause uncertainly, waiting to choose between the joy of Heaven and the misery of hell. ⁸Until you choose Heaven, you *are* in hell and misery.

8. There is no part of Heaven you can take and weave into illusions. ²Nor is there one illusion you can enter Heaven with. ³A savior cannot be a judge, nor mercy condemnation. ⁴And vision cannot damn, but only bless. ⁵Whose function is to save, will save. ⁶*How* He will do it is beyond your understanding, but *when* must be your choice. ⁷For time you made, and time you can command. ⁸You are no more a slave to time than to the world you made.

9. Let us look closer at the whole illusion that what you made has power to enslave its maker. ²This is the same belief that caused the separation. ³It is the meaningless idea that thoughts can leave the thinker's mind, be different from it and in opposition to it. ⁴If this were true, thoughts would not be the mind's extensions, but its enemies. ⁵And here we see again another form of the same fundamental illusion we have seen many times before. ⁶Only if it were possible the Son of God could leave his Father's Mind, make himself different and oppose His Will, would it be possible that the self he made, and all it made, should be his master.

10. Behold the great projection, but look on it with the decision that it must be healed, and not with fear. ²Nothing you made has any power over you unless you still would be apart from your Creator, and with a will opposed to His. ³For only if you would believe His Son could be His enemy does it seem possible that what you made is yours. ⁴You would condemn His joy to misery, and make Him different. ⁵And all the misery you made has been your own. ⁶Are you not glad to learn it is not true? ⁷Is it not welcome news to hear not one of the illusions that you made replaced the truth?

11. Only *your* thoughts have been impossible. ²Salvation cannot be. ³It *is* impossible to look upon your savior as your enemy and recognize him. ⁴Yet it is possible to recognize him for what he is, if God would have it so. ⁵What God has given to your holy relationship is there. ⁶For what He gave the Holy Spirit to give to you *He gave.* ⁷Would you not look upon the savior that has been given

you? [8]And would you not exchange, in gratitude, the function of an executioner you gave him for the one he has in truth? [9]Receive of him what God has given him for you, not what you tried to give yourself.

12. Beyond the body that you interposed between you and your brother, and shining in the golden light that reaches it from the bright, endless circle that extends forever, is your holy relationship, beloved of God Himself. [2]How still it rests, in time and yet beyond, immortal yet on earth. [3]How great the power that lies in it. [4]Time waits upon its will, and earth will be as it would have it be. [5]Here is no separate will, nor the desire that anything be separate. [6]Its will has no exceptions, and what it wills is true. [7]Every illusion brought to its forgiveness is gently overlooked and disappears. [8]For at its center Christ has been reborn, to light His home with vision that overlooks the world. [9]Would you not have this holy home be yours as well? [10]No misery is here, but only joy.

13. All you need do to dwell in quiet here with Christ is share His vision. [2]Quickly and gladly is His vision given anyone who is but willing to see his brother sinless. [3]And no one can remain beyond this willingness, if you would be released entirely from all effects of sin. [4]Would you have partial forgiveness for yourself? [5]Can you reach Heaven while a single sin still tempts you to remain in misery? [6]Heaven is the home of perfect purity, and God created it for you. [7]Look on your holy brother, sinless as yourself, and let him lead you there.

III. Reason and the Forms of Error

1. The introduction of reason into the ego's thought system is the beginning of its undoing, for reason and the ego are contradictory. [2]Nor is it possible for them to coexist in your awareness. [3]For reason's goal is to make plain, and therefore obvious. [4]You can *see* reason. [5]This is not a play on words, for here is the beginning of a vision that has meaning. [6]Vision is sense, quite literally. [7]If it is not the body's sight, it *must* be understood. [8]For it is plain, and what is obvious is not ambiguous. [9]It can be understood. [10]And here do reason and the ego separate, to go their separate ways.

2. The ego's whole continuance depends on its belief you cannot

learn this course. ²Share this belief, and reason will be unable to see your errors and make way for their correction. ³For reason sees through errors, telling you what you thought was real is not. ⁴Reason can see the difference between sin and mistakes, because it wants correction. ⁵Therefore, it tells you what you thought was uncorrectable can be corrected, and thus it must have been an error. ⁶The ego's opposition to correction leads to its fixed belief in sin and disregard of errors. ⁷It looks on nothing that can be corrected. ⁸Thus does the ego damn, and reason save.

3. Reason is not salvation in itself, but it makes way for peace and brings you to a state of mind in which salvation can be given you. ²Sin is a block, set like a heavy gate, locked and without a key, across the road to peace. ³No one who looks on it without the help of reason would try to pass it. ⁴The body's eyes behold it as solid granite, so thick it would be madness to attempt to pass it. ⁵Yet reason sees through it easily, because it is an error. ⁶The form it takes cannot conceal its emptiness from reason's eyes.

4. Only the form of error attracts the ego. ²Meaning it does not recognize, and does not see if it is there or not. ³Everything the body's eyes can see is a mistake, an error in perception, a distorted fragment of the whole without the meaning that the whole would give. ⁴And yet mistakes, regardless of their form, can be corrected. ⁵Sin is but error in a special form the ego venerates. ⁶It would preserve all errors and make them sins. ⁷For here is its own stability, its heavy anchor in the shifting world it made; the rock on which its church is built, and where its worshippers are bound to bodies, believing the body's freedom is their own.

5. Reason will tell you that the form of error is not what makes it a mistake. ²If what the form conceals is a mistake, the form cannot prevent correction. ³The body's eyes see only form. ⁴They cannot see beyond what they were made to see. ⁵And they were made to look on error and not see past it. ⁶Theirs is indeed a strange perception, for they can see only illusions, unable to look beyond the granite block of sin, and stopping at the outside form of nothing. ⁷To this distorted form of vision the outside of everything, the wall that stands between you and the truth, is wholly true. ⁸Yet how can sight that stops at nothingness, as if it were a solid wall, see truly? ⁹It is held back by form, having been made to guarantee that nothing else but form will be perceived.

6. These eyes, made not to see, will never see. ²For the idea they represent left not its maker, and it is their maker that sees through

them. ³What was its maker's goal but not to see? ⁴For this the body's eyes are perfect means, but not for seeing. ⁵See how the body's eyes rest on externals and cannot go beyond. ⁶Watch how they stop at nothingness, unable to go beyond the form to meaning. ⁷Nothing so blinding as perception of form. ⁸For sight of form means understanding has been obscured.

7. Only mistakes have different forms, and so they can deceive. ²You can change form *because* it is not true. ³It could not be reality *because* it can be changed. ⁴Reason will tell you that if form is not reality it must be an illusion, and is not there to see. ⁵And if you see it you must be mistaken, for you are seeing what can *not* be real as if it were. ⁶What cannot see beyond what is not there must be distorted perception, and must perceive illusions as the truth. ⁷Could it, then, recognize the truth?

8. Let not the form of his mistakes keep you from him whose holiness is yours. ²Let not the vision of his holiness, the sight of which would show you your forgiveness, be kept from you by what the body's eyes can see. ³Let your awareness of your brother not be blocked by your perception of his sins and of his body. ⁴What is there in him that you would attack except what you associate with his body, which you believe can sin? ⁵Beyond his errors is his holiness and your salvation. ⁶You gave him not his holiness, but tried to see your sins in him to save yourself. ⁷And yet, his holiness *is* your forgiveness. ⁸Can you be saved by making sinful the one whose holiness is your salvation?

9. A holy relationship, however newly born, must value holiness above all else. ²Unholy values will produce confusion, and in awareness. ³In an unholy relationship, each one is valued because he seems to justify the other's sin. ⁴Each sees within the other what impels him to sin against his will. ⁵And thus he lays his sins upon the other, and is attracted to him to perpetuate his sins. ⁶And so it must become impossible for each to see himself as causing sin by his desire to have sin real. ⁷Yet reason sees a holy relationship as what it is; a common state of mind, where both give errors gladly to correction, that both may happily be healed as one.

IV. The Branching of the Road

1. When you come to the place where the branch in the road is quite apparent, you cannot go ahead. ²You must go either one way or the other. ³For now if you go straight ahead, the way you went before you reached the branch, you will go nowhere. ⁴The whole purpose of coming this far was to decide which branch you will take now. ⁵The way you came no longer matters. ⁶It can no longer serve. ⁷No one who reaches this far can make the wrong decision, although he can delay. ⁸And there is no part of the journey that seems more hopeless and futile than standing where the road branches, and not deciding on which way to go.

2. It is but the first few steps along the right way that seem hard, for you have chosen, although you still may think you can go back and make the other choice. ²This is not so. ³A choice made with the power of Heaven to uphold it cannot be undone. ⁴Your way is decided. ⁵There will be nothing you will not be told, if you acknowledge this.

3. And so you and your brother stand, here in this holy place, before the veil of sin that hangs between you and the face of Christ. ²Let it be lifted! ³Raise it together with your brother, for it is but a veil that stands between you. ⁴Either you or your brother alone will see it as a solid block, nor realize how thin the drapery that separates you now. ⁵Yet it is almost over in your awareness, and peace has reached you even here, before the veil. ⁶Think what will happen after. ⁷The Love of Christ will light your face, and shine from it into a darkened world that needs the light. ⁸And from this holy place He will return with you, not leaving it nor you. ⁹You will become His messenger, returning Him unto Himself.

4. Think of the loveliness that you will see, who walk with Him! ²And think how beautiful will you and your brother look to the other! ³How happy you will be to be together, after such a long and lonely journey where you walked alone. ⁴The gates of Heaven, open now for you, will you now open to the sorrowful. ⁵And none who looks upon the Christ in you but will rejoice. ⁶How beautiful the sight you saw beyond the veil, which you will bring to light the tired eyes of those as weary now as once you were. ⁷How thankful will they be to see you come among them, offering Christ's forgiveness to dispel their faith in sin.

5. Every mistake you and your brother make, the other will gently

have corrected. ²For in his sight your loveliness is his salvation, which he would protect from harm. ³And you will be your brother's strong protector from everything that seems to rise between you both. ⁴So shall you walk the world with me, whose message has not yet been given everyone. ⁵For you are here to let it be received. ⁶God's offer still is open, yet it waits acceptance. ⁷From you who have accepted it is it received. ⁸Into your hand, joined with your brother's, is it safely given, for you who share it have become its willing guardian and protector.

6. To all who share the Love of God the grace is given to be the givers of what they have received. ²And so they learn that it is theirs forever. ³All barriers disappear before their coming, as every obstacle was finally surmounted that seemed to rise and block their way before. ⁴This veil you and your brother lift together opens the way to truth to more than you. ⁵Those who would let illusions be lifted from their minds are this world's saviors, walking the world with their Redeemer, and carrying His message of hope and freedom and release from suffering to everyone who needs a miracle to save him.

7. How easy is it to offer this miracle to everyone! ²No one who has received it for himself could find it difficult. ³For by receiving it, he learned it was not given him alone. ⁴Such is the function of a holy relationship; to receive together and give as you received. ⁵Standing before the veil, it still seems difficult. ⁶But hold out your hand, joined with your brother's, and touch this heavy-seeming block, and you will learn how easily your fingers slip through its nothingness. ⁷It is no solid wall. ⁸And only an illusion stands between you and your brother, and the holy Self you share together.

V. Weakness and Defensiveness

1. How does one overcome illusions? ²Surely not by force or anger, nor by opposing them in any way. ³Merely by letting reason tell you that they contradict reality. ⁴They go against what must be true. ⁵The opposition comes from them, and not reality. ⁶Reality opposes nothing. ⁷What merely is needs no defense, and offers none. ⁸Only illusions need defense because of weakness. ⁹And how can it be difficult to walk the way of truth when only weakness interferes? ¹⁰*You* are the strong one in this seeming

conflict. [11]And you need no defense. [12]Everything that needs defense you do not want, for anything that needs defense will weaken you.

2. Consider what the ego wants defenses for. [2]Always to justify what goes against the truth, flies in the face of reason and makes no sense. [3]Can this *be* justified? [4]What can this be except an invitation to insanity, to save you from the truth? [5]And what would you be saved from but what you fear? [6]Belief in sin needs great defense, and at enormous cost. [7]All that the Holy Spirit offers must be defended against and sacrificed. [8]For sin is carved into a block out of your peace, and laid between you and its return.

3. Yet how can peace be so fragmented? [2]It is still whole, and nothing has been taken from it. [3]See how the means and the material of evil dreams are nothing. [4]In truth you and your brother stand together, with nothing in between. [5]God holds your hands, and what can separate whom He has joined as one with Him? [6]It is your Father Whom you would defend against. [7]Yet it remains impossible to keep love out. [8]God rests with you in quiet, undefended and wholly undefending, for in this quiet state alone is strength and power. [9]Here can no weakness enter, for here is no attack and therefore no illusions. [10]Love rests in certainty. [11]Only uncertainty can be defensive. [12]And all uncertainty is doubt about yourself.

4. How weak is fear; how little and how meaningless. [2]How insignificant before the quiet strength of those whom love has joined! [3]This is your "enemy,"—a frightened mouse that would attack the universe. [4]How likely is it that it will succeed? [5]Can it be difficult to disregard its feeble squeaks that tell of its omnipotence, and would drown out the hymn of praise to its Creator that every heart throughout the universe forever sings as one? [6]Which is the stronger? [7]Is it this tiny mouse or everything that God created? [8]You and your brother are not joined together by this mouse, but by the Will of God. [9]And can a mouse betray whom God has joined?

5. If you but recognized how little stands between you and your awareness of your union with your brother! [2]Be not deceived by the illusions it presents of size and thickness, weight, solidity and firmness of foundation. [3]Yes, to the body's eyes it looks like an enormous solid body, immovable as is a mountain. [4]Yet within you is a Force that no illusions can resist. [5]This body only seems to be immovable; this Force is irresistible in truth. [6]What, then,

must happen when they come together? [7]Can the illusion of im-movability be long defended from what is quietly passed through and gone beyond?

6. Forget not, when you feel the need arise to be defensive about anything, you have identified yourself with an illusion. [2]And therefore feel that you are weak because you are alone. [3]This is the cost of all illusions. [4]Not one but rests on the belief that you are separate. [5]Not one that does not seem to stand, heavy and solid and immovable, between you and your brother. [6]And not one that truth cannot pass over lightly, and so easily that you must be convinced, in spite of what you thought it was, that it is nothing. [7]If you forgive your brother, this *must* happen. [8]For it is your unwillingness to overlook what seems to stand between you and your brother that makes it look impenetrable, and de-fends the illusion of its immovability.

VI. The Light of the Holy Relationship

1. Do you want freedom of the body or of the mind? [2]For both you cannot have. [3]Which do you value? [4]Which is your goal? [5]For one you see as means; the other, end. [6]And one must serve the other and lead to its predominance, increasing its importance by diminishing its own. [7]Means serve the end, and as the end is reached the value of the means decreases, eclipsed entirely when they are recognized as functionless. [8]No one but yearns for free-dom and tries to find it. [9]Yet he will seek for it where he believes it is and can be found. [10]He will believe it possible of mind or body, and he will make the other serve his choice as means to find it.

2. Where freedom of the body has been chosen, the mind is used as means whose value lies in its ability to contrive ways to achieve the body's freedom. [2]Yet freedom of the body has no meaning, and so the mind is dedicated to serve illusions. [3]This is a situation so contradictory and so impossible that anyone who chooses this has no idea of what is valuable. [4]Yet even in this confusion, so profound it cannot be described, the Holy Spirit waits in gentle patience, as certain of the outcome as He is sure of His Creator's Love. [5]He knows this mad decision was made by one as dear to His Creator as love is to itself.

3. Be not disturbed at all to think how He can change the role of

means and end so easily in what God loves, and would have free forever. ²But be you rather grateful that you can be the means to serve His end. ³This is the only service that leads to freedom. ⁴To serve this end the body must be perceived as sinless, because the goal is sinlessness. ⁵The lack of contradiction makes the soft transition from means to end as easy as is the shift from hate to gratitude before forgiving eyes. ⁶You will be sanctified by your brother, using your body only to serve the sinless. ⁷And it will be impossible for you to hate what serves whom you would heal.

4. This holy relationship, lovely in its innocence, mighty in strength, and blazing with a light far brighter than the sun that lights the sky you see, is chosen of your Father as a means for His Own plan. ²Be thankful that it serves yours not at all. ³Nothing entrusted to it can be misused, and nothing given it but will be used. ⁴This holy relationship has the power to heal all pain, regardless of its form. ⁵Neither you nor your brother alone can serve at all. ⁶Only in your joint will does healing lie. ⁷For here your healing is, and here will you accept Atonement. ⁸And in your healing is the Sonship healed *because* your will and your brother's are joined.

5. Before a holy relationship there is no sin. ²The form of error is no longer seen, and reason, joined with love, looks quietly on all confusion, observing merely, "This was a mistake." ³And then the same Atonement you accepted in your relationship corrects the error, and lays a part of Heaven in its place. ⁴How blessed are you who let this gift be given! ⁵Each part of Heaven that you bring is given you. ⁶And every empty place in Heaven that you fill again with the eternal light you bring, shines now on you. ⁷The means of sinlessness can know no fear because they carry only love with them.

6. Child of peace, the light *has* come to you. ²The light you bring you do not recognize, and yet you will remember. ³Who can deny himself the vision that he brings to others? ⁴And who would fail to recognize a gift he let be laid in Heaven through himself? ⁵The gentle service that you give the Holy Spirit is service to yourself. ⁶You who are now His means must love all that He loves. ⁷And what you bring is your remembrance of everything that is eternal. ⁸No trace of anything in time can long remain in a mind that serves the timeless. ⁹And no illusion can disturb the peace of a relationship that has become the means of peace.

7. When you have looked upon your brother with complete

forgiveness, from which no error is excluded and nothing kept hidden, what mistake can there be anywhere you cannot overlook? [2]What form of suffering could block your sight, preventing you from seeing past it? [3]And what illusion could there be you will not recognize as a mistake; a shadow through which you walk completely undismayed? [4]God would let nothing interfere with those whose wills are His, and they will recognize their wills are His, *because* they serve His Will. [5]And serve it willingly. [6]And could remembrance of what they are be long delayed?

8. You will see your value through your brother's eyes, and each one is released as he beholds his savior in place of the attacker who he thought was there. [2]Through this releasing is the world released. [3]This is your part in bringing peace. [4]For you have asked what is your function here, and have been answered. [5]Seek not to change it, nor to substitute another goal. [6]This one was given you, and only this. [7]Accept this one and serve it willingly, for what the Holy Spirit does with gifts you give your brother, to whom He offers them, and where and when, is up to Him. [8]He will bestow them where they are received and welcomed. [9]He will use every one of them for peace. [10]Nor will one little smile or willingness to overlook the tiniest mistake be lost to anyone.

9. What can it be but universal blessing to look on what your Father loves with charity? [2]Extension of forgiveness is the Holy Spirit's function. [3]Leave this to Him. [4]Let your concern be only that you give to Him that which can be extended. [5]Save no dark secrets that He cannot use, but offer Him the tiny gifts He can extend forever. [6]He will take each one and make of it a potent force for peace. [7]He will withhold no blessing from it, nor limit it in any way. [8]He will join to it all the power that God has given Him, to make each little gift of love a source of healing for everyone. [9]Each little gift you offer to your brother lights up the world. [10]Be not concerned with darkness; look away from it and toward your brother. [11]And let the darkness be dispelled by Him Who knows the light, and lays it gently in each quiet smile of faith and confidence with which you bless your brother.

10. On your learning depends the welfare of the world. [2]And it is only arrogance that would deny the power of your will. [3]Think you the Will of God is powerless? [4]Is this humility? [5]You do not see what this belief has done. [6]You see yourself as vulnerable, frail and easily destroyed, and at the mercy of countless attackers more powerful than you. [7]Let us look straight at how this error

came about, for here lies buried the heavy anchor that seems to keep the fear of God in place, immovable and solid as a rock. ⁸While this remains, so will it seem to be.

11. Who can attack the Son of God and not attack his Father? ²How can God's Son be weak and frail and easily destroyed unless his Father is? ³You do not see that every sin and every condemnation that you perceive and justify *is* an attack upon your Father. ⁴And that is why it has not happened, nor could be real. ⁵You do not see that this is your attempt because you think the Father and the Son are separate. ⁶And you must think that They are separate, because of fear. ⁷For it seems safer to attack another or yourself than to attack the great Creator of the universe, Whose power you know.

12. If you were one with God and recognized this oneness, you would know His power is yours. ²But you will not remember this while you believe attack of any kind means anything. ³It is unjustified in any form, because it has no meaning. ⁴The only way it could be justified is if you and your brother were separate from the other, and all were separate from your Creator. ⁵For only then would it be possible to attack a part of the creation without the whole, the Son without the Father; and to attack another without yourself, or hurt yourself without the other feeling pain. ⁶And this belief you want. ⁷Yet wherein lies its value, except in the desire to attack in safety? ⁸Attack is neither safe nor dangerous. ⁹It is impossible. ¹⁰And this is so because the universe is one. ¹¹You would not choose attack on its reality if it were not essential to attack to see it separated from its maker. ¹²And thus it seems as if love could attack and become fearful.

13. Only the different can attack. ²So you conclude *because* you can attack, you and your brother must be different. ³Yet does the Holy Spirit explain this differently. ⁴*Because* you and your brother are not different, you cannot attack. ⁵Either position is a logical conclusion. ⁶Either could be maintained, but never both. ⁷The only question to be answered in order to decide which must be true is whether you and your brother are different. ⁸From the position of what you understand you seem to be, and therefore can attack. ⁹Of the alternatives, this seems more natural and more in line with your experience. ¹⁰And therefore it is necessary that you have other experiences, more in line with truth, to teach you what *is* natural and true.

14. This is the function of your holy relationship. ²For what one

thinks, the other will experience with him. ³What can this mean except your mind and your brother's are one? ⁴Look not with fear upon this happy fact, and think not that it lays a heavy burden on you. ⁵For when you have accepted it with gladness, you will realize that your relationship is a reflection of the union of the Creator and His Son. ⁶From loving minds there *is* no separation. ⁷And every thought in one brings gladness to the other because they are the same. ⁸Joy is unlimited, because each shining thought of love extends its being and creates more of itself. ⁹There is no difference anywhere in it, for every thought is like itself.

15. The light that joins you and your brother shines throughout the universe, and because it joins you and him, so it makes you and him one with your Creator. ²And in Him is all creation joined. ³Would you regret you cannot fear alone, when your relationship can also teach the power of love is there, which makes all fear impossible? ⁴Do not attempt to keep a little of the ego with this gift. ⁵For it was given you to be used, and not obscured. ⁶What teaches you that you cannot separate denies the ego. ⁷Let truth decide if you and your brother be different or the same, and teach you which is true.

Chapter 23

THE WAR AGAINST YOURSELF

Introduction

1. Do you not see the opposite of frailty and weakness is sinlessness? [2]Innocence is strength, and nothing else is strong. [3]The sinless cannot fear, for sin of any kind is weakness. [4]The show of strength attack would use to cover frailty conceals it not, for how can the unreal be hidden? [5]No one is strong who has an enemy, and no one can attack unless he thinks he has. [6]Belief in enemies is therefore the belief in weakness, and what is weak is not the Will of God. [7]Being opposed to it, it is God's "enemy." [8]And God is feared as an opposing will.

2. How strange indeed becomes this war against yourself! [2]You will believe that everything you use for sin can hurt you and become your enemy. [3]And you will fight against it, and try to weaken it because of this; and you will think that you succeeded, and attack again. [4]It is as certain you will fear what you attack as it is sure that you will love what you perceive as sinless. [5]He walks in peace who travels sinlessly along the way love shows him. [6]For love walks with him there, protecting him from fear. [7]And he will see only the sinless, who can not attack.

3. Walk you in glory, with your head held high, and fear no evil. [2]The innocent are safe because they share their innocence. [3]Nothing they see is harmful, for their awareness of the truth releases everything from the illusion of harmfulness. [4]And what seemed harmful now stands shining in their innocence, released from sin and fear and happily returned to love. [5]They share the strength of love *because* they looked on innocence. [6]And every error disappeared because they saw it not. [7]Who looks for glory finds it where it is. [8]Where could it be but in the innocent?

4. Let not the little interferers pull you to littleness. [2]There can be no attraction of guilt in innocence. [3]Think what a happy world you walk, with truth beside you! [4]Do not give up this world of freedom for a little sigh of seeming sin, nor for a tiny stirring of guilt's attraction. [5]Would you, for all these meaningless distractions, lay Heaven aside? [6]Your destiny and purpose are far beyond them, in the clean place where littleness does not exist.

[7]Your purpose is at variance with littleness of any kind. [8]And so it is at variance with sin.

5.   Let us not let littleness lead God's Son into temptation. [2]His glory is beyond it, measureless and timeless as eternity. [3]Do not let time intrude upon your sight of him. [4]Leave him not frightened and alone in his temptation, but help him rise above it and perceive the light of which he is a part. [5]Your innocence will light the way to his, and so is yours protected and kept in your awareness. [6]For who can know his glory, and perceive the little and the weak about him? [7]Who can walk trembling in a fearful world, and realize that Heaven's glory shines on him?

6.   Nothing around you but is part of you. [2]Look on it lovingly, and see the light of Heaven in it. [3]So will you come to understand all that is given you. [4]In kind forgiveness will the world sparkle and shine, and everything you once thought sinful now will be reinterpreted as part of Heaven. [5]How beautiful it is to walk, clean and redeemed and happy, through a world in bitter need of the redemption that your innocence bestows upon it! [6]What can you value more than this? [7]For here is your salvation and your freedom. [8]And it must be complete if you would recognize it.

I. The Irreconcilable Beliefs

1.   The memory of God comes to the quiet mind. [2]It cannot come where there is conflict, for a mind at war against itself remembers not eternal gentleness. [3]The means of war are not the means of peace, and what the warlike would remember is not love. [4]War is impossible unless belief in victory is cherished. [5]Conflict within you must imply that you believe the ego has the power to be victorious. [6]Why else would you identify with it? [7]Surely you realize the ego is at war with God. [8]Certain it is it has no enemy. [9]Yet just as certain is its fixed belief it has an enemy that it must overcome and will succeed.

2.   Do you not realize a war against yourself would be a war on God? [2]Is victory conceivable? [3]And if it were, is this a victory that you would want? [4]The death of God, if it were possible, would be your death. [5]Is this a victory? [6]The ego always marches to defeat, because it thinks that triumph over you is possible. [7]And God thinks otherwise. [8]This is no war; only the mad belief the Will of God can be attacked and overthrown. [9]You may identify

with this belief, but never will it be more than madness. [10]And fear will reign in madness, and will seem to have replaced love there. [11]This is the conflict's purpose. [12]And to those who think that it is possible, the means seem real.

3. Be certain that it is impossible God and the ego, or yourself and it, will ever meet. [2]You seem to meet, and make your strange alliances on grounds that have no meaning. [3]For your beliefs converge upon the body, the ego's chosen home, which you believe is yours. [4]You meet at a mistake; an error in your self-appraisal. [5]The ego joins with an illusion of yourself you share with it. [6]And yet illusions cannot join. [7]They are the same, and they are nothing. [8]Their joining lies in nothingness; two are as meaningless as one or as a thousand. [9]The ego joins with nothing, being nothing. [10]The victory it seeks is meaningless as is itself.

4. Brother, the war against yourself is almost over. [2]The journey's end is at the place of peace. [3]Would you not now accept the peace offered you here? [4]This "enemy" you fought as an intruder on your peace is here transformed, before your sight, into the giver of your peace. [5]Your "enemy" was God Himself, to Whom all conflict, triumph and attack of any kind are all unknown. [6]He loves you perfectly, completely and eternally. [7]The Son of God at war with his Creator is a condition as ridiculous as nature roaring at the wind in anger, proclaiming it is part of itself no more. [8]Could nature possibly establish this, and make it true? [9]Nor is it up to you to say what shall be part of you and what is kept apart.

5. The war against yourself was undertaken to teach the Son of God that he is not himself, and *not* his Father's Son. [2]For this, the memory of his Father must be forgotten. [3]It *is* forgotten in the body's life, and if you think you are a body, you will believe you have forgotten it. [4]Yet truth can never be forgotten by itself, and you have not forgotten what you are. [5]Only a strange illusion of yourself, a wish to triumph over what you are, remembers not.

6. The war against yourself is but the battle of two illusions, struggling to make them different from each other, in the belief the one that conquers will be true. [2]There *is* no conflict between them and the truth. [3]Nor are they different from each other. [4]Both are not true. [5]And so it matters not what form they take. [6]What made them is insane, and they remain part of what made them. [7]Madness holds out no menace to reality, and has no influence upon it. [8]Illusions cannot triumph over truth, nor can they threaten it in any way. [9]And the reality that they deny

is not a part of them.

7. What *you* remember *is* a part of you. ²For you must be as God created you. ³Truth does not fight against illusions, nor do illusions fight against the truth. ⁴Illusions battle only with themselves. ⁵Being fragmented, they fragment. ⁶But truth is indivisible, and far beyond their little reach. ⁷You will remember what you know when you have learned you cannot be in conflict. ⁸One illusion about yourself can battle with another, yet the war of two illusions is a state where nothing happens. ⁹There is no victor and there is no victory. ¹⁰And truth stands radiant, apart from conflict, untouched and quiet in the peace of God.

8. Conflict must be between two forces. ²It cannot exist between one power and nothingness. ³There is nothing you could attack that is not part of you. ⁴And *by* attacking it you make two illusions of yourself, in conflict with each other. ⁵And this occurs whenever you look on anything that God created with anything but love. ⁶Conflict is fearful, for it is the birth of fear. ⁷Yet what is born of nothing cannot win reality through battle. ⁸Why would you fill your world with conflicts with yourself? ⁹Let all this madness be undone for you, and turn in peace to the rememberance of God, still shining in your quiet mind.

9. See how the conflict of illusions disappears when it is brought to truth! ²For it seems real only as long as it is seen as war between conflicting truths; the conqueror to be the truer, the more real, and the vanquisher of the illusion that was less real, made an illusion by defeat. ³Thus, conflict is the choice between illusions, one to be crowned as real, the other vanquished and despised. ⁴Here will the Father never be remembered. ⁵Yet no illusion can invade His home and drive Him out of what He loves forever. ⁶And what He loves must be forever quiet and at peace *because* it is His home.

10. You who are beloved of Him are no illusion, being as true and holy as Himself. ²The stillness of your certainty of Him and of yourself is home to Both of You, Who dwell as one and not apart. ³Open the door of His most holy home, and let forgiveness sweep away all trace of the belief in sin that keeps God homeless and His Son with Him. ⁴You are not a stranger in the house of God. ⁵Welcome your brother to the home where God has set him in serenity and peace, and dwells with him. ⁶Illusions have no place where love abides, protecting you from everything that is not true. ⁷You dwell in peace as limitless as its Creator, and

everything is given those who would remember Him. [8]Over His home the Holy Spirit watches, sure that its peace can never be disturbed.

11. How can the resting place of God turn on itself, and seek to overcome the One Who dwells there? [2]And think what happens when the house of God perceives itself divided. [3]The altar disappears, the light grows dim, the temple of the Holy One becomes a house of sin. [4]And nothing is remembered except illusions. [5]Illusions can conflict, because their forms are different. [6]And they do battle only to establish which form is true.

12. Illusion meets illusion; truth, itself. [2]The meeting of illusions leads to war. [3]Peace, looking on itself, extends itself. [4]War is the condition in which fear is born, and grows and seeks to dominate. [5]Peace is the state where love abides, and seeks to share itself. [6]Conflict and peace are opposites. [7]Where one abides the other cannot be; where either goes the other disappears. [8]So is the memory of God obscured in minds that have become illusions' battleground. [9]Yet far beyond this senseless war it shines, ready to be remembered when you side with peace.

II. The Laws of Chaos

1. The "laws" of chaos can be brought to light, though never understood. [2]Chaotic laws are hardly meaningful, and therefore out of reason's sphere. [3]Yet they appear to be an obstacle to reason and to truth. [4]Let us, then, look upon them calmly, that we may look beyond them, understanding what they are, not what they would maintain. [5]It is essential it be understood what they are for, because it is their purpose to make meaningless, and to attack the truth. [6]Here are the laws that rule the world you made. [7]And yet they govern nothing, and need not be broken; merely looked upon and gone beyond.

2. The *first* chaotic law is that the truth is different for everyone. [2]Like all these principles, this one maintains that each is separate and has a different set of thoughts that set him off from others. [3]This principle evolves from the belief there is a hierarchy of illusions; some are more valuable and therefore true. [4]Each one establishes this for himself, and makes it true by his attack on what another values. [5]And this is justified because the values differ, and those who hold them seem to be unlike, and therefore enemies.

3. Think how this seems to interfere with the first principle of miracles. ²For this establishes degrees of truth among illusions, making it seem that some of them are harder to overcome than others. ³If it were realized that they are all the same and equally untrue, it would be easy, then, to understand that miracles apply to all of them. ⁴Errors of any kind can be corrected *because* they are untrue. ⁵When brought to truth instead of to each other, they merely disappear. ⁶No part of nothing can be more resistant to the truth than can another.

4. The *second* law of chaos, dear indeed to every worshipper of sin, is that each one *must* sin, and therefore deserves attack and death. ²This principle, closely related to the first, is the demand that errors call for punishment and not correction. ³For the destruction of the one who makes the error places him beyond correction and beyond forgiveness. ⁴What he has done is thus interpreted as an irrevocable sentence upon himself, which God Himself is powerless to overcome. ⁵Sin cannot be remitted, being the belief the Son of God can make mistakes for which his own destruction becomes inevitable.

5. Think what this seems to do to the relationship between the Father and the Son. ²Now it appears that They can never be One again. ³For One must always be condemned, and by the Other. ⁴Now are They different, and enemies. ⁵And Their relationship is one of opposition, just as the separate aspects of the Son meet only to conflict but not to join. ⁶One becomes weak, the other strong by his defeat. ⁷And fear of God and of each other now appears as sensible, made real by what the Son of God has done both to himself and his Creator.

6. The arrogance on which the laws of chaos stand could not be more apparent than emerges here. ²Here is a principle that would define what the Creator of reality must be; what He must think and what He must believe; and how He must respond, believing it. ³It is not seen as even necessary that He be asked about the truth of what has been established for His belief. ⁴His Son can tell Him this, and He has but the choice whether to take his word for it or be mistaken. ⁵This leads directly to the *third* preposterous belief that seems to make chaos eternal. ⁶For if God cannot be mistaken, He must accept His Son's belief in what he is, and hate him for it.

7. See how the fear of God is reinforced by this third principle. ²Now it becomes impossible to turn to Him for help in misery.

³For now He has become the "enemy" Who caused it, to Whom appeal is useless. ⁴Nor can salvation lie within the Son, whose every aspect seems to be at war with Him, and justified in its attack. ⁵And now is conflict made inevitable, beyond the help of God. ⁶For now salvation must remain impossible, because the Savior has become the enemy.

8. There can be no release and no escape. ²Atonement thus becomes a myth, and vengeance, not forgiveness, is the Will of God. ³From where all this begins, there is no sight of help that can succeed. ⁴Only destruction can be the outcome. ⁵And God Himself seems to be siding with it, to overcome His Son. ⁶Think not the ego will enable you to find escape from what it wants. ⁷That is the function of this course, which does not value what the ego cherishes.

9. The ego values only what it takes. ²This leads to the *fourth* law of chaos, which, if the others are accepted, must be true. ³This seeming law is the belief you have what you have taken. ⁴By this, another's loss becomes your gain, and thus it fails to recognize that you can never take away save from yourself. ⁵Yet all the other laws must lead to this. ⁶For enemies do not give willingly to one another, nor would they seek to share the things they value. ⁷And what your enemies would keep from you must be worth having, because they keep it hidden from your sight.

10. All of the mechanisms of madness are seen emerging here: the "enemy" made strong by keeping hidden the valuable inheritance that should be yours; your justified position and attack for what has been withheld; and the inevitable loss the enemy must suffer to save yourself. ²Thus do the guilty ones protest their "innocence." ³Were they not forced into this foul attack by the unscrupulous behavior of the enemy, they would respond with only kindness. ⁴But in a savage world the kind cannot survive, so they must take or else be taken from.

11. And now there is a vague unanswered question, not yet "explained." ²What is this precious thing, this priceless pearl, this hidden secret treasure, to be wrested in righteous wrath from this most treacherous and cunning enemy? ³It must be what you want but never found. ⁴And now you "understand" the reason why you found it not. ⁵For it was taken from you by this enemy, and hidden where you would not think to look. ⁶He hid it in his body, making it the cover for his guilt, the hiding place for what belongs to you. ⁷Now must his body be destroyed and sacrificed,

that you may have that which belongs to you. [8]His treachery demands his death, that you may live. [9]And you attack only in self-defense.

12. But what is it you want that needs his death? [2]Can you be sure your murderous attack is justified unless you know what it is for? [3]And here a *final* principle of chaos comes to the "rescue." [4]It holds there is a substitute for love. [5]This is the magic that will cure all of your pain; the missing factor in your madness that makes it "sane." [6]This is the reason why you must attack. [7]Here is what makes your vengeance justified. [8]Behold, unveiled, the ego's secret gift, torn from your brother's body, hidden there in malice and in hatred for the one to whom the gift belongs. [9]He would deprive you of the secret ingredient that would give meaning to your life. [10]The substitute for love, born of your enmity to your brother, must be salvation. [11]It has no substitute, and there is only one. [12]And all your relationships have but the purpose of seizing it and making it your own.

13. Never is your possession made complete. [2]And never will your brother cease his attack on you for what you stole. [3]Nor will God end His vengeance upon both, for in His madness He must have this substitute for love, and kill you both. [4]You who believe you walk in sanity with feet on solid ground, and through a world where meaning can be found, consider this: These *are* the laws on which your "sanity" appears to rest. [5]These *are* the principles which make the ground beneath your feet seem solid. [6]And it *is* here you look for meaning. [7]These are the laws you made for your salvation. [8]They hold in place the substitute for Heaven which you prefer. [9]This is their purpose; they were made for this. [10]There is no point in asking what they mean. [11]That is apparent. [12]The means of madness must be insane. [13]Are you as certain that you realize the goal is madness?

14. No one wants madness, nor does anyone cling to his madness if he sees that this is what it is. [2]What protects madness is the belief that it is true. [3]It is the function of insanity to take the place of truth. [4]It must be seen as truth to be believed. [5]And if it is the truth, then must its opposite, which was the truth before, be madness now. [6]Such a reversal, completely turned around, with madness sanity, illusions true, attack a kindness, hatred love, and murder benediction, is the goal the laws of chaos serve. [7]These are the means by which the laws of God appear to be reversed. [8]Here do the laws of sin appear to hold love captive, and let sin go free.

15. These do not seem to be the goals of chaos, for by the great reversal they appear to be the laws of order. ²How could it not be so? ³Chaos is lawlessness, and has no laws. ⁴To be believed, its seeming laws must be perceived as real. ⁵Their goal of madness must be seen as sanity. ⁶And fear, with ashen lips and sightless eyes, blinded and terrible to look upon, is lifted to the throne of love, its dying conqueror, its substitute, the savior from salvation. ⁷How lovely do the laws of fear make death appear. ⁸Give thanks unto the hero on love's throne, who saved the Son of God for fear and death!

16. And yet, how can it be that laws like these can be believed? ²There is a strange device that makes it possible. ³Nor is it unfamiliar; we have seen how it appears to function many times before. ⁴In truth it does not function, yet in dreams, where only shadows play the major roles, it seems most powerful. ⁵No law of chaos could compel belief but for the emphasis on form and disregard of content. ⁶No one who thinks that one of these laws is true sees what it says. ⁷Some forms it takes seem to have meaning, and that is all.

17. How can some forms of murder not mean death? ²Can an attack in any form be love? ³What form of condemnation is a blessing? ⁴Who makes his savior powerless and finds salvation? ⁵Let not the form of the attack on him deceive you. ⁶You cannot seek to harm him and be saved. ⁷Who can find safety from attack by turning on himself? ⁸How can it matter what the form this madness takes? ⁹It is a judgment that defeats itself, condemning what it says it wants to save. ¹⁰Be not deceived when madness takes a form you think is lovely. ¹¹What is intent on your destruction is not your friend.

18. You would maintain, and think it true, that you do not believe these senseless laws, nor act upon them. ²And when you look at what they say, they cannot be believed. ³Brother, you *do* believe them. ⁴For how else could you perceive the form they take, with content such as this? ⁵Can any form of this be tenable? ⁶Yet you believe them *for* the form they take, and do not recognize the content. ⁷It never changes. ⁸Can you paint rosy lips upon a skeleton, dress it in loveliness, pet it and pamper it, and make it live? ⁹And can you be content with an illusion that you are living?

19. There is no life outside of Heaven. ²Where God created life, there life must be. ³In any state apart from Heaven life is illusion.

⁴At best it seems like life; at worst, like death. ⁵Yet both are judgments on what is not life, equal in their inaccuracy and lack of meaning. ⁶Life not in Heaven is impossible, and what is not in Heaven is not anywhere. ⁷Outside of Heaven, only the conflict of illusion stands; senseless, impossible and beyond all reason, and yet perceived as an eternal barrier to Heaven. ⁸Illusions are but forms. ⁹Their content is never true.

20.   The laws of chaos govern all illusions. ²Their forms conflict, making it seem quite possible to value some above the others. ³Yet each one rests as surely on the belief the laws of chaos are the laws of order as do the others. ⁴Each one upholds these laws completely, offering a certain witness that these laws are true. ⁵The seeming gentler forms of the attack are no less certain in their witnessing, or their results. ⁶Certain it is illusions will bring fear because of the beliefs that they imply, not for their form. ⁷And lack of faith in love, in any form, attests to chaos as reality.

21.   From the belief in sin, the faith in chaos must follow. ²It is because it follows that it seems to be a logical conclusion; a valid step in ordered thought. ³The steps to chaos do follow neatly from their starting point. ⁴Each is a different form in the progression of truth's reversal, leading still deeper into terror and away from truth. ⁵Think not one step is smaller than another, nor that return from one is easier. ⁶The whole descent from Heaven lies in each one. ⁷And where your thinking starts, there must it end.

22.   Brother, take not one step in the descent to hell. ²For having taken one, you will not recognize the rest for what they are. ³And they *will* follow. ⁴Attack in any form has placed your foot upon the twisted stairway that leads from Heaven. ⁵Yet any instant it is possible to have all this undone. ⁶How can you know whether you chose the stairs to Heaven or the way to hell? ⁷Quite easily. ⁸How do you feel? ⁹Is peace in your awareness? ¹⁰Are you certain which way you go? ¹¹And are you sure the goal of Heaven can be reached? ¹²If not, you walk alone. ¹³Ask, then, your Friend to join with you, and give you certainty of where you go.

III. Salvation without Compromise

1. Is it not true you do not recognize some of the forms attack can take? [2]If it is true attack in any form will hurt you, and will do so just as much as in another form that you *do* recognize, then it must follow that you do not always recognize the source of pain. [3]Attack in any form is equally destructive. [4]Its purpose does not change. [5]Its sole intent is murder, and what form of murder serves to cover the massive guilt and frantic fear of punishment the murderer must feel? [6]He may deny he is a murderer and justify his savagery with smiles as he attacks. [7]Yet he will suffer, and will look on his intent in nightmares where the smiles are gone, and where the purpose rises to meet his horrified awareness and pursue him still. [8]For no one thinks of murder and escapes the guilt the thought entails. [9]If the intent is death, what matter the form it takes?

2. Is death in any form, however lovely and charitable it may seem to be, a blessing and a sign the Voice for God speaks through you to your brother? [2]The wrapping does not make the gift you give. [3]An empty box, however beautiful and gently given, still contains nothing. [4]And neither the receiver nor the giver is long deceived. [5]Withhold forgiveness from your brother and you attack him. [6]You give him nothing, and receive of him but what you gave.

3. Salvation is no compromise of any kind. [2]To compromise is to accept but part of what you want; to take a little and give up the rest. [3]Salvation gives up nothing. [4]It is complete for everyone. [5]Let the idea of compromise but enter, and the awareness of salvation's purpose is lost because it is not recognized. [6]It is denied where compromise has been accepted, for compromise is the belief salvation is impossible. [7]It would maintain you can attack a little, love a little, and know the difference. [8]Thus it would teach a little of the same can still be different, and yet the same remain intact, as one. [9]Does this make sense? [10]Can it be understood?

4. This course is easy just because it makes no compromise. [2]Yet it seems difficult to those who still believe that compromise is possible. [3]They do not see that, if it is, salvation is attack. [4]Yet it is certain the belief that salvation is impossible cannot uphold a quiet, calm assurance it has come. [5]Forgiveness cannot be withheld a little. [6]Nor is it possible to attack for this and love for that

and understand forgiveness. [7]Would you not want to recognize assault upon your peace in any form, if only thus does it become impossible that you lose sight of it? [8]It can be kept shining before your vision, forever clear and never out of sight, if you defend it not.

5. Those who believe that peace can be defended, and that attack is justified on its behalf, cannot perceive it lies within them. [2]How could they know? [3]Could they accept forgiveness side by side with the belief that murder takes some forms by which their peace is saved? [4]Would they be willing to accept the fact their savage purpose is directed against themselves? [5]No one unites with enemies, nor is at one with them in purpose. [6]And no one compromises with an enemy but hates him still, for what he kept from him.

6. Mistake not truce for peace, nor compromise for the escape from conflict. [2]To be released from conflict means that it is over. [3]The door is open; you have left the battleground. [4]You have not lingered there in cowering hope that it will not return because the guns are stilled an instant, and the fear that haunts the place of death is not apparent. [5]There is no safety in a battleground. [6]You can look down on it in safety from above and not be touched. [7]But from within it you can find no safety. [8]Not one tree left still standing will shelter you. [9]Not one illusion of protection stands against the faith in murder. [10]Here stands the body, torn between the natural desire to communicate and the unnatural intent to murder and to die. [11]Think you the form that murder takes can offer safety? [12]Can guilt be absent from a battlefield?

IV. Above the Battleground

1. Do not remain in conflict, for there is no war without attack. [2]The fear of God is fear of life, and not of death. [3]Yet He remains the only place of safety. [4]In Him is no attack, and no illusion in any form stalks Heaven. [5]Heaven is wholly true. [6]No difference enters, and what is all the same cannot conflict. [7]You are not asked to fight against your wish to murder. [8]But you are asked to realize the form it takes conceals the same intent. [9]And it is this you fear, and not the form. [10]What is not love is murder. [11]What is not loving must be an attack. [12]Every illusion is an assault on truth, and every one does violence to the idea of love because it

seems to be of equal truth.

2.   What can be equal to the truth, yet different? ²Murder and love are incompatible. ³Yet if they both are true, then must they be the same, and indistinguishable from one another. ⁴So will they be to those who see God's Son a body. ⁵For it is not the body that is like the Son's Creator. ⁶And what is lifeless cannot be the Son of Life. ⁷How can a body be extended to hold the universe? ⁸Can it create, and be what it creates? ⁹And can it offer its creations all that it is and never suffer loss?

3.   God does not share His function with a body. ²He gave the function to create unto His Son because it is His Own. ³It is not sinful to believe the function of the Son is murder, but it *is* insanity. ⁴What is the same can have no different function. ⁵Creation is the means for God's extension, and what is His must be His Son's as well. ⁶Either the Father and the Son are murderers, or neither is. ⁷Life makes not death, creating like itself.

4.   The lovely light of your relationship is like the Love of God. ²It cannot yet assume the holy function God gave His Son, for your forgiveness of your brother is not complete as yet, and so it cannot be extended to all creation. ³Each form of murder and attack that still attracts you and that you do not recognize for what it is, limits the healing and the miracles you have the power to extend to all. ⁴Yet does the Holy Spirit understand how to increase your little gifts and make them mighty. ⁵Also He understands how your relationship is raised above the battleground, in it no more. ⁶This is your part; to realize that murder in any form is not your will. ⁷The overlooking of the battleground is now your purpose.

5.   Be lifted up, and from a higher place look down upon it. ²From there will your perspective be quite different. ³Here in the midst of it, it does seem real. ⁴Here you have chosen to be part of it. ⁵Here murder is your choice. ⁶Yet from above, the choice is miracles instead of murder. ⁷And the perspective coming from this choice shows you the battle is not real, and easily escaped. ⁸Bodies may battle, but the clash of forms is meaningless. ⁹And it is over when you realize it never was begun. ¹⁰How can a battle be perceived as nothingness when you engage in it? ¹¹How can the truth of miracles be recognized if murder is your choice?

6.   When the temptation to attack rises to make your mind darkened and murderous, remember you *can* see the battle from above. ²Even in forms you do not recognize, the signs you know. ³There is a stab of pain, a twinge of guilt, and above all, a loss of

peace. ⁴This you know well. ⁵When they occur leave not your place on high, but quickly choose a miracle instead of murder. ⁶And God Himself and all the lights of Heaven will gently lean to you, and hold you up. ⁷For you have chosen to remain where He would have you, and no illusion can attack the peace of God together with His Son.

7.   See no one from the battleground, for there you look on him from nowhere. ²You have no reference point from where to look, where meaning can be given what you see. ³For only bodies could attack and murder, and if this is your purpose, then you must be one with them. ⁴Only a purpose unifies, and those who share a purpose have a mind as one. ⁵The body has no purpose of itself, and must be solitary. ⁶From below, it cannot be surmounted. ⁷From above, the limits it exerts on those in battle still are gone, and not perceived. ⁸The body stands between the Father and the Heaven He created for His Son *because* it has no purpose.

8.   Think what is given those who share their Father's purpose, and who know that it is theirs. ²They want for nothing. ³Sorrow of any kind is inconceivable. ⁴Only the light they love is in awareness, and only love shines upon them forever. ⁵It is their past, their present and their future; always the same, eternally complete and wholly shared. ⁶They know it is impossible their happiness could ever suffer change of any kind. ⁷Perhaps you think the battleground can offer something you can win. ⁸Can it be anything that offers you a perfect calmness, and a sense of love so deep and quiet that no touch of doubt can ever mar your certainty? ⁹And that will last forever?

9.   Those with the strength of God in their awareness could never think of battle. ²What could they gain but loss of their perfection? ³For everything fought for on the battleground is of the body; something it seems to offer or to own. ⁴No one who knows that he has everything could seek for limitation, nor could he value the body's offerings. ⁵The senselessness of conquest is quite apparent from the quiet sphere above the battleground. ⁶What can conflict with everything? ⁷And what is there that offers less, yet could be wanted more? ⁸Who with the Love of God upholding him could find the choice of miracles or murder hard to make?

Chapter 24

THE GOAL OF SPECIALNESS

Introduction

1. Forget not that the motivation for this course is the attainment and the keeping of the state of peace. ²Given this state the mind is quiet, and the condition in which God is remembered is attained. ³It is not necessary to tell Him what to do. ⁴He will not fail. ⁵Where He can enter, there He is already. ⁶And can it be He cannot enter where He wills to be? ⁷Peace will be yours *because* it is His Will. ⁸Can you believe a shadow can hold back the Will that holds the universe secure? ⁹God does not wait upon illusions to let Him be Himself. ¹⁰No more His Son. ¹¹They *are*. ¹²And what illusion that idly seems to drift between Them has the power to defeat what is Their Will?

2. To learn this course requires willingness to question every value that you hold. ²Not one can be kept hidden and obscure but it will jeopardize your learning. ³No belief is neutral. ⁴Every one has the power to dictate each decision you make. ⁵For a decision is a conclusion based on everything that you believe. ⁶It is the outcome of belief, and follows it as surely as does suffering follow guilt and freedom sinlessness. ⁷There is no substitute for peace. ⁸What God creates has no alternative. ⁹The truth arises from what He knows. ¹⁰And your decisions come from your beliefs as certainly as all creation rose in His Mind *because* of what He knows.

I. Specialness as a Substitute for Love

1. Love is extension. ²To withhold the smallest gift is not to know love's purpose. ³Love offers everything forever. ⁴Hold back but one belief, one offering, and love is gone, because you asked a substitute to take its place. ⁵And now must war, the substitute for peace, come with the one alternative that you can choose for love. ⁶Your choosing it has given it all the reality it seems to have.

2. Beliefs will never openly attack each other because conflicting outcomes are impossible. ²But an unrecognized belief is a

decision to war in secret, where the results of conflict are kept unknown and never brought to reason, to be considered sensible or not. ³And many senseless outcomes have been reached, and meaningless decisions have been made and kept hidden, to become beliefs now given power to direct all subsequent decisions. ⁴Mistake you not the power of these hidden warriors to disrupt your peace. ⁵For it is at their mercy while you decide to leave it there. ⁶The secret enemies of peace, your least decision to choose attack instead of love, unrecognized and swift to challenge you to combat and to violence far more inclusive than you think, are there by your election. ⁷Do not deny their presence nor their terrible results. ⁸All that can be denied is their reality, but not their outcome.

3. All that is ever cherished as a hidden belief, to be defended though unrecognized, is faith in specialness. ²This takes many forms, but always clashes with the reality of God's creation and with the grandeur that He gave His Son. ³What else could justify attack? ⁴For who could hate someone whose Self is his, and Whom he knows? ⁵Only the special could have enemies, for they are different and not the same. ⁶And difference of any kind imposes orders of reality, and a need to judge that cannot be escaped.

4. What God created cannot be attacked, for there is nothing in the universe unlike itself. ²But what is different calls for judgment, and this must come from someone "better," someone incapable of being like what he condemns, "above" it, sinless by comparison with it. ³And thus does specialness become a means and end at once. ⁴For specialness not only sets apart, but serves as grounds from which attack on those who seem "beneath" the special one is "natural" and "just." ⁵The special ones feel weak and frail because of differences, for what would make them special *is* their enemy. ⁶Yet they protect its enmity and call it "friend." ⁷On its behalf they fight against the universe, for nothing in the world they value more.

5. Specialness is the great dictator of the wrong decisions. ²Here is the grand illusion of what you are and what your brother is. ³And here is what must make the body dear and worth preserving. ⁴Specialness must be defended. ⁵Illusions can attack it, and they do. ⁶For what your brother must become to keep your specialness *is* an illusion. ⁷He who is "worse" than you must be attacked, so that your specialness can live on his defeat. ⁸For specialness is triumph, and its victory is his defeat and shame.

[9]How can he live, with all your sins upon him? [10]And who must be his conqueror but you?

6. Would it be possible for you to hate your brother if you were like him? [2]Could you attack him if you realized you journey with him, to a goal that is the same? [3]Would you not help him reach it in every way you could, if his attainment of it were perceived as yours? [4]You are his enemy in specialness; his friend in a shared purpose. [5]Specialness can never share, for it depends on goals that you alone can reach. [6]And he must never reach them, or your goal is jeopardized. [7]Can love have meaning where the goal is triumph? [8]And what decision can be made for this that will not hurt you?

7. Your brother is your friend because his Father created him like you. [2]There is no difference. [3]You have been given to your brother that love might be extended, not cut off from him. [4]What you keep is lost to you. [5]God gave you and your brother Himself, and to remember this is now the only purpose that you share. [6]And so it is the only one you have. [7]Could you attack your brother if you chose to see no specialness of any kind between you and him? [8]Look fairly at whatever makes you give your brother only partial welcome, or would let you think that you are better off apart. [9]Is it not always your belief your specialness is limited by your relationship? [10]And is not this the "enemy" that makes you and your brother illusions to each other?

8. The fear of God and of your brother comes from each unrecognized belief in specialness. [2]For you demand your brother bow to it against his will. [3]And God Himself must honor it or suffer vengeance. [4]Every twinge of malice, or stab of hate or wish to separate arises here. [5]For here the purpose that you and your brother share becomes obscured from both of you. [6]You would oppose this course because it teaches you you and your brother are alike. [7]You have no purpose that is not the same, and none your Father does not share with you. [8]For your relationship has been made clean of special goals. [9]And would you now defeat the goal of holiness that Heaven gave it? [10]What perspective can the special have that does not change with every seeming blow, each slight, or fancied judgment on themselves?

9. Those who are special must defend illusions against the truth. [2]For what is specialness but an attack upon the Will of God? [3]You love your brother not while it is this you would defend against him. [4]This is what he attacks, and you protect. [5]Here is the

ground of battle which you wage against him. ⁶Here must he be your enemy and not your friend. ⁷Never can there be peace among the different. ⁸He is your friend *because* you are the same.

II. The Treachery of Specialness

1. Comparison must be an ego device, for love makes none. ²Specialness always makes comparisons. ³It is established by a lack seen in another, and maintained by searching for, and keeping clear in sight, all lacks it can perceive. ⁴This does it seek, and this it looks upon. ⁵And always whom it thus diminishes would be your savior, had you not chosen to make of him a tiny measure of your specialness instead. ⁶Against the littleness you see in him you stand as tall and stately, clean and honest, pure and unsullied, by comparison with what you see. ⁷Nor do you understand it is yourself that you diminish thus.

2. Pursuit of specialness is always at the cost of peace. ²Who can attack his savior and cut him down, yet recognize his strong support? ³Who can detract from his omnipotence, yet share his power? ⁴And who can use him as the gauge of littleness, and be released from limits? ⁵You have a function in salvation. ⁶Its pursuit will bring you joy. ⁷But the pursuit of specialness must bring you pain. ⁸Here is a goal that would defeat salvation, and thus run counter to the Will of God. ⁹To value specialness is to esteem an alien will to which illusions of yourself are dearer than the truth.

3. Specialness is the idea of sin made real. ²Sin is impossible even to imagine without this base. ³For sin arose from it, out of nothingness; an evil flower with no roots at all. ⁴Here is the self-made "savior," the "creator" who creates unlike the Father, and which made His Son like to itself and not like unto Him. ⁵His "special" sons are many, never one, each one in exile from himself, and Him of Whom they are a part. ⁶Nor do they love the Oneness which created them as one with Him. ⁷They chose their specialness instead of Heaven and instead of peace, and wrapped it carefully in sin, to keep it "safe" from truth.

4. You are not special. ²If you think you are, and would defend your specialness against the truth of what you really are, how can you know the truth? ³What answer that the Holy Spirit gives can reach you, when it is your specialness to which you listen, and

which asks and answers? [4]Its tiny answer, soundless in the melody that pours from God to you eternally in loving praise of what you are, is all you listen to. [5]And that vast song of honor and of love for what you are seems silent and unheard before its "mightiness." [6]You strain your ears to hear its soundless voice, and yet the Call of God Himself is soundless to you.

5. You can defend your specialness, but never will you hear the Voice for God beside it. [2]They speak a different language and they fall on different ears. [3]To every special one a different message, and one with different meaning, is the truth. [4]Yet how can truth be different to each one? [5]The special messages the special hear convince them they are different and apart; each in his special sins and "safe" from love, which does not see his specialness at all. [6]Christ's vision is their "enemy," for it sees not what they would look upon, and it would show them that the specialness they think they see is an illusion.

6. What would they see instead? [2]The shining radiance of the Son of God, so like his Father that the memory of Him springs instantly to mind. [3]And with this memory, the Son remembers his own creations, as like to him as he is to his Father. [4]And all the world he made, and all his specialness, and all the sins he held in its defense against himself, will vanish as his mind accepts the truth about himself, as it returns to take their place. [5]This is the only "cost" of truth: You will no longer see what never was, nor hear what makes no sound. [6]Is it a sacrifice to give up nothing, and to receive the Love of God forever?

7. You who have chained your savior to your specialness, and given it his place, remember this: He has not lost the power to forgive you all the sins you think you placed between him and the function of salvation given him for you. [2]Nor will you change his function, any more than you can change the truth in him and in yourself. [3]But be you certain that the truth is just the same in both. [4]It gives no different messages, and has one meaning. [5]And it is one you and your brother both can understand, and one that brings release to both of you. [6]Here stands your brother with the key to Heaven in his hand, held out to you. [7]Let not the dream of specialness remain between you. [8]What is one is joined in truth.

8. Think of the loveliness that you will see within yourself, when you have looked on him as on a friend. [2]He *is* the enemy of specialness, but only friend to what is real in you. [3]Not one attack you thought you made on him has taken from him the gift that

God would have him give to you. [4]His need to give it is as great as yours to have it. [5]Let him forgive you all your specialness, and make you whole in mind and one with him. [6]He waits for your forgiveness only that he may return it unto you. [7]It is not God Who has condemned His Son, but you, to save his specialness and kill his Self.

9. You have come far along the way of truth; too far to falter now. [2]Just one step more, and every vestige of the fear of God will melt away in love. [3]Your brother's specialness and yours *are* enemies, and bound in hate to kill each other and deny they are the same. [4]Yet it is not illusions that have reached this final obstacle which seems to make God and His Heaven so remote that They cannot be reached. [5]Here in this holy place does truth stand waiting to receive you and your brother in silent blessing, and in peace so real and so encompassing that nothing stands outside. [6]Leave all illusions of yourself outside this place, to which you come in hope and honesty.

10. Here is your savior *from* your specialness. [2]He is in need of your acceptance of himself as part of you, as you for his. [3]You are alike to God as God is to Himself. [4]He is not special, for He would not keep one part of what He is unto Himself, not given to His Son but kept for Him alone. [5]And it is this you fear, for if He is not special, then He willed His Son to be like Him, and your brother *is* like you. [6]Not special, but possessed of everything, including you. [7]Give him but what he has, remembering God gave Himself to you and your brother in equal love, that both might share the universe with Him Who chose that love could never be divided, and kept separate from what it is and must forever be.

11. You *are* your brother's; part of love was not denied to him. [2]But can it be that you have lost because he is complete? [3]What has been given him makes you complete, as it does him. [4]God's Love gave you to him and him to you because He gave Himself. [5]What is the same as God is one with Him. [6]And only specialness could make the truth of God and you as one seem anything but Heaven, with the hope of peace at last in sight.

12. Specialness is the seal of treachery upon the gift of love. [2]Whatever serves its purpose must be given to kill. [3]No gift that bears its seal but offers treachery to giver and receiver. [4]Not one glance from eyes it veils but looks on sight of death. [5]Not one believer in its potency but seeks for bargains and for compromise that would establish sin love's substitute, and serve it faithfully.

⁶And no relationship that holds its purpose dear but clings to murder as safety's weapon, and the great defender of all illusions from the "threat" of love.

13. The hope of specialness makes it seem possible God made the body as the prison house that keeps His Son from Him. ²For it demands a special place God cannot enter, and a hiding place where none is welcome but your tiny self. ³Nothing is sacred here but unto you, and you alone, apart and separate from all your brothers; safe from all intrusions of sanity upon illusions; safe from God and safe for conflict everlasting. ⁴Here are the gates of hell you closed upon yourself, to rule in madness and in loneliness your special kingdom, apart from God, away from truth and from salvation.

14. The key you threw away God gave your brother, whose holy hands would offer it to you when you were ready to accept His plan for your salvation in the place of yours. ²How could this readiness be reached save through the sight of all your misery, and the awareness that your plan has failed, and will forever fail to bring you peace and joy of any kind? ³Through this despair you travel now, yet it is but illusion of despair. ⁴The death of specialness is not your death, but your awaking into life eternal. ⁵You but emerge from an illusion of what you are to the acceptance of yourself as God created you.

III. The Forgiveness of Specialness

1. Forgiveness is the end of specialness. ²Only illusions can be forgiven, and then they disappear. ³Forgiveness is release from all illusions, and that is why it is impossible but partly to forgive. ⁴No one who clings to one illusion can see himself as sinless, for he holds one error to himself as lovely still. ⁵And so he calls it "unforgivable," and makes it sin. ⁶How can he then give his forgiveness wholly, when he would not receive it for himself? ⁷For it is sure he would receive it wholly the instant that he gave it so. ⁸And thus his secret guilt would disappear, forgiven by himself.

2. Whatever form of specialness you cherish, you have made sin. ²Inviolate it stands, strongly defended with all your puny might against the Will of God. ³And thus it stands against yourself; *your* enemy, not God's. ⁴So does it seem to split you off from God, and make you separate from Him as its defender. ⁵You would protect

505

what God created not. ⁶And yet, this idol that seems to give you power has taken it away. ⁷For you have given your brother's birthright to it, leaving him alone and unforgiven, and yourself in sin beside him, both in misery, before the idol that can save you not.

3. It is not *you* who are so vulnerable and open to attack that just a word, a little whisper that you do not like, a circumstance that suits you not, or an event that you did not anticipate upsets your world, and hurls it into chaos. ²Truth is not frail. ³Illusions leave it perfectly unmoved and undisturbed. ⁴But specialness is not the truth in you. ⁵*It* can be thrown off balance by anything. ⁶What rests on nothing never can be stable. ⁷However large and over-blown it seems to be, it still must rock and turn and whirl about with every breeze.

4. Without foundation nothing is secure. ²Would God have left His Son in such a state, where safety has no meaning? ³No, His Son is safe, resting on Him. ⁴It is your specialness that is attacked by everything that walks and breathes, or creeps or crawls, or even lives at all. ⁵Nothing is safe from its attack, and it is safe from nothing. ⁶It will forevermore be unforgiving, for that is what it is; a secret vow that what God wants for you will never be, and that you will oppose His Will forever. ⁷Nor is it possible the two can ever be the same, while specialness stands like a flaming sword of death between them, and makes them enemies.

5. God asks for your forgiveness. ²He would have no separation, like an alien will, rise between what He wills for you and what you will. ³They *are* the same, for neither One wills specialness. ⁴How could They will the death of love itself? ⁵Yet They are pow-erless to make attack upon illusions. ⁶They are not bodies; as one Mind They wait for all illusions to be brought to Them, and left behind. ⁷Salvation challenges not even death. ⁸And God Himself, Who knows that death is not your will, must say, "Thy will be done" because you think it is.

6. Forgive the great Creator of the universe, the Source of life, of love and holiness, the perfect Father of a perfect Son, for your illusions of your specialness. ²Here is the hell you chose to be your home. ³He chose not this for you. ⁴Ask not He enter this. ⁵The way is barred to love and to salvation. ⁶Yet if you would release your brother from the depths of hell, you have forgiven Him Whose Will it is you rest forever in the arms of peace, in perfect safety, and without the heat and malice of one thought of

specialness to mar your rest. ⁷Forgive the Holy One the specialness He could not give, and that you made instead.

7.   The special ones are all asleep, surrounded by a world of loveliness they do not see. ²Freedom and peace and joy stand there,
beside the bier on which they sleep, and call them to come forth
and waken from their dream of death. ³Yet they hear nothing.
⁴They are lost in dreams of specialness. ⁵They hate the call that
would awaken them, and they curse God because He did not
make their dream reality. ⁶Curse God and die, but not by Him
Who made not death; but only in the dream. ⁷Open your eyes a
little; see the savior God gave to you that you might look on him,
and give him back his birthright. ⁸It is yours.

8.   The slaves of specialness will yet be free. ²Such is the Will of
God and of His Son. ³Would God condemn Himself to hell and to
damnation? ⁴And do you will that this be done unto your savior?
⁵God calls to you from him to join His Will to save you both from
hell. ⁶Look on the print of nails upon his hands that he holds out
for your forgiveness. ⁷God asks your mercy on His Son and on
Himself. ⁸Deny Them not. ⁹They ask of you but that your will be
done. ¹⁰They seek your love that you may love yourself. ¹¹Love
not your specialness instead of Them. ¹²The print of nails is on
your hands as well. ¹³Forgive your Father it was not His Will that
you be crucified.

IV. Specialness versus Sinlessness

1.   Specialness is a lack of trust in anyone except yourself. ²Faith is
invested in yourself alone. ³Everything else becomes your enemy; feared and attacked, deadly and dangerous, hated and worthy only of destruction. ⁴Whatever gentleness it offers is but
deception, but its hate is real. ⁵In danger of destruction it must
kill, and you are drawn to it to kill it first. ⁶And such is guilt's
attraction. ⁷Here is death enthroned as savior; crucifixion is now
redemption, and salvation can only mean destruction of the
world, except yourself.

2.   What could the purpose of the body be but specialness? ²And
it is this that makes it frail and helpless in its own defense. ³It was
conceived to make *you* frail and helpless. ⁴The goal of separation
is its curse. ⁵Yet bodies have no goal. ⁶Purpose is of the mind.
⁷And minds can change as they desire. ⁸What they are, and all

their attributes, they cannot change. [9]But what they hold as purpose can be changed, and body states must shift accordingly. [10]Of itself the body can do nothing. [11]See it as means to hurt, and it is hurt. [12]See it as means to heal, and it is healed.

3. You can but hurt yourself. [2]This has been oft repeated, but is difficult to grasp as yet. [3]To minds intent on specialness it is impossible. [4]Yet to those who wish to heal and not attack, it is quite obvious. [5]The purpose of attack is in the mind, and its effects are felt but where it is. [6]Nor is the mind limited; so must it be that harmful purpose hurts the mind as one. [7]Nothing could make less sense to specialness. [8]Nothing could make more sense to miracles. [9]For miracles are merely change of purpose from hurt to healing. [10]This shift in purpose does "endanger" specialness, but only in the sense that all illusions are "threatened" by the truth. [11]They will not stand before it. [12]Yet what comfort has ever been in them, that you would keep the gift your Father asks from Him, and give it there instead? [13]Given to Him, the universe is yours. [14]Offered to them, no gifts can be returned. [15]What you have given specialness has left you bankrupt and your treasure house barren and empty, with an open door inviting everything that would disturb your peace to enter and destroy.

4. Earlier I said consider not the means by which salvation is attained, nor how to reach it. [2]But do consider, and consider well, whether it is your wish that you might see your brother sinless. [3]To specialness the answer must be "no." [4]A sinless brother *is* its enemy, while sin, if it were possible, would be its friend. [5]Your brother's sin would justify itself, and give it meaning that the truth denies. [6]All that is real proclaims his sinlessness. [7]All that is false proclaims his sins as real. [8]If he is sinful, then is your reality not real, but just a dream of specialness that lasts an instant, crumbling into dust.

5. Do not defend this senseless dream, in which God is bereft of what He loves, and you remain beyond salvation. [2]Only this is certain in this shifting world that has no meaning in reality: When peace is not with you entirely, and when you suffer pain of any kind, you have beheld some sin within your brother, and have rejoiced at what you thought was there. [3]Your specialness seemed safe because of it. [4]And thus you saved what you appointed to be your savior, and crucified the one whom God has given you instead. [5]So are you bound with him, for you are one. [6]And so is specialness his "enemy," and yours as well.

V. The Christ in You

1. The Christ in you is very still. [2]He looks on what He loves, and knows it as Himself. [3]And thus does He rejoice at what He sees, because He knows that it is one with Him and with His Father. [4]Specialness, too, takes joy in what it sees, although it is not true. [5]Yet what you seek for is a source of joy as you conceive it. [6]What you wish is true for you. [7]Nor is it possible that you can wish for something and lack faith that it is so. [8]Wishing makes real, as surely as does will create. [9]The power of a wish upholds illusions as strongly as does love extend itself. [10]Except that one deludes; the other heals.

2. There is no dream of specialness, however hidden or disguised the form, however lovely it may seem to be, however much it delicately offers the hope of peace and the escape from pain, in which you suffer not your condemnation. [2]In dreams effect and cause are interchanged, for here the maker of the dream believes that what he made is happening to him. [3]He does not realize he picked a thread from here, a scrap from there, and wove a picture out of nothing. [4]For the parts do not belong together, and the whole contributes nothing to the parts to give them meaning.

3. Where could your peace arise *but* from forgiveness? [2]The Christ in you looks only on the truth, and sees no condemnation that could need forgiveness. [3]He is at peace *because* He sees no sin. [4]Identify with Him, and what has He that you have not? [5]He is your eyes, your ears, your hands, your feet. [6]How gentle are the sights He sees, the sounds He hears. [7]How beautiful His hand that holds His brother's, and how lovingly He walks beside him, showing him what can be seen and heard, and where he will see nothing and there is no sound to hear.

4. Yet let your specialness direct his way, and you will follow. [2]And both will walk in danger, each intent, in the dark forest of the sightless, unlit but by the shifting tiny gleams that spark an instant from the fireflies of sin and then go out, to lead the other to a nameless precipice and hurl him over it. [3]For what can specialness delight in but to kill? [4]What does it seek for but the sight of death? [5]Where does it lead but to destruction? [6]Yet think not that it looked upon your brother first, nor hated him before it hated you. [7]The sin its eyes behold in him and love to look upon it saw in you, and looks on still with joy. [8]Yet is it joy to look upon decay and madness, and believe this crumbling thing, with flesh

already loosened from the bone and sightless holes for eyes, is like yourself?

5. Rejoice you have no eyes with which to see; no ears to listen, and no hands to hold nor feet to guide. ²Be glad that only Christ can lend you His, while you have need of them. ³They are illusions, too, as much as yours. ⁴And yet because they serve a different purpose, the strength their purpose holds is given them. ⁵And what they see and hear and hold and lead is given light, that you may lead as you were led.

6. The Christ in you is very still. ²He knows where you are going, and He leads you there in gentleness and blessing all the way. ³His Love for God replaces all the fear you thought you saw within yourself. ⁴His Holiness shows you Himself in him whose hand you hold, and whom you lead to Him. ⁵And what you see is like yourself. ⁶For what but Christ is there to see and hear and love and follow home? ⁷He looked upon you first, but recognized that you were not complete. ⁸And so He sought for your completion in each living thing that He beholds and loves. ⁹And seeks it still, that each might offer you the Love of God.

7. Yet is He quiet, for He knows that love is in you now, and safely held in you by that same hand that holds your brother's in your own. ²Christ's hand holds all His brothers in Himself. ³He gives them vision for their sightless eyes, and sings to them of Heaven, that their ears may hear no more the sound of battle and of death. ⁴He reaches through them, holding out His hand, that everyone may bless all living things, and see their holiness. ⁵And He rejoices that these sights are yours, to look upon with Him and share His joy. ⁶His perfect lack of specialness He offers you, that you may save all living things from death, receiving from each one the gift of life that your forgiveness offers to your Self. ⁷The sight of Christ is all there is to see. ⁸The song of Christ is all there is to hear. ⁹The hand of Christ is all there is to hold. ¹⁰There is no journey but to walk with Him.

8. You who would be content with specialness, and seek salvation in a war with love, consider this: The holy Lord of Heaven has Himself come down to you, to offer you your own completion. ²What is His is yours because in your completion is His Own. ³He Who willed not to be without His Son could never will that you be brotherless. ⁴And would He give a brother unto you except he be as perfect as yourself, and just as like to Him in holiness as you must be?

9. There must be doubt before there can be conflict. ²And every doubt must be about yourself. ³Christ has no doubt, and from His certainty His quiet comes. ⁴He will exchange His certainty for all your doubts, if you agree that He is One with you, and that this Oneness is endless, timeless, and within your grasp because your hands are His. ⁵He is within you, yet He walks beside you and before, leading the way that He must go to find Himself complete. ⁶His quietness becomes your certainty. ⁷And where is doubt when certainty has come?

VI. Salvation from Fear

1. Before your brother's holiness the world is still, and peace descends on it in gentleness and blessing so complete that not one trace of conflict still remains to haunt you in the darkness of the night. ²He is your savior from the dreams of fear. ³He is the healing of your sense of sacrifice and fear that what you have will scatter with the wind and turn to dust. ⁴In him is your assurance God is here, and with you now. ⁵While he is what he is, you can be sure that God is knowable and will be known to you. ⁶For He could never leave His Own creation. ⁷And the sign that this is so lies in your brother, offered you that all your doubts about yourself may disappear before his holiness. ⁸See in him God's creation. ⁹For in him his Father waits for your acknowledgment that He created you as part of Him.

2. Without you there would be a lack in God, a Heaven incomplete, a Son without a Father. ²There could be no universe and no reality. ³For what God wills is whole, and part of Him because His Will is One. ⁴Nothing alive that is not part of Him, and nothing is but is alive in Him. ⁵Your brother's holiness shows you that God is one with him and you; that what he has is yours because you are not separate from him nor from his Father.

3. Nothing is lost to you in all the universe. ²Nothing that God created has He failed to lay before you lovingly, as yours forever. ³And no Thought within His Mind is absent from your own. ⁴It is His Will you share His Love for you, and look upon yourself as lovingly as He conceived of you before the world began, and as He knows you still. ⁵God changes not His Mind about His Son with passing circumstance which has no meaning in eternity where He abides, and you with Him. ⁶Your brother *is* as He

511

created him. [7]And it is this that saves you from a world that He created not.

4. Forget not that the healing of God's Son is all the world is for. [2]That is the only purpose the Holy Spirit sees in it, and thus the only one it has. [3]Until you see the healing of the Son as all you wish to be accomplished by the world, by time and all appearances, you will not know the Father nor yourself. [4]For you will use the world for what is not its purpose, and will not escape its laws of violence and death. [5]Yet it is given you to be beyond its laws in all respects, in every way and every circumstance, in all temptation to perceive what is not there, and all belief God's Son can suffer pain because he sees himself as he is not.

5. Look on your brother, and behold in him the whole reversal of the laws that seem to rule this world. [2]See in his freedom yours, for such it is. [3]Let not his specialness obscure the truth in him, for not one law of death you bind him to will you escape. [4]And not one sin you see in him but keeps you both in hell. [5]Yet will his perfect sinlessness release you both, for holiness is quite impartial, with one judgment made for all it looks upon. [6]And that is made, not of itself, but through the Voice that speaks for God in everything that lives and shares His Being.

6. It is His sinlessness that eyes that see can look upon. [2]It is His loveliness they see in everything. [3]And it is He they look for everywhere, and find no sight nor place nor time where He is not. [4]Within your brother's holiness, the perfect frame for your salvation and the world's, is set the shining memory of Him in Whom your brother lives, and you along with him. [5]Let not your eyes be blinded by the veil of specialness that hides the face of Christ from him, and you as well. [6]And let the fear of God no longer hold the vision you were meant to see from you. [7]Your brother's body shows not Christ to you. [8]He *is* set forth within his holiness.

7. Choose, then, his body or his holiness as what you want to see, and which you choose is yours to look upon. [2]Yet will you choose in countless situations, and through time that seems to have no end, until the truth be your decision. [3]For eternity is not regained by still one more denial of Christ in him. [4]And where is your salvation, if he is but a body? [5]Where is your peace but in his holiness? [6]And where is God Himself but in that part of Him He set forever in your brother's holiness, that you might see the truth about yourself, set forth at last in terms you recognized and

understood?

8. Your brother's holiness is sacrament and benediction unto you. [2]His errors cannot withhold God's blessing from himself, nor you who see him truly. [3]His mistakes can cause delay, which it is given you to take from him, that both may end a journey that has never begun, and needs no end. [4]What never was is not a part of you. [5]Yet you will think it is, until you realize that it is not a part of him who stands beside you. [6]He is the mirror of yourself, wherein you see the judgment you have laid on both of you. [7]The Christ in you beholds his holiness. [8]Your specialness looks on his body and beholds him not.

9. See him as what he is, that your deliverance may not be long. [2]A senseless wandering, without a purpose and without accomplishment of any kind, is all the other choice can offer you. [3]Futility of function not fulfilled will haunt you while your brother lies asleep, till what has been assigned to you is done and he is risen from the past. [4]He who condemned himself, and you as well, is given you to save from condemnation, along with you. [5]And both shall see God's glory in His Son, whom you mistook as flesh, and bound to laws that have no power over him at all.

10. Would you not gladly realize these laws are not for you? [2]Then see him not as prisoner to them. [3]It cannot be what governs part of God holds not for all the rest. [4]You place yourself under the laws you see as ruling him. [5]Think, then, how great the Love of God for you must be, that He has given you a part of Him to save from pain and give you happiness. [6]And never doubt but that your specialness will disappear before the Will of God, Who loves each part of Him with equal love and care. [7]The Christ in you can see your brother truly. [8]Would you decide against the holiness He sees?

11. Specialness is the function that you gave yourself. [2]It stands for you alone, as self-created, self-maintained, in need of nothing, and unjoined with anything beyond the body. [3]In its eyes you are a separate universe, with all the power to hold itself complete within itself, with every entry shut against intrusion, and every window barred against the light. [4]Always attacked and always furious, with anger always fully justified, you have pursued this goal with vigilance you never thought to yield, and effort that you never thought to cease. [5]And all this grim determination was for this; you wanted specialness to be the truth.

12. Now you are merely asked that you pursue another goal with

far less vigilance; with little effort and with little time, and with the power of God maintaining it, and promising success. ²Yet of the two, it is this one you find more difficult. ³The "sacrifice" of self you understand, nor do you deem this cost too heavy. ⁴But a tiny willingness, a nod to God, a greeting to the Christ in you, you find a burden wearisome and tedious, too heavy to be borne. ⁵Yet to the dedication to the truth as God established it no sacrifice is asked, no strain called forth, and all the power of Heaven and the might of truth itself is given to provide the means, and guarantee the goal's accomplishment.

13.   You who believe it easier to see your brother's body than his holiness, be sure you understand what made this judgment. ²Here is the voice of specialness heard clearly, judging against the Christ and setting forth for you the purpose that you can attain, and what you cannot do. ³Forget not that this judgment must apply to what you do with it as your ally. ⁴For what you do through Christ it does not know. ⁵To Him this judgment makes no sense at all, for only what His Father wills is possible, and there is no alternative for Him to see. ⁶Out of His lack of conflict comes your peace. ⁷And from His purpose comes the means for effortless accomplishment and rest.

VII. The Meeting Place

1.   How bitterly does everyone tied to this world defend the specialness he wants to be the truth! ²His wish is law to him, and he obeys. ³Nothing his specialness demands does he withhold. ⁴Nothing it needs does he deny to what he loves. ⁵And while it calls to him he hears no other Voice. ⁶No effort is too great, no cost too much, no price too dear to save his specialness from the least slight, the tiniest attack, the whispered doubt, the hint of threat, or anything but deepest reverence. ⁷This is your son, beloved of you as you are to your Father. ⁸Yet it stands in place of your creations, who *are* son to you, that you might share the Fatherhood of God, not snatch it from Him. ⁹What is this son that you have made to be your strength? ¹⁰What is this child of earth on whom such love is lavished? ¹¹What is this parody of God's creation that takes the place of yours? ¹²And where are they, now that the host of God has found another son whom he prefers to them?

2. The memory of God shines not alone. ²What is within your brother still contains all of creation, everything created and creating, born and unborn as yet, still in the future or apparently gone by. ³What is in him is changeless, and your changelessness is recognized in its acknowledgment. ⁴The holiness in you belongs to him. ⁵And by your seeing it in him, returns to you. ⁶All of the tribute you have given specialness belongs to him, and thus returns to you. ⁷All of the love and care, the strong protection, the thought by day and night, the deep concern, the powerful conviction this is you, belong to him. ⁸Nothing you gave to specialness but is his due. ⁹And nothing due him is not due to you.

3. How can you know your worth while specialness claims you instead? ²How can you fail to know it in his holiness? ³Seek not to make your specialness the truth, for if it were you would be lost indeed. ⁴Be thankful, rather, it is given you to see his holiness *because* it is the truth. ⁵And what is true in him must be as true in you.

4. Ask yourself this: Can *you* protect the mind? ²The body, yes, a little; not from time, but temporarily. ³And much you think you save, you hurt. ⁴What would you save it *for?* ⁵For in that choice lie both its health and harm. ⁶Save it for show, as bait to catch another fish, to house your specialness in better style, or weave a frame of loveliness around your hate, and you condemn it to decay and death. ⁷And if you see this purpose in your brother's, such is your condemnation of your own. ⁸Weave, rather, then, a frame of holiness around him, that the truth may shine on him, and give *you* safety from decay.

5. The Father keeps what He created safe. ²You cannot touch it with the false ideas you made, because it was created not by you. ³Let not your foolish fancies frighten you. ⁴What is immortal cannot be attacked; what is but temporal has no effect. ⁵Only the purpose that you see in it has meaning, and if that is true, its safety rests secure. ⁶If not, it has no purpose, and is means for nothing. ⁷Whatever is perceived as means for truth shares in its holiness, and rests in light as safely as itself. ⁸Nor will that light go out when it is gone. ⁹Its holy purpose gave it immortality, setting another light in Heaven, where your creations recognize a gift from you, a sign that you have not forgotten them.

6. The test of everything on earth is simply this; "What is it *for?*" ²The answer makes it what it is for you. ³It has no meaning of itself, yet you can give reality to it, according to the purpose that

you serve. ⁴Here you are but means, along with it. ⁵God is a Means as well as End. ⁶In Heaven, means and end are one, and one with Him. ⁷This is the state of true creation, found not within time, but in eternity. ⁸To no one here is this describable. ⁹Nor is there any way to learn what this condition means. ¹⁰Not till you go past learning to the Given; not till you make again a holy home for your creations is it understood.

7. A co-creator with the Father must have a Son. ²Yet must this Son have been created like Himself. ³A perfect being, all-encompassing and all-encompassed, nothing to add and nothing taken from; not born of size nor place nor time, nor held to limits or uncertainties of any kind. ⁴Here do the means and end unite as one, nor does this one have any end at all. ⁵All this is true, and yet it has no meaning to anyone who still retains one unlearned lesson in his memory, one thought with purpose still uncertain, or one wish with a divided aim.

8. This course makes no attempt to teach what cannot easily be learned. ²Its scope does not exceed your own, except to say that what is yours will come to you when you are ready. ³Here are the means and the purpose separate because they were so made and so perceived. ⁴And therefore do we deal with them as if they were. ⁵It is essential it be kept in mind that all perception still is upside down until its purpose has been understood. ⁶Perception does not seem to be a means. ⁷And it is this that makes it hard to grasp the whole extent to which it must depend on what you see it for. ⁸Perception seems to teach you what you see. ⁹Yet it but witnesses to what you taught. ¹⁰It is the outward picture of a wish; an image that you wanted to be true.

9. Look at yourself, and you will see a body. ²Look at this body in a different light and it looks different. ³And without a light it seems that it is gone. ⁴Yet you are reassured that it is there because you still can feel it with your hands and hear it move. ⁵Here is an image that you want to be yourself. ⁶It is the means to make your wish come true. ⁷It gives the eyes with which you look on it, the hands that feel it, and the ears with which you listen to the sounds it makes. ⁸It proves its own reality to you.

10. Thus is the body made a theory of yourself, with no provisions made for evidence beyond itself, and no escape within its sight. ²Its course is sure, when seen through its own eyes. ³It grows and withers, flourishes and dies. ⁴And you cannot conceive of you apart from it. ⁵You brand it sinful and you hate its acts, judging it

evil. [6]Yet your specialness whispers, "Here is my own beloved son, in whom I am well pleased." [7]Thus does the "son" become the means to serve his "father's" purpose. [8]Not identical, not even like, but still a means to offer to the "father" what he wants. [9]Such is the travesty on God's creation. [10]For as His Son's creation gave Him joy and witness to His Love and shared His purpose, so does the body testify to the idea that made it, and speak for its reality and truth.

11. And thus are two sons made, and both appear to walk this earth without a meeting place and no encounter. [2]One do you perceive outside yourself, your own beloved son. [3]The other rests within, his Father's Son, within your brother as he is in you. [4]Their difference does not lie in how they look, nor where they go, nor even what they do. [5]They have a different purpose. [6]It is this that joins them to their like, and separates each from all aspects with a different purpose. [7]The Son of God retains his Father's Will. [8]The son of man perceives an alien will and wishes it were so. [9]And thus does his perception serve his wish by giving it appearances of truth. [10]Yet can perception serve another goal. [11]It is not bound to specialness but by your choice. [12]And it is given you to make a different choice, and use perception for a different purpose. [13]And what you see will serve that purpose well, and prove its own reality to you.

Chapter 25

THE JUSTICE OF GOD

Introduction

1. The Christ in you inhabits not a body. ²Yet He is in you. ³And thus it must be that you are not within a body. ⁴What is within you cannot be outside. ⁵And it is certain that you cannot be apart from what is at the very center of your life. ⁶What gives you life cannot be housed in death. ⁷No more can you. ⁸Christ is within a frame of Holiness whose only purpose is that He may be made manifest to those who know Him not, that He may call to them to come to Him and see Him where they thought their bodies were. ⁹Then will their bodies melt away, that they may frame His Holiness in them.

2. No one who carries Christ in him can fail to recognize Him everywhere. ²*Except* in bodies. ³And as long as he believes he is in a body, where he thinks he is He cannot be. ⁴And so he carries Him unknowingly, and does not make Him manifest. ⁵And thus he does not recognize Him where He is. ⁶The son of man is not the risen Christ. ⁷Yet does the Son of God abide exactly where he is, and walks with him within his holiness, as plain to see as is his specialness set forth within his body.

3. The body needs no healing. ²But the mind that thinks it is a body is sick indeed! ³And it is here that Christ sets forth the remedy. ⁴His purpose folds the body in His light, and fills it with the Holiness that shines from Him. ⁵And nothing that the body says or does but makes Him manifest. ⁶To those who know Him not it carries Him in gentleness and love, to heal their minds. ⁷Such is the mission that your brother has for you. ⁸And such it must be that your mission is for him.

I. The Link to Truth

1. It cannot be that it is hard to do the task that Christ appointed you to do, since it is He Who does it. ²And in the doing of it will you learn the body merely seems to be the means to do it. ³For the Mind is His. ⁴And so it must be yours. ⁵His Holiness directs

the body through the mind at one with Him. ⁶And you are manifest unto your holy brother, as he to you. ⁷Here is the meeting of the holy Christ unto Himself; nor any differences perceived to stand between the aspects of His Holiness, which meet and join and raise Him to His Father, whole and pure and worthy of His everlasting Love.

2. How can you manifest the Christ in you except to look on holiness and see Him there? ²Perception tells you *you* are manifest in what you see. ³Behold the body, and you will believe that you are there. ⁴And every body that you look upon reminds you of yourself; your sinfulness, your evil and, above all, your death. ⁵And would you not despise the one who tells you this, and seek his death instead? ⁶The message and the messenger are one. ⁷And you must see your brother as yourself. ⁸Framed in his body you will see your sinfulness, wherein you stand condemned. ⁹Set in his holiness, the Christ in him proclaims Himself as you.

3. Perception is a choice of what you want yourself to be; the world you want to live in, and the state in which you think your mind will be content and satisfied. ²It chooses where you think your safety lies, at your decision. ³It reveals yourself to you as you would have you be. ⁴And always is it faithful to your purpose, from which it never separates, nor gives the slightest witness unto anything the purpose in your mind upholdeth not. ⁵Perception is a part of what it is your purpose to behold, for means and end are never separate. ⁶And thus you learn what seems to have a life apart has none.

4. *You* are the means for God; not separate, nor with a life apart from His. ²His life is manifest in you who are His Son. ³Each aspect of Himself is framed in holiness and perfect purity, in love celestial and so complete it wishes only that it may release all that it looks upon unto itself. ⁴Its radiance shines through each body that it looks upon, and brushes all its darkness into light merely by looking past it *to* the light. ⁵The veil is lifted through its gentleness, and nothing hides the face of Christ from its beholders. ⁶You and your brother stand before Him now, to let Him draw aside the veil that seems to keep you separate and apart.

5. Since you believe that you are separate, Heaven presents itself to you as separate, too. ²Not that it is in truth, but that the link that has been given you to join the truth may reach to you through what you understand. ³Father and Son and Holy Spirit are as One, as all your brothers join as one in truth. ⁴Christ and

His Father never have been separate, and Christ abides within your understanding, in the part of you that shares His Father's Will. ⁵The Holy Spirit links the other part—the tiny, mad desire to be separate, different and special—to the Christ, to make the oneness clear to what is really one. ⁶In this world this is not understood, but can be taught.

6. The Holy Spirit serves Christ's purpose in your mind, so that the aim of specialness can be corrected where the error lies. ²Because His purpose still is one with both the Father and the Son, He knows the Will of God and what you really will. ³But this is understood by mind perceived as one, aware that it is one, and so experienced. ⁴It is the Holy Spirit's function to teach you how this oneness is experienced, what you must do that it can be experienced, and where you should go to do it.

7. All this takes note of time and place as if they were discrete, for while you think that part of you is separate, the concept of a Oneness joined as One is meaningless. ²It is apparent that a mind so split could never be the Teacher of a Oneness which unites all things within Itself. ³And so What is within this mind, and does unite all things together, must be its Teacher. ⁴Yet must It use the language that this mind can understand, in the condition in which it thinks it is. ⁵And It must use all learning to transfer illusions to the truth, taking all false ideas of what you are, and leading you beyond them to the truth that *is* beyond them. ⁶All this can very simply be reduced to this:

> ⁷*What is the same can not be different, and what is one can not have separate parts.*

II. The Savior from the Dark

1. Is it not evident that what the body's eyes perceive fills you with fear? ²Perhaps you think you find a hope of satisfaction there. ³Perhaps you fancy to attain some peace and satisfaction in the world as you perceive it. ⁴Yet it must be evident the outcome does not change. ⁵Despite your hopes and fancies, always does despair result. ⁶And there is no exception, nor will there ever be. ⁷The only value that the past can hold is that you learn it gave you no rewards which you would want to keep. ⁸For only thus will you be willing to relinquish it, and have it gone forever.

2. Is it not strange that you should cherish still some hope of satisfaction from the world you see? ²In no respect, at any time or place, has anything but fear and guilt been your reward. ³How long is needed for you to realize the chance of change in this respect is hardly worth delaying change that might result in better outcome? ⁴For one thing is sure; the way you see, and long have seen, gives no support to base your future hopes, and no suggestions of success at all. ⁵To place your hopes where no hope lies must make you hopeless. ⁶Yet is this hopelessness your choice, while you would seek for hope where none is ever found.

3. Is it not also true that you have found some hope apart from this; some glimmering,—inconstant, wavering, yet dimly seen,— that hopefulness is warranted on grounds that are not in this world? ²And yet your hope that they may still be here prevents you still from giving up the hopeless and unrewarding task you set yourself. ³Can it make sense to hold the fixed belief that there is reason to uphold pursuit of what has always failed, on grounds that it will suddenly succeed and bring what it has never brought before?

4. Its past *has* failed. ²Be glad that it is gone within your mind, to darken what is there. ³Take not the form for content, for the form is but a means for content. ⁴And the frame is but a means to hold the picture up, so that it can be seen. ⁵A frame that hides the picture has no purpose. ⁶It cannot be a frame if it is what you see. ⁷Without the picture is the frame without its meaning. ⁸Its purpose is to set the picture off, and not itself.

5. Who hangs an empty frame upon a wall and stands before it, deep in reverence, as if a masterpiece were there to see? ²Yet if you see your brother as a body, it is but this you do. ³The masterpiece that God has set within this frame is all there is to see. ⁴The body holds it for a while, without obscuring it in any way. ⁵Yet what God has created needs no frame, for what He has created He supports and frames within Himself. ⁶His masterpiece He offers you to see. ⁷And would you rather see the frame instead of this? ⁸And see the picture not at all?

6. The Holy Spirit is the frame God set around the part of Him that you would see as separate. ²Yet its frame is joined to its Creator, one with Him and with His masterpiece. ³This is its purpose, and you do not make the frame into the picture when you choose to see it in its place. ⁴The frame that God has given it but serves His purpose, not yours apart from His. ⁵It is your

separate purpose that obscures the picture, and cherishes the frame instead of it. ⁶Yet God has set His masterpiece within a frame that will endure forever, when yours has crumbled into dust. ⁷But think you not the picture is destroyed in any way. ⁸What God creates is safe from all corruption, unchanged and perfect in eternity.

7.   Accept God's frame instead of yours, and you will see the masterpiece. ²Look at its loveliness, and understand the Mind that thought it, not in flesh and bones, but in a frame as lovely as itself. ³Its holiness lights up the sinlessness the frame of darkness hides, and casts a veil of light across the picture's face which but reflects the light that shines from it to its Creator. ⁴Think not this face was ever darkened because you saw it in a frame of death. ⁵God kept it safe that you might look on it, and see the holiness that He has given it.

8.   Within the darkness see the savior *from* the dark, and understand your brother as his Father's Mind shows him to you. ²He will step forth from darkness as you look on him, and you will see the dark no more. ³The darkness touched him not, nor you who brought him forth for you to look upon. ⁴His sinlessness but pictures yours. ⁵His gentleness becomes your strength, and both will gladly look within, and see the holiness that must be there because of what you looked upon in him. ⁶He is the frame in which your holiness is set, and what God gave him must be given you. ⁷However much he overlooks the masterpiece in him and sees only a frame of darkness, it is still your only function to behold in him what he sees not. ⁸And in this seeing is the vision shared that looks on Christ instead of seeing death.

9.   How could the Lord of Heaven not be glad if you appreciate His masterpiece? ²What could He do but offer thanks to you who love His Son as He does? ³Would He not make known to you His Love, if you but share His praise of what He loves? ⁴God cherishes creation as the perfect Father that He is. ⁵And so His joy is made complete when any part of Him joins in His praise, to share His joy. ⁶This brother is His perfect gift to you. ⁷And He is glad and thankful when you thank His perfect Son for being what he is. ⁸And all His thanks and gladness shine on you who would complete His joy, along with Him. ⁹And thus is yours completed. ¹⁰Not one ray of darkness can be seen by those who will to make their Father's happiness complete, and theirs along with His. ¹¹The gratitude of God Himself is freely offered to everyone who

shares His purpose. [12]It is not His Will to be alone. [13]And neither is it yours.

10. Forgive your brother, and you cannot separate yourself from him nor from his Father. [2]You need no forgiveness, for the wholly pure have never sinned. [3]Give, then, what He has given you, that you may see His Son as one, and thank his Father as He thanks you. [4]Nor believe that all His praise is given not to you. [5]For what you give is His, and giving it, you learn to understand His gift to you. [6]And give the Holy Spirit what He offers unto the Father and the Son alike. [7]Nothing has power over you except His Will and yours, which but extends His Will. [8]It was for this you were created, and your brother with you and at one with you.

11. You and your brother are the same, as God Himself is One and not divided in His Will. [2]And you must have one purpose, since He gave the same to both of you. [3]His Will is brought together as you join in will, that you be made complete by offering completion to your brother. [4]See not in him the sinfulness he sees, but give him honor that you may esteem yourself and him. [5]To you and your brother is given the power of salvation, that escape from darkness into light be yours to share; that you may see as one what never has been separate, nor apart from all God's Love as given equally.

III. Perception and Choice

1. To the extent to which you value guilt, to that extent will you perceive a world in which attack is justified. [2]To the extent to which you recognize that guilt is meaningless, to that extent you will perceive attack cannot *be* justified. [3]This is in accord with perception's fundamental law: You see what you believe is there, and you believe it there because you want it there. [4]Perception has no other law than this. [5]The rest but stems from this, to hold it up and offer it support. [6]This is perception's form, adapted to this world, of God's more basic law; that love creates itself, and nothing but itself.

2. God's laws do not obtain directly to a world perception rules, for such a world could not have been created by the Mind to which perception has no meaning. [2]Yet are His laws reflected everywhere. [3]Not that the world where this reflection is, is real at all. [4]Only because His Son believes it is, and from His Son's belief

He could not let Himself be separate entirely. ⁵He could not enter His Son's insanity with him, but He could be sure His sanity went there with him, so he could not be lost forever in the madness of his wish.

3.   Perception rests on choosing; knowledge does not. ²Knowledge has but one law because it has but one Creator. ³But this world has two who made it, and they do not see it as the same. ⁴To each it has a different purpose, and to each it is a perfect means to serve the goal for which it is perceived. ⁵For specialness, it is the perfect frame to set it off; the perfect battleground to wage its wars, the perfect shelter for illusions which it would make real. ⁶Not one but it upholds in its perception; not one but can be fully justified.

4.   There is another Maker of the world, the simultaneous Corrector of the mad belief that anything could be established and maintained without some link that kept it still within the laws of God; not as the law itself upholds the universe as God created it, but in some form adapted to the need the Son of God believes he has. ²Corrected error is the error's end. ³And thus has God protected still His Son, even in error.

5.   There is another purpose in the world that error made, because it has another Maker Who can reconcile its goal with His Creator's purpose. ²In His perception of the world, nothing is seen but justifies forgiveness and the sight of perfect sinlessness. ³Nothing arises but is met with instant and complete forgiveness. ⁴Nothing remains an instant, to obscure the sinlessness that shines unchanged, beyond the pitiful attempts of specialness to put it out of mind, where it must be, and light the body up instead of it. ⁵The lamps of Heaven are not for mind to choose to see them where it will. ⁶If it elects to see them elsewhere from their home, as if they lit a place where they could never be, then must the Maker of the world correct your error, lest you remain in darkness where the lamps are not.

6.   Everyone here has entered darkness, yet no one has entered it alone. ²Nor need he stay more than an instant. ³For he has come with Heaven's Help within him, ready to lead him out of darkness into light at any time. ⁴The time he chooses can be any time, for help is there, awaiting but his choice. ⁵And when he chooses to avail himself of what is given him, then will he see each situation that he thought before was means to justify his anger turned to an event which justifies his love. ⁶He will hear plainly that the

calls to war he heard before are really calls to peace. ⁷He will perceive that where he gave attack is but another altar where he can, with equal ease and far more happiness, bestow forgiveness. ⁸And he will reinterpret all temptation as just another chance to bring him joy.

7. How can a misperception be a sin? ²Let all your brother's errors be to you nothing except a chance for you to see the workings of the Helper given you to see the world He made instead of yours. ³What, then, *is* justified? ⁴What do you want? ⁵For these two questions are the same. ⁶And when you see them as the same, your choice is made. ⁷For it is seeing them as one that brings release from the belief there are two ways to see. ⁸This world has much to offer to your peace, and many chances to extend your own forgiveness. ⁹Such its purpose is, to those who want to see peace and forgiveness descend on them, and offer them the light.

8. The Maker of the world of gentleness has perfect power to offset the world of violence and hate that seems to stand between you and His gentleness. ²It is not there in His forgiving eyes. ³And therefore it need not be there in yours. ⁴Sin is the fixed belief perception cannot change. ⁵What has been damned is damned and damned forever, being forever unforgivable. ⁶If, then, it is forgiven, sin's perception must have been wrong. ⁷And thus is change made possible. ⁸The Holy Spirit, too, sees what He sees as far beyond the chance of change. ⁹But on His vision sin cannot encroach, for sin has been corrected by His sight. ¹⁰And thus it must have been an error, not a sin. ¹¹For what it claimed could never be, has been. ¹²Sin is attacked by punishment, and so preserved. ¹³But to forgive it is to change its state from error into truth.

9. The Son of God could never sin, but he can wish for what would hurt him. ²And he has the power to think he can be hurt. ³What could this be except a misperception of himself? ⁴Is this a sin or a mistake, forgivable or not? ⁵Does he need help or condemnation? ⁶Is it your purpose that he be saved or damned? ⁷Forgetting not that what he is to you will make this choice your future? ⁸For you make it *now*, the instant when all time becomes a means to reach a goal. ⁹Make, then, your choice. ¹⁰But recognize that in this choice the purpose of the world you see is chosen, and will be justified.

IV. The Light You Bring

1. Minds that are joined and recognize they are, can feel no guilt. [2]For they cannot attack, and they rejoice that this is so, seeing their safety in this happy fact. [3]Their joy is in the innocence they see. [4]And thus they seek for it, because it is their purpose to behold it and rejoice. [5]Everyone seeks for what will bring him joy as he defines it. [6]It is not the aim, as such, that varies. [7]Yet it is the way in which the aim is seen that makes the choice of means inevitable, and beyond the hope of change unless the aim is changed. [8]And then the means are chosen once again, as what will bring rejoicing is defined another way and sought for differently.

2. Perception's basic law could thus be said, "You will rejoice at what you see because you see it to rejoice." [2]And while you think that suffering and sin will bring you joy, so long will they be there for you to see. [3]Nothing is harmful or beneficent apart from what you wish. [4]It is your wish that makes it what it is in its effects on you. [5]Because you chose it as a means to gain these same effects, believing them to be the bringers of rejoicing and of joy. [6]Even in Heaven does this law obtain. [7]The Son of God creates to bring him joy, sharing his Father's purpose in his own creation, that his joy might be increased, and God's along with his.

3. You maker of a world that is not so, take rest and comfort in another world where peace abides. [2]This world you bring with you to all the weary eyes and tired hearts that look on sin and beat its sad refrain. [3]From you can come their rest. [4]From you can rise a world they will rejoice to look upon, and where their hearts are glad. [5]In you there is a vision that extends to all of them, and covers them in gentleness and light. [6]And in this widening world of light the darkness that they thought was there is pushed away, until it is but distant shadows, far away, not long to be remembered as the sun shines them to nothingness. [7]And all their "evil" thoughts and "sinful" hopes, their dreams of guilt and merciless revenge, and every wish to hurt and kill and die, will disappear before the sun you bring.

4. Would you not do this for the Love of God? [2]And for *yourself*? [3]For think what it would do for you. [4]Your "evil" thoughts that haunt you now will seem increasingly remote and far away from you. [5]And they go farther and farther off, because the sun in you has risen that they may be pushed away before the light. [6]They

linger for a while, a little while, in twisted forms too far away for recognition, and are gone forever. ⁷And in the sunlight you will stand in quiet, in innocence and wholly unafraid. ⁸And from you will the rest you found extend, so that your peace can never fall away and leave you homeless. ⁹Those who offer peace to everyone have found a home in Heaven the world cannot destroy. ¹⁰For it is large enough to hold the world within its peace.

5. In you is all of Heaven. ²Every leaf that falls is given life in you. ³Each bird that ever sang will sing again in you. ⁴And every flower that ever bloomed has saved its perfume and its loveliness for you. ⁵What aim can supersede the Will of God and of His Son, that Heaven be restored to him for whom it was created as his only home? ⁶Nothing before and nothing after it. ⁷No other place; no other state nor time. ⁸Nothing beyond nor nearer. ⁹Nothing else. ¹⁰In any form. ¹¹This can you bring to all the world, and all the thoughts that entered it and were mistaken for a little while. ¹²How better could your own mistakes be brought to truth than by your willingness to bring the light of Heaven with you, as you walk beyond the world of darkness into light?

V. The State of Sinlessness

1. The state of sinlessness is merely this: The whole desire to attack is gone, and so there is no reason to perceive the Son of God as other than he is. ²The need for guilt is gone because it has no purpose, and is meaningless without the goal of sin. ³Attack and sin are bound as one illusion, each the cause and aim and justifier of the other. ⁴Each is meaningless alone, but seems to draw a meaning from the other. ⁵Each depends upon the other for whatever sense it seems to have. ⁶And no one could believe in one unless the other were the truth, for each attests the other must be true.

2. Attack makes Christ your enemy, and God along with Him. ²Must you not be afraid with "enemies" like these? ³And must you not be fearful of yourself? ⁴For you have hurt yourself, and made your Self your "enemy." ⁵And now you must believe you are not you, but something alien to yourself and "something else," a "something" to be feared instead of loved. ⁶Who would attack whatever he perceives as wholly innocent? ⁷And who,

because he wishes to attack, can fail to think he must be guilty to maintain the wish, while wanting innocence? [8]For who could see the Son of God as innocent and wish him dead? [9]Christ stands before you, each time you look upon your brother. [10]He has not gone because your eyes are closed. [11]But what is there to see by searching for your Savior, seeing Him through sightless eyes?

3. It is not Christ you see by looking thus. [2]It is the "enemy," confused with Christ, you look upon. [3]And hate because there is no sin in him for you to see. [4]Nor do you hear his plaintive call, unchanged in content in whatever form the call is made, that you unite with him, and join with him in innocence and peace. [5]And yet, beneath the ego's senseless shrieks, such is the call that God has given him, that you might hear in him His Call to you, and answer by returning unto God what is His Own.

4. The Son of God asks only this of you; that you return to him what is his due, that you may share in it with him. [2]Alone does neither have it. [3]So must it remain useless to both. [4]Together, it will give to each an equal strength to save the other, and save himself along with him. [5]Forgiven by you, your savior offers you salvation. [6]Condemned by you, he offers death to you. [7]In everyone you see but the reflection of what you choose to have him be to you. [8]If you decide against his proper function, the only one he has in truth, you are depriving him of all the joy he would have found if he fulfilled the role God gave to him. [9]But think not Heaven is lost to him alone. [10]Nor can it be regained unless the way is shown to him through you, that you may find it, walking by his side.

5. It is no sacrifice that he be saved, for by his freedom will you gain your own. [2]To let his function be fulfilled is but the means to let yours be. [3]And so you walk toward Heaven or toward hell, but not alone. [4]How beautiful his sinlessness will be when you perceive it! [5]And how great will be your joy, when he is free to offer you the gift of sight God gave to him for you! [6]He has no need but this; that you allow him freedom to complete the task God gave to him. [7]Remembering but this; that what he does you do, along with him. [8]And as you see him, so do you define the function he will have for you, until you see him differently and let him be what God appointed that he be to you.

6. Against the hatred that the Son of God may cherish toward himself, is God believed to be without the power to save what He created from the pain of hell. [2]But in the love he shows himself is

God made free to let His Will be done. ³In your brother you see the picture of your own belief in what the Will of God must be for you. ⁴In your forgiveness will you understand His Love for you; through your attack believe He hates you, thinking Heaven must be hell. ⁵Look once again upon your brother, not without the understanding that he is the way to Heaven or to hell, as you perceive him. ⁶But forget not this; the role you give to him is given you, and you will walk the way you pointed out to him because it is your judgment on yourself.

VI. The Special Function

1. The grace of God rests gently on forgiving eyes, and everything they look on speaks of Him to the beholder. ²He can see no evil; nothing in the world to fear, and no one who is different from himself. ³And as he loves them, so he looks upon himself with love and gentleness. ⁴He would no more condemn himself for his mistakes than damn another. ⁵He is not an arbiter of vengeance, nor a punisher of sin. ⁶The kindness of his sight rests on himself with all the tenderness it offers others. ⁷For he would only heal and only bless. ⁸And being in accord with what God wills, he has the power to heal and bless all those he looks on with the grace of God upon his sight.

2. Eyes become used to darkness, and the light of brilliant day seems painful to the eyes grown long accustomed to the dim effects perceived at twilight. ²And they turn away from sunlight and the clarity it brings to what they look upon. ³Dimness seems better; easier to see, and better recognized. ⁴Somehow the vague and more obscure seems easier to look upon; less painful to the eyes than what is wholly clear and unambiguous. ⁵Yet this is not what eyes are for, and who can say that he prefers the darkness and maintain he wants to see?

3. The wish to see calls down the grace of God upon your eyes, and brings the gift of light that makes sight possible. ²Would you behold your brother? ³God is glad to have you look on him. ⁴He does not will your savior be unrecognized by you. ⁵Nor does He will that he remain without the function that He gave to him. ⁶Let him no more be lonely, for the lonely ones are those who see no function in the world for them to fill; no place where they are needed, and no aim which only they can perfectly fulfill.

4. Such is the Holy Spirit's kind perception of specialness; His use of what you made, to heal instead of harm. ²To each He gives a special function in salvation he alone can fill; a part for only him. ³Nor is the plan complete until he finds his special function, and fulfills the part assigned to him, to make himself complete within a world where incompletion rules.

5. Here, where the laws of God do not prevail in perfect form, can he yet do *one* perfect thing and make *one* perfect choice. ²And by this act of special faithfulness to one perceived as other than himself, he learns the gift was given to himself, and so they must be one. ³Forgiveness is the only function meaningful in time. ⁴It is the means the Holy Spirit uses to translate specialness from sin into salvation. ⁵Forgiveness is for all. ⁶But when it rests on all it is complete, and every function of this world completed with it. ⁷Then is time no more. ⁸Yet while in time, there is still much to do. ⁹And each must do what is allotted him, for on his part does all the plan depend. ¹⁰He *has* a special part in time for so he chose, and choosing it, he made it for himself. ¹¹His wish was not denied but changed in form, to let it serve his brother and himself, and thus become a means to save instead of lose.

6. Salvation is no more than a reminder this world is not your home. ²Its laws are not imposed on you, its values are not yours. ³And nothing that you think you see in it is really there at all. ⁴This is seen and understood as each one takes his part in its undoing, as he did in making it. ⁵He has the means for either, as he always did. ⁶The specialness he chose to hurt himself did God appoint to be the means for his salvation, from the very instant that the choice was made. ⁷His special sin was made his special grace. ⁸His special hate became his special love.

7. The Holy Spirit needs your special function, that His may be fulfilled. ²Think not you lack a special value here. ³You wanted it, and it is given you. ⁴All that you made can serve salvation easily and well. ⁵The Son of God can make no choice the Holy Spirit cannot employ on his behalf, and not against himself. ⁶Only in darkness does your specialness appear to be attack. ⁷In light, you see it as your special function in the plan to save the Son of God from all attack, and let him understand that he is safe, as he has always been, and will remain in time and in eternity alike. ⁸This is the function given you for your brother. ⁹Take it gently, then, from your brother's hand, and let salvation be perfectly fulfilled in you. ¹⁰Do this *one* thing, that everything be given you.

VII. The Rock of Salvation

1. Yet if the Holy Spirit can commute each sentence that you laid upon yourself into a blessing, then it cannot be a sin. ²Sin is the only thing in all the world that cannot change. ³It is immutable. ⁴And on its changelessness the world depends. ⁵The magic of the world can seem to hide the pain of sin from sinners, and deceive with glitter and with guile. ⁶Yet each one knows the cost of sin is death. ⁷And so it is. ⁸For sin is a request for death, a wish to make this world's foundation sure as love, dependable as Heaven, and as strong as God Himself. ⁹The world is safe from love to everyone who thinks sin possible. ¹⁰Nor will it change. ¹¹Yet is it possible what God created not should share the attributes of His creation, when it opposes it in every way?

2. It cannot be the "sinner's" wish for death is just as strong as is God's Will for life. ²Nor can the basis of a world He did not make be firm and sure as Heaven. ³How could it be that hell and Heaven are the same? ⁴And is it possible that what He did not will cannot be changed? ⁵What is immutable besides His Will? ⁶And what can share its attributes except itself? ⁷What wish can rise against His Will, and be immutable? ⁸If you could realize nothing is changeless but the Will of God, this course would not be difficult for you. ⁹For it is this that you do not believe. ¹⁰Yet there is nothing else you could believe, if you but looked at what it really is.

3. Let us go back to what we said before, and think of it more carefully. ²It must be so that either God is mad, or is this world a place of madness. ³Not one Thought of His makes any sense at all within this world. ⁴And nothing that the world believes as true has any meaning in His Mind at all. ⁵What makes no sense and has no meaning is insanity. ⁶And what is madness cannot be the truth. ⁷If one belief so deeply valued here were true, then every Thought God ever had is an illusion. ⁸And if but one Thought of His is true, then all beliefs the world gives any meaning to are false, and make no sense at all. ⁹This is the choice you make. ¹⁰Do not attempt to see it differently, nor twist it into something it is not. ¹¹For only this decision can you make. ¹²The rest is up to God, and not to you.

4. To justify one value that the world upholds is to deny your Father's sanity and yours. ²For God and His beloved Son do not think differently. ³And it is the agreement of Their thought that

makes the Son a co-creator with the Mind Whose Thought created him. [4]So if he chooses to believe one thought opposed to truth, he has decided he is not his Father's Son because the Son is mad, and sanity must lie apart from both the Father and the Son. [5]This you believe. [6]Think not that this belief depends upon the form it takes. [7]Who thinks the world is sane in any way, is justified in anything it thinks, or is maintained by any form of reason, believes this to be true. [8]Sin is not real *because* the Father and the Son are not insane. [9]This world is meaningless *because* it rests on sin. [10]Who could create the changeless if it does not rest on truth?

5. The Holy Spirit has the power to change the whole foundation of the world you see to something else; a basis not insane, on which a sane perception can be based, another world perceived. [2]And one in which nothing is contradicted that would lead the Son of God to sanity and joy. [3]Nothing attests to death and cruelty; to separation and to differences. [4]For here is everything perceived as one, and no one loses that each one may gain.

6. Test everything that you believe against this one requirement, and understand that everything that meets this one demand is worthy of your faith. [2]But nothing else. [3]What is not love is sin, and either one perceives the other as insane and meaningless. [4]Love is the basis for a world perceived as wholly mad to sinners, who believe theirs is the way to sanity. [5]But sin is equally insane within the sight of love, whose gentle eyes would look beyond the madness and rest peacefully on truth. [6]Each sees a world immutable, as each defines the changeless and eternal truth of what you are. [7]And each reflects a view of what the Father and the Son must be, to make that viewpoint meaningful and sane.

7. Your special function is the special form in which the fact that God is not insane appears most sensible and meaningful to you. [2]The content is the same. [3]The form is suited to your special needs, and to the special time and place in which you think you find yourself, and where you can be free of place and time, and all that you believe must limit you. [4]The Son of God cannot be bound by time nor place nor anything God did not will. [5]Yet if His Will is seen as madness, then the form of sanity which makes it most acceptable to those who are insane requires special choice. [6]Nor can this choice be made by the insane, whose problem is their choices are not free, and made with reason in the light of sense.

8. It *would* be madness to entrust salvation to the insane. [2]Because He is not mad has God appointed One as sane as He to raise a saner world to meet the sight of everyone who chose insanity as his salvation. [3]To this One is given the choice of form most suitable to him; one which will not attack the world he sees, but enter into it in quietness and show him he is mad. [4]This One but points to an alternative, another way of looking at what he has seen before, and recognizes as the world in which he lives, and thought he understood before.

9. Now must he question this, because the form of the alternative is one which he cannot deny, nor overlook, nor fail completely to perceive at all. [2]To each his special function is designed to be perceived as possible, and more and more desired, as it proves to him that it is an alternative he really wants. [3]From this position does his sinfulness, and all the sin he sees within the world, offer him less and less. [4]Until he comes to understand it cost him his sanity, and stands between him and whatever hope he has of being sane. [5]Nor is he left without escape from madness, for he has a special part in everyone's escape. [6]He can no more be left outside, without a special function in the hope of peace, than could the Father overlook His Son, and pass him by in careless thoughtlessness.

10. What is dependable except God's Love? [2]And where does sanity abide except in Him? [3]The One Who speaks for Him can show you this, in the alternative He chose especially for you. [4]It is God's Will that you remember this, and so emerge from deepest mourning into perfect joy. [5]Accept the function that has been assigned to you in God's Own plan to show His Son that hell and Heaven are different, not the same. [6]And that in Heaven *They* are all the same, without the differences which would have made a hell of Heaven and a heaven of hell, had such insanity been possible.

11. The whole belief that someone loses but reflects the underlying tenet God must be insane. [2]For in this world it seems that one must gain *because* another lost. [3]If this were true, then God is mad indeed! [4]But what is this belief except a form of the more basic tenet, "Sin is real, and rules the world"? [5]For every little gain must someone lose, and pay exact amount in blood and suffering. [6]For otherwise would evil triumph, and destruction be the total cost of any gain at all. [7]You who believe that God is mad, look carefully at this, and understand that it must be either God

or this must be insane, but hardly both.

12.   Salvation is rebirth of the idea no one can lose for anyone to gain. [2]And everyone *must* gain, if anyone would be a gainer. [3]Here is sanity restored. [4]And on this single rock of truth can faith in God's eternal saneness rest in perfect confidence and perfect peace. [5]Reason is satisfied, for all insane beliefs can be corrected here. [6]And sin must be impossible, if this is true. [7]This is the rock on which salvation rests, the vantage point from which the Holy Spirit gives meaning and direction to the plan in which your special function has a part. [8]For here your special function is made whole, because it shares the function of the whole.

13.   Remember all temptation is but this; a mad belief that God's insanity would make you sane and give you what you want; that either God or you must lose to madness because your aims can not be reconciled. [2]Death demands life, but life is not maintained at any cost. [3]No one can suffer for the Will of God to be fulfilled. [4]Salvation is His Will *because* you share it. [5]Not for you alone, but for the Self that is the Son of God. [6]He cannot lose, for if he could the loss would be his Father's, and in Him no loss is possible. [7]And this is sane because it is the truth.

VIII. Justice Returned to Love

1.   The Holy Spirit can use all that you give to Him for your salvation. [2]But He cannot use what you withhold, for He cannot take it from you without your willingness. [3]For if He did, you would believe He wrested it from you against your will. [4]And so you would not learn it *is* your will to be without it. [5]You need not give it to Him wholly willingly, for if you could you had no need of Him. [6]But this He needs; that you prefer He take it than that you keep it for yourself alone, and recognize that what brings loss to no one you would not know. [7]This much is necessary to add to the idea no one can lose for you to gain. [8]And nothing more.

2.   Here is the only principle salvation needs. [2]Nor is it necessary that your faith in it be strong, unswerving, and without attack from all beliefs opposed to it. [3]You have no fixed allegiance. [4]But remember salvation is not needed by the saved. [5]You are not called upon to do what one divided still against himself would find impossible. [6]Have little faith that wisdom could be found in such a state of mind. [7]But be you thankful that only little faith is

asked of you. [8]What but a little faith remains to those who still believe in sin? [9]What could they know of Heaven and the justice of the saved?

3. There is a kind of justice in salvation of which the world knows nothing. [2]To the world, justice and vengeance are the same, for sinners see justice only as their punishment, perhaps sustained by someone else, but not escaped. [3]The laws of sin demand a victim. [4]Who it may be makes little difference. [5]But death must be the cost and must be paid. [6]This is not justice, but insanity. [7]Yet how could justice be defined without insanity where love means hate, and death is seen as victory and triumph over eternity and timelessness and life?

4. You who know not of justice still can ask, and learn the answer. [2]Justice looks on all in the same way. [3]It is not just that one should lack for what another has. [4]For that is vengeance in whatever form it takes. [5]Justice demands no sacrifice, for any sacrifice is made that sin may be preserved and kept. [6]It is a payment offered for the cost of sin, but not the total cost. [7]The rest is taken from another, to be laid beside your little payment, to "atone" for all that you would keep, and not give up. [8]So is the victim seen as partly you, with someone else by far the greater part. [9]And in the total cost, the greater his the less is yours. [10]And justice, being blind, is satisfied by being paid, it matters not by whom.

5. Can this be justice? [2]God knows not of this. [3]But justice does He know, and knows it well. [4]For He is wholly fair to everyone. [5]Vengeance is alien to God's Mind *because* He knows of justice. [6]To be just is to be fair, and not be vengeful. [7]Fairness and vengeance are impossible, for each one contradicts the other and denies that it is real. [8]It is impossible for you to share the Holy Spirit's justice with a mind that can conceive of specialness at all. [9]Yet how could He be just if He condemns a sinner for the crimes he did not do, but thinks he did? [10]And where would justice be if He demanded of the ones obsessed with the idea of punishment that they lay it aside, unaided, and perceive it is not true?

6. It is extremely hard for those who still believe sin meaningful to understand the Holy Spirit's justice. [2]They must believe He shares their own confusion, and cannot avoid the vengeance that their own belief in justice must entail. [3]And so they fear the Holy Spirit, and perceive the "wrath" of God in Him. [4]Nor can they trust Him not to strike them dead with lightning bolts torn from the "fires" of Heaven by God's Own angry Hand. [5]They *do*

believe that Heaven is hell, and *are* afraid of love. ⁶And deep suspicion and the chill of fear comes over them when they are told that they have never sinned. ⁷Their world depends on sin's stability. ⁸And they perceive the "threat" of what God knows as justice to be more destructive to themselves and to their world than vengeance, which they understand and love.

7. So do they think the loss of sin a curse. ²And flee the Holy Spirit as if He were a messenger from hell, sent from above, in treachery and guile, to work God's vengeance on them in the guise of a deliverer and friend. ³What could He be to them except a devil, dressed to deceive within an angel's cloak? ⁴And what escape has He for them except a door to hell that seems to look like Heaven's gate?

8. Yet justice cannot punish those who ask for punishment, but have a Judge Who knows that they are wholly innocent in truth. ²In justice He is bound to set them free, and give them all the honor they deserve and have denied themselves because they are not fair, and cannot understand that they are innocent. ³Love is not understandable to sinners because they think that justice is split off from love, and stands for something else. ⁴And thus is love perceived as weak, and vengeance strong. ⁵For love has lost when judgment left its side, and is too weak to save from punishment. ⁶But vengeance without love has gained in strength by being separate and apart from love. ⁷And what but vengeance now can help and save, while love stands feebly by with helpless hands, bereft of justice and vitality, and powerless to save?

9. What can Love ask of you who think that all of this is true? ²Could He, in justice and in love, believe in your confusion you have much to give? ³You are not asked to trust Him far. ⁴No more than what you see He offers you, and what you recognize you could not give yourself. ⁵In God's Own justice does He recognize all you deserve, but understands as well that you cannot accept it for yourself. ⁶It is His special function to hold out to you the gifts the innocent deserve. ⁷And every one that you accept brings joy to Him as well as you. ⁸He knows that Heaven is richer made by each one you accept. ⁹And God rejoices as His Son receives what loving justice knows to be his due. ¹⁰For love and justice are not different. ¹¹*Because* they are the same does mercy stand at God's right Hand, and gives the Son of God the power to forgive himself of sin.

10. To him who merits everything, how can it be that anything be

kept from him? ²For that would be injustice, and unfair indeed to all the holiness that is in him, however much he recognize it not. ³God knows of no injustice. ⁴He would not allow His Son be judged by those who seek his death, and could not see his worth at all. ⁵What honest witnesses could they call forth to speak on his behalf? ⁶And who would come to plead for him, and not against his life? ⁷No justice would be given him by you. ⁸Yet God ensured that justice would be done unto the Son He loves, and would protect from all unfairness you might seek to offer, believing vengeance is his proper due.

11. As specialness cares not who pays the cost of sin, so it be paid, the Holy Spirit heeds not who looks on innocence at last, provided it is seen and recognized. ²For just *one* witness is enough, if he sees truly. ³Simple justice asks no more. ⁴Of each one does the Holy Spirit ask if he will be that one, so justice may return to love and there be satisfied. ⁵Each special function He allots is but for this; that each one learn that love and justice are not separate. ⁶And both are strengthened by their union with each other. ⁷Without love is justice prejudiced and weak. ⁸And love without justice is impossible. ⁹For love is fair, and cannot chasten without cause. ¹⁰What cause can be to warrant an attack upon the innocent? ¹¹In justice, then, does love correct mistakes, but not in vengeance. ¹²For that would be unjust to innocence.

12. You can be perfect witness to the power of love and justice, if you understand it is impossible the Son of God could merit vengeance. ²You need not perceive, in every circumstance, that this is true. ³Nor need you look to your experience within the world, which is but shadows of all that is really happening within yourself. ⁴The understanding that you need comes not of you, but from a larger Self, so great and holy that He could not doubt His innocence. ⁵Your special function is a call to Him, that He may smile on you whose sinlessness He shares. ⁶His understanding will be yours. ⁷And so the Holy Spirit's special function has been fulfilled. ⁸God's Son has found a witness unto his sinlessness and not his sins. ⁹How little need you give the Holy Spirit that simple justice may be given you.

13. Without impartiality there is no justice. ²How can specialness be just? ³Judge not because you cannot, not because you are a miserable sinner too. ⁴How can the special really understand that justice is the same for everyone? ⁵To take from one to give

another must be an injustice to them both, since they are equal in the Holy Spirit's sight. [6]Their Father gave the same inheritance to both. [7]Who would have more or less is not aware that he has everything. [8]He is no judge of what must be another's due, because he thinks he is deprived. [9]And so must he be envious, and try to take away from whom he judges. [10]He is not impartial, and cannot fairly see another's rights because his own have been obscured to him.

14. You have the right to all the universe; to perfect peace, complete deliverance from all effects of sin, and to the life eternal, joyous and complete in every way, as God appointed for His holy Son. [2]This is the only justice Heaven knows, and all the Holy Spirit brings to earth. [3]Your special function shows you nothing else but perfect justice can prevail for you. [4]And you are safe from vengeance in all forms. [5]The world deceives, but it cannot replace God's justice with a version of its own. [6]For only love is just, and can perceive what justice must accord the Son of God. [7]Let love decide, and never fear that you, in your unfairness, will deprive yourself of what God's justice has allotted you.

IX. The Justice of Heaven

1. What can it be but arrogance to think your little errors cannot be undone by Heaven's justice? [2]And what could this mean except that they are sins and not mistakes, forever uncorrectable, and to be met with vengeance, not with justice? [3]Are you willing to be released from all effects of sin? [4]You cannot answer this until you see all that the answer must entail. [5]For if you answer "yes" it means you will forego all values of this world in favor of the peace of Heaven. [6]Not one sin would you retain. [7]And not one doubt that this is possible will you hold dear that sin be kept in place. [8]You mean that truth has greater value now than all illusions. [9]And you recognize that truth must be revealed to you, because you know not what it is.

2. To give reluctantly is not to gain the gift, because you are reluctant to accept it. [2]It is saved for you until reluctance to receive it disappears, and you are willing it be given you. [3]God's justice warrants gratitude, not fear. [4]Nothing you give is lost to you or anyone, but cherished and preserved in Heaven, where all of the treasures given to God's Son are kept for him, and offered

anyone who but holds out his hand in willingness they be received. [5]Nor is the treasure less as it is given out. [6]Each gift but adds to the supply. [7]For God is fair. [8]He does not fight against His Son's reluctance to perceive salvation as a gift from Him. [9]Yet would His justice not be satisfied until it is received by everyone.

3. Be certain any answer to a problem the Holy Spirit solves will always be one in which no one loses. [2]And this must be true, because He asks no sacrifice of anyone. [3]An answer which demands the slightest loss to anyone has not resolved the problem, but has added to it and made it greater, harder to resolve and more unfair. [4]It is impossible the Holy Spirit could see unfairness as a resolution. [5]To Him, what is unfair must be corrected *because* it is unfair. [6]And every error is a perception in which one, at least, is seen unfairly. [7]Thus is justice not accorded to the Son of God. [8]When anyone is seen as losing, he has been condemned. [9]And punishment becomes his due instead of justice.

4. The sight of innocence makes punishment impossible, and justice sure. [2]The Holy Spirit's perception leaves no ground for an attack. [3]Only a loss could justify attack, and loss of any kind He cannot see. [4]The world solves problems in another way. [5]It sees a resolution as a state in which it is decided who shall win and who shall lose; how much the one shall take, and how much can the loser still defend. [6]Yet does the problem still remain unsolved, for only justice can set up a state in which there is no loser; no one left unfairly treated and deprived, and thus with grounds for vengeance. [7]Problem solving cannot be vengeance, which at best can bring another problem added to the first, in which the murder is not obvious.

5. The Holy Spirit's problem solving is the way in which the problem ends. [2]It has been solved because it has been met with justice. [3]Until it has it will recur, because it has not yet been solved. [4]The principle that justice means no one can lose is crucial to this course. [5]For miracles depend on justice. [6]Not as it is seen through this world's eyes, but as God knows it and as knowledge is reflected in the sight the Holy Spirit gives.

6. No one deserves to lose. [2]And what would be unjust to him cannot occur. [3]Healing must be for everyone, because he does not merit an attack of any kind. [4]What order can there be in miracles, unless someone deserves to suffer more and others less? [5]And is this justice to the wholly innocent? [6]A miracle *is* justice. [7]It is not a special gift to some, to be withheld from others as less worthy,

more condemned, and thus apart from healing. [8]Who is there who can be separate from salvation, if its purpose is the end of specialness? [9]Where is salvation's justice if some errors are unforgivable, and warrant vengeance in place of healing and return of peace?

7. Salvation cannot seek to help God's Son be more unfair than he has sought to be. [2]If miracles, the Holy Spirit's gift, were given specially to an elect and special group, and kept apart from others as less deserving, then is He ally to specialness. [3]What He cannot perceive He bears no witness to. [4]And everyone is equally entitled to His gift of healing and deliverance and peace. [5]To give a problem to the Holy Spirit to solve for you means that you *want* it solved. [6]To keep it for yourself to solve without His help is to decide it should remain unsettled, unresolved, and lasting in its power of injustice and attack. [7]No one can be unjust to you, unless you have decided first to *be* unjust. [8]And then must problems rise to block your way, and peace be scattered by the winds of hate.

8. Unless you think that all your brothers have an equal right to miracles with you, you will not claim your right to them because you were unjust to one with equal rights. [2]Seek to deny and you will feel denied. [3]Seek to deprive, and you have been deprived. [4]A miracle can never be received because another could receive it not. [5]Only forgiveness offers miracles. [6]And pardon must be just to everyone.

9. The little problems that you keep and hide become your secret sins, because you did not choose to let them be removed for you. [2]And so they gather dust and grow, until they cover everything that you perceive and leave you fair to no one. [3]Not one right do you believe you have. [4]And bitterness, with vengeance justified and mercy lost, condemns you as unworthy of forgiveness. [5]The unforgiven have no mercy to bestow upon another. [6]That is why your sole responsibility must be to take forgiveness for yourself.

10. The miracle that you receive, you give. [2]Each one becomes an illustration of the law on which salvation rests; that justice must be done to all, if anyone is to be healed. [3]No one can lose, and everyone must benefit. [4]Each miracle is an example of what justice can accomplish when it is offered to everyone alike. [5]It is received and given equally. [6]It is awareness that giving and receiving are the same. [7]Because it does not make the same unlike,

it sees no differences where none exists. ⁸And thus it is the same for everyone, because it sees no differences in them. ⁹Its offering is universal, and it teaches but one message:

> ¹⁰*What is God's belongs to everyone, and is his due.*

Chapter 26

THE TRANSITION

I. The "Sacrifice" of Oneness

1. In the "dynamics" of attack is sacrifice a key idea. ²It is the pivot upon which all compromise, all desperate attempts to strike a bargain, and all conflicts achieve a seeming balance. ³It is the symbol of the central theme that *somebody must lose*. ⁴Its focus on the body is apparent, for it is always an attempt to limit loss. ⁵The body is itself a sacrifice; a giving up of power in the name of saving just a little for yourself. ⁶To see a brother in another body, separate from yours, is the expression of a wish to see a little part of him and sacrifice the rest. ⁷Look at the world, and you will see nothing attached to anything beyond itself. ⁸All seeming entities can come a little nearer, or go a little farther off, but cannot join.

2. The world you see is based on "sacrifice" of oneness. ²It is a picture of complete disunity and total lack of joining. ³Around each entity is built a wall so seeming solid that it looks as if what is inside can never reach without, and what is out can never reach and join with what is locked away within the wall. ⁴Each part must sacrifice the other part, to keep itself complete. ⁵For if they joined each one would lose its own identity, and by their separation are their selves maintained.

3. The little that the body fences off becomes the self, preserved through sacrifice of all the rest. ²And all the rest must lose this little part, remaining incomplete to keep its own identity intact. ³In this perception of yourself the body's loss would be a sacrifice indeed. ⁴For sight of bodies becomes the sign that sacrifice is limited, and something still remains for you alone. ⁵And for this little to belong to you are limits placed on everything outside, just as they are on everything you think is yours. ⁶For giving and receiving are the same. ⁷And to accept the limits of a body is to impose these limits on each brother whom you see. ⁸For you must see him as you see yourself.

4. The body *is* a loss, and *can* be made to sacrifice. ²And while you see your brother as a body, apart from you and separate in his cell, you are demanding sacrifice of him and you. ³What greater sacrifice could be demanded than that God's Son perceive

542

himself without his Father? [4]And his Father be without His Son? [5]Yet every sacrifice demands that They be separate and without the Other. [6]The memory of God must be denied if any sacrifice is asked of anyone. [7]What witness to the Wholeness of God's Son is seen within a world of separate bodies, however much he witnesses to truth? [8]He is invisible in such a world. [9]Nor can his song of union and of love be heard at all. [10]Yet is it given him to make the world recede before his song, and sight of him replace the body's eyes.

5. Those who would see the witnesses to truth instead of to illusion merely ask that they might see a purpose in the world that gives it sense and makes it meaningful. [2]Without your special function has this world no meaning for you. [3]Yet it can become a treasure house as rich and limitless as Heaven itself. [4]No instant passes here in which your brother's holiness cannot be seen, to add a limitless supply to every meager scrap and tiny crumb of happiness that you allot yourself.

6. You can lose sight of oneness, but can not make sacrifice of its reality. [2]Nor can you lose what you would sacrifice, nor keep the Holy Spirit from His task of showing you that it has not been lost. [3]Hear, then, the song your brother sings to you, and let the world recede, and take the rest his witness offers on behalf of peace. [4]But judge him not, for you will hear no song of liberation for yourself, nor see what it is given him to witness to, that you may see it and rejoice with him. [5]Make not his holiness a sacrifice to your belief in sin. [6]You sacrifice your innocence with his, and die each time you see in him a sin deserving death.

7. Yet every instant can you be reborn, and given life again. [2]His holiness gives life to you, who cannot die because his sinlessness is known to God; and can no more be sacrificed by you than can the light in you be blotted out because he sees it not. [3]You who would make a sacrifice of life, and make your eyes and ears bear witness to the death of God and of His holy Son, think not that you have power to make of Them what God willed not They be. [4]In Heaven, God's Son is not imprisoned in a body, nor is sacrificed in solitude to sin. [5]And as he is in Heaven, so must he be eternally and everywhere. [6]He is the same forever. [7]Born again each instant, untouched by time, and far beyond the reach of any sacrifice of life or death. [8]For neither did he make, and only one was given him by One Who knows His gifts can never suffer sacrifice and loss.

8. God's justice rests in gentleness upon His Son, and keeps him safe from all injustice the world would lay upon him. ²Could it be that you could make his sins reality, and sacrifice his Father's Will for him? ³Condemn him not by seeing him within the rotting prison where he sees himself. ⁴It is your special function to ensure the door be opened, that he may come forth to shine on you, and give you back the gift of freedom by receiving it of you. ⁵What is the Holy Spirit's special function but to release the holy Son of God from the imprisonment he made to keep himself from justice? ⁶Could your function be a task apart and separate from His Own?

II. Many Forms; One Correction

1. It is not difficult to understand the reasons why you do not ask the Holy Spirit to solve all problems for you. ²He has not greater difficulty in resolving some than others. ³Every problem is the same to Him, because each one is solved in just the same respect and through the same approach. ⁴The aspects that need solving do not change, whatever form the problem seems to take. ⁵A problem can appear in many forms, and it will do so while the problem lasts. ⁶It serves no purpose to attempt to solve it in a special form. ⁷It will recur and then recur again and yet again, until it has been answered for all time and will not rise again in any form. ⁸And only then are you released from it.

2. The Holy Spirit offers you release from every problem that you think you have. ²They are the same to Him because each one, regardless of the form it seems to take, is a demand that someone suffer loss and make a sacrifice that you might gain. ³And when the situation is worked out so no one loses is the problem gone, because it was an error in perception that now has been corrected. ⁴One mistake is not more difficult for Him to bring to truth than is another. ⁵For there *is* but one mistake; the whole idea that loss is possible, and could result in gain for anyone. ⁶If this were true, then God would be unfair; sin would be possible, attack be justified and vengeance fair.

3. This one mistake, in any form, has one correction. ²There is no loss; to think there is, is a mistake. ³You have no problems, though you think you have. ⁴And yet you could not think so if you saw them vanish one by one, without regard to size, com-

plexity, or place and time, or any attribute which you perceive that makes each one seem different from the rest. [5]Think not the limits you impose on what you see can limit God in any way.

4. The miracle of justice can correct all errors. [2]Every problem is an error. [3]It does injustice to the Son of God, and therefore is not true. [4]The Holy Spirit does not evaluate injustices as great or small, or more or less. [5]They have no properties to Him. [6]They are mistakes from which the Son of God is suffering, but needlessly. [7]And so He takes the thorns and nails away. [8]He does not pause to judge whether the hurt be large or little. [9]He makes but one judgment; that to hurt God's Son must be unfair and therefore is not so.

5. You who believe it safe to give but some mistakes to be corrected while you keep the others to yourself, remember this: Justice is total. [2]There is no such thing as partial justice. [3]If the Son of God is guilty then is he condemned, and he deserves no mercy from the God of justice. [4]But ask not God to punish him because *you* find him guilty and would have him die. [5]God offers you the means to see his innocence. [6]Would it be fair to punish him because you will not look at what is there to see? [7]Each time you keep a problem for yourself to solve, or judge that it is one that has no resolution, you have made it great, and past the hope of healing. [8]You deny the miracle of justice *can* be fair.

6. If God is just, then can there be no problems that justice cannot solve. [2]But you believe that some injustices are fair and good, and necessary to preserve yourself. [3]It is these problems that you think are great and cannot be resolved. [4]For there are those you want to suffer loss, and no one whom you wish to be preserved from sacrifice entirely. [5]Consider once again your special function. [6]One is given you to see in him his perfect sinlessness. [7]And you will ask no sacrifice of him because you could not will he suffer loss. [8]The miracle of justice you call forth will rest on you as surely as on him. [9]Nor will the Holy Spirit be content until it is received by everyone. [10]For what you give to Him is everyone's, and by your giving it can He ensure that everyone receives it equally.

7. Think, then, how great your own release will be when you are willing to receive correction for all your problems. [2]You will not keep one, for pain in any form you will not want. [3]And you will see each little hurt resolved before the Holy Spirit's gentle sight. [4]For all of them *are* little in His sight, and worth no more than just

a tiny sigh before they disappear, to be forever undone and unremembered. [5]What seemed once to be a special problem, a mistake without a remedy, or an affliction without a cure, has been transformed into a universal blessing. [6]Sacrifice is gone. [7]And in its place the Love of God can be remembered, and will shine away all memory of sacrifice and loss.

8. God cannot be remembered until justice is loved instead of feared. [2]He cannot be unjust to anyone or anything, because He knows that everything that is belongs to Him, and will forever be as He created it. [3]Nothing He loves but must be sinless and beyond attack. [4]Your special function opens wide the door beyond which is the memory of His Love kept perfectly intact and undefiled. [5]And all you need to do is but to wish that Heaven be given you instead of hell, and every bolt and barrier that seems to hold the door securely barred and locked will merely fall away and disappear. [6]For it is not your Father's Will that you should offer or receive less than He gave, when He created you in perfect love.

III. The Borderland

1. Complexity is not of God. [2]How could it be, when all He knows is one? [3]He knows of one creation, one reality, one truth and but one Son. [4]Nothing conflicts with oneness. [5]How, then, could there be complexity in Him? [6]What is there to decide? [7]For it is conflict that makes choice possible. [8]The truth is simple; it is one, without an opposite. [9]And how could strife enter in its simple presence, and bring complexity where oneness is? [10]The truth makes no decisions, for there is nothing to decide *between*. [11]And only if there were could choosing be a necessary step in the advance toward oneness. [12]What is everything leaves room for nothing else. [13]Yet is this magnitude beyond the scope of this curriculum. [14]Nor is it necessary we dwell on anything that cannot be immediately grasped.

2. There is a borderland of thought that stands between this world and Heaven. [2]It is not a place, and when you reach it is apart from time. [3]Here is the meeting place where thoughts are brought together; where conflicting values meet and all illusions are laid down beside the truth, where they are judged to be untrue. [4]This borderland is just beyond the gate of Heaven. [5]Here is

every thought made pure and wholly simple. ⁶Here is sin denied, and everything that *is* received instead.

3.   This is the journey's end. ²We have referred to it as the real world. ³And yet there is a contradiction here, in that the words imply a limited reality, a partial truth, a segment of the universe made true. ⁴This is because knowledge makes no attack upon perception. ⁵They are brought together, and only one continues past the gate where Oneness is. ⁶Salvation is a borderland where place and time and choice have meaning still, and yet it can be seen that they are temporary, out of place, and every choice has been already made.

4.   Nothing the Son of God believes can be destroyed. ²But what is truth to him must be brought to the last comparison that he will ever make; the last evaluation that will be possible, the final judgment upon this world. ³It is the judgment of the truth upon illusion, of knowledge on perception: "It has no meaning, and does not exist." ⁴This is not your decision. ⁵It is but a simple statement of a simple fact. ⁶But in this world there are no simple facts, because what is the same and what is different remain unclear. ⁷The one essential thing to make a choice at all is this distinction. ⁸And herein lies the difference between the worlds. ⁹In this one, choice is made impossible. ¹⁰In the real world is choosing simplified.

5.   Salvation stops just short of Heaven, for only perception needs salvation. ²Heaven was never lost, and so cannot be saved. ³Yet who can make a choice between the wish for Heaven and the wish for hell unless he recognizes they are not the same? ⁴This difference is the learning goal this course has set. ⁵It will not go beyond this aim. ⁶Its only purpose is to teach what is the same and what is different, leaving room to make the only choice that can be made.

6.   There is no basis for a choice in this complex and overcomplicated world. ²For no one understands what is the same, and seems to choose where no choice really is. ³The real world is the area of choice made real, not in the outcome, but in the perception of alternatives for choice. ⁴That there is choice is an illusion. ⁵Yet within this one lies the undoing of every illusion, not excepting this.

7.   Is not this like your special function, where the separation is undone by change of purpose in what once was specialness, and now is union? ²All illusions are but one. ³And in the recognition

this is so lies the ability to give up all attempts to choose between them, and to make them different. ⁴How simple is the choice between two things so clearly unalike. ⁵There is no conflict here. ⁶No sacrifice is possible in the relinquishment of an illusion recognized as such. ⁷Where all reality has been withdrawn from what was never true, can it be hard to give it up, and choose what *must* be true?

IV. Where Sin Has Left

1. Forgiveness is this world's equivalent of Heaven's justice. ²It translates the world of sin into a simple world, where justice can be reflected from beyond the gate behind which total lack of limits lies. ³Nothing in boundless love could need forgiveness. ⁴And what is charity within the world gives way to simple justice past the gate that opens into Heaven. ⁵No one forgives unless he has believed in sin, and still believes that he has much to be forgiven. ⁶Forgiveness thus becomes the means by which he learns he has done nothing to forgive. ⁷Forgiveness always rests upon the one who offers it, until he sees himself as needing it no more. ⁸And thus is he returned to his real function of creating, which his forgiveness offers him again.

2. Forgiveness turns the world of sin into a world of glory, wonderful to see. ²Each flower shines in light, and every bird sings of the joy of Heaven. ³There is no sadness and there is no parting here, for everything is totally forgiven. ⁴And what has been forgiven must join, for nothing stands between to keep them separate and apart. ⁵The sinless must perceive that they are one, for nothing stands between to push the other off. ⁶And in the space that sin left vacant do they join as one, in gladness recognizing what is part of them has not been kept apart and separate.

3. The holy place on which you stand is but the space that sin has left. ²And here you see the face of Christ, arising in its place. ³Who could behold the face of Christ and not recall His Father as He really is? ⁴Who could fear love, and stand upon the ground where sin has left a place for Heaven's altar to rise and tower far above the world, and reach beyond the universe to touch the Heart of all creation? ⁵What is Heaven but a song of gratitude and love and praise by everything created to the Source of its creation? ⁶The holiest of altars is set where once sin was believed

to be. [7]And here does every light of Heaven come, to be rekindled and increased in joy. [8]For here is what was lost restored to them, and all their radiance made whole again.

4. Forgiveness brings no little miracles to lay before the gate of Heaven. [2]Here the Son of God Himself comes to receive each gift that brings him nearer to his home. [3]Not one is lost, and none is cherished more than any other. [4]Each reminds him of his Father's Love as surely as the rest. [5]And each one teaches him that what he feared he loves the most. [6]What but a miracle could change his mind, so that he understands that love cannot be feared? [7]What other miracle is there but this? [8]And what else need there be to make the space between you disappear?

5. Where sin once was perceived will rise a world that will become an altar to the truth, and you will join the lights of Heaven there, and sing their song of gratitude and praise. [2]And as they come to you to be complete, so will you go with them. [3]For no one hears the song of Heaven and remains without a voice that adds its power to the song, and makes it sweeter still. [4]And each one joins the singing at the altar that was raised within the tiny spot that sin proclaimed to be its own. [5]And what was tiny then has soared into a magnitude of song in which the universe has joined with but a single voice.

6. This tiny spot of sin that stands between you and your brother still is holding back the happy opening of Heaven's gate. [2]How little is the hindrance that withholds the wealth of Heaven from you. [3]And how great will be the joy in Heaven when you join the mighty chorus to the Love of God!

V. The Little Hindrance

1. A little hindrance can seem large indeed to those who do not understand that miracles are all the same. [2]Yet teaching that is what this course is for. [3]This is its only purpose, for only that is all there is to learn. [4]And you can learn it in many different ways. [5]All learning is a help or hindrance to the gate of Heaven. [6]Nothing in between is possible. [7]There are two teachers only, who point in different ways. [8]And you will go along the way your chosen teacher leads. [9]There are but two directions you can take, while time remains and choice is meaningful. [10]For never will another road be made except the way to Heaven. [11]You but

choose whether to go toward Heaven, or away to nowhere. [12]There is nothing else to choose.

2. Nothing is ever lost but time, which in the end is meaningless. [2]For it is but a little hindrance to eternity, quite meaningless to the real Teacher of the world. [3]Yet since you do believe in it, why should you waste it going nowhere, when it can be used to reach a goal as high as learning can achieve? [4]Think not the way to Heaven's gate is difficult at all. [5]Nothing you undertake with certain purpose and high resolve and happy confidence, holding your brother's hand and keeping step to Heaven's song, is difficult to do. [6]But it is hard indeed to wander off, alone and miserable, down a road that leads to nothing and that has no purpose.

3. God gave His Teacher to replace the one you made, not to conflict with it. [2]And what He would replace has been replaced. [3]Time lasted but an instant in your mind, with no effect upon eternity. [4]And so is all time past, and everything exactly as it was before the way to nothingness was made. [5]The tiny tick of time in which the first mistake was made, and all of them within that one mistake, held also the Correction for that one, and all of them that came within the first. [6]And in that tiny instant time was gone, for that was all it ever was. [7]What God gave answer to is answered and is gone.

4. To you who still believe you live in time and know not it is gone, the Holy Spirit still guides you through the infinitely small and senseless maze you still perceive in time, though it has long since gone. [2]You think you live in what is past. [3]Each thing you look upon you saw but for an instant, long ago, before its unreality gave way to truth. [4]Not one illusion still remains unanswered in your mind. [5]Uncertainty was brought to certainty so long ago that it is hard indeed to hold it to your heart, as if it were before you still.

5. The tiny instant you would keep and make eternal, passed away in Heaven too soon for anything to notice it had come. [2]What disappeared too quickly to affect the simple knowledge of the Son of God can hardly still be there, for you to choose to be your teacher. [3]Only in the past,—an ancient past, too short to make a world in answer to creation,—did this world appear to rise. [4]So very long ago, for such a tiny interval of time, that not one note in Heaven's song was missed. [5]Yet in each unforgiving act or thought, in every judgment and in all belief in sin, is that

one instant still called back, as if it could be made again in time. ⁶You keep an ancient memory before your eyes. ⁷And he who lives in memories alone is unaware of where he is.

6. Forgiveness is the great release from time. ²It is the key to learning that the past is over. ³Madness speaks no more. ⁴There *is* no other teacher and no other way. ⁵For what has been undone no longer is. ⁶And who can stand upon a distant shore, and dream himself across an ocean, to a place and time that have long since gone by? ⁷How real a hindrance can this dream be to where he really is? ⁸For this is fact, and does not change whatever dreams he has. ⁹Yet can he still imagine he is elsewhere, and in another time. ¹⁰In the extreme, he can delude himself that this is true, and pass from mere imagining into belief and into madness, quite convinced that where he would prefer to be, he *is*.

7. Is this a hindrance to the place whereon he stands? ²Is any echo from the past that he may hear a fact in what is there to hear where he is now? ³And how much can his own illusions about time and place effect a change in where he really is?

8. The unforgiven is a voice that calls from out a past forevermore gone by. ²And everything that points to it as real is but a wish that what is gone could be made real again and seen as here and now, in place of what is *really* now and here. ³Is this a hindrance to the truth the past is gone, and cannot be returned to you? ⁴And do you want that fearful instant kept, when Heaven seemed to disappear and God was feared and made a symbol of your hate?

9. Forget the time of terror that has been so long ago corrected and undone. ²Can sin withstand the Will of God? ³Can it be up to you to see the past and put it in the present? ⁴You can *not* go back. ⁵And everything that points the way in the direction of the past but sets you on a mission whose accomplishment can only be unreal. ⁶Such is the justice your All-Loving Father has ensured must come to you. ⁷And from your own unfairness to yourself has He protected you. ⁸You cannot lose your way because there is no way but His, and nowhere can you go except to Him.

10. Would God allow His Son to lose his way along a road long since a memory of time gone by? ²This course will teach you only what is now. ³A dreadful instant in a distant past, now perfectly corrected, is of no concern nor value. ⁴Let the dead and gone be peacefully forgotten. ⁵Resurrection has come to take its place. ⁶And now you are a part of resurrection, not of death. ⁷No past

illusions have the power to keep you in a place of death, a vault God's Son entered an instant, to be instantly restored unto his Father's perfect Love. [8]And how can he be kept in chains long since removed and gone forever from his mind?

11.   The Son whom God created is as free as God created him. [2]He was reborn the instant that he chose to die instead of live. [3]And will you not forgive him now, because he made an error in the past that God remembers not, and is not there? [4]Now you are shifting back and forth between the past and present. [5]Sometimes the past seems real, as if it *were* the present. [6]Voices from the past are heard and then are doubted. [7]You are like to one who still hallucinates, but lacks conviction in what he perceives. [8]This is the borderland between the worlds, the bridge between the past and present. [9]Here. the shadow of the past remains, but still a present light is dimly recognized. [10]Once it is seen, this light can never be forgotten. [11]It must draw you from the past into the present, where you really are.

12.   The shadow voices do not change the laws of time nor of eternity. [2]They come from what is past and gone, and hinder not the true existence of the here and now. [3]The real world is the second part of the hallucination time and death are real, and have existence that can be perceived. [4]This terrible illusion was denied in but the time it took for God to give His Answer to illusion for all time and every circumstance. [5]And then it was no more to be experienced as there.

13.   Each day, and every minute in each day, and every instant that each minute holds, you but relive the single instant when the time of terror took the place of love. [2]And so you die each day to live again, until you cross the gap between the past and present, which is not a gap at all. [3]Such is each life; a seeming interval from birth to death and on to life again, a repetition of an instant gone by long ago that cannot be relived. [4]And all of time is but the mad belief that what is over is still here and now.

14.   Forgive the past and let it go, for it *is* gone. [2]You stand no longer on the ground that lies between the worlds. [3]You have gone on, and reached the world that lies at Heaven's gate. [4]There is no hindrance to the Will of God, nor any need that you repeat again a journey that was over long ago. [5]Look gently on your brother, and behold the world in which perception of your hate has been transformed into a world of love.

VI. The Appointed Friend

1. Anything in this world that you believe is good and valuable and worth striving for can hurt you, and will do so. ²Not because it has the power to hurt, but just because you have denied it is but an illusion, and made it real. ³And it is real to you. ⁴It is not nothing. ⁵And through its perceived reality has entered all the world of sick illusions. ⁶All belief in sin, in power of attack, in hurt and harm, in sacrifice and death, has come to you. ⁷For no one can make one illusion real, and still escape the rest. ⁸For who can choose to keep the ones that he prefers, and find the safety that the truth alone can give? ⁹Who can believe illusions are the same, and still maintain that even one is best?

2. Lead not your little life in solitude, with one illusion as your only friend. ²This is no friendship worthy of God's Son, nor one with which he could remain content. ³Yet God has given him a better Friend, in Whom all power in earth and Heaven rests. ⁴The one illusion that you think is friend obscures His grace and majesty from you, and keeps His friendship and forgiveness from your welcoming embrace. ⁵Without Him you are friendless. ⁶Seek not another friend to take His place. ⁷There *is* no other friend. ⁸What God appointed has no substitute, for what illusion can replace the truth?

3. Who dwells with shadows is alone indeed, and loneliness is not the Will of God. ²Would you allow one shadow to usurp the throne that God appointed for your Friend, if you but realized its emptiness has left yours empty and unoccupied? ³Make no illusion friend, for if you do, it can but take the place of Him Whom God has called your Friend. ⁴And it is He Who is your only Friend in truth. ⁵He brings you gifts that are not of this world, and only He to Whom they have been given can make sure that you receive them. ⁶He will place them on your throne, when you make room for Him on His.

VII. The Laws of Healing

1. This is a course in miracles. ²As such, the laws of healing must be understood before the purpose of the course can be accomplished. ³Let us review the principles that we have covered, and arrange them in a way that summarizes all that must occur

for healing to be possible. ⁴For when it once is possible it must occur.

2. All sickness comes from separation. ²When the separation is denied, it goes. ³For it is gone as soon as the idea that brought it has been healed, and been replaced by sanity. ⁴Sickness and sin are seen as consequence and cause, in a relationship kept hidden from awareness that it may be carefully preserved from reason's light.

3. Guilt asks for punishment, and its request is granted. ²Not in truth, but in the world of shadows and illusions built on sin. ³The Son of God perceived what he would see because perception is a wish fulfilled. ⁴Perception changes, made to take the place of changeless knowledge. ⁵Yet is truth unchanged. ⁶It cannot be perceived, but only known. ⁷What is perceived takes many forms, but none has meaning. ⁸Brought to truth, its senselessness is quite apparent. ⁹Kept apart from truth, it seems to have a meaning and be real.

4. Perception's laws are opposite to truth, and what is true of knowledge is not true of anything that is apart from it. ²Yet has God given answer to the world of sickness, which applies to all its forms. ³God's answer is eternal, though it works in time, where it is needed. ⁴Yet because it is of God, the laws of time do not affect its workings. ⁵It is in this world, but not a part of it. ⁶For it is real, and dwells where all reality must be. ⁷Ideas leave not their source, and their effects but seem to be apart from them. ⁸Ideas are of the mind. ⁹What is projected out, and seems to be external to the mind, is not outside at all, but an effect of what is in, and has not left its source.

5. God's answer lies where the belief in sin must be, for only there can its effects be utterly undone and without cause. ²Perception's laws must be reversed, because they *are* reversals of the laws of truth. ³The laws of truth forever will be true, and cannot be reversed; yet can be seen as upside down. ⁴And this must be corrected where the illusion of reversal lies.

6. It is impossible that one illusion be less amenable to truth than are the rest. ²But it is possible that some are given greater value, and less willingly offered to truth for healing and for help. ³No illusion has any truth in it. ⁴Yet it appears some are more true than others, although this clearly makes no sense at all. ⁵All that a hierarchy of illusions can show is preference, not reality. ⁶What relevance has preference to the truth? ⁷Illusions are illusions and

are false. ⁸Your preference gives them no reality. ⁹Not one is true in any way, and all must yield with equal ease to what God gave as answer to them all. ¹⁰God's Will is One. ¹¹And any wish that seems to go against His Will has no foundation in the truth.

7. Sin is not error, for it goes beyond correction to impossibility. ²Yet the belief that it is real has made some errors seem forever past the hope of healing, and the lasting grounds for hell. ³If this were so, would Heaven be opposed by its own opposite, as real as it. ⁴Then would God's Will be split in two, and all creation be subjected to the laws of two opposing powers, until God becomes impatient, splits the world apart, and relegates attack unto Himself. ⁵Thus has He lost His Mind, proclaiming sin has taken His reality from Him and brought His Love at last to vengeance's heels. ⁶For such an insane picture an insane defense can be expected, but can not establish that the picture must be true.

8. Nothing gives meaning where no meaning is. ²And truth needs no defense to make it true. ³Illusions have no witnesses and no effects. ⁴Who looks on them is but deceived. ⁵Forgiveness is the only function here, and serves to bring the joy this world denies to every aspect of God's Son where sin was thought to rule. ⁶Perhaps you do not see the role forgiveness plays in ending death and all beliefs that rise from mists of guilt. ⁷Sins are beliefs that you impose between your brother and yourself. ⁸They limit you to time and place, and give a little space to you, another little space to him. ⁹This separating off is symbolized, in your perception, by a body which is clearly separate and a thing apart. ¹⁰Yet what this symbol represents is but your wish to *be* apart and separate.

9. Forgiveness takes away what stands between your brother and yourself. ²It is the wish that you be joined with him, and not apart. ³We call it "wish" because it still conceives of other choices, and has not yet reached beyond the world of choice entirely. ⁴Yet is this wish in line with Heaven's state, and not in opposition to God's Will. ⁵Although it falls far short of giving you your full inheritance, it does remove the obstacles that you have placed between the Heaven where you are, and recognition of where and what you are. ⁶Facts are unchanged. ⁷Yet facts can be denied and thus unknown, though they were known before they were denied.

10. Salvation, perfect and complete, asks but a little wish that what is true be true; a little willingness to overlook what is not

there; a little sigh that speaks for Heaven as a preference to this world that death and desolation seem to rule. ²In joyous answer will creation rise within you, to replace the world you see with Heaven, wholly perfect and complete. ³What is forgiveness but a willingness that truth be true? ⁴What can remain unhealed and broken from a unity which holds all things within itself? ⁵There is no sin. ⁶And every miracle is possible the instant that the Son of God perceives his wishes and the Will of God are one.

11. What is the Will of God? ²He wills His Son have everything. ³And this He guaranteed when He created him *as* everything. ⁴It is impossible that anything be lost, if what you *have* is what you *are*. ⁵This is the miracle by which creation became your function, sharing it with God. ⁶It is not understood apart from Him, and therefore has no meaning in this world. ⁷Here does the Son of God ask not too much, but far too little. ⁸He would sacrifice his own identity with everything, to find a little treasure of his own. ⁹And this he cannot do without a sense of isolation, loss and loneliness. ¹⁰This is the treasure he has sought to find. ¹¹And he could only be afraid of it. ¹²Is fear a treasure? ¹³Can uncertainty be what you want? ¹⁴Or is it a mistake about your will, and what you really are?

12. Let us consider what the error is, so it can be corrected, not protected. ²Sin is belief attack can be projected outside the mind where the belief arose. ³Here is the firm conviction that ideas can leave their source made real and meaningful. ⁴And from this error does the world of sin and sacrifice arise. ⁵This world is an attempt to prove your innocence, while cherishing attack. ⁶Its failure lies in that you still feel guilty, though without understanding why. ⁷Effects are seen as separate from their source, and seem to be beyond you to control or to prevent. ⁸What is thus kept apart can never join.

13. Cause and effect are one, not separate. ²God wills you learn what always has been true: that He created you as part of Him, and this must still be true because ideas leave not their source. ³Such is creation's law; that each idea the mind conceives but adds to its abundance, never takes away. ⁴This is as true of what is idly wished as what is truly willed, because the mind can wish to be deceived, but cannot make it be what it is not. ⁵And to believe ideas can leave their source is to invite illusions to be true, without success. ⁶For never will success be possible in trying to deceive the Son of God.

14. The miracle is possible when cause and consequence are brought together, not kept separate. [2]The healing of effect without the cause can merely shift effects to other forms. [3]And this is not release. [4]God's Son could never be content with less than full salvation and escape from guilt. [5]For otherwise he still demands that he must make some sacrifice, and thus denies that everything is his, unlimited by loss of any kind. [6]A tiny sacrifice is just the same in its effects as is the whole idea of sacrifice. [7]If loss in any form is possible, then is God's Son made incomplete and not himself. [8]Nor will he know himself, nor recognize his will. [9]He has forsworn his Father and himself, and made Them both his enemies in hate.

15. Illusions serve the purpose they were made to serve. [2]And from their purpose they derive whatever meaning that they seem to have. [3]God gave to all illusions that were made another purpose that would justify a miracle whatever form they took. [4]In every miracle all healing lies, for God gave answer to them all as one. [5]And what is one to Him must be the same. [6]If you believe what is the same is different you but deceive yourself. [7]What God calls one will be forever one, not separate. [8]His Kingdom is united; thus it was created, and thus will it ever be.

16. The miracle but calls your ancient Name, which you will recognize because the truth is in your memory. [2]And to this Name your brother calls for his release and yours. [3]Heaven is shining on the Son of God. [4]Deny him not, that you may be released. [5]Each instant is the Son of God reborn until he chooses not to die again. [6]In every wish to hurt he chooses death instead of what his Father wills for him. [7]Yet every instant offers life to him because his Father wills that he should live.

17. In crucifixion is redemption laid, for healing is not needed where there is no pain or suffering. [2]Forgiveness is the answer to attack of any kind. [3]So is attack deprived of its effects, and hate is answered in the name of love. [4]To you to whom it has been given to save the Son of God from crucifixion and from hell and death, all glory be forever. [5]For you have power to save the Son of God because his Father willed that it be so. [6]And in your hands does all salvation lie, to be both offered and received as one.

18. To use the power God has given you as He would have it used is natural. [2]It is not arrogant to be as He created you, nor to make use of what He gave to answer all His Son's mistakes and set him free. [3]But it is arrogant to lay aside the power that He gave, and

choose a little senseless wish instead of what He wills. [4]The gift of God to you is limitless. [5]There is no circumstance it cannot answer, and no problem which is not resolved within its gracious light.

19.   Abide in peace, where God would have you be. [2]And be the means whereby your brother finds the peace in which your wishes are fulfilled. [3]Let us unite in bringing blessing to the world of sin and death. [4]For what can save each one of us can save us all. [5]There is no difference among the Sons of God. [6]The unity that specialness denies will save them all, for what is one can have no specialness. [7]And everything belongs to each of them. [8]No wishes lie between a brother and his own. [9]To get from one is to deprive them all. [10]And yet to bless but one gives blessing to them all as one.

20.   Your ancient Name belongs to everyone, as theirs to you. [2]Call on your brother's name and God will answer, for on Him you call. [3]Could He refuse to answer when He has already answered all who call on Him? [4]A miracle can make no change at all. [5]But it can make what always has been true be recognized by those who know it not; and by this little gift of truth but let to be itself, the Son of God allowed to be himself, and all creation freed to call upon the Name of God as one.

VIII. The Immediacy of Salvation

1.   The one remaining problem that you have is that you see an interval between the time when you forgive, and will receive the benefits of trusting in your brother. [2]This but reflects the little you would keep between you and your brother, that you and he might be a little separate. [3]For time and space are one illusion, which takes different forms. [4]If it has been projected beyond your mind you think of it as time. [5]The nearer it is brought to where it is, the more you think of it in terms of space.

2.   There is a distance you would keep apart from your brother, and this space you perceive as time because you still believe you are external to him. [2]This makes trust impossible. [3]And you cannot believe that trust would settle every problem now. [4]Thus do you think it safer to remain a little careful and a little watchful of interests perceived as separate. [5]From this perception you cannot conceive of gaining what forgiveness offers *now*. [6]The interval

you think lies in between the giving and receiving of the gift seems to be one in which you sacrifice and suffer loss. ⁷You see eventual salvation, not immediate results.

3. Salvation *is* immediate. ²Unless you so perceive it, you will be afraid of it, believing that the risk of loss is great between the time its purpose is made yours and its effects will come to you. ³In this form is the error still obscured that is the source of fear. ⁴Salvation *would* wipe out the space you see between you still, and let you instantly become as one. ⁵And it is here you fear the loss would lie. ⁶Do not project this fear to time, for time is not the enemy that you perceive. ⁷Time is as neutral as the body is, except in terms of what you see it for. ⁸If you would keep a little space between you and your brother still, you then would want a little time in which forgiveness is withheld a little while. ⁹And this but makes the interval between the time in which forgiveness is withheld from you and given seem dangerous, with terror justified.

4. Yet space between you and your brother is apparent only in the present, *now*, and cannot be perceived in future time. ²No more can it be overlooked except within the present. ³Future loss is not your fear. ⁴But present joining is your dread. ⁵Who can feel desolation except now? ⁶A future cause as yet has no effects. ⁷And therefore must it be that if you fear, there is a present cause. ⁸And it is *this* that needs correction, not a future state.

5. The plans you make for safety all are laid within the future, where you cannot plan. ²No purpose has been given it as yet, and what will happen has as yet no cause. ³Who can predict effects without a cause? ⁴And who could fear effects unless he thought they had been caused, and judged disastrous *now*? ⁵Belief in sin arouses fear, and like its cause, is looking forward, looking back, but overlooking what is here and now. ⁶Yet only here and now its cause must be, if its effects already have been judged as fearful. ⁷And in overlooking this, is it protected and kept separate from healing. ⁸For a miracle is *now*. ⁹It stands already here, in present grace, within the only interval of time that sin and fear have overlooked, but which is all there is to time.

6. The working out of all correction takes no time at all. ²Yet the acceptance of the working out can seem to take forever. ³The change of purpose the Holy Spirit brought to your relationship has in it all effects that you will see. ⁴They can be looked at *now*. ⁵Why wait till they unfold in time and fear they may not come,

although already there? [6]You have been told that everything brings good that comes from God. [7]And yet it seems as if this is not so. [8]Good in disaster's form is difficult to credit in advance. [9]Nor is there really sense in this idea.

7. Why should the good appear in evil's form? [2]And is it not deception if it does? [3]Its cause is here, if it appears at all. [4]Why are not its effects apparent, then? [5]Why in the future? [6]And you seek to be content with sighing, and with "reasoning" you do not understand it now, but will some day. [7]And then its meaning will be clear. [8]This is not reason, for it is unjust, and clearly hints at punishment until the time of liberation is at hand. [9]Given a change of purpose for the good, there is no reason for an interval in which disaster strikes, to be perceived as "good" some day but now in form of pain. [10]This is a sacrifice of *now*, which could not be the cost the Holy Spirit asks for what He gave without a cost at all.

8. Yet this illusion has a cause which, though untrue, must be already in your mind. [2]And this illusion is but one effect that it engenders, and one form in which its outcome is perceived. [3]This interval in time, when retribution is perceived to be the form in which the "good" appears, is but one aspect of the little space that lies between you, unforgiven still.

9. Be not content with future happiness. [2]It has no meaning, and is not your just reward. [3]For you have cause for freedom *now*. [4]What profits freedom in a prisoner's form? [5]Why should deliverance be disguised as death? [6]Delay is senseless, and the "reasoning" that would maintain effects of present cause must be delayed until a future time, is merely a denial of the fact that consequence and cause must come as one. [7]Look not to time, but to the little space between you still, to be delivered from. [8]And do not let it be disguised as time, and so preserved because its form is changed and what it is cannot be recognized. [9]The Holy Spirit's purpose now is yours. [10]Should not His happiness be yours as well?

IX. For They Have Come

1. Think but how holy you must be from whom the Voice for God calls lovingly unto your brother, that you may awake in him the Voice that answers to your call! [2]And think how holy he must be

when in him sleeps your own salvation, with his freedom joined! [3]However much you wish he be condemned, God is in him. [4]And never will you know He is in you as well while you attack His chosen home, and battle with His host. [5]Regard him gently. [6]Look with loving eyes on him who carries Christ within him, that you may behold his glory and rejoice that Heaven is not separate from you.

2. Is it too much to ask a little trust for him who carries Christ to you, that you may be forgiven all your sins, and left without a single one you cherish still? [2]Forget not that a shadow held between your brother and yourself obscures the face of Christ and memory of God. [3]And would you trade Them for an ancient hate? [4]The ground whereon you stand is holy ground because of Them Who, standing there with you, have blessed it with Their innocence and peace.

3. The blood of hatred fades to let the grass grow green again, and let the flowers be all white and sparkling in the summer sun. [2]What was a place of death has now become a living temple in a world of light. [3]Because of Them. [4]It is Their Presence which has lifted holiness again to take its ancient place upon an ancient throne. [5]Because of Them have miracles sprung up as grass and flowers on the barren ground that hate had scorched and rendered desolate. [6]What hate has wrought have They undone. [7]And now you stand on ground so holy Heaven leans to join with it, and make it like itself. [8]The shadow of an ancient hate has gone, and all the blight and withering have passed forever from the land where They have come.

4. What is a hundred or a thousand years to Them, or tens of thousands? [2]When They come, time's purpose is fulfilled. [3]What never was passes to nothingness when They have come. [4]What hatred claimed is given up to love, and freedom lights up every living thing and lifts it into Heaven, where the lights grow ever brighter as each one comes home. [5]The incomplete is made complete again, and Heaven's joy has been increased because what is its own has been restored to it. [6]The bloodied earth is cleansed, and the insane have shed their garments of insanity to join Them on the ground whereon you stand.

5. Heaven is grateful for this gift of what has been withheld so long. [2]For They have come to gather in Their Own. [3]What has been locked is opened; what was held apart from light is given up, that light may shine on it and leave no space nor distance

lingering between the light of Heaven and the world.

6.   The holiest of all the spots on earth is where an ancient hatred has become a present love. ²And They come quickly to the living temple, where a home for Them has been set up. ³There is no place in Heaven holier. ⁴And They have come to dwell within the temple offered Them, to be Their resting place as well as yours. ⁵What hatred has released to love becomes the brightest light in Heaven's radiance. ⁶And all the lights in Heaven brighter grow, in gratitude for what has been restored.

7.   Around you angels hover lovingly, to keep away all darkened thoughts of sin, and keep the light where it has entered in. ²Your footprints lighten up the world, for where you walk forgiveness gladly goes with you. ³No one on earth but offers thanks to one who has restored his home, and sheltered him from bitter winter and the freezing cold. ⁴And shall the Lord of Heaven and His Son give less in gratitude for so much more?

8.   Now is the temple of the living God rebuilt as host again to Him by Whom it was created. ²Where He dwells, His Son dwells with Him, never separate. ³And They give thanks that They are welcome made at last. ⁴Where stood a cross stands now the risen Christ, and ancient scars are healed within His sight. ⁵An ancient miracle has come to bless and to replace an ancient enmity that came to kill. ⁶In gentle gratitude do God the Father and the Son return to what is Theirs, and will forever be. ⁷Now is the Holy Spirit's purpose done. ⁸For They have come! ⁹For They have come at last!

X. The End of Injustice

1.   What, then, remains to be undone for you to realize Their Presence? ²Only this; you have a differential view of when attack is justified, and when you think it is unfair and not to be allowed. ³When you perceive it as unfair, you think that a response of anger now is just. ⁴And thus you see what is the same as different. ⁵Confusion is not limited. ⁶If it occurs at all it will be total. ⁷And its presence, in whatever form, will hide Their Presence. ⁸They are known with clarity or not at all. ⁹Confused perception will block knowledge. ¹⁰It is not a question of the size of the confusion, or how much it interferes. ¹¹Its simple presence shuts the door to Theirs, and keeps Them there unknown.

2. What does it mean if you perceive attack in certain forms to be unfair to you? ²It means that there must be some forms in which you think it fair. ³For otherwise, how could some be evaluated as unfair? ⁴Some, then, are given meaning and perceived as sensible. ⁵And only some are seen as meaningless. ⁶And this denies the fact that *all* are senseless, equally without a cause or consequence, and cannot have effects of any kind. ⁷Their Presence is obscured by any veil that stands between Their shining innocence, and your awareness that it is your own and equally belongs to every living thing along with you. ⁸God limits not. ⁹And what is limited cannot be Heaven. ¹⁰So it must be hell.

3. Unfairness and attack are one mistake, so firmly joined that where one is perceived the other must be seen. ²You cannot be unfairly treated. ³The belief you are is but another form of the idea you are deprived by someone not yourself. ⁴Projection of the cause of sacrifice is at the root of everything perceived to be unfair and not your just deserts. ⁵Yet it is you who ask this of yourself, in deep injustice to the Son of God. ⁶You have no enemy except yourself, and you are enemy indeed to him because you do not know him *as* yourself. ⁷What could be more unjust than that he be deprived of what he is, denied the right to be himself, and asked to sacrifice his Father's Love and yours as not his due?

4. Beware of the temptation to perceive yourself unfairly treated. ²In this view, you seek to find an innocence that is not Theirs but yours alone, and at the cost of someone else's guilt. ³Can innocence be purchased by the giving of your guilt to someone else? ⁴And *is* it innocence that your attack on him attempts to get? ⁵Is it not retribution for your own attack upon the Son of God you seek? ⁶Is it not safer to believe that you are innocent of this, and victimized despite your innocence? ⁷Whatever way the game of guilt is played, there must be loss. ⁸Someone must lose his innocence that someone else can take it from him, making it his own.

5. You think your brother is unfair to you because you think that one must be unfair to make the other innocent. ²And in this game do you perceive one purpose for your whole relationship. ³And this you seek to add unto the purpose given it. ⁴The Holy Spirit's purpose is to let the Presence of your holy Guests be known to you. ⁵And to this purpose nothing can be added, for the world is purposeless except for this. ⁶To add or take away from this one goal is but to take away all purpose from the world and from

563

yourself. [7]And each unfairness that the world appears to lay upon you, you have laid on it by rendering it purposeless, without the function that the Holy Spirit sees. [8]And simple justice has been thus denied to every living thing upon the earth.

6. What this injustice does to you who judge unfairly, and who see as you have judged, you cannot calculate. [2]The world grows dim and threatening, not a trace of all the happy sparkle that salvation brings can you perceive to lighten up your way. [3]And so you see yourself deprived of light, abandoned to the dark, unfairly left without a purpose in a futile world. [4]The world is fair because the Holy Spirit has brought injustice to the light within, and there has all unfairness been resolved and been replaced with justice and with love. [5]If you perceive injustice anywhere, you need but say:

> [6]*By this do I deny the Presence of the Father and the Son.*
> [7]*And I would rather know of Them than see injustice,*
> *which Their Presence shines away.*

564

Chapter 27

THE HEALING OF THE DREAM

I. The Picture of Crucifixion

1. The wish to be unfairly treated is a compromise attempt that would combine attack and innocence. ²Who can combine the wholly incompatible, and make a unity of what can never join? ³Walk you the gentle way, and you will fear no evil and no shadows in the night. ⁴But place no terror symbols on your path, or you will weave a crown of thorns from which your brother and yourself will not escape. ⁵You cannot crucify yourself alone. ⁶And if you are unfairly treated, he must suffer the unfairness that you see. ⁷You cannot sacrifice yourself alone. ⁸For sacrifice is total. ⁹If it could occur at all it would entail the whole of God's creation, and the Father with the sacrifice of His beloved Son.

2. In your release from sacrifice is his made manifest, and shown to be his own. ²But every pain you suffer do you see as proof that he is guilty of attack. ³Thus would you make yourself to be the sign that he has lost his innocence, and need but look on you to realize that he has been condemned. ⁴And what to you has been unfair will come to him in righteousness. ⁵The unjust vengeance that you suffer now belongs to him, and when it rests on him are you set free. ⁶Wish not to make yourself a living symbol of his guilt, for you will not escape the death you made for him. ⁷But in his innocence you find your own.

3. Whenever you consent to suffer pain, to be deprived, unfairly treated or in need of anything, you but accuse your brother of attack upon God's Son. ²You hold a picture of your crucifixion before his eyes, that he may see his sins are writ in Heaven in your blood and death, and go before him, closing off the gate and damning him to hell. ³Yet this is writ in hell and not in Heaven, where you are beyond attack and prove his innocence. ⁴The picture of yourself you offer him you show yourself, and give it all your faith. ⁵The Holy Spirit offers you, to give to him, a picture of yourself in which there is no pain and no reproach at all. ⁶And what was martyred to his guilt becomes the perfect witness to his innocence.

4. The power of witness is beyond belief because it brings convic-

tion in its wake. ²The witness is believed because he points beyond himself to what he represents. ³A sick and suffering you but represents your brother's guilt; the witness that you send lest he forget the injuries he gave, from which you swear he never will escape. ⁴This sick and sorry picture *you* accept, if only it can serve to punish him. ⁵The sick are merciless to everyone, and in contagion do they seek to kill. ⁶Death seems an easy price, if they can say, "Behold me, brother, at your hand I die." ⁷For sickness is the witness to his guilt, and death would prove his errors must be sins. ⁸Sickness is but a "little" death; a form of vengeance not yet total. ⁹Yet it speaks with certainty for what it represents. ¹⁰The bleak and bitter picture you have sent your brother *you* have looked upon in grief. ¹¹And everything that it has shown to him have you believed, because it witnessed to the guilt in him which you perceived and loved.

5. Now in the hands made gentle by His touch, the Holy Spirit lays a picture of a different you. ²It is a picture of a body still, for what you really are cannot be seen nor pictured. ³Yet this one has not been used for purpose of attack, and therefore never suffered pain at all. ⁴It witnesses to the eternal truth that you cannot be hurt, and points beyond itself to both your innocence and his. ⁵Show this unto your brother, who will see that every scar is healed, and every tear is wiped away in laughter and in love. ⁶And he will look on his forgiveness there, and with healed eyes will look beyond it to the innocence that he beholds in you. ⁷Here is the proof that he has never sinned; that nothing which his madness bid him do was ever done, or ever had effects of any kind. ⁸That no reproach he laid upon his heart was ever justified, and no attack can ever touch him with the poisoned and relentless sting of fear.

6. Attest his innocence and not his guilt. ²Your healing is his comfort and his health because it proves illusions are not true. ³It is not will for life but wish for death that is the motivation for this world. ⁴Its only purpose is to prove guilt real. ⁵No worldly thought or act or feeling has a motivation other than this one. ⁶These are the witnesses that are called forth to be believed, and lend conviction to the system they speak for and represent. ⁷And each has many voices, speaking to your brother and yourself in different tongues. ⁸And yet to both the message is the same. ⁹Adornment of the body seeks to show how lovely are the witnesses for guilt. ¹⁰Concerns about the body demonstrate how frail

and vulnerable is your life; how easily destroyed is what you love. ¹¹Depression speaks of death, and vanity of real concern with anything at all.

7. The strongest witness to futility, that bolsters all the rest and helps them paint the picture in which sin is justified, is sickness in whatever form it takes. ²The sick have reason for each one of their unnatural desires and strange needs. ³For who could live a life so soon cut short and not esteem the worth of passing joys? ⁴What pleasures could there be that will endure? ⁵Are not the frail entitled to believe that every stolen scrap of pleasure is their righteous payment for their little lives? ⁶Their death will pay the price for all of them, if they enjoy their benefits or not. ⁷The end of life must come, whatever way that life be spent. ⁸And so take pleasure in the quickly passing and ephemeral.

8. These are not sins, but witnesses unto the strange belief that sin and death are real, and innocence and sin will end alike within the termination of the grave. ²If this were true, there would be reason to remain content to seek for passing joys and cherish little pleasures where you can. ³Yet in this picture is the body not perceived as neutral and without a goal inherent in itself. ⁴For it becomes the symbol of reproach, the sign of guilt whose consequences still are there to see, so that the cause can never be denied.

9. Your function is to show your brother sin can have no cause. ²How futile must it be to see yourself a picture of the proof that what your function is can never be! ³The Holy Spirit's picture changes not the body into something it is not. ⁴It only takes away from it all signs of accusation and of blamefulness. ⁵Pictured without a purpose, it is seen as neither sick nor well, nor bad nor good. ⁶No grounds are offered that it may be judged in any way at all. ⁷It has no life, but neither is it dead. ⁸It stands apart from all experience of love or fear. ⁹For now it witnesses to nothing yet, its purpose being open, and the mind made free again to choose what it is for. ¹⁰Now is it not condemned, but waiting for a purpose to be given, that it may fulfill the function that it will receive.

10. Into this empty space, from which the goal of sin has been removed, is Heaven free to be remembered. ²Here its peace can come, and perfect healing take the place of death. ³The body can become a sign of life, a promise of redemption, and a breath of immortality to those grown sick of breathing in the fetid scent of

death. ⁴Let it have healing as its purpose. ⁵Then will it send forth the message it received, and by its health and loveliness proclaim the truth and value that it represents. ⁶Let it receive the power to represent an endless life, forever unattacked. ⁷And to your brother let its message be, "Behold me, brother, at your hand I live."

11. The simple way to let this be achieved is merely this; to let the body have no purpose from the past, when you were sure you knew its purpose was to foster guilt. ²For this insists your crippled picture is a lasting sign of what it represents. ³This leaves no space in which a different view, another purpose, can be given it. ⁴You do *not* know its purpose. ⁵You but gave illusions of a purpose to a thing you made to hide your function from yourself. ⁶This thing without a purpose cannot hide the function that the Holy Spirit gave. ⁷Let, then, its purpose and your function both be reconciled at last and seen as one.

II. The Fear of Healing

1. Is healing frightening? ²To many, yes. ³For accusation is a bar to love, and damaged bodies are accusers. ⁴They stand firmly in the way of trust and peace, proclaiming that the frail can have no trust and that the damaged have no grounds for peace. ⁵Who has been injured by his brother, and could love and trust him still? ⁶He has attacked and will attack again. ⁷Protect him not, because your damaged body shows that *you* must be protected from him. ⁸To forgive may be an act of charity, but not his due. ⁹He may be pitied for his guilt, but not exonerated. ¹⁰And if you forgive him his transgressions, you but add to all the guilt that he has really earned.

2. The unhealed cannot pardon. ²For they are the witnesses that pardon is unfair. ³They would retain the consequences of the guilt they overlook. ⁴Yet no one can forgive a sin that he believes is real. ⁵And what has consequences must be real, because what it has done is there to see. ⁶Forgiveness is not pity, which but seeks to pardon what it thinks to be the truth. ⁷Good cannot *be* returned for evil, for forgiveness does not first establish sin and then forgive it. ⁸Who can say and mean, "My brother, you have injured me, and yet, because I am the better of the two, I pardon you my hurt." ⁹His pardon and your hurt cannot exist together.

[10]One denies the other and must make it false.

3. To witness sin and yet forgive it is a paradox that reason cannot see. [2]For it maintains what has been done to you deserves no pardon. [3]And by giving it, you grant your brother mercy but retain the proof he is not really innocent. [4]The sick remain accusers. [5]They cannot forgive their brothers and themselves as well. [6]For no one in whom true forgiveness rests can suffer. [7]He holds not the proof of sin before his brother's eyes. [8]And thus he must have overlooked it and removed it from his own. [9]Forgiveness cannot be for one and not the other. [10]Who forgives is healed. [11]And in his healing lies the proof that he has truly pardoned, and retains no trace of condemnation that he still would hold against himself or any living thing.

4. Forgiveness is not real unless it brings a healing to your brother and yourself. [2]You must attest his sins have no effect on you to demonstrate they are not real. [3]How else could he be guiltless? [4]And how could his innocence be justified unless his sins have no effect to warrant guilt? [5]Sins are beyond forgiveness just because they would entail effects that cannot be undone and overlooked entirely. [6]In their undoing lies the proof that they are merely errors. [7]Let yourself be healed that you may be forgiving, offering salvation to your brother and yourself.

5. A broken body shows the mind has not been healed. [2]A miracle of healing proves that separation is without effect. [3]What you would prove to him you will believe. [4]The power of witness comes from your belief. [5]And everything you say or do or think but testifies to what you teach to him. [6]Your body can be means to teach that it has never suffered pain because of him. [7]And in its healing can it offer him mute testimony of his innocence. [8]It is this testimony that can speak with power greater than a thousand tongues. [9]For here is his forgiveness proved to him.

6. A miracle can offer nothing less to him than it has given unto you. [2]So does your healing show your mind is healed, and has forgiven what he did not do. [3]And so is he convinced his innocence was never lost, and healed along with you. [4]Thus does the miracle undo all things the world attests can never be undone. [5]And hopelessness and death must disappear before the ancient clarion call of life. [6]This call has power far beyond the weak and miserable cry of death and guilt. [7]The ancient calling of the Father to His Son, and of the Son unto His Own, will yet be the last trumpet that the world will ever hear. [8]Brother, there is no death.

⁹And this you learn when you but wish to show your brother that you had no hurt of him. ¹⁰He thinks your blood is on his hands, and so he stands condemned. ¹¹Yet it is given you to show him, by your healing, that his guilt is but the fabric of a senseless dream.

7. How just are miracles! ²For they bestow an equal gift of full deliverance from guilt upon your brother and yourself. ³Your healing saves him pain as well as you, and you are healed because you wished him well. ⁴This is the law the miracle obeys; that healing sees no specialness at all. ⁵It does not come from pity but from love. ⁶And love would prove all suffering is but a vain imagining, a foolish wish with no effects. ⁷Your health is a result of your desire to see your brother with no blood upon his hands, nor guilt upon his heart made heavy with the proof of sin. ⁸And what you wish is given you to see.

8. The "cost" of your serenity is his. ²This is the "price" the Holy Spirit and the world interpret differently. ³The world perceives it as a statement of the "fact" that your salvation sacrifices his. ⁴The Holy Spirit knows your healing is the witness unto his, and cannot be apart from his at all. ⁵As long as he consents to suffer, you will be unhealed. ⁶Yet you can show him that his suffering is purposeless and wholly without cause. ⁷Show him your healing, and he will consent no more to suffer. ⁸For his innocence has been established in your sight and his. ⁹And laughter will replace your sighs, because God's Son remembered that he *is* God's Son.

9. Who, then, fears healing? ²Only those to whom their brother's sacrifice and pain are seen to represent their own serenity. ³Their helplessness and weakness represent the grounds on which they justify his pain. ⁴The constant sting of guilt he suffers serves to prove that he is slave, but they are free. ⁵The constant pain they suffer demonstrates that they are free *because* they hold him bound. ⁶And sickness is desired to prevent a shift of balance in the sacrifice. ⁷How could the Holy Spirit be deterred an instant, even less, to reason with an argument for sickness such as this? ⁸And need your healing be delayed because you pause to listen to insanity?

10. Correction is not your function. ²It belongs to One Who knows of fairness, not of guilt. ³If you assume correction's role, you lose the function of forgiveness. ⁴No one can forgive until he learns correction is but to forgive, and never to accuse. ⁵Alone, you cannot see they are the same, and therefore is correction not of you.

⁶Identity and function are the same, and by your function do you know yourself. ⁷And thus, if you confuse your function with the function of Another, you must be confused about yourself and who you are. ⁸What is the separation but a wish to take God's function from Him and deny that it is His? ⁹Yet if it is not His it is not yours, for you must lose what you would take away.

11. In a split mind, identity must seem to be divided. ²Nor can anyone perceive a function unified which has conflicting purposes and different ends. ³Correction, to a mind so split, must be a way to punish sins you think are yours in someone else. ⁴And thus does he become your victim, not your brother, different from you in that he is more guilty, thus in need of your correction, as the one more innocent than he. ⁵This splits his function off from yours, and gives you both a different role. ⁶And so you cannot be perceived as one, and with a single function that would mean a shared identity with but one end.

12. Correction *you* would do must separate, because that is the function given it *by* you. ²When you perceive correction is the same as pardon, then you also know the Holy Spirit's Mind and yours are One. ³And so your own Identity is found. ⁴Yet must He work with what is given Him, and you allow Him only half your mind. ⁵And thus He represents the other half, and seems to have a different purpose from the one you cherish, and you think is yours. ⁶Thus does your function seem divided, with a half in opposition to a half. ⁷And these two halves appear to represent a split within a self perceived as two.

13. Consider how this self-perception must extend, and do not overlook the fact that every thought extends because that is its purpose, being what it really is. ²From an idea of self as two, there comes a necessary view of function split between the two. ³And what you would correct is only half the error, which you think is all of it. ⁴Your brother's sins become the central target for correction, lest your errors and his own be seen as one. ⁵Yours are mistakes, but his are sins and not the same as yours. ⁶His merit punishment, while yours, in fairness, should be overlooked.

14. In this interpretation of correction, your own mistakes you will not even see. ²The focus of correction has been placed outside yourself, on one who cannot be a part of you while this perception lasts. ³What is condemned can never be returned to its accuser, who had hated it, and hates it still as symbol of his fear. ⁴This is your brother, focus of your hate, unworthy to be

571

part of you and thus outside yourself; the other half, which is denied. ⁵And only what is left without his presence is perceived as all of you. ⁶To this remaining half the Holy Spirit must represent the other half until you recognize it *is* the other half. ⁷And this He does by giving you and him a function that is one, not different.

15.   Correction is the function given both, but neither one alone. ²And when it is fulfilled as shared, it must correct mistakes in you and him. ³It cannot leave mistakes in one unhealed and set the other free. ⁴That is divided purpose, which can not be shared, and so it cannot be the goal in which the Holy Spirit sees His Own. ⁵And you can rest assured that He will not fulfill a function that He does not see and recognize as His. ⁶For only thus can He keep yours preserved intact, despite Your separate views of what your function is. ⁷If He upheld divided function, you were lost indeed. ⁸His inability to see His goal divided and distinct for you and him, preserves yourself from the awareness of a function not your own. ⁹And thus is healing given you and him.

16.   Correction must be left to One Who knows correction and forgiveness are the same. ²With half a mind this is not understood. ³Leave, then, correction to the Mind that is united, functioning as one because it is not split in purpose, and conceives a single function as its only one. ⁴Here is the function given it conceived to be its Own, and not apart from that its Giver keeps *because* it has been shared. ⁵In His acceptance of this function lies the means whereby your mind is unified. ⁶His single purpose unifies the halves of you that you perceive as separate. ⁷And each forgives the other, that he may accept his other half as part of him.

III. Beyond All Symbols

1.   Power cannot oppose. ²For opposition would weaken it, and weakened power is a contradiction in ideas. ³Weak strength is meaningless, and power used to weaken is employed to limit. ⁴And therefore it must be limited and weak, because that is its purpose. ⁵Power is unopposed, to be itself. ⁶No weakness can intrude on it without changing it into something it is not. ⁷To weaken is to limit, and impose an opposite that contradicts the concept that it attacks. ⁸And by this does it join to the idea a something it is not, and make it unintelligible. ⁹Who can

understand a double concept, such as "weakened power" or "hateful love"?

2. You have decided that your brother is a symbol for a "hateful love," a "weakened power," and above all, a "living death." [2]And so he has no meaning to you, for he stands for what is meaningless. [3]He represents a double thought, where half is cancelled out by the remaining half. [4]Yet even this is quickly contradicted by the half it cancelled out, and so they both are gone. [5]And now he stands for nothing. [6]Symbols which but represent ideas that cannot be must stand for empty space and nothingness. [7]Yet nothingness and empty space can not be interference. [8]What can interfere with the awareness of reality is the belief that there is something there.

3. The picture of your brother that you see means nothing. [2]There is nothing to attack or to deny; to love or hate, or to endow with power or to see as weak. [3]The picture has been wholly cancelled out, because it symbolized a contradiction that cancelled out the thought it represents. [4]And thus the picture has no cause at all. [5]Who can perceive effect without a cause? [6]What can the causeless be but nothingness? [7]The picture of your brother that you see is wholly absent and has never been. [8]Let, then, the empty space it occupies be recognized as vacant, and the time devoted to its seeing be perceived as idly spent, a time unoccupied.

4. An empty space that is not seen as filled, an unused interval of time not seen as spent and fully occupied, become a silent invitation to the truth to enter, and to make itself at home. [2]No preparation can be made that would enhance the invitation's real appeal. [3]For what you leave as vacant God will fill, and where He is there must the truth abide. [4]Unweakened power, with no opposite, is what creation is. [5]For this there are no symbols. [6]Nothing points beyond the truth, for what can stand for more than everything? [7]Yet true undoing must be kind. [8]And so the first replacement for your picture is another picture of another kind.

5. As nothingness cannot be pictured, so there is no symbol for totality. [2]Reality is ultimately known without a form, unpictured and unseen. [3]Forgiveness is not yet a power known as wholly free of limits. [4]Yet it sets no limits you have chosen to impose. [5]Forgiveness is the means by which the truth is represented temporarily. [6]It lets the Holy Spirit make exchange of pictures possible, until the time when aids are meaningless and learning done. [7]No learning aid has use that can extend beyond the goal of

learning. [8]When its aim has been accomplished it is functionless. [9]Yet in the learning interval it has a use that now you fear, but yet will love.

6.   The picture of your brother given you to occupy the space so lately left unoccupied and vacant will not need defense of any kind. [2]For you will give it overwhelming preference. [3]Nor delay an instant in deciding that it is the only one you want. [4]It does not stand for double concepts. [5]Though it is but half the picture and is incomplete, within itself it is the same. [6]The other half of what it represents remains unknown, but is not cancelled out. [7]And thus is God left free to take the final step Himself. [8]For this you need no pictures and no learning aids. [9]And what will ultimately take the place of every learning aid will merely *be*.

7.   Forgiveness vanishes and symbols fade, and nothing that the eyes have ever seen or ears have heard remains to be perceived. [2]A power wholly limitless has come, not to destroy, but to receive its own. [3]There is no choice of function anywhere. [4]The choice you fear to lose you never had. [5]Yet only this appears to interfere with power unlimited and single thoughts, complete and happy, without opposite. [6]You do not know the peace of power that opposes nothing. [7]Yet no other kind can be at all. [8]Give welcome to the power beyond forgiveness, and beyond the world of symbols and of limitations. [9]He would merely be, and so He merely is.

IV. The Quiet Answer

1.   In quietness are all things answered, and is every problem quietly resolved. [2]In conflict there can be no answer and no resolution, for its purpose is to make no resolution possible, and to ensure no answer will be plain. [3]A problem set in conflict has no answer, for it is seen in different ways. [4]And what would be an answer from one point of view is not an answer in another light. [5]You *are* in conflict. [6]Thus it must be clear you cannot answer anything at all, for conflict has no limited effects. [7]Yet if God gave an answer there must be a way in which your problems are resolved, for what He wills already has been done.

2.   Thus it must be that time is not involved and every problem can be answered *now*. [2]Yet it must also be that, in your state of mind, solution is impossible. [3]Therefore, God must have given you a way of reaching to another state of mind in which the

answer is already there. ⁴Such is the holy instant. ⁵It is here that all your problems should be brought and left. ⁶Here they belong, for here their answer is. ⁷And where its answer is, a problem must be simple and be easily resolved. ⁸It must be pointless to attempt to solve a problem where the answer cannot be. ⁹Yet just as surely it must be resolved, if it is brought to where the answer is.

3. Attempt to solve no problems but within the holy instant's surety. ²For there the problem *will* be answered and resolved. ³Outside there will be no solution, for there is no answer there that could be found. ⁴Nowhere outside a single, simple question is ever asked. ⁵The world can only ask a double question. ⁶One with many answers can have no answers. ⁷None of them will do. ⁸It does not ask a question to be answered, but only to restate its point of view.

4. All questions asked within this world are but a way of looking, not a question asked. ²A question asked in hate cannot be answered, because it is an answer in itself. ³A double question asks and answers, both attesting the same thing in different form. ⁴The world asks but one question. ⁵It is this: "Of these illusions, which of them *is* true? ⁶Which ones establish peace and offer joy? ⁷And which can bring escape from all the pain of which this world is made?" ⁸Whatever form the question takes, its purpose is the same. ⁹It asks but to establish sin is real, and answers in the form of preference. ¹⁰"Which sin do you prefer? ¹¹That is the one that you should choose. ¹²The others are not true. ¹³What can the body get that you would want the most of all? ¹⁴It is your servant and also your friend. ¹⁵But tell it what you want, and it will serve you lovingly and well." ¹⁶And this is not a question, for it tells you what you want and where to go for it. ¹⁷It leaves no room to question its beliefs, except that what it states takes question's form.

5. A pseudo-question has no answer. ²It dictates the answer even as it asks. ³Thus is all questioning within the world a form of propaganda for itself. ⁴Just as the body's witnesses are but the senses from within itself, so are the answers to the questions of the world contained within the questions that are asked. ⁵Where answers represent the questions, they add nothing new and nothing has been learned. ⁶An honest question is a learning tool that asks for something that you do not know. ⁷It does not set conditions for response, but merely asks what the response should be.

[8]But no one in a conflict state is free to ask this question, for he does not *want* an honest answer where the conflict ends.

6.   Only within the holy instant can an honest question honestly be asked. [2]And from the meaning of the question does the meaningfulness of the answer come. [3]Here is it possible to separate your wishes from the answer, so it can be given you and also be received. [4]The answer is provided everywhere. [5]Yet it is only here it can be heard. [6]An honest answer asks no sacrifice because it answers questions truly asked. [7]The questions of the world but ask of whom is sacrifice demanded, asking not if sacrifice is meaningful at all. [8]And so, unless the answer tells "of whom," it will remain unrecognized, unheard, and thus the question is preserved intact because it gave the answer to itself. [9]The holy instant is the interval in which the mind is still enough to hear an answer that is not entailed within the question asked. [10]It offers something new and different from the question. [11]How could it be answered if it but repeats itself?

7.   Therefore, attempt to solve no problems in a world from which the answer has been barred. [2]But bring the problem to the only place that holds the answer lovingly for you. [3]Here are the answers that will solve your problems because they stand apart from them, and see what can be answered; what the question *is*. [4]Within the world the answers merely raise another question, though they leave the first unanswered. [5]In the holy instant, you can bring the question to the answer, and receive the answer that was made for you.

V. The Healing Example

1.   The only way to heal is to be healed. [2]The miracle extends without your help, but you are needed that it can begin. [3]Accept the miracle of healing, and it will go forth because of what it is. [4]It is its nature to extend itself the instant it is born. [5]And it is born the instant it is offered and received. [6]No one can ask another to be healed. [7]But he can let *himself* be healed, and thus offer the other what he has received. [8]Who can bestow upon another what he does not have? [9]And who can share what he denies himself? [10]The Holy Spirit speaks to *you*. [11]He does not speak to someone else. [12]Yet by your listening His Voice extends, because you have accepted what He says.

2. Health is the witness unto health. ²As long as it is unattested, it remains without conviction. ³Only when it has been demonstrated is it proved, and must provide a witness that compels belief. ⁴No one is healed through double messages. ⁵If you wish only to be healed, you heal. ⁶Your single purpose makes this possible. ⁷But if you are afraid of healing, then it cannot come through you. ⁸The only thing that is required for a healing is a lack of fear. ⁹The fearful are not healed, and cannot heal. ¹⁰This does not mean the conflict must be gone forever from your mind to heal. ¹¹For if it were, there were no need for healing then. ¹²But it does mean, if only for an instant, you love without attack. ¹³An instant is sufficient. ¹⁴Miracles wait not on time.

3. The holy instant is the miracle's abiding place. ²From there, each one is born into this world as witness to a state of mind that has transcended conflict, and has reached to peace. ³It carries comfort from the place of peace into the battleground, and demonstrates that war has no effects. ⁴For all the hurt that war has sought to bring, the broken bodies and the shattered limbs, the screaming dying and the silent dead, are gently lifted up and comforted.

4. There is no sadness where a miracle has come to heal. ²And nothing more than just one instant of your love without attack is necessary that all this occur. ³In that one instant you are healed, and in that single instant is all healing done. ⁴What stands apart from you, when you accept the blessing that the holy instant brings? ⁵Be not afraid of blessing, for the One Who blesses you loves all the world, and leaves nothing within the world that could be feared. ⁶But if you shrink from blessing, will the world indeed seem fearful, for you have withheld its peace and comfort, leaving it to die.

5. Would not a world so bitterly bereft be looked on as a condemnation by the one who could have saved it, but stepped back because he was afraid of being healed? ²The eyes of all the dying bring reproach, and suffering whispers, "What is there to fear?" ³Consider well its question. ⁴It is asked of you on your behalf. ⁵A dying world asks only that you rest an instant from attack upon yourself, that it be healed.

6. Come to the holy instant and be healed, for nothing that is there received is left behind on your returning to the world. ²And being blessed you will bring blessing. ³Life is given you to give the dying world. ⁴And suffering eyes no longer will accuse, but

shine in thanks to you who blessing gave. [5]The holy instant's radiance will light your eyes, and give them sight to see beyond all suffering and see Christ's face instead. [6]Healing replaces suffering. [7]Who looks on one cannot perceive the other, for they cannot both be there. [8]And what you see the world will witness, and will witness to.

7. Thus is your healing everything the world requires, that it may be healed. [2]It needs one lesson that has perfectly been learned. [3]And then, when you forget it, will the world remind you gently of what you have taught. [4]No reinforcement will its thanks withhold from you who let yourself be healed that it might live. [5]It will call forth its witnesses to show the face of Christ to you who brought the sight to them, by which they witnessed it. [6]The world of accusation is replaced by one in which all eyes look lovingly upon the Friend who brought them their release. [7]And happily your brother will perceive the many friends he thought were enemies.

8. Problems are not specific but they take specific forms, and these specific shapes make up the world. [2]And no one understands the nature of his problem. [3]If he did, it would be there no more for him to see. [4]Its very nature is that it is *not*. [5]And thus, while he perceives it he can not perceive it as it is. [6]But healing is apparent in specific instances, and generalizes to include them all. [7]This is because they really are the same, despite their different forms. [8]All learning aims at transfer, which becomes complete within two situations that are seen as one, for only common elements are there. [9]Yet this can only be attained by One Who does not see the differences you see. [10]The total transfer of your learning is not made by you. [11]But that it has been made in spite of all the differences you see, convinces you that they could not be real.

9. Your healing will extend, and will be brought to problems that you thought were not your own. [2]And it will also be apparent that your many different problems will be solved as any one of them has been escaped. [3]It cannot be their differences which made this possible, for learning does not jump from situations to their opposites and bring the same results. [4]All healing must proceed in lawful manner, in accord with laws that have been properly perceived but never violated. [5]Fear you not the way that you perceive them. [6]You are wrong, but there is One within you Who is right.

10. Leave, then, the transfer of your learning to the One Who really understands its laws, and Who will guarantee that they remain unviolated and unlimited. ²Your part is merely to apply what He has taught you to yourself, and He will do the rest. ³And it is thus the power of your learning will be proved to you by all the many different witnesses it finds. ⁴Your brother first among them will be seen, but thousands stand behind him, and beyond each one of them there are a thousand more. ⁵Each one may seem to have a problem that is different from the rest. ⁶Yet they are solved together. ⁷And their common answer shows the questions could not have been separate.

11. Peace be to you to whom is healing offered. ²And you will learn that peace is given you when you accept the healing for yourself. ³Its total value need not be appraised by you to let you understand that you have benefited from it. ⁴What occurred within the instant that love entered in without attack will stay with you forever. ⁵Your healing will be one of its effects, as will your brother's. ⁶Everywhere you go, will you behold its multiplied effects. ⁷Yet all the witnesses that you behold will be far less than all there really are. ⁸Infinity cannot be understood by merely counting up its separate parts. ⁹God thanks you for your healing, for He knows it is a gift of love unto His Son, and therefore is it given unto Him.

VI. The Witnesses to Sin

1. Pain demonstrates the body must be real. ²It is a loud, obscuring voice whose shrieks would silence what the Holy Spirit says, and keep His words from your awareness. ³Pain compels attention, drawing it away from Him and focusing upon itself. ⁴Its purpose is the same as pleasure, for they both are means to make the body real. ⁵What shares a common purpose is the same. ⁶This is the law of purpose, which unites all those who share in it within itself. ⁷Pleasure and pain are equally unreal, because their purpose cannot be achieved. ⁸Thus are they means for nothing, for they have a goal without a meaning. ⁹And they share the lack of meaning which their purpose has.

2. Sin shifts from pain to pleasure, and again to pain. ²For either witness is the same, and carries but one message: "You are here, within this body, and you can be hurt. ³You can have pleasure,

too, but only at the cost of pain." ⁴These witnesses are joined by many more. ⁵Each one seems different because it has a different name, and so it seems to answer to a different sound. ⁶Except for this, the witnesses of sin are all alike. ⁷Call pleasure pain, and it will hurt. ⁸Call pain a pleasure, and the pain behind the pleasure will be felt no more. ⁹Sin's witnesses but shift from name to name, as one steps forward and another back. ¹⁰Yet which is foremost makes no difference. ¹¹Sin's witnesses hear but the call of death.

3. This body, purposeless within itself, holds all your memories and all your hopes. ²You use its eyes to see, its ears to hear, and let it tell you what it is it feels. ³*It does not know.* ⁴It tells you but the names you gave to it to use, when you call forth the witnesses to its reality. ⁵You cannot choose among them which are real, for any one you choose is like the rest. ⁶This name or that, but nothing more, you choose. ⁷You do not make a witness true because you called him by truth's name. ⁸The truth is found in him if it is truth he represents. ⁹And otherwise he lies, if you should call him by the holy Name of God Himself.

4. God's Witness sees no witnesses against the body. ²Neither does He harken to the witnesses by other names that speak in other ways for its reality. ³He knows it is not real. ⁴For nothing could contain what you believe it holds within. ⁵Nor could it tell a part of God Himself what it should feel and what its function is. ⁶Yet must He love whatever you hold dear. ⁷And for each witness to the body's death He sends a witness to your life in Him Who knows no death. ⁸Each miracle He brings is witness that the body is not real. ⁹Its pains and pleasures does He heal alike, for all sin's witnesses do His replace.

5. The miracle makes no distinctions in the names by which sin's witnesses are called. ²It merely proves that what they represent has no effects. ³And this it proves because its own effects have come to take their place. ⁴It matters not the name by which you called your suffering. ⁵It is no longer there. ⁶The One Who brings the miracle perceives them all as one, and called by name of fear. ⁷As fear is witness unto death, so is the miracle the witness unto life. ⁸It is a witness no one can deny, for it is the effects of life it brings. ⁹The dying live, the dead arise, and pain has vanished. ¹⁰Yet a miracle speaks not but for itself, but what it represents.

6. Love, too, has symbols in a world of sin. ²The miracle forgives because it stands for what is past forgiveness and is true. ³How

foolish and insane it is to think a miracle is bound by laws that it came solely to undo! ⁴The laws of sin have different witnesses with different strengths. ⁵And they attest to different sufferings. ⁶Yet to the One Who sends forth miracles to bless the world, a tiny stab of pain, a little worldly pleasure, and the throes of death itself are but a single sound; a call for healing, and a plaintive cry for help within a world of misery. ⁷It is their sameness that the miracle attests. ⁸It is their sameness that it proves. ⁹The laws that call them different are dissolved, and shown as powerless. ¹⁰The purpose of a miracle is to accomplish this. ¹¹And God Himself has guaranteed the strength of miracles for what they witness to.

7. Be you then witness to the miracle, and not the laws of sin. ²There is no need to suffer any more. ³But there *is* need that you be healed, because the suffering and sorrow of the world have made it deaf to its salvation and deliverance.

8. The resurrection of the world awaits your healing and your happiness, that you may demonstrate the healing of the world. ²The holy instant will replace all sin if you but carry its effects with you. ³And no one will elect to suffer more. ⁴What better function could you serve than this? ⁵Be healed that you may heal, and suffer not the laws of sin to be applied to you. ⁶And truth will be revealed to you who chose to let love's symbols take the place of sin.

VII. The Dreamer of the Dream

1. Suffering is an emphasis upon all that the world has done to injure you. ²Here is the world's demented version of salvation clearly shown. ³Like to a dream of punishment, in which the dreamer is unconscious of what brought on the attack against himself, he sees himself attacked unjustly and by something not himself. ⁴He is the victim of this "something else," a thing outside himself, for which he has no reason to be held responsible. ⁵He must be innocent because he knows not what he does, but what is done to him. ⁶Yet is his own attack upon himself apparent still, for it is he who bears the suffering. ⁷And he cannot escape because its source is seen outside himself.

2. Now you are being shown you *can* escape. ²All that is needed is you look upon the problem as it is, and not the way that you have set it up. ³How could there be another way to solve a

problem that is very simple, but has been obscured by heavy clouds of complication, which were made to keep the problem unresolved? [4]Without the clouds the problem will emerge in all its primitive simplicity. [5]The choice will not be difficult, because the problem is absurd when clearly seen. [6]No one has difficulty making up his mind to let a simple problem be resolved if it is seen as hurting him, and also very easily removed.

3. The "reasoning" by which the world is made, on which it rests, by which it is maintained, is simply this: "*You* are the cause of what I do. [2]Your presence justifies my wrath, and you exist and think apart from me. [3]While you attack I must be innocent. [4]And what I suffer from is your attack." [5]No one who looks upon this "reasoning" exactly as it is could fail to see it does not follow and it makes no sense. [6]Yet it seems sensible, because it looks as if the world were hurting you. [7]And so it seems as if there is no need to go beyond the obvious in terms of cause.

4. There is indeed a need. [2]The world's escape from condemnation is a need which those within the world are joined in sharing. [3]Yet they do not recognize their common need. [4]For each one thinks that if he does his part, the condemnation of the world will rest on him. [5]And it is this that he perceives to *be* his part in its deliverance. [6]Vengeance must have a focus. [7]Otherwise is the avenger's knife in his own hand, and pointed to himself. [8]And he must see it in another's hand, if he would be a victim of attack he did not choose. [9]And thus he suffers from the wounds a knife he does not hold has made upon himself.

5. This is the purpose of the world he sees. [2]And looked at thus, the world provides the means by which this purpose seems to be fulfilled. [3]The means attest the purpose, but are not themselves a cause. [4]Nor will the cause be changed by seeing it apart from its effects. [5]The cause produces the effects, which then bear witness to the cause, and not themselves. [6]Look, then, beyond effects. [7]It is not here the cause of suffering and sin must lie. [8]And dwell not on the suffering and sin, for they are but reflections of their cause.

6. The part you play in salvaging the world from condemnation is your own escape. [2]Forget not that the witness to the world of evil cannot speak except for what has seen a need for evil in the world. [3]And this is where your guilt was first beheld. [4]In separation from your brother was the first attack upon yourself begun. [5]And it is this the world bears witness to. [6]Seek not another cause, nor look among the mighty legions of its witnesses for its

undoing. [7]They support its claim on your allegiance. [8]What conceals the truth is not where you should look to *find* the truth.

7. The witnesses to sin all stand within one little space. [2]And it is here you find the cause of your perspective on the world. [3]Once you were unaware of what the cause of everything the world appeared to thrust upon you, uninvited and unasked, must really be. [4]Of one thing you were sure: Of all the many causes you perceived as bringing pain and suffering to you, your guilt was not among them. [5]Nor did you in any way request them for yourself. [6]This is how all illusions came about. [7]The one who makes them does not see himself as making them, and their reality does not depend on him. [8]Whatever cause they have is something quite apart from him, and what he sees is separate from his mind. [9]He cannot doubt his dreams' reality, because he does not see the part he plays in making them and making them seem real.

8. No one can waken from a dream the world is dreaming for him. [2]He becomes a part of someone else's dream. [3]He cannot choose to waken from a dream he did not make. [4]Helpless he stands, a victim to a dream conceived and cherished by a separate mind. [5]Careless indeed of him this mind must be, as thoughtless of his peace and happiness as is the weather or the time of day. [6]It loves him not, but casts him as it will in any role that satisfies its dream. [7]So little is his worth that he is but a dancing shadow, leaping up and down according to a senseless plot conceived within the idle dreaming of the world.

9. This is the only picture you can see; the one alternative that you can choose, the other possibility of cause, if you be not the dreamer of your dreams. [2]And this is what you choose if you deny the cause of suffering is in your mind. [3]Be glad indeed it is, for thus are you the one decider of your destiny in time. [4]The choice is yours to make between a sleeping death and dreams of evil or a happy wakening and joy of life.

10. What could you choose between but life or death, waking or sleeping, peace or war, your dreams or your reality? [2]There is a risk of thinking death is peace, because the world equates the body with the Self which God created. [3]Yet a thing can never be its opposite. [4]And death is opposite to peace, because it is the opposite of life. [5]And life is peace. [6]Awaken and forget all thoughts of death, and you will find you have the peace of God. [7]Yet if the choice is really given you, then you must see the causes of the things you choose between exactly as they are and

where they are.

11. What choices can be made between two states, but one of which is clearly recognized? ²Who could be free to choose between effects, when only one is seen as up to him? ³An honest choice could never be perceived as one in which the choice is split between a tiny you and an enormous world, with different dreams about the truth in you. ⁴The gap between reality and dreams lies not between the dreaming of the world and what you dream in secret. ⁵They are one. ⁶The dreaming of the world is but a part of your own dream you gave away, and saw as if it were its start and ending, both. ⁷Yet was it started by your secret dream, which you do not perceive although it caused the part you see and do not doubt is real. ⁸How could you doubt it while you lie asleep, and dream in secret that its cause is real?

12. A brother separated from yourself, an ancient enemy, a murderer who stalks you in the night and plots your death, yet plans that it be lingering and slow; of this you dream. ²Yet underneath this dream is yet another, in which you become the murderer, the secret enemy, the scavenger and the destroyer of your brother and the world alike. ³Here is the cause of suffering, the space between your little dreams and your reality. ⁴The little gap you do not even see, the birthplace of illusions and of fear, the time of terror and of ancient hate, the instant of disaster, all are here. ⁵Here is the cause of unreality. ⁶And it is here that it will be undone.

13. *You* are the dreamer of the world of dreams. ²No other cause it has, nor ever will. ³Nothing more fearful than an idle dream has terrified God's Son, and made him think that he has lost his innocence, denied his Father, and made war upon himself. ⁴So fearful is the dream, so seeming real, he could not waken to reality without the sweat of terror and a scream of mortal fear, unless a gentler dream preceded his awaking, and allowed his calmer mind to welcome, not to fear, the Voice that calls with love to waken him; a gentler dream, in which his suffering was healed and where his brother was his friend. ⁵God willed he waken gently and with joy, and gave him means to waken without fear.

14. Accept the dream He gave instead of yours. ²It is not difficult to change a dream when once the dreamer has been recognized. ³Rest in the Holy Spirit, and allow His gentle dreams to take the place of those you dreamed in terror and in fear of death. ⁴He brings forgiving dreams, in which the choice is not who is the

murderer and who shall be the victim. ⁵In the dreams He brings there is no murder and there is no death. ⁶The dream of guilt is fading from your sight, although your eyes are closed. ⁷A smile has come to lighten up your sleeping face. ⁸The sleep is peaceful now, for these are happy dreams.

15. Dream softly of your sinless brother, who unites with you in holy innocence. ²And from this dream the Lord of Heaven will Himself awaken His beloved Son. ³Dream of your brother's kindnesses instead of dwelling in your dreams on his mistakes. ⁴Select his thoughtfulness to dream about instead of counting up the hurts he gave. ⁵Forgive him his illusions, and give thanks to him for all the helpfulness he gave. ⁶And do not brush aside his many gifts because he is not perfect in your dreams. ⁷He represents his Father, Whom you see as offering both life and death to you.

16. Brother, He gives but life. ²Yet what you see as gifts your brother offers represent the gifts you dream your Father gives to you. ³Let all your brother's gifts be seen in light of charity and kindness offered you. ⁴And let no pain disturb your dream of deep appreciation for his gifts to you.

VIII. The "Hero" of the Dream

1. The body is the central figure in the dreaming of the world. ²There is no dream without it, nor does it exist without the dream in which it acts as if it were a person to be seen and be believed. ³It takes the central place in every dream, which tells the story of how it was made by other bodies, born into the world outside the body, lives a little while and dies, to be united in the dust with other bodies dying like itself. ⁴In the brief time allotted it to live, it seeks for other bodies as its friends and enemies. ⁵Its safety is its main concern. ⁶Its comfort is its guiding rule. ⁷It tries to look for pleasure, and avoid the things that would be hurtful. ⁸Above all, it tries to teach itself its pains and joys are different and can be told apart.

2. The dreaming of the world takes many forms, because the body seeks in many ways to prove it is autonomous and real. ²It puts things on itself that it has bought with little metal discs or paper strips the world proclaims as valuable and real. ³It works to get them, doing senseless things, and tosses them away for senseless things it does not need and does not even want. ⁴It hires

other bodies, that they may protect it and collect more senseless things that it can call its own. ⁵It looks about for special bodies that can share its dream. ⁶Sometimes it dreams it is a conqueror of bodies weaker than itself. ⁷But in some phases of the dream, it is the slave of bodies that would hurt and torture it.

3. The body's serial adventures, from the time of birth to dying are the theme of every dream the world has ever had. ²The "hero" of this dream will never change, nor will its purpose. ³Though the dream itself takes many forms, and seems to show a great variety of places and events wherein its "hero" finds itself, the dream has but one purpose, taught in many ways. ⁴This single lesson does it try to teach again, and still again, and yet once more; that it is cause and not effect. ⁵And you are its effect, and cannot be its cause.

4. Thus are you not the dreamer, but the dream. ²And so you wander idly in and out of places and events that it contrives. ³That this is all the body does is true, for it is but a figure in a dream. ⁴But who reacts to figures in a dream unless he sees them as if they were real? ⁵The instant that he sees them as they are they have no more effects on him, because he understands he gave them their effects by causing them and making them seem real.

5. How willing are you to escape effects of all the dreams the world has ever had? ²Is it your wish to let no dream appear to be the cause of what it is you do? ³Then let us merely look upon the dream's beginning, for the part you see is but the second part, whose cause lies in the first. ⁴No one asleep and dreaming in the world remembers his attack upon himself. ⁵No one believes there really was a time when he knew nothing of a body, and could never have conceived this world as real. ⁶He would have seen at once that these ideas are one illusion, too ridiculous for anything but to be laughed away. ⁷How serious they now appear to be! ⁸And no one can remember when they would have met with laughter and with disbelief. ⁹We can remember this, if we but look directly at their cause. ¹⁰And we will see the grounds for laughter, not a cause for fear.

6. Let us return the dream he gave away unto the dreamer, who perceives the dream as separate from himself and done to him. ²Into eternity, where all is one, there crept a tiny, mad idea, at which the Son of God remembered not to laugh. ³In his forgetting did the thought become a serious idea, and possible of both

accomplishment and real effects. ⁴Together, we can laugh them both away, and understand that time cannot intrude upon eternity. ⁵It is a joke to think that time can come to circumvent eternity, which *means* there is no time.

7. A timelessness in which is time made real; a part of God that can attack itself; a separate brother as an enemy; a mind within a body all are forms of circularity whose ending starts at its beginning, ending at its cause. ²The world you see depicts exactly what you thought you did. ³Except that now you think that what you did is being done to you. ⁴The guilt for what you thought is being placed outside yourself, and on a guilty world that dreams your dreams and thinks your thoughts instead of you. ⁵It brings its vengeance, not your own. ⁶It keeps you narrowly confined within a body, which it punishes because of all the sinful things the body does within its dream. ⁷You have no power to make the body stop its evil deeds because you did not make it, and cannot control its actions nor its purpose nor its fate.

8. The world but demonstrates an ancient truth; you will believe that others do to you exactly what you think you did to them. ²But once deluded into blaming them you will not see the cause of what they do, because you *want* the guilt to rest on them. ³How childish is the petulant device to keep your innocence by pushing guilt outside yourself, but never letting go! ⁴It is not easy to perceive the jest when all around you do your eyes behold its heavy consequences, but without their trifling cause. ⁵Without the cause do its effects seem serious and sad indeed. ⁶Yet they but follow. ⁷And it is their cause that follows nothing and is but a jest.

9. In gentle laughter does the Holy Spirit perceive the cause, and looks not to effects. ²How else could He correct your error, who have overlooked the cause entirely? ³He bids you bring each terrible effect to Him that you may look together on its foolish cause and laugh with Him a while. ⁴*You* judge effects, but *He* has judged their cause. ⁵And by His judgment are effects removed. ⁶Perhaps you come in tears. ⁷But hear Him say, "My brother, holy Son of God, behold your idle dream, in which this could occur." ⁸And you will leave the holy instant with your laughter and your brother's joined with His.

10. The secret of salvation is but this: that you are doing this unto yourself. ²No matter what the form of the attack, this still is true. ³Whoever takes the role of enemy and of attacker, still is this the

truth. [4]Whatever seems to be the cause of any pain and suffering you feel, this is still true. [5]For you would not react at all to figures in a dream you knew that you were dreaming. [6]Let them be as hateful and as vicious as they may, they could have no effect on you unless you failed to recognize it is your dream.

11.   This single lesson learned will set you free from suffering, whatever form it takes. [2]The Holy Spirit will repeat this one inclusive lesson of deliverance until it has been learned, regardless of the form of suffering that brings you pain. [3]Whatever hurt you bring to Him He will make answer with this very simple truth. [4]For this one answer takes away the cause of every form of sorrow and of pain. [5]The form affects His answer not at all, for He would teach you but the single cause of all of them, no matter what their form. [6]And you will understand that miracles reflect the simple statement, "*I have done this thing, and it is this I would undo.*"

12.   Bring, then, all forms of suffering to Him Who knows that every one is like the rest. [2]He sees no differences where none exists, and He will teach you how each one is caused. [3]None has a different cause from all the rest, and all of them are easily undone by but a single lesson truly learned. [4]Salvation is a secret you have kept but from yourself. [5]The universe proclaims it so. [6]Yet to its witnesses you pay no heed at all. [7]For they attest the thing you do not want to know. [8]They seem to keep it secret from you. [9]Yet you need but learn you chose but not to listen, not to see.

13.   How differently will you perceive the world when this is recognized! [2]When you forgive the world your guilt, you will be free of it. [3]Its innocence does not demand your guilt, nor does your guiltlessness rest on its sins. [4]This is the obvious; a secret kept from no one but yourself. [5]And it is this that has maintained you separate from the world, and kept your brother separate from you. [6]Now need you but to learn that both of you are innocent or guilty. [7]The one thing that is impossible is that you be unlike each other; that they both be true. [8]This is the only secret yet to learn. [9]And it will be no secret you are healed.

Chapter 28

THE UNDOING OF FEAR

I. The Present Memory

1. The miracle does nothing. ²All it does is to undo. ³And thus it cancels out the interference to what has been done. ⁴It does not add, but merely takes away. ⁵And what it takes away is long since gone, but being kept in memory appears to have immediate effects. ⁶This world was over long ago. ⁷The thoughts that made it are no longer in the mind that thought of them and loved them for a little while. ⁸The miracle but shows the past is gone, and what has truly gone has no effects. ⁹Remembering a cause can but produce illusions of its presence, not effects.

2. All the effects of guilt are here no more. ²For guilt is over. ³In its passing went its consequences, left without a cause. ⁴Why would you cling to it in memory if you did not desire its effects? ⁵Remembering is as selective as perception, being its past tense. ⁶It is perception of the past as if it were occurring now, and still were there to see. ⁷Memory, like perception, is a skill made up by you to take the place of what God gave in your creation. ⁸And like all the things you made, it can be used to serve another purpose, and to be the means for something else. ⁹It can be used to heal and not to hurt, if you so wish it be.

3. Nothing employed for healing represents an effort to do anything at all. ²It is a recognition that you have no needs which mean that something must be done. ³It is an unselective memory, that is not used to interfere with truth. ⁴All things the Holy Spirit can employ for healing have been given Him, without the content and the purposes for which they have been made. ⁵They are but skills without an application. ⁶They await their use. ⁷They have no dedication and no aim.

4. The Holy Spirit can indeed make use of memory, for God Himself is there. ²Yet this is not a memory of past events, but only of a present state. ³You are so long accustomed to believe that memory holds only what is past, that it is hard for you to realize it is a skill that can remember *now*. ⁴The limitations on remembering the world imposes on it are as vast as those you let the world impose on you. ⁵There is no link of memory to the past. ⁶If you

would have it there, then there it is. [7]But only your desire made the link, and only you have held it to a part of time where guilt appears to linger still.

5.   The Holy Spirit's use of memory is quite apart from time. [2]He does not seek to use it as a means to keep the past, but rather as a way to let it go. [3]Memory holds the message it receives, and does what it is given it to do. [4]It does not write the message, nor appoint what it is for. [5]Like to the body, it is purposeless within itself. [6]And if it seems to serve to cherish ancient hate, and gives you pictures of injustices and hurts that you were saving, this is what you asked its message be and that it is. [7]Committed to its vaults, the history of all the body's past is hidden there. [8]All of the strange associations made to keep the past alive, the present dead, are stored within it, waiting your command that they be brought to you, and lived again. [9]And thus do their effects appear to be increased by time, which took away their cause.

6.   Yet time is but another phase of what does nothing. [2]It works hand in hand with all the other attributes with which you seek to keep concealed the truth about yourself. [3]Time neither takes away nor can restore. [4]And yet you make strange use of it, as if the past had caused the present, which is but a consequence in which no change can be made possible because its cause has gone. [5]Yet change must have a cause that will endure, or else it will not last. [6]No change can be made in the present if its cause is past. [7]Only the past is held in memory as you make use of it, and so it is a way to hold the past against the now.

7.   Remember nothing that you taught yourself, for you were badly taught. [2]And who would keep a senseless lesson in his mind, when he can learn and can preserve a better one? [3]When ancient memories of hate appear, remember that their cause is gone. [4]And so you cannot understand what they are for. [5]Let not the cause that you would give them now be what it was that made them what they were, or seemed to be. [6]Be glad that it is gone, for this is what you would be pardoned from. [7]And see, instead, the new effects of cause accepted *now*, with consequences *here*. [8]They will surprise you with their loveliness. [9]The ancient new ideas they bring will be the happy consequences of a Cause so ancient that It far exceeds the span of memory which your perception sees.

8.   This is the Cause the Holy Spirit has remembered for you, when you would forget. [2]It is not past because He let It not be

unremembered. ³It has never changed, because there never was a time in which He did not keep It safely in your mind. ⁴Its consequences will indeed seem new, because you thought that you remembered not their Cause. ⁵Yet was It never absent from your mind, for it was not your Father's Will that He be unremembered by His Son.

9. What *you* remember never was. ²It came from causelessness which you confused with cause. ³It can deserve but laughter, when you learn you have remembered consequences that were causeless and could never be effects. ⁴The miracle reminds you of a Cause forever present, perfectly untouched by time and interference. ⁵Never changed from what It is. ⁶And you are Its Effect, as changeless and as perfect as Itself. ⁷Its memory does not lie in the past, nor waits the future. ⁸It is not revealed in miracles. ⁹They but remind you that It has not gone. ¹⁰When you forgive It for your sins, It will no longer be denied.

10. You who have sought to lay a judgment on your own Creator cannot understand it is not He Who laid a judgment on His Son. ²You would deny Him His Effects, yet have They never been denied. ³There was no time in which His Son could be condemned for what was causeless and against His Will. ⁴What your remembering would witness to is but the fear of God. ⁵He has not done the thing you fear. ⁶No more have you. ⁷And so your innocence has not been lost. ⁸You need no healing to be healed. ⁹In quietness, see in the miracle a lesson in allowing Cause to have Its Own Effects, and doing nothing that would interfere.

11. The miracle comes quietly into the mind that stops an instant and is still. ²It reaches gently from that quiet time, and from the mind it healed in quiet then, to other minds to share its quietness. ³And they will join in doing nothing to prevent its radiant extension back into the Mind which caused all minds to be. ⁴Born out of sharing, there can be no pause in time to cause the miracle delay in hastening to all unquiet minds, and bringing them an instant's stillness, when the memory of God returns to them. ⁵Their own remembering is quiet now, and what has come to take its place will not be wholly unremembered afterwards.

12. He to Whom time is given offers thanks for every quiet instant given Him. ²For in that instant is God's memory allowed to offer all its treasures to the Son of God, for whom they have been kept. ³How gladly does He offer them unto the one for whom He has been given them! ⁴And His Creator shares His thanks, because

He would not be deprived of His Effects. [5]The instant's silence that His Son accepts gives welcome to eternity and Him, and lets Them enter where They would abide. [6]For in that instant does the Son of God do nothing that would make himself afraid.

13.   How instantly the memory of God arises in the mind that has no fear to keep the memory away! [2]Its own remembering has gone. [3]There is no past to keep its fearful image in the way of glad awakening to present peace. [4]The trumpets of eternity resound throughout the stillness, yet disturb it not. [5]And what is now remembered is not fear, but rather is the Cause that fear was made to render unremembered and undone. [6]The stillness speaks in gentle sounds of love the Son of God remembers from before his own remembering came in between the present and the past, to shut them out.

14.   Now is the Son of God at last aware of present Cause and Its benign Effects. [2]Now does he understand what he has made is causeless, having no effects at all. [3]He has done nothing. [4]And in seeing this, he understands he never had a need for doing anything, and never did. [5]His Cause *is* Its Effects. [6]There never was a cause beside It that could generate a different past or future. [7]Its Effects are changelessly eternal, beyond fear, and past the world of sin entirely.

15.   What has been lost, to see the causeless not? [2]And where is sacrifice, when memory of God has come to take the place of loss? [3]What better way to close the little gap between illusions and reality than to allow the memory of God to flow across it, making it a bridge an instant will suffice to reach beyond? [4]For God has closed it with Himself. [5]His memory has not gone by, and left a stranded Son forever on a shore where he can glimpse another shore that he can never reach. [6]His Father wills that he be lifted up and gently carried over. [7]He has built the bridge, and it is He Who will transport His Son across it. [8]Have no fear that He will fail in what He wills. [9]Nor that you be excluded from the Will that is for you.

II. Reversing Effect and Cause

1.   Without a cause there can be no effects, and yet without effects there is no cause. [2]The cause a cause is *made* by its effects; the Father *is* a Father by His Son. [3]Effects do not create their cause,

but they establish its causation. ⁴Thus, the Son gives Fatherhood to his Creator, and receives the gift that he has given Him. ⁵It is *because* he is God's Son that he must also be a father, who creates as God created him. ⁶The circle of creation has no end. ⁷Its starting and its ending are the same. ⁸But in itself it holds the universe of all creation, without beginning and without an end.

2.   Fatherhood *is* creation. ²Love must be extended. ³Purity is not confined. ⁴It is the nature of the innocent to be forever uncontained, without a barrier or limitation. ⁵Thus is purity not of the body. ⁶Nor can it be found where limitation is. ⁷The body can be healed by its effects, which are as limitless as is itself. ⁸Yet must all healing come about because the mind is recognized as not within the body, and its innocence is quite apart from it, and where all healing is. ⁹Where, then, is healing? ¹⁰Only where its cause is given its effects. ¹¹For sickness is a meaningless attempt to give effects to causelessness, and make it be a cause.

3.   Always in sickness does the Son of God attempt to make himself his cause, and not allow himself to be his Father's Son. ²For this impossible desire, he does not believe that he is Love's Effect, and must be cause because of what he is. ³The cause of healing is the only Cause of everything. ⁴It has but *one* Effect. ⁵And in that recognition, causelessness is given no effects and none is seen. ⁶A mind within a body and a world of other bodies, each with separate minds, are your "creations," you the "other" mind, creating with effects unlike yourself. ⁷And as their "father," you must be like them.

4.   Nothing at all has happened but that you have put yourself to sleep, and dreamed a dream in which you were an alien to yourself, and but a part of someone else's dream. ²The miracle does not awaken you, but merely shows you who the dreamer is. ³It teaches you there is a choice of dreams while you are still asleep, depending on the purpose of your dreaming. ⁴Do you wish for dreams of healing, or for dreams of death? ⁵A dream is like a memory in that it pictures what you wanted shown to you.

5.   An empty storehouse, with an open door, holds all your shreds of memories and dreams. ²Yet if you are the dreamer, you perceive this much at least: that you have caused the dream, and can accept another dream as well. ³But for this change in content of the dream, it must be realized that it is you who dreamed the dreaming that you do not like. ⁴It is but an effect that *you* have caused, and you would not be cause of this effect. ⁵In dreams of

murder and attack are you the victim in a dying body slain. ⁶But in forgiving dreams is no one asked to be the victim and the sufferer. ⁷These are the happy dreams the miracle exchanges for your own. ⁸It does not ask you make another; only that you see you made the one you would exchange for this.

6. This world is causeless, as is every dream that anyone has dreamed within the world. ²No plans are possible, and no design exists that could be found and understood. ³What else could be expected from a thing that has no cause? ⁴Yet if it has no cause, it has no purpose. ⁵You may cause a dream, but never will you give it real effects. ⁶For that would change its cause, and it is this you cannot do. ⁷The dreamer of a dream is not awake, but does not know he sleeps. ⁸He sees illusions of himself as sick or well, depressed or happy, but without a stable cause with guaranteed effects.

7. The miracle establishes you dream a dream, and that its content is not true. ²This is a crucial step in dealing with illusions. ³No one is afraid of them when he perceives he made them up. ⁴The fear was held in place because he did not see that he was author of the dream, and not a figure in the dream. ⁵He gives himself the consequences that he dreams he gave his brother. ⁶And it is but this the dream has put together and has offered him, to show him that his wishes have been done. ⁷Thus does he fear his own attack, but sees it at another's hands. ⁸As victim, he is suffering from its effects, but not their cause. ⁹He authored not his own attack, and he is innocent of what he caused. ¹⁰The miracle does nothing but to show him that he has done nothing. ¹¹What he fears is cause without the consequences that would make it cause. ¹²And so it never was.

8. The separation started with the dream the Father was deprived of His Effects, and powerless to keep them since He was no longer their Creator. ²In the dream, the dreamer made himself. ³But what he made has turned against him, taking on the role of its creator, as the dreamer had. ⁴And as he hated his Creator, so the figures in the dream have hated him. ⁵His body is their slave, which they abuse because the motives he has given it have they adopted as their own. ⁶And hate it for the vengeance it would offer them. ⁷It is their vengeance on the body which appears to prove the dreamer could not be the maker of the dream. ⁸Effect and cause are first split off, and then reversed, so that effect becomes a cause; the cause, effect.

9.   This is the separation's final step, with which salvation, which proceeds to go the other way, begins. ²This final step is an effect of what has gone before, appearing as a cause. ³The miracle is the first step in giving back to cause the function of causation, not effect. ⁴For this confusion has produced the dream, and while it lasts will wakening be feared. ⁵Nor will the call to wakening be heard, because it seems to be the call to fear.

10.   Like every lesson that the Holy Spirit requests you learn, the miracle is clear. ²It demonstrates what He would have you learn, and shows you its effects are what you want. ³In His forgiving dreams are the effects of yours undone, and hated enemies perceived as friends with merciful intent. ⁴Their enmity is seen as causeless now, because they did not make it. ⁵And you can accept the role of maker of their hate, because you see that it has no effects. ⁶Now are you freed from this much of the dream; the world is neutral, and the bodies that still seem to move about as separate things need not be feared. ⁷And so they are not sick.

11.   The miracle returns the cause of fear to you who made it. ²But it also shows that, having no effects, it is not cause, because the function of causation is to have effects. ³And where effects are gone, there is no cause. ⁴Thus is the body healed by miracles because they show the mind made sickness, and employed the body to be victim, or effect, of what it made. ⁵Yet half the lesson will not teach the whole. ⁶The miracle is useless if you learn but that the body can be healed, for this is not the lesson it was sent to teach. ⁷The lesson is the *mind* was sick that thought the body could be sick; projecting out its guilt caused nothing, and had no effects.

12.   This world is full of miracles. ²They stand in shining silence next to every dream of pain and suffering, of sin and guilt. ³They are the dream's alternative, the choice to be the dreamer, rather than deny the active role in making up the dream. ⁴They are the glad effects of taking back the consequence of sickness to its cause. ⁵The body is released because the mind acknowledges "this is not done to me, but *I* am doing this." ⁶And thus the mind is free to make another choice instead. ⁷Beginning here, salvation will proceed to change the course of every step in the descent to separation, until all the steps have been retraced, the ladder gone, and all the dreaming of the world undone.

III. The Agreement to Join

1. What waits in perfect certainty beyond salvation is not our concern. ²For you have barely started to allow your first, uncertain steps to be directed up the ladder separation led you down. ³The miracle alone is your concern at present. ⁴Here is where we must begin. ⁵And having started, will the way be made serene and simple in the rising up to waking and the ending of the dream. ⁶When you accept a miracle, you do not add your dream of fear to one that is already being dreamed. ⁷Without support, the dream will fade away without effects. ⁸For it is your support that strengthens it.

2. No mind is sick until another mind agrees that they are separate. ²And thus it is their joint decision to be sick. ³If you withhold agreement and accept the part you play in making sickness real, the other mind cannot project its guilt without your aid in letting it perceive itself as separate and apart from you. ⁴Thus is the body not perceived as sick by both your minds from separate points of view. ⁵Uniting with a brother's mind prevents the cause of sickness and perceived effects. ⁶Healing is the effect of minds that join, as sickness comes from minds that separate.

3. The miracle does nothing just *because* the minds are joined, and cannot separate. ²Yet in the dreaming has this been reversed, and separate minds are seen as bodies, which are separated and which cannot join. ³Do not allow your brother to be sick, for if he is, have you abandoned him to his own dream by sharing it with him. ⁴He has not seen the cause of sickness where it is, and you have overlooked the gap between you, where the sickness has been bred. ⁵Thus are you joined in sickness, to preserve the little gap unhealed, where sickness is kept carefully protected, cherished, and upheld by firm belief, lest God should come to bridge the little gap that leads to Him. ⁶Fight not His coming with illusions, for it is His coming that you want above all things that seem to glisten in the dream.

4. The end of dreaming is the end of fear, and love was never in the world of dreams. ²The gap *is* little. ³Yet it holds the seeds of pestilence and every form of ill, because it is a wish to keep apart and not to join. ⁴And thus it seems to give a cause to sickness which is not its cause. ⁵The purpose of the gap is all the cause that sickness has. ⁶For it was made to keep you separated, in a body which you see as if it were the cause of pain.

5. The cause of pain is separation, not the body, which is only its effect. ²Yet separation is but empty space, enclosing nothing, doing nothing, and as unsubstantial as the empty place between the ripples that a ship has made in passing by. ³And covered just as fast, as water rushes in to close the gap, and as the waves in joining cover it. ⁴Where is the gap between the waves when they have joined, and covered up the space which seemed to keep them separate for a little while? ⁵Where are the grounds for sickness when the minds have joined to close the little gap between them, where the seeds of sickness seemed to grow?

6. God builds the bridge, but only in the space left clean and vacant by the miracle. ²The seeds of sickness and the shame of guilt He cannot bridge, for He can not destroy the alien will that He created not. ³Let its effects be gone and clutch them not with eager hands, to keep them for yourself. ⁴The miracle will brush them all aside, and thus make room for Him Who wills to come and bridge His Son's returning to Himself.

7. Count, then, the silver miracles and golden dreams of happiness as all the treasures you would keep within the storehouse of the world. ²The door is open, not to thieves, but to your starving brothers, who mistook for gold the shining of a pebble, and who stored a heap of snow that shone like silver. ³They have nothing left behind the open door. ⁴What is the world except a little gap perceived to tear eternity apart, and break it into days and months and years? ⁵And what are you who live within the world except a picture of the Son of God in broken pieces, each concealed within a separate and uncertain bit of clay?

8. Be not afraid, my child, but let your world be gently lit by miracles. ²And where the little gap was seen to stand between you and your brother, join him there. ³And so sickness will now be seen without a cause. ⁴The dream of healing in forgiveness lies, and gently shows you that you never sinned. ⁵The miracle would leave no proof of guilt to bring you witness to what never was. ⁶And in your storehouse it will make a place of welcome for your Father and your Self. ⁷The door is open, that all those may come who would no longer starve, and would enjoy the feast of plenty set before them there. ⁸And they will meet with your invited Guests the miracle has asked to come to you.

9. This is a feast unlike indeed to those the dreaming of the world has shown. ²For here, the more that anyone receives, the more is left for all the rest to share. ³The Guests have brought unlimited

supply with Them. ⁴And no one is deprived or can deprive. ⁵Here is a feast the Father lays before His Son, and shares it equally with him. ⁶And in Their sharing there can be no gap in which abundance falters and grows thin. ⁷Here can the lean years enter not, for time waits not upon this feast, which has no end. ⁸For love has set its table in the space that seemed to keep your Guests apart from you.

IV. The Greater Joining

1.   Accepting the Atonement for yourself means not to give support to someone's dream of sickness and of death. ²It means that you share not his wish to separate, and let him turn illusions on himself. ³Nor do you wish that they be turned, instead, on you. ⁴Thus have they no effects. ⁵And you are free of dreams of pain because you let him be. ⁶Unless you help him, you will suffer pain with him because that is your wish. ⁷And you become a figure in his dream of pain, as he in yours. ⁸So do you and your brother both become illusions, and without identity. ⁹You could be anyone or anything, depending on whose evil dream you share. ¹⁰You can be sure of just one thing; that you are evil, for you share in dreams of fear.

2.   There is a way of finding certainty right here and now. ²Refuse to be a part of fearful dreams whatever form they take, for you will lose identity in them. ³You find yourself by not accepting them as causing you, and giving you effects. ⁴You stand apart from them, but not apart from him who dreams them. ⁵Thus you separate the dreamer from the dream, and join in one, but let the other go. ⁶The dream is but illusion in the mind. ⁷And with the mind you would unite, but never with the dream. ⁸It is the dream you fear, and not the mind. ⁹You see them as the same, because you think that *you* are but a dream. ¹⁰And what is real and what is but illusion in yourself you do not know and cannot tell apart.

3.   Like you, your brother thinks he is a dream. ²Share not in his illusion of himself, for your Identity depends on his reality. ³Think, rather, of him as a mind in which illusions still persist, but as a mind which brother is to you. ⁴He is not brother made by what he dreams, nor is his body, "hero" of the dream, your brother. ⁵It is his reality that is your brother, as is yours to him. ⁶Your mind and his are joined in brotherhood. ⁷His body and his

dreams but seem to make a little gap, where yours have joined with his.

4. And yet, between your minds there is no gap. ²To join his dreams is thus to meet him not, because his dreams would separate from you. ³Therefore release him, merely by your claim on brotherhood, and not on dreams of fear. ⁴Let him acknowledge who he is, by not supporting his illusions by your faith, for if you do, you will have faith in yours. ⁵With faith in yours, he will not be released, and you are kept in bondage to his dreams. ⁶And dreams of fear will haunt the little gap, inhabited but by illusions which you have supported in your brother's mind.

5. Be certain, if you do your part, he will do his, for he will join you where you stand. ²Call not to him to meet you in the gap between you, or you must believe that it is your reality as well as his. ³You cannot do his part, but this you *do* when you become a passive figure in his dreams, instead of dreamer of your own. ⁴Identity in dreams is meaningless because the dreamer and the dream are one. ⁵Who shares a dream must be the dream he shares, because by sharing is a cause produced.

6. You share confusion and you are confused, for in the gap no stable self exists. ²What is the same seems different, because what is the same appears to be unlike. ³His dreams are yours because you let them be. ⁴But if you took your own away would he be free of them, and of his own as well. ⁵Your dreams are witnesses to his, and his attest the truth of yours. ⁶Yet if you see there is no truth in yours, his dreams will go, and he will understand what made the dream.

7. The Holy Spirit is in both your minds, and He is One because there is no gap that separates His Oneness from Itself. ²The gap between your bodies matters not, for what is joined in Him is always one. ³No one is sick if someone else accepts his union with him. ⁴His desire to be a sick and separated mind can not remain without a witness or a cause. ⁵And both are gone if someone wills to be united with him. ⁶He has dreams that he was separated from his brother who, by sharing not his dream, has left the space between them vacant. ⁷And the Father comes to join His Son the Holy Spirit joined.

8. The Holy Spirit's function is to take the broken picture of the Son of God and put the pieces into place again. ²This holy picture, healed entirely, does He hold out to every separate piece that thinks it is a picture in itself. ³To each He offers his Identity,

which the whole picture represents, instead of just a little, broken bit that he insisted was himself. ⁴And when he sees this picture he will recognize himself. ⁵If you share not your brother's evil dream, this is the picture that the miracle will place within the little gap, left clean of all the seeds of sickness and of sin. ⁶And here the Father will receive His Son, because His Son was gracious to himself.

9.   I thank You, Father, knowing You will come to close each little gap that lies between the broken pieces of Your holy Son. ²Your Holiness, complete and perfect, lies in every one of them. ³And they are joined because what is in one is in them all. ⁴How holy is the smallest grain of sand, when it is recognized as being part of the completed picture of God's Son! ⁵The forms the broken pieces seem to take mean nothing. ⁶For the whole is in each one. ⁷And every aspect of the Son of God is just the same as every other part.

10.   Join not your brother's dreams but join with him, and where you join His Son the Father is. ²Who seeks for substitutes when he perceives he has lost nothing? ³Who would want to have the "benefits" of sickness when he has received the simple happiness of health? ⁴What God has given cannot be a loss, and what is not of Him has no effects. ⁵What, then, would you perceive within the gap? ⁶The seeds of sickness come from the belief that there is joy in separation, and its giving up would be a sacrifice. ⁷But miracles are the result when you do not insist on seeing in the gap what is not there. ⁸Your willingness to let illusions go is all the Healer of God's Son requires. ⁹He will place the miracle of healing where the seeds of sickness were. ¹⁰And there will be no loss, but only gain.

V. The Alternate to Dreams of Fear

1.   What is a sense of sickness but a sense of limitation? ²Of a splitting *off* and separating *from*? ³A gap that is perceived between you and your brother, and what is now seen as health? ⁴And so the good is seen to be outside; the evil, in. ⁵And thus is sickness separating off the self from good, and keeping evil in. ⁶God is the Alternate to dreams of fear. ⁷Who shares in them can never share in Him. ⁸But who withdraws his mind from sharing them *is* sharing Him. ⁹There is no other choice. ¹⁰Except you share it, nothing can exist. ¹¹And you exist because God shared His Will

with you, that His creation might create.

2.   It is the sharing of the evil dreams of hate and malice, bitterness and death, of sin and suffering and pain and loss, that makes them real. ²Unshared, they are perceived as meaningless. ³The fear is gone from them because you did not give them your support. ⁴Where fear has gone there love must come, because there are but these alternatives. ⁵Where one appears, the other disappears. ⁶And which you share becomes the only one you have. ⁷You have the one that you accept, because it is the only one you wish to have.

3.   You share no evil dreams if you forgive the dreamer, and perceive that he is not the dream he made. ²And so he cannot be a part of yours, from which you both are free. ³Forgiveness separates the dreamer from the evil dream, and thus releases him. ⁴Remember if you share an evil dream, you will believe you are the dream you share. ⁵And fearing it, you will not want to know your own Identity, because you think that It is fearful. ⁶And you will deny your Self, and walk upon an alien ground which your Creator did not make, and where you seem to be a something you are not. ⁷You will make war upon your Self, which seems to be your enemy; and will attack your brother, as a part of what you hate. ⁸There is no compromise. ⁹You are your Self or an illusion. ¹⁰What can be between illusion and the truth? ¹¹A middle ground, where you can be a thing that is not you, must be a dream and cannot be the truth.

4.   You have conceived a little gap between illusions and the truth to be the place where all your safety lies, and where your Self is safely hidden by what you have made. ²Here is a world established that is sick, and this the world the body's eyes perceive. ³Here are the sounds it hears; the voices that its ears were made to hear. ⁴Yet sights and sounds the body can perceive are meaningless. ⁵It cannot see nor hear. ⁶It does not know what seeing *is*; what listening is *for*. ⁷It is as little able to perceive as it can judge or understand or know. ⁸Its eyes are blind; its ears are deaf. ⁹It can not think, and so it cannot have effects.

5.   What is there God created to be sick? ²And what that He created not can be? ³Let not your eyes behold a dream; your ears bear witness to illusion. ⁴They were made to look upon a world that is not there; to hear the voices that can make no sound. ⁵Yet are there other sounds and other sights that *can* be seen and heard and understood. ⁶For eyes and ears are senses without

601

sense, and what they see and hear they but report. [7]It is not they that hear and see, but you, who put together every jagged piece, each senseless scrap and shred of evidence, and make a witness to the world you want. [8]Let not the body's ears and eyes perceive these countless fragments seen within the gap that you imagined, and let them persuade their maker his imaginings are real.

6. Creation proves reality because it shares the function all creation shares. [2]It is not made of little bits of glass, a piece of wood, a thread or two, perhaps, all put together to attest its truth. [3]Reality does not depend on this. [4]There is no gap that separates the truth from dreams and from illusions. [5]Truth has left no room for them in any place or time. [6]For it fills every place and every time, and makes them wholly indivisible.

7. You who believe there is a little gap between you and your brother, do not see that it is here you are as prisoners in a world perceived to be existing here. [2]The world you see does not exist, because the place where you perceive it is not real. [3]The gap is carefully concealed in fog, and misty pictures rise to cover it with vague uncertain forms and changing shapes, forever unsubstantial and unsure. [4]Yet in the gap is nothing. [5]And there are no awesome secrets and no darkened tombs where terror rises from the bones of death. [6]Look at the little gap, and you behold the innocence and emptiness of sin that you will see within yourself, when you have lost the fear of recognizing love.

VI. The Secret Vows

1. Who punishes the body is insane. [2]For here the little gap is seen, and yet it is not here. [3]It has not judged itself, nor made itself to be what it is not. [4]It does not seek to make of pain a joy and look for lasting pleasure in the dust. [5]It does not tell you what its purpose is and cannot understand what it is for. [6]It does not victimize, because it has no will, no preferences and no doubts. [7]It does not wonder what it is. [8]And so it has no need to be competitive. [9]It can be victimized, but cannot feel itself as victim. [10]It accepts no role, but does what it is told, without attack.

2. It is indeed a senseless point of view to hold responsible for sight a thing that cannot see, and blame it for the sounds you do not like, although it cannot hear. [2]It suffers not the punishment you give because it has no feeling. [3]It behaves in ways you want,

but never makes the choice. ⁴It is not born and does not die. ⁵It can but follow aimlessly the path on which it has been set. ⁶And if that path is changed, it walks as easily another way. ⁷It takes no sides and judges not the road it travels. ⁸It perceives no gap, because it does not hate. ⁹It can be used for hate, but it cannot be hateful made thereby.

3. The thing you hate and fear and loathe and want, the body does not know. ²You send it forth to seek for separation and be separate. ³And then you hate it, not for what it is, but for the uses you have made of it. ⁴You shrink from what it sees and what it hears, and hate its frailty and littleness. ⁵And you despise its acts, but not your own. ⁶It sees and acts for *you*. ⁷It hears your voice. ⁸And it is frail and little by your wish. ⁹It seems to punish you, and thus deserve your hatred for the limitations that it brings to you. ¹⁰Yet you have made of it a symbol for the limitations that you want your mind to have and see and keep.

4. The body represents the gap between the little bit of mind you call your own and all the rest of what is really yours. ²You hate it, yet you think it is your self, and that, without it, would your self be lost. ³This is the secret vow that you have made with every brother who would walk apart. ⁴This is the secret oath you take again, whenever you perceive yourself attacked. ⁵No one can suffer if he does not see himself attacked, and losing by attack. ⁶Unstated and unheard in consciousness is every pledge to sickness. ⁷Yet it is a promise to another to be hurt by him, and to attack him in return.

5. Sickness is anger taken out upon the body, so that it will suffer pain. ²It is the obvious effect of what was made in secret, in agreement with another's secret wish to be apart from you, as you would be apart from him. ³Unless you both agree that is your wish, it can have no effects. ⁴Whoever says, "There is no gap between my mind and yours" has kept God's promise, not his tiny oath to be forever faithful unto death. ⁵And by his healing is his brother healed.

6. Let this be your agreement with each one; that you be one with him and not apart. ²And he will keep the promise that you make with him, because it is the one that he has made to God, as God has made to him. ³God keeps His promises; His Son keeps his. ⁴In his creation did his Father say, "You are beloved of Me and I of you forever. ⁵Be you perfect as Myself, for you can never be apart from Me." ⁶His Son remembers not that

he replied "I will," though in that promise he was born. [7]Yet God reminds him of it every time he does not share a promise to be sick, but lets his mind be healed and unified. [8]His secret vows are powerless before the Will of God, Whose promises he shares. [9]And what he substitutes is not his will, who has made promise of himself to God.

VII. The Ark of Safety

1. God asks for nothing, and His Son, like Him, need ask for nothing. [2]For there is no lack in him. [3]An empty space, a little gap, would be a lack. [4]And it is only there that he could want for something he has not. [5]A space where God is not, a gap between the Father and the Son is not the Will of Either, Who have promised to be one. [6]God's promise is a promise to Himself, and there is no one who could be untrue to what He wills as part of what He is. [7]The promise that there is no gap between Himself and what He is cannot be false. [8]What will can come between what must be one, and in Whose Wholeness there can be no gap?

2. The beautiful relationship you have with all your brothers is a part of you because it is a part of God Himself. [2]Are you not sick, if you deny yourself your wholeness and your health, the Source of help, the Call to healing and the Call to heal? [3]Your savior waits for healing, and the world waits with him. [4]Nor are you apart from it. [5]For healing will be one or not at all, its oneness being where the healing is. [6]What could correct for separation but its opposite? [7]There is no middle ground in any aspect of salvation. [8]You accept it wholly or accept it not. [9]What is unseparated must be joined. [10]And what is joined cannot be separate.

3. Either there is a gap between you and your brother, or you are as one. [2]There is no in between, no other choice, and no allegiance to be split between the two. [3]A split allegiance is but faithlessness to both, and merely sets you spinning round, to grasp uncertainly at any straw that seems to hold some promise of relief. [4]Yet who can build his home upon a straw, and count on it as shelter from the wind? [5]The body can be made a home like this, because it lacks foundation in the truth. [6]And yet, because it does, it can be seen as not your home, but merely as an aid to help you reach the home where God abides.

4. With *this* as purpose is the body healed. [2]It is not used to

witness to the dream of separation and disease. [3]Nor is it idly blamed for what it did not do. [4]It serves to help the healing of God's Son, and for this purpose it cannot be sick. [5]It will not join a purpose not your own, and you have chosen that it not be sick. [6]All miracles are based upon this choice, and given you the instant it is made. [7]No forms of sickness are immune, because the choice cannot be made in terms of form. [8]The choice of sickness seems to be of form, yet it is one, as is its opposite. [9]And you are sick or well, accordingly.

5. But never you alone. [2]This world is but the dream that you can be alone, and think without affecting those apart from you. [3]To be alone must mean you are apart, and if you are, you cannot but be sick. [4]This seems to prove that you must be apart. [5]Yet all it means is that you tried to keep a promise to be true to faithlessness. [6]Yet faithlessness is sickness. [7]It is like the house set upon straw. [8]It seems to be quite solid and substantial in itself. [9]Yet its stability cannot be judged apart from its foundation. [10]If it rests on straw, there is no need to bar the door and lock the windows and make fast the bolts. [11]The wind will topple it, and rain will come and carry it into oblivion.

6. What is the sense in seeking to be safe in what was made for danger and for fear? [2]Why burden it with further locks and chains and heavy anchors, when its weakness lies, not in itself, but in the frailty of the little gap of nothingness whereon it stands? [3]What can be safe that rests upon a shadow? [4]Would you build your home upon what will collapse beneath a feather's weight?

7. Your home is built upon your brother's health, upon his happiness, his sinlessness, and everything his Father promised him. [2]No secret promise you have made instead has shaken the Foundation of his home. [3]The winds will blow upon it and the rain will beat against it, but with no effect. [4]The world will wash away and yet this house will stand forever, for its strength lies not within itself alone. [5]It is an ark of safety, resting on God's promise that His Son is safe forever in Himself. [6]What gap can interpose itself between the safety of this shelter and its Source? [7]From here the body can be seen as what it is, and neither less nor more in worth than the extent to which it can be used to liberate God's Son unto his home. [8]And with this holy purpose is it made a home of holiness a little while, because it shares your Father's Will with you.

Chapter 29

THE AWAKENING

I. The Closing of the Gap

1.   There is no time, no place, no state where God is absent. ²There is nothing to be feared. ³There is no way in which a gap could be conceived of in the Wholeness that is His. ⁴The compromise the least and littlest gap would represent in His eternal Love is quite impossible. ⁵For it would mean His Love could harbor just a hint of hate, His gentleness turn sometimes to attack, and His eternal patience sometimes fail. ⁶All this do you believe, when you perceive a gap between your brother and yourself. ⁷How could you trust Him, then? ⁸For He must be deceptive in His Love. ⁹Be wary, then; let Him not come too close, and leave a gap between you and His Love, through which you can escape if there be need for you to flee.

2.   Here is the fear of God most plainly seen. ²For love *is* treacherous to those who fear, since fear and hate can never be apart. ³No one who hates but is afraid of love, and therefore must he be afraid of God. ⁴Certain it is he knows not what love means. ⁵He fears to love and loves to hate, and so he thinks that love is fearful; hate is love. ⁶This is the consequence the little gap must bring to those who cherish it, and think that it is their salvation and their hope.

3.   The fear of God! ²The greatest obstacle that peace must flow across has not yet gone. ³The rest are past, but this one still remains to block your path, and make the way to light seem dark and fearful, perilous and bleak. ⁴You had decided that your brother is your enemy. ⁵Sometimes a friend, perhaps, provided that your separate interests made your friendship possible a little while. ⁶But not without a gap perceived between you and him, lest he turn again into an enemy. ⁷Let him come close to you, and you jumped back; as you approached, did he but instantly withdraw. ⁸A cautious friendship, and limited in scope and carefully restricted in amount, became the treaty that you had made with him. ⁹Thus you and your brother but shared a qualified entente, in which a clause of separation was a point you both agreed to keep intact. ¹⁰And violating this was thought to

be a breach of treaty not to be allowed.

4. The gap between you and your brother is not one of space between two separate bodies. ²And this but seems to be dividing off your separate minds. ³It is the symbol of a promise made to meet when you prefer, and separate till you and he elect to meet again. ⁴And then your bodies seem to get in touch, and thereby signify a meeting place to join. ⁵But always is it possible for you and him to go your separate ways. ⁶Conditional upon the "right" to separate will you and he agree to meet from time to time, and keep apart in intervals of separation, which do protect you from the "sacrifice" of love. ⁷The body saves you, for it gets away from total sacrifice and gives to you the time in which to build again your separate self, which you truly believe diminishes as you and your brother meet.

5. The body could not separate your mind from your brother's unless you wanted it to be a cause of separation and of distance seen between you and him. ²Thus do you endow it with a power that lies not within itself. ³And herein lies its power over you. ⁴For now you think that it determines when your brother and you meet, and limits your ability to make communion with your brother's mind. ⁵And now it tells you where to go and how to go there, what is feasible for you to undertake, and what you cannot do. ⁶It dictates what its health can tolerate, and what will tire it and make it sick. ⁷And its "inherent" weaknesses set up the limitations on what you would do, and keep your purpose limited and weak.

6. The body will accommodate to this, if you would have it so. ²It will allow but limited indulgences in "love," with intervals of hatred in between. ³And it will take command of when to "love," and when to shrink more safely into fear. ⁴It will be sick because you do not know what loving means. ⁵And so you must misuse each circumstance and everyone you meet, and see in them a purpose not your own.

7. It is not love that asks a sacrifice. ²But fear demands the sacrifice of love, for in love's presence fear cannot abide. ³For hate to be maintained, love must be feared; and only sometimes present, sometimes gone. ⁴Thus is love seen as treacherous, because it seems to come and go uncertainly, and offer no stability to you. ⁵You do not see how limited and weak is your allegiance, and how frequently you have demanded that love go away, and leave you quietly alone in "peace."

8.   The body, innocent of goals, is your excuse for variable goals you hold, and force the body to maintain. ²You do not fear its weakness, but its lack of strength *or* weakness. ³Would you know that nothing stands between you and your brother? ⁴Would you know there is no gap behind which you can hide? ⁵There is a shock that comes to those who learn their savior is their enemy no more. ⁶There is a wariness that is aroused by learning that the body is not real. ⁷And there are overtones of seeming fear around the happy message, "God is Love."

9.   Yet all that happens when the gap is gone is peace eternal. ²Nothing more than that, and nothing less. ³Without the fear of God, what could induce you to abandon Him? ⁴What toys or trinkets in the gap could serve to hold you back an instant from His Love? ⁵Would you allow the body to say "no" to Heaven's calling, were you not afraid to find a loss of self in finding God? ⁶Yet can your self be lost by being found?

II. The Coming of the Guest

1.   Why would you not perceive it as release from suffering to learn that you are free? ²Why would you not acclaim the truth instead of looking on it as an enemy? ³Why does an easy path, so clearly marked it is impossible to lose the way, seem thorny, rough and far too difficult for you to follow? ⁴Is it not because you see it as the road to hell instead of looking on it as a simple way, without a sacrifice or any loss, to find yourself in Heaven and in God? ⁵Until you realize you give up nothing, until you understand there is no loss, you will have some regrets about the way that you have chosen. ⁶And you will not see the many gains your choice has offered you. ⁷Yet though you do not see them, they are there. ⁸Their cause has been effected, and they must be present where their cause has entered in.

2.   You have accepted healing's cause, and so it must be you are healed. ²And being healed, the power to heal must also now be yours. ³The miracle is not a separate thing that happens suddenly, as an effect without a cause. ⁴Nor is it, in itself, a cause. ⁵But where its cause is must it be. ⁶Now is it caused, though not as yet perceived. ⁷And its effects are there, though not yet seen. ⁸Look inward now, and you will not behold a reason for regret, but cause indeed for glad rejoicing and for hope of peace.

3.   It has been hopeless to attempt to find the hope of peace upon a battleground. ²It has been futile to demand escape from sin and pain of what was made to serve the function of retaining sin and pain. ³For pain and sin are one illusion, as are hate and fear, attack and guilt but one. ⁴Where they are causeless their effects are gone, and love must come wherever they are not. ⁵Why are you not rejoicing? ⁶You are free of pain and sickness, misery and loss, and all effects of hatred and attack. ⁷No more is pain your friend and guilt your god, and you should welcome the effects of love.

4.   Your Guest *has* come. ²You asked Him, and He came. ³You did not hear Him enter, for you did not wholly welcome Him. ⁴And yet His gifts came with Him. ⁵He has laid them at your feet, and asks you now that you will look on them and take them for your own. ⁶He needs your help in giving them to all who walk apart, believing they are separate and alone. ⁷They will be healed when you accept your gifts, because your Guest will welcome everyone whose feet have touched the holy ground whereon you stand, and where His gifts for them are laid.

5.   You do not see how much you now can give, because of everything you have received. ²Yet He Who entered in but waits for you to come where you invited Him to be. ³There is no other place where He can find His host, nor where His host can meet with Him. ⁴And nowhere else His gifts of peace and joy, and all the happiness His Presence brings, can be obtained. ⁵For they are where He is Who brought them with Him, that they might be yours. ⁶You cannot see your Guest, but you can see the gifts He brought. ⁷And when you look on them, you will believe His Presence must be there. ⁸For what you now can do could not be done without the love and grace His Presence holds.

6.   Such is the promise of the living God; His Son have life and every living thing be part of him, and nothing else have life. ²What you have given "life" is not alive, and symbolizes but your wish to be alive apart from life; alive in death, with death perceived as life, and living, death. ³Confusion follows on confusion here, for on confusion has this world been based, and there is nothing else it rests upon. ⁴Its basis does not change, although it seems to be in constant change. ⁵Yet what is that except the state confusion really means? ⁶Stability to those who are confused is meaningless, and shift and change become the law on which they predicate their lives.

7.   The body does not change. ²It represents the larger dream that

change is possible. [3]To change is to attain a state unlike the one in which you found yourself before. [4]There is no change in immortality, and Heaven knows it not. [5]Yet here on earth it has a double purpose, for it can be made to teach opposing things. [6]And they reflect the teacher who is teaching them. [7]The body can appear to change with time, with sickness or with health, and with events that seem to alter it. [8]Yet this but means the mind remains unchanged in its belief of what the purpose of the body is.

8. Sickness is a demand the body be a thing that it is not. [2]Its nothingness is guarantee that it can *not* be sick. [3]In your demand that it be more than this lies the idea of sickness. [4]For it asks that God be less than all He really is. [5]What, then, becomes of you, for it is you of whom the sacrifice is asked? [6]For He is told that part of Him belongs to Him no longer. [7]He must sacrifice your self, and in His sacrifice are you made more and He is lessened by the loss of you. [8]And what is gone from Him becomes your god, protecting you from being part of Him.

9. The body that is asked to be a god will be attacked, because its nothingness has not been recognized. [2]And so it seems to be a thing with power in itself. [3]As something, it can be perceived and thought to feel and act, and hold you in its grasp as prisoner to itself. [4]And it can fail to be what you demanded that it be. [5]And you will hate it for its littleness, unmindful that the failure does not lie in that it is not more than it should be, but only in your failure to perceive that it is nothing. [6]Yet its nothingness is your salvation, from which you would flee.

10. As "something" is the body asked to be God's enemy, replacing what He is with littleness and limit and despair. [2]It is His loss you celebrate when you behold the body as a thing you love, or look upon it as a thing you hate. [3]For if He be the sum of everything, then what is not in Him does not exist, and His completion is its nothingness. [4]Your savior is not dead, nor does he dwell in what was built as temple unto death. [5]He lives in God, and it is this that makes him savior unto you, and only this. [6]His body's nothingness releases yours from sickness and from death. [7]For what is yours cannot be more or less than what is his.

III. God's Witnesses

1. Condemn your savior not because he thinks he is a body. [2]For beyond his dreams is his reality. [3]But he must learn he is a savior first, before he can remember what he is. [4]And he must save who would be saved. [5]On saving you depends his happiness. [6]For who is savior but the one who gives salvation? [7]Thus he learns it must be his to give. [8]Unless he gives he will not know he has, for giving is the proof of having. [9]Only those who think that God is lessened by their strength could fail to understand this must be so. [10]For who could give unless he has, and who could lose by giving what must be increased thereby?

2. Think you the Father lost Himself when He created you? [2]Was He made weak because He shared His Love? [3]Was He made incomplete by your perfection? [4]Or are you the proof that He is perfect and complete? [5]Deny Him not His witness in the dream His Son prefers to his reality. [6]He must be savior from the dream he made, that he be free of it. [7]He must see someone else as not a body, one with him without the wall the world has built to keep apart all living things who know not that they live.

3. Within the dream of bodies and of death is yet one theme of truth; no more, perhaps, than just a tiny spark, a space of light created in the dark, where God still shines. [2]You cannot wake yourself. [3]Yet you can let yourself be wakened. [4]You can overlook your brother's dreams. [5]So perfectly can you forgive him his illusions he becomes your savior from your dreams. [6]And as you see him shining in the space of light where God abides within the darkness, you will see that God Himself is where his body is. [7]Before this light the body disappears, as heavy shadows must give way to light. [8]The darkness cannot choose that it remain. [9]The coming of the light means it is gone. [10]In glory will you see your brother then, and understand what really fills the gap so long perceived as keeping you apart. [11]There, in its place, God's witness has set forth the gentle way of kindness to God's Son. [12]Whom you forgive is given power to forgive you your illusions. [13]By your gift of freedom is it given unto you.

4. Make way for love, which you did not create, but which you can extend. [2]On earth this means forgive your brother, that the darkness may be lifted from your mind. [3]When light has come to him through your forgiveness, he will not forget his savior, leaving him unsaved. [4]For it was in your face he saw the light that he

611

would keep beside him, as he walks through darkness to the everlasting light.

5.   How holy are you, that the Son of God can be your savior in the midst of dreams of desolation and disaster. ²See how eagerly he comes, and steps aside from heavy shadows that have hidden him, and shines on you in gratitude and love. ³He is himself, but not himself alone. ⁴And as his Father lost not part of him in your creation, so the light in him is brighter still because you gave your light to him, to save him from the dark. ⁵And now the light in you must be as bright as shines in him. ⁶This is the spark that shines within the dream; that you can help him waken, and be sure his waking eyes will rest on you. ⁷And in his glad salvation you are saved.

IV. Dream Roles

1.   Do you believe that truth can be but some illusions? ²They are dreams *because* they are not true. ³Their equal lack of truth becomes the basis for the miracle, which means that you have understood that dreams are dreams; and that escape depends, not on the dream, but only on awaking. ⁴Could it be some dreams are kept, and others wakened from? ⁵The choice is not between which dreams to keep, but only if you want to live in dreams or to awaken from them. ⁶Thus it is the miracle does not select some dreams to leave untouched by its beneficence. ⁷You cannot dream some dreams and wake from some, for you are either sleeping or awake. ⁸And dreaming goes with only one of these.

2.   The dreams you think you like would hold you back as much as those in which the fear is seen. ²For every dream is but a dream of fear, no matter what the form it seems to take. ³The fear is seen within, without, or both. ⁴Or it can be disguised in pleasant form. ⁵But never is it absent from the dream, for fear is the material of dreams, from which they all are made. ⁶Their form can change, but they cannot be made of something else. ⁷The miracle were treacherous indeed if it allowed you still to be afraid because you did not recognize the fear. ⁸You would not then be willing to awake, for which the miracle prepares the way.

3.   In simplest form, it can be said attack is a response to function unfulfilled as you perceive the function. ²It can be in you or someone else, but where it is perceived it will be there it is

attacked. [3]Depression or assault must be the theme of every dream, for they are made of fear. [4]The thin disguise of pleasure and of joy in which they may be wrapped but slightly veils the heavy lump of fear that is their core. [5]And it is this the miracle perceives, and not the wrappings in which it is bound.

4. When you are angry, is it not because someone has failed to fill the function you allotted him? [2]And does not this become the "reason" your attack is justified? [3]The dreams you think you like are those in which the functions you have given have been filled; the needs which you ascribe to you are met. [4]It does not matter if they be fulfilled or merely wanted. [5]It is the idea that they exist from which the fears arise. [6]Dreams are not wanted more or less. [7]They are desired or not. [8]And each one represents some function that you have assigned; some goal which an event, or body, or a thing *should* represent, and *should* achieve for you. [9]If it succeeds you think you like the dream. [10]If it should fail you think the dream is sad. [11]But whether it succeeds or fails is not its core, but just the flimsy covering.

5. How happy would your dreams become if you were not the one who gave the "proper" role to every figure which the dream contains. [2]No one can fail but your idea of him, and there is no betrayal but of this. [3]The core of dreams the Holy Spirit gives is never one of fear. [4]The coverings may not appear to change, but what they mean has changed because they cover something else. [5]Perceptions are determined by their purpose, in that they seem to be what they are for. [6]A shadow figure who attacks becomes a brother giving you a chance to help, if this becomes the function of the dream. [7]And dreams of sadness thus are turned to joy.

6. What is your brother for? [2]You do not know, because your function is obscure to you. [3]Do not ascribe a role to him that you imagine would bring happiness to you. [4]And do not try to hurt him when he fails to take the part that you assigned to him, in what you dream your life was meant to be. [5]He asks for help in every dream he has, and you have help to give him if you see the function of the dream as He perceives its function, Who can utilize all dreams as means to serve the function given Him. [6]Because He loves the dreamer, not the dream, each dream becomes an offering of love. [7]For at its center is His Love for you, which lights whatever form it takes with love.

V. The Changeless Dwelling Place

1. There is a place in you where this whole world has been forgotten; where no memory of sin and of illusion lingers still. ²There is a place in you which time has left, and echoes of eternity are heard. ³There is a resting place so still no sound except a hymn to Heaven rises up to gladden God the Father and the Son. ⁴Where Both abide are They remembered, Both. ⁵And where They are is Heaven and is peace.

2. Think not that you can change Their dwelling place. ²For your Identity abides in Them, and where They are, forever must you be. ³The changelessness of Heaven is in you, so deep within that nothing in this world but passes by, unnoticed and unseen. ⁴The still infinity of endless peace surrounds you gently in its soft embrace, so strong and quiet, tranquil in the might of its Creator, nothing can intrude upon the sacred Son of God within.

3. Here is the role the Holy Spirit gives to you who wait upon the Son of God, and would behold him waken and be glad. ²He is a part of you and you of him, because he is his Father's Son, and not for any purpose you may see in him. ³Nothing is asked of you but to accept the changeless and eternal that abide in him, for your Identity is there. ⁴The peace in you can but be found in him. ⁵And every thought of love you offer him but brings you nearer to your wakening to peace eternal and to endless joy.

4. This sacred Son of God is like yourself; the mirror of his Father's Love for you, the soft reminder of his Father's Love by which he was created and which still abides in him as it abides in you. ²Be very still and hear God's Voice in him, and let It tell you what his function is. ³He was created that you might be whole, for only the complete can be a part of God's completion, which created you.

5. There is no gift the Father asks of you but that you see in all creation but the shining glory of His gift to you. ²Behold His Son, His perfect gift, in whom his Father shines forever, and to whom is all creation given as his own. ³Because he has it is it given you, and where it lies in him behold your peace. ⁴The quiet that surrounds you dwells in him, and from this quiet come the happy dreams in which your hands are joined in innocence. ⁵These are not hands that grasp in dreams of pain. ⁶They hold no sword, for they have left their hold on every vain illusion of the world. ⁷And being empty they receive, instead, a

brother's hand in which completion lies.

6. If you but knew the glorious goal that lies beyond forgiveness, you would not keep hold on any thought, however light the touch of evil on it may appear to be. [2]For you would understand how great the cost of holding anything God did not give in minds that can direct the hand to bless, and lead God's Son unto his Father's house. [3]Would you not want to be a friend to him, created by his Father as His home? [4]If God esteems him worthy of Himself, would you attack him with the hands of hate? [5]Who would lay bloody hands on Heaven itself, and hope to find its peace? [6]Your brother thinks he holds the hand of death. [7]Believe him not. [8]But learn, instead, how blessed are you who can release him, just by offering him yours.

7. A dream is given you in which he is your savior, not your enemy in hate. [2]A dream is given you in which you have forgiven him for all his dreams of death; a dream of hope you share with him, instead of dreaming evil separate dreams of hate. [3]Why does it seem so hard to share this dream? [4]Because unless the Holy Spirit gives the dream its function, it was made for hate, and will continue in death's services. [5]Each form it takes in some way calls for death. [6]And those who serve the lord of death have come to worship in a separated world, each with his tiny spear and rusted sword, to keep his ancient promises to die.

8. Such is the core of fear in every dream that has been kept apart from use by Him Who sees a different function for a dream. [2]When dreams are shared they lose the function of attack and separation, even though it was for this that every dream was made. [3]Yet nothing in the world of dreams remains without the hope of change and betterment, for here is not where changelessness is found. [4]Let us be glad indeed that this is so, and seek not the eternal in this world. [5]Forgiving dreams are means to step aside from dreaming of a world outside yourself. [6]And leading finally beyond all dreams, unto the peace of everlasting life.

VI. Forgiveness and the End of Time

1. How willing are you to forgive your brother? [2]How much do you desire peace instead of endless strife and misery and pain? [3]These questions are the same, in different form. [4]Forgiveness is your peace, for herein lies the end of separation and the dream of

615

danger and destruction, sin and death; of madness and of murder, grief and loss. [5]This is the "sacrifice" salvation asks, and gladly offers peace instead of this.

2. Swear not to die, you holy Son of God! [2]You make a bargain that you cannot keep. [3]The Son of Life cannot be killed. [4]He is immortal as his Father. [5]What he is cannot be changed. [6]He is the only thing in all the universe that must be one. [7]What *seems* eternal all will have an end. [8]The stars will disappear, and night and day will be no more. [9]All things that come and go, the tides, the seasons and the lives of men; all things that change with time and bloom and fade will not return. [10]Where time has set an end is not where the eternal is. [11]God's Son can never change by what men made of him. [12]He will be as he was and as he is, for time appointed not his destiny, nor set the hour of his birth and death. [13]Forgiveness will not change him. [14]Yet time waits upon forgiveness that the things of time may disappear because they have no use.

3. Nothing survives its purpose. [2]If it be conceived to die, then die it must unless it does not take this purpose as its own. [3]Change is the only thing that can be made a blessing here, where purpose is not fixed, however changeless it appears to be. [4]Think not that you can set a goal unlike God's purpose for you, and establish it as changeless and eternal. [5]You can give yourself a purpose that you do not have. [6]But you can not remove the power to change your mind, and see another purpose there.

4. Change is the greatest gift God gave to all that you would make eternal, to ensure that only Heaven would not pass away. [2]You were not born to die. [3]You cannot change, because your function has been fixed by God. [4]All other goals are set in time and change that time might be preserved, excepting one. [5]Forgiveness does not aim at keeping time, but at its ending, when it has no use. [6]Its purpose ended, it is gone. [7]And where it once held seeming sway is now restored the function God established for His Son in full awareness. [8]Time can set no end to its fulfillment nor its changelessness. [9]There is no death because the living share the function their Creator gave to them. [10]Life's function cannot be to die. [11]It must be life's extension, that it be as one forever and forever, without end.

5. This world will bind your feet and tie your hands and kill your body only if you think that it was made to crucify God's Son. [2]For even though it was a dream of death, you need not let it stand for

this to you. ³Let *this* be changed, and nothing in the world but must be changed as well. ⁴For nothing here but is defined as what you see it for.

6. How lovely is the world whose purpose is forgiveness of God's Son! ²How free from fear, how filled with blessing and with happiness! ³And what a joyous thing it is to dwell a little while in such a happy place! ⁴Nor can it be forgot, in such a world, it *is* a little while till timelessness comes quietly to take the place of time.

VII. Seek Not Outside Yourself

1. Seek not outside yourself. ²For it will fail, and you will weep each time an idol falls. ³Heaven cannot be found where it is not, and there can be no peace excepting there. ⁴Each idol that you worship when God calls will never answer in His place. ⁵There is no other answer you can substitute, and find the happiness His answer brings. ⁶Seek not outside yourself. ⁷For all your pain comes simply from a futile search for what you want, insisting where it must be found. ⁸What if it is not there? ⁹Do you prefer that you be right or happy? ¹⁰Be you glad that you are told where happiness abides, and seek no longer elsewhere. ¹¹You will fail. ¹²But it is given you to know the truth, and not to seek for it outside yourself.

2. No one who comes here but must still have hope, some lingering illusion, or some dream that there is something outside of himself that will bring happiness and peace to him. ²If everything is in him this cannot be so. ³And therefore by his coming, he denies the truth about himself, and seeks for something more than everything, as if a part of it were separated off and found where all the rest of it is not. ⁴This is the purpose he bestows upon the body; that it seek for what he lacks, and give him what would make himself complete. ⁵And thus he wanders aimlessly about, in search of something that he cannot find, believing that he is what he is not.

3. The lingering illusion will impel him to seek out a thousand idols, and to seek beyond them for a thousand more. ²And each will fail him, all excepting one; for he will die, and does not understand the idol that he seeks *is* but his death. ³Its form appears to be outside himself. ⁴Yet does he seek to kill God's Son within,

617

and prove that he is victor over him. ⁵This is the purpose every idol has, for this the role that is assigned to it, and this the role that cannot be fulfilled.

4.   Whenever you attempt to reach a goal in which the body's betterment is cast as major beneficiary, you try to bring about your death. ²For you believe that you can suffer lack, and lack *is* death. ³To sacrifice is to give up, and thus to be without and to have suffered loss. ⁴And by this giving up is life renounced. ⁵Seek not outside yourself. ⁶The search implies you are not whole within and fear to look upon your devastation, but prefer to seek outside yourself for what you are.

5.   Idols must fall *because* they have no life, and what is lifeless is a sign of death. ²You came to die, and what would you expect but to perceive the signs of death you seek? ³No sadness and no suffering proclaim a message other than an idol found that represents a parody of life which, in its lifelessness, is really death, conceived as real and given living form. ⁴Yet each must fail and crumble and decay, because a form of death cannot be life, and what is sacrificed cannot be whole.

6.   All idols of this world were made to keep the truth within from being known to you, and to maintain allegiance to the dream that you must find what is outside yourself to be complete and happy. ²It is vain to worship idols in the hope of peace. ³God dwells within, and your completion lies in Him. ⁴No idol takes His place. ⁵Look not to idols. ⁶Do not seek outside yourself.

7.   Let us forget the purpose of the world the past has given it. ²For otherwise, the future will be like the past, and but a series of depressing dreams, in which all idols fail you, one by one, and you see death and disappointment everywhere.

8.   To change all this, and open up a road of hope and of release in what appeared to be an endless circle of despair, you need but to decide you do not know the purpose of the world. ²You give it goals it does not have, and thus do you decide what it is for. ³You try to see in it a place of idols found outside yourself, with power to make complete what is within by splitting what you are between the two. ⁴You choose your dreams, for they are what you wish, perceived as if it had been given you. ⁵Your idols do what you would have them do, and have the power you ascribe to them. ⁶And you pursue them vainly in the dream, because you want their power as your own.

9.   Yet where are dreams but in a mind asleep? ²And can a dream

succeed in making real the picture it projects outside itself? ³Save time, my brother; learn what time is for. ⁴And speed the end of idols in a world made sad and sick by seeing idols there. ⁵Your holy mind is altar unto God, and where He is no idols can abide. ⁶The fear of God is but the fear of loss of idols. ⁷It is not the fear of loss of your reality. ⁸But you have made of your reality an idol, which you must protect against the light of truth. ⁹And all the world becomes the means by which this idol can be saved. ¹⁰Salvation thus appears to threaten life and offer death.

10. It is not so. ²Salvation seeks to prove there is no death, and only life exists. ³The sacrifice of death is nothing lost. ⁴An idol cannot take the place of God. ⁵Let Him remind you of His Love for you, and do not seek to drown His Voice in chants of deep despair to idols of yourself. ⁶Seek not outside your Father for your hope. ⁷For hope of happiness is *not* despair.

VIII. The Anti-Christ

1. What is an idol? ²Do you think you know? ³For idols are unrecognized as such, and never seen for what they really are. ⁴That is the only power that they have. ⁵Their purpose is obscure, and they are feared and worshipped, both, *because* you do not know what they are for, and why they have been made. ⁶An idol is an image of your brother that you would value more than what he is. ⁷Idols are made that he may be replaced, no matter what their form. ⁸And it is this that never is perceived and recognized. ⁹Be it a body or a thing, a place, a situation or a circumstance, an object owned or wanted, or a right demanded or achieved, it is the same.

2. Let not their form deceive you. ²Idols are but substitutes for your reality. ³In some way, you believe they will complete your little self, for safety in a world perceived as dangerous, with forces massed against your confidence and peace of mind. ⁴They have the power to supply your lacks, and add the value that you do not have. ⁵No one believes in idols who has not enslaved himself to littleness and loss. ⁶And thus must seek beyond his little self for strength to raise his head, and stand apart from all the misery the world reflects. ⁷This is the penalty for looking not within for certainty and quiet calm that liberates you from the world, and lets you stand apart, in quiet and in peace.

3.　An idol is a false impression, or a false belief; some form of anti-Christ, that constitutes a gap between the Christ and what you see. ²An idol is a wish, made tangible and given form, and thus perceived as real and seen outside the mind. ³Yet it is still a thought, and cannot leave the mind that is its source. ⁴Nor is its form apart from the idea it represents. ⁵All forms of anti-Christ oppose the Christ. ⁶And fall before His face like a dark veil that seems to shut you off from Him, alone in darkness. ⁷Yet the light is there. ⁸A cloud does not put out the sun. ⁹No more a veil can banish what it seems to separate, nor darken by one whit the light itself.

4.　This world of idols *is* a veil across the face of Christ, because its purpose is to separate your brother from yourself. ²A dark and fearful purpose, yet a thought without the power to change one blade of grass from something living to a sign of death. ³Its form is nowhere, for its source abides within your mind where God abideth not. ⁴Where is this place where what is everywhere has been excluded and been kept apart? ⁵What hand could be held up to block God's way? ⁶Whose voice could make demand He enter not? ⁷The "more-than-everything" is not a thing to make you tremble and to quail in fear. ⁸Christ's enemy is nowhere. ⁹He can take no form in which he ever will be real.

5.　What is an idol? ²Nothing! ³It must be believed before it seems to come to life, and given power that it may be feared. ⁴Its life and power are its believer's gift, and this is what the miracle restores to what *has* life and power worthy of the gift of Heaven and eternal peace. ⁵The miracle does not restore the truth, the light the veil between has not put out. ⁶It merely lifts the veil, and lets the truth shine unencumbered, being what it is. ⁷It does not need belief to be itself, for it has been created; so it *is*.

6.　An idol is established by belief, and when it is withdrawn the idol "dies." ²This is the anti-Christ; the strange idea there is a power past omnipotence, a place beyond the infinite, a time transcending the eternal. ³Here the world of idols has been set by the idea this power and place and time are given form, and shape the world where the impossible has happened. ⁴Here the deathless come to die, the all-encompassing to suffer loss, the timeless to be made the slaves of time. ⁵Here does the changeless change; the peace of God, forever given to all living things, give way to chaos. ⁶And the Son of God, as perfect, sinless and as loving as his Father, come to hate a little while; to suffer pain and finally to die.

7. Where is an idol? [2]Nowhere! [3]Can there be a gap in what is infinite, a place where time can interrupt eternity? [4]A place of darkness set where all is light, a dismal alcove separated off from what is endless, *has* no place to be. [5]An idol is beyond where God has set all things forever, and has left no room for anything to be except His Will. [6]Nothing and nowhere must an idol be, while God is everything and everywhere.

8. What purpose has an idol, then? [2]What is it for? [3]This is the only question that has many answers, each depending on the one of whom the question has been asked. [4]The world believes in idols. [5]No one comes unless he worshipped them, and still attempts to seek for one that yet might offer him a gift reality does not contain. [6]Each worshipper of idols harbors hope his special deities will give him more than other men possess. [7]It must be more. [8]It does not really matter more of what; more beauty, more intelligence, more wealth, or even more affliction and more pain. [9]But more of something is an idol for. [10]And when one fails another takes its place, with hope of finding more of something else. [11]Be not deceived by forms the "something" takes. [12]An idol is a means for getting more. [13]And it is this that is against God's Will.

9. God has not many Sons, but only One. [2]Who can have more, and who be given less? [3]In Heaven would the Son of God but laugh, if idols could intrude upon his peace. [4]It is for him the Holy Spirit speaks, and tells you idols have no purpose here. [5]For more than Heaven can you never have. [6]If Heaven is within, why would you seek for idols that would make of Heaven less, to give you more than God bestowed upon your brother and on you, as one with Him? [7]God gave you all there is. [8]And to be sure you could not lose it, did He also give the same to every living thing as well. [9]And thus is every living thing a part of you, as of Himself. [10]No idol can establish you as more than God. [11]But you will never be content with being less.

IX. The Forgiving Dream

1. The slave of idols is a willing slave. ²For willing he must be to let himself bow down in worship to what has no life, and seek for power in the powerless. ³What happened to the holy Son of God that this could be his wish; to let himself fall lower than the stones upon the ground, and look to idols that they raise him up? ⁴Hear, then, your story in the dream you made, and ask yourself if it be not the truth that you believe that it is not a dream.

2. A dream of judgment came into the mind that God created perfect as Himself. ²And in that dream was Heaven changed to hell, and God made enemy unto His Son. ³How can God's Son awaken from the dream? ⁴It is a dream of judgment. ⁵So must he judge not, and he will waken. ⁶For the dream will seem to last while he is part of it. ⁷Judge not, for he who judges will have need of idols, which will hold the judgment off from resting on himself. ⁸Nor can he know the Self he has condemned. ⁹Judge not, because you make yourself a part of evil dreams, where idols are your "true" identity, and your salvation from the judgment laid in terror and in guilt upon yourself.

3. All figures in the dream are idols, made to save you from the dream. ²Yet they are part of what they have been made to save you *from*. ³Thus does an idol keep the dream alive and terrible, for who could wish for one unless he were in terror and despair? ⁴And this the idol represents, and so its worship is the worship of despair and terror, and the dream from which they come. ⁵Judgment is an injustice to God's Son, and it *is* justice that who judges him will not escape the penalty he laid upon himself within the dream he made. ⁶God knows of justice, not of penalty. ⁷But in the dream of judgment you attack and are condemned; and wish to be the slave of idols, which are interposed between your judgment and the penalty it brings.

4. There can be no salvation in the dream as you are dreaming it. ²For idols must be part of it, to save you from what you believe you have accomplished, and have done to make you sinful and put out the light within you. ³Little child, the light is there. ⁴You do but dream, and idols are the toys you dream you play with. ⁵Who has need of toys but children? ⁶They pretend they rule the world, and give their toys the power to move about, and talk and think and feel and speak for them. ⁷Yet everything their toys appear to do is in the minds of those who play with them. ⁸But they

are eager to forget that they made up the dream in which their toys are real, nor recognize their wishes are their own.

5. Nightmares are childish dreams. ²The toys have turned against the child who thought he made them real. ³Yet can a dream attack? ⁴Or can a toy grow large and dangerous and fierce and wild? ⁵This does the child believe, because he fears his thoughts and gives them to the toys instead. ⁶And their reality becomes his own, because they seem to save him from his thoughts. ⁷Yet do they keep his thoughts alive and real, but seen outside himself, where they can turn against him for his treachery to them. ⁸He thinks he needs them that he may escape his thoughts, because he thinks the thoughts are real. ⁹And so he makes of anything a toy, to make his world remain outside himself, and play that he is but a part of it.

6. There is a time when childhood should be passed and gone forever. ²Seek not to retain the toys of children. ³Put them all away, for you have need of them no more. ⁴The dream of judgment is a children's game, in which the child becomes the father, powerful, but with the little wisdom of a child. ⁵What hurts him is destroyed; what helps him, blessed. ⁶Except he judges this as does a child, who does not know what hurts and what will heal. ⁷And bad things seem to happen, and he is afraid of all the chaos in a world he thinks is governed by the laws he made. ⁸Yet is the real world unaffected by the world he thinks is real. ⁹Nor have its laws been changed because he does not understand.

7. The real world still is but a dream. ²Except the figures have been changed. ³They are not seen as idols which betray. ⁴It is a dream in which no one is used to substitute for something else, nor interposed between the thoughts the mind conceives and what it sees. ⁵No one is used for something he is not, for childish things have all been put away. ⁶And what was once a dream of judgment now has changed into a dream where all is joy, because that is the purpose that it has. ⁷Only forgiving dreams can enter here, for time is almost over. ⁸And the forms that enter in the dream are now perceived as brothers, not in judgment, but in love.

8. Forgiving dreams have little need to last. ²They are not made to separate the mind from what it thinks. ³They do not seek to prove the dream is being dreamed by someone else. ⁴And in these dreams a melody is heard that everyone remembers, though he has not heard it since before all time began. ⁵Forgive-

ness, once complete, brings timelessness so close the song of Heaven can be heard, not with the ears, but with the holiness that never left the altar that abides forever deep within the Son of God. ⁶And when he hears this song again, he knows he never heard it not. ⁷And where is time, when dreams of judgment have been put away?

9.   Whenever you feel fear in any form,—and you *are* fearful if you do not feel a deep content, a certainty of help, a calm assurance Heaven goes with you,—be sure you made an idol, and believe it will betray you. ²For beneath your hope that it will save you lie the guilt and pain of self-betrayal and uncertainty, so deep and bitter that the dream cannot conceal completely all your sense of doom. ³Your self-betrayal must result in fear, for fear *is* judgment, leading surely to the frantic search for idols and for death.

10.   Forgiving dreams remind you that you live in safety and have not attacked yourself. ²So do your childish terrors melt away, and dreams become a sign that you have made a new beginning, not another try to worship idols and to keep attack. ³Forgiving dreams are kind to everyone who figures in the dream. ⁴And so they bring the dreamer full release from dreams of fear. ⁵He does not fear his judgment for he has judged no one, nor has sought to be released through judgment from what judgment must impose. ⁶And all the while he is remembering what he forgot, when judgment seemed to be the way to save him from its penalty.

Chapter 30

THE NEW BEGINNING

Introduction

1.   The new beginning now becomes the focus of the curriculum. ²The goal is clear, but now you need specific methods for attaining it. ³The speed by which it can be reached depends on this one thing alone; your willingness to practice every step. ⁴Each one will help a little, every time it is attempted. ⁵And together will these steps lead you from dreams of judgment to forgiving dreams and out of pain and fear. ⁶They are not new to you, but they are more ideas than rules of thought to you as yet. ⁷So now we need to practice them awhile, until they are the rules by which you live. ⁸We seek to make them habits now, so you will have them ready for whatever need.

I. Rules for Decision

1.   Decisions are continuous. ²You do not always know when you are making them. ³But with a little practice with the ones you recognize, a set begins to form which sees you through the rest. ⁴It is not wise to let yourself become preoccupied with every step you take. ⁵The proper set, adopted consciously each time you wake, will put you well ahead. ⁶And if you find resistance strong and dedication weak, you are not ready. ⁷*Do not fight yourself.* ⁸But think about the kind of day you want, and tell yourself there is a way in which this very day can happen just like that. ⁹Then try again to have the day you want.
2.   (1) The outlook starts with this:

²*Today I will make no decisions by myself.*

³This means that you are choosing not to be the judge of what to do. ⁴But it must also mean you will not judge the situations where you will be called upon to make response. ⁵For if you judge them, you have set the rules for how you should react to them. ⁶And then another answer cannot but produce confusion

625

and uncertainty and fear.

3. This is your major problem now. ²You still make up your mind, and *then* decide to ask what you should do. ³And what you hear may not resolve the problem as you saw it first. ⁴This leads to fear, because it contradicts what you perceive and so you feel attacked. ⁵And therefore angry. ⁶There are rules by which this will not happen. ⁷But it does occur at first, while you are learning how to hear.

4. (2) Throughout the day, at any time you think of it and have a quiet moment for reflection, tell yourself again the kind of day you want; the feelings you would have, the things you want to happen to you, and the things you would experience, and say:

> ²*If I make no decisions by myself, this is the day that will be given me.*

³These two procedures, practiced well, will serve to let you be directed without fear, for opposition will not first arise and then become a problem in itself.

5. But there will still be times when you have judged already. ²Now the answer will provoke attack, unless you quickly straighten out your mind to want an answer that will work. ³Be certain this has happened if you feel yourself unwilling to sit by and ask to have the answer given you. ⁴This means you have decided by yourself, and can not see the question. ⁵Now you need a quick restorative before you ask again.

6. (3) Remember once again the day you want, and recognize that something has occurred that is not part of it. ²Then realize that you have asked a question by yourself, and must have set an answer in your terms. ³Then say:

> ⁴*I have no question.* ⁵*I forgot what to decide.*

⁶This cancels out the terms that you have set, and lets the answer show you what the question must have really been.

7. Try to observe this rule without delay, despite your opposition. ²For you have already gotten angry. ³And your fear of being answered in a different way from what your version of the question asks will gain momentum, until you believe the day you want is one in which you get *your* answer to *your* question. ⁴And you will not get it, for it would destroy the day by robbing you of what

you really want. [5]This can be very hard to realize, when once you have decided by yourself the rules that promise you a happy day. [6]Yet this decision still can be undone, by simple methods that you can accept.

8. (4) If you are so unwilling to receive you cannot even let your question go, you can begin to change your mind with this:

[2]*At least I can decide I do not like what I feel now.*

[3]This much is obvious, and paves the way for the next easy step.

9. (5) Having decided that you do not like the way you feel, what could be easier than to continue with:

[2]*And so I hope I have been wrong.*

[3]This works against the sense of opposition, and reminds you that help is not being thrust upon you but is something that you want and that you need, because you do not like the way you feel. [4]This tiny opening will be enough to let you go ahead with just a few more steps you need to let yourself be helped.

10. Now you have reached the turning point, because it has occurred to you that you will gain if what you have decided is not so. [2]Until this point is reached, you will believe your happiness depends on being right. [3]But this much reason have you now attained; you would be better off if you were wrong.

11. (6) This tiny grain of wisdom will suffice to take you further. [2]You are not coerced, but merely hope to get a thing you want. [3]And you can say in perfect honesty:

[4]*I want another way to look at this.*

[5]Now you have changed your mind about the day, and have remembered what you really want. [6]Its purpose has no longer been obscured by the insane belief you want it for the goal of being right when you are wrong. [7]Thus is the readiness for asking brought to your awareness, for you cannot be in conflict when you ask for what you want, and see that it is this for which you ask.

12. (7) This final step is but acknowledgment of lack of opposition to be helped. [2]It is a statement of an open mind, not certain yet, but willing to be shown:

^{3}*Perhaps there is another way to look at this.* ^{4}*What can I lose by asking?*

^{5}Thus you now can ask a question that makes sense, and so the answer will make sense as well. ^{6}Nor will you fight against it, for you see that it is you who will be helped by it.

13. It must be clear that it is easier to have a happy day if you prevent unhappiness from entering at all. ^{2}But this takes practice in the rules that will protect you from the ravages of fear. ^{3}When this has been achieved, the sorry dream of judgment has forever been undone. ^{4}But meanwhile, you have need for practicing the rules for its undoing. ^{5}Let us, then, consider once again the very first of the decisions which are offered here.

14. We said you can begin a happy day with the determination not to make decisions by yourself. ^{2}This seems to be a real decision in itself. ^{3}And yet, you *cannot* make decisions by yourself. ^{4}The only question really is with what you choose to make them. ^{5}That is really all. ^{6}The first rule, then, is not coercion, but a simple statement of a simple fact. ^{7}You will not make decisions by yourself whatever you decide. ^{8}For they are made with idols or with God. ^{9}And you ask help of anti-Christ or Christ, and which you choose will join with you and tell you what to do.

15. Your day is not at random. ^{2}It is set by what you choose to live it with, and how the friend whose counsel you have sought perceives your happiness. ^{3}You always ask advice before you can decide on anything. ^{4}Let this be understood, and you can see there cannot be coercion here, nor grounds for opposition that you may be free. ^{5}There is no freedom from what must occur. ^{6}And if you think there is, you must be wrong.

16. The second rule as well is but a fact. ^{2}For you and your adviser must agree on what you want before it can occur. ^{3}It is but this agreement that permits all things to happen. ^{4}Nothing can be caused without some form of union, be it with a dream of judgment or the Voice for God. ^{5}Decisions cause results *because* they are not made in isolation. ^{6}They are made by you and your adviser, for yourself and for the world as well. ^{7}The day you want you offer to the world, for it will be what you have asked for, and will reinforce the rule of your adviser in the world. ^{8}Whose kingdom is the world for you today? ^{9}What kind of day will you decide to have?

17. It needs but two who would have happiness this day to

promise it to all the world. ²It needs but two to understand that they cannot decide alone, to guarantee the joy they asked for will be wholly shared. ³For they have understood the basic law that makes decision powerful, and gives it all effects that it will ever have. ⁴It needs but two. ⁵These two are joined before there can be a decision. ⁶Let this be the one reminder that you keep in mind, and you will have the day you want, and give it to the world by having it yourself. ⁷Your judgment has been lifted from the world by your decision for a happy day. ⁸And as you have received, so must you give.

II. Freedom of Will

1. Do you not understand that to oppose the Holy Spirit is to fight *yourself*? ²He tells you but your will; He speaks for you. ³In His Divinity is but your own. ⁴And all He knows is but your knowledge, saved for you that you may do your will through Him. ⁵God *asks* you do your will. ⁶He joins with *you*. ⁷He did not set His Kingdom up alone. ⁸And Heaven itself but represents your will, where everything created is for you. ⁹No spark of life but was created with your glad consent, as you would have it be. ¹⁰And not one Thought that God has ever had but waited for your blessing to be born. ¹¹God is no enemy to you. ¹²He asks no more than that He hear you call Him "Friend."

2. How wonderful it is to do your will! ²For that is freedom. ³There is nothing else that ever should be called by freedom's name. ⁴Unless you do your will you are not free. ⁵And would God leave His Son without what he has chosen for himself? ⁶God but ensured that you would never lose your will when He gave you His perfect Answer. ⁷Hear It now, that you may be reminded of His Love and learn your will. ⁸God would not have His Son made prisoner to what he does not want. ⁹He joins with you in willing you be free. ¹⁰And to oppose Him is to make a choice against yourself, and choose that you be bound.

3. Look once again upon your enemy, the one you chose to hate instead of love. ²For thus was hatred born into the world, and thus the rule of fear established there. ³Now hear God speak to you, through Him Who is His Voice and yours as well, reminding you that it is not your will to hate and be a prisoner to fear, a slave to death, a little creature with a little life. ⁴Your will is

boundless; it is not your will that it be bound. [5]What lies in you has joined with God Himself in all creation's birth. [6]Remember Him Who has created you, and through your will created everything. [7]Not one created thing but gives you thanks, for it is by your will that it was born. [8]No light of Heaven shines except for you, for it was set in Heaven by your will.

4. What cause have you for anger in a world that merely waits your blessing to be free? [2]If you be prisoner, then God Himself could not be free. [3]For what is done to him whom God so loves is done to God Himself. [4]Think not He wills to bind you, Who has made you co-creator of the universe along with Him. [5]He would but keep your will forever and forever limitless. [6]This world awaits the freedom you will give when you have recognized that you are free. [7]But you will not forgive the world until you have forgiven Him Who gave your will to you. [8]For it is by your will the world is given freedom. [9]Nor can you be free apart from Him Whose holy Will you share.

5. God turns to you to ask the world be saved, for by your own salvation is it healed. [2]And no one walks upon the earth but must depend on your decision, that he learn death has no power over him, because he shares your freedom as he shares your will. [3]It *is* your will to heal him, and because you have decided with him, he is healed. [4]And now is God forgiven, for you chose to look upon your brother as a friend.

III. Beyond All Idols

1. Idols are quite specific. [2]But your will is universal, being limitless. [3]And so it has no form, nor is content for its expression in the terms of form. [4]Idols are limits. [5]They are the belief that there are forms that will bring happiness, and that, by limiting, is all attained. [6]It is as if you said, "I have no need of everything. [7]This little thing I want, and it will be as everything to me." [8]And this must fail to satisfy, because it is your will that everything be yours. [9]Decide for idols and you ask for loss. [10]Decide for truth and everything is yours.

2. It is not form you seek. [2]What form can be a substitute for God the Father's Love? [3]What form can take the place of all the love in the Divinity of God the Son? [4]What idol can make two of what is one? [5]And can the limitless be limited? [6]You do not want an idol.

⁷It is not your will to have one. ⁸It will not bestow on you the gift you seek. ⁹When you decide upon the form of what you want, you lose the understanding of its purpose. ¹⁰So you see your will within the idol, thus reducing it to a specific form. ¹¹Yet this could never be your will, because what shares in all creation cannot be content with small ideas and little things.

3.   Behind the search for every idol lies the yearning for completion. ²Wholeness has no form because it is unlimited. ³To seek a special person or a thing to add to you to make yourself complete, can only mean that you believe some form is missing. ⁴And by finding this, you will achieve completion in a form you like. ⁵This is the purpose of an idol; that you will not look beyond it, to the source of the belief that you are incomplete. ⁶Only if you had sinned could this be so. ⁷For sin is the idea you are alone and separated off from what is whole. ⁸And thus it would be necessary for the search for wholeness to be made beyond the boundaries of limits on yourself.

4.   It never is the idol that you want. ²But what you think it offers you, you want indeed and have the right to ask for. ³Nor could it be possible it be denied. ⁴Your will to be complete is but God's Will, and this is given you by being His. ⁵God knows not form. ⁶He cannot answer you in terms that have no meaning. ⁷And your will could not be satisfied with empty forms, made but to fill a gap that is not there. ⁸It is not this you want. ⁹Creation gives no separate person and no separate thing the power to complete the Son of God. ¹⁰What idol can be called upon to give the Son of God what he already has?

5.   Completion is the *function* of God's Son. ²He has no need to seek for it at all. ³Beyond all idols stands his holy will to be but what he is. ⁴For more than whole is meaningless. ⁵If there were change in him, if he could be reduced to any form and limited to what is not in him, he would not be as God created him. ⁶What idol can he need to be himself? ⁷For can he give a part of him away? ⁸What is not whole cannot make whole. ⁹But what is really asked for cannot be denied. ¹⁰Your will *is* granted. ¹¹Not in any form that would content you not, but in the whole completely lovely Thought God holds of you.

6.   Nothing that God knows not exists. ²And what He knows exists forever, changelessly. ³For thoughts endure as long as does the mind that thought of them. ⁴And in the Mind of God there is no ending, nor a time in which His Thoughts were absent or

could suffer change. [5]Thoughts are not born and cannot die. [6]They share the attributes of their creator, nor have they a separate life apart from his. [7]The thoughts you think are in your mind, as you are in the Mind which thought of you. [8]And so there are no separate parts in what exists within God's Mind. [9]It is forever One, eternally united and at peace.

7.   Thoughts seem to come and go. [2]Yet all this means is that you are sometimes aware of them, and sometimes not. [3]An unremembered thought is born again to you when it returns to your awareness. [4]Yet it did not die when you forgot it. [5]It was always there, but you were unaware of it. [6]The Thought God holds of you is perfectly unchanged by your forgetting. [7]It will always be exactly as it was before the time when you forgot, and will be just the same when you remember. [8]And it is the same within the interval when you forgot.

8.   The Thoughts of God are far beyond all change, and shine forever. [2]They await not birth. [3]They wait for welcome and remembering. [4]The Thought God holds of you is like a star, unchangeable in an eternal sky. [5]So high in Heaven is it set that those outside of Heaven know not it is there. [6]Yet still and white and lovely will it shine through all eternity. [7]There was no time it was not there; no instant when its light grew dimmer or less perfect ever was.

9.   Who knows the Father knows this light, for He is the eternal sky that holds it safe, forever lifted up and anchored sure. [2]Its perfect purity does not depend on whether it is seen on earth or not. [3]The sky embraces it and softly holds it in its perfect place, which is as far from earth as earth from Heaven. [4]It is not the distance nor the time that keeps this star invisible to earth. [5]But those who seek for idols cannot know the star is there.

10.   Beyond all idols is the Thought God holds of you. [2]Completely unaffected by the turmoil and the terror of the world, the dreams of birth and death that here are dreamed, the myriad of forms that fear can take; quite undisturbed, the Thought God holds of you remains exactly as it always was. [3]Surrounded by a stillness so complete no sound of battle comes remotely near, it rests in certainty and perfect peace. [4]Here is your one reality kept safe, completely unaware of all the world that worships idols, and that knows not God. [5]In perfect sureness of its changelessness and of its rest in its eternal home, the Thought God holds of you has never left the Mind of its Creator Whom it knows, as its Creator

knows that it is there.

11. Where could the Thought God holds of you exist but where you are? ²Is your reality a thing apart from you, and in a world which your reality knows nothing of? ³Outside you there is no eternal sky, no changeless star and no reality. ⁴The mind of Heaven's Son in Heaven is, for there the Mind of Father and of Son joined in creation which can have no end. ⁵You have not two realities, but one. ⁶Nor can you be aware of more than one. ⁷An idol *or* the Thought God holds of you is your reality. ⁸Forget not, then, that idols must keep hidden what you are, not from the Mind of God, but from your own. ⁹The star shines still; the sky has never changed. ¹⁰But you, the holy Son of God Himself, are unaware of your reality.

IV. The Truth behind Illusions

1. You will attack what does not satisfy, and thus you will not see you made it up. ²You always fight illusions. ³For the truth behind them is so lovely and so still in loving gentleness, were you aware of it you would forget defensiveness entirely, and rush to its embrace. ⁴The truth could never be attacked. ⁵And this you knew when you made idols. ⁶They were made that this might be forgotten. ⁷You attack but false ideas, and never truthful ones. ⁸All idols are the false ideas you made to fill the gap you think arose between yourself and what is true. ⁹And you attack them for the things you think they represent. ¹⁰What lies beyond them cannot be attacked.

2. The wearying, dissatisfying gods you made are blown-up children's toys. ²A child is frightened when a wooden head springs up as a closed box is opened suddenly, or when a soft and silent woolly bear begins to squeak as he takes hold of it. ³The rules he made for boxes and for bears have failed him, and have broken his "control" of what surrounds him. ⁴And he is afraid, because he thought the rules protected him. ⁵Now must he learn the boxes and the bears did not deceive him, broke no rules, nor mean his world is made chaotic and unsafe. ⁶He was mistaken. ⁷He misunderstood what made him safe, and thought that it had left.

3. The gap that is not there is filled with toys in countless forms. ²And each one seems to break the rules you set for it. ³It never

was the thing you thought. ⁴It must appear to break your rules for safety, since the rules were wrong. ⁵But *you* are not endangered. ⁶You can laugh at popping heads and squeaking toys, as does the child who learns they are no threat to him. ⁷Yet while he likes to play with them, he still perceives them as obeying rules he made for his enjoyment. ⁸So there still are rules that they can seem to break and frighten him. ⁹Yet *is* he at the mercy of his toys? ¹⁰And *can* they represent a threat to him?

4. Reality observes the laws of God, and not the rules you set. ²It is His laws that guarantee your safety. ³All illusions that you believe about yourself obey no laws. ⁴They seem to dance a little while, according to the rules you set for them. ⁵But then they fall and cannot rise again. ⁶They are but toys, my child, so do not grieve for them. ⁷Their dancing never brought you joy. ⁸But neither were they things to frighten you, nor make you safe if they obeyed your rules. ⁹They must be neither cherished nor attacked, but merely looked upon as children's toys without a single meaning of their own. ¹⁰See one in them and you will see them all. ¹¹See none in them and they will touch you not.

5. Appearances deceive *because* they are appearances and not reality. ²Dwell not on them in any form. ³They but obscure reality, and they bring fear *because* they hide the truth. ⁴Do not attack what you have made to let you be deceived, for thus you prove that you have been deceived. ⁵Attack has power to make illusions real. ⁶Yet what it makes is nothing. ⁷Who could be made fearful by a power that can have no real effects at all? ⁸What could it be but an illusion, making things appear like to itself? ⁹Look calmly at its toys, and understand that they are idols which but dance to vain desires. ¹⁰Give them not your worship, for they are not there. ¹¹Yet this is equally forgotten in attack. ¹²God's Son needs no defense against his dreams. ¹³His idols do not threaten him at all. ¹⁴His one mistake is that he thinks them real. ¹⁵What can the power of illusions do?

6. Appearances can but deceive the mind that wants to be deceived. ²And you can make a simple choice that will forever place you far beyond deception. ³You need not concern yourself with how this will be done, for this you cannot understand. ⁴But you will understand that mighty changes have been quickly brought about, when you decide one very simple thing; you do not want whatever you believe an idol gives. ⁵For thus the Son of God declares that he is free of idols. ⁶And thus *is* he free.

7. Salvation is a paradox indeed! ²What could it be except a happy dream? ³It asks you but that you forgive all things that no one ever did; to overlook what is not there, and not to look upon the unreal as reality. ⁴You are but asked to let your will be done, and seek no longer for the things you do not want. ⁵And you are asked to let yourself be free of all the dreams of what you never were, and seek no more to substitute the strength of idle wishes for the Will of God.

8. Here does the dream of separation start to fade and disappear. ²For here the gap that is not there begins to be perceived without the toys of terror that you made. ³No more than this is asked. ⁴Be glad indeed salvation asks so little, not so much. ⁵It asks for nothing in reality. ⁶And even in illusions it but asks forgiveness be the substitute for fear. ⁷Such is the only rule for happy dreams. ⁸The gap is emptied of the toys of fear, and then its unreality is plain. ⁹Dreams are for nothing. ¹⁰And the Son of God can have no need of them. ¹¹They offer him no single thing that he could ever want. ¹²He is delivered from illusions by his will, and but restored to what he is. ¹³What could God's plan for his salvation be, except a means to give him to Himself?

V. The Only Purpose

1. The real world is the state of mind in which the only purpose of the world is seen to be forgiveness. ²Fear is not its goal, for the escape from guilt becomes its aim. ³The value of forgiveness is perceived and takes the place of idols, which are sought no longer, for their "gifts" are not held dear. ⁴No rules are idly set, and no demands are made of anyone or anything to twist and fit into the dream of fear. ⁵Instead, there is a wish to understand all things created as they really are. ⁶And it is recognized that all things must be first forgiven, and *then* understood.

2. Here, it is thought that understanding is acquired by attack. ²There, it is clear that by attack is understanding lost. ³The folly of pursuing guilt as goal is fully recognized. ⁴And idols are not wanted there, for guilt is understood as the sole cause of pain in any form. ⁵No one is tempted by its vain appeal, for suffering and death have been perceived as things not wanted and not striven for. ⁶The possibility of freedom has been grasped and welcomed, and the means by which it can be gained can now be understood.

⁷The world becomes a place of hope, because its only purpose is to be a place where hope of happiness can be fulfilled. ⁸And no one stands outside this hope, because the world has been united in belief the purpose of the world is one which all must share, if hope be more than just a dream.

3.   Not yet is Heaven quite remembered, for the purpose of forgiveness still remains. ²Yet everyone is certain he will go beyond forgiveness, and he but remains until it is made perfect in himself. ³He has no wish for anything but this. ⁴And fear has dropped away, because he is united in his purpose with himself. ⁵There is a hope of happiness in him so sure and constant he can barely stay and wait a little longer, with his feet still touching earth. ⁶Yet is he glad to wait till every hand is joined, and every heart made ready to arise and go with him. ⁷For thus is he made ready for the step in which is all forgiveness left behind.

4.   The final step is God's, because it is but God Who could create a perfect Son and share His Fatherhood with him. ²No one outside of Heaven knows how this can be, for understanding this is Heaven itself. ³Even the real world has a purpose still beneath creation and eternity. ⁴But fear is gone because its purpose is forgiveness, not idolatry. ⁵And so is Heaven's Son prepared to be himself, and to remember that the Son of God knows everything his Father understands, and understands it perfectly with Him.

5.   The real world still falls short of this, for this is God's Own purpose; only His, and yet completely shared and perfectly fulfilled. ²The real world is a state in which the mind has learned how easily do idols go when they are still perceived but wanted not. ³How willingly the mind can let them go when it has understood that idols are nothing and nowhere, and are purposeless. ⁴For only then can guilt and sin be seen without a purpose, and as meaningless.

6.   Thus is the real world's purpose gently brought into awareness, to replace the goal of sin and guilt. ²And all that stood between your image of yourself and what you are, forgiveness washes joyfully away. ³Yet God need not create His Son again, that what is his be given back to him. ⁴The gap between your brother and yourself was never there. ⁵And what the Son of God knew in creation he must know again.

7.   When brothers join in purpose in the world of fear, they stand already at the edge of the real world. ²Perhaps they still look back, and think they see an idol that they want. ³Yet has their

path been surely set away from idols toward reality. ⁴For when they joined their hands it was Christ's hand they took, and they will look on Him Whose hand they hold. ⁵The face of Christ is looked upon before the Father is remembered. ⁶For He must be unremembered till His Son has reached beyond forgiveness to the Love of God. ⁷Yet is the Love of Christ accepted first. ⁸And then will come the knowledge They are one.

8. How light and easy is the step across the narrow boundaries of the world of fear when you have recognized Whose hand you hold! ²Within your hand is everything you need to walk with perfect confidence away from fear forever, and to go straight on, and quickly reach the gate of Heaven itself. ³For He Whose hand you hold was waiting but for you to join Him. ⁴Now that you have come, would He delay in showing you the way that He must walk with you? ⁵His blessing lies on you as surely as His Father's Love rests upon Him. ⁶His gratitude to you is past your understanding, for you have enabled Him to rise from chains and go with you, together, to His Father's house.

9. An ancient hate is passing from the world. ²And with it goes all hatred and all fear. ³Look back no longer, for what lies ahead is all you ever wanted in your heart. ⁴Give up the world! ⁵But not to sacrifice. ⁶You never wanted it. ⁷What happiness have you sought here that did not bring you pain? ⁸What moment of content has not been bought at fearful price in coins of suffering? ⁹Joy has no cost. ¹⁰It is your sacred right, and what you pay for is not happiness. ¹¹Be speeded on your way by honesty, and let not your experiences here deceive in retrospect. ¹²They were not free from bitter cost and joyless consequence.

10. Do not look back except in honesty. ²And when an idol tempts you, think of this:

> ³*There never was a time an idol brought you anything*
> *except the "gift" of guilt. ⁴Not one was bought except*
> *at cost of pain, nor was it ever paid by you alone.*

⁵Be merciful unto your brother, then. ⁶And do not choose an idol thoughtlessly, remembering that he will pay the cost as well as you. ⁷For he will be delayed when you look back, and you will not perceive Whose loving hand you hold. ⁸Look forward, then; in confidence walk with a happy heart that beats in hope and does not pound in fear.

11.   The Will of God forever lies in those whose hands are joined. ²Until they joined, they thought He was their enemy. ³But when they joined and shared a purpose, they were free to learn their will is one. ⁴And thus the Will of God must reach to their awareness. ⁵Nor can they forget for long that it is but their own.

VI. The Justification for Forgiveness

1.   Anger is *never* justified. ²Attack has *no* foundation. ³It is here escape from fear begins, and will be made complete. ⁴Here is the real world given in exchange for dreams of terror. ⁵For it is on this forgiveness rests, and is but natural. ⁶You are not asked to offer pardon where attack is due, and would be justified. ⁷For that would mean that you forgive a sin by overlooking what is really there. ⁸This is not pardon. ⁹For it would assume that, by responding in a way which is not justified, your pardon will become the answer to attack that has been made. ¹⁰And thus is pardon inappropriate, by being granted where it is not due.

2.   Pardon is *always* justified. ²It has a sure foundation. ³You do not forgive the unforgivable, nor overlook a real attack that calls for punishment. ⁴Salvation does not lie in being asked to make unnatural responses which are inappropriate to what is real. ⁵Instead, it merely asks that you respond appropriately to what is not real by not perceiving what has not occurred. ⁶If pardon were unjustified, you would be asked to sacrifice your rights when you return forgiveness for attack. ⁷But you are merely asked to see forgiveness as the natural reaction to distress that rests on error, and thus calls for help. ⁸Forgiveness is the only sane response. ⁹It *keeps* your rights from being sacrificed.

3.   This understanding is the only change that lets the real world rise to take the place of dreams of terror. ²Fear cannot arise unless attack is justified, and if it had a real foundation pardon would have none. ³The real world is achieved when you perceive the basis of forgiveness is quite real and fully justified. ⁴While you regard it as a gift unwarranted, it must uphold the guilt you would "forgive." ⁵Unjustified forgiveness is attack. ⁶And this is all the world can ever give. ⁷It pardons "sinners" sometimes, but remains aware that they have sinned. ⁸And so they do not merit the forgiveness that it gives.

4.   This is the false forgiveness which the world employs to keep

the sense of sin alive. [2]And recognizing God is just, it seems impossible His pardon could be real. [3]Thus is the fear of God the sure result of seeing pardon as unmerited. [4]No one who sees himself as guilty can avoid the fear of God. [5]But he is saved from this dilemma if he can forgive. [6]The mind must think of its Creator as it looks upon itself. [7]If you can see your brother merits pardon, you have learned forgiveness is your right as much as his. [8]Nor will you think that God intends for you a fearful judgment that your brother does not merit. [9]For it is the truth that you can merit neither more nor less than he.

5. Forgiveness recognized as merited will heal. [2]It gives the miracle its strength to overlook illusions. [3]This is how you learn that you must be forgiven too. [4]There can be no appearance that can not be overlooked. [5]For if there were, it would be necessary first there be some sin that stands beyond forgiveness. [6]There would be an error that is more than a mistake; a special form of error that remains unchangeable, eternal, and beyond correction or escape. [7]There would be one mistake that had the power to undo creation, and to make a world that could replace it and destroy the Will of God. [8]Only if this were possible could there be some appearances that could withstand the miracle, and not be healed by it.

6. There is no surer proof idolatry is what you wish than a belief there are some forms of sickness and of joylessness forgiveness cannot heal. [2]This means that you prefer to keep some idols, and are not prepared, as yet, to let all idols go. [3]And thus you think that some appearances are real and not appearances at all. [4]Be not deceived about the meaning of a fixed belief that some appearances are harder to look past than others are. [5]It always means you think forgiveness must be limited. [6]And you have set a goal of partial pardon and a limited escape from guilt for you. [7]What can this be except a false forgiveness of yourself, and everyone who seems apart from you?

7. It must be true the miracle can heal all forms of sickness, or it cannot heal. [2]Its purpose cannot be to judge which forms are real, and which appearances are true. [3]If one appearance must remain apart from healing, one illusion must be part of truth. [4]And you could not escape all guilt, but only some of it. [5]You must forgive God's Son entirely. [6]Or you will keep an image of yourself that is not whole, and will remain afraid to look within and find escape from every idol there. [7]Salvation rests on faith there cannot be

some forms of guilt that you cannot forgive. ⁸And so there cannot be appearances that have replaced the truth about God's Son.

8.   Look on your brother with the willingness to see him as he is. ²And do not keep a part of him outside your willingness that he be healed. ³To heal is to make whole. ⁴And what is whole can have no missing parts that have been kept outside. ⁵Forgiveness rests on recognizing this, and being glad there cannot be some forms of sickness which the miracle must lack the power to heal.

9.   God's Son is perfect, or he cannot be God's Son. ²Nor will you know him, if you think he does not merit the escape from guilt in all its consequences and its forms. ³There is no way to think of him but this, if you would know the truth about yourself.

> ⁴I thank You, Father, for Your perfect Son,
> and in his glory will I see my own.

⁵Here is the joyful statement that there are no forms of evil that can overcome the Will of God; the glad acknowledgment that guilt has not succeeded by your wish to make illusions real. ⁶And what is this except a simple statement of the truth?

10.   Look on your brother with this hope in you, and you will understand he could not make an error that could change the truth in him. ²It is not difficult to overlook mistakes that have been given no effects. ³But what you see as having power to make an idol of the Son of God you will not pardon. ⁴For he has become to you a graven image and a sign of death. ⁵Is this your savior? ⁶Is his Father wrong about His Son? ⁷Or have you been deceived in him who has been given you to heal, for your salvation and deliverance?

VII. The New Interpretation

1.   Would God have left the meaning of the world to your interpretation? ²If He had, it *has* no meaning. ³For it cannot be that meaning changes constantly, and yet is true. ⁴The Holy Spirit looks upon the world as with one purpose, changelessly established. ⁵And no situation can affect its aim, but must be in accord with it. ⁶For only if its aim could change with every situation could each one be open to interpretation which is different every time you think of it. ⁷You add an element into the script you write

for every minute in the day, and all that happens now means something else. [8]You take away another element, and every meaning shifts accordingly.

2. What do your scripts reflect except your plans for what the day *should* be? [2]And thus you judge disaster and success, advance, retreat, and gain and loss. [3]These judgments all are made according to the roles the script assigns. [4]The fact they have no meaning in themselves is demonstrated by the ease with which these labels change with other judgments, made on different aspects of experience. [5]And then, in looking back, you think you see another meaning in what went before. [6]What have you really done, except to show there was no meaning there? [7]But you assigned a meaning in the light of goals that change, with every meaning shifting as they change.

3. Only a constant purpose can endow events with stable meaning. [2]But it must accord *one* meaning to them all. [3]If they are given different meanings, it must be that they reflect but different purposes. [4]And this is all the meaning that they have. [5]Can this be meaning? [6]Can confusion be what meaning means? [7]Perception cannot be in constant flux, and make allowance for stability of meaning anywhere. [8]Fear is a judgment never justified. [9]Its presence has no meaning but to show you wrote a fearful script, and are afraid accordingly. [10]But not because the thing you fear has fearful meaning in itself.

4. A common purpose is the only means whereby perception can be stabilized, and one interpretation given to the world and all experiences here. [2]In this shared purpose is one judgment shared by everyone and everything you see. [3]You do not have to judge, for you have learned one meaning has been given everything, and you are glad to see it everywhere. [4]It cannot change *because* you would perceive it everywhere, unchanged by circumstance. [5]And so you offer it to all events, and let them offer you stability.

5. Escape from judgment simply lies in this; all things have but one purpose, which you share with all the world. [2]And nothing in the world can be opposed to it, for it belongs to everything, as it belongs to you. [3]In single purpose is the end of all ideas of sacrifice, which must assume a different purpose for the one who gains and him who loses. [4]There could be no thought of sacrifice apart from this idea. [5]And it is this idea of different goals that makes perception shift and meaning change. [6]In one united goal does this become impossible, for your agreement makes interpre-

tation stabilize and last.

6.   How can communication really be established while the symbols that are used mean different things? ²The Holy Spirit's goal gives one interpretation, meaningful to you and to your brother. ³Thus can you communicate with him, and he with you. ⁴In symbols that you both can understand the sacrifice of meaning is undone. ⁵All sacrifice entails the loss of your ability to see relationships among events. ⁶And looked at separately they have no meaning. ⁷For there is no light by which they can be seen and understood. ⁸They have no purpose. ⁹And what they are for cannot be seen. ¹⁰In any thought of loss there is no meaning. ¹¹No one has agreed with you on what it means. ¹²It is a part of a distorted script, which cannot be interpreted with meaning. ¹³It must be forever unintelligible. ¹⁴This is not communication. ¹⁵Your dark dreams are but the senseless, isolated scripts you write in sleep. ¹⁶Look not to separate dreams for meaning. ¹⁷Only dreams of pardon can be shared. ¹⁸They mean the same to both of you.

7.   Do not interpret out of solitude, for what you see means nothing. ²It will shift in what it stands for, and you will believe the world is an uncertain place, in which you walk in danger and uncertainty. ³It is but your interpretations which are lacking in stability, for they are not in line with what you really are. ⁴This is a state so seemingly unsafe that fear must rise. ⁵Do not continue thus, my brother. ⁶We have one Interpreter. ⁷And through His use of symbols are we joined, so that they mean the same to all of us. ⁸Our common language lets us speak to all our brothers, and to understand with them forgiveness has been given to us all, and thus we can communicate again.

VIII. Changeless Reality

1.   Appearances deceive, but can be changed. ²Reality is changeless. ³It does not deceive at all, and if you fail to see beyond appearances you *are* deceived. ⁴For everything you see will change, and yet you thought it real before, and now you think it real again. ⁵Reality is thus reduced to form, and capable of change. ⁶Reality is changeless. ⁷It is this that makes it real, and keeps it separate from all appearances. ⁸It must transcend all form to be itself. ⁹It cannot change.

2.   The miracle is means to demonstrate that all appearances can

change because they *are* appearances, and cannot have the changelessness reality entails. [2]The miracle attests salvation from appearances by showing they can change. [3]Your brother has a changelessness in him beyond appearance and deception, both. [4]It is obscured by changing views of him that you perceive as his reality. [5]The happy dream about him takes the form of the appearance of his perfect health, his perfect freedom from all forms of lack, and safety from disaster of all kinds. [6]The miracle is proof he is not bound by loss or suffering in any form, because it can so easily be changed. [7]This demonstrates that it was never real, and could not stem from his reality. [8]For that is changeless, and has no effects that anything in Heaven or on earth could ever alter. [9]But appearances are shown to be unreal *because* they change.

3. What is temptation but a wish to make illusions real? [2]It does not seem to be the wish that no reality be so. [3]Yet it is an assertion that some forms of idols have a powerful appeal that makes them harder to resist than those you would not want to have reality. [4]Temptation, then, is nothing more than this; a prayer the miracle touch not some dreams, but keep their unreality obscure and give to them reality instead. [5]And Heaven gives no answer to the prayer, nor can a miracle be given you to heal appearances you do not like. [6]You have established limits. [7]What you ask *is* given you, but not of God Who knows no limits. [8]You have limited yourself.

4. Reality is changeless. [2]Miracles but show what you have interposed between reality and your awareness is unreal, and does not interfere at all. [3]The cost of the belief there must be some appearances beyond the hope of change is that the miracle cannot come forth from you consistently. [4]For you have asked it be withheld from power to heal all dreams. [5]There is no miracle you cannot have when you desire healing. [6]But there is no miracle that can be given you unless you want it. [7]Choose what you would heal, and He Who gives all miracles has not been given freedom to bestow His gifts upon God's Son. [8]When he is tempted, he denies reality. [9]And he becomes the willing slave of what he chose instead.

5. *Because* reality is changeless is a miracle already there to heal all things that change, and offer them to you to see in happy form, devoid of fear. [2]It will be given you to look upon your brother thus. [3]But not while you would have it otherwise in some

respects. [4]For this but means you would not have him healed and whole. [5]The Christ in him is perfect. [6]Is it this that you would look upon? [7]Then let there be no dreams about him that you would prefer to seeing this. [8]And you will see the Christ in him because you let Him come to you. [9]And when He has appeared to you, you will be certain you are like Him, for He is the changeless in your brother and in you.

6.   This will you look upon when you decide there is not one appearance you would hold in place of what your brother really is. [2]Let no temptation to prefer a dream allow uncertainty to enter here. [3]Be not made guilty and afraid when you are tempted by a dream of what he is. [4]But do not give it power to replace the changeless in him in your sight of him. [5]There is no false appearance but will fade, if you request a miracle instead. [6]There is no pain from which he is not free, if you would have him be but what he is. [7]Why should you fear to see the Christ in him? [8]You but behold yourself in what you see. [9]As he is healed are you made free of guilt, for his appearance is your own to you.

Chapter 31

THE FINAL VISION

I. The Simplicity of Salvation

1. How simple is salvation! ²All it says is what was never true is not true now, and never will be. ³The impossible has not occurred, and can have no effects. ⁴And that is all. ⁵Can this be hard to learn by anyone who wants it to be true? ⁶Only unwillingness to learn it could make such an easy lesson difficult. ⁷How hard is it to see that what is false can not be true, and what is true can not be false? ⁸You can no longer say that you perceive no differences in false and true. ⁹You have been told exactly how to tell one from the other, and just what to do if you become confused. ¹⁰Why, then, do you persist in learning not such simple things?

2. There is a reason. ²But confuse it not with difficulty in the simple things salvation asks you learn. ³It teaches but the very obvious. ⁴It merely goes from one apparent lesson to the next, in easy steps that lead you gently from one to another, with no strain at all. ⁵This cannot be confusing, yet you are confused. ⁶For somehow you believe that what is totally confused is easier to learn and understand. ⁷What you have taught yourself is such a giant learning feat it is indeed incredible. ⁸But you accomplished it because you wanted to, and did not pause in diligence to judge it hard to learn or too complex to grasp.

3. No one who understands what you have learned, how carefully you learned it, and the pains to which you went to practice and repeat the lessons endlessly, in every form you could conceive of them, could ever doubt the power of your learning skill. ²There is no greater power in the world. ³The world was made by it, and even now depends on nothing else. ⁴The lessons you have taught yourself have been so overlearned and fixed they rise like heavy curtains to obscure the simple and the obvious. ⁵Say not you cannot learn them. ⁶For your power to learn is strong enough to teach you that your will is not your own, your thoughts do not belong to you, and even you are someone else.

4. Who could maintain that lessons such as these are easy? ²Yet you have learned more than this. ³You have continued, taking every step, however difficult, without complaint, until a world

was built that suited you. ⁴And every lesson that makes up the world arises from the first accomplishment of learning; an enormity so great the Holy Spirit's Voice seems small and still before its magnitude. ⁵The world began with one strange lesson, powerful enough to render God forgotten, and His Son an alien to himself, in exile from the home where God Himself established him. ⁶You who have taught yourself the Son of God is guilty, say not that you cannot learn the simple things salvation teaches you!

5. Learning is an ability you made and gave yourself. ²It was not made to do the Will of God, but to uphold a wish that it could be opposed, and that a will apart from it was yet more real than it. ³And this has learning sought to demonstrate, and you have learned what it was made to teach. ⁴Now does your ancient overlearning stand implacable before the Voice of truth, and teach you that Its lessons are not true; too hard to learn, too difficult to see, and too opposed to what is really true. ⁵Yet you will learn them, for their learning is the only purpose for your learning skill the Holy Spirit sees in all the world. ⁶His simple lessons in forgiveness have a power mightier than yours, because they call from God and from your Self to you.

6. Is this a little Voice, so small and still It cannot rise above the senseless noise of sounds that have no meaning? ²God willed not His Son forget Him. ³And the power of His Will is in the Voice that speaks for Him. ⁴Which lesson will you learn? ⁵What outcome is inevitable, sure as God, and far beyond all doubt and question? ⁶Can it be your little learning, strange in outcome and incredible in difficulty will withstand the simple lessons being taught to you in every moment of each day, since time began and learning had been made?

7. The lessons to be learned are only two. ²Each has its outcome in a different world. ³And each world follows surely from its source. ⁴The certain outcome of the lesson that God's Son is guilty is the world you see. ⁵It is a world of terror and despair. ⁶Nor is there hope of happiness in it. ⁷There is no plan for safety you can make that ever will succeed. ⁸There is no joy that you can seek for here and hope to find. ⁹Yet this is not the only outcome which your learning can produce. ¹⁰However much you may have overlearned your chosen task, the lesson that reflects the Love of God is stronger still. ¹¹And you will learn God's Son is innocent, and see another world.

8.   The outcome of the lesson that God's Son is guiltless is a world in which there is no fear, and everything is lit with hope and sparkles with a gentle friendliness. ²Nothing but calls to you in soft appeal to be your friend, and let it join with you. ³And never does a call remain unheard, misunderstood, nor left unanswered in the selfsame tongue in which the call was made. ⁴And you will understand it was this call that everyone and everything within the world has always made, but you had not perceived it as it was. ⁵And now you see you were mistaken. ⁶You had been deceived by forms the call was hidden in. ⁷And so you did not hear it, and had lost a friend who always wanted to be part of you. ⁸The soft eternal calling of each part of God's creation to the whole is heard throughout the world this second lesson brings.

9.   There is no living thing that does not share the universal Will that it be whole, and that you do not leave its call unheard. ²Without your answer is it left to die, as it is saved from death when you have heard its calling as the ancient call to life, and understood that it is but your own. ³The Christ in you remembers God with all the certainty with which He knows His Love. ⁴But only if His Son is innocent can He be Love. ⁵For God were fear indeed if he whom He created innocent could be a slave to guilt. ⁶God's perfect Son remembers his creation. ⁷But in guilt he has forgotten what he really is.

10.   The fear of God results as surely from the lesson that His Son is guilty as God's Love must be remembered when he learns his innocence. ²For hate must father fear, and look upon its father as itself. ³How wrong are you who fail to hear the call that echoes past each seeming call to death, that sings behind each murderous attack and pleads that love restore the dying world. ⁴You do not understand Who calls to you beyond each form of hate; each call to war. ⁵Yet you will recognize Him as you give Him answer in the language that He calls. ⁶He will appear when you have answered Him, and you will know in Him that God is Love.

11.   What is temptation but a wish to make the wrong decision on what you would learn, and have an outcome that you do not want? ²It is the recognition that it is a state of mind unwanted that becomes the means whereby the choice is reassessed; another outcome seen to be preferred. ³You are deceived if you believe you want disaster and disunity and pain. ⁴Hear not the call

for this within yourself. [5]But listen, rather, to the deeper call beyond it that appeals for peace and joy. [6]And all the world will give you joy and peace. [7]For as you hear, you answer. [8]And behold! [9]Your answer is the proof of what you learned. [10]Its outcome is the world you look upon.

12. Let us be still an instant, and forget all things we ever learned, all thoughts we had, and every preconception that we hold of what things mean and what their purpose is. [2]Let us remember not our own ideas of what the world is for. [3]We do not know. [4]Let every image held of everyone be loosened from our minds and swept away.

13. Be innocent of judgment, unaware of any thoughts of evil or of good that ever crossed your mind of anyone. [2]Now do you know him not. [3]But you are free to learn of him, and learn of him anew. [4]Now is he born again to you, and you are born again to him, without the past that sentenced him to die, and you with him. [5]Now is he free to live as you are free, because an ancient learning passed away, and left a place for truth to be reborn.

II. Walking with Christ

1. An ancient lesson is not overcome by the opposing of the new and old. [2]It is not vanquished that the truth be known, nor fought against to lose to truth's appeal. [3]There is no battle that must be prepared; no time to be expended, and no plans that need be laid for bringing in the new. [4]There *is* an ancient battle being waged against the truth, but truth does not respond. [5]Who could be hurt in such a war, unless he hurts himself? [6]He has no enemy in truth. [7]And can he be assailed by dreams?

2. Let us review again what seems to stand between you and the truth of what you are. [2]For there are steps in its relinquishment. [3]The first is a decision that you make. [4]But afterwards, the truth is given you. [5]You would establish truth. [6]And by your wish you set two choices to be made, each time you think you must decide on anything. [7]Neither is true. [8]Nor are they different. [9]Yet must we see them both, before you can look past them to the one alternative that *is* a different choice. [10]But not in dreams you made, that this might be obscured to you.

3. What you would choose between is not a choice and gives but the illusion it is free, for it will have one outcome either way.

²Thus is it really not a choice at all. ³The leader and the follower emerge as separate roles, each seeming to possess advantages you would not want to lose. ⁴So in their fusion there appears to be the hope of satisfaction and of peace. ⁵You see yourself divided into both these roles, forever split between the two. ⁶And every friend or enemy becomes a means to help you save yourself from this.

4. Perhaps you call it love. ²Perhaps you think that it is murder justified at last. ³You hate the one you gave the leader's role when you would have it, and you hate as well his not assuming it at times you want to let the follower in you arise, and give away the role of leadership. ⁴And this is what you made your brother for, and learned to think that this his purpose is. ⁵Unless he serves it, he has not fulfilled the function that was given him by you. ⁶And thus he merits death, because he has no purpose and no usefulness to you.

5. And what of him? ²What does he want of you? ³What could he want, but what you want of him? ⁴Herein is life as easily as death, for what you choose you choose as well for him. ⁵Two calls you make to him, as he to you. ⁶Between these two *is* choice, because from them there is a different outcome. ⁷If he be the leader or the follower to you it matters not, for you have chosen death. ⁸But if he calls for death or calls for life, for hate or for forgiveness and for help, is not the same in outcome. ⁹Hear the one, and you are separate from him and are lost. ¹⁰But hear the other, and you join with him and in your answer is salvation found. ¹¹The voice you hear in him is but your own. ¹²What does he ask you for? ¹³And listen well! ¹⁴For he is asking what will come to you, because you see an image of yourself and hear your voice requesting what you want.

6. Before you answer, pause to think of this:

> ²*The answer that I give my brother is what I am asking for.* ³*And what I learn of him is what I learn about myself.*

⁴Then let us wait an instant and be still, forgetting everything we thought we heard; remembering how much we do not know. ⁵This brother neither leads nor follows us, but walks beside us on the selfsame road. ⁶He is like us, as near or far away from what we want as we will let him be. ⁷We make no gains he does not

make with us, and we fall back if he does not advance. ⁸Take not his hand in anger but in love, for in his progress do you count your own. ⁹And we go separately along the way unless you keep him safely by your side.

7.   Because he is your equal in God's Love, you will be saved from all appearances and answer to the Christ Who calls to you. ²Be still and listen. ³Think not ancient thoughts. ⁴Forget the dismal lessons that you learned about this Son of God who calls to you. ⁵Christ calls to all with equal tenderness, seeing no leaders and no followers, and hearing but one answer to them all. ⁶Because He hears one Voice, He cannot hear a different answer from the one He gave when God appointed Him His only Son.

8.   Be very still an instant. ²Come without all thought of what you ever learned before, and put aside all images you made. ³The old will fall away before the new without your opposition or intent. ⁴There will be no attack upon the things you thought were precious and in need of care. ⁵There will be no assault upon your wish to hear a call that never has been made. ⁶Nothing will hurt you in this holy place, to which you come to listen silently and learn the truth of what you really want. ⁷No more than this will you be asked to learn. ⁸But as you hear it, you will understand you need but come away without the thoughts you did not want, and that were never true.

9.   Forgive your brother all appearances, that are but ancient lessons you have taught yourself about the sinfulness in you. ²Hear but his call for mercy and release from all the fearful images he holds of what he is and of what you must be. ³He is afraid to walk with you, and thinks perhaps a bit behind, a bit ahead would be a safer place for him to be. ⁴Can you make progress if you think the same, advancing only when he would step back, and falling back when he would go ahead? ⁵For so do you forget the journey's goal, which is but to decide to walk with him, so neither leads nor follows. ⁶Thus it is a way you go together, not alone. ⁷And in this choice is learning's outcome changed, for Christ has been reborn to both of you.

10.   An instant spent without your old ideas of who your great companion is and what he should be asking for, will be enough to let this happen. ²And you will perceive his purpose is the same as yours. ³He asks for what you want, and needs the same as you. ⁴It takes, perhaps, a different form in him, but it is not the form you answer to. ⁵He asks and you receive, for you have come with

but one purpose; that you learn you love your brother with a brother's love. ⁶And as a brother, must his Father be the same as yours, as he is like yourself in truth.

11. Together is your joint inheritance remembered and accepted by you both. ²Alone it is denied to both of you. ³Is it not clear that while you still insist on leading or on following, you think you walk alone, with no one by your side? ⁴This is the road to nowhere, for the light cannot be given while you walk alone, and so you cannot see which way you go. ⁵And thus there is confusion, and a sense of endless doubting as you stagger back and forward in the darkness and alone. ⁶Yet these are but appearances of what the journey is, and how it must be made. ⁷For next to you is One Who holds the light before you, so that every step is made in certainty and sureness of the road. ⁸A blindfold can indeed obscure your sight, but cannot make the way itself grow dark. ⁹And He Who travels with you *has* the light.

III. The Self-Accused

1. Only the self-accused condemn. ²As you prepare to make a choice that will result in different outcomes, there is first one thing that must be overlearned. ³It must become a habit of response so typical of everything you do that it becomes your first response to all temptation, and to every situation that occurs. ⁴Learn this, and learn it well, for it is here delay of happiness is shortened by a span of time you cannot realize. ⁵You never hate your brother for his sins, but only for your own. ⁶Whatever form his sins appear to take, it but obscures the fact that you believe them to be yours, and therefore meriting a "just" attack.

2. Why should his sins be sins, if you did not believe they could not be forgiven in you? ²Why are they real in him, if you did not believe that they are your reality? ³And why do you attack them everywhere except you hate yourself? ⁴Are *you* a sin? ⁵You answer "yes" whenever you attack, for by attack do you assert that you are guilty, and must give as you deserve. ⁶And what can you deserve but what you are? ⁷If you did not believe that you deserved attack, it never would occur to you to give attack to anyone at all. ⁸Why should you? ⁹What would be the gain to you? ¹⁰What could the outcome be that you would want? ¹¹And how could murder bring you benefit?

3.   Sins are in bodies. [2]They are not perceived in minds. [3]They are not seen as purposes, but actions. [4]Bodies act, and minds do not. [5]And therefore must the body be at fault for what it does. [6]It is not seen to be a passive thing, obeying your commands, and doing nothing of itself at all. [7]If you are sin you *are* a body, for the mind acts not. [8]And purpose must be in the body, not the mind. [9]The body must act on its own, and motivate itself. [10]If you are sin you lock the mind within the body, and you give its purpose to its prison house, which acts instead of it. [11]A jailer does not follow orders, but enforces orders on the prisoner.

4.   Yet is the *body* prisoner, and not the mind. [2]The body thinks no thoughts. [3]It has no power to learn, to pardon, nor enslave. [4]It gives no orders that the mind need serve, nor sets conditions that it must obey. [5]It holds in prison but the willing mind that would abide in it. [6]It sickens at the bidding of the mind that would become its prisoner. [7]And it grows old and dies, because that mind is sick within itself. [8]Learning is all that causes change. [9]And so the body, where no learning can occur, could never change unless the mind preferred the body change in its appearances, to suit the purpose given by the mind. [10]For mind can learn, and there is all change made.

5.   The mind that thinks it is a sin has but one purpose; that the body be the source of sin, to keep it in the prison house it chose and guards and holds itself at bay, a sleeping prisoner to the snarling dogs of hate and evil, sickness and attack; of pain and age, of grief and suffering. [2]Here are the thoughts of sacrifice preserved, for here guilt rules, and orders that the world be like itself; a place where nothing can find mercy, nor survive the ravages of fear except in murder and in death. [3]For here are you made sin, and sin cannot abide the joyous and the free, for they are enemies which sin must kill. [4]In death is sin preserved, and those who think that they are sin must die for what they think they are.

6.   Let us be glad that you will see what you believe, and that it has been given you to change what you believe. [2]The body will but follow. [3]It can never lead you where you would not be. [4]It does not guard your sleep, nor interfere with your awakening. [5]Release your body from imprisonment, and you will see no one as prisoner to what you have escaped. [6]You will not want to hold in guilt your chosen enemies, nor keep in chains, to the illusion of a changing love, the ones you think are friends.

7. The innocent release in gratitude for their release. ²And what they see upholds their freedom from imprisonment and death. ³Open your mind to change, and there will be no ancient penalty exacted from your brother or yourself. ⁴For God has said there *is* no sacrifice that can be asked; there *is* no sacrifice that can be made.

IV. The Real Alternative

1. There is a tendency to think the world can offer consolation and escape from problems that its purpose is to keep. ²Why should this be? ³Because it is a place where choice among illusions seems to be the only choice. ⁴And you are in control of outcomes of your choosing. ⁵Thus you think, within the narrow band from birth to death, a little time is given you to use for you alone; a time when everyone conflicts with you, but you can choose which road will lead you out of conflict, and away from difficulties that concern you not. ⁶Yet they *are* your concern. ⁷How, then, can you escape from them by leaving them behind? ⁸What must go with you, you will take with you whatever road you choose to walk along.

2. Real choice is no illusion. ²But the world has none to offer. ³All its roads but lead to disappointment, nothingness and death. ⁴There is no choice in its alternatives. ⁵Seek not escape from problems here. ⁶The world was made that problems could not *be* escaped. ⁷Be not deceived by all the different names its roads are given. ⁸They have but one end. ⁹And each is but the means to gain that end, for it is here that all its roads will lead, however differently they seem to start; however differently they seem to go. ¹⁰Their end is certain, for there is no choice among them. ¹¹All of them will lead to death. ¹²On some you travel gaily for a while, before the bleakness enters. ¹³And on some the thorns are felt at once. ¹⁴The choice is not what will the ending be, but when it comes.

3. There is no choice where every end is sure. ²Perhaps you would prefer to try them all, before you really learn they are but one. ³The roads this world can offer seem to be quite large in number, but the time must come when everyone begins to see how like they are to one another. ⁴Men have died on seeing this, because they saw no way except the pathways offered by the

world. ⁵And learning they led nowhere, lost their hope. ⁶And yet this was the time they could have learned their greatest lesson. ⁷All must reach this point, and go beyond it. ⁸It is true indeed there is no choice at all within the world. ⁹But this is not the lesson in itself. ¹⁰The lesson has a purpose, and in this you come to understand what it is for.

4. Why would you seek to try another road, another person or another place, when you have learned the way the lesson starts, but do not yet perceive what it is for? ²Its purpose is the answer to the search that all must undertake who still believe there is another answer to be found. ³Learn now, without despair, there is no hope of answer in the world. ⁴But do not judge the lesson that is but begun with this. ⁵Seek not another signpost in the world that seems to point to still another road. ⁶No longer look for hope where there is none. ⁷Make fast your learning now, and understand you but waste time unless you go beyond what you have learned to what is yet to learn. ⁸For from this lowest point will learning lead to heights of happiness, in which you see the purpose of the lesson shining clear, and perfectly within your learning grasp.

5. Who would be willing to be turned away from all the roadways of the world, unless he understood their real futility? ²Is it not needful that he should begin with this, to seek another way instead? ³For while he sees a choice where there is none, what power of decision can he use? ⁴The great release of power must begin with learning where it really has a use. ⁵And what decision has power if it be applied in situations without choice?

6. The learning that the world can offer but one choice, no matter what its form may be, is the beginning of acceptance that there is a real alternative instead. ²To fight against this step is to defeat your purpose here. ³You did not come to learn to find a road the world does not contain. ⁴The search for different pathways in the world is but the search for different forms of truth. ⁵And this would *keep* the truth from being reached.

7. Think not that happiness is ever found by following a road away from it. ²This makes no sense, and cannot be the way. ³To you who seem to find this course to be too difficult to learn, let me repeat that to achieve a goal you must proceed in its direction, not away from it. ⁴And every road that leads the other way will not advance the purpose to be found. ⁵If this be difficult to understand, then is this course impossible to learn. ⁶But only

then. [7]For otherwise, it is a simple teaching in the obvious.

8. There *is* a choice that you have power to make when you have seen the real alternatives. [2]Until that point is reached you have no choice, and you can but decide how you would choose the better to deceive yourself again. [3]This course attempts to teach no more than that the power of decision cannot lie in choosing different forms of what is still the same illusion and the same mistake. [4]All choices in the world depend on this; you choose between your brother and yourself, and you will gain as much as he will lose, and what you lose is what is given him. [5]How utterly opposed to truth is this, when all the lesson's purpose is to teach that what your brother loses *you* have lost, and what he gains is what is given *you*.

9. He has not left His Thoughts! [2]But you forgot His Presence and remembered not His Love. [3]No pathway in the world can lead to Him, nor any worldly goal be one with His. [4]What road in all the world will lead within, when every road was made to separate the journey from the purpose it must have unless it be but futile wandering? [5]All roads that lead away from what you are will lead you to confusion and despair. [6]Yet has He never left His Thoughts to die, without their Source forever in themselves.

10. He has not left His Thoughts! [2]He could no more depart from them than they could keep Him out. [3]In unity with Him do they abide, and in Their Oneness Both are kept complete. [4]There is no road that leads away from Him. [5]A journey from yourself does not exist. [6]How foolish and insane it is to think that there could be a road with such an aim! [7]Where could it go? [8]And how could you be made to travel on it, walking there without your own reality at one with you?

11. Forgive yourself your madness, and forget all senseless journeys and all goal-less aims. [2]They have no meaning. [3]You can not escape from what you are. [4]For God is merciful, and did not let His Son abandon Him. [5]For what He is be thankful, for in that is your escape from madness and from death. [6]Nowhere but where He is can you be found. [7]There *is* no path that does not lead to Him.

V. Self-Concept versus Self

1. The learning of the world is built upon a concept of the self adjusted to the world's reality. [2]It fits it well. [3]For this an image is that suits a world of shadows and illusions. [4]Here it walks at home, where what it sees is one with it. [5]The building of a concept of the self is what the learning of the world is for. [6]This is its purpose; that you come without a self, and make one as you go along. [7]And by the time you reach "maturity" you have perfected it, to meet the world on equal terms, at one with its demands.

2. A concept of the self is made by you. [2]It bears no likeness to yourself at all. [3]It is an idol, made to take the place of your reality as Son of God. [4]The concept of the self the world would teach is not the thing that it appears to be. [5]For it is made to serve two purposes, but one of which the mind can recognize. [6]The first presents the face of innocence, the aspect acted on. [7]It is this face that smiles and charms and even seems to love. [8]It searches for companions and it looks, at times with pity, on the suffering, and sometimes offers solace. [9]It believes that it is good within an evil world.

3. This aspect can grow angry, for the world is wicked and unable to provide the love and shelter innocence deserves. [2]And so this face is often wet with tears at the injustices the world accords to those who would be generous and good. [3]This aspect never makes the first attack. [4]But every day a hundred little things make small assaults upon its innocence, provoking it to irritation, and at last to open insult and abuse.

4. The face of innocence the concept of the self so proudly wears can tolerate attack in self-defense, for is it not a well-known fact the world deals harshly with defenseless innocence? [2]No one who makes a picture of himself omits this face, for he has need of it. [3]The other side he does not want to see. [4]Yet it is here the learning of the world has set its sights, for it is here the world's "reality" is set, to see to it the idol lasts.

5. Beneath the face of innocence there is a lesson that the concept of the self was made to teach. [2]It is a lesson in a terrible displacement, and a fear so devastating that the face that smiles above it must forever look away, lest it perceive the treachery it hides. [3]The lesson teaches this: "I am the thing you made of me, and as you look on me, you stand condemned because of what I am." [4]On this conception of the self the world smiles with approval,

for it guarantees the pathways of the world are safely kept, and those who walk on them will not escape.

6. Here is the central lesson that ensures your brother is condemned eternally. [2]For what you are has now become his sin. [3]For this is no forgiveness possible. [4]No longer does it matter what he does, for your accusing finger points to him, unwavering and deadly in its aim. [5]It points to you as well, but this is kept still deeper in the mists below the face of innocence. [6]And in these shrouded vaults are all his sins and yours preserved and kept in darkness, where they cannot be perceived as errors, which the light would surely show. [7]You can be neither blamed for what you are, nor can you change the things it makes you do. [8]Your brother then is symbol of your sins to you who are but silently, and yet with ceaseless urgency, condemning still your brother for the hated thing you are.

7. Concepts are learned. [2]They are not natural. [3]Apart from learning they do not exist. [4]They are not given, so they must be made. [5]Not one of them is true, and many come from feverish imaginations, hot with hatred and distortions born of fear. [6]What is a concept but a thought to which its maker gives a meaning of his own? [7]Concepts maintain the world. [8]But they can not be used to demonstrate the world is real. [9]For all of them are made within the world, born in its shadow, growing in its ways and finally "maturing" in its thought. [10]They are ideas of idols, painted with the brushes of the world, which cannot make a single picture representing truth.

8. A concept of the self is meaningless, for no one here can see what it is for, and therefore cannot picture what it is. [2]Yet is all learning that the world directs begun and ended with the single aim of teaching you this concept of yourself, that you will choose to follow this world's laws, and never seek to go beyond its roads nor realize the way you see yourself. [3]Now must the Holy Spirit find a way to help you see this concept of the self must be undone, if any peace of mind is to be given you. [4]Nor can it be unlearned except by lessons aimed to teach that you are something else. [5]For otherwise, you would be asked to make exchange of what you now believe for total loss of self, and greater terror would arise in you.

9. Thus are the Holy Spirit's lesson plans arranged in easy steps, that though there be some lack of ease at times and some distress, there is no shattering of what was learned, but just a

re-translation of what seems to be the evidence on its behalf. [2]Let us consider, then, what proof there is that you are what your brother made of you. [3]For even though you do not yet perceive that this is what you think, you surely learned by now that you behave as if it were. [4]Does he react for you? [5]And does he know exactly what would happen? [6]Can he see your future and ordain, before it comes, what you should do in every circumstance? [7]He must have made the world as well as you to have such prescience in the things to come.

10. That you are what your brother made of you seems most unlikely. [2]Even if he did, who gave the face of innocence to you? [3]Is this your contribution? [4]Who is, then, the "you" who made it? [5]And who is deceived by all your goodness, and attacks it so? [6]Let us forget the concept's foolishness, and merely think of this; there are two parts to what you think yourself to be. [7]If one were generated by your brother, who was there to make the other? [8]And from whom must something be kept hidden? [9]If the world be evil, there is still no need to hide what you are made of. [10]Who is there to see? [11]And what but is attacked could need defense?

11. Perhaps the reason why this concept must be kept in darkness is that, in the light, the one who would not think it true is you. [2]And what would happen to the world you see, if all its underpinnings were removed? [3]Your concept of the world depends upon this concept of the self. [4]And both would go, if either one were ever raised to doubt. [5]The Holy Spirit does not seek to throw you into panic. [6]So He merely asks if just a little question might be raised.

12. There are alternatives about the thing that you must be. [2]You might, for instance, be the thing you chose to have your brother be. [3]This shifts the concept of the self from what is wholly passive, and at least makes way for active choice, and some acknowledgment that interaction must have entered in. [4]There is some understanding that you chose for both of you, and what he represents has meaning that was given it by you. [5]It also shows some glimmering of sight into perception's law that what you see reflects the state of the perceiver's mind. [6]Yet who was it that did the choosing first? [7]If you are what you chose your brother be, alternatives were there to choose among, and someone must have first decided on the one to choose, and let the other go.

13. Although this step has gains, it does not yet approach a basic question. [2]Something must have gone before these concepts of

the self. [3]And something must have done the learning which gave rise to them. [4]Nor can this be explained by either view. [5]The main advantage of the shifting to the second from the first is that you somehow entered in the choice by your decision. [6]But this gain is paid in almost equal loss, for now you stand accused of guilt for what your brother is. [7]And you must share his guilt, because you chose it for him in the image of your own. [8]While only he was treacherous before, now must you be condemned along with him.

14. The concept of the self has always been the great preoccupation of the world. [2]And everyone believes that he must find the answer to the riddle of himself. [3]Salvation can be seen as nothing more than the escape from concepts. [4]It does not concern itself with content of the mind, but with the simple statement that it thinks. [5]And what can think has choice, and can be shown that different thoughts have different consequence. [6]So it can learn that everything it thinks reflects the deep confusion that it feels about how it was made and what it is. [7]And vaguely does the concept of the self appear to answer what it does not know.

15. Seek not your Self in symbols. [2]There can be no concept that can stand for what you are. [3]What matters it which concept you accept while you perceive a self that interacts with evil, and reacts to wicked things? [4]Your concept of yourself will still remain quite meaningless. [5]And you will not perceive that you can interact but with yourself. [6]To see a guilty world is but the sign your learning has been guided by the world, and you behold it as you see yourself. [7]The concept of the self embraces all you look upon, and nothing is outside of this perception. [8]If you can be hurt by anything, you see a picture of your secret wishes. [9]Nothing more than this. [10]And in your suffering of any kind you see your own concealed desire to kill.

16. You will make many concepts of the self as learning goes along. [2]Each one will show the changes in your own relationships, as your perception of yourself is changed. [3]There will be some confusion every time there is a shift, but be you thankful that the learning of the world is loosening its grasp upon your mind. [4]And be you sure and happy in the confidence that it will go at last, and leave your mind at peace. [5]The role of the accuser will appear in many places and in many forms. [6]And each will seem to be accusing you. [7]Yet have no fear it will not be undone.

17.   The world can teach no images of you unless you want to learn them. ²There will come a time when images have all gone by, and you will see you know not what you are. ³It is to this unsealed and open mind that truth returns, unhindered and unbound. ⁴Where concepts of the self have been laid by is truth revealed exactly as it is. ⁵When every concept has been raised to doubt and question, and been recognized as made on no assumptions that would stand the light, then is the truth left free to enter in its sanctuary, clean and free of guilt. ⁶There is no statement that the world is more afraid to hear than this:

> ⁷*I do not know the thing I am, and therefore do not know what I am doing, where I am, or how to look upon the world or on myself.*

⁸Yet in this learning is salvation born. ⁹And What you are will tell you of Itself.

VI. Recognizing the Spirit

1.   You see the flesh or recognize the spirit. ²There is no compromise between the two. ³If one is real the other must be false, for what is real denies its opposite. ⁴There is no choice in vision but this one. ⁵What you decide in this determines all you see and think is real and hold as true. ⁶On this one choice does all your world depend, for here have you established what you are, as flesh or spirit in your own belief. ⁷If you choose flesh, you never will escape the body as your own reality, for you have chosen that you want it so. ⁸But choose the spirit, and all Heaven bends to touch your eyes and bless your holy sight, that you may see the world of flesh no more except to heal and comfort and to bless.

2.   Salvation is undoing. ²If you choose to see the body, you behold a world of separation, unrelated things, and happenings that make no sense at all. ³This one appears and disappears in death; that one is doomed to suffering and loss. ⁴And no one is exactly as he was an instant previous, nor will he be the same as he is now an instant hence. ⁵Who could have trust where so much change is seen, for who is worthy if he be but dust? ⁶Salvation is

undoing of all this. [7]For constancy arises in the sight of those whose eyes salvation has released from looking at the cost of keeping guilt, because they chose to let it go instead.

3. Salvation does not ask that you behold the spirit and perceive the body not. [2]It merely asks that this should be your choice. [3]For you can see the body without help, but do not understand how to behold a world apart from it. [4]It is your world salvation will undo, and let you see another world your eyes could never find. [5]Be not concerned how this could ever be. [6]You do not understand how what you see arose to meet your sight. [7]For if you did, it would be gone. [8]The veil of ignorance is drawn across the evil and the good, and must be passed that both may disappear, so that perception finds no hiding place. [9]How is this done? [10]It is not done at all. [11]What could there be within the universe that God created that must still be done?

4. Only in arrogance could you conceive that you must make the way to Heaven plain. [2]The means are given you by which to see the world that will replace the one you made. [3]Your will be done! [4]In Heaven as on earth this is forever true. [5]It matters not where you believe you are, nor what you think the truth about yourself must really be. [6]It makes no difference what you look upon, nor what you choose to feel or think or wish. [7]For God Himself has said, "Your will be done." [8]And it is done to you accordingly.

5. You who believe that you can choose to see the Son of God as you would have him be, forget not that no concept of yourself will stand against the truth of what you are. [2]Undoing truth would be impossible. [3]But concepts are not difficult to change. [4]One vision, clearly seen, that does not fit the picture as it was perceived before will change the world for eyes that learn to see, because the concept of the self has changed.

6. Are you invulnerable? [2]Then the world is harmless in your sight. [3]Do you forgive? [4]Then is the world forgiving, for you have forgiven it its trespasses, and so it looks on you with eyes that see as yours. [5]Are you a body? [6]So is all the world perceived as treacherous, and out to kill. [7]Are you a spirit, deathless, and without the promise of corruption and the stain of sin upon you? [8]So the world is seen as stable, fully worthy of your trust; a happy place to rest in for a while, where nothing need be feared, but only loved. [9]Who is unwelcome to the kind in heart? [10]And what could hurt the truly innocent?

7.   Your will be done, you holy child of God. ²It does not matter if you think you are in earth or Heaven. ³What your Father wills of you can never change. ⁴The truth in you remains as radiant as a star, as pure as light, as innocent as love itself. ⁵And you *are* worthy that your will be done!

VII. The Savior's Vision

1.   Learning is change. ²Salvation does not seek to use a means as yet too alien to your thinking to be helpful, nor to make the kinds of change you could not recognize. ³Concepts are needed while perception lasts, and changing concepts is salvation's task. ⁴For it must deal in contrasts, not in truth, which has no opposite and cannot change. ⁵In this world's concepts are the guilty "bad"; the "good" are innocent. ⁶And no one here but holds a concept of himself in which he counts the "good" to pardon him the "bad." ⁷Nor does he trust the "good" in anyone, believing that the "bad" must lurk behind. ⁸This concept emphasizes treachery, and trust becomes impossible. ⁹Nor could it change while you perceive the "bad" in you.

2.   You could not recognize your "evil" thoughts as long as you see value in attack. ²You will perceive them sometimes, but will not see them as meaningless. ³And so they come in fearful form, with content still concealed, to shake your sorry concept of yourself and blacken it with still another "crime." ⁴You cannot give yourself your innocence, for you are too confused about yourself. ⁵But should *one* brother dawn upon your sight as wholly worthy of forgiveness, then your concept of yourself is wholly changed. ⁶Your "evil" thoughts have been forgiven with his, because you let them all affect you not. ⁷No longer do you choose that you should be the sign of evil and of guilt in him. ⁸And as you give your trust to what is good in him, you give it to the good in you.

3.   In terms of concepts, it is thus you see him more than just a body, for the good is never what the body seems to be. ²The actions of the body are perceived as coming from the "baser" part of you, and thus of him as well. ³By focusing upon the good in him, the body grows decreasingly persistent in your sight, and will at length be seen as little more than just a shadow circling round the good. ⁴And this will be your concept of yourself, when

you have reached the world beyond the sight your eyes alone can offer you to see. [5]For you will not interpret what you see without the Aid that God has given you. [6]And in His sight there *is* another world.

4. You live in that world just as much as this. [2]For both are concepts of yourself, which can be interchanged but never jointly held. [3]The contrast is far greater than you think, for you will love this concept of yourself, because it was not made for you alone. [4]Born as a gift for someone not perceived to be yourself, it has been given you. [5]For your forgiveness, offered unto him, has been accepted now for both of you.

5. Have faith in him who walks with you, so that your fearful concept of yourself may change. [2]And look upon the good in him, that you may not be frightened by your "evil" thoughts because they do not cloud your view of him. [3]And all this shift requires is that you be willing that this happy change occur. [4]No more than this is asked. [5]On its behalf, remember what the concept of yourself that now you hold has brought you in its wake, and welcome the glad contrast offered you. [6]Hold out your hand, that you may have the gift of kind forgiveness which you offer one whose need for it is just the same as yours. [7]And let the cruel concept of yourself be changed to one that brings the peace of God.

6. The concept of yourself that now you hold would guarantee your function here remain forever unaccomplished and undone. [2]And thus it dooms you to a bitter sense of deep depression and futility. [3]Yet it need not be fixed, unless you choose to hold it past the hope of change and keep it static and concealed within your mind. [4]Give it instead to Him Who understands the changes that it needs to let it serve the function given you to bring you peace, that you may offer peace to have it yours. [5]Alternatives are in your mind to use, and you can see yourself another way. [6]Would you not rather look upon yourself as needed for salvation of the world, instead of as salvation's enemy?

7. The concept of the self stands like a shield, a silent barricade before the truth, and hides it from your sight. [2]All things you see are images, because you look on them as through a barrier that dims your sight and warps your vision, so that you behold nothing with clarity. [3]The light is kept from everything you see. [4]At most, you glimpse a shadow of what lies beyond. [5]At least, you merely look on darkness, and perceive the terrified imaginings

that come from guilty thoughts and concepts born of fear. [6]And what you see is hell, for fear *is* hell. [7]All that is given you is for release; the sight, the vision and the inner Guide all lead you out of hell with those you love beside you, and the universe with them.

8. Behold your role within the universe! [2]To every part of true creation has the Lord of Love and life entrusted all salvation from the misery of hell. [3]And to each one has He allowed the grace to be a savior to the holy ones especially entrusted to his care. [4]And this he learns when first he looks upon one brother as he looks upon himself, and sees the mirror of himself in him. [5]Thus is the concept of himself laid by, for nothing stands between his sight and what he looks upon, to judge what he beholds. [6]And in this single vision does he see the face of Christ, and understands he looks on everyone as he beholds this one. [7]For there is light where darkness was before, and now the veil is lifted from his sight.

9. The veil across the face of Christ, the fear of God and of salvation, and the love of guilt and death, they all are different names for just one error; that there is a space between you and your brother, kept apart by an illusion of yourself that holds him off from you, and you away from him. [2]The sword of judgment is the weapon that you give to the illusion of yourself, that it may fight to keep the space that holds your brother off unoccupied by love. [3]Yet while you hold this sword, you must perceive the body as yourself, for you are bound to separation from the sight of him who holds the mirror to another view of what he is, and thus what you must be.

10. What is temptation but the wish to stay in hell and misery? [2]And what could this give rise to but an image of yourself that can be miserable, and remain in hell and torment? [3]Who has learned to see his brother not as this has saved himself, and thus is he a savior to the rest. [4]To everyone has God entrusted all, because a partial savior would be one who is but partly saved. [5]The holy ones whom God has given you to save are but everyone you meet or look upon, not knowing who they are; all those you saw an instant and forgot, and those you knew a long while since, and those you will yet meet; the unremembered and the not yet born. [6]For God has given you His Son to save from every concept that he ever held.

11. Yet while you wish to stay in hell, how could you be the savior of the Son of God? [2]How would you know his holiness while you

see him apart from yours? ³For holiness is seen through holy eyes that look upon the innocence within, and thus expect to see it everywhere. ⁴And so they call it forth in everyone they look upon, that he may be what they expect of him. ⁵This is the savior's vision; that he see his innocence in all he looks upon, and see his own salvation everywhere. ⁶He holds no concept of himself between his calm and open eyes and what he sees. ⁷He brings the light to what he looks upon, that he may see it as it really is.

12. Whatever form temptation seems to take, it always but reflects a wish to be a self that you are not. ²And from that wish a concept rises, teaching that you are the thing you wish to be. ³It will remain your concept of yourself until the wish that fathered it no longer is held dear. ⁴But while you cherish it, you will behold your brother in the likeness of the self whose image has the wish begot of you. ⁵For seeing can but represent a wish, because it has no power to create. ⁶Yet it can look with love or look with hate, depending only on the simple choice of whether you would join with what you see, or keep yourself apart and separate.

13. The savior's vision is as innocent of what your brother is as it is free of any judgment made upon yourself. ²It sees no past in anyone at all. ³And thus it serves a wholly open mind, unclouded by old concepts, and prepared to look on only what the present holds. ⁴It cannot judge because it does not know. ⁵And recognizing this, it merely asks, "What is the meaning of what I behold?" ⁶Then is the answer given. ⁷And the door held open for the face of Christ to shine upon the one who asks, in innocence, to see beyond the veil of old ideas and ancient concepts held so long and dear against the vision of the Christ in you.

14. Be vigilant against temptation, then, remembering that it is but a wish, insane and meaningless, to make yourself a thing that you are not. ²And think as well upon the thing that you would be instead. ³It is a thing of madness, pain and death; a thing of treachery and black despair, of failing dreams and no remaining hope except to die, and end the dream of fear. ⁴*This* is temptation; nothing more than this. ⁵Can this be difficult to choose *against*? ⁶Consider what temptation is, and see the real alternatives you choose between. ⁷There are but two. ⁸Be not deceived by what appears as many choices. ⁹There is hell or Heaven, and of these you choose but one.

15. Let not the world's light, given unto you, be hidden from the

world. [2]It needs the light, for it is dark indeed, and men despair because the savior's vision is withheld and what they see is death. [3]Their savior stands, unknowing and unknown, beholding them with eyes unopened. [4]And they cannot see until he looks on them with seeing eyes, and offers them forgiveness with his own. [5]Can you to whom God says, "Release My Son!" be tempted not to listen, when you learn that it is you for whom He asks release? [6]And what but this is what this course would teach? [7]And what but this is there for you to learn?

VIII. Choose Once Again

1. Temptation has one lesson it would teach, in all its forms, wherever it occurs. [2]It would persuade the holy Son of God he is a body, born in what must die, unable to escape its frailty, and bound by what it orders him to feel. [3]It sets the limits on what he can do; its power is the only strength he has; his grasp cannot exceed its tiny reach. [4]Would you be this, if Christ appeared to you in all His glory, asking you but this:

> [5]Choose once again if you would take your place
> among the saviors of the world, or would remain in
> hell, and hold your brothers there.

[6]For He *has* come, and He *is* asking this.

2. How do you make the choice? [2]How easily is this explained! [3]You always choose between your weakness and the strength of Christ in you. [4]And what you choose is what you think is real. [5]Simply by never using weakness to direct your actions, you have given it no power. [6]And the light of Christ in you is given charge of everything you do. [7]For you have brought your weakness unto Him, and He has given you His strength instead.

3. Trials are but lessons that you failed to learn presented once again, so where you made a faulty choice before you now can make a better one, and thus escape all pain that what you chose before has brought to you. [2]In every difficulty, all distress, and each perplexity Christ calls to you and gently says, "My brother, choose again." [3]He would not leave one source of pain unhealed, nor any image left to veil the truth. [4]He would remove all misery from you whom God created altar unto joy. [5]He would not leave

you comfortless, alone in dreams of hell, but would release your mind from everything that hides His face from you. ⁶His Holiness is yours because He is the only power that is real in you. ⁷His strength is yours because He is the Self that God created as His only Son.

4. The images you make cannot prevail against what God Himself would have you be. ²Be never fearful of temptation, then, but see it as it is; another chance to choose again, and let Christ's strength prevail in every circumstance and every place you raised an image of yourself before. ³For what appears to hide the face of Christ is powerless before His majesty, and disappears before His holy sight. ⁴The saviors of the world, who see like Him, are merely those who choose His strength instead of their own weakness, seen apart from Him. ⁵They will redeem the world, for they are joined in all the power of the Will of God. ⁶And what they will is only what He wills.

5. Learn, then, the happy habit of response to all temptation to perceive yourself as weak and miserable with these words:

> ²I am as God created me. ³His Son can suffer
> nothing. ⁴And I am His Son.

⁵Thus is Christ's strength invited to prevail, replacing all your weakness with the strength that comes from God and that can never fail. ⁶And thus are miracles as natural as fear and agony appeared to be before the choice for holiness was made. ⁷For in that choice are false distinctions gone, illusory alternatives laid by, and nothing left to interfere with truth.

6. You *are* as God created you, and so is every living thing you look upon, regardless of the images you see. ²What you behold as sickness and as pain, as weakness and as suffering and loss, is but temptation to perceive yourself defenseless and in hell. ³Yield not to this, and you will see all pain, in every form, wherever it occurs, but disappear as mists before the sun. ⁴A miracle has come to heal God's Son, and close the door upon his dreams of weakness, opening the way to his salvation and release. ⁵Choose once again what you would have him be, remembering that every choice you make establishes your own identity as you will see it and believe it is.

7. Deny me not the little gift I ask, when in exchange I lay before your feet the peace of God, and power to bring this peace to

everyone who wanders in the world uncertain, lonely, and in constant fear. [2]For it is given you to join with him, and through the Christ in you unveil his eyes, and let him look upon the Christ in him.

8.   My brothers in salvation, do not fail to hear my voice and listen to my words. [2]I ask for nothing but your own release. [3]There is no place for hell within a world whose loveliness can yet be so intense and so inclusive it is but a step from there to Heaven. [4]To your tired eyes I bring a vision of a different world, so new and clean and fresh you will forget the pain and sorrow that you saw before. [5]Yet this a vision is which you must share with everyone you see, for otherwise you will behold it not. [6]To give this gift is how to make it yours. [7]And God ordained, in loving kindness, that it be for you.

9.   Let us be glad that we can walk the world, and find so many chances to perceive another situation where God's gift can once again be recognized as ours! [2]And thus will all the vestiges of hell, the secret sins and hidden hates be gone. [3]And all the loveliness which they concealed appear like lawns of Heaven to our sight, to lift us high above the thorny roads we travelled on before the Christ appeared. [4]Hear me, my brothers, hear and join with me. [5]God has ordained I cannot call in vain, and in His certainty I rest content. [6]For you *will* hear, and you *will* choose again. [7]And in this choice is everyone made free.

10.   I thank You, Father, for these holy ones who are my brothers as they are Your Sons. [2]My faith in them is Yours. [3]I am as sure that they will come to me as You are sure of what they are, and will forever be. [4]They will accept the gift I offer them, because You gave it me on their behalf. [5]And as I would but do Your holy Will, so will they choose. [6]And I give thanks for them. [7]Salvation's song will echo through the world with every choice they make. [8]For we are one in purpose, and the end of hell is near.

11.   In joyous welcome is my hand outstretched to every brother who would join with me in reaching past temptation, and who looks with fixed determination toward the light that shines beyond in perfect constancy. [2]Give me my own, for they belong to You. [3]And can You fail in what is but Your Will? [4]I give You thanks for what my brothers are. [5]And as each one elects to join with me, the song of thanks from earth to Heaven grows from tiny scattered threads of melody to one inclusive chorus from a world redeemed from hell, and giving thanks to You.

12.   And now we say "Amen." [2]For Christ has come to dwell in the abode You set for Him before time was, in calm eternity. [3]The journey closes, ending at the place where it began. [4]No trace of it remains. [5]Not one illusion is accorded faith, and not one spot of darkness still remains to hide the face of Christ from anyone. [6]Thy Will is done, complete and perfectly, and all creation recognizes You, and knows You as the only Source it has. [7]Clear in Your likeness does the light shine forth from everything that lives and moves in You. [8]For we have reached where all of us are one, and we are home, where You would have us be.

A COURSE IN MIRACLES

WORKBOOK FOR STUDENTS

FOUNDATION FOR INNER PEACE

CONTENTS

PART II

xii

INTRODUCTION

1. A theoretical foundation such as the text provides is necessary as a framework to make the exercises in this workbook meaningful. ²Yet it is doing the exercises that will make the goal of the course possible. ³An untrained mind can accomplish nothing. ⁴It is the purpose of this workbook to train your mind to think along the lines the text sets forth.

2. The exercises are very simple. ²They do not require a great deal of time, and it does not matter where you do them. ³They need no preparation. ⁴The training period is one year. ⁵The exercises are numbered from 1 to 365. ⁶Do not undertake to do more than one set of exercises a day.

3. The workbook is divided into two main sections, the first dealing with the undoing of the way you see now, and the second with the acquisition of true perception. ²With the exception of the review periods, each day's exercises are planned around one central idea, which is stated first. ³This is followed by a description of the specific procedures by which the idea for the day is to be applied.

4. The purpose of the workbook is to train your mind in a systematic way to a different perception of everyone and everything in the world. ²The exercises are planned to help you generalize the lessons, so that you will understand that each of them is equally applicable to everyone and everything you see.

5. Transfer of training in true perception does not proceed as does transfer of the training of the world. ²If true perception has been achieved in connection with any person, situation or event, total transfer to everyone and everything is certain. ³On the other hand, one exception held apart from true perception makes its accomplishments anywhere impossible.

6. The only general rules to be observed throughout, then, are: First, that the exercises be practiced with great specificity, as will be indicated. ²This will help you to generalize the ideas involved to every situation in which you find yourself, and to everyone and everything in it. ³Second, be sure that you do not decide for yourself that there are some people, situations or things to which the ideas are inapplicable. ⁴This will interfere with transfer of training. ⁵The very nature of true perception is that it has no limits. ⁶It is the opposite of the way you see now.

7. The overall aim of the exercises is to increase your ability to extend the ideas you will be practicing to include everything. [2]This will require no effort on your part. [3]The exercises themselves meet the conditions necessary for this kind of transfer.

8. Some of the ideas the workbook presents you will find hard to believe, and others may seem to be quite startling. [2]This does not matter. [3]You are merely asked to apply the ideas as you are directed to do. [4]You are not asked to judge them at all. [5]You are asked only to use them. [6]It is their use that will give them meaning to you, and will show you that they are true.

9. Remember only this; you need not believe the ideas, you need not accept them, and you need not even welcome them. [2]Some of them you may actively resist. [3]None of this will matter, or decrease their efficacy. [4]But do not allow yourself to make exceptions in applying the ideas the workbook contains, and whatever your reactions to the ideas may be, use them. [5]Nothing more than that is required.

PART I

LESSON 1

Nothing I see in this room [on this street, from this window, in this place] means anything.

1. Now look slowly around you, and practice applying this idea very specifically to whatever you see:

    > [2]*This table does not mean anything.*
    > [3]*This chair does not mean anything.*
    > [4]*This hand does not mean anything.*
    > [5]*This foot does not mean anything.*
    > [6]*This pen does not mean anything.*

2. Then look farther away from your immediate area, and apply the idea to a wider range:

    > [2]*That door does not mean anything.*
    > [3]*That body does not mean anything.*
    > [4]*That lamp does not mean anything.*
    > [5]*That sign does not mean anything.*
    > [6]*That shadow does not mean anything.*

3. Notice that these statements are not arranged in any order, and make no allowance for differences in the kinds of things to which they are applied. [2]That is the purpose of the exercise. [3]The statement should merely be applied to anything you see. [4]As you practice the idea for the day, use it totally indiscriminately. [5]Do not attempt to apply it to everything you see, for these exercises should not become ritualistic. [6]Only be sure that nothing you see is specifically excluded. [7]One thing is like another as far as the application of the idea is concerned.

4. Each of the first three lessons should not be done more than twice a day each, preferably morning and evening. [2]Nor should they be attempted for more than a minute or so, unless that entails a sense of hurry. [3]A comfortable sense of leisure is essential.

LESSON 2

**I have given everything I see in this room
[on this street, from this window, in this place]
all the meaning that it has for me.**

1.   The exercises with this idea are the same as those for the first one. [2]Begin with the things that are near you, and apply the idea to whatever your glance rests on. [3]Then increase the range outward. [4]Turn your head so that you include whatever is on either side. [5]If possible, turn around and apply the idea to what was behind you. [6]Remain as indiscriminate as possible in selecting subjects for its application, do not concentrate on anything in particular, and do not attempt to include everything you see in a given area, or you will introduce strain.

2.   Merely glance easily and fairly quickly around you, trying to avoid selection by size, brightness, color, material, or relative importance to you. [2]Take the subjects simply as you see them. [3]Try to apply the exercise with equal ease to a body or a button, a fly or a floor, an arm or an apple. [4]The sole criterion for applying the idea to anything is merely that your eyes have lighted on it. [5]Make no attempt to include anything particular, but be sure that nothing is specifically excluded.

LESSON 3

**I do not understand anything I see in this room
[on this street, from this window, in this place].**

1. Apply this idea in the same way as the previous ones, without making distinctions of any kind. ²Whatever you see becomes a proper subject for applying the idea. ³Be sure that you do not question the suitability of anything for application of the idea. ⁴These are not exercises in judgment. ⁵Anything is suitable if you see it. ⁶Some of the things you see may have emotionally charged meaning for you. ⁷Try to lay such feelings aside, and merely use these things exactly as you would anything else.

2. The point of the exercises is to help you clear your mind of all past associations, to see things exactly as they appear to you now, and to realize how little you really understand about them. ²It is therefore essential that you keep a perfectly open mind, unhampered by judgment, in selecting the things to which the idea for the day is to be applied. ³For this purpose one thing is like another; equally suitable and therefore equally useful.

LESSON 4

**These thoughts do not mean anything. They are like
the things I see in this room [on this street,
from this window, in this place].**

1. Unlike the preceding ones, these exercises do not begin with
the idea for the day. ²In these practice periods, begin with noting
the thoughts that are crossing your mind for about a minute.
³Then apply the idea to them. ⁴If you are already aware of unhappy thoughts, use them as subjects for the idea. ⁵Do not, however, select only the thoughts you think are "bad." ⁶You will find,
if you train yourself to look at your thoughts, that they represent
such a mixture that, in a sense, none of them can be called "good"
or "bad." ⁷This is why they do not mean anything.

2. In selecting the subjects for the application of today's idea, the
usual specificity is required. ²Do not be afraid to use "good"
thoughts as well as "bad." ³None of them represents your real
thoughts, which are being covered up by them. ⁴The "good" ones
are but shadows of what lies beyond, and shadows make sight
difficult. ⁵The "bad" ones are blocks to sight, and make seeing
impossible. ⁶You do not want either.

3. This is a major exercise, and will be repeated from time to time
in somewhat different form. ²The aim here is to train you in the
first steps toward the goal of separating the meaningless from the
meaningful. ³It is a first attempt in the long-range purpose of
learning to see the meaningless as outside you, and the meaningful within. ⁴It is also the beginning of training your mind to recognize what is the same and what is different.

4. In using your thoughts for application of the idea for today,
identify each thought by the central figure or event it contains;
for example:

> ²*This thought about* _____ *does not mean anything.*
> ³*It is like the things I see in this room [on this street,
> and so on].*

5. You can also use the idea for a particular thought that you
recognize as harmful. ²This practice is useful, but is not a substitute for the more random procedures to be followed for the

exercises. [3]Do not, however, examine your mind for more than a minute or so. [4]You are too inexperienced as yet to avoid a tendency to become pointlessly preoccupied.

6. Further, since these exercises are the first of their kind, you may find the suspension of judgment in connection with thoughts particularly difficult. [2]Do not repeat these exercises more than three or four times during the day. [3]We will return to them later.

LESSON 5

I am never upset for the reason I think.

1. This idea, like the preceding one, can be used with any person, situation or event you think is causing you pain. ²Apply it specifically to whatever you believe is the cause of your upset, using the description of the feeling in whatever term seems accurate to you. ³The upset may seem to be fear, worry, depression, anxiety, anger, hatred, jealousy or any number of forms, all of which will be perceived as different. ⁴This is not true. ⁵However, until you learn that form does not matter, each form becomes a proper subject for the exercises for the day. ⁶Applying the same idea to each of them separately is the first step in ultimately recognizing they are all the same.

2. When using the idea for today for a specific perceived cause of an upset in any form, use both the name of the form in which you see the upset, and the cause which you ascribe to it. ²For example:

> ³I am not angry at _____ for the reason I think.
> ⁴I am not afraid of _____ for the reason I think.

3. But again, this should not be substituted for practice periods in which you first search your mind for "sources" of upset in which you believe, and forms of upset which you think result.

4. In these exercises, more than in the preceding ones, you may find it hard to be indiscriminate, and to avoid giving greater weight to some subjects than to others. ²It might help to precede the exercises with the statement:

> ³There are no small upsets. ⁴They are all equally
> disturbing to my peace of mind.

5. Then examine your mind for whatever is distressing you, regardless of how much or how little you think it is doing so.

6. You may also find yourself less willing to apply today's idea to some perceived sources of upset than to others. ²If this occurs, think first of this:

>*[3]I cannot keep this form of upset and let the others
go. [4]For the purposes of these exercises, then, I will
regard them all as the same.*

7. Then search your mind for no more than a minute or so, and try to identify a number of different forms of upset that are disturbing you, regardless of the relative importance you may give them. [2]Apply the idea for today to each of them, using the name of both the source of the upset as you perceive it, and of the feeling as you experience it. [3]Further examples are:

>*[4]I am not worried about _____ for the reason I think.*
>*[5]I am not depressed about _____ for the reason I think.*

[6]Three or four times during the day is enough.

LESSON 6

I am upset because I see something that is not there.

1. The exercises with this idea are very similar to the preceding ones. [2]Again, it is necessary to name both the form of upset (anger, fear, worry, depression and so on) and the perceived source very specifically for any application of the idea. [3]For example:

> [4]*I am angry at _____ because I see something that is not there.*
> [5]*I am worried about _____ because I see something that is not there.*

2. Today's idea is useful for application to anything that seems to upset you, and can profitably be used throughout the day for that purpose. [2]However, the three or four practice periods which are required should be preceded by a minute or so of mind searching, as before, and the application of the idea to each upsetting thought uncovered in the search.

3. Again, if you resist applying the idea to some upsetting thoughts more than to others, remind yourself of the two cautions stated in the previous lesson:

> [2]*There are no small upsets. [3]They are all equally disturbing to my peace of mind.*

> [4]And:

> [5]*I cannot keep this form of upset and let the others go. [6]For the purposes of these exercises, then, I will regard them all as the same.*

10

LESSON 7

I see only the past.

1. This idea is particularly difficult to believe at first. ²Yet it is the rationale for all of the preceding ones.

   ³It is the reason why nothing that you see means anything.
   ⁴It is the reason why you have given everything you see all the meaning that it has for you.
   ⁵It is the reason why you do not understand anything you see.
   ⁶It is the reason why your thoughts do not mean anything, and why they are like the things you see.
   ⁷It is the reason why you are never upset for the reason you think.
   ⁸It is the reason why you are upset because you see something that is not there.

2. Old ideas about time are very difficult to change, because everything you believe is rooted in time, and depends on your not learning these new ideas about it. ²Yet that is precisely why you need new ideas about time. ³This first time idea is not really so strange as it may sound at first.

3. Look at a cup, for example. ²Do you see a cup, or are you merely reviewing your past experiences of picking up a cup, being thirsty, drinking from a cup, feeling the rim of a cup against your lips, having breakfast and so on? ³Are not your aesthetic reactions to the cup, too, based on past experiences? ⁴How else would you know whether or not this kind of cup will break if you drop it? ⁵What do you know about this cup except what you learned in the past? ⁶You would have no idea what this cup is, except for your past learning. ⁷Do you, then, really see it?

4. Look about you. ²This is equally true of whatever you look at. ³Acknowledge this by applying the idea for today indiscriminately to whatever catches your eye. ⁴For example:

   > ⁵*I see only the past in this pencil.*
   > ⁶*I see only the past in this shoe.*
   > ⁷*I see only the past in this hand.*
   > ⁸*I see only the past in that body.*
   > ⁹*I see only the past in that face.*

11

5. Do not linger over any one thing in particular, but remember to omit nothing specifically. ²Glance briefly at each subject, and then move on to the next. ³Three or four practice periods, each to last a minute or so, will be enough.

LESSON 8

My mind is preoccupied with past thoughts.

1. This idea is, of course, the reason why you see only the past. ²No one really sees anything. ³He sees only his thoughts projected outward. ⁴The mind's preoccupation with the past is the cause of the misconception about time from which your seeing suffers. ⁵Your mind cannot grasp the present, which is the only time there is. ⁶It therefore cannot understand time, and cannot, in fact, understand anything.

2. The one wholly true thought one can hold about the past is that it is not here. ²To think about it at all is therefore to think about illusions. ³Very few have realized what is actually entailed in picturing the past or in anticipating the future. ⁴The mind is actually blank when it does this, because it is not really thinking about anything.

3. The purpose of the exercises for today is to begin to train your mind to recognize when it is not really thinking at all. ²While thoughtless ideas preoccupy your mind, the truth is blocked. ³Recognizing that your mind has been merely blank, rather than believing that it is filled with real ideas, is the first step to opening the way to vision.

4. The exercises for today should be done with eyes closed. ²This is because you actually cannot see anything, and it is easier to recognize that no matter how vividly you may picture a thought, you are not seeing anything. ³With as little investment as possible, search your mind for the usual minute or so, merely noting the thoughts you find there. ⁴Name each one by the central figure or theme it contains, and pass on to the next. ⁵Introduce the practice period by saying:

⁶I seem to be thinking about _____.

5. Then name each of your thoughts specifically, for example:

²I seem to be thinking about [name of a person], about [name of an object], about [name of an emotion],

13

and so on, concluding at the end of the mind-searching period with:

> [3]But my mind is preoccupied with past thoughts.

6. This can be done four or five times during the day, unless you find it irritates you. [2]If you find it trying, three or four times is sufficient. [3]You might find it helpful, however, to include your irritation, or any emotion that the idea for today may induce, in the mind searching itself.

LESSON 9

I see nothing as it is now.

1. This idea obviously follows from the two preceding ones. [2]But while you may be able to accept it intellectually, it is unlikely that it will mean anything to you as yet. [3]However, understanding is not necessary at this point. [4]In fact, the recognition that you do not understand is a prerequisite for undoing your false ideas. [5]These exercises are concerned with practice, not with understanding. [6]You do not need to practice what you already understand. [7]It would indeed be circular to aim at understanding, and assume that you have it already.

2. It is difficult for the untrained mind to believe that what it seems to picture is not there. [2]This idea can be quite disturbing, and may meet with active resistance in any number of forms. [3]Yet that does not preclude applying it. [4]No more than that is required for these or any other exercises. [5]Each small step will clear a little of the darkness away, and understanding will finally come to lighten every corner of the mind that has been cleared of the debris that darkens it.

3. These exercises, for which three or four practice periods are sufficient, involve looking about you and applying the idea for the day to whatever you see, remembering the need for its indiscriminate application, and the essential rule of excluding nothing. [2]For example:

> [3]*I do not see this typewriter as it is now.*
> [4]*I do not see this telephone as it is now.*
> [5]*I do not see this arm as it is now.*

4. Begin with things that are nearest you, and then extend the range outward:

> [2]*I do not see that coat rack as it is now.*
> [3]*I do not see that door as it is now.*
> [4]*I do not see that face as it is now.*

5. It is emphasized again that while complete inclusion should not be attempted, specific exclusion must be avoided. [2]Be sure you are honest with yourself in making this distinction. [3]You may be tempted to obscure it.

15

LESSON 10

My thoughts do not mean anything.

1. This idea applies to all the thoughts of which you are aware, or become aware in the practice periods. ²The reason the idea is applicable to all of them is that they are not your real thoughts. ³We have made this distinction before, and will do so again. ⁴You have no basis for comparison as yet. ⁵When you do, you will have no doubt that what you once believed were your thoughts did not mean anything.

2. This is the second time we have used this kind of idea. ²The form is only slightly different. ³This time the idea is introduced with "My thoughts" instead of "These thoughts," and no link is made overtly with the things around you. ⁴The emphasis is now on the lack of reality of what you think you think.

3. This aspect of the correction process began with the idea that the thoughts of which you are aware are meaningless, outside rather than within; and then stressed their past rather than their present status. ²Now we are emphasizing that the presence of these "thoughts" means that you are not thinking. ³This is merely another way of repeating our earlier statement that your mind is really a blank. ⁴To recognize this is to recognize nothingness when you think you see it. ⁵As such, it is the prerequisite for vision.

4. Close your eyes for these exercises, and introduce them by repeating the idea for today quite slowly to yourself. ²Then add:

   ³*This idea will help to release me from all that I now believe.*

⁴The exercises consist, as before, in searching your mind for all the thoughts that are available to you, without selection or judgment. ⁵Try to avoid classification of any kind. ⁶In fact, if you find it helpful to do so, you might imagine that you are watching an oddly assorted procession going by, which has little if any personal meaning to you. ⁷As each one crosses your mind, say:

   ⁸*My thought about _____ does not mean anything.*
   ⁹*My thought about _____ does not mean anything.*

5. Today's thought can obviously serve for any thought that distresses you at any time. ²In addition, five practice periods are recommended, each involving no more than a minute or so of mind searching. ³It is not recommended that this time period be extended, and it should be reduced to half a minute or less if you experience discomfort. ⁴Remember, however, to repeat the idea slowly before applying it specifically, and also to add:

     ⁵*This idea will help to release me from all that I now believe.*

LESSON 11

My meaningless thoughts are showing me a meaningless world.

1. This is the first idea we have had that is related to a major phase of the correction process; the reversal of the thinking of the world. [2]It seems as if the world determines what you perceive. [3]Today's idea introduces the concept that your thoughts determine the world you see. [4]Be glad indeed to practice the idea in its initial form, for in this idea is your release made sure. [5]The key to forgiveness lies in it.

2. The practice periods for today's idea are to be undertaken somewhat differently from the previous ones. [2]Begin with your eyes closed, and repeat the idea slowly to yourself. [3]Then open your eyes and look about, near and far, up and down,—anywhere. [4]During the minute or so to be spent in using the idea merely repeat it to yourself, being sure to do so without haste, and with no sense of urgency or effort.

3. To do these exercises for maximum benefit, the eyes should move from one thing to another fairly rapidly, since they should not linger on anything in particular. [2]The words, however, should be used in an unhurried, even leisurely fashion. [3]The introduction to this idea, in particular, should be practiced as casually as possible. [4]It contains the foundation for the peace, relaxation and freedom from worry that we are trying to achieve. [5]On concluding the exercises, close your eyes and repeat the idea once more slowly to yourself.

4. Three practice periods today will probably be sufficient. [2]However, if there is little or no uneasiness and an inclination to do more, as many as five may be undertaken. [3]More than this is not recommended.

LESSON 12

I am upset because I see a meaningless world.

1. The importance of this idea lies in the fact that it contains a correction for a major perceptual distortion. [2]You think that what upsets you is a frightening world, or a sad world, or a violent world, or an insane world. [3]All these attributes are given it by you. [4]The world is meaningless in itself.

2. These exercises are done with eyes open. [2]Look around you, this time quite slowly. [3]Try to pace yourself so that the slow shifting of your glance from one thing to another involves a fairly constant time interval. [4]Do not allow the time of the shift to become markedly longer or shorter, but try, instead, to keep a measured, even tempo throughout. [5]What you see does not matter. [6]You teach yourself this as you give whatever your glance rests on equal attention and equal time. [7]This is a beginning step in learning to give them all equal value.

3. As you look about you, say to yourself:

> [2]*I think I see a fearful world, a dangerous world, a hostile world, a sad world, a wicked world, a crazy world,*

and so on, using whatever descriptive terms happen to occur to you. [3]If terms which seem positive rather than negative occur to you, include them. [4]For example, you might think of "a good world," or "a satisfying world." [5]If such terms occur to you, use them along with the rest. [6]You may not yet understand why these "nice" adjectives belong in these exercises but remember that a "good world" implies a "bad" one, and a "satisfying world" implies an "unsatisfying" one. [7]All terms which cross your mind are suitable subjects for today's exercises. [8]Their seeming quality does not matter.

4. Be sure that you do not alter the time intervals between applying today's idea to what you think is pleasant and what you think is unpleasant. [2]For the purposes of these exercises, there is no difference between them. [3]At the end of the practice period, add:

> [4]*But I am upset because I see a meaningless world.*

19

5. What is meaningless is neither good nor bad. [2]Why, then, should a meaningless world upset you? [3]If you could accept the world as meaningless and let the truth be written upon it for you, it would make you indescribably happy. [4]But because it is meaningless, you are impelled to write upon it what you would have it be. [5]It is this you see in it. [6]It is this that is meaningless in truth. [7]Beneath your words is written the Word of God. [8]The truth upsets you now, but when your words have been erased, you will see His. [9]That is the ultimate purpose of these exercises.

6. Three or four times is enough for practicing the idea for today. [2]Nor should the practice periods exceed a minute. [3]You may find even this too long. [4]Terminate the exercises whenever you experience a sense of strain.

LESSON 13

A meaningless world engenders fear.

1. Today's idea is really another form of the preceding one, except that it is more specific as to the emotion aroused. ²Actually, a meaningless world is impossible. ³Nothing without meaning exists. ⁴However, it does not follow that you will not think you perceive something that has no meaning. ⁵On the contrary, you will be particularly likely to think you do perceive it.

2. Recognition of meaninglessness arouses intense anxiety in all the separated ones. ²It represents a situation in which God and the ego "challenge" each other as to whose meaning is to be written in the empty space that meaninglessness provides. ³The ego rushes in frantically to establish its own ideas there, fearful that the void may otherwise be used to demonstrate its own impotence and unreality. ⁴And on this alone it is correct.

3. It is essential, therefore, that you learn to recognize the meaningless, and accept it without fear. ²If you are fearful, it is certain that you will endow the world with attributes that it does not possess, and crowd it with images that do not exist. ³To the ego illusions are safety devices, as they must also be to you who equate yourself with the ego.

4. The exercises for today, which should be done about three or four times for not more than a minute or so at most each time, are to be practiced in a somewhat different way from the preceding ones. ²With eyes closed, repeat today's idea to yourself. ³Then open your eyes, and look about you slowly, saying:

⁴*I am looking at a meaningless world.*

⁵Repeat this statement to yourself as you look about. ⁶Then close your eyes, and conclude with:

⁷*A meaningless world engenders fear because I think I am in competition with God.*

5. You may find it difficult to avoid resistance, in one form or another, to this concluding statement. ²Whatever form such resistance may take, remind yourself that you are really afraid of such

21

a thought because of the "vengeance" of the "enemy." [3]You are not expected to believe the statement at this point, and will probably dismiss it as preposterous. [4]Note carefully, however, any signs of overt or covert fear which it may arouse.

6. This is our first attempt at stating an explicit cause and effect relationship of a kind which you are very inexperienced in recognizing. [2]Do not dwell on the concluding statement, and try not even to think of it except during the practice periods. [3]That will suffice at present.

LESSON 14

God did not create a meaningless world.

1. The idea for today is, of course, the reason why a meaningless world is impossible. ²What God did not create does not exist. ³And everything that does exist exists as He created it. ⁴The world you see has nothing to do with reality. ⁵It is of your own making, and it does not exist.

2. The exercises for today are to be practiced with eyes closed throughout. ²The mind-searching period should be short, a minute at most. ³Do not have more than three practice periods with today's idea unless you find them comfortable. ⁴If you do, it will be because you really understand what they are for.

3. The idea for today is another step in learning to let go the thoughts that you have written on the world, and see the Word of God in their place. ²The early steps in this exchange, which can truly be called salvation, can be quite difficult and even quite painful. ³Some of them will lead you directly into fear. ⁴You will not be left there. ⁵You will go far beyond it. ⁶Our direction is toward perfect safety and perfect peace.

4. With eyes closed, think of all the horrors in the world that cross your mind. ²Name each one as it occurs to you, and then deny its reality. ³God did not create it, and so it is not real. ⁴Say, for example:

⁵*God did not create that war, and so it is not real.*
⁶*God did not create that airplane crash, and so it is not real.*
⁷*God did not create that disaster [specify], and so it is not real.*

5. Suitable subjects for the application of today's idea also include anything you are afraid might happen to you, or to anyone about whom you are concerned. ²In each case, name the "disaster" quite specifically. ³Do not use general terms. ⁴For example, do not say, "God did not create illness," but, "God did not create cancer," or heart attacks, or whatever may arouse fear in you.

6. This is your personal repertory of horrors at which you are looking. ²These things are part of the world you see. ³Some of them are shared illusions, and others are part of your personal hell. ⁴It does not matter. ⁵What God did not create can only be in

your own mind apart from His. ⁶Therefore, it has no meaning. ⁷In recognition of this fact, conclude the practice periods by repeating today's idea:

⁸*God did not create a meaningless world.*

7. The idea for today can, of course, be applied to anything that disturbs you during the day, aside from the practice periods. ²Be very specific in applying it. ³Say:

⁴*God did not create a meaningless world.* ⁵*He did not create [specify the situation which is disturbing you], and so it is not real.*

24

LESSON 15

My thoughts are images that I have made.

1. It is because the thoughts you think you think appear as images that you do not recognize them as nothing. ²You think you think them, and so you think you see them. ³This is how your "seeing" was made. ⁴This is the function you have given your body's eyes. ⁵It is not seeing. ⁶It is image making. ⁷It takes the place of seeing, replacing vision with illusions.

2. This introductory idea to the process of image making that you call seeing will not have much meaning for you. ²You will begin to understand it when you have seen little edges of light around the same familiar objects which you see now. ³That is the beginning of real vision. ⁴You can be certain that real vision will come quickly when this has occurred.

3. As we go along, you may have many "light episodes." ²They may take many different forms, some of them quite unexpected. ³Do not be afraid of them. ⁴They are signs that you are opening your eyes at last. ⁵They will not persist, because they merely symbolize true perception, and they are not related to knowledge. ⁶These exercises will not reveal knowledge to you. ⁷But they will prepare the way to it.

4. In practicing the idea for today, repeat it first to yourself, and then apply it to whatever you see around you, using its name and letting your eyes rest on it as you say:

> ²This _____ is an image that I have made.
> ³That _____ is an image that I have made.

⁴It is not necessary to include a large number of specific subjects for the application of today's idea. ⁵It is necessary, however, to continue to look at each subject while you repeat the idea to yourself. ⁶The idea should be repeated quite slowly each time.

5. Although you will obviously not be able to apply the idea to very many things during the minute or so of practice that is recommended, try to make the selection as random as possible. ²Less than a minute will do for the practice periods, if you begin to feel uneasy. ³Do not have more than three application periods for today's idea unless you feel completely comfortable with it, and do not exceed four. ⁴However, the idea can be applied as needed throughout the day.

LESSON 16

I have no neutral thoughts.

1. The idea for today is a beginning step in dispelling the belief that your thoughts have no effect. [2]Everything you see is the result of your thoughts. [3]There is no exception to this fact. [4]Thoughts are not big or little; powerful or weak. [5]They are merely true or false. [6]Those that are true create their own likeness. [7]Those that are false make theirs.

2. There is no more self-contradictory concept than that of "idle thoughts." [2]What gives rise to the perception of a whole world can hardly be called idle. [3]Every thought you have contributes to truth or to illusion; either it extends the truth or it multiplies illusions. [4]You can indeed multiply nothing, but you will not extend it by doing so.

3. Besides your recognizing that thoughts are never idle, salvation requires that you also recognize that every thought you have brings either peace or war; either love or fear. [2]A neutral result is impossible because a neutral thought is impossible. [3]There is such a temptation to dismiss fear thoughts as unimportant, trivial and not worth bothering about that it is essential you recognize them all as equally destructive, but equally unreal. [4]We will practice this idea in many forms before you really understand it.

4. In applying the idea for today, search your mind for a minute or so with eyes closed, and actively seek not to overlook any "little" thought that may tend to elude the search. [2]This is quite difficult until you get used to it. [3]You will find that it is still hard for you not to make artificial distinctions. [4]Every thought that occurs to you, regardless of the qualities that you assign to it, is a suitable subject for applying today's idea.

5. In the practice periods, first repeat the idea to yourself, and then as each one crosses your mind hold it in awareness while you tell yourself:

> [2]*This thought about _____ is not a neutral thought.*
> [3]*That thought about _____ is not a neutral thought.*

[4]As usual, use today's idea whenever you are aware of a particu-

lar thought that arouses uneasiness. [5]The following form is suggested for this purpose:

> [6]*This thought about _____ is not a neutral thought,*
> *because I have no neutral thoughts.*

6. Four or five practice periods are recommended, if you find them relatively effortless. [2]If strain is experienced, three will be enough. [3]The length of the exercise period should also be reduced if there is discomfort.

LESSON 17

I see no neutral things.

1.   This idea is another step in the direction of identifying cause and effect as it really operates in the world. ²You see no neutral things because you have no neutral thoughts. ³It is always the thought that comes first, despite the temptation to believe that it is the other way around. ⁴This is not the way the world thinks, but you must learn that it is the way you think. ⁵If it were not so, perception would have no cause, and would itself be the cause of reality. ⁶In view of its highly variable nature, this is hardly likely.

2.   In applying today's idea, say to yourself, with eyes open:

> ²*I see no neutral things because I have no neutral thoughts.*

³Then look about you, resting your glance on each thing you note long enough to say:

> ⁴*I do not see a neutral _____ , because my thoughts about _____ are not neutral.*

⁵For example, you might say:

> ⁶*I do not see a neutral wall, because my thoughts about walls are not neutral.*
> ⁷*I do not see a neutral body, because my thoughts about bodies are not neutral.*

3.   As usual, it is essential to make no distinctions between what you believe to be animate or inanimate; pleasant or unpleasant. ²Regardless of what you may believe, you do not see anything that is really alive or really joyous. ³That is because you are unaware as yet of any thought that is really true, and therefore really happy.

4.   Three or four specific practice periods are recommended, and no less than three are required for maximum benefit, even if you experience resistance. ²However, if you do, the length of the practice period may be reduced to less than the minute or so that is otherwise recommended.

LESSON 18

I am not alone in experiencing the effects of my seeing.

1. The idea for today is another step in learning that the thoughts which give rise to what you see are never neutral or unimportant. [2]It also emphasizes the idea that minds are joined, which will be given increasing stress later on.
2. Today's idea does not refer to what you see as much as to how you see it. [2]Therefore, the exercises for today emphasize this aspect of your perception. [3]The three or four practice periods which are recommended should be done as follows:
3. Look about you, selecting subjects for the application of the idea for today as randomly as possible, and keeping your eyes on each one long enough to say:

> [2]*I am not alone in experiencing the effects of how I see _____.*

[3]Conclude each practice period by repeating the more general statement:

> [4]*I am not alone in experiencing the effects of my seeing.*

[5]A minute or so, or even less, will be sufficient for each practice period.

LESSON 19

I am not alone in experiencing the effects of my thoughts.

1. The idea for today is obviously the reason why your seeing does not affect you alone. ²You will notice that at times the ideas related to thinking precede those related to perceiving, while at other times the order is reversed. ³The reason is that the order does not matter. ⁴Thinking and its results are really simultaneous, for cause and effect are never separate.

2. Today we are again emphasizing the fact that minds are joined. ²This is rarely a wholly welcome idea at first, since it seems to carry with it an enormous sense of responsibility, and may even be regarded as an "invasion of privacy." ³Yet it is a fact that there are no private thoughts. ⁴Despite your initial resistance to this idea, you will yet understand that it must be true if salvation is possible at all. ⁵And salvation must be possible because it is the Will of God.

3. The minute or so of mind searching which today's exercises require is to be undertaken with eyes closed. ²The idea for today is to be repeated first, and then the mind should be carefully searched for the thoughts it contains at that time. ³As you consider each one, name it in terms of the central person or theme it contains, and holding it in your mind as you do so, say:

> ⁴*I am not alone in experiencing the effects of this*
> *thought about _____ .*

4. The requirement of as much indiscriminateness as possible in selecting subjects for the practice periods should be quite familiar to you by now, and will no longer be repeated each day, although it will occasionally be included as a reminder. ²Do not forget, however, that random selection of subjects for all practice periods remains essential throughout. ³Lack of order in this connection will ultimately make the recognition of lack of order in miracles meaningful to you.

5. Apart from the "as needed" application of today's idea, at least three practice periods are required, shortening the length of time involved, if necessary. ²Do not attempt more than four.

LESSON 20

I am determined to see.

1. We have been quite casual about our practice periods thus far. ²There has been virtually no attempt to direct the time for undertaking them, minimal effort has been required, and not even active cooperation and interest have been asked. ³This approach has been intentional, and very carefully planned. ⁴We have not lost sight of the crucial importance of the reversal of your thinking. ⁵The salvation of the world depends on it. ⁶Yet you will not see if you regard yourself as being coerced, and if you give in to resentment and opposition.

2. This is our first attempt to introduce structure. ²Do not misconstrue it as an effort to exert force or pressure. ³You want salvation. ⁴You want to be happy. ⁵You want peace. ⁶You do not have them now, because your mind is totally undisciplined, and you cannot distinguish between joy and sorrow, pleasure and pain, love and fear. ⁷You are now learning how to tell them apart. ⁸And great indeed will be your reward.

3. Your decision to see is all that vision requires. ²What you want is yours. ³Do not mistake the little effort that is asked of you for an indication that our goal is of little worth. ⁴Can the salvation of the world be a trivial purpose? ⁵And can the world be saved if you are not? ⁶God has one Son, and he is the resurrection and the life. ⁷His will is done because all power is given him in Heaven and on earth. ⁸In your determination to see is vision given you.

4. The exercises for today consist in reminding yourself throughout the day that you want to see. ²Today's idea also tacitly implies the recognition that you do not see now. ³Therefore, as you repeat the idea, you are stating that you are determined to change your present state for a better one, and one you really want.

5. Repeat today's idea slowly and positively at least twice an hour today, attempting to do so every half hour. ²Do not be distressed if you forget to do so, but make a real effort to remember. ³The extra repetitions should be applied to any situation, person or event that upsets you. ⁴You can see them differently, and you will. ⁵What you desire you will see. ⁶Such is the real law of cause and effect as it operates in the world.

LESSON 21

I am determined to see things differently.

1. The idea for today is obviously a continuation and extension of the preceding one. ²This time, however, specific mind-searching periods are necessary, in addition to applying the idea to particular situations as they may arise. ³Five practice periods are urged, allowing a full minute for each.
2. In the practice periods, begin by repeating the idea to yourself. ²Then close your eyes and search your mind carefully for situations past, present or anticipated that arouse anger in you. ³The anger may take the form of any reaction ranging from mild irritation to rage. ⁴The degree of the emotion you experience does not matter. ⁵You will become increasingly aware that a slight twinge of annoyance is nothing but a veil drawn over intense fury.
3. Try, therefore, not to let the "little" thoughts of anger escape you in the practice periods. ²Remember that you do not really recognize what arouses anger in you, and nothing that you believe in this connection means anything. ³You will probably be tempted to dwell more on some situations or persons than on others, on the fallacious grounds that they are more "obvious." ⁴This is not so. ⁵It is merely an example of the belief that some forms of attack are more justified than others.
4. As you search your mind for all the forms in which attack thoughts present themselves, hold each one in mind while you tell yourself:

    ²*I am determined to see* _____ *[name of person] differently.*
    ³*I am determined to see* _____ *[specify the situation] differently.*

5. Try to be as specific as possible. ²You may, for example, focus your anger on a particular attribute of a particular person, believing that the anger is limited to this aspect. ³If your perception is suffering from this form of distortion, say:

    ⁴*I am determined to see* _____ *[specify the attribute] in* _____ *[name of person] differently.*

32

LESSON 22

What I see is a form of vengeance.

1. Today's idea accurately describes the way anyone who holds attack thoughts in his mind must see the world. ²Having projected his anger onto the world, he sees vengeance about to strike at him. ³His own attack is thus perceived as self defense. ⁴This becomes an increasingly vicious circle until he is willing to change how he sees. ⁵Otherwise, thoughts of attack and counter-attack will preoccupy him and people his entire world. ⁶What peace of mind is possible to him then?

2. It is from this savage fantasy that you want to escape. ²Is it not joyous news to hear that it is not real? ³Is it not a happy discovery to find that you can escape? ⁴You made what you would destroy; everything that you hate and would attack and kill. ⁵All that you fear does not exist.

3. Look at the world about you at least five times today, for at least a minute each time. ²As your eyes move slowly from one object to another, from one body to another, say to yourself:

> ³*I see only the perishable.*
> ⁴*I see nothing that will last.*
> ⁵*What I see is not real.*
> ⁶*What I see is a form of vengeance.*

⁷At the end of each practice period, ask yourself:

> ⁸*Is this the world I really want to see?*

⁹The answer is surely obvious.

LESSON 23

I can escape from the world I see
by giving up attack thoughts.

1. The idea for today contains the only way out of fear that will ever succeed. [2]Nothing else will work; everything else is meaningless. [3]But this way cannot fail. [4]Every thought you have makes up some segment of the world you see. [5]It is with your thoughts, then, that we must work, if your perception of the world is to be changed.

2. If the cause of the world you see is attack thoughts, you must learn that it is these thoughts which you do not want. [2]There is no point in lamenting the world. [3]There is no point in trying to change the world. [4]It is incapable of change because it is merely an effect. [5]But there is indeed a point in changing your thoughts about the world. [6]Here you are changing the cause. [7]The effect will change automatically.

3. The world you see is a vengeful world, and everything in it is a symbol of vengeance. [2]Each of your perceptions of "external reality" is a pictorial representation of your own attack thoughts. [3]One can well ask if this can be called seeing. [4]Is not fantasy a better word for such a process, and hallucination a more appropriate term for the result?

4. You see the world that you have made, but you do not see yourself as the image maker. [2]You cannot be saved from the world, but you can escape from its cause. [3]This is what salvation means, for where is the world you see when its cause is gone? [4]Vision already holds a replacement for everything you think you see now. [5]Loveliness can light your images, and so transform them that you will love them, even though they were made of hate. [6]For you will not be making them alone.

5. The idea for today introduces the thought that you are not trapped in the world you see, because its cause can be changed. [2]This change requires, first, that the cause be identified and then let go, so that it can be replaced. [3]The first two steps in this process require your cooperation. [4]The final one does not. [5]Your images have already been replaced. [6]By taking the first two steps, you will see that this is so.

6. Besides using it throughout the day as the need arises, five

practice periods are required in applying today's idea. ²As you look about you, repeat the idea slowly to yourself first, and then close your eyes and devote about a minute to searching your mind for as many attack thoughts as occur to you. ³As each one crosses your mind say:

⁴*I can escape from the world I see by giving up attack thoughts about _____ .*

⁵Hold each attack thought in mind as you say this, and then dismiss that thought and go on to the next.

7. In the practice periods, be sure to include both your thoughts of attacking and of being attacked. ²Their effects are exactly the same because they are exactly the same. ³You do not recognize this as yet, and you are asked at this time only to treat them as the same in today's practice periods. ⁴We are still at the stage of identifying the cause of the world you see. ⁵When you finally learn that thoughts of attack and of being attacked are not different, you will be ready to let the cause go.

35

LESSON 24

I do not perceive my own best interests.

1. In no situation that arises do you realize the outcome that would make you happy. ²Therefore, you have no guide to appropriate action, and no way of judging the result. ³What you do is determined by your perception of the situation, and that perception is wrong. ⁴It is inevitable, then, that you will not serve your own best interests. ⁵Yet they are your only goal in any situation which is correctly perceived. ⁶Otherwise, you will not recognize what they are.

2. If you realized that you do not perceive your own best interests, you could be taught what they are. ²But in the presence of your conviction that you do know what they are, you cannot learn. ³The idea for today is a step toward opening your mind so that learning can begin.

3. The exercises for today require much more honesty than you are accustomed to using. ²A few subjects, honestly and carefully considered in each of the five practice periods which should be undertaken today, will be more helpful than a more cursory examination of a large number. ³Two minutes are suggested for each of the mind-searching periods which the exercises involve.

4. The practice periods should begin with repeating today's idea, followed by searching the mind, with closed eyes, for unresolved situations about which you are currently concerned. ²The emphasis should be on uncovering the outcome you want. ³You will quickly realize that you have a number of goals in mind as part of the desired outcome, and also that these goals are on different levels and often conflict.

5. In applying the idea for today, name each situation that occurs to you, and then enumerate carefully as many goals as possible that you would like to be met in its resolution. ²The form of each application should be roughly as follows:

> ³*In the situation involving _____ , I would like _____ to happen, and _____ to happen,*

and so on. ⁴Try to cover as many different kinds of outcomes as may honestly occur to you, even if some of them do not appear to be directly related to the situation, or even to be inherent in it at all.

6. If these exercises are done properly, you will quickly recognize that you are making a large number of demands of the situation which have nothing to do with it. [2]You will also recognize that many of your goals are contradictory, that you have no unified outcome in mind, and that you must experience disappointment in connection with some of your goals, however the situation turns out.

7. After covering the list of as many hoped-for goals as possible, for each unresolved situation that crosses your mind say to yourself:

> [2]*I do not perceive my own best interests in this situation,*

and go on to the next one.

LESSON 25

I do not know what anything is for.

1. Purpose is meaning. [2]Today's idea explains why nothing you see means anything. [3]You do not know what it is for. [4]Therefore, it is meaningless to you. [5]Everything is for your own best interests. [6]That is what it is for; that is its purpose; that is what it means. [7]It is in recognizing this that your goals become unified. [8]It is in recognizing this that what you see is given meaning.

2. You perceive the world and everything in it as meaningful in terms of ego goals. [2]These goals have nothing to do with your own best interests, because the ego is not you. [3]This false identification makes you incapable of understanding what anything is for. [4]As a result, you are bound to misuse it. [5]When you believe this, you will try to withdraw the goals you have assigned to the world, instead of attempting to reinforce them.

3. Another way of describing the goals you now perceive is to say that they are all concerned with "personal" interests. [2]Since you have no personal interests, your goals are really concerned with nothing. [3]In cherishing them, therefore, you have no goals at all. [4]And thus you do not know what anything is for.

4. Before you can make any sense out of the exercises for today, one more thought is necessary. [2]At the most superficial levels, you do recognize purpose. [3]Yet purpose cannot be understood at these levels. [4]For example, you do understand that a telephone is for the purpose of talking to someone who is not physically in your immediate vicinity. [5]What you do not understand is what you want to reach him for. [6]And it is this that makes your contact with him meaningful or not.

5. It is crucial to your learning to be willing to give up the goals you have established for everything. [2]The recognition that they are meaningless, rather than "good" or "bad," is the only way to accomplish this. [3]The idea for today is a step in this direction.

6. Six practice periods, each of two-minutes duration, are required. [2]Each practice period should begin with a slow repetition of the idea for today, followed by looking about you and letting your glance rest on whatever happens to catch your eye, near or far, "important" or "unimportant," "human" or "nonhuman." [3]With your eyes resting on each subject you so select, say, for example:

> ⁴*I do not know what this chair is for.*
> ⁵*I do not know what this pencil is for.*
> ⁶*I do not know what this hand is for.*

⁷Say this quite slowly, without shifting your eyes from the subject until you have completed the statement about it. ⁸Then move on to the next subject, and apply today's idea as before.

39

LESSON 26

My attack thoughts are attacking my invulnerability.

1. It is surely obvious that if you can be attacked you are not invulnerable. ²You see attack as a real threat. ³That is because you believe that you can really attack. ⁴And what would have effects through you must also have effects on you. ⁵It is this law that will ultimately save you, but you are misusing it now. ⁶You must therefore learn how it can be used for your own best interests, rather than against them.

2. Because your attack thoughts will be projected, you will fear attack. ²And if you fear attack, you must believe that you are not invulnerable. ³Attack thoughts therefore make you vulnerable in your own mind, which is where the attack thoughts are. ⁴Attack thoughts and invulnerability cannot be accepted together. ⁵They contradict each other.

3. The idea for today introduces the thought that you always attack yourself first. ²If attack thoughts must entail the belief that you are vulnerable, their effect is to weaken you in your own eyes. ³Thus they have attacked your perception of yourself. ⁴And because you believe in them, you can no longer believe in yourself. ⁵A false image of yourself has come to take the place of what you are.

4. Practice with today's idea will help you to understand that vulnerability or invulnerability is the result of your own thoughts. ²Nothing except your thoughts can attack you. ³Nothing except your thoughts can make you think you are vulnerable. ⁴And nothing except your thoughts can prove to you this is not so.

5. Six practice periods are required in applying today's idea. ²A full two minutes should be attempted for each of them, although the time may be reduced to a minute if the discomfort is too great. ³Do not reduce it further.

6. The practice period should begin with repeating the idea for today, then closing your eyes and reviewing the unresolved questions whose outcomes are causing you concern. ²The concern may take the form of depression, worry, anger, a sense of imposition, fear, foreboding or preoccupation. ³Any problem as yet unsettled that tends to recur in your thoughts during the day is a

suitable subject. [4]You will not be able to use very many for any one practice period, because a longer time than usual should be spent with each one. [5]Today's idea should be applied as follows:

7. First, name the situation:

²I am concerned about _____ .

³Then go over every possible outcome that has occurred to you in that connection and which has caused you concern, referring to each one quite specifically, saying:

⁴I am afraid _____ will happen.

8. If you are doing the exercises properly, you should have some five or six distressing possibilities available for each situation you use, and quite possibly more. ²It is much more helpful to cover a few situations thoroughly than to touch on a larger number. ³As the list of anticipated outcomes for each situation continues, you will probably find some of them, especially those that occur to you toward the end, less acceptable to you. ⁴Try, however, to treat them all alike to whatever extent you can.

9. After you have named each outcome of which you are afraid, tell yourself:

²That thought is an attack upon myself.

³Conclude each practice period by repeating today's idea to yourself once more.

LESSON 27

Above all else I want to see.

1. Today's idea expresses something stronger than mere determination. [2]It gives vision priority among your desires. [3]You may feel hesitant about using the idea, on the grounds that you are not sure you really mean it. [4]This does not matter. [5]The purpose of today's exercises is to bring the time when the idea will be wholly true a little nearer.

2. There may be a great temptation to believe that some sort of sacrifice is being asked of you when you say you want to see above all else. [2]If you become uneasy about the lack of reservation involved, add:

   [3]*Vision has no cost to anyone.*

   [4]If fear of loss still persists, add further:

   [5]*It can only bless.*

3. The idea for today needs many repetitions for maximum benefit. [2]It should be used at least every half hour, and more if possible. [3]You might try for every fifteen or twenty minutes. [4]It is recommended that you set a definite time interval for using the idea when you wake or shortly afterwards, and attempt to adhere to it throughout the day. [5]It will not be difficult to do this, even if you are engaged in conversation, or otherwise occupied at the time. [6]You can still repeat one short sentence to yourself without disturbing anything.

4. The real question is, how often will you remember? [2]How much do you want today's idea to be true? [3]Answer one of these questions, and you have answered the other. [4]You will probably miss several applications, and perhaps quite a number. [5]Do not be disturbed by this, but do try to keep on your schedule from then on. [6]If only once during the day you feel that you were perfectly sincere while you were repeating today's idea, you can be sure that you have saved yourself many years of effort.

LESSON 28

Above all else I want to see things differently.

1. Today we are really giving specific application to the idea for yesterday. ²In these practice periods, you will be making a series of definite commitments. ³The question of whether you will keep them in the future is not our concern here. ⁴If you are willing at least to make them now, you have started on the way to keeping them. ⁵And we are still at the beginning.

2. You may wonder why it is important to say, for example, "Above all else I want to see this table differently." ²In itself it is not important at all. ³Yet what is by itself? ⁴And what does "in itself" mean? ⁵You see a lot of separate things about you, which really means you are not seeing at all. ⁶You either see or not. ⁷When you have seen one thing differently, you will see all things differently. ⁸The light you will see in any one of them is the same light you will see in them all.

3. When you say, "Above all else I want to see this table differently," you are making a commitment to withdraw your preconceived ideas about the table, and open your mind to what it is, and what it is for. ²You are not defining it in past terms. ³You are asking what it is, rather than telling it what it is. ⁴You are not binding its meaning to your tiny experience of tables, nor are you limiting its purpose to your little personal thoughts.

4. You will not question what you have already defined. ²And the purpose of these exercises is to ask questions and receive the answers. ³In saying, "Above all else I want to see this table differently," you are committing yourself to seeing. ⁴It is not an exclusive commitment. ⁵It is a commitment that applies to the table just as much as to anything else, neither more nor less.

5. You could, in fact, gain vision from just that table, if you would withdraw all your own ideas from it, and look upon it with a completely open mind. ²It has something to show you; something beautiful and clean and of infinite value, full of happiness and hope. ³Hidden under all your ideas about it is its real purpose, the purpose it shares with all the universe.

6. In using the table as a subject for applying the idea for today, you are therefore really asking to see the purpose of the universe. ²You will be making this same request of each subject that you

use in the practice periods. ³And you are making a commitment to each of them to let its purpose be revealed to you, instead of placing your own judgment upon it.

7. We will have six two-minute practice periods today, in which the idea for the day is stated first, and then applied to whatever you see about you. ²Not only should the subjects be chosen randomly, but each one should be accorded equal sincerity as today's idea is applied to it, in an attempt to acknowledge the equal value of them all in their contribution to your seeing.

8. As usual, the applications should include the name of the subject your eyes happen to light on, and you should rest your eyes on it while saying:

²*Above all else I want to see this _____ differently.*

³Each application should be made quite slowly, and as thoughtfully as possible. ⁴There is no hurry.

LESSON 29

God is in everything I see.

1. The idea for today explains why you can see all purpose in everything. ²It explains why nothing is separate, by itself or in itself. ³And it explains why nothing you see means anything. ⁴In fact, it explains every idea we have used thus far, and all subsequent ones as well. ⁵Today's idea is the whole basis for vision.

2. You will probably find this idea very difficult to grasp at this point. ²You may find it silly, irreverent, senseless, funny and even objectionable. ³Certainly God is not in a table, for example, as you see it. ⁴Yet we emphasized yesterday that a table shares the purpose of the universe. ⁵And what shares the purpose of the universe shares the purpose of its Creator.

3. Try then, today, to begin to learn how to look on all things with love, appreciation and open-mindedness. ²You do not see them now. ³Would you know what is in them? ⁴Nothing is as it appears to you. ⁵Its holy purpose stands beyond your little range. ⁶When vision has shown you the holiness that lights up the world, you will understand today's idea perfectly. ⁷And you will not understand how you could ever have found it difficult.

4. Our six two-minute practice periods for today should follow a now familiar pattern: Begin with repeating the idea to yourself, and then apply it to randomly chosen subjects about you, naming each one specifically. ²Try to avoid the tendency toward self-directed selection, which may be particularly tempting in connection with today's idea because of its wholly alien nature. ³Remember that any order you impose is equally alien to reality.

5. Your list of subjects should therefore be as free of self-selection as possible. ²For example, a suitable list might include:

> ³*God is in this coat hanger.*
> ⁴*God is in this magazine.*
> ⁵*God is in this finger.*
> ⁶*God is in this lamp.*
> ⁷*God is in that body.*
> ⁸*God is in that door.*
> ⁹*God is in that waste basket.*

[10]In addition to the assigned practice periods, repeat the idea for today at least once an hour, looking slowly about you as you say the words unhurriedly to yourself. [11]At least once or twice, you should experience a sense of restfulness as you do this.

LESSON 30

God is in everything I see because God is in my mind.

1. The idea for today is the springboard for vision. [2]From this idea will the world open up before you, and you will look upon it and see in it what you have never seen before. [3]Nor will what you saw before be even faintly visible to you.

2. Today we are trying to use a new kind of "projection." [2]We are not attempting to get rid of what we do not like by seeing it outside. [3]Instead, we are trying to see in the world what is in our minds, and what we want to recognize is there. [4]Thus, we are trying to join with what we see, rather than keeping it apart from us. [5]That is the fundamental difference between vision and the way you see.

3. Today's idea should be applied as often as possible throughout the day. [2]Whenever you have a moment or so, repeat it to yourself slowly, looking about you, and trying to realize that the idea applies to everything you do see now, or could see now if it were within the range of your sight.

4. Real vision is not limited to concepts such as "near" and "far." [2]To help you begin to get used to this idea, try to think of things beyond your present range as well as those you can actually see, as you apply today's idea.

5. Real vision is not only unlimited by space and distance, but it does not depend on the body's eyes at all. [2]The mind is its only source. [3]To aid in helping you to become more accustomed to this idea as well, devote several practice periods to applying today's idea with your eyes closed, using whatever subjects come to mind, and looking within rather than without. [4]Today's idea applies equally to both.

LESSON 31

I am not the victim of the world I see.

1. Today's idea is the introduction to your declaration of release. [2]Again, the idea should be applied to both the world you see without and the world you see within. [3]In applying the idea, we will use a form of practice which will be used more and more, with changes as indicated. [4]Generally speaking, the form includes two aspects; one in which you apply the idea on a more sustained basis, and the other consisting of frequent applications of the idea throughout the day.

2. Two longer periods of practice with the idea for today are needed, one in the morning and one at night. [2]Three to five minutes for each of these are recommended. [3]During that time, look about you slowly while repeating the idea two or three times. [4]Then close your eyes, and apply the same idea to your inner world. [5]You will escape from both together, for the inner is the cause of the outer.

3. As you survey your inner world, merely let whatever thoughts cross your mind come into your awareness, each to be considered for a moment, and then replaced by the next. [2]Try not to establish any kind of hierarchy among them. [3]Watch them come and go as dispassionately as possible. [4]Do not dwell on any one in particular, but try to let the stream move on evenly and calmly, without any special investment on your part. [5]As you sit and quietly watch your thoughts, repeat today's idea to yourself as often as you care to, but with no sense of hurry.

4. In addition, repeat the idea for today as often as possible during the day. [2]Remind yourself that you are making a declaration of independence in the name of your own freedom. [3]And in your freedom lies the freedom of the world.

5. The idea for today is also a particularly useful one to use as a response to any form of temptation that may arise. [2]It is a declaration that you will not yield to it, and put yourself in bondage.

LESSON 32

I have invented the world I see.

1. Today we are continuing to develop the theme of cause and effect. ²You are not the victim of the world you see because you invented it. ³You can give it up as easily as you made it up. ⁴You will see it or not see it, as you wish. ⁵While you want it you will see it; when you no longer want it, it will not be there for you to see.

2. The idea for today, like the preceding ones, applies to your inner and outer worlds, which are actually the same. ²However, since you see them as different, the practice periods for today will again include two phases, one involving the world you see outside you, and the other the world you see in your mind. ³In today's exercises, try to introduce the thought that both are in your own imagination.

3. Again we will begin the practice periods for the morning and evening by repeating the idea for today two or three times while looking around at the world you see as outside yourself. ²Then close your eyes and look around your inner world. ³Try to treat them both as equally as possible. ⁴Repeat the idea for today unhurriedly as often as you wish, as you watch the images your imagination presents to your awareness.

4. For the two longer practice periods three to five minutes are recommended, with not less than three required. ²More than five can be utilized, if you find the exercise restful. ³To facilitate this, select a time when few distractions are anticipated, and when you yourself feel reasonably ready.

5. These exercises are also to be continued during the day, as often as possible. ²The shorter applications consist of repeating the idea slowly, as you survey either your inner or outer world. ³It does not matter which you choose.

6. The idea for today should also be applied immediately to any situation that may distress you. ²Apply the idea by telling yourself:

³*I have invented this situation as I see it.*

LESSON 33

There is another way of looking at the world.

1. Today's idea is an attempt to recognize that you can shift your perception of the world in both its outer and inner aspects. [2]A full five minutes should be devoted to the morning and evening applications. [3]In these practice periods, the idea should be repeated as often as you find comfortable, though unhurried applications are essential. [4]Alternate between surveying your outer and inner perceptions, but without an abrupt sense of shifting.

2. Merely glance casually around the world you perceive as outside yourself, then close your eyes and survey your inner thoughts with equal casualness. [2]Try to remain equally uninvolved in both, and to maintain this detachment as you repeat the idea throughout the day.

3. The shorter exercise periods should be as frequent as possible. [2]Specific applications of today's idea should also be made immediately, when any situation arises which tempts you to become disturbed. [3]For these applications, say:

[4]*There is another way of looking at this.*

4. Remember to apply today's idea the instant you are aware of distress. [2]It may be necessary to take a minute or so to sit quietly and repeat the idea to yourself several times. [3]Closing your eyes will probably help in this form of application.

LESSON 34

I could see peace instead of this.

1. The idea for today begins to describe the conditions that prevail in the other way of seeing. ²Peace of mind is clearly an internal matter. ³It must begin with your own thoughts, and then extend outward. ⁴It is from your peace of mind that a peaceful perception of the world arises.

2. Three longer practice periods are required for today's exercises. ²One in the morning and one in the evening are advised, with an additional one to be undertaken at any time in between that seems most conducive to readiness. ³All applications should be done with your eyes closed. ⁴It is your inner world to which the applications of today's idea should be made.

3. Some five minutes of mind searching are required for each of the longer practice periods. ²Search your mind for fear thoughts, anxiety-provoking situations, "offending" personalities or events, or anything else about which you are harboring unloving thoughts. ³Note them all casually, repeating the idea for today slowly as you watch them arise in your mind, and let each one go, to be replaced by the next.

4. If you begin to experience difficulty in thinking of specific subjects, continue to repeat the idea to yourself in an unhurried manner, without applying it to anything in particular. ²Be sure, however, not to make any specific exclusions.

5. The shorter applications are to be frequent, and made whenever you feel your peace of mind is threatened in any way. ²The purpose is to protect yourself from temptation throughout the day. ³If a specific form of temptation arises in your awareness, the exercise should take this form:

⁴*I could see peace in this situation instead of what I now see in it.*

6. If the inroads on your peace of mind take the form of more generalized adverse emotions, such as depression, anxiety or worry, use the idea in its original form. ²If you find you need more than one application of today's idea to help you change your mind in any specific context, try to take several minutes and devote them to repeating the idea until you feel some sense of

relief. [3]It will help you if you tell yourself specifically:

> [4]I can replace my feelings of depression, anxiety or worry [or my thoughts about this situation, personality or event] with peace.

LESSON 35

My mind is part of God's. I am very holy.

1. Today's idea does not describe the way you see yourself now. ²It does, however, describe what vision will show you. ³It is difficult for anyone who thinks he is in this world to believe this of himself. ⁴Yet the reason he thinks he is in this world is because he does not believe it.

2. You will believe that you are part of where you think you are. ²That is because you surround yourself with the environment you want. ³And you want it to protect the image of yourself that you have made. ⁴The image is part of this environment. ⁵What you see while you believe you are in it is seen through the eyes of the image. ⁶This is not vision. ⁷Images cannot see.

3. The idea for today presents a very different view of yourself. ²By establishing your Source it establishes your Identity, and it describes you as you must really be in truth. ³We will use a somewhat different kind of application for today's idea because the emphasis for today is on the perceiver, rather than on what he perceives.

4. For each of the three five-minute practice periods today, begin by repeating today's idea to yourself, and then close your eyes and search your mind for the various kinds of descriptive terms in which you see yourself. ²Include all the ego-based attributes which you ascribe to yourself, positive or negative, desirable or undesirable, grandiose or debased. ³All of them are equally unreal, because you do not look upon yourself through the eyes of holiness.

5. In the earlier part of the mind-searching period, you will probably emphasize what you consider to be the more negative aspects of your perception of yourself. ²Toward the latter part of the exercise period, however, more self-inflating descriptive terms may well cross your mind. ³Try to recognize that the direction of your fantasies about yourself does not matter. ⁴Illusions have no direction in reality. ⁵They are merely not true.

6. A suitable unselected list for applying the idea for today might be as follows:

> [2]*I see myself as imposed on.*
> [3]*I see myself as depressed.*
> [4]*I see myself as failing.*
> [5]*I see myself as endangered.*
> [6]*I see myself as helpless.*
> [7]*I see myself as victorious.*
> [8]*I see myself as losing out.*
> [9]*I see myself as charitable.*
> [10]*I see myself as virtuous.*

7. You should not think of these terms in an abstract way. [2]They will occur to you as various situations, personalities and events in which you figure cross your mind. [3]Pick up any specific situation that occurs to you, identify the descriptive term or terms you feel are applicable to your reactions to that situation, and use them in applying today's idea. [4]After you have named each one, add:

> [5]*But my mind is part of God's.* [6]*I am very holy.*

8. During the longer exercise periods, there will probably be intervals in which nothing specific occurs to you. [2]Do not strain to think up specific things to fill the interval, but merely relax and repeat today's idea slowly until something occurs to you. [3]Although nothing that does occur should be omitted from the exercises, nothing should be "dug out" with effort. [4]Neither force nor discrimination should be used.

9. As often as possible during the day, pick up a specific attribute or attributes you are ascribing to yourself at the time and apply the idea for today to them, adding the idea in the form stated above to each of them. [2]If nothing particular occurs to you, merely repeat the idea to yourself, with closed eyes.

LESSON 36

My holiness envelops everything I see.

1. Today's idea extends the idea for yesterday from the perceiver to the perceived. ²You are holy because your mind is part of God's. ³And because you are holy, your sight must be holy as well. ⁴"Sinless" means without sin. ⁵You cannot be without sin a little. ⁶You are sinless or not. ⁷If your mind is part of God's you must be sinless, or a part of His Mind would be sinful. ⁸Your sight is related to His Holiness, not to your ego, and therefore not to your body.

2. Four three-to-five-minute practice periods are required for today. ²Try to distribute them fairly evenly, and make the shorter applications frequently, to protect your protection throughout the day. ³The longer practice periods should take this form:

3. First, close your eyes and repeat the idea for today several times, slowly. ²Then open your eyes and look quite slowly about you, applying the idea specifically to whatever you note in your casual survey. ³Say, for example:

> ⁴*My holiness envelops that rug.*
> ⁵*My holiness envelops that wall.*
> ⁶*My holiness envelops these fingers.*
> ⁷*My holiness envelops that chair.*
> ⁸*My holiness envelops that body.*
> ⁹*My holiness envelops this pen.*

¹⁰Several times during these practice periods, close your eyes and repeat the idea to yourself. ¹¹Then open your eyes, and continue as before.

4. For the shorter exercise periods, close your eyes and repeat the idea; look about you as you repeat it again; and conclude with one more repetition with your eyes closed. ²All applications should, of course, be made quite slowly, as effortlessly and unhurriedly as possible.

LESSON 37

My holiness blesses the world.

1. This idea contains the first glimmerings of your true function in the world, or why you are here. [2]Your purpose is to see the world through your own holiness. [3]Thus are you and the world blessed together. [4]No one loses; nothing is taken away from anyone; everyone gains through your holy vision. [5]It signifies the end of sacrifice because it offers everyone his full due. [6]And he is entitled to everything because it is his birthright as a Son of God.

2. There is no other way in which the idea of sacrifice can be removed from the world's thinking. [2]Any other way of seeing will inevitably demand payment of someone or something. [3]As a result, the perceiver will lose. [4]Nor will he have any idea why he is losing. [5]Yet is his wholeness restored to his awareness through your vision. [6]Your holiness blesses him by asking nothing of him. [7]Those who see themselves as whole make no demands.

3. Your holiness is the salvation of the world. [2]It lets you teach the world that it is one with you, not by preaching to it, not by telling it anything, but merely by your quiet recognition that in your holiness are all things blessed along with you.

4. Today's four longer exercise periods, each to involve three to five minutes of practice, begin with the repetition of the idea for today, followed by a minute or so of looking about you as you apply the idea to whatever you see:

> [2]*My holiness blesses this chair.*
> [3]*My holiness blesses that window.*
> [4]*My holiness blesses this body.*

[5]Then close your eyes and apply the idea to any person who occurs to you, using his name and saying:

> [6]*My holiness blesses you, [name].*

5. You may continue the practice period with your eyes closed; you may open your eyes again and apply the idea for today to your outer world if you so desire; you may alternate between applying the idea to what you see around you and to those who

are in your thoughts; or you may use any combination of these two phases of application that you prefer. [2]The practice period should conclude with a repetition of the idea with your eyes closed, and another, following immediately, with your eyes open.

6. The shorter exercises consist of repeating the idea as often as you can. [2]It is particularly helpful to apply it silently to anyone you meet, using his name as you do so. [3]It is essential to use the idea if anyone seems to cause an adverse reaction in you. [4]Offer him the blessing of your holiness immediately, that you may learn to keep it in your own awareness.

57

LESSON 38

There is nothing my holiness cannot do.

1. Your holiness reverses all the laws of the world. ²It is beyond every restriction of time, space, distance and limits of any kind. ³Your holiness is totally unlimited in its power because it establishes you as a Son of God, at one with the Mind of his Creator.

2. Through your holiness the power of God is made manifest. ²Through your holiness the power of God is made available. ³And there is nothing the power of God cannot do. ⁴Your holiness, then, can remove all pain, can end all sorrow, and can solve all problems. ⁵It can do so in connection with yourself and with anyone else. ⁶It is equal in its power to help anyone because it is equal in its power to save anyone.

3. If you are holy, so is everything God created. ²You are holy because all things He created are holy. ³And all things He created are holy because you are. ⁴In today's exercises, we will apply the power of your holiness to all problems, difficulties or suffering in any form that you happen to think of, in yourself or in someone else. ⁵We will make no distinctions because there are no distinctions.

4. In the four longer practice periods, each preferably to last a full five minutes, repeat the idea for today, close your eyes, and then search your mind for any sense of loss or unhappiness of any kind as you see it. ²Try to make as little distinction as possible between a situation that is difficult for you, and one that is difficult for someone else. ³Identify the situation specifically, and also the name of the person concerned. ⁴Use this form in applying the idea for today:

> ⁵*In the situation involving _____ in which I see myself, there is nothing that my holiness cannot do.*
> ⁶*In the situation involving _____ in which _____ sees himself, there is nothing my holiness cannot do.*

5. From time to time you may want to vary this procedure, and add some relevant thoughts of your own. ²You might like, for example, to include thoughts such as:

3There is nothing my holiness cannot do because
the power of God lies in it.

4Introduce whatever variations appeal to you, but keep the exercises focused on the theme, "There is nothing my holiness cannot do." 5The purpose of today's exercises is to begin to instill in you a sense that you have dominion over all things because of what you are.

6. In the frequent shorter applications, apply the idea in its original form unless a specific problem concerning you or someone else arises, or comes to mind. 2In that event, use the more specific form in applying the idea to it.

59

LESSON 39

My holiness is my salvation.

1. If guilt is hell, what is its opposite? [2]Like the text for which this workbook was written, the ideas used for the exercises are very simple, very clear and totally unambiguous. [3]We are not concerned with intellectual feats nor logical toys. [4]We are dealing only in the very obvious, which has been overlooked in the clouds of complexity in which you think you think.

2. If guilt is hell, what is its opposite? [2]This is not difficult, surely. [3]The hesitation you may feel in answering is not due to the ambiguity of the question. [4]But do you believe that guilt is hell? [5]If you did, you would see at once how direct and simple the text is, and you would not need a workbook at all. [6]No one needs practice to gain what is already his.

3. We have already said that your holiness is the salvation of the world. [2]What about your own salvation? [3]You cannot give what you do not have. [4]A savior must be saved. [5]How else can he teach salvation? [6]Today's exercises will apply to you, recognizing that your salvation is crucial to the salvation of the world. [7]As you apply the exercises to your world, the whole world stands to benefit.

4. Your holiness is the answer to every question that was ever asked, is being asked now, or will be asked in the future. [2]Your holiness means the end of guilt, and therefore the end of hell. [3]Your holiness is the salvation of the world, and your own. [4]How could you to whom your holiness belongs be excluded from it? [5]God does not know unholiness. [6]Can it be He does not know His Son?

5. A full five minutes are urged for the four longer practice periods for today, and longer and more frequent practice sessions are encouraged. [2]If you want to exceed the minimum requirements, more rather than longer sessions are recommended, although both are suggested.

6. Begin the practice periods as usual, by repeating today's idea to yourself. [2]Then, with closed eyes, search out your unloving thoughts in whatever form they appear; uneasiness, depression, anger, fear, worry, attack, insecurity and so on. [3]Whatever form they take, they are unloving and therefore fearful. [4]And so it is

from them that you need to be saved.

7. Specific situations, events or personalities you associate with unloving thoughts of any kind are suitable subjects for today's exercises. ²It is imperative for your salvation that you see them differently. ³And it is your blessing on them that will save you and give you vision.

8. Slowly, without conscious selection and without undue emphasis on any one in particular, search your mind for every thought that stands between you and your salvation. ²Apply the idea for today to each of them in this way:

   ³*My unloving thoughts about _____ are keeping me in hell.*
   ⁴*My holiness is my salvation.*

9. You may find these practice periods easier if you intersperse them with several short periods during which you merely repeat today's idea to yourself slowly a few times. ²You may also find it helpful to include a few short intervals in which you just relax and do not seem to be thinking of anything. ³Sustained concentration is very difficult at first. ⁴It will become much easier as your mind becomes more disciplined and less distractible.

10. Meanwhile, you should feel free to introduce variety into the exercise periods in whatever form appeals to you. ²Do not, however, change the idea itself as you vary the method of applying it. ³However you elect to use it, the idea should be stated so that its meaning is the fact that your holiness is your salvation. ⁴End each practice period by repeating the idea in its original form once more, and adding:

   ⁵*If guilt is hell, what is its opposite?*

11. In the shorter applications, which should be made some three or four times an hour and more if possible, you may ask yourself this question, repeat today's idea, and preferably both. ²If temptations arise, a particularly helpful form of the idea is:

   ³*My holiness is my salvation from this.*

LESSON 40

I am blessed as a Son of God.

1. Today we will begin to assert some of the happy things to which you are entitled, being what you are. [2]No long practice periods are required today, but very frequent short ones are necessary. [3]Once every ten minutes would be highly desirable, and you are urged to attempt this schedule and to adhere to it whenever possible. [4]If you forget, try again. [5]If there are long interruptions, try again. [6]Whenever you remember, try again.

2. You need not close your eyes for the exercise periods, although you will probably find it more helpful if you do. [2]However, you may be in a number of situations during the day when closing your eyes would not be feasible. [3]Do not miss a practice period because of this. [4]You can practice quite well under any circumstances, if you really want to.

3. Today's exercises take little time and no effort. [2]Repeat the idea for today, and then add several of the attributes you associate with being a Son of God, applying them to yourself. [3]One practice period might, for example, consist of the following:

[4]I am blessed as a Son of God.
[5]I am happy, peaceful, loving and contented.

[6]Another might take this form:

[7]I am blessed as a Son of God.
[8]I am calm, quiet, assured and confident.

[9]If only a brief period is available, merely telling yourself that you are blessed as a Son of God will do.

LESSON 41

God goes with me wherever I go.

1. Today's idea will eventually overcome completely the sense of loneliness and abandonment all the separated ones experience. [2]Depression is an inevitable consequence of separation. [3]So are anxiety, worry, a deep sense of helplessness, misery, suffering and intense fear of loss.

2. The separated ones have invented many "cures" for what they believe to be "the ills of the world." [2]But the one thing they do not do is to question the reality of the problem. [3]Yet its effects cannot be cured because the problem is not real. [4]The idea for today has the power to end all this foolishness forever. [5]And foolishness it is, despite the serious and tragic forms it may take.

3. Deep within you is everything that is perfect, ready to radiate through you and out into the world. [2]It will cure all sorrow and pain and fear and loss because it will heal the mind that thought these things were real, and suffered out of its allegiance to them.

4. You can never be deprived of your perfect holiness because its Source goes with you wherever you go. [2]You can never suffer because the Source of all joy goes with you wherever you go. [3]You can never be alone because the Source of all life goes with you wherever you go. [4]Nothing can destroy your peace of mind because God goes with you wherever you go.

5. We understand that you do not believe all this. [2]How could you, when the truth is hidden deep within, under a heavy cloud of insane thoughts, dense and obscuring, yet representing all you see? [3]Today we will make our first real attempt to get past this dark and heavy cloud, and to go through it to the light beyond.

6. There will be only one long practice period today. [2]In the morning, as soon as you get up if possible, sit quietly for some three to five minutes, with your eyes closed. [3]At the beginning of the practice period, repeat today's idea very slowly. [4]Then make no effort to think of anything. [5]Try, instead, to get a sense of turning inward, past all the idle thoughts of the world. [6]Try to enter very deeply into your own mind, keeping it clear of any thoughts that might divert your attention.

7. From time to time, you may repeat the idea if you find it helpful. [2]But most of all, try to sink down and inward, away from the

world and all the foolish thoughts of the world. ³You are trying to reach past all these things. ⁴You are trying to leave appearances and approach reality.

8. It is quite possible to reach God. ²In fact it is very easy, because it is the most natural thing in the world. ³You might even say it is the only natural thing in the world. ⁴The way will open, if you believe that it is possible. ⁵This exercise can bring very startling results even the first time it is attempted, and sooner or later it is always successful. ⁶We will go into more detail about this kind of practice as we go along. ⁷But it will never fail completely, and instant success is possible.

9. Throughout the day use today's idea often, repeating it very slowly, preferably with eyes closed. ²Think of what you are saying; what the words mean. ³Concentrate on the holiness that they imply about you; on the unfailing companionship that is yours; on the complete protection that surrounds you.

10. You can indeed afford to laugh at fear thoughts, remembering that God goes with you wherever you go.

LESSON 42

God is my strength. Vision is His gift.

1. The idea for today combines two very powerful thoughts, both of major importance. [2]It also sets forth a cause and effect relationship that explains why you cannot fail in your efforts to achieve the goal of the course. [3]You will see because it is the Will of God. [4]It is His strength, not your own, that gives you power. [5]And it is His gift, rather than your own, that offers vision to you.

2. God is indeed your strength, and what He gives is truly given. [2]This means that you can receive it any time and anywhere, wherever you are, and in whatever circumstance you find yourself. [3]Your passage through time and space is not at random. [4]You cannot but be in the right place at the right time. [5]Such is the strength of God. [6]Such are His gifts.

3. We will have two three-to-five-minute practice periods today, one as soon as possible after you wake, and another as close as possible to the time you go to sleep. [2]It is better, however, to wait until you can sit quietly by yourself, at a time when you feel ready, than it is to be concerned with the time as such.

4. Begin these practice periods by repeating the idea for today slowly, with your eyes open, looking about you. [2]Then close your eyes and repeat the idea again, even slower than before. [3]After this, try to think of nothing except thoughts that occur to you in relation to the idea for the day. [4]You might think, for example:

[5]Vision must be possible. [6]God gives truly,

or:

[7]God's gifts to me must be mine, because He gave them to me.

5. Any thought that is clearly related to the idea for today is suitable. [2]You may, in fact, be astonished at the amount of course-related understanding some of your thoughts contain. [3]Let them come without censoring unless you find your mind is merely wandering, and you have let obviously irrelevant thoughts intrude. [4]You may also reach a point where no thoughts at all seem to come to mind. [5]If such interferences occur, open your eyes and repeat the thought once more while looking slowly

about; close your eyes, repeat the idea once more, and then continue to look for related thoughts in your mind.

6. Remember, however, that active searching for relevant thoughts is not appropriate for today's exercises. [2]Try merely to step back and let the thoughts come. [3]If you find this difficult, it is better to spend the practice period alternating between slow repetitions of the idea with eyes open, then with eyes closed, than it is to strain to find suitable thoughts.

7. There is no limit on the number of short practice periods that would be beneficial today. [2]The idea for the day is a beginning step in bringing thoughts together, and teaching you that you are studying a unified thought system in which nothing is lacking that is needed, and nothing is included that is contradictory or irrelevant.

8. The more often you repeat the idea during the day, the more often you will be reminding yourself that the goal of the course is important to you, and that you have not forgotten it.

LESSON 43

God is my Source. I cannot see apart from Him.

1. Perception is not an attribute of God. ²His is the realm of knowledge. ³Yet He has created the Holy Spirit as the Mediator between perception and knowledge. ⁴Without this link with God, perception would have replaced knowledge forever in your mind. ⁵With this link with God, perception will become so changed and purified that it will lead to knowledge. ⁶That is its function as the Holy Spirit sees it. ⁷Therefore, that is its function in truth.

2. In God you cannot see. ²Perception has no function in God, and does not exist. ³Yet in salvation, which is the undoing of what never was, perception has a mighty purpose. ⁴Made by the Son of God for an unholy purpose, it must become the means for the restoration of his holiness to his awareness. ⁵Perception has no meaning. ⁶Yet does the Holy Spirit give it a meaning very close to God's. ⁷Healed perception becomes the means by which the Son of God forgives his brother, and thus forgives himself.

3. You cannot see apart from God because you cannot be apart from God. ²Whatever you do you do in Him, because whatever you think, you think with His Mind. ³If vision is real, and it is real to the extent to which it shares the Holy Spirit's purpose, then you cannot see apart from God.

4. Three five-minute practice periods are required today, one as early and one as late as possible in the day. ²The third may be undertaken at the most convenient and suitable time that circumstances and readiness permit. ³At the beginning of these practice periods, repeat the idea for today to yourself with eyes open. ⁴Then glance around you for a short time, applying the idea specifically to what you see. ⁵Four or five subjects for this phase of the practice period are sufficient. ⁶You might say, for example:

⁷*God is my Source. ⁸I cannot see this desk apart from Him.*
⁹*God is my Source. ¹⁰I cannot see that picture apart from Him.*

5. Although this part of the exercise period should be relatively short, be sure that you select the subjects for this phase of practice indiscriminately, without self-directed inclusion or exclusion.

²For the second and longer phase, close your eyes, repeat today's idea again, and then let whatever relevant thoughts occur to you add to the idea in your own personal way. ³Thoughts such as:

> ⁴*I see through the eyes of forgiveness.*
> ⁵*I see the world as blessed.*
> ⁶*The world can show me myself.*
> ⁷*I see my own thoughts, which are like God's.*

⁸Any thought related more or less directly to today's idea is suitable. ⁹The thoughts need not bear any obvious relationship to the idea, but they should not be in opposition to it.

6.   If you find your mind wandering; if you begin to be aware of thoughts which are clearly out of accord with today's idea, or if you seem to be unable to think of anything, open your eyes, repeat the first phase of the exercise period, and then attempt the second phase again. ²Do not allow any protracted period to occur in which you become preoccupied with irrelevant thoughts. ³Return to the first phase of the exercises as often as necessary to prevent this.

7.   In applying today's idea in the shorter practice periods, the form may vary according to the circumstances and situations in which you find yourself during the day. ²When you are with someone else, for example, try to remember to tell him silently:

> ³*God is my Source.* ⁴*I cannot see you apart from Him.*

⁵This form is equally applicable to strangers as it is to those you think are closer to you. ⁶In fact, try not to make distinctions of this kind at all.

8.   Today's idea should also be applied throughout the day to various situations and events that may occur, particularly to those which seem to distress you in any way. ²For this purpose, apply the idea in this form:

> ³*God is my Source.* ⁴*I cannot see this apart from Him.*

9.   If no particular subject presents itself to your awareness at the time, merely repeat the idea in its original form. ²Try today not to allow any long periods of time to slip by without remembering today's idea, and thus remembering your function.

LESSON 44

God is the light in which I see.

1. Today we are continuing the idea for yesterday, adding an-other dimension to it. ²You cannot see in darkness, and you can-not make light. ³You can make darkness and then think you see in it, but light reflects life, and is therefore an aspect of creation. ⁴Creation and darkness cannot coexist, but light and· life must go together, being but different aspects of creation.

2. In order to see, you must recognize that light is within, not without. ²You do not see outside yourself, nor is the equipment for seeing outside you. ³An essential part of this equipment is the light that makes seeing possible. ⁴It is with you always, making vision possible in every circumstance.

3. Today we are going to attempt to reach that light. ²For this purpose, we will use a form of exercise which has been suggested before, and which we will utilize increasingly. ³It is a particularly difficult form for the undisciplined mind, and represents a major goal of mind training. ⁴It requires precisely what the untrained mind lacks. ⁵Yet this training must be accomplished if you are to see.

4. Have at least three practice periods today, each lasting three to five minutes. ²A longer time is highly recommended, but only if you find the time slipping by with little or no sense of strain. ³The form of practice we will use today is the most natural and easy one in the world for the trained mind, just as it seems to be the most unnatural and difficult for the untrained mind.

5. Your mind is no longer wholly untrained. ²You are quite ready to learn the form of exercise we will use today, but you may find that you will encounter strong resistance. ³The reason is very sim-ple. ⁴While you practice in this way, you leave behind everything that you now believe, and all the thoughts that you have made up. ⁵Properly speaking, this is the release from hell. ⁶Yet per-ceived through the ego's eyes, it is loss of identity and a descent into hell.

6. If you can stand aside from the ego by ever so little, you will have no difficulty in recognizing that its opposition and its fears are meaningless. ²You might find it helpful to remind yourself, from time to time, that to reach light is to escape from darkness,

whatever you may believe to the contrary. [3]God is the light in which you see. [4]You are attempting to reach Him.

7. Begin the practice period by repeating today's idea with your eyes open, and close them slowly, repeating the idea several times more. [2]Then try to sink into your mind, letting go every kind of interference and intrusion by quietly sinking past them. [3]Your mind cannot be stopped in this unless you choose to stop it. [4]It is merely taking its natural course. [5]Try to observe your passing thoughts without involvement, and slip quietly by them.

8. While no particular approach is advocated for this form of exercise, what is needful is a sense of the importance of what you are doing; its inestimable value to you, and an awareness that you are attempting something very holy. [2]Salvation is your happiest accomplishment. [3]It is also the only one that has any meaning, because it is the only one that has any real use to you at all.

9. If resistance rises in any form, pause long enough to repeat today's idea, keeping your eyes closed unless you are aware of fear. [2]In that case, you will probably find it more reassuring to open your eyes briefly. [3]Try, however, to return to the exercises with eyes closed as soon as possible.

10. If you are doing the exercises correctly, you should experience some sense of relaxation, and even a feeling that you are approaching, if not actually entering into light. [2]Try to think of light, formless and without limit, as you pass by the thoughts of this world. [3]And do not forget that they cannot hold you to the world unless you give them the power to do so.

11. Throughout the day repeat the idea often, with eyes open or closed as seems better to you at the time. [2]But do not forget. [3]Above all, be determined not to forget today.

LESSON 45

God is the Mind with which I think.

1. Today's idea holds the key to what your real thoughts are. [2]They are nothing that you think you think, just as nothing that you think you see is related to vision in any way. [3]There is no relationship between what is real and what you think is real. [4]Nothing that you think are your real thoughts resemble your real thoughts in any respect. [5]Nothing that you think you see bears any resemblance to what vision will show you.

2. You think with the Mind of God. [2]Therefore you share your thoughts with Him, as He shares His with you. [3]They are the same thoughts, because they are thought by the same Mind. [4]To share is to make alike, or to make one. [5]Nor do the thoughts you think with the Mind of God leave your mind, because thoughts do not leave their source. [6]Therefore, your thoughts are in the Mind of God, as you are. [7]They are in your mind as well, where He is. [8]As you are part of His Mind, so are your thoughts part of His Mind.

3. Where, then, are your real thoughts? [2]Today we will attempt to reach them. [3]We will have to look for them in your mind, because that is where they are. [4]They must still be there, because they cannot have left their source. [5]What is thought by the Mind of God is eternal, being part of creation.

4. Our three five-minute practice periods for today will take the same general form that we used in applying yesterday's idea. [2]We will attempt to leave the unreal and seek for the real. [3]We will deny the world in favor of truth. [4]We will not let the thoughts of the world hold us back. [5]We will not let the beliefs of the world tell us that what God would have us do is impossible. [6]Instead, we will try to recognize that only what God would have us do is possible.

5. We will also try to understand that only what God would have us do is what we want to do. [2]And we will also try to remember that we cannot fail in doing what He would have us do. [3]There is every reason to feel confident that we will succeed today. [4]It is the Will of God.

6. Begin the exercises for today by repeating the idea to yourself, closing your eyes as you do so. [2]Then spend a fairly short period

71

in thinking a few relevant thoughts of your own, keeping the idea in mind. ³After you have added some four or five thoughts of your own to the idea, repeat it again and tell yourself gently:

⁴*My real thoughts are in my mind.* ⁵*I would like to find them.*

⁶Then try to go past all the unreal thoughts that cover the truth in your mind, and reach to the eternal.

7. Under all the senseless thoughts and mad ideas with which you have cluttered up your mind are the thoughts that you thought with God in the beginning. ²They are there in your mind now, completely unchanged. ³They will always be in your mind, exactly as they always were. ⁴Everything you have thought since then will change, but the Foundation on which it rests is wholly changeless.

8. It is this Foundation toward which the exercises for today are directed. ²Here is your mind joined with the Mind of God. ³Here are your thoughts one with His. ⁴For this kind of practice only one thing is necessary; approach it as you would an altar dedicated in Heaven to God the Father and to God the Son. ⁵For such is the place you are trying to reach. ⁶You will probably be unable as yet to realize how high you are trying to go. ⁷Yet even with the little understanding you have already gained, you should be able to remind yourself that this is no idle game, but an exercise in holiness and an attempt to reach the Kingdom of Heaven.

9. In the shorter exercise periods for today, try to remember how important it is to you to understand the holiness of the mind that thinks with God. ²Take a minute or two, as you repeat the idea throughout the day, to appreciate your mind's holiness. ³Stand aside, however briefly, from all thoughts that are unworthy of Him Whose host you are. ⁴And thank Him for the Thoughts He is thinking with you.

LESSON 46

God is the Love in which I forgive.

1. God does not forgive because He has never condemned. ²And there must be condemnation before forgiveness is necessary. ³Forgiveness is the great need of this world, but that is because it is a world of illusions. ⁴Those who forgive are thus releasing themselves from illusions, while those who withhold forgiveness are binding themselves to them. ⁵As you condemn only yourself, so do you forgive only yourself.

2. Yet although God does not forgive, His Love is nevertheless the basis of forgiveness. ²Fear condemns and love forgives. ³Forgiveness thus undoes what fear has produced, returning the mind to the awareness of God. ⁴For this reason, forgiveness can truly be called salvation. ⁵It is the means by which illusions disappear.

3. Today's exercises require at least three full five-minute practice periods, and as many shorter ones as possible. ²Begin the longer practice periods by repeating today's idea to yourself, as usual. ³Close your eyes as you do so, and spend a minute or two in searching your mind for those whom you have not forgiven. ⁴It does not matter "how much" you have not forgiven them. ⁵You have forgiven them entirely or not at all.

4. If you are doing the exercises well you should have no difficulty in finding a number of people you have not forgiven. ²It is a safe rule that anyone you do not like is a suitable subject. ³Mention each one by name, and say:

    ⁴*God is the Love in which I forgive you, [name].*

5. The purpose of the first phase of today's practice periods is to put you in a position to forgive yourself. ²After you have applied the idea to all those who have come to mind, tell yourself:

    ³*God is the Love in which I forgive myself.*

⁴Then devote the remainder of the practice period to adding related ideas such as:

> [5]*God is the Love with which I love myself.*
> [6]*God is the Love in which I am blessed.*

6. The form of the application may vary considerably, but the central idea should not be lost sight of. [2]You might say, for example:

> [3]*I cannot be guilty because I am a Son of God.*
> [4]*I have already been forgiven.*
> [5]*No fear is possible in a mind beloved of God.*
> [6]*There is no need to attack because love has forgiven me.*

[7]The practice period should end, however, with a repetition of today's idea as originally stated.

7. The shorter practice periods may consist either of a repetition of the idea for today in the original or in a related form, as you prefer. [2]Be sure, however, to make more specific applications if they are needed. [3]They will be needed at any time during the day when you become aware of any kind of negative reaction to anyone, present or not. [4]In that event, tell him silently:

> [5]*God is the Love in which I forgive you.*

74

LESSON 47

God is the strength in which I trust.

1. If you are trusting in your own strength, you have every reason to be apprehensive, anxious and fearful. ²What can you predict or control? ³What is there in you that can be counted on? ⁴What would give you the ability to be aware of all the facets of any problem, and to resolve them in such a way that only good can come of it? ⁵What is there in you that gives you the recognition of the right solution, and the guarantee that it will be accomplished?

2. Of yourself you can do none of these things. ²To believe that you can is to put your trust where trust is unwarranted, and to justify fear, anxiety, depression, anger and sorrow. ³Who can put his faith in weakness and feel safe? ⁴Yet who can put his faith in strength and feel weak?

3. God is your safety in every circumstance. ²His Voice speaks for Him in all situations and in every aspect of all situations, telling you exactly what to do to call upon His strength and His protection. ³There are no exceptions because God has no exceptions. ⁴And the Voice which speaks for Him thinks as He does.

4. Today we will try to reach past your own weakness to the Source of real strength. ²Four five-minute practice periods are necessary today, and longer and more frequent ones are urged. ³Close your eyes and begin, as usual, by repeating the idea for the day. ⁴Then spend a minute or two in searching for situations in your life which you have invested with fear, dismissing each one by telling yourself:

⁵*God is the strength in which I trust.*

5. Now try to slip past all concerns related to your own sense of inadequacy. ²It is obvious that any situation that causes you concern is associated with feelings of inadequacy, for otherwise you would believe that you could deal with the situation successfully. ³It is not by trusting yourself that you will gain confidence. ⁴But the strength of God in you is successful in all things.

6. The recognition of your own frailty is a necessary step in the correction of your errors, but it is hardly a sufficient one in giving

you the confidence which you need, and to which you are entitled. ²You must also gain an awareness that confidence in your real strength is fully justified in every respect and in all circumstances.

7. In the latter phase of the practice period, try to reach down into your mind to a place of real safety. ²You will recognize that you have reached it if you feel a sense of deep peace, however briefly. ³Let go all the trivial things that churn and bubble on the surface of your mind, and reach down and below them to the Kingdom of Heaven. ⁴There is a place in you where there is perfect peace. ⁵There is a place in you where nothing is impossible. ⁶There is a place in you where the strength of God abides.

8. During the day, repeat the idea often. ²Use it as your answer to any disturbance. ³Remember that peace is your right, because you are giving your trust to the strength of God.

LESSON 48

There is nothing to fear.

1. The idea for today simply states a fact. [2]It is not a fact to those who believe in illusions, but illusions are not facts. [3]In truth there is nothing to fear. [4]It is very easy to recognize this. [5]But it is very difficult to recognize it for those who want illusions to be true.

2. Today's practice periods will be very short, very simple and very frequent. [2]Merely repeat the idea as often as possible. [3]You can use it with your eyes open at any time and in any situation. [4]It is strongly recommended, however, that you take a minute or so whenever possible to close your eyes and repeat the idea slowly to yourself several times. [5]It is particularly important that you use the idea immediately, should anything disturb your peace of mind.

3. The presence of fear is a sure sign that you are trusting in your own strength. [2]The awareness that there is nothing to fear shows that somewhere in your mind, though not necessarily in a place you recognize as yet, you have remembered God, and let His strength take the place of your weakness. [3]The instant you are willing to do this there is indeed nothing to fear.

LESSON 49

God's Voice speaks to me all through the day.

1. It is quite possible to listen to God's Voice all through the day without interrupting your regular activities in any way. ²The part of your mind in which truth abides is in constant communication with God, whether you are aware of it or not. ³It is the other part of your mind that functions in the world and obeys the world's laws. ⁴It is this part that is constantly distracted, disorganized and highly uncertain.

2. The part that is listening to the Voice for God is calm, always at rest and wholly certain. ²It is really the only part there is. ³The other part is a wild illusion, frantic and distraught, but without reality of any kind. ⁴Try today not to listen to it. ⁵Try to identify with the part of your mind where stillness and peace reign forever. ⁶Try to hear God's Voice call to you lovingly, reminding you that your Creator has not forgotten His Son.

3. We will need at least four five-minute practice periods today, and more if possible. ²We will try actually to hear God's Voice reminding you of Him and of your Self. ³We will approach this happiest and holiest of thoughts with confidence, knowing that in doing so we are joining our will with the Will of God. ⁴He wants you to hear His Voice. ⁵He gave It to you to be heard.

4. Listen in deep silence. ²Be very still and open your mind. ³Go past all the raucous shrieks and sick imaginings that cover your real thoughts and obscure your eternal link with God. ⁴Sink deep into the peace that waits for you beyond the frantic, riotous thoughts and sights and sounds of this insane world. ⁵You do not live here. ⁶We are trying to reach your real home. ⁷We are trying to reach the place where you are truly welcome. ⁸We are trying to reach God.

5. Do not forget to repeat today's idea very frequently. ²Do so with your eyes open when necessary, but closed when possible. ³And be sure to sit quietly and repeat the idea for today whenever you can, closing your eyes on the world, and realizing that you are inviting God's Voice to speak to you.

LESSON 50

I am sustained by the Love of God.

1. Here is the answer to every problem that will confront you, today and tomorrow and throughout time. ²In this world, you believe you are sustained by everything but God. ³Your faith is placed in the most trivial and insane symbols; pills, money, "protective" clothing, influence, prestige, being liked, knowing the "right" people, and an endless list of forms of nothingness that you endow with magical powers.

2. All these things are your replacements for the Love of God. ²All these things are cherished to ensure a body identification. ³They are songs of praise to the ego. ⁴Do not put your faith in the worthless. ⁵It will not sustain you.

3. Only the Love of God will protect you in all circumstances. ²It will lift you out of every trial, and raise you high above all the perceived dangers of this world into a climate of perfect peace and safety. ³It will transport you into a state of mind that nothing can threaten, nothing can disturb, and where nothing can intrude upon the eternal calm of the Son of God.

4. Put not your faith in illusions. ²They will fail you. ³Put all your faith in the Love of God within you; eternal, changeless and forever unfailing. ⁴This is the answer to whatever confronts you today. ⁵Through the Love of God within you, you can resolve all seeming difficulties without effort and in sure confidence. ⁶Tell yourself this often today. ⁷It is a declaration of release from the belief in idols. ⁸It is your acknowledgment of the truth about yourself.

5. For ten minutes, twice today, morning and evening, let the idea for today sink deep into your consciousness. ²Repeat it, think about it, let related thoughts come to help you recognize its truth, and allow peace to flow over you like a blanket of protection and surety. ³Let no idle and foolish thoughts enter to disturb the holy mind of the Son of God. ⁴Such is the Kingdom of Heaven. ⁵Such is the resting place where your Father has placed you forever.

REVIEW I

Introduction

1. Beginning with today we will have a series of review periods. ²Each of them will cover five of the ideas already presented, starting with the first and ending with the fiftieth. ³There will be a few short comments after each of the ideas, which you should consider in your review. ⁴In the practice periods, the exercises should be done as follows:

2. Begin the day by reading the five ideas, with the comments included. ²Thereafter, it is not necessary to follow any particular order in considering them, though each one should be practiced at least once. ³Devote two minutes or more to each practice period, thinking about the idea and the related comments after reading them over. ⁴Do this as often as possible during the day. ⁵If any one of the five ideas appeals to you more than the others, concentrate on that one. ⁶At the end of the day, however, be sure to review all of them once more.

3. It is not necessary to cover the comments that follow each idea either literally or thoroughly in the practice periods. ²Try, rather, to emphasize the central point, and think about it as part of your review of the idea to which it relates. ³After you have read the idea and the related comments, the exercises should be done with your eyes closed and when you are alone in a quiet place, if possible.

4. This is emphasized for practice periods at your stage of learning. ²It will be necessary, however, that you learn to require no special settings in which to apply what you have learned. ³You will need your learning most in situations that appear to be upsetting, rather than in those that already seem to be calm and quiet. ⁴The purpose of your learning is to enable you to bring the quiet with you, and to heal distress and turmoil. ⁵This is not done by avoiding them and seeking a haven of isolation for yourself.

5. You will yet learn that peace is part of you, and requires only that you be there to embrace any situation in which you are. ²And finally you will learn that there is no limit to where you are, so that your peace is everywhere, as you are.

6. You will note that, for review purposes, some of the ideas are not given in quite their original form. ²Use them as they are given

80

here. ³It is not necessary to return to the original statements, nor to apply the ideas as was suggested then. ⁴We are now emphasizing the relationships among the first fifty of the ideas we have covered, and the cohesiveness of the thought system to which they are leading you.

LESSON 51

The review for today covers the following ideas:

1. (1) **Nothing I see means anything.**

²The reason this is so is that I see nothing, and nothing has no meaning. ³It is necessary that I recognize this, that I may learn to see. ⁴What I think I see now is taking the place of vision. ⁵I must let it go by realizing it has no meaning, so that vision may take its place.

2. (2) **I have given what I see all the meaning it has for me.**

²I have judged everything I look upon, and it is this and only this I see. ³This is not vision. ⁴It is merely an illusion of reality, because my judgments have been made quite apart from reality. ⁵I am willing to recognize the lack of validity in my judgments, because I want to see. ⁶My judgments have hurt me, and I do not want to see according to them.

3. (3) **I do not understand anything I see.**

²How could I understand what I see when I have judged it amiss? ³What I see is the projection of my own errors of thought. ⁴I do not understand what I see because it is not understandable. ⁵There is no sense in trying to understand it. ⁶But there is every reason to let it go, and make room for what can be seen and understood and loved. ⁷I can exchange what I see now for this merely by being willing to do so. ⁸Is not this a better choice than the one I made before?

4. (4) **These thoughts do not mean anything.**

²The thoughts of which I am aware do not mean anything because I am trying to think without God. ³What I call "my" thoughts are not my real thoughts. ⁴My real thoughts are the thoughts I think with God. ⁵I am not aware of them because I have made my thoughts to take their place. ⁶I am willing to recognize that my thoughts do not mean anything, and to let them go. ⁷I choose to have them be replaced by what they were intended to replace. ⁸My thoughts are meaningless, but all creation lies in the thoughts I think with God.

5. (5) **I am never upset for the reason I think.**

²I am never upset for the reason I think because I am constantly trying to justify my thoughts. ³I am constantly trying to make them true. ⁴I make all things my enemies, so that my anger is justified and my attacks are warranted. ⁵I have not realized how much I have misused everything I see by assigning this role to it. ⁶I have done this to defend a thought system that has hurt me, and that I no longer want. ⁷I am willing to let it go.

LESSON 52

Today's review covers these ideas:

1. (6) **I am upset because I see what is not there.**

²Reality is never frightening. ³It is impossible that it could upset me. ⁴Reality brings only perfect peace. ⁵When I am upset, it is always because I have replaced reality with illusions I made up. ⁶The illusions are upsetting because I have given them reality, and thus regard reality as an illusion. ⁷Nothing in God's creation is affected in any way by this confusion of mine. ⁸I am always upset by nothing.

2. (7) **I see only the past.**

²As I look about, I condemn the world I look upon. ³I call this seeing. ⁴I hold the past against everyone and everything, making them my enemies. ⁵When I have forgiven myself and remembered Who I am, I will bless everyone and everything I see. ⁶There will be no past, and therefore no enemies. ⁷And I will look with love on all that I failed to see before.

3. (8) **My mind is preoccupied with past thoughts.**

²I see only my own thoughts, and my mind is preoccupied with the past. ³What, then, can I see as it is? ⁴Let me remember that I look on the past to prevent the present from dawning on my mind. ⁵Let me understand that I am trying to use time against God. ⁶Let me learn to give the past away, realizing that in so doing I am giving up nothing.

4. (9) **I see nothing as it is now.**

²If I see nothing as it is now, it can truly be said that I see nothing. ³I can see only what is now. ⁴The choice is not whether to see the past or the present; the choice is merely whether to see or not. ⁵What I have chosen to see has cost me vision. ⁶Now I would choose again, that I may see.

5. (10) **My thoughts do not mean anything.**

²I have no private thoughts. ³Yet it is only private thoughts of which I am aware. ⁴What can these thoughts mean? ⁵They do not exist, and so they mean nothing. ⁶Yet my mind is part of creation and part of its Creator. ⁷Would I not rather join the thinking of the universe than to obscure all that is really mine with my pitiful and meaningless "private" thoughts?

LESSON 53

Today we will review the following:

1. (11) **My meaningless thoughts are showing me a meaningless world.**

²Since the thoughts of which I am aware do not mean anything, the world that pictures them can have no meaning. ³What is producing this world is insane, and so is what it produces. ⁴Reality is not insane, and I have real thoughts as well as insane ones. ⁵I can therefore see a real world, if I look to my real thoughts as my guide for seeing.

2. (12) **I am upset because I see a meaningless world.**

²Insane thoughts are upsetting. ³They produce a world in which there is no order anywhere. ⁴Only chaos rules a world that represents chaotic thinking, and chaos has no laws. ⁵I cannot live in peace in such a world. ⁶I am grateful that this world is not real, and that I need not see it at all unless I choose to value it. ⁷And I do not choose to value what is totally insane and has no meaning.

3. (13) **A meaningless world engenders fear.**

²The totally insane engenders fear because it is completely undependable, and offers no grounds for trust. ³Nothing in madness is dependable. ⁴It holds out no safety and no hope. ⁵But such a world is not real. ⁶I have given it the illusion of reality, and have suffered from my belief in it. ⁷Now I choose to withdraw this belief, and place my trust in reality. ⁸In choosing this, I will escape all the effects of the world of fear, because I am acknowledging that it does not exist.

4. (14) **God did not create a meaningless world.**

²How can a meaningless world exist if God did not create it? ³He is the Source of all meaning, and everything that is real is in His Mind. ⁴It is in my mind too, because He created it with me. ⁵Why should I continue to suffer from the effects of my own insane thoughts, when the perfection of creation is my home? ⁶Let me remember the power of my decision, and recognize where I really abide.

5. (15) **My thoughts are images that I have made.**

²Whatever I see reflects my thoughts. ³It is my thoughts that tell me where I am and what I am. ⁴The fact that I see a world in which there is suffering and loss and death shows me that I am seeing only the representation of my insane thoughts, and am not allowing my real thoughts to cast their beneficent light on what I see. ⁵Yet God's way is sure. ⁶The images I have made cannot prevail against Him because it is not my will that they do so. ⁷My will is His, and I will place no other gods before Him.

LESSON 54

These are the review ideas for today:

1. (16) **I have no neutral thoughts.**

[2]Neutral thoughts are impossible because all thoughts have power. [3]They will either make a false world or lead me to the real one. [4]But thoughts cannot be without effects. [5]As the world I see arises from my thinking errors, so will the real world rise before my eyes as I let my errors be corrected. [6]My thoughts cannot be neither true nor false. [7]They must be one or the other. [8]What I see shows me which they are.

2. (17) **I see no neutral things.**

[2]What I see witnesses to what I think. [3]If I did not think I would not exist, because life is thought. [4]Let me look on the world I see as the representation of my own state of mind. [5]I know that my state of mind can change. [6]And so I also know the world I see can change as well.

3. (18) **I am not alone in experiencing the effects of my seeing.**

[2]If I have no private thoughts, I cannot see a private world. [3]Even the mad idea of separation had to be shared before it could form the basis of the world I see. [4]Yet that sharing was a sharing of nothing. [5]I can also call upon my real thoughts, which share everything with everyone. [6]As my thoughts of separation call to the separation thoughts of others, so my real thoughts awaken the real thoughts in them. [7]And the world my real thoughts show me will dawn on their sight as well as mine.

4. (19) **I am not alone in experiencing the effects of my thoughts.**

²I am alone in nothing. ³Everything I think or say or do teaches all the universe. ⁴A Son of God cannot think or speak or act in vain. ⁵He cannot be alone in anything. ⁶It is therefore in my power to change every mind along with mine, for mine is the power of God.

5. (20) **I am determined to see.**

²Recognizing the shared nature of my thoughts, I am determined to see. ³I would look upon the witnesses that show me the thinking of the world has been changed. ⁴I would behold the proof that what has been done through me has enabled love to replace fear, laughter to replace tears, and abundance to replace loss. ⁵I would look upon the real world, and let it teach me that my will and the Will of God are one.

LESSON 55

Today's review includes the following:

1. (21) **I am determined to see things differently.**

²What I see now are but signs of disease, disaster and death. ³This cannot be what God created for His beloved Son. ⁴The very fact that I see such things is proof that I do not understand God. ⁵Therefore I also do not understand His Son. ⁶What I see tells me that I do not know who I am. ⁷I am determined to see the witnesses to the truth in me, rather than those which show me an illusion of myself.

2. (22) **What I see is a form of vengeance.**

²The world I see is hardly the representation of loving thoughts. ³It is a picture of attack on everything by everything. ⁴It is anything but a reflection of the Love of God and the Love of His Son. ⁵It is my own attack thoughts that give rise to this picture. ⁶My loving thoughts will save me from this perception of the world, and give me the peace God intended me to have.

3. (23) **I can escape from this world by giving up attack thoughts.**

²Herein lies salvation, and nowhere else. ³Without attack thoughts I could not see a world of attack. ⁴As forgiveness allows love to return to my awareness, I will see a world of peace and safety and joy. ⁵And it is this I choose to see, in place of what I look on now.

4. (24) **I do not perceive my own best interests.**

[2]How could I recognize my own best interests when I do not know who I am? [3]What I think are my best interests would merely bind me closer to the world of illusions. [4]I am willing to follow the Guide God has given me to find out what my own best interests are, recognizing that I cannot perceive them by myself.

5. (25) **I do not know what anything is for.**

[2]To me, the purpose of everything is to prove that my illusions about myself are real. [3]It is for this purpose that I attempt to use everyone and everything. [4]It is for this that I believe the world is for. [5]Therefore I do not recognize its real purpose. [6]The purpose I have given the world has led to a frightening picture of it. [7]Let me open my mind to the world's real purpose by withdrawing the one I have given it, and learning the truth about it.

LESSON 56

Our review for today covers the following:

1. (26) **My attack thoughts are attacking my invulnerability.**

²How can I know who I am when I see myself as under constant attack? ³Pain, illness, loss, age and death seem to threaten me. ⁴All my hopes and wishes and plans appear to be at the mercy of a world I cannot control. ⁵Yet perfect security and complete fulfillment are my inheritance. ⁶I have tried to give my inheritance away in exchange for the world I see. ⁷But God has kept my inheritance safe for me. ⁸My own real thoughts will teach me what it is.

2. (27) **Above all else I want to see.**

²Recognizing that what I see reflects what I think I am, I realize that vision is my greatest need. ³The world I see attests to the fearful nature of the self-image I have made. ⁴If I would remember who I am, it is essential that I let this image of myself go. ⁵As it is replaced by truth, vision will surely be given me. ⁶And with this vision, I will look upon the world and on myself with charity and love.

3. (28) **Above all else I want to see differently.**

²The world I see holds my fearful self-image in place, and guarantees its continuance. ³While I see the world as I see it now, truth cannot enter my awareness. ⁴I would let the door behind this world be opened for me, that I may look past it to the world that reflects the Love of God.

4. (29) **God is in everything I see.**

²Behind every image I have made, the truth remains unchanged. ³Behind every veil I have drawn across the face of love, its light remains undimmed. ⁴Beyond all my insane wishes is my will, united with the Will of my Father. ⁵God is still everywhere and in everything forever. ⁶And we who are part of Him will yet look past all appearances, and recognize the truth beyond them all.

5. (30) **God is in everything I see because God is in my mind.**

²In my own mind, behind all my insane thoughts of separation and attack, is the knowledge that all is one forever. ³I have not lost the knowledge of Who I am because I have forgotten it. ⁴It has been kept for me in the Mind of God, Who has not left His Thoughts. ⁵And I, who am among them, am one with them and one with Him.

LESSON 57

Today let us review these ideas:

1. (31) **I am not the victim of the world I see.**

²How can I be the victim of a world that can be completely undone if I so choose? ³My chains are loosened. ⁴I can drop them off merely by desiring to do so. ⁵The prison door is open. ⁶I can leave simply by walking out. ⁷Nothing holds me in this world. ⁸Only my wish to stay keeps me a prisoner. ⁹I would give up my insane wishes and walk into the sunlight at last.

2. (32) **I have invented the world I see.**

²I made up the prison in which I see myself. ³All I need do is recognize this and I am free. ⁴I have deluded myself into believing it is possible to imprison the Son of God. ⁵I was bitterly mistaken in this belief, which I no longer want. ⁶The Son of God must be forever free. ⁷He is as God created him, and not what I would make of him. ⁸He is where God would have him be, and not where I thought to hold him prisoner.

3. (33) **There is another way of looking at the world.**

²Since the purpose of the world is not the one I ascribed to it, there must be another way of looking at it. ³I see everything upside down, and my thoughts are the opposite of truth. ⁴I see the world as a prison for God's Son. ⁵It must be, then, that the world is really a place where he can be set free. ⁶I would look upon the world as it is, and see it as a place where the Son of God finds his freedom.

4. (34) **I could see peace instead of this.**

²When I see the world as a place of freedom, I realize that it reflects the laws of God instead of the rules I made up for it to obey. ³I will understand that peace, not war, abides in it. ⁴And I will perceive that peace also abides in the hearts of all who share this place with me.

5. (35) **My mind is part of God's.** ²**I am very holy.**

³As I share the peace of the world with my brothers, I begin to understand that this peace comes from deep within myself. ⁴The world I look upon has taken on the light of my forgiveness, and shines forgiveness back at me. ⁵In this light I begin to see what my illusions about myself kept hidden. ⁶I begin to understand the holiness of all living things, including myself, and their oneness with me.

LESSON 58

These ideas are for review today:

1. (36) My holiness envelops everything I see.

²From my holiness does the perception of the real world come. ³Having forgiven, I no longer see myself as guilty. ⁴I can accept the innocence that is the truth about me. ⁵Seen through understanding eyes, the holiness of the world is all I see, for I can picture only the thoughts I hold about myself.

2. (37) My holiness blesses the world.

²The perception of my holiness does not bless me alone. ³Everyone and everything I see in its light shares in the joy it brings to me. ⁴There is nothing that is apart from this joy, because there is nothing that does not share my holiness. ⁵As I recognize my holiness, so does the holiness of the world shine forth for everyone to see.

3. (38) There is nothing my holiness cannot do.

²My holiness is unlimited in its power to heal, because it is unlimited in its power to save. ³What is there to be saved from except illusions? ⁴And what are all illusions except false ideas about myself? ⁵My holiness undoes them all by asserting the truth about me. ⁶In the presence of my holiness, which I share with God Himself, all idols vanish.

4. (39) **My holiness is my salvation.**

²Since my holiness saves me from all guilt, recognizing my holiness is recognizing my salvation. ³It is also recognizing the salvation of the world. ⁴Once I have accepted my holiness, nothing can make me afraid. ⁵And because I am unafraid, everyone must share in my understanding, which is the gift of God to me and to the world.

5. (40) **I am blessed as a Son of God.**

²Herein lies my claim to all good and only good. ³I am blessed as a Son of God. ⁴All good things are mine, because God intended them for me. ⁵I cannot suffer any loss or deprivation or pain because of Who I am. ⁶My Father supports me, protects me, and directs me in all things. ⁷His care for me is infinite, and is with me forever. ⁸I am eternally blessed as His Son.

LESSON 59

The following ideas are for review today:

1. (41) **God goes with me wherever I go.**

[2]How can I be alone when God always goes with me? [3]How can I be doubtful and unsure of myself when perfect certainty abides in Him? [4]How can I be disturbed by anything when He rests in me in absolute peace? [5]How can I suffer when love and joy surround me through Him? [6]Let me not cherish illusions about myself. [7]I am perfect because God goes with me wherever I go.

2. (42) **God is my strength. [2]Vision is His gift.**

[3]Let me not look to my own eyes to see today. [4]Let me be willing to exchange my pitiful illusion of seeing for the vision that is given by God. [5]Christ's vision is His gift, and He has given it to me. [6]Let me call upon this gift today, so that this day may help me to understand eternity.

3. (43) **God is my Source. [2]I cannot see apart from Him.**

[3]I can see what God wants me to see. [4]I cannot see anything else. [5]Beyond His Will lie only illusions. [6]It is these I choose when I think I can see apart from Him. [7]It is these I choose when I try to see through the body's eyes. [8]Yet the vision of Christ has been given me to replace them. [9]It is through this vision that I choose to see.

4. (44) **God is the light in which I see.**

[2]I cannot see in darkness. [3]God is the only light. [4]Therefore, if I am to see, it must be through Him. [5]I have tried to define what seeing is, and I have been wrong. [6]Now it is given me to understand that God is the light in which I see. [7]Let me welcome vision and the happy world it will show me.

5. (45) **God is the Mind with which I think.**

[2]I have no thoughts I do not share with God. [3]I have no thoughts apart from Him, because I have no mind apart from His. [4]As part of His Mind, my thoughts are His and His Thoughts are mine.

99

LESSON 60

These ideas are for today's review:

1. (46) God is the Love in which I forgive.

[2]God does not forgive because He has never condemned. [3]The blameless cannot blame, and those who have accepted their innocence see nothing to forgive. [4]Yet forgiveness is the means by which I will recognize my innocence. [5]It is the reflection of God's Love on earth. [6]It will bring me near enough to Heaven that the Love of God can reach down to me and raise me up to Him.

2. (47) God is the strength in which I trust.

[2]It is not my own strength through which I forgive. [3]It is through the strength of God in me, which I am remembering as I forgive. [4]As I begin to see, I recognize His reflection on earth. [5]I forgive all things because I feel the stirring of His strength in me. [6]And I begin to remember the Love I chose to forget, but which has not forgotten me.

3. (48) There is nothing to fear.

[2]How safe the world will look to me when I can see it! [3]It will not look anything like what I imagine I see now. [4]Everyone and everything I see will lean toward me to bless me. [5]I will recognize in everyone my dearest Friend. [6]What could there be to fear in a world that I have forgiven, and that has forgiven me?

4. (49) God's Voice speaks to me all through the day.

²There is not a moment in which God's Voice ceases to call on my forgiveness to save me. ³There is not a moment in which His Voice fails to direct my thoughts, guide my actions and lead my feet. ⁴I am walking steadily on toward truth. ⁵There is nowhere else I can go, because God's Voice is the only Voice and the only Guide that has been given to His Son.

5. (50) I am sustained by the Love of God.

²As I listen to God's Voice, I am sustained by His Love. ³As I open my eyes, His Love lights up the world for me to see. ⁴As I forgive, His Love reminds me that His Son is sinless. ⁵And as I look upon the world with the vision He has given me, I remember that I am His Son.

LESSON 61

I am the light of the world.

1.   Who is the light of the world except God's Son? ²This, then, is merely a statement of the truth about yourself. ³It is the opposite of a statement of pride, of arrogance, or of self-deception. ⁴It does not describe the self-concept you have made. ⁵It does not refer to any of the characteristics with which you have endowed your idols. ⁶It refers to you as you were created by God. ⁷It simply states the truth.

2.   To the ego, today's idea is the epitome of self-glorification. ²But the ego does not understand humility, mistaking it for self-debasement. ³Humility consists of accepting your role in salvation and in taking no other. ⁴It is not humility to insist you cannot be the light of the world if that is the function God assigned to you. ⁵It is only arrogance that would assert this function cannot be for you, and arrogance is always of the ego.

3.   True humility requires that you accept today's idea because it is God's Voice which tells you it is true. ²This is a beginning step in accepting your real function on earth. ³It is a giant stride toward taking your rightful place in salvation. ⁴It is a positive assertion of your right to be saved, and an acknowledgment of the power that is given you to save others.

4.   You will want to think about this idea as often as possible today. ²It is the perfect answer to all illusions, and therefore to all temptation. ³It brings all the images you have made about yourself to the truth, and helps you depart in peace, unburdened and certain of your purpose.

5.   As many practice periods as possible should be undertaken today, although each one need not exceed a minute or two. ²They should begin with telling yourself:

> ³*I am the light of the world.* ⁴*That is my only function.*
> ⁵*That is why I am here.*

⁶Then think about these statements for a short while, preferably with your eyes closed if the situation permits. ⁷Let a few related thoughts come to you, and repeat the idea to yourself if your mind wanders away from the central thought.

6. Be sure both to begin and end the day with a practice period. [2]Thus you will awaken with an acknowledgment of the truth about yourself, reinforce it throughout the day, and turn to sleep as you reaffirm your function and your only purpose here. [3]These two practice periods may be longer than the rest, if you find them helpful and want to extend them.

7. Today's idea goes far beyond the ego's petty views of what you are and what your purpose is. [2]As a bringer of salvation, this is obviously necessary. [3]This is the first of a number of giant steps we will take in the next few weeks. [4]Try today to begin to build a firm foundation for these advances. [5]You are the light of the world. [6]God has built His plan for the salvation of His Son on you.

LESSON 62

Forgiveness is my function as the light of the world.

1.   It is your forgiveness that will bring the world of darkness to the light. ²It is your forgiveness that lets you recognize the light in which you see. ³Forgiveness is the demonstration that you are the light of the world. ⁴Through your forgiveness does the truth about yourself return to your memory. ⁵Therefore, in your forgiveness lies your salvation.

2.   Illusions about yourself and the world are one. ²That is why all forgiveness is a gift to yourself. ³Your goal is to find out who you are, having denied your Identity by attacking creation and its Creator. ⁴Now you are learning how to remember the truth. ⁵For this attack must be replaced by forgiveness, so that thoughts of life may replace thoughts of death.

3.   Remember that in every attack you call upon your own weakness, while each time you forgive you call upon the strength of Christ in you. ²Do you not then begin to understand what forgiveness will do for you? ³It will remove all sense of weakness, strain and fatigue from your mind. ⁴It will take away all fear and guilt and pain. ⁵It will restore the invulnerability and power God gave His Son to your awareness.

4.   Let us be glad to begin and end this day by practicing today's idea, and to use it as frequently as possible throughout the day. ²It will help to make the day as happy for you as God wants you to be. ³And it will help those around you, as well as those who seem to be far away in space and time, to share this happiness with you.

5.   As often as you can, closing your eyes if possible, say to yourself today:

²*Forgiveness is my function as the light of the world.*
³*I would fulfill my function that I may be happy.*

⁴Then devote a minute or two to considering your function and the happiness and release it will bring you. ⁵Let related thoughts come freely, for your heart will recognize these words, and in your mind is the awareness they are true. ⁶Should your attention wander, repeat the idea and add:

⁷*I would remember this because I want to be happy.*

104

LESSON 63

The light of the world brings peace to every mind through my forgiveness.

1. How holy are you who have the power to bring peace to every mind! ²How blessed are you who can learn to recognize the means for letting this be done through you! ³What purpose could you have that would bring you greater happiness?

2. You are indeed the light of the world with such a function. ²The Son of God looks to you for his redemption. ³It is yours to give him, for it belongs to you. ⁴Accept no trivial purpose or meaningless desire in its place, or you will forget your function and leave the Son of God in hell. ⁵This is no idle request that is being asked of you. ⁶You are being asked to accept salvation that it may be yours to give.

3. Recognizing the importance of this function, we will be happy to remember it very often today. ²We will begin the day by acknowledging it, and close the day with the thought of it in our awareness. ³And throughout the day we will repeat this as often as we can:

> ⁴*The light of the world brings peace to every mind*
> *through my forgiveness.* ⁵*I am the means God has*
> *appointed for the salvation of the world.*

4. If you close your eyes, you will probably find it easier to let the related thoughts come to you in the minute or two that you should devote to considering this. ²Do not, however, wait for such an opportunity. ³No chance should be lost for reinforcing today's idea. ⁴Remember that God's Son looks to you for his salvation. ⁵And Who but your Self must be His Son?

105

LESSON 64

Let me not forget my function.

1. Today's idea is merely another way of saying "Let me not wander into temptation." ²The purpose of the world you see is to obscure your function of forgiveness, and provide you with a justification for forgetting it. ³It is the temptation to abandon God and His Son by taking on a physical appearance. ⁴It is this the body's eyes look upon.

2. Nothing the body's eyes seem to see can be anything but a form of temptation, since this was the purpose of the body itself. ²Yet we have learned that the Holy Spirit has another use for all the illusions you have made, and therefore He sees another purpose in them. ³To the Holy Spirit, the world is a place where you learn to forgive yourself what you think of as your sins. ⁴In this perception, the physical appearance of temptation becomes the spiritual recognition of salvation.

3. To review our last few lessons, your function here is to be the light of the world, a function given you by God. ²It is only the arrogance of the ego that leads you to question this, and only the fear of the ego that induces you to regard yourself as unworthy of the task assigned to you by God Himself. ³The world's salvation awaits your forgiveness, because through it does the Son of God escape from all illusions, and thus from all temptation. ⁴The Son of God is you.

4. Only by fulfilling the function given you by God will you be happy. ²That is because your function is to be happy by using the means by which happiness becomes inevitable. ³There is no other way. ⁴Therefore, every time you choose whether or not to fulfill your function, you are really choosing whether or not to be happy.

5. Let us remember this today. ²Let us remind ourselves of it in the morning and again at night, and all through the day as well. ³Prepare yourself in advance for all the decisions you will make today by remembering they are all really very simple. ⁴Each one will lead to happiness or unhappiness. ⁵Can such a simple decision really be difficult to make? ⁶Let not the form of the decision deceive you. ⁷Complexity of form does not imply complexity of content. ⁸It is impossible that any decision on earth can have a

content different from just this one simple choice. [9]That is the only choice the Holy Spirit sees. [10]Therefore it is the only choice there is.

6. Today, then, let us practice with these thoughts:

> [2]*Let me not forget my function.*
> [3]*Let me not try to substitute mine for God's.*
> [4]*Let me forgive and be happy.*

[5]At least once devote ten or fifteen minutes today to reflecting on this with closed eyes. [6]Related thoughts will come to help you, if you remember the crucial importance of your function to you and to the world.

7. In the frequent applications of today's idea throughout the day, devote several minutes to reviewing these thoughts, and then thinking about them and about nothing else. [2]This will be difficult, at first particularly, since you are not proficient in the mind discipline that it requires. [3]You may need to repeat "Let me not forget my function" quite often to help you concentrate.

8. Two forms of shorter practice periods are required. [2]At times, do the exercises with your eyes closed, trying to concentrate on the thoughts you are using. [3]At other times, keep your eyes open after reviewing the thoughts, and then look slowly and unselectively around you, telling yourself:

> [4]*This is the world it is my function to save.*

LESSON 65

My only function is the one God gave me.

1. The idea for today reaffirms your commitment to salvation. ²It also reminds you that you have no function other than that. ³Both these thoughts are obviously necessary for a total commitment. ⁴Salvation cannot be the only purpose you hold while you still cherish others. ⁵The full acceptance of salvation as your only function necessarily entails two phases; the recognition of salvation as your function, and the relinquishment of all the other goals you have invented for yourself.

2. This is the only way in which you can take your rightful place among the saviors of the world. ²This is the only way in which you can say and mean, "My only function is the one God gave me." ³This is the only way in which you can find peace of mind.

3. Today, and for a number of days to follow, set aside ten to fifteen minutes for a more sustained practice period, in which you try to understand and accept what the idea for the day really means. ²Today's idea offers you escape from all your perceived difficulties. ³It places the key to the door of peace, which you have closed upon yourself, in your own hands. ⁴It gives you the answer to all the searching you have done since time began.

4. Try, if possible, to undertake the daily extended practice periods at approximately the same time each day. ²Try, also, to determine this time in advance, and then adhere to it as closely as possible. ³The purpose of this is to arrange your day so that you have set apart the time for God, as well as for all the trivial purposes and goals you will pursue. ⁴This is part of the long-range disciplinary training your mind needs, so that the Holy Spirit can use it consistently for the purpose He shares with you.

5. For the longer practice period, begin by reviewing the idea for the day. ²Then close your eyes, repeat the idea to yourself once again, and watch your mind carefully to catch whatever thoughts cross it. ³At first, make no attempt to concentrate only on thoughts related to the idea for the day. ⁴Rather, try to uncover each thought that arises to interfere with it. ⁵Note each one as it comes to you, with as little involvement or concern as possible, dismissing each one by telling yourself:

> ⁶*This thought reflects a goal that is preventing me from accepting my only function.*

6. After a while, interfering thoughts will become harder to find. ²Try, however, to continue a minute or so longer, attempting to catch a few of the idle thoughts that escaped your attention before, but do not strain or make undue effort in doing this. ³Then tell yourself:

> ⁴*On this clean slate let my true function be written for me.*

⁵You need not use these exact words, but try to get the sense of being willing to have your illusions of purpose be replaced by truth.

7. Finally, repeat the idea for today once more, and devote the rest of the practice period to trying to focus on its importance to you, the relief its acceptance will bring you by resolving your conflicts once and for all, and the extent to which you really want salvation in spite of your own foolish ideas to the contrary.

8. In the shorter practice periods, which should be undertaken at least once an hour, use this form in applying today's idea:

> ²*My only function is the one God gave me.* ³*I want no other and I have no other.*

⁴Sometimes close your eyes as you practice this, and sometimes keep them open and look about you. ⁵It is what you see now that will be totally changed when you accept today's idea completely.

LESSON 66

My happiness and my function are one.

1. You have surely noticed an emphasis throughout our recent lessons on the connection between fulfilling your function and achieving happiness. ²This is because you do not really see the connection. ³Yet there is more than just a connection between them; they are the same. ⁴Their forms are different, but their content is completely one.

2. The ego does constant battle with the Holy Spirit on the fundamental question of what your function is. ²So does it do constant battle with the Holy Spirit about what your happiness is. ³It is not a two-way battle. ⁴The ego attacks and the Holy Spirit does not respond. ⁵He knows what your function is. ⁶He knows that it is your happiness.

3. Today we will try to go past this wholly meaningless battle and arrive at the truth about your function. ²We will not engage in senseless arguments about what it is. ³We will not become hopelessly involved in defining happiness and determining the means for achieving it. ⁴We will not indulge the ego by listening to its attacks on truth. ⁵We will merely be glad that we can find out what truth is.

4. Our longer practice period today has as its purpose your acceptance of the fact that not only is there a very real connection between the function God gave you and your happiness, but that they are actually identical. ²God gives you only happiness. ³Therefore, the function He gave you must be happiness, even if it appears to be different. ⁴Today's exercises are an attempt to go beyond these differences in appearance, and recognize a common content where it exists in truth.

5. Begin the ten-to-fifteen-minute practice period by reviewing these thoughts:

> ²God gives me only happiness.
> ³He has given my function to me.
> ⁴Therefore my function must be happiness.

⁵Try to see the logic in this sequence, even if you do not yet accept the conclusion. ⁶It is only if the first two thoughts are wrong that

the conclusion could be false. [7]Let us, then, think about the premises for a while, as we are practicing.

6. The first premise is that God gives you only happiness. [2]This could be false, of course, but in order to be false it is necessary to define God as something He is not. [3]Love cannot give evil, and what is not happiness is evil. [4]God cannot give what He does not have, and He cannot have what He is not. [5]Unless God gives you only happiness, He must be evil. [6]And it is this definition of Him you are believing if you do not accept the first premise.

7. The second premise is that God has given you your function. [2]We have seen that there are only two parts of your mind. [3]One is ruled by the ego, and is made up of illusions. [4]The other is the home of the Holy Spirit, where truth abides. [5]There are no other guides but these to choose between, and no other outcomes possible as a result of your choice but the fear that the ego always engenders, and the love that the Holy Spirit always offers to replace it.

8. Thus, it must be that your function is established by God through His Voice, or is made by the ego which you have made to replace Him. [2]Which is true? [3]Unless God gave your function to you, it must be the gift of the ego. [4]Does the ego really have gifts to give, being itself an illusion and offering only the illusion of gifts?

9. Think about this during the longer practice period today. [2]Think also about the many forms the illusion of your function has taken in your mind, and the many ways in which you tried to find salvation under the ego's guidance. [3]Did you find it? [4]Were you happy? [5]Did they bring you peace? [6]We need great honesty today. [7]Remember the outcomes fairly, and consider also whether it was ever reasonable to expect happiness from anything the ego ever proposed. [8]Yet the ego is the only alternative to the Holy Spirit's Voice.

10. You will listen to madness or hear the truth. [2]Try to make this choice as you think about the premises on which our conclusion rests. [3]We can share in this conclusion, but in no other. [4]For God Himself shares it with us. [5]Today's idea is another giant stride in the perception of the same as the same, and the different as different. [6]On one side stand all illusions. [7]All truth stands on the other. [8]Let us try today to realize that only the truth is true.

11. In the shorter practice periods, which would be most helpful

today if undertaken twice an hour, this form of the application is suggested:

> [2] *My happiness and function are one, because God has given me both.*

[3] It will not take more than a minute, and probably less, to repeat these words slowly and think about them a little while as you say them.

LESSON 67

Love created me like itself.

1. Today's idea is a complete and accurate statement of what you are. ²This is why you are the light of the world. ³This is why God appointed you as the world's savior. ⁴This is why the Son of God looks to you for his salvation. ⁵He is saved by what you are. ⁶We will make every effort today to reach this truth about you, and to realize fully, if only for a moment, that it is the truth.

2. In the longer practice period, we will think about your reality and its wholly unchanged and unchangeable nature. ²We will begin by repeating this truth about you, and then spend a few minutes adding some relevant thoughts, such as:

> ³*Holiness created me holy.*
> ⁴*Kindness created me kind.*
> ⁵*Helpfulness created me helpful.*
> ⁶*Perfection created me perfect.*

⁷Any attribute which is in accord with God as He defines Himself is appropriate for use. ⁸We are trying today to undo your definition of God and replace it with His Own. ⁹We are also trying to emphasize that you are part of His definition of Himself.

3. After you have gone over several such related thoughts, try to let all thoughts drop away for a brief preparatory interval, and then try to reach past all your images and preconceptions about yourself to the truth in you. ²If love created you like itself, this Self must be in you. ³And somewhere in your mind It is there for you to find.

4. You may find it necessary to repeat the idea for today from time to time to replace distracting thoughts. ²You may also find that this is not sufficient, and that you need to continue adding other thoughts related to the truth about yourself. ³Yet perhaps you will succeed in going past that, and through the interval of thoughtlessness to the awareness of a blazing light in which you recognize yourself as love created you. ⁴Be confident that you will do much today to bring that awareness nearer, whether you feel you have succeeded or not.

5. It will be particularly helpful today to practice the idea for the

day as often as you can. ²You need to hear the truth about yourself as frequently as possible, because your mind is so preoccupied with false self-images. ³Four or five times an hour, and perhaps even more, it would be most beneficial to remind yourself that love created you like itself. ⁴Hear the truth about yourself in this.

6. Try to realize in the shorter practice periods that this is not your tiny, solitary voice that tells you this. ²This is the Voice for God, reminding you of your Father and of your Self. ³This is the Voice of truth, replacing everything that the ego tells you about yourself with the simple truth about the Son of God. ⁴You were created by love like itself.

LESSON 68

Love holds no grievances.

1. You who were created by love like itself can hold no grievances and know your Self. ²To hold a grievance is to forget who you are. ³To hold a grievance is to see yourself as a body. ⁴To hold a grievance is to let the ego rule your mind and to condemn the body to death. ⁵Perhaps you do not yet fully realize just what holding grievances does to your mind. ⁶It seems to split you off from your Source and make you unlike Him. ⁷It makes you believe that He is like what you think you have become, for no one can conceive of his Creator as unlike himself.

2. Shut off from your Self, which remains aware of Its likeness to Its Creator, your Self seems to sleep, while the part of your mind that weaves illusions in its sleep appears to be awake. ²Can all this arise from holding grievances? ³Oh, yes! ⁴For he who holds grievances denies he was created by love, and his Creator has become fearful to him in his dream of hate. ⁵Who can dream of hatred and not fear God?

3. It is as sure that those who hold grievances will redefine God in their own image, as it is certain that God created them like Himself, and defined them as part of Him. ²It is as sure that those who hold grievances will suffer guilt, as it is certain that those who forgive will find peace. ³It is as sure that those who hold grievances will forget who they are, as it is certain that those who forgive will remember.

4. Would you not be willing to relinquish your grievances if you believed all this were so? ²Perhaps you do not think you can let your grievances go. ³That, however, is simply a matter of motivation. ⁴Today we will try to find out how you would feel without them. ⁵If you succeed even by ever so little, there will never be a problem in motivation ever again.

5. Begin today's extended practice period by searching your mind for those against whom you hold what you regard as major grievances. ²Some of these will be quite easy to find. ³Then think of the seemingly minor grievances you hold against those you like and even think you love. ⁴It will quickly become apparent that there is no one against whom you do not cherish grievances of some sort. ⁵This has left you alone in all the universe in your perception of yourself.

6.   Determine now to see all these people as friends. ²Say to them all, thinking of each one in turn as you do so:

> ³*I would see you as my friend, that I may remember you are part of me and come to know myself.*

⁴Spend the remainder of the practice period trying to think of yourself as completely at peace with everyone and everything, safe in a world that protects you and loves you, and that you love in return. ⁵Try to feel safety surrounding you, hovering over you and holding you up. ⁶Try to believe, however briefly, that nothing can harm you in any way. ⁷At the end of the practice period tell yourself:

> ⁸*Love holds no grievances. ⁹When I let all my grievances go I will know I am perfectly safe.*

7.   The short practice periods should include a quick application of today's idea in this form, whenever any thought of grievance arises against anyone, physically present or not:

> ²*Love holds no grievances. ³Let me not betray my Self.*

⁴In addition, repeat the idea several times an hour in this form:

> ⁵*Love holds no grievances. ⁶I would wake to my Self by laying all my grievances aside and wakening in Him.*

LESSON 69

My grievances hide the light of the world in me.

1. No one can look upon what your grievances conceal. ²Because your grievances are hiding the light of the world in you, everyone stands in darkness, and you beside him. ³But as the veil of your grievances is lifted, you are released with him. ⁴Share your salvation now with him who stood beside you when you were in hell. ⁵He is your brother in the light of the world that saves you both.

2. Today let us make another real attempt to reach the light in you. ²Before we undertake this in our more extended practice period, let us devote several minutes to thinking about what we are trying to do. ³We are literally attempting to get in touch with the salvation of the world. ⁴We are trying to see past the veil of darkness that keeps it concealed. ⁵We are trying to let the veil be lifted, and to see the tears of God's Son disappear in the sunlight.

3. Let us begin our longer practice period today with the full realization that this is so, and with real determination to reach what is dearer to us than all else. ²Salvation is our only need. ³There is no other purpose here, and no other function to fulfill. ⁴Learning salvation is our only goal. ⁵Let us end the ancient search today by finding the light in us, and holding it up for everyone who searches with us to look upon and rejoice.

4. Very quietly now, with your eyes closed, try to let go of all the content that generally occupies your consciousness. ²Think of your mind as a vast circle, surrounded by a layer of heavy, dark clouds. ³You can see only the clouds because you seem to be standing outside the circle and quite apart from it.

5. From where you stand, you can see no reason to believe there is a brilliant light hidden by the clouds. ²The clouds seem to be the only reality. ³They seem to be all there is to see. ⁴Therefore, you do not attempt to go through them and past them, which is the only way in which you would be really convinced of their lack of substance. ⁵We will make this attempt today.

6. After you have thought about the importance of what you are trying to do for yourself and the world, try to settle down in perfect stillness, remembering only how much you want to reach the light in you today,—now! ²Determine to go past the clouds.

³Reach out and touch them in your mind. ⁴Brush them aside with your hand; feel them resting on your cheeks and forehead and eyelids as you go through them. ⁵Go on; clouds cannot stop you.

7. If you are doing the exercises properly, you will begin to feel a sense of being lifted up and carried ahead. ²Your little effort and small determination call on the power of the universe to help you, and God Himself will raise you from darkness into light. ³You are in accord with His Will. ⁴You cannot fail because your will is His.

8. Have confidence in your Father today, and be certain that He has heard you and answered you. ²You may not recognize His answer yet, but you can indeed be sure that it is given you and you will yet receive it. ³Try, as you attempt to go through the clouds to the light, to hold this confidence in your mind. ⁴Try to remember that you are at last joining your will to God's. ⁵Try to keep the thought clearly in mind that what you undertake with God must succeed. ⁶Then let the power of God work in you and through you, that His Will and yours be done.

9. In the shorter practice periods, which you will want to do as often as possible in view of the importance of today's idea to you and your happiness, remind yourself that your grievances are hiding the light of the world from your awareness. ²Remind yourself also that you are not searching for it alone, and that you do know where to look for it. ³Say, then:

⁴My grievances hide the light of the world in me. ⁵I cannot see what I have hidden. ⁶Yet I want to let it be revealed to me, for my salvation and the salvation of the world.

⁷Also, be sure to tell yourself:

⁸If I hold this grievance the light of the world will be hidden from me,

if you are tempted to hold anything against anyone today.

LESSON 70

My salvation comes from me.

1. All temptation is nothing more than some form of the basic temptation not to believe the idea for today. [2]Salvation seems to come from anywhere except from you. [3]So, too, does the source of guilt. [4]You see neither guilt nor salvation as in your own mind and nowhere else. [5]When you realize that all guilt is solely an invention of your mind, you also realize that guilt and salvation must be in the same place. [6]In understanding this you are saved.

2. The seeming cost of accepting today's idea is this: It means that nothing outside yourself can save you; nothing outside yourself can give you peace. [2]But it also means that nothing outside yourself can hurt you, or disturb your peace or upset you in any way. [3]Today's idea places you in charge of the universe, where you belong because of what you are. [4]This is not a role that can be partially accepted. [5]And you must surely begin to see that accepting it is salvation.

3. It may not, however, be clear to you why the recognition that guilt is in your own mind entails the realization that salvation is there as well. [2]God would not have put the remedy for the sickness where it cannot help. [3]That is the way your mind has worked, but hardly His. [4]He wants you to be healed, so He has kept the Source of healing where the need for healing lies.

4. You have tried to do just the opposite, making every attempt, however distorted and fantastic it might be, to separate healing from the sickness for which it was intended, and thus keep the sickness. [2]Your purpose was to ensure that healing did not occur. [3]God's purpose was to ensure that it did.

5. Today we practice realizing that God's Will and ours are really the same in this. [2]God wants us to be healed, and we do not really want to be sick, because it makes us unhappy. [3]Therefore, in accepting the idea for today, we are really in agreement with God. [4]He does not want us to be sick. [5]Neither do we. [6]He wants us to be healed. [7]So do we.

6. We are ready for two longer practice periods today, each of which should last some ten to fifteen minutes. [2]We will, however, still let you decide when to undertake them. [3]We will follow this practice for a number of lessons, and it would again be well to

119

decide in advance when would be a good time to lay aside for each of them, and then adhering to your own decisions as closely as possible.

7. Begin these practice periods by repeating the idea for today, adding a statement signifying your recognition that salvation comes from nothing outside of you. ²You might put it this way:

> ³*My salvation comes from me.* ⁴*It cannot come from anywhere else.*

⁵Then devote a few minutes, with your eyes closed, to reviewing some of the external places where you have looked for salvation in the past;—in other people, in possessions, in various situations and events, and in self-concepts that you sought to make real. ⁶Recognize that it is not there, and tell yourself:

> ⁷*My salvation cannot come from any of these things.* ⁸*My salvation comes from me and only from me.*

8. Now we will try again to reach the light in you, which is where your salvation is. ²You cannot find it in the clouds that surround the light, and it is in them you have been looking for it. ³It is not there. ⁴It is past the clouds and in the light beyond. ⁵Remember that you will have to go through the clouds before you can reach the light. ⁶But remember also that you have never found anything in the cloud patterns you imagined that endured, or that you wanted.

9. Since all illusions of salvation have failed you, surely you do not want to remain in the clouds, looking vainly for idols there, when you could so easily walk on into the light of real salvation. ²Try to pass the clouds by whatever means appeals to you. ³If it helps you, think of me holding your hand and leading you. ⁴And I assure you this will be no idle fantasy.

10. For the short and frequent practice periods today, remind yourself that your salvation comes from you, and nothing but your own thoughts can hamper your progress. ²You are free from all external interference. ³You are in charge of your salvation. ⁴You are in charge of the salvation of the world. ⁵Say, then:

> ⁶*My salvation comes from me.* ⁷*Nothing outside of me can hold me back.* ⁸*Within me is the world's salvation and my own.*

LESSON 71

Only God's plan for salvation will work.

1.   You may not realize that the ego has set up a plan for salvation in opposition to God's. [2]It is this plan in which you believe. [3]Since it is the opposite of God's, you also believe that to accept God's plan in place of the ego's is to be damned. [4]This sounds preposterous, of course. [5]Yet after we have considered just what the ego's plan is, perhaps you will realize that, however preposterous it may be, you do believe in it.

2.   The ego's plan for salvation centers around holding grievances. [2]It maintains that, if someone else spoke or acted differently, if some external circumstance or event were changed, you would be saved. [3]Thus, the source of salvation is constantly perceived as outside yourself. [4]Each grievance you hold is a declaration, and an assertion in which you believe, that says, "If this were different, I would be saved." [5]The change of mind necessary for salvation is thus demanded of everyone and everything except yourself.

3.   The role assigned to your own mind in this plan, then, is simply to determine what, other than itself, must change if you are to be saved. [2]According to this insane plan, any perceived source of salvation is acceptable provided that it will not work. [3]This ensures that the fruitless search will continue, for the illusion persists that, although this hope has always failed, there is still grounds for hope in other places and in other things. [4]Another person will yet serve better; another situation will yet offer success.

4.   Such is the ego's plan for your salvation. [2]Surely you can see how it is in strict accord with the ego's basic doctrine, "Seek but do not find." [3]For what could more surely guarantee that you will not find salvation than to channelize all your efforts in searching for it where it is not?

5.   God's plan for salvation works simply because, by following His direction, you seek for salvation where it is. [2]But if you are to succeed, as God promises you will, you must be willing to seek there only. [3]Otherwise, your purpose is divided and you will attempt to follow two plans for salvation that are diametrically opposed in all ways. [4]The result can only bring confusion, misery

121

and a deep sense of failure and despair.

6. How can you escape all this? [2]Very simply. [3]The idea for today is the answer. [4]Only God's plan for salvation will work. [5]There can be no real conflict about this, because there is no possible alternative to God's plan that will save you. [6]His is the only plan that is certain in its outcome. [7]His is the only plan that must succeed.

7. Let us practice recognizing this certainty today. [2]And let us rejoice that there is an answer to what seems to be a conflict with no resolution possible. [3]All things are possible to God. [4]Salvation must be yours because of His plan, which cannot fail.

8. Begin the two longer practice periods for today by thinking about today's idea, and realizing that it contains two parts, each making equal contribution to the whole. [2]God's plan for your salvation will work, and other plans will not. [3]Do not allow yourself to become depressed or angry at the second part; it is inherent in the first. [4]And in the first is your full release from all your own insane attempts and mad proposals to free yourself. [5]They have led to depression and anger; but God's plan will succeed. [6]It will lead to release and joy.

9. Remembering this, let us devote the remainder of the extended practice periods to asking God to reveal His plan to us. [2]Ask Him very specifically:

[3]*What would You have me do?*
[4]*Where would You have me go?*
[5]*What would You have me say, and to whom?*

[6]Give Him full charge of the rest of the practice period, and let Him tell you what needs to be done by you in His plan for your salvation. [7]He will answer in proportion to your willingness to hear His Voice. [8]Refuse not to hear. [9]The very fact that you are doing the exercises proves that you have some willingness to listen. [10]This is enough to establish your claim to God's answer.

10. In the shorter practice periods, tell yourself often that God's plan for salvation, and only His, will work. [2]Be alert to all temptation to hold grievances today, and respond to them with this form of today's idea:

[3]*Holding grievances is the opposite of God's plan*
for salvation. [4]And only His plan will work.

[5]Try to remember today's idea some six or seven times an hour. [6]There could be no better way to spend a half minute or less than to remember the Source of your salvation, and to see It where It is.

LESSON 72

Holding grievances is an attack on God's plan for salvation.

1.   While we have recognized that the ego's plan for salvation is the opposite of God's, we have not yet emphasized that it is an active attack on His plan, and a deliberate attempt to destroy it. [2]In the attack, God is assigned the attributes which are actually associated with the ego, while the ego appears to take on the attributes of God.

2.   The ego's fundamental wish is to replace God. [2]In fact, the ego is the physical embodiment of that wish. [3]For it is that wish that seems to surround the mind with a body, keeping it separate and alone, and unable to reach other minds except through the body that was made to imprison it. [4]The limit on communication cannot be the best means to expand communication. [5]Yet the ego would have you believe that it is.

3.   Although the attempt to keep the limitations that a body would impose is obvious here, it is perhaps not so apparent why holding grievances is an attack on God's plan for salvation. [2]But let us consider the kinds of things you are apt to hold grievances for. [3]Are they not always associated with something a body does? [4]A person says something you do not like. [5]He does something that displeases you. [6]He "betrays" his hostile thoughts in his behavior.

4.   You are not dealing here with what the person is. [2]On the contrary, you are exclusively concerned with what he does in a body. [3]You are doing more than failing to help in freeing him from the body's limitations. [4]You are actively trying to hold him to it by confusing it with him, and judging them as one. [5]Herein is God attacked, for if His Son is only a body, so must He be as well. [6]A creator wholly unlike his creation is inconceivable.

5.   If God is a body, what must His plan for salvation be? [2]What could it be but death? [3]In trying to present Himself as the Author of life and not of death, He is a liar and a deceiver, full of false promises and offering illusions in place of truth. [4]The body's apparent reality makes this view of God quite convincing. [5]In fact, if the body were real, it would be difficult indeed to escape this conclusion. [6]And every grievance that you hold insists that the body is real. [7]It overlooks entirely what your brother is. [8]It rein-

forces your belief that he is a body, and condemns him for it.
9And it asserts that his salvation must be death, projecting this
attack onto God, and holding Him responsible for it.

6. To this carefully prepared arena, where angry animals seek for
prey and mercy cannot enter, the ego comes to save you. 2God
made you a body. 3Very well. 4Let us accept this and be glad. 5As
a body, do not let yourself be deprived of what the body offers.
6Take the little you can get. 7God gave you nothing. 8The body is
your only savior. 9It is the death of God and your salvation.

7. This is the universal belief of the world you see. 2Some hate the
body, and try to hurt and humiliate it. 3Others love the body, and
try to glorify and exalt it. 4But while the body stands at the center
of your concept of yourself, you are attacking God's plan for salvation, and holding your grievances against Him and His creation, that you may not hear the Voice of truth and welcome It as
Friend. 5Your chosen savior takes His place instead. 6It is your
friend; He is your enemy.

8. We will try today to stop these senseless attacks on salvation.
2We will try to welcome it instead. 3Your upside-down perception
has been ruinous to your peace of mind. 4You have seen yourself
in a body and the truth outside you, locked away from your
awareness by the body's limitations. 5Now we are going to try to
see this differently.

9. The light of truth is in us, where it was placed by God. 2It is the
body that is outside us, and is not our concern. 3To be without a
body is to be in our natural state. 4To recognize the light of truth
in us is to recognize ourselves as we are. 5To see our Self as separate from the body is to end the attack on God's plan for salvation, and to accept it instead. 6And wherever His plan is accepted,
it is accomplished already.

10. Our goal in the longer practice periods today is to become
aware that God's plan for salvation has already been accomplished in us. 2To achieve this goal, we must replace attack with
acceptance. 3As long as we attack it, we cannot understand what
God's plan for us is. 4We are therefore attacking what we do not
recognize. 5Now we are going to try to lay judgment aside, and
ask what God's plan for us is:

> 6What is salvation, Father? 7I do not know. 8Tell me, that I
> may understand.

⁹Then we will wait in quiet for His answer. ¹⁰We have attacked God's plan for salvation without waiting to hear what it is. ¹¹We have shouted our grievances so loudly that we have not listened to His Voice. ¹²We have used our grievances to close our eyes and stop our ears.

11. Now we would see and hear and learn. ²"What is salvation, Father?" ³Ask and you will be answered. ⁴Seek and you will find. ⁵We are no longer asking the ego what salvation is and where to find it. ⁶We are asking it of truth. ⁷Be certain, then, that the answer will be true because of Whom you ask.

12. Whenever you feel your confidence wane and your hope of success flicker and go out, repeat your question and your request, remembering that you are asking of the infinite Creator of infinity, Who created you like Himself:

> ²*What is salvation, Father?* ³*I do not know.* ⁴*Tell me, that I may understand.*

⁵He will answer. ⁶Be determined to hear.

13. One or perhaps two shorter practice periods an hour will be enough for today, since they will be somewhat longer than usual. ²These exercises should begin with this:

> ³*Holding grievances is an attack on God's plan for salvation.*
> ⁴*Let me accept it instead.* ⁵*What is salvation, Father?*

⁶Then wait a minute or so in silence, preferably with your eyes closed, and listen for His answer.

LESSON 73

I will there be light.

1. Today we are considering the will you share with God. [2]This is not the same as the ego's idle wishes, out of which darkness and nothingness arise. [3]The will you share with God has all the power of creation in it. [4]The ego's idle wishes are unshared, and therefore have no power at all. [5]Its wishes are not idle in the sense that they can make a world of illusions in which your belief can be very strong. [6]But they are idle indeed in terms of creation. [7]They make nothing that is real.

2. Idle wishes and grievances are partners or co-makers in picturing the world you see. [2]The wishes of the ego gave rise to it, and the ego's need for grievances, which are necessary to maintain it, peoples it with figures that seem to attack you and call for "righteous" judgment. [3]These figures become the middlemen the ego employs to traffic in grievances. [4]They stand between your awareness and your brothers' reality. [5]Beholding them, you do not know your brothers or your Self.

3. Your will is lost to you in this strange bartering, in which guilt is traded back and forth, and grievances increase with each exchange. [2]Can such a world have been created by the Will the Son of God shares with his Father? [3]Did God create disaster for His Son? [4]Creation is the Will of Both together. [5]Would God create a world that kills Himself?

4. Today we will try once more to reach the world that is in accordance with your will. [2]The light is in it because it does not oppose the Will of God. [3]It is not Heaven, but the light of Heaven shines on it. [4]Darkness has vanished. [5]The ego's idle wishes have been withdrawn. [6]Yet the light that shines upon this world reflects your will, and so it must be in you that we will look for it.

5. Your picture of the world can only mirror what is within. [2]The source of neither light nor darkness can be found without. [3]Grievances darken your mind, and you look out on a darkened world. [4]Forgiveness lifts the darkness, reasserts your will, and lets you look upon a world of light. [5]We have repeatedly emphasized that the barrier of grievances is easily passed, and cannot stand between you and your salvation. [6]The reason is very

simple. [7]Do you really want to be in hell? [8]Do you really want to weep and suffer and die?

6.   Forget the ego's arguments which seek to prove all this is really Heaven. [2]You know it is not so. [3]You cannot want this for yourself. [4]There is a point beyond which illusions cannot go. [5]Suffering is not happiness, and it is happiness you really want. [6]Such is your will in truth. [7]And so salvation is your will as well. [8]You want to succeed in what we are trying to do today. [9]We undertake it with your blessing and your glad accord.

7.   We will succeed today if you remember that you want salvation for yourself. [2]You want to accept God's plan because you share in it. [3]You have no will that can really oppose it, and you do not want to do so. [4]Salvation is for you. [5]Above all else, you want the freedom to remember Who you really are. [6]Today it is the ego that stands powerless before your will. [7]Your will is free, and nothing can prevail against it.

8.   Therefore, we undertake the exercises for today in happy confidence, certain that we will find what it is your will to find, and remember what it is your will to remember. [2]No idle wishes can detain us, nor deceive us with an illusion of strength. [3]Today let your will be done, and end forever the insane belief that it is hell in place of Heaven that you choose.

9.   We will begin our longer practice periods with the recognition that God's plan for salvation, and only His, is wholly in accord with your will. [2]It is not the purpose of an alien power, thrust upon you unwillingly. [3]It is the one purpose here on which you and your Father are in perfect accord. [4]You will succeed today, the time appointed for the release of the Son of God from hell and from all idle wishes. [5]His will is now restored to his awareness. [6]He is willing this very day to look upon the light in him and be saved.

10.   After reminding yourself of this, and determining to keep your will clearly in mind, tell yourself with gentle firmness and quiet certainty:

> [2]*I will there be light. [3]Let me behold the light that reflects God's Will and mine.*

[4]Then let your will assert itself, joined with the power of God and united with your Self. [5]Put the rest of the practice period under Their guidance. [6]Join with Them as They lead the way.

11.   In the shorter practice periods, again make a declaration of what you really want. ²Say:

> ³*I will there be light.* ⁴*Darkness is not my will.*

⁵This should be repeated several times an hour. ⁶It is most important, however, to apply today's idea in this form immediately you are tempted to hold a grievance of any kind. ⁷This will help you let your grievances go, instead of cherishing them and hiding them in darkness.

LESSON 74

There is no will but God's.

1. The idea for today can be regarded as the central thought toward which all our exercises are directed. ²God's is the only Will. ³When you have recognized this, you have recognized that your will is His. ⁴The belief that conflict is possible has gone. ⁵Peace has replaced the strange idea that you are torn by conflicting goals. ⁶As an expression of the Will of God, you have no goal but His.

2. There is great peace in today's idea, and the exercises for today are directed towards finding it. ²The idea itself is wholly true. ³Therefore it cannot give rise to illusions. ⁴Without illusions conflict is impossible. ⁵Let us try to recognize this today, and experience the peace this recognition brings.

3. Begin the longer practice periods by repeating these thoughts several times, slowly and with firm determination to understand what they mean, and to hold them in mind:

> ²*There is no will but God's. ³I cannot be in conflict.*

⁴Then spend several minutes in adding some related thoughts, such as:

> ⁵*I am at peace.*
> ⁶*Nothing can disturb me. ⁷My will is God's.*
> ⁸*My will and God's are one.*
> ⁹*God wills peace for His Son.*

¹⁰During this introductory phase, be sure to deal quickly with any conflict thoughts that may cross your mind. ¹¹Tell yourself immediately:

> ¹²*There is no will but God's. ¹³These conflict thoughts are meaningless.*

4. If there is one conflict area that seems particularly difficult to resolve, single it out for special consideration. ²Think about it briefly but very specifically, identify the particular person or per-

sons and the situation or situations involved, and tell yourself:

> ³*There is no will but God's.* ⁴*I share it with Him.*
> ⁵*My conflicts about _____ cannot be real.*

5. After you have cleared your mind in this way, close your eyes and try to experience the peace to which your reality entitles you. ²Sink into it and feel it closing around you. ³There may be some temptation to mistake these attempts for withdrawal, but the difference is easily detected. ⁴If you are succeeding, you will feel a deep sense of joy and an increased alertness, rather than a feeling of drowsiness and enervation.

6. Joy characterizes peace. ²By this experience will you recognize that you have reached it. ³If you feel yourself slipping off into withdrawal, quickly repeat the idea for today and try again. ⁴Do this as often as necessary. ⁵There is definite gain in refusing to allow retreat into withdrawal, even if you do not experience the peace you seek.

7. In the shorter periods, which should be undertaken at regular and predetermined intervals today, say to yourself:

> ²*There is no will but God's.* ³*I seek His peace today.*

⁴Then try to find what you are seeking. ⁵A minute or two every half an hour, with eyes closed if possible, would be well spent on this today.

131

LESSON 75

The light has come.

1. The light has come. ²You are healed and you can heal. ³The light has come. ⁴You are saved and you can save. ⁵You are at peace, and you bring peace with you wherever you go. ⁶Darkness and turmoil and death have disappeared. ⁷The light has come.

2. Today we celebrate the happy ending to your long dream of disaster. ²There are no dark dreams now. ³The light has come. ⁴Today the time of light begins for you and everyone. ⁵It is a new era, in which a new world is born. ⁶The old one has left no trace upon it in its passing. ⁷Today we see a different world, because the light has come.

3. Our exercises for today will be happy ones, in which we offer thanks for the passing of the old and the beginning of the new. ²No shadows from the past remain to darken our sight and hide the world forgiveness offers us. ³Today we will accept the new world as what we want to see. ⁴We will be given what we desire. ⁵We will to see the light; the light has come.

4. Our longer practice periods will be devoted to looking at the world that our forgiveness shows us. ²This is what we want to see, and only this. ³Our single purpose makes our goal inevitable. ⁴Today the real world rises before us in gladness, to be seen at last. ⁵Sight is given us, now that the light has come.

5. We do not want to see the ego's shadow on the world today. ²We see the light, and in it we see Heaven's reflection lie across the world. ³Begin the longer practice periods by telling yourself the glad tidings of your release:

⁴*The light has come.* ⁵*I have forgiven the world.*

6. Dwell not upon the past today. ²Keep a completely open mind, washed of all past ideas and clean of every concept you have made. ³You have forgiven the world today. ⁴You can look upon it now as if you never saw it before. ⁵You do not know yet what it looks like. ⁶You merely wait to have it shown to you. ⁷While you wait, repeat several times, slowly and in complete patience:

⁸*The light has come.* ⁹*I have forgiven the world.*

7.   Realize that your forgiveness entitles you to vision. ²Understand that the Holy Spirit never fails to give the gift of sight to the forgiving. ³Believe He will not fail you now. ⁴You have forgiven the world. ⁵He will be with you as you watch and wait. ⁶He will show you what true vision sees. ⁷It is His Will, and you have joined with Him. ⁸Wait patiently for Him. ⁹He will be there. ¹⁰The light has come. ¹¹You have forgiven the world.

8.   Tell Him you know you cannot fail because you trust in Him. ²And tell yourself you wait in certainty to look upon the world He promised you. ³From this time forth you will see differently. ⁴Today the light has come. ⁵And you will see the world that has been promised you since time began, and in which is the end of time ensured.

9.   The shorter practice periods, too, will be joyful reminders of your release. ²Remind yourself every quarter of an hour or so that today is a time for special celebration. ³Give thanks for mercy and the Love of God. ⁴Rejoice in the power of forgiveness to heal your sight completely. ⁵Be confident that on this day there is a new beginning. ⁶Without the darkness of the past upon your eyes, you cannot fail to see today. ⁷And what you see will be so welcome that you will gladly extend today forever.

10. Say, then:

> ²*The light has come.* ³*I have forgiven the world.*

⁴Should you be tempted, say to anyone who seems to pull you back into darkness:

> ⁵*The light has come.* ⁶*I have forgiven you.*

11. We dedicate this day to the serenity in which God would have you be. ²Keep it in your awareness of yourself and see it everywhere today, as we celebrate the beginning of your vision and the sight of the real world, which has come to replace the unforgiven world you thought was real.

LESSON 76

I am under no laws but God's.

1. We have observed before how many senseless things have seemed to you to be salvation. [2]Each has imprisoned you with laws as senseless as itself. [3]You are not bound by them. [4]Yet to understand that this is so, you must first realize salvation lies not there. [5]While you would seek for it in things that have no meaning, you bind yourself to laws that make no sense. [6]Thus do you seek to prove salvation is where it is not.

2. Today we will be glad you cannot prove it. [2]For if you could, you would forever seek salvation where it is not, and never find it. [3]The idea for today tells you once again how simple is salvation. [4]Look for it where it waits for you, and there it will be found. [5]Look nowhere else, for it is nowhere else.

3. Think of the freedom in the recognition that you are not bound by all the strange and twisted laws you have set up to save you. [2]You really think that you would starve unless you have stacks of green paper strips and piles of metal discs. [3]You really think a small round pellet or some fluid pushed into your veins through a sharpened needle will ward off disease and death. [4]You really think you are alone unless another body is with you.

4. It is insanity that thinks these things. [2]You call them laws, and put them under different names in a long catalogue of rituals that have no use and serve no purpose. [3]You think you must obey the "laws" of medicine, of economics and of health. [4]Protect the body, and you will be saved.

5. These are not laws, but madness. [2]The body is endangered by the mind that hurts itself. [3]The body suffers just in order that the mind will fail to see it is the victim of itself. [4]The body's suffering is a mask the mind holds up to hide what really suffers. [5]It would not understand it is its own enemy; that it attacks itself and wants to die. [6]It is from this your "laws" would save the body. [7]It is for this you think you are a body.

6. There are no laws except the laws of God. [2]This needs repeating, over and over, until you realize it applies to everything that you have made in opposition to God's Will. [3]Your magic has no meaning. [4]What it is meant to save does not exist. [5]Only what it is meant to hide will save you.

7. The laws of God can never be replaced. ²We will devote today to rejoicing that this is so. ³It is no longer a truth that we would hide. ⁴We realize instead it is a truth that keeps us free forever. ⁵Magic imprisons, but the laws of God make free. ⁶The light has come because there are no laws but His.

8. We will begin the longer practice periods today with a short review of the different kinds of "laws" we have believed we must obey. ²These would include, for example, the "laws" of nutrition, of immunization, of medication, and of the body's protection in innumerable ways. ³Think further; you believe in the "laws" of friendship, of "good" relationships and reciprocity. ⁴Perhaps you even think that there are laws which set forth what is God's and what is yours. ⁵Many "religions" have been based on this. ⁶They would not save but damn in Heaven's name. ⁷Yet they are no more strange than other "laws" you hold must be obeyed to make you safe.

9. There are no laws but God's. ²Dismiss all foolish magical beliefs today, and hold your mind in silent readiness to hear the Voice that speaks the truth to you. ³You will be listening to One Who says there is no loss under the laws of God. ⁴Payment is neither given nor received. ⁵Exchange cannot be made; there are no substitutes; and nothing is replaced by something else. ⁶God's laws forever give and never take.

10. Hear Him Who tells you this, and realize how foolish are the "laws" you thought upheld the world you thought you saw. ²Then listen further. ³He will tell you more. ⁴About the Love your Father has for you. ⁵About the endless joy He offers you. ⁶About His yearning for His only Son, created as His channel for creation; denied to Him by his belief in hell.

11. Let us today open God's channels to Him, and let His Will extend through us to Him. ²Thus is creation endlessly increased. ³His Voice will speak of this to us, as well as of the joys of Heaven which His laws keep limitless forever. ⁴We will repeat today's idea until we have listened and understood there are no laws but God's. ⁵Then we will tell ourselves, as a dedication with which the practice period concludes:

⁶*I am under no laws but God's.*

12. We will repeat this dedication as often as possible today; at least four or five times an hour, as well as in response to any

135

temptation to experience ourselves as subject to other laws throughout the day. [2]It is our statement of freedom from all danger and all tyranny. [3]It is our acknowledgment that God is our Father, and that His Son is saved.

LESSON 77

I am entitled to miracles.

1. You are entitled to miracles because of what you are. ²You will receive miracles because of what God is. ³And you will offer miracles because you are one with God. ⁴Again, how simple is salvation! ⁵It is merely a statement of your true Identity. ⁶It is this that we will celebrate today.

2. Your claim to miracles does not lie in your illusions about yourself. ²It does not depend on any magical powers you have ascribed to yourself, nor on any of the rituals you have devised. ³It is inherent in the truth of what you are. ⁴It is implicit in what God your Father is. ⁵It was ensured in your creation, and guaranteed by the laws of God.

3. Today we will claim the miracles which are your right, since they belong to you. ²You have been promised full release from the world you made. ³You have been assured that the Kingdom of God is within you, and can never be lost. ⁴We ask no more than what belongs to us in truth. ⁵Today, however, we will also make sure that we will not content ourselves with less.

4. Begin the longer practice periods by telling yourself quite confidently that you are entitled to miracles. ²Closing your eyes, remind yourself that you are asking only for what is rightfully yours. ³Remind yourself also that miracles are never taken from one and given to another, and that in asking for your rights, you are upholding the rights of everyone. ⁴Miracles do not obey the laws of this world. ⁵They merely follow from the laws of God.

5. After this brief introductory phase, wait quietly for the assurance that your request is granted. ²You have asked for the salvation of the world, and for your own. ³You have requested that you be given the means by which this is accomplished. ⁴You cannot fail to be assured in this. ⁵You are but asking that the Will of God be done.

6. In doing this, you do not really ask for anything. ²You state a fact that cannot be denied. ³The Holy Spirit cannot but assure you that your request is granted. ⁴The fact that you accepted must be so. ⁵There is no room for doubt and uncertainty today. ⁶We are asking a real question at last. ⁷The answer is a simple

statement of a simple fact. [8]You will receive the assurance that you seek.

7.   Our shorter practice periods will be frequent, and will also be devoted to a reminder of a simple fact. [2]Tell yourself often today:

[3]*I am entitled to miracles.*

[4]Ask for them whenever a situation arises in which they are called for. [5]You will recognize these situations. [6]And since you are not relying on yourself to find the miracle, you are fully entitled to receive it whenever you ask.

8.   Remember, too, not to be satisfied with less than the perfect answer. [2]Be quick to tell yourself, should you be tempted:

[3]*I will not trade miracles for grievances. [4]I want only what belongs to me. [5]God has established miracles as my right.*

LESSON 78

Let miracles replace all grievances.

1. Perhaps it is not yet quite clear to you that each decision that you make is one between a grievance and a miracle. ²Each grievance stands like a dark shield of hate before the miracle it would conceal. ³And as you raise it up before your eyes, you will not see the miracle beyond. ⁴Yet all the while it waits for you in light, but you behold your grievances instead.

2. Today we go beyond the grievances, to look upon the miracle instead. ²We will reverse the way you see by not allowing sight to stop before it sees. ³We will not wait before the shield of hate, but lay it down and gently lift our eyes in silence to behold the Son of God.

3. He waits for you behind your grievances, and as you lay them down he will appear in shining light where each one stood before. ²For every grievance is a block to sight, and as it lifts you see the Son of God where he has always been. ³He stands in light, but you were in the dark. ⁴Each grievance made the darkness deeper, and you could not see.

4. Today we will attempt to see God's Son. ²We will not let ourselves be blind to him; we will not look upon our grievances. ³So is the seeing of the world reversed, as we look out toward truth, away from fear. ⁴We will select one person you have used as target for your grievances, and lay the grievances aside and look at him. ⁵Someone, perhaps, you fear and even hate; someone you think you love who angered you; someone you call a friend, but whom you see as difficult at times or hard to please, demanding, irritating or untrue to the ideal he should accept as his, according to the role you set for him.

5. You know the one to choose; his name has crossed your mind already. ²He will be the one of whom we ask God's Son be shown to you. ³Through seeing him behind the grievances that you have held against him, you will learn that what lay hidden while you saw him not is there in everyone, and can be seen. ⁴He who was enemy is more than friend when he is freed to take the holy role the Holy Spirit has assigned to him. ⁵Let him be savior unto you today. ⁶Such is his role in God your Father's plan.

6. Our longer practice periods today will see him in this role.

139

²You will attempt to hold him in your mind, first as you now consider him. ³You will review his faults, the difficulties you have had with him, the pain he caused you, his neglect, and all the little and the larger hurts he gave. ⁴You will regard his body with its flaws and better points as well, and you will think of his mistakes and even of his "sins."

7. Then let us ask of Him Who knows this Son of God in his reality and truth, that we may look on him a different way, and see our savior shining in the light of true forgiveness, given unto us. ²We ask Him in the holy Name of God and of His Son, as holy as Himself:

> ³*Let me behold my savior in this one You have appointed as the one for me to ask to lead me to the holy light in which he stands, that I may join with him.*

⁴The body's eyes are closed, and as you think of him who grieved you, let your mind be shown the light in him beyond your grievances.

8. What you have asked for cannot be denied. ²Your savior has been waiting long for this. ³He would be free, and make his freedom yours. ⁴The Holy Spirit leans from him to you, seeing no separation in God's Son. ⁵And what you see through Him will free you both. ⁶Be very quiet now, and look upon your shining savior. ⁷No dark grievances obscure the sight of him. ⁸You have allowed the Holy Spirit to express through him the role God gave Him that you might be saved.

9. God thanks you for these quiet times today in which you laid your images aside, and looked upon the miracle of love the Holy Spirit showed you in their place. ²The world and Heaven join in thanking you, for not one Thought of God but must rejoice as you are saved, and all the world with you.

10. We will remember this throughout the day, and take the role assigned to us as part of God's salvation plan, and not our own. ²Temptation falls away when we allow each one we meet to save us, and refuse to hide his light behind our grievances. ³To everyone you meet, and to the ones you think of or remember from the past, allow the role of savior to be given, that you may share it with him. ⁴For you both, and all the sightless ones as well, we pray:

> ⁵*Let miracles replace all grievances.*

LESSON 79

Let me recognize the problem so it can be solved.

1. A problem cannot be solved if you do not know what it is. ²Even if it is really solved already you will still have the problem, because you will not recognize that it has been solved. ³This is the situation of the world. ⁴The problem of separation, which is really the only problem, has already been solved. ⁵Yet the solution is not recognized because the problem is not recognized.

2. Everyone in this world seems to have his own special problems. ²Yet they are all the same, and must be recognized as one if the one solution that solves them all is to be accepted. ³Who can see that a problem has been solved if he thinks the problem is something else? ⁴Even if he is given the answer, he cannot see its relevance.

3. That is the position in which you find yourself now. ²You have the answer, but you are still uncertain about what the problem is. ³A long series of different problems seems to confront you, and as one is settled the next one and the next arise. ⁴There seems to be no end to them. ⁵There is no time in which you feel completely free of problems and at peace.

4. The temptation to regard problems as many is the temptation to keep the problem of separation unsolved. ²The world seems to present you with a vast number of problems, each requiring a different answer. ³This perception places you in a position in which your problem solving must be inadequate, and failure is inevitable.

5. No one could solve all the problems the world appears to hold. ²They seem to be on so many levels, in such varying forms and with such varied content, that they confront you with an impossible situation. ³Dismay and depression are inevitable as you regard them. ⁴Some spring up unexpectedly, just as you think you have resolved the previous ones. ⁵Others remain unsolved under a cloud of denial, and rise to haunt you from time to time, only to be hidden again but still unsolved.

6. All this complexity is but a desperate attempt not to recognize the problem, and therefore not to let it be resolved. ²If you could recognize that your only problem is separation, no matter what form it takes, you could accept the answer because you would

see its relevance. [3]Perceiving the underlying constancy in all the problems that seem to confront you, you would understand that you have the means to solve them all. [4]And you would use the means, because you recognize the problem.

7. In our longer practice periods today we will ask what the problem is, and what is the answer to it. [2]We will not assume that we already know. [3]We will try to free our minds of all the many different kinds of problems we think we have. [4]We will try to realize that we have only one problem, which we have failed to recognize. [5]We will ask what it is, and wait for the answer. [6]We will be told. [7]Then we will ask for the solution to it. [8]And we will be told.

8. The exercises for today will be successful to the extent to which you do not insist on defining the problem. [2]Perhaps you will not succeed in letting all your preconceived notions go, but that is not necessary. [3]All that is necessary is to entertain some doubt about the reality of your version of what your problems are. [4]You are trying to recognize that you have been given the answer by recognizing the problem, so that the problem and the answer can be brought together and you can be at peace.

9. The shorter practice periods for today will not be set by time, but by need. [2]You will see many problems today, each one calling for an answer. [3]Our efforts will be directed toward recognizing that there is only one problem and one answer. [4]In this recognition are all problems resolved. [5]In this recognition there is peace.

10. Be not deceived by the form of problems today. [2]Whenever any difficulty seems to rise, tell yourself quickly:

[3]*Let me recognize this problem so it can be solved.*

[4]Then try to suspend all judgment about what the problem is. [5]If possible, close your eyes for a moment and ask what it is. [6]You will be heard and you will be answered.

LESSON 80

Let me recognize my problems have been solved.

1. If you are willing to recognize your problems, you will recognize that you have no problems. ²Your one central problem has been answered, and you have no other. ³Therefore, you must be at peace. ⁴Salvation thus depends on recognizing this one problem, and understanding that it has been solved. ⁵One problem, one solution. ⁶Salvation is accomplished. ⁷Freedom from conflict has been given you. ⁸Accept that fact, and you are ready to take your rightful place in God's plan for salvation.

2. Your only problem has been solved! ²Repeat this over and over to yourself today, with gratitude and conviction. ³You have recognized your only problem, opening the way for the Holy Spirit to give you God's answer. ⁴You have laid deception aside, and seen the light of truth. ⁵You have accepted salvation for yourself by bringing the problem to the answer. ⁶And you can recognize the answer, because the problem has been identified.

3. You are entitled to peace today. ²A problem that has been resolved cannot trouble you. ³Only be certain you do not forget that all problems are the same. ⁴Their many forms will not deceive you while you remember this. ⁵One problem, one solution. ⁶Accept the peace this simple statement brings.

4. In our longer practice periods today, we will claim the peace that must be ours when the problem and the answer have been brought together. ²The problem must be gone, because God's answer cannot fail. ³Having recognized one, you have recognized the other. ⁴The solution is inherent in the problem. ⁵You are answered, and have accepted the answer. ⁶You are saved.

5. Now let the peace that your acceptance brings be given you. ²Close your eyes, and receive your reward. ³Recognize that your problems have been solved. ⁴Recognize that you are out of conflict; free and at peace. ⁵Above all, remember that you have one problem, and that the problem has one solution. ⁶It is in this that the simplicity of salvation lies. ⁷It is because of this that it is guaranteed to work.

6. Assure yourself often today that your problems have been solved. ²Repeat the idea with deep conviction, as frequently as possible. ³And be particularly sure to apply the idea for today to

any specific problem that may arise. ⁴Say quickly:

> ⁵*Let me recognize this problem has been solved.*

7. Let us be determined not to collect grievances today. ²Let us be determined to be free of problems that do not exist. ³The means is simple honesty. ⁴Do not deceive yourself about what the problem is, and you must recognize it has been solved.

REVIEW II

Introduction

1.   We are now ready for another review. ²We will begin where our last review left off, and cover two ideas each day. ³The earlier part of each day will be devoted to one of these ideas, and the latter part of the day to the other. ⁴We will have one longer exercise period, and frequent shorter ones in which we practice each of them.

2.   The longer practice periods will follow this general form: Take about fifteen minutes for each of them, and begin by thinking about the ideas for the day, and the comments that are included in the assignments. ²Devote some three or four minutes to reading them over slowly, several times if you wish, and then close your eyes and listen.

3.   Repeat the first phase of the exercise period if you find your mind wandering, but try to spend the major part of the time listening quietly but attentively. ²There is a message waiting for you. ³Be confident that you will receive it. ⁴Remember that it belongs to you, and that you want it.

4.   Do not allow your intent to waver in the face of distracting thoughts. ²Realize that, whatever form such thoughts may take, they have no meaning and no power. ³Replace them with your determination to succeed. ⁴Do not forget that your will has power over all fantasies and dreams. ⁵Trust it to see you through, and carry you beyond them all.

5.   Regard these practice periods as dedications to the way, the truth and the life. ²Refuse to be sidetracked into detours, illusions and thoughts of death. ³You are dedicated to salvation. ⁴Be determined each day not to leave your function unfulfilled.

6.   Reaffirm your determination in the shorter practice periods as well, using the original form of the idea for general applications, and more specific forms when needed. ²Some specific forms are included in the comments which follow the statement of the ideas. ³These, however, are merely suggestions. ⁴It is not the particular words you use that matter.

LESSON 81

Our ideas for review today are:

1. (61) **I am the light of the world.**

²How holy am I, who have been given the function of lighting up the world! ³Let me be still before my holiness. ⁴In its calm light let all my conflicts disappear. ⁵In its peace let me remember Who I am.

2. Some specific forms for applying this idea when special difficulties seem to arise might be:

> ²*Let me not obscure the light of the world in me.*
> ³*Let the light of the world shine through this appearance.*
> ⁴*This shadow will vanish before the light.*

3. (62) **Forgiveness is my function as the light of the world.**

²It is through accepting my function that I will see the light in me. ³And in this light will my function stand clear and perfectly unambiguous before my sight. ⁴My acceptance does not depend on my recognizing what my function is, for I do not yet understand forgiveness. ⁵Yet I will trust that, in the light, I will see it as it is.

4. Specific forms for using this idea might include:

> ²*Let this help me learn what forgiveness means.*
> ³*Let me not separate my function from my will.*
> ⁴*I will not use this for an alien purpose.*

LESSON 82

We will review these ideas today:

1. (63) **The light of the world brings peace to every mind through my forgiveness.**

²My forgiveness is the means by which the light of the world finds expression through me. ³My forgiveness is the means by which I become aware of the light of the world in me. ⁴My forgiveness is the means by which the world is healed, together with myself. ⁵Let me, then, forgive the world, that it may be healed along with me.

2. Suggestions for specific forms for applying this idea are:

> ²*Let peace extend from my mind to yours, [name].*
> ³*I share the light of the world with you, [name].*
> ⁴*Through my forgiveness I can see this as it is.*

3. (64) **Let me not forget my function.**

²I would not forget my function, because I would remember my Self. ³I cannot fulfill my function if I forget it. ⁴And unless I fulfill my function, I will not experience the joy that God intends for me.

4. Suitable specific forms of this idea include:

> ²*Let me not use this to hide my function from me.*
> ³*I would use this as an opportunity to fulfill my function.*
> ⁴*This may threaten my ego, but cannot change my function in any way.*

LESSON 83

Today let us review these ideas:

1. (65) **My only function is the one God gave me.**

[2]I have no function but the one God gave me. [3]This recognition releases me from all conflict, because it means I cannot have conflicting goals. [4]With one purpose only, I am always certain what to do, what to say and what to think. [5]All doubt must disappear as I acknowledge that my only function is the one God gave me.

2. More specific applications of this idea might take these forms:

> [2]*My perception of this does not change my function.*
> [3]*This does not give me a function other than the one God gave me.*
> [4]*Let me not use this to justify a function God did not give me.*

3. (66) **My happiness and my function are one.**

[2]All things that come from God are one. [3]They come from Oneness, and must be received as one. [4]Fulfilling my function is my happiness because both come from the same Source. [5]And I must learn to recognize what makes me happy, if I would find happiness.

4. Some useful forms for specific applications of this idea are:

> [2]*This cannot separate my happiness from my function.*
> [3]*The oneness of my happiness and my function remains wholly unaffected by this.*
> [4]*Nothing, including this, can justify the illusion of happiness apart from my function.*

LESSON 84

These are the ideas for today's review:

1. (67) **Love created me like itself.**

[2]I am in the likeness of my Creator. [3]I cannot suffer, I cannot experience loss and I cannot die. [4]I am not a body. [5]I would recognize my reality today. [6]I will worship no idols, nor raise my own self-concept to replace my Self. [7]I am in the likeness of my Creator. [8]Love created me like itself.

2. You might find these specific forms helpful in applying the idea:

> [2]*Let me not see an illusion of myself in this.*
> [3]*As I look on this, let me remember my Creator.*
> [4]*My Creator did not create this as I see it.*

3. (68) **Love holds no grievances.**

[2]Grievances are completely alien to love. [3]Grievances attack love and keep its light obscure. [4]If I hold grievances I am attacking love, and therefore attacking my Self. [5]My Self thus becomes alien to me. [6]I am determined not to attack my Self today, so that I can remember Who I am.

4. These specific forms for applying this idea would be helpful:

> [2]*This is no justification for denying my Self.*
> [3]*I will not use this to attack love.*
> [4]*Let this not tempt me to attack myself.*

LESSON 85

Today's review will cover these ideas:

1. (69) **My grievances hide the light of the world in me.**

²My grievances show me what is not there, and hide from me what I would see. ³Recognizing this, what do I want my grievances for? ⁴They keep me in darkness and hide the light. ⁵Grievances and light cannot go together, but light and vision must be joined for me to see. ⁶To see, I must lay grievances aside. ⁷I want to see, and this will be the means by which I will succeed.

2. Specific applications for this idea might be made in these forms:

> ²Let me not use this as a block to sight.
> ³The light of the world will shine all this away.
> ⁴I have no need for this. ⁵I want to see.

3. (70) **My salvation comes from me.**

²Today I will recognize where my salvation is. ³It is in me because its Source is there. ⁴It has not left its Source, and so it cannot have left my mind. ⁵I will not look for it outside myself. ⁶It is not found outside and then brought in. ⁷But from within me it will reach beyond, and everything I see will but reflect the light that shines in me and in itself.

4. These forms of the idea are suitable for more specific applications:

> ²Let this not tempt me to look away from me for
>   my salvation.
> ³I will not let this interfere with my awareness
>   of the Source of my salvation.
> ⁴This has no power to remove salvation from me.

LESSON 86

These ideas are for review today:

1. (71) **Only God's plan for salvation will work.**

²It is senseless for me to search wildly about for salvation. ³I have seen it in many people and in many things, but when I reached for it, it was not there. ⁴I was mistaken about where it is. ⁵I was mistaken about what it is. ⁶I will undertake no more idle seeking. ⁷Only God's plan for salvation will work. ⁸And I will rejoice because His plan can never fail.

2. These are some suggested forms for applying this idea specifically:

²*God's plan for salvation will save me from my perception of this.*
³*This is no exception in God's plan for my salvation.*
⁴*Let me perceive this only in the light of God's plan for salvation.*

3. (72) **Holding grievances is an attack on God's plan for salvation.**

²Holding grievances is an attempt to prove that God's plan for salvation will not work. ³Yet only His plan will work. ⁴By holding grievances, I am therefore excluding my only hope of salvation from my awareness. ⁵I would no longer defeat my own best interests in this insane way. ⁶I would accept God's plan for salvation, and be happy.

4. Specific applications for this idea might be in these forms:

²*I am choosing between misperception and salvation as I look on this.*
³*If I see grounds for grievances in this, I will not see the grounds for my salvation.*
⁴*This calls for salvation, not attack.*

LESSON 87

Our review today will cover these ideas:

1. (73) **I will there be light.**

²I will use the power of my will today. ³It is not my will to grope about in darkness, fearful of shadows and afraid of things unseen and unreal. ⁴Light shall be my guide today. ⁵I will follow it where it leads me, and I will look only on what it shows me. ⁶This day I will experience the peace of true perception.

2. These forms of this idea would be helpful for specific applications:

> ²*This cannot hide the light I will to see.*
> ³*You stand with me in light, [name].*
> ⁴*In the light this will look different.*

3. (74) **There is no will but God's.**

²I am safe today because there is no will but God's. ³I can become afraid only when I believe there is another will. ⁴I try to attack only when I am afraid, and only when I try to attack can I believe that my eternal safety is threatened. ⁵Today I will recognize that all this has not occurred. ⁶I am safe because there is no will but God's.

4. These are some useful forms of this idea for specific applications:

> ²*Let me perceive this in accordance with the Will of God.*
> ³*It is God's Will you are His Son, [name], and mine as well.*
> ⁴*This is part of God's Will for me, however I may see it.*

LESSON 88

Today we will review these ideas:

1. (75) **The light has come.**

[2]In choosing salvation rather than attack, I merely choose to recognize what is already there. [3]Salvation is a decision made already. [4]Attack and grievances are not there to choose. [5]That is why I always choose between truth and illusion; between what is there and what is not. [6]The light has come. [7]I can but choose the light, for it has no alternative. [8]It has replaced the darkness, and the darkness has gone.

2. These would prove useful forms for specific applications of this idea:

> [2]*This cannot show me darkness, for the light has come.*
> [3]*The light in you is all that I would see, [name].*
> [4]*I would see in this only what is there.*

3. (76) **I am under no laws but God's.**

[2]Here is the perfect statement of my freedom. [3]I am under no laws but God's. [4]I am constantly tempted to make up other laws and give them power over me. [5]I suffer only because of my belief in them. [6]They have no real effect on me at all. [7]I am perfectly free of the effects of all laws save God's. [8]And His are the laws of freedom.

4. For specific forms in applying this idea, these would be useful:

> [2]*My perception of this shows me I believe in laws that do not exist.*
> [3]*I see only the laws of God at work in this.*
> [4]*Let me allow God's laws to work in this, and not my own.*

LESSON 89

These are our review ideas for today:

1. (77) **I am entitled to miracles.**

²I am entitled to miracles because I am under no laws but God's. ³His laws release me from all grievances, and replace them with miracles. ⁴And I would accept the miracles in place of the grievances, which are but illusions that hide the miracles beyond. ⁵Now I would accept only what the laws of God entitle me to have, that I may use it on behalf of the function He has given me.

2. You might use these suggestions for specific applications of this idea:

> ²*Behind this is a miracle to which I am entitled.*
> ³*Let me not hold a grievance against you, [name], but*
>   *offer you the miracle that belongs to you instead.*
> ⁴*Seen truly, this offers me a miracle.*

3. (78) **Let miracles replace all grievances.**

²By this idea do I unite my will with the Holy Spirit's, and perceive them as one. ³By this idea do I accept my release from hell. ⁴By this idea do I express my willingness to have all my illusions be replaced with truth, according to God's plan for my salvation. ⁵I would make no exceptions and no substitutes. ⁶I want all of Heaven and only Heaven, as God wills me to have.

4. Useful specific forms for applying this idea would be:

> ²*I would not hold this grievance apart from my salvation.*
> ³*Let our grievances be replaced by miracles, [name].*
> ⁴*Beyond this is the miracle by which all my grievances*
>   *are replaced.*

154

LESSON 90

For this review we will use these ideas:

1. (79) **Let me recognize the problem so it can be solved.**

[2]Let me realize today that the problem is always some form of grievance that I would cherish. [3]Let me also understand that the solution is always a miracle with which I let the grievance be replaced. [4]Today I would remember the simplicity of salvation by reinforcing the lesson that there is one problem and one solution. [5]The problem is a grievance; the solution is a miracle. [6]And I invite the solution to come to me through my forgiveness of the grievance, and my welcome of the miracle that takes its place.

2. Specific applications of this idea might be in these forms:

> [2]*This presents a problem to me which I would have resolved.*
> [3]*The miracle behind this grievance will resolve it for me.*
> [4]*The answer to this problem is the miracle that it conceals.*

3. (80) **Let me recognize my problems have been solved.**

[2]I seem to have problems only because I am misusing time. [3]I believe that the problem comes first, and time must elapse before it can be worked out. [4]I do not see the problem and the answer as simultaneous in their occurrence. [5]That is because I do not yet realize that God has placed the answer together with the problem, so that they cannot be separated by time. [6]The Holy Spirit will teach me this, if I will let Him. [7]And I will understand it is impossible that I could have a problem which has not been solved already.

4. These forms of the idea will be useful for specific applications:

> [2]*I need not wait for this to be resolved.*
> [3]*The answer to this problem is already given me, if I will accept it.*
> [4]*Time cannot separate this problem from its solution.*

LESSON 91

Miracles are seen in light.

1. It is important to remember that miracles and vision necessarily go together. ²This needs repeating, and frequent repeating. ³It is a central idea in your new thought system, and the perception that it produces. ⁴The miracle is always there. ⁵Its presence is not caused by your vision; its absence is not the result of your failure to see. ⁶It is only your awareness of miracles that is affected. ⁷You will see them in the light; you will not see them in the dark.

2. To you, then, light is crucial. ²While you remain in darkness, the miracle remains unseen. ³Thus you are convinced it is not there. ⁴This follows from the premises from which the darkness comes. ⁵Denial of light leads to failure to perceive it. ⁶Failure to perceive light is to perceive darkness. ⁷The light is useless to you then, even though it is there. ⁸You cannot use it because its presence is unknown to you. ⁹And the seeming reality of the darkness makes the idea of light meaningless.

3. To be told that what you do not see is there sounds like insanity. ²It is very difficult to become convinced that it is insanity not to see what is there, and to see what is not there instead. ³You do not doubt that the body's eyes can see. ⁴You do not doubt the images they show you are reality. ⁵Your faith lies in the darkness, not the light. ⁶How can this be reversed? ⁷For you it is impossible, but you are not alone in this.

4. Your efforts, however little they may be, have strong support. ²Did you but realize how great this strength, your doubts would vanish. ³Today we will devote ourselves to the attempt to let you feel this strength. ⁴When you have felt the strength in you, which makes all miracles within your easy reach, you will not doubt. ⁵The miracles your sense of weakness hides will leap into awareness as you feel the strength in you.

5. Three times today, set aside about ten minutes for a quiet time in which you try to leave your weakness behind. ²This is accomplished very simply, as you instruct yourself that you are not a body. ³Faith goes to what you want, and you instruct your mind accordingly. ⁴Your will remains your teacher, and your will has all the strength to do what it desires. ⁵You can escape the body if you choose. ⁶You can experience the strength in you.

6. Begin the longer practice periods with this statement of true cause and effect relationships:

> ²*Miracles are seen in light.*
> ³*The body's eyes do not perceive the light.*
> ⁴*But I am not a body.* ⁵*What am I?*

⁶The question with which this statement ends is needed for our exercises today. ⁷What you think you are is a belief to be undone. ⁸But what you really are must be revealed to you. ⁹The belief you are a body calls for correction, being a mistake. ¹⁰The truth of what you are calls on the strength in you to bring to your awareness what the mistake conceals.

7. If you are not a body, what are you? ²You need to be aware of what the Holy Spirit uses to replace the image of a body in your mind. ³You need to feel something to put your faith in, as you lift it from the body. ⁴You need a real experience of something else, something more solid and more sure; more worthy of your faith, and really there.

8. If you are not a body, what are you? ²Ask this in honesty, and then devote several minutes to allowing your mistaken thoughts about your attributes to be corrected, and their opposites to take their place. ³Say, for example:

> ⁴*I am not weak, but strong.*
> ⁵*I am not helpless, but all powerful.*
> ⁶*I am not limited, but unlimited.*
> ⁷*I am not doubtful, but certain.*
> ⁸*I am not an illusion, but a reality.*
> ⁹*I cannot see in darkness, but in light.*

9. In the second phase of the exercise period, try to experience these truths about yourself. ²Concentrate particularly on the experience of strength. ³Remember that all sense of weakness is associated with the belief you are a body, a belief that is mistaken and deserves no faith. ⁴Try to remove your faith from it, if only for a moment. ⁵You will be accustomed to keeping faith with the more worthy in you as we go along.

10. Relax for the rest of the practice period, confident that your efforts, however meager, are fully supported by the strength of God and all His Thoughts. ²It is from Them that your strength

will come. ³It is through Their strong support that you will feel the strength in you. ⁴They are united with you in this practice period, in which you share a purpose like Their Own. ⁵Theirs is the light in which you will see miracles, because Their strength is yours. ⁶Their strength becomes your eyes, that you may see.

11. Five or six times an hour, at reasonably regular intervals, remind yourself that miracles are seen in light. ²Also, be sure to meet temptation with today's idea. ³This form would be helpful for this special purpose:

> ⁴*Miracles are seen in light.* ⁵*Let me not close my eyes because of this.*

158

LESSON 92

Miracles are seen in light, and light and strength are one.

1. The idea for today is an extension of the previous one. ²You do not think of light in terms of strength, and darkness in terms of weakness. ³That is because your idea of what seeing means is tied up with the body and its eyes and brain. ⁴Thus you believe that you can change what you see by putting little bits of glass before your eyes. ⁵This is among the many magical beliefs that come from the conviction you are a body, and the body's eyes can see.

2. You also believe the body's brain can think. ²If you but understood the nature of thought, you could but laugh at this insane idea. ³It is as if you thought you held the match that lights the sun and gives it all its warmth; or that you held the world within your hand, securely bound until you let it go. ⁴Yet this is no more foolish than to believe the body's eyes can see; the brain can think.

3. It is God's strength in you that is the light in which you see, as it is His Mind with which you think. ²His strength denies your weakness. ³It is your weakness that sees through the body's eyes, peering about in darkness to behold the likeness of itself; the small, the weak, the sickly and the dying, those in need, the helpless and afraid, the sad, the poor, the starving and the joyless. ⁴These are seen through eyes that cannot see and cannot bless.

4. Strength overlooks these things by seeing past appearances. ²It keeps its steady gaze upon the light that lies beyond them. ³It unites with light, of which it is a part. ⁴It sees itself. ⁵It brings the light in which your Self appears. ⁶In darkness you perceive a self that is not there. ⁷Strength is the truth about you; weakness is an idol falsely worshipped and adored that strength may be dispelled, and darkness rule where God appointed that there should be light.

5. Strength comes from truth, and shines with light its Source has given it; weakness reflects the darkness of its maker. ²It is sick and looks on sickness, which is like itself. ³Truth is a savior and can only will for happiness and peace for everyone. ⁴It gives its strength to everyone who asks, in limitless supply. ⁵It sees that lack in anyone would be a lack in all. ⁶And so it gives its light that all may see and benefit as one. ⁷Its strength is shared, that it may

159

bring to all the miracle in which they will unite in purpose and forgiveness and in love.

6. Weakness, which looks in darkness, cannot see a purpose in forgiveness and in love. ²It sees all others different from itself, and nothing in the world that it would share. ³It judges and condemns, but does not love. ⁴In darkness it remains to hide itself, and dreams that it is strong and conquering, a victor over limitations that but grow in darkness to enormous size.

7. It fears and it attacks and hates itself, and darkness covers everything it sees, leaving its dreams as fearful as itself. ²No miracles are here, but only hate. ³It separates itself from what it sees, while light and strength perceive themselves as one. ⁴The light of strength is not the light you see. ⁵It does not change and flicker and go out. ⁶It does not shift from night to day, and back to darkness till the morning comes again.

8. The light of strength is constant, sure as love, forever glad to give itself away, because it cannot give but to itself. ²No one can ask in vain to share its sight, and none who enters its abode can leave without a miracle before his eyes, and strength and light abiding in his heart.

9. The strength in you will offer you the light, and guide your seeing so you do not dwell on idle shadows that the body's eyes provide for self-deception. ²Strength and light unite in you, and where they meet, your Self stands ready to embrace you as Its Own. ³Such is the meeting place we try today to find and rest in, for the peace of God is where your Self, His Son, is waiting now to meet Itself again, and be as one.

10. Let us give twenty minutes twice today to join this meeting. ²Let yourself be brought unto your Self. ³Its strength will be the light in which the gift of sight is given you. ⁴Leave, then, the dark a little while today, and we will practice seeing in the light, closing the body's eyes and asking truth to show us how to find the meeting place of self and Self, where light and strength are one.

11. Morning and evening we will practice thus. ²After the morning meeting, we will use the day in preparation for the time at night when we will meet again in trust. ³Let us repeat as often as we can the idea for today, and recognize that we are being introduced to sight, and led away from darkness to the light where only miracles can be perceived.

LESSON 93

Light and joy and peace abide in me.

1. You think you are the home of evil, darkness and sin. ²You think if anyone could see the truth about you he would be repelled, recoiling from you as if from a poisonous snake. ³You think if what is true about you were revealed to you, you would be struck with horror so intense that you would rush to death by your own hand, living on after seeing this being impossible.

2. These are beliefs so firmly fixed that it is difficult to help you see that they are based on nothing. ²That you have made mistakes is obvious. ³That you have sought salvation in strange ways; have been deceived, deceiving and afraid of foolish fantasies and savage dreams; and have bowed down to idols made of dust,—all this is true by what you now believe.

3. Today we question this, not from the point of view of what you think, but from a very different reference point, from which such idle thoughts are meaningless. ²These thoughts are not according to God's Will. ³These weird beliefs He does not share with you. ⁴This is enough to prove that they are wrong, but you do not perceive that this is so.

4. Why would you not be overjoyed to be assured that all the evil that you think you did was never done, that all your sins are nothing, that you are as pure and holy as you were created, and that light and joy and peace abide in you? ²Your image of yourself cannot withstand the Will of God. ³You think that this is death, but it is life. ⁴You think you are destroyed, but you are saved.

5. The self you made is not the Son of God. ²Therefore, this self does not exist at all. ³And anything it seems to do and think means nothing. ⁴It is neither bad nor good. ⁵It is unreal, and nothing more than that. ⁶It does not battle with the Son of God. ⁷It does not hurt him, nor attack his peace. ⁸It has not changed creation, nor reduced eternal sinlessness to sin, and love to hate. ⁹What power can this self you made possess, when it would contradict the Will of God?

6. Your sinlessness is guaranteed by God. ²Over and over this must be repeated, until it is accepted. ³It is true. ⁴Your sinlessness is guaranteed by God. ⁵Nothing can touch it, or change what God

created as eternal. [6]The self you made, evil and full of sin, is meaningless. [7]Your sinlessness is guaranteed by God, and light and joy and peace abide in you.

7. Salvation requires the acceptance of but one thought;—you are as God created you, not what you made of yourself. [2]Whatever evil you may think you did, you are as God created you. [3]Whatever mistakes you made, the truth about you is unchanged. [4]Creation is eternal and unalterable. [5]Your sinlessness is guaranteed by God. [6]You are and will forever be exactly as you were created. [7]Light and joy and peace abide in you because God put them there.

8. In our longer exercise periods today, which would be most profitable if done for the first five minutes of every waking hour, begin by stating the truth about your creation:

[2]*Light and joy and peace abide in me.*
[3]*My sinlessness is guaranteed by God.*

[4]Then put away your foolish self-images, and spend the rest of the practice period in trying to experience what God has given you, in place of what you have decreed for yourself.

9. You are what God created or what you made. [2]One Self is true; the other is not there. [3]Try to experience the unity of your one Self. [4]Try to appreciate Its Holiness and the love from which It was created. [5]Try not to interfere with the Self which God created as you, by hiding Its majesty behind the tiny idols of evil and sinfulness you have made to replace It. [6]Let It come into Its Own. [7]Here you are; This is You. [8]And light and joy and peace abide in you because this is so.

10. You may not be willing or even able to use the first five minutes of each hour for these exercises. [2]Try, however, to do so when you can. [3]At least remember to repeat these thoughts each hour:

[4]*Light and joy and peace abide in me.*
[5]*My sinlessness is guaranteed by God.*

[6]Then try to devote at least a minute or so to closing your eyes and realizing that this is a statement of the truth about you.

11. If a situation arises that seems to be disturbing, quickly dispel the illusion of fear by repeating these thoughts again. [2]Should you be tempted to become angry with someone, tell him silently:

> ³*Light and joy and peace abide in you.*
> ⁴*Your sinlessness is guaranteed by God.*

⁵You can do much for the world's salvation today. ⁶You can do much today to bring you closer to the part in salvation that God has assigned to you. ⁷And you can do much today to bring the conviction to your mind that the idea for the day is true indeed.

LESSON 94

I am as God created me.

1. Today we continue with the one idea which brings complete salvation; the one statement which makes all forms of temptation powerless; the one thought which renders the ego silent and entirely undone. ²You are as God created you. ³The sounds of this world are still, the sights of this world disappear, and all the thoughts that this world ever held are wiped away forever by this one idea. ⁴Here is salvation accomplished. ⁵Here is sanity restored.

2. True light is strength, and strength is sinlessness. ²If you remain as God created you, you must be strong and light must be in you. ³He Who ensured your sinlessness must be the guarantee of strength and light as well. ⁴You are as God created you. ⁵Darkness cannot obscure the glory of God's Son. ⁶You stand in light, strong in the sinlessness in which you were created, and in which you will remain throughout eternity.

3. Today we will again devote the first five minutes of each waking hour to the attempt to feel the truth in you. ²Begin these times of searching with these words:

³*I am as God created me.*
⁴*I am His Son eternally.*

⁵Now try to reach the Son of God in you. ⁶This is the Self that never sinned, nor made an image to replace reality. ⁷This is the Self that never left Its home in God to walk the world uncertainly. ⁸This is the Self that knows no fear, nor could conceive of loss or suffering or death.

4. Nothing is required of you to reach this goal except to lay all idols and self-images aside; go past the list of attributes, both good and bad, you have ascribed to yourself; and wait in silent expectancy for the truth. ²God has Himself promised that it will be revealed to all who ask for it. ³You are asking now. ⁴You cannot fail because He cannot fail.

5. If you do not meet the requirement of practicing for the first five minutes of every hour, at least remind yourself hourly:

²I am as God created me.
³I am His Son eternally.

⁴Tell yourself frequently today that you are as God created you.
⁵And be sure to respond to anyone who seems to irritate you with
these words:

⁶You are as God created you.
⁷You are His Son eternally.

⁸Make every effort to do the hourly exercises today. ⁹Each one
you do will be a giant stride toward your release, and a milestone
in learning the thought system which this course sets forth.

LESSON 95

I am one Self, united with my Creator.

1. Today's idea accurately describes you as God created you. ²You are one within yourself, and one with Him. ³Yours is the unity of all creation. ⁴Your perfect unity makes change in you impossible. ⁵You do not accept this, and you fail to realize it must be so, only because you believe that you have changed yourself already.

2. You see yourself as a ridiculous parody on God's creation; weak, vicious, ugly and sinful, miserable and beset with pain. ²Such is your version of yourself; a self divided into many warring parts, separate from God, and tenuously held together by its erratic and capricious maker, to which you pray. ³It does not hear your prayers, for it is deaf. ⁴It does not see the oneness in you, for it is blind. ⁵It does not understand you are the Son of God, for it is senseless and understands nothing.

3. We will attempt today to be aware only of what can hear and see, and what makes perfect sense. ²We will again direct our exercises towards reaching your one Self, which is united with Its Creator. ³In patience and in hope we try again today.

4. The use of the first five minutes of every waking hour for practicing the idea for the day has special advantages at the stage of learning in which you are at present. ²It is difficult at this point not to allow your mind to wander, if it undertakes extended practice. ³You have surely realized this by now. ⁴You have seen the extent of your lack of mental discipline, and of your need for mind training. ⁵It is necessary that you be aware of this, for it is indeed a hindrance to your advance.

5. Frequent but shorter practice periods have other advantages for you at this time. ²In addition to recognizing your difficulties with sustained attention, you must also have noticed that, unless you are reminded of your purpose frequently, you tend to forget about it for long periods of time. ³You often fail to remember the short applications of the idea for the day, and you have not yet formed the habit of using the idea as an automatic response to temptation.

6. Structure, then, is necessary for you at this time, planned to include frequent reminders of your goal and regular attempts to

reach it. ²Regularity in terms of time is not the ideal requirement for the most beneficial form of practice in salvation. ³It is advantageous, however, for those whose motivation is inconsistent, and who remain heavily defended against learning.

7. We will, therefore, keep to the five-minutes-an-hour practice periods for a while, and urge you to omit as few as possible. ²Using the first five minutes of the hour will be particularly helpful, since it imposes firmer structure. ³Do not, however, use your lapses from this schedule as an excuse not to return to it again as soon as you can. ⁴There may well be a temptation to regard the day as lost because you have already failed to do what is required. ⁵This should, however, merely be recognized as what it is; a refusal to let your mistake be corrected, and an unwillingness to try again.

8. The Holy Spirit is not delayed in His teaching by your mistakes. ²He can be held back only by your unwillingness to let them go. ³Let us therefore be determined, particularly for the next week or so, to be willing to forgive ourselves for our lapses in diligence, and our failures to follow the instructions for practicing the day's idea. ⁴This tolerance for weakness will enable us to overlook it, rather than give it power to delay our learning. ⁵If we give it power to do this, we are regarding it as strength, and are confusing strength with weakness.

9. When you fail to comply with the requirements of this course, you have merely made a mistake. ²This calls for correction, and for nothing else. ³To allow a mistake to continue is to make additional mistakes, based on the first and reinforcing it. ⁴It is this process that must be laid aside, for it is but another way in which you would defend illusions against the truth.

10. Let all these errors go by recognizing them for what they are. ²They are attempts to keep you unaware you are one Self, united with your Creator, at one with every aspect of creation, and limitless in power and in peace. ³This is the truth, and nothing else is true. ⁴Today we will affirm this truth again, and try to reach the place in you in which there is no doubt that only this is true.

11. Begin the practice periods today with this assurance, offered to your mind with all the certainty that you can give:

> ²*I am one Self, united with my Creator, at one with every aspect of creation, and limitless in power and in peace.*

167

³Then close your eyes and tell yourself again, slowly and thought-fully, attempting to allow the meaning of the words to sink into your mind, replacing false ideas:

⁴*I am one Self.*

⁵Repeat this several times, and then attempt to feel the meaning that the words convey.

12. You are one Self, united and secure in light and joy and peace. ²You are God's Son, one Self, with one Creator and one goal; to bring awareness of this oneness to all minds, that true creation may extend the allness and the unity of God. ³You are one Self, complete and healed and whole, with power to lift the veil of darkness from the world, and let the light in you come through to teach the world the truth about yourself.

13. You are one Self, in perfect harmony with all there is, and all that there will be. ²You are one Self, the holy Son of God, united with your brothers in that Self; united with your Father in His Will. ³Feel this one Self in you, and let It shine away all your illusions and your doubts. ⁴This is your Self, the Son of God Himself, sinless as Its Creator, with His strength within you and His Love forever yours. ⁵You are one Self, and it is given you to feel this Self within you, and to cast all your illusions out of the one Mind that is this Self, the holy truth in you.

14. Do not forget today. ²We need your help; your little part in bringing happiness to all the world. ³And Heaven looks to you in confidence that you will try today. ⁴Share, then, its surety, for it is yours. ⁵Be vigilant. ⁶Do not forget today. ⁷Throughout the day do not forget your goal. ⁸Repeat today's idea as frequently as possible, and understand each time you do so, someone hears the voice of hope, the stirring of the truth within his mind, the gentle rustling of the wings of peace.

15. Your own acknowledgment you are one Self, united with your Father, is a call to all the world to be at one with you. ²To everyone you meet today, be sure to give the promise of today's idea and tell him this:

> ³*You are one Self with me, united with our Creator in this Self. ⁴I honor you because of What I am, and What He is, Who loves us both as One.*

LESSON 96

Salvation comes from my one Self.

1. Although you are one Self, you experience yourself as two; as both good and evil, loving and hating, mind and body. ²This sense of being split into opposites induces feelings of acute and constant conflict, and leads to frantic attempts to reconcile the contradictory aspects of this self-perception. ³You have sought many such solutions, and none of them has worked. ⁴The opposites you see in you will never be compatible. ⁵But one exists.

2. The fact that truth and illusion cannot be reconciled, no matter how you try, what means you use and where you see the problem, must be accepted if you would be saved. ²Until you have accepted this, you will attempt an endless list of goals you cannot reach; a senseless series of expenditures of time and effort, hopefulness and doubt, each one as futile as the one before, and failing as the next one surely will.

3. Problems that have no meaning cannot be resolved within the framework they are set. ²Two selves in conflict could not be resolved, and good and evil have no meeting place. ³The self you made can never be your Self, nor can your Self be split in two, and still be what It is and must forever be. ⁴A mind and body cannot both exist. ⁵Make no attempt to reconcile the two, for one denies the other can be real. ⁶If you are physical, your mind is gone from your self-concept, for it has no place in which it could be really part of you. ⁷If you are spirit, then the body must be meaningless to your reality.

4. Spirit makes use of mind as means to find its Self expression. ²And the mind which serves the spirit is at peace and filled with joy. ³Its power comes from spirit, and it is fulfilling happily its function here. ⁴Yet mind can also see itself divorced from spirit, and perceive itself within a body it confuses with itself. ⁵Without its function then it has no peace, and happiness is alien to its thoughts.

5. Yet mind apart from spirit cannot think. ²It has denied its Source of strength, and sees itself as helpless, limited and weak. ³Dissociated from its function now, it thinks it is alone and separate, attacked by armies massed against itself and hiding in the body's frail support. ⁴Now must it reconcile unlike with like, for

this is what it thinks that it is for.

6. Waste no more time on this. ²Who can resolve the senseless conflicts which a dream presents? ³What could the resolution mean in truth? ⁴What purpose could it serve? ⁵What is it for? ⁶Salvation cannot make illusions real, nor solve a problem that does not exist. ⁷Perhaps you hope it can. ⁸Yet would you have God's plan for the release of His dear Son bring pain to him, and fail to set him free?

7. Your Self retains Its Thoughts, and they remain within your mind and in the Mind of God. ²The Holy Spirit holds salvation in your mind, and offers it the way to peace. ³Salvation is a thought you share with God, because His Voice accepted it for you and answered in your name that it was done. ⁴Thus is salvation kept among the Thoughts your Self holds dear and cherishes for you.

8. We will attempt today to find this thought, whose presence in your mind is guaranteed by Him Who speaks to you from your one Self. ²Our hourly five-minute practicing will be a search for Him within your mind. ³Salvation comes from this one Self through Him Who is the Bridge between your mind and It. ⁴Wait patiently, and let Him speak to you about your Self, and what your mind can do, restored to It and free to serve Its Will.

9. Begin with saying this:

> ²Salvation comes from my one Self. ³Its Thoughts are mine to use.

⁴Then seek Its Thoughts, and claim them as your own. ⁵These are your own real thoughts you have denied, and let your mind go wandering in a world of dreams, to find illusions in their place. ⁶Here are your thoughts, the only ones you have. ⁷Salvation is among them; find it there.

10. If you succeed, the thoughts that come to you will tell you you are saved, and that your mind has found the function that it sought to lose. ²Your Self will welcome it and give it peace. ³Restored in strength, it will again flow out from spirit to the spirit in all things created by the Spirit as Itself. ⁴Your mind will bless all things. ⁵Confusion done, you are restored, for you have found your Self.

11. Your Self knows that you cannot fail today. ²Perhaps your mind remains uncertain yet a little while. ³Be not dismayed by this. ⁴The joy your Self experiences It will save for you, and it will

yet be yours in full awareness. [5]Every time you spend five minutes of the hour seeking Him Who joins your mind and Self, you offer Him another treasure to be kept for you.

12. Each time today you tell your frantic mind salvation comes from your one Self, you lay another treasure in your growing store. [2]And all of it is given everyone who asks for it, and will accept the gift. [3]Think, then, how much is given unto you to give this day, that it be given you!

LESSON 97

I am spirit.

1. Today's idea identifies you with your one Self. ²It accepts no split identity, nor tries to weave opposing factors into unity. ³It simply states the truth. ⁴Practice this truth today as often as you can, for it will bring your mind from conflict to the quiet fields of peace. ⁵No chill of fear can enter, for your mind has been absolved from madness, letting go illusions of a split identity.

2. We state again the truth about your Self, the holy Son of God Who rests in you, whose mind has been restored to sanity. ²You are the spirit lovingly endowed with all your Father's Love and peace and joy. ³You are the spirit which completes Himself, and shares His function as Creator. ⁴He is with you always, as you are with Him.

3. Today we try to bring reality still closer to your mind. ²Each time you practice, awareness is brought a little nearer at least; sometimes a thousand years or more are saved. ³The minutes which you give are multiplied over and over, for the miracle makes use of time, but is not ruled by it. ⁴Salvation is a miracle, the first and last; the first that is the last, for it is one.

4. You are the spirit in whose mind abides the miracle in which all time stands still; the miracle in which a minute spent in using these ideas becomes a time that has no limit and that has no end. ²Give, then, these minutes willingly, and count on Him Who promised to lay timelessness beside them. ³He will offer all His strength to every little effort that you make. ⁴Give Him the minutes which He needs today, to help you understand with Him you are the spirit that abides in Him, and that calls through His Voice to every living thing; offers His sight to everyone who asks; replaces error with the simple truth.

5. The Holy Spirit will be glad to take five minutes of each hour from your hands, and carry them around this aching world where pain and misery appear to rule. ²He will not overlook one open mind that will accept the healing gifts they bring, and He will lay them everywhere He knows they will be welcome. ³And they will increase in healing power each time someone accepts them as his thoughts, and uses them to heal.

6. Thus will each gift to Him be multiplied a thousandfold and

tens of thousands more. [2]And when it is returned to you, it will surpass in might the little gift you gave as much as does the radiance of the sun outshine the tiny gleam a firefly makes an uncertain moment and goes out. [3]The steady brilliance of this light remains and leads you out of darkness, nor will you be able to forget the way again.

7. Begin these happy exercises with the words the Holy Spirit speaks to you, and let them echo round the world through Him:

> [2]*Spirit am I, a holy Son of God, free of all limits, safe and healed and whole, free to forgive, and free to save the world.*

[3]Expressed through you, the Holy Spirit will accept this gift that you received of Him, increase its power and give it back to you.

8. Offer each practice period today gladly to Him. [2]And He will speak to you, reminding you that you are spirit, one with Him and God, your brothers and your Self. [3]Listen for His assurance every time you speak the words He offers you today, and let Him tell your mind that they are true. [4]Use them against temptation, and escape its sorry consequences if you yield to the belief that you are something else. [5]The Holy Spirit gives you peace today. [6]Receive His words, and offer them to Him.

173

LESSON 98

I will accept my part in God's plan for salvation.

1. Today is a day of special dedication. ²We take a stand on but one side today. ³We side with truth and let illusions go. ⁴We will not vacillate between the two, but take a firm position with the One. ⁵We dedicate ourselves to truth today, and to salvation as God planned it be. ⁶We will not argue it is something else. ⁷We will not seek for it where it is not. ⁸In gladness we accept it as it is, and take the part assigned to us by God.

2. How happy to be certain! ²All our doubts we lay aside today, and take our stand with certainty of purpose, and with thanks that doubt is gone and surety has come. ³We have a mighty purpose to fulfill, and have been given everything we need with which to reach the goal. ⁴Not one mistake stands in our way. ⁵For we have been absolved from errors. ⁶All our sins are washed away by realizing they were but mistakes.

3. The guiltless have no fear, for they are safe and recognize their safety. ²They do not appeal to magic, nor invent escapes from fancied threats without reality. ³They rest in quiet certainty that they will do what it is given them to do. ⁴They do not doubt their own ability because they know their function will be filled completely in the perfect time and place. ⁵They took the stand which we will take today, that we may share their certainty and thus increase it by accepting it ourselves.

4. They will be with us; all who took the stand we take today will gladly offer us all that they learned and every gain they made. ²Those still uncertain, too, will join with us, and, borrowing our certainty, will make it stronger still. ³While those as yet unborn will hear the call we heard, and answer it when they have come to make their choice again. ⁴We do not choose but for ourselves today.

5. Is it not worth five minutes of your time each hour to be able to accept the happiness that God has given you? ²Is it not worth five minutes hourly to recognize your special function here? ³Is not five minutes but a small request to make in terms of gaining a reward so great it has no measure? ⁴You have made a thousand losing bargains at the least.

6.   Here is an offer guaranteeing you your full release from pain of every kind, and joy the world does not contain. ²You can exchange a little of your time for peace of mind and certainty of purpose, with the promise of complete success. ³And since time has no meaning, you are being asked for nothing in return for everything. ⁴Here is a bargain that you cannot lose. ⁵And what you gain is limitless indeed!

7.   Each hour today give Him your tiny gift of but five minutes. ²He will give the words you use in practicing today's idea the deep conviction and the certainty you lack. ³His words will join with yours, and make each repetition of today's idea a total dedication, made in faith as perfect and as sure as His in you. ⁴His confidence in you will bring the light to all the words you say, and you will go beyond their sound to what they really mean. ⁵Today you practice with Him, as you say:

⁶I will accept my part in God's plan for salvation.

8.   In each five minutes that you spend with Him, He will accept your words and give them back to you all bright with faith and confidence so strong and steady they will light the world with hope and gladness. ²Do not lose one chance to be the glad receiver of His gifts, that you may give them to the world today.

9.   Give Him the words, and He will do the rest. ²He will enable you to understand your special function. ³He will open up the way to happiness, and peace and trust will be His gifts; His answer to your words. ⁴He will respond with all His faith and joy and certainty that what you say is true. ⁵And you will have conviction then of Him Who knows the function that you have on earth as well as Heaven. ⁶He will be with you each practice period you share with Him, exchanging every instant of the time you offer Him for timelessness and peace.

10.   Throughout the hour, let your time be spent in happy preparation for the next five minutes you will spend again with Him. ²Repeat today's idea while you wait for the glad time to come to you again. ³Repeat it often, and do not forget each time you do so, you have let your mind be readied for the happy time to come.

11.   And when the hour goes and He is there once more to spend a little time with you, be thankful and lay down all earthly tasks, all little thoughts and limited ideas, and spend a happy time

again with Him. ²Tell Him once more that you accept the part that He would have you take and help you fill, and He will make you sure you want this choice, which He has made with you and you with Him.

LESSON 99

Salvation is my only function here.

1. Salvation and forgiveness are the same. ²They both imply that something has gone wrong; something to be saved from, forgiven for; something amiss that needs corrective change; something apart or different from the Will of God. ³Thus do both terms imply a thing impossible but yet which has occurred, resulting in a state of conflict seen between what is and what could never be.

2. Truth and illusions both are equal now, for both have happened. ²The impossible becomes the thing you need forgiveness for, salvation from. ³Salvation now becomes the borderland between the truth and the illusion. ⁴It reflects the truth because it is the means by which you can escape illusions. ⁵Yet it is not yet the truth because it undoes what was never done.

3. How could there be a meeting place at all where earth and Heaven can be reconciled within a mind where both of them exist? ²The mind that sees illusions thinks them real. ³They have existence in that they are thoughts. ⁴And yet they are not real, because the mind that thinks these thoughts is separate from God.

4. What joins the separated mind and thoughts with Mind and Thought which are forever one? ²What plan could hold the truth inviolate, yet recognize the need illusions bring, and offer means by which they are undone without attack and with no touch of pain? ³What but a Thought of God could be this plan, by which the never done is overlooked, and sins forgotten which were never real?

5. The Holy Spirit holds this plan of God exactly as it was received of Him within the Mind of God and in your own. ²It is apart from time in that its Source is timeless. ³Yet it operates in time, because of your belief that time is real. ⁴Unshaken does the Holy Spirit look on what you see; on sin and pain and death, on grief and separation and on loss. ⁵Yet does He know one thing must still be true; God is still Love, and this is not His Will.

6. This is the Thought that brings illusions to the truth, and sees them as appearances behind which is the changeless and the sure. ²This is the Thought that saves and that forgives, because it lays no faith in what is not created by the only Source it knows.

[3]This is the Thought whose function is to save by giving you its function as your own. [4]Salvation is your function, with the One to Whom the plan was given. [5]Now are you entrusted with this plan, along with Him. [6]He has one answer to appearances; regardless of their form, their size, their depth or any attribute they seem to have:

> [7]*Salvation is my only function here.*
> [8]*God still is Love, and this is not His Will.*

7. You who will yet work miracles, be sure you practice well the idea for today. [2]Try to perceive the strength in what you say, for these are words in which your freedom lies. [3]Your Father loves you. [4]All the world of pain is not His Will. [5]Forgive yourself the thought He wanted this for you. [6]Then let the Thought with which He has replaced all your mistakes enter the darkened places of your mind that thought the thoughts that never were His Will.

8. This part belongs to God, as does the rest. [2]It does not think its solitary thoughts, and make them real by hiding them from Him. [3]Let in the light, and you will look upon no obstacle to what He wills for you. [4]Open your secrets to His kindly light, and see how bright this light still shines in you.

9. Practice His Thought today, and let His light seek out and lighten up all darkened spots, and shine through them to join them to the rest. [2]It is God's Will your mind be one with His. [3]It is God's Will that He has but one Son. [4]It is God's Will that His one Son is you. [5]Think of these things in practicing today, and start the lesson that we learn today with this instruction in the way of truth:

> [6]*Salvation is my only function here.*
> [7]*Salvation and forgiveness are the same.*

[8]Then turn to Him Who shares your function here, and let Him teach you what you need to learn to lay all fear aside, and know your Self as Love which has no opposite in you.

10. Forgive all thoughts which would oppose the truth of your completion, unity and peace. [2]You cannot lose the gifts your Father gave. [3]You do not want to be another self. [4]You have no function that is not of God. [5]Forgive yourself the one you think

178

you made. ⁶Forgiveness and salvation are the same. ⁷Forgive what you have made and you are saved.

11.   There is a special message for today which has the power to remove all forms of doubt and fear forever from your mind. ²If you are tempted to believe them true, remember that appearances can not withstand the truth these mighty words contain:

>   ³*Salvation is my only function here.*
>   ⁴*God still is Love, and this is not His Will.*

12.   Your only function tells you you are one. ²Remind yourself of this between the times you give five minutes to be shared with Him Who shares God's plan with you. ³Remind yourself:

>   ⁴*Salvation is my only function here.*

⁵Thus do you lay forgiveness on your mind and let all fear be gently laid aside, that love may find its rightful place in you and show you that you are the Son of God.

LESSON 100

My part is essential to God's plan for salvation.

1. Just as God's Son completes his Father, so your part in it completes your Father's plan. [2]Salvation must reverse the mad belief in separate thoughts and separate bodies, which lead separate lives and go their separate ways. [3]One function shared by separate minds unites them in one purpose, for each one of them is equally essential to them all.

2. God's Will for you is perfect happiness. [2]Why should you choose to go against His Will? [3]The part that He has saved for you to take in working out His plan is given you that you might be restored to what He wills. [4]This part is as essential to His plan as to your happiness. [5]Your joy must be complete to let His plan be understood by those to whom He sends you. [6]They will see their function in your shining face, and hear God calling to them in your happy laugh.

3. You are indeed essential to God's plan. [2]Without your joy, His joy is incomplete. [3]Without your smile, the world cannot be saved. [4]While you are sad, the light that God Himself appointed as the means to save the world is dim and lusterless, and no one laughs because all laughter can but echo yours.

4. You are indeed essential to God's plan. [2]Just as your light increases every light that shines in Heaven, so your joy on earth calls to all minds to let their sorrows go, and take their place beside you in God's plan. [3]God's messengers are joyous, and their joy heals sorrow and despair. [4]They are the proof that God wills perfect happiness for all who will accept their Father's gifts as theirs.

5. We will not let ourselves be sad today. [2]For if we do, we fail to take the part that is essential to God's plan, as well as to our vision. [3]Sadness is the sign that you would play another part, instead of what has been assigned to you by God. [4]Thus do you fail to show the world how great the happiness He wills for you. [5]And so you do not recognize that it is yours.

6. Today we will attempt to understand joy is our function here. [2]If you are sad, your part is unfulfilled, and all the world is thus deprived of joy, along with you. [3]God asks you to be happy, so the world can see how much He loves His Son, and wills no

sorrow rises to abate his joy; no fear besets him to disturb his peace. ⁴You are God's messenger today. ⁵You bring His happiness to all you look upon; His peace to everyone who looks on you and sees His message in your happy face.

7. We will prepare ourselves for this today, in our five-minute practice periods, by feeling happiness arise in us according to our Father's Will and ours. ²Begin the exercises with the thought today's idea contains. ³Then realize your part is to be happy. ⁴Only this is asked of you or anyone who wants to take his place among God's messengers. ⁵Think what this means. ⁶You have indeed been wrong in your belief that sacrifice is asked. ⁷You but receive according to God's plan, and never lose or sacrifice or die.

8. Now let us try to find that joy that proves to us and all the world God's Will for us. ²It is your function that you find it here, and that you find it now. ³For this you came. ⁴Let this one be the day that you succeed! ⁵Look deep within you, undismayed by all the little thoughts and foolish goals you pass as you ascend to meet the Christ in you.

9. He will be there. ²And you can reach Him now. ³What could you rather look upon in place of Him Who waits that you may look on Him? ⁴What little thought has power to hold you back? ⁵What foolish goal can keep you from success when He Who calls to you is God Himself?

10. He will be there. ²You are essential to His plan. ³You are His messenger today. ⁴And you must find what He would have you give. ⁵Do not forget the idea for today between your hourly practice periods. ⁶It is your Self Who calls to you today. ⁷And it is Him you answer, every time you tell yourself you are essential to God's plan for the salvation of the world.

LESSON 101

God's Will for me is perfect happiness.

1. Today we will continue with the theme of happiness. ²This is a key idea in understanding what salvation means. ³You still believe it asks for suffering as penance for your "sins." ⁴This is not so. ⁵Yet you must think it so while you believe that sin is real, and that God's Son can sin.

2. If sin is real, then punishment is just and cannot be escaped. ²Salvation thus cannot be purchased but through suffering. ³If sin is real, then happiness must be illusion, for they cannot both be true. ⁴The sinful warrant only death and pain, and it is this they ask for. ⁵For they know it waits for them, and it will seek them out and find them somewhere, sometime, in some form that evens the account they owe to God. ⁶They would escape Him in their fear. ⁷And yet He will pursue, and they can not escape.

3. If sin is real, salvation must be pain. ²Pain is the cost of sin, and suffering can never be escaped, if sin is real. ³Salvation must be feared, for it will kill, but slowly, taking everything away before it grants the welcome boon of death to victims who are little more than bones before salvation is appeased. ⁴Its wrath is boundless, merciless, but wholly just.

4. Who would seek out such savage punishment? ²Who would not flee salvation, and attempt in every way he can to drown the Voice which offers it to him? ³Why would he try to listen and accept Its offering? ⁴If sin is real, its offering is death, and meted out in cruel form to match the vicious wishes in which sin is born. ⁵If sin is real, salvation has become your bitter enemy, the curse of God upon you who have crucified His Son.

5. You need the practice periods today. ²The exercises teach sin is not real, and all that you believe must come from sin will never happen, for it has no cause. ³Accept Atonement with an open mind, which cherishes no lingering belief that you have made a devil of God's Son. ⁴There is no sin. ⁵We practice with this thought as often as we can today, because it is the basis for to-day's idea.

6. God's Will for you is perfect happiness because there is no sin, and suffering is causeless. ²Joy is just, and pain is but the sign you have misunderstood yourself. ³Fear not the Will of God. ⁴But turn

to it in confidence that it will set you free from all the consequences sin has wrought in feverish imagination. [5]Say:

> [6]*God's Will for me is perfect happiness.*
> [7]*There is no sin; it has no consequence.*

[8]So should you start your practice periods, and then attempt again to find the joy these thoughts will introduce into your mind.

7. Give these five minutes gladly, to remove the heavy load you lay upon yourself with the insane belief that sin is real. [2]Today escape from madness. [3]You are set on freedom's road, and now today's idea brings wings to speed you on, and hope to go still faster to the waiting goal of peace. [4]There is no sin. [5]Remember this today, and tell yourself as often as you can:

> [6]*God's Will for me is perfect happiness.*
> [7]*This is the truth, because there is no sin.*

LESSON 102

I share God's Will for happiness for me.

1.   You do not want to suffer. ²You may think it buys you something, and may still believe a little that it buys you what you want. ³Yet this belief is surely shaken now, at least enough to let you question it, and to suspect it really makes no sense. ⁴It has not gone as yet, but lacks the roots that once secured it tightly to the dark and hidden secret places of your mind.

2.   Today we try to loose its weakened hold still further, and to realize that pain is purposeless, without a cause and with no power to accomplish anything. ²It cannot purchase anything at all. ³It offers nothing, and does not exist. ⁴And everything you think it offers you is lacking in existence, like itself. ⁵You have been slave to nothing. ⁶Be you free today to join the happy Will of God.

3.   For several days we will continue to devote our periods of practicing to exercises planned to help you reach the happiness God's Will has placed in you. ²Here is your home, and here your safety is. ³Here is your peace, and here there is no fear. ⁴Here is salvation. ⁵Here is rest at last.

4.   Begin your practice periods today with this acceptance of God's Will for you:

> ²*I share God's Will for happiness for me, and I accept it as my function now.*

³Then seek this function deep within your mind, for it is there, awaiting but your choice. ⁴You cannot fail to find it when you learn it is your choice, and that you share God's Will.

5.   Be happy, for your only function here is happiness. ²You have no need to be less loving to God's Son than He Whose Love created him as loving as Himself. ³Besides these hourly five-minute rests, pause frequently today, to tell yourself that you have now accepted happiness as your one function. ⁴And be sure that you are joining with God's Will in doing this.

LESSON 103

God, being Love, is also happiness.

1.   Happiness is an attribute of love. ²It cannot be apart from it. ³Nor can it be experienced where love is not. ⁴Love has no limits, being everywhere. ⁵And therefore joy is everywhere as well. ⁶Yet can the mind deny that this is so, believing there are gaps in love where sin can enter, bringing pain instead of joy. ⁷This strange belief would limit happiness by redefining love as limited, and introducing opposition in what has no limit and no opposite.

2.   Fear is associated then with love, and its results become the heritage of minds that think what they have made is real. ²These images, with no reality in truth, bear witness to the fear of God, forgetting being Love, He must be joy. ³This basic error we will try again to bring to truth today, and teach ourselves:

> ⁴*God, being Love, is also happiness.*
> ⁵*To fear Him is to be afraid of joy.*

⁶Begin your periods of practicing today with this association, which corrects the false belief that God is fear. ⁷It also emphasizes happiness belongs to you, because of what He is.

3.   Allow this one correction to be placed within your mind each waking hour today. ²Then welcome all the happiness it brings as truth replaces fear, and joy becomes what you expect to take the place of pain. ³God, being Love, it will be given you. ⁴Bolster this expectation frequently throughout the day, and quiet all your fears with this assurance, kind and wholly true:

> ⁵*God, being Love, is also happiness.*
> ⁶*And it is happiness I seek today.*
> ⁷*I cannot fail, because I seek the truth.*

LESSON 104

I seek but what belongs to me in truth.

1. Today's idea continues with the thought that joy and peace are not but idle dreams. ²They are your right, because of what you are. ³They come to you from God, Who cannot fail to give you what He wills. ⁴Yet must there be a place made ready to receive His gifts. ⁵They are not welcomed gladly by a mind that has instead received the gifts it made where His belong, as substitutes for them.

2. Today we would remove all meaningless and self-made gifts which we have placed upon the holy altar where God's gifts belong. ²His are the gifts that are our own in truth. ³His are the gifts that we inherited before time was, and that will still be ours when time has passed into eternity. ⁴His are the gifts that are within us now, for they are timeless. ⁵And we need not wait to have them. ⁶They belong to us today.

3. Therefore, we choose to have them now, and know, in choosing them in place of what we made, we but unite our will with what God wills, and recognize the same as being one. ²Our longer practice periods today, the hourly five minutes given truth for your salvation, should begin with this:

> ³I seek but what belongs to me in truth,
> And joy and peace are my inheritance.

⁴Then lay aside the conflicts of the world that offer other gifts and other goals made of illusions, witnessed to by them, and sought for only in a world of dreams.

4. All this we lay aside, and seek instead that which is truly ours, as we ask to recognize what God has given us. ²We clear a holy place within our minds before His altar, where His gifts of peace and joy are welcome, and to which we come to find what has been given us by Him. ³We come in confidence today, aware that what belongs to us in truth is what He gives. ⁴And we would wish for nothing else, for nothing else belongs to us in truth.

5. So do we clear the way for Him today by simply recognizing that His Will is done already, and that joy and peace belong to us as His eternal gifts. ²We will not let ourselves lose sight of them

between the times we come to seek for them where He has laid them. ³This reminder will we bring to mind as often as we can:

> ⁴*I seek but what belongs to me in truth.*
> ⁵*God's gifts of joy and peace are all I want.*

LESSON 105

God's peace and joy are mine.

1. God's peace and joy are yours. ²Today we will accept them, knowing they belong to us. ³And we will try to understand these gifts increase as we receive them. ⁴They are not like to the gifts the world can give, in which the giver loses as he gives the gift; the taker is the richer by his loss. ⁵Such are not gifts, but bargains made with guilt. ⁶The truly given gift entails no loss. ⁷It is impossible that one can gain because another loses. ⁸This implies a limit and an insufficiency.

2. No gift is given thus. ²Such "gifts" are but a bid for a more valuable return; a loan with interest to be paid in full; a temporary lending, meant to be a pledge of debt to be repaid with more than was received by him who took the gift. ³This strange distortion of what giving means pervades all levels of the world you see. ⁴It strips all meaning from the gifts you give, and leaves you nothing in the ones you take.

3. A major learning goal this course has set is to reverse your view of giving, so you can receive. ²For giving has become a source of fear, and so you would avoid the only means by which you can receive. ³Accept God's peace and joy, and you will learn a different way of looking at a gift. ⁴God's gifts will never lessen when they are given away. ⁵They but increase thereby.

4. As Heaven's peace and joy intensify when you accept them as God's gift to you, so does the joy of your Creator grow when you accept His joy and peace as yours. ²True giving is creation. ³It extends the limitless to the unlimited, eternity to timelessness, and love unto itself. ⁴It adds to all that is complete already, not in simple terms of adding more, for that implies that it was less before. ⁵It adds by letting what cannot contain itself fulfill its aim of giving everything it has away, securing it forever for itself.

5. Today accept God's peace and joy as yours. ²Let Him complete Himself as He defines completion. ³You will understand that what completes Him must complete His Son as well. ⁴He cannot give through loss. ⁵No more can you. ⁶Receive His gift of joy and peace today, and He will thank you for your gift to Him.

6. Today our practice periods will start a little differently. ²Begin today by thinking of those brothers who have been denied by

you the peace and joy that are their right under the equal laws of God. ³Here you denied them to yourself. ⁴And here you must return to claim them as your own.

7. Think of your "enemies" a little while, and tell each one, as he occurs to you:

> ²*My brother, peace and joy I offer you,*
> *That I may have God's peace and joy as mine.*

³Thus you prepare yourself to recognize God's gifts to you, and let your mind be free of all that would prevent success today. ⁴Now are you ready to accept the gift of peace and joy that God has given you. ⁵Now are you ready to experience the joy and peace you have denied yourself. ⁶Now you can say, "God's peace and joy are mine," for you have given what you would receive.

8. You must succeed today, if you prepare your mind as we suggest. ²For you have let all bars to peace and joy be lifted up, and what is yours can come to you at last. ³So tell yourself, "God's peace and joy are mine," and close your eyes a while, and let His Voice assure you that the words you speak are true.

9. Spend your five minutes thus with Him each time you can today, but do not think that less is worthless when you cannot give Him more. ²At least remember hourly to say the words which call to Him to give you what He wills to give, and wills you to receive. ³Determine not to interfere today with what He wills. ⁴And if a brother seems to tempt you to deny God's gift to him, see it as but another chance to let yourself receive the gifts of God as yours. ⁵Then bless your brother thankfully, and say:

> ⁶*My brother, peace and joy I offer you,*
> *That I may have God's peace and joy as mine.*

LESSON 106

Let me be still and listen to the truth.

1. If you will lay aside the ego's voice, however loudly it may seem to call; if you will not accept its petty gifts that give you nothing that you really want; if you will listen with an open mind, that has not told you what salvation is; then you will hear the mighty Voice of truth, quiet in power, strong in stillness, and completely certain in Its messages.

2. Listen, and hear your Father speak to you through His appointed Voice, which silences the thunder of the meaningless, and shows the way to peace to those who cannot see. ²Be still today and listen to the truth. ³Be not deceived by voices of the dead, which tell you they have found the source of life and offer it to you for your belief. ⁴Attend them not, but listen to the truth.

3. Be not afraid today to circumvent the voices of the world. ²Walk lightly past their meaningless persuasion. ³Hear them not. ⁴Be still today and listen to the truth. ⁵Go past all things which do not speak of Him Who holds your happiness within His Hand, held out to you in welcome and in love. ⁶Hear only Him today, and do not wait to reach Him longer. ⁷Hear one Voice today.

4. Today the promise of God's Word is kept. ²Hear and be silent. ³He would speak to you. ⁴He comes with miracles a thousand times as happy and as wonderful as those you ever dreamed or wished for in your dreams. ⁵His miracles are true. ⁶They will not fade when dreaming ends. ⁷They end the dream instead; and last forever, for they come from God to His dear Son, whose other name is you. ⁸Prepare yourself for miracles today. ⁹Today allow your Father's ancient pledge to you and all your brothers to be kept.

5. Hear Him today, and listen to the Word which lifts the veil that lies upon the earth, and wakes all those who sleep and cannot see. ²God calls to them through you. ³He needs your voice to speak to them, for who could reach God's Son except his Father, calling through your Self? ⁴Hear Him today, and offer Him your voice to speak to all the multitude who wait to hear the Word that He will speak today.

6. Be ready for salvation. ²It is here, and will today be given unto you. ³And you will learn your function from the One Who chose

it in your Father's Name for you. ⁴Listen today, and you will hear a Voice which will resound throughout the world through you. ⁵The bringer of all miracles has need that you receive them first, and thus become the joyous giver of what you received.

7.   Thus does salvation start and thus it ends; when everything is yours and everything is given away, it will remain with you forever. ²And the lesson has been learned. ³Today we practice giving, not the way you understand it now, but as it is. ⁴Each hour's exercises should begin with this request for your enlightenment:

> ⁵*I will be still and listen to the truth.*
> ⁶*What does it mean to give and to receive?*

8.   Ask and expect an answer. ²Your request is one whose answer has been waiting long to be received by you. ³It will begin the ministry for which you came, and which will free the world from thinking giving is a way to lose. ⁴And so the world becomes ready to understand and to receive.

9.   Be still and listen to the truth today. ²For each five minutes spent in listening, a thousand minds are opened to the truth and they will hear the holy Word you hear. ³And when the hour is past, you will again release a thousand more who pause to ask that truth be given them, along with you.

10.   Today the holy Word of God is kept through your receiving it to give away, so you can teach the world what giving means by listening and learning it of Him. ²Do not forget today to reinforce your choice to hear and to receive the Word by this reminder, given to yourself as often as is possible today:

> ³*Let me be still and listen to the truth.*
> ⁴*I am the messenger of God today,*
> *My voice is His, to give what I receive.*

LESSON 107

Truth will correct all errors in my mind.

1. What can correct illusions but the truth? ²And what are errors but illusions that remain unrecognized for what they are? ³Where truth has entered errors disappear. ⁴They merely vanish, leaving not a trace by which to be remembered. ⁵They are gone because, without belief, they have no life. ⁶And so they disappear to nothingness, returning whence they came. ⁷From dust to dust they come and go, for only truth remains.

2. Can you imagine what a state of mind without illusions is? ²How it would feel? ³Try to remember when there was a time,—perhaps a minute, maybe even less—when nothing came to interrupt your peace; when you were certain you were loved and safe. ⁴Then try to picture what it would be like to have that moment be extended to the end of time and to eternity. ⁵Then let the sense of quiet that you felt be multiplied a hundred times, and then be multiplied another hundred more.

3. And now you have a hint, not more than just the faintest intimation of the state your mind will rest in when the truth has come. ²Without illusions there could be no fear, no doubt and no attack. ³When truth has come all pain is over, for there is no room for transitory thoughts and dead ideas to linger in your mind. ⁴Truth occupies your mind completely, liberating you from all beliefs in the ephemeral. ⁵They have no place because the truth has come, and they are nowhere. ⁶They can not be found, for truth is everywhere forever, now.

4. When truth has come it does not stay a while, to disappear or change to something else. ²It does not shift and alter in its form, nor come and go and go and come again. ³It stays exactly as it always was, to be depended on in every need, and trusted with a perfect trust in all the seeming difficulties and the doubts that the appearances the world presents engender. ⁴They will merely blow away, when truth corrects the errors in your mind.

5. When truth has come it harbors in its wings the gift of perfect constancy, and love which does not falter in the face of pain, but looks beyond it, steadily and sure. ²Here is the gift of healing, for the truth needs no defense, and therefore no attack is possible. ³Illusions can be brought to truth to be corrected. ⁴But the truth

stands far beyond illusions, and can not be brought to them to turn them into truth.

6. Truth does not come and go nor shift nor change, in this appearance now and then in that, evading capture and escaping grasp. ²It does not hide. ³It stands in open light, in obvious accessibility. ⁴It is impossible that anyone could seek it truly, and would not succeed. ⁵Today belongs to truth. ⁶Give truth its due, and it will give you yours. ⁷You were not meant to suffer and to die. ⁸Your Father wills these dreams be gone. ⁹Let truth correct them all.

7. We do not ask for what we do not have. ²We merely ask for what belongs to us, that we may recognize it as our own. ³Today we practice on the happy note of certainty that has been born of truth. ⁴The shaky and unsteady footsteps of illusion are not our approach today. ⁵We are as certain of success as we are sure we live and hope and breathe and think. ⁶We do not doubt we walk with truth today, and count on it to enter into all the exercises that we do this day.

8. Begin by asking Him Who goes with you upon this undertaking that He be in your awareness as you go with Him. ²You are not made of flesh and blood and bone, but were created by the selfsame Thought which gave the gift of life to Him as well. ³He is your Brother, and so like to you your Father knows that You are both the same. ⁴It is your Self you ask to go with you, and how could He be absent where you are?

9. Truth will correct all errors in your mind which tell you you could be apart from Him. ²You speak to Him today, and make your pledge to let His function be fulfilled through you. ³To share His function is to share His joy. ⁴His confidence is with you, as you say:

> ⁵*Truth will correct all errors in my mind,*
> *And I will rest in Him Who is my Self.*

⁶Then let Him lead you gently to the truth, which will envelop you and give you peace so deep and tranquil that you will return to the familiar world reluctantly.

10. And yet you will be glad to look again upon this world. ²For you will bring with you the promise of the changes which the truth that goes with you will carry to the world. ³They will increase with every gift you give of five small minutes, and the

errors that surround the world will be corrected as you let them be corrected in your mind.

11. Do not forget your function for today. ²Each time you tell yourself with confidence, "Truth will correct all errors in my mind," you speak for all the world and Him Who would release the world, as He would set you free.

194

LESSON 108

To give and to receive are one in truth.

1.   Vision depends upon today's idea. ²The light is in it, for it reconciles all seeming opposites. ³And what is light except the resolution, born of peace, of all your conflicts and mistaken thoughts into one concept which is wholly true? ⁴Even that one will disappear, because the Thought behind it will appear instead to take its place. ⁵And now you are at peace forever, for the dream is over then.

2.   True light that makes true vision possible is not the light the body's eyes behold. ²It is a state of mind that has become so unified that darkness cannot be perceived at all. ³And thus what is the same is seen as one, while what is not the same remains unnoticed, for it is not there.

3.   This is the light that shows no opposites, and vision, being healed, has power to heal. ²This is the light that brings your peace of mind to other minds, to share it and be glad that they are one with you and with themselves. ³This is the light that heals because it brings single perception, based upon one frame of reference, from which one meaning comes.

4.   Here are both giving and receiving seen as different aspects of one Thought whose truth does not depend on which is seen as first, nor which appears to be in second place. ²Here it is understood that both occur together, that the Thought remain complete. ³And in this understanding is the base on which all opposites are reconciled, because they are perceived from the same frame of reference which unifies this Thought.

5.   One thought, completely unified, will serve to unify all thought. ²This is the same as saying one correction will suffice for all correction, or that to forgive one brother wholly is enough to bring salvation to all minds. ³For these are but some special cases of one law which holds for every kind of learning, if it be directed by the One Who knows the truth.

6.   To learn that giving and receiving are the same has special usefulness, because it can be tried so easily and seen as true. ²And when this special case has proved it always works, in every circumstance where it is tried, the thought behind it can be generalized to other areas of doubt and double vision. ³And from there

it will extend, and finally arrive at the one Thought which underlies them all.

7. Today we practice with the special case of giving and receiving. [2]We will use this simple lesson in the obvious because it has results we cannot miss. [3]To give is to receive. [4]Today we will attempt to offer peace to everyone, and see how quickly peace returns to us. [5]Light is tranquility, and in that peace is vision given us, and we can see.

8. So we begin the practice periods with the instruction for today, and say:

[2]*To give and to receive are one in truth.*
[3]*I will receive what I am giving now.*

[4]Then close your eyes, and for five minutes think of what you would hold out to everyone, to have it yours. [5]You might, for instance, say:

[6]*To everyone I offer quietness.*
[7]*To everyone I offer peace of mind.*
[8]*To everyone I offer gentleness.*

9. Say each one slowly and then pause a while, expecting to receive the gift you gave. [2]And it will come to you in the amount in which you gave it. [3]You will find you have exact return, for that is what you asked. [4]It might be helpful, too, to think of one to whom to give your gifts. [5]He represents the others, and through him you give to all.

10. Our very simple lesson for today will teach you much. [2]Effect and cause will be far better understood from this time on, and we will make much faster progress now. [3]Think of the exercises for today as quick advances in your learning, made still faster and more sure each time you say, "To give and to receive are one in truth."

LESSON 109

I rest in God.

1. We ask for rest today, and quietness unshaken by the world's appearances. ²We ask for peace and stillness, in the midst of all the turmoil born of clashing dreams. ³We ask for safety and for happiness, although we seem to look on danger and on sorrow. ⁴And we have the thought that will answer our asking with what we request.

2. "I rest in God." ²This thought will bring to you the rest and quiet, peace and stillness, and the safety and the happiness you seek. ³"I rest in God." ⁴This thought has power to wake the sleeping truth in you, whose vision sees beyond appearances to that same truth in everyone and everything there is. ⁵Here is the end of suffering for all the world, and everyone who ever came and yet will come to linger for a while. ⁶Here is the thought in which the Son of God is born again, to recognize himself.

3. "I rest in God." ²Completely undismayed, this thought will carry you through storms and strife, past misery and pain, past loss and death, and onward to the certainty of God. ³There is no suffering it cannot heal. ⁴There is no problem that it cannot solve. ⁵And no appearance but will turn to truth before the eyes of you who rest in God.

4. This is the day of peace. ²You rest in God, and while the world is torn by winds of hate your rest remains completely undisturbed. ³Yours is the rest of truth. ⁴Appearances cannot intrude on you. ⁵You call to all to join you in your rest, and they will hear and come to you because you rest in God. ⁶They will not hear another voice than yours because you gave your voice to God, and now you rest in Him and let Him speak through you.

5. In Him you have no cares and no concerns, no burdens, no anxiety, no pain, no fear of future and no past regrets. ²In timelessness you rest, while time goes by without its touch upon you, for your rest can never change in any way at all. ³You rest today. ⁴And as you close your eyes, sink into stillness. ⁵Let these periods of rest and respite reassure your mind that all its frantic fantasies were but the dreams of fever that has passed away. ⁶Let it be still and thankfully accept its healing. ⁷No more fearful dreams will come, now that you rest in God. ⁸Take time today to slip away

from dreams and into peace.

6. Each hour that you take your rest today, a tired mind is suddenly made glad, a bird with broken wings begins to sing, a stream long dry begins to flow again. [2]The world is born again each time you rest, and hourly remember that you came to bring the peace of God into the world, that it might take its rest along with you.

7. With each five minutes that you rest today, the world is nearer waking. [2]And the time when rest will be the only thing there is comes closer to all worn and tired minds, too weary now to go their way alone. [3]And they will hear the bird begin to sing and see the stream begin to flow again, with hope reborn and energy restored to walk with lightened steps along the road that suddenly seems easy as they go.

8. You rest within the peace of God today, and call upon your brothers from your rest to draw them to their rest, along with you. [2]You will be faithful to your trust today, forgetting no one, bringing everyone into the boundless circle of your peace, the holy sanctuary where you rest. [3]Open the temple doors and let them come from far across the world, and near as well; your distant brothers and your closest friends; bid them all enter here and rest with you.

9. You rest within the peace of God today, quiet and unafraid. [2]Each brother comes to take his rest, and offer it to you. [3]We rest together here, for thus our rest is made complete, and what we give today we have received already. [4]Time is not the guardian of what we give today. [5]We give to those unborn and those passed by, to every Thought of God, and to the Mind in which these Thoughts were born and where they rest. [6]And we remind them of their resting place each time we tell ourselves, "I rest in God."

LESSON 110

I am as God created me.

1.   We will repeat today's idea from time to time. [2]For this one thought would be enough to save you and the world, if you believed that it is true. [3]Its truth would mean that you have made no changes in yourself that have reality, nor changed the universe so that what God created was replaced by fear and evil, misery and death. [4]If you remain as God created you fear has no meaning, evil is not real, and misery and death do not exist.

2.   Today's idea is therefore all you need to let complete correction heal your mind, and give you perfect vision that will heal all the mistakes that any mind has made at any time or place. [2]It is enough to heal the past and make the future free. [3]It is enough to let the present be accepted as it is. [4]It is enough to let time be the means for all the world to learn escape from time, and every change that time appears to bring in passing by.

3.   If you remain as God created you, appearances cannot replace the truth, health cannot turn to sickness, nor can death be substitute for life, or fear for love. [2]All this has not occurred, if you remain as God created you. [3]You need no thought but just this one, to let redemption come to light the world and free it from the past.

4.   In this one thought is all the past undone; the present saved to quietly extend into a timeless future. [2]If you are as God created you, then there has been no separation of your mind from His, no split between your mind and other minds, and only unity within your own.

5.   The healing power of today's idea is limitless. [2]It is the birthplace of all miracles, the great restorer of the truth to the awareness of the world. [3]Practice today's idea with gratitude. [4]This is the truth that comes to set you free. [5]This is the truth that God has promised you. [6]This is the Word in which all sorrow ends.

6.   For your five-minute practice periods, begin with this quotation from the text:

> [2]*I am as God created me. [3]His Son can suffer nothing.*
> [4]*And I **am** His Son.*

7. Then, with this statement firmly in your mind, try to discover in your mind the Self Who is the holy Son of God Himself.

8. Seek Him within you Who is Christ in you, the Son of God and brother to the world; the Savior Who has been forever saved, with power to save whoever touches Him, however lightly, asking for the Word that tells him he is brother unto Him.

9. You are as God created you. ²Today honor your Self. ³Let graven images you made to be the Son of God instead of what he is be worshipped not today. ⁴Deep in your mind the holy Christ in you is waiting your acknowledgment as you. ⁵And you are lost and do not know yourself while He is unacknowledged and unknown.

10. Seek Him today, and find Him. ²He will be your Savior from all idols you have made. ³For when you find Him, you will understand how worthless are your idols, and how false the images which you believed were you. ⁴Today we make a great advance to truth by letting idols go, and opening our hands and hearts and minds to God today.

11. We will remember Him throughout the day with thankful hearts and loving thoughts for all who meet with us today. ²For it is thus that we remember Him. ³And we will say, that we may be reminded of His Son, our holy Self, the Christ in each of us:

⁴*I am as God created me.*

⁵Let us declare this truth as often as we can. ⁶This is the Word of God that sets you free. ⁷This is the key that opens up the gate of Heaven, and that lets you enter in the peace of God and His eternity.

REVIEW III

Introduction

1. Our next review begins today. [2]We will review two recent lessons every day for ten successive days of practicing. [3]We will observe a special format for these practice periods, that you are urged to follow just as closely as you can.

2. We understand, of course, that it may be impossible for you to undertake what is suggested here as optimal each day and every hour of the day. [2]Learning will not be hampered when you miss a practice period because it is impossible at the appointed time. [3]Nor is it necessary that you make excessive efforts to be sure that you catch up in terms of numbers. [4]Rituals are not our aim, and would defeat our goal.

3. But learning will be hampered when you skip a practice period because you are unwilling to devote the time to it that you are asked to give. [2]Do not deceive yourself in this. [3]Unwillingness can be most carefully concealed behind a cloak of situations you cannot control. [4]Learn to distinguish situations that are poorly suited to your practicing from those that you establish to uphold a camouflage for your unwillingness.

4. Those practice periods that you have lost because you did not want to do them, for whatever reason, should be done as soon as you have changed your mind about your goal. [2]You are unwilling to cooperate in practicing salvation only if it interferes with goals you hold more dear. [3]When you withdraw the value given them, allow your practice periods to be replacements for your litanies to them. [4]They gave you nothing. [5]But your practicing can offer everything to you. [6]And so accept their offering and be at peace.

5. The format you should use for these reviews is this: Devote five minutes twice a day, or longer if you would prefer it, to considering the thoughts that are assigned. [2]Read over the ideas and comments that are written down for each day's exercise. [3]And then begin to think about them, while letting your mind relate them to your needs, your seeming problems and all your concerns.

6. Place the ideas within your mind, and let it use them as it chooses. [2]Give it faith that it will use them wisely, being helped in its decisions by the One Who gave the thoughts to you. [3]What

can you trust but what is in your mind? ⁴Have faith, in these reviews, the means the Holy Spirit uses will not fail. ⁵The wisdom of your mind will come to your assistance. ⁶Give direction at the outset; then lean back in quiet faith, and let the mind employ the thoughts you gave as they were given you for it to use.

7. You have been given them in perfect trust; in perfect confidence that you would use them well; in perfect faith that you would see their messages and use them for yourself. ²Offer them to your mind in that same trust and confidence and faith. ³It will not fail. ⁴It is the Holy Spirit's chosen means for your salvation. ⁵Since it has His trust, His means must surely merit yours as well.

8. We emphasize the benefits to you if you devote the first five minutes of the day to your reviews, and also give the last five minutes of your waking day to them. ²If this cannot be done, at least try to divide them so you undertake one in the morning, and the other in the hour just before you go to sleep.

9. The exercises to be done throughout the day are equally important, and perhaps of even greater value. ²You have been inclined to practice only at appointed times, and then go on your way to other things, without applying what you learned to them. ³As a result, you have gained little reinforcement, and have not given your learning a fair chance to prove how great are its potential gifts to you. ⁴Here is another chance to use it well.

10. In these reviews, we stress the need to let your learning not lie idly by between your longer practice periods. ²Attempt to give your daily two ideas a brief but serious review each hour. ³Use one on the hour, and the other one a half an hour later. ⁴You need not give more than just a moment to each one. ⁵Repeat it, and allow your mind to rest a little time in silence and in peace. ⁶Then turn to other things, but try to keep the thought with you, and let it serve to help you keep your peace throughout the day as well.

11. If you are shaken, think of it again. ²These practice periods are planned to help you form the habit of applying what you learn each day to everything you do. ³Do not repeat the thought and lay it down. ⁴Its usefulness is limitless to you. ⁵And it is meant to serve you in all ways, all times and places, and whenever you need help of any kind. ⁶Try, then, to take it with you in the business of the day and make it holy, worthy of God's Son, acceptable to God and to your Self.

12. Each day's review assignments will conclude with a restatement of the thought to use each hour, and the one to be applied on each half hour as well. [2]Forget them not. [3]This second chance with each of these ideas will bring such large advances that we come from these reviews with learning gains so great we will continue on more solid ground, with firmer footsteps and with stronger faith.

13. Do not forget how little you have learned.
    [2]Do not forget how much you can learn now.
    [3]Do not forget your Father's need of you,
    As you review these thoughts He gave to you.

LESSON 111

For morning and evening review:

1. (91) **Miracles are seen in light.**

> [2]*I cannot see in darkness.* [3]*Let the light of holiness and truth light up my mind, and let me see the innocence within.*

2. (92) **Miracles are seen in light, and light and strength are one.**

> [2]*I see through strength, the gift of God to me.* [3]*My weakness is the dark His gift dispels, by giving me His strength to take its place.*

3. On the hour:
   [2]**Miracles are seen in light.**

   [3]On the half hour:
   [4]**Miracles are seen in light, and light and strength are one.**

LESSON 112

For morning and evening review:

1. (93) **Light and joy and peace abide in me.**

> ²*I am the home of light and joy and peace.* ³*I welcome them into the home I share with God, because I am a part of Him.*

2. (94) **I am as God created me.**

> ²*I will remain forever as I was, created by the Changeless like Himself.* ³*And I am one with Him, and He with me.*

3. On the hour:
   ²Light and joy and peace abide in me.

   ³On the half hour:
   ⁴I am as God created me.

LESSON 113

For morning and evening review:

1. (95) **I am one Self, united with my Creator.**

> [2]*Serenity and perfect peace are mine, because I am one Self, completely whole, at one with all creation and with God.*

2. (96) **Salvation comes from my one Self.**

> [2]*From my one Self, Whose knowledge still remains within my mind, I see God's perfect plan for my salvation perfectly fulfilled.*

3. On the hour:
   [2]**I am one Self, united with my Creator.**

   [3]On the half hour:
   [4]**Salvation comes from my one Self.**

LESSON 114

For morning and evening review:

1. (97) **I am spirit.**

> [2]*I am the Son of God.* [3]*No body can contain my spirit, nor impose on me a limitation God created not.*

2. (98) **I will accept my part in God's plan for salvation.**

> [2]*What can my function be but to accept the Word of God, Who has created me for what I am and will forever be?*

3. On the hour:
   [2]**I am spirit.**

   [3]On the half hour:
   [4]**I will accept my part in God's plan for salvation.**

LESSON 115

For morning and evening review:

1. (99) **Salvation is my only function here.**

> [2]*My function here is to forgive the world for all the errors I have made.* [3]*For thus am I released from them with all the world.*

2. (100) **My part is essential to God's plan for salvation.**

> [2]*I am essential to the plan of God for the salvation of the world.* [3]*For He gave me His plan that I might save the world.*

3. On the hour:
   [2]Salvation is my only function here.

   [3]On the half hour:
   [4]My part is essential to God's plan for salvation.

LESSON 116

For morning and evening review:

1. (101) **God's Will for me is perfect happiness.**

   [2]*God's Will is perfect happiness for me.* [3]*And I can suffer but from the belief there is another will apart from His.*

2. (102) **I share God's Will for happiness for me.**

   [2]*I share my Father's Will for me, His Son.* [3]*What He has given me is all I want.* [4]*What He has given me is all there is.*

3. On the hour:
   [2]**God's Will for me is perfect happiness.**

   [3]On the half hour:
   [4]**I share God's Will for happiness for me.**

LESSON 117

For morning and evening review:

1. (103) **God, being Love, is also happiness.**

> [2]*Let me remember love is happiness, and nothing else brings joy.* [3]*And so I choose to entertain no substitutes for love.*

2. (104) **I seek but what belongs to me in truth.**

> [2]*Love is my heritage, and with it joy.* [3]*These are the gifts my Father gave to me.* [4]*I would accept all that is mine in truth.*

3. On the hour:
[2]**God, being Love, is also happiness.**

[3]On the half hour:
[4]**I seek but what belongs to me in truth.**

LESSON 118

For morning and evening review:

1. (105) **God's peace and joy are mine.**

   > [2]*Today I will accept God's peace and joy, in glad exchange for all the substitutes that I have made for happiness and peace.*

2. (106) **Let me be still and listen to the truth.**

   > [2]*Let my own feeble voice be still, and let me hear the mighty Voice for Truth Itself assure me that I am God's perfect Son.*

3. On the hour:
   [2]**God's peace and joy are mine.**

   [3]On the half hour:
   [4]**Let me be still and listen to the truth.**

LESSON 119

For morning and evening review:

1. (107) **Truth will correct all errors in my mind.**

    [2]*I am mistaken when I think I can be hurt in any way.* [3]*I am God's Son, whose Self rests safely in the Mind of God.*

2. (108) **To give and to receive are one in truth.**

    [2]*I will forgive all things today, that I may learn how to accept the truth in me, and come to recognize my sinlessness.*

3. On the hour:
   [2]**Truth will correct all errors in my mind.**

   [3]On the half hour:
   [4]**To give and to receive are one in truth.**

LESSON 120

For morning and evening review:

1. (109) **I rest in God.**

> ^{2}*I rest in God today, and let Him work in me and through me, while I rest in Him in quiet and in perfect certainty.*

2. (110) **I am as God created me.**

> ^{2}*I am God's Son. ^{3}Today I lay aside all sick illusions of myself, and let my Father tell me Who I really am.*

3. On the hour:
   ^{2}**I rest in God.**

   ^{3}On the half hour:
   ^{4}**I am as God created me.**

LESSON 121

Forgiveness is the key to happiness.

1. Here is the answer to your search for peace. ²Here is the key to meaning in a world that seems to make no sense. ³Here is the way to safety in apparent dangers that appear to threaten you at every turn, and bring uncertainty to all your hopes of ever finding quietness and peace. ⁴Here are all questions answered; here the end of all uncertainty ensured at last.

2. The unforgiving mind is full of fear, and offers love no room to be itself; no place where it can spread its wings in peace and soar above the turmoil of the world. ²The unforgiving mind is sad, without the hope of respite and release from pain. ³It suffers and abides in misery, peering about in darkness, seeing not, yet certain of the danger lurking there.

3. The unforgiving mind is torn with doubt, confused about itself and all it sees; afraid and angry, weak and blustering, afraid to go ahead, afraid to stay, afraid to waken or to go to sleep, afraid of every sound, yet more afraid of stillness; terrified of darkness, yet more terrified at the approach of light. ²What can the unforgiving mind perceive but its damnation? ³What can it behold except the proof that all its sins are real?

4. The unforgiving mind sees no mistakes, but only sins. ²It looks upon the world with sightless eyes, and shrieks as it beholds its own projections rising to attack its miserable parody of life. ³It wants to live, yet wishes it were dead. ⁴It wants forgiveness, yet it sees no hope. ⁵It wants escape, yet can conceive of none because it sees the sinful everywhere.

5. The unforgiving mind is in despair, without the prospect of a future which can offer anything but more despair. ²Yet it regards its judgment of the world as irreversible, and does not see it has condemned itself to this despair. ³It thinks it cannot change, for what it sees bears witness that its judgment is correct. ⁴It does not ask, because it thinks it knows. ⁵It does not question, certain it is right.

6. Forgiveness is acquired. ²It is not inherent in the mind, which cannot sin. ³As sin is an idea you taught yourself, forgiveness must be learned by you as well, but from a Teacher other than yourself, Who represents the other Self in you. ⁴Through Him

you learn how to forgive the self you think you made, and let it disappear. [5]Thus you return your mind as one to Him Who is your Self, and Who can never sin.

7. Each unforgiving mind presents you with an opportunity to teach your own how to forgive itself. [2]Each one awaits release from hell through you, and turns to you imploringly for Heaven here and now. [3]It has no hope, but you become its hope. [4]And as its hope, do you become your own. [5]The unforgiving mind must learn through your forgiveness that it has been saved from hell. [6]And as you teach salvation, you will learn. [7]Yet all your teaching and your learning will be not of you, but of the Teacher Who was given you to show the way to you.

8. Today we practice learning to forgive. [2]If you are willing, you can learn today to take the key to happiness, and use it on your own behalf. [3]We will devote ten minutes in the morning, and at night another ten, to learning how to give forgiveness and receive forgiveness, too.

9. The unforgiving mind does not believe that giving and receiving are the same. [2]Yet we will try to learn today that they are one through practicing forgiveness toward one whom you think of as an enemy, and one whom you consider as a friend. [3]And as you learn to see them both as one, we will extend the lesson to yourself, and see that their escape included yours.

10. Begin the longer practice periods by thinking of someone you do not like, who seems to irritate you, or to cause regret in you if you should meet him; one you actively despise, or merely try to overlook. [2]It does not matter what the form your anger takes. [3]You probably have chosen him already. [4]He will do.

11. Now close your eyes and see him in your mind, and look at him a while. [2]Try to perceive some light in him somewhere; a little gleam which you had never noticed. [3]Try to find some little spark of brightness shining through the ugly picture that you hold of him. [4]Look at this picture till you see a light somewhere within it, and then try to let this light extend until it covers him, and makes the picture beautiful and good.

12. Look at this changed perception for a while, and turn your mind to one you call a friend. [2]Try to transfer the light you learned to see around your former "enemy" to him. [3]Perceive him now as more than friend to you, for in that light his holiness shows you your savior, saved and saving, healed and whole.

13. Then let him offer you the light you see in him, and let your

"enemy" and friend unite in blessing you with what you gave. [2]Now are you one with them, and they with you. [3]Now have you been forgiven by yourself. [4]Do not forget, throughout the day, the role forgiveness plays in bringing happiness to every unforgiving mind, with yours among them. [5]Every hour tell yourself:

> [6]*Forgiveness is the key to happiness.* [7]*I will awaken from the dream that I am mortal, fallible and full of sin, and know I am the perfect Son of God.*

LESSON 122

Forgiveness offers everything I want.

1. What could you want forgiveness cannot give? [2]Do you want peace? [3]Forgiveness offers it. [4]Do you want happiness, a quiet mind, a certainty of purpose, and a sense of worth and beauty that transcends the world? [5]Do you want care and safety, and the warmth of sure protection always? [6]Do you want a quietness that cannot be disturbed, a gentleness that never can be hurt, a deep abiding comfort, and a rest so perfect it can never be upset?

2. All this forgiveness offers you, and more. [2]It sparkles on your eyes as you awake, and gives you joy with which to meet the day. [3]It soothes your forehead while you sleep, and rests upon your eyelids so you see no dreams of fear and evil, malice and attack. [4]And when you wake again, it offers you another day of happiness and peace. [5]All this forgiveness offers you, and more.

3. Forgiveness lets the veil be lifted up that hides the face of Christ from those who look with unforgiving eyes upon the world. [2]It lets you recognize the Son of God, and clears your memory of all dead thoughts so that remembrance of your Father can arise across the threshold of your mind. [3]What would you want forgiveness cannot give? [4]What gifts but these are worthy to be sought? [5]What fancied value, trivial effect or transient promise, never to be kept, can hold more hope than what forgiveness brings?

4. Why would you seek an answer other than the answer that will answer everything? [2]Here is the perfect answer, given to imperfect questions, meaningless requests, halfhearted willingness to hear, and less than halfway diligence and partial trust. [3]Here is the answer! [4]Seek for it no more. [5]You will not find another one instead.

5. God's plan for your salvation cannot change, nor can it fail. [2]Be thankful it remains exactly as He planned it. [3]Changelessly it stands before you like an open door, with warmth and welcome calling from beyond the doorway, bidding you to enter in and make yourself at home, where you belong.

6. Here is the answer! [2]Would you stand outside while all of Heaven waits for you within? [3]Forgive and be forgiven. [4]As you give you will receive. [5]There is no plan but this for the salvation

of the Son of God. [6]Let us today rejoice that this is so, for here we have an answer, clear and plain, beyond deceit in its simplicity. [7]All the complexities the world has spun of fragile cobwebs disappear before the power and the majesty of this extremely simple statement of the truth.

7. Here is the answer! [2]Do not turn away in aimless wandering again. [3]Accept salvation now. [4]It is the gift of God, and not the world. [5]The world can give no gifts of any value to a mind that has received what God has given as its own. [6]God wills salvation be received today, and that the intricacies of your dreams no longer hide their nothingness from you.

8. Open your eyes today and look upon a happy world of safety and of peace. [2]Forgiveness is the means by which it comes to take the place of hell. [3]In quietness it rises up to greet your open eyes, and fill your heart with deep tranquility as ancient truths, forever newly born, arise in your awareness. [4]What you will remember then can never be described. [5]Yet your forgiveness offers it to you.

9. Remembering the gifts forgiveness gives, we undertake our practicing today with hope and faith that this will be the day salvation will be ours. [2]Earnestly and gladly will we seek for it today, aware we hold the key within our hands, accepting Heaven's answer to the hell we made, but where we would remain no more.

10. Morning and evening do we gladly give a quarter of an hour to the search in which the end of hell is guaranteed. [2]Begin in hopefulness, for we have reached the turning point at which the road becomes far easier. [3]And now the way is short that yet we travel. [4]We are close indeed to the appointed ending of the dream.

11. Sink into happiness as you begin these practice periods, for they hold out the sure rewards of questions answered and what your acceptance of the answer brings. [2]Today it will be given you to feel the peace forgiveness offers, and the joy the lifting of the veil holds out to you.

12. Before the light you will receive today the world will fade until it disappears, and you will see another world arise you have no words to picture. [2]Now we walk directly into light, and we receive the gifts that have been held in store for us since time began, kept waiting for today.

13. Forgiveness offers everything you want. [2]Today all things you

want are given you. ³Let not your gifts recede throughout the day, as you return again to meet a world of shifting change and bleak appearances. ⁴Retain your gifts in clear awareness as you see the changeless in the heart of change; the light of truth behind appearances.

14. Be tempted not to let your gifts slip by and drift into forgetfulness, but hold them firmly in your mind by your attempts to think of them at least a minute as each quarter of an hour passes by. ²Remind yourself how precious are these gifts with this reminder, which has power to hold your gifts in your awareness through the day:

> ³*Forgiveness offers everything I want.*
> ⁴*Today I have accepted this as true.*
> ⁵*Today I have received the gifts of God.*

LESSON 123

I thank my Father for His gifts to me.

1. Today let us be thankful. ²We have come to gentler pathways and to smoother roads. ³There is no thought of turning back, and no implacable resistance to the truth. ⁴A bit of wavering remains, some small objections and a little hesitance, but you can well be grateful for your gains, which are far greater than you realize.

2. A day devoted now to gratitude will add the benefit of some insight into the real extent of all the gains which you have made; the gifts you have received. ²Be glad today, in loving thankfulness, your Father has not left you to yourself, nor let you wander in the dark alone. ³Be grateful He has saved you from the self you thought you made to take the place of Him and His creation. ⁴Give Him thanks today.

3. Give thanks that He has not abandoned you, and that His Love forever will remain shining on you, forever without change. ²Give thanks as well that you are changeless, for the Son He loves is changeless as Himself. ³Be grateful you are saved. ⁴Be glad you have a function in salvation to fulfill. ⁵Be thankful that your value far transcends your meager gifts and petty judgments of the one whom God established as His Son.

4. Today in gratitude we lift our hearts above despair, and raise our thankful eyes, no longer looking downward to the dust. ²We sing the song of thankfulness today, in honor of the Self that God has willed to be our true Identity in Him. ³Today we smile on everyone we see, and walk with lightened footsteps as we go to do what is appointed us to do.

5. We do not go alone. ²And we give thanks that in our solitude a Friend has come to speak the saving Word of God to us. ³And thanks to you for listening to Him. ⁴His Word is soundless if it be not heard. ⁵In thanking Him the thanks are yours as well. ⁶An unheard message will not save the world, however mighty be the Voice that speaks, however loving may the message be.

6. Thanks be to you who heard, for you become the messenger who brings His Voice with you, and lets It echo round and round the world. ²Receive the thanks of God today, as you give thanks to Him. ³For He would offer you the thanks you give, since He receives your gifts in loving gratitude, and gives them back a

thousand and a hundred thousand more than they were given. ⁴He will bless your gifts by sharing them with you. ⁵And so they grow in power and in strength, until they fill the world with gladness and with gratitude.

7. Receive His thanks and offer yours to Him for fifteen minutes twice today. ²And you will realize to Whom you offer thanks, and Whom He thanks as you are thanking Him. ³This holy half an hour given Him will be returned to you in terms of years for every second; power to save the world eons more quickly for your thanks to Him.

8. Receive His thanks, and you will understand how lovingly He holds you in His Mind, how deep and limitless His care for you, how perfect is His gratitude to you. ²Remember hourly to think of Him, and give Him thanks for everything He gave His Son, that he might rise above the world, remembering his Father and his Self.

LESSON 124

Let me remember I am one with God.

1. Today we will again give thanks for our Identity in God. ²Our home is safe, protection guaranteed in all we do, power and strength available to us in all our undertakings. ³We can fail in nothing. ⁴Everything we touch takes on a shining light that blesses and that heals. ⁵At one with God and with the universe we go our way rejoicing, with the thought that God Himself goes everywhere with us.

2. How holy are our minds! ²And everything we see reflects the holiness within the mind at one with God and with itself. ³How easily do errors disappear, and death give place to everlasting life. ⁴Our shining footprints point the way to truth, for God is our Companion as we walk the world a little while. ⁵And those who come to follow us will recognize the way because the light we carry stays behind, yet still remains with us as we walk on.

3. What we receive is our eternal gift to those who follow after, and to those who went before or stayed with us a while. ²And God, Who loves us with the equal love in which we were created, smiles on us and offers us the happiness we gave.

4. Today we will not doubt His Love for us, nor question His protection and His care. ²No meaningless anxieties can come between our faith and our awareness of His Presence. ³We are one with Him today in recognition and rememberance. ⁴We feel Him in our hearts. ⁵Our minds contain His Thoughts; our eyes behold His loveliness in all we look upon. ⁶Today we see only the loving and the lovable.

5. We see it in appearances of pain, and pain gives way to peace. ²We see it in the frantic, in the sad and the distressed, the lonely and afraid, who are restored to the tranquility and peace of mind in which they were created. ³And we see it in the dying and the dead as well, restoring them to life. ⁴All this we see because we saw it first within ourselves.

6. No miracle can ever be denied to those who know that they are one with God. ²No thought of theirs but has the power to heal all forms of suffering in anyone, in times gone by and times as yet to come, as easily as in the ones who walk beside them

now. ³Their thoughts are timeless, and apart from distance as apart from time.

7. We join in this awareness as we say that we are one with God. ²For in these words we say as well that we are saved and healed; that we can save and heal accordingly. ³We have accepted, and we now would give. ⁴For we would keep the gifts our Father gave. ⁵Today we would experience ourselves at one with Him, so that the world may share our recognition of reality. ⁶In our experience the world is freed. ⁷As we deny our separation from our Father, it is healed along with us.

8. Peace be to you today. ²Secure your peace by practicing awareness you are one with your Creator, as He is with you. ³Sometime today, whenever it seems best, devote a half an hour to the thought that you are one with God. ⁴This is our first attempt at an extended period for which we give no rules nor special words to guide your meditation. ⁵We will trust God's Voice to speak as He sees fit today, certain He will not fail. ⁶Abide with Him this half an hour. ⁷He will do the rest.

9. Your benefit will not be less if you believe that nothing happens. ²You may not be ready to accept the gain today. ³Yet sometime, somewhere, it will come to you, nor will you fail to recognize it when it dawns with certainty upon your mind. ⁴This half an hour will be framed in gold, with every minute like a diamond set around the mirror that this exercise will offer you. ⁵And you will see Christ's face upon it, in reflection of your own.

10. Perhaps today, perhaps tomorrow, you will see your own transfiguration in the glass this holy half an hour will hold out to you, to look upon yourself. ²When you are ready you will find it there, within your mind and waiting to be found. ³You will remember then the thought to which you gave this half an hour, thankfully aware no time was ever better spent.

11. Perhaps today, perhaps tomorrow, you will look into this glass, and understand the sinless light you see belongs to you; the loveliness you look on is your own. ²Count this half hour as your gift to God, in certainty that His return will be a sense of love you cannot understand, a joy too deep for you to comprehend, a sight too holy for the body's eyes to see. ³And yet you can be sure someday, perhaps today, perhaps tomorrow, you will understand and comprehend and see.

12.   Add further jewels to the golden frame that holds the mirror offered you today, by hourly repeating to yourself:

> [2]Let me remember I am one with God, at one with all my
> brothers and my Self, in everlasting holiness and peace.

LESSON 125

In quiet I receive God's Word today.

1. Let this day be a day of stillness and of quiet listening. ²Your Father wills you hear His Word today. ³He calls to you from deep within your mind where He abides. ⁴Hear Him today. ⁵No peace is possible until His Word is heard around the world; until your mind, in quiet listening, accepts the message that the world must hear to usher in the quiet time of peace.

2. This world will change through you. ²No other means can save it, for God's plan is simply this: The Son of God is free to save himself, given the Word of God to be his Guide, forever in his mind and at his side to lead him surely to his Father's house by his own will, forever free as God's. ³He is not led by force, but only love. ⁴He is not judged, but only sanctified.

3. In stillness we will hear God's Voice today without intrusion of our petty thoughts, without our personal desires, and without all judgment of His holy Word. ²We will not judge ourselves today, for what we are can not be judged. ³We stand apart from all the judgments which the world has laid upon the Son of God. ⁴It knows him not. ⁵Today we will not listen to the world, but wait in silence for the Word of God.

4. Hear, holy Son of God, your Father speak. ²His Voice would give to you His holy Word, to spread across the world the tidings of salvation and the holy time of peace. ³We gather at the throne of God today, the quiet place within the mind where He abides forever, in the holiness that He created and will never leave.

5. He has not waited until you return your mind to Him to give His Word to you. ²He has not hid Himself from you, while you have wandered off a little while from Him. ³He does not cherish the illusions which you hold about yourself. ⁴He knows His Son, and wills that he remain as part of Him regardless of his dreams; regardless of his madness that his will is not his own.

6. Today He speaks to you. ²His Voice awaits your silence, for His Word can not be heard until your mind is quiet for a while, and meaningless desires have been stilled. ³Await His Word in quiet. ⁴There is peace within you to be called upon today, to help make ready your most holy mind to hear the Voice for its Creator speak.

7. Three times today, at times most suitable for silence, give ten

minutes set apart from listening to the world, and choose instead a gentle listening to the Word of God. [2]He speaks from nearer than your heart to you. [3]His Voice is closer than your hand. [4]His Love is everything you are and that He is; the same as you, and you the same as He.

8. It is your voice to which you listen as He speaks to you. [2]It is your word He speaks. [3]It is the Word of freedom and of peace, of unity of will and purpose, with no separation nor division in the single Mind of Father and of Son. [4]In quiet listen to your Self today, and let Him tell you God has never left His Son, and you have never left your Self.

9. Only be quiet. [2]You will need no rule but this, to let your practicing today lift you above the thinking of the world, and free your vision from the body's eyes. [3]Only be still and listen. [4]You will hear the Word in which the Will of God the Son joins in His Father's Will, at one with it, with no illusions interposed between the wholly indivisible and true. [5]As every hour passes by today, be still a moment and remind yourself you have a special purpose for this day; in quiet to receive the Word of God.

LESSON 126

All that I give is given to myself.

1. Today's idea, completely alien to the ego and the thinking of the world, is crucial to the thought reversal that this course will bring about. ²If you believed this statement, there would be no problem in complete forgiveness, certainty of goal, and sure direction. ³You would understand the means by which salvation comes to you, and would not hesitate to use it now.

2. Let us consider what you do believe, in place of this idea. ²It seems to you that other people are apart from you, and able to behave in ways which have no bearing on your thoughts, nor yours on theirs. ³Therefore, your attitudes have no effect on them, and their appeals for help are not in any way related to your own. ⁴You further think that they can sin without affecting your perception of yourself, while you can judge their sin, and yet remain apart from condemnation and at peace.

3. When you "forgive" a sin, there is no gain to you directly. ²You give charity to one unworthy, merely to point out that you are better, on a higher plane than he whom you forgive. ³He has not earned your charitable tolerance, which you bestow on one unworthy of the gift, because his sins have lowered him beneath a true equality with you. ⁴He has no claim on your forgiveness. ⁵It holds out a gift to him, but hardly to yourself.

4. Thus is forgiveness basically unsound; a charitable whim, benevolent yet undeserved, a gift bestowed at times, at other times withheld. ²Unmerited, withholding it is just, nor is it fair that you should suffer when it is withheld. ³The sin that you forgive is not your own. ⁴Someone apart from you committed it. ⁵And if you then are gracious unto him by giving him what he does not deserve, the gift is no more yours than was his sin.

5. If this be true, forgiveness has no grounds on which to rest dependably and sure. ²It is an eccentricity, in which you sometimes choose to give indulgently an undeserved reprieve. ³Yet it remains your right to let the sinner not escape the justified repayment for his sin. ⁴Think you the Lord of Heaven would allow the world's salvation to depend on this? ⁵Would not His care for you be small indeed, if your salvation rested on a whim?

6. You do not understand forgiveness. ²As you see it, it is but a

check upon overt attack, without requiring correction in your mind. ³It cannot give you peace as you perceive it. ⁴It is not a means for your release from what you see in someone other than yourself. ⁵It has no power to restore your unity with him to your awareness. ⁶It is not what God intended it to be for you.

7. Not having given Him the gift He asks of you, you cannot recognize His gifts, and think He has not given them to you. ²Yet would He ask you for a gift unless it was for you? ³Could He be satisfied with empty gestures, and evaluate such petty gifts as worthy of His Son? ⁴Salvation is a better gift than this. ⁵And true forgiveness, as the means by which it is attained, must heal the mind that gives, for giving is receiving. ⁶What remains as unreceived has not been given, but what has been given must have been received.

8. Today we try to understand the truth that giver and receiver are the same. ²You will need help to make this meaningful, because it is so alien to the thoughts to which you are accustomed. ³But the Help you need is there. ⁴Give Him your faith today, and ask Him that He share your practicing in truth today. ⁵And if you only catch a tiny glimpse of the release that lies in the idea we practice for today, this is a day of glory for the world.

9. Give fifteen minutes twice today to the attempt to understand today's idea. ²It is the thought by which forgiveness takes its proper place in your priorities. ³It is the thought that will release your mind from every bar to what forgiveness means, and let you realize its worth to you.

10. In silence, close your eyes upon the world that does not understand forgiveness, and seek sanctuary in the quiet place where thoughts are changed and false beliefs laid by. ²Repeat today's idea, and ask for help in understanding what it really means. ³Be willing to be taught. ⁴Be glad to hear the Voice of truth and healing speak to you, and you will understand the words He speaks, and recognize He speaks your words to you.

11. As often as you can, remind yourself you have a goal today; an aim which makes this day of special value to yourself and all your brothers. ²Do not let your mind forget this goal for long, but tell yourself:

> ³All that I give is given to myself. ⁴The Help I need to learn
> that this is true is with me now. ⁵And I will trust in Him.

⁶Then spend a quiet moment, opening your mind to His correction and His Love. ⁷And what you hear of Him you will believe, for what He gives will be received by you.

LESSON 127

There is no love but God's.

1. Perhaps you think that different kinds of love are possible. ²Perhaps you think there is a kind of love for this, a kind for that; a way of loving one, another way of loving still another. ³Love is one. ⁴It has no separate parts and no degrees; no kinds nor levels, no divergencies and no distinctions. ⁵It is like itself, unchanged throughout. ⁶It never alters with a person or a circumstance. ⁷It is the Heart of God, and also of His Son.

2. Love's meaning is obscure to anyone who thinks that love can change. ²He does not see that changing love must be impossible. ³And thus he thinks that he can love at times, and hate at other times. ⁴He also thinks that love can be bestowed on one, and yet remain itself although it is withheld from others. ⁵To believe these things of love is not to understand it. ⁶If it could make such distinctions, it would have to judge between the righteous and the sinner, and perceive the Son of God in separate parts.

3. Love cannot judge. ²As it is one itself, it looks on all as one. ³Its meaning lies in oneness. ⁴And it must elude the mind that thinks of it as partial or in part. ⁵There is no love but God's, and all of love is His. ⁶There is no other principle that rules where love is not. ⁷Love is a law without an opposite. ⁸Its wholeness is the power holding everything as one, the link between the Father and the Son which holds Them both forever as the same.

4. No course whose purpose is to teach you to remember what you really are could fail to emphasize that there can never be a difference in what you really are and what love is. ²Love's meaning is your own, and shared by God Himself. ³For what you are is what He is. ⁴There is no love but His, and what He is, is everything there is. ⁵There is no limit placed upon Himself, and so are you unlimited as well.

5. No law the world obeys can help you grasp love's meaning. ²What the world believes was made to hide love's meaning, and to keep it dark and secret. ³There is not one principle the world upholds but violates the truth of what love is, and what you are as well.

6. Seek not within the world to find your Self. ²Love is not found in darkness and in death. ³Yet it is perfectly apparent to the eyes

that see and ears that hear love's Voice. ⁴Today we practice making free your mind of all the laws you think you must obey; of all the limits under which you live, and all the changes that you think are part of human destiny. ⁵Today we take the largest single step this course requests in your advance towards its established goal.

7.   If you achieve the faintest glimmering of what love means today, you have advanced in distance without measure and in time beyond the count of years to your release. ²Let us together, then, be glad to give some time to God today, and understand there is no better use for time than this.

8.   For fifteen minutes twice today escape from every law in which you now believe. ²Open your mind and rest. ³The world that seems to hold you prisoner can be escaped by anyone who does not hold it dear. ⁴Withdraw all value you have placed upon its meager offerings and senseless gifts, and let the gift of God replace them all.

9.   Call to your Father, certain that His Voice will answer. ²He Himself has promised this. ³And He Himself will place a spark of truth within your mind wherever you give up a false belief, a dark illusion of your own reality and what love means. ⁴He will shine through your idle thoughts today, and help you understand the truth of love. ⁵In loving gentleness He will abide with you, as you allow His Voice to teach love's meaning to your clean and open mind. ⁶And He will bless the lesson with His Love.

10.   Today the legion of the future years of waiting for salvation disappears before the timelessness of what you learn. ²Let us give thanks today that we are spared a future like the past. ³Today we leave the past behind us, nevermore to be remembered. ⁴And we raise our eyes upon a different present, where a future dawns unlike the past in every attribute.

11.   The world in infancy is newly born. ²And we will watch it grow in health and strength, to shed its blessing upon all who come to learn to cast aside the world they thought was made in hate to be love's enemy. ³Now are they all made free, along with us. ⁴Now are they all our brothers in God's Love.

12.   We will remember them throughout the day, because we cannot leave a part of us outside our love if we would know our Self. ²At least three times an hour think of one who makes the journey

with you, and who came to learn what you must learn. ³And as he comes to mind, give him this message from your Self:

⁴*I bless you, brother, with the Love of God, which I would share with you. ⁵For I would learn the joyous lesson that there is no love but God's and yours and mine and everyone's.*

LESSON 128

The world I see holds nothing that I want.

1. The world you see holds nothing that you need to offer you; nothing that you can use in any way, nor anything at all that serves to give you joy. ²Believe this thought, and you are saved from years of misery, from countless disappointments, and from hopes that turn to bitter ashes of despair. ³No one but must accept this thought as true, if he would leave the world behind and soar beyond its petty scope and little ways.

2. Each thing you value here is but a chain that binds you to the world, and it will serve no other end but this. ²For everything must serve the purpose you have given it, until you see a different purpose there. ³The only purpose worthy of your mind this world contains is that you pass it by, without delaying to perceive some hope where there is none. ⁴Be you deceived no more. ⁵The world you see holds nothing that you want.

3. Escape today the chains you place upon your mind when you perceive salvation here. ²For what you value you make part of you as you perceive yourself. ³All things you seek to make your value greater in your sight limit you further, hide your worth from you, and add another bar across the door that leads to true awareness of your Self.

4. Let nothing that relates to body thoughts delay your progress to salvation, nor permit temptation to believe the world holds anything you want to hold you back. ²Nothing is here to cherish. ³Nothing here is worth one instant of delay and pain; one moment of uncertainty and doubt. ⁴The worthless offer nothing. ⁵Certainty of worth can not be found in worthlessness.

5. Today we practice letting go all thought of values we have given to the world. ²We leave it free of purposes we gave its aspects and its phases and its dreams. ³We hold it purposeless within our minds, and loosen it from all we wish it were. ⁴Thus do we lift the chains that bar the door to freedom from the world, and go beyond all little values and diminished goals.

6. Pause and be still a little while, and see how far you rise above the world, when you release your mind from chains and let it seek the level where it finds itself at home. ²It will be grateful to be free a while. ³It knows where it belongs. ⁴But free its wings,

and it will fly in sureness and in joy to join its holy purpose. [5]Let it rest in its Creator, there to be restored to sanity, to freedom and to love.

7. Give it ten minutes rest three times today. [2]And when your eyes are opened afterwards, you will not value anything you see as much as when you looked at it before. [3]Your whole perspective on the world will shift by just a little, every time you let your mind escape its chains. [4]The world is not where it belongs. [5]And you belong where it would be, and where it goes to rest when you release it from the world. [6]Your Guide is sure. [7]Open your mind to Him. [8]Be still and rest.

8. Protect your mind throughout the day as well. [2]And when you think you see some value in an aspect or an image of the world, refuse to lay this chain upon your mind, but tell yourself with quiet certainty:

[3]*This will not tempt me to delay myself.*
[4]*The world I see holds nothing that I want.*

LESSON 129

Beyond this world there is a world I want.

1. This is the thought that follows from the one we practiced yesterday. ²You cannot stop with the idea the world is worthless, for unless you see that there is something else to hope for, you will only be depressed. ³Our emphasis is not on giving up the world, but on exchanging it for what is far more satisfying, filled with joy, and capable of offering you peace. ⁴Think you this world can offer that to you?

2. It might be worth a little time to think once more about the value of this world. ²Perhaps you will concede there is no loss in letting go all thought of value here. ³The world you see is merciless indeed, unstable, cruel, unconcerned with you, quick to avenge and pitiless with hate. ⁴It gives but to rescind, and takes away all things that you have cherished for a while. ⁵No lasting love is found, for none is here. ⁶This is the world of time, where all things end.

3. Is it a loss to find a world instead where losing is impossible; where love endures forever, hate cannot exist and vengeance has no meaning? ²Is it loss to find all things you really want, and know they have no ending and they will remain exactly as you want them throughout time? ³Yet even they will be exchanged at last for what we cannot speak of, for you go from there to where words fail entirely, into a silence where the language is unspoken and yet surely understood.

4. Communication, unambiguous and plain as day, remains unlimited for all eternity. ²And God Himself speaks to His Son, as His Son speaks to Him. ³Their language has no words, for what They say cannot be symbolized. ⁴Their knowledge is direct and wholly shared and wholly one. ⁵How far away from this are you who stay bound to this world. ⁶And yet how near are you, when you exchange it for the world you want.

5. Now is the last step certain; now you stand an instant's space away from timelessness. ²Here can you but look forward, never back to see again the world you do not want. ³Here is the world that comes to take its place, as you unbind your mind from little things the world sets forth to keep you prisoner. ⁴Value them not, and they will disappear. ⁵Esteem them, and

they will seem real to you.

6. Such is the choice. ²What loss can be for you in choosing not to value nothingness? ³This world holds nothing that you really want, but what you choose instead you want indeed! ⁴Let it be given you today. ⁵It waits but for your choosing it, to take the place of all the things you seek but do not want.

7. Practice your willingness to make this change ten minutes in the morning and at night, and once more in between. ²Begin with this:

> ³Beyond this world there is a world I want. ⁴I choose to see that world instead of this, for here is nothing that I really want.

⁵Then close your eyes upon the world you see, and in the silent darkness watch the lights that are not of this world light one by one, until where one begins another ends loses all meaning as they blend in one.

8. Today the lights of Heaven bend to you, to shine upon your eyelids as you rest beyond the world of darkness. ²Here is light your eyes can not behold. ³And yet your mind can see it plainly, and can understand. ⁴A day of grace is given you today, and we give thanks. ⁵This day we realize that what you feared to lose was only loss.

9. Now do we understand there is no loss. ²For we have seen its opposite at last, and we are grateful that the choice is made. ³Remember your decision hourly, and take a moment to confirm your choice by laying by whatever thoughts you have, and dwelling briefly only upon this:

> ⁴The world I see holds nothing that I want.
> ⁵Beyond this world there is a world I want.

LESSON 130

It is impossible to see two worlds.

1. Perception is consistent. ²What you see reflects your thinking. ³And your thinking but reflects your choice of what you want to see. ⁴Your values are determiners of this, for what you value you must want to see, believing what you see is really there. ⁵No one can see a world his mind has not accorded value. ⁶And no one can fail to look upon what he believes he wants.

2. Yet who can really hate and love at once? ²Who can desire what he does not want to have reality? ³And who can choose to see a world of which he is afraid? ⁴Fear must make blind, for this its weapon is: That which you fear to see you cannot see. ⁵Love and perception thus go hand in hand, but fear obscures in darkness what is there.

3. What, then, can fear project upon the world? ²What can be seen in darkness that is real? ³Truth is eclipsed by fear, and what remains is but imagined. ⁴Yet what can be real in blind imaginings of panic born? ⁵What would you want that this is shown to you? ⁶What would you wish to keep in such a dream?

4. Fear has made everything you think you see. ²All separation, all distinctions, and the multitude of differences you believe make up the world. ³They are not there. ⁴Love's enemy has made them up. ⁵Yet love can have no enemy, and so they have no cause, no being and no consequence. ⁶They can be valued, but remain unreal. ⁷They can be sought, but they can not be found. ⁸Today we will not seek for them, nor waste this day in seeking what can not be found.

5. It is impossible to see two worlds which have no overlap of any kind. ²Seek for the one; the other disappears. ³But one remains. ⁴They are the range of choice beyond which your decision cannot go. ⁵The real and the unreal are all there are to choose between, and nothing more than these.

6. Today we will attempt no compromise where none is possible. ²The world you see is proof you have already made a choice as all-embracing as its opposite. ³What we would learn today is more than just the lesson that you cannot see two worlds. ⁴It also teaches that the one you see is quite consistent from the point of view from which you see it. ⁵It is all a piece because it stems from

one emotion, and reflects its source in everything you see.

7. Six times today, in thanks and gratitude, we gladly give five minutes to the thought that ends all compromise and doubt, and go beyond them all as one. ²We will not make a thousand meaningless distinctions, nor attempt to bring with us a little part of unreality, as we devote our minds to finding only what is real.

8. Begin your searching for the other world by asking for a strength beyond your own, and recognizing what it is you seek. ²You do not want illusions. ³And you come to these five minutes emptying your hands of all the petty treasures of this world. ⁴You wait for God to help you, as you say:

⁵*It is impossible to see two worlds. ⁶Let me accept the strength God offers me and see no value in this world, that I may find my freedom and deliverance.*

9. God will be there. ²For you have called upon the great unfailing power which will take this giant step with you in gratitude. ³Nor will you fail to see His thanks expressed in tangible perception and in truth. ⁴You will not doubt what you will look upon, for though it is perception, it is not the kind of seeing that your eyes alone have ever seen before. ⁵And you will know God's strength upheld you as you made this choice.

10. Dismiss temptation easily today whenever it arises, merely by remembering the limits of your choice. ²The unreal or the real, the false or true is what you see and only what you see. ³Perception is consistent with your choice, and hell or Heaven comes to you as one.

11. Accept a little part of hell as real, and you have damned your eyes and cursed your sight, and what you will behold is hell indeed. ²Yet the release of Heaven still remains within your range of choice, to take the place of everything that hell would show to you. ³All you need say to any part of hell, whatever form it takes, is simply this:

⁴*It is impossible to see two worlds. ⁵I seek my freedom and deliverance, and this is not a part of what I want.*

238

LESSON 131

No one can fail who seeks to reach the truth.

1. Failure is all about you while you seek for goals that cannot be achieved. [2]You look for permanence in the impermanent, for love where there is none, for safety in the midst of danger; immortality within the darkness of the dream of death. [3]Who could succeed where contradiction is the setting of his searching, and the place to which he comes to find stability?

2. Goals that are meaningless are not attained. [2]There is no way to reach them, for the means by which you strive for them are meaningless as they are. [3]Who can use such senseless means, and hope through them to gain in anything? [4]Where can they lead? [5]And what could they achieve that offers any hope of being real? [6]Pursuit of the imagined leads to death because it is the search for nothingness, and while you seek for life you ask for death. [7]You look for safety and security, while in your heart you pray for danger and protection for the little dream you made.

3. Yet searching is inevitable here. [2]For this you came, and you will surely do the thing you came for. [3]But the world can not dictate the goal for which you search, unless you give it power to do so. [4]Otherwise, you still are free to choose a goal that lies beyond the world and every worldly thought, and one that comes to you from an idea relinquished yet remembered, old yet new; an echo of a heritage forgot, yet holding everything you really want.

4. Be glad that search you must. [2]Be glad as well to learn you search for Heaven, and must find the goal you really want. [3]No one can fail to want this goal and reach it in the end. [4]God's Son can not seek vainly, though he try to force delay, deceive himself and think that it is hell he seeks. [5]When he is wrong, he finds correction. [6]When he wanders off, he is led back to his appointed task.

5. No one remains in hell, for no one can abandon his Creator, nor affect His perfect, timeless and unchanging Love. [2]You will find Heaven. [3]Everything you seek but this will fall away. [4]Yet not because it has been taken from you. [5]It will go because you do not want it. [6]You will reach the goal you really want as certainly as God created you in sinlessness.

6. Why wait for Heaven? ²It is here today. ³Time is the great illusion it is past or in the future. ⁴Yet this cannot be, if it is where God wills His Son to be. ⁵How could the Will of God be in the past, or yet to happen? ⁶What He wills is now, without a past and wholly futureless. ⁷It is as far removed from time as is a tiny candle from a distant star, or what you chose from what you really want.

7. Heaven remains your one alternative to this strange world you made and all its ways; its shifting patterns and uncertain goals, its painful pleasures and its tragic joys. ²God made no contradictions. ³What denies its own existence and attacks itself is not of Him. ⁴He did not make two minds, with Heaven as the glad effect of one, and earth the other's sorry outcome which is Heaven's opposite in every way.

8. God does not suffer conflict. ²Nor is His creation split in two. ³How could it be His Son could be in hell, when God Himself established him in Heaven? ⁴Could he lose what the Eternal Will has given him to be his home forever? ⁵Let us not try longer to impose an alien will upon God's single purpose. ⁶He is here because He wills to be, and what He wills is present now, beyond the reach of time.

9. Today we will not choose a paradox in place of truth. ²How could the Son of God make time to take away the Will of God? ³He thus denies himself, and contradicts what has no opposite. ⁴He thinks he made a hell opposing Heaven, and believes that he abides in what does not exist, while Heaven is the place he cannot find.

10. Leave foolish thoughts like these behind today, and turn your mind to true ideas instead. ²No one can fail who seeks to reach the truth, and it is truth we seek to reach today. ³We will devote ten minutes to this goal three times today, and we will ask to see the rising of the real world to replace the foolish images that we hold dear, with true ideas arising in the place of thoughts that have no meaning, no effect, and neither source nor substance in the truth.

11. This we acknowledge as we start upon our practice periods. ²Begin with this:

> ³I ask to see a different world, and think a different kind of thought from those I made. ⁴The world I seek I did not make alone, the thoughts I want to think are not my own.

⁵For several minutes watch your mind and see, although your eyes are closed, the senseless world you think is real. ⁶Review the thoughts as well which are compatible with such a world, and which you think are true. ⁷Then let them go, and sink below them to the holy place where they can enter not. ⁸There is a door beneath them in your mind, which you could not completely lock to hide what lies beyond.

12. Seek for that door and find it. ²But before you try to open it, remind yourself no one can fail who seeks to reach the truth. ³And it is this request you make today. ⁴Nothing but this has any meaning now; no other goal is valued now nor sought, nothing before this door you really want, and only what lies past it do you seek.

13. Put out your hand, and see how easily the door swings open with your one intent to go beyond it. ²Angels light the way, so that all darkness vanishes, and you are standing in a light so bright and clear that you can understand all things you see. ³A tiny moment of surprise, perhaps, will make you pause before you realize the world you see before you in the light reflects the truth you knew, and did not quite forget in wandering away in dreams.

14. You cannot fail today. ²There walks with you the Spirit Heaven sent you, that you might approach this door some day, and through His aid slip effortlessly past it, to the light. ³Today that day has come. ⁴Today God keeps His ancient promise to His holy Son, as does His Son remember his to Him. ⁵This is a day of gladness, for we come to the appointed time and place where you will find the goal of all your searching here, and all the seeking of the world, which end together as you pass beyond the door.

15. Remember often that today should be a time of special gladness, and refrain from dismal thoughts and meaningless laments. ²Salvation's time has come. ³Today is set by Heaven itself to be a time of grace for you and for the world. ⁴If you forget this happy fact, remind yourself with this:

> ⁵*Today I seek and find all that I want.*
> ⁶*My single purpose offers it to me.*
> ⁷*No one can fail who seeks to reach the truth.*

LESSON 132

I loose the world from all I thought it was.

1. What keeps the world in chains but your beliefs? [2]And what can save the world except your Self? [3]Belief is powerful indeed. [4]The thoughts you hold are mighty, and illusions are as strong in their effects as is the truth. [5]A madman thinks the world he sees is real, and does not doubt it. [6]Nor can he be swayed by questioning his thoughts' effects. [7]It is but when their source is raised to question that the hope of freedom comes to him at last.

2. Yet is salvation easily achieved, for anyone is free to change his mind, and all his thoughts change with it. [2]Now the source of thought has shifted, for to change your mind means you have changed the source of all ideas you think or ever thought or yet will think. [3]You free the past from what you thought before. [4]You free the future from all ancient thoughts of seeking what you do not want to find.

3. The present now remains the only time. [2]Here in the present is the world set free. [3]For as you let the past be lifted and release the future from your ancient fears, you find escape and give it to the world. [4]You have enslaved the world with all your fears, your doubts and miseries, your pain and tears; and all your sorrows press on it, and keep the world a prisoner to your beliefs. [5]Death strikes it everywhere because you hold the bitter thoughts of death within your mind.

4. The world is nothing in itself. [2]Your mind must give it meaning. [3]And what you behold upon it are your wishes, acted out so you can look on them and think them real. [4]Perhaps you think you did not make the world, but came unwillingly to what was made already, hardly waiting for your thoughts to give it meaning. [5]Yet in truth you found exactly what you looked for when you came.

5. There is no world apart from what you wish, and herein lies your ultimate release. [2]Change but your mind on what you want to see, and all the world must change accordingly. [3]Ideas leave not their source. [4]This central theme is often stated in the text, and must be borne in mind if you would understand the lesson for today. [5]It is not pride which tells you that you made the world you see, and that it changes as you change your mind.

242

6. But it is pride that argues you have come into a world quite separate from yourself, impervious to what you think, and quite apart from what you chance to think it is. ²There is no world! ³This is the central thought the course attempts to teach. ⁴Not everyone is ready to accept it, and each one must go as far as he can let himself be led along the road to truth. ⁵He will return and go still farther, or perhaps step back a while and then return again.

7. But healing is the gift of those who are prepared to learn there is no world, and can accept the lesson now. ²Their readiness will bring the lesson to them in some form which they can understand and recognize. ³Some see it suddenly on point of death, and rise to teach it. ⁴Others find it in experience that is not of this world, which shows them that the world does not exist because what they behold must be the truth, and yet it clearly contradicts the world.

8. And some will find it in this course, and in the exercises that we do today. ²Today's idea is true because the world does not exist. ³And if it is indeed your own imagining, then you can loose it from all things you ever thought it was by merely changing all the thoughts that gave it these appearances. ⁴The sick are healed as you let go all thoughts of sickness, and the dead arise when you let thoughts of life replace all thoughts you ever held of death.

9. A lesson earlier repeated once must now be stressed again, for it contains the firm foundation for today's idea. ²You are as God created you. ³There is no place where you can suffer, and no time that can bring change to your eternal state. ⁴How can a world of time and place exist, if you remain as God created you?

10. What is the lesson for today except another way of saying that to know your Self is the salvation of the world? ²To free the world from every kind of pain is but to change your mind about yourself. ³There is no world apart from your ideas because ideas leave not their source, and you maintain the world within your mind in thought.

11. Yet if you are as God created you, you cannot think apart from Him, nor make what does not share His timelessness and Love. ²Are these inherent in the world you see? ³Does it create like Him? ⁴Unless it does, it is not real, and cannot be at all. ⁵If you are real the world you see is false, for God's creation is unlike the world in every way. ⁶And as it was His Thought by which you

were created, so it is your thoughts which made it and must set it free, that you may know the Thoughts you share with God.

12. Release the world! ²Your real creations wait for this release to give you fatherhood, not of illusions, but as God in truth. ³God shares His Fatherhood with you who are His Son, for He makes no distinctions in what is Himself and what is still Himself. ⁴What He creates is not apart from Him, and nowhere does the Father end, the Son begin as something separate from Him.

13. There is no world because it is a thought apart from God, and made to separate the Father and the Son, and break away a part of God Himself and thus destroy His Wholeness. ²Can a world which comes from this idea be real? ³Can it be anywhere? ⁴Deny illusions, but accept the truth. ⁵Deny you are a shadow briefly laid upon a dying world. ⁶Release your mind, and you will look upon a world released.

14. Today our purpose is to free the world from all the idle thoughts we ever held about it, and about all living things we see upon it. ²They can not be there. ³No more can we. ⁴For we are in the home our Father set for us, along with them. ⁵And we who are as He created us would loose the world this day from every one of our illusions, that we may be free.

15. Begin the fifteen-minute periods in which we practice twice today with this:

> ²I who remain as God created me would loose the world from all I thought it was. ³For I am real because the world is not, and I would know my own reality.

⁴Then merely rest, alert but with no strain, and let your mind in quietness be changed so that the world is freed, along with you.

16. You need not realize that healing comes to many brothers far across the world, as well as to the ones you see nearby, as you send out these thoughts to bless the world. ²But you will sense your own release, although you may not fully understand as yet that you could never be released alone.

17. Throughout the day, increase the freedom sent through your ideas to all the world, and say whenever you are tempted to deny the power of your simple change of mind:

> ²I loose the world from all I thought it was, and choose my own reality instead.

LESSON 133

I will not value what is valueless.

1. Sometimes in teaching there is benefit, particularly after you have gone through what seems theoretical and far from what the student has already learned, to bring him back to practical concerns. ²This we will do today. ³We will not speak of lofty, world-encompassing ideas, but dwell instead on benefits to you.

2. You do not ask too much of life, but far too little. ²When you let your mind be drawn to bodily concerns, to things you buy, to eminence as valued by the world, you ask for sorrow, not for happiness. ³This course does not attempt to take from you the little that you have. ⁴It does not try to substitute utopian ideas for satisfactions which the world contains. ⁵There are no satisfactions in the world.

3. Today we list the real criteria by which to test all things you think you want. ²Unless they meet these sound requirements, they are not worth desiring at all, for they can but replace what offers more. ³The laws that govern choice you cannot make, no more than you can make alternatives from which to choose. ⁴The choosing you can do; indeed, you must. ⁵But it is wise to learn the laws you set in motion when you choose, and what alternatives you choose between.

4. We have already stressed there are but two, however many there appear to be. ²The range is set, and this we cannot change. ³It would be most ungenerous to you to let alternatives be limitless, and thus delay your final choice until you had considered all of them in time; and not been brought so clearly to the place where there is but one choice that must be made.

5. Another kindly and related law is that there is no compromise in what your choice must bring. ²It cannot give you just a little, for there is no in between. ³Each choice you make brings everything to you or nothing. ⁴Therefore, if you learn the tests by which you can distinguish everything from nothing, you will make the better choice.

6. First, if you choose a thing that will not last forever, what you chose is valueless. ²A temporary value is without all value. ³Time can never take away a value that is real. ⁴What fades and dies was never there, and makes no offering to him who chooses it.

⁵He is deceived by nothing in a form he thinks he likes.

7. Next, if you choose to take a thing away from someone else, you will have nothing left. ²This is because, when you deny his right to everything, you have denied your own. ³You therefore will not recognize the things you really have, denying they are there. ⁴Who seeks to take away has been deceived by the illusion loss can offer gain. ⁵Yet loss must offer loss, and nothing more.

8. Your next consideration is the one on which the others rest. ²Why is the choice you make of value to you? ³What attracts your mind to it? ⁴What purpose does it serve? ⁵Here it is easiest of all to be deceived. ⁶For what the ego wants it fails to recognize. ⁷It does not even tell the truth as it perceives it, for it needs to keep the halo which it uses to protect its goals from tarnish and from rust, that you may see how "innocent" it is.

9. Yet is its camouflage a thin veneer, which could deceive but those who are content to be deceived. ²Its goals are obvious to anyone who cares to look for them. ³Here is deception doubled, for the one who is deceived will not perceive that he has merely failed to gain. ⁴He will believe that he has served the ego's hidden goals.

10. Yet though he tries to keep its halo clear within his vision, still must he perceive its tarnished edges and its rusted core. ²His ineffectual mistakes appear as sins to him, because he looks upon the tarnish as his own; the rust a sign of deep unworthiness within himself. ³He who would still preserve the ego's goals and serve them as his own makes no mistakes, according to the dictates of his guide. ⁴This guidance teaches it is error to believe that sins are but mistakes, for who would suffer for his sins if this were so?

11. And so we come to the criterion for choice that is the hardest to believe, because its obviousness is overlaid with many levels of obscurity. ²If you feel any guilt about your choice, you have allowed the ego's goals to come between the real alternatives. ³And thus you do not realize there are but two, and the alternative you think you chose seems fearful, and too dangerous to be the nothingness it actually is.

12. All things are valuable or valueless, worthy or not of being sought at all, entirely desirable or not worth the slightest effort to obtain. ²Choosing is easy just because of this. ³Complexity is nothing but a screen of smoke, which hides the very simple fact that no decision can be difficult. ⁴What is the gain to you in learn-

ing this? ⁵It is far more than merely letting you make choices easily and without pain.

13. Heaven itself is reached with empty hands and open minds, which come with nothing to find everything and claim it as their own. ²We will attempt to reach this state today, with self-deception laid aside, and with an honest willingness to value but the truly valuable and the real. ³Our two extended practice periods of fifteen minutes each begin with this:

> ⁴*I will not value what is valueless, and only what has value do I seek, for only that do I desire to find.*

14. And then receive what waits for everyone who reaches, unencumbered, to the gate of Heaven, which swings open as he comes. ²Should you begin to let yourself collect some needless burdens, or believe you see some difficult decisions facing you, be quick to answer with this simple thought:

> ³*I will not value what is valueless, for what is valuable belongs to me.*

LESSON 134

Let me perceive forgiveness as it is.

1. Let us review the meaning of "forgive," for it is apt to be distorted and to be perceived as something that entails an unfair sacrifice of righteous wrath, a gift unjustified and undeserved, and a complete denial of the truth. ²In such a view, forgiveness must be seen as mere eccentric folly, and this course appear to rest salvation on a whim.

2. This twisted view of what forgiveness means is easily corrected, when you can accept the fact that pardon is not asked for what is true. ²It must be limited to what is false. ³It is irrelevant to everything except illusions. ⁴Truth is God's creation, and to pardon that is meaningless. ⁵All truth belongs to Him, reflects His laws and radiates His Love. ⁶Does this need pardon? ⁷How can you forgive the sinless and eternally benign?

3. The major difficulty that you find in genuine forgiveness on your part is that you still believe you must forgive the truth, and not illusions. ²You conceive of pardon as a vain attempt to look past what is there; to overlook the truth, in an unfounded effort to deceive yourself by making an illusion true. ³This twisted viewpoint but reflects the hold that the idea of sin retains as yet upon your mind, as you regard yourself.

4. Because you think your sins are real, you look on pardon as deception. ²For it is impossible to think of sin as true and not believe forgiveness is a lie. ³Thus is forgiveness really but a sin, like all the rest. ⁴It says the truth is false, and smiles on the corrupt as if they were as blameless as the grass; as white as snow. ⁵It is delusional in what it thinks it can accomplish. ⁶It would see as right the plainly wrong; the loathsome as the good.

5. Pardon is no escape in such a view. ²It merely is a further sign that sin is unforgivable, at best to be concealed, denied or called another name, for pardon is a treachery to truth. ³Guilt cannot be forgiven. ⁴If you sin, your guilt is everlasting. ⁵Those who are forgiven from the view their sins are real are pitifully mocked and twice condemned; first, by themselves for what they think they did, and once again by those who pardon them.

6. It is sin's unreality that makes forgiveness natural and wholly sane, a deep relief to those who offer it; a quiet blessing where it is received. ²It does not countenance illusions, but collects them lightly, with a little laugh, and gently lays them at the feet of truth. ³And there they disappear entirely.

7. Forgiveness is the only thing that stands for truth in the illusions of the world. ²It sees their nothingness, and looks straight through the thousand forms in which they may appear. ³It looks on lies, but it is not deceived. ⁴It does not heed the self-accusing shrieks of sinners mad with guilt. ⁵It looks on them with quiet eyes, and merely says to them, "My brother, what you think is not the truth."

8. The strength of pardon is its honesty, which is so uncorrupted that it sees illusions as illusions, not as truth. ²It is because of this that it becomes the undeceiver in the face of lies; the great restorer of the simple truth. ³By its ability to overlook what is not there, it opens up the way to truth, which has been blocked by dreams of guilt. ⁴Now are you free to follow in the way your true forgiveness opens up to you. ⁵For if one brother has received this gift of you, the door is open to yourself.

9. There is a very simple way to find the door to true forgiveness, and perceive it open wide in welcome. ²When you feel that you are tempted to accuse someone of sin in any form, do not allow your mind to dwell on what you think he did, for that is self-deception. ³Ask instead, "Would I accuse myself of doing this?"

10. Thus will you see alternatives for choice in terms that render choosing meaningful, and keep your mind as free of guilt and pain as God Himself intended it to be, and as it is in truth. ²It is but lies that would condemn. ³In truth is innocence the only thing there is. ⁴Forgiveness stands between illusions and the truth; between the world you see and that which lies beyond; between the hell of guilt and Heaven's gate.

11. Across this bridge, as powerful as love which laid its blessing on it, are all dreams of evil and of hatred and attack brought silently to truth. ²They are not kept to swell and bluster, and to terrify the foolish dreamer who believes in them. ³He has been gently wakened from his dream by understanding what he thought he saw was never there. ⁴And now he cannot feel that all escape has been denied to him.

12. He does not have to fight to save himself. ²He does not have to kill the dragons which he thought pursued him. ³Nor need he erect the heavy walls of stone and iron doors he thought would make him safe. ⁴He can remove the ponderous and useless armor made to chain his mind to fear and misery. ⁵His step is light, and as he lifts his foot to stride ahead a star is left behind, to point the way to those who follow him.

13. Forgiveness must be practiced, for the world cannot perceive its meaning, nor provide a guide to teach you its beneficence. ²There is no thought in all the world that leads to any understanding of the laws it follows, nor the Thought that it reflects. ³It is as alien to the world as is your own reality. ⁴And yet it joins your mind with the reality in you.

14. Today we practice true forgiveness, that the time of joining be no more delayed. ²For we would meet with our reality in freedom and in peace. ³Our practicing becomes the footsteps lighting up the way for all our brothers, who will follow us to the reality we share with them. ⁴That this may be accomplished, let us give a quarter of an hour twice today, and spend it with the Guide Who understands the meaning of forgiveness, and was sent to us to teach it. ⁵Let us ask of Him:

⁶*Let me perceive forgiveness as it is.*

15. Then choose one brother as He will direct, and catalogue his "sins," as one by one they cross your mind. ²Be certain not to dwell on any one of them, but realize that you are using his "offenses" but to save the world from all ideas of sin. ³Briefly consider all the evil things you thought of him, and each time ask yourself, "Would I condemn myself for doing this?"

16. Let him be freed from all the thoughts you had of sin in him. ²And now you are prepared for freedom. ³If you have been practicing thus far in willingness and honesty, you will begin to sense a lifting up, a lightening of weight across your chest, a deep and certain feeling of relief. ⁴The time remaining should be given to experiencing the escape from all the heavy chains you sought to lay upon your brother, but were laid upon yourself.

17. Forgiveness should be practiced through the day, for there will still be many times when you forget its meaning and attack yourself. ²When this occurs, allow your mind to see through this illusion as you tell yourself:

³*Let me perceive forgiveness as it is.* ⁴*Would I accuse myself of doing this?* ⁵*I will not lay this chain upon myself.*

⁶In everything you do remember this:

⁷*No one is crucified alone, and yet no one can enter Heaven by himself.*

LESSON 135

If I defend myself I am attacked.

1. Who would defend himself unless he thought he were attacked, that the attack were real, and that his own defense could save himself? [2]And herein lies the folly of defense; it gives illusions full reality, and then attempts to handle them as real. [3]It adds illusions to illusions, thus making correction doubly difficult. [4]And it is this you do when you attempt to plan the future, activate the past, or organize the present as you wish.

2. You operate from the belief you must protect yourself from what is happening because it must contain what threatens you. [2]A sense of threat is an acknowledgment of an inherent weakness; a belief that there is danger which has power to call on you to make appropriate defense. [3]The world is based on this insane belief. [4]And all its structures, all its thoughts and doubts, its penalties and heavy armaments, its legal definitions and its codes, its ethics and its leaders and its gods, all serve but to preserve its sense of threat. [5]For no one walks the world in armature but must have terror striking at his heart.

3. Defense is frightening. [2]It stems from fear, increasing fear as each defense is made. [3]You think it offers safety. [4]Yet it speaks of fear made real and terror justified. [5]Is it not strange you do not pause to ask, as you elaborate your plans and make your armor thicker and your locks more tight, what you defend, and how, and against what?

4. Let us consider first what you defend. [2]It must be something that is very weak and easily assaulted. [3]It must be something made easy prey, unable to protect itself and needing your defense. [4]What but the body has such frailty that constant care and watchful, deep concern are needful to protect its little life? [5]What but the body falters and must fail to serve the Son of God as worthy host?

5. Yet it is not the body that can fear, nor be a thing of fear. [2]It has no needs but those which you assign to it. [3]It needs no complicated structures of defense, no health-inducing medicine, no care and no concern at all. [4]Defend its life, or give it gifts to make it beautiful or walls to make it safe, and you but say your home is open to the thief of time, corruptible and crumbling, so unsafe it

must be guarded with your very life.

6. Is not this picture fearful? ²Can you be at peace with such a concept of your home? ³Yet what endowed the body with the right to serve you thus except your own belief? ⁴It is your mind which gave the body all the functions that you see in it, and set its value far beyond a little pile of dust and water. ⁵Who would make defense of something that he recognized as this?

7. The body is in need of no defense. ²This cannot be too often emphasized. ³It will be strong and healthy if the mind does not abuse it by assigning it to roles it cannot fill, to purposes beyond its scope, and to exalted aims which it cannot accomplish. ⁴Such attempts, ridiculous yet deeply cherished, are the sources for the many mad attacks you make upon it. ⁵For it seems to fail your hopes, your needs, your values and your dreams.

8. The "self" that needs protection is not real. ²The body, value-less and hardly worth the least defense, need merely be perceived as quite apart from you, and it becomes a healthy, serviceable instrument through which the mind can operate until its usefulness is over. ³Who would want to keep it when its usefulness is done?

9. Defend the body and you have attacked your mind. ²For you have seen in it the faults, the weaknesses, the limits and the lacks from which you think the body must be saved. ³You will not see the mind as separate from bodily conditions. ⁴And you will impose upon the body all the pain that comes from the conception of the mind as limited and fragile, and apart from other minds and separate from its Source.

10. These are the thoughts in need of healing, and the body will respond with health when they have been corrected and replaced with truth. ²This is the body's only real defense. ³Yet is this where you look for its defense? ⁴You offer it protection of a kind from which it gains no benefit at all, but merely adds to your distress of mind. ⁵You do not heal, but merely take away the hope of healing, for you fail to see where hope must lie if it be meaningful.

11. A healed mind does not plan. ²It carries out the plans that it receives through listening to wisdom that is not its own. ³It waits until it has been taught what should be done, and then proceeds to do it. ⁴It does not depend upon itself for anything except its adequacy to fulfill the plans assigned to it. ⁵It is secure in certainty that obstacles can not impede its progress to accomplishment of

any goal that serves the greater plan established for the good of everyone.

12. A healed mind is relieved of the belief that it must plan, although it cannot know the outcome which is best, the means by which it is achieved, nor how to recognize the problem that the plan is made to solve. [2]It must misuse the body in its plans until it recognizes this is so. [3]But when it has accepted this as true, then is it healed, and lets the body go.

13. Enslavement of the body to the plans the unhealed mind sets up to save itself must make the body sick. [2]It is not free to be the means of helping in a plan which far exceeds its own protection, and which needs its service for a little while. [3]In this capacity is health assured. [4]For everything the mind employs for this will function flawlessly, and with the strength that has been given it and cannot fail.

14. It is, perhaps, not easy to perceive that self-initiated plans are but defenses, with the purpose all of them were made to realize. [2]They are the means by which a frightened mind would undertake its own protection, at the cost of truth. [3]This is not difficult to realize in some forms which these self-deceptions take, where the denial of reality is very obvious. [4]Yet planning is not often recognized as a defense.

15. The mind engaged in planning for itself is occupied in setting up control of future happenings. [2]It does not think that it will be provided for, unless it makes its own provisions. [3]Time becomes a future emphasis, to be controlled by learning and experience obtained from past events and previous beliefs. [4]It overlooks the present, for it rests on the idea the past has taught enough to let the mind direct its future course.

16. The mind that plans is thus refusing to allow for change. [2]What it has learned before becomes the basis for its future goals. [3]Its past experience directs its choice of what will happen. [4]And it does not see that here and now is everything it needs to guarantee a future quite unlike the past, without a continuity of any old ideas and sick beliefs. [5]Anticipation plays no part at all, for present confidence directs the way.

17. Defenses are the plans you undertake to make against the truth. [2]Their aim is to select what you approve, and disregard what you consider incompatible with your beliefs of your reality. [3]Yet what remains is meaningless indeed. [4]For it is your reality that is the "threat" which your defenses would attack, obscure,

and take apart and crucify.

18. What could you not accept, if you but knew that everything that happens, all events, past, present and to come, are gently planned by One Whose only purpose is your good? ²Perhaps you have misunderstood His plan, for He would never offer pain to you. ³But your defenses did not let you see His loving blessing shine in every step you ever took. ⁴While you made plans for death, He led you gently to eternal life.

19. Your present trust in Him is the defense that promises a future undisturbed, without a trace of sorrow, and with joy that constantly increases, as this life becomes a holy instant, set in time, but heeding only immortality. ²Let no defenses but your present trust direct the future, and this life becomes a meaningful encounter with the truth that only your defenses would conceal.

20. Without defenses, you become a light which Heaven gratefully acknowledges to be its own. ²And it will lead you on in ways appointed for your happiness according to the ancient plan, begun when time was born. ³Your followers will join their light with yours, and it will be increased until the world is lighted up with joy. ⁴And gladly will our brothers lay aside their cumbersome defenses, which availed them nothing and could only terrify.

21. We will anticipate that time today with present confidence, for this is part of what was planned for us. ²We will be sure that everything we need is given us for our accomplishment of this today. ³We make no plans for how it will be done, but realize that our defenselessness is all that is required for the truth to dawn upon our minds with certainty.

22. For fifteen minutes twice today we rest from senseless planning, and from every thought that blocks the truth from entering our minds. ²Today we will receive instead of plan, that we may give instead of organize. ³And we are given truly, as we say:

> ⁴*If I defend myself I am attacked.* ⁵*But in defenselessness I will be strong, and I will learn what my defenses hide.*

23. Nothing but that. ²If there are plans to make, you will be told of them. ³They may not be the plans you thought were needed, nor indeed the answers to the problems which you thought confronted you. ⁴But they are answers to another kind of question, which remains unanswered yet in need of answering until the

Answer comes to you at last.

24. All your defenses have been aimed at not receiving what you will receive today. [2]And in the light and joy of simple trust, you will but wonder why you ever thought that you must be defended from release. [3]Heaven asks nothing. [4]It is hell that makes extravagant demands for sacrifice. [5]You give up nothing in these times today when, undefended, you present yourself to your Creator as you really are.

25. He has remembered you. [2]Today we will remember Him. [3]For this is Eastertime in your salvation. [4]And you rise again from what was seeming death and hopelessness. [5]Now is the light of hope reborn in you, for now you come without defense, to learn the part for you within the plan of God. [6]What little plans or magical beliefs can still have value, when you have received your function from the Voice for God Himself?

26. Try not to shape this day as you believe would benefit you most. [2]For you can not conceive of all the happiness that comes to you without your planning. [3]Learn today. [4]And all the world will take this giant stride, and celebrate your Eastertime with you. [5]Throughout the day, as foolish little things appear to raise defensiveness in you and tempt you to engage in weaving plans, remind yourself this is a special day for learning, and acknowledge it with this:

> [6]*This is my Easthertime. [7]And I would keep it holy. [8]I will not defend myself, because the Son of God needs no defense against the truth of his reality.*

LESSON 136

Sickness is a defense against the truth.

1. No one can heal unless he understands what purpose sickness seems to serve. [2]For then he understands as well its purpose has no meaning. [3]Being causeless and without a meaningful intent of any kind, it cannot be at all. [4]When this is seen, healing is automatic. [5]It dispels this meaningless illusion by the same approach that carries all of them to truth, and merely leaves them there to disappear.

2. Sickness is not an accident. [2]Like all defenses, it is an insane device for self-deception. [3]And like all the rest, its purpose is to hide reality, attack it, change it, render it inept, distort it, twist it, or reduce it to a little pile of unassembled parts. [4]The aim of all defenses is to keep the truth from being whole. [5]The parts are seen as if each one were whole within itself.

3. Defenses are not unintentional, nor are they made without awareness. [2]They are secret, magic wands you wave when truth appears to threaten what you would believe. [3]They seem to be unconscious but because of the rapidity with which you choose to use them. [4]In that second, even less, in which the choice is made, you recognize exactly what you would attempt to do, and then proceed to think that it is done.

4. Who but yourself evaluates a threat, decides escape is necessary, and sets up a series of defenses to reduce the threat that has been judged as real? [2]All this cannot be done unconsciously. [3]But afterwards, your plan requires that you must forget you made it, so it seems to be external to your own intent; a happening beyond your state of mind, an outcome with a real effect on you, instead of one effected by yourself.

5. It is this quick forgetting of the part you play in making your "reality" that makes defenses seem to be beyond your own control. [2]But what you have forgot can be remembered, given willingness to reconsider the decision which is doubly shielded by oblivion. [3]Your not remembering is but the sign that this decision still remains in force, as far as your desires are concerned. [4]Mistake not this for fact. [5]Defenses must make facts unrecognizable. [6]They aim at doing this, and it is this they do.

6. Every defense takes fragments of the whole, assembles them

without regard to all their true relationships, and thus constructs illusions of a whole that is not there. [2]It is this process that imposes threat, and not whatever outcome may result. [3]When parts are wrested from the whole and seen as separate and wholes within themselves, they become symbols standing for attack upon the whole; successful in effect, and never to be seen as whole again. [4]And yet you have forgotten that they stand but for your own decision of what should be real, to take the place of what is real.

7. Sickness is a decision. [2]It is not a thing that happens to you, quite unsought, which makes you weak and brings you suffering. [3]It is a choice you make, a plan you lay, when for an instant truth arises in your own deluded mind, and all your world appears to totter and prepare to fall. [4]Now are you sick, that truth may go away and threaten your establishments no more.

8. How do you think that sickness can succeed in shielding you from truth? [2]Because it proves the body is not separate from you, and so you must be separate from the truth. [3]You suffer pain because the body does, and in this pain are you made one with it. [4]Thus is your "true" identity preserved, and the strange, haunting thought that you might be something beyond this little pile of dust silenced and stilled. [5]For see, this dust can make you suffer, twist your limbs and stop your heart, commanding you to die and cease to be.

9. Thus is the body stronger than the truth, which asks you live, but cannot overcome your choice to die. [2]And so the body is more powerful than everlasting life, Heaven more frail than hell, and God's design for the salvation of His Son opposed by a decision stronger than His Will. [3]His Son is dust, the Father incomplete, and chaos sits in triumph on His throne.

10. Such is your planning for your own defense. [2]And you believe that Heaven quails before such mad attacks as these, with God made blind by your illusions, truth turned into lies, and all the universe made slave to laws which your defenses would impose on it. [3]Yet who believes illusions but the one who made them up? [4]Who else can see them and react to them as if they were the truth?

11. God knows not of your plans to change His Will. [2]The universe remains unheeding of the laws by which you thought to govern it. [3]And Heaven has not bowed to hell, nor life to death. [4]You can but choose to think you die, or suffer sickness or distort the truth

in any way. [5]What is created is apart from all of this. [6]Defenses are plans to defeat what cannot be attacked. [7]What is unalterable cannot change. [8]And what is wholly sinless cannot sin.

12. Such is the simple truth. [2]It does not make appeal to might nor triumph. [3]It does not command obedience, nor seek to prove how pitiful and futile your attempts to plan defenses that would alter it. [4]Truth merely wants to give you happiness, for such its purpose is. [5]Perhaps it sighs a little when you throw away its gifts, and yet it knows, with perfect certainty, that what God wills for you must be received.

13. It is this fact that demonstrates that time is an illusion. [2]For time lets you think what God has given you is not the truth right now, as it must be. [3]The Thoughts of God are quite apart from time. [4]For time is but another meaningless defense you made against the truth. [5]Yet what He wills is here, and you remain as He created you.

14. Truth has a power far beyond defense, for no illusions can remain where truth has been allowed to enter. [2]And it comes to any mind that would lay down its arms, and cease to play with folly. [3]It is found at any time; today, if you will choose to practice giving welcome to the truth.

15. This is our aim today. [2]And we will give a quarter of an hour twice to ask the truth to come to us and set us free. [3]And truth will come, for it has never been apart from us. [4]It merely waits for just this invitation which we give today. [5]We introduce it with a healing prayer, to help us rise above defensiveness, and let truth be as it has always been:

> [6]*Sickness is a defense against the truth.* [7]*I will accept the truth of what I am, and let my mind be wholly healed today.*

16. Healing will flash across your open mind, as peace and truth arise to take the place of war and vain imaginings. [2]There will be no dark corners sickness can conceal, and keep defended from the light of truth. [3]There will be no dim figures from your dreams, nor their obscure and meaningless pursuits with double purposes insanely sought, remaining in your mind. [4]It will be healed of all the sickly wishes that it tried to authorize the body to obey.

17. Now is the body healed, because the source of sickness has been opened to relief. [2]And you will recognize you practiced well

by this: The body should not feel at all. ³If you have been success-ful, there will be no sense of feeling ill or feeling well, of pain or pleasure. ⁴No response at all is in the mind to what the body does. ⁵Its usefulness remains and nothing more.

18. Perhaps you do not realize that this removes the limits you had placed upon the body by the purposes you gave to it. ²As these are laid aside, the strength the body has will always be enough to serve all truly useful purposes. ³The body's health is fully guar-anteed, because it is not limited by time, by weather or fatigue, by food and drink, or any laws you made it serve before. ⁴You need do nothing now to make it well, for sickness has become impossible.

19. Yet this protection needs to be preserved by careful watching. ²If you let your mind harbor attack thoughts, yield to judgment or make plans against uncertainties to come, you have again mis-placed yourself, and made a bodily identity which will attack the body, for the mind is sick.

20. Give instant remedy, should this occur, by not allowing your defensiveness to hurt you longer. ²Do not be confused about what must be healed, but tell yourself:

> ³I have forgotten what I really am, for I mistook my body for
> myself. ⁴Sickness is a defense against the truth. ⁵But I am not
> a body. ⁶And my mind cannot attack. ⁷So I can not be sick.

LESSON 137

When I am healed I am not healed alone.

1. Today's idea remains the central thought on which salvation rests. [2]For healing is the opposite of all the world's ideas which dwell on sickness and on separate states. [3]Sickness is a retreat from others, and a shutting off of joining. [4]It becomes a door that closes on a separate self, and keeps it isolated and alone.

2. Sickness is isolation. [2]For it seems to keep one self apart from all the rest, to suffer what the others do not feel. [3]It gives the body final power to make the separation real, and keep the mind in solitary prison, split apart and held in pieces by a solid wall of sickened flesh, which it can not surmount.

3. The world obeys the laws that sickness serves, but healing operates apart from them. [2]It is impossible that anyone be healed alone. [3]In sickness must he be apart and separate. [4]But healing is his own decision to be one again, and to accept his Self with all Its parts intact and unassailed. [5]In sickness does his Self appear to be dismembered, and without the unity that gives It life. [6]But healing is accomplished as he sees the body has no power to attack the universal Oneness of God's Son.

4. Sickness would prove that lies must be the truth. [2]But healing demonstrates that truth is true. [3]The separation sickness would impose has never really happened. [4]To be healed is merely to accept what always was the simple truth, and always will remain exactly as it has forever been. [5]Yet eyes accustomed to illusions must be shown that what they look upon is false. [6]So healing, never needed by the truth, must demonstrate that sickness is not real.

5. Healing might thus be called a counter-dream, which cancels out the dream of sickness in the name of truth, but not in truth itself. [2]Just as forgiveness overlooks all sins that never were accomplished, healing but removes illusions that have not occurred. [3]Just as the real world will arise to take the place of what has never been at all, healing but offers restitution for imagined states and false ideas which dreams embroider into pictures of the truth.

6. Yet think not healing is unworthy of your function here. [2]For anti-Christ becomes more powerful than Christ to those who

dream the world is real. ³The body seems to be more solid and more stable than the mind. ⁴And love becomes a dream, while fear remains the one reality that can be seen and justified and fully understood.

7. Just as forgiveness shines away all sin and the real world will occupy the place of what you made, so healing must replace the fantasies of sickness which you hold before the simple truth. ²When sickness has been seen to disappear in spite of all the laws that hold it cannot but be real, then questions have been answered. ³And the laws can be no longer cherished nor obeyed.

8. Healing is freedom. ²For it demonstrates that dreams will not prevail against the truth. ³Healing is shared. ⁴And by this attribute it proves that laws unlike the ones which hold that sickness is inevitable are more potent than their sickly opposites. ⁵Healing is strength. ⁶For by its gentle hand is weakness overcome, and minds that were walled off within a body free to join with other minds, to be forever strong.

9. Healing, forgiveness, and the glad exchange of all the world of sorrow for a world where sadness cannot enter, are the means by which the Holy Spirit urges you to follow Him. ²His gentle lessons teach how easily salvation can be yours; how little practice you need undertake to let His laws replace the ones you made to hold yourself a prisoner to death. ³His life becomes your own, as you extend the little help He asks in freeing you from everything that ever caused you pain.

10. And as you let yourself be healed, you see all those around you, or who cross your mind, or whom you touch or those who seem to have no contact with you, healed along with you. ²Perhaps you will not recognize them all, nor realize how great your offering to all the world, when you let healing come to you. ³But you are never healed alone. ⁴And legions upon legions will receive the gift that you receive when you are healed.

11. Those who are healed become the instruments of healing. ²Nor does time elapse between the instant they are healed, and all the grace of healing it is given them to give. ³What is opposed to God does not exist, and who accepts it not within his mind becomes a haven where the weary can remain to rest. ⁴For here is truth bestowed, and here are all illusions brought to truth.

12. Would you not offer shelter to God's Will? ²You but invite your Self to be at home. ³And can this invitation be refused? ⁴Ask the inevitable to occur, and you will never fail. ⁵The other choice is

but to ask what cannot be to be, and this can not succeed. [6]Today we ask that only truth will occupy our minds; that thoughts of healing will this day go forth from what is healed to what must yet be healed, aware that they will both occur as one.

13.   We will remember, as the hour strikes, our function is to let our minds be healed, that we may carry healing to the world, exchanging curse for blessing, pain for joy, and separation for the peace of God. [2]Is not a minute of the hour worth the giving to receive a gift like this? [3]Is not a little time a small expense to offer for the gift of everything?

14.   Yet must we be prepared for such a gift. [2]And so we will begin the day with this, and give ten minutes to these thoughts with which we will conclude today at night as well:

> [3]*When I am healed I am not healed alone.* [4]*And I would share my healing with the world, that sickness may be banished from the mind of God's one Son, Who is my only Self.*

15.   Let healing be through you this very day. [2]And as you rest in quiet, be prepared to give as you receive, to hold but what you give, and to receive the Word of God to take the place of all the foolish thoughts that ever were imagined. [3]Now we come together to make well all that was sick, and offer blessing where there was attack. [4]Nor will we let this function be forgot as every hour of the day slips by, remembering our purpose with this thought:

> [5]*When I am healed I am not healed alone.* [6]*And I would bless my brothers, for I would be healed with them, as they are healed with me.*

LESSON 138

Heaven is the decision I must make.

1. In this world Heaven is a choice, because here we believe there are alternatives to choose between. [2]We think that all things have an opposite, and what we want we choose. [3]If Heaven exists there must be hell as well, for contradiction is the way we make what we perceive, and what we think is real.

2. Creation knows no opposite. [2]But here is opposition part of being "real." [3]It is this strange perception of the truth that makes the choice of Heaven seem to be the same as the relinquishment of hell. [4]It is not really thus. [5]Yet what is true in God's creation cannot enter here until it is reflected in some form the world can understand. [6]Truth cannot come where it could only be perceived with fear. [7]For this would be the error truth can be brought to illusions. [8]Opposition makes the truth unwelcome, and it cannot come.

3. Choice is the obvious escape from what appears as opposites. [2]Decision lets one of conflicting goals become the aim of effort and expenditure of time. [3]Without decision, time is but a waste and effort dissipated. [4]It is spent for nothing in return, and time goes by without results. [5]There is no sense of gain, for nothing is accomplished; nothing learned.

4. You need to be reminded that you think a thousand choices are confronting you, when there is really only one to make. [2]And even this but seems to be a choice. [3]Do not confuse yourself with all the doubts that myriad decisions would induce. [4]You make but one. [5]And when that one is made, you will perceive it was no choice at all. [6]For truth is true, and nothing else is true. [7]There is no opposite to choose instead. [8]There is no contradiction to the truth.

5. Choosing depends on learning. [2]And the truth cannot be learned, but only recognized. [3]In recognition its acceptance lies, and as it is accepted it is known. [4]But knowledge is beyond the goals we seek to teach within the framework of this course. [5]Ours are teaching goals, to be attained through learning how to reach them, what they are, and what they offer you. [6]Decisions are the outcome of your learning, for they rest on what you have accepted as the truth of what you are, and what your needs must be.

6. In this insanely complicated world, Heaven appears to take the form of choice, rather than merely being what it is. [2]Of all the choices you have tried to make this is the simplest, most definitive and prototype of all the rest, the one which settles all decisions. [3]If you could decide the rest, this one remains unsolved. [4]But when you solve this one, the others are resolved with it, for all decisions but conceal this one by taking different forms. [5]Here is the final and the only choice in which is truth accepted or denied.

7. So we begin today considering the choice that time was made to help us make. [2]Such is its holy purpose, now transformed from the intent you gave it; that it be a means for demonstrating hell is real, hope changes to despair, and life itself must in the end be overcome by death. [3]In death alone are opposites resolved, for ending opposition is to die. [4]And thus salvation must be seen as death, for life is seen as conflict. [5]To resolve the conflict is to end your life as well.

8. These mad beliefs can gain unconscious hold of great intensity, and grip the mind with terror and anxiety so strong that it will not relinquish its ideas about its own protection. [2]It must be saved from salvation, threatened to be safe, and magically armored against truth. [3]And these decisions are made unaware, to keep them safely undisturbed; apart from question and from reason and from doubt.

9. Heaven is chosen consciously. [2]The choice cannot be made until alternatives are accurately seen and understood. [3]All that is veiled in shadows must be raised to understanding, to be judged again, this time with Heaven's help. [4]And all mistakes in judgment that the mind had made before are open to correction, as the truth dismisses them as causeless. [5]Now are they without effects. [6]They cannot be concealed, because their nothingness is recognized.

10. The conscious choice of Heaven is as sure as is the ending of the fear of hell, when it is raised from its protective shield of unawareness, and is brought to light. [2]Who can decide between the clearly seen and the unrecognized? [3]Yet who can fail to make a choice between alternatives when only one is seen as valuable; the other as a wholly worthless thing, a but imagined source of guilt and pain? [4]Who hesitates to make a choice like this? [5]And shall we hesitate to choose today?

11. We make the choice for Heaven as we wake, and spend five minutes making sure that we have made the one decision that is

sane. [2]We recognize we make a conscious choice between what has existence and what has nothing but an appearance of the truth. [3]Its pseudo-being, brought to what is real, is flimsy and transparent in the light. [4]It holds no terror now, for what was made enormous, vengeful, pitiless with hate, demands obscurity for fear to be invested there. [5]Now it is recognized as but a foolish, trivial mistake.

12. Before we close our eyes in sleep tonight, we reaffirm the choice that we have made each hour in between. [2]And now we give the last five minutes of our waking day to the decision with which we awoke. [3]As every hour passed, we have declared our choice again, in a brief quiet time devoted to maintaining sanity. [4]And finally, we close the day with this, acknowledging we chose but what we want:

> [5]*Heaven is the decision I must make.* [6]*I make it now, and will not change my mind, because it is the only thing I want.*

LESSON 139

I will accept Atonement for myself.

1. Here is the end of choice. [2]For here we come to a decision to accept ourselves as God created us. [3]And what is choice except uncertainty of what we are? [4]There is no doubt that is not rooted here. [5]There is no question but reflects this one. [6]There is no conflict that does not entail the single, simple question, "What am I?"

2. Yet who could ask this question except one who has refused to recognize himself? [2]Only refusal to accept yourself could make the question seem to be sincere. [3]The only thing that can be surely known by any living thing is what it is. [4]From this one point of certainty, it looks on other things as certain as itself.

3. Uncertainty about what you must be is self-deception on a scale so vast, its magnitude can hardly be conceived. [2]To be alive and not to know yourself is to believe that you are really dead. [3]For what is life except to be yourself, and what but you can be alive instead? [4]Who is the doubter? [5]What is it he doubts? [6]Whom does he question? [7]Who can answer him?

4. He merely states that he is not himself, and therefore, being something else, becomes a questioner of what that something is. [2]Yet he could never be alive at all unless he knew the answer. [3]If he asks as if he does not know, it merely shows he does not want to be the thing he is. [4]He has accepted it because he lives; has judged against it and denied its worth, and has decided that he does not know the only certainty by which he lives.

5. Thus he becomes uncertain of his life, for what it is has been denied by him. [2]It is for this denial that you need Atonement. [3]Your denial made no change in what you are. [4]But you have split your mind into what knows and does not know the truth. [5]You are yourself. [6]There is no doubt of this. [7]And yet you doubt it. [8]But you do not ask what part of you can really doubt yourself. [9]It cannot really be a part of you that asks this question. [10]For it asks of one who knows the answer. [11]Were it part of you, then certainty would be impossible.

6. Atonement remedies the strange idea that it is possible to doubt yourself, and be unsure of what you really are. [2]This is the depth of madness. [3]Yet it is the universal question of the world. [4]What does this mean except the world is mad? [5]Why share its

madness in the sad belief that what is universal here is true?

7. Nothing the world believes is true. ²It is a place whose purpose is to be a home where those who claim they do not know themselves can come to question what it is they are. ³And they will come again until the time Atonement is accepted, and they learn it is impossible to doubt yourself, and not to be aware of what you are.

8. Only acceptance can be asked of you, for what you are is certain. ²It is set forever in the holy Mind of God, and in your own. ³It is so far beyond all doubt and question that to ask what it must be is all the proof you need to show that you believe the contradiction that you know not what you cannot fail to know. ⁴Is this a question, or a statement which denies itself in statement? ⁵Let us not allow our holy minds to occupy themselves with senseless musings such as this.

9. We have a mission here. ²We did not come to reinforce the madness that we once believed in. ³Let us not forget the goal that we accepted. ⁴It is more than just our happiness alone we came to gain. ⁵What we accept as what we are proclaims what everyone must be, along with us. ⁶Fail not your brothers, or you fail yourself. ⁷Look lovingly on them, that they may know that they are part of you, and you of them.

10. This does Atonement teach, and demonstrates the Oneness of God's Son is unassailed by his belief he knows not what he is. ²Today accept Atonement, not to change reality, but merely to accept the truth about yourself, and go your way rejoicing in the endless Love of God. ³It is but this that we are asked to do. ⁴It is but this that we will do today.

11. Five minutes in the morning and at night we will devote to dedicate our minds to our assignment for today. ²We start with this review of what our mission is:

> ³*I will accept Atonement for myself,*
> *For I remain as God created me.*

⁴We have not lost the knowledge that God gave to us when He created us like Him. ⁵We can remember it for everyone, for in creation are all minds as one. ⁶And in our memory is the recall how dear our brothers are to us in truth, how much a part of us is every mind, how faithful they have really been to us, and how our Father's Love contains them all.

12. In thanks for all creation, in the Name of its Creator and His Oneness with all aspects of creation, we repeat our dedication to our cause today each hour, as we lay aside all thoughts that would distract us from our holy aim. ²For several minutes let your mind be cleared of all the foolish cobwebs which the world would weave around the holy Son of God. ³And learn the fragile nature of the chains that seem to keep the knowledge of yourself apart from your awareness, as you say:

> ⁴*I will accept Atonement for myself,*
> *For I remain as God created me.*

LESSON 140

Only salvation can be said to cure.

1. "Cure" is a word that cannot be applied to any remedy the world accepts as beneficial. ²What the world perceives as therapeutic is but what will make the body "better." ³When it tries to heal the mind, it sees no separation from the body, where it thinks the mind exists. ⁴Its forms of healing thus must substitute illusion for illusion. ⁵One belief in sickness takes another form, and so the patient now perceives himself as well.

2. He is not healed. ²He merely had a dream that he was sick, and in the dream he found a magic formula to make him well. ³Yet he has not awakened from the dream, and so his mind remains exactly as it was before. ⁴He has not seen the light that would awaken him and end the dream. ⁵What difference does the content of a dream make in reality? ⁶One either sleeps or wakens. ⁷There is nothing in between.

3. The happy dreams the Holy Spirit brings are different from the dreaming of the world, where one can merely dream he is awake. ²The dreams forgiveness lets the mind perceive do not induce another form of sleep, so that the dreamer dreams another dream. ³His happy dreams are heralds of the dawn of truth upon the mind. ⁴They lead from sleep to gentle waking, so that dreams are gone. ⁵And thus they cure for all eternity.

4. Atonement heals with certainty, and cures all sickness. ²For the mind which understands that sickness can be nothing but a dream is not deceived by forms the dream may take. ³Sickness where guilt is absent cannot come, for it is but another form of guilt. ⁴Atonement does not heal the sick, for that is not a cure. ⁵It takes away the guilt that makes the sickness possible. ⁶And that is cure indeed. ⁷For sickness now is gone, with nothing left to which it can return.

5. Peace be to you who have been cured in God, and not in idle dreams. ²For cure must come from holiness, and holiness can not be found where sin is cherished. ³God abides in holy temples. ⁴He is barred where sin has entered. ⁵Yet there is no place where He is not. ⁶And therefore sin can have no home in which to hide from His beneficence. ⁷There is no place where holiness is not, and nowhere sin and sickness can abide.

6. This is the thought that cures. ²It does not make distinctions among unrealities. ³Nor does it seek to heal what is not sick, unmindful where the need for healing is. ⁴This is no magic. ⁵It is merely an appeal to truth, which cannot fail to heal and heal forever. ⁶It is not a thought that judges an illusion by its size, its seeming gravity, or anything that is related to the form it takes. ⁷It merely focuses on what it is, and knows that no illusion can be real.

7. Let us not try today to seek to cure what cannot suffer sickness. ²Healing must be sought but where it is, and then applied to what is sick, so that it can be cured. ³There is no remedy the world provides that can effect a change in anything. ⁴The mind that brings illusions to the truth is really changed. ⁵There is no change but this. ⁶For how can one illusion differ from another but in attributes that have no substance, no reality, no core, and nothing that is truly different?

8. Today we seek to change our minds about the source of sickness, for we seek a cure for all illusions, not another shift among them. ²We will try today to find the source of healing, which is in our minds because our Father placed it there for us. ³It is not farther from us than ourselves. ⁴It is as near to us as our own thoughts; so close it is impossible to lose. ⁵We need but seek it and it must be found.

9. We will not be misled today by what appears to us as sick. ²We go beyond appearances today and reach the source of healing, from which nothing is exempt. ³We will succeed to the extent to which we realize that there can never be a meaningful distinction made between what is untrue and equally untrue. ⁴Here there are no degrees, and no beliefs that what does not exist is truer in some forms than others. ⁵All of them are false, and can be cured because they are not true.

10. So do we lay aside our amulets, our charms and medicines, our chants and bits of magic in whatever form they take. ²We will be still and listen for the Voice of healing, which will cure all ills as one, restoring saneness to the Son of God. ³No voice but this can cure. ⁴Today we hear a single Voice which speaks to us of truth, where all illusions end, and peace returns to the eternal, quiet home of God.

11. We waken hearing Him, and let Him speak to us five minutes as the day begins, and end the day by listening again five minutes more before we go to sleep. ²Our only preparation is to let

our interfering thoughts be laid aside, not separately, but all of them as one. ³They are the same. ⁴We have no need to make them different, and thus delay the time when we can hear our Father speak to us. ⁵We hear Him now. ⁶We come to Him today.

12.　With nothing in our hands to which we cling, with lifted hearts and listening minds we pray:

> ²*Only salvation can be said to cure.*
> ³*Speak to us, Father, that we may be healed.*

⁴And we will feel salvation cover us with soft protection, and with peace so deep that no illusion can disturb our minds, nor offer proof to us that it is real. ⁵This will we learn today. ⁶And we will say our prayer for healing hourly, and take a minute as the hour strikes, to hear the answer to our prayer be given us as we attend in silence and in joy. ⁷This is the day when healing comes to us. ⁸This is the day when separation ends, and we remember Who we really are.

REVIEW IV

Introduction

1. Now we review again, this time aware we are preparing for the second part of learning how the truth can be applied. ²Today we will begin to concentrate on readiness for what will follow next. ³Such is our aim for this review, and for the lessons following. ⁴Thus, we review the recent lessons and their central thoughts in such a way as will facilitate the readiness that we would now achieve.

2. There is a central theme that unifies each step in the review we undertake, which can be simply stated in these words:

> ²*My mind holds only what I think with God.*

³That is a fact, and represents the truth of What you are and What your Father is. ⁴It is this thought by which the Father gave creation to the Son, establishing the Son as co-creator with Himself. ⁵It is this thought that fully guarantees salvation to the Son. ⁶For in his mind no thoughts can dwell but those his Father shares. ⁷Lack of forgiveness blocks this thought from his awareness. ⁸Yet it is forever true.

3. Let us begin our preparation with some understanding of the many forms in which the lack of true forgiveness may be carefully concealed. ²Because they are illusions, they are not perceived to be but what they are; defenses that protect your unforgiving thoughts from being seen and recognized. ³Their purpose is to show you something else, and hold correction off through self-deceptions made to take its place.

4. And yet, your mind holds only what you think with God. ²Your self-deceptions cannot take the place of truth. ³No more than can a child who throws a stick into the ocean change the coming and the going of the tides, the warming of the water by the sun, the silver of the moon on it by night. ⁴So do we start each practice period in this review with readying our minds to understand the lessons that we read, and see the meaning that they offer us.

5. Begin each day with time devoted to the preparation of your mind to learn what each idea you will review that day can offer

you in freedom and in peace. ²Open your mind, and clear it of all thoughts that would deceive, and let this thought alone engage it fully, and remove the rest:

³My mind holds only what I think with God.

⁴Five minutes with this thought will be enough to set the day along the lines which God appointed, and to place His Mind in charge of all the thoughts you will receive that day.

6. They will not come from you alone, for they will all be shared with Him. ²And so each one will bring the message of His Love to you, returning messages of yours to Him. ³So will communion with the Lord of Hosts be yours, as He Himself has willed it be. ⁴And as His Own completion joins with Him, so will He join with you who are complete as you unite with Him, and He with you.

7. After your preparation, merely read each of the two ideas assigned to you to be reviewed that day. ²Then close your eyes, and say them slowly to yourself. ³There is no hurry now, for you are using time for its intended purpose. ⁴Let each word shine with the meaning God has given it, as it was given to you through His Voice. ⁵Let each idea which you review that day give you the gift that He has laid in it for you to have of Him. ⁶And we will use no format for our practicing but this:

8. Each hour of the day, bring to your mind the thought with which the day began, and spend a quiet moment with it. ²Then repeat the two ideas you practice for the day unhurriedly, with time enough to see the gifts that they contain for you, and let them be received where they were meant to be.

9. We add no other thoughts, but let these be the messages they are. ²We need no more than this to give us happiness and rest, and endless quiet, perfect certainty, and all our Father wills that we receive as the inheritance we have of Him. ³Each day of practicing, as we review, we close as we began, repeating first the thought that made the day a special time of blessing and of happiness for us; and through our faithfulness restored the world from darkness to the light, from grief to joy, from pain to peace, from sin to holiness.

10. God offers thanks to you who practice thus the keeping of His Word. ²And as you give your mind to the ideas for the day again before you sleep, His gratitude surrounds you in the peace wherein He wills you be forever, and are learning now to claim again as your inheritance.

LESSON 141

My mind holds only what I think with God.

(121) Forgiveness is the key to happiness.
(122) Forgiveness offers everything I want.

LESSON 142

My mind holds only what I think with God.

(123) I thank my Father for His gifts to me.
(124) Let me remember I am one with God.

LESSON 143

My mind holds only what I think with God.

(125) In quiet I receive God's Word today.
(126) All that I give is given to myself.

LESSON 144

My mind holds only what I think with God.

(127) There is no love but God's.
(128) The world I see holds nothing that I want.

LESSON 145

My mind holds only what I think with God.

(129) Beyond this world there is a world I want.
(130) It is impossible to see two worlds.

LESSON 146

My mind holds only what I think with God.

(131) No one can fail who seeks to reach the truth.
(132) I loose the world from all I thought it was.

LESSON 147

My mind holds only what I think with God.

(133) I will not value what is valueless.
(134) Let me perceive forgiveness as it is.

LESSON 148

My mind holds only what I think with God.

(135) If I defend myself I am attacked.
(136) Sickness is a defense against the truth.

LESSON 149

My mind holds only what I think with God.

(137) When I am healed I am not healed alone.
(138) Heaven is the decision I must make.

LESSON 150

My mind holds only what I think with God.

(139) I will accept Atonement for myself.
(140) Only salvation can be said to cure.

LESSON 151

All things are echoes of the Voice for God.

1.   No one can judge on partial evidence. ²That is not judgment. ³It is merely an opinion based on ignorance and doubt. ⁴Its seeming certainty is but a cloak for the uncertainty it would conceal. ⁵It needs irrational defense because it is irrational. ⁶And its defense seems strong, convincing, and without a doubt because of all the doubting underneath.

2.   You do not seem to doubt the world you see. ²You do not really question what is shown you through the body's eyes. ³Nor do you ask why you believe it, even though you learned a long while since your senses do deceive. ⁴That you believe them to the last detail which they report is even stranger, when you pause to recollect how frequently they have been faulty witnesses indeed! ⁵Why would you trust them so implicitly? ⁶Why but because of underlying doubt, which you would hide with show of certainty?

3.   How can you judge? ²Your judgment rests upon the witness that your senses offer you. ³Yet witness never falser was than this. ⁴But how else do you judge the world you see? ⁵You place pathetic faith in what your eyes and ears report. ⁶You think your fingers touch reality, and close upon the truth. ⁷This is awareness that you understand, and think more real than what is witnessed to by the eternal Voice for God Himself.

4.   Can this be judgment? ²You have often been urged to refrain from judging, not because it is a right to be withheld from you. ³You cannot judge. ⁴You merely can believe the ego's judgments, all of which are false. ⁵It guides your senses carefully, to prove how weak you are; how helpless and afraid, how apprehensive of just punishment, how black with sin, how wretched in your guilt.

5.   This thing it speaks of, and would yet defend, it tells you is yourself. ²And you believe that this is so with stubborn certainty. ³Yet underneath remains the hidden doubt that what it shows you as reality with such conviction it does not believe. ⁴It is itself alone that it condemns. ⁵It is within itself it sees the guilt. ⁶It is its own despair it sees in you.

6.   Hear not its voice. ²The witnesses it sends to prove to you its evil is your own are false, and speak with certainty of what they

278

do not know. ³Your faith in them is blind because you would not share the doubts their lord can not completely vanquish. ⁴You believe to doubt his vassals is to doubt yourself.

7.. Yet you must learn to doubt their evidence will clear the way to recognize yourself, and let the Voice for God alone be Judge of what is worthy of your own belief. ²He will not tell you that your brother should be judged by what your eyes behold in him, nor what his body's mouth says to your ears, nor what your fingers' touch reports of him. ³He passes by such idle witnesses, which merely bear false witness to God's Son. ⁴He recognizes only what God loves, and in the holy light of what He sees do all the ego's dreams of what you are vanish before the splendor He beholds.

8. Let Him be Judge of what you are, for He has certainty in which there is no doubt, because it rests on Certainty so great that doubt is meaningless before Its face. ²Christ cannot doubt Himself. ³The Voice for God can only honor Him, rejoicing in His perfect, everlasting sinlessness. ⁴Whom He has judged can only laugh at guilt, unwilling now to play with toys of sin; unheeding of the body's witnesses before the rapture of Christ's holy face.

9. And thus He judges you. ²Accept His Word for what you are, for He bears witness to your beautiful creation, and the Mind Whose Thought created your reality. ³What can the body mean to Him Who knows the glory of the Father and the Son? ⁴What whispers of the ego can He hear? ⁵What could convince Him that your sins are real? ⁶Let Him be Judge as well of everything that seems to happen to you in this world. ⁷His lessons will enable you to bridge the gap between illusions and the truth.

10. He will remove all faith that you have placed in pain, disaster, suffering and loss. ²He gives you vision which can look beyond these grim appearances, and can behold the gentle face of Christ in all of them. ³You will no longer doubt that only good can come to you who are beloved of God, for He will judge all happenings, and teach the single lesson that they all contain.

11. He will select the elements in them which represent the truth, and disregard those aspects which reflect but idle dreams. ²And He will reinterpret all you see, and all occurrences, each circumstance, and every happening that seems to touch on you in any way from His one frame of reference, wholly unified and sure. ³And you will see the love beyond the hate, the constancy in change, the pure in sin, and only Heaven's blessing on the world.

12. Such is your resurrection, for your life is not a part of anything

you see. ²It stands beyond the body and the world, past every witness for unholiness, within the Holy, holy as Itself. ³In everyone and everything His Voice would speak to you of nothing but your Self and your Creator, Who is one with Him. ⁴So will you see the holy face of Christ in everything, and hear in everything no sound except the echo of God's Voice.

13. We practice wordlessly today, except at the beginning of the time we spend with God. ²We introduce these times with but a single, slow repeating of the thought with which the day begins. ³And then we watch our thoughts, appealing silently to Him Who sees the elements of truth in them. ⁴Let Him evaluate each thought that comes to mind, remove the elements of dreams, and give them back again as clean ideas that do not contradict the Will of God.

14. Give Him your thoughts, and He will give them back as miracles which joyously proclaim the wholeness and the happiness God wills His Son, as proof of His eternal Love. ²And as each thought is thus transformed, it takes on healing power from the Mind which saw the truth in it, and failed to be deceived by what was falsely added. ³All the threads of fantasy are gone. ⁴And what remains is unified into a perfect Thought that offers its perfection everywhere.

15. Spend fifteen minutes thus when you awake, and gladly give another fifteen more before you go to sleep. ²Your ministry begins as all your thoughts are purified. ³So are you taught to teach the Son of God the holy lesson of his sanctity. ⁴No one can fail to listen, when you hear the Voice for God give honor to God's Son. ⁵And everyone will share the thoughts with you which He has retranslated in your mind.

16. Such is your Eastertide. ²And so you lay the gift of snow-white lilies on the world, replacing witnesses to sin and death. ³Through your transfiguration is the world redeemed, and joyfully released from guilt. ⁴Now do we lift our resurrected minds in gladness and in gratitude to Him Who has restored our sanity to us.

17. And we will hourly remember Him Who is salvation and deliverance. ²As we give thanks, the world unites with us and happily accepts our holy thoughts, which Heaven has corrected and made pure. ³Now has our ministry begun at last, to carry round the world the joyous news that truth has no illusions, and the peace of God, through us, belongs to everyone.

LESSON 152

The power of decision is my own.

1.   No one can suffer loss unless it be his own decision. ²No one suffers pain except his choice elects this state for him. ³No one can grieve nor fear nor think him sick unless these are the outcomes that he wants. ⁴And no one dies without his own consent. ⁵Nothing occurs but represents your wish, and nothing is omitted that you choose. ⁶Here is your world, complete in all details. ⁷Here is its whole reality for you. ⁸And it is only here salvation is.

2.   You may believe that this position is extreme, and too inclusive to be true. ²Yet can truth have exceptions? ³If you have the gift of everything, can loss be real? ⁴Can pain be part of peace, or grief of joy? ⁵Can fear and sickness enter in a mind where love and perfect holiness abide? ⁶Truth must be all-inclusive, if it be the truth at all. ⁷Accept no opposites and no exceptions, for to do so is to contradict the truth entirely.

3.   Salvation is the recognition that the truth is true, and nothing else is true. ²This you have heard before, but may not yet accept both parts of it. ³Without the first, the second has no meaning. ⁴But without the second, is the first no longer true. ⁵Truth cannot have an opposite. ⁶This can not be too often said and thought about. ⁷For if what is not true is true as well as what is true, then part of truth is false. ⁸And truth has lost its meaning. ⁹Nothing but the truth is true, and what is false is false.

4.   This is the simplest of distinctions, yet the most obscure. ²But not because it is a difficult distinction to perceive. ³It is concealed behind a vast array of choices that do not appear to be entirely your own. ⁴And thus the truth appears to have some aspects that belie consistency, but do not seem to be but contradictions introduced by you.

5.   As God created you, you must remain unchangeable, with transitory states by definition false. ²And that includes all shifts in feeling, alterations in conditions of the body and the mind; in all awareness and in all response. ³This is the all-inclusiveness which sets the truth apart from falsehood, and the false kept separate from the truth, as what it is.

6.   Is it not strange that you believe to think you made the world

you see is arrogance? [2]God made it not. [3]Of this you can be sure. [4]What can He know of the ephemeral, the sinful and the guilty, the afraid, the suffering and lonely, and the mind that lives within a body that must die? [5]You but accuse Him of insanity, to think He made a world where such things seem to have reality. [6]He is not mad. [7]Yet only madness makes a world like this.

7. To think that God made chaos, contradicts His Will, invented opposites to truth, and suffers death to triumph over life; all this is arrogance. [2]Humility would see at once these things are not of Him. [3]And can you see what God created not? [4]To think you can is merely to believe you can perceive what God willed not to be. [5]And what could be more arrogant than this?

8. Let us today be truly humble, and accept what we have made as what it is. [2]The power of decision is our own. [3]Decide but to accept your rightful place as co-creator of the universe, and all you think you made will disappear. [4]What rises to awareness then will be all that there ever was, eternally as it is now. [5]And it will take the place of self-deceptions made but to usurp the altar to the Father and the Son.

9. Today we practice true humility, abandoning the false pretense by which the ego seeks to prove it arrogant. [2]Only the ego can be arrogant. [3]But truth is humble in acknowledging its mightiness, its changelessness and its eternal wholeness, all-encompassing, God's perfect gift to His beloved Son. [4]We lay aside the arrogance which says that we are sinners, guilty and afraid, ashamed of what we are; and lift our hearts in true humility instead to Him Who has created us immaculate, like to Himself in power and in love.

10. The power of decision is our own. [2]And we accept of Him that which we are; and humbly recognize the Son of God. [3]To recognize God's Son implies as well that all self-concepts have been laid aside, and recognized as false. [4]Their arrogance has been perceived. [5]And in humility the radiance of God's Son, his gentleness, his perfect sinlessness, his Father's Love, his right to Heaven and release from hell, are joyously accepted as our own.

11. Now do we join in glad acknowledgment that lies are false, and only truth is true. [2]We think of truth alone as we arise, and spend five minutes practicing its ways, encouraging our frightened minds with this:

³*The power of decision is my own.* ⁴*This day I will accept myself as what my Father's Will created me to be.*

⁵Then will we wait in silence, giving up all self-deceptions, as we humbly ask our Self that He reveal Himself to us. ⁶And He Who never left will come again to our awareness, grateful to restore His home to God, as it was meant to be.

12. In patience wait for Him throughout the day, and hourly invite Him with the words with which the day began, concluding it with this same invitation to your Self. ²God's Voice will answer, for He speaks for you and for your Father. ³He will substitute the peace of God for all your frantic thoughts, the truth of God for self-deceptions, and God's Son for your illusions of yourself.

LESSON 153

In my defenselessness my safety lies.

1. You who feel threatened by this changing world, its twists of fortune and its bitter jests, its brief relationships and all the "gifts" it merely lends to take away again; attend this lesson well. ²The world provides no safety. ³It is rooted in attack, and all its "gifts" of seeming safety are illusory deceptions. ⁴It attacks, and then attacks again. ⁵No peace of mind is possible where danger threatens thus.

2. The world gives rise but to defensiveness. ²For threat brings anger, anger makes attack seem reasonable, honestly provoked, and righteous in the name of self-defense. ³Yet is defensiveness a double threat. ⁴For it attests to weakness, and sets up a system of defense that cannot work. ⁵Now are the weak still further undermined, for there is treachery without and still a greater treachery within. ⁶The mind is now confused, and knows not where to turn to find escape from its imaginings.

3. It is as if a circle held it fast, wherein another circle bound it and another one in that, until escape no longer can be hoped for nor obtained. ²Attack, defense; defense, attack, become the circles of the hours and the days that bind the mind in heavy bands of steel with iron overlaid, returning but to start again. ³There seems to be no break nor ending in the ever-tightening grip of the imprisonment upon the mind.

4. Defenses are the costliest of all the prices which the ego would exact. ²In them lies madness in a form so grim that hope of sanity seems but to be an idle dream, beyond the possible. ³The sense of threat the world encourages is so much deeper, and so far beyond the frenzy and intensity of which you can conceive, that you have no idea of all the devastation it has wrought.

5. You are its slave. ²You know not what you do, in fear of it. ³You do not understand how much you have been made to sacrifice, who feel its iron grip upon your heart. ⁴You do not realize what you have done to sabotage the holy peace of God by your defensiveness. ⁵For you behold the Son of God as but a victim to attack by fantasies, by dreams, and by illusions he has made; yet helpless in their presence, needful only of defense by still more fantasies, and dreams by which illusions of his safety comfort him.

6. Defenselessness is strength. ²It testifies to recognition of the Christ in you. ³Perhaps you will recall the text maintains that choice is always made between Christ's strength and your own weakness, seen apart from Him. ⁴Defenselessness can never be attacked, because it recognizes strength so great attack is folly, or a silly game a tired child might play, when he becomes too sleepy to remember what he wants.

7. Defensiveness is weakness. ²It proclaims you have denied the Christ and come to fear His Father's anger. ³What can save you now from your delusion of an angry god, whose fearful image you believe you see at work in all the evils of the world? ⁴What but illusions could defend you now, when it is but illusions that you fight?

8. We will not play such childish games today. ²For our true purpose is to save the world, and we would not exchange for foolishness the endless joy our function offers us. ³We would not let our happiness slip by because a fragment of a senseless dream happened to cross our minds, and we mistook the figures in it for the Son of God; its tiny instant for eternity.

9. We look past dreams today, and recognize that we need no defense because we are created unassailable, without all thought or wish or dream in which attack has any meaning. ²Now we cannot fear, for we have left all fearful thoughts behind. ³And in defenselessness we stand secure, serenely certain of our safety now, sure of salvation; sure we will fulfill our chosen purpose, as our ministry extends its holy blessing through the world.

10. Be still a moment, and in silence think how holy is your purpose, how secure you rest, untouchable within its light. ²God's ministers have chosen that the truth be with them. ³Who is holier than they? ⁴Who could be surer that his happiness is fully guaranteed? ⁵And who could be more mightily protected? ⁶What defense could possibly be needed by the ones who are among the chosen ones of God, by His election and their own as well?

11. It is the function of God's ministers to help their brothers choose as they have done. ²God has elected all, but few have come to realize His Will is but their own. ³And while you fail to teach what you have learned, salvation waits and darkness holds the world in grim imprisonment. ⁴Nor will you learn that light has come to you, and your escape has been accomplished. ⁵For you will not see the light, until you offer it to all your brothers. ⁶As they take it from your hands, so will you recognize it as your own.

12. Salvation can be thought of as a game that happy children play. ²It was designed by One Who loves His children, and Who would replace their fearful toys with joyous games, which teach them that the game of fear is gone. ³His game instructs in happiness because there is no loser. ⁴Everyone who plays must win, and in his winning is the gain to everyone ensured. ⁵The game of fear is gladly laid aside, when children come to see the benefits salvation brings.

13. You who have played that you are lost to hope, abandoned by your Father, left alone in terror in a fearful world made mad by sin and guilt; be happy now. ²That game is over. ³Now a quiet time has come, in which we put away the toys of guilt, and lock our quaint and childish thoughts of sin forever from the pure and holy minds of Heaven's children and the Son of God.

14. We pause but for a moment more, to play our final, happy game upon this earth. ²And then we go to take our rightful place where truth abides and games are meaningless. ³So is the story ended. ⁴Let this day bring the last chapter closer to the world, that everyone may learn the tale he reads of terrifying destiny, defeat of all his hopes, his pitiful defense against a vengeance he can not escape, is but his own deluded fantasy. ⁵God's ministers have come to waken him from the dark dreams this story has evoked in his confused, bewildered memory of this distorted tale. ⁶God's Son can smile at last, on learning that it is not true.

15. Today we practice in a form we will maintain for quite a while. ²We will begin each day by giving our attention to the daily thought as long as possible. ³Five minutes now becomes the least we give to preparation for a day in which salvation is the only goal we have. ⁴Ten would be better; fifteen better still. ⁵And as distraction ceases to arise to turn us from our purpose, we will find that half an hour is too short a time to spend with God. ⁶Nor will we willingly give less at night, in gratitude and joy.

16. Each hour adds to our increasing peace, as we remember to be faithful to the Will we share with God. ²At times, perhaps, a minute, even less, will be the most that we can offer as the hour strikes. ³Sometimes we will forget. ⁴At other times the business of the world will close on us, and we will be unable to withdraw a little while, and turn our thoughts to God.

17. Yet when we can, we will observe our trust as ministers of God, in hourly remembrance of our mission and His Love. ²And we will quietly sit by and wait on Him and listen to His Voice,

and learn what He would have us do the hour that is yet to come; while thanking Him for all the gifts He gave us in the one gone by.

18. In time, with practice, you will never cease to think of Him, and hear His loving Voice guiding your footsteps into quiet ways, where you will walk in true defenselessness. ²For you will know that Heaven goes with you. ³Nor would you keep your mind away from Him a moment, even though your time is spent in offering salvation to the world. ⁴Think you He will not make this possible, for you who chose to carry out His plan for the salvation of the world and yours?

19. Today our theme is our defenselessness. ²We clothe ourselves in it, as we prepare to meet the day. ³We rise up strong in Christ, and let our weakness disappear, as we remember that His strength abides in us. ⁴We will remind ourselves that He remains beside us through the day, and never leaves our weakness unsupported by His strength. ⁵We call upon His strength each time we feel the threat of our defenses undermine our certainty of purpose. ⁶We will pause a moment, as He tells us, "I am here."

20. Your practicing will now begin to take the earnestness of love, to help you keep your mind from wandering from its intent. ²Be not afraid nor timid. ³There can be no doubt that you will reach your final goal. ⁴The ministers of God can never fail, because the love and strength and peace that shine from them to all their brothers come from Him. ⁵These are His gifts to you. ⁶Defenselessness is all you need to give Him in return. ⁷You lay aside but what was never real, to look on Christ and see His sinlessness.

LESSON 154

I am among the ministers of God.

1. Let us today be neither arrogant nor falsely humble. ²We have gone beyond such foolishness. ³We cannot judge ourselves, nor need we do so. ⁴These are but attempts to hold decision off, and to delay commitment to our function. ⁵It is not our part to judge our worth, nor can we know what role is best for us; what we can do within a larger plan we cannot see in its entirety. ⁶Our part is cast in Heaven, not in hell. ⁷And what we think is weakness can be strength; what we believe to be our strength is often arrogance.

2. Whatever your appointed role may be, it was selected by the Voice for God, Whose function is to speak for you as well. ²Seeing your strengths exactly as they are, and equally aware of where they can be best applied, for what, to whom and when, He chooses and accepts your part for you. ³He does not work without your own consent. ⁴But He is not deceived in what you are, and listens only to His Voice in you.

3. It is through His ability to hear one Voice which is His Own that you become aware at last there is one Voice in you. ²And that one Voice appoints your function, and relays it to you, giving you the strength to understand it, do what it entails, and to succeed in everything you do that is related to it. ³God has joined His Son in this, and thus His Son becomes His messenger of unity with Him.

4. It is this joining, through the Voice for God, of Father and of Son, that sets apart salvation from the world. ²It is this Voice which speaks of laws the world does not obey; which promises salvation from all sin, with guilt abolished in the mind that God created sinless. ³Now this mind becomes aware again of Who created it, and of His lasting union with itself. ⁴So is its Self the one reality in which its will and that of God are joined.

5. A messenger is not the one who writes the message he delivers. ²Nor does he question the right of him who does, nor ask why he has chosen those who will receive the message that he brings. ³It is enough that he accept it, give it to the ones for whom it is intended, and fulfill his role in its delivery. ⁴If he determines what the messages should be, or what their purpose is, or where they should be carried, he is failing to perform his

proper part as bringer of the Word.

6. There is one major difference in the role of Heaven's messengers, which sets them off from those the world appoints. ²The messages that they deliver are intended first for them. ³And it is only as they can accept them for themselves that they become able to bring them further, and to give them everywhere that they were meant to be. ⁴Like earthly messengers, they did not write the messages they bear, but they become their first receivers in the truest sense, receiving to prepare themselves to give.

7. An earthly messenger fulfills his role by giving all his messages away. ²The messengers of God perform their part by their acceptance of His messages as for themselves, and show they understand the messages by giving them away. ³They choose no roles that are not given them by His authority. ⁴And so they gain by every message that they give away.

8. Would you receive the messages of God? ²For thus do you become His messenger. ³You are appointed now. ⁴And yet you wait to give the messages you have received. ⁵And so you do not know that they are yours, and do not recognize them. ⁶No one can receive and understand he has received until he gives. ⁷For in the giving is his own acceptance of what he received.

9. You who are now the messenger of God, receive His messages. ²For that is part of your appointed role. ³God has not failed to offer what you need, nor has it been left unaccepted. ⁴Yet another part of your appointed task is yet to be accomplished. ⁵He Who has received for you the messages of God would have them be received by you as well. ⁶For thus do you identify with Him and claim your own.

10. It is this joining that we undertake to recognize today. ²We will not seek to keep our minds apart from Him Who speaks for us, for it is but our voice we hear as we attend Him. ³He alone can speak to us and for us, joining in one Voice the getting and the giving of God's Word; the giving and receiving of His Will.

11. We practice giving Him what He would have, that we may recognize His gifts to us. ²He needs our voice that He may speak through us. ³He needs our hands to hold His messages, and carry them to those whom He appoints. ⁴He needs our feet to bring us where He wills, that those who wait in misery may be at last delivered. ⁵And He needs our will united with His Own, that we may be the true receivers of the gifts He gives.

12. Let us but learn this lesson for today: We will not recognize

what we receive until we give it. ²You have heard this said a hundred ways, a hundred times, and yet belief is lacking still. ³But this is sure; until belief is given it, you will receive a thousand miracles and then receive a thousand more, but will not know that God Himself has left no gift beyond what you already have; nor has denied the tiniest of blessings to His Son. ⁴What can this mean to you, until you have identified with Him and with His Own?

13. Our lesson for today is stated thus:

> ²I am among the ministers of God, and I am grateful that
> I have the means by which to recognize that I am free.

14. The world recedes as we light up our minds, and realize these holy words are true. ²They are the message sent to us today from our Creator. ³Now we demonstrate how they have changed our minds about ourselves, and what our function is. ⁴For as we prove that we accept no will we do not share, our many gifts from our Creator will spring to our sight and leap into our hands, and we will recognize what we received.

LESSON 155

I will step back and let Him lead the way.

1. There is a way of living in the world that is not here, although it seems to be. ²You do not change appearance, though you smile more frequently. ³Your forehead is serene; your eyes are quiet. ⁴And the ones who walk the world as you do recognize their own. ⁵Yet those who have not yet perceived the way will recognize you also, and believe that you are like them, as you were before.

2. The world is an illusion. ²Those who choose to come to it are seeking for a place where they can be illusions, and avoid their own reality. ³Yet when they find their own reality is even here, then they step back and let it lead the way. ⁴What other choice is really theirs to make? ⁵To let illusions walk ahead of truth is madness. ⁶But to let illusion sink behind the truth and let the truth stand forth as what it is, is merely sanity.

3. This is the simple choice we make today. ²The mad illusion will remain awhile in evidence, for those to look upon who chose to come, and have not yet rejoiced to find they were mistaken in their choice. ³They cannot learn directly from the truth, because they have denied that it is so. ⁴And so they need a Teacher Who perceives their madness, but Who still can look beyond illusion to the simple truth in them.

4. If truth demanded they give up the world, it would appear to them as if it asked the sacrifice of something that is real. ²Many have chosen to renounce the world while still believing its reality. ³And they have suffered from a sense of loss, and have not been released accordingly. ⁴Others have chosen nothing but the world, and they have suffered from a sense of loss still deeper, which they did not understand.

5. Between these paths there is another road that leads away from loss of every kind, for sacrifice and deprivation both are quickly left behind. ²This is the way appointed for you now. ³You walk this path as others walk, nor do you seem to be distinct from them, although you are indeed. ⁴Thus can you serve them while you serve yourself, and set their footsteps on the way that God has opened up to you, and them through you.

6. Illusion still appears to cling to you, that you may reach them.

²Yet it has stepped back. ³And it is not illusion that they hear you speak of, nor illusion that you bring their eyes to look on and their minds to grasp. ⁴Nor can the truth, which walks ahead of you, speak to them through illusions, for the road leads past illusion now, while on the way you call to them, that they may follow you.

7. All roads will lead to this one in the end. ²For sacrifice and deprivation are paths that lead nowhere, choices for defeat, and aims that will remain impossible. ³All this steps back as truth comes forth in you, to lead your brothers from the ways of death, and set them on the way to happiness. ⁴Their suffering is but illusion. ⁵Yet they need a guide to lead them out of it, for they mistake illusion for the truth.

8. Such is salvation's call, and nothing more. ²It asks that you accept the truth, and let it go before you, lighting up the path of ransom from illusion. ³It is not a ransom with a price. ⁴There is no cost, but only gain. ⁵Illusion can but seem to hold in chains the holy Son of God. ⁶It is but from illusions he is saved. ⁷As they step back, he finds himself again.

9. Walk safely now, yet carefully, because this path is new to you. ²And you may find that you are tempted still to walk ahead of truth, and let illusions be your guide. ³Your holy brothers have been given you, to follow in your footsteps as you walk with certainty of purpose to the truth. ⁴It goes before you now, that they may see something with which they can identify; something they understand to lead the way.

10. Yet at the journey's ending there will be no gap, no distance between truth and you. ²And all illusions walking in the way you travelled will be gone from you as well, with nothing left to keep the truth apart from God's completion, holy as Himself. ³Step back in faith and let truth lead the way. ⁴You know not where you go. ⁵But One Who knows goes with you. ⁶Let Him lead you with the rest.

11. When dreams are over, time has closed the door on all the things that pass and miracles are purposeless, the holy Son of God will make no journeys. ²There will be no wish to be illusion rather than the truth. ³And we step forth toward this, as we progress along the way that truth points out to us. ⁴This is our final journey, which we make for everyone. ⁵We must not lose our way. ⁶For as truth goes before us, so it goes before our brothers who will follow us.

12.   We walk to God. ²Pause and reflect on this. ³Could any way be holier, or more deserving of your effort, of your love and of your full intent? ⁴What way could give you more than everything, or offer less and still content the holy Son of God? ⁵We walk to God. ⁶The truth that walks before us now is one with Him, and leads us to where He has always been. ⁷What way but this could be a path that you would choose instead?

13.   Your feet are safely set upon the road that leads the world to God. ²Look not to ways that seem to lead you elsewhere. ³Dreams are not a worthy guide for you who are God's Son. ⁴Forget not He has placed His Hand in yours, and given you your brothers in His trust that you are worthy of His trust in you. ⁵He cannot be deceived. ⁶His trust has made your pathway certain and your goal secure. ⁷You will not fail your brothers nor your Self.

14.   And now He asks but that you think of Him a while each day, that He may speak to you and tell you of His Love, reminding you how great His trust; how limitless His Love. ²In your Name and His Own, which are the same, we practice gladly with this thought today:

> ³I will step back and let Him lead the way,
> For I would walk along the road to Him.

LESSON 156

I walk with God in perfect holiness.

1. Today's idea but states the simple truth that makes the thought of sin impossible. ²It promises there is no cause for guilt, and being causeless it does not exist. ³It follows surely from the basic thought so often mentioned in the text; ideas leave not their source. ⁴If this be true, how can you be apart from God? ⁵How could you walk the world alone and separate from your Source?

2. We are not inconsistent in the thoughts that we present in our curriculum. ²Truth must be true throughout, if it be true. ³It cannot contradict itself, nor be in parts uncertain and in others sure. ⁴You cannot walk the world apart from God, because you could not be without Him. ⁵He is what your life is. ⁶Where you are He is. ⁷There is one life. ⁸That life you share with Him. ⁹Nothing can be apart from Him and live.

3. Yet where He is, there must be holiness as well as life. ²No attribute of His remains unshared by everything that lives. ³What lives is holy as Himself, because what shares His life is part of Holiness, and could no more be sinful than the sun could choose to be of ice; the sea elect to be apart from water, or the grass to grow with roots suspended in the air.

4. There is a light in you which cannot die; whose presence is so holy that the world is sanctified because of you. ²All things that live bring gifts to you, and offer them in gratitude and gladness at your feet. ³The scent of flowers is their gift to you. ⁴The waves bow down before you, and the trees extend their arms to shield you from the heat, and lay their leaves before you on the ground that you may walk in softness, while the wind sinks to a whisper round your holy head.

5. The light in you is what the universe longs to behold. ²All living things are still before you, for they recognize Who walks with you. ³The light you carry is their own. ⁴And thus they see in you their holiness, saluting you as savior and as God. ⁵Accept their reverence, for it is due to Holiness Itself, which walks with you, transforming in Its gentle light all things unto Its likeness and Its purity.

6. This is the way salvation works. ²As you step back, the light in you steps forward and encompasses the world. ³It heralds not the

end of sin in punishment and death. ⁴In lightness and in laughter is sin gone, because its quaint absurdity is seen. ⁵It is a foolish thought, a silly dream, not frightening, ridiculous perhaps, but who would waste an instant in approach to God Himself for such a senseless whim?

7. Yet you have wasted many, many years on just this foolish thought. ²The past is gone, with all its fantasies. ³They keep you bound no longer. ⁴The approach to God is near. ⁵And in the little interval of doubt that still remains, you may perhaps lose sight of your Companion, and mistake Him for the senseless, ancient dream that now is past.

8. "Who walks with me?" ²This question should be asked a thousand times a day, till certainty has ended doubting and established peace. ³Today let doubting cease. ⁴God speaks for you in answering your question with these words:

> ⁵*I walk with God in perfect holiness.* ⁶*I light the world, I light my mind and all the minds which God created one with me.*

LESSON 157

Into His Presence would I enter now.

1. This is a day of silence and of trust. ²It is a special time of promise in your calendar of days. ³It is a time Heaven has set apart to shine upon, and cast a timeless light upon this day, when echoes of eternity are heard. ⁴This day is holy, for it ushers in a new experience; a different kind of feeling and awareness. ⁵You have spent long days and nights in celebrating death. ⁶Today you learn to feel the joy of life.

2. This is another crucial turning point in the curriculum. ²We add a new dimension now; a fresh experience that sheds a light on all that we have learned already, and prepares us for what we have yet to learn. ³It brings us to the door where learning ceases, and we catch a glimpse of what lies past the highest reaches it can possibly attain. ⁴It leaves us here an instant, and we go beyond it, sure of our direction and our only goal.

3. Today it will be given you to feel a touch of Heaven, though you will return to paths of learning. ²Yet you have come far enough along the way to alter time sufficiently to rise above its laws, and walk into eternity a while. ³This you will learn to do increasingly, as every lesson, faithfully rehearsed, brings you more swiftly to this holy place and leaves you, for a moment, to your Self.

4. He will direct your practicing today, for what you ask for now is what He wills. ²And having joined your will with His this day, what you are asking must be given you. ³Nothing is needed but today's idea to light your mind, and let it rest in still anticipation and in quiet joy, wherein you quickly leave the world behind.

5. From this day forth, your ministry takes on a genuine devotion, and a glow that travels from your fingertips to those you touch, and blesses those you look upon. ²A vision reaches everyone you meet, and everyone you think of, or who thinks of you. ³For your experience today will so transform your mind that it becomes the touchstone for the holy Thoughts of God.

6. Your body will be sanctified today, its only purpose being now to bring the vision of what you experience this day to light the world. ²We cannot give experience like this directly. ³Yet it leaves a vision in our eyes which we can offer everyone, that he may

come the sooner to the same experience in which the world is quietly forgot, and Heaven is remembered for a while.

7. As this experience increases and all goals but this become of little worth, the world to which you will return becomes a little closer to the end of time; a little more like Heaven in its ways; a little nearer its deliverance. ²And you who bring it light will come to see the light more sure; the vision more distinct. ³The time will come when you will not return in the same form in which you now appear, for you will have no need of it. ⁴Yet now it has a purpose, and will serve it well.

8. Today we will embark upon a course you have not dreamed of. ²But the Holy One, the Giver of the happy dreams of life, Translator of perception into truth, the holy Guide to Heaven given you, has dreamed for you this journey which you make and start today, with the experience this day holds out to you to be your own.

9. Into Christ's Presence will we enter now, serenely unaware of everything except His shining face and perfect Love. ²The vision of His face will stay with you, but there will be an instant which transcends all vision, even this, the holiest. ³This you will never teach, for you attained it not through learning. ⁴Yet the vision speaks of your rememberance of what you knew that instant, and will surely know again.

LESSON 158

Today I learn to give as I receive.

1. What has been given you? [2]The knowledge that you are a mind, in Mind and purely mind, sinless forever, wholly unafraid, because you were created out of love. [3]Nor have you left your Source, remaining as you were created. [4]This was given you as knowledge which you cannot lose. [5]It was given as well to every living thing, for by that knowledge only does it live.

2. You have received all this. [2]No one who walks the world but has received it. [3]It is not this knowledge which you give, for that is what creation gave. [4]All this cannot be learned. [5]What, then, are you to learn to give today? [6]Our lesson yesterday evoked a theme found early in the text. [7]Experience cannot be shared directly, in the way that vision can. [8]The revelation that the Father and the Son are one will come in time to every mind. [9]Yet is that time determined by the mind itself, not taught.

3. The time is set already. [2]It appears to be quite arbitrary. [3]Yet there is no step along the road that anyone takes but by chance. [4]It has already been taken by him, although he has not yet embarked on it. [5]For time but seems to go in one direction. [6]We but undertake a journey that is over. [7]Yet it seems to have a future still unknown to us.

4. Time is a trick, a sleight of hand, a vast illusion in which figures come and go as if by magic. [2]Yet there is a plan behind appearances that does not change. [3]The script is written. [4]When experience will come to end your doubting has been set. [5]For we but see the journey from the point at which it ended, looking back on it, imagining we make it once again; reviewing mentally what has gone by.

5. A teacher does not give experience, because he did not learn it. [2]It revealed itself to him at its appointed time. [3]But vision is his gift. [4]This he can give directly, for Christ's knowledge is not lost, because He has a vision He can give to anyone who asks. [5]The Father's Will and His are joined in knowledge. [6]Yet there is a vision which the Holy Spirit sees because the Mind of Christ beholds it too.

6. Here is the joining of the world of doubt and shadows made with the intangible. [2]Here is a quiet place within the world made

holy by forgiveness and by love. ³Here are all contradictions reconciled, for here the journey ends. ⁴Experience—unlearned, untaught, unseen—is merely there. ⁵This is beyond our goal, for it transcends what needs to be accomplished. ⁶Our concern is with Christ's vision. ⁷This we can attain.

7.   Christ's vision has one law. ²It does not look upon a body, and mistake it for the Son whom God created. ³It beholds a light beyond the body; an idea beyond what can be touched, a purity undimmed by errors, pitiful mistakes, and fearful thoughts of guilt from dreams of sin. ⁴It sees no separation. ⁵And it looks on everyone, on every circumstance, all happenings and all events, without the slightest fading of the light it sees.

8.   This can be taught; and must be taught by all who would achieve it. ²It requires but the recognition that the world can not give anything that faintly can compare with this in value; nor set up a goal that does not merely disappear when this has been perceived. ³And this you give today: See no one as a body. ⁴Greet him as the Son of God he is, acknowledging that he is one with you in holiness.

9.   Thus are his sins forgiven him, for Christ has vision that has power to overlook them all. ²In His forgiveness are they gone. ³Unseen by One they merely disappear, because a vision of the holiness that lies beyond them comes to take their place. ⁴It matters not what form they took, nor how enormous they appeared to be, nor who seemed to be hurt by them. ⁵They are no more. ⁶And all effects they seemed to have are gone with them, undone and never to be done.

10.   Thus do you learn to give as you receive. ²And thus Christ's vision looks on you as well. ³This lesson is not difficult to learn, if you remember in your brother you but see yourself. ⁴If he be lost in sin, so must you be; if you see light in him, your sins have been forgiven by yourself. ⁵Each brother whom you meet today provides another chance to let Christ's vision shine on you, and offer you the peace of God.

11.   It matters not when revelation comes, for that is not of time. ²Yet time has still one gift to give, in which true knowledge is reflected in a way so accurate its image shares its unseen holiness; its likeness shines with its immortal love. ³We practice seeing with the eyes of Christ today. ⁴And by the holy gifts we give, Christ's vision looks upon ourselves as well.

LESSON 159

I give the miracles I have received.

1. No one can give what he has not received. ²To give a thing requires first you have it in your own possession. ³Here the laws of Heaven and the world agree. ⁴But here they also separate. ⁵The world believes that to possess a thing, it must be kept. ⁶Salvation teaches otherwise. ⁷To give is how to recognize you have received. ⁸It is the proof that what you have is yours.

2. You understand that you are healed when you give healing. ²You accept forgiveness as accomplished in yourself when you forgive. ³You recognize your brother as yourself, and thus do you perceive that you are whole. ⁴There is no miracle you cannot give, for all are given you. ⁵Receive them now by opening the storehouse of your mind where they are laid, and giving them away.

3. Christ's vision is a miracle. ²It comes from far beyond itself, for it reflects eternal love and the rebirth of love which never dies, but has been kept obscure. ³Christ's vision pictures Heaven, for it sees a world so like to Heaven that what God created perfect can be mirrored there. ⁴The darkened glass the world presents can show but twisted images in broken parts. ⁵The real world pictures Heaven's innocence.

4. Christ's vision is the miracle in which all miracles are born. ²It is their source, remaining with each miracle you give, and yet remaining yours. ³It is the bond by which the giver and receiver are united in extension here on earth, as they are one in Heaven. ⁴Christ beholds no sin in anyone. ⁵And in His sight the sinless are as one. ⁶Their holiness was given by His Father and Himself.

5. Christ's vision is the bridge between the worlds. ²And in its power can you safely trust to carry you from this world into one made holy by forgiveness. ³Things which seem quite solid here are merely shadows there; transparent, faintly seen, at times forgot, and never able to obscure the light that shines beyond them. ⁴Holiness has been restored to vision, and the blind can see.

6. This is the Holy Spirit's single gift; the treasure house to which you can appeal with perfect certainty for all the things that can contribute to your happiness. ²All are laid here already. ³All can be received but for the asking. ⁴Here the door is never locked,

and no one is denied his least request or his most urgent need. [5]There is no sickness not already healed, no lack unsatisfied, no need unmet within this golden treasury of Christ.

7. Here does the world remember what was lost when it was made. [2]For here it is repaired, made new again, but in a different light. [3]What was to be the home of sin becomes the center of redemption and the hearth of mercy, where the suffering are healed and welcome. [4]No one will be turned away from this new home, where his salvation waits. [5]No one is stranger to him. [6]No one asks for anything of him except the gift of his acceptance of his welcoming.

8. Christ's vision is the holy ground in which the lilies of forgiveness set their roots. [2]This is their home. [3]They can be brought from here back to the world, but they can never grow in its unnourishing and shallow soil. [4]They need the light and warmth and kindly care Christ's charity provides. [5]They need the love with which He looks on them. [6]And they become His messengers, who give as they received.

9. Take from His storehouse, that its treasures may increase. [2]His lilies do not leave their home when they are carried back into the world. [3]Their roots remain. [4]They do not leave their source, but carry its beneficence with them, and turn the world into a garden like the one they came from, and to which they go again with added fragrance. [5]Now are they twice blessed. [6]The messages they brought from Christ have been delivered, and returned to them. [7]And they return them gladly unto Him.

10. Behold the store of miracles set out for you to give. [2]Are you not worth the gift, when God appointed it be given you? [3]Judge not God's Son, but follow in the way He has established. [4]Christ has dreamed the dream of a forgiven world. [5]It is His gift, whereby a sweet transition can be made from death to life; from hopelessness to hope. [6]Let us an instant dream with Him. [7]His dream awakens us to truth. [8]His vision gives the means for a return to our unlost and everlasting sanctity in God.

LESSON 160

I am at home. Fear is the stranger here.

1. Fear is a stranger to the ways of love. [2]Identify with fear, and you will be a stranger to yourself. [3]And thus you are unknown to you. [4]What is your Self remains an alien to the part of you which thinks that it is real, but different from yourself. [5]Who could be sane in such a circumstance? [6]Who but a madman could believe he is what he is not, and judge against himself?

2. There is a stranger in our midst, who comes from an idea so foreign to the truth he speaks a different language, looks upon a world truth does not know, and understands what truth regards as senseless. [2]Stranger yet, he does not recognize to whom he comes, and yet maintains his home belongs to him, while he is alien now who is at home. [3]And yet, how easy it would be to say, "This is my home. [4]Here I belong, and will not leave because a madman says I must."

3. What reason is there for not saying this? [2]What could the reason be except that you had asked this stranger in to take your place, and let you be a stranger to yourself? [3]No one would let himself be dispossessed so needlessly, unless he thought there were another home more suited to his tastes.

4. Who is the stranger? [2]Is it fear or you who are unsuited to the home which God provided for His Son? [3]Is fear His Own, created in His likeness? [4]Is it fear that love completes, and is completed by? [5]There is no home can shelter love and fear. [6]They cannot coexist. [7]If you are real, then fear must be illusion. [8]And if fear is real, then you do not exist at all.

5. How simply, then, the question is resolved. [2]Who fears has but denied himself and said, "I am the stranger here. [3]And so I leave my home to one more like me than myself, and give him all I thought belonged to me." [4]Now is he exiled of necessity, not knowing who he is, uncertain of all things but this; that he is not himself, and that his home has been denied to him.

6. What does he search for now? [2]What can he find? [3]A stranger to himself can find no home wherever he may look, for he has made return impossible. [4]His way is lost, except a miracle will search him out and show him that he is no stranger now. [5]The miracle will come. [6]For in his home his Self remains. [7]It asked no

stranger in, and took no alien thought to be Itself. ⁸And It will call Its Own unto Itself in recognition of what is Its Own.

7. Who is the stranger? ²Is he not the one your Self calls not? ³You are unable now to recognize this stranger in your midst, for you have given him your rightful place. ⁴Yet is your Self as certain of Its Own as God is of His Son. ⁵He cannot be confused about creation. ⁶He is sure of what belongs to Him. ⁷No stranger can be interposed between His knowledge and His Son's reality. ⁸He does not know of strangers. ⁹He is certain of His Son.

8. God's certainty suffices. ²Whom He knows to be His Son belongs where He has set His Son forever. ³He has answered you who ask, "Who is the stranger?" ⁴Hear His Voice assure you, quietly and sure, that you are not a stranger to your Father, nor is your Creator stranger made to you. ⁵Whom God has joined remain forever one, at home in Him, no stranger to Himself.

9. Today we offer thanks that Christ has come to search the world for what belongs to Him. ²His vision sees no strangers, but beholds His Own and joyously unites with them. ³They see Him as a stranger, for they do not recognize themselves. ⁴Yet as they give Him welcome, they remember. ⁵And He leads them gently home again, where they belong.

10. Not one does Christ forget. ²Not one He fails to give you to remember, that your home may be complete and perfect as it was established. ³He has not forgotten you. ⁴But you will not remember Him until you look on all as He does. ⁵Who denies his brother is denying Him, and thus refusing to accept the gift of sight by which his Self is clearly recognized, his home remembered and salvation come.

LESSON 161

Give me your blessing, holy Son of God.

1. Today we practice differently, and take a stand against our anger, that our fears may disappear and offer room to love. ²Here is salvation in the simple words in which we practice with today's idea. ³Here is the answer to temptation which can never fail to welcome in the Christ where fear and anger had prevailed before. ⁴Here is Atonement made complete, the world passed safely by and Heaven now restored. ⁵Here is the answer of the Voice for God.

2. Complete abstraction is the natural condition of the mind. ²But part of it is now unnatural. ³It does not look on everything as one. ⁴It sees instead but fragments of the whole, for only thus could it invent the partial world you see. ⁵The purpose of all seeing is to show you what you wish to see. ⁶All hearing but brings to your mind the sounds it wants to hear.

3. Thus were specifics made. ²And now it is specifics we must use in practicing. ³We give them to the Holy Spirit, that He may employ them for a purpose which is different from the one we gave to them. ⁴Yet He can use but what we made, to teach us from a different point of view, so we can see a different use in everything.

4. One brother is all brothers. ²Every mind contains all minds, for every mind is one. ³Such is the truth. ⁴Yet do these thoughts make clear the meaning of creation? ⁵Do these words bring perfect clarity with them to you? ⁶What can they seem to be but empty sounds; pretty, perhaps, correct in sentiment, yet fundamentally not understood nor understandable. ⁷The mind that taught itself to think specifically can no longer grasp abstraction in the sense that it is all-encompassing. ⁸We need to see a little, that we learn a lot.

5. It seems to be the body that we feel limits our freedom, makes us suffer, and at last puts out our life. ²Yet bodies are but symbols for a concrete form of fear. ³Fear without symbols calls for no response, for symbols can stand for the meaningless. ⁴Love needs no symbols, being true. ⁵But fear attaches to specifics, being false.

6. Bodies attack, but minds do not. ²This thought is surely reminiscent of our text, where it is often emphasized. ³This is the

reason bodies easily become fear's symbols. ⁴You have many times been urged to look beyond the body, for its sight presents the symbol of love's "enemy" Christ's vision does not see. ⁵The body is the target for attack, for no one thinks he hates a mind. ⁶Yet what but mind directs the body to attack? ⁷What else could be the seat of fear except what thinks of fear?

7. Hate is specific. ²There must be a thing to be attacked. ³An enemy must be perceived in such a form he can be touched and seen and heard, and ultimately killed. ⁴When hatred rests upon a thing, it calls for death as surely as God's Voice proclaims there is no death. ⁵Fear is insatiable, consuming everything its eyes behold, seeing itself in everything, compelled to turn upon itself and to destroy.

8. Who sees a brother as a body sees him as fear's symbol. ²And he will attack, because what he beholds is his own fear external to himself, poised to attack, and howling to unite with him again. ³Mistake not the intensity of rage projected fear must spawn. ⁴It shrieks in wrath, and claws the air in frantic hope it can reach to its maker and devour him.

9. This do the body's eyes behold in one whom Heaven cherishes, the angels love and God created perfect. ²This is his reality. ³And in Christ's vision is his loveliness reflected in a form so holy and so beautiful that you could scarce refrain from kneeling at his feet. ⁴Yet you will take his hand instead, for you are like him in the sight that sees him thus. ⁵Attack on him is enemy to you, for you will not perceive that in his hands is your salvation. ⁶Ask him but for this, and he will give it to you. ⁷Ask him not to symbolize your fear. ⁸Would you request that love destroy itself? ⁹Or would you have it be revealed to you and set you free?

10. Today we practice in a form we have attempted earlier. ²Your readiness is closer now, and you will come today nearer Christ's vision. ³If you are intent on reaching it, you will succeed today. ⁴And once you have succeeded, you will not be willing to accept the witnesses your body's eyes call forth. ⁵What you will see will sing to you of ancient melodies you will remember. ⁶You are not forgot in Heaven. ⁷Would you not remember it?

11. Select one brother, symbol of the rest, and ask salvation of him. ²See him first as clearly as you can, in that same form to which you are accustomed. ³See his face, his hands and feet, his clothing. ⁴Watch him smile, and see familiar gestures which he makes so frequently. ⁵Then think of this: What you are seeing now conceals

from you the sight of one who can forgive you all your sins; whose sacred hands can take away the nails which pierce your own, and lift the crown of thorns which you have placed upon your bleeding head. ⁶Ask this of him, that he may set you free:

> ⁷*Give me your blessing, holy Son of God.* ⁸*I would behold you with the eyes of Christ, and see my perfect sinlessness in you.*

12. And He will answer Whom you called upon. ²For He will hear the Voice for God in you, and answer in your own. ³Behold him now, whom you have seen as merely flesh and bone, and recognize that Christ has come to you. ⁴Today's idea is your safe escape from anger and from fear. ⁵Be sure you use it instantly, should you be tempted to attack a brother and perceive in him the symbol of your fear. ⁶And you will see him suddenly transformed from enemy to savior; from the devil into Christ.

LESSON 162

I am as God created me.

1. This single thought, held firmly in the mind, would save the world. ²From time to time we will repeat it, as we reach another stage in learning. ³It will mean far more to you as you advance. ⁴These words are sacred, for they are the words God gave in answer to the world you made. ⁵By them it disappears, and all things seen within its misty clouds and vaporous illusions vanish as these words are spoken. ⁶For they come from God.

2. Here is the Word by which the Son became his Father's happiness, His Love and His completion. ²Here creation is proclaimed, and honored as it is. ³There is no dream these words will not dispel; no thought of sin and no illusion which the dream contains that will not fade away before their might. ⁴They are the trumpet of awakening that sounds around the world. ⁵The dead awake in answer to its call. ⁶And those who live and hear this sound will never look on death.

3. Holy indeed is he who makes these words his own; arising with them in his mind, recalling them throughout the day, at night bringing them with him as he goes to sleep. ²His dreams are happy and his rest secure, his safety certain and his body healed, because he sleeps and wakens with the truth before him always. ³He will save the world, because he gives the world what he receives each time he practices the words of truth.

4. Today we practice simply. ²For the words we use are mighty, and they need no thoughts beyond themselves to change the mind of him who uses them. ³So wholly is it changed that it is now the treasury in which God places all His gifts and all His Love, to be distributed to all the world, increased in giving; kept complete because its sharing is unlimited. ⁴And thus you learn to think with God. ⁵Christ's vision has restored your sight by salvaging your mind.

5. We honor you today. ²Yours is the right to perfect holiness you now accept. ³With this acceptance is salvation brought to everyone, for who could cherish sin when holiness like this has blessed the world? ⁴Who could despair when perfect joy is yours, available to all as remedy for grief and misery, all sense of loss, and for complete escape from sin and guilt?

6.   And who would not be brother to you now; you, his redeemer and his savior. [2]Who could fail to welcome you into his heart with loving invitation, eager to unite with one like him in holiness? [3]You are as God created you. [4]These words dispel the night, and darkness is no more. [5]The light is come today to bless the world. [6]For you have recognized the Son of God, and in that recognition is the world's.

LESSON 163

There is no death. The Son of God is free.

1. Death is a thought that takes on many forms, often unrecognized. [2]It may appear as sadness, fear, anxiety or doubt; as anger, faithlessness and lack of trust; concern for bodies, envy, and all forms in which the wish to be as you are not may come to tempt you. [3]All such thoughts are but reflections of the worshipping of death as savior and as giver of release.

2. Embodiment of fear, the host of sin, god of the guilty and the lord of all illusions and deceptions, does the thought of death seem mighty. [2]For it seems to hold all living things within its withered hand; all hopes and wishes in its blighting grasp; all goals perceived but in its sightless eyes. [3]The frail, the helpless and the sick bow down before its image, thinking it alone is real, inevitable, worthy of their trust. [4]For it alone will surely come.

3. All things but death are seen to be unsure, too quickly lost however hard to gain, uncertain in their outcome, apt to fail the hopes they once engendered, and to leave the taste of dust and ashes in their wake, in place of aspirations and of dreams. [2]But death is counted on. [3]For it will come with certain footsteps when the time has come for its arrival. [4]It will never fail to take all life as hostage to itself.

4. Would you bow down to idols such as this? [2]Here is the strength and might of God Himself perceived within an idol made of dust. [3]Here is the opposite of God proclaimed as lord of all creation, stronger than God's Will for life, the endlessness of love and Heaven's perfect, changeless constancy. [4]Here is the Will of Father and of Son defeated finally, and laid to rest beneath the headstone death has placed upon the body of the holy Son of God.

5. Unholy in defeat, he has become what death would have him be. [2]His epitaph, which death itself has written, gives no name to him, for he has passed to dust. [3]It says but this: "Here lies a witness God is dead." [4]And this it writes again and still again, while all the while its worshippers agree, and kneeling down with foreheads to the ground, they whisper fearfully that it is so.

6. It is impossible to worship death in any form, and still select a few you would not cherish and would yet avoid, while still

believing in the rest. [2]For death is total. [3]Either all things die, or else they live and cannot die. [4]No compromise is possible. [5]For here again we see an obvious position, which we must accept if we be sane; what contradicts one thought entirely can not be true, unless its opposite is proven false.

7.   The idea of the death of God is so preposterous that even the insane have difficulty in believing it. [2]For it implies that God was once alive and somehow perished; killed, apparently, by those who did not want Him to survive. [3]Their stronger will could triumph over His, and so eternal life gave way to death. [4]And with the Father died the Son as well.

8.   Death's worshippers may be afraid. [2]And yet, can thoughts like these be fearful? [3]If they saw that it is only this which they believe, they would be instantly released. [4]And you will show them this today. [5]There is no death, and we renounce it now in every form, for their salvation and our own as well. [6]God made not death. [7]Whatever form it takes must therefore be illusion. [8]This the stand we take today. [9]And it is given us to look past death, and see the life beyond.

9.   *Our Father, bless our eyes today. [2]We are Your messengers, and we would look upon the glorious reflection of Your Love which shines in everything. [3]We live and move in You alone. [4]We are not separate from Your eternal life. [5]There is no death, for death is not Your Will. [6]And we abide where You have placed us, in the life we share with You and with all living things, to be like You and part of You forever. [7]We accept Your Thoughts as ours, and our will is one with Yours eternally. [8]Amen.*

LESSON 164

Now are we one with Him Who is our Source.

1. What time but now can truth be recognized? [2]The present is the only time there is. [3]And so today, this instant, now, we come to look upon what is forever there; not in our sight, but in the eyes of Christ. [4]He looks past time, and sees eternity as represented there. [5]He hears the sounds the senseless, busy world engenders, yet He hears them faintly. [6]For beyond them all He hears the song of Heaven, and the Voice for God more clear, more meaningful, more near.

2. The world fades easily away before His sight. [2]Its sounds grow dim. [3]A melody from far beyond the world increasingly is more and more distinct; an ancient call to which He gives an ancient answer. [4]You will recognize them both, for they are but your answer to your Father's Call to you. [5]Christ answers for you, echoing your Self, using your voice to give His glad consent; accepting your deliverance for you.

3. How holy is your practicing today, as Christ gives you His sight and hears for you, and answers in your name the Call He hears! [2]How quiet is the time you give to spend with Him, beyond the world. [3]How easily are all your seeming sins forgot, and all your sorrows unremembered. [4]On this day is grief laid by, for sights and sounds that come from nearer than the world are clear to you who will today accept the gifts He gives.

4. There is a silence into which the world can not intrude. [2]There is an ancient peace you carry in your heart and have not lost. [3]There is a sense of holiness in you the thought of sin has never touched. [4]All this today you will remember. [5]Faithfulness in practicing today will bring rewards so great and so completely different from all things you sought before, that you will know that here your treasure is, and here your rest.

5. This is the day when vain imaginings part like a curtain, to reveal what lies beyond them. [2]Now is what is really there made visible, while all the shadows which appeared to hide it merely sink away. [3]Now is the balance righted, and the scale of judgment left to Him Who judges true. [4]And in His judgment will a world unfold in perfect innocence before your eyes. [5]Now will you see it with the eyes of Christ. [6]Now is its transformation clear to you.

6. Brother, this day is sacred to the world. ²Your vision, given you from far beyond all things within the world, looks back on them in a new light. ³And what you see becomes the healing and salvation of the world. ⁴The valuable and valueless are both perceived and recognized for what they are. ⁵And what is worthy of your love receives your love, while nothing to be feared remains.

7. We will not judge today. ²We will receive but what is given us from judgment made beyond the world. ³Our practicing today becomes our gift of thankfulness for our release from blindness and from misery. ⁴All that we see will but increase our joy, because its holiness reflects our own. ⁵We stand forgiven in the sight of Christ, with all the world forgiven in our own. ⁶We bless the world, as we behold it in the light in which our Savior looks on us, and offer it the freedom given us through His forgiving vision, not our own.

8. Open the curtain in your practicing by merely letting go all things you think you want. ²Your trifling treasures put away, and leave a clean and open space within your mind where Christ can come, and offer you the treasure of salvation. ³He has need of your most holy mind to save the world. ⁴Is not this purpose worthy to be yours? ⁵Is not Christ's vision worthy to be sought above the world's unsatisfying goals?

9. Let not today slip by without the gifts it holds for you receiving your consent and your acceptance. ²We can change the world, if you acknowledge them. ³You may not see the value your acceptance gives the world. ⁴But this you surely want; you can exchange all suffering for joy this very day. ⁵Practice in earnest, and the gift is yours. ⁶Would God deceive you? ⁷Can His promise fail? ⁸Can you withhold so little, when His Hand holds out complete salvation to His Son?

LESSON 165

Let not my mind deny the Thought of God.

1. What makes this world seem real except your own denial of the truth that lies beyond? ²What but your thoughts of misery and death obscure the perfect happiness and the eternal life your Father wills for you? ³And what could hide what cannot be concealed except illusion? ⁴What could keep from you what you already have except your choice to see it not, denying it is there?

2. The Thought of God created you. ²It left you not, nor have you ever been apart from it an instant. ³It belongs to you. ⁴By it you live. ⁵It is your Source of life, holding you one with it, and everything is one with you because it left you not. ⁶The Thought of God protects you, cares for you, makes soft your resting place and smooth your way, lighting your mind with happiness and love. ⁷Eternity and everlasting life shine in your mind, because the Thought of God has left you not, and still abides with you.

3. Who would deny his safety and his peace, his joy, his healing and his peace of mind, his quiet rest, his calm awakening, if he but recognized where they abide? ²Would he not instantly prepare to go where they are found, abandoning all else as worthless in comparison with them? ³And having found them, would he not make sure they stay with him, and he remain with them?

4. Deny not Heaven. ²It is yours today, but for the asking. ³Nor need you perceive how great the gift, how changed your mind will be before it comes to you. ⁴Ask to receive, and it is given you. ⁵Conviction lies within it. ⁶Till you welcome it as yours, uncertainty remains. ⁷Yet God is fair. ⁸Sureness is not required to receive what only your acceptance can bestow.

5. Ask with desire. ²You need not be sure that you request the only thing you want. ³But when you have received, you will be sure you have the treasure you have always sought. ⁴What would you then exchange for it? ⁵What would induce you now to let it fade away from your ecstatic vision? ⁶For this sight proves that you have exchanged your blindness for the seeing eyes of Christ; your mind has come to lay aside denial, and accept the Thought of God as your inheritance.

6. Now is all doubting past, the journey's end made certain, and

salvation given you. [2]Now is Christ's power in your mind, to heal as you were healed. [3]For now you are among the saviors of the world. [4]Your destiny lies there and nowhere else. [5]Would God consent to let His Son remain forever starved by his denial of the nourishment he needs to live? [6]Abundance dwells in him, and deprivation cannot cut him off from God's sustaining Love and from his home.

7. Practice today in hope. [2]For hope indeed is justified. [3]Your doubts are meaningless, for God is certain. [4]And the Thought of Him is never absent. [5]Sureness must abide within you who are host to Him. [6]This course removes all doubts which you have interposed between Him and your certainty of Him.

8. We count on God, and not upon ourselves, to give us certainty. [2]And in His Name we practice as His Word directs we do. [3]His sureness lies beyond our every doubt. [4]His Love remains beyond our every fear. [5]The Thought of Him is still beyond all dreams and in our minds, according to His Will.

LESSON 166

I am entrusted with the gifts of God.

1. All things are given you. ²God's trust in you is limitless. ³He knows His Son. ⁴He gives without exception, holding nothing back that can contribute to your happiness. ⁵And yet, unless your will is one with His, His gifts are not received. ⁶But what would make you think there is another will than His?

2. Here is the paradox that underlies the making of the world. ²This world is not the Will of God, and so it is not real. ³Yet those who think it real must still believe there is another will, and one that leads to opposite effects from those He wills. ⁴Impossible indeed; but every mind that looks upon the world and judges it as certain, solid, trustworthy and true believes in two creators; or in one, himself alone. ⁵But never in one God.

3. The gifts of God are not acceptable to anyone who holds such strange beliefs. ²He must believe that to accept God's gifts, however evident they may become, however urgently he may be called to claim them as his own, is to be pressed to treachery against himself. ³He must deny their presence, contradict the truth, and suffer to preserve the world he made.

4. Here is the only home he thinks he knows. ²Here is the only safety he believes that he can find. ³Without the world he made is he an outcast; homeless and afraid. ⁴He does not realize that it is here he is afraid indeed, and homeless, too; an outcast wandering so far from home, so long away, he does not realize he has forgotten where he came from, where he goes, and even who he really is.

5. Yet in his lonely, senseless wanderings, God's gifts go with him, all unknown to him. ²He cannot lose them. ³But he will not look at what is given him. ⁴He wanders on, aware of the futility he sees about him everywhere, perceiving how his little lot but dwindles, as he goes ahead to nowhere. ⁵Still he wanders on in misery and poverty, alone though God is with him, and a treasure his so great that everything the world contains is valueless before its magnitude.

6. He seems a sorry figure; weary, worn, in threadbare clothing, and with feet that bleed a little from the rocky road he walks. ²No one but has identified with him, for everyone who comes here

315

has pursued the path he follows, and has felt defeat and hope-lessness as he is feeling them. ³Yet is he really tragic, when you see that he is following the way he chose, and need but realize Who walks with him and open up his treasures to be free?

7.   This is your chosen self, the one you made as a replacement for reality. ²This is the self you savagely defend against all reason, every evidence, and all the witnesses with proof to show this is not you. ³You heed them not. ⁴You go on your appointed way, with eyes cast down lest you might catch a glimpse of truth, and be released from self-deception and set free.

8.   You cower fearfully lest you should feel Christ's touch upon your shoulder, and perceive His gentle hand directing you to look upon your gifts. ²How could you then proclaim your poverty in exile? ³He would make you laugh at this perception of yourself. ⁴Where is self-pity then? ⁵And what becomes of all the tragedy you sought to make for him whom God intended only joy?

9.   Your ancient fear has come upon you now, and justice has caught up with you at last. ²Christ's hand has touched your shoulder, and you feel that you are not alone. ³You even think the miserable self you thought was you may not be your Identity. ⁴Perhaps God's Word is truer than your own. ⁵Perhaps His gifts to you are real. ⁶Perhaps He has not wholly been outwitted by your plan to keep His Son in deep oblivion, and go the way you chose without your Self.

10.   God's Will does not oppose. ²It merely is. ³It is not God you have imprisoned in your plan to lose your Self. ⁴He does not know about a plan so alien to His Will. ⁵There was a need He did not understand, to which He gave an Answer. ⁶That is all. ⁷And you who have this Answer given you have need no more of any-thing but this.

11.   Now do we live, for now we cannot die. ²The wish for death is answered, and the sight that looked upon it now has been re-placed by vision which perceives that you are not what you pre-tend to be. ³One walks with you Who gently answers all your fears with this one merciful reply, "It is not so." ⁴He points to all the gifts you have each time the thought of poverty oppresses you, and speaks of His Companionship when you perceive your-self as lonely and afraid.

12.   Yet He reminds you still of one thing more you had forgotten. ²For His touch on you has made you like Himself. ³The gifts you have are not for you alone. ⁴What He has come to offer you, you

now must learn to give. ⁵This is the lesson that His giving holds, for He has saved you from the solitude you sought to make in which to hide from God. ⁶He has reminded you of all the gifts that God has given you. ⁷He speaks as well of what becomes your will when you accept these gifts, and recognize they are your own.

13. The gifts are yours, entrusted to your care, to give to all who chose the lonely road you have escaped. ²They do not understand they but pursue their wishes. ³It is you who teach them now. ⁴For you have learned of Christ there is another way for them to walk. ⁵Teach them by showing them the happiness that comes to those who feel the touch of Christ, and recognize God's gifts. ⁶Let sorrow not tempt you to be unfaithful to your trust.

14. Your sighs will now betray the hopes of those who look to you for their release. ²Your tears are theirs. ³If you are sick, you but withhold their healing. ⁴What you fear but teaches them their fears are justified. ⁵Your hand becomes the giver of Christ's touch; your change of mind becomes the proof that who accepts God's gifts can never suffer anything. ⁶You are entrusted with the world's release from pain.

15. Betray it not. ²Become the living proof of what Christ's touch can offer everyone. ³God has entrusted all His gifts to you. ⁴Be witness in your happiness to how transformed the mind becomes which chooses to accept His gifts, and feel the touch of Christ. ⁵Such is your mission now. ⁶For God entrusts the giving of His gifts to all who have received them. ⁷He has shared His joy with you. ⁸And now you go to share it with the world.

LESSON 167

There is one life, and that I share with God.

1.   There are not different kinds of life, for life is like the truth. ²It does not have degrees. ³It is the one condition in which all that God created share. ⁴Like all His Thoughts, it has no opposite. ⁵There is no death because what God created shares His life. ⁶There is no death because an opposite to God does not exist. ⁷There is no death because the Father and the Son are one.

2.   In this world, there appears to be a state that is life's opposite. ²You call it death. ³Yet we have learned that the idea of death takes many forms. ⁴It is the one idea which underlies all feelings that are not supremely happy. ⁵It is the alarm to which you give response of any kind that is not perfect joy. ⁶All sorrow, loss, anxiety and suffering and pain, even a little sigh of weariness, a slight discomfort or the merest frown, acknowledge death. ⁷And thus deny you live.

3.   You think that death is of the body. ²Yet it is but an idea, irrelevant to what is seen as physical. ³A thought is in the mind. ⁴It can be then applied as mind directs it. ⁵But its origin is where it must be changed, if change occurs. ⁶Ideas leave not their source. ⁷The emphasis this course has placed on that idea is due to its centrality in our attempts to change your mind about yourself. ⁸It is the reason you can heal. ⁹It is the cause of healing. ¹⁰It is why you cannot die. ¹¹Its truth established you as one with God.

4.   Death is the thought that you are separate from your Creator. ²It is the belief conditions change, emotions alternate because of causes you cannot control, you did not make, and you can never change. ³It is the fixed belief ideas can leave their source, and take on qualities the source does not contain, becoming different from their own origin, apart from it in kind as well as distance, time and form.

5.   Death cannot come from life. ²Ideas remain united to their source. ³They can extend all that their source contains. ⁴In that, they can go far beyond themselves. ⁵But they can not give birth to what was never given them. ⁶As they are made, so will their making be. ⁷As they were born, so will they then give birth. ⁸And where they come from, there will they return.

6.   The mind can think it sleeps, but that is all. ²It cannot change

what is its waking state. [3]It cannot make a body, nor abide within a body. [4]What is alien to the mind does not exist, because it has no source. [5]For mind creates all things that are, and cannot give them attributes it lacks, nor change its own eternal, mindful state. [6]It cannot make the physical. [7]What seems to die is but the sign of mind asleep.

7. The opposite of life can only be another form of life. [2]As such, it can be reconciled with what created it, because it is not opposite in truth. [3]Its form may change; it may appear to be what it is not. [4]Yet mind is mind, awake or sleeping. [5]It is not its opposite in anything created, nor in what it seems to make when it believes it sleeps.

8. God creates only mind awake. [2]He does not sleep, and His creations cannot share what He gives not, nor make conditions which He does not share with them. [3]The thought of death is not the opposite to thoughts of life. [4]Forever unopposed by opposites of any kind, the Thoughts of God remain forever changeless, with the power to extend forever changelessly, but yet within themselves, for they are everywhere.

9. What seems to be the opposite of life is merely sleeping. [2]When the mind elects to be what it is not, and to assume an alien power which it does not have, a foreign state it cannot enter, or a false condition not within its Source, it merely seems to go to sleep a while. [3]It dreams of time; an interval in which what seems to happen never has occurred, the changes wrought are substance-less, and all events are nowhere. [4]When the mind awakes, it but continues as it always was.

10. Let us today be children of the truth, and not deny our holy heritage. [2]Our life is not as we imagine it. [3]Who changes life because he shuts his eyes, or makes himself what he is not because he sleeps, and sees in dreams an opposite to what he is? [4]We will not ask for death in any form today. [5]Nor will we let imagined opposites to life abide even an instant where the Thought of life eternal has been set by God Himself.

11. His holy home we strive to keep today as He established it, and wills it be forever and forever. [2]He is Lord of what we think today. [3]And in His Thoughts, which have no opposite, we understand there is one life, and that we share with Him, with all creation, with their thoughts as well, whom He created in a unity of life that cannot separate in death and leave the Source of life from where it came.

12. We share one life because we have one Source, a Source from which perfection comes to us, remaining always in the holy minds which He created perfect. ²As we were, so are we now and will forever be. ³A sleeping mind must waken, as it sees its own perfection mirroring the Lord of life so perfectly it fades into what is reflected there. ⁴And now it is no more a mere reflection. ⁵It becomes the thing reflected, and the light which makes reflection possible. ⁶No vision now is needed. ⁷For the wakened mind is one that knows its Source, its Self, its Holiness.

LESSON 168

Your grace is given me. I claim it now.

1.   God speaks to us. ²Shall we not speak to Him? ³He is not distant. ⁴He makes no attempt to hide from us. ⁵We try to hide from Him, and suffer from deception. ⁶He remains entirely accessible. ⁷He loves His Son. ⁸There is no certainty but this, yet this suffices. ⁹He will love His Son forever. ¹⁰When his mind remains asleep, He loves him still. ¹¹And when his mind awakes, He loves him with a never-changing Love.

2.   If you but knew the meaning of His Love, hope and despair would be impossible. ²For hope would be forever satisfied; despair of any kind unthinkable. ³His grace His answer is to all despair, for in it lies remembrance of His Love. ⁴Would He not gladly give the means by which His Will is recognized? ⁵His grace is yours by your acknowledgment. ⁶And memory of Him awakens in the mind that asks the means of Him whereby its sleep is done.

3.   Today we ask of God the gift He has most carefully preserved within our hearts, waiting to be acknowledged. ²This the gift by which God leans to us and lifts us up, taking salvation's final step Himself. ³All steps but this we learn, instructed by His Voice. ⁴But finally He comes Himself, and takes us in His Arms and sweeps away the cobwebs of our sleep. ⁵His gift of grace is more than just an answer. ⁶It restores all memories the sleeping mind forgot; all certainty of what Love's meaning is.

4.   God loves His Son. ²Request Him now to give the means by which this world will disappear, and vision first will come, with knowledge but an instant later. ³For in grace you see a light that covers all the world in love, and watch fear disappear from every face as hearts rise up and claim the light as theirs. ⁴What now remains that Heaven be delayed an instant longer? ⁵What is still undone when your forgiveness rests on everything?

5.   It is a new and holy day today, for we receive what has been given us. ²Our faith lies in the Giver, not our own acceptance. ³We acknowledge our mistakes, but He to Whom all error is unknown is yet the One Who answers our mistakes by giving us the means to lay them down, and rise to Him in gratitude and love.

6.   And He descends to meet us, as we come to Him. ²For what He

has prepared for us He gives and we receive. ³Such is His Will, because He loves His Son. ⁴To Him we pray today, returning but the word He gave to us through His Own Voice, His Word, His Love:

⁵*Your grace is given me.* ⁶*I claim it now.* ⁷*Father, I come to You.* ⁸*And You will come to me who ask.* ⁹*I am the Son You love.*

LESSON 169

By grace I live. By grace I am released.

1. Grace is an aspect of the Love of God which is most like the state prevailing in the unity of truth. [2]It is the world's most lofty aspiration, for it leads beyond the world entirely. [3]It is past learning, yet the goal of learning, for grace cannot come until the mind prepares itself for true acceptance. [4]Grace becomes inevitable instantly in those who have prepared a table where it can be gently laid and willingly received; an altar clean and holy for the gift.

2. Grace is acceptance of the Love of God within a world of seeming hate and fear. [2]By grace alone the hate and fear are gone, for grace presents a state so opposite to everything the world contains, that those whose minds are lighted by the gift of grace can not believe the world of fear is real.

3. Grace is not learned. [2]The final step must go beyond all learning. [3]Grace is not the goal this course aspires to attain. [4]Yet we prepare for grace in that an open mind can hear the Call to waken. [5]It is not shut tight against God's Voice. [6]It has become aware that there are things it does not know, and thus is ready to accept a state completely different from experience with which it is familiarly at home.

4. We have perhaps appeared to contradict our statement that the revelation of the Father and the Son as one has been already set. [2]But we have also said the mind determines when that time will be, and has determined it. [3]And yet we urge you to bear witness to the Word of God to hasten the experience of truth, and speed its advent into every mind that recognizes truth's effects on you.

5. Oneness is simply the idea God is. [2]And in His Being, He encompasses all things. [3]No mind holds anything but Him. [4]We say "God is," and then we cease to speak, for in that knowledge words are meaningless. [5]There are no lips to speak them, and no part of mind sufficiently distinct to feel that it is now aware of something not itself. [6]It has united with its Source. [7]And like its Source Itself, it merely is.

6. We cannot speak nor write nor even think of this at all. [2]It comes to every mind when total recognition that its will is God's has been completely given and received completely. [3]It returns the mind into the endless present, where the past and future

cannot be conceived. ⁴It lies beyond salvation; past all thought of time, forgiveness and the holy face of Christ. ⁵The Son of God has merely disappeared into his Father, as his Father has in him. ⁶The world has never been at all. ⁷Eternity remains a constant state.

7. This is beyond experience we try to hasten. ²Yet forgiveness, taught and learned, brings with it the experiences which bear witness that the time the mind itself determined to abandon all but this is now at hand. ³We do not hasten it, in that what you will offer was concealed from Him Who teaches what forgiveness means.

8. All learning was already in His Mind, accomplished and complete. ²He recognized all that time holds, and gave it to all minds that each one might determine, from a point where time was ended, when it is released to revelation and eternity. ³We have repeated several times before that you but make a journey that is done.

9. For oneness must be here. ²Whatever time the mind has set for revelation is entirely irrelevant to what must be a constant state, forever as it always was; forever to remain as it is now. ³We merely take the part assigned long since, and fully recognized as perfectly fulfilled by Him Who wrote salvation's script in His Creator's Name, and in the Name of His Creator's Son.

10. There is no need to further clarify what no one in the world can understand. ²When revelation of your oneness comes, it will be known and fully understood. ³Now we have work to do, for those in time can speak of things beyond, and listen to words which explain what is to come is past already. ⁴Yet what meaning can the words convey to those who count the hours still, and rise and work and go to sleep by them?

11. Suffice it, then, that you have work to do to play your part. ²The ending must remain obscure to you until your part is done. ³It does not matter. ⁴For your part is still what all the rest depends on. ⁵As you take the role assigned to you, salvation comes a little nearer each uncertain heart that does not beat as yet in tune with God.

12. Forgiveness is the central theme that runs throughout salvation, holding all its parts in meaningful relationships, the course it runs directed and its outcome sure. ²And now we ask for grace, the final gift salvation can bestow. ³Experience that grace provides will end in time, for grace foreshadows Heaven, yet does not replace the thought of time but for a little while.

13. The interval suffices. ²It is here that miracles are laid; to be

returned by you from holy instants you receive, through grace in your experience, to all who see the light that lingers in your face. ³What is the face of Christ but his who went a moment into timelessness, and brought a clear reflection of the unity he felt an instant back to bless the world? ⁴How could you finally attain to it forever, while a part of you remains outside, unknowing, unawakened, and in need of you as witness to the truth?

14. Be grateful to return, as you were glad to go an instant, and accept the gifts that grace provided you. ²You carry them back to yourself. ³And revelation stands not far behind. ⁴Its coming is ensured. ⁵We ask for grace, and for experience that comes from grace. ⁶We welcome the release it offers everyone. ⁷We do not ask for the unaskable. ⁸We do not look beyond what grace can give. ⁹For this we can give in the grace that has been given us.

15. Our learning goal today does not exceed this prayer. ²Yet in the world, what could be more than what we ask this day of Him Who gives the grace we ask, as it was given Him?

> ³*By grace I live.* ⁴*By grace I am released.*
> ⁵*By grace I give.* ⁶*By grace I will release.*

LESSON 170

There is no cruelty in God and none in me.

1. No one attacks without intent to hurt. ²This can have no exception. ³When you think that you attack in self-defense, you mean that to be cruel is protection; you are safe because of cruelty. ⁴You mean that you believe to hurt another brings you freedom. ⁵And you mean that to attack is to exchange the state in which you are for something better, safer, more secure from dangerous invasion and from fear.

2. How thoroughly insane is the idea that to defend from fear is to attack! ²For here is fear begot and fed with blood, to make it grow and swell and rage. ³And thus is fear protected, not escaped. ⁴Today we learn a lesson which can save you more delay and needless misery than you can possibly imagine. ⁵It is this:

> ⁶*You make what you defend against, and by your own*
> *defense against it is it real and inescapable.* ⁷*Lay down*
> *your arms, and only then do you perceive it false.*

3. It seems to be the enemy without that you attack. ²Yet your defense sets up an enemy within; an alien thought at war with you, depriving you of peace, splitting your mind into two camps which seem wholly irreconcilable. ³For love now has an "enemy," an opposite; and fear, the alien, now needs your defense against the threat of what you really are.

4. If you consider carefully the means by which your fancied self-defense proceeds on its imagined way, you will perceive the premises on which the idea stands. ²First, it is obvious ideas must leave their source, for it is you who make attack, and must have first conceived of it. ³Yet you attack outside yourself, and separate your mind from him who is to be attacked, with perfect faith the split you made is real.

5. Next, are the attributes of love bestowed upon its "enemy." ²For fear becomes your safety and protector of your peace, to which you turn for solace and escape from doubts about your strength, and hope of rest in dreamless quiet. ³And as love is shorn of what belongs to it and it alone, love is endowed with attributes of fear. ⁴For love would ask you lay down all defense as

merely foolish. ⁵And your arms indeed would crumble into dust. ⁶For such they are.

6. With love as enemy, must cruelty become a god. ²And gods demand that those who worship them obey their dictates, and refuse to question them. ³Harsh punishment is meted out relentlessly to those who ask if the demands are sensible or even sane. ⁴It is their enemies who are unreasonable and insane, while they are always merciful and just.

7. Today we look upon this cruel god dispassionately. ²And we note that though his lips are smeared with blood, and fire seems to flame from him, he is but made of stone. ³He can do nothing. ⁴We need not defy his power. ⁵He has none. ⁶And those who see in him their safety have no guardian, no strength to call upon in danger, and no mighty warrior to fight for them.

8. This moment can be terrible. ²But it can also be the time of your release from abject slavery. ³You make a choice, standing before this idol, seeing him exactly as he is. ⁴Will you restore to love what you have sought to wrest from it and lay before this mindless piece of stone? ⁵Or will you make another idol to replace it? ⁶For the god of cruelty takes many forms. ⁷Another can be found.

9. Yet do not think that fear is the escape from fear. ²Let us remember what the text has stressed about the obstacles to peace. ³The final one, the hardest to believe is nothing, and a seeming obstacle with the appearance of a solid block, impenetrable, fearful and beyond surmounting, is the fear of God Himself. ⁴Here is the basic premise which enthrones the thought of fear as god. ⁵For fear is loved by those who worship it, and love appears to be invested now with cruelty.

10. Where does the totally insane belief in gods of vengeance come from? ²Love has not confused its attributes with those of fear. ³Yet must the worshippers of fear perceive their own confusion in fear's "enemy"; its cruelty as now a part of love. ⁴And what becomes more fearful than the Heart of Love Itself? ⁵The blood appears to be upon His Lips; the fire comes from Him. ⁶And He is terrible above all else, cruel beyond conception, striking down all who acknowledge Him to be their God.

11. The choice you make today is certain. ²For you look for the last time upon this bit of carven stone you made, and call it god no longer. ³You have reached this place before, but you have chosen that this cruel god remain with you in still another form. ⁴And so

the fear of God returned with you. ⁵This time you leave it there. ⁶And you return to a new world, unburdened by its weight; beheld not in its sightless eyes, but in the vision that your choice restored to you.

12. Now do your eyes belong to Christ, and He looks through them. ²Now your voice belongs to God and echoes His. ³And now your heart remains at peace forever. ⁴You have chosen Him in place of idols, and your attributes, given by your Creator, are restored to you at last. ⁵The Call for God is heard and answered. ⁶Now has fear made way for love, as God Himself replaces cruelty.

13. *Father, we are like You. ²No cruelty abides in us, for there is none in You. ³Your peace is ours. ⁴And we bless the world with what we have received from You alone. ⁵We choose again, and make our choice for all our brothers, knowing they are one with us. ⁶We bring them Your salvation as we have received it now. ⁷And we give thanks for them who render us complete. ⁸In them we see Your glory, and in them we find our peace. ⁹Holy are we because Your Holiness has set us free. ¹⁰And we give thanks. ¹¹Amen.*

REVIEW V

Introduction

1. We now review again. ²This time we are ready to give more effort and more time to what we undertake. ³We recognize we are preparing for another phase of understanding. ⁴We would take this step completely, that we may go on again more certain, more sincere, with faith upheld more surely. ⁵Our footsteps have not been unwavering, and doubts have made us walk uncertainly and slowly on the road this course sets forth. ⁶But now we hasten on, for we approach a greater certainty, a firmer purpose and a surer goal.

2. *Steady our feet, our Father. ²Let our doubts be quiet and our holy minds be still, and speak to us. ³We have no words to give to You. ⁴We would but listen to Your Word, and make it ours. ⁵Lead our practicing as does a father lead a little child along a way he does not understand. ⁶Yet does he follow, sure that he is safe because his father leads the way for him.*

3. *So do we bring our practicing to You. ²And if we stumble, You will raise us up. ³If we forget the way, we count upon Your sure remembering. ⁴We wander off, but You will not forget to call us back. ⁵Quicken our footsteps now, that we may walk more certainly and quickly unto You. ⁶And we accept the Word You offer us to unify our practicing, as we review the thoughts that You have given us.*

4. This is the thought which should precede the thoughts that we review. ²Each one but clarifies some aspect of this thought, or helps it be more meaningful, more personal and true, and more descriptive of the holy Self we share and now prepare to know again:

    ³*God is but Love, and therefore so am I.*

⁴This Self alone knows Love. ⁵This Self alone is perfectly consistent in Its Thoughts; knows Its Creator, understands Itself, is perfect in Its knowledge and Its Love, and never changes from Its constant state of union with Its Father and Itself.

5. And it is this that waits to meet us at the journey's ending.

²Every step we take brings us a little nearer. ³This review will shorten time immeasurably, if we keep in mind that this remains our goal, and as we practice it is this to which we are approaching. ⁴Let us raise our hearts from dust to life, as we remember this is promised us, and that this course was sent to open up the path of light to us, and teach us, step by step, how to return to the eternal Self we thought we lost.

6. I take the journey with you. ²For I share your doubts and fears a little while, that you may come to me who recognize the road by which all fears and doubts are overcome. ³We walk together. ⁴I must understand uncertainty and pain, although I know they have no meaning. ⁵Yet a savior must remain with those he teaches, seeing what they see, but still retaining in his mind the way that led him out, and now will lead you out with him. ⁶God's Son is crucified until you walk along the road with me.

7. My resurrection comes again each time I lead a brother safely to the place at which the journey ends and is forgot. ²I am renewed each time a brother learns there is a way from misery and pain. ³I am reborn each time a brother's mind turns to the light in him and looks for me. ⁴I have forgotten no one. ⁵Help me now to lead you back to where the journey was begun, to make another choice with me.

8. Release me as you practice once again the thoughts I brought to you from Him Who sees your bitter need, and knows the answer God has given Him. ²Together we review these thoughts. ³Together we devote our time and effort to them. ⁴And together we will teach them to our brothers. ⁵God would not have Heaven incomplete. ⁶It waits for you, as I do. ⁷I am incomplete without your part in me. ⁸And as I am made whole we go together to our ancient home, prepared for us before time was and kept unchanged by time, immaculate and safe, as it will be at last when time is done.

9. Let this review be then your gift to me. ²For this alone I need; that you will hear the words I speak, and give them to the world. ³You are my voice, my eyes, my feet, my hands through which I save the world. ⁴The Self from which I call to you is but your own. ⁵To Him we go together. ⁶Take your brother's hand, for this is not a way we walk alone. ⁷In him I walk with you, and you with me. ⁸Our Father wills His Son be one with Him. ⁹What lives but must not then be one with you?

10. Let this review become a time in which we share a new experi-

ence for you, yet one as old as time and older still. ²Hallowed your Name. ³Your glory undefiled forever. ⁴And your wholeness now complete, as God established it. ⁵You are His Son, completing His extension in your own. ⁶We practice but an ancient truth we knew before illusion seemed to claim the world. ⁷And we remind the world that it is free of all illusions every time we say:

⁸*God is but Love, and therefore so am I.*

11.   With this we start each day of our review. ²With this we start and end each period of practice time. ³And with this thought we sleep, to waken once again with these same words upon our lips, to greet another day. ⁴No thought that we review but we surround with it, and use the thoughts to hold it up before our minds, and keep it clear in our rememberance throughout the day. ⁵And thus, when we have finished this review, we will have recognized the words we speak are true.

12.   Yet are the words but aids, and to be used, except at the beginning and the end of practice periods, but to recall the mind, as needed, to its purpose. ²We place faith in the experience that comes from practice, not the means we use. ³We wait for the experience, and recognize that it is only here conviction lies. ⁴We use the words, and try and try again to go beyond them to their meaning, which is far beyond their sound. ⁵The sound grows dim and disappears, as we approach the Source of meaning. ⁶It is Here that we find rest.

LESSON 171

God is but Love, and therefore so am I.

1. (151) All things are echoes of the Voice for God.
   ²**God is but Love, and therefore so am I.**

2. (152) The power of decision is my own.
   ²**God is but Love, and therefore so am I.**

LESSON 172

God is but Love, and therefore so am I.

1. (153) In my defenselessness my safety lies.
   ²**God is but Love, and therefore so am I.**

2. (154) I am among the ministers of God.
   ²**God is but Love, and therefore so am I.**

LESSON 173

God is but Love, and therefore so am I.

1. (155) I will step back and let Him lead the way.
   ²**God is but Love, and therefore so am I.**

2. (156) I walk with God in perfect holiness.
   ²**God is but Love, and therefore so am I.**

LESSON 174

God is but Love, and therefore so am I.

1. (157) Into His Presence would I enter now.
   ²**God is but Love, and therefore so am I.**

2. (158) Today I learn to give as I receive.
   ²**God is but Love, and therefore so am I.**

LESSON 175

God is but Love, and therefore so am I.

1. (159) I give the miracles I have received.
   ²**God is but Love, and therefore so am I.**

2. (160) I am at home. ²Fear is the stranger here.
   ³**God is but Love, and therefore so am I.**

LESSON 176

God is but Love, and therefore so am I.

1. (161) Give me your blessing, holy Son of God.
   ²**God is but Love, and therefore so am I.**

2. (162) I am as God created me.
   ²**God is but Love, and therefore so am I.**

LESSON 177

God is but Love, and therefore so am I.

1. (163) There is no death. ²The Son of God is free.
   ³**God is but Love, and therefore so am I.**

2. (164) Now are we one with Him Who is our Source.
   ²**God is but Love, and therefore so am I.**

LESSON 178

God is but Love, and therefore so am I.

1. (165) Let not my mind deny the Thought of God.
   ²**God is but Love, and therefore so am I.**

2. (166) I am entrusted with the gifts of God.
   ²**God is but Love, and therefore so am I.**

LESSON 179

God is but Love, and therefore so am I.

1. (167) There is one life, and that I share with God.
   ²**God is but Love, and therefore so am I.**

2. (168) Your grace is given me. ²I claim it now.
   ³**God is but Love, and therefore so am I.**

LESSON 180

God is but Love, and therefore so am I.

1. (169) By grace I live. ²By grace I am released.
   ³God is but Love, and therefore so am I.

2. (170) There is no cruelty in God and none in me.
   ²God is but Love, and therefore so am I.

Introduction to Lessons 181–200

1. Our next few lessons make a special point of firming up your willingness to make your weak commitment strong; your scattered goals blend into one intent. ²You are not asked for total dedication all the time as yet. ³But you are asked to practice now in order to attain the sense of peace such unified commitment will bestow, if only intermittently. ⁴It is experiencing this that makes it sure that you will give your total willingness to following the way the course sets forth.

2. Our lessons now are geared specifically to widening horizons, and direct approaches to the special blocks that keep your vision narrow, and too limited to let you see the value of our goal. ²We are attempting now to lift these blocks, however briefly. ³Words alone can not convey the sense of liberation which their lifting brings. ⁴But the experience of freedom and of peace that comes as you give up your tight control of what you see speaks for itself. ⁵Your motivation will be so intensified that words become of little consequence. ⁶You will be sure of what you want, and what is valueless.

3. And so we start our journey beyond words by concentrating first on what impedes your progress still. ²Experience of what exists beyond defensiveness remains beyond achievement while it is denied. ³It may be there, but you cannot accept its presence. ⁴So we now attempt to go past all defenses for a little while each day. ⁵No more than this is asked, because no more than this is needed. ⁶It will be enough to guarantee the rest will come.

LESSON 181

I trust my brothers, who are one with me.

1. Trusting your brothers is essential to establishing and holding up your faith in your ability to transcend doubt and lack of sure conviction in yourself. ²When you attack a brother, you proclaim that he is limited by what you have perceived in him. ³You do not look beyond his errors. ⁴Rather, they are magnified, becoming blocks to your awareness of the Self that lies beyond your own mistakes, and past his seeming sins as well as yours.

2. Perception has a focus. ²It is this that gives consistency to what you see. ³Change but this focus, and what you behold will change accordingly. ⁴Your vision now will shift, to give support to the intent which has replaced the one you held before. ⁵Remove your focus on your brother's sins, and you experience the peace that comes from faith in sinlessness. ⁶This faith receives its only sure support from what you see in others past their sins. ⁷For their mistakes, if focused on, are witnesses to sins in you. ⁸And you will not transcend their sight and see the sinlessness that lies beyond.

3. Therefore, in practicing today, we first let all such little focuses give way to our great need to let our sinlessness become apparent. ²We instruct our minds that it is this we seek, and only this, for just a little while. ³We do not care about our future goals. ⁴And what we saw an instant previous has no concern for us within this interval of time wherein we practice changing our intent. ⁵We seek for innocence and nothing else. ⁶We seek for it with no concern but now.

4. A major hazard to success has been involvement with your past and future goals. ²You have been quite preoccupied with how extremely different the goals this course is advocating are from those you held before. ³And you have also been dismayed by the depressing and restricting thought that, even if you should succeed, you will inevitably lose your way again.

5. How could this matter? ²For the past is gone; the future but imagined. ³These concerns are but defenses against present change of focus in perception. ⁴Nothing more. ⁵We lay these pointless limitations by a little while. ⁶We do not look to past beliefs, and what we will believe will not intrude upon us now.

[7]We enter in the time of practicing with one intent; to look upon the sinlessness within.

6. We recognize that we have lost this goal if anger blocks our way in any form. [2]And if a brother's sins occur to us, our narrowed focus will restrict our sight, and turn our eyes upon our own mistakes, which we will magnify and call our "sins." [3]So, for a little while, without regard to past or future, should such blocks arise we will transcend them with instructions to our minds to change their focus, as we say:

[4]*It is not this that I would look upon.*
[5]*I trust my brothers, who are one with me.*

7. And we will also use this thought to keep us safe throughout the day. [2]We do not seek for long-range goals. [3]As each obstruction seems to block the vision of our sinlessness, we seek but for surcease an instant from the misery the focus upon sin will bring, and uncorrected will remain.

8. Nor do we ask for fantasies. [2]For what we seek to look upon is really there. [3]And as our focus goes beyond mistakes, we will behold a wholly sinless world. [4]When seeing this is all we want to see, when this is all we seek for in the name of true perception, are the eyes of Christ inevitably ours. [5]And the Love He feels for us becomes our own as well. [6]This will become the only thing we see reflected in the world and in ourselves.

9. The world which once proclaimed our sins becomes the proof that we are sinless. [2]And our love for everyone we look upon attests to our remembrance of the holy Self which knows no sin, and never could conceive of anything without Its sinlessness. [3]We seek for this remembrance as we turn our minds to practicing today. [4]We look neither ahead nor backwards. [5]We look straight into the present. [6]And we give our trust to the experience we ask for now. [7]Our sinlessness is but the Will of God. [8]This instant is our willing one with His.

LESSON 182

I will be still an instant and go home.

1. This world you seem to live in is not home to you. ²And some-where in your mind you know that this is true. ³A memory of home keeps haunting you, as if there were a place that called you to return, although you do not recognize the voice, nor what it is the voice reminds you of. ⁴Yet still you feel an alien here, from somewhere all unknown. ⁵Nothing so definite that you could say with certainty you are an exile here. ⁶Just a persistent feeling, sometimes not more than a tiny throb, at other times hardly re-membered, actively dismissed, but surely to return to mind again.

2. No one but knows whereof we speak. ²Yet some try to put by their suffering in games they play to occupy their time, and keep their sadness from them. ³Others will deny that they are sad, and do not recognize their tears at all. ⁴Still others will maintain that what we speak of is illusion, not to be considered more than but a dream. ⁵Yet who, in simple honesty, without defensiveness and self-deception, would deny he understands the words we speak?

3. We speak today for everyone who walks this world, for he is not at home. ²He goes uncertainly about in endless search, seek-ing in darkness what he cannot find; not recognizing what it is he seeks. ³A thousand homes he makes, yet none contents his rest-less mind. ⁴He does not understand he builds in vain. ⁵The home he seeks can not be made by him. ⁶There is no substitute for Heaven. ⁷All he ever made was hell.

4. Perhaps you think it is your childhood home that you would find again. ²The childhood of your body, and its place of shelter, are a memory now so distorted that you merely hold a picture of a past that never happened. ³Yet there is a Child in you Who seeks His Father's house, and knows that He is alien here. ⁴This childhood is eternal, with an innocence that will endure forever. ⁵Where this Child shall go is holy ground. ⁶It is His Holiness that lights up Heaven, and that brings to earth the pure reflection of the light above, wherein are earth and Heaven joined as one.

5. It is this Child in you your Father knows as His Own Son. ²It is this Child Who knows His Father. ³He desires to go home so deeply, so unceasingly, His voice cries unto you to let Him rest a

while. ⁴He does not ask for more than just a few instants of respite; just an interval in which He can return to breathe again the holy air that fills His Father's house. ⁵You are His home as well. ⁶He will return. ⁷But give Him just a little time to be Himself, within the peace that is His home, resting in silence and in peace and love.

6. This Child needs your protection. ²He is far from home. ³He is so little that He seems so easily shut out, His tiny voice so readily obscured, His call for help almost unheard amid the grating sounds and harsh and rasping noises of the world. ⁴Yet does He know that in you still abides His sure protection. ⁵You will fail Him not. ⁶He will go home, and you along with Him.

7. This Child is your defenselessness; your strength. ²He trusts in you. ³He came because He knew you would not fail. ⁴He whispers of His home unceasingly to you. ⁵For He would bring you back with Him, that He Himself might stay, and not return again where He does not belong, and where He lives an outcast in a world of alien thoughts. ⁶His patience has no limits. ⁷He will wait until you hear His gentle Voice within you, calling you to let Him go in peace, along with you, to where He is at home and you with Him.

8. When you are still an instant, when the world recedes from you, when valueless ideas cease to have value in your restless mind, then will you hear His Voice. ²So poignantly He calls to you that you will not resist Him longer. ³In that instant He will take you to His home, and you will stay with Him in perfect stillness, silent and at peace, beyond all words, untouched by fear and doubt, sublimely certain that you are at home.

9. Rest with Him frequently today. ²For He was willing to become a little Child that you might learn of Him how strong is he who comes without defenses, offering only love's messages to those who think he is their enemy. ³He holds the might of Heaven in His hand and calls them friend, and gives His strength to them, that they may see He would be Friend to them. ⁴He asks that they protect Him, for His home is far away, and He will not return to it alone.

10. Christ is reborn as but a little Child each time a wanderer would leave his home. ²For he must learn that what he would protect is but this Child, Who comes defenseless and Who is protected by defenselessness. ³Go home with Him from time to time today. ⁴You are as much an alien here as He.

11. Take time today to lay aside your shield which profits nothing, and lay down the spear and sword you raised against an enemy without existence. ²Christ has called you friend and brother. ³He has even come to ask your help in letting Him go home today, completed and completely. ⁴He has come as does a little child, who must beseech his father for protection and for love. ⁵He rules the universe, and yet He asks unceasingly that you return with Him, and take illusions as your gods no more.

12. You have not lost your innocence. ²It is for this you yearn. ³This is your heart's desire. ⁴This is the voice you hear, and this the call which cannot be denied. ⁵The holy Child remains with you. ⁶His home is yours. ⁷Today He gives you His defenselessness, and you accept it in exchange for all the toys of battle you have made. ⁸And now the way is open, and the journey has an end in sight at last. ⁹Be still an instant and go home with Him, and be at peace a while.

LESSON 183

I call upon God's Name and on my own.

1. God's Name is holy, but no holier than yours. ²To call upon His Name is but to call upon your own. ³A father gives his son his name, and thus identifies the son with him. ⁴His brothers share his name, and thus are they united in a bond to which they turn for their identity. ⁵Your Father's Name reminds you who you are, even within a world that does not know; even though you have not remembered it.

2. God's Name can not be heard without response, nor said without an echo in the mind that calls you to remember. ²Say His Name, and you invite the angels to surround the ground on which you stand, and sing to you as they spread out their wings to keep you safe, and shelter you from every worldly thought that would intrude upon your holiness.

3. Repeat God's Name, and all the world responds by laying down illusions. ²Every dream the world holds dear has suddenly gone by, and where it seemed to stand you find a star; a miracle of grace. ³The sick arise, healed of their sickly thoughts. ⁴The blind can see; the deaf can hear. ⁵The sorrowful cast off their mourning, and the tears of pain are dried as happy laughter comes to bless the world.

4. Repeat the Name of God, and little names have lost their meaning. ²No temptation but becomes a nameless and unwanted thing before God's Name. ³Repeat His Name, and see how easily you will forget the names of all the gods you valued. ⁴They have lost the name of god you gave them. ⁵They become anonymous and valueless to you, although before you let the Name of God replace their little names, you stood before them worshipfully, naming them as gods.

5. Repeat the Name of God, and call upon your Self, Whose Name is His. ²Repeat His Name, and all the tiny, nameless things on earth slip into right perspective. ³Those who call upon the Name of God can not mistake the nameless for the Name, nor sin for grace, nor bodies for the holy Son of God. ⁴And should you join a brother as you sit with him in silence, and repeat God's Name along with him within your quiet mind, you have established there an altar which reaches to God Himself and to His Son.

6. Practice but this today; repeat God's Name slowly again and still again. [2]Become oblivious to every name but His. [3]Hear nothing else. [4]Let all your thoughts become anchored on this. [5]No other word we use except at the beginning, when we say today's idea but once. [6]And then God's Name becomes our only thought, our only word, the only thing that occupies our minds, the only wish we have, the only sound with any meaning, and the only Name of everything that we desire to see; of everything that we would call our own.

7. Thus do we give an invitation which can never be refused. [2]And God will come, and answer it Himself. [3]Think not He hears the little prayers of those who call on Him with names of idols cherished by the world. [4]They cannot reach Him thus. [5]He cannot hear requests that He be not Himself, or that His Son receive another name than His.

8. Repeat God's Name, and you acknowledge Him as sole Creator of reality. [2]And you acknowledge also that His Son is part of Him, creating in His Name. [3]Sit silently, and let His Name become the all-encompassing idea that holds your mind completely. [4]Let all thoughts be still except this one. [5]And to all other thoughts respond with this, and see God's Name replace the thousand little names you gave your thoughts, not realizing that there is one Name for all there is, and all that there will be.

9. Today you can achieve a state in which you will experience the gift of grace. [2]You can escape all bondage of the world, and give the world the same release you found. [3]You can remember what the world forgot, and offer it your own remembering. [4]You can accept today the part you play in its salvation, and your own as well. [5]And both can be accomplished perfectly.

10. Turn to the Name of God for your release, and it is given you. [2]No prayer but this is necessary, for it holds them all within it. [3]Words are insignificant, and all requests unneeded when God's Son calls on his Father's Name. [4]His Father's Thoughts become his own. [5]He makes his claim to all his Father gave, is giving still, and will forever give. [6]He calls on Him to let all things he thought he made be nameless now, and in their place the holy Name of God becomes his judgment of their worthlessness.

11. All little things are silent. [2]Little sounds are soundless now. [3]The little things of earth have disappeared. [4]The universe consists of nothing but the Son of God, who calls upon his Father. [5]And his Father's Voice gives answer in his Father's holy Name.

[6]In this eternal, still relationship, in which communication far transcends all words, and yet exceeds in depth and height whatever words could possibly convey, is peace eternal. [7]In our Father's Name, we would experience this peace today. [8]And in His Name, it shall be given us.

LESSON 184

The Name of God is my inheritance.

1. You live by symbols. ²You have made up names for everything you see. ³Each one becomes a separate entity, identified by its own name. ⁴By this you carve it out of unity. ⁵By this you designate its special attributes, and set it off from other things by emphasizing space surrounding it. ⁶This space you lay between all things to which you give a different name; all happenings in terms of place and time; all bodies which are greeted by a name.

2. This space you see as setting off all things from one another is the means by which the world's perception is achieved. ²You see something where nothing is, and see as well nothing where there is unity; a space between all things, between all things and you. ³Thus do you think that you have given life in separation. ⁴By this split you think you are established as a unity which functions with an independent will.

3. What are these names by which the world becomes a series of discrete events, of things ununified, of bodies kept apart and holding bits of mind as separate awarenesses? ²You gave these names to them, establishing perception as you wished to have perception be. ³The nameless things were given names, and thus reality was given them as well. ⁴For what is named is given meaning and will then be seen as meaningful; a cause of true effect, with consequence inherent in itself.

4. This is the way reality is made by partial vision, purposefully set against the given truth. ²Its enemy is wholeness. ³It conceives of little things and looks upon them. ⁴And a lack of space, a sense of unity or vision that sees differently, become the threats which it must overcome, conflict with and deny.

5. Yet does this other vision still remain a natural direction for the mind to channel its perception. ²It is hard to teach the mind a thousand alien names, and thousands more. ³Yet you believe this is what learning means; its one essential goal by which communication is achieved, and concepts can be meaningfully shared.

6. This is the sum of the inheritance the world bestows. ²And everyone who learns to think that it is so accepts the signs and symbols that assert the world is real. ³It is for this they stand.

⁴They leave no doubt that what is named is there. ⁵It can be seen, as is anticipated. ⁶What denies that it is true is but illusion, for it is the ultimate reality. ⁷To question it is madness; to accept its presence is the proof of sanity.

7. Such is the teaching of the world. ²It is a phase of learning everyone who comes must go through. ³But the sooner he perceives on what it rests, how questionable are its premises, how doubtful its results, the sooner does he question its effects. ⁴Learning that stops with what the world would teach stops short of meaning. ⁵In its proper place, it serves but as a starting point from which another kind of learning can begin, a new perception can be gained, and all the arbitrary names the world bestows can be withdrawn as they are raised to doubt.

8. Think not you made the world. ²Illusions, yes! ³But what is true in earth and Heaven is beyond your naming. ⁴When you call upon a brother, it is to his body that you make appeal. ⁵His true Identity is hidden from you by what you believe he really is. ⁶His body makes response to what you call him, for his mind consents to take the name you give him as his own. ⁷And thus his unity is twice denied, for you perceive him separate from you, and he accepts this separate name as his.

9. It would indeed be strange if you were asked to go beyond all symbols of the world, forgetting them forever; yet were asked to take a teaching function. ²You have need to use the symbols of the world a while. ³But be you not deceived by them as well. ⁴They do not stand for anything at all, and in your practicing it is this thought that will release you from them. ⁵They become but means by which you can communicate in ways the world can understand, but which you recognize is not the unity where true communication can be found.

10. Thus what you need are intervals each day in which the learning of the world becomes a transitory phase; a prison house from which you go into the sunlight and forget the darkness. ²Here you understand the Word, the Name which God has given you; the one Identity which all things share; the one acknowledgment of what is true. ³And then step back to darkness, not because you think it real, but only to proclaim its unreality in terms which still have meaning in the world that darkness rules.

11. Use all the little names and symbols which delineate the world of darkness. ²Yet accept them not as your reality. ³The Holy Spirit uses all of them, but He does not forget creation has one Name,

one meaning, and a single Source which unifies all things within Itself. ⁴Use all the names the world bestows on them but for convenience, yet do not forget they share the Name of God along with you.

12. God has no name. ²And yet His Name becomes the final lesson that all things are one, and at this lesson does all learning end. ³All names are unified; all space is filled with truth's reflection. ⁴Every gap is closed, and separation healed. ⁵The Name of God is the inheritance He gave to those who chose the teaching of the world to take the place of Heaven. ⁶In our practicing, our purpose is to let our minds accept what God has given as the answer to the pitiful inheritance you made as fitting tribute to the Son He loves.

13. No one can fail who seeks the meaning of the Name of God. ²Experience must come to supplement the Word. ³But first you must accept the Name for all reality, and realize the many names you gave its aspects have distorted what you see, but have not interfered with truth at all. ⁴One Name we bring into our practicing. ⁵One Name we use to unify our sight.

14. And though we use a different name for each awareness of an aspect of God's Son, we understand that they have but one Name, which He has given them. ²It is this Name we use in practicing. ³And through Its use, all foolish separations disappear which kept us blind. ⁴And we are given strength to see beyond them. ⁵Now our sight is blessed with blessings we can give as we receive.

15. *Father, our Name is Yours. ²In It we are united with all living things, and You Who are their one Creator. ³What we made and call by many different names is but a shadow we have tried to cast across Your Own reality. ⁴And we are glad and thankful we were wrong. ⁵All our mistakes we give to You, that we may be absolved from all effects our errors seemed to have. ⁶And we accept the truth You give, in place of every one of them. ⁷Your Name is our salvation and escape from what we made. ⁸Your Name unites us in the oneness which is our inheritance and peace. ⁹Amen.*

LESSON 185

I want the peace of God.

1. To say these words is nothing. ²But to mean these words is everything. ³If you could but mean them for just an instant, there would be no further sorrow possible for you in any form; in any place or time. ⁴Heaven would be completely given back to full awareness, memory of God entirely restored, the resurrection of all creation fully recognized.

2. No one can mean these words and not be healed. ²He cannot play with dreams, nor think he is himself a dream. ³He cannot make a hell and think it real. ⁴He wants the peace of God, and it is given him. ⁵For that is all he wants, and that is all he will receive. ⁶Many have said these words. ⁷But few indeed have meant them. ⁸You have but to look upon the world you see around you to be sure how very few they are. ⁹The world would be completely changed, should any two agree these words express the only thing they want.

3. Two minds with one intent become so strong that what they will becomes the Will of God. ²For minds can only join in truth. ³In dreams, no two can share the same intent. ⁴To each, the hero of the dream is different; the outcome wanted not the same for both. ⁵Loser and gainer merely shift about in changing patterns, as the ratio of gain to loss and loss to gain takes on a different aspect or another form.

4. Yet compromise alone a dream can bring. ²Sometimes it takes the form of union, but only the form. ³The meaning must escape the dream, for compromising is the goal of dreaming. ⁴Minds cannot unite in dreams. ⁵They merely bargain. ⁶And what bargain can give them the peace of God? ⁷Illusions come to take His place. ⁸And what He means is lost to sleeping minds intent on compromise, each to his gain and to another's loss.

5. To mean you want the peace of God is to renounce all dreams. ²For no one means these words who wants illusions, and who therefore seeks the means which bring illusions. ³He has looked on them, and found them wanting. ⁴Now he seeks to go beyond them, recognizing that another dream would offer nothing more than all the others. ⁵Dreams are one to him. ⁶And he has learned their only difference is one of form, for one will bring the same

despair and misery as do the rest.

6. The mind which means that all it wants is peace must join with other minds, for that is how peace is obtained. ²And when the wish for peace is genuine, the means for finding it is given, in a form each mind that seeks for it in honesty can understand. ³Whatever form the lesson takes is planned for him in such a way that he can not mistake it, if his asking is sincere. ⁴But if he asks without sincerity, there is no form in which the lesson will meet with acceptance and be truly learned.

7. Let us today devote our practicing to recognizing that we really mean the words we say. ²We want the peace of God. ³This is no idle wish. ⁴These words do not request another dream be given us. ⁵They do not ask for compromise, nor try to make another bargain in the hope that there may yet be one that can succeed where all the rest have failed. ⁶To mean these words acknowledges illusions are in vain, requesting the eternal in the place of shifting dreams which seem to change in what they offer, but are one in nothingness.

8. Today devote your practice periods to careful searching of your mind, to find the dreams you cherish still. ²What do you ask for in your heart? ³Forget the words you use in making your requests. ⁴Consider but what you believe will comfort you, and bring you happiness. ⁵But be you not dismayed by lingering illusions, for their form is not what matters now. ⁶Let not some dreams be more acceptable, reserving shame and secrecy for others. ⁷They are one. ⁸And being one, one question should be asked of all of them, "Is this what I would have, in place of Heaven and the peace of God?"

9. This is the choice you make. ²Be not deceived that it is otherwise. ³No compromise is possible in this. ⁴You choose God's peace, or you have asked for dreams. ⁵And dreams will come as you requested them. ⁶Yet will God's peace come just as certainly, and to remain with you forever. ⁷It will not be gone with every twist and turning of the road, to reappear, unrecognized, in forms which shift and change with every step you take.

10. You want the peace of God. ²And so do all who seem to seek for dreams. ³For them as well as for yourself, you ask but this when you make this request with deep sincerity. ⁴For thus you reach to what they really want, and join your own intent with what they seek above all things, perhaps unknown to them, but sure to you. ⁵You have been weak at times, uncertain in your

purpose, and unsure of what you wanted, where to look for it, and where to turn for help in the attempt. [6]Help has been given you. [7]And would you not avail yourself of it by sharing it?

11. No one who truly seeks the peace of God can fail to find it. [2]For he merely asks that he deceive himself no longer by denying to himself what is God's Will. [3]Who can remain unsatisfied who asks for what he has already? [4]Who could be unanswered who requests an answer which is his to give? [5]The peace of God is yours.

12. For you was peace created, given you by its Creator, and established as His Own eternal gift. [2]How can you fail, when you but ask for what He wills for you? [3]And how could your request be limited to you alone? [4]No gift of God can be unshared. [5]It is this attribute that sets the gifts of God apart from every dream that ever seemed to take the place of truth.

13. No one can lose and everyone must gain whenever any gift of God has been requested and received by anyone. [2]God gives but to unite. [3]To take away is meaningless to Him. [4]And when it is as meaningless to you, you can be sure you share one Will with Him, and He with you. [5]And you will also know you share one Will with all your brothers, whose intent is yours.

14. It is this one intent we seek today, uniting our desires with the need of every heart, the call of every mind, the hope that lies beyond despair, the love attack would hide, the brotherhood that hate has sought to sever, but which still remains as God created it. [2]With Help like this beside us, can we fail today as we request the peace of God be given us?

LESSON 186

Salvation of the world depends on me.

1. Here is the statement that will one day take all arrogance away from every mind. ²Here is the thought of true humility, which holds no function as your own but that which has been given you. ³It offers your acceptance of a part assigned to you, without insisting on another role. ⁴It does not judge your proper role. ⁵It but acknowledges the Will of God is done on earth as well as Heaven. ⁶It unites all wills on earth in Heaven's plan to save the world, restoring it to Heaven's peace.

2. Let us not fight our function. ²We did not establish it. ³It is not our idea. ⁴The means are given us by which it will be perfectly accomplished. ⁵All that we are asked to do is to accept our part in genuine humility, and not deny with self-deceiving arrogance that we are worthy. ⁶What is given us to do, we have the strength to do. ⁷Our minds are suited perfectly to take the part assigned to us by One Who knows us well.

3. Today's idea may seem quite sobering, until you see its meaning. ²All it says is that your Father still remembers you, and offers you the perfect trust He holds in you who are His Son. ³It does not ask that you be different in any way from what you are. ⁴What could humility request but this? ⁵And what could arrogance deny but this? ⁶Today we will not shrink from our assignment on the specious grounds that modesty is outraged. ⁷It is pride that would deny the Call for God Himself.

4. All false humility we lay aside today, that we may listen to God's Voice reveal to us what He would have us do. ²We do not doubt our adequacy for the function He will offer us. ³We will be certain only that He knows our strengths, our wisdom and our holiness. ⁴And if He deems us worthy, so we are. ⁵It is but arrogance that judges otherwise.

5. There is one way, and only one, to be released from the imprisonment your plan to prove the false is true has brought to you. ²Accept the plan you did not make instead. ³Judge not your value to it. ⁴If God's Voice assures you that salvation needs your part, and that the whole depends on you, be sure that it is so. ⁵The arrogant must cling to words, afraid to go beyond them to experience which might affront their stance. ⁶Yet are the humble

free to hear the Voice which tells them what they are, and what to do.

6. Arrogance makes an image of yourself that is not real. [2]It is this image which quails and retreats in terror, as the Voice for God assures you that you have the strength, the wisdom and the holiness to go beyond all images. [3]You are not weak, as is the image of yourself. [4]You are not ignorant and helpless. [5]Sin can not tarnish the truth in you, and misery can come not near the holy home of God.

7. All this the Voice for God relates to you. [2]And as He speaks, the image trembles and seeks to attack the threat it does not know, sensing its basis crumble. [3]Let it go. [4]Salvation of the world depends on you, and not upon this little pile of dust. [5]What can it tell the holy Son of God? [6]Why need he be concerned with it at all?

8. And so we find our peace. [2]We will accept the function God has given us, for all illusions rest upon the weird belief that we can make another for ourselves. [3]Our self-made roles are shifting, and they seem to change from mourner to ecstatic bliss of love and loving. [4]We can laugh or weep, and greet the day with welcome or with tears. [5]Our very being seems to change as we experience a thousand shifts in mood, and our emotions raise us high indeed, or dash us to the ground in hopelessness.

9. Is this the Son of God? [2]Could He create such instability and call it Son? [3]He Who is changeless shares His attributes with His creation. [4]All the images His Son appears to make have no effect on what he is. [5]They blow across his mind like wind-swept leaves that form a patterning an instant, break apart to group again, and scamper off. [6]Or like mirages seen above a desert, rising from the dust.

10. These unsubstantial images will go, and leave your mind unclouded and serene, when you accept the function given you. [2]The images you make give rise to but conflicting goals, impermanent and vague, uncertain and ambiguous. [3]Who could be constant in his efforts, or direct his energies and concentrated drive toward goals like these? [4]The functions which the world esteems are so uncertain that they change ten times an hour at their most secure. [5]What hope of gain can rest on goals like this?

11. In lovely contrast, certain as the sun's return each morning to dispel the night, your truly given function stands out clear and wholly unambiguous. [2]There is no doubt of its validity. [3]It comes

from One Who knows no error, and His Voice is certain of Its messages. ⁴They will not change, nor be in conflict. ⁵All of them point to one goal, and one you can attain. ⁶Your plan may be impossible, but God's can never fail because He is its Source.

12. Do as God's Voice directs. ²And if It asks a thing of you which seems impossible, remember Who it is that asks, and who would make denial. ³Then consider this; which is more likely to be right? ⁴The Voice that speaks for the Creator of all things, Who knows all things exactly as they are, or a distorted image of yourself, confused, bewildered, inconsistent and unsure of everything? ⁵Let not its voice direct you. ⁶Hear instead a certain Voice, which tells you of a function given you by your Creator Who remembers you, and urges that you now remember Him.

13. His gentle Voice is calling from the known to the unknowing. ²He would comfort you, although He knows no sorrow. ³He would make a restitution, though He is complete; a gift to you, although He knows that you have everything already. ⁴He has Thoughts which answer every need His Son perceives, although He sees them not. ⁵For Love must give, and what is given in His Name takes on the form most useful in a world of form.

14. These are the forms which never can deceive, because they come from Formlessness Itself. ²Forgiveness is an earthly form of love, which as it is in Heaven has no form. ³Yet what is needed here is given here as it is needed. ⁴In this form you can fulfill your function even here, although what love will mean to you when formlessness has been restored to you is greater still. ⁵Salvation of the world depends on you who can forgive. ⁶Such is your function here.

LESSON 187

I bless the world because I bless myself.

1.   No one can give unless he has. ²In fact, giving is proof of having. ³We have made this point before. ⁴What seems to make it hard to credit is not this. ⁵No one can doubt that you must first possess what you would give. ⁶It is the second phase on which the world and true perception differ. ⁷Having had and given, then the world asserts that you have lost what you possessed. ⁸The truth maintains that giving will increase what you possess.

2.   How is this possible? ²For it is sure that if you give a finite thing away, your body's eyes will not perceive it yours. ³Yet we have learned that things but represent the thoughts that make them. ⁴And you do not lack for proof that when you give ideas away, you strengthen them in your own mind. ⁵Perhaps the form in which the thought seems to appear is changed in giving. ⁶Yet it must return to him who gives. ⁷Nor can the form it takes be less acceptable. ⁸It must be more.

3.   Ideas must first belong to you, before you give them. ²If you are to save the world, you first accept salvation for yourself. ³But you will not believe that this is done until you see the miracles it brings to everyone you look upon. ⁴Herein is the idea of giving clarified and given meaning. ⁵Now you can perceive that by your giving is your store increased.

4.   Protect all things you value by the act of giving them away, and you are sure that you will never lose them. ²What you thought you did not have is thereby proven yours. ³Yet value not its form. ⁴For this will change and grow unrecognizable in time, however much you try to keep it safe. ⁵No form endures. ⁶It is the thought behind the form of things that lives unchangeable.

5.   Give gladly. ²You can only gain thereby. ³The thought remains, and grows in strength as it is reinforced by giving. ⁴Thoughts extend as they are shared, for they can not be lost. ⁵There is no giver and receiver in the sense the world conceives of them. ⁶There is a giver who retains; another who will give as well. ⁷And both must gain in this exchange, for each will have the thought in form most helpful to him. ⁸What he seems to lose is always something he will value less than what will surely be returned to him.

6.   Never forget you give but to yourself. ²Who understands what

giving means must laugh at the idea of sacrifice. [3]Nor can he fail to recognize the many forms which sacrifice may take. [4]He laughs as well at pain and loss, at sickness and at grief, at poverty, starvation and at death. [5]He recognizes sacrifice remains the one idea that stands behind them all, and in his gentle laughter are they healed.

7. Illusion recognized must disappear. [2]Accept not suffering, and you remove the thought of suffering. [3]Your blessing lies on everyone who suffers, when you choose to see all suffering as what it is. [4]The thought of sacrifice gives rise to all the forms that suffering appears to take. [5]And sacrifice is an idea so mad that sanity dismisses it at once.

8. Never believe that you can sacrifice. [2]There is no place for sacrifice in what has any value. [3]If the thought occurs, its very presence proves that error has arisen and correction must be made. [4]Your blessing will correct it. [5]Given first to you, it now is yours to give as well. [6]No form of sacrifice and suffering can long endure before the face of one who has forgiven and has blessed himself.

9. The lilies that your brother offers you are laid upon your altar, with the ones you offer him beside them. [2]Who could fear to look upon such lovely holiness? [3]The great illusion of the fear of God diminishes to nothingness before the purity that you will look on here. [4]Be not afraid to look. [5]The blessedness you will behold will take away all thought of form, and leave instead the perfect gift forever there, forever to increase, forever yours, forever given away.

10. Now are we one in thought, for fear has gone. [2]And here, before the altar to one God, one Father, one Creator and one Thought, we stand together as one Son of God. [3]Not separate from Him Who is our Source; not distant from one brother who is part of our one Self Whose innocence has joined us all as one, we stand in blessedness, and give as we receive. [4]The Name of God is on our lips. [5]And as we look within, we see the purity of Heaven shine in our reflection of our Father's Love.

11. Now are we blessed, and now we bless the world. [2]What we have looked upon we would extend, for we would see it everywhere. [3]We would behold it shining with the grace of God in everyone. [4]We would not have it be withheld from anything we look upon. [5]And to ensure this holy sight is ours, we offer it to

everything we see. [6]For where we see it, it will be returned to us in form of lilies we can lay upon our altar, making it a home for Innocence Itself, Who dwells in us and offers us His Holiness as ours.

LESSON 188

The peace of God is shining in me now.

1. Why wait for Heaven? ²Those who seek the light are merely covering their eyes. ³The light is in them now. ⁴Enlightenment is but a recognition, not a change at all. ⁵Light is not of the world, yet you who bear the light in you are alien here as well. ⁶The light came with you from your native home, and stayed with you because it is your own. ⁷It is the only thing you bring with you from Him Who is your Source. ⁸It shines in you because it lights your home, and leads you back to where it came from and you are at home.

2. This light can not be lost. ²Why wait to find it in the future, or believe it has been lost already, or was never there? ³It can so easily be looked upon that arguments which prove it is not there become ridiculous. ⁴Who can deny the presence of what he beholds in him? ⁵It is not difficult to look within, for there all vision starts. ⁶There is no sight, be it of dreams or from a truer Source, that is not but the shadow of the seen through inward vision. ⁷There perception starts, and there it ends. ⁸It has no source but this.

3. The peace of God is shining in you now, and from your heart extends around the world. ²It pauses to caress each living thing, and leaves a blessing with it that remains forever and forever. ³What it gives must be eternal. ⁴It removes all thoughts of the ephemeral and valueless. ⁵It brings renewal to all tired hearts, and lights all vision as it passes by. ⁶All of its gifts are given everyone, and everyone unites in giving thanks to you who give, and you who have received.

4. The shining in your mind reminds the world of what it has forgotten, and the world restores the memory to you as well. ²From you salvation radiates with gifts beyond all measure, given and returned. ³To you, the giver of the gift, does God Himself give thanks. ⁴And in His blessing does the light in you shine brighter, adding to the gifts you have to offer to the world.

5. The peace of God can never be contained. ²Who recognizes it within himself must give it. ³And the means for giving it are in his understanding. ⁴He forgives because he recognized the truth in him. ⁵The peace of God is shining in you now, and in all living

things. ⁶In quietness is it acknowledged universally. ⁷For what your inward vision looks upon is your perception of the universe.

6. Sit quietly and close your eyes. ²The light within you is sufficient. ³It alone has power to give the gift of sight to you. ⁴Exclude the outer world, and let your thoughts fly to the peace within. ⁵They know the way. ⁶For honest thoughts, untainted by the dream of worldly things outside yourself, become the holy messengers of God Himself.

7. These thoughts you think with Him. ²They recognize their home. ³And they point surely to their Source, Where God the Father and the Son are one. ⁴God's peace is shining on them, but they must remain with you as well, for they were born within your mind, as yours was born in God's. ⁵They lead you back to peace, from where they came but to remind you how you must return.

8. They heed your Father's Voice when you refuse to listen. ²And they urge you gently to accept His Word for what you are, instead of fantasies and shadows. ³They remind you that you are the co-creator of all things that live. ⁴For as the peace of God is shining in you, it must shine on them.

9. We practice coming nearer to the light in us today. ²We take our wandering thoughts, and gently bring them back to where they fall in line with all the thoughts we share with God. ³We will not let them stray. ⁴We let the light within our minds direct them to come home. ⁵We have betrayed them, ordering that they depart from us. ⁶But now we call them back, and wash them clean of strange desires and disordered wishes. ⁷We restore to them the holiness of their inheritance.

10. Thus are our minds restored with them, and we acknowledge that the peace of God still shines in us, and from us to all living things that share our life. ²We will forgive them all, absolving all the world from what we thought it did to us. ³For it is we who make the world as we would have it. ⁴Now we choose that it be innocent, devoid of sin and open to salvation. ⁵And we lay our saving blessing on it, as we say:

> ⁶The peace of God is shining in me now.
> ⁷Let all things shine upon me in that peace,
> And let me bless them with the light in me.

LESSON 189

I feel the Love of God within me now.

1. There is a light in you the world can not perceive. ²And with its eyes you will not see this light, for you are blinded by the world. ³Yet you have eyes to see it. ⁴It is there for you to look upon. ⁵It was not placed in you to be kept hidden from your sight. ⁶This light is a reflection of the thought we practice now. ⁷To feel the Love of God within you is to see the world anew, shining in innocence, alive with hope, and blessed with perfect charity and love.

2. Who could feel fear in such a world as this? ²It welcomes you, rejoices that you came, and sings your praises as it keeps you safe from every form of danger and of pain. ³It offers you a warm and gentle home in which to stay a while. ⁴It blesses you throughout the day, and watches through the night as silent guardian of your holy sleep. ⁵It sees salvation in you, and protects the light in you, in which it sees its own. ⁶It offers you its flowers and its snow, in thankfulness for your benevolence.

3. This is the world the Love of God reveals. ²It is so different from the world you see through darkened eyes of malice and of fear, that one belies the other. ³Only one can be perceived at all. ⁴The other one is wholly meaningless. ⁵A world in which forgiveness shines on everything, and peace offers its gentle light to everyone, is inconceivable to those who see a world of hatred rising from attack, poised to avenge, to murder and destroy.

4. Yet is the world of hatred equally unseen and inconceivable to those who feel God's Love in them. ²Their world reflects the quietness and peace that shines in them; the gentleness and innocence they see surrounding them; the joy with which they look out from the endless wells of joy within. ³What they have felt in them they look upon, and see its sure reflection everywhere.

5. What would you see? ²The choice is given you. ³But learn and do not let your mind forget this law of seeing: You will look upon that which you feel within. ⁴If hatred finds a place within your heart, you will perceive a fearful world, held cruelly in death's sharp-pointed, bony fingers. ⁵If you feel the Love of God within you, you will look out on a world of mercy and of love.

6. Today we pass illusions, as we seek to reach to what is true in

us, and feel its all-embracing tenderness, its Love which knows us perfect as itself, its sight which is the gift its Love bestows on us. ²We learn the way today. ³It is as sure as Love itself, to which it carries us. ⁴For its simplicity avoids the snares the foolish convolutions of the world's apparent reasoning but serve to hide.

7. Simply do this: Be still, and lay aside all thoughts of what you are and what God is; all concepts you have learned about the world; all images you hold about yourself. ²Empty your mind of everything it thinks is either true or false, or good or bad, of every thought it judges worthy, and all the ideas of which it is ashamed. ³Hold onto nothing. ⁴Do not bring with you one thought the past has taught, nor one belief you ever learned before from anything. ⁵Forget this world, forget this course, and come with wholly empty hands unto your God.

8. Is it not He Who knows the way to you? ²You need not know the way to Him. ³Your part is simply to allow all obstacles that you have interposed between the Son and God the Father to be quietly removed forever. ⁴God will do His part in joyful and immediate response. ⁵Ask and receive. ⁶But do not make demands, nor point the road to God by which He should appear to you. ⁷The way to reach Him is merely to let Him be. ⁸For in that way is your reality proclaimed as well.

9. And so today we do not choose the way in which we go to Him. ²But we do choose to let Him come. ³And with this choice we rest. ⁴And in our quiet hearts and open minds, His Love will blaze its pathway of itself. ⁵What has not been denied is surely there, if it be true and can be surely reached. ⁶God knows His Son, and knows the way to him. ⁷He does not need His Son to show Him how to find His way. ⁸Through every opened door His Love shines outward from its home within, and lightens up the world in innocence.

10. *Father, we do not know the way to You. ²But we have called, and You have answered us. ³We will not interfere. ⁴Salvation's ways are not our own, for they belong to You. ⁵And it is unto You we look for them. ⁶Our hands are open to receive Your gifts. ⁷We have no thoughts we think apart from You, and cherish no beliefs of what we are, or Who created us. ⁸Yours is the way that we would find and follow. ⁹And we ask but that Your Will, which is our own as well, be done in us and in the world, that it become a part of Heaven now. ¹⁰Amen.*

LESSON 190

I choose the joy of God instead of pain.

1. Pain is a wrong perspective. ²When it is experienced in any form, it is a proof of self-deception. ³It is not a fact at all. ⁴There is no form it takes that will not disappear if seen aright. ⁵For pain proclaims God cruel. ⁶How could it be real in any form? ⁷It witnesses to God the Father's hatred of His Son, the sinfulness He sees in him, and His insane desire for revenge and death.

2. Can such projections be attested to? ²Can they be anything but wholly false? ³Pain is but witness to the Son's mistakes in what he thinks he is. ⁴It is a dream of fierce retaliation for a crime that could not be committed; for attack on what is wholly unassailable. ⁵It is a nightmare of abandonment by an Eternal Love, which could not leave the Son whom It created out of love.

3. Pain is a sign illusions reign in place of truth. ²It demonstrates God is denied, confused with fear, perceived as mad, and seen as traitor to Himself. ³If God is real, there is no pain. ⁴If pain is real, there is no God. ⁵For vengeance is not part of love. ⁶And fear, denying love and using pain to prove that God is dead, has shown that death is victor over life. ⁷The body is the Son of God, corruptible in death, as mortal as the Father he has slain.

4. Peace to such foolishness! ²The time has come to laugh at such insane ideas. ³There is no need to think of them as savage crimes, or secret sins with weighty consequence. ⁴Who but a madman could conceive of them as cause of anything? ⁵Their witness, pain, is mad as they, and no more to be feared than the insane illusions which it shields, and tries to demonstrate must still be true.

5. It is your thoughts alone that cause you pain. ²Nothing external to your mind can hurt or injure you in any way. ³There is no cause beyond yourself that can reach down and bring oppression. ⁴No one but yourself affects you. ⁵There is nothing in the world that has the power to make you ill or sad, or weak or frail. ⁶But it is you who have the power to dominate all things you see by merely recognizing what you are. ⁷As you perceive the harmlessness in them, they will accept your holy will as theirs. ⁸And what was seen as fearful now becomes a source of innocence and holiness.

6. My holy brother, think of this awhile: The world you see does nothing. [2]It has no effects at all. [3]It merely represents your thoughts. [4]And it will change entirely as you elect to change your mind, and choose the joy of God as what you really want. [5]Your Self is radiant in this holy joy, unchanged, unchanging and unchangeable, forever and forever. [6]And would you deny a little corner of your mind its own inheritance, and keep it as a hospital for pain; a sickly place where living things must come at last to die?

7. The world may seem to cause you pain. [2]And yet the world, as causeless, has no power to cause. [3]As an effect, it cannot make effects. [4]As an illusion, it is what you wish. [5]Your idle wishes represent its pains. [6]Your strange desires bring it evil dreams. [7]Your thoughts of death envelop it in fear, while in your kind forgiveness does it live.

8. Pain is the thought of evil taking form, and working havoc in your holy mind. [2]Pain is the ransom you have gladly paid not to be free. [3]In pain is God denied the Son He loves. [4]In pain does fear appear to triumph over love, and time replace eternity and Heaven. [5]And the world becomes a cruel and a bitter place, where sorrow rules and little joys give way before the onslaught of the savage pain that waits to end all joy in misery.

9. Lay down your arms, and come without defense into the quiet place where Heaven's peace holds all things still at last. [2]Lay down all thoughts of danger and of fear. [3]Let no attack enter with you. [4]Lay down the cruel sword of judgment that you hold against your throat, and put aside the withering assaults with which you seek to hide your holiness.

10. Here will you understand there is no pain. [2]Here does the joy of God belong to you. [3]This is the day when it is given you to realize the lesson that contains all of salvation's power. [4]It is this: Pain is illusion; joy, reality. [5]Pain is but sleep; joy is awakening. [6]Pain is deception; joy alone is truth.

11. And so again we make the only choice that ever can be made; we choose between illusions and the truth, or pain and joy, or hell and Heaven. [2]Let our gratitude unto our Teacher fill our hearts, as we are free to choose our joy instead of pain, our holiness in place of sin, the peace of God instead of conflict, and the light of Heaven for the darkness of the world.

LESSON 191

I am the holy Son of God Himself.

1. Here is your declaration of release from bondage of the world.
²And here as well is all the world released. ³You do not see what
you have done by giving to the world the role of jailer to the Son
of God. ⁴What could it be but vicious and afraid, fearful of shadows, punitive and wild, lacking all reason, blind, insane with
hate?

2. What have you done that this should be your world? ²What
have you done that this is what you see? ³Deny your own Identity, and this is what remains. ⁴You look on chaos and proclaim it
is yourself. ⁵There is no sight that fails to witness this to you.
⁶There is no sound that does not speak of frailty within you and
without; no breath you draw that does not seem to bring you
nearer death; no hope you hold but will dissolve in tears.

3. Deny your own Identity, and you will not escape the madness
which induced this weird, unnatural and ghostly thought that
mocks creation and that laughs at God. ²Deny your own Identity,
and you assail the universe alone, without a friend, a tiny particle
of dust against the legions of your enemies. ³Deny your own
Identity, and look on evil, sin and death, and watch despair
snatch from your fingers every scrap of hope, leaving you nothing but the wish to die.

4. Yet what is it except a game you play in which Identity can be
denied? ²You are as God created you. ³All else but this one thing
is folly to believe. ⁴In this one thought is everyone set free. ⁵In this
one truth are all illusions gone. ⁶In this one fact is sinlessness
proclaimed to be forever part of everything, the central core of its
existence and its guarantee of immortality.

5. But let today's idea find a place among your thoughts and you
have risen far above the world, and all the worldly thoughts that
hold it prisoner. ²And from this place of safety and escape you
will return and set it free. ³For he who can accept his true Identity
is truly saved. ⁴And his salvation is the gift he gives to everyone,
in gratitude to Him Who pointed out the way to happiness that
changed his whole perspective of the world.

6. One holy thought like this and you are free: You are the holy
Son of God Himself. ²And with this holy thought you learn as

well that you have freed the world. ³You have no need to use it cruelly, and then perceive this savage need in it. ⁴You set it free of your imprisonment. ⁵You will not see a devastating image of yourself walking the world in terror, with the world twisting in agony because your fears have laid the mark of death upon its heart.

7. Be glad today how very easily is hell undone. ²You need but tell yourself:

> ³*I am the holy Son of God Himself.* ⁴*I cannot suffer,*
> *cannot be in pain; I cannot suffer loss, nor fail to do all*
> *that salvation asks.*

⁵And in that thought is everything you look on wholly changed.

8. A miracle has lighted up all dark and ancient caverns, where the rites of death echoed since time began. ²For time has lost its hold upon the world. ³The Son of God has come in glory to redeem the lost, to save the helpless, and to give the world the gift of his forgiveness. ⁴Who could see the world as dark and sinful, when God's Son has come again at last to set it free?

9. You who perceive yourself as weak and frail, with futile hopes and devastated dreams, born but to die, to weep and suffer pain, hear this: All power is given unto you in earth and Heaven. ²There is nothing that you cannot do. ³You play the game of death, of being helpless, pitifully tied to dissolution in a world which shows no mercy to you. ⁴Yet when you accord it mercy, will its mercy shine on you.

10. Then let the Son of God awaken from his sleep, and opening his holy eyes, return again to bless the world he made. ²In error it began, but it will end in the reflection of his holiness. ³And he will sleep no more and dream of death. ⁴Then join with me today. ⁵Your glory is the light that saves the world. ⁶Do not withhold salvation longer. ⁷Look about the world, and see the suffering there. ⁸Is not your heart willing to bring your weary brothers rest?

11. They must await your own release. ²They stay in chains till you are free. ³They cannot see the mercy of the world until you find it in yourself. ⁴They suffer pain until you have denied its hold on you. ⁵They die till you accept your own eternal life. ⁶You are the holy Son of God Himself. ⁷Remember this, and all the world is free. ⁸Remember this, and earth and Heaven are one.

LESSON 192

I have a function God would have me fill.

1. It is your Father's holy Will that you complete Himself, and that your Self shall be His sacred Son, forever pure as He, of love created and in love preserved, extending love, creating in its name, forever one with God and with your Self. ²Yet what can such a function mean within a world of envy, hatred and attack?

2. Therefore, you have a function in the world in its own terms. ²For who can understand a language far beyond his simple grasp? ³Forgiveness represents your function here. ⁴It is not God's creation, for it is the means by which untruth can be undone. ⁵And who would pardon Heaven? ⁶Yet on earth, you need the means to let illusions go. ⁷Creation merely waits for your return to be acknowledged, not to be complete.

3. Creation cannot even be conceived of in the world. ²It has no meaning here. ³Forgiveness is the closest it can come to earth. ⁴For being Heaven-born, it has no form at all. ⁵Yet God created One Who has the power to translate in form the wholly form-less. ⁶What He makes are dreams, but of a kind so close to waking that the light of day already shines in them, and eyes already opening behold the joyful sights their offerings contain.

4. Forgiveness gently looks upon all things unknown in Heaven, sees them disappear, and leaves the world a clean and unmarked slate on which the Word of God can now replace the senseless symbols written there before. ²Forgiveness is the means by which the fear of death is overcome, because it holds no fierce attraction now and guilt is gone. ³Forgiveness lets the body be perceived as what it is; a simple teaching aid, to be laid by when learning is complete, but hardly changing him who learns at all.

5. The mind without the body cannot make mistakes. ²It cannot think that it will die, nor be the prey of merciless attack. ³Anger becomes impossible, and where is terror then? ⁴What fears could still assail those who have lost the source of all attack, the core of anguish and the seat of fear? ⁵Only forgiveness can relieve the mind of thinking that the body is its home. ⁶Only forgiveness can restore the peace that God intended for His holy Son. ⁷Only forgiveness can persuade the Son to look again upon his holiness.

6. With anger gone, you will indeed perceive that, for Christ's vision and the gift of sight, no sacrifice was asked, and only pain was lifted from a sick and tortured mind. [2]Is this unwelcome? [3]Is it to be feared? [4]Or is it to be hoped for, met with thanks and joyously accepted? [5]We are one, and therefore give up nothing. [6]But we have indeed been given everything by God.

7. Yet do we need forgiveness to perceive that this is so. [2]Without its kindly light we grope in darkness, using reason but to justify our rage and our attack. [3]Our understanding is so limited that what we think we understand is but confusion born of error. [4]We are lost in mists of shifting dreams and fearful thoughts, our eyes shut tight against the light; our minds engaged in worshipping what is not there.

8. Who can be born again in Christ but him who has forgiven everyone he sees or thinks of or imagines? [2]Who could be set free while he imprisons anyone? [3]A jailer is not free, for he is bound together with his prisoner. [4]He must be sure that he does not escape, and so he spends his time in keeping watch on him. [5]The bars that limit him become the world in which his jailer lives, along with him. [6]And it is on his freedom that the way to liberty depends for both of them.

9. Therefore, hold no one prisoner. [2]Release instead of bind, for thus are you made free. [3]The way is simple. [4]Every time you feel a stab of anger, realize you hold a sword above your head. [5]And it will fall or be averted as you choose to be condemned or free. [6]Thus does each one who seems to tempt you to be angry represent your savior from the prison house of death. [7]And so you owe him thanks instead of pain.

10. Be merciful today. [2]The Son of God deserves your mercy. [3]It is he who asks that you accept the way to freedom now. [4]Deny him not. [5]His Father's Love for him belongs to you. [6]Your function here on earth is only to forgive him, that you may accept him back as your Identity. [7]He is as God created him. [8]And you are what he is. [9]Forgive him now his sins, and you will see that you are one with him.

LESSON 193

All things are lessons God would have me learn.

1. God does not know of learning. ²Yet His Will extends to what He does not understand, in that He wills the happiness His Son inherited of Him be undisturbed; eternal and forever gaining scope, eternally expanding in the joy of full creation, and eternally open and wholly limitless in Him. ³That is His Will. ⁴And thus His Will provides the means to guarantee that it is done.

2. God sees no contradictions. ²Yet His Son believes he sees them. ³Thus he has a need for One Who can correct his erring sight, and give him vision that will lead him back to where perception ceases. ⁴God does not perceive at all. ⁵Yet it is He Who gives the means by which perception is made true and beautiful enough to let the light of Heaven shine upon it. ⁶It is He Who answers what His Son would contradict, and keeps his sinlessness forever safe.

3. These are the lessons God would have you learn. ²His Will reflects them all, and they reflect His loving kindness to the Son He loves. ³Each lesson has a central thought, the same in all of them. ⁴The form alone is changed, with different circumstances and events; with different characters and different themes, apparent but not real. ⁵They are the same in fundamental content. ⁶It is this:

⁷*Forgive, and you will see this differently.*

4. Certain it is that all distress does not appear to be but unforgiveness. ²Yet that is the content underneath the form. ³It is this sameness which makes learning sure, because the lesson is so simple that it cannot be rejected in the end. ⁴No one can hide forever from a truth so very obvious that it appears in countless forms, and yet is recognized as easily in all of them, if one but wants to see the simple lesson there.

5. *Forgive, and you will see this differently.*

²These are the words the Holy Spirit speaks in all your tribulations, all your pain, all suffering regardless of its form. ³These are the words with which temptation ends, and guilt, abandoned, is

revered no more. ⁴These are the words which end the dream of sin, and rid the mind of fear. ⁵These are the words by which salvation comes to all the world.

6. Shall we not learn to say these words when we are tempted to believe that pain is real, and death becomes our choice instead of life? ²Shall we not learn to say these words when we have understood their power to release all minds from bondage? ³These are words which give you power over all events that seem to have been given power over you. ⁴You see them rightly when you hold these words in full awareness, and do not forget these words apply to everything you see or any brother looks upon amiss.

7. How can you tell when you are seeing wrong, or someone else is failing to perceive the lesson he should learn? ²Does pain seem real in the perception? ³If it does, be sure the lesson is not learned. ⁴And there remains an unforgiveness hiding in the mind that sees the pain through eyes the mind directs.

8. God would not have you suffer thus. ²He would help you forgive yourself. ³His Son does not remember who he is. ⁴And God would have him not forget His Love, and all the gifts His Love brings with it. ⁵Would you now renounce your own salvation? ⁶Would you fail to learn the simple lessons Heaven's Teacher sets before you, that all pain may disappear and God may be remembered by His Son?

9. All things are lessons God would have you learn. ²He would not leave an unforgiving thought without correction, nor one thorn or nail to hurt His holy Son in any way. ³He would ensure his holy rest remain untroubled and serene, without a care, in an eternal home which cares for him. ⁴And He would have all tears be wiped away, with none remaining yet unshed, and none but waiting their appointed time to fall. ⁵For God has willed that laughter should replace each one, and that His Son be free again.

10. We will attempt today to overcome a thousand seeming obstacles to peace in just one day. ²Let mercy come to you more quickly. ³Do not try to hold it off another day, another minute or another instant. ⁴Time was made for this. ⁵Use it today for what its purpose is. ⁶Morning and night, devote what time you can to serve its proper aim, and do not let the time be less than meets your deepest need.

11. Give all you can, and give a little more. ²For now we would arise in haste and go unto our Father's house. ³We have been gone too long, and we would linger here no more. ⁴And as we

practice, let us think about all things we saved to settle by ourselves, and kept apart from healing. [5]Let us give them all to Him Who knows the way to look upon them so that they will disappear. [6]Truth is His message; truth His teaching is. [7]His are the lessons God would have us learn.

12.   Each hour, spend a little time today, and in the days to come, in practicing the lesson in forgiveness in the form established for the day. [2]And try to give it application to the happenings the hour brought, so that the next one is free of the one before. [3]The chains of time are easily unloosened in this way. [4]Let no one hour cast its shadow on the one that follows, and when that one goes, let everything that happened in its course go with it. [5]Thus will you remain unbound, in peace eternal in the world of time.

13.   This is the lesson God would have you learn: There is a way to look on everything that lets it be to you another step to Him, and to salvation of the world. [2]To all that speaks of terror, answer thus:

[3]*I will forgive, and this will disappear.*

[4]To every apprehension, every care and every form of suffering, repeat these selfsame words. [5]And then you hold the key that opens Heaven's gate, and brings the Love of God the Father down to earth at last, to raise it up to Heaven. [6]God will take this final step Himself. [7]Do not deny the little steps He asks you take to Him.

LESSON 194

I place the future in the Hands of God.

1. Today's idea takes another step toward quick salvation, and a giant stride it is indeed! ²So great the distance is that it encompasses, it sets you down just short of Heaven, with the goal in sight and obstacles behind. ³Your foot has reached the lawns that welcome you to Heaven's gate; the quiet place of peace, where you await with certainty the final step of God. ⁴How far are we progressing now from earth! ⁵How close are we approaching to our goal! ⁶How short the journey still to be pursued!

2. Accept today's idea, and you have passed all anxiety, all pits of hell, all blackness of depression, thoughts of sin, and devastation brought about by guilt. ²Accept today's idea, and you have released the world from all imprisonment by loosening the heavy chains that locked the door to freedom on it. ³You are saved, and your salvation thus becomes the gift you give the world, because you have received.

3. In no one instant is depression felt, or pain experienced or loss perceived. ²In no one instant sorrow can be set upon a throne, and worshipped faithfully. ³In no one instant can one even die. ⁴And so each instant given unto God in passing, with the next one given Him already, is a time of your release from sadness, pain and even death itself.

4. God holds your future as He holds your past and present. ²They are one to Him, and so they should be one to you. ³Yet in this world, the temporal progression still seems real. ⁴And so you are not asked to understand the lack of sequence really found in time. ⁵You are but asked to let the future go, and place it in God's Hands. ⁶And you will see by your experience that you have laid the past and present in His Hands as well, because the past will punish you no more, and future dread will now be meaningless.

5. Release the future. ²For the past is gone, and what is present, freed from its bequest of grief and misery, of pain and loss, becomes the instant in which time escapes the bondage of illusions where it runs its pitiless, inevitable course. ³Then is each instant which was slave to time transformed into a holy instant, when the light that was kept hidden in God's Son is freed to bless the world. ⁴Now is he free, and all his glory shines upon a world

made free with him, to share his holiness.

6. If you can see the lesson for today as the deliverance it really is, you will not hesitate to give as much consistent effort as you can, to make it be a part of you. ²As it becomes a thought that rules your mind, a habit in your problem-solving repertoire, a way of quick reaction to temptation, you extend your learning to the world. ³And as you learn to see salvation in all things, so will the world perceive that it is saved.

7. What worry can beset the one who gives his future to the loving Hands of God? ²What can he suffer? ³What can cause him pain, or bring experience of loss to him? ⁴What can he fear? ⁵And what can he regard except with love? ⁶For he who has escaped all fear of future pain has found his way to present peace, and certainty of care the world can never threaten. ⁷He is sure that his perception may be faulty, but will never lack correction. ⁸He is free to choose again when he has been deceived; to change his mind when he has made mistakes.

8. Place, then, your future in the Hands of God. ²For thus you call the memory of Him to come again, replacing all your thoughts of sin and evil with the truth of love. ³Think you the world could fail to gain thereby, and every living creature not respond with healed perception? ⁴Who entrusts himself to God has also placed the world within the Hands to which he has himself appealed for comfort and security. ⁵He lays aside the sick illusions of the world along with his, and offers peace to both.

9. Now are we saved indeed. ²For in God's Hands we rest untroubled, sure that only good can come to us. ³If we forget, we will be gently reassured. ⁴If we accept an unforgiving thought, it will be soon replaced by love's reflection. ⁵And if we are tempted to attack, we will appeal to Him Who guards our rest to make the choice for us that leaves temptation far behind. ⁶No longer is the world our enemy, for we have chosen that we be its friend.

LESSON 195

Love is the way I walk in gratitude.

1. Gratitude is a lesson hard to learn for those who look upon the world amiss. [2]The most that they can do is see themselves as better off than others. [3]And they try to be content because another seems to suffer more than they. [4]How pitiful and deprecating are such thoughts! [5]For who has cause for thanks while others have less cause? [6]And who could suffer less because he sees another suffer more? [7]Your gratitude is due to Him alone Who made all cause of sorrow disappear throughout the world.

2. It is insane to offer thanks because of suffering. [2]But it is equally insane to fail in gratitude to One Who offers you the certain means whereby all pain is healed, and suffering replaced with laughter and with happiness. [3]Nor could the even partly sane refuse to take the steps which He directs, and follow in the way He sets before them, to escape a prison that they thought contained no door to the deliverance they now perceive.

3. Your brother is your "enemy" because you see in him the rival for your peace; a plunderer who takes his joy from you, and leaves you nothing but a black despair so bitter and relentless that there is no hope remaining. [2]Now is vengeance all there is to wish for. [3]Now can you but try to bring him down to lie in death with you, as useless as yourself; as little left within his grasping fingers as in yours.

4. You do not offer God your gratitude because your brother is more slave than you, nor could you sanely be enraged if he seems freer. [2]Love makes no comparisons. [3]And gratitude can only be sincere if it be joined to love. [4]We offer thanks to God our Father that in us all things will find their freedom. [5]It will never be that some are loosed while others still are bound. [6]For who can bargain in the name of love?

5. Therefore give thanks, but in sincerity. [2]And let your gratitude make room for all who will escape with you; the sick, the weak, the needy and afraid, and those who mourn a seeming loss or feel apparent pain, who suffer cold or hunger, or who walk the way of hatred and the path of death. [3]All these go with you. [4]Let us not compare ourselves with them, for thus we split them off from our awareness of the unity we share with them, as they

must share with us.

6. We thank our Father for one thing alone; that we are separate from no living thing, and therefore one with Him. ²And we rejoice that no exceptions ever can be made which would reduce our wholeness, nor impair or change our function to complete the One Who is Himself completion. ³We give thanks for every living thing, for otherwise we offer thanks for nothing, and we fail to recognize the gifts of God to us.

7. Then let our brothers lean their tired heads against our shoulders as they rest a while. ²We offer thanks for them. ³For if we can direct them to the peace that we would find, the way is opening at last to us. ⁴An ancient door is swinging free again; a long forgotten Word re-echoes in our memory, and gathers clarity as we are willing once again to hear.

8. Walk, then, in gratitude the way of love. ²For hatred is forgotten when we lay comparisons aside. ³What more remains as obstacles to peace? ⁴The fear of God is now undone at last, and we forgive without comparing. ⁵Thus we cannot choose to overlook some things, and yet retain some other things still locked away as "sins." ⁶When your forgiveness is complete you will have total gratitude, for you will see that everything has earned the right to love by being loving, even as your Self.

9. Today we learn to think of gratitude in place of anger, malice and revenge. ²We have been given everything. ³If we refuse to recognize it, we are not entitled therefore to our bitterness, and to a self-perception which regards us in a place of merciless pursuit, where we are badgered ceaselessly, and pushed about without a thought or care for us or for our future. ⁴Gratitude becomes the single thought we substitute for these insane perceptions. ⁵God has cared for us, and calls us Son. ⁶Can there be more than this?

10. Our gratitude will pave the way to Him, and shorten our learning time by more than you could ever dream of. ²Gratitude goes hand in hand with love, and where one is the other must be found. ³For gratitude is but an aspect of the Love which is the Source of all creation. ⁴God gives thanks to you, His Son, for being what you are; His Own completion and the Source of love, along with Him. ⁵Your gratitude to Him is one with His to you. ⁶For love can walk no road except the way of gratitude, and thus we go who walk the way to God.

LESSON 196

It can be but myself I crucify.

1. When this is firmly understood and kept in full awareness, you will not attempt to harm yourself, nor make your body slave to vengeance. ²You will not attack yourself, and you will realize that to attack another is but to attack yourself. ³You will be free of the insane belief that to attack a brother saves yourself. ⁴And you will understand his safety is your own, and in his healing you are healed.

2. Perhaps at first you will not understand how mercy, limitless and with all things held in its sure protection, can be found in the idea we practice for today. ²It may, in fact, appear to be a sign that punishment can never be escaped because the ego, under what it sees as threat, is quick to cite the truth to save its lies. ³Yet must it fail to understand the truth it uses thus. ⁴But you can learn to see these foolish applications, and deny the meaning they appear to have.

3. Thus do you also teach your mind that you are not an ego. ²For the ways in which the ego would distort the truth will not deceive you longer. ³You will not believe you are a body to be crucified. ⁴And you will see within today's idea the light of resurrection, looking past all thoughts of crucifixion and of death, to thoughts of liberation and of life.

4. Today's idea is one step we take in leading us from bondage to the state of perfect freedom. ²Let us take this step today, that we may quickly go the way salvation shows us, taking every step in its appointed sequence, as the mind relinquishes its burdens one by one. ³It is not time we need for this. ⁴It is but willingness. ⁵For what would seem to need a thousand years can easily be done in just one instant by the grace of God.

5. The dreary, hopeless thought that you can make attacks on others and escape yourself has nailed you to the cross. ²Perhaps it seemed to be salvation. ³Yet it merely stood for the belief the fear of God is real. ⁴And what is that but hell? ⁵Who could believe his Father is his deadly enemy, separate from him, and waiting to destroy his life and blot him from the universe, without the fear of hell upon his heart?

6. Such is the form of madness you believe, if you accept the

fearful thought you can attack another and be free yourself. ²Until this form is changed, there is no hope. ³Until you see that this, at least, must be entirely impossible, how could there be escape? ⁴The fear of God is real to anyone who thinks this thought is true. ⁵And he will not perceive its foolishness, or even see that it is there, so that it would be possible to question it.

7. To question it at all, its form must first be changed at least as much as will permit fear of retaliation to abate, and the responsibility returned to some extent to you. ²From there you can at least consider if you want to go along this painful path. ³Until this shift has been accomplished, you can not perceive that it is but your thoughts that bring you fear, and your deliverance depends on you.

8. Our next steps will be easy, if you take this one today. ²From there we go ahead quite rapidly. ³For once you understand it is impossible that you be hurt except by your own thoughts, the fear of God must disappear. ⁴You cannot then believe that fear is caused without. ⁵And God, Whom you had thought to banish, can be welcomed back within the holy mind He never left.

9. Salvation's song can certainly be heard in the idea we practice for today. ²If it can but be you you crucify, you did not hurt the world, and need not fear its vengeance and pursuit. ³Nor need you hide in terror from the deadly fear of God projection hides behind. ⁴The thing you dread the most is your salvation. ⁵You are strong, and it is strength you want. ⁶And you are free, and glad of freedom. ⁷You have sought to be both weak and bound, because you feared your strength and freedom. ⁸Yet salvation lies in them.

10. There is an instant in which terror seems to grip your mind so wholly that escape appears quite hopeless. ²When you realize, once and for all, that it is you you fear, the mind perceives itself as split. ³And this had been concealed while you believed attack could be directed outward, and returned from outside to within. ⁴It seemed to be an enemy outside you had to fear. ⁵And thus a god outside yourself became your mortal enemy; the source of fear.

11. Now, for an instant, is a murderer perceived within you, eager for your death, intent on plotting punishment for you until the time when it can kill at last. ²Yet in this instant is the time as well in which salvation comes. ³For fear of God has disappeared. ⁴And you can call on Him to save you from illusions by His Love,

calling Him Father and yourself His Son. ⁵Pray that the instant may be soon,—today. ⁶Step back from fear, and make advance to love.

12. There is no Thought of God that does not go with you to help you reach that instant, and to go beyond it quickly, surely and forever. ²When the fear of God is gone, there are no obstacles that still remain between you and the holy peace of God. ³How kind and merciful is the idea we practice! ⁴Give it welcome, as you should, for it is your release. ⁵It is indeed but you your mind can try to crucify. ⁶Yet your redemption, too, will come from you.

LESSON 197

It can be but my gratitude I earn.

1. Here is the second step we take to free your mind from the belief in outside force pitted against your own. ²You make attempts at kindness and forgiveness. ³Yet you turn them to attack again, unless you find external gratitude and lavish thanks. ⁴Your gifts must be received with honor, lest they be withdrawn. ⁵And so you think God's gifts are loans at best; at worst, deceptions which would cheat you of defenses, to ensure that when He strikes He will not fail to kill.

2. How easily are God and guilt confused by those who know not what their thoughts can do. ²Deny your strength, and weakness must become salvation to you. ³See yourself as bound, and bars become your home. ⁴Nor will you leave the prison house, or claim your strength, until guilt and salvation are not seen as one, and freedom and salvation are perceived as joined, with strength beside them, to be sought and claimed, and found and fully recognized.

3. The world must thank you when you offer it release from your illusions. ²Yet your thanks belong to you as well, for its release can only mirror yours. ³Your gratitude is all your gifts require, that they be a lasting offering of a thankful heart, released from hell forever. ⁴Is it this you would undo by taking back your gifts, because they were not honored? ⁵It is you who honor them and give them fitting thanks, for it is you who have received the gifts.

4. It does not matter if another thinks your gifts unworthy. ²In his mind there is a part that joins with yours in thanking you. ³It does not matter if your gifts seem lost and ineffectual. ⁴They are received where they are given. ⁵In your gratitude are they accepted universally, and thankfully acknowledged by the Heart of God Himself. ⁶And would you take them back, when He has gratefully accepted them?

5. God blesses every gift you give to Him, and every gift is given Him, because it can be given only to yourself. ²And what belongs to God must be His Own. ³Yet you will never realize His gifts are sure, eternal, changeless, limitless, forever giving out, extending love and adding to your never-ending joy while you forgive but to attack again.

6. Withdraw the gifts you give, and you will think that what is given you has been withdrawn. [2]But learn to let forgiveness take away the sins you think you see outside yourself, and you can never think the gifts of God are lent but for a little while, before He snatches them away again in death. [3]For death will have no meaning for you then.

7. And with the end of this belief is fear forever over. [2]Thank your Self for this, for He is grateful only unto God, and He gives thanks for you unto Himself. [3]To everyone who lives will Christ yet come, for everyone must live and move in Him. [4]His Being in His Father is secure, because Their Will is One. [5]Their gratitude to all They have created has no end, for gratitude remains a part of love.

8. Thanks be to you, the holy Son of God. [2]For as you were created, you contain all things within your Self. [3]And you are still as God created you. [4]Nor can you dim the light of your perfection. [5]In your heart the Heart of God is laid. [6]He holds you dear, because you are Himself. [7]All gratitude belongs to you, because of what you are.

9. Give thanks as you receive it. [2]Be you free of all ingratitude to anyone who makes your Self complete. [3]And from this Self is no one left outside. [4]Give thanks for all the countless channels which extend this Self. [5]All that you do is given unto Him. [6]All that you think can only be His Thoughts, sharing with Him the holy Thoughts of God. [7]Earn now the gratitude you have denied yourself when you forgot the function God has given you. [8]But never think that He has ever ceased to offer thanks to you.

LESSON 198

Only my condemnation injures me.

1. Injury is impossible. [2]And yet illusion makes illusion. [3]If you can condemn, you can be injured. [4]For you have believed that you can injure, and the right you have established for yourself can be now used against you, till you lay it down as valueless, unwanted and unreal. [5]Then does illusion cease to have effects, and those it seemed to have will be undone. [6]Then are you free, for freedom is your gift, and you can now receive the gift you gave.

2. Condemn and you are made a prisoner. [2]Forgive and you are freed. [3]Such is the law that rules perception. [4]It is not a law that knowledge understands, for freedom is a part of knowledge. [5]To condemn is thus impossible in truth. [6]What seems to be its influence and its effects have not occurred at all. [7]Yet must we deal with them a while as if they had. [8]Illusion makes illusion. [9]Except one. [10]Forgiveness is illusion that is answer to the rest.

3. Forgiveness sweeps all other dreams away, and though it is itself a dream, it breeds no others. [2]All illusions save this one must multiply a thousandfold. [3]But this is where illusions end. [4]Forgiveness is the end of dreams, because it is a dream of waking. [5]It is not itself the truth. [6]Yet does it point to where the truth must be, and gives direction with the certainty of God Himself. [7]It is a dream in which the Son of God awakens to his Self and to his Father, knowing They are one.

4. Forgiveness is the only road that leads out of disaster, past all suffering, and finally away from death. [2]How could there be another way, when this one is the plan of God Himself? [3]And why would you oppose it, quarrel with it, seek to find a thousand ways in which it must be wrong; a thousand other possibilities?

5. Is it not wiser to be glad you hold the answer to your problems in your hand? [2]Is it not more intelligent to thank the One Who gives salvation, and accept His gift with gratitude? [3]And is it not a kindness to yourself to hear His Voice and learn the simple lessons He would teach, instead of trying to dismiss His words, and substitute your own in place of His?

6. His words will work. [2]His words will save. [3]His words contain all hope, all blessing and all joy that ever can be found upon this earth. [4]His words are born in God, and come to you with

Heaven's love upon them. ⁵Those who hear His words have heard the song of Heaven. ⁶For these are the words in which all merge as one at last. ⁷And as this one will fade away, the Word of God will come to take its place, for it will be remembered then and loved.

7. This world has many seeming separate haunts where mercy has no meaning, and attack appears as justified. ²Yet all are one; a place where death is offered to God's Son and to his Father. ³You may think They have accepted. ⁴But if you will look again upon the place where you beheld Their blood, you will perceive a miracle instead. ⁵How foolish to believe that They could die! ⁶How foolish to believe you can attack! ⁷How mad to think that you could be condemned, and that the holy Son of God can die!

8. The stillness of your Self remains unmoved, untouched by thoughts like these, and unaware of any condemnation which could need forgiveness. ²Dreams of any kind are strange and alien to the truth. ³And what but truth could have a Thought which builds a bridge to it that brings illusions to the other side?

9. Today we practice letting freedom come to make its home with you. ²The truth bestows these words upon your mind, that you may find the key to light and let the darkness end:

³Only my condemnation injures me.
⁴Only my own forgiveness sets me free.

⁵Do not forget today that there can be no form of suffering that fails to hide an unforgiving thought. ⁶Nor can there be a form of pain forgiveness cannot heal.

10. Accept the one illusion which proclaims there is no condemnation in God's Son, and Heaven is remembered instantly; the world forgotten, all its weird beliefs forgotten with it, as the face of Christ appears unveiled at last in this one dream. ²This is the gift the Holy Spirit holds for you from God your Father. ³Let today be celebrated both on earth and in your holy home as well. ⁴Be kind to Both, as you forgive the trespasses you thought Them guilty of, and see your innocence shining upon you from the face of Christ.

11. Now is there silence all around the world. ²Now is there stillness where before there was a frantic rush of thoughts that made no sense. ³Now is there tranquil light across the face of earth, made quiet in a dreamless sleep. ⁴And now the Word of God

alone remains upon it. ⁵Only that can be perceived an instant longer. ⁶Then are symbols done, and everything you ever thought you made completely vanished from the mind that God forever knows to be His only Son.

12. There is no condemnation in him. ²He is perfect in his holiness. ³He needs no thoughts of mercy. ⁴Who could give him gifts when everything is his? ⁵And who could dream of offering forgiveness to the Son of Sinlessness Itself, so like to Him Whose Son he is, that to behold the Son is to perceive no more, and only know the Father? ⁶In this vision of the Son, so brief that not an instant stands between this single sight and timelessness itself, you see the vision of yourself, and then you disappear forever into God.

13. Today we come still nearer to the end of everything that yet would stand between this vision and our sight. ²And we are glad that we have come this far, and recognize that He Who brought us here will not forsake us now. ³For He would give to us the gift that God has given us through Him today. ⁴Now is the time for your deliverance. ⁵The time has come. ⁶The time has come today.

LESSON 199

I am not a body. I am free.

1. Freedom must be impossible as long as you perceive a body as yourself. [2]The body is a limit. [3]Who would seek for freedom in a body looks for it where it can not be found. [4]The mind can be made free when it no longer sees itself as in a body, firmly tied to it and sheltered by its presence. [5]If this were the truth, the mind were vulnerable indeed!

2. The mind that serves the Holy Spirit is unlimited forever, in all ways, beyond the laws of time and space, unbound by any preconceptions, and with strength and power to do whatever it is asked. [2]Attack thoughts cannot enter such a mind, because it has been given to the Source of love, and fear can never enter in a mind that has attached itself to love. [3]It rests in God. [4]And who can be afraid who lives in Innocence, and only loves?

3. It is essential for your progress in this course that you accept today's idea, and hold it very dear. [2]Be not concerned that to the ego it is quite insane. [3]The ego holds the body dear because it dwells in it, and lives united with the home that it has made. [4]It is a part of the illusion that has sheltered it from being found illusory itself.

4. Here does it hide, and here it can be seen as what it is. [2]Declare your innocence and you are free. [3]The body disappears, because you have no need of it except the need the Holy Spirit sees. [4]For this, the body will appear as useful form for what the mind must do. [5]It thus becomes a vehicle which helps forgiveness be extended to the all-inclusive goal that it must reach, according to God's plan.

5. Cherish today's idea, and practice it today and every day. [2]Make it a part of every practice period you take. [3]There is no thought that will not gain thereby in power to help the world, and none which will not gain in added gifts to you as well. [4]We sound the call of freedom round the world with this idea. [5]And would you be exempt from the acceptance of the gifts you give?

6. The Holy Spirit is the home of minds that seek for freedom. [2]In Him they have found what they have sought. [3]The body's purpose now is unambiguous. [4]And it becomes perfect in the ability to serve an undivided goal. [5]In conflict-free and unequivocal

response to mind with but the thought of freedom as its goal, the body serves, and serves its purpose well. ⁶Without the power to enslave, it is a worthy servant of the freedom which the mind within the Holy Spirit seeks.

7. Be free today. ²And carry freedom as your gift to those who still believe they are enslaved within a body. ³Be you free, so that the Holy Spirit can make use of your escape from bondage, to set free the many who perceive themselves as bound and helpless and afraid. ⁴Let love replace their fears through you. ⁵Accept salvation now, and give your mind to Him Who calls to you to make this gift to Him. ⁶For He would give you perfect freedom, perfect joy, and hope that finds its full accomplishment in God.

8. You are God's Son. ²In immortality you live forever. ³Would you not return your mind to this? ⁴Then practice well the thought the Holy Spirit gives you for today. ⁵Your brothers stand released with you in it; the world is blessed along with you, God's Son will weep no more, and Heaven offers thanks for the increase of joy your practice brings even to it. ⁶And God Himself extends His Love and happiness each time you say:

> ⁷*I am not a body. ⁸I am free. ⁹I hear the Voice that God has given me, and it is only this my mind obeys.*

LESSON 200

There is no peace except the peace of God.

1. Seek you no further. ²You will not find peace except the peace of God. ³Accept this fact, and save yourself the agony of yet more bitter disappointments, bleak despair, and sense of icy hopelessness and doubt. ⁴Seek you no further. ⁵There is nothing else for you to find except the peace of God, unless you seek for misery and pain.

2. This is the final point to which each one must come at last, to lay aside all hope of finding happiness where there is none; of being saved by what can only hurt; of making peace of chaos, joy of pain, and Heaven out of hell. ²Attempt no more to win through losing, nor to die to live. ³You cannot but be asking for defeat.

3. Yet you can ask as easily for love, for happiness, and for eternal life in peace that has no ending. ²Ask for this, and you can only win. ³To ask for what you have already must succeed. ⁴To ask that what is false be true can only fail. ⁵Forgive yourself for vain imaginings, and seek no longer what you cannot find. ⁶For what could be more foolish than to seek and seek and seek again for hell, when you have but to look with open eyes to find that Heaven lies before you, through a door that opens easily to welcome you?

4. Come home. ²You have not found your happiness in foreign places and in alien forms that have no meaning to you, though you sought to make them meaningful. ³This world is not where you belong. ⁴You are a stranger here. ⁵But it is given you to find the means whereby the world no longer seems to be a prison house or jail for anyone.

5. Freedom is given you where you beheld but chains and iron doors. ²But you must change your mind about the purpose of the world, if you would find escape. ³You will be bound till all the world is seen by you as blessed, and everyone made free of your mistakes and honored as he is. ⁴You made him not; no more yourself. ⁵And as you free the one, the other is accepted as he is.

6. What does forgiveness do? ²In truth it has no function, and does nothing. ³For it is unknown in Heaven. ⁴It is only hell where it is needed, and where it must serve a mighty function. ⁵Is not the escape of God's beloved Son from evil dreams that he imagines,

yet believes are true, a worthy purpose? ⁶Who could hope for more, while there appears to be a choice to make between success and failure; love and fear?

7.   There is no peace except the peace of God, because He has one Son who cannot make a world in opposition to God's Will and to his own, which is the same as His. ²What could he hope to find in such a world? ³It cannot have reality, because it never was created. ⁴Is it here that he would seek for peace? ⁵Or must he see that, as he looks on it, the world can but deceive? ⁶Yet can he learn to look on it another way, and find the peace of God.

8.   Peace is the bridge that everyone will cross, to leave this world behind. ²But peace begins within the world perceived as different, and leading from this fresh perception to the gate of Heaven and the way beyond. ³Peace is the answer to conflicting goals, to senseless journeys, frantic, vain pursuits, and meaningless endeavors. ⁴Now the way is easy, sloping gently toward the bridge where freedom lies within the peace of God.

9.   Let us not lose our way again today. ²We go to Heaven, and the path is straight. ³Only if we attempt to wander can there be delay, and needless wasted time on thorny byways. ⁴God alone is sure, and He will guide our footsteps. ⁵He will not desert His Son in need, nor let him stray forever from his home. ⁶The Father calls; the Son will hear. ⁷And that is all there is to what appears to be a world apart from God, where bodies have reality.

10. Now is there silence. ²Seek no further. ³You have come to where the road is carpeted with leaves of false desires, fallen from the trees of hopelessness you sought before. ⁴Now are they underfoot. ⁵And you look up and on toward Heaven, with the body's eyes but serving for an instant longer now. ⁶Peace is already recognized at last, and you can feel its soft embrace surround your heart and mind with comfort and with love.

11. Today we seek no idols. ²Peace can not be found in them. ³The peace of God is ours, and only this will we accept and want. ⁴Peace be to us today. ⁵For we have found a simple, happy way to leave the world of ambiguity, and to replace our shifting goals and solitary dreams with single purpose and companionship. ⁶For peace is union, if it be of God. ⁷We seek no further. ⁸We are close to home, and draw still nearer every time we say:

> ⁹*There is no peace except the peace of God,*
> *And I am glad and thankful it is so.*

REVIEW VI

Introduction

1. For this review we take but one idea each day, and practice it as often as is possible. ²Besides the time you give morning and evening, which should not be less than fifteen minutes, and the hourly remembrances you make throughout the day, use the idea as often as you can between them. ³Each of these ideas alone would be sufficient for salvation, if it were learned truly. ⁴Each would be enough to give release to you and to the world from every form of bondage, and invite the memory of God to come again.

2. With this in mind we start our practicing, in which we carefully review the thoughts the Holy Spirit has bestowed on us in our last twenty lessons. ²Each contains the whole curriculum if understood, practiced, accepted, and applied to all the seeming happenings throughout the day. ³One is enough. ⁴But from that one, there must be no exceptions made. ⁵And so we need to use them all and let them blend as one, as each contributes to the whole we learn.

3. These practice sessions, like our last review, are centered round a central theme with which we start and end each lesson. ²It is this:

*³I am not a body. ⁴I am free.
⁵For I am still as God created me.*

⁶The day begins and ends with this. ⁷And we repeat it every time the hour strikes, or we remember, in between, we have a function that transcends the world we see. ⁸Beyond this, and a repetition of the special thought we practice for the day, no form of exercise is urged, except a deep relinquishment of everything that clutters up the mind, and makes it deaf to reason, sanity and simple truth.

4. We will attempt to get beyond all words and special forms of practicing for this review. ²For we attempt, this time, to reach a quickened pace along a shorter path to the serenity and peace of God. ³We merely close our eyes, and then forget all that we thought we knew and understood. ⁴For thus is freedom given us from all we did not know and failed to understand.

386

5. There is but one exception to this lack of structuring. ²Permit no idle thought to go unchallenged. ³If you notice one, deny its hold and hasten to assure your mind that this is not what it would have. ⁴Then gently let the thought which you denied be given up, in sure and quick exchange for the idea we practice for the day.

6. When you are tempted, hasten to proclaim your freedom from temptation, as you say:

> ²*This thought I do not want.* ³*I choose instead* ____.

⁴And then repeat the idea for the day, and let it take the place of what you thought. ⁵Beyond such special applications of each day's idea, we will add but a few formal expressions or specific thoughts to aid in practicing. ⁶Instead, we give these times of quiet to the Teacher Who instructs in quiet, speaks of peace, and gives our thoughts whatever meaning they may have.

7. To Him I offer this review for you. ²I place you in His charge, and let Him teach you what to do and say and think, each time you turn to Him. ³He will not fail to be available to you, each time you call to Him to help you. ⁴Let us offer Him the whole review we now begin, and let us also not forget to Whom it has been given, as we practice day by day, advancing toward the goal He set for us; allowing Him to teach us how to go, and trusting Him completely for the way each practice period can best become a loving gift of freedom to the world.

LESSON 201

I am not a body. I am free.
For I am still as God created me.

1. (181) I trust my brothers, who are one with me.

> [2]*No one but is my brother.* [3]*I am blessed with oneness with the universe and God, my Father, one Creator of the whole that is my Self, forever One with me.*

> [4]**I am not a body.** [5]**I am free.**
> [6]**For I am still as God created me.**

LESSON 202

I am not a body. I am free.
For I am still as God created me.

1. (182) I will be still an instant and go home.

> [2]*Why would I choose to stay an instant more where I do not belong, when God Himself has given me His Voice to call me home?*

> [3]**I am not a body.** [4]**I am free.**
> [5]**For I am still as God created me.**

LESSON 203

**I am not a body. I am free.
For I am still as God created me.**

1. (183) I call upon God's Name and on my own.

> [2]*The Name of God is my deliverance from every thought of
> evil and of sin, because it is my own as well as His.*

**[3]I am not a body. [4]I am free.
[5]For I am still as God created me.**

LESSON 204

**I am not a body. I am free.
For I am still as God created me.**

1. (184) The Name of God is my inheritance.

> [2]*God's Name reminds me that I am His Son, not slave to
> time, unbound by laws which rule the world of sick illu-
> sions, free in God, forever and forever one with Him.*

**[3]I am not a body. [4]I am free.
[5]For I am still as God created me.**

LESSON 205

I am not a body. I am free.
For I am still as God created me.

1. (185) I want the peace of God.

   ²The peace of God is everything I want. ³The peace of God is my one goal; the aim of all my living here, the end I seek, my purpose and my function and my life, while I abide where I am not at home.

   ⁴I am not a body. ⁵I am free.
   ⁶For I am still as God created me.

LESSON 206

I am not a body. I am free.
For I am still as God created me.

1. (186) Salvation of the world depends on me.

   ²I am entrusted with the gifts of God, because I am His Son. ³And I would give His gifts where He intended them to be.

   ⁴I am not a body. ⁵I am free.
   ⁶For I am still as God created me.

LESSON 207

I am not a body. I am free.
For I am still as God created me.

1. (187) I bless the world because I bless myself.

   [2]*God's blessing shines upon me from within my heart, where He abides.* [3]*I need but turn to Him, and every sorrow melts away, as I accept His boundless Love for me.*

   [4]I am not a body. [5]I am free.
   [6]For I am still as God created me.

LESSON 208

I am not a body. I am free.
For I am still as God created me.

1. (188) The peace of God is shining in me now.

   [2]*I will be still, and let the earth be still along with me.* [3]*And in that stillness we will find the peace of God.* [4]*It is within my heart, which witnesses to God Himself.*

   [5]I am not a body. [6]I am free.
   [7]For I am still as God created me.

LESSON 209

I am not a body. I am free.
For I am still as God created me.

1. (189) I feel the Love of God within me now.

   [2]The Love of God is what created me. [3]The Love of God is everything I am. [4]The Love of God proclaimed me as His Son. [5]The Love of God within me sets me free.

   [6]I am not a body. [7]I am free.
   [8]For I am still as God created me.

LESSON 210

I am not a body. I am free.
For I am still as God created me.

1. (190) I choose the joy of God instead of pain.

   [2]Pain is my own idea. [3]It is not a Thought of God, but one I thought apart from Him and from His Will. [4]His Will is joy, and only joy for His beloved Son. [5]And that I choose, instead of what I made.

   [6]I am not a body. [7]I am free.
   [8]For I am still as God created me.

LESSON 211

I am not a body. I am free.
For I am still as God created me.

1. (191) I am the holy Son of God Himself.

   [2]*In silence and in true humility I seek God's glory, to behold it in the Son whom He created as my Self.*

[3]I am not a body. [4]I am free.
[5]For I am still as God created me.

LESSON 212

I am not a body. I am free.
For I am still as God created me.

1. (192) I have a function God would have me fill.

   [2]*I seek the function that would set me free from all the vain illusions of the world.* [3]*Only the function God has given me can offer freedom.* [4]*Only this I seek, and only this will I accept as mine.*

[5]I am not a body. [6]I am free.
[7]For I am still as God created me.

LESSON 213

**I am not a body. I am free.
For I am still as God created me.**

1. (193) All things are lessons God would have me learn.

   ²A lesson is a miracle which God offers to me, in place of thoughts I made that hurt me. ³What I learn of Him becomes the way I am set free. ⁴And so I choose to learn His lessons and forget my own.

   **⁵I am not a body. ⁶I am free.
   ⁷For I am still as God created me.**

LESSON 214

**I am not a body. I am free.
For I am still as God created me.**

1. (194) I place the future in the Hands of God.

   ²The past is gone; the future is not yet. ³Now am I freed from both. ⁴For what God gives can only be for good. ⁵And I accept but what He gives as what belongs to me.

   **⁶I am not a body. ⁷I am free.
   ⁸For I am still as God created me.**

LESSON 215

**I am not a body. I am free.
For I am still as God created me.**

1. (195) Love is the way I walk in gratitude.

   ²The Holy Spirit is my only Guide. ³He walks with me in love. ⁴And I give thanks to Him for showing me the way to go.

   **⁵I am not a body. ⁶I am free.
   ⁷For I am still as God created me.**

LESSON 216

**I am not a body. I am free.
For I am still as God created me.**

1. (196) It can be but myself I crucify.

   ²All that I do I do unto myself. ³If I attack, I suffer. ⁴But if I forgive, salvation will be given me.

   **⁵I am not a body. ⁶I am free.
   ⁷For I am still as God created me.**

LESSON 217

I am not a body. I am free.
For I am still as God created me.

1. (197) It can be but my gratitude I earn.

   ²Who should give thanks for my salvation but myself? ³And how but through salvation can I find the Self to Whom my thanks are due?

   ⁴I am not a body. ⁵I am free.
   ⁶For I am still as God created me.

LESSON 218

I am not a body. I am free.
For I am still as God created me.

1. (198) Only my condemnation injures me.

   ²My condemnation keeps my vision dark, and through my sightless eyes I cannot see the vision of my glory. ³Yet today I can behold this glory and be glad.

   ⁴I am not a body. ⁵I am free.
   ⁶For I am still as God created me.

LESSON 219

I am not a body. I am free.
For I am still as God created me.

1. (199) I am not a body. [2]I am free.

[3]*I am God's Son.* [4]*Be still, my mind, and think a moment upon this.* [5]*And then return to earth, without confusion as to what my Father loves forever as His Son.*

[6]I am not a body. [7]I am free.
[8]For I am still as God created me.

LESSON 220

I am not a body. I am free.
For I am still as God created me.

1. (200) There is no peace except the peace of God.

[2]*Let me not wander from the way of peace, for I am lost on other roads than this.* [3]*But let me follow Him Who leads me home, and peace is certain as the Love of God.*

[4]I am not a body. [5]I am free.
[6]For I am still as God created me.

397

PART II

Introduction

1.   Words will mean little now. ²We use them but as guides on which we do not now depend. ³For now we seek direct experience of truth alone. ⁴The lessons that remain are merely introductions to the times in which we leave the world of pain, and go to enter peace. ⁵Now we begin to reach the goal this course has set, and find the end toward which our practicing was always geared.

2.   Now we attempt to let the exercise be merely a beginning. ²For we wait in quiet expectation for our God and Father. ³He has promised He will take the final step Himself. ⁴And we are sure His promises are kept. ⁵We have come far along the road, and now we wait for Him. ⁶We will continue spending time with Him each morning and at night, as long as makes us happy. ⁷We will not consider time a matter of duration now. ⁸We use as much as we will need for the result that we desire. ⁹Nor will we forget our hourly remembrance in between, calling to God when we have need of Him as we are tempted to forget our goal.

3.   We will continue with a central thought for all the days to come, and we will use that thought to introduce our times of rest, and calm our minds at need. ²Yet we will not content ourselves with simple practicing in the remaining holy instants which conclude the year that we have given God. ³We say some simple words of welcome, and expect our Father to reveal Himself, as He has promised. ⁴We have called on Him, and He has promised that His Son will not remain unanswered when he calls His Name.

4.   Now do we come to Him with but His Word upon our minds and hearts, and wait for Him to take the step to us that He has told us, through His Voice, He would not fail to take when we invited Him. ²He has not left His Son in all his madness, nor betrayed his trust in Him. ³Has not His faithfulness earned Him the invitation that He seeks to make us happy? ⁴We will offer it, and it will be accepted. ⁵So our times with Him will now be spent. ⁶We say the words of invitation that His Voice suggests, and then we wait for Him to come to us.

5.   Now is the time of prophecy fulfilled. ²Now are all ancient

promises upheld and fully kept. ³No step remains for time to separate from its accomplishment. ⁴For now we cannot fail. ⁵Sit silently and wait upon your Father. ⁶He has willed to come to you when you have recognized it is your will He do so. ⁷And you could have never come this far unless you saw, however dimly, that it is your will.

6. I am so close to you we cannot fail. ²Father, we give these holy times to You, in gratitude to Him Who taught us how to leave the world of sorrow in exchange for its replacement, given us by You. ³We look not backward now. ⁴We look ahead, and fix our eyes upon the journey's end. ⁵Accept these little gifts of thanks from us, as through Christ's vision we behold a world beyond the one we made, and take that world to be the full replacement of our own.

7. And now we wait in silence, unafraid and certain of Your coming. ²We have sought to find our way by following the Guide You sent to us. ³We did not know the way, but You did not forget us. ⁴And we know that You will not forget us now. ⁵We ask but that Your ancient promises be kept which are Your Will to keep. ⁶We will with You in asking this. ⁷The Father and the Son, Whose holy Will created all that is, can fail in nothing. ⁸In this certainty, we undertake these last few steps to You, and rest in confidence upon Your Love, which will not fail the Son who calls to You.

8. And so we start upon the final part of this one holy year, which we have spent together in the search for truth and God, Who is its one Creator. ²We have found the way He chose for us, and made the choice to follow it as He would have us go. ³His Hand has held us up. ⁴His Thoughts have lit the darkness of our minds. ⁵His Love has called to us unceasingly since time began.

9. We had a wish that God would fail to have the Son whom He created for Himself. ²We wanted God to change Himself, and be what we would make of Him. ³And we believed that our insane desires were the truth. ⁴Now we are glad that this is all undone, and we no longer think illusions true. ⁵The memory of God is shimmering across the wide horizons of our minds. ⁶A moment more, and it will rise again. ⁷A moment more, and we who are God's Sons are safely home, where He would have us be.

10. Now is the need for practice almost done. ²For in this final section, we will come to understand that we need only call to God, and all temptations disappear. ³Instead of words, we need but feel His Love. ⁴Instead of prayers, we need but call His Name. ⁵Instead of judging, we need but be still and let all things

be healed. ⁶We will accept the way God's plan will end, as we received the way it started. ⁷Now it is complete. ⁸This year has brought us to eternity.

11.   One further use for words we still retain. ²From time to time, instructions on a theme of special relevance will intersperse our daily lessons and the periods of wordless, deep experience which should come afterwards. ³These special thoughts should be reviewed each day, each one of them to be continued till the next is given you. ⁴They should be slowly read and thought about a little while, preceding one of the holy and blessed instants in the day. ⁵We give the first of these instructions now.

1. What Is Forgiveness?

1. Forgiveness recognizes what you thought your brother did to you has not occurred. [2]It does not pardon sins and make them real. [3]It sees there was no sin. [4]And in that view are all your sins forgiven. [5]What is sin, except a false idea about God's Son? [6]Forgiveness merely sees its falsity, and therefore lets it go. [7]What then is free to take its place is now the Will of God.

2. An unforgiving thought is one which makes a judgment that it will not raise to doubt, although it is not true. [2]The mind is closed, and will not be released. [3]The thought protects projection, tightening its chains, so that distortions are more veiled and more obscure; less easily accessible to doubt, and further kept from reason. [4]What can come between a fixed projection and the aim that it has chosen as its wanted goal?

3. An unforgiving thought does many things. [2]In frantic action it pursues its goal, twisting and overturning what it sees as interfering with its chosen path. [3]Distortion is its purpose, and the means by which it would accomplish it as well. [4]It sets about its furious attempts to smash reality, without concern for anything that would appear to pose a contradiction to its point of view.

4. Forgiveness, on the other hand, is still, and quietly does nothing. [2]It offends no aspect of reality, nor seeks to twist it to appearances it likes. [3]It merely looks, and waits, and judges not. [4]He who would not forgive must judge, for he must justify his failure to forgive. [5]But he who would forgive himself must learn to welcome truth exactly as it is.

5. Do nothing, then, and let forgiveness show you what to do, through Him Who is your Guide, your Savior and Protector, strong in hope, and certain of your ultimate success. [2]He has forgiven you already, for such is His function, given Him by God. [3]Now must you share His function, and forgive whom He has saved, whose sinlessness He sees, and whom He honors as the Son of God.

LESSON 221

Peace to my mind. Let all my thoughts be still.

1. *Father, I come to You today to seek the peace that You alone can give.* ²*I come in silence.* ³*In the quiet of my heart, the deep recesses of my mind, I wait and listen for Your Voice.* ⁴*My Father, speak to me today.* ⁵*I come to hear Your Voice in silence and in certainty and love, sure You will hear my call and answer me.*

2. Now do we wait in quiet. ²God is here, because we wait together. ³I am sure that He will speak to you, and you will hear. ⁴Accept my confidence, for it is yours. ⁵Our minds are joined. ⁶We wait with one intent; to hear our Father's answer to our call, to let our thoughts be still and find His peace, to hear Him speak to us of what we are, and to reveal Himself unto His Son.

LESSON 222

God is with me. I live and move in Him.

1. God is with me. ²He is my Source of life, the life within, the air I breathe, the food by which I am sustained, the water which renews and cleanses me. ³He is my home, wherein I live and move; the Spirit which directs my actions, offers me Its Thoughts, and guarantees my safety from all pain. ⁴He covers me with kindness and with care, and holds in love the Son He shines upon, who also shines on Him. ⁵How still is he who knows the truth of what He speaks today!

2. *Father, we have no words except Your Name upon our lips and in our minds, as we come quietly into Your Presence now, and ask to rest with You in peace a while.*

LESSON 223

God is my life. I have no life but His.

1. I was mistaken when I thought I lived apart from God, a separate entity that moved in isolation, unattached, and housed within a body. ²Now I know my life is God's, I have no other home, and I do not exist apart from Him. ³He has no Thoughts that are not part of me, and I have none but those which are of Him.

2. *Our Father, let us see the face of Christ instead of our mistakes. ²For we who are Your holy Son are sinless. ³We would look upon our sinlessness, for guilt proclaims that we are not Your Son. ⁴And we would not forget You longer. ⁵We are lonely here, and long for Heaven, where we are at home. ⁶Today we would return. ⁷Our Name is Yours, and we acknowledge that we are Your Son.*

LESSON 224

God is my Father, and He loves His Son.

1. My true Identity is so secure, so lofty, sinless, glorious and great, wholly beneficent and free from guilt, that Heaven looks to It to give it light. ²It lights the world as well. ³It is the gift my Father gave to me; the one as well I give the world. ⁴There is no gift but this that can be either given or received. ⁵This is reality, and only this. ⁶This is illusion's end. ⁷It is the truth.

2. *My Name, O Father, still is known to You. ²I have forgotten It, and do not know where I am going, who I am, or what it is I do. ³Remind me, Father, now, for I am weary of the world I see. ⁴Reveal what You would have me see instead.*

LESSON 225

God is my Father, and His Son loves Him.

1. *Father, I must return Your Love for me, for giving and receiving are the same, and You have given all Your Love to me.* [2]*I must return it, for I want it mine in full awareness, blazing in my mind and keeping it within its kindly light, inviolate, beloved, with fear behind and only peace ahead.* [3]*How still the way Your loving Son is led along to You!*

2. Brother, we find that stillness now. [2]The way is open. [3]Now we follow it in peace together. [4]You have reached your hand to me, and I will never leave you. [5]We are one, and it is but this oneness that we seek, as we accomplish these few final steps which end a journey that was not begun.

LESSON 226

My home awaits me. I will hasten there.

1. If I so choose, I can depart this world entirely. [2]It is not death which makes this possible, but it is change of mind about the purpose of the world. [3]If I believe it has a value as I see it now, so will it still remain for me. [4]But if I see no value in the world as I behold it, nothing that I want to keep as mine or search for as a goal, it will depart from me. [5]For I have not sought for illusions to replace the truth.

2. *Father, my home awaits my glad return.* [2]*Your Arms are open and I hear Your Voice.* [3]*What need have I to linger in a place of vain desires and of shattered dreams, when Heaven can so easily be mine?*

LESSON 227

This is my holy instant of release.

1. *Father, it is today that I am free, because my will is Yours. ²I thought to make another will. ³Yet nothing that I thought apart from You exists. ⁴And I am free because I was mistaken, and did not affect my own reality at all by my illusions. ⁵Now I give them up, and lay them down before the feet of truth, to be removed forever from my mind. ⁶This is my holy instant of release. ⁷Father, I know my will is one with Yours.*

2. And so today we find our glad return to Heaven, which we never really left. ²The Son of God this day lays down his dreams. ³The Son of God this day comes home again, released from sin and clad in holiness, with his right mind restored to him at last.

LESSON 228

God has condemned me not. No more do I.

1. My Father knows my holiness. ²Shall I deny His knowledge, and believe in what His knowledge makes impossible? ³Shall I accept as true what He proclaims as false? ⁴Or shall I take His Word for what I am, since He is my Creator, and the One Who knows the true condition of His Son?

2. *Father, I was mistaken in myself, because I failed to realize the Source from which I came. ²I have not left that Source to enter in a body and to die. ³My holiness remains a part of me, as I am part of You. ⁴And my mistakes about myself are dreams. ⁵I let them go today. ⁶And I stand ready to receive Your Word alone for what I really am.*

LESSON 229

Love, which created me, is what I am.

1. I seek my own Identity, and find It in these words: "Love, which created me, is what I am." ²Now need I seek no more. ³Love has prevailed. ⁴So still It waited for my coming home, that I will turn away no longer from the holy face of Christ. ⁵And what I look upon attests the truth of the Identity I sought to lose, but which my Father has kept safe for me.

2. *Father, my thanks to You for what I am; for keeping my Identity untouched and sinless, in the midst of all the thoughts of sin my foolish mind made up. ²And thanks to You for saving me from them. ³Amen.*

LESSON 230

Now will I seek and find the peace of God.

1. In peace I was created. ²And in peace do I remain. ³It is not given me to change my Self. ⁴How merciful is God my Father, that when He created me He gave me peace forever. ⁵Now I ask but to be what I am. ⁶And can this be denied me, when it is forever true?

2. *Father, I seek the peace You gave as mine in my creation. ²What was given then must be here now, for my creation was apart from time, and still remains beyond all change. ³The peace in which Your Son was born into Your Mind is shining there unchanged. ⁴I am as You created me. ⁵I need but call on You to find the peace You gave. ⁶It is Your Will that gave it to Your Son.*

2. What Is Salvation?

1.   Salvation is a promise, made by God, that you would find your way to Him at last. ²It cannot but be kept. ³It guarantees that time will have an end, and all the thoughts that have been born in time will end as well. ⁴God's Word is given every mind which thinks that it has separate thoughts, and will replace these thoughts of conflict with the Thought of peace.

2.   The Thought of peace was given to God's Son the instant that his mind had thought of war. ²There was no need for such a Thought before, for peace was given without opposite, and merely was. ³But when the mind is split there is a need of healing. ⁴So the Thought that has the power to heal the split became a part of every fragment of the mind that still was one, but failed to recognize its oneness. ⁵Now it did not know itself, and thought its own Identity was lost.

3.   Salvation is undoing in the sense that it does nothing, failing to support the world of dreams and malice. ²Thus it lets illusions go. ³By not supporting them, it merely lets them quietly go down to dust. ⁴And what they hid is now revealed; an altar to the holy Name of God whereon His Word is written, with the gifts of your forgiveness laid before it, and the memory of God not far behind.

4.   Let us come daily to this holy place, and spend a while together. ²Here we share our final dream. ³It is a dream in which there is no sorrow, for it holds a hint of all the glory given us by God. ⁴The grass is pushing through the soil, the trees are budding now, and birds have come to live within their branches. ⁵Earth is being born again in new perspective. ⁶Night has gone, and we have come together in the light.

5.   From here we give salvation to the world, for it is here salvation was received. ²The song of our rejoicing is the call to all the world that freedom is returned, that time is almost over, and God's Son has but an instant more to wait until his Father is remembered, dreams are done, eternity has shined away the world, and only Heaven now exists at all.

LESSON 231

Father, I will but to remember You.

1. *What can I seek for, Father, but Your Love? ²Perhaps I think I seek for something else; a something I have called by many names. ³Yet is Your Love the only thing I seek, or ever sought. ⁴For there is nothing else that I could ever really want to find. ⁵Let me remember You. ⁶What else could I desire but the truth about myself?*

2. This is your will, my brother. ²And you share this will with me, and with the One as well Who is our Father. ³To remember Him is Heaven. ⁴This we seek. ⁵And only this is what it will be given us to find.

LESSON 232

Be in my mind, my Father, through the day.

1. *Be in my mind, my Father, when I wake, and shine on me throughout the day today. ²Let every minute be a time in which I dwell with You. ³And let me not forget my hourly thanksgiving that You have remained with me, and always will be there to hear my call to You and answer me. ⁴As evening comes, let all my thoughts be still of You and of Your Love. ⁵And let me sleep sure of my safety, certain of Your care, and happily aware I am Your Son.*

2. This is as every day should be. ²Today, practice the end of fear. ³Have faith in Him Who is your Father. ⁴Trust all things to Him. ⁵Let Him reveal all things to you, and be you undismayed because you are His Son.

408

LESSON 233

I give my life to God to guide today.

1. *Father, I give You all my thoughts today.* ²*I would have none of mine.* ³*In place of them, give me Your Own.* ⁴*I give You all my acts as well, that I may do Your Will instead of seeking goals which cannot be obtained, and wasting time in vain imaginings.* ⁵*Today I come to You.* ⁶*I will step back and merely follow You.* ⁷*Be You the Guide, and I the follower who questions not the wisdom of the Infinite, nor Love whose tenderness I cannot comprehend, but which is yet Your perfect gift to me.*

2. Today we have one Guide to lead us on. ²And as we walk together, we will give this day to Him with no reserve at all. ³This is His day. ⁴And so it is a day of countless gifts and mercies unto us.

LESSON 234

Father, today I am Your Son again.

1. Today we will anticipate the time when dreams of sin and guilt are gone, and we have reached the holy peace we never left. ²Merely a tiny instant has elapsed between eternity and timelessness. ³So brief the interval there was no lapse in continuity, nor break in thoughts which are forever unified as one. ⁴Nothing has ever happened to disturb the peace of God the Father and the Son. ⁵This we accept as wholly true today.

2. *We thank You, Father, that we cannot lose the memory of You and of Your Love.* ²*We recognize our safety, and give thanks for all the gifts You have bestowed on us, for all the loving help we have received, for Your eternal patience, and the Word which You have given us that we are saved.*

LESSON 235

God in His mercy wills that I be saved.

1. I need but look upon all things that seem to hurt me, and with perfect certainty assure myself, "God wills that I be saved from this," and merely watch them disappear. [2]I need but keep in mind my Father's Will for me is only happiness, to find that only happiness has come to me. [3]And I need but remember that God's Love surrounds His Son and keeps his sinlessness forever perfect, to be sure that I am saved and safe forever in His Arms. [4]I am the Son He loves. [5]And I am saved because God in His mercy wills it so.

2. *Father, Your Holiness is mine. [2]Your Love created me, and made my sinlessness forever part of You. [3]I have no guilt nor sin in me, for there is none in You.*

LESSON 236

I rule my mind, which I alone must rule.

1. I have a kingdom I must rule. [2]At times, it does not seem I am its king at all. [3]It seems to triumph over me, and tell me what to think, and what to do and feel. [4]And yet it has been given me to serve whatever purpose I perceive in it. [5]My mind can only serve. [6]Today I give its service to the Holy Spirit to employ as He sees fit. [7]I thus direct my mind, which I alone can rule. [8]And thus I set it free to do the Will of God.

2. *Father, my mind is open to Your Thoughts, and closed today to every thought but Yours. [2]I rule my mind, and offer it to You. [3]Accept my gift, for it is Yours to me.*

LESSON 237

Now would I be as God created me.

1. Today I will accept the truth about myself. ²I will arise in glory, and allow the light in me to shine upon the world throughout the day. ³I bring the world the tidings of salvation which I hear as God my Father speaks to me. ⁴And I behold the world that Christ would have me see, aware it ends the bitter dream of death; aware it is my Father's Call to me.

2. *Christ is my eyes today, and He the ears that listen to the Voice for God today. ²Father, I come to You through Him Who is Your Son, and my true Self as well. ³Amen.*

LESSON 238

On my decision all salvation rests.

1. *Father, Your trust in me has been so great, I must be worthy. ²You created me, and know me as I am. ³And yet You placed Your Son's salvation in my hands, and let it rest on my decision. ⁴I must be beloved of You indeed. ⁵And I must be steadfast in holiness as well, that You would give Your Son to me in certainty that he is safe Who still is part of You, and yet is mine, because He is my Self.*

2. And so, again today, we pause to think how much our Father loves us. ²And how dear His Son, created by His Love, remains to Him Whose Love is made complete in him.

LESSON 239

The glory of my Father is my own.

1. Let not the truth about ourselves today be hidden by a false humility. ²Let us instead be thankful for the gifts our Father gave us. ³Can we see in those with whom He shares His glory any trace of sin and guilt? ⁴And can it be that we are not among them, when He loves His Son forever and with perfect constancy, knowing he is as He created him?

2. *We thank You, Father, for the light that shines forever in us. ²And we honor it, because You share it with us. ³We are one, united in this light and one with You, at peace with all creation and ourselves.*

LESSON 240

Fear is not justified in any form.

1. Fear is deception. ²It attests that you have seen yourself as you could never be, and therefore look upon a world which is impossible. ³Not one thing in this world is true. ⁴It does not matter what the form in which it may appear. ⁵It witnesses but to your own illusions of yourself. ⁶Let us not be deceived today. ⁷We are the Sons of God. ⁸There is no fear in us, for we are each a part of Love Itself.

2. *How foolish are our fears! ²Would You allow Your Son to suffer? ³Give us faith today to recognize Your Son, and set him free. ⁴Let us forgive him in Your Name, that we may understand his holiness, and feel the love for him which is Your Own as well.*

412

3. What Is the World?

1.   The world is false perception. ²It is born of error, and it has not left its source. ³It will remain no longer than the thought that gave it birth is cherished. ⁴When the thought of separation has been changed to one of true forgiveness, will the world be seen in quite another light; and one which leads to truth, where all the world must disappear and all its errors vanish. ⁵Now its source has gone, and its effects are gone as well.

2.   The world was made as an attack on God. ²It symbolizes fear. ³And what is fear except love's absence? ⁴Thus the world was meant to be a place where God could enter not, and where His Son could be apart from Him. ⁵Here was perception born, for knowledge could not cause such insane thoughts. ⁶But eyes deceive, and ears hear falsely. ⁷Now mistakes become quite possible, for certainty has gone.

3.   The mechanisms of illusion have been born instead. ²And now they go to find what has been given them to seek. ³Their aim is to fulfill the purpose which the world was made to witness and make real. ⁴They see in its illusions but a solid base where truth exists, upheld apart from lies. ⁵Yet everything that they report is but illusion which is kept apart from truth.

4.   As sight was made to lead away from truth, it can be redirected. ²Sounds become the call for God, and all perception can be given a new purpose by the One Whom God appointed Savior to the world. ³Follow His light, and see the world as He beholds it. ⁴Hear His Voice alone in all that speaks to you. ⁵And let Him give you peace and certainty, which you have thrown away, but Heaven has preserved for you in Him.

5.   Let us not rest content until the world has joined our changed perception. ²Let us not be satisfied until forgiveness has been made complete. ³And let us not attempt to change our function. ⁴We must save the world. ⁵For we who made it must behold it through the eyes of Christ, that what was made to die can be restored to everlasting life.

LESSON 241

This holy instant is salvation come.

1. What joy there is today! ²It is a time of special celebration. ³For today holds out the instant to the darkened world where its release is set. ⁴The day has come when sorrows pass away and pain is gone. ⁵The glory of salvation dawns today upon a world set free. ⁶This is the time of hope for countless millions. ⁷They will be united now, as you forgive them all. ⁸For I will be forgiven by you today.

2. *We have forgiven one another now, and so we come at last to You again. ²Father, Your Son, who never left, returns to Heaven and his home. ³How glad are we to have our sanity restored to us, and to remember that we all are one.*

LESSON 242

This day is God's. It is my gift to Him.

1. I will not lead my life alone today. ²I do not understand the world, and so to try to lead my life alone must be but foolishness. ³But there is One Who knows all that is best for me. ⁴And He is glad to make no choices for me but the ones that lead to God. ⁵I give this day to Him, for I would not delay my coming home, and it is He Who knows the way to God.

2. *And so we give today to You. ²We come with wholly open minds. ³We do not ask for anything that we may think we want. ⁴Give us what You would have received by us. ⁵You know all our desires and our wants. ⁶And You will give us everything we need in helping us to find the way to You.*

LESSON 243

Today I will judge nothing that occurs.

1. I will be honest with myself today. ²I will not think that I already know what must remain beyond my present grasp. ³I will not think I understand the whole from bits of my perception, which are all that I can see. ⁴Today I recognize that this is so. ⁵And so I am relieved of judgments that I cannot make. ⁶Thus do I free myself and what I look upon, to be in peace as God created us.

2. *Father, today I leave creation free to be itself. ²I honor all its parts, in which I am included. ³We are one because each part contains Your memory, and truth must shine in all of us as one.*

LESSON 244

I am in danger nowhere in the world.

1. *Your Son is safe wherever he may be, for You are there with him. ²He need but call upon Your Name, and he will recollect his safety and Your Love, for they are one. ³How can he fear or doubt or fail to know he cannot suffer, be endangered, or experience unhappiness, when he belongs to You, beloved and loving, in the safety of Your Fatherly embrace?*

2. And there we are in truth. ²No storms can come into the hallowed haven of our home. ³In God we are secure. ⁴For what can come to threaten God Himself, or make afraid what will forever be a part of Him?

415

LESSON 245

Your peace is with me, Father. I am safe.

1. *Your peace surrounds me, Father.* ²*Where I go, Your peace goes there with me.* ³*It sheds its light on everyone I meet.* ⁴*I bring it to the desolate and lonely and afraid.* ⁵*I give Your peace to those who suffer pain, or grieve for loss, or think they are bereft of hope and happiness.* ⁶*Send them to me, my Father.* ⁷*Let me bring Your peace with me.* ⁸*For I would save Your Son, as is Your Will, that I may come to recognize my Self.*

2. And so we go in peace. ²To all the world we give the message that we have received. ³And thus we come to hear the Voice for God, Who speaks to us as we relate His Word; Whose Love we recognize because we share the Word that He has given unto us.

LESSON 246

To love my Father is to love His Son.

1. Let me not think that I can find the way to God, if I have hatred in my heart. ²Let me not try to hurt God's Son, and think that I can know his Father or my Self. ³Let me not fail to recognize myself, and still believe that my awareness can contain my Father, or my mind conceive of all the love my Father has for me, and all the love which I return to Him.

2. *I will accept the way You choose for me to come to You, my Father.* ²*For in that will I succeed, because it is Your Will.* ³*And I would recognize that what You will is what I will as well, and only that.* ⁴*And so I choose to love Your Son.* ⁵*Amen.*

LESSON 247

Without forgiveness I will still be blind.

1. Sin is the symbol of attack. ²Behold it anywhere, and I will suffer. ³For forgiveness is the only means whereby Christ's vision comes to me. ⁴Let me accept what His sight shows me as the simple truth, and I am healed completely. ⁵Brother, come and let me look on you. ⁶Your loveliness reflects my own. ⁷Your sinlessness is mine. ⁸You stand forgiven, and I stand with you.

2. *So would I look on everyone today. ²My brothers are Your Sons. ³Your Fatherhood created them, and gave them all to me as part of You, and my own Self as well. ⁴Today I honor You through them, and thus I hope this day to recognize my Self.*

LESSON 248

Whatever suffers is not part of me.

1. I have disowned the truth. ²Now let me be as faithful in disowning falsity. ³Whatever suffers is not part of me. ⁴What grieves is not myself. ⁵What is in pain is but illusion in my mind. ⁶What dies was never living in reality, and did but mock the truth about myself. ⁷Now I disown self-concepts and deceits and lies about the holy Son of God. ⁸Now am I ready to accept him back as God created him, and as he is.

2. *Father, my ancient love for You returns, and lets me love Your Son again as well. ²Father, I am as You created me. ³Now is Your Love remembered, and my own. ⁴Now do I understand that they are one.*

LESSON 249

Forgiveness ends all suffering and loss.

1. Forgiveness paints a picture of a world where suffering is over, loss becomes impossible and anger makes no sense. [2]Attack is gone, and madness has an end. [3]What suffering is now conceivable? [4]What loss can be sustained? [5]The world becomes a place of joy, abundance, charity and endless giving. [6]It is now so like to Heaven that it quickly is transformed into the light that it reflects. [7]And so the journey which the Son of God began has ended in the light from which he came.

2. *Father, we would return our minds to You. [2]We have betrayed them, held them in a vise of bitterness, and frightened them with thoughts of violence and death. [3]Now would we rest again in You, as You created us.*

LESSON 250

Let me not see myself as limited.

1. Let me behold the Son of God today, and witness to his glory. [2]Let me not try to obscure the holy light in him, and see his strength diminished and reduced to frailty; nor perceive the lacks in him with which I would attack his sovereignty.

2. *He is Your Son, my Father. [2]And today I would behold his gentleness instead of my illusions. [3]He is what I am, and as I see him so I see myself. [4]Today I would see truly, that this day I may at last identify with him.*

4. What Is Sin?

1. Sin is insanity. ²It is the means by which the mind is driven mad, and seeks to let illusions take the place of truth. ³And being mad, it sees illusions where the truth should be, and where it really is. ⁴Sin gave the body eyes, for what is there the sinless would behold? ⁵What need have they of sights or sounds or touch? ⁶What would they hear or reach to grasp? ⁷What would they sense at all? ⁸To sense is not to know. ⁹And truth can be but filled with knowledge, and with nothing else.

2. The body is the instrument the mind made in its efforts to deceive itself. ²Its purpose is to strive. ³Yet can the goal of striving change. ⁴And now the body serves a different aim for striving. ⁵What it seeks for now is chosen by the aim the mind has taken as replacement for the goal of self-deception. ⁶Truth can be its aim as well as lies. ⁷The senses then will seek instead for witnesses to what is true.

3. Sin is the home of all illusions, which but stand for things imagined, issuing from thoughts that are untrue. ²They are the "proof" that what has no reality is real. ³Sin "proves" God's Son is evil; timelessness must have an end; eternal life must die. ⁴And God Himself has lost the Son He loves, with but corruption to complete Himself, His Will forever overcome by death, love slain by hate, and peace to be no more.

4. A madman's dreams are frightening, and sin appears indeed to terrify. ²And yet what sin perceives is but a childish game. ³The Son of God may play he has become a body, prey to evil and to guilt, with but a little life that ends in death. ⁴But all the while his Father shines on him, and loves him with an everlasting Love which his pretenses cannot change at all.

5. How long, O Son of God, will you maintain the game of sin? ²Shall we not put away these sharp-edged children's toys? ³How soon will you be ready to come home? ⁴Perhaps today? ⁵There is no sin. ⁶Creation is unchanged. ⁷Would you still hold return to Heaven back? ⁸How long, O holy Son of God, how long?

LESSON 251

I am in need of nothing but the truth.

1. I sought for many things, and found despair. [2]Now do I seek but one, for in that one is all I need, and only what I need. [3]All that I sought before I needed not, and did not even want. [4]My only need I did not recognize. [5]But now I see that I need only truth. [6]In that all needs are satisfied, all cravings end, all hopes are finally fulfilled and dreams are gone. [7]Now have I everything that I could need. [8]Now have I everything that I could want. [9]And now at last I find myself at peace.

2. *And for that peace, our Father, we give thanks. [2]What we denied ourselves You have restored, and only that is what we really want.*

LESSON 252

The Son of God is my Identity.

1. My Self is holy beyond all the thoughts of holiness of which I now conceive. [2]Its shimmering and perfect purity is far more brilliant than is any light that I have ever looked upon. [3]Its love is limitless, with an intensity that holds all things within it, in the calm of quiet certainty. [4]Its strength comes not from burning impulses which move the world, but from the boundless Love of God Himself. [5]How far beyond this world my Self must be, and yet how near to me and close to God!

2. *Father, You know my true Identity. [2]Reveal It now to me who am Your Son, that I may waken to the truth in You, and know that Heaven is restored to me.*

LESSON 253

My Self is ruler of the universe.

1. It is impossible that anything should come to me unbidden by myself. ²Even in this world, it is I who rule my destiny. ³What happens is what I desire. ⁴What does not occur is what I do not want to happen. ⁵This must I accept. ⁶For thus am I led past this world to my creations, children of my will, in Heaven where my holy Self abides with them and Him Who has created me.

2. *You are the Self Whom You created Son, creating like Yourself and One with You. ²My Self, which rules the universe, is but Your Will in perfect union with my own, which can but offer glad assent to Yours, that it may be extended to Itself.*

LESSON 254

Let every voice but God's be still in me.

1. *Father, today I would but hear Your Voice. ²In deepest silence I would come to You, to hear Your Voice and to receive Your Word. ³I have no prayer but this: I come to You to ask You for the truth. ⁴And truth is but Your Will, which I would share with You today.*

2. Today we let no ego thoughts direct our words or actions. ²When such thoughts occur, we quietly step back and look at them, and then we let them go. ³We do not want what they would bring with them. ⁴And so we do not choose to keep them. ⁵They are silent now. ⁶And in the stillness, hallowed by His Love, God speaks to us and tells us of our will, as we have chosen to remember Him.

LESSON 255

This day I choose to spend in perfect peace.

1. It does not seem to me that I can choose to have but peace today. ²And yet, my God assures me that His Son is like Himself. ³Let me this day have faith in Him Who says I am God's Son. ⁴And let the peace I choose be mine today bear witness to the truth of what He says. ⁵God's Son can have no cares, and must remain forever in the peace of Heaven. ⁶In His Name, I give today to finding what my Father wills for me, accepting it as mine, and giving it to all my Father's Sons, along with me.

2. *And so, my Father, would I pass this day with You. ²Your Son has not forgotten You. ³The peace You gave him still is in his mind, and it is there I choose to spend today.*

LESSON 256

God is the only goal I have today.

1. The way to God is through forgiveness here. ²There is no other way. ³If sin had not been cherished by the mind, what need would there have been to find the way to where you are? ⁴Who would still be uncertain? ⁵Who could be unsure of who he is? ⁶And who would yet remain asleep, in heavy clouds of doubt about the holiness of him whom God created sinless? ⁷Here we can but dream. ⁸But we can dream we have forgiven him in whom all sin remains impossible, and it is this we choose to dream today. ⁹God is our goal; forgiveness is the means by which our minds return to Him at last.

2. *And so, our Father, would we come to You in Your appointed way. ²We have no goal except to hear Your Voice, and find the way Your sacred Word has pointed out to us.*

422

LESSON 257

Let me remember what my purpose is.

1.   If I forget my goal I can be but confused, unsure of what I am, and thus conflicted in my actions. ²No one can serve contradicting goals and serve them well. ³Nor can he function without deep distress and great depression. ⁴Let us therefore be determined to remember what we want today, that we may unify our thoughts and actions meaningfully, and achieve only what God would have us do this day.

2.   *Father, forgiveness is Your chosen means for our salvation. ²Let us not forget today that we can have no will but Yours. ³And thus our purpose must be Yours as well, if we would reach the peace You will for us.*

LESSON 258

Let me remember that my goal is God.

1.   All that is needful is to train our minds to overlook all little senseless aims, and to remember that our goal is God. ²His memory is hidden in our minds, obscured but by our pointless little goals which offer nothing, and do not exist. ³Shall we continue to allow God's grace to shine in unawareness, while the toys and trinkets of the world are sought instead? ⁴God is our only goal, our only Love. ⁵We have no aim but to remember Him.

2.   *Our goal is but to follow in the way that leads to You. ²We have no goal but this. ³What could we want but to remember You? ⁴What could we seek but our Identity?*

LESSON 259

Let me remember that there is no sin.

1. Sin is the only thought that makes the goal of God seem unattainable. ²What else could blind us to the obvious, and make the strange and the distorted seem more clear? ³What else but sin engenders our attacks? ⁴What else but sin could be the source of guilt, demanding punishment and suffering? ⁵And what but sin could be the source of fear, obscuring God's creation; giving love the attributes of fear and of attack?

2. *Father, I would not be insane today. ²I would not be afraid of love, nor seek for refuge in its opposite. ³For love can have no opposite. ⁴You are the Source of everything there is. ⁵And everything that is remains with You, and You with it.*

LESSON 260

Let me remember God created me.

1. *Father, I did not make myself, although in my insanity I thought I did. ²Yet, as Your Thought, I have not left my Source, remaining part of Who created me. ³Your Son, my Father, calls on You today. ⁴Let me remember You created me. ⁵Let me remember my Identity. ⁶And let my sinlessness arise again before Christ's vision, through which I would look upon my brothers and myself today.*

2. Now is our Source remembered, and Therein we find our true Identity at last. ²Holy indeed are we, because our Source can know no sin. ³And we who are His Sons are like each other, and alike to Him.

5. What Is the Body?

1. The body is a fence the Son of God imagines he has built, to separate parts of his Self from other parts. ²It is within this fence he thinks he lives, to die as it decays and crumbles. ³For within this fence he thinks that he is safe from love. ⁴Identifying with his safety, he regards himself as what his safety is. ⁵How else could he be certain he remains within the body, keeping love outside?

2. The body will not stay. ²Yet this he sees as double safety. ³For the Son of God's impermanence is "proof" his fences work, and do the task his mind assigns to them. ⁴For if his oneness still remained untouched, who could attack and who could be attacked? ⁵Who could be victor? ⁶Who could be his prey? ⁷Who could be victim? ⁸Who the murderer? ⁹And if he did not die, what "proof" is there that God's eternal Son can be destroyed?

3. The body is a dream. ²Like other dreams it sometimes seems to picture happiness, but can quite suddenly revert to fear, where every dream is born. ³For only love creates in truth, and truth can never fear. ⁴Made to be fearful, must the body serve the purpose given it. ⁵But we can change the purpose that the body will obey by changing what we think that it is for.

4. The body is the means by which God's Son returns to sanity. ²Though it was made to fence him into hell without escape, yet has the goal of Heaven been exchanged for the pursuit of hell. ³The Son of God extends his hand to reach his brother, and to help him walk along the road with him. ⁴Now is the body holy. ⁵Now it serves to heal the mind that it was made to kill.

5. You will identify with what you think will make you safe. ²Whatever it may be, you will believe that it is one with you. ³Your safety lies in truth, and not in lies. ⁴Love is your safety. ⁵Fear does not exist. ⁶Identify with love, and you are safe. ⁷Identify with love, and you are home. ⁸Identify with love, and find your Self.

LESSON 261

God is my refuge and security.

1. I will identify with what I think is refuge and security. ²I will behold myself where I perceive my strength, and think I live within the citadel where I am safe and cannot be attacked. ³Let me today seek not security in danger, nor attempt to find my peace in murderous attack. ⁴I live in God. ⁵In Him I find my refuge and my strength. ⁶In Him is my Identity. ⁷In Him is everlasting peace. ⁸And only there will I remember Who I really am.

2. *Let me not seek for idols.* ²*I would come, my Father, home to You today.* ³*I choose to be as You created me, and find the Son whom You created as my Self.*

LESSON 262

Let me perceive no differences today.

1. *Father, You have one Son.* ²*And it is he that I would look upon today.* ³*He is Your one creation.* ⁴*Why should I perceive a thousand forms in what remains as one?* ⁵*Why should I give this one a thousand names, when only one suffices?* ⁶*For Your Son must bear Your Name, for You created him.* ⁷*Let me not see him as a stranger to his Father, nor as stranger to myself.* ⁸*For he is part of me and I of him, and we are part of You Who are our Source, eternally united in Your Love; eternally the holy Son of God.*

2. We who are one would recognize this day the truth about ourselves. ²We would come home, and rest in unity. ³For there is peace, and nowhere else can peace be sought and found.

LESSON 263

My holy vision sees all things as pure.

1. *Father, Your Mind created all that is, Your Spirit entered into it, Your Love gave life to it. ²And would I look upon what You created as if it could be made sinful? ³I would not perceive such dark and fearful images. ⁴A madman's dream is hardly fit to be my choice, instead of all the loveliness with which You blessed creation; all its purity, its joy, and its eternal, quiet home in You.*

2. And while we still remain outside the gate of Heaven, let us look on all we see through holy vision and the eyes of Christ. ²Let all appearances seem pure to us, that we may pass them by in innocence, and walk together to our Father's house as brothers and the holy Sons of God.

LESSON 264

I am surrounded by the Love of God.

1. *Father, You stand before me and behind, beside me, in the place I see myself, and everywhere I go. ²You are in all the things I look upon, the sounds I hear, and every hand that reaches for my own. ³In You time disappears, and place becomes a meaningless belief. ⁴For what surrounds Your Son and keeps him safe is Love itself. ⁵There is no source but this, and nothing is that does not share its holiness; that stands beyond Your one creation, or without the Love which holds all things within itself. ⁶Father, Your Son is like Yourself. ⁷We come to You in Your Own Name today, to be at peace within Your everlasting Love.*

2. My brothers, join with me in this today. ²This is salvation's prayer. ³Must we not join in what will save the world, along with us?

LESSON 265

Creation's gentleness is all I see.

1.   I have indeed misunderstood the world, because I laid my sins on it and saw them looking back at me. ²How fierce they seemed! ³And how deceived was I to think that what I feared was in the world, instead of in my mind alone. ⁴Today I see the world in the celestial gentleness with which creation shines. ⁵There is no fear in it. ⁶Let no appearance of my sins obscure the light of Heaven shining on the world. ⁷What is reflected there is in God's Mind. ⁸The images I see reflect my thoughts. ⁹Yet is my mind at one with God's. ¹⁰And so I can perceive creation's gentleness.

2.   *In quiet would I look upon the world, which but reflects Your Thoughts, and mine as well. ²Let me remember that they are the same, and I will see creation's gentleness.*

LESSON 266

My holy Self abides in you, God's Son.

1.   *Father, You gave me all Your Sons, to be my saviors and my counselors in sight; the bearers of Your holy Voice to me. ²In them are You reflected, and in them does Christ look back upon me from my Self. ³Let not Your Son forget Your holy Name. ⁴Let not Your Son forget his holy Source. ⁵Let not Your Son forget his Name is Yours.*

2.   This day we enter into Paradise, calling upon God's Name and on our own, acknowledging our Self in each of us; united in the holy Love of God. ²How many saviors God has given us! ³How can we lose the way to Him, when He has filled the world with those who point to Him, and given us the sight to look on them?

LESSON 267

My heart is beating in the peace of God.

1.   Surrounding me is all the life that God created in His Love. ²It calls to me in every heartbeat and in every breath; in every action and in every thought. ³Peace fills my heart, and floods my body with the purpose of forgiveness. ⁴Now my mind is healed, and all I need to save the world is given me. ⁵Each heartbeat brings me peace; each breath infuses me with strength. ⁶I am a messenger of God, directed by His Voice, sustained by Him in love, and held forever quiet and at peace within His loving Arms. ⁷Each heartbeat calls His Name, and every one is answered by His Voice, assuring me I am at home in Him.

2.   *Let me attend Your Answer, not my own. ²Father, my heart is beating in the peace the Heart of Love created. ³It is there and only there that I can be at home.*

LESSON 268

Let all things be exactly as they are.

1.   *Let me not be Your critic, Lord, today, and judge against You. ²Let me not attempt to interfere with Your creation, and distort it into sickly forms. ³Let me be willing to withdraw my wishes from its unity, and thus to let it be as You created it. ⁴For thus will I be able, too, to recognize my Self as You created me. ⁵In love was I created, and in love will I remain forever. ⁶What can frighten me, when I let all things be exactly as they are?*

2.   Let not our sight be blasphemous today, nor let our ears attend to lying tongues. ²Only reality is free of pain. ³Only reality is free of loss. ⁴Only reality is wholly safe. ⁵And it is only this we seek today.

LESSON 269

My sight goes forth to look upon Christ's face.

1. *I ask Your blessing on my sight today. ²It is the means which You have chosen to become the way to show me my mistakes, and look beyond them. ³It is given me to find a new perception through the Guide You gave to me, and through His lessons to surpass perception and return to truth. ⁴I ask for the illusion which transcends all those I made. ⁵Today I choose to see a world forgiven, in which everyone shows me the face of Christ, and teaches me that what I look upon belongs to me; that nothing is, except Your holy Son.*

2. Today our sight is blessed indeed. ²We share one vision, as we look upon the face of Him Whose Self is ours. ³We are one because of Him Who is the Son of God; of Him Who is our own Identity.

LESSON 270

I will not use the body's eyes today.

1. *Father, Christ's vision is Your gift to me, and it has power to translate all that the body's eyes behold into the sight of a forgiven world. ²How glorious and gracious is this world! ³Yet how much more will I perceive in it than sight can give. ⁴The world forgiven signifies Your Son acknowledges his Father, lets his dreams be brought to truth, and waits expectantly the one remaining instant more of time which ends forever, as Your memory returns to him. ⁵And now his will is one with Yours. ⁶His function now is but Your Own, and every thought except Your Own is gone.*

2. The quiet of today will bless our hearts, and through them peace will come to everyone. ²Christ is our eyes today. ³And through His sight we offer healing to the world through Him, the holy Son whom God created whole; the holy Son whom God created one.

6. What Is the Christ?

1. Christ is God's Son as He created Him. ²He is the Self we share, uniting us with one another, and with God as well. ³He is the Thought which still abides within the Mind that is His Source. ⁴He has not left His holy home, nor lost the innocence in which He was created. ⁵He abides unchanged forever in the Mind of God.

2. Christ is the link that keeps you one with God, and guarantees that separation is no more than an illusion of despair, for hope forever will abide in Him. ²Your mind is part of His, and His of yours. ³He is the part in which God's Answer lies; where all decisions are already made, and dreams are over. ⁴He remains untouched by anything the body's eyes perceive. ⁵For though in Him His Father placed the means for your salvation, yet does He remain the Self Who, like His Father, knows no sin.

3. Home of the Holy Spirit, and at home in God alone, does Christ remain at peace within the Heaven of your holy mind. ²This is the only part of you that has reality in truth. ³The rest is dreams. ⁴Yet will these dreams be given unto Christ, to fade before His glory and reveal your holy Self, the Christ, to you at last.

4. The Holy Spirit reaches from the Christ in you to all your dreams, and bids them come to Him, to be translated into truth. ²He will exchange them for the final dream which God appointed as the end of dreams. ³For when forgiveness rests upon the world and peace has come to every Son of God, what could there be to keep things separate, for what remains to see except Christ's face?

5. And how long will this holy face be seen, when it is but the symbol that the time for learning now is over, and the goal of the Atonement has been reached at last? ²So therefore let us seek to find Christ's face and look on nothing else. ³As we behold His glory, will we know we have no need of learning or perception or of time, or anything except the holy Self, the Christ Whom God created as His Son.

LESSON 271

Christ's is the vision I will use today.

1. Each day, each hour, every instant, I am choosing what I want to look upon, the sounds I want to hear, the witnesses to what I want to be the truth for me. [2]Today I choose to look upon what Christ would have me see, to listen to God's Voice, and seek the witnesses to what is true in God's creation. [3]In Christ's sight, the world and God's creation meet, and as they come together all perception disappears. [4]His kindly sight redeems the world from death, for nothing that He looks on but must live, remembering the Father and the Son; Creator and creation unified.

2. *Father, Christ's vision is the way to You. [2]What He beholds invites Your memory to be restored to me. [3]And this I choose, to be what I would look upon today.*

LESSON 272

How can illusions satisfy God's Son?

1. *Father, the truth belongs to me. [2]My home is set in Heaven by Your Will and mine. [3]Can dreams content me? [4]Can illusions bring me happiness? [5]What but Your memory can satisfy Your Son? [6]I will accept no less than You have given me. [7]I am surrounded by Your Love, forever still, forever gentle and forever safe. [8]God's Son must be as You created him.*

2. Today we pass illusions by. [2]And if we hear temptation call to us to stay and linger in a dream, we turn aside and ask ourselves if we, the Sons of God, could be content with dreams, when Heaven can be chosen just as easily as hell, and love will happily replace all fear.

LESSON 273

The stillness of the peace of God is mine.

1. Perhaps we are now ready for a day of undisturbed tranquility. ²If this is not yet feasible, we are content and even more than satisfied to learn how such a day can be achieved. ³If we give way to a disturbance, let us learn how to dismiss it and return to peace. ⁴We need but tell our minds, with certainty, "The stillness of the peace of God is mine," and nothing can intrude upon the peace that God Himself has given to His Son.

2. *Father, Your peace is mine. ²What need have I to fear that anything can rob me of what You would have me keep? ³I cannot lose Your gifts to me. ⁴And so the peace You gave Your Son is with me still, in quietness and in my own eternal love for You.*

LESSON 274

Today belongs to love. Let me not fear.

1. *Father, today I would let all things be as You created them, and give Your Son the honor due his sinlessness; the love of brother to his brother and his Friend. ²Through this I am redeemed. ³Through this as well the truth will enter where illusions were, light will replace all darkness, and Your Son will know he is as You created him.*

2. A special blessing comes to us today, from Him Who is our Father. ²Give this day to Him, and there will be no fear today, because the day is given unto love.

LESSON 275

God's healing Voice protects all things today.

1. Let us today attend the Voice for God, which speaks an ancient lesson, no more true today than any other day. ²Yet has this day been chosen as the time when we will seek and hear and learn and understand. ³Join me in hearing. ⁴For the Voice for God tells us of things we cannot understand alone, nor learn apart. ⁵It is in this that all things are protected. ⁶And in this the healing of the Voice for God is found.

2. *Your healing Voice protects all things today, and so I leave all things to You. ²I need be anxious over nothing. ³For Your Voice will tell me what to do and where to go; to whom to speak and what to say to him, what thoughts to think, what words to give the world. ⁴The safety that I bring is given me. ⁵Father, Your Voice protects all things through me.*

LESSON 276

The Word of God is given me to speak.

1. What is the Word of God? ²"My Son is pure and holy as Myself." ³And thus did God become the Father of the Son He loves, for thus was he created. ⁴This the Word His Son did not create with Him, because in this His Son was born. ⁵Let us accept His Fatherhood, and all is given us. ⁶Deny we were created in His Love and we deny our Self, to be unsure of Who we are, of Who our Father is, and for what purpose we have come. ⁷And yet, we need but to acknowledge Him Who gave His Word to us in our creation, to remember Him and so recall our Self.

2. *Father, Your Word is mine. ²And it is this that I would speak to all my brothers, who are given me to cherish as my own, as I am loved and blessed and saved by You.*

LESSON 277

Let me not bind Your Son with laws I made.

1.   *Your Son is free, my Father.* ²*Let me not imagine I have bound him with the laws I made to rule the body.* ³*He is not subject to any laws I made by which I try to make the body more secure.* ⁴*He is not changed by what is changeable.* ⁵*He is not slave to any laws of time.* ⁶*He is as You created him, because he knows no law except the law of love.*

2.   Let us not worship idols, nor believe in any law idolatry would make to hide the freedom of the Son of God. ²He is not bound except by his beliefs. ³Yet what he is, is far beyond his faith in slavery or freedom. ⁴He is free because he is his Father's Son. ⁵And he cannot be bound unless God's truth can lie, and God can will that He deceive Himself.

LESSON 278

If I am bound, my Father is not free.

1.   If I accept that I am prisoner within a body, in a world in which all things that seem to live appear to die, then is my Father prisoner with me. ²And this do I believe, when I maintain the laws the world obeys must I obey; the frailties and the sins which I perceive are real, and cannot be escaped. ³If I am bound in any way, I do not know my Father nor my Self. ⁴And I am lost to all reality. ⁵For truth is free, and what is bound is not a part of truth.

2.   *Father, I ask for nothing but the truth.* ²*I have had many foolish thoughts about myself and my creation, and have brought a dream of fear into my mind.* ³*Today, I would not dream.* ⁴*I choose the way to You instead of madness and instead of fear.* ⁵*For truth is safe, and only love is sure.*

LESSON 279

Creation's freedom promises my own.

1. The end of dreams is promised me, because God's Son is not abandoned by His Love. [2]Only in dreams is there a time when he appears to be in prison, and awaits a future freedom, if it be at all. [3]Yet in reality his dreams are gone, with truth established in their place. [4]And now is freedom his already. [5]Should I wait in chains which have been severed for release, when God is offering me freedom now?

2. *I will accept Your promises today, and give my faith to them.* [2]*My Father loves the Son Whom He created as His Own.* [3]*Would You withhold the gifts You gave to me?*

LESSON 280

What limits can I lay upon God's Son?

1. Whom God created limitless is free. [2]I can invent imprisonment for him, but only in illusions, not in truth. [3]No Thought of God has left its Father's Mind. [4]No Thought of God is limited at all. [5]No Thought of God but is forever pure. [6]Can I lay limits on the Son of God, whose Father willed that he be limitless, and like Himself in freedom and in love?

2. *Today let me give honor to Your Son, for thus alone I find the way to You.* [2]*Father, I lay no limits on the Son You love and You created limitless.* [3]*The honor that I give to him is Yours, and what is Yours belongs to me as well.*

7. What Is the Holy Spirit?

1. The Holy Spirit mediates between illusions and the truth. ²Since He must bridge the gap between reality and dreams, perception leads to knowledge through the grace that God has given Him, to be His gift to everyone who turns to Him for truth. ³Across the bridge that He provides are dreams all carried to the truth, to be dispelled before the light of knowledge. ⁴There are sights and sounds forever laid aside. ⁵And where they were perceived before, forgiveness has made possible perception's tranquil end.

2. The goal the Holy Spirit's teaching sets is just this end of dreams. ²For sights and sounds must be translated from the witnesses of fear to those of love. ³And when this is entirely accomplished, learning has achieved the only goal it has in truth. ⁴For learning, as the Holy Spirit guides it to the outcome He perceives for it, becomes the means to go beyond itself, to be replaced by the eternal truth.

3. If you but knew how much your Father yearns to have you recognize your sinlessness, you would not let His Voice appeal in vain, nor turn away from His replacement for the fearful images and dreams you made. ²The Holy Spirit understands the means you made, by which you would attain what is forever unattainable. ³And if you offer them to Him, He will employ the means you made for exile to restore your mind to where it truly is at home.

4. From knowledge, where He has been placed by God, the Holy Spirit calls to you, to let forgiveness rest upon your dreams, and be restored to sanity and peace of mind. ²Without forgiveness will your dreams remain to terrify you. ³And the memory of all your Father's Love will not return to signify the end of dreams has come.

5. Accept your Father's gift. ²It is a Call from Love to Love, that It be but Itself. ³The Holy Spirit is His gift, by which the quietness of Heaven is restored to God's beloved Son. ⁴Would you refuse to take the function of completing God, when all He wills is that you be complete?

LESSON 281

I can be hurt by nothing but my thoughts.

1. *Father, Your Son is perfect.* ²*When I think that I am hurt in any way, it is because I have forgotten who I am, and that I am as You created me.* ³*Your Thoughts can only bring me happiness.* ⁴*If ever I am sad or hurt or ill, I have forgotten what You think, and put my little meaningless ideas in place of where Your Thoughts belong, and where they are.* ⁵*I can be hurt by nothing but my thoughts.* ⁶*The Thoughts I think with You can only bless.* ⁷*The Thoughts I think with You alone are true.*

2. I will not hurt myself today. ²For I am far beyond all pain. ³My Father placed me safe in Heaven, watching over me. ⁴And I would not attack the Son He loves, for what He loves is also mine to love.

LESSON 282

I will not be afraid of love today.

1. If I could realize but this today, salvation would be reached for all the world. ²This the decision not to be insane, and to accept myself as God Himself, my Father and my Source, created me. ³This the determination not to be asleep in dreams of death, while truth remains forever living in the joy of love. ⁴And this the choice to recognize the Self Whom God created as the Son He loves, and Who remains my one Identity.

2. *Father, Your Name is Love and so is mine.* ²*Such is the truth.* ³*And can the truth be changed by merely giving it another name?* ⁴*The name of fear is simply a mistake.* ⁵*Let me not be afraid of truth today.*

LESSON 283

My true Identity abides in You.

1. *Father, I made an image of myself, and it is this I call the Son of God.* ²*Yet is creation as it always was, for Your creation is unchangeable.* ³*Let me not worship idols.* ⁴*I am he my Father loves.* ⁵*My holiness remains the light of Heaven and the Love of God.* ⁶*Is not what is beloved of You secure?* ⁷*Is not the light of Heaven infinite?* ⁸*Is not Your Son my true Identity, when You created everything that is?*

2. Now are we one in shared Identity, with God our Father as our only Source, and everything created part of us. ²And so we offer blessing to all things, uniting lovingly with all the world, which our forgiveness has made one with us.

LESSON 284

I can elect to change all thoughts that hurt.

1. Loss is not loss when properly perceived. ²Pain is impossible. ³There is no grief with any cause at all. ⁴And suffering of any kind is nothing but a dream. ⁵This is the truth, at first to be but said and then repeated many times; and next to be accepted as but partly true, with many reservations. ⁶Then to be considered seriously more and more, and finally accepted as the truth. ⁷I can elect to change all thoughts that hurt. ⁸And I would go beyond these words today, and past all reservations, and arrive at full acceptance of the truth in them.

2. *Father, what You have given cannot hurt, so grief and pain must be impossible.* ²*Let me not fail to trust in You today, accepting but the joyous as Your gifts; accepting but the joyous as the truth.*

LESSON 285

My holiness shines bright and clear today.

1. Today I wake with joy, expecting but the happy things of God to come to me. ²I ask but them to come, and realize my invitation will be answered by the thoughts to which it has been sent by me. ³And I will ask for only joyous things the instant I accept my holiness. ⁴For what would be the use of pain to me, what purpose would my suffering fulfill, and how would grief and loss avail me if insanity departs from me today, and I accept my holiness instead?

2. *Father, my holiness is Yours. ²Let me rejoice in it, and through forgiveness be restored to sanity. ³Your Son is still as You created him. ⁴My holiness is part of me, and also part of You. ⁵And what can alter Holiness Itself?*

LESSON 286

The hush of Heaven holds my heart today.

1. *Father, how still today! ²How quietly do all things fall in place! ³This is the day that has been chosen as the time in which I come to understand the lesson that there is no need that I do anything. ⁴In You is every choice already made. ⁵In You has every conflict been resolved. ⁶In You is everything I hope to find already given me. ⁷Your peace is mine. ⁸My heart is quiet, and my mind at rest. ⁹Your Love is Heaven, and Your Love is mine.*

2. The stillness of today will give us hope that we have found the way, and travelled far along it to a wholly certain goal. ²Today we will not doubt the end which God Himself has promised us. ³We trust in Him, and in our Self, Who still is one with Him.

LESSON 287

You are my goal, my Father. Only You.

1.   Where would I go but Heaven? ²What could be a substitute for happiness? ³What gift could I prefer before the peace of God? ⁴What treasure would I seek and find and keep that can compare with my Identity? ⁵And would I rather live with fear than love?

2.   *You are my goal, my Father. ²What but You could I desire to have? ³What way but that which leads to You could I desire to walk? ⁴And what except the memory of You could signify to me the end of dreams and futile substitutions for the truth? ⁵You are my only goal. ⁶Your Son would be as You created him. ⁷What way but this could I expect to recognize my Self, and be at one with my Identity?*

LESSON 288

Let me forget my brother's past today.

1.   *This is the thought that leads the way to You, and brings me to my goal. ²I cannot come to You without my brother. ³And to know my Source, I first must recognize what You created one with me. ⁴My brother's is the hand that leads me on the way to You. ⁵His sins are in the past along with mine, and I am saved because the past is gone. ⁶Let me not cherish it within my heart, or I will lose the way to walk to You. ⁷My brother is my savior. ⁸Let me not attack the savior You have given me. ⁹But let me honor him who bears Your Name, and so remember that It is my own.*

2.   Forgive me, then, today. ²And you will know you have forgiven me if you behold your brother in the light of holiness. ³He cannot be less holy than can I, and you can not be holier than he.

LESSON 289

The past is over. It can touch me not.

1.   Unless the past is over in my mind, the real world must escape my sight. ²For I am really looking nowhere; seeing but what is not there. ³How can I then perceive the world forgiveness offers? ⁴This the past was made to hide, for this the world that can be looked on only now. ⁵It has no past. ⁶For what can be forgiven but the past, and if it is forgiven it is gone.

2.   *Father, let me not look upon a past that is not there. ²For You have offered me Your Own replacement, in a present world the past has left untouched and free of sin. ³Here is the end of guilt. ⁴And here am I made ready for Your final step. ⁵Shall I demand that You wait longer for Your Son to find the loveliness You planned to be the end of all his dreams and all his pain?*

LESSON 290

My present happiness is all I see.

1.   Unless I look upon what is not there, my present happiness is all I see. ²Eyes that begin to open see at last. ³And I would have Christ's vision come to me this very day. ⁴What I perceive without God's Own Correction for the sight I made is frightening and painful to behold. ⁵Yet I would not allow my mind to be deceived by the belief the dream I made is real an instant longer. ⁶This the day I seek my present happiness, and look on nothing else except the thing I seek.

2.   *With this resolve I come to You, and ask Your strength to hold me up today, while I but seek to do Your Will. ²You cannot fail to hear me, Father. ³What I ask have You already given me. ⁴And I am sure that I will see my happiness today.*

8. What Is the Real World?

1.   The real world is a symbol, like the rest of what perception offers. ²Yet it stands for what is opposite to what you made. ³Your world is seen through eyes of fear, and brings the witnesses of terror to your mind. ⁴The real world cannot be perceived except through eyes forgiveness blesses, so they see a world where terror is impossible, and witnesses to fear can not be found.

2.   The real world holds a counterpart for each unhappy thought reflected in your world; a sure correction for the sights of fear and sounds of battle which your world contains. ²The real world shows a world seen differently, through quiet eyes and with a mind at peace. ³Nothing but rest is there. ⁴There are no cries of pain and sorrow heard, for nothing there remains outside forgiveness. ⁵And the sights are gentle. ⁶Only happy sights and sounds can reach the mind that has forgiven itself.

3.   What need has such a mind for thoughts of death, attack and murder? ²What can it perceive surrounding it but safety, love and joy? ³What is there it would choose to be condemned, and what is there that it would judge against? ⁴The world it sees arises from a mind at peace within itself. ⁵No danger lurks in anything it sees, for it is kind, and only kindness does it look upon.

4.   The real world is the symbol that the dream of sin and guilt is over, and God's Son no longer sleeps. ²His waking eyes perceive the sure reflection of his Father's Love; the certain promise that he is redeemed. ³The real world signifies the end of time, for its perception makes time purposeless.

5.   The Holy Spirit has no need of time when it has served His purpose. ²Now He waits but that one instant more for God to take His final step, and time has disappeared, taking perception with it as it goes, and leaving but the truth to be itself. ³That instant is our goal, for it contains the memory of God. ⁴And as we look upon a world forgiven, it is He Who calls to us and comes to take us home, reminding us of our Identity which our forgiveness has restored to us.

LESSON 291

This is a day of stillness and of peace.

1. Christ's vision looks through me today. ²His sight shows me all things forgiven and at peace, and offers this same vision to the world. ³And I accept this vision in its name, both for myself and for the world as well. ⁴What loveliness we look upon today! ⁵What holiness we see surrounding us! ⁶And it is given us to recognize it is a holiness in which we share; it is the Holiness of God Himself.

2. *This day my mind is quiet, to receive the Thoughts You offer me. ²And I accept what comes from You, instead of from myself. ³I do not know the way to You. ⁴But You are wholly certain. ⁵Father, guide Your Son along the quiet path that leads to You. ⁶Let my forgiveness be complete, and let the memory of You return to me.*

LESSON 292

A happy outcome to all things is sure.

1. God's promises make no exceptions. ²And He guarantees that only joy can be the final outcome found for everything. ³Yet it is up to us when this is reached; how long we let an alien will appear to be opposing His. ⁴And while we think this will is real, we will not find the end He has appointed as the outcome of all problems we perceive, all trials we see, and every situation that we meet. ⁵Yet is the ending certain. ⁶For God's Will is done in earth and Heaven. ⁷We will seek and we will find according to His Will, which guarantees that our will is done.

2. *We thank You, Father, for Your guarantee of only happy outcomes in the end. ²Help us not interfere, and so delay the happy endings You have promised us for every problem that we can perceive; for every trial we think we still must meet.*

LESSON 293

All fear is past and only love is here.

1. All fear is past, because its source is gone, and all its thoughts gone with it. ²Love remains the only present state, whose Source is here forever and forever. ³Can the world seem bright and clear and safe and welcoming, with all my past mistakes oppressing it, and showing me distorted forms of fear? ⁴Yet in the present love is obvious, and its effects apparent. ⁵All the world shines in reflection of its holy light, and I perceive a world forgiven at last.

2. *Father, let not Your holy world escape my sight today. ²Nor let my ears be deaf to all the hymns of gratitude the world is singing underneath the sounds of fear. ³There is a real world which the present holds safe from all past mistakes. ⁴And I would see only this world before my eyes today.*

LESSON 294

My body is a wholly neutral thing.

1. I am a Son of God. ²And can I be another thing as well? ³Did God create the mortal and corruptible? ⁴What use has God's beloved Son for what must die? ⁵And yet a neutral thing does not see death, for thoughts of fear are not invested there, nor is a mockery of love bestowed upon it. ⁶Its neutrality protects it while it has a use. ⁷And afterwards, without a purpose, it is laid aside. ⁸It is not sick nor old nor hurt. ⁹It is but functionless, unneeded and cast off. ¹⁰Let me not see it more than this today; of service for a while and fit to serve, to keep its usefulness while it can serve, and then to be replaced for greater good.

2. *My body, Father, cannot be Your Son. ²And what is not created cannot be sinful nor sinless; neither good nor bad. ³Let me, then, use this dream to help Your plan that we awaken from all dreams we made.*

LESSON 295

The Holy Spirit looks through me today.

1. Christ asks that He may use my eyes today, and thus redeem the world. ²He asks this gift that He may offer peace of mind to me, and take away all terror and all pain. ³And as they are removed from me, the dreams that seemed to settle on the world are gone. ⁴Redemption must be one. ⁵As I am saved, the world is saved with me. ⁶For all of us must be redeemed together. ⁷Fear appears in many different forms, but love is one.

2. *My Father, Christ has asked a gift of me, and one I give that it be given me. ²Help me to use the eyes of Christ today, and thus allow the Holy Spirit's Love to bless all things which I may look upon, that His forgiving Love may rest on me.*

LESSON 296

The Holy Spirit speaks through me today.

1. *The Holy Spirit needs my voice today, that all the world may listen to Your Voice, and hear Your Word through me. ²I am resolved to let You speak through me, for I would use no words but Yours, and have no thoughts which are apart from Yours, for only Yours are true. ³I would be savior to the world I made. ⁴For having damned it I would set it free, that I may find escape, and hear the Word Your holy Voice will speak to me today.*

2. We teach today what we would learn, and that alone. ²And so our learning goal becomes an unconflicted one, and possible of easy reach and quick accomplishment. ³How gladly does the Holy Spirit come to rescue us from hell, when we allow His teaching to persuade the world, through us, to seek and find the easy path to God.

LESSON 297

Forgiveness is the only gift I give.

1. Forgiveness is the only gift I give, because it is the only gift I want. ²And everything I give I give myself. ³This is salvation's simple formula. ⁴And I, who would be saved, would make it mine, to be the way I live within a world that needs salvation, and that will be saved as I accept Atonement for myself.

2. *Father, how certain are Your ways; how sure their final outcome, and how faithfully is every step in my salvation set already, and accomplished by Your grace. ²Thanks be to You for Your eternal gifts, and thanks to You for my Identity.*

LESSON 298

I love You, Father, and I love Your Son.

1. My gratitude permits my love to be accepted without fear. ²And thus am I restored to my reality at last. ³All that intruded on my holy sight forgiveness takes away. ⁴And I draw near the end of senseless journeys, mad careers and artificial values. ⁵I accept instead what God establishes as mine, sure that in that alone I will be saved; sure that I go through fear to meet my Love.

2. *Father, I come to You today, because I would not follow any way but Yours. ²You are beside me. ³Certain is Your way. ⁴And I am grateful for Your holy gifts of certain sanctuary, and escape from everything that would obscure my love for God my Father and His holy Son.*

LESSON 299

Eternal holiness abides in me.

1.   My holiness is far beyond my own ability to understand or know. ²Yet God, my Father, Who created it, acknowledges my holiness as His. ³Our Will, together, understands it. ⁴And Our Will, together, knows that it is so.

2.   *Father, my holiness is not of me. ²It is not mine to be destroyed by sin. ³It is not mine to suffer from attack. ⁴Illusions can obscure it, but can not put out its radiance, nor dim its light. ⁵It stands forever perfect and untouched. ⁶In it are all things healed, for they remain as You created them. ⁷And I can know my holiness. ⁸For Holiness Itself created me, and I can know my Source because it is Your Will that You be known.*

LESSON 300

Only an instant does this world endure.

1.   This is a thought which can be used to say that death and sorrow are the certain lot of all who come here, for their joys are gone before they are possessed, or even grasped. ²Yet this is also the idea that lets no false perception keep us in its hold, nor represent more than a passing cloud upon a sky eternally serene. ³And it is this serenity we seek, unclouded, obvious and sure, today.

2.   *We seek Your holy world today. ²For we, Your loving Sons, have lost our way a while. ³But we have listened to Your Voice, and learned exactly what to do to be restored to Heaven and our true Identity. ⁴And we give thanks today the world endures but for an instant. ⁵We would go beyond that tiny instant to eternity.*

9. What Is the Second Coming?

1. Christ's Second Coming, which is sure as God, is merely the correction of mistakes, and the return of sanity. [2]It is a part of the condition that restores the never lost, and re-establishes what is forever and forever true. [3]It is the invitation to God's Word to take illusion's place; the willingness to let forgiveness rest upon all things without exception and without reserve.
2. It is the all-inclusive nature of Christ's Second Coming that permits it to embrace the world and hold you safe within its gentle advent, which encompasses all living things with you. [2]There is no end to the release the Second Coming brings, as God's creation must be limitless. [3]Forgiveness lights the Second Coming's way, because it shines on everything as one. [4]And thus is oneness recognized at last.
3. The Second Coming ends the lessons that the Holy Spirit teaches, making way for the Last Judgment, in which learning ends in one last summary that will extend beyond itself, and reaches up to God. [2]The Second Coming is the time in which all minds are given to the hands of Christ, to be returned to spirit in the name of true creation and the Will of God.
4. The Second Coming is the one event in time which time itself can not affect. [2]For every one who ever came to die, or yet will come or who is present now, is equally released from what he made. [3]In this equality is Christ restored as one Identity, in which the Sons of God acknowledge that they all are one. [4]And God the Father smiles upon His Son, His one creation and His only joy.
5. Pray that the Second Coming will be soon, but do not rest with that. [2]It needs your eyes and ears and hands and feet. [3]It needs your voice. [4]And most of all it needs your willingness. [5]Let us rejoice that we can do God's Will, and join together in its holy light. [6]Behold, the Son of God is one in us, and we can reach our Father's Love through Him.

LESSON 301

And God Himself shall wipe away all tears.

1. *Father, unless I judge I cannot weep.* ²*Nor can I suffer pain, or feel I am abandoned or unneeded in the world.* ³*This is my home because I judge it not, and therefore is it only what You will.* ⁴*Let me today behold it uncondemned, through happy eyes forgiveness has released from all distortion.* ⁵*Let me see Your world instead of mine.* ⁶*And all the tears I shed will be forgotten, for their source is gone.* ⁷*Father, I will not judge Your world today.*

2. God's world is happy. ²Those who look on it can only add their joy to it, and bless it as a cause of further joy in them. ³We wept because we did not understand. ⁴But we have learned the world we saw was false, and we will look upon God's world today.

LESSON 302

Where darkness was I look upon the light.

1. *Father, our eyes are opening at last.* ²*Your holy world awaits us, as our sight is finally restored and we can see.* ³*We thought we suffered.* ⁴*But we had forgot the Son whom You created.* ⁵*Now we see that darkness is our own imagining, and light is there for us to look upon.* ⁶*Christ's vision changes darkness into light, for fear must disappear when love has come.* ⁷*Let me forgive Your holy world today, that I may look upon its holiness and understand it but reflects my own.*

2. Our Love awaits us as we go to Him, and walks beside us showing us the way. ²He fails in nothing. ³He the End we seek, and He the Means by which we go to Him.

LESSON 303

The holy Christ is born in me today.

1. Watch with me, angels, watch with me today. [2]Let all God's holy Thoughts surround me, and be still with me while Heaven's Son is born. [3]Let earthly sounds be quiet, and the sights to which I am accustomed disappear. [4]Let Christ be welcomed where He is at home. [5]And let Him hear the sounds He understands, and see but sights that show His Father's Love. [6]Let Him no longer be a stranger here, for He is born again in me today.

2. *Your Son is welcome, Father. [2]He has come to save me from the evil self I made. [3]He is the Self that You have given me. [4]He is but what I really am in truth. [5]He is the Son You love above all things. [6]He is my Self as You created me. [7]It is not Christ that can be crucified. [8]Safe in Your Arms let me receive Your Son.*

LESSON 304

Let not my world obscure the sight of Christ.

1. I can obscure my holy sight, if I intrude my world upon it. [2]Nor can I behold the holy sights Christ looks upon, unless it is His vision that I use. [3]Perception is a mirror, not a fact. [4]And what I look on is my state of mind, reflected outward. [5]I would bless the world by looking on it through the eyes of Christ. [6]And I will look upon the certain signs that all my sins have been forgiven me.

2. *You lead me from the darkness to the light; from sin to holiness. [2]Let me forgive, and thus receive salvation for the world. [3]It is Your gift, my Father, given me to offer to Your holy Son, that he may find again the memory of You, and of Your Son as You created him.*

LESSON 305

There is a peace that Christ bestows on us.

1. Who uses but Christ's vision finds a peace so deep and quiet, undisturbable and wholly changeless, that the world contains no counterpart. ²Comparisons are still before this peace. ³And all the world departs in silence as this peace envelops it, and gently carries it to truth, no more to be the home of fear. ⁴For love has come, and healed the world by giving it Christ's peace.

2. *Father, the peace of Christ is given us, because it is Your Will that we be saved. ²Help us today but to accept Your gift, and judge it not. ³For it has come to us to save us from our judgment on ourselves.*

LESSON 306

The gift of Christ is all I seek today.

1. What but Christ's vision would I use today, when it can offer me a day in which I see a world so like to Heaven that an ancient memory returns to me? ²Today I can forget the world I made. ³Today I can go past all fear, and be restored to love and holiness and peace. ⁴Today I am redeemed, and born anew into a world of mercy and of care; of loving kindness and the peace of God.

2. *And so, our Father, we return to You, remembering we never went away; remembering Your holy gifts to us. ²In gratitude and thankfulness we come, with empty hands and open hearts and minds, asking but what You give. ³We cannot make an offering sufficient for Your Son. ⁴But in Your Love the gift of Christ is his.*

LESSON 307

Conflicting wishes cannot be my will.

1. *Father, Your Will is mine, and only that.* ²*There is no other will for me to have.* ³*Let me not try to make another will, for it is senseless and will cause me pain.* ⁴*Your Will alone can bring me happiness, and only Yours exists.* ⁵*If I would have what only You can give, I must accept Your Will for me, and enter into peace where conflict is impossible, Your Son is one with You in being and in will, and nothing contradicts the holy truth that I remain as You created me.*

2. And with this prayer we enter silently into a state where conflict cannot come, because we join our holy will with God's, in recognition that they are the same.

LESSON 308

This instant is the only time there is.

1. I have conceived of time in such a way that I defeat my aim. ²If I elect to reach past time to timelessness, I must change my perception of what time is for. ³Time's purpose cannot be to keep the past and future one. ⁴The only interval in which I can be saved from time is now. ⁵For in this instant has forgiveness come to set me free. ⁶The birth of Christ is now, without a past or future. ⁷He has come to give His present blessing to the world, restoring it to timelessness and love. ⁸And love is ever-present, here and now.

2. *Thanks for this instant, Father.* ²*It is now I am redeemed.* ³*This instant is the time You have appointed for Your Son's release, and for salvation of the world in him.*

LESSON 309

I will not fear to look within today.

1. Within me is eternal innocence, because it is God's Will that it be there forever and forever. ²I, His Son, whose will is limitless as is His Own, can will no change in this. ³For to deny my Father's Will is to deny my own. ⁴To look within is but to find my will as God created it, and as it is. ⁵I fear to look within because I think I made another will that is not true, and made it real. ⁶Yet it has no effects. ⁷Within me is the Holiness of God. ⁸Within me is the memory of Him.

2. *The step I take today, my Father, is my sure release from idle dreams of sin. ²Your altar stands serene and undefiled. ³It is the holy altar to my Self, and there I find my true Identity.*

LESSON 310

In fearlessness and love I spend today.

1. *This day, my Father, would I spend with You, as You have chosen all my days should be. ²And what I will experience is not of time at all. ³The joy that comes to me is not of days nor hours, for it comes from Heaven to Your Son. ⁴This day will be Your sweet reminder to remember You, Your gracious calling to Your holy Son, the sign Your grace has come to me, and that it is Your Will I be set free today.*

2. We spend this day together, you and I. ²And all the world joins with us in our song of thankfulness and joy to Him Who gave salvation to us, and Who set us free. ³We are restored to peace and holiness. ⁴There is no room in us for fear today, for we have welcomed love into our hearts.

10. What Is the Last Judgment?

1. Christ's Second Coming gives the Son of God this gift: to hear the Voice for God proclaim that what is false is false, and what is true has never changed. ²And this the judgment is in which perception ends. ³At first you see a world that has accepted this as true, projected from a now corrected mind. ⁴And with this holy sight, perception gives a silent blessing and then disappears, its goal accomplished and its mission done.

2. The final judgment on the world contains no condemnation. ²For it sees the world as totally forgiven, without sin and wholly purposeless. ³Without a cause, and now without a function in Christ's sight, it merely slips away to nothingness. ⁴There it was born, and there it ends as well. ⁵And all the figures in the dream in which the world began go with it. ⁶Bodies now are useless, and will therefore fade away, because the Son of God is limitless.

3. You who believed that God's Last Judgment would condemn the world to hell along with you, accept this holy truth: God's Judgment is the gift of the Correction He bestowed on all your errors, freeing you from them, and all effects they ever seemed to have. ²To fear God's saving grace is but to fear complete release from suffering, return to peace, security and happiness, and union with your own Identity.

4. God's Final Judgment is as merciful as every step in His appointed plan to bless His Son, and call him to return to the eternal peace He shares with him. ²Be not afraid of love. ³For it alone can heal all sorrow, wipe away all tears, and gently waken from his dream of pain the Son whom God acknowledges as His. ⁴Be not afraid of this. ⁵Salvation asks you give it welcome. ⁶And the world awaits your glad acceptance, which will set it free.

5. This is God's Final Judgment: "You are still My holy Son, forever innocent, forever loving and forever loved, as limitless as your Creator, and completely changeless and forever pure. ²Therefore awaken and return to Me. ³I am your Father and you are My Son."

LESSON 311

I judge all things as I would have them be.

1. Judgment was made to be a weapon used against the truth. ²It separates what it is being used against, and sets it off as if it were a thing apart. ³And then it makes of it what you would have it be. ⁴It judges what it cannot understand, because it cannot see totality and therefore judges falsely. ⁵Let us not use it today, but make a gift of it to Him Who has a different use for it. ⁶He will relieve us of the agony of all the judgments we have made against ourselves, and re-establish peace of mind by giving us God's Judgment of His Son.

2. *Father, we wait with open mind today, to hear Your Judgment of the Son You love. ²We do not know him, and we cannot judge. ³And so we let Your Love decide what he whom You created as Your Son must be.*

LESSON 312

I see all things as I would have them be.

1. Perception follows judgment. ²Having judged, we therefore see what we would look upon. ³For sight can merely serve to offer us what we would have. ⁴It is impossible to overlook what we would see, and fail to see what we have chosen to behold. ⁵How surely, therefore, must the real world come to greet the holy sight of anyone who takes the Holy Spirit's purpose as his goal for seeing. ⁶And he cannot fail to look upon what Christ would have him see, and share Christ's Love for what he looks upon.

2. *I have no purpose for today except to look upon a liberated world, set free from all the judgments I have made. ²Father, this is Your Will for me today, and therefore it must be my goal as well.*

LESSON 313

Now let a new perception come to me.

1. *Father, there is a vision which beholds all things as sinless, so that fear has gone, and where it was is love invited in.* ²*And love will come wherever it is asked.* ³*This vision is Your gift.* ⁴*The eyes of Christ look on a world forgiven.* ⁵*In His sight are all its sins forgiven, for He sees no sin in anything He looks upon.* ⁶*Now let His true perception come to me, that I may waken from the dream of sin and look within upon my sinlessness, which You have kept completely undefiled upon the altar to Your holy Son, the Self with which I would identify.*

2. Let us today behold each other in the sight of Christ. ²How beautiful we are! ³How holy and how loving! ⁴Brother, come and join with me today. ⁵We save the world when we have joined. ⁶For in our vision it becomes as holy as the light in us.

LESSON 314

I seek a future different from the past.

1. From new perception of the world there comes a future very different from the past. ²The future now is recognized as but extension of the present. ³Past mistakes can cast no shadows on it, so that fear has lost its idols and its images, and being formless, it has no effects. ⁴Death will not claim the future now, for life is now its goal, and all the needed means are happily provided. ⁵Who can grieve or suffer when the present has been freed, extending its security and peace into a quiet future filled with joy?

2. *Father, we were mistaken in the past, and choose to use the present to be free.* ²*Now do we leave the future in Your Hands, leaving behind our past mistakes, and sure that You will keep Your present promises, and guide the future in their holy light.*

LESSON 315

All gifts my brothers give belong to me.

1. Each day a thousand treasures come to me with every passing moment. ²I am blessed with gifts throughout the day, in value far beyond all things of which I can conceive. ³A brother smiles upon another, and my heart is gladdened. ⁴Someone speaks a word of gratitude or mercy, and my mind receives this gift and takes it as its own. ⁵And everyone who finds the way to God becomes my savior, pointing out the way to me, and giving me his certainty that what he learned is surely mine as well.

2. *I thank You, Father, for the many gifts that come to me today and every day from every Son of God. ²My brothers are unlimited in all their gifts to me. ³Now may I offer them my thankfulness, that gratitude to them may lead me on to my Creator and His memory.*

LESSON 316

All gifts I give my brothers are my own.

1. As every gift my brothers give is mine, so every gift I give belongs to me. ²Each one allows a past mistake to go, and leave no shadow on the holy mind my Father loves. ³His grace is given me in every gift a brother has received throughout all time, and past all time as well. ⁴My treasure house is full, and angels watch its open doors that not one gift is lost, and only more are added. ⁵Let me come to where my treasures are, and enter in where I am truly welcome and at home, among the gifts that God has given me.

2. *Father, I would accept Your gifts today. ²I do not recognize them. ³Yet I trust that You Who gave them will provide the means by which I can behold them, see their worth, and cherish only them as what I want.*

LESSON 317

I follow in the way appointed me.

1.   I have a special place to fill; a role for me alone. ²Salvation waits until I take this part as what I choose to do. ³Until I make this choice, I am the slave of time and human destiny. ⁴But when I willingly and gladly go the way my Father's plan appointed me to go, then will I recognize salvation is already here, already given all my brothers and already mine as well.

2.   *Father, Your way is what I choose today. ²Where it would lead me do I choose to go; what it would have me do I choose to do. ³Your way is certain, and the end secure. ⁴The memory of You awaits me there. ⁵And all my sorrows end in Your embrace, which You have promised to Your Son, who thought mistakenly that he had wandered from the sure protection of Your loving Arms.*

LESSON 318

In me salvation's means and end are one.

1.   In me, God's holy Son, are reconciled all parts of Heaven's plan to save the world. ²What could conflict, when all the parts have but one purpose and one aim? ³How could there be a single part that stands alone, or one of more or less importance than the rest? ⁴I am the means by which God's Son is saved, because salvation's purpose is to find the sinlessness that God has placed in me. ⁵I was created as the thing I seek. ⁶I am the goal the world is searching for. ⁷I am God's Son, His one eternal Love. ⁸I am salvation's means and end as well.

2.   *Let me today, my Father, take the role You offer me in Your request that I accept Atonement for myself. ²For thus does what is thereby reconciled in me become as surely reconciled to You.*

LESSON 319

I came for the salvation of the world.

1. Here is a thought from which all arrogance has been removed, and only truth remains. ²For arrogance opposes truth. ³But when there is no arrogance the truth will come immediately, and fill up the space the ego left unoccupied by lies. ⁴Only the ego can be limited, and therefore it must seek for aims which are curtailed and limiting. ⁵The ego thinks that what one gains, totality must lose. ⁶And yet it is the Will of God I learn that what one gains is given unto all.

2. *Father, Your Will is total.* ²*And the goal which stems from it shares its totality.* ³*What aim but the salvation of the world could You have given me?* ⁴*And what but this could be the Will my Self has shared with You?*

LESSON 320

My Father gives all power unto me.

1. The Son of God is limitless. ²There are no limits on his strength, his peace, his joy, nor any attributes his Father gave in his creation. ³What he wills with his Creator and Redeemer must be done. ⁴His holy will can never be denied, because his Father shines upon his mind, and lays before it all the strength and love in earth and Heaven. ⁵I am he to whom all this is given. ⁶I am he in whom the power of my Father's Will abides.

2. *Your Will can do all things in me, and then extend to all the world as well through me.* ²*There is no limit on Your Will.* ³*And so all power has been given to Your Son.*

11. What Is Creation?

1. Creation is the sum of all God's Thoughts, in number infinite, and everywhere without all limit. ²Only love creates, and only like itself. ³There was no time when all that it created was not there. ⁴Nor will there be a time when anything that it created suffers any loss. ⁵Forever and forever are God's Thoughts exactly as they were and as they are, unchanged through time and after time is done.

2. God's Thoughts are given all the power that their own Creator has. ²For He would add to love by its extension. ³Thus His Son shares in creation, and must therefore share in power to create. ⁴What God has willed to be forever One will still be One when time is over; and will not be changed throughout the course of time, remaining as it was before the thought of time began.

3. Creation is the opposite of all illusions, for creation is the truth. ²Creation is the holy Son of God, for in creation is His Will complete in every aspect, making every part container of the whole. ³Its oneness is forever guaranteed inviolate; forever held within His holy Will, beyond all possibility of harm, of separation, imperfection and of any spot upon its sinlessness.

4. We are creation; we the Sons of God. ²We seem to be discrete, and unaware of our eternal unity with Him. ³Yet back of all our doubts, past all our fears, there still is certainty. ⁴For love remains with all its Thoughts, its sureness being theirs. ⁵God's memory is in our holy minds, which know their oneness and their unity with their Creator. ⁶Let our function be only to let this memory return, only to let God's Will be done on earth, only to be restored to sanity, and to be but as God created us.

5. Our Father calls to us. ²We hear His Voice, and we forgive creation in the Name of its Creator, Holiness Itself, Whose Holiness His Own creation shares; Whose Holiness is still a part of us.

LESSON 321

Father, my freedom is in You alone.

1.   *I did not understand what made me free, nor what my freedom is, nor where to look to find it. ²Father, I have searched in vain until I heard Your Voice directing me. ³Now I would guide myself no more. ⁴For I have neither made nor understood the way to find my freedom. ⁵But I trust in You. ⁶You Who endowed me with my freedom as Your holy Son will not be lost to me. ⁷Your Voice directs me, and the way to You is opening and clear to me at last. ⁸Father, my freedom is in You alone. ⁹Father, it is my will that I return.*

2.   Today we answer for the world, which will be freed along with us. ²How glad are we to find our freedom through the certain way our Father has established. ³And how sure is all the world's salvation, when we learn our freedom can be found in God alone.

LESSON 322

I can give up but what was never real.

1.   I sacrifice illusions; nothing more. ²And as illusions go I find the gifts illusions tried to hide, awaiting me in shining welcome, and in readiness to give God's ancient messages to me. ³His memory abides in every gift that I receive of Him. ⁴And every dream serves only to conceal the Self which is God's only Son, the likeness of Himself, the Holy One Who still abides in Him forever, as He still abides in me.

2.   *Father, to You all sacrifice remains forever inconceivable. ²And so I cannot sacrifice except in dreams. ³As You created me, I can give up nothing You gave me. ⁴What You did not give has no reality. ⁵What loss can I anticipate except the loss of fear, and the return of love into my mind?*

462

LESSON 323

I gladly make the "sacrifice" of fear.

1. *Here is the only "sacrifice" You ask of Your beloved Son; You ask him to give up all suffering, all sense of loss and sadness, all anxiety and doubt, and freely let Your Love come streaming in to his awareness, healing him of pain, and giving him Your Own eternal joy.* ²*Such is the "sacrifice" You ask of me, and one I gladly make; the only "cost" of restoration of Your memory to me, for the salvation of the world.*

2. And as we pay the debt we owe to truth,—a debt that merely is the letting go of self-deceptions and of images we worshipped falsely—truth returns to us in wholeness and in joy. ²We are deceived no longer. ³Love has now returned to our awareness. ⁴And we are at peace again, for fear has gone and only love remains.

LESSON 324

I merely follow, for I would not lead.

1. *Father, You are the One Who gave the plan for my salvation to me.* ²*You have set the way I am to go, the role to take, and every step in my appointed path.* ³*I cannot lose the way.* ⁴*I can but choose to wander off a while, and then return.* ⁵*Your loving Voice will always call me back, and guide my feet aright.* ⁶*My brothers all can follow in the way I lead them.* ⁷*Yet I merely follow in the way to You, as You direct me and would have me go.*

2. So let us follow One Who knows the way. ²We need not tarry, and we cannot stray except an instant from His loving Hand. ³We walk together, for we follow Him. ⁴And it is He Who makes the ending sure, and guarantees a safe returning home.

LESSON 325

All things I think I see reflect ideas.

1. This is salvation's keynote: What I see reflects a process in my mind, which starts with my idea of what I want. [2]From there, the mind makes up an image of the thing the mind desires, judges valuable, and therefore seeks to find. [3]These images are then projected outward, looked upon, esteemed as real and guarded as one's own. [4]From insane wishes comes an insane world. [5]From judgment comes a world condemned. [6]And from forgiving thoughts a gentle world comes forth, with mercy for the holy Son of God, to offer him a kindly home where he can rest a while before he journeys on, and help his brothers walk ahead with him, and find the way to Heaven and to God.

2. *Our Father, Your ideas reflect the truth, and mine apart from Yours but make up dreams. [2]Let me behold what only Yours reflect, for Yours and Yours alone establish truth.*

LESSON 326

I am forever an Effect of God.

1. *Father, I was created in Your Mind, a holy Thought that never left its home. [2]I am forever Your Effect, and You forever and forever are my Cause. [3]As You created me I have remained. [4]Where You established me I still abide. [5]And all Your attributes abide in me, because it is Your Will to have a Son so like his Cause that Cause and Its Effect are indistinguishable. [6]Let me know that I am an Effect of God, and so I have the power to create like You. [7]And as it is in Heaven, so on earth. [8]Your plan I follow here, and at the end I know that You will gather Your effects into the tranquil Heaven of Your Love, where earth will vanish, and all separate thoughts unite in glory as the Son of God.*

2. Let us today behold earth disappear, at first transformed, and then, forgiven, fade entirely into God's holy Will.

LESSON 327

I need but call and You will answer me.

1.   I am not asked to take salvation on the basis of an unsupported faith. ²For God has promised He will hear my call, and answer me Himself. ³Let me but learn from my experience that this is true, and faith in Him must surely come to me. ⁴This is the faith that will endure, and take me farther and still farther on the road that leads to Him. ⁵For thus I will be sure that He has not abandoned me and loves me still, awaiting but my call to give me all the help I need to come to Him.

2.   *Father, I thank You that Your promises will never fail in my experience, if I but test them out. ²Let me attempt therefore to try them, and to judge them not. ³Your Word is one with You. ⁴You give the means whereby conviction comes, and surety of Your abiding Love is gained at last.*

LESSON 328

I choose the second place to gain the first.

1.   What seems to be the second place is first, for all things we perceive are upside down until we listen to the Voice for God. ²It seems that we will gain autonomy but by our striving to be separate, and that our independence from the rest of God's creation is the way in which salvation is obtained. ³Yet all we find is sickness, suffering and loss and death. ⁴This is not what our Father wills for us, nor is there any second to His Will. ⁵To join with His is but to find our own. ⁶And since our will is His, it is to Him that we must go to recognize our will.

2.   *There is no will but Yours. ²And I am glad that nothing I imagine contradicts what You would have me be. ³It is Your Will that I be wholly safe, eternally at peace. ⁴And happily I share that Will which You, my Father, gave as part of me.*

LESSON 329

I have already chosen what You will.

1. *Father, I thought I wandered from Your Will, defied it, broke its laws, and interposed a second will more powerful than Yours. ²Yet what I am in truth is but Your Will, extended and extending. ³This am I, and this will never change. ⁴As You are One, so am I one with You. ⁵And this I chose in my creation, where my will became forever one with Yours. ⁶That choice was made for all eternity. ⁷It cannot change, and be in opposition to itself. ⁸Father, my will is Yours. ⁹And I am safe, untroubled and serene, in endless joy, because it is Your Will that it be so.*

2. Today we will accept our union with each other and our Source. ²We have no will apart from His, and all of us are one because His Will is shared by all of us. ³Through it we recognize that we are one. ⁴Through it we find our way at last to God.

LESSON 330

I will not hurt myself again today.

1. Let us this day accept forgiveness as our only function. ²Why should we attack our minds, and give them images of pain? ³Why should we teach them they are powerless, when God holds out His power and His Love, and bids them take what is already theirs? ⁴The mind that is made willing to accept God's gifts has been restored to spirit, and extends its freedom and its joy, as is the Will of God united with its own. ⁵The Self which God created cannot sin, and therefore cannot suffer. ⁶Let us choose today that He be our Identity, and thus escape forever from all things the dream of fear appears to offer us.

2. *Father, Your Son can not be hurt. ²And if we think we suffer, we but fail to know our one Identity we share with You. ³We would return to It today, to be made free forever from all our mistakes, and to be saved from what we thought we were.*

466

12. What Is the Ego?

1. The ego is idolatry; the sign of limited and separated self, born in a body, doomed to suffer and to end its life in death. [2]It is the "will" that sees the Will of God as enemy, and takes a form in which it is denied. [3]The ego is the "proof" that strength is weak and love is fearful, life is really death, and what opposes God alone is true.

2. The ego is insane. [2]In fear it stands beyond the Everywhere, apart from All, in separation from the Infinite. [3]In its insanity it thinks it has become a victor over God Himself. [4]And in its terrible autonomy it "sees" the Will of God has been destroyed. [5]It dreams of punishment, and trembles at the figures in its dreams; its enemies, who seek to murder it before it can ensure its safety by attacking them.

3. The Son of God is egoless. [2]What can he know of madness and the death of God, when he abides in Him? [3]What can he know of sorrow and of suffering, when he lives in eternal joy? [4]What can he know of fear and punishment, of sin and guilt, of hatred and attack, when all there is surrounding him is everlasting peace, forever conflict-free and undisturbed, in deepest silence and tranquility?

4. To know reality is not to see the ego and its thoughts, its works, its acts, its laws and its beliefs, its dreams, its hopes, its plans for its salvation, and the cost belief in it entails. [2]In suffering, the price for faith in it is so immense that crucifixion of the Son of God is offered daily at its darkened shrine, and blood must flow before the altar where its sickly followers prepare to die.

5. Yet will one lily of forgiveness change the darkness into light; the altar to illusions to the shrine of Life Itself. [2]And peace will be restored forever to the holy minds which God created as His Son, His dwelling place, His joy, His love, completely His, completely one with Him.

LESSON 331

There is no conflict, for my will is Yours.

1. *How foolish, Father, to believe Your Son could cause himself to suffer!* ²*Could he make a plan for his damnation, and be left without a certain way to his release?* ³*You love me, Father.* ⁴*You could never leave me desolate, to die within a world of pain and cruelty.* ⁵*How could I think that Love has left Itself?* ⁶*There is no will except the Will of Love.* ⁷*Fear is a dream, and has no will that can conflict with Yours.* ⁸*Conflict is sleep, and peace awakening.* ⁹*Death is illusion; life, eternal truth.* ¹⁰*There is no opposition to Your Will.* ¹¹*There is no conflict, for my will is Yours.*

2. Forgiveness shows us that God's Will is One, and that we share it. ²Let us look upon the holy sights forgiveness shows today, that we may find the peace of God. ³Amen.

LESSON 332

Fear binds the world. Forgiveness sets it free.

1. The ego makes illusions. ²Truth undoes its evil dreams by shining them away. ³Truth never makes attack. ⁴It merely is. ⁵And by its presence is the mind recalled from fantasies, awaking to the real. ⁶Forgiveness bids this presence enter in, and take its rightful place within the mind. ⁷Without forgiveness is the mind in chains, believing in its own futility. ⁸Yet with forgiveness does the light shine through the dream of darkness, offering it hope, and giving it the means to realize the freedom that is its inheritance.

2. *We would not bind the world again today.* ²*Fear holds it prisoner.* ³*And yet Your Love has given us the means to set it free.* ⁴*Father, we would release it now.* ⁵*For as we offer freedom, it is given us.* ⁶*And we would not remain as prisoners, while You are holding freedom out to us.*

LESSON 333

Forgiveness ends the dream of conflict here.

1. Conflict must be resolved. ²It cannot be evaded, set aside, denied, disguised, seen somewhere else, called by another name, or hidden by deceit of any kind, if it would be escaped. ³It must be seen exactly as it is, where it is thought to be, in the reality which has been given it, and with the purpose that the mind accorded it. ⁴For only then are its defenses lifted, and the truth can shine upon it as it disappears.

2. *Father, forgiveness is the light You chose to shine away all conflict and all doubt, and light the way for our return to You. ²No light but this can end our evil dream. ³No light but this can save the world. ⁴For this alone will never fail in anything, being Your gift to Your beloved Son.*

LESSON 334

Today I claim the gifts forgiveness gives.

1. I will not wait another day to find the treasures that my Father offers me. ²Illusions are all vain, and dreams are gone even while they are woven out of thoughts that rest on false perceptions. ³Let me not accept such meager gifts again today. ⁴God's Voice is offering the peace of God to all who hear and choose to follow Him. ⁵This is my choice today. ⁶And so I go to find the treasures God has given me.

2. *I seek but the eternal. ²For Your Son can be content with nothing less than this. ³What, then, can be his solace but what You are offering to his bewildered mind and frightened heart, to give him certainty and bring him peace? ⁴Today I would behold my brother sinless. ⁵This Your Will for me, for so will I behold my sinlessness.*

LESSON 335

I choose to see my brother's sinlessness.

1. Forgiveness is a choice. ²I never see my brother as he is, for that is far beyond perception. ³What I see in him is merely what I wish to see, because it stands for what I want to be the truth. ⁴It is to this alone that I respond, however much I seem to be impelled by outside happenings. ⁵I choose to see what I would look upon, and this I see, and only this. ⁶My brother's sinlessness shows me that I would look upon my own. ⁷And I will see it, having chosen to behold my brother in its holy light.

2. *What could restore Your memory to me, except to see my brother's sinlessness? ²His holiness reminds me that he was created one with me, and like myself. ³In him I find my Self, and in Your Son I find the memory of You as well.*

LESSON 336

Forgiveness lets me know that minds are joined.

1. Forgiveness is the means appointed for perception's ending. ²Knowledge is restored after perception first is changed, and then gives way entirely to what remains forever past its highest reach. ³For sights and sounds, at best, can serve but to recall the memory that lies beyond them all. ⁴Forgiveness sweeps away distortions, and opens the hidden altar to the truth. ⁵Its lilies shine into the mind, and call it to return and look within, to find what it has vainly sought without. ⁶For here, and only here, is peace of mind restored, for this the dwelling place of God Himself.

2. *In quiet may forgiveness wipe away my dreams of separation and of sin. ²Then let me, Father, look within, and find Your promise of my sinlessness is kept; Your Word remains unchanged within my mind, Your Love is still abiding in my heart.*

LESSON 337

My sinlessness protects me from all harm.

1. My sinlessness ensures me perfect peace, eternal safety, everlasting love, freedom forever from all thought of loss; complete deliverance from suffering. ²And only happiness can be my state, for only happiness is given me. ³What must I do to know all this is mine? ⁴I must accept Atonement for myself, and nothing more. ⁵God has already done all things that need be done. ⁶And I must learn I need do nothing of myself, for I need but accept my Self, my sinlessness, created for me, now already mine, to feel God's Love protecting me from harm, to understand my Father loves His Son; to know I am the Son my Father loves.

2. *You Who created me in sinlessness are not mistaken about what I am.* ²*I was mistaken when I thought I sinned, but I accept Atonement for myself.* ³*Father, my dream is ended now.* ⁴*Amen.*

LESSON 338

I am affected only by my thoughts.

1. It needs but this to let salvation come to all the world. ²For in this single thought is everyone released at last from fear. ³Now has he learned that no one frightens him, and nothing can endanger him. ⁴He has no enemies, and he is safe from all external things. ⁵His thoughts can frighten him, but since these thoughts belong to him alone, he has the power to change them and exchange each fear thought for a happy thought of love. ⁶He crucified himself. ⁷Yet God has planned that His beloved Son will be redeemed.

2. *Your plan is sure, my Father,—only Yours.* ²*All other plans will fail.* ³*And I will have thoughts that will frighten me, until I learn that You have given me the only Thought that leads me to salvation.* ⁴*Mine alone will fail, and lead me nowhere.* ⁵*But the Thought You gave me promises to lead me home, because it holds Your promise to Your Son.*

LESSON 339

I will receive whatever I request.

1. No one desires pain. ²But he can think that pain is pleasure. ³No one would avoid his happiness. ⁴But he can think that joy is painful, threatening and dangerous. ⁵Everyone will receive what he requests. ⁶But he can be confused indeed about the things he wants; the state he would attain. ⁷What can he then request that he would want when he receives it? ⁸He has asked for what will frighten him, and bring him suffering. ⁹Let us resolve today to ask for what we really want, and only this, that we may spend this day in fearlessness, without confusing pain with joy, or fear with love.

2. *Father, this is Your day. ²It is a day in which I would do nothing by myself, but hear Your Voice in everything I do; requesting only what You offer me, accepting only Thoughts You share with me.*

LESSON 340

I can be free of suffering today.

1. *Father, I thank You for today, and for the freedom I am certain it will bring. ²This day is holy, for today Your Son will be redeemed. ³His suffering is done. ⁴For he will hear Your Voice directing him to find Christ's vision through forgiveness, and be free forever from all suffering. ⁵Thanks for today, my Father. ⁶I was born into this world but to achieve this day, and what it holds in joy and freedom for Your holy Son and for the world he made, which is released along with him today.*

2. Be glad today! ²Be glad! ³There is no room for anything but joy and thanks today. ⁴Our Father has redeemed His Son this day. ⁵Not one of us but will be saved today. ⁶Not one who will remain in fear, and none the Father will not gather to Himself, awake in Heaven in the Heart of Love.

13. What Is a Miracle?

1. A miracle is a correction. ²It does not create, nor really change at all. ³It merely looks on devastation, and reminds the mind that what it sees is false. ⁴It undoes error, but does not attempt to go beyond perception, nor exceed the function of forgiveness. ⁵Thus it stays within time's limits. ⁶Yet it paves the way for the return of timelessness and love's awakening, for fear must slip away under the gentle remedy it brings.

2. A miracle contains the gift of grace, for it is given and received as one. ²And thus it illustrates the law of truth the world does not obey, because it fails entirely to understand its ways. ³A miracle inverts perception which was upside down before, and thus it ends the strange distortions that were manifest. ⁴Now is perception open to the truth. ⁵Now is forgiveness seen as justified.

3. Forgiveness is the home of miracles. ²The eyes of Christ deliver them to all they look upon in mercy and in love. ³Perception stands corrected in His sight, and what was meant to curse has come to bless. ⁴Each lily of forgiveness offers all the world the silent miracle of love. ⁵And each is laid before the Word of God, upon the universal altar to Creator and creation in the light of perfect purity and endless joy.

4. The miracle is taken first on faith, because to ask for it implies the mind has been made ready to conceive of what it cannot see and does not understand. ²Yet faith will bring its witnesses to show that what it rested on is really there. ³And thus the miracle will justify your faith in it, and show it rested on a world more real than what you saw before; a world redeemed from what you thought was there.

5. Miracles fall like drops of healing rain from Heaven on a dry and dusty world, where starved and thirsty creatures come to die. ²Now they have water. ³Now the world is green. ⁴And everywhere the signs of life spring up, to show that what is born can never die, for what has life has immortality.

LESSON 341

I can attack but my own sinlessness,
And it is only that which keeps me safe.

1. *Father, Your Son is holy.* [2]*I am he on whom You smile in love and tenderness so dear and deep and still the universe smiles back on You, and shares Your Holiness.* [3]*How pure, how safe, how holy, then, are we, abiding in Your Smile, with all Your Love bestowed upon us, living one with You, in brotherhood and Fatherhood complete; in sinlessness so perfect that the Lord of Sinlessness conceives us as His Son, a universe of Thought completing Him.*

2. Let us not, then, attack our sinlessness, for it contains the Word of God to us. [2]And in its kind reflection we are saved.

LESSON 342

I let forgiveness rest upon all things,
For thus forgiveness will be given me.

1. *I thank You, Father, for Your plan to save me from the hell I made.* [2]*It is not real.* [3]*And You have given me the means to prove its unreality to me.* [4]*The key is in my hand, and I have reached the door beyond which lies the end of dreams.* [5]*I stand before the gate of Heaven, wondering if I should enter in and be at home.* [6]*Let me not wait again today.* [7]*Let me forgive all things, and let creation be as You would have it be and as it is.* [8]*Let me remember that I am Your Son, and opening the door at last, forget illusions in the blazing light of truth, as memory of You returns to me.*

2. Brother, forgive me now. [2]I come to you to take you home with me. [3]And as we go, the world goes with us on our way to God.

LESSON 343

I am not asked to make a sacrifice
To find the mercy and the peace of God.

1.   *The end of suffering can not be loss. ²The gift of everything can be but gain. ³You only give. ⁴You never take away. ⁵And You created me to be like You, so sacrifice becomes impossible for me as well as You. ⁶I, too, must give. ⁷And so all things are given unto me forever and forever. ⁸As I was created I remain. ⁹Your Son can make no sacrifice, for he must be complete, having the function of completing You. ¹⁰I am complete because I am Your Son. ¹¹I cannot lose, for I can only give, and everything is mine eternally.*

2.   The mercy and the peace of God are free. ²Salvation has no cost. ³It is a gift that must be freely given and received. ⁴And it is this that we would learn today.

LESSON 344

Today I learn the law of love; that what
I give my brother is my gift to me.

1.   *This is Your law, my Father, not my own. ²I have not understood what giving means, and thought to save what I desired for myself alone. ³And as I looked upon the treasure that I thought I had, I found an empty place where nothing ever was or is or will be. ⁴Who can share a dream? ⁵And what can an illusion offer me? ⁶Yet he whom I forgive will give me gifts beyond the worth of anything on earth. ⁷Let my forgiven brothers fill my store with Heaven's treasures, which alone are real. ⁸Thus is the law of love fulfilled. ⁹And thus Your Son arises and returns to You.*

2.   How near we are to one another, as we go to God. ²How near is He to us. ³How close the ending of the dream of sin, and the redemption of the Son of God.

LESSON 345

I offer only miracles today,
For I would have them be returned to me.

1. *Father, a miracle reflects Your gifts to me, Your Son.* ²*And every one I give returns to me, reminding me the law of love is universal.* ³*Even here, it takes a form which can be recognized and seen to work.* ⁴*The miracles I give are given back in just the form I need to help me with the problems I perceive.* ⁵*Father, in Heaven it is different, for there, there are no needs.* ⁶*But here on earth, the miracle is closer to Your gifts than any other gift that I can give.* ⁷*Then let me give this gift alone today, which, born of true forgiveness, lights the way that I must travel to remember You.*

2. Peace to all seeking hearts today. ²The light has come to offer miracles to bless the tired world. ³It will find rest today, for we will offer what we have received.

LESSON 346

Today the peace of God envelops me,
And I forget all things except His Love.

1. *Father, I wake today with miracles correcting my perception of all things.* ²*And so begins the day I share with You as I will share eternity, for time has stepped aside today.* ³*I do not seek the things of time, and so I will not look upon them.* ⁴*What I seek today transcends all laws of time and things perceived in time.* ⁵*I would forget all things except Your Love.* ⁶*I would abide in You, and know no laws except Your law of love.* ⁷*And I would find the peace which You created for Your Son, forgetting all the foolish toys I made as I behold Your glory and my own.*

2. And when the evening comes today, we will remember nothing but the peace of God. ²For we will learn today what peace is ours, when we forget all things except God's Love.

LESSON 347

**Anger must come from judgment. Judgment is
The weapon I would use against myself,
To keep the miracle away from me.**

1.   *Father, I want what goes against my will, and do not want what is my will to have.* ²*Straighten my mind, my Father.* ³*It is sick.* ⁴*But You have offered freedom, and I choose to claim Your gift today.* ⁵*And so I give all judgment to the One You gave to me to judge for me.* ⁶*He sees what I behold, and yet He knows the truth.* ⁷*He looks on pain, and yet He understands it is not real, and in His understanding it is healed.* ⁸*He gives the miracles my dreams would hide from my awareness.* ⁹*Let Him judge today.* ¹⁰*I do not know my will, but He is sure it is Your Own.* ¹¹*And He will speak for me, and call Your miracles to come to me.*

2.   Listen today. ²Be very still, and hear the gentle Voice for God assuring you that He has judged you as the Son He loves.

LESSON 348

**I have no cause for anger or for fear,
For You surround me. And in every need
That I perceive, Your grace suffices me.**

1.   *Father, let me remember You are here, and I am not alone.* ²*Surrounding me is everlasting Love.* ³*I have no cause for anything except the perfect peace and joy I share with You.* ⁴*What need have I for anger or for fear?* ⁵*Surrounding me is perfect safety.* ⁶*Can I be afraid, when Your eternal promise goes with me?* ⁷*Surrounding me is perfect sinlessness.* ⁸*What can I fear, when You created me in holiness as perfect as Your Own?*

2.   God's grace suffices us in everything that He would have us do. ²And only that we choose to be our will as well as His.

LESSON 349

Today I let Christ's vision look upon
All things for me and judge them not, but give
Each one a miracle of love instead.

1.   *So would I liberate all things I see, and give to them the freedom that I seek. ²For thus do I obey the law of love, and give what I would find and make my own. ³It will be given me, because I have chosen it as the gift I want to give. ⁴Father, Your gifts are mine. ⁵Each one that I accept gives me a miracle to give. ⁶And giving as I would receive, I learn Your healing miracles belong to me.*

2.   Our Father knows our needs. ²He gives us grace to meet them all. ³And so we trust in Him to send us miracles to bless the world, and heal our minds as we return to Him.

LESSON 350

Miracles mirror God's eternal Love.
To offer them is to remember Him,
And through His memory to save the world.

1.   *What we forgive becomes a part of us, as we perceive ourselves. ²The Son of God incorporates all things within himself as You created him. ³Your memory depends on his forgiveness. ⁴What he is, is unaffected by his thoughts. ⁵But what he looks upon is their direct result. ⁶Therefore, my Father, I would turn to You. ⁷Only Your memory will set me free. ⁸And only my forgiveness teaches me to let Your memory return to me, and give it to the world in thankfulness.*

2.   And as we gather miracles from Him, we will indeed be grateful. ²For as we remember Him, His Son will be restored to us in the reality of Love.

14. What Am I?

1. *I am God's Son, complete and healed and whole, shining in the reflection of His Love. [2]In me is His creation sanctified and guaranteed eternal life. [3]In me is love perfected, fear impossible, and joy established without opposite. [4]I am the holy home of God Himself. [5]I am the Heaven where His Love resides. [6]I am His holy Sinlessness Itself, for in my purity abides His Own.*

2. Our use for words is almost over now. [2]Yet in the final days of this one year we gave to God together, you and I, we found a single purpose that we shared. [3]And thus you joined with me, so what I am are you as well. [4]The truth of what we are is not for words to speak of nor describe. [5]Yet we can realize our function here, and words can speak of this and teach it, too, if we exemplify the words in us.

3. We are the bringers of salvation. [2]We accept our part as saviors of the world, which through our joint forgiveness is redeemed. [3]And this, our gift, is therefore given us. [4]We look on everyone as brother, and perceive all things as kindly and as good. [5]We do not seek a function that is past the gate of Heaven. [6]Knowledge will return when we have done our part. [7]We are concerned only with giving welcome to the truth.

4. Ours are the eyes through which Christ's vision sees a world redeemed from every thought of sin. [2]Ours are the ears that hear the Voice for God proclaim the world as sinless. [3]Ours the minds that join together as we bless the world. [4]And from the oneness that we have attained we call to all our brothers, asking them to share our peace and consummate our joy.

5. We are the holy messengers of God who speak for Him, and carrying His Word to everyone whom He has sent to us, we learn that it is written on our hearts. [2]And thus our minds are changed about the aim for which we came, and which we seek to serve. [3]We bring glad tidings to the Son of God, who thought he suffered. [4]Now is he redeemed. [5]And as he sees the gate of Heaven stand open before him, he will enter in and disappear into the Heart of God.

LESSON 351

My sinless brother is my guide to peace.
My sinful brother is my guide to pain.
And which I choose to see I will behold.

1.   *Who is my brother but Your holy Son?* [2]*And if I see him sinful I proclaim myself a sinner, not a Son of God; alone and friendless in a fearful world.* [3]*Yet this perception is a choice I make, and can relinquish.* [4]*I can also see my brother sinless, as Your holy Son.* [5]*And with this choice I see my sinlessness, my everlasting Comforter and Friend beside me, and my way secure and clear.* [6]*Choose, then, for me, my Father, through Your Voice.* [7]*For He alone gives judgment in Your Name.*

LESSON 352

Judgment and love are opposites. From one
Come all the sorrows of the world. But from
The other comes the peace of God Himself.

1.   *Forgiveness looks on sinlessness alone, and judges not.* [2]*Through this I come to You.* [3]*Judgment will bind my eyes and make me blind.* [4]*Yet love, reflected in forgiveness here, reminds me You have given me a way to find Your peace again.* [5]*I am redeemed when I elect to follow in this way.* [6]*You have not left me comfortless.* [7]*I have within me both the memory of You, and One Who leads me to it.* [8]*Father, I would hear Your Voice and find Your peace today.* [9]*For I would love my own Identity, and find in It the memory of You.*

LESSON 353

**My eyes, my tongue, my hands, my feet today
Have but one purpose; to be given Christ
To use to bless the world with miracles.**

1. *Father, I give all that is mine today to Christ, to use in any way that best will serve the purpose that I share with Him.* ²*Nothing is mine alone, for He and I have joined in purpose.* ³*Thus has learning come almost to its appointed end.* ⁴*A while I work with Him to serve His purpose.* ⁵*Then I lose myself in my Identity, and recognize that Christ is but my Self.*

LESSON 354

**We stand together, Christ and I, in peace
And certainty of purpose. And in Him
Is His Creator, as He is in me.**

1. *My oneness with the Christ establishes me as Your Son, beyond the reach of time, and wholly free of every law but Yours.* ²*I have no self except the Christ in me.* ³*I have no purpose but His Own.* ⁴*And He is like His Father.* ⁵*Thus must I be one with You as well as Him.* ⁶*For who is Christ except Your Son as You created Him?* ⁷*And what am I except the Christ in me?*

LESSON 355

There is no end to all the peace and joy,
And all the miracles that I will give,
When I accept God's Word. Why not today?

1. *Why should I wait, my Father, for the joy You promised me?* ²*For You will keep Your Word You gave Your Son in exile.* ³*I am sure my treasure waits for me, and I need but reach out my hand to find it.* ⁴*Even now my fingers touch it.* ⁵*It is very close.* ⁶*I need not wait an instant more to be at peace forever.* ⁷*It is You I choose, and my Identity along with You.* ⁸*Your Son would be Himself, and know You as his Father and Creator, and his Love.*

LESSON 356

Sickness is but another name for sin.
Healing is but another name for God.
The miracle is thus a call to Him.

1. *Father, You promised You would never fail to answer any call Your Son might make to You.* ²*It does not matter where he is, what seems to be his problem, nor what he believes he has become.* ³*He is Your Son, and You will answer him.* ⁴*The miracle reflects Your Love, and thus it answers him.* ⁵*Your Name replaces every thought of sin, and who is sinless cannot suffer pain.* ⁶*Your Name gives answer to Your Son, because to call Your Name is but to call his own.*

LESSON 357

**Truth answers every call we make to God,
Responding first with miracles, and then
Returning unto us to be itself.**

1.   *Forgiveness, truth's reflection, tells me how to offer miracles, and thus escape the prison house in which I think I live. ²Your holy Son is pointed out to me, first in my brother; then in me. ³Your Voice instructs me patiently to hear Your Word, and give as I receive. ⁴And as I look upon Your Son today, I hear Your Voice instructing me to find the way to You, as You appointed that the way shall be:*

   ⁵"Behold his sinlessness, and be you healed."

LESSON 358

**No call to God can be unheard nor left
Unanswered. And of this I can be sure;
His answer is the one I really want.**

1.   *You Who remember what I really am alone remember what I really want. ²You speak for God, and so You speak for me. ³And what You give me comes from God Himself. ⁴Your Voice, my Father, then is mine as well, and all I want is what You offer me, in just the form You choose that it be mine. ⁵Let me remember all I do not know, and let my voice be still, remembering. ⁶But let me not forget Your Love and care, keeping Your promise to Your Son in my awareness always. ⁷Let me not forget myself is nothing, but my Self is all.*

LESSON 359

God's answer is some form of peace. All pain
Is healed; all misery replaced with joy.
All prison doors are opened. And all sin
Is understood as merely a mistake.

1. *Father, today we will forgive Your world, and let creation be Your Own.* ²*We have misunderstood all things.* ³*But we have not made sinners of the holy Sons of God.* ⁴*What You created sinless so abides forever and forever.* ⁵*Such are we.* ⁶*And we rejoice to learn that we have made mistakes which have no real effects on us.* ⁷*Sin is impossible, and on this fact forgiveness rests upon a certain base more solid than the shadow world we see.* ⁸*Help us forgive, for we would be redeemed.* ⁹*Help us forgive, for we would be at peace.*

LESSON 360

Peace be to me, the holy Son of God.
Peace to my brother, who is one with me.
Let all the world be blessed with peace through us.

1. *Father, it is Your peace that I would give, receiving it of You.* ²*I am Your Son, forever just as You created me, for the Great Rays remain forever still and undisturbed within me.* ³*I would reach to them in silence and in certainty, for nowhere else can certainty be found.* ⁴*Peace be to me, and peace to all the world.* ⁵*In holiness were we created, and in holiness do we remain.* ⁶*Your Son is like to You in perfect sinlessness.* ⁷*And with this thought we gladly say "Amen."*

FINAL LESSONS

Introduction

1.   Our final lessons will be left as free of words as possible. ²We use them but at the beginning of our practicing, and only to remind us that we seek to go beyond them. ³Let us turn to Him Who leads the way and makes our footsteps sure. ⁴To Him we leave these lessons, as to Him we give our lives henceforth. ⁵For we would not return again to the belief in sin that made the world seem ugly and unsafe, attacking and destroying, dangerous in all its ways, and treacherous beyond the hope of trust and the escape from pain.

2.   His is the only way to find the peace that God has given us. ²It is His way that everyone must travel in the end, because it is this ending God Himself appointed. ³In the dream of time it seems to be far off. ⁴And yet, in truth, it is already here; already serving us as gracious guidance in the way to go. ⁵Let us together follow in the way that truth points out to us. ⁶And let us be the leaders of our many brothers who are seeking for the way, but find it not.

3.   And to this purpose let us dedicate our minds, directing all our thoughts to serve the function of salvation. ²Unto us the aim is given to forgive the world. ³It is the goal that God has given us. ⁴It is His ending to the dream we seek, and not our own. ⁵For all that we forgive we will not fail to recognize as part of God Himself. ⁶And thus His memory is given back, completely and complete.

4.   It is our function to remember Him on earth, as it is given us to be His Own completion in reality. ²So let us not forget our goal is shared, for it is that remembrance which contains the memory of God, and points the way to Him and to the Heaven of His peace. ³And shall we not forgive our brother, who can offer this to us? ⁴He is the way, the truth and life that shows the way to us. ⁵In him resides salvation, offered us through our forgiveness, given unto him.

5.   We will not end this year without the gift our Father promised to His holy Son. ²We are forgiven now. ³And we are saved from all the wrath we thought belonged to God, and found it was a dream. ⁴We are restored to sanity, in which we understand that anger is insane, attack is mad, and vengeance merely foolish fantasy. ⁵We have been saved from wrath because we learned we

were mistaken. [6]Nothing more than that. [7]And is a father angry at his son because he failed to understand the truth?

6.   We come in honesty to God and say we did not understand, and ask Him to help us to learn His lessons, through the Voice of His Own Teacher. [2]Would He hurt His Son? [3]Or would He rush to answer him, and say, "This is My Son, and all I have is his"? [4]Be certain He will answer thus, for these are His Own words to you. [5]And more than that can no one ever have, for in these words is all there is, and all that there will be throughout all time and in eternity.

LESSONS 361 to 365

This holy instant would I give to You.
Be You in charge. For I would follow You,
Certain that Your direction gives me peace.

1.   And if I need a word to help me, He will give it to me. [2]If I need a thought, that will He also give. [3]And if I need but stillness and a tranquil, open mind, these are the gifts I will receive of Him. [4]He is in charge by my request. [5]And He will hear and answer me, because He speaks for God my Father and His holy Son.

EPILOGUE

1. This course is a beginning, not an end. [2]Your Friend goes with you. [3]You are not alone. [4]No one who calls on Him can call in vain. [5]Whatever troubles you, be certain that He has the answer, and will gladly give it to you, if you simply turn to Him and ask it of Him. [6]He will not withhold all answers that you need for anything that seems to trouble you. [7]He knows the way to solve all problems, and resolve all doubts. [8]His certainty is yours. [9]You need but ask it of Him, and it will be given you.

2. You are as certain of arriving home as is the pathway of the sun laid down before it rises, after it has set, and in the half-lit hours in between. [2]Indeed, your pathway is more certain still. [3]For it can not be possible to change the course of those whom God has called to Him. [4]Therefore obey your will, and follow Him Whom you accepted as your voice, to speak of what you really want and really need. [5]His is the Voice for God and also yours. [6]And thus He speaks of freedom and of truth.

3. No more specific lessons are assigned, for there is no more need of them. [2]Henceforth, hear but the Voice for God and for your Self when you retire from the world, to seek reality instead. [3]He will direct your efforts, telling you exactly what to do, how to direct your mind, and when to come to Him in silence, asking for His sure direction and His certain Word. [4]His is the Word that God has given you. [5]His is the Word you chose to be your own.

4. And now I place you in His hands, to be His faithful follower, with Him as Guide through every difficulty and all pain that you may think is real. [2]Nor will He give you pleasures that will pass away, for He gives only the eternal and the good. [3]Let Him prepare you further. [4]He has earned your trust by speaking daily to you of your Father and your brother and your Self. [5]He will continue. [6]Now you walk with Him, as certain as is He of where you go; as sure as He of how you should proceed; as confident as He is of the goal, and of your safe arrival in the end.

5. The end is certain, and the means as well. [2]To this we say "Amen." [3]You will be told exactly what God wills for you each time there is a choice to make. [4]And He will speak for God and for your Self, thus making sure that hell will claim you not, and that each choice you make brings Heaven nearer to your reach. [5]And so we walk with Him from this time on, and turn to Him for

guidance and for peace and sure direction. ⁶Joy attends our way. ⁷For we go homeward to an open door which God has held unclosed to welcome us.

6. We trust our ways to Him and say "Amen." ²In peace we will continue in His way, and trust all things to Him. ³In confidence we wait His answers, as we ask His Will in everything we do. ⁴He loves God's Son as we would love him. ⁵And He teaches us how to behold him through His eyes, and love him as He does. ⁶You do not walk alone. ⁷God's angels hover near and all about. ⁸His Love surrounds you, and of this be sure; that I will never leave you comfortless.

A COURSE IN MIRACLES

MANUAL FOR TEACHERS

FOUNDATION FOR INNER PEACE

CONTENTS

MANUAL FOR TEACHERS

CLARIFICATION OF TERMS

MANUAL FOR TEACHERS

INTRODUCTION

1. The role of teaching and learning is actually reversed in the thinking of the world. ²The reversal is characteristic. ³It seems as if the teacher and the learner are separated, the teacher giving something to the learner rather than to himself. ⁴Further, the act of teaching is regarded as a special activity, in which one engages only a relatively small proportion of one's time. ⁵The course, on the other hand, emphasizes that to teach *is* to learn, so that teacher and learner are the same. ⁶It also emphasizes that teaching is a constant process; it goes on every moment of the day, and continues into sleeping thoughts as well.

2. To teach is to demonstrate. ²There are only two thought systems, and you demonstrate that you believe one or the other is true all the time. ³From your demonstration others learn, and so do you. ⁴The question is not whether you will teach, for in that there is no choice. ⁵The purpose of the course might be said to provide you with a means of choosing what you want to teach on the basis of what you want to learn. ⁶You cannot give to someone else, but only to yourself, and this you learn through teaching. ⁷Teaching is but a call to witnesses to attest to what you believe. ⁸It is a method of conversion. ⁹This is not done by words alone. ¹⁰Any situation must be to you a chance to teach others what you are, and what they are to you. ¹¹No more than that, but also never less.

3. The curriculum you set up is therefore determined exclusively by what you think you are, and what you believe the relationship of others is to you. ²In the formal teaching situation, these questions may be totally unrelated to what you think you are teaching. ³Yet it is impossible not to use the content of any situation on behalf of what you really teach, and therefore really learn. ⁴To this the verbal content of your teaching is quite irrelevant. ⁵It may coincide with it, or it may not. ⁶It is the teaching underlying what you say that teaches you. ⁷Teaching but reinforces what you believe about yourself. ⁸Its fundamental purpose is to diminish self-doubt. ⁹This does not mean that the self you are trying to protect is real. ¹⁰But it does mean that the self you think is real is what you teach.

4. This is inevitable. ²There is no escape from it. ³How could it be otherwise? ⁴Everyone who follows the world's curriculum, and

everyone here does follow it until he changes his mind, teaches solely to convince himself that he is what he is not. [5]Herein is the purpose of the world. [6]What else, then, would its curriculum be? [7]Into this hopeless and closed learning situation, which teaches nothing but despair and death, God sends His teachers. [8]And as they teach His lessons of joy and hope, their learning finally becomes complete.

5. Except for God's teachers there would be little hope of salvation, for the world of sin would seem forever real. [2]The self-deceiving must deceive, for they must teach deception. [3]And what else is hell? [4]This is a manual for the teachers of God. [5]They are not perfect, or they would not be here. [6]Yet it is their mission to become perfect here, and so they teach perfection over and over, in many, many ways, until they have learned it. [7]And then they are seen no more, although their thoughts remain a source of strength and truth forever. [8]Who are they? [9]How are they chosen? [10]What do they do? [11]How can they work out their own salvation and the salvation of the world? [12]This manual attempts to answer these questions.

1. WHO ARE GOD'S TEACHERS?

1. A teacher of God is anyone who chooses to be one. [2]His qualifications consist solely in this; somehow, somewhere he has made a deliberate choice in which he did not see his interests as apart from someone else's. [3]Once he has done that, his road is established and his direction is sure. [4]A light has entered the darkness. [5]It may be a single light, but that is enough. [6]He has entered an agreement with God even if he does not yet believe in Him. [7]He has become a bringer of salvation. [8]He has become a teacher of God.

2. They come from all over the world. [2]They come from all religions and from no religion. [3]They are the ones who have answered. [4]The Call is universal. [5]It goes on all the time everywhere. [6]It calls for teachers to speak for It and redeem the world. [7]Many hear It, but few will answer. [8]Yet it is all a matter of time. [9]Everyone will answer in the end, but the end can be a long, long way off. [10]It is because of this that the plan of the teachers was established. [11]Their function is to save time. [12]Each one begins as a single light, but with the Call at its center it is a light that cannot be limited. [13]And each one saves a thousand years of time as the world judges it. [14]To the Call Itself time has no meaning.

3. There is a course for every teacher of God. [2]The form of the course varies greatly. [3]So do the particular teaching aids involved. [4]But the content of the course never changes. [5]Its central theme is always, "God's Son is guiltless, and in his innocence is his salvation." [6]It can be taught by actions or thoughts; in words or soundlessly; in any language or in no language; in any place or time or manner. [7]It does not matter who the teacher was before he heard the Call. [8]He has become a savior by his answering. [9]He has seen someone else as himself. [10]He has therefore found his own salvation and the salvation of the world. [11]In his rebirth is the world reborn.

4. This is a manual for a special curriculum, intended for teachers of a special form of the universal course. [2]There are many thousands of other forms, all with the same outcome. [3]They merely save time. [4]Yet it is time alone that winds on wearily, and the world is very tired now. [5]It is old and worn and without hope. [6]There was never a question of outcome, for what can change the Will of God? [7]But time, with its illusions of change and death,

wears out the world and all things in it. [8]Yet time has an ending, and it is this that the teachers of God are appointed to bring about. [9]For time is in their hands. [10]Such was their choice, and it is given them.

2. WHO ARE THEIR PUPILS?

1. Certain pupils have been assigned to each of God's teachers, and they will begin to look for him as soon as he has answered the Call. [2]They were chosen for him because the form of the universal curriculum that he will teach is best for them in view of their level of understanding. [3]His pupils have been waiting for him, for his coming is certain. [4]Again, it is only a matter of time. [5]Once he has chosen to fulfill his role, they are ready to fulfill theirs. [6]Time waits on his choice, but not on whom he will serve. [7]When he is ready to learn, the opportunities to teach will be provided for him.

2. In order to understand the teaching-learning plan of salvation, it is necessary to grasp the concept of time that the course sets forth. [2]Atonement corrects illusions, not truth. [3]Therefore, it corrects what never was. [4]Further, the plan for this correction was established and completed simultaneously, for the Will of God is entirely apart from time. [5]So is all reality, being of Him. [6]The instant the idea of separation entered the mind of God's Son, in that same instant was God's Answer given. [7]In time this happened very long ago. [8]In reality it never happened at all.

3. The world of time is the world of illusion. [2]What happened long ago seems to be happening now. [3]Choices made long since appear to be open; yet to be made. [4]What has been learned and understood and long ago passed by is looked upon as a new thought, a fresh idea, a different approach. [5]Because your will is free you can accept what has already happened at any time you choose, and only then will you realize that it was always there. [6]As the course emphasizes, you are not free to choose the curriculum, or even the form in which you will learn it. [7]You are free, however, to decide when you want to learn it. [8]And as you accept it, it is already learned.

4. Time really, then, goes backward to an instant so ancient that it is beyond all memory, and past even the possibility of remembering. [2]Yet because it is an instant that is relived again and again and still again, it seems to be now. [3]And thus it is that pupil and teacher seem to come together in the present, finding each other as if they had not met before. [4]The pupil comes at the right time to the right place. [5]This is inevitable, because he made the right choice in that ancient instant which he now relives. [6]So has the

teacher, too, made an inevitable choice out of an ancient past. [7]God's Will in everything but seems to take time in the working-out. [8]What could delay the power of eternity?

5.   When pupil and teacher come together, a teaching-learning situation begins. [2]For the teacher is not really the one who does the teaching. [3]God's Teacher speaks to any two who join together for learning purposes. [4]The relationship is holy because of that purpose, and God has promised to send His Spirit into any holy relationship. [5]In the teaching-learning situation, each one learns that giving and receiving are the same. [6]The demarcations they have drawn between their roles, their minds, their bodies, their needs, their interests, and all the differences they thought separated them from one another, fade and grow dim and disappear. [7]Those who would learn the same course share one interest and one goal. [8]And thus he who was the learner becomes a teacher of God himself, for he has made the one decision that gave his teacher to him. [9]He has seen in another person the same interests as his own.

3. WHAT ARE THE LEVELS OF TEACHING?

1. The teachers of God have no set teaching level. [2]Each teaching-learning situation involves a different relationship at the beginning, although the ultimate goal is always the same; to make of the relationship a holy relationship, in which both can look upon the Son of God as sinless. [3]There is no one from whom a teacher of God cannot learn, so there is no one whom he cannot teach. [4]However, from a practical point of view he cannot meet everyone, nor can everyone find him. [5]Therefore, the plan includes very specific contacts to be made for each teacher of God. [6]There are no accidents in salvation. [7]Those who are to meet will meet, because together they have the potential for a holy relationship. [8]They are ready for each other.

2. The simplest level of teaching appears to be quite superficial. [2]It consists of what seem to be very casual encounters; a "chance" meeting of two apparent strangers in an elevator, a child who is not looking where he is going running into an adult "by chance," two students "happening" to walk home together. [3]These are not chance encounters. [4]Each of them has the potential for becoming a teaching-learning situation. [5]Perhaps the seeming strangers in the elevator will smile to one another; perhaps the adult will not scold the child for bumping into him; perhaps the students will become friends. [6]Even at the level of the most casual encounter, it is possible for two people to lose sight of separate interests, if only for a moment. [7]That moment will be enough. [8]Salvation has come.

3. It is difficult to understand that levels of teaching the universal course is a concept as meaningless in reality as is time. [2]The illusion of one permits the illusion of the other. [3]In time, the teacher of God seems to begin to change his mind about the world with a single decision, and then learns more and more about the new direction as he teaches it. [4]We have covered the illusion of time already, but the illusion of levels of teaching seems to be something different. [5]Perhaps the best way to demonstrate that these levels cannot exist is simply to say that any level of the teaching-learning situation is part of God's plan for Atonement, and His plan can have no levels, being a reflection of His Will. [6]Salvation is always ready and always there. [7]God's teachers work at different levels, but the result is always the same.

4. Each teaching-learning situation is maximal in the sense that

each person involved will learn the most that he can from the other person at that time. [2]In this sense, and in this sense only, we can speak of levels of teaching. [3]Using the term in this way, the second level of teaching is a more sustained relationship, in which, for a time, two people enter into a fairly intense teaching-learning situation and then appear to separate. [4]As with the first level, these meetings are not accidental, nor is what appears to be the end of the relationship a real end. [5]Again, each has learned the most he can at the time. [6]Yet all who meet will someday meet again, for it is the destiny of all relationships to become holy. [7]God is not mistaken in His Son.

5. The third level of teaching occurs in relationships which, once they are formed, are lifelong. [2]These are teaching-learning situations in which each person is given a chosen learning partner who presents him with unlimited opportunities for learning. [3]These relationships are generally few, because their existence implies that those involved have reached a stage simultaneously in which the teaching-learning balance is actually perfect. [4]This does not mean that they necessarily recognize this; in fact, they generally do not. [5]They may even be quite hostile to each other for some time, and perhaps for life. [6]Yet should they decide to learn it, the perfect lesson is before them and can be learned. [7]And if they decide to learn that lesson, they become the saviors of the teachers who falter and may even seem to fail. [8]No teacher of God can fail to find the Help he needs.

8

4. WHAT ARE THE CHARACTERISTICS OF GOD'S TEACHERS?

1. The surface traits of God's teachers are not at all alike. [2]They do not look alike to the body's eyes, they come from vastly different backgrounds, their experiences of the world vary greatly, and their superficial "personalities" are quite distinct. [3]Nor, at the beginning stages of their functioning as teachers of God, have they as yet acquired the deeper characteristics that will establish them as what they are. [4]God gives special gifts to His teachers, because they have a special role in His plan for Atonement. [5]Their specialness is, of course, only temporary; set in time as a means of leading out of time. [6]These special gifts, born in the holy relationship toward which the teaching-learning situation is geared, become characteristic of all teachers of God who have advanced in their own learning. [7]In this respect they are all alike.

2. All differences among the Sons of God are temporary. [2]Nevertheless, in time it can be said that the advanced teachers of God have the following characteristics:

I. Trust

1. This is the foundation on which their ability to fulfill their function rests. [2]Perception is the result of learning. [3]In fact, perception *is* learning, because cause and effect are never separated. [4]The teachers of God have trust in the world, because they have learned it is not governed by the laws the world made up. [5]It is governed by a power that is *in* them but not *of* them. [6]It is this power that keeps all things safe. [7]It is through this power that the teachers of God look on a forgiven world.

2. When this power has once been experienced, it is impossible to trust one's own petty strength again. [2]Who would attempt to fly with the tiny wings of a sparrow when the mighty power of an eagle has been given him? [3]And who would place his faith in the shabby offerings of the ego when the gifts of God are laid before him? [4]What is it that induces them to make the shift?

9

A. Development of Trust

3. First, they must go through what might be called "a period of undoing." [2]This need not be painful, but it usually is so experienced. [3]It seems as if things are being taken away, and it is rarely understood initially that their lack of value is merely being recognized. [4]How can lack of value be perceived unless the perceiver is in a position where he must see things in a different light? [5]He is not yet at a point at which he can make the shift entirely internally. [6]And so the plan will sometimes call for changes in what seem to be external circumstances. [7]These changes are always helpful. [8]When the teacher of God has learned that much, he goes on to the second stage.

4. Next, the teacher of God must go through "a period of sorting out." [2]This is always somewhat difficult because, having learned that the changes in his life are always helpful, he must now decide all things on the basis of whether they increase the helpfulness or hamper it. [3]He will find that many, if not most of the things he valued before will merely hinder his ability to transfer what he has learned to new situations as they arise. [4]Because he has valued what is really valueless, he will not generalize the lesson for fear of loss and sacrifice. [5]It takes great learning to understand that all things, events, encounters and circumstances are helpful. [6]It is only to the extent to which they are helpful that any degree of reality should be accorded them in this world of illusion. [7]The word "value" can apply to nothing else.

5. The third stage through which the teacher of God must go can be called "a period of relinquishment." [2]If this is interpreted as giving up the desirable, it will engender enormous conflict. [3]Few teachers of God escape this distress entirely. [4]There is, however, no point in sorting out the valuable from the valueless unless the next obvious step is taken. [5]Therefore, the period of overlap is apt to be one in which the teacher of God feels called upon to sacrifice his own best interests on behalf of truth. [6]He has not realized as yet how wholly impossible such a demand would be. [7]He can learn this only as he actually does give up the valueless. [8]Through this, he learns that where he anticipated grief, he finds a happy lightheartedness instead; where he thought something was asked of him, he finds a gift bestowed on him.

6. Now comes "a period of settling down." [2]This is a quiet time, in which the teacher of God rests a while in reasonable peace. [3]Now

10

he consolidates his learning. ⁴Now he begins to see the transfer value of what he has learned. ⁵Its potential is literally staggering, and the teacher of God is now at the point in his progress at which he sees in it his whole way out. ⁶"Give up what you do not want, and keep what you do." ⁷How simple is the obvious! ⁸And how easy to do! ⁹The teacher of God needs this period of respite. ¹⁰He has not yet come as far as he thinks. ¹¹Yet when he is ready to go on, he goes with mighty companions beside him. ¹²Now he rests a while, and gathers them before going on. ¹³He will not go on from here alone.

7. The next stage is indeed "a period of unsettling." ²Now must the teacher of God understand that he did not really know what was valuable and what was valueless. ³All that he really learned so far was that he did not want the valueless, and that he did want the valuable. ⁴Yet his own sorting out was meaningless in teaching him the difference. ⁵The idea of sacrifice, so central to his own thought system, had made it impossible for him to judge. ⁶He thought he learned willingness, but now he sees that he does not know what the willingness is for. ⁷And now he must attain a state that may remain impossible to reach for a long, long time. ⁸He must learn to lay all judgment aside, and ask only what he really wants in every circumstance. ⁹Were not each step in this direction so heavily reinforced, it would be hard indeed!

8. And finally, there is "a period of achievement." ²It is here that learning is consolidated. ³Now what was seen as merely shadows before become solid gains, to be counted on in all "emergencies" as well as tranquil times. ⁴Indeed, the tranquility is their result; the outcome of honest learning, consistency of thought and full transfer. ⁵This is the stage of real peace, for here is Heaven's state fully reflected. ⁶From here, the way to Heaven is open and easy. ⁷In fact, it is here. ⁸Who would "go" anywhere, if peace of mind is already complete? ⁹And who would seek to change tranquility for something more desirable? ¹⁰What could be more desirable than this?

II. Honesty

1. All other traits of God's teachers rest on trust. ²Once that has been achieved, the others cannot fail to follow. ³Only the trusting can afford honesty, for only they can see its value. ⁴Honesty does not apply only to what you say. ⁵The term actually means consistency. ⁶There is nothing you say that contradicts what you think

or do; no thought opposes any other thought; no act belies your word; and no word lacks agreement with another. ⁷Such are the truly honest. ⁸At no level are they in conflict with themselves. ⁹Therefore it is impossible for them to be in conflict with anyone or anything.

2. The peace of mind which the advanced teachers of God experience is largely due to their perfect honesty. ²It is only the wish to deceive that makes for war. ³No one at one with himself can even conceive of conflict. ⁴Conflict is the inevitable result of self-deception, and self-deception is dishonesty. ⁵There is no challenge to a teacher of God. ⁶Challenge implies doubt, and the trust on which God's teachers rest secure makes doubt impossible. ⁷Therefore they can only succeed. ⁸In this, as in all things, they are honest. ⁹They can only succeed, because they never do their will alone. ¹⁰They choose for all mankind; for all the world and all things in it; for the unchanging and unchangeable beyond appearances; and for the Son of God and his Creator. ¹¹How could they not succeed? ¹²They choose in perfect honesty, sure of their choice as of themselves.

III. Tolerance

1. God's teachers do not judge. ²To judge is to be dishonest, for to judge is to assume a position you do not have. ³Judgment without self-deception is impossible. ⁴Judgment implies that you have been deceived in your brothers. ⁵How, then, could you not have been deceived in yourself? ⁶Judgment implies a lack of trust, and trust remains the bedrock of the teacher of God's whole thought system. ⁷Let this be lost, and all his learning goes. ⁸Without judgment are all things equally acceptable, for who could judge otherwise? ⁹Without judgment are all men brothers, for who is there who stands apart? ¹⁰Judgment destroys honesty and shatters trust. ¹¹No teacher of God can judge and hope to learn.

IV. Gentleness

1. Harm is impossible for God's teachers. ²They can neither harm nor be harmed. ³Harm is the outcome of judgment. ⁴It is the dishonest act that follows a dishonest thought. ⁵It is a verdict of guilt

upon a brother, and therefore on oneself. ⁶It is the end of peace and the denial of learning. ⁷It demonstrates the absence of God's curriculum, and its replacement by insanity. ⁸No teacher of God but must learn,—and fairly early in his training,—that harmfulness completely obliterates his function from his awareness. ⁹It will make him confused, fearful, angry and suspicious. ¹⁰It will make the Holy Spirit's lessons impossible to learn. ¹¹Nor can God's Teacher be heard at all, except by those who realize that harm can actually achieve nothing. ¹²No gain can come of it.

2. Therefore, God's teachers are wholly gentle. ²They need the strength of gentleness, for it is in this that the function of salvation becomes easy. ³To those who would do harm, it is impossible. ⁴To those to whom harm has no meaning, it is merely natural. ⁵What choice but this has meaning to the sane? ⁶Who chooses hell when he perceives a way to Heaven? ⁷And who would choose the weakness that must come from harm in place of the unfailing, all-encompassing and limitless strength of gentleness? ⁸The might of God's teachers lies in their gentleness, for they have understood their evil thoughts came neither from God's Son nor his Creator. ⁹Thus did they join their thoughts with Him Who is their Source. ¹⁰And so their will, which always was His Own, is free to be itself.

V. Joy

1. Joy is the inevitable result of gentleness. ²Gentleness means that fear is now impossible, and what could come to interfere with joy? ³The open hands of gentleness are always filled. ⁴The gentle have no pain. ⁵They cannot suffer. ⁶Why would they not be joyous? ⁷They are sure they are beloved and must be safe. ⁸Joy goes with gentleness as surely as grief attends attack. ⁹God's teachers trust in Him. ¹⁰And they are sure His Teacher goes before them, making sure no harm can come to them. ¹¹They hold His gifts and follow in His way, because God's Voice directs them in all things. ¹²Joy is their song of thanks. ¹³And Christ looks down on them in thanks as well. ¹⁴His need of them is just as great as theirs of Him. ¹⁵How joyous it is to share the purpose of salvation!

VI. Defenselessness

1. God's teachers have learned how to be simple. ²They have no dreams that need defense against the truth. ³They do not try to make themselves. ⁴Their joy comes from their understanding Who created them. ⁵And does what God created need defense? ⁶No one can become an advanced teacher of God until he fully understands that defenses are but foolish guardians of mad illusions. ⁷The more grotesque the dream, the fiercer and more powerful its defenses seem to be. ⁸Yet when the teacher of God finally agrees to look past them, he finds that nothing was there. ⁹Slowly at first he lets himself be undeceived. ¹⁰But he learns faster as his trust increases. ¹¹It is not danger that comes when defenses are laid down. ¹²It is safety. ¹³It is peace. ¹⁴It is joy. ¹⁵And it is God.

VII. Generosity

1. The term generosity has special meaning to the teacher of God. ²It is not the usual meaning of the word; in fact, it is a meaning that must be learned and learned very carefully. ³Like all the other attributes of God's teachers this one rests ultimately on trust, for without trust no one can be generous in the true sense. ⁴To the world, generosity means "giving away" in the sense of "giving up." ⁵To the teachers of God, it means giving away in order to keep. ⁶This has been emphasized throughout the text and the workbook, but it is perhaps more alien to the thinking of the world than many other ideas in our curriculum. ⁷Its greater strangeness lies merely in the obviousness of its reversal of the world's thinking. ⁸In the clearest way possible, and at the simplest of levels, the word means the exact opposite to the teachers of God and to the world.

2. The teacher of God is generous out of Self interest. ²This does not refer, however, to the self of which the world speaks. ³The teacher of God does not want anything he cannot give away, because he realizes it would be valueless to him by definition. ⁴What would he want it *for*? ⁵He could only lose because of it. ⁶He could not gain. ⁷Therefore he does not seek what only he could keep, because that is a guarantee of loss. ⁸He does not want to suffer. ⁹Why should he ensure himself pain? ¹⁰But he does want to keep for himself all things that are of God, and therefore for His Son. ¹¹These are the things that belong to him. ¹²These he can give away in true generosity, protecting them forever for himself.

VIII. Patience

1. Those who are certain of the outcome can afford to wait, and wait without anxiety. [2]Patience is natural to the teacher of God. [3]All he sees is certain outcome, at a time perhaps unknown to him as yet, but not in doubt. [4]The time will be as right as is the answer. [5]And this is true for everything that happens now or in the future. [6]The past as well held no mistakes; nothing that did not serve to benefit the world, as well as him to whom it seemed to happen. [7]Perhaps it was not understood at the time. [8]Even so, the teacher of God is willing to reconsider all his past decisions, if they are causing pain to anyone. [9]Patience is natural to those who trust. [10]Sure of the ultimate interpretation of all things in time, no outcome already seen or yet to come can cause them fear.

IX. Faithfulness

1. The extent of the teacher of God's faithfulness is the measure of his advancement in the curriculum. [2]Does he still select some aspects of his life to bring to his learning, while keeping others apart? [3]If so, his advancement is limited, and his trust not yet firmly established. [4]Faithfulness is the teacher of God's trust in the Word of God to set all things right; not some, but all. [5]Generally, his faithfulness begins by resting on just some problems, remaining carefully limited for a time. [6]To give up all problems to one Answer is to reverse the thinking of the world entirely. [7]And that alone is faithfulness. [8]Nothing but that really deserves the name. [9]Yet each degree, however small, is worth achieving. [10]Readiness, as the text notes, is not mastery.

2. True faithfulness, however, does not deviate. [2]Being consistent, it is wholly honest. [3]Being unswerving, it is full of trust. [4]Being based on fearlessness, it is gentle. [5]Being certain, it is joyous. [6]And being confident, it is tolerant. [7]Faithfulness, then, combines in itself the other attributes of God's teachers. [8]It implies acceptance of the Word of God and His definition of His Son. [9]It is to Them that faithfulness in the true sense is always directed. [10]Toward Them it looks, seeking until it finds. [11]Defenselessness attends it naturally, and joy is its condition. [12]And having found, it rests in quiet certainty on that alone to which all faithfulness is due.

X. Open-Mindedness

1. The centrality of open-mindedness, perhaps the last of the attributes the teacher of God acquires, is easily understood when its relation to forgiveness is recognized. [2]Open-mindedness comes with lack of judgment. [3]As judgment shuts the mind against God's Teacher, so open-mindedness invites Him to come in. [4]As condemnation judges the Son of God as evil, so open-mindedness permits him to be judged by the Voice for God on His behalf. [5]As the projection of guilt upon him would send him to hell, so open-mindedness lets Christ's image be extended to him. [6]Only the open-minded can be at peace, for they alone see reason for it.

2. How do the open-minded forgive? [2]They have let go all things that would prevent forgiveness. [3]They have in truth abandoned the world, and let it be restored to them in newness and in joy so glorious they could never have conceived of such a change. [4]Nothing is now as it was formerly. [5]Nothing but sparkles now which seemed so dull and lifeless before. [6]And above all are all things welcoming, for threat is gone. [7]No clouds remain to hide the face of Christ. [8]Now is the goal achieved. [9]Forgiveness is the final goal of the curriculum. [10]It paves the way for what goes far beyond all learning. [11]The curriculum makes no effort to exceed its legitimate goal. [12]Forgiveness is its single aim, at which all learning ultimately converges. [13]It is indeed enough.

3. You may have noticed that the list of attributes of God's teachers does not include things that are the Son of God's inheritance. [2]Terms like love, sinlessness, perfection, knowledge and eternal truth do not appear in this context. [3]They would be most inappropriate here. [4]What God has given is so far beyond our curriculum that learning but disappears in its presence. [5]Yet while its presence is obscured, the focus properly belongs on the curriculum. [6]It is the function of God's teachers to bring true learning to the world. [7]Properly speaking it is unlearning that they bring, for that is "true learning" in the world. [8]It is given to the teachers of God to bring the glad tidings of complete forgiveness to the world. [9]Blessed indeed are they, for they are the bringers of salvation.

5. HOW IS HEALING ACCOMPLISHED?

1. Healing involves an understanding of what the illusion of sickness is for. ²Healing is impossible without this.

I. The Perceived Purpose of Sickness

1. Healing is accomplished the instant the sufferer no longer sees any value in pain. ²Who would choose suffering unless he thought it brought him something, and something of value to him? ³He must think it is a small price to pay for something of greater worth. ⁴For sickness is an election; a decision. ⁵It is the choice of weakness, in the mistaken conviction that it is strength. ⁶When this occurs, real strength is seen as threat and health as danger. ⁷Sickness is a method, conceived in madness, for placing God's Son on his Father's throne. ⁸God is seen as outside, fierce and powerful, eager to keep all power for Himself. ⁹Only by His death can He be conquered by His Son.

2. And what, in this insane conviction, does healing stand for? ²It symbolizes the defeat of God's Son and the triumph of his Father over him. ³It represents the ultimate defiance in a direct form which the Son of God is forced to recognize. ⁴It stands for all that he would hide from himself to protect his "life." ⁵If he is healed, he is responsible for his thoughts. ⁶And if he is responsible for his thoughts, he will be killed to prove to him how weak and pitiful he is. ⁷But if he chooses death himself, his weakness is his strength. ⁸Now has he given himself what God would give to him, and thus entirely usurped the throne of his Creator.

II. The Shift in Perception

1. Healing must occur in exact proportion to which the valuelessness of sickness is recognized. ²One need but say, "There is no gain at all to me in this" and he is healed. ³But to say this, one first must recognize certain facts. ⁴First, it is obvious that decisions are of the mind, not of the body. ⁵If sickness is but a faulty problem-solving approach, it is a decision. ⁶And if it is a decision, it is the mind and not the body that makes it. ⁷The resistance to recognizing this is enormous, because the existence of the world as you perceive it depends on the body being the decision maker.

17

[8]Terms like "instincts," "reflexes" and the like represent attempts to endow the body with non-mental motivators. [9]Actually, such terms merely state or describe the problem. [10]They do not answer it.

2. The acceptance of sickness as a decision of the mind, for a purpose for which it would use the body, is the basis of healing. [2]And this is so for healing in all forms. [3]A patient decides that this is so, and he recovers. [4]If he decides against recovery, he will not be healed. [5]Who is the physician? [6]Only the mind of the patient himself. [7]The outcome is what he decides that it is. [8]Special agents seem to be ministering to him, yet they but give form to his own choice. [9]He chooses them in order to bring tangible form to his desires. [10]And it is this they do, and nothing else. [11]They are not actually needed at all. [12]The patient could merely rise up without their aid and say, "I have no use for this." [13]There is no form of sickness that would not be cured at once.

3. What is the single requisite for this shift in perception? [2]It is simply this; the recognition that sickness is of the mind, and has nothing to do with the body. [3]What does this recognition "cost"? [4]It costs the whole world you see, for the world will never again appear to rule the mind. [5]For with this recognition is responsibility placed where it belongs; not with the world, but on him who looks on the world and sees it as it is not. [6]He looks on what he chooses to see. [7]No more and no less. [8]The world does nothing to him. [9]He only thought it did. [10]Nor does he do anything to the world, because he was mistaken about what it is. [11]Herein is the release from guilt and sickness both, for they are one. [12]Yet to accept this release, the insignificance of the body must be an acceptable idea.

4. With this idea is pain forever gone. [2]But with this idea goes also all confusion about creation. [3]Does not this follow of necessity? [4]Place cause and effect in their true sequence in one respect, and the learning will generalize and transform the world. [5]The transfer value of one true idea has no end or limit. [6]The final outcome of this lesson is the remembrance of God. [7]What do guilt and sickness, pain, disaster and all suffering mean now? [8]Having no purpose, they are gone. [9]And with them also go all the effects they seemed to cause. [10]Cause and effect but replicate creation. [11]Seen in their proper perspective, without distortion and without fear, they re-establish Heaven.

III. The Function of the Teacher of God

1. If the patient must change his mind in order to be healed, what does the teacher of God do? ²Can he change the patient's mind for him? ³Certainly not. ⁴For those already willing to change their minds he has no function except to rejoice with them, for they have become teachers of God with him. ⁵He has, however, a more specific function for those who do not understand what healing is. ⁶These patients do not realize they have chosen sickness. ⁷On the contrary, they believe that sickness has chosen them. ⁸Nor are they open-minded on this point. ⁹The body tells them what to do and they obey. ¹⁰They have no idea how insane this concept is. ¹¹If they even suspected it, they would be healed. ¹²Yet they suspect nothing. ¹³To them the separation is quite real.

2. To them God's teachers come, to represent another choice which they had forgotten. ²The simple presence of a teacher of God is a reminder. ³His thoughts ask for the right to question what the patient has accepted as true. ⁴As God's messengers, His teachers are the symbols of salvation. ⁵They ask the patient for forgiveness for God's Son in his own Name. ⁶They stand for the Alternative. ⁷With God's Word in their minds they come in benediction, not to heal the sick but to remind them of the remedy God has already given them. ⁸It is not their hands that heal. ⁹It is not their voice that speaks the Word of God. ¹⁰They merely give what has been given them. ¹¹Very gently they call to their brothers to turn away from death: "Behold, you Son of God, what life can offer you. ¹²Would you choose sickness in place of this?"

3. Not once do the advanced teachers of God consider the forms of sickness in which their brother believes. ²To do this is to forget that all of them have the same purpose, and therefore are not really different. ³They seek for God's Voice in this brother who would so deceive himself as to believe God's Son can suffer. ⁴And they remind him that he did not make himself, and must remain as God created him. ⁵They recognize illusions can have no effect. ⁶The truth in their minds reaches out to the truth in the minds of their brothers, so that illusions are not reinforced. ⁷They are thus brought to truth; truth is not brought to them. ⁸So are they dispelled, not by the will of another, but by the union of the one Will with itself. ⁹And this is the function of God's teachers; to see no will as separate from their own, nor theirs as separate from God's.

19

6. IS HEALING CERTAIN?

1. Healing is always certain. [2]It is impossible to let illusions be brought to truth and keep the illusions. [3]Truth demonstrates illusions have no value. [4]The teacher of God has seen the correction of his errors in the mind of the patient, recognizing it for what it is. [5]Having accepted the Atonement for himself, he has also accepted it for the patient. [6]Yet what if the patient uses sickness as a way of life, believing healing is the way to death? [7]When this is so, a sudden healing might precipitate intense depression, and a sense of loss so deep that the patient might even try to destroy himself. [8]Having nothing to live for, he may ask for death. [9]Healing must wait, for his protection.

2. Healing will always stand aside when it would be seen as threat. [2]The instant it is welcome it is there. [3]Where healing has been given it will be received. [4]And what is time before the gifts of God? [5]We have referred many times in the text to the storehouse of treasures laid up equally for the giver and the receiver of God's gifts. [6]Not one is lost, for they can but increase. [7]No teacher of God should feel disappointed if he has offered healing and it does not appear to have been received. [8]It is not up to him to judge when his gift should be accepted. [9]Let him be certain it has been received, and trust that it will be accepted when it is recognized as a blessing and not a curse.

3. It is not the function of God's teachers to evaluate the outcome of their gifts. [2]It is merely their function to give them. [3]Once they have done that they have also given the outcome, for that is part of the gift. [4]No one can give if he is concerned with the result of giving. [5]That is a limitation on the giving itself, and neither the giver nor the receiver would have the gift. [6]Trust is an essential part of giving; in fact, it is the part that makes sharing possible, the part that guarantees the giver will not lose, but only gain. [7]Who gives a gift and then remains with it, to be sure it is used as the giver deems appropriate? [8]Such is not giving but imprisoning.

4. It is the relinquishing of all concern about the gift that makes it truly given. [2]And it is trust that makes true giving possible. [3]Healing is the change of mind that the Holy Spirit in the patient's mind is seeking for him. [4]And it is the Holy Spirit in the mind of the giver Who gives the gift to him. [5]How can it be lost? [6]How can it be ineffectual? [7]How can it be wasted? [8]God's treasure house can

never be empty. [9]And if one gift is missing, it would not be full. [10]Yet is its fullness guaranteed by God. [11]What concern, then, can a teacher of God have about what becomes of his gifts? [12]Given by God to God, who in this holy exchange can receive less than everything?

7. SHOULD HEALING BE REPEATED?

1. This question really answers itself. [2]Healing cannot be repeated. [3]If the patient is healed, what remains to heal him from? [4]And if the healing is certain, as we have already said it is, what is there to repeat? [5]For a teacher of God to remain concerned about the result of healing is to limit the healing. [6]It is now the teacher of God himself whose mind needs to be healed. [7]And it is this he must facilitate. [8]He is now the patient, and he must so regard himself. [9]He has made a mistake, and must be willing to change his mind about it. [10]He lacked the trust that makes for giving truly, and so he has not received the benefit of his gift.

2. Whenever a teacher of God has tried to be a channel for healing he has succeeded. [2]Should he be tempted to doubt this, he should not repeat his previous effort. [3]That was already maximal, because the Holy Spirit so accepted it and so used it. [4]Now the teacher of God has only one course to follow. [5]He must use his reason to tell himself that he has given the problem to One Who cannot fail, and must recognize that his own uncertainty is not love but fear, and therefore hate. [6]His position has thus become untenable, for he is offering hate to one to whom he offered love. [7]This is impossible. [8]Having offered love, only love can be received.

3. It is in this that the teacher of God must trust. [2]This is what is really meant by the statement that the one responsibility of the miracle worker is to accept the Atonement for himself. [3]The teacher of God is a miracle worker because he gives the gifts he has received. [4]Yet he must first accept them. [5]He need do no more, nor is there more that he could do. [6]By accepting healing he can give it. [7]If he doubts this, let him remember Who gave the gift and Who received it. [8]Thus is his doubt corrected. [9]He thought the gifts of God could be withdrawn. [10]That was a mistake, but hardly one to stay with. [11]And so the teacher of God can only recognize it for what it is, and let it be corrected for him.

4. One of the most difficult temptations to recognize is that to doubt a healing because of the appearance of continuing symptoms is a mistake in the form of lack of trust. [2]As such it is an attack. [3]Usually it seems to be just the opposite. [4]It does appear unreasonable at first to be told that continued concern is attack. [5]It has all the appearances of love. [6]Yet love without trust is impossible, and doubt and trust cannot coexist. [7]And hate must be

the opposite of love, regardless of the form it takes. ⁸Doubt not the gift and it is impossible to doubt its result. ⁹This is the certainty that gives God's teachers the power to be miracle workers, for they have put their trust in Him.

5. The real basis for doubt about the outcome of any problem that has been given to God's Teacher for resolution is always self-doubt. ²And that necessarily implies that trust has been placed in an illusory self, for only such a self can be doubted. ³This illusion can take many forms. ⁴Perhaps there is a fear of weakness and vulnerability. ⁵Perhaps there is a fear of failure and shame associated with a sense of inadequacy. ⁶Perhaps there is a guilty embarrassment stemming from false humility. ⁷The form of the mistake is not important. ⁸What is important is only the recognition of a mistake as a mistake.

6. The mistake is always some form of concern with the self to the exclusion of the patient. ²It is a failure to recognize him as part of the Self, and thus represents a confusion in identity. ³Conflict about what you are has entered your mind, and you have become deceived about yourself. ⁴And you are deceived about yourself because you have denied the Source of your creation. ⁵If you are offering only healing, you cannot doubt. ⁶If you really want the problem solved, you cannot doubt. ⁷If you are certain what the problem is, you cannot doubt. ⁸Doubt is the result of conflicting wishes. ⁹Be sure of what you want, and doubt becomes impossible.

8. HOW CAN PERCEPTION OF ORDER OF DIFFICULTIES BE AVOIDED?

1. The belief in order of difficulties is the basis for the world's perception. [2]It rests on differences; on uneven background and shifting foreground, on unequal heights and diverse sizes, on varying degrees of darkness and light, and thousands of contrasts in which each thing seen competes with every other in order to be recognized. [3]A larger object overshadows a smaller one. [4]A brighter thing draws the attention from another with less intensity of appeal. [5]And a more threatening idea, or one conceived of as more desirable by the world's standards, completely upsets the mental balance. [6]What the body's eyes behold is only conflict. [7]Look not to them for peace and understanding.

2. Illusions are always illusions of differences. [2]How could it be otherwise? [3]By definition, an illusion is an attempt to make something real that is regarded as of major importance, but is recognized as being untrue. [4]The mind therefore seeks to make it true out of its intensity of desire to have it for itself. [5]Illusions are travesties of creation; attempts to bring truth to lies. [6]Finding truth unacceptable, the mind revolts against truth and gives itself an illusion of victory. [7]Finding health a burden, it retreats into feverish dreams. [8]And in these dreams the mind is separate, different from other minds, with different interests of its own, and able to gratify its needs at the expense of others.

3. Where do all these differences come from? [2]Certainly they seem to be in the world outside. [3]Yet it is surely the mind that judges what the eyes behold. [4]It is the mind that interprets the eyes' messages and gives them "meaning." [5]And this meaning does not exist in the world outside at all. [6]What is seen as "reality" is simply what the mind prefers. [7]Its hierarchy of values is projected outward, and it sends the body's eyes to find it. [8]The body's eyes will never see except through differences. [9]Yet it is not the messages they bring on which perception rests. [10]Only the mind evaluates their messages, and so only the mind is responsible for seeing. [11]It alone decides whether what is seen is real or illusory, desirable or undesirable, pleasurable or painful.

4. It is in the sorting out and categorizing activities of the mind that errors in perception enter. [2]And it is here correction must be made. [3]The mind classifies what the body's eyes bring to it according to its preconceived values, judging where each sense

datum fits best. ⁴What basis could be faultier than this? ⁵Unrecognized by itself, it has itself asked to be given what will fit into these categories. ⁶And having done so, it concludes that the categories must be true. ⁷On this the judgment of all differences rests, because it is on this that judgments of the world depend. ⁸Can this confused and senseless "reasoning" be depended on for anything?

5. There can be no order of difficulty in healing merely because all sickness is illusion. ²Is it harder to dispel the belief of the insane in a larger hallucination as opposed to a smaller one? ³Will he agree more quickly to the unreality of a louder voice he hears than to that of a softer one? ⁴Will he dismiss more easily a whispered demand to kill than a shout? ⁵And do the number of pitchforks the devils he sees carrying affect their credibility in his perception? ⁶His mind has categorized them all as real, and so they are all real to him. ⁷When he realizes they are all illusions they will disappear. ⁸And so it is with healing. ⁹The properties of illusions which seem to make them different are really irrelevant, for their properties are as illusory as they are.

6. The body's eyes will continue to see differences. ²But the mind that has let itself be healed will no longer acknowledge them. ³There will be those who seem to be "sicker" than others, and the body's eyes will report their changed appearances as before. ⁴But the healed mind will put them all in one category; they are unreal. ⁵This is the gift of its Teacher; the understanding that only two categories are meaningful in sorting out the messages the mind receives from what appears to be the outside world. ⁶And of these two, but one is real. ⁷Just as reality is wholly real, apart from size and shape and time and place—for differences cannot exist within it—so too are illusions without distinctions. ⁸The one answer to sickness of any kind is healing. ⁹The one answer to all illusions is truth.

9. ARE CHANGES REQUIRED IN THE LIFE SITUATION
OF GOD'S TEACHERS?

1. Changes are required in the *minds* of God's teachers. [2]This may or may not involve changes in the external situation. [3]Remember that no one is where he is by accident, and chance plays no part in God's plan. [4]It is most unlikely that changes in attitudes would not be the first step in the newly made teacher of God's training. [5]There is, however, no set pattern, since training is always highly individualized. [6]There are those who are called upon to change their life situation almost immediately, but these are generally special cases. [7]By far the majority are given a slowly evolving training program, in which as many previous mistakes as possible are corrected. [8]Relationships in particular must be properly perceived, and all dark cornerstones of unforgiveness removed. [9]Otherwise the old thought system still has a basis for return.

2. As the teacher of God advances in his training, he learns one lesson with increasing thoroughness. [2]He does not make his own decisions; he asks his Teacher for His answer, and it is this he follows as his guide for action. [3]This becomes easier and easier, as the teacher of God learns to give up his own judgment. [4]The giving up of judgment, the obvious prerequisite for hearing God's Voice, is usually a fairly slow process, not because it is difficult, but because it is apt to be perceived as personally insulting. [5]The world's training is directed toward achieving a goal in direct opposition to that of our curriculum. [6]The world trains for reliance on one's judgment as the criterion for maturity and strength. [7]Our curriculum trains for the relinquishment of judgment as the necessary condition of salvation.

10. HOW IS JUDGMENT RELINQUISHED?

1. Judgment, like other devices by which the world of illusions is maintained, is totally misunderstood by the world. [2]It is actually confused with wisdom, and substitutes for truth. [3]As the world uses the term, an individual is capable of "good" and "bad" judgment, and his education aims at strengthening the former and minimizing the latter. [4]There is, however, considerable confusion about what these categories mean. [5]What is "good" judgment to one is "bad" judgment to another. [6]Further, even the same person classifies the same action as showing "good" judgment at one time and "bad" judgment at another time. [7]Nor can any consistent criteria for determining what these categories are be really taught. [8]At any time the student may disagree with what his would-be teacher says about them, and the teacher himself may well be inconsistent in what he believes. [9]"Good" judgment, in these terms, does not mean anything. [10]No more does "bad."

2. It is necessary for the teacher of God to realize, not that he should not judge, but that he cannot. [2]In giving up judgment, he is merely giving up what he did not have. [3]He gives up an illusion; or better, he has an illusion of giving up. [4]He has actually merely become more honest. [5]Recognizing that judgment was always impossible for him, he no longer attempts it. [6]This is no sacrifice. [7]On the contrary, he puts himself in a position where judgment *through* him rather than *by* him can occur. [8]And this judgment is neither "good" nor "bad." [9]It is the only judgment there is, and it is only one: "God's Son is guiltless, and sin does not exist."

3. The aim of our curriculum, unlike the goal of the world's learning, is the recognition that judgment in the usual sense is impossible. [2]This is not an opinion but a fact. [3]In order to judge anything rightly, one would have to be fully aware of an inconceivably wide range of things; past, present and to come. [4]One would have to recognize in advance all the effects of his judgments on everyone and everything involved in them in any way. [5]And one would have to be certain there is no distortion in his perception, so that his judgment would be wholly fair to everyone on whom it rests now and in the future. [6]Who is in a position to do this? [7]Who except in grandiose fantasies would claim this for himself?

4. Remember how many times you thought you knew all the "facts" you needed for judgment, and how wrong you were! [2]Is there anyone who has not had this experience? [3]Would you know how many times you merely thought you were right, without ever realizing you were wrong? [4]Why would you choose such an arbitrary basis for decision making? [5]Wisdom is not judgment; it is the relinquishment of judgment. [6]Make then but one more judgment. [7]It is this: There is Someone with you Whose judgment is perfect. [8]He does know all the facts; past, present and to come. [9]He does know all the effects of His judgment on everyone and everything involved in any way. [10]And He is wholly fair to everyone, for there is no distortion in His perception.

5. Therefore lay judgment down, not with regret but with a sigh of gratitude. [2]Now are you free of a burden so great that you could merely stagger and fall down beneath it. [3]And it was all illusion. [4]Nothing more. [5]Now can the teacher of God rise up unburdened, and walk lightly on. [6]Yet it is not only this that is his benefit. [7]His sense of care is gone, for he has none. [8]He has given it away, along with judgment. [9]He gave himself to Him Whose judgment he has chosen now to trust, instead of his own. [10]Now he makes no mistakes. [11]His Guide is sure. [12]And where he came to judge, he comes to bless. [13]Where now he laughs, he used to come to weep.

6. It is not difficult to relinquish judgment. [2]But it is difficult indeed to try to keep it. [3]The teacher of God lays it down happily the instant he recognizes its cost. [4]All of the ugliness he sees about him is its outcome. [5]All of the pain he looks upon is its result. [6]All of the loneliness and sense of loss; of passing time and growing hopelessness; of sickening despair and fear of death; all these have come of it. [7]And now he knows that these things need not be. [8]Not one is true. [9]For he has given up their cause, and they, which never were but the effects of his mistaken choice, have fallen from him. [10]Teacher of God, this step will bring you peace. [11]Can it be difficult to want but this?

11. HOW IS PEACE POSSIBLE IN THIS WORLD?

1. This is a question everyone must ask. ²Certainly peace seems to be impossible here. ³Yet the Word of God promises other things that seem impossible, as well as this. ⁴His Word has promised peace. ⁵It has also promised that there is no death, that resurrection must occur, and that rebirth is man's inheritance. ⁶The world you see cannot be the world God loves, and yet His Word assures us that He loves the world. ⁷God's Word has promised that peace is possible here, and what He promises can hardly be impossible. ⁸But it is true that the world must be looked at differently, if His promises are to be accepted. ⁹What the world is, is but a fact. ¹⁰You cannot choose what this should be. ¹¹But you can choose how you would see it. ¹²Indeed, you *must* choose this.

2. Again we come to the question of judgment. ²This time ask yourself whether your judgment or the Word of God is more likely to be true. ³For they say different things about the world, and things so opposite that it is pointless to try to reconcile them. ⁴God offers the world salvation; your judgment would condemn it. ⁵God says there is no death; your judgment sees but death as the inevitable end of life. ⁶God's Word assures you that He loves the world; your judgment says it is unlovable. ⁷Who is right? ⁸For one of you is wrong. ⁹It must be so.

3. The text explains that the Holy Spirit is the Answer to all problems you have made. ²These problems are not real, but that is meaningless to those who believe in them. ³And everyone believes in what he made, for it was made by his believing it. ⁴Into this strange and paradoxical situation,—one without meaning and devoid of sense, yet out of which no way seems possible,— God has sent His Judgment to answer yours. ⁵Gently His Judgment substitutes for yours. ⁶And through this substitution is the un-understandable made understandable. ⁷How is peace possible in this world? ⁸In your judgment it is not possible, and can never be possible. ⁹But in the Judgment of God what is reflected here is only peace.

4. Peace is impossible to those who look on war. ²Peace is inevitable to those who offer peace. ³How easily, then, is your judgment of the world escaped! ⁴It is not the world that makes peace seem impossible. ⁵It is the world you see that is impossible. ⁶Yet has

29

God's Judgment on this distorted world redeemed it and made it fit to welcome peace. [7]And peace descends on it in joyous answer. [8]Peace now belongs here, because a Thought of God has entered. [9]What else but a Thought of God turns hell to Heaven merely by being what it is? [10]The earth bows down before its gracious Presence, and it leans down in answer, to raise it up again. [11]Now is the question different. [12]It is no longer, "Can peace be possible in this world?" but instead, "Is it not impossible that peace be absent here?"

12. HOW MANY TEACHERS OF GOD ARE NEEDED TO SAVE THE WORLD?

1. The answer to this question is—one. [2]One wholly perfect teacher, whose learning is complete, suffices. [3]This one, sanctified and redeemed, becomes the Self Who is the Son of God. [4]He who was always wholly spirit now no longer sees himself as a body, or even as in a body. [5]Therefore he is limitless. [6]And being limitless, his thoughts are joined with God's forever and ever. [7]His perception of himself is based upon God's Judgment, not his own. [8]Thus does he share God's Will, and bring His Thoughts to still deluded minds. [9]He is forever one, because he is as God created him. [10]He has accepted Christ, and he is saved.

2. Thus does the son of man become the Son of God. [2]It is not really a change; it is a change of mind. [3]Nothing external alters, but everything internal now reflects only the Love of God. [4]God can no longer be feared, for the mind sees no cause for punishment. [5]God's teachers appear to be many, for that is what is the world's need. [6]Yet being joined in one purpose, and one they share with God, how could they be separate from each other? [7]What does it matter if they then appear in many forms? [8]Their minds are one; their joining is complete. [9]And God works through them now as one, for that is what they are.

3. Why is the illusion of many necessary? [2]Only because reality is not understandable to the deluded. [3]Only very few can hear God's Voice at all, and even they cannot communicate His messages directly through the Spirit which gave them. [4]They need a medium through which communication becomes possible to those who do not realize that they are spirit. [5]A body they can see. [6]A voice they understand and listen to, without the fear that truth would encounter in them. [7]Do not forget that truth can come only where it is welcomed without fear. [8]So do God's teachers need a body, for their unity could not be recognized directly.

4. Yet what makes God's teachers is their recognition of the proper purpose of the body. [2]As they advance in their profession, they become more and more certain that the body's function is but to let God's Voice speak through it to human ears. [3]And these ears will carry to the mind of the hearer messages that are not of this world, and the mind will understand because of their Source. [4]From this understanding will come the recognition, in this new teacher of God, of what the body's purpose really is; the only use

31

there really is for it. [5]This lesson is enough to let the thought of unity come in, and what is one is recognized as one. [6]The teachers of God appear to share the illusion of separation, but because of what they use the body for, they do not believe in the illusion despite appearances.

5. The central lesson is always this; that what you use the body for it will become to you. [2]Use it for sin or for attack, which is the same as sin, and you will see it as sinful. [3]Because it is sinful it is weak, and being weak, it suffers and it dies. [4]Use it to bring the Word of God to those who have it not, and the body becomes holy. [5]Because it is holy it cannot be sick, nor can it die. [6]When its usefulness is done it is laid by, and that is all. [7]The mind makes this decision, as it makes all decisions that are responsible for the body's condition. [8]Yet the teacher of God does not make this decision alone. [9]To do that would be to give the body another purpose from the one that keeps it holy. [10]God's Voice will tell him when he has fulfilled his role, just as It tells him what his function is. [11]He does not suffer either in going or remaining. [12]Sickness is now impossible to him.

6. Oneness and sickness cannot coexist. [2]God's teachers choose to look on dreams a while. [3]It is a conscious choice. [4]For they have learned that all choices are made consciously, with full awareness of their consequences. [5]The dream says otherwise, but who would put his faith in dreams once they are recognized for what they are? [6]Awareness of dreaming is the real function of God's teachers. [7]They watch the dream figures come and go, shift and change, suffer and die. [8]Yet they are not deceived by what they see. [9]They recognize that to behold a dream figure as sick and separate is no more real than to regard it as healthy and beautiful. [10]Unity alone is not a thing of dreams. [11]And it is this God's teachers acknowledge as behind the dream, beyond all seeming and yet surely theirs.

13. WHAT IS THE REAL MEANING OF SACRIFICE?

1. Although in truth the term sacrifice is altogether meaningless, it does have meaning in the world. ²Like all things in the world, its meaning is temporary and will ultimately fade into the nothingness from which it came when there is no more use for it. ³Now its real meaning is a lesson. ⁴Like all lessons it is an illusion, for in reality there is nothing to learn. ⁵Yet this illusion must be replaced by a corrective device; another illusion that replaces the first, so both can finally disappear. ⁶The first illusion, which must be displaced before another thought system can take hold, is that it is a sacrifice to give up the things of this world. ⁷What could this be but an illusion, since this world itself is nothing more than that?

2. It takes great learning both to realize and to accept the fact that the world has nothing to give. ²What can the sacrifice of nothing mean? ³It cannot mean that you have less because of it. ⁴There is no sacrifice in the world's terms that does not involve the body. ⁵Think a while about what the world calls sacrifice. ⁶Power, fame, money, physical pleasure; who is the "hero" to whom all these things belong? ⁷Could they mean anything except to a body? ⁸Yet a body cannot evaluate. ⁹By seeking after such things the mind associates itself with the body, obscuring its Identity and losing sight of what it really is.

3. Once this confusion has occurred, it becomes impossible for the mind to understand that all the "pleasures" of the world are nothing. ²But what a sacrifice,—and it is sacrifice indeed! — all this entails. ³Now has the mind condemned itself to seek without finding; to be forever dissatisfied and discontented; to know not what it really wants to find. ⁴Who can escape this self-condemnation? ⁵Only through God's Word could this be possible. ⁶For self-condemnation is a decision about identity, and no one doubts what he believes he is. ⁷He can doubt all things, but never this.

4. God's teachers can have no regret on giving up the pleasures of the world. ²Is it a sacrifice to give up pain? ³Does an adult resent the giving up of children's toys? ⁴Does one whose vision has already glimpsed the face of Christ look back with longing on a slaughter house? ⁵No one who has escaped the world and all its ills looks back on it with condemnation. ⁶Yet he must rejoice that he is free of all the sacrifice its values would demand of him. ⁷To

them he sacrifices all his peace. [8]To them he sacrifices all his freedom. [9]And to possess them must he sacrifice his hope of Heaven and remembrance of his Father's Love. [10]Who in his sane mind chooses nothing as a substitute for everything?

5. What is the real meaning of sacrifice? [2]It is the cost of believing in illusions. [3]It is the price that must be paid for the denial of truth. [4]There is no pleasure of the world that does not demand this, for otherwise the pleasure would be seen as pain, and no one asks for pain if he recognizes it. [5]It is the idea of sacrifice that makes him blind. [6]He does not see what he is asking for. [7]And so he seeks it in a thousand ways and in a thousand places, each time believing it is there, and each time disappointed in the end. [8]"Seek but do not find" remains this world's stern decree, and no one who pursues the world's goals can do otherwise.

6. You may believe this course requires sacrifice of all you really hold dear. [2]In one sense this is true, for you hold dear the things that crucify God's Son, and it is the course's aim to set him free. [3]But do not be mistaken about what sacrifice means. [4]It always means the giving up of what you want. [5]And what, O teacher of God, is it that you want? [6]You have been called by God, and you have answered. [7]Would you now sacrifice that Call? [8]Few have heard it as yet, and they can but turn to you. [9]There is no other hope in all the world that they can trust. [10]There is no other voice in all the world that echoes God's. [11]If you would sacrifice the truth, they stay in hell. [12]And if they stay, you will remain with them.

7. Do not forget that sacrifice is total. [2]There are no half sacrifices. [3]You cannot give up Heaven partially. [4]You cannot be a little bit in hell. [5]The Word of God has no exceptions. [6]It is this that makes it holy and beyond the world. [7]It is its holiness that points to God. [8]It is its holiness that makes you safe. [9]It is denied if you attack any brother for anything. [10]For it is here the split with God occurs. [11]A split that is impossible. [12]A split that cannot happen. [13]Yet a split in which you surely will believe, because you have set up a situation that is impossible. [14]And in this situation the impossible can seem to happen. [15]It seems to happen at the "sacrifice" of truth.

8. Teacher of God, do not forget the meaning of sacrifice, and remember what each decision you make must mean in terms of cost. [2]Decide for God, and everything is given you at no cost at all. [3]Decide against Him, and you choose nothing, at the expense

of the awareness of everything. [4]What would you teach? [5]Remember only what you would learn. [6]For it is here that your concern should be. [7]Atonement is for you. [8]Your learning claims it and your learning gives it. [9]The world contains it not. [10]But learn this course and it is yours. [11]God holds out His Word to you, for He has need of teachers. [12]What other way is there to save His Son?

14. HOW WILL THE WORLD END?

1. Can what has no beginning really end? ²The world will end in an illusion, as it began. ³Yet will its ending be an illusion of mercy. ⁴The illusion of forgiveness, complete, excluding no one, limitless in gentleness, will cover it, hiding all evil, concealing all sin and ending guilt forever. ⁵So ends the world that guilt had made, for now it has no purpose and is gone. ⁶The father of illusions is the belief that they have a purpose; that they serve a need or gratify a want. ⁷Perceived as purposeless, they are no longer seen. ⁸Their uselessness is recognized, and they are gone. ⁹How but in this way are all illusions ended? ¹⁰They have been brought to truth, and truth saw them not. ¹¹It merely overlooked the meaningless.

2. Until forgiveness is complete, the world does have a purpose. ²It becomes the home in which forgiveness is born, and where it grows and becomes stronger and more all-embracing. ³Here is it nourished, for here it is needed. ⁴A gentle Savior, born where sin was made and guilt seemed real. ⁵Here is His home, for here there is need of Him indeed. ⁶He brings the ending of the world with Him. ⁷It is His Call God's teachers answer, turning to Him in silence to receive His Word. ⁸The world will end when all things in it have been rightly judged by His judgment. ⁹The world will end with the benediction of holiness upon it. ¹⁰When not one thought of sin remains, the world is over. ¹¹It will not be destroyed nor attacked nor even touched. ¹²It will merely cease to seem to be.

3. Certainly this seems to be a long, long while away. ²"When not one thought of sin remains" appears to be a long-range goal indeed. ³But time stands still, and waits on the goal of God's teachers. ⁴Not one thought of sin will remain the instant any one of them accepts Atonement for himself. ⁵It is not easier to forgive one sin than to forgive all of them. ⁶The illusion of orders of difficulty is an obstacle the teacher of God must learn to pass by and leave behind. ⁷One sin perfectly forgiven by one teacher of God can make salvation complete. ⁸Can you understand this? ⁹No; it is meaningless to anyone here. ¹⁰Yet it is the final lesson in which unity is restored. ¹¹It goes against all the thinking of the world, but so does Heaven.

4. The world will end when its thought system has been com-

pletely reversed. [2]Until then, bits and pieces of its thinking will still seem sensible. [3]The final lesson, which brings the ending of the world, cannot be grasped by those not yet prepared to leave the world and go beyond its tiny reach. [4]What, then, is the function of the teacher of God in this concluding lesson? [5]He need merely learn how to approach it; to be willing to go in its direction. [6]He need merely trust that, if God's Voice tells him it is a lesson he can learn, he can learn it. [7]He does not judge it either as hard or easy. [8]His Teacher points to it, and he trusts that He will show him how to learn it.

5. The world will end in joy, because it is a place of sorrow. [2]When joy has come, the purpose of the world has gone. [3]The world will end in peace, because it is a place of war. [4]When peace has come, what is the purpose of the world? [5]The world will end in laughter, because it is a place of tears. [6]Where there is laughter, who can longer weep? [7]And only complete forgiveness brings all this to bless the world. [8]In blessing it departs, for it will not end as it began. [9]To turn hell into Heaven is the function of God's teachers, for what they teach are lessons in which Heaven is reflected. [10]And now sit down in true humility, and realize that all God would have you do you can do. [11]Do not be arrogant and say you cannot learn His Own curriculum. [12]His Word says otherwise. [13]His Will be done. [14]It cannot be otherwise. [15]And be you thankful it is so.

15. IS EACH ONE TO BE JUDGED IN THE END?

1. Indeed, yes! [2]No one can escape God's Final Judgment. [3]Who could flee forever from the truth? [4]But the Final Judgment will not come until it is no longer associated with fear. [5]One day each one will welcome it, and on that very day it will be given him. [6]He will hear his sinlessness proclaimed around and around the world, setting it free as God's Final Judgment on him is received. [7]This is the Judgment in which salvation lies. [8]This is the Judgment that will set him free. [9]This is the Judgment in which all things are freed with him. [10]Time pauses as eternity comes near, and silence lies across the world that everyone may hear this Judgment of the Son of God:

> [11]*Holy are you, eternal, free and whole, at peace forever in the Heart of God.* [12]*Where is the world, and where is sorrow now?*

2. Is this your judgment on yourself, teacher of God? [2]Do you believe that this is wholly true? [3]No; not yet, not yet. [4]But this is still your goal; why you are here. [5]It is your function to prepare yourself to hear this Judgment and to recognize that it is true. [6]One instant of complete belief in this, and you will go beyond belief to Certainty. [7]One instant out of time can bring time's end. [8]Judge not, for you but judge yourself, and thus delay this Final Judgment. [9]What is your judgment of the world, teacher of God? [10]Have you yet learned to stand aside and hear the Voice of Judgment in yourself? [11]Or do you still attempt to take His role from Him? [12]Learn to be quiet, for His Voice is heard in stillness. [13]And His Judgment comes to all who stand aside in quiet listening, and wait for Him.

3. You who are sometimes sad and sometimes angry; who sometimes feel your just due is not given you, and your best efforts meet with lack of appreciation and even contempt; give up these foolish thoughts! [2]They are too small and meaningless to occupy your holy mind an instant longer. [3]God's Judgment waits for you to set you free. [4]What can the world hold out to you, regardless of your judgments on its gifts, that you would rather have? [5]You will be judged, and judged in fairness and in honesty. [6]There is no deceit in God. [7]His promises are sure. [8]Only remember that.

[9]His promises have guaranteed His Judgment, and His alone, will be accepted in the end. [10]It is your function to make that end be soon. [11]It is your function to hold it to your heart, and offer it to all the world to keep it safe.

16. HOW SHOULD THE TEACHER OF GOD SPEND HIS DAY?

1. To the advanced teacher of God this question is meaningless. ²There is no program, for the lessons change each day. ³Yet the teacher of God is sure of but one thing; they do not change at random. ⁴Seeing this and understanding that it is true, he rests content. ⁵He will be told all that his role should be, this day and every day. ⁶And those who share that role with him will find him, so they can learn the lessons for the day together. ⁷Not one is absent whom he needs; not one is sent without a learning goal already set, and one which can be learned that very day. ⁸For the advanced teacher of God, then, this question is superfluous. ⁹It has been asked and answered, and he keeps in constant contact with the Answer. ¹⁰He is set, and sees the road on which he walks stretch surely and smoothly before him.

2. But what about those who have not reached his certainty? ²They are not yet ready for such lack of structuring on their own part. ³What must they do to learn to give the day to God? ⁴There are some general rules which do apply, although each one must use them as best he can in his own way. ⁵Routines as such are dangerous, because they easily become gods in their own right, threatening the very goals for which they were set up. ⁶Broadly speaking, then, it can be said that it is well to start the day right. ⁷It is always possible to begin again, should the day begin with error. ⁸Yet there are obvious advantages in terms of saving time.

3. At the beginning, it is wise to think in terms of time. ²This is by no means the ultimate criterion, but at the outset it is probably the simplest to observe. ³The saving of time is an essential early emphasis which, although it remains important throughout the learning process, becomes less and less emphasized. ⁴At the outset, we can safely say that time devoted to starting the day right does indeed save time. ⁵How much time should be so spent? ⁶This must depend on the teacher of God himself. ⁷He cannot claim that title until he has gone through the workbook, since we are learning within the framework of our course. ⁸After completion of the more structured practice periods, which the workbook contains, individual need becomes the chief consideration.

4. This course is always practical. ²It may be that the teacher of God is not in a situation that fosters quiet thought as he awakes. ³If this is so, let him but remember that he chooses to spend time

with God as soon as possible, and let him do so. ⁴Duration is not the major concern. ⁵One can easily sit still an hour with closed eyes and accomplish nothing. ⁶One can as easily give God only an instant, and in that instant join with Him completely. ⁷Perhaps the one generalization that can be made is this; as soon as possible after waking take your quiet time, continuing a minute or two after you begin to find it difficult. ⁸You may find that the difficulty will diminish and drop away. ⁹If not, that is the time to stop.

5. The same procedures should be followed at night. ²Perhaps your quiet time should be fairly early in the evening, if it is not feasible for you to take it just before going to sleep. ³It is not wise to lie down for it. ⁴It is better to sit up, in whatever position you prefer. ⁵Having gone through the workbook, you must have come to some conclusions in this respect. ⁶If possible, however, just before going to sleep is a desirable time to devote to God. ⁷It sets your mind into a pattern of rest, and orients you away from fear. ⁸If it is expedient to spend this time earlier, at least be sure that you do not forget a brief period,—not more than a moment will do,—in which you close your eyes and think of God.

6. There is one thought in particular that should be remembered throughout the day. ²It is a thought of pure joy; a thought of peace, a thought of limitless release, limitless because all things are freed within it. ³You think you made a place of safety for yourself. ⁴You think you made a power that can save you from all the fearful things you see in dreams. ⁵It is not so. ⁶Your safety lies not there. ⁷What you give up is merely the illusion of protecting illusions. ⁸And it is this you fear, and only this. ⁹How foolish to be so afraid of nothing! ¹⁰Nothing at all! ¹¹Your defenses will not work, but you are not in danger. ¹²You have no need of them. ¹³Recognize this, and they will disappear. ¹⁴And only then will you accept your real protection.

7. How simply and how easily does time slip by for the teacher of God who has accepted His protection! ²All that he did before in the name of safety no longer interests him. ³For he is safe, and knows it to be so. ⁴He has a Guide Who will not fail. ⁵He need make no distinctions among the problems he perceives, for He to Whom he turns with all of them recognizes no order of difficulty in resolving them. ⁶He is as safe in the present as he was before illusions were accepted into his mind, and as he will be when he has let them go. ⁷There is no difference in his state at different times and different places, because they are all one to God. ⁸This

is his safety. [9]And he has no need for more than this.

8. Yet there will be temptations along the way the teacher of God has yet to travel, and he has need of reminding himself throughout the day of his protection. [2]How can he do this, particularly during the time when his mind is occupied with external things? [3]He can but try, and his success depends on his conviction that he will succeed. [4]He must be sure success is not of him, but will be given him at any time, in any place and circumstance he calls for it. [5]There are times his certainty will waver, and the instant this occurs he will return to earlier attempts to place reliance on himself alone. [6]Forget not this is magic, and magic is a sorry substitute for true assistance. [7]It is not good enough for God's teacher, because it is not enough for God's Son.

9. The avoidance of magic is the avoidance of temptation. [2]For all temptation is nothing more than the attempt to substitute another will for God's. [3]These attempts may indeed seem frightening, but they are merely pathetic. [4]They can have no effects; neither good nor bad, neither rewarding nor demanding sacrifice, healing nor destructive, quieting nor fearful. [5]When all magic is recognized as merely nothing, the teacher of God has reached the most advanced state. [6]All intermediate lessons will but lead to this, and bring this goal nearer to recognition. [7]For magic of any kind, in all its forms, simply does nothing. [8]Its powerlessness is the reason it can be so easily escaped. [9]What has no effects can hardly terrify.

10. There is no substitute for the Will of God. [2]In simple statement, it is to this fact that the teacher of God devotes his day. [3]Each substitute he may accept as real can but deceive him. [4]But he is safe from all deception if he so decides. [5]Perhaps he needs to remember, "God is with me. [6]I cannot be deceived." [7]Perhaps he prefers other words, or only one, or none at all. [8]Yet each temptation to accept magic as true must be abandoned through his recognition, not that it is fearful, not that it is sinful, not that it is dangerous, but merely that it is meaningless. [9]Rooted in sacrifice and separation, two aspects of one error and no more, he merely chooses to give up all that he never had. [10]And for this "sacrifice" is Heaven restored to his awareness.

11. Is not this an exchange that you would want? [2]The world would gladly make it, if it knew it could be made. [3]It is God's teachers who must teach it that it can. [4]And so it is their function to make sure that they have learned it. [5]No risk is possible throughout the day except to put your trust in magic, for it is

only this that leads to pain. [6]"There is no will but God's." [7]His teachers know that this is so, and have learned that everything but this is magic. [8]All belief in magic is maintained by just one simple-minded illusion;—that it works. [9]All through their training, every day and every hour, and even every minute and second, must God's teachers learn to recognize the forms of magic and perceive their meaninglessness. [10]Fear is withdrawn from them, and so they go. [11]And thus the gate of Heaven is reopened, and its light can shine again on an untroubled mind.

17. HOW DO GOD'S TEACHERS DEAL WITH MAGIC THOUGHTS?

1. This is a crucial question both for teacher and pupil. ²If this issue is mishandled, the teacher of God has hurt himself and has also attacked his pupil. ³This strengthens fear, and makes the magic seem quite real to both of them. ⁴How to deal with magic thus becomes a major lesson for the teacher of God to master. ⁵His first responsibility in this is not to attack it. ⁶If a magic thought arouses anger in any form, God's teacher can be sure that he is strengthening his own belief in sin and has condemned himself. ⁷He can be sure as well that he has asked for depression, pain, fear and disaster to come to him. ⁸Let him remember, then, it is not this that he would teach, because it is not this that he would learn.

2. There is, however, a temptation to respond to magic in a way that reinforces it. ²Nor is this always obvious. ³It can, in fact, be easily concealed beneath a wish to help. ⁴It is this double wish that makes the help of little value, and must lead to undesired outcomes. ⁵Nor should it be forgotten that the outcome that results will always come to teacher and to pupil alike. ⁶How many times has it been emphasized that you give but to yourself? ⁷And where could this be better shown than in the kinds of help the teacher of God gives to those who need his aid? ⁸Here is his gift most clearly given him. ⁹For he will give only what he has chosen for himself. ¹⁰And in this gift is his judgment upon the holy Son of God.

3. It is easiest to let error be corrected where it is most apparent, and errors can be recognized by their results. ²A lesson truly taught can lead to nothing but release for teacher and pupil, who have shared in one intent. ³Attack can enter only if perception of separate goals has entered. ⁴And this must indeed have been the case if the result is anything but joy. ⁵The single aim of the teacher turns the divided goal of the pupil into one direction, with the call for help becoming his one appeal. ⁶This then is easily responded to with just one answer, and this answer will enter the teacher's mind unfailingly. ⁷From there it shines into his pupil's mind, making it one with his.

4. Perhaps it will be helpful to remember that no one can be angry at a fact. ²It is always an interpretation that gives rise to negative emotions, regardless of their seeming justification by what

appears as facts. [3]Regardless, too, of the intensity of the anger that is aroused. [4]It may be merely slight irritation, perhaps too mild to be even clearly recognized. [5]Or it may also take the form of intense rage, accompanied by thoughts of violence, fantasied or apparently acted out. [6]It does not matter. [7]All of these reactions are the same. [8]They obscure the truth, and this can never be a matter of degree. [9]Either truth is apparent, or it is not. [10]It cannot be partially recognized. [11]Who is unaware of truth must look upon illusions.

5. Anger in response to perceived magic thoughts is a basic cause of fear. [2]Consider what this reaction means, and its centrality in the world's thought system becomes apparent. [3]A magic thought, by its mere presence, acknowledges a separation from God. [4]It states, in the clearest form possible, that the mind which believes it has a separate will that can oppose the Will of God, also believes it can succeed. [5]That this can hardly be a fact is obvious. [6]Yet that it can be believed as fact is equally obvious. [7]And herein lies the birthplace of guilt. [8]Who usurps the place of God and takes it for himself now has a deadly "enemy." [9]And he must stand alone in his protection, and make himself a shield to keep him safe from fury that can never be abated, and vengeance that can never be satisfied.

6. How can this unfair battle be resolved? [2]Its ending is inevitable, for its outcome must be death. [3]How, then, can one believe in one's defenses? [4]Magic again must help. [5]Forget the battle. [6]Accept it as a fact, and then forget it. [7]Do not remember the impossible odds against you. [8]Do not remember the immensity of the "enemy," and do not think about your frailty in comparison. [9]Accept your separation, but do not remember how it came about. [10]Believe that you have won it, but do not retain the slightest memory of Who your great "opponent" really is. [11]Projecting your "forgetting" onto Him, it seems to you He has forgotten, too.

7. But what will now be your reaction to all magic thoughts? [2]They can but reawaken sleeping guilt, which you have hidden but have not let go. [3]Each one says clearly to your frightened mind, "You have usurped the place of God. [4]Think not He has forgotten." [5]Here we have the fear of God most starkly represented. [6]For in that thought has guilt already raised madness to the throne of God Himself. [7]And now there is no hope. [8]Except to kill. [9]Here is salvation now. [10]An angry father pursues his guilty

son. [11]Kill or be killed, for here alone is choice. [12]Beyond this there is none, for what was done cannot be done without. [13]The stain of blood can never be removed, and anyone who bears this stain on him must meet with death.

8. Into this hopeless situation God sends His teachers. [2]They bring the light of hope from God Himself. [3]There is a way in which escape is possible. [4]It can be learned and taught, but it requires patience and abundant willingness. [5]Given that, the lesson's manifest simplicity stands out like an intense white light against a black horizon, for such it is. [6]If anger comes from an interpretation and not a fact, it is never justified. [7]Once this is even dimly grasped, the way is open. [8]Now it is possible to take the next step. [9]The interpretation can be changed at last. [10]Magic thoughts need not lead to condemnation, for they do not really have the power to give rise to guilt. [11]And so they can be overlooked, and thus forgotten in the truest sense.

9. Madness but seems terrible. [2]In truth it has no power to make anything. [3]Like the magic which becomes its servant, it neither attacks nor protects. [4]To see it and to recognize its thought system is to look on nothing. [5]Can nothing give rise to anger? [6]Hardly so. [7]Remember, then, teacher of God, that anger recognizes a reality that is not there; yet is the anger certain witness that you do believe in it as fact. [8]Now is escape impossible, until you see you have responded to your own interpretation, which you have projected on an outside world. [9]Let this grim sword be taken from you now. [10]There is no death. [11]This sword does not exist. [12]The fear of God is causeless. [13]But His Love is Cause of everything beyond all fear, and thus forever real and always true.

18. HOW IS CORRECTION MADE?

1. Correction of a lasting nature,—and only this is true correction,—cannot be made until the teacher of God has ceased to confuse interpretation with fact, or illusion with truth. ²If he argues with his pupil about a magic thought, attacks it, tries to establish its error or demonstrate its falsity, he is but witnessing to its reality. ³Depression is then inevitable, for he has "proved," both to his pupil and himself, that it is their task to escape from what is real. ⁴And this can only be impossible. ⁵Reality is changeless. ⁶Magic thoughts are but illusions. ⁷Otherwise salvation would be only the same age-old impossible dream in but another form. ⁸Yet the dream of salvation has new content. ⁹It is not the form alone in which the difference lies.

2. God's teachers' major lesson is to learn how to react to magic thoughts wholly without anger. ²Only in this way can they proclaim the truth about themselves. ³Through them, the Holy Spirit can now speak of the reality of the Son of God. ⁴Now He can remind the world of sinlessness, the one unchanged, unchangeable condition of all that God created. ⁵Now He can speak the Word of God to listening ears, and bring Christ's vision to eyes that see. ⁶Now is He free to teach all minds the truth of what they are, so they will gladly be returned to Him. ⁷And now is guilt forgiven, overlooked completely in His sight and in God's Word.

3. Anger but screeches, "Guilt is real!" ²Reality is blotted out as this insane belief is taken as replacement for God's Word. ³The body's eyes now "see"; its ears alone can "hear." ⁴Its little space and tiny breath become the measure of reality. ⁵And truth becomes diminutive and meaningless. ⁶Correction has one answer to all this, and to the world that rests on this:

> ⁷*You but mistake interpretation for the truth. ⁸And you are wrong. ⁹But a mistake is not a sin, nor has reality been taken from its throne by your mistakes. ¹⁰God reigns forever, and His laws alone prevail upon you and upon the world. ¹¹His Love remains the only thing there is. ¹²Fear is illusion, for you are like Him.*

4. In order to heal, it thus becomes essential for the teacher of God to let all his own mistakes be corrected. [2]If he senses even the faintest hint of irritation in himself as he responds to anyone, let him instantly realize that he has made an interpretation that is not true. [3]Then let him turn within to his eternal Guide, and let Him judge what the response should be. [4]So is he healed, and in his healing is his pupil healed with him. [5]The sole responsibility of God's teacher is to accept the Atonement for himself. [6]Atonement means correction, or the undoing of errors. [7]When this has been accomplished, the teacher of God becomes a miracle worker by definition. [8]His sins have been forgiven him, and he no longer condemns himself. [9]How can he then condemn anyone? [10]And who is there whom his forgiveness can fail to heal?

19. WHAT IS JUSTICE?

1. Justice is the divine correction for injustice. [2]Injustice is the basis for all the judgments of the world. [3]Justice corrects the interpretations to which injustice gives rise, and cancels them out. [4]Neither justice nor injustice exists in Heaven, for error is impossible and correction meaningless. [5]In this world, however, forgiveness depends on justice, since all attack can only be unjust. [6]Justice is the Holy Spirit's verdict upon the world. [7]Except in His judgment justice is impossible, for no one in the world is capable of making only just interpretations and laying all injustices aside. [8]If God's Son were fairly judged, there would be no need for salvation. [9]The thought of separation would have been forever inconceivable.

2. Justice, like its opposite, is an interpretation. [2]It is, however, the one interpretation that leads to truth. [3]This becomes possible because, while it is not true in itself, justice includes nothing that opposes truth. [4]There is no inherent conflict between justice and truth; one is but the first small step in the direction of the other. [5]The path becomes quite different as one goes along. [6]Nor could all the magnificence, the grandeur of the scene and the enormous opening vistas that rise to meet one as the journey continues, be foretold from the outset. [7]Yet even these, whose splendor reaches indescribable heights as one proceeds, fall short indeed of all that wait when the pathway ceases and time ends with it. [8]But somewhere one must start. [9]Justice is the beginning.

3. All concepts of your brothers and yourself; all fears of future states and all concerns about the past, stem from injustice. [2]Here is the lens which, held before the body's eyes, distorts perception and brings witness of the distorted world back to the mind that made the lens and holds it very dear. [3]Selectively and arbitrarily is every concept of the world built up in just this way. [4]"Sins" are perceived and justified by careful selectivity in which all thought of wholeness must be lost. [5]Forgiveness has no place in such a scheme, for not one "sin" but seems forever true.

4. Salvation is God's justice. [2]It restores to your awareness the wholeness of the fragments you perceive as broken off and separate. [3]And it is this that overcomes the fear of death. [4]For separate fragments must decay and die, but wholeness is immortal. [5]It remains forever and forever like its Creator, being one with Him.

⁶God's Judgment is His justice. ⁷Onto this,—a Judgment wholly lacking in condemnation; an evaluation based entirely on love,— you have projected your injustice, giving God the lens of warped perception through which you look. ⁸Now it belongs to Him and not to you. ⁹You are afraid of Him, and do not see you hate and fear your Self as enemy.

5.　Pray for God's justice, and do not confuse His mercy with your own insanity. ²Perception can make whatever picture the mind desires to see. ³Remember this. ⁴In this lies either Heaven or hell, as you elect. ⁵God's justice points to Heaven just because it is entirely impartial. ⁶It accepts all evidence that is brought before it, omitting nothing and assessing nothing as separate and apart from all the rest. ⁷From this one standpoint does it judge, and this alone. ⁸Here all attack and condemnation becomes meaningless and indefensible. ⁹Perception rests, the mind is still, and light returns again. ¹⁰Vision is now restored. ¹¹What had been lost has now been found. ¹²The peace of God descends on all the world, and we can see. ¹³And we can see!

20. WHAT IS THE PEACE OF GOD?

1. It has been said that there is a kind of peace that is not of this world. [2]How is it recognized? [3]How is it found? [4]And being found, how can it be retained? [5]Let us consider each of these questions separately, for each reflects a different step along the way.

2. First, how can the peace of God be recognized? [2]God's peace is recognized at first by just one thing; in every way it is totally unlike all previous experiences. [3]It calls to mind nothing that went before. [4]It brings with it no past associations. [5]It is a new thing entirely. [6]There is a contrast, yes, between this thing and all the past. [7]But strangely, it is not a contrast of true differences. [8]The past just slips away, and in its place is everlasting quiet. [9]Only that. [10]The contrast first perceived has merely gone. [11]Quiet has reached to cover everything.

3. How is this quiet found? [2]No one can fail to find it who but seeks out its conditions. [3]God's peace can never come where anger is, for anger must deny that peace exists. [4]Who sees anger as justified in any way or any circumstance proclaims that peace is meaningless, and must believe that it cannot exist. [5]In this condition, peace cannot be found. [6]Therefore, forgiveness is the necessary condition for finding the peace of God. [7]More than this, given forgiveness there *must* be peace. [8]For what except attack will lead to war? [9]And what but peace is opposite to war? [10]Here the initial contrast stands out clear and apparent. [11]Yet when peace is found, the war is meaningless. [12]And it is conflict now that is perceived as nonexistent and unreal.

4. How is the peace of God retained, once it is found? [2]Returning anger, in whatever form, will drop the heavy curtain once again, and the belief that peace cannot exist will certainly return. [3]War is again accepted as the one reality. [4]Now must you once again lay down your sword, although you do not recognize that you have picked it up again. [5]But you will learn, as you remember even faintly now what happiness was yours without it, that you must have taken it again as your defense. [6]Stop for a moment now and think of this: Is conflict what you want, or is God's peace the better choice? [7]Which gives you more? [8]A tranquil mind is not a little gift. [9]Would you not rather live than choose to die?

5. Living is joy, but death can only weep. [2]You see in death escape from what you made. [3]But this you do not see; that you made

51

death, and it is but illusion of an end. ⁴Death cannot be escape, because it is not life in which the problem lies. ⁵Life has no opposite, for it is God. ⁶Life and death seem to be opposites because you have decided death ends life. ⁷Forgive the world, and you will understand that everything that God created cannot have an end, and nothing He did not create is real. ⁸In this one sentence is our course explained. ⁹In this one sentence is our practicing given its one direction. ¹⁰And in this one sentence is the Holy Spirit's whole curriculum specified exactly as it is.

6. What is the peace of God? ²No more than this; the simple understanding that His Will is wholly without opposite. ³There is no thought that contradicts His Will, yet can be true. ⁴The contrast between His Will and yours but seemed to be reality. ⁵In truth there was no conflict, for His Will is yours. ⁶Now is the mighty Will of God Himself His gift to you. ⁷He does not seek to keep it for Himself. ⁸Why would you seek to keep your tiny frail imaginings apart from Him? ⁹The Will of God is One and all there is. ¹⁰This is your heritage. ¹¹The universe beyond the sun and stars, and all the thoughts of which you can conceive, belongs to you. ¹²God's peace is the condition for His Will. ¹³Attain His peace, and you remember Him.

21. WHAT IS THE ROLE OF WORDS IN HEALING?

1. Strictly speaking, words play no part at all in healing. [2]The motivating factor is prayer, or asking. [3]What you ask for you receive. [4]But this refers to the prayer of the heart, not to the words you use in praying. [5]Sometimes the words and the prayer are contradictory; sometimes they agree. [6]It does not matter. [7]God does not understand words, for they were made by separated minds to keep them in the illusion of separation. [8]Words can be helpful, particularly for the beginner, in helping concentration and facilitating the exclusion, or at least the control, of extraneous thoughts. [9]Let us not forget, however, that words are but symbols of symbols. [10]They are thus twice removed from reality.

2. As symbols, words have quite specific references. [2]Even when they seem most abstract, the picture that comes to mind is apt to be very concrete. [3]Unless a specific referent does occur to the mind in conjunction with the word, the word has little or no practical meaning, and thus cannot help the healing process. [4]The prayer of the heart does not really ask for concrete things. [5]It always requests some kind of experience, the specific things asked for being the bringers of the desired experience in the opinion of the asker. [6]The words, then, are symbols for the things asked for, but the things themselves but stand for the experiences that are hoped for.

3. The prayer for things of this world will bring experiences of this world. [2]If the prayer of the heart asks for this, this will be given because this will be received. [3]It is impossible that the prayer of the heart remain unanswered in the perception of the one who asks. [4]If he asks for the impossible, if he wants what does not exist or seeks for illusions in his heart, all this becomes his own. [5]The power of his decision offers it to him as he requests. [6]Herein lie hell and Heaven. [7]The sleeping Son of God has but this power left to him. [8]It is enough. [9]His words do not matter. [10]Only the Word of God has any meaning, because it symbolizes that which has no human symbols at all. [11]The Holy Spirit alone understands what this Word stands for. [12]And this, too, is enough.

4. Is the teacher of God, then, to avoid the use of words in his teaching? [2]No, indeed! [3]There are many who must be reached through words, being as yet unable to hear in silence. [4]The teacher of God must, however, learn to use words in a new way.

⁵Gradually, he learns how to let his words be chosen for him by ceasing to decide for himself what he will say. ⁶This process is merely a special case of the lesson in the workbook that says, "I will step back and let Him lead the way." ⁷The teacher of God accepts the words which are offered him, and gives as he receives. ⁸He does not control the direction of his speaking. ⁹He listens and hears and speaks.

5.　A major hindrance in this aspect of his learning is the teacher of God's fear about the validity of what he hears. ²And what he hears may indeed be quite startling. ³It may also seem to be quite irrelevant to the presented problem as he perceives it, and may, in fact, confront the teacher with a situation that appears to be very embarrassing to him. ⁴All these are judgments that have no value. ⁵They are his own, coming from a shabby self-perception which he would leave behind. ⁶Judge not the words that come to you, but offer them in confidence. ⁷They are far wiser than your own. ⁸God's teachers have God's Word behind their symbols. ⁹And He Himself gives to the words they use the power of His Spirit, raising them from meaningless symbols to the Call of Heaven itself.

22. HOW ARE HEALING AND ATONEMENT RELATED?

1. Healing and Atonement are not related; they are identical. ²There is no order of difficulty in miracles because there are no degrees of Atonement. ³It is the one complete concept possible in this world, because it is the source of a wholly unified perception. ⁴Partial Atonement is a meaningless idea, just as special areas of hell in Heaven are inconceivable. ⁵Accept Atonement and you are healed. ⁶Atonement is the Word of God. ⁷Accept His Word and what remains to make sickness possible? ⁸Accept His Word and every miracle has been accomplished. ⁹To forgive is to heal. ¹⁰The teacher of God has taken accepting the Atonement for himself as his only function. ¹¹What is there, then, he cannot heal? ¹²What miracle can be withheld from him?

2. The progress of the teacher of God may be slow or rapid, depending on whether he recognizes the Atonement's inclusiveness, or for a time excludes some problem areas from it. ²In some cases, there is a sudden and complete awareness of the perfect applicability of the lesson of the Atonement to all situations, but this is comparatively rare. ³The teacher of God may have accepted the function God has given him long before he has learned all that his acceptance holds out to him. ⁴It is only the end that is certain. ⁵Anywhere along the way, the necessary realization of inclusiveness may reach him. ⁶If the way seems long, let him be content. ⁷He has decided on the direction he wants to take. ⁸What more was asked of him? ⁹And having done what was required, would God withhold the rest?

3. That forgiveness is healing needs to be understood, if the teacher of God is to make progress. ²The idea that a body can be sick is a central concept in the ego's thought system. ³This thought gives the body autonomy, separates it from the mind, and keeps the idea of attack inviolate. ⁴If the body could be sick Atonement would be impossible. ⁵A body that can order a mind to do as it sees fit could merely take the place of God and prove salvation is impossible. ⁶What, then, is left to heal? ⁷The body has become lord of the mind. ⁸How could the mind be returned to the Holy Spirit unless the body is killed? ⁹And who would want salvation at such a price?

4. Certainly sickness does not appear to be a decision. ²Nor would anyone actually believe he wants to be sick. ³Perhaps he

can accept the idea in theory, but it is rarely if ever consistently applied to all specific forms of sickness, both in the individual's perception of himself and of all others as well. [4]Nor is it at this level that the teacher of God calls forth the miracle of healing. [5]He overlooks the mind *and* body, seeing only the face of Christ shining in front of him, correcting all mistakes and healing all perception. [6]Healing is the result of the recognition, by God's teacher, of who it is that is in need of healing. [7]This recognition has no special reference. [8]It is true of all things that God created. [9]In it are all illusions healed.

5. When a teacher of God fails to heal, it is because he has forgotten Who he is. [2]Another's sickness thus becomes his own. [3]In allowing this to happen, he has identified with another's ego, and has thus confused him with a body. [4]In so doing, he has refused to accept the Atonement for himself, and can hardly offer it to his brother in Christ's Name. [5]He will, in fact, be unable to recognize his brother at all, for his Father did not create bodies, and so he is seeing in his brother only the unreal. [6]Mistakes do not correct mistakes, and distorted perception does not heal. [7]Step back now, teacher of God. [8]You have been wrong. [9]Lead not the way, for you have lost it. [10]Turn quickly to your Teacher, and let yourself be healed.

6. The offer of Atonement is universal. [2]It is equally applicable to all individuals in all circumstances. [3]And in it is the power to heal all individuals of all forms of sickness. [4]Not to believe this is to be unfair to God, and thus unfaithful to Him. [5]A sick person perceives himself as separate from God. [6]Would you see him as separate from you? [7]It is your task to heal the sense of separation that has made him sick. [8]It is your function to recognize for him that what he believes about himself is not the truth. [9]It is your forgiveness that must show him this. [10]Healing is very simple. [11]Atonement is received and offered. [12]Having been received, it must be accepted. [13]It is in the receiving, then, that healing lies. [14]All else must follow from this single purpose.

7. Who can limit the power of God Himself? [2]Who, then, can say which one can be healed of what, and what must remain beyond God's power to forgive? [3]This is insanity indeed. [4]It is not up to God's teachers to set limits upon Him, because it is not up to them to judge His Son. [5]And to judge His Son is to limit his Father. [6]Both are equally meaningless. [7]Yet this will not be understood until God's teacher recognizes that they are the same mistake.

[8]Herein does he receive Atonement, for he withdraws his judgment from the Son of God, accepting him as God created him. [9]No longer does he stand apart from God, determining where healing should be given and where it should be withheld. [10]Now can he say with God, "This is my beloved Son, created perfect and forever so."

23. DOES JESUS HAVE A SPECIAL PLACE IN HEALING?

1. God's gifts can rarely be received directly. [2]Even the most advanced of God's teachers will give way to temptation in this world. [3]Would it be fair if their pupils were denied healing because of this? [4]The Bible says, "Ask in the name of Jesus Christ." [5]Is this merely an appeal to magic? [6]A name does not heal, nor does an invocation call forth any special power. [7]What does it mean to call on Jesus Christ? [8]What does calling on his name confer? [9]Why is the appeal to him part of healing?

2. We have repeatedly said that one who has perfectly accepted the Atonement for himself can heal the world. [2]Indeed, he has already done so. [3]Temptation may recur to others, but never to this One. [4]He has become the risen Son of God. [5]He has overcome death because he has accepted life. [6]He has recognized himself as God created him, and in so doing he has recognized all living things as part of him. [7]There is now no limit on his power, because it is the power of God. [8]So has his name become the Name of God, for he no longer sees himself as separate from Him.

3. What does this mean for you? [2]It means that in remembering Jesus you are remembering God. [3]The whole relationship of the Son to the Father lies in him. [4]His part in the Sonship is also yours, and his completed learning guarantees your own success. [5]Is he still available for help? [6]What did he say about this? [7]Remember his promises, and ask yourself honestly whether it is likely that he will fail to keep them. [8]Can God fail His Son? [9]And can one who is one with God be unlike Him? [10]Who transcends the body has transcended limitation. [11]Would the greatest teacher be unavailable to those who follow him?

4. The name of Jesus Christ as such is but a symbol. [2]But it stands for love that is not of this world. [3]It is a symbol that is safely used as a replacement for the many names of all the gods to which you pray. [4]It becomes the shining symbol for the Word of God, so close to what it stands for that the little space between the two is lost, the moment that the name is called to mind. [5]Remembering the name of Jesus Christ is to give thanks for all the gifts that God has given you. [6]And gratitude to God becomes the way in which He is remembered, for love cannot be far behind a grateful heart and thankful mind. [7]God enters easily, for these are the true conditions for your homecoming.

5. Jesus has led the way. [2]Why would you not be grateful to him? [3]He has asked for love, but only that he might give it to you. [4]You do not love yourself. [5]But in his eyes your loveliness is so complete and flawless that he sees in it an image of his Father. [6]You become the symbol of his Father here on earth. [7]To you he looks for hope, because in you he sees no limit and no stain to mar your beautiful perfection. [8]In his eyes Christ's vision shines in perfect constancy. [9]He has remained with you. [10]Would you not learn the lesson of salvation through his learning? [11]Why would you choose to start again, when he has made the journey for you?

6. No one on earth can grasp what Heaven is, or what its one Creator really means. [2]Yet we have witnesses. [3]It is to them that wisdom should appeal. [4]There have been those whose learning far exceeds what we can learn. [5]Nor would we teach the limitations we have laid on us. [6]No one who has become a true and dedicated teacher of God forgets his brothers. [7]Yet what he can offer them is limited by what he learns himself. [8]Then turn to one who laid all limits by, and went beyond the farthest reach of learning. [9]He will take you with him, for he did not go alone. [10]And you were with him then, as you are now.

7. This course has come from him because his words have reached you in a language you can love and understand. [2]Are other teachers possible, to lead the way to those who speak in different tongues and appeal to different symbols? [3]Certainly there are. [4]Would God leave anyone without a very present help in time of trouble; a savior who can symbolize Himself? [5]Yet do we need a many-faceted curriculum, not because of content differences, but because symbols must shift and change to suit the need. [6]Jesus has come to answer yours. [7]In him you find God's Answer. [8]Do you, then, teach with him, for he is with you; he is always here.

24. IS REINCARNATION SO?

1. In the ultimate sense, reincarnation is impossible. [2]There is no past or future, and the idea of birth into a body has no meaning either once or many times. [3]Reincarnation cannot, then, be true in any real sense. [4]Our only question should be, "Is the concept helpful?" [5]And that depends, of course, on what it is used for. [6]If it is used to strengthen the recognition of the eternal nature of life, it is helpful indeed. [7]Is any other question about it really useful in lighting up the way? [8]Like many other beliefs, it can be bitterly misused. [9]At least, such misuse offers preoccupation and perhaps pride in the past. [10]At worst, it induces inertia in the present. [11]In between, many kinds of folly are possible.

2. Reincarnation would not, under any circumstances, be the problem to be dealt with *now*. [2]If it were responsible for some of the difficulties the individual faces now, his task would still be only to escape from them now. [3]If he is laying the groundwork for a future life, he can still work out his salvation only now. [4]To some, there may be comfort in the concept, and if it heartens them its value is self-evident. [5]It is certain, however, that the way to salvation can be found by those who believe in reincarnation and by those who do not. [6]The idea cannot, therefore, be regarded as essential to the curriculum. [7]There is always some risk in seeing the present in terms of the past. [8]There is always some good in any thought which strengthens the idea that life and the body are not the same.

3. For our purposes, it would not be helpful to take any definite stand on reincarnation. [2]A teacher of God should be as helpful to those who believe in it as to those who do not. [3]If a definite stand were required of him, it would merely limit his usefulness, as well as his own decision making. [4]Our course is not concerned with any concept that is not acceptable to anyone, regardless of his formal beliefs. [5]His ego will be enough for him to cope with, and it is not the part of wisdom to add sectarian controversies to his burdens. [6]Nor would there be an advantage in his premature acceptance of the course merely because it advocates a long-held belief of his own.

4. It cannot be too strongly emphasized that this course aims at a complete reversal of thought. [2]When this is finally accomplished, issues such as the validity of reincarnation become meaningless.

³Until then, they are likely to be merely controversial. ⁴The teacher of God is, therefore, wise to step away from all such questions, for he has much to teach and learn apart from them. ⁵He should both learn and teach that theoretical issues but waste time, draining it away from its appointed purpose. ⁶If there are aspects to any concept or belief that will be helpful, he will be told about it. ⁷He will also be told how to use it. ⁸What more need he know?

5. Does this mean that the teacher of God should not believe in reincarnation himself, or discuss it with others who do? ²The answer is, certainly not! ³If he does believe in reincarnation, it would be a mistake for him to renounce the belief unless his internal Teacher so advised. ⁴And this is most unlikely. ⁵He might be advised that he is misusing the belief in some way that is detrimental to his pupil's advance or his own. ⁶Reinterpretation would then be recommended, because it is necessary. ⁷All that must be recognized, however, is that birth was not the beginning, and death is not the end. ⁸Yet even this much is not required of the beginner. ⁹He need merely accept the idea that what he knows is not necessarily all there is to learn. ¹⁰His journey has begun.

6. The emphasis of this course always remains the same;—it is at this moment that complete salvation is offered you, and it is at this moment that you can accept it. ²This is still your one responsibility. ³Atonement might be equated with total escape from the past and total lack of interest in the future. ⁴Heaven is here. ⁵There is nowhere else. ⁶Heaven is now. ⁷There is no other time. ⁸No teaching that does not lead to this is of concern to God's teachers. ⁹All beliefs will point to this if properly interpreted. ¹⁰In this sense, it can be said that their truth lies in their usefulness. ¹¹All beliefs that lead to progress should be honored. ¹²This is the sole criterion this course requires. ¹³No more than this is necessary.

25. ARE "PSYCHIC" POWERS DESIRABLE?

1. The answer to this question is much like the preceding one. ²There are, of course, no "unnatural" powers, and it is obviously merely an appeal to magic to make up a power that does not exist. ³It is equally obvious, however, that each individual has many abilities of which he is unaware. ⁴As his awareness increases, he may well develop abilities that seem quite startling to him. ⁵Yet nothing he can do can compare even in the slightest with the glorious surprise of remembering Who he is. ⁶Let all his learning and all his efforts be directed toward this one great final surprise, and he will not be content to be delayed by the little ones that may come to him on the way.

2. Certainly there are many "psychic" powers that are clearly in line with this course. ²Communication is not limited to the small range of channels the world recognizes. ³If it were, there would be little point in trying to teach salvation. ⁴It would be impossible to do so. ⁵The limits the world places on communication are the chief barriers to direct experience of the Holy Spirit, Whose Presence is always there and Whose Voice is available but for the hearing. ⁶These limits are placed out of fear, for without them the walls that surround all the separate places of the world would fall at the holy sound of His Voice. ⁷Who transcends these limits in any way is merely becoming more natural. ⁸He is doing nothing special, and there is no magic in his accomplishments.

3. The seemingly new abilities that may be gathered on the way can be very helpful. ²Given to the Holy Spirit, and used under His direction, they are valuable teaching aids. ³To this, the question of how they arise is irrelevant. ⁴The only important consideration is how they are used. ⁵Taking them as ends in themselves, no matter how this is done, will delay progress. ⁶Nor does their value lie in proving anything; achievements from the past, unusual attunement with the "unseen," or "special" favors from God. ⁷God gives no special favors, and no one has any powers that are not available to everyone. ⁸Only by tricks of magic are special powers "demonstrated."

4. Nothing that is genuine is used to deceive. ²The Holy Spirit is incapable of deception, and He can use only genuine abilities. ³What is used for magic is useless to Him. ⁴But what He uses cannot be used for magic. ⁵There is, however, a particular appeal

in unusual abilities that can be curiously tempting. ⁶Here are strengths which the Holy Spirit wants and needs. ⁷Yet the ego sees in these same strengths an opportunity to glorify itself. ⁸Strengths turned to weakness are tragedy indeed. ⁹Yet what is not given to the Holy Spirit must be given to weakness, for what is withheld from love is given to fear, and will be fearful in consequence.

5.   Even those who no longer value the material things of the world may still be deceived by "psychic" powers. ²As investment has been withdrawn from the world's material gifts, the ego has been seriously threatened. ³It may still be strong enough to rally under this new temptation to win back strength by guile. ⁴Many have not seen through the ego's defenses here, although they are not particularly subtle. ⁵Yet, given a remaining wish to be deceived, deception is made easy. ⁶Now the "power" is no longer a genuine ability, and cannot be used dependably. ⁷It is almost inevitable that, unless the individual changes his mind about its purpose, he will bolster his "power's" uncertainties with increasing deception.

6.   Any ability that anyone develops has the potentiality for good. ²To this there is no exception. ³And the more unusual and unexpected the power, the greater its potential usefulness. ⁴Salvation has need of all abilities, for what the world would destroy the Holy Spirit would restore. ⁵"Psychic" abilities have been used to call upon the devil, which merely means to strengthen the ego. ⁶Yet here is also a great channel of hope and healing in the Holy Spirit's service. ⁷Those who have developed "psychic" powers have simply let some of the limitations they laid upon their minds be lifted. ⁸It can be but further limitations they lay upon themselves if they utilize their increased freedom for greater imprisonment. ⁹The Holy Spirit needs these gifts, and those who offer them to Him and Him alone go with Christ's gratitude upon their hearts, and His holy sight not far behind.

26. CAN GOD BE REACHED DIRECTLY?

1. God indeed can be reached directly, for there is no distance between Him and His Son. ²His awareness is in everyone's memory, and His Word is written on everyone's heart. ³Yet this awareness and this memory can arise across the threshold of recognition only where all barriers to truth have been removed. ⁴In how many is this the case? ⁵Here, then, is the role of God's teachers. ⁶They, too, have not attained the necessary understanding as yet, but they have joined with others. ⁷This is what sets them apart from the world. ⁸And it is this that enables others to leave the world with them. ⁹Alone they are nothing. ¹⁰But in their joining is the power of God.

2. There are those who have reached God directly, retaining no trace of worldly limits and remembering their own Identity perfectly. ²These might be called the Teachers of teachers because, although they are no longer visible, their image can yet be called upon. ³And they will appear when and where it is helpful for them to do so. ⁴To those to whom such appearances would be frightening, they give their ideas. ⁵No one can call on them in vain. ⁶Nor is there anyone of whom they are unaware. ⁷All needs are known to them, and all mistakes are recognized and overlooked by them. ⁸The time will come when this is understood. ⁹And meanwhile, they give all their gifts to the teachers of God who look to them for help, asking all things in their name and in no other.

3. Sometimes a teacher of God may have a brief experience of direct union with God. ²In this world, it is almost impossible that this endure. ³It can, perhaps, be won after much devotion and dedication, and then be maintained for much of the time on earth. ⁴But this is so rare that it cannot be considered a realistic goal. ⁵If it happens, so be it. ⁶If it does not happen, so be it as well. ⁷All worldly states must be illusory. ⁸If God were reached directly in sustained awareness, the body would not be long maintained. ⁹Those who have laid the body down merely to extend their helpfulness to those remaining behind are few indeed. ¹⁰And they need helpers who are still in bondage and still asleep, so that by their awakening can God's Voice be heard.

4. Do not despair, then, because of limitations. ²It is your function to escape from them, but not to be without them. ³If you would

64

be heard by those who suffer, you must speak their language. [4]If you would be a savior, you must understand what needs to be escaped. [5]Salvation is not theoretical. [6]Behold the problem, ask for the answer, and then accept it when it comes. [7]Nor will its coming be long delayed. [8]All the help you can accept will be provided, and not one need you have will not be met. [9]Let us not, then, be too concerned with goals for which you are not ready. [10]God takes you where you are and welcomes you. [11]What more could you desire, when this is all you need?

27. WHAT IS DEATH?

1. Death is the central dream from which all illusions stem. ²Is it not madness to think of life as being born, aging, losing vitality, and dying in the end? ³We have asked this question before, but now we need to consider it more carefully. ⁴It is the one fixed, unchangeable belief of the world that all things in it are born only to die. ⁵This is regarded as "the way of nature," not to be raised to question, but to be accepted as the "natural" law of life. ⁶The cyclical, the changing and unsure; the undependable and the unsteady, waxing and waning in a certain way upon a certain path,—all this is taken as the Will of God. ⁷And no one asks if a benign Creator could will this.

2. In this perception of the universe as God created it, it would be impossible to think of Him as loving. ²For who has decreed that all things pass away, ending in dust and disappointment and despair, can but be feared. ³He holds your little life in his hand but by a thread, ready to break it off without regret or care, perhaps today. ⁴Or if he waits, yet is the ending certain. ⁵Who loves such a god knows not of love, because he has denied that life is real. ⁶Death has become life's symbol. ⁷His world is now a battleground, where contradiction reigns and opposites make endless war. ⁸Where there is death is peace impossible.

3. Death is the symbol of the fear of God. ²His Love is blotted out in the idea, which holds it from awareness like a shield held up to obscure the sun. ³The grimness of the symbol is enough to show it cannot coexist with God. ⁴It holds an image of the Son of God in which he is "laid to rest" in devastation's arms, where worms wait to greet him and to last a little while by his destruction. ⁵Yet the worms as well are doomed to be destroyed as certainly. ⁶And so do all things live because of death. ⁷Devouring is nature's "law of life." ⁸God is insane, and fear alone is real.

4. The curious belief that there is part of dying things that may go on apart from what will die, does not proclaim a loving God nor re-establish any grounds for trust. ²If death is real for anything, there is no life. ³Death denies life. ⁴But if there is reality in life, death is denied. ⁵No compromise in this is possible. ⁶There is either a god of fear or One of Love. ⁷The world attempts a thousand compromises, and will attempt a thousand more. ⁸Not one can be acceptable to God's teachers, because not one could be

acceptable to God. [9]He did not make death because He did not make fear. [10]Both are equally meaningless to Him.

5. The "reality" of death is firmly rooted in the belief that God's Son is a body. [2]And if God created bodies, death would indeed be real. [3]But God would not be loving. [4]There is no point at which the contrast between the perception of the real world and that of the world of illusions becomes more sharply evident. [5]Death is indeed the death of God, if He is Love. [6]And now His Own creation must stand in fear of Him. [7]He is not Father, but destroyer. [8]He is not Creator, but avenger. [9]Terrible His Thoughts and fearful His image. [10]To look on His creations is to die.

6. "And the last to be overcome will be death." [2]Of course! [3]Without the idea of death there is no world. [4]All dreams will end with this one. [5]This is salvation's final goal; the end of all illusions. [6]And in death are all illusions born. [7]What can be born of death and still have life? [8]But what is born of God and still can die? [9]The inconsistencies, the compromises and the rituals the world fosters in its vain attempts to cling to death and yet to think love real are mindless magic, ineffectual and meaningless. [10]God is, and in Him all created things must be eternal. [11]Do you not see that otherwise He has an opposite, and fear would be as real as love?

7. Teacher of God, your one assignment could be stated thus: Accept no compromise in which death plays a part. [2]Do not believe in cruelty, nor let attack conceal the truth from you. [3]What seems to die has but been misperceived and carried to illusion. [4]Now it becomes your task to let the illusion be carried to the truth. [5]Be steadfast but in this; be not deceived by the "reality" of any changing form. [6]Truth neither moves nor wavers nor sinks down to death and dissolution. [7]And what is the end of death? [8]Nothing but this; the realization that the Son of God is guiltless now and forever. [9]Nothing but this. [10]But do not let yourself forget it is not less than this.

28. WHAT IS THE RESURRECTION?

1. Very simply, the resurrection is the overcoming or surmounting of death. [2]It is a reawakening or a rebirth; a change of mind about the meaning of the world. [3]It is the acceptance of the Holy Spirit's interpretation of the world's purpose; the acceptance of the Atonement for oneself. [4]It is the end of dreams of misery, and the glad awareness of the Holy Spirit's final dream. [5]It is the recognition of the gifts of God. [6]It is the dream in which the body functions perfectly, having no function except communication. [7]It is the lesson in which learning ends, for it is consummated and surpassed with this. [8]It is the invitation to God to take His final step. [9]It is the relinquishment of all other purposes, all other interests, all other wishes and all other concerns. [10]It is the single desire of the Son for the Father.

2. The resurrection is the denial of death, being the assertion of life. [2]Thus is all the thinking of the world reversed entirely. [3]Life is now recognized as salvation, and pain and misery of any kind perceived as hell. [4]Love is no longer feared, but gladly welcomed. [5]Idols have disappeared, and the remembrance of God shines unimpeded across the world. [6]Christ's face is seen in every living thing, and nothing is held in darkness, apart from the light of forgiveness. [7]There is no sorrow still upon the earth. [8]The joy of Heaven has come upon it.

3. Here the curriculum ends. [2]From here on, no directions are needed. [3]Vision is wholly corrected and all mistakes undone. [4]Attack is meaningless and peace has come. [5]The goal of the curriculum has been achieved. [6]Thoughts turn to Heaven and away from hell. [7]All longings are satisfied, for what remains unanswered or incomplete? [8]The last illusion spreads across the world, forgiving all things and replacing all attack. [9]The whole reversal is accomplished. [10]Nothing is left to contradict the Word of God. [11]There is no opposition to the truth. [12]And now the truth can come at last. [13]How quickly will it come as it is asked to enter and envelop such a world!

4. All living hearts are tranquil with a stir of deep anticipation, for the time of everlasting things is now at hand. [2]There is no death. [3]The Son of God is free. [4]And in his freedom is the end of fear. [5]No hidden places now remain on earth to shelter sick illusions, dreams of fear and misperceptions of the universe. [6]All things are

seen in light, and in the light their purpose is transformed and understood. [7]And we, God's children, rise up from the dust and look upon our perfect sinlessness. [8]The song of Heaven sounds around the world, as it is lifted up and brought to truth.

5. Now there are no distinctions. [2]Differences have disappeared and Love looks on Itself. [3]What further sight is needed? [4]What remains that vision could accomplish? [5]We have seen the face of Christ, His sinlessness, His Love behind all forms, beyond all purposes. [6]Holy are we because His Holiness has set us free indeed! [7]And we accept His Holiness as ours; as it is. [8]As God created us so will we be forever and forever, and we wish for nothing but His Will to be our own. [9]Illusions of another will are lost, for unity of purpose has been found.

6. These things await us all, but we are not prepared as yet to welcome them with joy. [2]As long as any mind remains possessed of evil dreams, the thought of hell is real. [3]God's teachers have the goal of wakening the minds of those asleep, and seeing there the vision of Christ's face to take the place of what they dream. [4]The thought of murder is replaced with blessing. [5]Judgment is laid by, and given Him Whose function judgment is. [6]And in His Final Judgment is restored the truth about the holy Son of God. [7]He is redeemed, for he has heard God's Word and understood its meaning. [8]He is free because he let God's Voice proclaim the truth. [9]And all he sought before to crucify are resurrected with him, by his side, as he prepares with them to meet his God.

29. AS FOR THE REST...

1. This manual is not intended to answer all questions that both teacher and pupil may raise. [2]In fact, it covers only a few of the more obvious ones, in terms of a brief summary of some of the major concepts in the text and workbook. [3]It is not a substitute for either, but merely a supplement. [4]While it is called a manual for teachers, it must be remembered that only time divides teacher and pupil, so that the difference is temporary by definition. [5]In some cases, it may be helpful for the pupil to read the manual first. [6]Others might do better to begin with the workbook. [7]Still others may need to start at the more abstract level of the text.

2. Which is for which? [2]Who would profit more from prayers alone? [3]Who needs but a smile, being as yet unready for more? [4]No one should attempt to answer these questions alone. [5]Surely no teacher of God has come this far without realizing that. [6]The curriculum is highly individualized, and all aspects are under the Holy Spirit's particular care and guidance. [7]Ask and He will answer. [8]The responsibility is His, and He alone is fit to assume it. [9]To do so is His function. [10]To refer the questions to Him is yours. [11]Would you want to be responsible for decisions about which you understand so little? [12]Be glad you have a Teacher Who cannot make a mistake. [13]His answers are always right. [14]Would you say that of yours?

3. There is another advantage,—and a very important one,—in referring decisions to the Holy Spirit with increasing frequency. [2]Perhaps you have not thought of this aspect, but its centrality is obvious. [3]To follow the Holy Spirit's guidance is to let yourself be absolved of guilt. [4]It is the essence of the Atonement. [5]It is the core of the curriculum. [6]The imagined usurping of functions not your own is the basis of fear. [7]The whole world you see reflects the illusion that you have done so, making fear inevitable. [8]To return the function to the One to Whom it belongs is thus the escape from fear. [9]And it is this that lets the memory of love return to you. [10]Do not, then, think that following the Holy Spirit's guidance is necessary merely because of your own inadequacies. [11]It is the way out of hell for you.

4. Here again is the paradox often referred to in the course. [2]To say, "Of myself I can do nothing" is to gain all power. [3]And yet it is but a seeming paradox. [4]As God created you, you *have* all

70

power. ⁵The image you made of yourself has none. ⁶The Holy Spirit knows the truth about you. ⁷The image you made does not. ⁸Yet, despite its obvious and complete ignorance, this image assumes it knows all things because you have given that belief to it. ⁹Such is your teaching, and the teaching of the world that was made to uphold it. ¹⁰But the Teacher Who knows the truth has not forgotten it. ¹¹His decisions bring benefit to all, being wholly devoid of attack. ¹²And therefore incapable of arousing guilt.

5. Who assumes a power that he does not possess is deceiving himself. ²Yet to accept the power given him by God is but to acknowledge his Creator and accept His gifts. ³And His gifts have no limit. ⁴To ask the Holy Spirit to decide for you is simply to accept your true inheritance. ⁵Does this mean that you cannot say anything without consulting Him? ⁶No, indeed! ⁷That would hardly be practical, and it is the practical with which this course is most concerned. ⁸If you have made it a habit to ask for help when and where you can, you can be confident that wisdom will be given you when you need it. ⁹Prepare for this each morning, remember God when you can throughout the day, ask the Holy Spirit's help when it is feasible to do so, and thank Him for His guidance at night. ¹⁰And your confidence will be well founded indeed.

6. Never forget that the Holy Spirit does not depend on your words. ²He understands the requests of your heart, and answers them. ³Does this mean that, while attack remains attractive to you, He will respond with evil? ⁴Hardly! ⁵For God has given Him the power to translate your prayers of the heart into His language. ⁶He understands that an attack is a call for help. ⁷And He responds with help accordingly. ⁸God would be cruel if He let your words replace His Own. ⁹A loving father does not let his child harm himself, or choose his own destruction. ¹⁰He may ask for injury, but his father will protect him still. ¹¹And how much more than this does your Father love His Son?

7. Remember you are His completion and His Love. ²Remember your weakness is His strength. ³But do not read this hastily or wrongly. ⁴If His strength is in you, what you perceive as your weakness is but illusion. ⁵And He has given you the means to prove it so. ⁶Ask all things of His Teacher, and all things are given you. ⁷Not in the future but immediately; now. ⁸God does not wait, for waiting implies time and He is timeless. ⁹Forget your foolish images, your sense of frailty and your fear of harm, your

dreams of danger and selected "wrongs." [10]God knows but His Son, and as he was created so he is. [11]In confidence I place you in His Hands, and I give thanks for you that this is so.

8. And now in all your doings be you blessed.
   [2]God turns to you for help to save the world.
   [3]Teacher of God, His thanks He offers you,
   And all the world stands silent in the grace
   You bring from Him. [4]You are the Son He loves,
   And it is given you to be the means
   Through which His Voice is heard around the world,
   To close all things of time; to end the sight
   Of all things visible; and to undo
   All things that change. [5]Through you is ushered in
   A world unseen, unheard, yet truly there.
   [6]Holy are you, and in your light the world
   Reflects your holiness, for you are not
   Alone and friendless. [7]I give thanks for you,
   And join your efforts on behalf of God,
   Knowing they are on my behalf as well,
   And for all those who walk to God with me.

[8]AMEN

CLARIFICATION OF TERMS

INTRODUCTION

1. This is not a course in philosophical speculation, nor is it concerned with precise terminology. ²It is concerned only with Atonement, or the correction of perception. ³The means of the Atonement is forgiveness. ⁴The structure of "individual consciousness" is essentially irrelevant because it is a concept representing the "original error" or the "original sin." ⁵To study the error itself does not lead to correction, if you are indeed to succeed in overlooking the error. ⁶And it is just this process of overlooking at which the course aims.

2. All terms are potentially controversial, and those who seek controversy will find it. ²Yet those who seek clarification will find it as well. ³They must, however, be willing to overlook controversy, recognizing that it is a defense against truth in the form of a delaying maneuver. ⁴Theological considerations as such are necessarily controversial, since they depend on belief and can therefore be accepted or rejected. ⁵A universal theology is impossible, but a universal experience is not only possible but necessary. ⁶It is this experience toward which the course is directed. ⁷Here alone consistency becomes possible because here alone uncertainty ends.

3. This course remains within the ego framework, where it is needed. ²It is not concerned with what is beyond all error because it is planned only to set the direction towards it. ³Therefore it uses words, which are symbolic, and cannot express what lies beyond symbols. ⁴It is merely the ego that questions because it is only the ego that doubts. ⁵The course merely gives another answer, once a question has been raised. ⁶However, this answer does not attempt to resort to inventiveness or ingenuity. ⁷These are attributes of the ego. ⁸*The course is simple.* ⁹It has one function and one goal. ¹⁰Only in that does it remain wholly consistent because only that can *be* consistent.

4. The ego will demand many answers that this course does not give. ²It does not recognize as questions the mere form of a question to which an answer is impossible. ³The ego may ask, "How did the impossible occur?", "To what did the impossible happen?", and may ask this in many forms. ⁴Yet there is no answer; only an experience. ⁵Seek only this, and do not let theology delay you.

5. You will notice that the emphasis on structural issues in the

course is brief and early. [2]Afterwards and soon, it drops away to make way for the central teaching. [3]Since you have asked for clarification, however, these are some of the terms that are used.

1. MIND – SPIRIT

1. The term *mind* is used to represent the activating agent of spirit, supplying its creative energy. ²When the term is capitalized it refers to God or Christ (i.e., the Mind of God or the Mind of Christ). ³*Spirit* is the Thought of God which He created like Himself. ⁴The unified spirit is God's one Son, or Christ.

2. In this world, because the mind is split, the Sons of God appear to be separate. ²Nor do their minds seem to be joined. ³In this illusory state, the concept of an "individual mind" seems to be meaningful. ⁴It is therefore described in the course *as if* it has two parts; spirit and ego.

3. Spirit is the part that is still in contact with God through the Holy Spirit, Who abides in this part but sees the other part as well. ²The term "soul" is not used except in direct biblical quotations because of its highly controversial nature. ³It would, however, be an equivalent of "spirit," with the understanding that, being of God, it is eternal and was never born.

4. The other part of the mind is entirely illusory and makes only illusions. ²Spirit retains the potential for creating, but its Will, which is God's, seems to be imprisoned while the mind is not unified. ³Creation continues unabated because that is the Will of God. ⁴This Will is always unified and therefore has no meaning in this world. ⁵It has no opposite and no degrees.

5. The mind can be right or wrong, depending on the voice to which it listens. ²*Right-mindedness* listens to the Holy Spirit, forgives the world, and through Christ's vision sees the real world in its place. ³This is the final vision, the last perception, the condition in which God takes the final step Himself. ⁴Here time and illusions end together.

6. *Wrong-mindedness* listens to the ego and makes illusions; perceiving sin and justifying anger, and seeing guilt, disease and death as real. ²Both this world and the real world are illusions because right-mindedness merely overlooks, or forgives, what never happened. ³Therefore it is not the *One-mindedness* of the Christ Mind, Whose Will is one with God's.

7. In this world the only remaining freedom is the freedom of choice; always between two choices or two voices. ²Will is not involved in perception at any level, and has nothing to do with choice. ³*Consciousness* is the receptive mechanism, receiving

messages from above or below; from the Holy Spirit or the ego. [4]Consciousness has levels and awareness can shift quite dramatically, but it cannot transcend the perceptual realm. [5]At its highest it becomes aware of the real world, and can be trained to do so increasingly. [6]Yet the very fact that it has levels and can be trained demonstrates that it cannot reach knowledge.

2. THE EGO – THE MIRACLE

1. Illusions will not last. ²Their death is sure and this alone is certain in their world. ³It is the ego's world because of this. ⁴What is the *ego*? ⁵But a dream of what you really are. ⁶A thought you are apart from your Creator and a wish to be what He created not. ⁷It is a thing of madness, not reality at all. ⁸A name for namelessness is all it is. ⁹A symbol of impossibility; a choice for options that do not exist. ¹⁰We name it but to help us understand that it is nothing but an ancient thought that what is made has immortality. ¹¹But what could come of this except a dream which, like all dreams, can only end in death?

2. What is the ego? ²Nothingness, but in a form that seems like something. ³In a world of form the ego cannot be denied for it alone seems real. ⁴Yet could God's Son as He created him abide in form or in a world of form? ⁵Who asks you to define the ego and explain how it arose can be but he who thinks it real, and seeks by definition to ensure that its illusive nature is concealed behind the words that seem to make it so.

3. There is no definition for a lie that serves to make it true. ²Nor can there be a truth that lies conceal effectively. ³The ego's unreality is not denied by words nor is its meaning clear because its nature seems to have a form. ⁴Who can define the undefinable? ⁵And yet there is an answer even here.

4. We cannot really make a definition for what the ego is, but we *can* say what it is not. ²And this is shown to us with perfect clarity. ³It is from this that we deduce all that the ego is. ⁴Look at its opposite and you can see the only answer that is meaningful.

5. The ego's opposite in every way,—in origin, effect and consequence—we call a miracle. ²And here we find all that is not the ego in this world. ³Here is the ego's opposite and here alone we look on what the ego was, for here we see all that it seemed to do, and cause and its effects must still be one.

6. Where there was darkness now we see the light. ²What is the ego? ³What the darkness was. ⁴Where is the ego? ⁵Where the darkness was. ⁶What is it now and where can it be found? ⁷Nothing and nowhere. ⁸Now the light has come: Its opposite has gone without a trace. ⁹Where evil was there now is holiness. ¹⁰What is the ego? ¹¹What the evil was. ¹²Where is the ego? ¹³In an evil dream that but seemed real while you were dreaming it. ¹⁴Where

there was crucifixion stands God's Son. [15]What is the ego? [16]Who has need to ask? [17]Where is the ego? [18]Who has need to seek for an illusion now that dreams are gone?

7. What is a *miracle*? [2]A dream as well. [3]But look at all the aspects of *this* dream and you will never question any more. [4]Look at the kindly world you see extend before you as you walk in gentleness. [5]Look at the helpers all along the way you travel, happy in the certainty of Heaven and the surety of peace. [6]And look an instant, too, on what you left behind at last and finally passed by.

8. This was the ego—all the cruel hate, the need for vengeance and the cries of pain, the fear of dying and the urge to kill, the brotherless illusion and the self that seemed alone in all the universe. [2]This terrible mistake about yourself the miracle corrects as gently as a loving mother sings her child to rest. [3]Is not a song like this what you would hear? [4]Would it not answer all you thought to ask, and even make the question meaningless?

9. Your questions have no answer, being made to still God's Voice, which asks of everyone one question only: "Are you ready yet to help Me save the world?" [2]Ask this instead of what the ego is, and you will see a sudden brightness cover up the world the ego made. [3]No miracle is now withheld from anyone. [4]The world is saved from what you thought it was. [5]And what it is, is wholly uncondemned and wholly pure.

10. The miracle forgives; the ego damns. [2]Neither need be defined except by this. [3]Yet could a definition be more sure, or more in line with what salvation is? [4]Problem and answer lie together here, and having met at last the choice is clear. [5]Who chooses hell when it is recognized? [6]And who would not go on a little while when it is given him to understand the way is short and Heaven is his goal?

3. FORGIVENESS – THE FACE OF CHRIST

1. *Forgiveness* is for God and toward God but not of Him. ²It is impossible to think of anything He created that could need forgiveness. ³Forgiveness, then, is an illusion, but because of its purpose, which is the Holy Spirit's, it has one difference. ⁴Unlike all other illusions it leads away from error and not towards it.

2. Forgiveness might be called a kind of happy fiction; a way in which the unknowing can bridge the gap between their perception and the truth. ²They cannot go directly from perception to knowledge because they do not think it is their will to do so. ³This makes God appear to be an enemy instead of what He really is. ⁴And it is just this insane perception that makes them unwilling merely to rise up and to return to Him in peace.

3. And so they need an illusion of help because they are helpless; a Thought of peace because they are in conflict. ²God knows what His Son needs before he asks. ³He is not at all concerned with form, but having given the content it is His Will that it be understood. ⁴And that suffices. ⁵The form adapts itself to need; the content is unchanging, as eternal as its Creator.

4. *The face of Christ* has to be seen before the memory of God can return. ²The reason is obvious. ³Seeing the face of Christ involves perception. ⁴No one can look on knowledge. ⁵But the face of Christ is the great symbol of forgiveness. ⁶It is salvation. ⁷It is the symbol of the real world. ⁸Whoever looks on this no longer sees the world. ⁹He is as near to Heaven as is possible outside the gate. ¹⁰Yet from this gate it is no more than just a step inside. ¹¹It is the final step. ¹²And this we leave to God.

5. Forgiveness is a symbol, too, but as the symbol of His Will alone it cannot be divided. ²And so the unity that it reflects becomes His Will. ³It is the only thing still in the world in part, and yet the bridge to Heaven.

6. God's Will is all there is. ²We can but go from nothingness to everything; from hell to Heaven. ³Is this a journey? ⁴No, not in truth, for truth goes nowhere. ⁵But illusions shift from place to place; from time to time. ⁶The final step is also but a shift. ⁷As a perception it is part unreal. ⁸And yet this part will vanish. ⁹What remains is peace eternal and the Will of God.

7. There are no wishes now for wishes change. ²Even the wished-for can become unwelcome. ³That must be so because the ego

cannot be at peace. [4]But Will is constant, as the gift of God. [5]And what He gives is always like Himself. [6]This is the purpose of the face of Christ. [7]It is the gift of God to save His Son. [8]But look on this and you have been forgiven.

8. How lovely does the world become in just that single instant when you see the truth about yourself reflected there. [2]Now you are sinless and behold your sinlessness. [3]Now you are holy and perceive it so. [4]And now the mind returns to its Creator; the joining of the Father and the Son, the Unity of unities that stands behind all joining but beyond them all. [5]God is not seen but only understood. [6]His Son is not attacked but recognized.

4. TRUE PERCEPTION – KNOWLEDGE

1. The world you see is an illusion of a world. ²God did not create it, for what He creates must be eternal as Himself. ³Yet there is nothing in the world you see that will endure forever. ⁴Some things will last in time a little while longer than others. ⁵But the time will come when all things visible will have an end.

2. The body's eyes are therefore not the means by which the real world can be seen, for the illusions that they look upon must lead to more illusions of reality. ²And so they do. ³For everything they see not only will not last, but lends itself to thoughts of sin and guilt. ⁴While everything that God created is forever without sin and therefore is forever without guilt.

3. Knowledge is not the remedy for false perception since, being another level, they can never meet. ²The one correction possible for false perception must be *true perception*. ³It will not endure. ⁴But for the time it lasts it comes to heal. ⁵For true perception is a remedy with many names. ⁶Forgiveness, salvation, Atonement, true perception, all are one. ⁷They are the one beginning, with the end to lead to Oneness far beyond themselves. ⁸True perception is the means by which the world is saved from sin, for sin does not exist. ⁹And it is this that true perception sees.

4. The world stands like a block before Christ's face. ²But true perception looks on it as nothing more than just a fragile veil, so easily dispelled that it can last no longer than an instant. ³It is seen at last for only what it is. ⁴And now it cannot fail to disappear, for now there is an empty place made clean and ready. ⁵Where destruction was perceived the face of Christ appears, and in that instant is the world forgot, with time forever ended as the world spins into nothingness from where it came.

5. A world forgiven cannot last. ²It was the home of bodies. ³But forgiveness looks past bodies. ⁴This is its holiness; this is how it heals. ⁵The world of bodies is the world of sin, for only if there were a body is sin possible. ⁶From sin comes guilt as surely as forgiveness takes all guilt away. ⁷And once all guilt is gone what more remains to keep a separated world in place? ⁸For place has gone as well, along with time. ⁹Only the body makes the world seem real, for being separate it could not remain where separation is impossible. ¹⁰Forgiveness proves it is impossible because it sees it not. ¹¹And what you then will overlook will not be under-

standable to you, just as its presence once had been your certainty.

6. This is the shift that true perception brings: What was projected out is seen within, and there forgiveness lets it disappear. [2]For there the altar to the Son is set, and there his Father is remembered. [3]Here are all illusions brought to truth and laid upon the altar. [4]What is seen outside must lie beyond forgiveness, for it seems to be forever sinful. [5]Where is hope while sin is seen as outside? [6]What remedy can guilt expect? [7]But seen within your mind, guilt and forgiveness for an instant lie together, side by side, upon one altar. [8]There at last are sickness and its single remedy joined in one healing brightness. [9]God has come to claim His Own. [10]Forgiveness is complete.

7. And now God's *knowledge*, changeless, certain, pure and wholly understandable, enters its kingdom. [2]Gone is perception, false and true alike. [3]Gone is forgiveness, for its task is done. [4]And gone are bodies in the blazing light upon the altar to the Son of God. [5]God knows it is His Own, as it is his. [6]And here They join, for here the face of Christ has shone away time's final instant, and now is the last perception of the world without a purpose and without a cause. [7]For where God's memory has come at last there is no journey, no belief in sin, no walls, no bodies, and the grim appeal of guilt and death is there snuffed out forever.

8. O my brothers, if you only knew the peace that will envelop you and hold you safe and pure and lovely in the Mind of God, you could but rush to meet Him where His altar is. [2]Hallowed your Name and His, for they are joined here in this holy place. [3]Here He leans down to lift you up to Him, out of illusions into holiness; out of the world and to eternity; out of all fear and given back to love.

5. JESUS – CHRIST

1. There is no need for help to enter Heaven for you have never left. ²But there is need for help beyond yourself as you are circumscribed by false beliefs of your Identity, which God alone established in reality. ³Helpers are given you in many forms, although upon the altar they are one. ⁴Beyond each one there is a Thought of God, and this will never change. ⁵But they have names which differ for a time, for time needs symbols, being itself unreal. ⁶Their names are legion, but we will not go beyond the names the course itself employs. ⁷God does not help because He knows no need. ⁸But He creates all Helpers of His Son while he believes his fantasies are true. ⁹Thank God for them for they will lead you home.

2. The name of *Jesus* is the name of one who was a man but saw the face of Christ in all his brothers and remembered God. ²So he became identified with *Christ*, a man no longer, but at one with God. ³The man was an illusion, for he seemed to be a separate being, walking by himself, within a body that appeared to hold his self from Self, as all illusions do. ⁴Yet who can save unless he sees illusions and then identifies them as what they are? ⁵Jesus remains a Savior because he saw the false without accepting it as true. ⁶And Christ needed his form that He might appear to men and save them from their own illusions.

3. In his complete identification with the Christ—the perfect Son of God, His one creation and His happiness, forever like Himself and one with Him—Jesus became what all of you must be. ²He led the way for you to follow him. ³He leads you back to God because he saw the road before him, and he followed it. ⁴He made a clear distinction, still obscure to you, between the false and true. ⁵He offered you a final demonstration that it is impossible to kill God's Son; nor can his life in any way be changed by sin and evil, malice, fear or death.

4. And therefore all your sins have been forgiven because they carried no effects at all. ²And so they were but dreams. ³Arise with him who showed you this because you owe him this who shared your dreams that they might be dispelled. ⁴And shares them still, to be at one with you.

5. Is he the Christ? ²O yes, along with you. ³His little life on earth was not enough to teach the mighty lesson that he learned for all

of you. [4]He will remain with you to lead you from the hell you made to God. [5]And when you join your will with his, your sight will be his vision, for the eyes of Christ are shared. [6]Walking with him is just as natural as walking with a brother whom you knew since you were born, for such indeed he is. [7]Some bitter idols have been made of him who would be only brother to the world. [8]Forgive him your illusions, and behold how dear a brother he would be to you. [9]For he will set your mind at rest at last and carry it with you unto your God.

6. Is he God's only Helper? [2]No, indeed. [3]For Christ takes many forms with different names until their oneness can be recognized. [4]But Jesus is for you the bearer of Christ's single message of the Love of God. [5]You need no other. [6]It is possible to read his words and benefit from them without accepting him into your life. [7]Yet he would help you yet a little more if you will share your pains and joys with him, and leave them both to find the peace of God. [8]Yet still it is his lesson most of all that he would have you learn, and it is this:

> [9]*There is no death because the Son of God is like his Father.* [10]*Nothing you can do can change Eternal Love.* [11]*Forget your dreams of sin and guilt, and come with me instead to share the resurrection of God's Son.* [12]*And bring with you all those whom He has sent to you to care for as I care for you.*

6. THE HOLY SPIRIT

1. Jesus is the manifestation of the *Holy Spirit*, Whom he called down upon the earth after he ascended into Heaven, or became completely identified with the Christ, the Son of God as He created Him. ²The Holy Spirit, being a creation of the one Creator, creating with Him and in His likeness or spirit, is eternal and has never changed. ³He was "called down upon the earth" in the sense that it was now possible to accept Him and to hear His Voice. ⁴His is the Voice for God, and has therefore taken form. ⁵This form is not His reality, which God alone knows along with Christ, His real Son, Who is part of Him.

2. The Holy Spirit is described throughout the course as giving us the answer to the separation and bringing the plan of the Atonement to us, establishing our particular part in it and showing us exactly what it is. ²He has established Jesus as the leader in carrying out His plan since he was the first to complete his own part perfectly. ³All power in Heaven and earth is therefore given him and he will share it with you when you have completed yours. ⁴The Atonement principle was given to the Holy Spirit long before Jesus set it in motion.

3. The Holy Spirit is described as the remaining Communication Link between God and His separated Sons. ²In order to fulfill this special function the Holy Spirit has assumed a dual function. ³He knows because He is part of God; He perceives because He was sent to save humanity. ⁴He is the great correction principle; the bringer of true perception, the inherent power of the vision of Christ. ⁵He is the light in which the forgiven world is perceived; in which the face of Christ alone is seen. ⁶He never forgets the Creator or His creation. ⁷He never forgets the Son of God. ⁸He never forgets you. ⁹And He brings the Love of your Father to you in an eternal shining that will never be obliterated because God has put it there.

4. The Holy Spirit abides in the part of your mind that is part of the Christ Mind. ²He represents your Self and your Creator, Who are One. ³He speaks for God and also for you, being joined with Both. ⁴And therefore it is He Who proves Them One. ⁵He seems to be a Voice, for in that form He speaks God's Word to you. ⁶He seems to be a Guide through a far country, for you need that form of help. ⁷He seems to be whatever meets the needs you think you

have. ⁸But He is not deceived when you perceive your self entrapped in needs you do not have. ⁹It is from these He would deliver you. ¹⁰It is from these that He would make you safe.

5.   You are His manifestation in this world. ²Your brother calls to you to be His Voice along with him. ³Alone he cannot be the Helper of God's Son for he alone is functionless. ⁴But joined with you he is the shining Savior of the world, Whose part in its redemption you have made complete. ⁵He offers thanks to you as well as him for you arose with him when he began to save the world. ⁶And you will be with him when time is over and no trace remains of dreams of spite in which you dance to death's thin melody. ⁷For in its place the hymn to God is heard a little while. ⁸And then the Voice is gone, no longer to take form but to return to the eternal formlessness of God.

EPILOGUE

1. Forget not once this journey is begun the end is certain. ²Doubt along the way will come and go and go to come again. ³Yet is the ending sure. ⁴No one can fail to do what God appointed him to do. ⁵When you forget, remember that you walk with Him and with His Word upon your heart. ⁶Who could despair when hope like this is his? ⁷Illusions of despair may seem to come, but learn how not to be deceived by them. ⁸Behind each one there is reality and there is God. ⁹Why would you wait for this and trade it for illusions, when His Love is but an instant farther on the road where all illusions end? ¹⁰The end *is* sure and guaranteed by God. ¹¹Who stands before a lifeless image when a step away the Holy of the Holies opens up an ancient door that leads beyond the world?

2. You *are* a stranger here. ²But you belong to Him Who loves you as He loves Himself. ³Ask but my help to roll the stone away, and it is done according to His Will. ⁴We *have* begun the journey. ⁵Long ago the end was written in the stars and set into the Heavens with a shining Ray that held it safe within eternity and through all time as well. ⁶And holds it still; unchanged, unchanging and unchangeable.

3. Be not afraid. ²We only start again an ancient journey long ago begun that but seems new. ³We have begun again upon a road we travelled on before and lost our way a little while. ⁴And now we try again. ⁵Our new beginning has the certainty the journey lacked till now. ⁶Look up and see His Word among the stars, where He has set your Name along with His. ⁷Look up and find your certain destiny the world would hide but God would have you see.

4. Let us wait here in silence, and kneel down an instant in our gratitude to Him Who called to us and helped us hear His Call. ²And then let us arise and go in faith along the way to Him. ³Now we are sure we do not walk alone. ⁴For God is here, and with Him all our brothers. ⁵Now we know that we will never lose the way again. ⁶The song begins again which had been stopped only an instant, though it seems to be unsung forever. ⁷What is here begun will grow in life and strength and hope, until the world is still an instant and forgets all that the dream of sin had made of it.

5. Let us go out and meet the newborn world, knowing that

Christ has been reborn in it, and that the holiness of this rebirth will last forever. [2]We had lost our way but He has found it for us. [3]Let us go and bid Him welcome Who returns to us to celebrate salvation and the end of all we thought we made. [4]The morning star of this new day looks on a different world where God is welcomed and His Son with Him. [5]We who complete Him offer thanks to Him, as He gives thanks to us. [6]The Son is still, and in the quiet God has given him enters his home and is at peace at last.

Supplements to
A Course in Miracles

PSYCHOTHERAPY:
Purpose, Process and Practice

THE SONG OF PRAYER
Prayer, Forgiveness, Healing

FOUNDATION FOR INNER PEACE

The two supplements *Psychotherapy: Purpose, Process, Practice* and *The Song of Prayer* were scribed by Dr. Helen Schucman, as was *A Course in Miracles*, and are extensions of its principles.

Psychotherapy, begun in 1973 and completed in 1975, offers a summary of the Course's principles of healing: two people joined in sharing a common interest or goal. While ostensibly written for psychotherapists, all readers can benefit from its teachings.

The Song of Prayer was scribed in 1977, and its three chapters summarize the Course's teachings on *prayer, forgiveness,* and *healing.* It first presents the ego's wrong-minded understanding of these terms, which is then contrasted with the Holy Spirit's right-minded view.

These supplements presuppose a basic understanding of the Course's teachings, and are helpful adjuncts to a student's study and practice of *A Course in Miracles.*

PSYCHOTHERAPY:
Purpose, Process and Practice

An Extension of the Principles of
A Course in Miracles

FOUNDATION FOR INNER PEACE

CONTENTS

CONTENTS

INTRODUCTION

1. Psychotherapy is the only form of therapy there is. ²Since only the mind can be sick, only the mind can be healed. ³Only the mind is in need of healing. ⁴This does not appear to be the case, for the manifestations of this world seem real indeed. ⁵Psychotherapy is necessary so that an individual can begin to question their reality. ⁶Sometimes he is able to start to open his mind without formal help, but even then it is always some change in his perception of interpersonal relationships that enables him to do so. ⁷Sometimes he needs a more structured, extended relationship with an "official" therapist. ⁸Either way, the task is the same; the patient must be helped to change his mind about the "reality" of illusions.

1. THE PURPOSE OF PSYCHOTHERAPY

1. Very simply, the purpose of psychotherapy is to remove the blocks to truth. [2]Its aim is to aid the patient in abandoning his fixed delusional system, and to begin to reconsider the spurious cause and effect relationships on which it rests. [3]No one in this world escapes fear, but everyone can reconsider its causes and learn to evaluate them correctly. [4]God has given everyone a Teacher Whose wisdom and help far exceed whatever contributions an earthly therapist can provide. [5]Yet there are times and situations in which an earthly patient-therapist relationship becomes the means through which He offers His greater gifts to both.

2. What better purpose could any relationship have than to invite the Holy Spirit to enter into it and give it His Own great gift of rejoicing? [2]What higher goal could there be for anyone than to learn to call upon God and hear His Answer? [3]And what more transcendent aim can there be than to recall the way, the truth and the life, and to remember God? [4]To help in this is the proper purpose of psychotherapy. [5]Could anything be holier? [6]For psychotherapy, correctly understood, teaches forgiveness and helps the patient to recognize and accept it. [7]And in his healing is the therapist forgiven with him.

3. Everyone who needs help, regardless of the form of his distress, is attacking himself, and his peace of mind is suffering in consequence. [2]These tendencies are often described as "self-destructive," and the patient often regards them in that way himself. [3]What he does not realize and needs to learn is that this "self," which can attack and be attacked as well, is a concept he made up. [4]Further, he cherishes it, defends it, and is sometimes even willing to "sacrifice" his "life" on its behalf. [5]For he regards it as himself. [6]This self he sees as being acted on, reacting to external forces as they demand, and helpless midst the power of the world.

4. Psychotherapy, then, must restore to his awareness the ability to make his own decisions. [2]He must become willing to reverse his thinking, and to understand that what he thought projected its effects on him were made by his projections on the world. [3]The world he sees does therefore not exist. [4]Until this is at least

in part accepted, the patient cannot see himself as really capable of making decisions. [5]And he will fight against his freedom because he thinks that it is slavery.

5. The patient need not think of truth as God in order to make progress in salvation. [2]But he must begin to separate truth from illusion, recognizing that they are not the same, and becoming increasingly willing to see illusions as false and to accept the truth as true. [3]His Teacher will take him on from there, as far as he is ready to go. [4]Psychotherapy can only save him time. [5]The Holy Spirit uses time as He thinks best, and He is never wrong. [6]Psychotherapy under His direction is one of the means He uses to save time, and to prepare additional teachers for His work. [7]There is no end to the help that He begins and He directs. [8]By whatever routes He chooses, all psychotherapy leads to God in the end. [9]But that is up to Him. [10]We are all His psychotherapists, for He would have us all be healed in Him.

2. THE PROCESS OF PSYCHOTHERAPY

Introduction

1. Psychotherapy is a process that changes the view of the self. [2]At best this "new" self is a more beneficent self-concept, but psychotherapy can hardly be expected to establish reality. [3]That is not its function. [4]If it can make way for reality, it has achieved its ultimate success. [5]Its whole function, in the end, is to help the patient deal with one fundamental error; the belief that anger brings him something he really wants, and that by justifying attack he is protecting himself. [6]To whatever extent he comes to realize that this is an error, to that extent is he truly saved.

2. Patients do not enter the therapeutic relationship with this goal in mind. [2]On the contrary, such concepts mean little to them, or they would not need help. [3]Their aim is to be able to retain their self-concept exactly as it is, but without the suffering that it entails. [4]Their whole equilibrium rests on the insane belief that this is possible. [5]And because to the sane mind it is so clearly impossible, what they seek is magic. [6]In illusions the impossible is easily accomplished, but only at the cost of making illusions true. [7]The patient has already paid this price. [8]Now he wants a "better" illusion.

3. At the beginning, then, the patient's goal and the therapist's are at variance. [2]The therapist as well as the patient may cherish false self-concepts, but their respective perceptions of "improvement" still must differ. [3]The patient hopes to learn how to get the changes he wants without changing his self-concept to any significant extent. [4]He hopes, in fact, to stabilize it sufficiently to include within it the magical powers he seeks in psychotherapy. [5]He wants to make the vulnerable invulnerable and the finite limitless. [6]The self he sees is his god, and he seeks only to serve it better.

4. Regardless of how sincere the therapist himself may be, he must want to change the patient's self-concept in some way that he believes is real. [2]The task of therapy is one of reconciling these differences. [3]Hopefully, both will learn to give up their original goals, for it is only in relationships that salvation can be found. [4]At the beginning, it is inevitable that patients and therapists alike accept unrealistic goals not completely free of magical overtones. [5]They are finally given up in the minds of both.

4

I. The Limits on Psychotherapy

1. Yet the ideal outcome is rarely achieved. [2]Therapy begins with the realization that healing is of the mind, and in psychotherapy those have come together who already believe this. [3]It may be they will not get much further, for no one learns beyond his own readiness. [4]Yet levels of readiness change, and when therapist or patient has reached the next one, there will be a relationship held out to them that meets the changing need. [5]Perhaps they will come together again and advance in the same relationship, making it holier. [6]Or perhaps each of them will enter into another commitment. [7]Be assured of this; each will progress. [8]Retrogression is temporary. [9]The overall direction is one of progress toward the truth.

2. Psychotherapy itself cannot be creative. [2]This is one of the errors which the ego fosters; that it is capable of true change, and therefore of true creativity. [3]When we speak of "the saving illusion" or "the final dream," this is not what we mean, but here is the ego's last defense. [4]"Resistance" is its way of looking at things; its interpretation of progress and growth. [5]These interpretations will be wrong of necessity, because they are delusional. [6]The changes the ego seeks to make are not really changes. [7]They are but deeper shadows, or perhaps different cloud patterns. [8]Yet what is made of nothingness cannot be called new or different. [9]Illusions are illusions; truth is truth.

3. Resistance as defined here can be characteristic of a therapist as well as of a patient. [2]Either way, it sets a limit on psychotherapy because it restricts its aims. [3]Nor can the Holy Spirit fight against the intrusions of the ego on the therapeutic process. [4]But He will wait, and His patience is infinite. [5]His goal is wholly undivided always. [6]Whatever resolutions patient and therapist reach in connection with their own divergent goals, they cannot become completely reconciled as one until they join with His. [7]Only then is all conflict over, for only then can there be certainty.

4. Ideally, psychotherapy is a series of holy encounters in which brothers meet to bless each other and to receive the peace of God. [2]And this will one day come to pass for every "patient" on the face of this earth, for who except a patient could possibly have come here? [3]The therapist is only a somewhat more specialized teacher of God. [4]He learns through teaching, and the more advanced he is the more he teaches and the more he learns. [5]But

whatever stage he is in, there are patients who need him just that way. [6]They cannot take more than he can give for now. [7]Yet both will find sanity at last.

II. The Place of Religion in Psychotherapy

1. To be a teacher of God, it is not necessary to be religious or even to believe in God to any recognizable extent. [2]It is necessary, however, to teach forgiveness rather than condemnation. [3]Even in this, complete consistency is not required, for one who had achieved that point could teach salvation completely, within an instant and without a word. [4]Yet he who has learned all things does not need a teacher, and the healed have no need for a therapist. [5]Relationships are still the temple of the Holy Spirit, and they will be made perfect in time and restored to eternity.

2. Formal religion has no place in psychotherapy, but it also has no real place in religion. [2]In this world, there is an astonishing tendency to join contradictory words into one term without perceiving the contradiction at all. [3]The attempt to formalize religion is so obviously an ego attempt to reconcile the irreconcilable that it hardly requires elaboration here. [4]Religion is experience; psychotherapy is experience. [5]At the highest levels they become one. [6]Neither is truth itself, but both can lead to truth. [7]What can be necessary to find truth, which remains perfectly obvious, but to remove the seeming obstacles to true awareness?

3. No one who learns to forgive can fail to remember God. [2]Forgiveness, then, is all that need be taught, because it is all that need be learned. [3]All blocks to the remembrance of God are forms of unforgiveness, and nothing else. [4]This is never apparent to the patient, and only rarely so to the therapist. [5]The world has marshalled all its forces against this one awareness, for in it lies the ending of the world and all it stands for.

4. Yet it is not the awareness of God that constitutes a reasonable goal for psychotherapy. [2]This will come when psychotherapy is complete, for where there is forgiveness truth must come. [3]It would be unfair indeed if belief in God were necessary to psychotherapeutic success. [4]Nor is belief in God a really meaningful concept, for God can be but known. [5]Belief implies that unbelief is possible, but knowledge of God has no true opposite. [6]Not to know God is to have no knowledge, and it is to this that all

6

unforgiveness leads. [7]And without knowledge one can have only belief.

5. Different teaching aids appeal to different people. [2]Some forms of religion have nothing to do with God, and some forms of psychotherapy have nothing to do with healing. [3]Yet if pupil and teacher join in sharing one goal, God will enter into their relationship because He has been invited to come in. [4]In the same way, a union of purpose between patient and therapist restores the place of God to ascendance, first through Christ's vision and then through the memory of God Himself. [5]The process of psychotherapy is the return to sanity. [6]Teacher and pupil, therapist and patient, are all insane or they would not be here. [7]Together they can find a pathway out, for no one will find sanity alone.

6. If healing is an invitation to God to enter into His Kingdom, what difference does it make how the invitation is written? [2]Does the paper matter, or the ink, or the pen? [3]Or is it he who writes that gives the invitation? [4]God comes to those who would restore His world, for they have found the way to call to Him. [5]If any two are joined, He must be there. [6]It does not matter what their purpose is, but they must share it wholly to succeed. [7]It is impossible to share a goal not blessed by Christ, for what is unseen through His eyes is too fragmented to be meaningful.

7. As true religion heals, so must true psychotherapy be religious. [2]But both have many forms, because no good teacher uses one approach to every pupil. [3]On the contrary, he listens patiently to each one, and lets him formulate his own curriculum; not the curriculum's goal, but how he can best reach the aim it sets for him. [4]Perhaps the teacher does not think of God as part of teaching. [5]Perhaps the psychotherapist does not understand that healing comes from God. [6]They can succeed where many who believe they have found God will fail.

8. What must the teacher do to ensure learning? [2]What must the therapist do to bring healing about? [3]Only one thing; the same requirement salvation asks of everyone. [4]Each one must share one goal with someone else, and in so doing, lose all sense of separate interests. [5]Only by doing this is it possible to transcend the narrow boundaries the ego would impose upon the self. [6]Only by doing this can teacher and pupil, therapist and patient, you and I, accept Atonement and learn to give it as it was received.

9. Communion is impossible alone. [2]No one who stands apart can receive Christ's vision. [3]It is held out to him, but he cannot hold

out his hand to receive it. ⁴Let him be still and recognize his brother's need is his own. ⁵And let him then meet his brother's need as his and see that they are met as one, for such they are. ⁶What is religion but an aid in helping him to see that this is so? ⁷And what is psychotherapy except a help in just this same direction? ⁸It is the goal that makes these processes the same, for they are one in purpose and must thus be one in means.

III. The Role of the Psychotherapist

1. The psychotherapist is a leader in the sense that he walks slightly ahead of the patient, and helps him to avoid a few of the pitfalls along the road by seeing them first. ²Ideally, he is also a follower, for One should walk ahead of him to give him light to see. ³Without this One, both will merely stumble blindly on to nowhere. ⁴It is, however, impossible that this One be wholly absent if the goal is healing. ⁵He may, however, not be recognized. ⁶And so the little light that can be then accepted is all there is to light the way to truth.

2. Healing is limited by the limitations of the psychotherapist, as it is limited by those of the patient. ²The aim of the process, therefore, is to transcend these limits. ³Neither can do this alone, but when they join, the potentiality for transcending all limitations has been given them. ⁴Now the extent of their success depends on how much of this potentiality they are willing to use. ⁵The willingness may come from either one at the beginning, and as the other shares it, it will grow. ⁶Progress becomes a matter of decision; it can reach almost to Heaven or go no further than a step or two from hell.

3. It is quite possible for psychotherapy to seem to fail. ²It is even possible for the result to look like retrogression. ³But in the end there must be some success. ⁴One asks for help; another hears and tries to answer in the form of help. ⁵This is the formula for salvation, and must heal. ⁶Divided goals alone can interfere with perfect healing. ⁷One wholly egoless therapist could heal the world without a word, merely by being there. ⁸No one need see him or talk to him or even know of his existence. ⁹His simple Presence is enough to heal.

4. The ideal therapist is one with Christ. ²But healing is a process, not a fact. ³The therapist cannot progress without the patient, and

the patient cannot be ready to receive the Christ or he could not be sick. ⁴In a sense, the egoless psychotherapist is an abstraction that stands at the end of the process of healing, too advanced to believe in sickness and too near to God to keep his feet on earth. ⁵Now he can help through those in need of help, for thus he carries out the plan established for salvation. ⁶The psychotherapist becomes his patient, working through other patients to express his thoughts as he receives them from the Mind of Christ.

IV. The Process of Illness

1. As all therapy is psychotherapy, so all illness is mental illness. ²It is a judgment on the Son of God, and judgment is a mental activity. ³Judgment is a decision, made again and again, against creation and its Creator. ⁴It is a decision to perceive the universe as you would have created it. ⁵It is a decision that truth can lie and must be lies. ⁶What, then, can illness be except an expression of sorrow and of guilt? ⁷And who could weep but for his innocence?

2. Once God's Son is seen as guilty, illness becomes inevitable. ²It has been asked for and will be received. ³And all who ask for illness have now condemned themselves to seek for remedies that cannot help, because their faith is in the illness and not in salvation. ⁴There can be nothing that a change of mind cannot effect, for all external things are only shadows of a decision already made. ⁵Change the decision, and how can its shadow be unchanged? ⁶Illness can be but guilt's shadow, grotesque and ugly since it mimics deformity. ⁷If a deformity is seen as real, what could its shadow be except deformed?

3. The descent into hell follows step by step in an inevitable course, once the decision that guilt is real has been made. ²Sickness and death and misery now stalk the earth in unrelenting waves, sometimes together and sometimes in grim succession. ³Yet all these things, however real they seem, are but illusions. ⁴Who could have faith in them once this is realized? ⁵And who could not have faith in them until he realizes this? ⁶Healing is therapy or correction, and we have said already and will say again, all therapy is psychotherapy. ⁷To heal the sick is but to bring this realization to them.

4. The word "cure" has come into disrepute among the more "respectable" therapists of the world, and justly so. ²For not one of

them can cure, and not one of them understands healing. ³At worst, they but make the body real in their own minds, and having done so, seek for magic by which to heal the ills with which their minds endow it. ⁴How could such a process cure? ⁵It is ridiculous from start to finish. ⁶Yet having started, it must finish thus. ⁷It is as if God were the devil and must be found in evil. ⁸How could love be there? ⁹And how could sickness cure? ¹⁰Are not these both one question?

5. At best, and the word is perhaps questionable here, the "healers" of the world may recognize the mind as the source of illness. ²But their error lies in the belief that it can cure itself. ³This has some merit in a world where "degrees of error" is a meaningful concept. ⁴Yet must their cures remain temporary, or another illness rise instead, for death has not been overcome until the meaning of love is understood. ⁵And who can understand this without the Word of God, given by Him to the Holy Spirit as His gift to you?

6. Illness of any kind may be defined as the result of a view of the self as weak, vulnerable, evil and endangered, and thus in need of constant defense. ²Yet if such were really the self, defense would be impossible. ³Therefore, the defenses sought for must be magical. ⁴They must overcome all limits perceived in the self, at the same time making a new self-concept into which the old one cannot return. ⁵In a word, error is accepted as real and dealt with by illusions. ⁶Truth being brought to illusions, reality now becomes a threat and is perceived as evil. ⁷Love becomes feared because reality is love. ⁸Thus is the circle closed against the "inroads" of salvation.

7. Illness is therefore a mistake and needs correction. ²And as we have already emphasized, correction cannot be achieved by first establishing the "rightness" of the mistake and then overlooking it. ³If illness is real it cannot be overlooked in truth, for to overlook reality is insanity. ⁴Yet that is magic's purpose; to make illusions true through false perception. ⁵This cannot heal, for it opposes truth. ⁶Perhaps an illusion of health is substituted for a little while, but not for long. ⁷Fear cannot long be hidden by illusions, for it is part of them. ⁸It will escape and take another form, being the source of all illusions.

8. Sickness is insanity because all sickness is mental illness, and in it there are no degrees. ²One of the illusions by which sickness is perceived as real is the belief that illness varies in intensity; that

the degree of threat differs according to the form it takes. ³Herein lies the basis of all errors, for all of them are but attempts to compromise by seeing just a little bit of hell. ⁴This is a mockery so alien to God that it must be forever inconceivable. ⁵But the insane believe it because they are insane.

9. A madman will defend his own illusions because in them he sees his own salvation. ²Thus, he will attack the one who tries to save him from them, believing that he is attacking him. ³This curious circle of attack-defense is one of the most difficult problems with which the psychotherapist must deal. ⁴In fact, this is his central task; the core of psychotherapy. ⁵The therapist is seen as one who is attacking the patient's most cherished possession; his picture of himself. ⁶And since this picture has become the patient's security as he perceives it, the therapist cannot but be seen as a real source of danger, to be attacked and even killed.

10. The psychotherapist, then, has a tremendous responsibility. ²He must meet attack without attack, and therefore without defense. ³It is his task to demonstrate that defenses are not necessary, and that defenselessness is strength. ⁴This must be his teaching, if his lesson is to be that sanity is safe. ⁵It cannot be too strongly emphasized that the insane believe that sanity is threat. ⁶This is the corollary of the "original sin"; the belief that guilt is real and fully justified. ⁷It is therefore the psychotherapist's function to teach that guilt, being unreal, cannot be justified. ⁸But neither is it safe. ⁹And thus it must remain unwanted as well as unreal.

11. Salvation's single doctrine is the goal of all therapy. ²Relieve the mind of the insane burden of guilt it carries so wearily, and healing is accomplished. ³The body is not cured. ⁴It is merely recognized as what it is. ⁵Seen rightly, its purpose can be understood. ⁶What is the need for sickness then? ⁷Given this single shift, all else will follow. ⁸There is no need for complicated change. ⁹There is no need for long analyses and wearying discussion and pursuits. ¹⁰The truth is simple, being one for all.

V. The Process of Healing

1. While truth is simple, it must still be taught to those who have already lost their way in endless mazes of complexity. ²This is the great illusion. ³In its wake comes the inevitable belief that, to be safe, one must control the unknown. ⁴This strange belief relies on

certain steps which never reach to consciousness. [5]First, it is ushered in by the belief that there are forces to be overcome to be alive at all. [6]And next, it seems as if these forces can be held at bay only by an inflated sense of self that holds in darkness what is truly felt, and seeks to raise illusions to the light.

2. Let us remember that the ones who come to us for help are bitterly afraid. [2]What they believe will help can only harm; what they believe will harm alone can help. [3]Progress becomes impossible until the patient is persuaded to reverse his twisted way of looking at the world; his twisted way of looking at himself. [4]The truth is simple. [5]Yet it must be taught to those who think it will endanger them. [6]It must be taught to those who will attack because they feel endangered, and to those who need the lesson of defenselessness above all else, to show them what is strength.

3. If this world were ideal, there could perhaps be ideal therapy. [2]And yet it would be useless in an ideal state. [3]We speak of ideal teaching in a world in which the perfect teacher could not long remain; the perfect psychotherapist is but a glimmer of a thought not yet conceived. [4]But still we speak of what can yet be done in helping the insane within the bounds of the attainable. [5]While they are sick, they can and must be helped. [6]No more than that is asked of psychotherapy; no less than all he has to give is worthy of the therapist. [7]For God Himself holds out his brother as his savior from the world.

4. Healing is holy. [2]Nothing in the world is holier than helping one who asks for help. [3]And two come very close to God in this attempt, however limited, however lacking in sincerity. [4]Where two have joined for healing, God is there. [5]And He has guaranteed that He will hear and answer them in truth. [6]They can be sure that healing is a process He directs, because it is according to His Will. [7]We have His Word to guide us, as we try to help our brothers. [8]Let us not forget that we are helpless of ourselves, and lean upon a strength beyond our little scope for what to teach as well as what to learn.

5. A brother seeking aid can bring us gifts beyond the heights perceived in any dream. [2]He offers us salvation, for he comes to us as Christ and Savior. [3]What he asks is asked by God through him. [4]And what we do for him becomes the gift we give to God. [5]The sacred calling of God's holy Son for help in his perceived distress can be but answered by his Father. [6]Yet He needs a voice through which to speak His holy Word; a hand to reach His Son and touch

his heart. ⁷In such a process, who could not be healed? ⁸This holy interaction is the plan of God Himself, by which His Son is saved.

6. For two have joined. ²And now God's promises are kept by Him. ³The limits laid on both the patient and the therapist will count as nothing, for the healing has begun. ⁴What they must start their Father will complete. ⁵For He has never asked for more than just the smallest willingness, the least advance, the tiniest of whispers of His Name. ⁶To ask for help, whatever form it takes, is but to call on Him. ⁷And He will send His Answer through the therapist who best can serve His Son in all his present needs. ⁸Perhaps the answer does not seem to be a gift from Heaven. ⁹It may even seem to be a worsening and not a help. ¹⁰Yet let the outcome not be judged by us.

7. Somewhere all gifts of God must be received. ²In time no effort can be made in vain. ³It is not our perfection that is asked in our attempts to heal. ⁴We are deceived already, if we think there is a need of healing. ⁵And the truth will come to us only through one who seems to share our dream of sickness. ⁶Let us help him to forgive himself for all the trespasses with which he would condemn himself without a cause. ⁷His healing is our own. ⁸And as we see the sinlessness in him come shining through the veil of guilt that shrouds the Son of God, we will behold in him the face of Christ, and understand that it is but our own.

8. Let us stand silently before God's Will, and do what it has chosen that we do. ²There is one way alone by which we come to where all dreams began. ³And it is there that we will lay them down, to come away in peace forever. ⁴Hear a brother call for help and answer him. ⁵It will be God to Whom you answer, for you called on Him. ⁶There is no other way to hear His Voice. ⁷There is no other way to seek His Son. ⁸There is no other way to find your Self. ⁹Holy is healing, for the Son of God returns to Heaven through its kind embrace. ¹⁰For healing tells him, in the Voice for God, that all his sins have been forgiven him.

VI. The Definition of Healing

1. The process of psychotherapy, then, can be defined simply as forgiveness, for no healing can be anything else. ²The unforgiving are sick, believing they are unforgiven. ³The hanging-on to guilt, its hugging-close and sheltering, its loving protection and alert

defense,—all this is but the grim refusal to forgive. [4]"God may not enter here" the sick repeat, over and over, while they mourn their loss and yet rejoice in it. [5]Healing occurs as a patient begins to hear the dirge he sings, and questions its validity. [6]Until he hears it, he cannot understand that it is he who sings it to himself. [7]To hear it is the first step in recovery. [8]To question it must then become his choice.

2. There is a tendency, and it is very strong, to hear this song of death only an instant, and then dismiss it uncorrected. [2]These fleeting awarenesses represent the many opportunities given us literally "to change our tune." [3]The sound of healing can be heard instead. [4]But first the willingness to question the "truth" of the song of condemnation must arise. [5]The strange distortions woven inextricably into the self-concept, itself but a pseudo-creation, make this ugly sound seem truly beautiful. [6]"The rhythm of the universe," "the herald angel's song," all these and more are heard instead of loud discordant shrieks.

3. The ear translates; it does not hear. [2]The eye reproduces; it does not see. [3]Their task is to make agreeable whatever is called on, however disagreeable it may be. [4]They answer the decisions of the mind, reproducing its desires and translating them into acceptable and pleasant forms. [5]Sometimes the thought behind the form breaks through, but only very briefly, and the mind grows fearful and begins to doubt its sanity. [6]Yet it will not permit its slaves to change the forms they look upon; the sounds they hear. [7]These are its "remedies"; its "safeguards" from insanity.

4. These testimonies which the senses bring have but one purpose; to justify attack and thus keep unforgiveness unrecognized for what it is. [2]Seen undisguised it is intolerable. [3]Without protection it could not endure. [4]Here is all sickness cherished, but without the recognition that this is so. [5]For when an unforgiveness is not recognized, the form it takes seems to be something else. [6]And now it is the "something else" that seems to terrify. [7]But it is not the "something else" that can be healed. [8]It is not sick, and needs no remedy. [9]To concentrate your healing efforts here is but futility. [10]Who can cure what cannot be sick and make it well?

5. Sickness takes many forms, and so does unforgiveness. [2]The forms of one but reproduce the forms of the other, for they are the same illusion. [3]So closely is one translated into the other, that a careful study of the form a sickness takes will point quite clearly to the form of unforgiveness that it represents. [4]Yet seeing this

will not effect a cure. ⁵That is achieved by only one recognition; that only forgiveness heals an unforgiveness, and only an unforgiveness can possibly give rise to sickness of any kind.

6. This realization is the final goal of psychotherapy. ²How is it reached? ³The therapist sees in the patient all that he has not forgiven in himself, and is thus given another chance to look at it, open it to re-evaluation and forgive it. ⁴When this occurs, he sees his sins as gone into a past that is no longer here. ⁵Until he does this, he must think of evil as besetting him here and now. ⁶The patient is his screen for the projection of his sins, enabling him to let them go. ⁷Let him retain one spot of sin in what he looks upon, and his release is partial and will not be sure.

7. No one is healed alone. ²This is the joyous song salvation sings to all who hear its Voice. ³This statement cannot be too often remembered by all who see themselves as therapists. ⁴Their patients can but be seen as the bringers of forgiveness, for it is they who come to demonstrate their sinlessness to eyes that still believe that sin is there to look upon. ⁵Yet will the proof of sinlessness, seen in the patient and accepted in the therapist, offer the mind of both a covenant in which they meet and join and are as one.

VII. The Ideal Patient-Therapist Relationship

1. Who, then, is the therapist, and who is the patient? ²In the end, everyone is both. ³He who needs healing must heal. ⁴Physician, heal thyself. ⁵Who else is there to heal? ⁶And who else is in need of healing? ⁷Each patient who comes to a therapist offers him a chance to heal himself. ⁸He is therefore his therapist. ⁹And every therapist must learn to heal from each patient who comes to him. ¹⁰He thus becomes his patient. ¹¹God does not know of separation. ¹²What He knows is only that He has one Son. ¹³His knowledge is reflected in the ideal patient-therapist relationship. ¹⁴God comes to him who calls, and in Him he recognizes Himself.

2. Think carefully, teacher and therapist, for whom you pray, and who is in need of healing. ²For therapy is prayer, and healing is its aim and its result. ³What is prayer except the joining of minds in a relationship which Christ can enter? ⁴This is His home, into which psychotherapy invites Him. ⁵What is symptom cure, when another is always there to choose? ⁶But once Christ enters in, what choice is there except to have Him stay? ⁷There is no need for

more than this, for it is everything. [8]Healing is here, and happiness and peace. [9]These are the "symptoms" of the ideal patient-therapist relationship, replacing those with which the patient came to ask for help.

3. The process that takes place in this relationship is actually one in which the therapist in his heart tells the patient that all his sins have been forgiven him, along with his own. [2]What could be the difference between healing and forgiveness? [3]Only Christ forgives, knowing His sinlessness. [4]His vision heals perception and sickness disappears. [5]Nor will it return again, once its cause has been removed. [6]This, however, needs the help of a very advanced therapist, capable of joining with the patient in a holy relationship in which all sense of separation finally is overcome.

4. For this, one thing and one thing only is required: The therapist in no way confuses himself with God. [2]All "unhealed healers" make this fundamental confusion in one form or another, because they must regard themselves as self-created rather than God-created. [3]This confusion is rarely if ever in awareness, or the unhealed healer would instantly become a teacher of God, devoting his life to the function of true healing. [4]Before he reached this point, he thought he was in charge of the therapeutic process and was therefore responsible for its outcome. [5]His patient's errors thus became his own failures, and guilt became the cover, dark and strong, for what should be the Holiness of Christ. [6]Guilt is inevitable in those who use their judgment in making their decisions. [7]Guilt is impossible in those through whom the Holy Spirit speaks.

5. The passing of guilt is the true aim of therapy and the obvious aim of forgiveness. [2]In this their oneness can be clearly seen. [3]Yet who could experience the end of guilt who feels responsible for his brother in the role of guide for him? [4]Such a function presupposes a knowledge that no one here can have; a certainty of past, present and future, and of all the effects that may occur in them. [5]Only from this omniscient point of view would such a role be possible. [6]Yet no perception is omniscient, nor is the tiny self of one alone against the universe able to assume he has such wisdom except in madness. [7]That many therapists are mad is obvious. [8]No unhealed healer can be wholly sane.

6. Yet it is as insane not to accept a function God has given you as to invent one He has not. [2]The advanced therapist in no way can ever doubt the power that is in him. [3]Nor does he doubt its Source.

[4]He understands all power in earth and Heaven belongs to him because of who he is. [5]And he is this because of his Creator, Whose Love is in him and Who cannot fail. [6]Think what this means; he has the gifts of God Himself to give away. [7]His patients are God's saints, who call upon his sanctity to make it theirs. [8]And as he gives it to them, they behold Christ's shining face as it looks back at them.

7. The insane, thinking they are God, are not afraid to offer weakness to God's Son. [2]But what they see in him because of this they fear indeed. [3]The unhealed healer cannot but be fearful of his patients, and suspect them of the treachery he sees in him. [4]He tries to heal, and thus at times he may. [5]But he will not succeed except to some extent and for a little while. [6]He does not see the Christ in him who calls. [7]What answer can he give to one who seems to be a stranger; alien to the truth and poor in wisdom, without the god who must be given him? [8]Behold your God in him, for what you see will be your Answer.

8. Think what the joining of two brothers really means. [2]And then forget the world and all its little triumphs and its dreams of death. [3]The same are one, and nothing now can be remembered of the world of guilt. [4]The room becomes a temple, and the street a stream of stars that brushes lightly past all sickly dreams. [5]Healing is done, for what is perfect needs no healing, and what remains to be forgiven where there is no sin?

9. Be thankful, therapist, that you can see such things as this, if you but understand your proper role. [2]But if you fail in this, you have denied that God created you, and so you will not know you are His Son. [3]Who is your brother now? [4]What saint can come to take you home with him? [5]You lost the way. [6]And can you now expect to see in him an answer that you have refused to give? [7]Heal and be healed. [8]There is no other choice of pathways that can ever lead to peace. [9]O let your patient in, for he has come to you from God. [10]Is not his holiness enough to wake your memory of Him?

3. THE PRACTICE OF PSYCHOTHERAPY

I. The Selection of Patients

1. Everyone who is sent to you is a patient of yours. ²This does not mean that you select him, nor that you choose the kind of treatment that is suitable. ³But it does mean that no one comes to you by mistake. ⁴There are no errors in God's plan. ⁵It would be an error, however, to assume that you know what to offer everyone who comes. ⁶This is not up to you to decide. ⁷There is a tendency to assume that you are being called on constantly to make sacrifices of yourself for those who come. ⁸This could hardly be true. ⁹To demand sacrifice of yourself is to demand a sacrifice of God, and He knows nothing of sacrifice. ¹⁰Who could ask of Perfection that He be imperfect?

2. Who, then, decides what each brother needs? ²Surely not you, who do not yet recognize who he is who asks. ³There is Something in him that will tell you, if you listen. ⁴And that is the answer; listen. ⁵Do not demand, do not decide, do not sacrifice. ⁶Listen. ⁷What you hear is true. ⁸Would God send His Son to you and not be sure you recognize his needs? ⁹Think what God is telling you; He needs your voice to speak for Him. ¹⁰Could anything be holier? ¹¹Or a greater gift to you? ¹²Would you rather choose who would be god, or hear the Voice of Him Who is God in you?

3. Your patients need not be physically present for you to serve them in the Name of God. ²This may be hard to remember, but God will not have His gifts to you limited to the few you actually see. ³You can see others as well, for seeing is not limited to the body's eyes. ⁴Some do not need your physical presence. ⁵They need you as much, and perhaps even more, at the instant they are sent. ⁶You will recognize them in whatever way can be most helpful to both of you. ⁷It does not matter how they come. ⁸They will be sent in whatever form is most helpful; a name, a thought, a picture, an idea, or perhaps just a feeling of reaching out to someone somewhere. ⁹The joining is in the hands of the Holy Spirit. ¹⁰It cannot fail to be accomplished.

4. A holy therapist, an advanced teacher of God, never forgets one thing; he did not make the curriculum of salvation, nor did he establish his part in it. ²He understands that his part is necessary to the whole, and that through it he will recognize the whole when

his part is complete. ³Meanwhile he must learn, and his patients are the means sent to him for his learning. ⁴What could he be but grateful for them and to them? ⁵They come bearing God. ⁶Would he refuse this Gift for a pebble, or would he close the door on the savior of the world to let in a ghost? ⁷Let him not betray the Son of God. ⁸Who calls on him is far beyond his understanding. ⁹Yet would he not rejoice that he can answer, when only thus will he be able to hear the call and understand that it is his?

II. Is Psychotherapy a Profession?

1. Strictly speaking the answer is no. ²How could a separate profession be one in which everyone is engaged? ³And how could any limits be laid on an interaction in which everyone is both patient and therapist in every relationship in which he enters? ⁴Yet practically speaking, it can still be said that there are those who devote themselves primarily to healing of one sort or another as their chief function. ⁵And it is to them that a large number of others turn for help. ⁶That, in effect, is the practice of therapy. ⁷These are therefore "officially" helpers. ⁸They are devoted to certain kinds of needs in their professional activities, although they may be far more able teachers outside of them. ⁹These people need no special rules, of course, but they may be called upon to use special applications of the general principles of healing.

2. First, the professional therapist is in an excellent position to demonstrate that there is no order of difficulty in healing. ²For this, however, he needs special training, because the curriculum by which he became a therapist probably taught him little or nothing about the real principles of healing. ³In fact, it probably taught him how to make healing impossible. ⁴Most of the world's teaching follows a curriculum in judgment, with the aim of making the therapist a judge.

3. Even this the Holy Spirit can use, and will use, given the slightest invitation. ²The unhealed healer may be arrogant, selfish, unconcerned, and actually dishonest. ³He may be uninterested in healing as his major goal. ⁴Yet something happened to him, however slight it may have been, when he chose to be a healer, however misguided the direction he may have chosen. ⁵That "something" is enough. ⁶Sooner or later that something will rise and grow; a patient will touch his heart, and the therapist will silently ask him for

help. 7He has himself found a therapist. 8He has asked the Holy Spirit to enter the relationship and heal it. 9He has accepted the Atonement for himself.

4. God is said to have looked on all He created and pronounced it good. 2No, He declared it perfect, and so it was. 3And since His creations do not change and last forever, so it is now. 4Yet neither a perfect therapist nor a perfect patient can possibly exist. 5Both must have denied their perfection, for their very need for each other implies a sense of lack. 6A one-to-one relationship is not One Relationship. 7Yet it is the means of return; the way God chose for the return of His Son. 8In that strange dream a strange correction must enter, for only that is the call to awake. 9And what else should therapy be? 10Awake and be glad, for all your sins have been forgiven you. 11This is the only message that any two should ever give each other.

5. Something good must come from every meeting of patient and therapist. 2And that good is saved for both, against the day when they can recognize that only that was real in their relationship. 3At that moment the good is returned to them, blessed by the Holy Spirit as a gift from their Creator as a sign of His Love. 4For the therapeutic relationship must become like the relationship of the Father and the Son. 5There is no other, for there is nothing else. 6The therapists of this world do not expect this outcome, and many of their patients would not be able to accept help from them if they did. 7Yet no therapist really sets the goal for the relationships of which he is a part. 8His understanding begins with recognizing this, and then goes on from there.

6. It is in the instant that the therapist forgets to judge the patient that healing occurs. 2In some relationships this point is never reached, although both patient and therapist may change their dreams in the process. 3Yet it will not be the same dream for both of them, and so it is not the dream of forgiveness in which both will someday wake. 4The good is saved; indeed is cherished. 5But only little time is saved. 6The new dreams will lose their temporary appeal and turn to dreams of fear, which is the content of all dreams. 7Yet no patient can accept more than he is ready to receive, and no therapist can offer more than he believes he has. 8And so there is a place for all relationships in this world, and they will bring as much good as each can accept and use.

7. Yet it is when judgment ceases that healing occurs, because only then it can be understood that there is no order of difficulty in

healing. ²This is a necessary understanding for the healed healer. ³He has learned that it is no harder to wake a brother from one dream than from another. ⁴No professional therapist can hold this understanding consistently in his mind, offering it to all who come to him. ⁵There are some in this world who have come very close, but they have not accepted the gift entirely in order to stay and let their understanding remain on earth until the closing of time. ⁶They could hardly be called professional therapists. ⁷They are the Saints of God. ⁸They are the Saviors of the world. ⁹Their image remains, because they have chosen that it be so. ¹⁰They take the place of other images, and help with kindly dreams.

8. Once the professional therapist has realized that minds are joined, he can also recognize that order of difficulty in healing is meaningless. ²Yet well before he reaches this in time he can go towards it. ³Many holy instants can be his along the way. ⁴A goal marks the end of a journey, not the beginning, and as each goal is reached another can be dimly seen ahead. ⁵Most professional therapists are still at the very start of the beginning stage of the first journey. ⁶Even those who have begun to understand what they must do may still oppose the setting-out. ⁷Yet all the laws of healing can be theirs in just an instant. ⁸The journey is not long except in dreams.

9. The professional therapist has one advantage that can save enormous time if it is properly used. ²He has chosen a road in which there is great temptation to misuse his role. ³This enables him to pass by many obstacles to peace quite quickly, if he escapes the temptation to assume a function that has not been given him. ⁴To understand there is no order of difficulty in healing, he must also recognize the equality of himself and the patient. ⁵There is no halfway point in this. ⁶Either they are equal or not. ⁷The attempts of therapists to compromise in this respect are strange indeed. ⁸Some utilize the relationship merely to collect bodies to worship at their shrine, and this they regard as healing. ⁹Many patients, too, consider this strange procedure as salvation. ¹⁰Yet at each meeting there is One Who says, "My brother, choose again."

10. Do not forget that any form of specialness must be defended, and will be. ²The defenseless therapist has the strength of God with him, but the defensive therapist has lost sight of the Source of his salvation. ³He does not see and he does not hear. ⁴How, then, can he teach? ⁵Because it is the Will of God that he take his place in the plan for salvation. ⁶Because it is the Will of God that

his patient be helped to join with him there. [7]Because his inability to see and hear does not limit the Holy Spirit in any way. [8]Except in time. [9]In time there can be a great lag between the offering and the acceptance of healing. [10]This is the veil across the face of Christ. [11]Yet it can be but an illusion, because time does not exist and the Will of God has always been exactly as it is.

III. The Question of Payment

1. No one can pay for therapy, for healing is of God and He asks for nothing. [2]It is, however, part of His plan that everything in this world be used by the Holy Spirit to help in carrying out the plan. [3]Even an advanced therapist has some earthly needs while he is here. [4]Should he need money it will be given him, not in payment, but to help him better serve the plan. [5]Money is not evil. [6]It is nothing. [7]But no one here can live with no illusions, for he must yet strive to have the last illusion be accepted by everyone everywhere. [8]He has a mighty part in this one purpose, for which he came. [9]He stays here but for this. [10]And while he stays he will be given what he needs to stay.

2. Only an unhealed healer would try to heal for money, and he will not succeed to the extent to which he values it. [2]Nor will he find his healing in the process. [3]There will be those of whom the Holy Spirit asks some payment for His purpose. [4]There will be those from whom He does not ask. [5]It should not be the therapist who makes these decisions. [6]There is a difference between payment and cost. [7]To give money where God's plan allots it has no cost. [8]To withhold it from where it rightfully belongs has enormous cost. [9]The therapist who would do this loses the name of healer, for he could never understand what healing is. [10]He cannot give it, and so he does not have it.

3. The therapists of this world are indeed useless to the world's salvation. [2]They make demands, and so they cannot give. [3]Patients can pay only for the exchange of illusions. [4]This, indeed, must demand payment, and the cost is great. [5]A "bought" relationship cannot offer the only gift whereby all healing is accomplished. [6]Forgiveness, the Holy Spirit's only dream, must have no cost. [7]For if it does, it merely crucifies God's Son again. [8]Can this be how he is forgiven? [9]Can this be how the dream of sin will end?

4. The right to live is something no one need fight for. [2]It is promised him, and guaranteed by God. [3]Therefore it is a right the therapist and patient share alike. [4]If their relationship is to be holy, whatever one needs is given by the other; whatever one lacks the other supplies. [5]Herein is the relationship made holy, for herein both are healed. [6]The therapist repays the patient in gratitude, as does the patient repay him. [7]There is no cost to either. [8]But thanks are due to both, for the release from long imprisonment and doubt. [9]Who would not be grateful for such a gift? [10]Yet who could possibly imagine that it could be bought?

5. It has well been said that to him who hath shall be given. [2]Because he has, he can give. [3]And because he gives, he shall be given. [4]This is the law of God, and not of the world. [5]So it is with God's healers. [6]They give because they have heard His Word and understood it. [7]All that they need will thus be given them. [8]But they will lose this understanding unless they remember that all they have comes only from God. [9]If they believe they need anything from a brother, they will recognize him as a brother no longer. [10]And if they do this, a light goes out even in Heaven. [11]Where God's Son turns against himself, he can look only upon darkness. [12]He has himself denied the light, and cannot see.

6. One rule should always be observed: No one should be turned away because he cannot pay. [2]No one is sent by accident to anyone. [3]Relationships are always purposeful. [4]Whatever their purpose may have been before the Holy Spirit entered them, they are always His potential temple; the resting place of Christ and home of God Himself. [5]Whoever comes has been sent. [6]Perhaps he was sent to give his brother the money he needed. [7]Both will be blessed thereby. [8]Perhaps he was sent to teach the therapist how much he needs forgiveness, and how valueless is money in comparison. [9]Again will both be blessed. [10]Only in terms of cost could one have more. [11]In sharing, everyone must gain a blessing without cost.

7. This view of payment may well seem impractical, and in the eyes of the world it would be so. [2]Yet not one worldly thought is really practical. [3]How much is gained by striving for illusions? [4]How much is lost by throwing God away? [5]And is it possible to do so? [6]Surely it is impractical to strive for nothing, and to attempt to do what is impossible. [7]Then stop a while, long enough to think of this: You have perhaps been seeking for salvation without recognizing where to look. [8]Whoever asks your help can show

23

you where. ⁹What greater gift than this could you be given? ¹⁰What greater gift is there that you would give?

8. Physician, healer, therapist, teacher, heal thyself. ²Many will come to you carrying the gift of healing, if you so elect. ³The Holy Spirit never refuses an invitation to enter and abide with you. ⁴He will give you endless opportunities to open the door to your salvation, for such is His function. ⁵He will also tell you exactly what your function is in every circumstance and at all times. ⁶Whoever He sends you will reach you, holding out his hand to his Friend. ⁷Let the Christ in you bid him welcome, for that same Christ is in him as well. ⁸Deny him entrance, and you have denied the Christ in you. ⁹Remember the sorrowful story of the world, and the glad tidings of salvation. ¹⁰Remember the plan of God for the restoration of joy and peace. ¹¹And do not forget how very simple are the ways of God:

> ¹²*You were lost in the darkness of the world until you asked for light. ¹³And then God sent His Son to give it to you.*

24

THE SONG OF PRAYER

Prayer, Forgiveness, Healing

An Extension of the Principles of
A Course in Miracles

FOUNDATION FOR INNER PEACE

CONTENTS

CONTENTS

1. PRAYER

Introduction

1. Prayer is the greatest gift with which God blessed His Son at his creation. [2]It was then what it is to become; the single voice Creator and creation share; the song the Son sings to the Father, Who returns the thanks it offers Him unto the Son. [3]Endless the harmony, and endless, too, the joyous concord of the Love They give forever to Each Other. [4]And in this, creation is extended. [5]God gives thanks to His extension in His Son. [6]His Son gives thanks for his creation, in the song of his creating in his Father's Name. [7]The Love They share is what all prayer will be throughout eternity, when time is done. [8]For such it was before time seemed to be.

2. To you who are in time a little while, prayer takes the form that best will suit your need. [2]You have but one. [3]What God created one must recognize its oneness, and rejoice that what illusions seemed to separate is one forever in the Mind of God. [4]Prayer now must be the means by which God's Son leaves separate goals and separate interests by, and turns in holy gladness to the truth of union in his Father and himself.

3. Lay down your dreams, you holy Son of God, and rising up as God created you, dispense with idols and remember Him. [2]Prayer will sustain you now, and bless you as you lift your heart to Him in rising song that reaches higher and then higher still, until both high and low have disappeared. [3]Faith in your goal will grow and hold you up as you ascend the shining stairway to the lawns of Heaven and the gate of peace. [4]For this is prayer, and here salvation is. [5]This is the way. [6]It is God's gift to you.

I. True Prayer

1. Prayer is a way offered by the Holy Spirit to reach God. [2]It is not merely a question or an entreaty. [3]It cannot succeed until you realize that it asks for nothing. [4]How else could it serve its purpose? [5]It is impossible to pray for idols and hope to reach God. [6]True prayer must avoid the pitfall of asking to entreat. [7]Ask, rather, to receive what is already given; to accept what is already there.

2. You have been told to ask the Holy Spirit for the answer to any

specific problem, and that you will receive a specific answer if such is your need. ²You have also been told that there is only one problem and one answer. ³In prayer this is not contradictory. ⁴There are decisions to make here, and they must be made whether they be illusions or not. ⁵You cannot be asked to accept answers which are beyond the level of need that you can recognize. ⁶Therefore, it is not the form of the question that matters, nor how it is asked. ⁷The form of the answer, if given by God, will suit your need as you see it. ⁸This is merely an echo of the reply of His Voice. ⁹The real sound is always a song of thanksgiving and of Love.

3. You cannot, then, ask for the echo. ²It is the song that is the gift. ³Along with it come the overtones, the harmonics, the echoes, but these are secondary. ⁴In true prayer you hear only the song. ⁵All the rest is merely added. ⁶You have sought first the Kingdom of Heaven, and all else has indeed been given you.

4. The secret of true prayer is to forget the things you think you need. ²To ask for the specific is much the same as to look on sin and then forgive it. ³Also in the same way, in prayer you overlook your specific needs as you see them, and let them go into God's Hands. ⁴There they become your gifts to Him, for they tell Him that you would have no gods before Him; no love but His. ⁵What could His answer be but your remembrance of Him? ⁶Can this be traded for a bit of trifling advice about a problem of an instant's duration? ⁷God answers only for eternity. ⁸But still all little answers are contained in this.

5. Prayer is a stepping aside; a letting go, a quiet time of listening and loving. ²It should not be confused with supplication of any kind, because it is a way of remembering your holiness. ³Why should holiness entreat, being fully entitled to everything Love has to offer? ⁴And it is to Love you go in prayer. ⁵Prayer is an offering; a giving up of yourself to be at one with Love. ⁶There is nothing to ask because there is nothing left to want. ⁷That nothingness becomes the altar of God. ⁸It disappears in Him.

6. This is not a level of prayer that everyone can attain as yet. ²Those who have not reached it still need your help in prayer because their asking is not yet based upon acceptance. ³Help in prayer does not mean that another mediates between you and God. ⁴But it does mean that another stands beside you and helps to raise you up to Him. ⁵One who has realized the goodness of God prays without fear. ⁶And one who prays without fear cannot

but reach Him. [7]He can therefore also reach His Son, wherever he may be and whatever form he may seem to take.

7. Praying to Christ in anyone is true prayer because it is a gift of thanks to His Father. [2]To ask that Christ be but Himself is not an entreaty. [3]It is a song of thanksgiving for what you are. [4]Herein lies the power of prayer. [5]It asks nothing and receives everything. [6]This prayer can be shared because it receives for everyone. [7]To pray with one who knows that this is true is to be answered. [8]Perhaps the specific form of resolution for a specific problem will occur to either of you; it does not matter which. [9]Perhaps it will reach both, if you are genuinely attuned to one another. [10]It will come because you have realized that Christ is in both of you. [11]That is its only truth.

II. The Ladder of Prayer

1. Prayer has no beginning and no end. [2]It is a part of life. [3]But it does change in form, and grow with learning until it reaches its formless state, and fuses into total communication with God. [4]In its asking form it need not, and often does not, make appeal to God, or even involve belief in Him. [5]At these levels prayer is merely wanting, out of a sense of scarcity and lack.

2. These forms of prayer, or asking-out-of-need, always involve feelings of weakness and inadequacy, and could never be made by a Son of God who knows Who he is. [2]No one, then, who is sure of his Identity could pray in these forms. [3]Yet it is also true that no one who is uncertain of his Identity can avoid praying in this way. [4]And prayer is as continual as life. [5]Everyone prays without ceasing. [6]Ask and you have received, for you have established what it is you want.

3. It is also possible to reach a higher form of asking-out-of-need, for in this world prayer is reparative, and so it must entail levels of learning. [2]Here, the asking may be addressed to God in honest belief, though not yet with understanding. [3]A vague and usually unstable sense of identification has generally been reached, but tends to be blurred by a deep-rooted sense of sin. [4]It is possible at this level to continue to ask for things of this world in various forms, and it is also possible to ask for gifts such as honesty or goodness, and particularly for forgiveness for the many sources of guilt that inevitably underlie any prayer of need. [5]Without

3

guilt there is no scarcity. ⁶The sinless have no needs.

4. At this level also comes that curious contradiction in terms known as "praying for one's enemies." ²The contradiction lies not in the actual words, but rather in the way in which they are usually interpreted. ³While you believe you have enemies, you have limited prayer to the laws of this world, and have also limited your ability to receive and to accept to the same narrow margins. ⁴And yet, if you have enemies you have need of prayer, and great need, too. ⁵What does the phrase really mean? ⁶Pray for yourself, that you may not seek to imprison Christ and thereby lose the recognition of your own Identity. ⁷Be traitor to no one, or you will be treacherous to yourself.

5. An enemy is the symbol of an imprisoned Christ. ²And who could He be except yourself? ³The prayer for enemies thus becomes a prayer for your own freedom. ⁴Now it is no longer a contradiction in terms. ⁵It has become a statement of the unity of Christ and a recognition of His sinlessness. ⁶And now it has become holy, for it acknowledges the Son of God as he was created.

6. Let it never be forgotten that prayer at any level is always for yourself. ²If you unite with anyone in prayer, you make him part of you. ³The enemy is you, as is the Christ. ⁴Before it can become holy, then, prayer becomes a choice. ⁵You do not choose for another. ⁶You can but choose for yourself. ⁷Pray truly for your enemies, for herein lies your own salvation. ⁸Forgive them for your sins, and you will be forgiven indeed.

7. Prayer is a ladder reaching up to Heaven. ²At the top there is a transformation much like your own, for prayer is part of you. ³The things of earth are left behind, all unremembered. ⁴There is no asking, for there is no lack. ⁵Identity in Christ is fully recognized as set forever, beyond all change and incorruptible. ⁶The light no longer flickers, and will never go out. ⁷Now, without needs of any kind, and clad forever in the pure sinlessness that is the gift of God to you, His Son, prayer can again become what it was meant to be. ⁸For now it rises as a song of thanks to your Creator, sung without words, or thoughts, or vain desires, unneedful now of anything at all. ⁹So it extends, as it was meant to do. ¹⁰And for this giving God Himself gives thanks.

8. God is the goal of every prayer, giving it timelessness instead of end. ²Nor has it a beginning, because the goal has never changed. ³Prayer in its earlier forms is an illusion, because there is no need for a ladder to reach what one has never left. ⁴Yet prayer is part of

forgiveness as long as forgiveness, itself an illusion, remains unattained. [5]Prayer is tied up with learning until the goal of learning has been reached. [6]And then all things will be transformed together, and returned unblemished into the Mind of God. [7]Being beyond learning, this state cannot be described. [8]The stages necessary to its attainment, however, need to be understood, if peace is to be restored to God's Son, who lives now with the illusion of death and the fear of God.

III. Praying for Others

1. We said that prayer is always for yourself, and this is so. [2]Why, then, should you pray for others at all? [3]And if you should, how should you do it? [4]Praying for others, if rightly understood, becomes a means for lifting your projections of guilt from your brother, and enabling you to recognize it is not he who is hurting you. [5]The poisonous thought that he *is* your enemy, your evil counterpart, your nemesis, must be relinquished before *you* can be saved from guilt. [6]For this the means is prayer, of rising power and with ascending goals, until it reaches even up to God.

2. The earlier forms of prayer, at the bottom of the ladder, will not be free from envy and malice. [2]They call for vengeance, not for love. [3]Nor do they come from one who understands that they are calls for death, made out of fear by those who cherish guilt. [4]They call upon a vengeful god, and it is he who seems to answer them. [5]Hell cannot be asked for another, and then escaped by him who asks for it. [6]Only those who are in hell can ask for hell. [7]Those who have been forgiven, and who accepted their forgiveness, could never make a prayer like that.

3. At these levels, then, the learning goal must be to recognize that prayer will bring an answer only in the form in which the prayer was made. [2]This is enough. [3]From here it will be an easy step to the next levels. [4]The next ascent begins with this:

> [5]*What I have asked for for my brother is not what I would have.* [6]*Thus have I made of him my enemy.*

[7]It is apparent that this step cannot be reached by anyone who sees no value or advantage to himself in setting others free. [8]This may be long delayed, because it may seem to be dangerous

instead of merciful. ⁹To the guilty there seems indeed to be a real advantage in having enemies, and this imagined gain must go, if enemies are to be set free.

4. Guilt must be given up, and not concealed. ²Nor can this be done without some pain, and a glimpse of the merciful nature of this step may for some time be followed by a deep retreat into fear. ³For fear's defenses are fearful in themselves, and when they are recognized they bring their fear with them. ⁴Yet what advantage has an illusion of escape ever brought a prisoner? ⁵His real escape from guilt can lie only in the recognition that the guilt has gone. ⁶And how can this be recognized as long as he hides it in another, and does not see it as his own? ⁷Fear of escape makes it difficult to welcome freedom, and to make a jailer of an enemy seems to be safety. ⁸How, then, can he be released without an insane fear for yourself? ⁹You have made of him your salvation and your escape from guilt. ¹⁰Your investment in this escape is heavy, and your fear of letting it go is strong.

5. Stand still an instant, now, and think what you have done. ²Do not forget that it is you who did it, and who can therefore let it go. ³Hold out your hand. ⁴This enemy has come to bless you. ⁵Take his blessing, and feel how your heart is lifted and your fear released. ⁶Do not hold on to it, nor onto him. ⁷He is a Son of God, along with you. ⁸He is no jailer, but a messenger of Christ. ⁹Be this to him, that you may see him thus.

6. It is not easy to realize that prayers for things, for status, for human love, for external "gifts" of any kind, are always made to set up jailers and to hide from guilt. ²These things are used for goals that substitute for God, and therefore distort the purpose of prayer. ³The desire for them *is* the prayer. ⁴One need not ask explicitly. ⁵The goal of God is lost in the quest for lesser goals of any kind, and prayer becomes requests for enemies. ⁶The power of prayer can be quite clearly recognized even in this. ⁷No one who wants an enemy will fail to find one. ⁸But just as surely will he lose the only true goal that is given him. ⁹Think of the cost, and understand it well. ¹⁰All other goals are at the cost of God.

IV. Praying with Others

1. Until the second level at least begins, one cannot share in prayer. ²For until that point, each one must ask for different things. ³But once the need to hold the other as an enemy has been questioned, and the reason for doing so has been recognized if only for an instant, it becomes possible to join in prayer. ⁴Enemies do not share a goal. ⁵It is in this their enmity is kept. ⁶Their separate wishes are their arsenals; their fortresses in hate. ⁷The key to rising further still in prayer lies in this simple thought; this change of mind:

⁸We go together, you and I.

2. Now it is possible to help in prayer, and so reach up yourself. ²This step begins the quicker ascent, but there are still many lessons to learn. ³The way is open, and hope is justified. ⁴Yet it is likely at first that what is asked for even by those who join in prayer is not the goal that prayer should truly seek. ⁵Even together you may ask for things, and thus set up but an illusion of a goal you share. ⁶You may ask together for specifics, and not realize that you are asking for effects without the cause. ⁷And this you cannot have. ⁸For no one can receive effects alone, asking a cause from which they do not come to offer them to him.

3. Even the joining, then, is not enough, if those who pray together do not ask, before all else, what is the Will of God. ²From this Cause only can the answer come in which are all specifics satisfied; all separate wishes unified in one. ³Prayer for specifics always asks to have the past repeated in some way. ⁴What was enjoyed before, or seemed to be; what was another's and he seemed to love,—all these are but illusions from the past. ⁵The aim of prayer is to release the present from its chains of past illusions; to let it be a freely chosen remedy from every choice that stood for a mistake. ⁶What prayer can offer now so far exceeds all that you asked before that it is pitiful to be content with less.

4. You have chosen a newborn chance each time you pray. ²And would you stifle and imprison it in ancient prisons, when the chance has come to free yourself from all of them at once? ³Do not restrict your asking. ⁴Prayer can bring the peace of God. ⁵What time-bound thing can give you more than this, in just the little space that lasts until it crumbles into dust?

7

V. The Ladder Ends

1. Prayer is a way to true humility. [2]And here again it rises slowly up, and grows in strength and love and holiness. [3]Let it but leave the ground where it begins to rise to God, and true humility will come at last to grace the mind that thought it was alone and stood against the world. [4]Humility brings peace because it does not claim that you must rule the universe, nor judge all things as you would have them be. [5]All little gods it gladly lays aside, not in resentment, but in honesty and recognition that they do not serve.

2. Illusions and humility have goals so far apart they cannot co-exist, nor share a dwelling place where they can meet. [2]Where one has come the other disappears. [3]The truly humble have no goal but God because they need no idols, and defense no longer serves a purpose. [4]Enemies are useless now, because humility does not oppose. [5]It does not hide in shame because it is content with what it is, knowing creation is the Will of God. [6]Its selflessness is Self, and this it sees in every meeting, where it gladly joins with every Son of God, whose purity it recognizes that it shares with him.

3. Now prayer is lifted from the world of things, of bodies, and of gods of every kind, and you can rest in holiness at last. [2]Humility has come to teach you how to understand your glory as God's Son, and recognize the arrogance of sin. [3]A dream has veiled the face of Christ from you. [4]Now can you look upon His sinlessness. [5]High has the ladder risen. [6]You have come almost to Heaven. [7]There is little more to learn before the journey is complete. [8]Now can you say to everyone who comes to join in prayer with you:

    [9]*I cannot go without you, for you are a part of me.*

    [10]And so he is in truth. [11]Now can you pray only for what you truly share with him. [12]For you have understood he never left, and you, who seemed alone, are one with him.

4. The ladder ends with this, for learning is no longer needed. [2]Now you stand before the gate of Heaven, and your brother stands beside you there. [3]The lawns are deep and still, for here the place appointed for the time when you should come has waited long for you. [4]Here will time end forever. [5]At this gate eternity itself will join with you. [6]Prayer has become what it was meant to be, for you have recognized the Christ in you.

2. FORGIVENESS

Introduction

1. Forgiveness offers wings to prayer, to make its rising easy and its progress swift. ²Without its strong support it would be vain to try to rise above prayer's bottom step, or even to attempt to climb at all. ³Forgiveness is prayer's ally; sister in the plan for your salvation. ⁴Both must come to hold you up and keep your feet secure; your purpose steadfast and unchangeable. ⁵Behold the greatest help that God ordained to be with you until you reach to Him. ⁶Illusion's end will come with this. ⁷Unlike the timeless nature of its sister, prayer, forgiveness has an end. ⁸For it becomes unneeded when the rising up is done. ⁹Yet now it has a purpose beyond which you cannot go, nor have you need to go. ¹⁰Accomplish this and you have been redeemed. ¹¹Accomplish this and you have been transformed. ¹²Accomplish this and you will save the world.

I. Forgiveness of Yourself

1. No gift of Heaven has been more misunderstood than has forgiveness. ²It has, in fact, become a scourge; a curse where it was meant to bless, a cruel mockery of grace, a parody upon the holy peace of God. ³Yet those who have not yet chosen to begin the steps of prayer cannot but use it thus. ⁴Forgiveness' kindness is obscure at first, because salvation is not understood, *nor truly sought for.* ⁵What was meant to heal is used to hurt because forgiveness is not wanted. ⁶Guilt becomes salvation, and the remedy appears to be a terrible alternative to life.

2. Forgiveness-to-destroy will therefore suit the purpose of the world far better than its true objective, and the honest means by which this goal is reached. ²Forgiveness-to-destroy will overlook no sin, no crime, no guilt that it can seek and find and "love." ³Dear to its heart is error, and mistakes loom large and grow and swell within its sight. ⁴It carefully picks out all evil things, and overlooks the loving as a plague; a hateful thing of danger and of death. ⁵Forgiveness-to-destroy *is* death, and this it sees in all it looks upon and hates. ⁶God's mercy has become a twisted knife

9

that would destroy the holy Son He loves.

3. Would you forgive yourself for doing this? ²Then learn that God has given you the means by which you can return to Him in peace. ³*Do not see error.* ⁴Do not make it real. ⁵Select the loving and forgive the sin by choosing in its place the face of Christ. ⁶How otherwise can prayer return to God? ⁷He loves His Son. ⁸Can you remember Him and hate what He created? ⁹You will hate his Father if you hate the Son He loves. ¹⁰For as you see the Son you see yourself, and as you see yourself is God to you.

4. As prayer is always for yourself, so is forgiveness always given you. ²It is impossible to forgive another, for it is only your sins you see in him. ³You want to see them there, and not in you. ⁴That is why forgiveness of another is an illusion. ⁵Yet it is the only happy dream in all the world; the only one that does not lead to death. ⁶Only in someone else can you forgive yourself, for you have called him guilty of your sins, and in him must your innocence now be found. ⁷Who but the sinful need to be forgiven? ⁸And do not ever think you can see sin in anyone except yourself.

5. This is the great deception of the world, and you the great deceiver of yourself. ²It always seems to be another who is evil, and in his sin you are the injured one. ³How could freedom be possible if this were so? ⁴You would be slave to everyone, for what he does entails your fate, your feelings, your despair or hope, your misery or joy. ⁵You have no freedom unless he gives it to you. ⁶And being evil, he can only give of what he is. ⁷You cannot see his sins and not your own. ⁸But you can free him and yourself as well.

6. Forgiveness, truly given, is the way in which your only hope of freedom lies. ²Others will make mistakes and so will you, as long as this illusion of a world appears to be your home. ³Yet God Himself has given all His Sons a remedy for all illusions that they think they see. ⁴Christ's vision does not use your eyes, but you can look through His and learn to see like Him. ⁵Mistakes are tiny shadows, quickly gone, that for an instant only seem to hide the face of Christ, which still remains unchanged behind them all. ⁶His constancy remains in tranquil silence and in perfect peace. ⁷He does not know of shadows. ⁸His the eyes that look past error to the Christ in you.

7. Ask, then, His help, and ask Him how to learn forgiveness as His vision lets it be. ²You are in need of what He gives, and your salvation rests on learning this of Him. ³Prayer cannot be released to Heaven while forgiveness-to-destroy remains with you. ⁴God's

mercy would remove this withering and poisoned thinking from your holy mind. [5]Christ has forgiven you, and in His sight the world becomes as holy as Himself. [6]Who sees no evil in it sees like Him. [7]For what He has forgiven has not sinned, and guilt can be no more. [8]Salvation's plan is made complete, and sanity has come.

8. Forgiveness is the call to sanity, for who but the insane would look on sin when he could see the face of Christ instead? [2]This is the choice you make; the simplest one, and yet the only one that you *can* make. [3]God calls on you to save His Son from death by offering Christ's Love to him. [4]This is your need, and God holds out this gift to you. [5]As He would give, so must you give as well. [6]And thus is prayer restored to formlessness, beyond all limits into timelessness, with nothing of the past to hold it back from reuniting with the ceaseless song that all creation sings unto its God.

9. But to achieve this end you first must learn, before you reach where learning cannot go. [2]Forgiveness is the key, but who can use a key when he has lost the door for which the key was made, and where alone it fits? [3]Therefore we make distinctions, so that prayer can be released from darkness into light. [4]Forgiveness' role must be reversed, and cleansed from evil usages and hateful goals. [5]Forgiveness-to-destroy must be unveiled in all its treachery, and then let go forever and forever. [6]There can be no trace of it remaining, if the plan that God established for returning be achieved at last, and learning be complete.

10. This is the world of opposites. [2]And you must choose between them every instant while this world retains reality for you. [3]Yet you must learn alternatives for choice, or you will not be able to attain your freedom. [4]Let it then be clear to you exactly what forgiveness means to you, and learn what it should be to set you free. [5]The level of your prayer depends on this, for here it waits its freedom to ascend above the world of chaos into peace.

II. Forgiveness-to-Destroy

1. Forgiveness-to-destroy has many forms, being a weapon of the world of form. [2]Not all of them are obvious, and some are carefully concealed beneath what seems like charity. [3]Yet all the forms that it may seem to take have but this single goal; their purpose is to separate and make what God created equal, different. [4]The difference is clear in several forms where the designed comparison cannot be

missed, nor is it really meant to be.

2. In this group, first, there are the forms in which a "better" person deigns to stoop to save a "baser" one from what he truly is. [2]Forgiveness here rests on an attitude of gracious lordliness so far from love that arrogance could never be dislodged. [3]Who can forgive and yet despise? [4]And who can tell another he is steeped in sin, and yet perceive him as the Son of God? [5]Who makes a slave to teach what freedom is? [6]There is no union here, but only grief. [7]This is not really mercy. [8]This is death.

3. Another form, still very like the first if it is understood, does not appear in quite such blatant arrogance. [2]The one who would forgive the other does not claim to be the better. [3]Now he says instead that here is one whose sinfulness he shares, since both have been unworthy and deserve the retribution of the wrath of God. [4]This can appear to be a humble thought, and may indeed induce a rivalry in sinfulness and guilt. [5]It is not love for God's creation and the holiness that is His gift forever. [6]Can His Son condemn himself and still remember Him?

4. Here the goal is to separate from God the Son He loves, and keep him from his Source. [2]This goal is also sought by those who seek the role of martyr at another's hand. [3]Here must the aim be clearly seen, for this may pass as meekness and as charity instead of cruelty. [4]Is it not kind to be accepting of another's spite, and not respond except with silence and a gentle smile? [5]Behold, how good are you who bear with patience and with saintliness the anger and the hurt another gives, and do not show the bitter pain you feel.

5. Forgiveness-to-destroy will often hide behind a cloak like this. [2]It shows the face of suffering and pain, in silent proof of guilt and of the ravages of sin. [3]Such is the witness that it offers one who could be savior, not an enemy. [4]But having been made enemy, he must accept the guilt and heavy-laid reproach that thus is put upon him. [5]Is this love? [6]Or is it rather treachery to one who needs salvation from the pain of guilt? [7]What could the purpose be, except to keep the witnesses of guilt away from love?

6. Forgiveness-to-destroy can also take the form of bargaining and compromise. [2]"I will forgive you if you meet my needs, for in your slavery is my release." [3]Say this to anyone and you are slave. [4]And you will seek to rid yourself of guilt in further bargains which can give no hope, but only greater pain and misery. [5]How fearful has forgiveness now become, and how distorted is the end

it seeks. ⁶Have mercy on yourself who bargains thus. ⁷God gives and does not ask for recompense. ⁸There is no giving but to give like Him. ⁹All else is mockery. ¹⁰For who would try to strike a bargain with the Son of God, and thank his Father for his holiness?

7. What would you show your brother? ²Would you try to reinforce his guilt and thus your own? ³Forgiveness is the means for your escape. ⁴How pitiful it is to make of it the means for further slavery and pain. ⁵Within the world of opposites there is a way to use forgiveness for the goal of God, and find the peace He offers you. ⁶Take nothing else, or you have sought your death, and prayed for separation from your Self. ⁷Christ is for all because He is in all. ⁸It is His face forgiveness lets you see. ⁹It is His face in which you see your own.

8. All forms forgiveness takes that do not lead away from anger, condemnation and comparisons of every kind are death. ²For that is what their purposes have set. ³Be not deceived by them, but lay them by as worthless in their tragic offerings. ⁴You do not want to stay in slavery. ⁵You do not want to be afraid of God. ⁶You want to see the sunlight and the glow of Heaven shining on the face of earth, redeemed from sin and in the Love of God. ⁷From here is prayer released, along with you. ⁸Your wings are free, and prayer will lift you up and bring you home where God would have you be.

III. Forgiveness-for-Salvation

1. Forgiveness-for-salvation has one form, and only one. ²It does not ask for proof of innocence, nor pay of any kind. ³It does not argue, nor evaluate the errors that it wants to overlook. ⁴It does not offer gifts in treachery, nor promise freedom while it asks for death. ⁵Would God deceive you? ⁶He but asks for trust and willingness to learn how to be free. ⁷He gives His Teacher to whoever asks, and seeks to understand the Will of God. ⁸His readiness to give lies far beyond your understanding and your simple grasp. ⁹Yet He has willed you learn the way to Him, and in His willing there is certainty.

2. You child of God, the gifts of God are yours, not by your plans but by His holy Will. ²His Voice will teach you what forgiveness is, and how to give it as He wills it be. ³Do not, then, seek to understand what is beyond you yet, but let it be a way to draw you up to

where the eyes of Christ become the sight you choose. ⁴Give up all else, for there *is* nothing else. ⁵When someone calls for help in any form, He is the One to answer for you. ⁶All that you need do is to step back and not to interfere. ⁷Forgiveness-for-salvation is His task, and it is He Who will respond for you.

3. Do not establish what the form should be that Christ's forgiveness takes. ²He knows the way to make of every call a help to you, as you arise in haste to go at last unto your Father's house. ³Now can He make your footsteps sure, your words sincere; not with your own sincerity, but with His Own. ⁴Let Him take charge of how you would forgive, and each occasion then will be to you another step to Heaven and to peace.

4. Are you not weary of imprisonment? ²God did not choose this sorry path for you. ³What you have chosen still can be undone, for prayer is merciful and God is just. ⁴His is a justice He can understand, but you cannot as yet. ⁵Still will He give the means to you to learn of Him, and know at last that condemnation is not real and makes illusions in its evil name. ⁶And yet it matters not the form that dreams may seem to take. ⁷Illusions are untrue. ⁸God's Will is truth, and you are one with Him in Will and purpose. ⁹Here all dreams are done.

5. "What should I do for him, Your holy Son?" should be the only thing you ever ask when help is needed and forgiveness sought. ²The form the seeking takes you need not judge. ³And let it not be you who sets the form in which forgiveness comes to save God's Son. ⁴The light of Christ in him is his release, and it is this that answers to his call. ⁵Forgive him as the Christ decides you should, and be His eyes through which you look on him, and speak for Him as well. ⁶He knows the need; the question and the answer. ⁷He will say exactly what to do, in words that you can understand and you can also use. ⁸Do not confuse His function with your own. ⁹He is the Answer. ¹⁰You the one who hears.

6. And what is it He speaks to you about? ²About salvation and the gift of peace. ³About the end of sin and guilt and death. ⁴About the role forgiveness has in Him. ⁵Do you but listen. ⁶For He will be heard by anyone who calls upon His Name, and places his forgiveness in His hands. ⁷Forgiveness has been given Him to teach, to save it from destruction and to make the means for separation, sin and death become again the holy gift of God. ⁸Prayer is His Own right Hand, made free to save as true forgiveness is allowed to come from His eternal vigilance and Love. ⁹Listen and learn, and

do not judge. [10]It is to God you turn to hear what you should do. [11]His answer will be clear as morning, nor is His forgiveness what you think it is.

7. Still does He know, and that should be enough. [2]Forgiveness has a Teacher Who will fail in nothing. [3]Rest a while in this; do not attempt to judge forgiveness, nor to set it in an earthly frame. [4]Let it arise to Christ, Who welcomes it as gift to Him. [5]He will not leave you comfortless, nor fail to send His angels down to answer you in His Own Name. [6]He stands beside the door to which forgiveness is the only key. [7]Give it to Him to use instead of you, and you will see the door swing silently open upon the shining face of Christ. [8]Behold your brother there beyond the door; the Son of God as He created him.

3. HEALING

Introduction

1. Prayer has both aids and witnesses which make the steep ascent more gentle and more sure, easing the pain of fear and offering the comfort and the promises of hope. ²Forgiveness' witness and an aid to prayer, a giver of assurance of success in ultimate attainment of the goal, is healing. ³Its importance should not be too strongly emphasized, for healing is a sign or symbol of forgiveness' strength, and only an effect or shadow of a change of mind about the goal of prayer.

I. The Cause of Sickness

1. Do not mistake effect for cause, nor think that sickness is apart and separate from what its cause must be. ²It is a sign, a shadow of an evil thought that seems to have reality and to be just, according to the usage of the world. ³It is external proof of inner "sins," and witnesses to unforgiving thoughts that injure and would hurt the Son of God. ⁴Healing the body is impossible, and this is shown by the brief nature of the "cure." ⁵The body yet must die, and so its healing but delays its turning back to dust, where it was born and will return.

2. The body's cause is unforgiveness of the Son of God. ²It has not left its source, and in its pain and aging and the mark of death upon it this is clearly shown. ³Fearful and frail it seems to be to those who think their life is tied to its command and linked to its unstable, tiny breath. ⁴Death stares at them as every moment goes irrevocably past their grasping hands, which cannot hold them back. ⁵And they feel fear as bodies change and sicken. ⁶For they sense the heavy scent of death upon their hearts.

3. The body can be healed as an effect of true forgiveness. ²Only that can give rememberance of immortality, which is the gift of holiness and love. ³Forgiveness must be given by a mind which understands that it must overlook all shadows on the holy face of Christ, among which sickness should be seen as one. ⁴Nothing but that; the sign of judgment made by brother upon brother, and the Son of God upon himself. ⁵For he has damned his body

16

as his prison, and forgot that it is he who gave this role to it. 4. What he has done now must God's Son undo. ²But not alone. ³For he has thrown away the prison's key; his holy sinlessness and the remembrance of his Father's Love. ⁴Yet help is given to him in the Voice his Father placed in him. ⁵The power to heal is now his Father's gift, for through His Voice He still can reach His Son, reminding him the body may become his chosen home, but it will never be his home in truth.

5. Distinctions therefore must be made between true healing and its faulty counterpart. ²The world of opposites is healing's place, for what in Heaven could there be to heal? ³As prayer within the world can ask amiss and seeming charity forgive to kill, so healing can be false as well as true; a witness to the power of the world or to the everlasting Love of God.

II. False versus True Healing

1. False healing merely makes a poor exchange of one illusion for a "nicer" one; a dream of sickness for a dream of health. ²This can occur at lower forms of prayer, combining with forgiveness kindly meant but not completely understood as yet. ³Only false healing can give way to fear, so sickness will be free to strike again. ⁴False healing can indeed remove a form of pain and sickness. ⁵But the cause remains, and will not lack effects. ⁶The cause is still the wish to die and overcome the Christ. ⁷And with this wish is death a certainty, for prayer *is* answered. ⁸Yet there is a kind of seeming death that has a different source. ⁹It does not come because of hurtful thoughts and raging anger at the universe. ¹⁰It merely signifies the end has come for usefulness of body functioning. ¹¹And so it is discarded as a choice, as one lays by a garment now outworn.

2. This is what death should be; a quiet choice, made joyfully and with a sense of peace, because the body has been kindly used to help the Son of God along the way he goes to God. ²We thank the body, then, for all the service it has given us. ³But we are thankful, too, the need is done to walk the world of limits, and to reach the Christ in hidden forms and clearly seen at most in lovely flashes. ⁴Now we can behold Him without blinders, in the light that we have learned to look upon again.

3. We call it death, but it is liberty. ²It does not come in forms that

seem to be thrust down in pain upon unwilling flesh, but as a gentle welcome to release. [3]If there has been true healing, this can be the form in which death comes when it is time to rest a while from labor gladly done and gladly ended. [4]Now we go in peace to freer air and gentler climate, where it is not hard to see the gifts we gave were saved for us. [5]For Christ is clearer now; His vision more sustained in us; His Voice, the Word of God, more certainly our own.

4. This gentle passage to a higher prayer, a kind forgiveness of the ways of earth, can only be received with thankfulness. [2]Yet first true healing must have come to bless the mind with loving pardon for the sins it dreamed about and laid upon the world. [3]Now are its dreams dispelled in quiet rest. [4]Now its forgiveness comes to heal the world and it is ready to depart in peace, the journey over and the lessons learned.

5. This is not death according to the world, for death is cruel in its frightened eyes and takes the form of punishment for sin. [2]How could it be a blessing, then? [3]And how could it be welcome when it must be feared? [4]What healing has occurred in such a view of what is merely opening the gate to higher prayer and kindly justice done? [5]Death is reward and not a punishment. [6]But such a viewpoint must be fostered by the healing that the world cannot conceive. [7]There is no partial healing. [8]What but shifts illusions has done nothing. [9]What is false cannot be partly true. [10]If you are healed your healing is complete. [11]Forgiveness is the only gift you give and would receive.

6. False healing rests upon the body's cure, leaving the cause of illness still unchanged, ready to strike again until it brings a cruel death in seeming victory. [2]It can be held at bay a little while, and there can be brief respite as it waits to take its vengeance on the Son of God. [3]Yet it cannot be overcome until all faith in it has been laid by, and placed upon God's substitute for evil dreams; a world in which there is no veil of sin to keep it dark and comfortless. [4]At last the gate of Heaven opens and God's Son is free to enter in the home that stands ready to welcome him, and was prepared before time was and still but waits for him.

III. Separation versus Union

1. False healing heals the body in a part, but never as a whole. ²Its separate goals become quite clear in this, for it has not removed the curse of sin that lies on it. ³Therefore it still deceives. ⁴Nor is it made by one who understands the other is exactly like himself. ⁵For it is this that makes true healing possible. ⁶When false, there is some power that another has, not equally bestowed on both as one. ⁷Here is the separation shown. ⁸And here the meaning of true healing has been lost, and idols have arisen to obscure the unity that is the Son of God.

2. Healing-to-separate may seem to be a strange idea. ²And yet it can be said of any form of healing that is based on inequality of any kind. ³These forms may heal the body, and indeed are generally limited to this. ⁴Someone knows better, has been better trained, or is perhaps more talented and wise. ⁵Therefore, he can give healing to the one who stands beneath him in his patronage. ⁶The healing of the body can be done by this because, in dreams, equality cannot be permanent. ⁷The shifts and change are what the dream is made of. ⁸To be healed appears to be to find a wiser one who, by his arts and learning, will succeed.

3. Someone knows better; this the magic phrase by which the body seems to be the aim of healing as the world conceives of it. ²And to this wiser one another goes to profit by his learning and his skill; to find in him the remedy for pain. ³How can that be? ⁴True healing cannot come from inequality assumed and then accepted as the truth, and used to help restore the wounded and to calm the mind that suffers from the agony of doubt.

4. Is there a role for healing, then, that one can use to offer help for someone else? ²In arrogance the answer must be "no." ³But in humility there is indeed a place for helpers. ⁴It is like the role that helps in prayer, and lets forgiveness be what it is meant to be. ⁵You do not make yourself the bearer of the special gift that brings the healing. ⁶You but recognize your oneness with the one who calls for help. ⁷For in this oneness is his separate sense dispelled, and it is this that made him sick. ⁸There is no point in giving remedy apart from where the source of sickness is, for never thus can it be truly healed.

5. Healers there are, for they are Sons of God who recognize their Source, and understand that all their Source creates is one with them. ²This is the remedy that brings relief which cannot fail. ³It

will remain to bless for all eternity. ⁴It heals no part, but wholly and forever. ⁵Now the cause of every malady has been revealed exactly as it is. ⁶And in that place is written now the holy Word of God. ⁷Sickness and separation must be healed by love and union. ⁸Nothing else can heal as God established healing. ⁹Without Him there is no healing, for there is no love.

6. God's Voice alone can tell you how to heal. ²Listen, and you will never fail to bring His kindly remedy to those He sends to you, to let Him heal them, and to bless all those who serve with Him in healing's name. ³The body's healing will occur because its cause has gone. ⁴And now without a cause, it cannot come again in different form. ⁵Nor will death any more be feared because it has been understood. ⁶There is no fear in one who has been truly healed, for love has entered now where idols used to stand, and fear has given way at last to God.

IV. The Holiness of Healing

1. How holy are the healed! ²For in their sight their brothers share their healing and their love. ³Bringers of peace,—the Holy Spirit's voice, through whom He speaks for God, Whose Voice He is,—such are God's healers. ⁴They but speak for Him and never for themselves. ⁵They have no gifts but those they have from God. ⁶And these they share because they know that this is what He wills. ⁷They are not special. ⁸They are holy. ⁹They have chosen holiness, and given up all separate dreams of special attributes through which they can bestow unequal gifts on those less fortunate. ¹⁰Their healing has restored their wholeness so they can forgive, and join the song of prayer in which the healed sing of their union and their thanks to God.

2. As witness to forgiveness, aid to prayer, and the effect of mercy truly taught, healing is blessing. ²And the world responds in quickened chorus through the voice of prayer. ³Forgiveness shines its merciful reprieve upon each blade of grass and feathered wing and all the living things upon the earth. ⁴Fear has no haven here, for love has come in all its holy oneness. ⁵Time remains only to let the last embrace of prayer rest on the earth an instant, as the world is shined away. ⁶This instant is the goal of all true healers, whom the Christ has taught to see His likeness and to teach like Him.

3. Think what it means to help the Christ to heal! ²Can anything be holier than this? ³God thanks His healers, for He knows the Cause of healing is Himself, His Love, His Son, restored as His completion and returned to share with Him creation's holy joy. ⁴Do not ask partial healing, nor accept an idol for rememberance of Him Whose Love has never changed and never will. ⁵You are as dear to Him as is the whole of His creation, for it lies in you as His eternal gift. ⁶What need have you for shifting dreams within a sorry world? ⁷Do not forget the gratitude of God. ⁸Do not forget the holy grace of prayer. ⁹Do not forget forgiveness of God's Son.

4. You first forgive, then pray, and you are healed. ²Your prayer has risen up and called to God, Who hears and answers. ³You have understood that you forgive and pray but for yourself. ⁴And in this understanding you are healed. ⁵In prayer you have united with your Source, and understood that you have never left. ⁶This level cannot be attained until there is no hatred in your heart, and no desire to attack the Son of God.

5. Never forget this; it is you who are God's Son, and as you choose to be to him so are you to yourself, and God to you. ²Nor will your judgment fail to reach to God, for you will give the role to Him you see in His creation. ³Do not choose amiss, or you will think that it is you who are creator in His place, and He is then no longer Cause but only an effect. ⁴Now healing is impossible, for He is blamed for your deception and your guilt. ⁵He Who is Love becomes the source of fear, for only fear can now be justified. ⁶Vengeance is His. ⁷His great destroyer, death. ⁸And sickness, suffering and grievous loss become the lot of everyone on earth, which He abandoned to the devil's care, swearing He will deliver it no more.

6. Come unto Me, My children, once again, without such twisted thoughts upon your hearts. ²You still are holy with the Holiness Which fathered you in perfect sinlessness, and still surrounds you with the Arms of peace. ³Dream now of healing. ⁴Then arise and lay all dreaming down forever. ⁵You are he your Father loves, who never left his home, nor wandered in a savage world with feet that bleed, and with a heavy heart made hard against the love that is the truth in you. ⁶Give all your dreams to Christ and let Him be your Guide to healing, leading you in prayer beyond the sorry reaches of the world.

7. He comes for Me and speaks My Word to you. ²I would recall

My weary Son to Me from dreams of malice to the sweet embrace of everlasting Love and perfect peace. ³My Arms are open to the Son I love, who does not understand that he is healed, and that his prayers have never ceased to sing his joyful thanks in unison with all creation, in the holiness of Love. ⁴Be still an instant. ⁵Underneath the sounds of harsh and bitter striving and defeat there is a Voice that speaks to you of Me. ⁶Hear this an instant and you will be healed. ⁷Hear this an instant and you have been saved.

8. Help Me to wake My children from the dream of retribution and a little life beset with fear, that ends so soon it might as well have never been. ²Let Me instead remind you of eternity, in which your joy grows greater as your love extends along with Mine beyond infinity, where time and distance have no meaning. ³While you wait in sorrow Heaven's melody is incomplete, because your song is part of the eternal harmony of love. ⁴Without you is creation unfulfilled. ⁵Return to Me Who never left My Son. ⁶Listen, My child, your Father calls to you. ⁷Do not refuse to hear the Call for Love. ⁸Do not deny to Christ what is His Own. ⁹Heaven is here and Heaven is your home.

9. Creation leans across the bars of time to lift the heavy burden from the world. ²Lift up your hearts to greet its advent. ³See the shadows fade away in gentleness; the thorns fall softly from the bleeding brow of him who is the holy Son of God. ⁴How lovely are you, child of Holiness! ⁵How like to Me! ⁶How lovingly I hold you in My Heart and in My Arms. ⁷How dear is every gift to Me that you have made, who healed My Son and took him from the cross. ⁸Arise and let My thanks be given you. ⁹And with My gratitude will come the gift first of forgiveness, then eternal peace.

10. So now return your holy voice to Me. ²The song of prayer is silent without you. ³The universe is waiting your release because it is its own. ⁴Be kind to it and to yourself, and then be kind to Me. ⁵I ask but this; that you be comforted and live no more in terror and in pain. ⁶Do not abandon Love. ⁷Remember this; whatever you may think about yourself, whatever you may think about the world, your Father needs you and will call to you until you come to Him in peace at last.

A Course in Miracles Related Material
Available from The Foundation for Inner Peace

For those interested in obtaining materials related to *A Course in Miracles* please see the following list. These materials can be purchased from the Foundation for Inner Peace, P.O. Box 598, Mill Valley, CA 94942 or ordered directly from the Foundation's Online Store at: WWW.ACIM.ORG.

Print Editions:

The Combined Volume, Third Edition of *A Course in Miracles*, is the only edition that contains in one place all of the writings that Dr. Helen Schucman, its Scribe, authorized to be printed. It is published solely by The Foundation for Inner Peace, the not-for-profit organization chosen by Dr. Schucman for this purpose.

The Combined Volume also includes the Supplements to *A Course in Miracles*, "Psychotherapy: Purpose, Process and Practice " and " The Song of Prayer." These sections are extensions of the Course principles, which were dictated to Dr. Schucman shortly after she completed *A Course in Miracles*.

Hardcover $37.50
Quality Softcover $32.50
Mass Market Paperback $26.00

• *Un Curso de Milagros*

Our Spanish language edition is the culmination of a lengthy process of candidate evaluation before the selection of the most qualified candidate for the task. The team's education, experience, study of the Course and many years of work have rewarded us with a fluent, accurate translation of the only English version authorized by the scribes.   Hardcover $37.50

Supplements to *A Course in Miracles*

• Psychotherapy: Purpose, Process and Practice

Taken down by Helen Schucman in the same manner as *A Course in Miracles* this twenty-three page booklet discusses the

Course's principles of healing and forgiveness in the context of psychotherapy. Written for professional therapists, the booklet nonetheless will be of help to anyone interested in how the Course's theoretical principle of healing—joining with another through the Holy Spirit—is applied to the field of psychotherapy.

$6.00

• The Song of Prayer

Taken down by Helen Schucman in the same manner as *A Course in Miracles*, this twenty-two page booklet discusses forgiveness and healing in the context of prayer, contrasting the meaning of true prayer, forgiveness, and healing with their opposites. The process of prayer is described in the booklet as "growth in forgiveness," with healing seen as the effect of the mind's undoing of the belief in separation.

$6.00

• Anexo a *Un Curso en Milagros* - booklet

Spanish language edition of Supplements to *A Course in Miracles*, "Psychotherapy: Purpose, Process and Practice " and " The Song of Prayer."

$17.00

Digital Editions

• ACIM Ebooks

ACIM ebooks can be purchased from ebook distributors such as Amazon.com, BN.com and ebookstore.sony.com. These ebook distributors have developed free reader apps that allow the ACIM ebook to be read on the PC and Mac, and many reading devices, including but not limited to the Amazon Kindle, Apple iPhone, Apple iPad, Apple iPod touch, Barnes & Noble Nook, Sony Readers, Blackberry, Motorola Droid and other Android devices. Visit the Foundation's website at WWW.ACIM.ORG to find the latest information about new reader apps and reading devices supported.

• Fully Searchable Electronic Version of ACIM (EACIM) - CD

A powerful search program allows users to do complex, Boolean, multiple and single-word searches across the three volumes of *A Course in Miracles* and the two Supplements: *Psycho-*

therapy: Purpose, Process, and Practice and *The Song of Prayer: Prayer, Forgiveness, Healing*. Results are displayed within seconds. Users can add notes and highlighters, copy and paste selected text into a word processor, and print selected text directly to a printer. Users can also search to find words within their notes and highlighted text.

EACIM is available for the PC on Vista and all Windows operating systems, including Windows 7 and Windows 8. $33.00

EACIM-Mac runs only on OS 9 and earlier systems $33.00

Apps for the Apple Devices

• :ACIM Workbook App WITH Reminders

The Foundation has joined with CDE Solutions to bring you an ACIM Workbook with Reminders app for the iPhone and iPad. The app includes the entire Workbook for Students. Remembering when to do the Workbook's daily lessons can sometimes be difficult, especially during a busy day. Therefore this app will remind you when to do your daily lessons, with a system of alerts based on the intervals suggested within each lesson in the Workbook.

You can choose to use the preset reminders, or set them with intervals of your choosing. Alerts can be set with various tones and pop-ups. In addition, this App highlights the specific portion of the wording from each lesson that is to be declared for the day. $5.99

• ACIM: Workbook Lessons and Audio Affirmations

Developed by Studio Six in cooperation with the Foundation for Inner Peace, this app is a companion to *A Course In Miracles*. Designed to be used in conjunction with the Workbook for Students, use of this app will enhance your study, and add another dimension to the work that you are doing with the Course.

Text of all 365 Workbook lessons and introductions to lessons are included. Play the official Foundation-produced audio of the affirmations included for each lesson, or record your own personalized affirmation.

You can follow your studies with a handy pocket reminder of the lesson of the day that you can reference several times per day. For each lesson, you can add your own text notes, and even record your own personalized affirmation. By personalizing the

Course in this way, as you progress through the lessons, you will create a living record of your journey.

Also, to help you appreciate the breadth and scope of the Course, we have included a beautiful rendition of the Earth, with points marked on the Earth showing all of the people who are working on the Course through this app. We have color-coded the points so that you can see who is working on the same lesson that you are, and who is currently online.

Note that if you have a 2nd gen Touch, you will need an external microphone for recording.

Available for the iPad (Requires iOS 2.2.1 or later), iPhone, iPod touch (2nd & 3rd generation), iPod touch (3rd & 4th generation) This app will soon become available for the 1st generation iPod.

App for Android Devices

• ACIM: Workbook Lessons

Developed by the Foundation for Inner Peace, this app is a companion to *A Course In Miracles*. Designed to be used in conjunction with the Workbook for Students, use of this app will enhance your study, and add another dimension to the work that you are doing with the Course. The complete Workbook is included.

This app can be purchased and downloaded from Google Play.

You will find announcements on the Foundation's website (WWW.ACIM.ORG) about current and future digital editions.

Translations of ACIM

As of October 2013, the Foundation has produced the Course in twenty-one languages — Afrikaans, Bulgarian, Chinese, Croatian, Czech, Danish, Dutch, Finnish, French, German, Hebrew, Hungarian, Italian, Norwegian, Polish, Portuguese, Romanian, Russian, Slovene, Spanish, Swedish, and . These can be purchased at various prices from the Foundation's Online Store at: WWW.ACIM.ORG.

Additional languages currently in the Foundation's translation process — and being readied for future publication — include

Greek, Japanese, Korean, Yoruba, with still others to be added as qualified translators become ready for the task.

- Afrikaans - Electronic Book of ACIM on CD

  The Afrikaans language edition is available as a PDF. $23.00

Audio CDs

- *A Course in Miracles* CD Set

  A Course in Miracles Audio CD Set contains 59 CDs, approximately 63 hours, containing the complete Course including the Text, Workbook and Manual for Teachers. This audio version is read by Mr. Jim Stewart, a longtime student of the Course.

  The set includes a small booklet that lists the contents of each disc and comes packaged in an attractive blue and gold carrying case. $170.00

- Also available as a 5-CD MP3 Set $65.00

- Readings from *A Course in Miracles* - CD

  A one-hour CD of selected readings from the Course. Chosen and read by Dr. William Thetford, these readings add a moving dimension to the inspirational and poetic quality of the printed words. This recording is also available as a one hour audio cassette. $17.00

- A Recently Discovered Recording

  Excerpts from *A Course in Miracles* read by Dr. William Thetford (one of the Scribes of the Course) and his close friend, Dr. Gerald Jampolsky. $17.00

- What It Says – Audio CD

  This CD is the audio soundtrack of a 45 minute lecture by Dr. Kenneth Wapnick. It is an extraordinary summary of the principal themes in *A Course in Miracles*. Dr. Wapnick was an associate of Dr. Helen Schucman and has studied the Course since before it was published. He currently leads workshops and seminars on the content of the Course at The Foundation for *A Course in Miracles* in Temecula, California. $17.00

This lecture is also available as a video DVD. $26.00

• *Un Curso de Milagros* - MP3

A single disc of approximately 70 hours, contains the complete Spanish translation of the Course read by Mr. Javier Saenz Messia. This digital audio recording is the revised edition (2008) by Rosa Maria Wynn and Fernando Gómez with Lector: Javier Sánez Messia. $47.50

Videos on DVDs

• Memories of Helen & Bill – 2-disc DVD
We are thrilled to announce the release of our brand new 2-disc DVD set that focuses on the Scribes of *A Course in Miracles*. In this three-hour celebration of the 25th anniversary of the Course's publication, held in Anaheim, California in 2001, Dr. Kenneth Wapnick and Judith Skutch Whitson share their experiences with and recollections of Drs. Helen Schucman and William Thetford. Augmented by more than a hundred photos, this DVD set gives an intimate view of the lives of the two people responsible for bringing the Course to the world. $33.00

• The Story of *A Course in Miracles* – DVD
A remarkable 2-1/4 hour documentary film.

Part One: "The Forgotten Song" (also available separately) is the inspiring story of how the Course came to be. It features Dr. William Thetford, and spans a 70-year period in the life of Dr. Helen Schucman, "scribe" of the Course.

Part Two: "The Song Remembered" contains first-hand accounts of various psychologists, businesspeople, educators, physicians, prison inmates, and others who relate how the Course has affected their lives. $33.00

• The Forgotten Song – DVD
This DVD is Part One (the first hour only) of the 2-1/4 hour documentary film, "The Story of *A Course in Miracles*," produced by Bridget Winter. Featuring Dr. William Thetford, it spans a 70-year period in the life of Dr. Helen Schucman, "scribe" of the Course, and tells the inspiring story of how the Course came to be. $26.00

• The Cave Vision – DVD

This DVD contains a recreation of "The Vision of the Cave" as portrayed in the "Story of *A Course in Miracles*" DVD. Dr. Helen Schucman's own words, taken from her autobiography, are narrated by actress Glynis Johns. Includes an inner vision experienced by Helen that preceded her scribing of the Course. $17.00

• Rare Interview with Helen Schucman – DVD

A rare interview in which Dr. Helen Schucman, "Scribe" of *A Course in Miracles* discusses the Inner Voice responsible for the dictation.
This DVD also includes the transcript of her words. $17.00

• Recollections about Dr. Helen Schucman – DVD

In this DVD, Dr. William Thetford, Dr. Kenneth Wapnick and Judith Skutch Whitson discuss their personal memories of Dr. Helen Schucman, "Scribe" of *A Course in Miracles*.

This film was produced in 1987 by Bridget Winter during the period that she made "The Story of *A Course in Miracles*" and is the only time these three people shared their views of Helen in such a format. $17.00

• What It Says – DVD

This 45-minute video recording of a lecture by Dr. Kenneth Wapnick, is an extraordinary summary of the principal themes in *A Course in Miracles*. Dr. Wapnick was an associate of Dr. Helen Schucman and has studied the Course since before it was published. He currently leads workshops and seminars on the content of the Course at The Foundation for *A Course in Miracles* in Temecula, California. $26.00

Other Related Materials

• *Choose Once Again*

Selections from *A Course in Miracles* in blank verse form. Short inspirational selections that highlight the beauty of language which illuminates the concepts presented, 128 pages of personal messages that help turn each moment into a joyous experience.
 $15.00

- *Journey Without Distance* – Softcover

  The complete inspirational story of how the Course came to be, taking the reader on a fascinating journey that spans more than seventy years. Meet Dr. Helen Schucman, the highly respected research psychologist who heard a "voice" dictating the material to her. Learn how Dr. William Thetford, the head of her Psychology Department, aided and supported her. Written by Robert Skutch, co-founder of the Foundation for Inner Peace, 142 pages.

  $18.00

- *The Gifts of God* – Softcover

  The inspired poetry of Dr. Helen Schucman, scribe of *A Course in Miracles*. One hundred and fourteen poems written over a ten-year period that share the spiritual content of the Course.

  $18.00

- Workbook Lesson Cards

  All 365 lessons from the Workbook for Students reproduced on heavy 3-3/8" x 4-7/8" cards enabling you to carry your current lesson with you for easy reference throughout the day. $26.00

- Helen Schucman Autobiography - PDF Download

  Dr. Helen Schucman's autobiography, completed in 1975, includes selected highlights of her remarkable life that she felt would offer a flavor of her role as Scribe of *A Course in Miracles*. This stylized account was not meant to be published during her lifetime and indeed does not truly represent her amazing contribution. Nevertheless, her 50-page autobiography has now been made available for the first time since her death in 1981 by the Foundation for *A Course in Miracles* and the Foundation for Inner Peace as a downloadable PDF. $9.95

- William Thetford Life Story - PDF Download

  Bill Thetford's Life Story stems from a lengthy series of taped interviews conducted in 1982 that recorded a narrated version of his extraordinary life and career. The memoir spans from his childhood through the scribing of *A Course in Miracles* and includes reminiscences of how he applied the Course himself. The interviews, together with other significant biographical material about him, were later assembled into an autobiography following his death in 1988. This 48-page PDF electronic download of William Thetford's Life Story is published by the Foundation for Inner Peace. $9.95